Cisco IOS Cookbook™

Other resources from O'Reilly

Related titles

Cisco IOS in a Nusthell

Cisco IOS Access Lists

DNS and BIND

Ethernet: The Definitive
   Guide

Hardening Cisco Routers

IP Routing

IPv6 Essentials

IPv6 Network Administration

SSH, The Secure Shell: The
   Definitive Guide

oreilly.com

oreilly.com is more than a complete catalog of O'Reilly books. You'll also find links to news, events, articles, weblogs, sample chapters, and code examples.

oreillynet.com is the essential portal for developers interested in open and emerging technologies, including new platforms, programming languages, and operating systems.

Conferences

O'Reilly brings diverse innovators together to nurture the ideas that spark revolutionary industries. We specialize in documenting the latest tools and systems, translating the innovator's knowledge into useful skills for those in the trenches. Visit *conferences.oreilly.com* for our upcoming events.

Safari Bookshelf (*safari.oreilly.com*) is the premier online reference library for programmers and IT professionals. Conduct searches across more than 1,000 books. Subscribers can zero in on answers to time-critical questions in a matter of seconds. Read the books on your Bookshelf from cover to cover or simply flip to the page you need. Try it today for free.

SECOND EDITION

Cisco IOS Cookbook™

Kevin Dooley and Ian J. Brown

Beijing · Cambridge · Farnham · Köln · Sebastopol · Taipei · Tokyo

Cisco IOS Cookbook™, Second Edition
by Kevin Dooley and Ian J. Brown

Published by O'Reilly Media, Inc., 1005 Gravenstein Highway North, Sebastopol, CA 95472.

O'Reilly books may be purchased for educational, business, or sales promotional use. Online editions are also available for most titles (*safari.oreilly.com*). For more information, contact our corporate/institutional sales department: (800) 998-9938 or *corporate@oreilly.com*.

Editor: Mike Loukides	**Cover Designer:** Ellie Volckhausen
Production Editor: Colleen Gorman	**Interior Designer:** David Futato
Proofreader: Ann Atalla	**Illustrators:** Robert Romano and Jessamyn Read
Indexer: John Bickelhaupt	

Printing History:

July 2003:	First Edition.
December 2006:	Second Edition.

ISBN: 978-0-596-52722-8
[LSI]

Table of Contents

Preface

Cicso routers are nearly ubiquitous in IP networks. They are extremely flexible and reliable devices. The number and variety of features grows with each new release of the Internetwork Operating System (IOS). And while Cisco Press and several other publishers supply excellent documentation of these features both online and in a variety of books, it is often difficult to know when, why, and how to use these features. There are often many different ways to solve any given networking problem using Cisco devices. Some of these solutions are clearly more effective than others.

The most pressing question in the mind of you, the network engineer, is which of the many potential solutions is the most appropriate for your particular situation. And once you have decided to use a particular feature, the next question is how to actually implement it. Unfortunately, the feature documentation that describes a particular command or feature frequently does very little to answer either of these questions.

Indeed, there are many cases in which the Cisco IOS and documentation offers solutions that will make the network extremely difficult to support in the long term. These solutions are legitimate in odd special situations, but we strongly believe that they should be avoided in most production networks. In some cases this is because there are features that open potentially serious security holes in their default modes. In other cases, there are features that can render the network exceedingly difficult to manage effectively (policy-based routing is the classic example of this problem). Everybody who has worked with Cisco routers for any length of time has at one time or another had to ask their friends and co-workers for example router configuration files that show how to actually solve a common problem. A good working configuration example can often save huge amounts of time and frustration when implementing a feature that you've never used before. This is often true even when you already understand the theory behind this feature. This is why we have written this book.

We don't intend the *Cisco IOS Cookbook* to replace the detailed feature documentation included in books like *Cisco IOS in a Nutshell,* Second Edition, by James Boney (O'Reilly), or information available on Cisco's web site (*http://www.cisco.com*). We don't have the space to tell you in detail about how particular protocols actually work.

This is information that you can find in places like the Internet Engineering Task Force (IETF) Request for Comment (RFC) documents, as well as a wide variety of books.

Instead, this book is a complement to those sources of information. They will tell you things like what a routing protocol is, how it works, and which command turns it on. We will help you select the right routing protocol and configure it in the most efficient way for your network.

This book includes a collection of sample router configurations and scripts that we have found useful in real-world networks. It also includes, wherever possible, our advice on what features to use in which situations and how to use them most effectively. There are many common mistakes that we have seen before (although we rarely make mistakes ourselves), and we want to help you to avoid making these same mistakes yourself.

What's New in This Edition

The first important difference between the first and second editions of this book is visible right on the cover: we changed the title from *Cisco Cookbook* to *Cisco IOS Cookbook*. We had two main reasons for making this change. First, it's more accurate. Cisco has several different product lines with completely different configuration interfaces. This book just covers the Cisco Internetwork Operating System (IOS), the software that runs on most of Cisco's routers and switches. It doesn't cover PIX or ASA firewall configuration or content switching or Cisco's Intrusion Detection Systems (IDS), for example.

The second reason for the change is that somebody might one day want to write a Cisco firewall or content switching or IDS cookbook. In fact, several readers have written to us asking for such things, although having just completed the marathon process of updating this book, neither of us feels a burning desire to undertake such a project right away.

For the second edition, we had two main goals. The first was to update the information for the first edition so that it now reflects IOS Version 12.4. And our second goal was to add some of the new topics, like MPLS and IPv6, which have become more relevant since the first edition was published. Many of these ideas came from reader suggestions. However, Cisco rarely deletes features from its software when it creates a new version, so we have also retained most of the content from the first edition of this book.

This means that much of the content in this book is also relevant to lower IOS versions. We have tried to make it clear when certain features were introduced, or if they are only available with certain IOS feature sets.

In each chapter, whenever there were relevant and useful new features, we have added new recipes showing how to use these features effectively. And when there were modifications to existing features, we have added information to the existing recipes.

We have also written four new chapters on topics that either were requested by readers, or that we felt were interesting and important. The new chapters cover IP Mobility, IP Version 6, MPLS, and Security, respectively.

In all, this edition contains 89 entirely new recipes, and we have deleted two old ones, one because we didn't feel it was still the best solution to the problem, and the other because it made sense to absorb its content into another recipe. We have made significant updates to existing recipes in every chapter, mostly to describe useful new options to existing commands.

We welcome feedback from our readers. If you have comments, suggestions, or ideas for other recipes or topics that you'd like to see covered, please let us know. Just as we did with this edition, if there are addtional future editions of the *Cisco IOS Cookbook*, we will include any suggestions that we think are especially useful. You can reach us at *kevind@manageablenetworks.com* or *ijbrown@hotmail.com*.

Organization

As the name suggests, the *Cisco Cookbook* is organized as a series of recipes. Each recipe begins with a problem statement that describes a common situation that you might be faced with. After each problem statement is a brief solution that shows a sample router configuration or a script that you can use to resolve this particular problem. Then we turn to a discussion section where we describe the solution, how it works, and when you should or should not use it.

We have tried to construct the recipes so you can turn directly to the one that addresses your specific problem and find a useful solution without needing to read the entire book. If the solution includes terms or concepts that you are not familiar with, the chapter introductions should help to bridge the gap. And many recipes refer to other recipes or chapters that discuss related topics. We have also included a variety of references to other sources in case you need more background information on a particular subject.

The chapters are organized by the feature or protocol discussed. So, if you are looking for information on a particular feature such as NAT, NTP, or SNMP, you can turn to that chapter and find a variety of related recipes. Most of the chapters list the more basic problems first, and any unusual or complicated situations last. But there are some exceptions to this, when we have opted instead to group related recipes together.

What's in This Book

The first four chapters cover what would be considered essential system administration functions if a router were a server. Chapter 1 covers router configuration and file management issues. In Chapter 2, we turn to useful router management tricks. such as command aliases, how to use CDP and DNS, as well as how to tune buffers and create exception dumps. This chapter ends with a set of four scripts that generate various useful reports to help you manage your routers. Then Chapter 3 discusses user access and privileges on the router. Chapter 4 extends this discussion on using TACACS+ to provide centralized management of user access to your routers.

The next five chapters look at various aspects of IP routing. Chapter 5 looks at IP routing in general, including static routes and administrative distances. In Chapter 6, we focus on RIP, including both versions 1 and 2. Chapter 7 looks at EIGRP, and Chapter 8 at OSPF. And, in Chapter 9 we discuss the BGP protocol, which controls all IP routing through the backbone of the Internet.

The remaining chapters all cover separate topics. We look at the popular Frame Relay WAN protocol in Chapter 10. Chapter 11 discusses queuing and congestion. This chapter also goes into some detail on various IP Quality of Service issues. In Chapter 12, we look at IP tunnels and VPNs. This chapter includes a discussion of Cisco's IPSec implementation.

We turn to issues related to Dial Backup in Chapter 13. Then, in Chapter 14, we look at time. We include a relatively detailed discussion of the NTP protocol, which you can use to synchronize the clocks of all your routers. You can then use the synchronized routers as a time source for other equipment, including application servers on your network.

Chapter 15 is primarily concerned with configuring the DLSw protocol. It also looks SNA and SDLC protocols, which often are carried over IP networks using DLSw. In Chapter 16, we show how to configure several of the most popular interface types on a Cisco router.

Chapters 17 and 18 look at the closely related issues of network management and logging. In Chapter 17, we discuss SNMP in particular. This chapter includes several router configuration examples to use with SNMP, as well as a number of useful scripts that you can use to help manage your Cisco equipment. Chapter 18 looks at issues related to managing the router's event logs, as well how to use the syslog protocol to send these log messages to a central server.

It's impossible to do much on a Cisco router without having a good understanding of Access Lists. There are several different kinds of Access Lists, and Chapter 19 shows several useful and interesting applications of the various IP specific Access Lists.

In Chapter 20, we look at DHCP. Routers usually just act as DHCP proxy devices, but we also show how to use the router as a DHCP server, or even as a client.

Chapter 21 talks about NAT, which allows you to use private IP addresses, and even resolve conflicting address ranges between networks.

One of the best ways to build a fault-tolerant LAN is to configure two or more routers to share a single IP address using HSRP. We show several different HSRP configurations in Chapter 22. Then, in Chapter 23, we look at how to implement multicast routing functionality on a Cisco router.

The four new chapters appear at the end of the book. Chapter 24 covers IP Mobility. There also is a recipe on the related but much simpler topic of Local Area Mobility. IP Mobility is something of a fringe topic in the TCP/IP protocol suite, but we believe it is becoming more common for two reasons. First, there has been a marked increase in the number of wireless mobile devices. The second reason is increased demand for consumer access to the public Internet.

In Chapter 25, we look at another subject that is not widely deployed in Enterprise networks, but which we nonetheless think is increasingly important: IPv6. Most people today still mean IPv4 when they talk about TCP/IP. But there are some large service provider networks, particularly for third generation cell phones, in which the number of end devices demands IPv6. We expect to see the number of IPv6 installations expand rapidly over the next few years.

Then Chapter 26 turns to a protocol that has exploded in popularity since the first edition of this book: MPLS. When we wrote the first edition, just three years ago, Frame Relay and ATM still were the WAN protocols of choice in most regions. While these protocols are still present, particularly inside carrier networks, MPLS has largely replaced them as a delivery mode for IP WANs.

And finally, in Chapter 27, we look at Security. Most of the features discussed in this chapter concern the IOS Firewall feature set (also called Advanced Security). Many of these features are not new. Indeed, one of the recipes in this new chapter was in the previous edition, and has been relocated from the Access List chapter. However, we have seen such an increase in concern about network security since then that it seemed wise to include an entire chapter on the subject. We should also point out that security as a general topic is discussed in several other chapters in this book. For example, the security of the router itself is discussed in Chapters 2, 3, and 4. Another popular security topic, VPNs, is found in Chapter 12.

We also include two appendices. Appendix A discusses the various external software tools that we use throughout the book, and shows how to obtain your own copies of these packages. Appendix B gives some helpful background on IP Quality of Service, as well as various queueing algorithms that you can use on Cisco routers.

Conventions Used in This Book

The following typographical conventions are used in this book:

Constant width
> Indicates command-line elements, computer output, and code examples.

Constant width italic
> Indicates placeholders (for which you substitute an actual name) in examples and in registry keys.

Constant width bold

    Indicates user input and is used to highlight key portions of code.

Italic

    Introduces new terms and example URLs, interfaces, keywords, commands, file extensions, filenames, and directory or folder names

 Indicates a tip, suggestion, or general note.

 Indicates a warning or caution.

Using Code Examples

This book is here to help you get your job done. In general, you may use the code in this book in your programs and documentation. You do not need to contact us for permission unless you're reproducing a significant portion of the code. For example, writing a program that uses several chunks of code from this book does not require permission. Selling or distributing a CD-ROM of examples from O'Reilly books *does* require permission. Answering a question by citing this book and quoting example code does not require permission. Incorporating a significant amount of example code from this book into your product's documentation *does* require permission.

We appreciate, but do not require, attribution. An attribution usually includes the title, author, publisher, and ISBN. For example: "*Cisco IOS Cookbook*, Second Edition, by Kevin Dooley and Ian J. Brown. Copyright 2007 O'Reilly Media, Inc., 978-0-596-52722-8."

If you feel your use of code examples falls outside fair use or the permission given above, feel free to contact us at *permissions@oreilly.com*.

We'd Like Your Feedback!

We at O'Reilly have tested and verified the information in this book to the best of our ability, but mistakes and oversights do occur. Please let us know about errors you may find, as well as your suggestions for future editions, by writing to:

O'Reilly Media, Inc.
1005 Gravenstein Highway North
Sebastopol, CA 95472
800-998-9938 (in the United States or Canada)
707-829-0515 (international or local)
707-829-0104 (fax)

There is a web page for the book where we list errata, examples, or any additional information. You can access this page at:

>*http://www.oreilly.com/catalog/9780596527228*

To comment or ask technical questions about this book, send email to:

>*bookquestions@oreilly.com*

For more information about our books, conferences, software, Resource Centers, and the O'Reilly Network, see our web site at:

>*http://www.oreilly.com*

Safari® Enabled

 When you see a Safari® Enabled icon on the cover of your favorite technology book, that means the book is available online through the O'Reilly Network Safari Bookshelf.

Safari offers a solution that's better than e-books. It's a virtual library that lets you easily search thousands of top tech books, cut and paste code samples, download chapters, and find quick answers when you need the most accurate, current information. Try it for free at *http://safari.oreilly.com*.

Acknowledgments

Although this book has been significantly updated since the first edition, it was built on the bones of that earlier book, and so we need to start by repeating our gratitude to everybody who helped in the production of the first edition: John Karek, Jackman Chan, David Close, Jim Sumser, Mike Loukides, Phil Dangler, Jessamyn Read, Ellie Volckhausen, and our insightful technical reviewers Peter Rybaczyk, Ravi Malhotra, and Iljitsch van Beijnum.

For the second edition, we'd like to say thanks again to everybody at O'Reilly, particularly our editor, Mike Loukides, who must have seriously wondered how we were going to pull our rapidly slipping writing schedule out of the dirt. He took us at our rather cavalier word that we had it under control. A lesser editor would surely have run screaming. So thanks for believing our bravado.

We had only one technical reviewer for the second edition. Ravi Malhotra had the unenviable task of reading this enormous new book and pointing out the many rough spots. Thanks Ravi, and thanks also for your encouraging words. Although this is a second edition, it contains as much new material as many first editions, so we do know how much we asked you to do and with what time constraints, and we really appreciate it.

Kevin Dooley

I'd like to thank my ceaselessly supportive wife, Sherry Biscope. We dated while I wrote my first book. You agreed to marry me during the writing of the first edition of this book, and we're still together as this massive second edition goes out the door. You've also cheered me on through marathons and a thousand other crazy, life-consuming projects. And I'd also like to thank my lovely daughter, Alice. You are a constant delight. My life was bright before you came into it, and then the sun rose. I love you both more than I ever thought was possible.

And thanks to Ginger the beagle, the best dog in the world, despite the occasional bit of late-night-writing-snack thievery.

Ian J. Brown

I would like to thank my beautiful and understanding wife, Lisa, who supported me (almost) unconditionally throughout this project. Special thanks also to my son, Ethan, and daughter, Darby, who provided me with endless amounts of encouragement throughout. Without the assistance and encouragement of my family, this book would not have been possible. You guys mean the world to me and I will love you always and forever.

I would also like to thank our friends at Cisco, who provided equipment, cards, and cables throughout so we could build, configure, and test our solutions. Special thanks to the No Ma'am organization for their support throughout the years.

## CHAPTER 1

Router Configuration and File Management

1.0 Introduction

The Internet Protocol (IP) seemed ubiquitous three years ago when we wrote the first edition of this book. It was then, as it still is today, the basis of the public Internet as well as nearly all corporate, institutional, educational, and home networks. But somehow it has managed to take on an even more important role than it ever had before.

It now seems almost quaint to find a cellphone that doesn't have its own web browser, for example. And while the delivery method of choice for WANs was Frame Relay and ATM when we wrote the first edition, it is now MPLS, an IP protocol.

For its part, Cisco has continued to be the dominant network hardware vendor in all but a few niches, and has even edged out a few of its competitors. This has been partly due to excellent marketing, but we see a large part of its success in the Internetwork Operating System (IOS) that runs on most of their routers and switches. Cisco has done a great job of producing new IOS versions with new features, and in keeping this software relatively stable and bug free through frequent incremental software releases.

Of course, these new features and new software versions mean that writing books like this one is a little bit like running a dairy; nobody wants last week's product. Keeping up with Cisco is hard work, but we think that this new edition has captured many of the most important and useful new IOS features.

Our benchmark software version for this edition is 12.4. The vast majority of the recipes in the book will in fact run on earlier versions, and we have noted version numbers when features have been introduced recently. Many of the recipes in this edition were also present in the previous edition, but we have reviewed and updated every chapter. We also added 89 new recipes throughout the book.

Many people wrote to us after the first edition with comments and suggestions. We have been able to include just about all of these suggestions in the current edition, and we sincerely hope that you will find this new edition as useful as the previous one.

IOS

You can think of a Cisco router as essentially a special purpose computer. It has its own operating system, which is called Internetwork Operating System (IOS), and even has files and filesystems. So we will start this book with a discussion of the basic system administration functions that a router engineer needs to know. This will include important matters such as how to manage your router's filesystems, upgrading the operating system, doing backups, and restoring the system configuration.

Cisco routers use flash memory, rather than disks, for storing information. Flash storage media is significantly more expensive and slower than disk storage, but the amount of storage needed to run a router is relatively small, compared to the amount needed to run a general-purpose computer. So this is not a serious problem. Flash has the important benefit that it tends to be more reliable than disk storage.

Flash storage is similar to Random Access Memory (RAM), but it doesn't need power to retain information, so it is called nonvolatile. Unlike Read Only Memory (ROM), you can erase and rewrite flash easily. Technically, there are other types of nonvolatile solid state storage, such as Erasable Programmable Read Only Memory (EPROM) and Electronically Erasable Programmable Read Only Memory (EEPROM). EPROM is not suitable for routers because it generally requires an external device, such as an ultraviolet light shone through a window on the chip to erase it. EEPROM, on the other hand, can be erased by simply sending an erase signal to the chip. But there is a key difference between EEPROM and flash memory. When you erase something from an EEPROM device, you must erase the entire device, while flash devices allow selective deletion of parts of the medium.

This is an important feature for routers because you don't always want to erase the entire storage medium just because you want to erase a single file. In Recipes 1.11 and 1.12, we will discuss ways that you can erase single files on some types of routers, depending on the type of filesystem used.

There are at least two main pieces of nonvolatile storage in a Cisco router. The router's configuration information is stored in a device called the Nonvolatile RAM (NVRAM), and the IOS images are stored in a device called the flash. It's important to keep these names straight because, of course, all flash memory is nonvolatile RAM. And, in fact, most routers use Flash technology for their nonvolatile RAM. So it's easy to get confused by the terms.

On most Cisco routers, the NVRAM area is between 16 Kb and 256 Kb, depending on the size and function of the router. Larger routers are expected to have larger configuration files, so they need more NVRAM. The Flash, on the other hand, is usually upgradeable, and can be anywhere from a few Megabytes to hundreds of Megabytes.

We often talk about a router's configuration file, but in fact there are two important configuration files on any router. There is the configuration file that describes the current running state of the router, which is called the *running-config*. Then there is the configuration file that the router uses to boot, which is called the *startup-config*. Only the *startup-config* is stored in NVRAM. So it is important to periodically check that the version of the configuration in the NVRAM is synchronized with the version that the router is currently running. Otherwise you could get a surprise from ancient history the next time the router reboots. You can synchronize the two configuration files by simply copying the *running-config* onto the *startup-config* file:

```
Router1#copy running-config startup-config
```

Many Cisco engineers, including the authors, still use the old-fashioned version of this command out of force of habit:

```
Router1#write memory
```

This command is not only deprecated, however, but is also less descriptive of what the router is doing.

The router uses the larger flash storage device for holding the operating system, or IOS. Unlike the operating systems on most computers, the IOS is a single file containing all of the features and functions available on the router. You can obtain the IOS image files from Cisco either on CD or, if you have an account on their system, you can download IOS files from the Cisco web site by using File Transfer Protocol (FTP) over the public Internet.

Most examples throughout this book assume that you have IOS Version 12. However, many features we discuss are available in earlier versions. And we expect that Cisco will continue to support all of the features we describe well into the future, although there may be slight syntax changes. It is important to be flexible because, if you work with Cisco routers a lot, you will encounter a large variety of different IOS versions, with various subtle differences. Unfortunately, some of these subtle differences are actually bugs. Cisco offers a detailed bug tracking system on their web site for registered users.

When you go to change an IOS version on a router, there are several important things to consider. First is the feature set. For each IOS release, Cisco produces several different versions. There is usually an Enterprise Feature Set, which includes essentially all of the different feature options available at a given time. But because the IOS is a monolithic file containing all features and all commands, the Enterprise IOS files are usually quite large. The Enterprise version is also usually much more expensive than the various stripped-down versions.

The simplest IOS versions are usually the IP Only Feature Set. As the name suggestions, this only includes TCP/IP based functionality. In most networks, you will find that the IP Only Feature Set is more than sufficient. In fact, almost all of the recipes in this book will work with the IP Only version of IOS.

There are several other important variations such as IP Plus, IP Plus IPSec 56, IP Plus IPSec 3DES, and so forth. The contents of these different versions (and even their names, to some extent) vary from release to release. We encourage you to consult Cisco's feature matrices to ensure the features you need are in the IOS version you have.

One of the most important considerations with any IOS release is whether you have sufficient RAM and Flash memory to support the new version. You can see how much storage your router has by looking at the output of the *show version* command.

The other important thing to remember about IOS images on Cisco routers is that every router has a fallback image located in the router's Read Only Memory (ROM). This IOS image cannot be changed or upgraded without physically replacing the ROM chips in the router.

The router's ROM contains three items: the power on self test (POST), the bootstrap program, and a stripped-down version of the router's Operating System. The router uses the bootstrap program while booting. The IOS image in ROM is usually an extremely stripped-down version that frequently doesn't support common features such as routing protocols, for example. In the normal boot cycle, the router will first load the POST, and then the bootstrap program, followed by the appropriate IOS image. Please refer to Recipe 1.7 for more information about booting from different IOS files.

Recipe 1.7 also shows how to adjust the configuration register values. These values tell the router a variety of boot options, and even allow you to force the router to stop its boot process before loading the IOS. This can be useful if the IOS image is corrupted, or if you need to do password recovery.

1.1 Configuring the Router via TFTP

Problem

You want to load configuration commands via TFTP.

Solution

You can use the *copy tftp:* command to configure the router via the Trivial File Transfer Protocol (TFTP):

```
Router1#copy tftp://172.25.1.1/NEWCONFIG running-config
Destination filename [running-config]? <enter>
Accessing tftp://172.25.1.1/NEWCONFIG...
Loading NEWCONFIG from 172.25.1.1 (via FastEthernet0/0.1): !
[OK - 24 bytes]

24 bytes copied in 0.192 secs (125 bytes/sec)
Router1#
```

 IOS versions before 12.0 used the command *configure network*. This command is still available in more recent versions, but it is now deprecated and may not continue to be available in the future.

Discussion

Generally, most people configure their routers by using *Telnet* and the *configure terminal* command. For large configuration changes, people tend to resort to cutting and pasting a large set of commands. While this method works, it is inefficient and slow, particularly if you have to configure large numbers of routers. When you use TFTP to download a large set of configuration commands, the router doesn't need to echo each character to your screen, which reduces the overhead and increases the speed.

In our example, we configured the router by making it download the file called NEWCONFIG from the server at 172.25.1.1 by using the Trivial File Transfer Protocol (TFTP). The router will copy the entire file via TFTP before entering the commands into the running configuration. This is extremely useful because sometimes some commands in the middle of a configuration could disrupt your access to the router, but the rest of the commands might fix the problem. If you tried to enter them manually using *TELNET* and *configure terminal*, you would simply lock yourself out of the router and not be able to continue. A typical example of this problem happens when you replace an active access-list. When you enter the first line, the router puts an implicit *deny all* at the end, which could break your session. However, entering commands by using TFTP avoids this problem.

We mention in passing that the last line of any configuration file that you copy into the router like this should be the *end* command so the router knows that it has reached the end of the file. If you don't do this, the router still will accept all of the commands normally, but will put the following error into its logs:

```
Jan 19 11:26:38: %PARSER-4-BADCFG: Unexpected end of configuration file.
```

If you have the *end* command in your configuration file, then seeing this message will tell you that the router didn't get all of the configuration commands. But if you don't terminate the file properly, it's impossible to tell if the transfer was successful.

Instead of TFTP, you can use the FTP protocol to download configuration files. FTP has a number of advantages over TFTP in terms of reliability and security. Recipe 1.14 shows how to load configuration commands by using FTP instead of TFTP.

See Also

Recipe 1.14

1.2 Saving Router Configuration to Server

Problem

You want to store a backup copy of your router's configuration on a TFTP server.

Solution

This example shows how to use TFTP to upload a copy of the router's active configuration to a remote server:

```
Freebsd% touch /tftpboot/router1-confg
Freebsd% chmod 666 /tftpboot/router1-confg
Freebsd% telnet Router1
Trying 172.25.1.5...
Connected to Router1.
Escape character is '^]'.

User Access Verification

Password: <vtypassword>

Router1>enable
Password: <enablepassword>
Router1#copy running-config tftp://172.25.1.1/router1-confg
Address or name of remote host [172.25.1.1]? <enter>
Destination filename [router1-confg]? <enter>
!!!
9640 bytes copied in 3.956 secs (2437 bytes/sec)
Router1#
```

Discussion

We cannot overstress the importance of making regular backups of your router configuration files and keeping copies in a safe place. If you have a serious failure that damages a router's hardware or software, the configuration will be destroyed. And anybody who has had to reconstruct a complex router configuration file from memory will tell you how difficult and stressful this task is. But if you have a backup of the last working configuration file, you can usually get a router working again within minutes of fixing any hardware problems.

Typical Mean Time Between Failure (MTBF) estimates for Cisco routers tend to be about 16 years. This sounds like a long time, but in a large network it means that you can expect to see a few failures every year. Unfortunately, human error is far more common than a device failure, and these human errors can result in complete or partial loss of the configuration file.

In the example, we created an empty backup configuration file on the TFTP server and then instructed the router to send its running configuration to this server. It is important to adjust the file permissions with the Unix *chmod* command. The transfer will fail if the configuration file is not *world writable*. We highly recommend moving the configuration files out of the TFTP directory to ensure that the file isn't read by unauthorized people or accidentally overwritten.

Reading files located in the TFTP directory is trivial because the TFTP program needs this directory to be both *world readable* and *world writeable*. Since router

---

configuration files contain passwords and IP addresses, you should take steps to protect these files as much as possible. In fact, you don't even need to be logged into the TFTP server to read these files. In the following example, we are able to access the TFTP server and read a router configuration file from another router:

```
Router1#more tftp://172.25.1.1/router1-confg
!
! Last configuration change at 11:23:59 EST Sat Jan 11 2003 by ijbrown
! NVRAM config last updated at 00:37:16 EST Sat Jan 11 2003 by ijbrown
!
Version 12.2
service tcp-keepalives-in
service timestamps debug datetime msec
service timestamps log datetime localtime
service password-encryption
!
hostname Router1
<removed for brevity>
```

As you can see, any files left in the TFTP directory can be easily viewed or even deliberately corrupted. TFTP is notoriously insecure, so we recommend using care whenever you work with this protocol.

Recipe 1.18 provides an automated script that gathers the configuration files for a list of routers on a nightly basis and stores these files for 30 days, by default.

See Also

Recipe 1.14; Recipe 1.18

1.3   Booting the Router Using a Remote Configuration File

Problem

You want to boot the router using an alternate configuration.

Solution

The following set of commands allows you to automatically load a configuration file located on a remote TFTP server when the router boots:

```
Router1#configure terminal
Enter configuration commands, one per line.  End with CNTL/Z.
Router1(config)#service config
Router1(config)#boot network tftp Network-auto 172.25.1.1
Router1(config)#boot host tftp Router8-auto 172.25.1.1
Router1(config)#end
Router1#
```

Discussion

By default, when the router reloads, it will read the configuration information from a file in its Nonvolatile Random Access Memory (NVRAM). Cisco commonly refers to this file as the startup configuration file. However, you can configure the router to load all or part of its configuration from a remote server via TFTP. This feature does not prevent the router from loading its startup configuration from NVRAM. In fact, the router will load its local startup file first before proceeding to the TFTP server files.

Uses for this feature vary, although most people who implement it do so because their configuration file has grown too large for their NVRAM to handle. It can also be a useful way of keeping an access-list that is shared by a number of routers, centralized and up to date. And we have sometimes used it as a temporary measure when the NVRAM in a router is damaged.

However, we consider this feature to be highly risky and recommend avoiding it in most cases. If the problem is simply one of NVRAM capacity, Recipe 1.4 shows how to compress the startup configuration file to help fit more information into your existing NVRAM. Also, since routers can operate for years without reloading, using this feature to keep your routers up to date seems pointless.

If you choose to implement remote configuration despite these cautions, we should mention a few other items. First, the router will attempt to load a host and a network file. The router will assume that network files are common to all routers, while the host files contain router specific information. When you enable the *service config* option, the router will attempt to first load a network file and then a host file. If it can't find these files, the router will generate error messages:

```
%Error opening tftp://255.255.255.255/network-confg (Timed out)
%Error opening tftp://255.255.255.255/cisconet.cfg (Timed out)
%Error opening tftp://255.255.255.255/router1-confg (Timed out)
%Error opening tftp://255.255.255.255/router1.cfg (Timed out)
```

Here you can see what happened when we enabled the *service config* option and reloaded our router, which was called router1. It attempted to load several different files automatically. The first two files have generic network filenames. Then it looks for the host file under two different names. The router attempts to load these configuration files from IP address 255.255.255.255 by default.

Then, when we added the *boot* commands, the router looks for the specified files from the appropriate TFTP server. Again, notice the order in which the router loaded the files, with the network file first followed by the host file:

```
Loading Network-auto from 172.25.1.1 (via Ethernet0): !
[OK - 27/4096 bytes]

Loading Router8-auto from 172.25.1.1 (via Ethernet0): !
[OK - 71/4096 bytes]
```

If you do not configure the router to load specific network or host filenames, it will try to load the default files, shown in the trace above. If these files don't exist, the router will pause for a significant amount of time while it tries to find them. So when you use this feature, you should always include both a network and a host file to load. If you don't need a network file, for example, you can put a file on the server that only contains the keyword "end".

This feature only loads configuration commands into the running configuration. It does not copy them into the startup configuration file.

The *show version* command tells you whether the router was able to load these files successfully:

```
Router1#show version
Cisco Internetwork Operating System Software
IOS (tm) 2500 Software (C2500-IO-L), Version 12.2(7a), RELEASE SOFTWARE (fc2)
Copyright (c) 1986-2002 by cisco Systems, Inc.
Compiled Thu 21-Feb-02 02:07 by pwade
Image text-base: 0x0304CF80, data-base: 0x00001000

ROM: System Bootstrap, Version 5.2(8a), RELEASE SOFTWARE
BOOTLDR: 3000 Bootstrap Software (IGS-RXBOOT), Version 10.2(8a), RELEASE SOFTWAR
E (fc1)

Router1 uptime is 4 minutes
System returned to ROM by reload
System image file is "flash:c2500-io-l.122-7a.bin"
Host configuration file is "tftp://172.25.1.1/Router1-auto"
Network configuration file is "tftp://172.25.1.1/Network-auto"

cisco 2500 (68030) processor (revision D) with 16384K/2048K bytes of memory.
Processor board ID 04915359, with hardware revision 00000000
Bridging software.
X.25 software, Version 3.0.0.
2 Ethernet/IEEE 802.3 interface(s)
2 Serial network interface(s)
32K bytes of nonvolatile configuration memory.
16384K bytes of processor board System flash (Read ONLY)

Configuration register is 0x2102
```

The *service config* option is disabled by default. However, if the router tries to boot but cannot find its startup configuration file, it will automatically enable this option to attempt to find a configuration file through the network:

```
00:00:25: AUTOINSTALL: Ethernet0 is assigned 172.25.1.30
00:00:25: AUTOINSTALL: Obtain siaddr 172.25.1.3 (as config server)
00:00:25: AUTOINSTALL: Obtain default router (opt 3) 172.25.1.3
%Error opening tftp://172.25.1.3/network-confg (No such file or directory)
%Error opening tftp://172.25.1.3/cisconet.cfg (No such file or directory)
%Error opening tftp://172.25.1.3/router-confg (No such file or directory)
%Error opening tftp://172.25.1.3/ciscortr.cfg (No such file or directory)
%Error opening tftp://172.25.1.3/network-confg (No such file or directory)
%Error opening tftp://172.25.1.3/cisconet.cfg (No such file or directory)
```

Two interesting things happen if you reload a router with an empty configuration file. First, the router enables its *autoinstall* option and attempts to acquire an IP address via DHCP. In this example, the router obtained a DHCP address of 172.25.1.30. Second, after it obtains a dynamic address, it attempts to load a configuration file via TFTP.

Notice the filenames that the router cycles through in an attempt to load a configuration file. If there happened to be a file with one of these names in the TFTP directory for some other reason, this router will have downloaded it and used its contents to configure itself, which could have caused serious problems.

See Also

Recipe 1.4; Recipe 1.5

1.4 Storing Configuration Files Larger Than NVRAM

Problem

Your configuration file has become larger than the router's available NVRAM.

Solution

You can compress your router's configuration file before saving it to NVRAM to allow you to save more configuration information. The command service *compress-config* will compress the configuration information when the router saves the file, and uncompress it when it is required:

```
Router1#configure terminal
Enter configuration commands, one per line.  End with CNTL/Z.
Router1(config)#service compress-config
Router1(config)#end
Router1#
```

Discussion

Cisco generally ships its routers with more than enough NVRAM to store an average configuration file. However, there are times when configuration files exceed the available NVRAM. For instance, some routers contain large access-lists that could be hundreds of lines in length. Eventually, some configuration files will grow beyond the finite amount of NVRAM and you will begin to have problems.

The first sign of serious problems with an overly large configuration file is usually when the router refuses to save its configuration because of size. This is a dangerous problem because the router can no longer keep a copy of the whole running-configuration file in its NVRAM storage, and it is difficult to predict how much of your configuration will be lost if you were to reload the router.

Turning on compression roughly doubles the size of the configuration file you can store. You have to put the command *service compress-config* into the configuration

with a configure terminal. Then, for this command to take effect, you need to copy
the running configuration file to NVRAM as follows:

```
Router1#copy running-config startup-config
Destination filename [startup-config]? <enter>
Building configuration...
Compressed configuration from 9664 bytes to 4903 bytes[OK]
Router1#
```

In this case, you can see that the compression reduced the configuration file to less
than half of its original size. This compression algorithm will not attempt to compress a file that is three times larger than the available NVRAM space. Although this
limit exists, we have never seen a router approach a 3-to-1 ratio in practice anyway.

The actual amount of available NVRAM storage varies between different router
models. You can see how much total NVRAM storage is available on a particular
router with the *show version* command:

```
Router1#show version
Cisco Internetwork Operating System Software
IOS (tm) C2600 Software (C2600-IK9O3S-M), Version 12.2(12a), RELEASE SOFTWARE (fc1)
Copyright (c) 1986-2002 by cisco Systems, Inc.
Compiled Tue 24-Sep-02 02:05 by pwade
Image text-base: 0x8000808C, data-base: 0x8127FF40

ROM: System Bootstrap, Version 11.3(2)XA4, RELEASE SOFTWARE (fc1)

Router1 uptime is 12 hours, 15 minutes
System returned to ROM by reload
System restarted at 23:18:45 EST Fri Jan 10 2003
System image file is "flash:c2600-ik9o3s-mz.122-12a.bin"

cisco 2621 (MPC860) processor (revision 0x102) with 45056K/4096K bytes of memory.
Processor board ID JABO4130B2Q (1293133440)
M860 processor: part number 0, mask 49
Bridging software.
X.25 software, Version 3.0.0.
2 FastEthernet/IEEE 802.3 interface(s)
2 Serial network interface(s)
32K bytes of nonvolatile configuration memory.
16384K bytes of processor board System flash (Read/Write)

Configuration register is 0x2102

Router1#
```

This router contains 32 Kb of NVRAM to store configuration files. The top of the
output from the *show startup-config* command shows how much NVRAM storage is
available, and how much this particular configuration file requires. Iif you enable
compression, it will also show the compressed and uncompressed sizes:

```
Router1#show startup-config
Using 5068 out of 29688 bytes, uncompressed size = 9969 bytes
Uncompressed configuration from 5068 bytes to 9969 bytes
```

```
!
! Last configuration change at 12:36:22 EST Sat Jan 11 2003 by ijbrown
! NVRAM config last updated at 13:34:57 EST Sat Jan 11 2003 by ijbrown
!
version 12.2
<removed for brevity>
```

In this case, we have used about 5Kb of the available 29Kb for this router's configuration file. But the show version output said that there was 32Kb of NVRAM in total, which leaves 3Kb unaccounted for. The router's NVRAM used to contain the startup configuration file only, but this is no longer strictly the case. Recent IOS releases also use the same NVRAM space to store information such as private keys for SSH or IPSec, and interface numbers for SNMP. You can see information about all of these files with the *dir nvram:* command:

```
Router1#dir nvram:
Directory of nvram:/

   20  -rw-        5068             <no date>  startup-config
   21  ----        2302             <no date>  private-config
    1  ----           0             <no date>  persistent-data
    2  -rw-         133             <no date>  ifIndex-table

29688 bytes total (20218 bytes free)
Router1#
```

Note that the second column from the left in this output contains file attributes similar to those used by the Unix *ls* command. In this case, both the *startup-config* and *ifIndex-table* files are readable and writeable. For example, you could look at your router's *startup-config* file by using the following command:

```
Router1#more nvram:/startup-config
```

You can view any file that has an "r" and modify any file that has a "w". But the two files in this router's NVRAM that have neither "r" nor "w" can't be displayed, modified, or deleted. Note that the file *ifIndex-table* in particular is in a binary format that isn't very meaningful when you display it with the more command like this.

See Also

Recipe 1.3

1.5   Clearing the Startup Configuration

Problem

You want to clear an old configuration out of your router and return it to a factory default configuration.

Solution

You can delete the current startup configuration files and return the router to its factory default settings with the *erase nvram:* command:

```
Router1#erase nvram:
Erasing the nvram filesystem will remove all files! Continue? [confirm] <enter>
[OK]
Erase of nvram: complete
Router1#reload

System configuration has been modified. Save? [yes/no]: no
Proceed with reload? [confirm] <enter>
```

You can achieve the same result with the erase *startup-config* command:

```
Router1#erase startup-config
Erasing the nvram filesystem will remove all files! Continue? [confirm] <enter>
[OK]
Erase of nvram: complete
Router1#reload
Proceed with reload? [confirm] <enter>
```

Discussion

Before you redeploy an old router that you have previously used for some other purpose, it is a good idea to completely erase the old configuration. This ensures that the router starts with a clean configuration. However, if you did this on a production router, it would wipe out the configuration and leave it with all of its interfaces down. Fortunately, completely deleting your configuration requires two steps: erasing the startup configuration file, followed by a *reload*.

After you erase your startup configuration file and reload the router, it will enter its configuration dialog mode. Most experienced Cisco engineers prefer to skip this mode:

```
--- System Configuration Dialog ---

Would you like to enter the initial configuration dialog? [yes/no]: no

Would you like to terminate autoinstall? [yes]: yes


Press RETURN to get started!
Router>
```

At this point, the router's configuration has been returned to the factory defaults:

```
Router#show running-config
Building configuration...

Current configuration : 431 bytes
!
version 12.2
service timestamps debug uptime
service timestamps log uptime
```

```
no service password-encryption
!
hostname Router
!
!
ip subnet-zero
!
!
!
!
interface Ethernet0
 no ip address
 shutdown
!
interface Ethernet1
 no ip address
 shutdown
!
interface Serial0
 no ip address
 shutdown
!
interface Serial1
 no ip address
 shutdown
!
ip classless
ip http server
ip pim bidir-enable
!
!
line con 0
line aux 0
line vty 0 4
!
end

Router#
```

You can now safely reconfigure the router for its new function. We note in passing that the factory defaults are slightly different, depending on the level of IOS you are running and the hardware installed in the router.

If you accidentally erase the startup configuration file, you can still recover if the router has not yet been reloaded. Simply copy the running configuration back to the startup configuration, and the router will be returned to normal:

```
Router1#show startup-config
startup-config is not present
Router1#copy running-config startup-config
Building configuration...
[OK]
Router1#show startup-config
```

```
version 12.2
service timestamps debug datetime msec
service timestamps log datetime localtime
service password-encryption
!
hostname Router1
<removed for brevity>
```

But, if the router's configuration is erased and the router is reloaded, it will either need to be reconfigured manually from memory, or preferably, from a backup copy, as in Recipe 1.2.

See Also

Recipe 1.2

1.6   Loading a New IOS Image

Problem

You want to upgrade the IOS image that your router uses.

Solution

The *copy tftp* command allows you to use TFTP to download a new IOS version into the router's flash memory:

```
Router1#copy tftp://172.25.1.1/c2600-ik9o3s-mz.122-12a.bin flash:
Destination filename [c2600-ik9o3s-mz.122-12a.bin]? <enter>
Accessing tftp://172.25.1.1/c2600-ik9o3s-mz.122-12a.bin...
Erase flash: before copying? [confirm] <enter>
Erasing the flash filesystem will remove all files! Continue? [confirm] <enter>
Erasing device... eeeeeeeeeeeeeeeeeeeeeeeeeeeeeeeeeeeeeeeeeeeeeeeeeeeeeeeeeeeeeeeeee ...
erased
Erase of flash: complete
Loading c2600-ik9o3s-mz.122-12a.bin from 172.25.1.1 (via FastEthernet0/0.1):
!!!!!!!!!!!!!!!!!!!!!!!!!!!!!!!!!!!!!!!!!!!!!!!!!!!!!!!!!!!!!!!!!!!!!!!!!!!!!!!!!!
!!!!!!!!!!!!!!!!!!!!!!!!!!!!!!!!!!!!!!!!!!!!!!!!!!!!!!!!!!!!!!!!!!!!!!!!!!!!!!!!!!
!!!!!!!!!!!!!!!!!!!!!!!!!!!!!!!!!!!!!!!!!!!!!!!!!!!!!!!!!!!!!!!!!!!!!!!!!!!!!!!!!!
!!!!!!!!!!!!!!!!!!!!!!!!!!!!!!!!!!!!!!!!!!!!!!!!!!!!!!!
[OK - 11135588 bytes]

Verifying checksum... OK (0xE643)
11135588 bytes copied in 82.236 secs (135410 bytes/sec)
Router1# reload
Proceed with reload? [confirm] <enter>
```

Discussion

Sooner or later you will need to upgrade your router's IOS image. Common reasons for upgrading the IOS include new features, bug fixes, and security vulnerabilities.

Before you attempt to upgrade your IOS, you should save a backup copy of your current IOS to your TFTP server, as discussed in Recipe 1.9.

You should always start by analyzing how much free space is available in your router's flash to ensure that there is enough space to load the new IOS image. If there isn't enough, then you may have to erase existing image(s) from flash as we did in our example. And in some cases, you may not have enough flash to load the new image at all. You can use the *show flash* command to see how much flash memory is available:

```
Router1#show flash

System flash directory:
File  Length    Name/status
  1   11135588  c2600-ik9o3s-mz.122-12a.bin
[11135652 bytes used, 5117276 available, 16252928 total]
16384K bytes of processor board System flash (Read/Write)

Router1#
```

Some routers can support additional flash memory in the form of PCMCIA cards. The *show slot0:* and *show slot1:* commands will give you details about these additional storage locations. You can store IOS images on the flash cards, but keep in mind that the router will load the first available IOS image in the router's main flash by default. Recipe 1.7 shows how to boot the router by using IOS images located on flash cards.

Before you can load an IOS image to your router, you must, of course, download the appropriate image from Cisco or purchase it on CD media. You will then need to move the new image into the TFTP directory to ensure that the file is world readable. On Unix systems, you can use the *chmod* command to do this. If the file is not world readable, the TFTP process will not be able to access it, and the IOS upgrade will fail. You should also do some simple sanity checks on the file by confirming the file size is correct and that the checksum or MD5 "fingerprint" match the values provided by Cisco. We note in passing that it would be extremely unwise to use an IOS image that was not created and supported by Cisco.

The router will do several tests while loading a new IOS image to ensure that the process goes smoothly. The first test is to see whether the TFTP server has the specified file:

```
Router1#copy tftp://172.25.1.1/c2600-ik9o3s-mz.122-14.bin flash:
Destination filename [c2600-ik9o3s-mz.122-14.bin]? <enter>
Accessing tftp://172.25.1.1/c2600-ik9o3s-mz.122-14.bin...
%Error opening tftp://172.25.1.1/c2600-ik9o3s-mz.122-14.bin (No such file or
directory)
Router1#
```

Here you can see that the router tried to find the file on the TFTP server before going any further, and discovered that it was not present. If the file exists and the permissions are correct, then the router will continue with the dialogue. If your TFTP server keeps detailed logs of activity, you will see an aborted TFTP file transfer as the router checked to see if the file was available. These aborted attempts are normal and shouldn't cause concern. If the requested file is present but not world-readable, the router will show an error message and abort the upgrade process:

```
Router1#copy tftp://172.25.1.1/c2600-ik9o3s-mz.122-12a.bin flash:
Destination filename [c2600-ik9o3s-mz.122-12a.bin]? <enter>
Accessing tftp://172.25.1.1/c2600-ik9o3s-mz.122-12a.bin...
%Error opening tftp://172.25.1.1/c2600-ik9o3s-mz.122-12a.bin (Permission denied)
Router1#
```

Aborting the upgrade early in the process like this ensures that you don't erase the flash unless there is a suitable replacement image available for download.

In the next step in the download process, you must tell the router whether or not to erase the flash before downloading a new image. If there is enough room available in flash then you can load the new image without erasing the existing image or images. However, if you attempt to download an image and you don't have enough flash space available, then the router will protest and abort the procedure:

```
Router1#copy tftp://172.25.1.1/c2600-ik9o3s-mz.122-12a.bin flash:
Destination filename [c2600-ik9o3s-mz.122-12a.bin]? <enter>
Accessing tftp://172.25.1.1/c2600-ik9o3s-mz.122-12a.bin...
Erase flash: before copying? [confirm]n
Loading c2600-ik9o3s-mz.122-12a.bin from 172.25.1.1 (via FastEthernet0/0.1): !
%Error copying tftp://172.25.1.1/c2600-ik9o3s-mz.122-12a.bin (Not enough space on
device)
Router1#
```

The process of upgrading your router's IOS image is fairly forgiving. The router performs sanity checks throughout the process to ensure that image integrity is maintained. After downloading the image, the router does one final sanity check and verifies the image's checksum. This ensures that the IOS image was not corrupted during transmission. If the image does not pass the verification test, attempt your download again and do not reload the router.

You can manually check to see if the IOS checksum is correct by using the *verify* command. We show how to use the *verify* command in Recipe 1.10.

If the IOS upgrade goes smoothly and the checksum verifies correctly, then it is safe to reboot your router to load the new IOS image. Once the router becomes reachable again, you should verify the new IOS loaded correctly with the *show version* command:

```
Router1#show version
Cisco Internetwork Operating System Software
IOS (tm) C2600 Software (C2600-IK9O3S-M), Version 12.2(12a), RELEASE SOFTWARE (fc1)
Copyright (c) 1986-2002 by cisco Systems, Inc.
Compiled Tue 24-Sep-02 02:05 by pwade
Image text-base: 0x8000808C, data-base: 0x8127FF40

ROM: System Bootstrap, Version 11.3(2)XA4, RELEASE SOFTWARE (fc1)

Router1 uptime is 2 minutes
System returned to ROM by reload
System restarted at 11:53:26 EST Sat Jan 11 2003
System image file is "flash:c2600-ik9o3s-mz.122-12a.bin"
```

```
cisco 2621 (MPC860) processor (revision 0x102) with 45056K/4096K bytes of memory.
Processor board ID JAB04130B2Q (1293133440)
M860 processor: part number 0, mask 49
Bridging software.
X.25 software, Version 3.0.0.
2 FastEthernet/IEEE 802.3 interface(s)
2 Serial network interface(s)
32K bytes of nonvolatile configuration memory.
16384K bytes of processor board System flash (Read/Write)

Configuration register is 0x2102

Router1#
```

In this example, you can see that the router's boot sequence completed successfully correctly and that it's running the new IOS version. Also, notice that the router's new system image file matches the name of the file we just downloaded. This indicates the IOS upgrade was completely successful.

See Also

Recipe 1.7; Recipe 1.9; Recipe 1.10

1.7   Booting a Different IOS Image

Problem

You want to boot using an alternate IOS image.

Solution

To specify which IOS image the router should load next time it reboots, use the boot system command:

```
Router1#configure terminal
Enter configuration commands, one per line.  End with CNTL/Z.
Router1(config)#boot system flash:c3620-jk9o3s-mz.122-7a.bin
Router1(config)#boot system flash:c3620-jos56i-l.120-11.bin
Router1(config)#boot system slot0:c3620-ik9s-mz.122-13.bin
Router1(config)#boot system rom
Router1(config)#end
```

 The sequence of the *boot system* commands is extremely important, as the router will attempt to load the IOS images in the order that they appear in the configuration file.

Discussion

The router can store as many IOS images in its flash memory as there is space to hold. If there is only one file, it can safely assume that this must be the IOS image to

load. However, if the router has several images in its flash storage, you need to specify which one it should load, or the router will simply select one. This is particularly
true on routers that have additional flash memory in the form of PCMCIA cards,
which can hold many files, not all of which are even necessarily IOS images.

With the default configuration register settings, the router will attempt to load the
first accessible IOS image it finds in its flash storage. However, loading the first available image might not be appropriate. For instance, in our last recipe we showed that,
if you have space, you can download a new IOS image without erasing old images. In
this case, you probably want the router to load the newer IOS image. And it would
be better still if the router would try the new image first, and revert to the old image
if the first one failed to load correctly for any reason. The boot system command
allows you to specify not only which IOS images to boot from, but also the order to
try them in if it has trouble booting.

In the example, this router will try a succession of three different IOS images. If they
all fail, it will resort to using its boot ROM image.

As we noted earlier, the sequence of the boot system commands is important since
the router will attempt to load the IOS images in order of entry. This means that the
only way to add a new IOS image to load is to remove all of the old *boot system* commands and reenter them again in the order of preference. You can remove all of the
boot system commands at once with the following command:

```
Router1#configure terminal
Enter configuration commands, one per line.  End with CNTL/Z.
Router1(config)#no boot system
Router1(config)#end
Router1#
```

Once the old *boot system* commands have been removed, you can configure a new
set in whatever order you require.

In addition to allowing you to boot from IOS images in the router's flash storage,
you can also use the the boot system to boot from the IOS image in its ROM storage, or even using the TFTP or Remote Copy (RCP) protocols across the network.
Recipe 1.8 shows an example of booting across the network, using TFTP. Table 1-1
shows all of the different options for the *boot system* command.

Table 1-1. Boot system command target options

Keyword	Description
flash:	On-board flash
slot0:	PCMCIA flash card in slot0
slot1:	PCMCIA flash card in slot1
mop:	Load an image using the MOP protocol
bootflash:	Load bootflash image (not available on all systems)
rom:	Load the image from ROM

Table 1-1. Boot system command target options (continued)

Keyword	Description
rcp:	Load an image using the remote copy protocol
tftp:	Load an image using the TFTP protocol
ftp:	Load an image using the FTP protocol

In addition to the *boot system* commands, you can change which image the router will boot from using the router's configuration register. The last octet in the configuration register must be set to 2, or the router will ignore the boot system commands completely. For instance, if the last octet of the configuration register is set to 1, the router will boot from ROM and ignore the *boot system* commands. In our example, the test router's configuration register was set to 0x2102. The *config-register* command allows you to set the appropriate configuration register values:

```
Router1#configure terminal
Enter configuration commands, one per line.  End with CNTL/Z.
Router1(config)#config-register 0x2102
Router1(config)#end
Router1#
```

It is important to remember that unlike any other configuration command, you don't need to save the running configuration to NVRAM when you change the configuration register setting. It will survive a reload without being saved. In fact, the new setting will not take effect until after the next reload:

```
Router1#show version
Cisco Internetwork Operating System Software
IOS (tm) 3000 Bootstrap Software (IGS-RXBOOT), Version 10.2(8a), RELEASE SOFTWAR
E (fc1)
Copyright (c) 1986-1995 by cisco Systems, Inc.
Compiled Tue 24-Oct-95 15:46 by mkamson
Image text-base: 0x01020000, data-base: 0x00001000

ROM: System Bootstrap, Version 5.2(8a), RELEASE SOFTWARE

Router1 uptime is 2 minutes
System restarted by reload
Running default software

cisco 2500 (68030) processor (revision D) with 16380K/2048K bytes of memory.
Processor board serial number 04915359 with hardware revision 00000000
X.25 software, Version 2.0, NET2, BFE and GOSIP compliant.
2 Ethernet/IEEE 802.3 interfaces.
2 Serial network interfaces.
32K bytes of nonvolatile configuration memory.
16384K bytes of processor board System flash (Read/Write)

Configuration register is 0x2101 (will be 0x2102 at next reload)

Router1#
```

After setting the appropriate *boot system* commands and reloading the router, you can see which image file the router used to boot with the *show version* command:

```
Router2#show version
Cisco Internetwork Operating System Software
IOS (tm) 3600 Software (C3620-IK9S-M), Version 12.2(13), RELEASE SOFTWARE (fc1)
Copyright (c) 1986-2002 by cisco Systems, Inc.
Compiled Tue 19-Nov-02 19:04 by pwade
Image text-base: 0x60008930, data-base: 0x61276000

ROM: System Bootstrap, Version 11.1(19)AA, EARLY DEPLOYMENT RELEASE SOFTWARE (fc1)

Router2 uptime is 2 hours, 4 minutes
System returned to ROM by reload
System restarted at 21:13:13 EST Wed Jan 15 2003
System image file is "slot0:c3620-ik9s-mz.122-13.bin"

cisco 3620 (R4700) processor (revision 0x81) with 41984K/7168K bytes of memory.
Processor board ID 05969532
R4700 CPU at 80Mhz, Implementation 33, Rev 1.0
Bridging software.
X.25 software, Version 3.0.0.
SuperLAT software (copyright 1990 by Meridian Technology Corp).
Basic Rate ISDN software, Version 1.1.
1 Ethernet/IEEE 802.3 interface(s)
1 FastEthernet/IEEE 802.3 interface(s)
1 Serial network interface(s)
1 ISDN Basic Rate interface(s)
DRAM configuration is 32 bits wide with parity disabled.
29K bytes of nonvolatile configuration memory.
16384K bytes of processor board System flash (Read/Write)
16384K bytes of processor board PCMCIA Slot0 flash (Read/Write)
16384K bytes of processor board PCMCIA Slot1 flash (Read/Write)

Configuration register is 0x2102

Router2#
```

In this case, the router says that it loaded its IOS image from slot0:, as configured. After changing your *boot system* commands, you should be sure to reboot and verify that it behaved as expected. You don't want the wrong IOS image to accidentally get loaded the next time the router reboots. If you do have problems with the *boot system* command, connect to the console and reload the router. This will display any error messages as the router boots. The router does not capture these messages anywhere, so this is the only way to see them.

Beginning with IOS Version 12.3(4)T, Cisco introduced the concept of boot markers. Essentially, all *boot system* command lines are now placed between two permanent boot markers located within the configuration file. These markers cannot be erased and make locating the *boot system* commands easy. The following is an example of a router using boot markers:

```
Router1#show running-config | include ^boot
boot-start-marker
```

```
boot system slot0:c3745-ipbasek9-mz.124-6.T.bin
boot system slot0:c3745-ipbasek9-mz.124-7.bin
boot system flash:
boot-end-marker
Router1#
```

Notice that all of the *boot system* commands have been automatically placed between the start boot marker and the end boot marker. The files are also listed in order of boot preference. If you don't configure the router with explicit *boot system* commands, then the router will load the first available IOS image in flash by default. In this case, the boot markers will still appear in the configuration file, but no *boot system* commands will accompany them:

```
Router2#show running-config | include ^boot
boot-start-marker
boot-end-marker
Router2#
```

See Also

Recipe 1.6; Recipe 1.8

1.8   Booting over the Network

Problem

You want to load an IOS image that is too large to store on your router's local flash.

Solution

You can load an IOS image that is larger than your router's flash by configuring the router to first use TFTP to download the image and before booting:

```
Router1#configure terminal
Enter configuration commands, one per line.  End with CNTL/Z.
Router1(config)#boot system tftp c2500-io-l.122-7a.bin 172.25.1.1
Router1(config)#boot system flash
Router1(config)#end
Router1#
```

Discussion

We mentioned in Recipe 1.7 that it is possible to load IOS images over the network at boot time. However, booting from remote IOS images presents some unique challenges. Therefore, we decided to dedicate an entire recipe to remote booting.

One of the most important advantages of booting an IOS image over the network is that it allows you to use images that are larger than your router's flash. Like any other software, each new IOS image tends to be slightly larger than the previous versions. So it is relatively common to discover that you can't load the latest IOS version because it is too big to fit in an older router's flash.

Booting over the network also provides a way of loading a backup IOS image if the primary image fails. As we discussed Recipe 1.7, it's a good idea to configure your router with at least one backup IOS image to load in case the primary fails for any reason. Even if you have a lot of flash storage, you may find that you can't store two IOS images at once. So booting over the network is actually a reasonable way of providing a backup image.

Booting over the network also poses an important security problem because, as we discussed in Recipe 1.2, it is virtually impossible to secure a UDP-based service like TFTP. In addition, it makes the router dependant on the TFTP server for its boot images. Network booting also has performance issues. Loading an IOS over the network can significantly increase the time it takes your router to reload, particularly if it has to traverse slower WAN links. We certainly do not recommend relying solely on remote booting in a production environment.

However, in a lab or testing environment, it can be extremely useful to be able to load an IOS image that is larger than your router's flash. This lets you work with IOS versions that you could not otherwise load and test. The following *show version* command output was taken from a router that was booted in this way:

```
Router1#show version
Cisco Internetwork Operating System Software
IOS (tm) 2500 Software (C2500-IO-L), Version 12.2(7a), RELEASE SOFTWARE (fc2)
Copyright (c) 1986-2002 by cisco Systems, Inc.
Compiled Thu 21-Feb-02 02:07 by pwade
Image text-base: 0x0000144C, data-base: 0x0082E874

ROM: System Bootstrap, Version 5.2(8a), RELEASE SOFTWARE
BOOTLDR: 3000 Bootstrap Software (IGS-RXBOOT), Version 10.2(8a), RELEASE SOFTWARE
(fc1)

Router1 uptime is 10 hours, 16 minutes
System returned to ROM by reload
System restarted at 01:57:47 EST Sat Jan 11 2003
System image file is "tftp://172.25.1.1/c2500-io-l.122-7a.bin"

cisco 2520 (68030) processor (revision E) with 16384K/2048K bytes of memory.
Processor board ID 03870281, with hardware revision 00000002
Bridging software.
X.25 software, Version 3.0.0.
Basic Rate ISDN software, Version 1.1.
1 Ethernet/IEEE 802.3 interface(s)
2 Serial network interface(s)
2 Low-speed serial(sync/async) network interface(s)
1 ISDN Basic Rate interface(s)
32K bytes of nonvolatile configuration memory.
16384K bytes of processor board System flash (Read/Write)

Configuration register is 0x2102

Router1#
```

This shows that the router is running the new version of IOS, which it loaded by using TFTP. In this example, we put the TFTP boot first:

```
Router1(config)#boot system tftp c2500-io-l.122-7a.bin 172.25.1.1
Router1(config)#boot system flash
```

If the TFTP file transfer had failed, the router would have loaded its old IOS image from its local flash. If we had reversed the order of these commands, the router would have tried first to boot from flash, and would have resorted to TFTP if the router had trouble with the file on the flash.

For redundancy purposes, you can configure the router to boot from multiple TFTP servers. Simply copy the same IOS image to an alternate set of TFTP servers and include a *boot system* command per server. This reduces the dependency of the router to a single TFTP server, although the router has to try each successive server and time out before moving on to the next one, which can increase the boot time.

See Also

Recipe 1.2; Recipe 1.7

1.9   Copying an IOS Image to a Server

Problem

You want to save a backup copy of your IOS image on a TFTP server.

Solution

You can upload a copy of your router's IOS image to a TFTP server with the following set of commands:

```
Freebsd% touch /tftpboot/c2600-ik9o3s-mz.122-12a.bin
Freebsd% chmod 666 /tftpboot/c2600-ik9o3s-mz.122-12a.bin
Freebsd% telnet Router1
Trying 172.25.1.5...
Connected to Router1.
Escape character is '^]'.

User Access Verification

Password: <vtypassword>

Router1>enable
Password: <enablepassword>
Router1#copy flash:c2600-ik9o3s-mz.122-12a.bin  tftp
Address or name of remote host []? 172.25.1.1
Destination filename [c2600-ik9o3s-mz.122-12a.bin]? <enter>
```

```
!!!!!!!!!!!!!!!!!!!!!!!!!!!!!!!!!!!!!!!!!!!!!!!!!!!!!!!!!!!!!!!!!!!!!!!!!!!!!!!!!!!!!!!!!
!!!!!!!!!!!!!!!!!!!!!!!!!!!!!!!!!!!!!!!!!!!!!!!!!!!!!!!!!!!!!!!!!!!!!!!!!!!!!!!!!!!!!!!!!!
!!!!!!!!!!!!!!!!!!!!!!!!!!!!!!!!!!!!!!!!!!!!!!!!!!!!!!!!!!!!!!!!!!!!!!!!!!!!!!!!!!!!!!!!!!
!!!!!!!!!!!!!!!!!!!!!!!!!!!!!!!!!!!!!!!!!!!!!!!!!!!!!!!!!!!!!!!!!!!!!!!!!!!!!!!!!!!!!!!!!!
!!!!!!!!!!!!!!!!!!!!!!!!!!!!!!!!!!!!!
11135588 bytes copied in 52.588 secs (211752 bytes/sec)
Router1#
```

Discussion

Before attempting to upgrade the IOS version of a router it's a good idea to save a copy of the current IOS image. This way, if an upgrade fails or if you have problems with the new IOS version, you can revert back to the old proven IOS version. The procedure to copy an IOS image to a TFTP server is very similar to the way we backed up a configuration file in Recipe 1.2. The only real difference is the size of the file involved, since IOS images are quite a bit larger than configuration files.

As we mentioned in Recipe 1.2, you have to watch out for the file permissions on your TFTP server. The transfer will fail if this file isn't world writable. We highly recommend that you remove the world-writable attribute on this file after uploading it. On Unix systems, you can use the *chmod* command to change the file attributes. This will ensure that the file isn't accidentally overwritten. Unlike configuration files, which you should never store in your TFTP directory, IOS images pose no security concerns, as long as they are not world writeable.

See Also

Recipe 1.2; Recipe 1.6

1.10   Copying an IOS Image Through the Console

Problem

You want to load an IOS image into your router through a serial connection to the console or AUX ports.

Solution

You can use the following set of commands to copy an IOS image onto a router through either the console or the AUX port:

```
Router1#copy xmodem: slot1:
                    **** WARNING ****
x/ymodem is a slow transfer protocol limited to the current speed
settings of the auxiliary/console ports. The use of the auxilary
port for this download is strongly recommended.
During the course of the download no exec input/output will be
available.
                    ---- ****** ----
```

```
Proceed? [confirm] <enter>
Destination filename []? c3620-ik9s-mz.122-12a.bin
Erase slot1: before copying? [confirm] <enter>
Use crc block checksumming? [confirm] <enter>
Max Retry Count [10]: <enter>
Perform image validation checks? [confirm] <enter>
Xmodem download using crc checksumming with image validation
Continue? [confirm]  <enter>
Ready to receive file..........CC  <start xmodem file transfer here>
4294967295 bytes copied in 1450.848 secs (1271445669961 bytes/sec)
Router1#
```

 Cisco highly recommends using the AUX port for this procedure rather than the console port because the AUX port supports hardware flow control.

Discussion

It can be quite useful to be able to load an IOS image through a serial connection, particularly if you don't have access to a TFTP server, or if the router doesn't have any accessible LAN interfaces. Although this feature is rarely used, Cisco does support *xmodem* and *ymodem* file transfers through a serial connection.

We also recommend enabling the CRC checksum feature when you use *xmodem* to download an IOS image through a serial connection. This will help ensure the integrity of the file transfer.

We should stress that this process can be extremely slow. Don't even attempt to download an IOS image at the default speed of 9,600 bps unless you have an entire day to kill. We highly recommend increasing the speed to the highest value that your terminal emulation package will support. We have found that 115,200 bps provides the maximum throughput with the most reliability. The *speed* command allows you to change the speed of an asynchronous serial port:

```
Router1#configure terminal
Enter configuration commands, one per line.  End with CNTL/Z.
Router1(config)#line aux 0
Router1(config-line)#speed 115200
Router1(config-line)#end
Router1#
```

In this example, we used *Hyperterminal* because it is included with the Windows operating system. However, almost any terminal emulation program that supports *xmodem* or *ymodem* protocols will work. In fact, we have found significant differences in download times between the various emulation packages, and Hyperterminal tends to be one of the slowest. Other packages such as ProComm tend to be somewhat faster. But they all work.

Even after we increased the speed of the Aux port to 115,200 bps, the file transfer took nearly 25 minutes to complete. By comparison, loading the same IOS version via

TFTP through an Ethernet connection took less than four minutes. So, in general, we don't recommend using this method unless you can't use TFTP for some reason.

The first step, once you have a copy of the IOS image on your computer, is to connect to the router's AUX port. Set the line speed to 115,200 bps on both the console port and the terminal emulator, and issue the *copy* command. The router will prompt you to begin the file transfer with the text "Ready to receive file."

At this point, you should begin your file transfer protocol. If you are using Hyperterminal, select the "Transfer" drop-down menu, and then click on "Send-file." It will prompt you for the file name and location, and protocol type. Enter the name of the IOS image, and then select "Xmodem" to start the file transfer.

During the file transfer, the connection is busy transferring the file, so the router can't display any messages. This is normal. However, most terminal emulator programs provide a status window to let you keep track of the file transfer.

When the transfer is complete, the terminal emulator will drop out of the file transfer mode and the router will put up its normal prompt again. At this point, we highly recommend checking the new IOS image to make sure that it copied successfully. You can verify the file size as follows:

```
Router1#show slot1:

PCMCIA Slot1 flash directory:
File  Length   Name/status
  1   11922512  c3620-ik9s-mz.122-12a.bin
[11922576 bytes used, 4592496 available, 16515072 total]
16384K bytes of processor board PCMCIA Slot1 flash (Read/Write)
```

In this case, we loaded the image into the PCMCIA device in slot 1. If you put the image somewhere else, such as the internal flash memory, you would use the command *show flash:* instead.

If the file size is correct, check the image's checksum by using the *verify* command:

```
Router1#verify slot1:c3620-ik9s-mz.122-12a.bin
Verified slot1:c3620-ik9s-mz.122-12a.bin
Router1#
```

1.11   Deleting Files from Flash

Problem

You want to erase files from your router's flash.

Solution

To delete all of the files from your router's flash memory, use the erase command:

```
Router1#erase slot1:
Erasing the slot1 filesystem will remove all files! Continue? [confirm] <enter>
```

```
Erasing device...
eeeeeeeeeeeeeeeeeeeeeeeeeeeeeeeeeeeeeeeeeeeeeeeeeeeeeeeeeeeeeeeeeeeeeeeeeeeeeeee
eeeeeeeeeeeeeeeeeeeeeeeeeeeeeeeeeeeeeeeeeeeeeee ...erased
Erase of slot1: complete
Router1#
```

    Not all router types support the *erase* command.

You can remove individual files from the router's flash memory with the *delete* command:

```
Router1#delete slot1:c3620-ik9s-mz.122-13.bin
Delete filename [c3620-ik9s-mz.122-13.bin]? <enter>
Delete slot1:c3620-ik9s-mz.122-13.bin? [confirm] <enter>
Router1#
```

Discussion

As we have indicated, there are two ways to delete files from flash, depending on the type of router. The difference arose because Cisco routers use three different kinds of filesystems, called Class A, Class B, and Class C. Table 1-2 shows the filesystems that Cisco's most common routers use.

Table 1-2. Supported filesystems of common Cisco routers

Router type	Filesystem type
7000 (RSP)	Class A
7500 (RSP 2 ,4, and 8)	Class A
12000	Class A
Route Switch Module (RSM)	Class A
1600	Class B
2500	Class B
3600	Class B
4000	Class B
AS5300	Class B
AS5800	Class C
7100	Class C
7200	Class C

Table 1-3 lists some of the different filesystem commands, their meanings, and the filesystems that they work with.

Table 1-3. Filesystem commands and their meanings

Command	Filesystem	Description
Delete	All	Marks the files as deleted, but does not permanently remove them from flash.
Squeeze	A	Permanently removes all files that have been marked as deleted.
Format	A and C	Erases the entire flash device.
Verify	All	Verifies that the IOS file's checksum matches the value encoded in the image.
Undelete	A and B	Recovers deleted files.
Erase	A and B	Erases the entire flash device.

The *erase* command is not available on all router types. On routers that use the Class C filesystem, you can remove files from the flash only with the *delete* command.

The *delete* command marks files as deleted, but does not permanently remove them:

```
Router1#show slot1:

PCMCIA Slot1 flash directory:
File  Length    Name/status
  1   11992088  c3620-ik9s-mz.122-13.bin [deleted]
[16515072 bytes used, 0 available, 16515072 total]
16384K bytes of processor board PCMCIA Slot1 flash (Read/Write)

Router1#
```

You can permanently remove this file and reclaim the space on the flash device with the *squeeze* command. Note, however, that only routers with the type A filesystem support this command:

```
Router1#squeeze slot1:
Squeeze operation may take a while. Continue? [confirm] <enter>
squeeze in progress...
Squeeze of slot1 complete
Router1#
```

The *squeeze* function can take up to several minutes, so be patient. Once the *squeeze* command is complete, you can view the flash device to verify that the file is gone:

```
Router1#show slot1:

PCMCIA Slot1 flash directory:
No files in PCMCIA Slot1 flash
[0 bytes used, 16515072 available, 16515072 total]
16384K bytes of processor board PCMCIA Slot1 flash (Read/Write)

Router1#
```

The file is has now been permanently removed, and you can no longer recover it with the *undelete* command. On routers with filesystems that do not support the *squeeze* command, the only way to permanently remove deleted files is to use the *erase* command. However, the *erase* command deletes the entire flash system and will not permit you to delete individual files. It's all or nothing. In the next recipe, we will look at ways to partition flash devices to reduce the impact of the *erase* command.

See Also

Recipe 1.12

1.12   Partitioning Flash

Problem

You want to change how your router's flash memory is partitioned.

Solution

The *partition* command allows you to create a partition in the router's flash memory:

```
Router1#configure terminal
Enter configuration commands, one per line.  End with CNTL/Z.
Router1(config)#partition slot1: 2 8 8
Router1(config)#end
Router1#
```

Discussion

As we discussed in Recipe 1.11, the *erase* command deletes the entire contents of a flash device. On routers that don't support the *delete* and *squeeze* commands, there is no way to delete an individual file from flash without erasing all of the files in the flash device. Fortunately, you can use the *partition* command on flash devices to shelter some files from the effects of the *erase* command.

After you have partitioned a flash device, the *erase* command only affects one partition at a time. This command doesn't affect any of the other partitions on the same flash device. You can use it to allow you to delete individual files without having to wipe out the entire flash device.

In the next example, we partitioned a flash device into two equal parts. We then stored an IOS image on each of the partitions. You can see the partitions and their contents with the following command:

```
Router1#show slot1:

PCMCIA Slot1 flash directory, partition 1:
File  Length   Name/status
  1   7723664  c3620-ajs56i-mz.120-25.bin
[7723728 bytes used, 664880 available, 8388608 total]
8192K bytes of processor board PCMCIA Slot1 flash (Read/Write)
```

```
PCMCIA Slot1 flash directory, partition 2:
File  Length   Name/status
  1   7723664  c3620-ajs56i-mz.120-25.bin
[7723728 bytes used, 402736 available, 8126464 total]
8192K bytes of processor board PCMCIA Slot1 flash (Read/Write)

Router1#
```

Notice that the router treats the two partitions as if they were separate flash devices. You can erase the contents a particular partition by specifying the flash device name, followed by the partition number and a colon as follows:

```
Router1#erase slot1:2:
Erasing the slot1:2 filesystem will remove all files! Continue? [confirm] <enter>
Erasing device... eeeeeeeeeeeeeeeeeeeeeeeeeeeeeeeeeeeeeeeeeeeeeeeeeeeeeeeeeeeeeeeeee ...
erased
Erase of slot1:2: complete
Router1#
```

Then, if you view the entire flash device again, you can see that the file in partition 2 has been erased, while the contents of partition 1 remain untouched:

```
Router1#show slot1:

PCMCIA Slot1 flash directory, partition 1:
File  Length   Name/status
  1   7723664  c3620-ajs56i-mz.120-25.bin
[7723728 bytes used, 664880 available, 8388608 total]
8192K bytes of processor board PCMCIA Slot1 flash (Read/Write)

PCMCIA Slot1 flash directory, partition 2:
No files in PCMCIA Slot1 flash
[0 bytes used, 8126464 available, 8126464 total]
8192K bytes of processor board PCMCIA Slot1 flash (Read/Write)

Router1#
```

As we mentioned in Recipe 1.11, if you attempt to erase one file from this flash device without partitioning it first, the router will erase both IOS images.

You can remove an existing set of partitions with the *no partition* command:

```
Router1#configure terminal
Enter configuration commands, one per line.  End with CNTL/Z.
Router1(config)#no partition slot1: 2 8 8
ee
Router1(config)#end
Router1#
```

Finally, you can safely partition a flash device that already contains files, as long as you don't attempt to create a partition partway through an existing file. If you do attempt create a partition that partitions an existing file, then the router will identify it as a problem.

See Also

Recipe 1.6; Recipe 1.11

1.13   Using the Router as a TFTP Server

Problem

You want to configure your router to act as a TFTP server.

Solution

The *tftp-server* command configures the router to act as a TFTP server:

```
Router1#configure terminal
Enter configuration commands, one per line.  End with CNTL/Z.
Router1(config)#tftp-server flash:c2600-ik9o3s-mz.122-12a.bin
Router1(config)#end
Router1#
```

Discussion

The ability to use a router as a TFTP server can be quite useful. We have often used this feature to upgrade several routers that are separated from the TFTP server by slow WAN connections. In situations like this, you can upgrade one of the remote routers by using TFTP over the slow WAN connection as we described in Recipe 1.6. Then you can configure the first router to act as a TFTP server, and use it to upgrade the remaining routers over high-speed local links.

The router is not a fully functional TFTP server. It can only serve files for download. You cannot use this feature to upload files into the serving router's local flash. However, the router is not limited to just serving IOS images. You can use your router's flash to store configuration files and make them available for download via TFTP as well. Moreover, you can even use it to hold configuration files for nonCisco equipment.

Security is a concern whenever you enable services on a router. Every extra service you enable provides the wily hacker with a new potential avenue to exploit against your network. Therefore, we certainly don't recommend using the TFTP server feature on routers facing the public Internet or other unfriendly networks. However, for internal use, we believe it is reasonably safe. You can increase the security of the router's TFTP server by using an access-list like this:

```
Router1#configure terminal
Enter configuration commands, one per line.  End with CNTL/Z.
Router1(config)#access-list 99 permit 172.25.1.0 0.0.0.255
Router1(config)#access-list 99 deny any
Router1(config)#tftp-server flash:c2600-ik9o3s-mz.122-12a.bin 99
Router1(config)#end
Router1#
```

In this example, we defined an access-list 99 that will allow all devices on the 172.25.1.0 network to access the router's TFTP server. Then we applied the access-list to the TFTP service by specifying the access-list number at the end of the *tftp-server* command line. This will help to ensure that only the authorized devices permitted by the access-list may download the specified file via TFTP.

You can configure the router to serve multiple files via TFTP by simply adding more *tftp-server* commands. And, if security is a concern, you can configure each file to use its own access-list.

Although this feature can be useful, we recommend enabling it only when you need to do a download, and then disabling the service as soon as the download has completed. This will help to mitigate the security concerns of running extra services from your router.

See Also

Recipe 1.6

1.14 Using FTP from the Router

Problem

You want to use FTP directly from your router to download configuration or IOS files.

Solution

The *copy ftp:* command lets the router exchange files using FTP:

```
Router1#configure terminal
Enter configuration commands, one per line.  End with CNTL/Z.
Router1(config)#ip ftp username ijbrown
Router1(config)#ip ftp password ianpassword
Router1(config)#end
Router1#copy ftp: running-config
Address or name of remote host [172.25.1.1]? 172.25.1.1
Source filename []? test
Destination filename [running-config]? <enter>
Accessing ftp://172.25.1.1/test...
Loading /test
[OK - 24/4096 bytes]

24 bytes copied in 0.276 secs (87 bytes/sec)
Router1#
```

Notice that we explicitly defined a username and password in this example. If you don't specify a username, the router will try to connect to the server's anonymous FTP service.

Discussion

Several recipes in this chapter have shown how to transfer files between your router and server by using TFTP. However, Cisco routers also support FTP. We find that FTP is better suited for transferring files over busy and congested links. While TFTP file transfers tend to abort if they encounter persistent congestion, FTP appears to be more resilient.

FTP is also somewhat more secure than TFTP because it uses usernames and passwords. TFTP has no user-level security features. However, FTP sends its passwords across the network in unencrypted cleartext, so it is still not highly secure.

In the example, we explicitly configured a FTP username and password on the router. Once this information is defined, using FTP is as easy as using TFTP. You can also override the username and password settings defined in the configuration file by including them on the command line:

```
Router1#copy ftp://ijbrown:ianpassword@172.25.1.1/c3620-ik9s-mz.122-10a.bin slot1:
Destination filename [c3620-ik9s-mz.122-10a.bin]? <enter>
Accessing ftp://ijbrown:ianpassword@172.25.1.1/c3620-ik9s-mz.122-10a.bin...
Loading pub/c3620-ik9s-mz.122-10a.bin !!!!
Erase slot1: before copying? [confirm] <enter>
Erasing the slot1 filesystem will remove all files! Continue? [confirm] <enter>
Erasing device... eeeeeeeeeeeeeeeeeeeeeeeeeeeeeeeeee ...erased
Erase of slot1: complete
Loading pub/c3620-ik9s-mz.122-10a.bin
!!!!!!!!!!!!!!!!!!!!!!!!!!!!!!!!!!!!!!!!!!!!!!!!!!!!!!!!!!!!!!!!!!!!!!!!!!!!!!!!!!!!!
!!!!!!!!!!!!!!!!!!!!!!!!!!!!!!!!!!!!!!!!!!!!!!!!!!!!!!!!!!!!!!!!!!!!!!!!!!!!!!!!!!!!!
!!!!!!!!!!!!!!!!!!!!!!!!!!!!!!!!!!!!!!!!!!!!!!!!!!!!!!!!!!!!!!!!!!!!!
[OK - 11819052/4096 bytes]

Verifying checksum...  OK (0x3238)
11819052 bytes copied in 266.956 secs (44273 bytes/sec)
Router1#
```

Notice that we used URL format to specify the username and password as well as the server address and the filename that we wanted to download. The format of the FTP URL looks like this:

ftp://ijbrown:ianpassword@172.25.1.1/c3620-ik9s-mz.122-10a.bin

A colon separates the username, ijbrown, from the password, ianpassword. An @ sign then separates the user information from the server information, which can be either an IP address or a DNS name. Then a forward slash, /, separates the filename from the directory and filename.

If you don't include an FTP username in the configuration or the command line, the router will default to using anonymous FTP. And, if no password is specified in either the router's configuration or on the command line, the router will send a default password of *router@cisco.com*.

It is important to remember that if you specify a username and password on the command line, it will override whatever values you have configured. If you don't specify a username or password on the command line, the router will use the configured FTP username and password. If you don't specify a username and password in either place, the router will resort to anonymous FTP.

See Also

Recipe 1.1; Recipe 1.2; Recipe 1.6; Recipe 1.10

1.15 Generating Large Numbers of Router Configurations

Problem

You need to generate hundreds of router configuration files for a big network rollout.

Solution

When building a large WAN, you will usually configure the remote branch routers similarly, according to a template. This is a good basic design principle, but it also makes it relatively easy to create the router configuration files. The Perl script in Example 1-1 merges a CSV file containing basic router information with a standard template file. It takes the CSV file as input on STDIN.

Example 1-1. create-configs.pl

```perl
#!/usr/local/bin/perl
#
$template_file_name="rtr-template.txt";
while(<>) {

    ($location, $name, $loOip, $frameip, $framedlci, $ethOip, $x)
        = split (/,/);

    open(TFILE, "< $template_file_name") || die "config template file $template_file_name:
$!\n";
    $ofile_name = $name . ".txt";
    open(OFILE, "> $ofile_name") || die "output config file $ofile_name: $!\n";

    while (<TFILE>) {

      s/##location##/$location/;
      s/##rtrname##/$name/;
      s/##eth0-ip##/$ethOip/;
      s/##loop0-ip##/$loOip/;
      s/##frame-ip##/$frameip/;
      s/##frame-DLCI##/$framedlci/;
```

Example 1-1. create-configs.pl (continued)

```
    printf OFILE $_;
    }
}
```

Discussion

This Perl script is a simplified version of much larger scripts that we have used to create the configuration files for some very large networks. We then loaded these configuration files into the routers and shipped them to the remote locations, along with a hard copy of the configuration, in case there were problems during shipment. The technician doing the router installation could then simply connect the appropriate cables and power on the router, and never need to even connect to the router's console unless there were unexpected problems. This methodology can save hundreds of hours in a network installation project.

The script does a relatively simple merge function. It expects the input data in CSV format on STDIN. So if the input file is named RTR-DATA.CSV, you would run the script as follows:

```
Freebsd% create-configs.pl < RTR-DATA.CSV
```

The input file in this case might look something like this:

```
Toronto, Router1, 172.25.15.1, 172.25.16.6, 101, 172.25.100.1,
Boston, Router2, 172.25.15.2, 172.25.16.10, 102, 172.25.101.1,
San Francisco, Router3, 172.25.15.3, 172.25.16.14, 103, 172.25.102.1,
```

Using a CSV file like this is convenient because you can keep track of the entire network in a spreadsheet, and then just create a CSV file containing the data you need for the router configurations.

The template configuration needs to include unique variable names that the script will replace with values from the CSV file. For example, the template configuration file might look like this:

```
!
version 12.1
service timestamps debug datetime msec
service timestamps log datetime msec
service password-encryption
!
hostname ##rtrname##
!
enable password cisco
enable secret cisco
!
interface Loopback0
 ip address ##loop0-ip## 255.255.255.255
!
interface Serial0/0
 description Frame-Relay Circuit
```

```
  no ip address
  encapsulation frame-relay
  ip route-cache policy
  frame-relay lmi-type ansi
  no shutdown
 !
 interface Serial0/0.1 point-to-point
  ip address ##frame-ip## 255.255.255.252
  frame-relay interface-dlci ##frame-DLCI##
 !
 interface FastEthernet0/1
  description User LAN Segment
  ip address ##eth0-ip## 255.255.255.0
  no shutdown
 !
 router eigrp 99
  network 172.25.0.0
 !
 snmp-server location ##location##
 !
 line con 0
  password cisco
  login
  transport input none
 line aux 0
  password cisco
  login
 line vty 0 4
  password cisco
  login
  transport input telnet
 !
 end
```

The script expects to find this template file located in the current directory with the name rtr-template.txt by default, but you can change it easily by modifying the variable called template_file_name.

Naturally, your router templates will not look like this one, and your CSV file will almost certainly contain other data that is important to your network. So we expect that this script will need significant local modification every time you use it on a new network. But the amount of time required to modify the script is usually far less than the amount of time needed to create all of the configuration files by hand.

The output of this script will be a series of files whose names are the same as the router names, but with .txt added to the end. You can then use a terminal emulator to cut and paste the router configuration files into the routers prior to shipping them to their destinations. Always remember to save the configuration to the router's NVRAM before powering it off:

```
Router1#copy running-config startup-config
```

See Also

Recipe 1.16

1.16 Changing the Configurations of Many Routers at Once

Problem

You want to make a configuration change to a large number of routers.

Solution

The *Expect* script in Example 1-2 makes the same configuration changes to a list of routers by using Telnet. When it finishes running, the script produces a status report to identify which devices, if any, failed to update properly. No arguments are required or expected.

Example 1-2. rtrchg.exp

```
#!/usr/local/bin/expect
#
#    rtrcfg.exp -- a script to perform mass configuration changes to
#                  a list of routers using telnet and Expect
#
#
# Set Behavior
set tftp "172.25.1.1"
set workingdir /home/cisco/rtr
#
puts stdout "Enter user name:"
gets stdin userid
system stty -echo
puts stdout "Enter login password:"
gets stdin vtypasswd
puts stdout "\nEnter enable password:"
gets stdin enablepwd
system stty echo
system "cp $workingdir/NEWCONFIG /tftpboot/NEWCONFIG"
set RTR [open "$workingdir/RTR_LIST" r]
set LOG [open "$workingdir/RESULT" w]
while {[gets $RTR router] != -1} {
    if {[ string range $router 0 0 ] != "#"} {
        set timeout 10
        spawn telnet; expect "telnet>"; send "open $router\n"
        expect {
                {Username}    { send "$userid\r"
                            expect {
                                    {*Password*} { send "$vtypasswd\r" }
                            }
```

Example 1-2. rtrchg.exp (continued)

```
                          }
            {Password}    { send "$vtypasswd\r" }
            timeout       { puts $LOG "$router - telnet failed"
                            close; wait; continue
                          }
        }

    expect {
            {Password}    { puts $LOG "$router - vty login failed"
                            close; wait; continue
                          }

            {Username}    { puts $LOG "$router - vty login failed"
                            close; wait; continue
                          }

            {>}           { puts $LOG "$router - vty login ok" }

            timeout       { puts $LOG "$router - vty login failed"
                            close; wait; continue
                          }
        }

    send "enable\r"
    expect "Password"
    send "$enablepwd\r"
    #
    expect {
            {*#}          { puts $LOG "$router - enable login ok" }

            {*>}          { puts $LOG "$router - enable login failed"
                            close; wait; continue
                          }

            timeout       { puts $LOG "$router - enable login failed"
                            close; wait; continue
                          }
        }
    # CMDs
    set timeout 30
    send "copy tftp://$tftp/NEWCONFIG running-config\r"
    expect "running-config"
    send "\r"
    expect {
            {OK}          { puts $LOG "$router - TFTP successful"}
            timeout       { puts $LOG "$router - TFTP failed"
                            close; wait; continue }
        }
    send "copy running-config startup-config\r\r\r"
    expect {
            {OK}          { puts $LOG "$router - config saved"}
            timeout       { puts $LOG "$router - config failed"
                            close; wait; continue }
        }
```

Example 1-2. rtrchg.exp (continued)

```
    #CMDs
    send "exit\r"; close; wait
    }
}
close $RTR; close $LOG
system "rm /tftpboot/NEWCONFIG"
```

Discussion

This script uses the *Expect* language to emulate how a performing human router engineer would do a series of configuration updates via TFTP. The script logs into each router in a list and uses TFTP to download a set of configuration changes into the router's running configuration. It then saves the new configuration file to NVRAM to make sure that it will survive any power failures, and moves on to the next router in the list. Automating a routine but time-consuming procedure with a script like this saves time and decreases the chances of fatigue-induced errors.

The script is designed to work with either normal router passwords or AAA-enabled username and password combinations, which we describe in Chapter 3. The script begins by asking you to supply a username. If one or more of your routers aren't configured to use AAA or local authentication, the script will simply ignore this username and insert the password instead.

After asking for the username, the script will prompt you to enter a login password that will either be your VTY password or AAA password. Then the script will ask for the enable password, and it will then begin to perform its task.

> The script is designed to work with IOS Versions 12.0 and greater. Unfortunately, Cisco changed the command sequence prior to 12.0, meaning the script will not work correctly with old IOS versions.

You must change two variables in this script for it to work in your network. The first variable is called `tftp`. You must set this value to your TFTP server's IP address. The second variable you need to change is `workingdir`, which must contain the name of the directory that holds the list of routers, the file of configuration changes, and the location where the script will put its report.

The script is written in the Expect language and requires Expect to be loaded on your server and available in the `/usr/local/bin` directory. For more information on the Expect language, please see Appendix A or *Exploring Expect* by Don Libes (O'Reilly).

The script expects to find two special files in the working directory. The first is called `RTR_LIST`, and contains a list of router names, with one name on each line. The second file is called `NEWCONFIG`, which contains all required configuration changes. We also recommend you put the configuration command *end* on that the last line of the NEWCONFIG file to avoid the error messages that we mentioned in Recipe 1.1.

Here is a typical example of the sort of things you might put in the configuration file:

```
Freebsd% cat NEWCONFIG
enable secret cisco
end
```

Using this file, the script will log into all routers and change the *enable secret* password. You could put any number of commands in this configuration file, but naturally the script will download the exact same set of configuration commands into every router, so you should never change anything that is unique to a particular router, such as an IP address, this way. This method is perfect for changing things like passwords, SNMP community strings, and access-lists, which can be the same on all routers.

The script will copy the NEWCONFIG file into the /tftpboot directory so it can then use TFTP to transfer it to each of the routers. It is a good idea to ensure that your server's TFTP is working correctly before launching the script.

When the script finishes, it will create a status file called RESULT in the working directory. This status file will contain detailed status reports of what happened on each router. The easiest way to see a list of the routers that the script failed to change is to use the Unix *grep* command to search for the keyword "fail", as follows:

```
Freebsd% grep fail RESULT
toronto - enable login failed
boston  - telnet failed
test    - enable login failed
frame   - enable login failed
```

See Also

Recipe 1.1; Appendix A; *Exploring Expect* by Don Libes (O'Reilly)

1.17 Extracting Hardware Inventory Information

Problem

You need an up-to-date list of the hardware configurations and IOS levels of all of your routers.

Solution

The *Bourne Shell* script in Example 1-3 uses *SNMP* to extract useful version information from a list of routers. By default, the script will store this data in CSV format so you can easily import it into a spreadsheet for analysis. No arguments are required or expected.

Example 1-3. inventory.sh

```
#!/bin/sh
#
#     inventory.sh -- a script to extract valuable information
#                     from a list of routers. (Name, Type, IOS version)
#
#
# Set behaviour
public="ORARO"
workingdir="/home/cisco"
#
LOG=$workingdir/RESULT.csv
infile=$workingdir/RTR_LIST
snmp="/usr/local/bin/snmpget -v1 -c $public"
#
while read device
do
  $snmp $device sysName.0 > /dev/null
  if [ "$?" = "0" ] ; then
    rtr=`$snmp $device .1.3.6.1.4.1.9.2.1.3.0 | cut -f2 -d\" `
    type2=`$snmp $device .1.3.6.1.4.1.9.9.25.1.1.1.2.3 | cut -f2 -d$ `
    ios=`$snmp $device .1.3.6.1.4.1.9.9.25.1.1.1.2.5 | cut -f2 -d$ `
    prot=`$snmp $device .1.3.6.1.4.1.9.9.25.1.1.1.2.4 | cut -f2 -d$ `
    echo "$device, $rtr, $type2, $ios, $prot" >> $LOG
  fi
done < $infile
```

Discussion

The *inventory.sh* script extracts hardware and IOS version information directly from the routers using SNMP. This ensures that the data is up to date. You can even automate this script so it runs periodically to make sure that your inventory information is always accurate. In a large network, this is much easier than keeping track of this information manually.

By default, the script captures the device name, router type, IOS version, and IOS feature set from each router. It stores this information gathered in a CSV format file called RESULT.csv.

This script requires *NET-SNMP* to gather the information via SNMP. You could use a different SNMP package if you prefer, but then you will need to modify the syntax appropriately. The script expects to find the executable *snmpget* in the directory /usr/local/bin. Again, if you keep this file in a different location, you will need to define the correct location in the variable snmp. For more information on NET-SNMP, see Chapter 17 or Appendix A.

Before running this script in your network, you will need to modify two variables. The first is the variable called public. This value must contain your read-only SNMP *community string*. The script assumes that you have the same community string on all of the routers in the list. The second variable that you will need to set is workingdir, which must contain the name of the directory that you wish to run the script from.

Finally, you will need to build a file called RTR_LIST that contains the names of all of your routers, with one name on each line. The script expects to find this file in the working directory.

The output of the script is a CSV file, which you can import into a spreadsheet to analyze and sort the results as required. Table 1-4 shows an example of the script's output as it might look in a spreadsheet.

Table 1-4. Output results from the inventory.sh script

Router	Router name	Type	IOS version	IOS feature set
Toronto	toronto	C2500	12.2(1d)	ENTERPRISE|FIREWALL PLUS IPSEC 56
Boston	boston	C2600	12.4(10)	IP|VOICE
Newyork	newyork	C2600	12.2(31)	ENTERPRISE PLUS
Tampa	tampa	C2600	12.4(10)	IP|VOICE
Sanfran	sanfran	C2500	12.3(16)	IP PLUS

See Also

Chapter 17; Appendix A

1.18 Backing Up Router Configurations

Problem

You need to download all of the active router configurations to see what has changed recently.

Solution

The Perl script in Example 1-4 automatically retrieves and stores router configuration files on a nightly basis. By default, it retains these configuration files for 30 days. The script should be run through the Unix *cron* utility to get the automatic nightly updates, but you can also run it manually if required. No arguments are required or expected.

Example 1-4. backup.pl

```
#!/usr/local/bin/perl
#
#       backup.pl -- a script to automatically backup a list of
#                    router configuraton files on a nightly basis.
#
#
```

Example 1-4. backup.pl (continued)

```perl
# Set behavior
$workingdir="/home/cisco/bkup";
$snmprw="ORARW";
$ipaddress="172.25.1.1";
$days="30";
#
#
$rtrlist="$workingdir/RTR_LIST";
$storage="$workingdir/storage";
$latest="$storage/LATEST";
$prev="$storage/PREV";
if (! -d $storage) {mkdir ($storage, 0755)};
if (! -d $prev) {mkdir ($prev, 0755)};
if (! -d $latest) {mkdir ($latest, 0755)};
($sec, $min, $hr, $mday, $mon, $year, @etc) = localtime(time);
$mon++; $year=$year+1900;
$today1=sprintf("%.4d_%.2d_%.2d", $year, $mon, $mday);
$today="$storage/$today1";
system("cp -p $latest/* $prev/");
unlink <$latest/*>;
mkdir ($today, 0755);

open (RTR, "$rtrlist") || die "Can't open $rtrlist file";
open (LOG, ">$workingdir/RESULT") || die "Can't open $workingdir/RESULT file";
print LOG "Router Configuration Backup Report for $year/$mon/$mday\n";
print LOG "======================================================\n";
print LOG "Device Name                           Status\n";
print LOG "======================================================\n";
while (<RTR>) {
  chomp($rtr="$_");
  $oid=".1.3.6.1.4.1.9.2.1.55.$ipaddress";
  $snmpset ="/usr/local/bin/snmpset -v1 -c $snmprw -t60 -r2 $rtr";
  $rtrfile="/tftpboot/$rtr.cfg";
  unlink $rtrfile;
  open (CFG, ">$rtrfile"); print CFG " ";close CFG;
  chmod 0666, $rtrfile;
  chop ($status=`$snmpset $oid s $rtr.cfg`);
  $status=~/.+ = "(.+)".*$/;
  if($1 eq "$rtr.cfg") {
     if( -z "$rtrfile" ) {
        $result="not ok (File empty)";
        unlink $rtrfile;
     }
     else {
        $result="ok";
        chmod 0444, $rtrfile;
        system("mv $rtrfile $latest");
     }
  }
  else {
     $result="not ok";
     unlink $rtrfile;
```

Example 1-4. backup.pl (continued)

```
    }

printf LOG ("%-28s        %-28s\n", $rtr,$result);


}
system ("cp -p $latest/*cfg $today");
$time=$days*86400;
print "$time\n";
($sec, $min, $hr, $mday, $mon, $year, @etc) = localtime(time-$time);
$mon++; $year=$year+1900;
$rmdir=sprintf("%s/%.4d_%.2d_%.2d",$configs, $year, $mon, $mday);
system ("rm -r -f $storage/$rmdir");
```

Discussion

As we mentioned earlier in the chapter, it is extremely important to make regular backup copies of your router configuration files. However, as the size of your network grows, it becomes quite tedious to maintain a useful archive of these backups. This script automates the task of collecting and storing router configuration files on a Unix-based TFTP server.

This script will maintain 30 days worth of configuration files. We have found that this is a reasonable length of time, allowing engineers to recover router configuration files that are up to one month old. However, if you prefer, you can change the $days variable to increase or decrease how long the script will store these files before deleting them. If you increase the length of time that the server must store these files, it will obviously increase the amount of disk space you need to hold the extra configuration files. But router configuration files are generally quite small, so this is usually not a serious problem unless you support thousands of routers.

Before executing this script, you will need to modify a few variables. First, the $workingdir variable should contain the name of the directory that the server will run the script in. Then the $snmprw variable must contain your SNMP read-write community string. Please note that the read-only community string will not allow you to copy a configuration file—it must be the read-write string. The other variable you need to change is $ipaddress, which should contain the IP address of your TFTP server.

The script is written in Perl, and it makes a few system calls out to Bourne Shell commands. The script expects to find the Perl executable in the /usr/local/bin directory. The script is also dependent on NET-SNMP, and it expects to find the executable *snmpset* in the /usr/local/bin directory as well. If these files are in different locations on your local system, you will need to modify these paths. For more information on Perl or NET-SNMP, please see Appendix A.

Finally, you will need a file called RTR_LIST that contains the list of router names. This file must be in the working directory.

As we mentioned earlier, you should run this backup script should from the Unix *cron* utility on a nightly basis. This will ensure that you have an up-to-date backup of your configuration files. We recommend launching this script during off hours, since it does generate traffic across your network, as well as a small amount of CPU loading on the routers, although neither of these should be large. Here is an example *crontab* entry to start the script every night at 1:30AM.

```
30 1 * * * /home/cisco/bkup/backup.pl
```

When the script runs, it will create a new directory, called storage, under the working directory. Under this directory, the script will create several subdirectories, including LATEST, PREV, and dated directory names, such as 2003_01_28. The directory LATEST will always contain the most up-to-date router configuration files. And you can find the previous stored version of each router's configuration in the directory called PREV. The dated directories will contain all of the router configuration files that were captured on the date indicated in the directory name.

You can use the Unix *diff* command to see what changes have occurred on a given router.

Finally, the script will create a nightly status report that it stores in a file called RESULT in the working directory:

```
Freebsd% cat RESULT
Router Configuration Backup Report for 2003/1/28
=========================================================
Device Name                     Status
=========================================================
toronto                         ok
boston                          not ok
test                            ok
frame                           ok
```

With slight modification, you can configure the script to email this report to the responsible engineer. However, since each different Unix flavor uses a different mail program, we chose not to include it here in the interest of compatibility. On a Solaris server, for example, you could add the following line to the bottom of the script to mail this report:

```
system ("/usr/ucb/mail -s \"Config Report for $today1\" `/bin/cat $mail` <
$workingdir/RESULT");
```

In this case, you would need to define the variable $mail to be email distribution list for the report. For other Unix or Linux variants, please consult you man pages for more information on your local mail program.

See Also

Recipe 1.2; Appendix A

1.19 Warm Reload

Problem

You want to reload the router with minimal service interruption.

Solution

To enable warm reload, use the *warm-reboot* command:

```
Router1#configure terminal
Enter configuration commands, one per line.  End with CNTL/Z.
Router1(config)#warm-reboot
Router1(config)#end
Router1#
```

 After enabling this feature, you must perform a cold reboot before it will take effect.

Discussion

Beginning with IOS Version 12.3(2)T, Cisco introduced the ability to perform a warm reload of the router. The primary benefit of this feature is increased system availability, since the router is able to load the IOS version directly from memory without the need to copy the image from flash to RAM or wait for decompression of the IOS image. In addition, the router is able to reload without ROM monitor mode (ROMMON) intervention. This allows the router to complete its reload significantly quicker than a normal cold reload. For example, a cold reboot took more than four minutes longer than a warm reboot on our test router.

Although this feature requires addition memory to be consumed, its impact is minimized by the compressing of initialized variables store in RAM. To prevent corruption of the initial variables, they are marked "read-only."

This feature not only allows you to perform manual warm reloads, but also allows the router to recover from software forced crashes. Since software forced crashes are unplanned outages, the ability to recover quickly is quite useful. By default, the router will allow five warm reboots due to software forced crashes before forcing the router to perform a cold reboot. In addition, by default the router must remain up and active for a minimum of five minutes before the next warm reboot is allowed due to software forced error. If a software forced error is experienced before the five minute period elapses then the router will perform a cold reboot.

The number of permitted warm reboots and the time duration are adjustable, as seen in the example:

```
Router1#configure terminal
Enter configuration commands, one per line.  End with CNTL/Z.
```

```
Router1(config)#warm-reboot count 4 uptime 6
Warm reboot will be possible after the next cold reboot
Router1(config)#end
Router1#
```

In this example, we've modified the router to allow only four warm reboots before performing a cold reboot. Also notice, we've configured the router to wait at least six minutes before allowing another reboot due to software forced error.

To view the configuration status of the warm reboot feature, use the *show warm-reboot* command:

```
Router1#show warm-reboot
Warm Reboot is enabled
Maximum warm reboot count is 4
Uptime after which warm reboot is safe in case of a crash is 6 (min)

Statistics:

0 warm reboots due to crashes and 1 warm reboots due to requests have taken
place since the last cold reboot
2872 KB taken up by warm reboot storage
Router1#
```

The output of this command shows that the warm-reboot feature is enabled on this router and that no warm reloads have taken place due to software forced crashes. Also notice that 2,872 KB of memory is used by this feature to store the initialized variables.

To perform a manual warm reboot of the router use the *warm* keyword when issuing a reload. If you don't include the *warm* keyword, then a normal cold reboot will take place:

```
Router1#reload warm
Proceed with reload? [confirm] <enter>
Connection closed by foreign host.
Freebsd%
```

See Also

Recipe 1.20

1.20 Warm Upgrade

Problem

You want to upgrade the router IOS version with minimal service interruption.

Solution

To perform a warm IOS upgrade, use the following commands:

```
Router1#configure terminal
Enter configuration commands, one per line.  End with CNTL/Z.
Router1(config)#warm-reboot
Router1(config)#end
Router1#reload warm file slot0:c3745-ipbasek9-mz.124-7.bin
```

 In order to perform a warm IOS upgrade, you must enable the warm reboot feature. For more information regarding the warm reboot feature, please see the previous recipe.

Discussion

Beginning with IOS Version 12.3(11)T, Cisco introduced the ability to perform warm IOS upgrades. The warm IOS upgrade feature allows the router to load a new IOS version into memory and decompress it before transferring control to the new image. Since the router continues to operate normally while the new image is loaded and decompressed, it greatly reduces service interruption.

 The warm upgrade also can be used to downgrade an IOS version.

Before you can use the warm IOS upgrade feature, you must first enable the warm reboot feature and perform a cold reboot. For more information on enabling the warm reboot feature, please see the previous recipe, Recipe 1.19.

Once you've enable the warm reboot feature, you can perform a warm IOS upgrade by using the *reload warm file* command. Note that the command can load the new IOS image from a variety of locations including flash, slot0, slot1, a TFTP server, and so on:

```
Router1#reload warm file slot0:c3745-ipbasek9-mz.124-7.bin
Proceed with reload? [confirm] <enter>
Decompressing the image :
##################################################################################
################################################################# [OK]
<Removed for brevity>
```

Once you issue the warm upgrade command and confirm it, the router will begin to load the image and decompress it. Once the image is loaded into memory, the router will transfer control to the new image. The overall down time is minimized.

If there isn't sufficient memory to load and decompress the new IOS image, then the warm IOS upgrade will terminate. In the next example, we attempt to upgrade to a very large image:

```
Router1#reload warm file slot0:c3745-entservicesk9-mz.124-8a.bin
Proceed with reload? [confirm] <enter>
Router1#
```

```
Sep  2 21:58:40.135 EDT: %SYS-2-NOMEMORY: No memory available for warm upgrade
58197272
Router1
```

Notice that router aborted the upgrade and created a log message.

We note in passing that it is possible to downgrade the router to an IOS version that does not support the warm upgrade feature. However, it is not possible to upgrade to a new IOS image if the current IOS version does not support the warm upgrade feature.

See Also

Recipe 1.19; Recipe 1.6

1.21 Configuration Archiving

Problem

You want to automatically maintain an archive of router configuration files.

Solution

To create an archive of old configuration files, use the following set of commands:

```
Router1#configure terminal
Enter configuration commands, one per line.  End with CNTL/Z.
Router1(config)#archive
Router1(config-archive)#path slot0:/configs/$h
Router1(config-archive)#write-memory
Router1(config-archive)#time-period 1440
Router1(config-archive)#end
Router1#
```

Discussion

Starting with IOS Version 12.3(4)T, Cisco introduced the ability to archive IOS configuration files. Once the feature is enabled, the router's configuration is stored in the archive each time you issue a *write memory* or *copy running-config startup-config*. In our example, we chose to save the archive configuration files on the flash card in slot0; however, you can also store the configuration files remotely using such protocols as TFTP.

Before the router can store the files in the location we've configured, we first need to create the directory configs. You don't need to store the archive files within a directory, but it's a good idea to keep the archive files together and away from other files such as IOS images. To create a directory in flash, use the *mkdir* command:

```
Router1#cd slot0:
Router1#mkdir configs
Create directory filename [configs]? <enter>
Created dir slot0:/configs
Router1#
```

Once the directory is created, the router will begin to automatically store its router configuration files each time you save the configuration file to NVRAM. In addition, you will notice that we configured a periodic archive every 1,440 minutes, or once a day. This is purely optional, but is a nice feature to enable—especially if you're saving the router configuration files to a remote server.

To view the archive configuration, use the *show archive* command:

```
Router1#show archive
There are currently 5 archive configurations saved.
The next archive file will be named slot0:/configs/Router1-5
 Archive #  Name
    0
    1        slot0:/configs/Router1-1
    2        slot0:/configs/Router1-2
    3        slot0:/configs/Router1-3
    4        slot0:/configs/Router1-4 <- Most Recent
    5
    6
    7
    8
    9
   10
   11
   12
   13
   14
Router1#
```

Notice that we already have five archived configurations saved. Also notice the name of each file begins with the hostname and has a suffix of "-" and a number. If you recall, we configured the path to include "$h", which automatically uses the hostname to name the archive files. You can choose to explicitly name the archive files yourself but this provides a nice easy way to name the files, especially if you're configuring a group or routers at once using a script. You can also choose to include a date/time stamp in the filename as well by including the "$t" variable in the filename:

```
Router1(config-archive)#path slot0:/configs/$h$t
```

The file numbering is automatically tagged on to the end of each filename to ensure uniqueness and allow you to determine the order of creation. By default, 14 archive files are stored; however, you can adjust the number of archive files by using the *maximum* command:

```
Router1#configure terminal
Enter configuration commands, one per line.  End with CNTL/Z.
Router1(config)#archive
Router1(config-archive)#maximum 10
Router1(config-archive)#end
Router1#
```

The router automatically overwrites the oldest archive once the maximum number of archives is reached to ensure you always have the more recent archive files available.

Another useful feature of maintaining a configuration files archive is the ability to view the differences between archive files and the ability to perform a configuration rollback. For instance, to view the configuration differences between the current running configuration and a particular archive file, use the following command:

```
Router1#show archive config differences slot0:/configs/Router1-1
Contextual Config Diffs:
+ip cef
-no ip cef

Router1#
```

In this simple example, the only difference is that we've disabled *ip cef*. Notice that commands added to the configuration file are marked with a "+" sign and commands removed from the file are marked with a "-" sign.

Say you wish to resort back to a previous configuration archive file. We recommend that you first store the current running configuration file by using the *archive config* EXEC command, and then issue the *configure replace* command. In the next example we chose to roll back the configuration to the archive file named "Router1-1":

```
Router1#archive config
Router1#configure replace slot0:/configs/Router1-1
This will apply all necessary additions and deletions
to replace the current running configuration with the
contents of the specified configuration file, which is
assumed to be a complete configuration, not a partial
configuration. Enter Y if you are sure you want to proceed. ? [no]: y
Total number of passes: 1
Rollback Done

Router1#
```

This is a nice feature, since it provides an elegent method of rolling back the configuration file in case you make a mistake or a new feature didn't work as planned.

See Also

Recipe 1.18

1.22 Locking Configuration Access

Problem

You want to prevent multiple concurrent users from making configuration changes at the same time.

Solution

To automatically prevent other users from making configuration changes at the same time as you, use the following command:

```
Router1#configure terminal
Enter configuration commands, one per line.  End with CNTL/Z.
Router1(config)#configuration mode exclusive auto
Router1(config)#end
Router1#
```

To enable the ability to lock the configuration file, on an as-needed basis, use the following command:

```
Router1#configure terminal
Enter configuration commands, one per line.  End with CNTL/Z.
Router1(config)#configuration mode exclusive manual
Router1(config)#end
Router1#
```

 This feature was introduced in IOS Version 12.3(14)T.

Discussion

By default, the router running IOS software allows multiple concurrent users to change the running configuration files at once. In some operating environments, preventing multiple concurrent users from making changes is beneficial. Being able to prevent two users attempting to modify the same portion of the configuration file is desired. By enabling this feature, you temporarily prevent multiple users from modifying the router configuration at the same time.

Essentially, this feature allows only a single user to enter the configuration mode at a time. All other users on the router are effectively locked out of the configuration mode until the first user exits it. As we've seen in our examples, this feature runs in two modes, auto and manual. In auto mode, the configuration mode is automatically locked each time a user enters the configuration mode. In manual mode, users have the ability to manually lock the configuration mode each time they change the router configuration by using the *lock* keyword:

```
Router1#configure terminal lock
Enter configuration commands, one per line.  End with CNTL/Z.
Router1(config)#
```

If you don't issue the *lock* keyword, then the router will not lock the configuration mode and the router will function as normal. In auto mode, you don't need to issue the *lock* keyword, since it is implicitly enabled.

If you attempt to enter the configuration mode and someone has already locked it, then you will receive the following message informing you that the configuration mode is locked and by whom:

```
Router1#configure terminal
Configuration mode locked exclusively by user 'ijbrown' process '31' from terminal
'162'. Please try later.
Router1#
```

You can always show the status of the configuration lock by issuing the following command:

```
Router1#show configuration lock
Parser Configure Lock
---------------------
Owner PID        : 31
User             : ijbrown
TTY              : 162
Type             : EXCLUSIVE
State            : LOCKED
Class            : EXPOSED
Count            : 1
Pending Requests : 0
User debug info  : configure terminal lock
Router1#
```

If you absolutely need to change the router configuration and someone has locked you out, then you always have the option of terminating his or her session. Notice that user ijbrown has currently locked the configuration mode, and he is using TTY 162. In the next example, we will clear the TTY session and view the status of the configuration lock:

```
Router1#clear line 162
[confirm] <enter>
 [OK]
Router1#show configuration lock
Parser Configure Lock
---------------------
Owner PID        : -1
User             : unknown
TTY              : -1
Type             : NO LOCK
State            : FREE
Class            : unknown
Count            : 0
Pending Requests : 0
User debug info  :
Router1#
```

Notice that once we clear the user's session, the lock is removed and we are then free to make configuration changes. In addition, once someone does lock the configuration mode, a system message is sent to inform all other users:

```
Sep  2 22:39:03.304 EDT:  Configuration mode locked exclusively. The lock will be
cleared once you exit out of configuration mode using end/exit
```

## CHAPTER 2

Router Management

2.0 Introduction

This chapter, like the previous one, looks at system management issues on the router. But unlike the previous chapter, which looked primarily at general system administration issues such as filesystem management, here we will talk about how to manage and tune issues related to router performance, as well as deal with disaster scenarios such as creating exception dumps.

Cisco's IOS supports a variety of special-purpose protocols and services. Some of them are useful for network management and administration, while others are more useful for testing purposes. One of the most useful of these features is the *Cisco Discovery Protocol* (CDP), which allows you to see useful information about the Layer 2 connections between Cisco devices. This chapter shows how to use CDP, but it also discusses some of the well known security problems with the protocol. It is best to simply disable this service.

Disabling is often the best strategy for several of the other services. Some, like the HTTP management interface and the various test protocols lumped together under the title of the TCP and UDP *small servers*, serve no real purpose in most production networks, so they are disabled by default. But others, like DNS, do have useful functions, and are enabled by default.

We will discuss several important administrative features, such as different methods for handling the hostnames of other network devices and command aliases that make complex commands easier to remember and type. The chapter concludes with a set of four useful scripts for gathering important information from your network devices.

2.1 Creating Command Aliases

Problem

You want to create aliases for commonly used or complex commands.

Solution

You can create command aliases on your router with the *alias* command:

```
Router1#configure terminal
Enter configuration commands, one per line.  End with CNTL/Z.
Router1(config)#alias exec rt show ip route
Router1(config)#alias exec on show ip ospf neighbor
Router1(config)#end
Router1#
```

Discussion

Unix system administrators have been using command aliases for many years to help reduce typing and save time. These shortcut commands allow you to reduce long or complex command sequences to a few simple characters. This is most useful for extremely common commands, and for commands that are complex or difficult to remember. You can create an alias for any command, including some or all of its associated keywords or variables.

Here we have created the alias, rt, for one of the most common commands we use everyday, *show ip route*:

```
Router1(config)#alias exec rt show ip route
```

We can now use this simple two-letter command to display the routing table, saving time and typing:

```
Router1#rt
Codes: C - connected, S - static, I - IGRP, R - RIP, M - mobile, B - BGP
       D - EIGRP, EX - EIGRP external, O - OSPF, IA - OSPF inter area
       N1 - OSPF NSSA external type 1, N2 - OSPF NSSA external type 2
       E1 - OSPF external type 1, E2 - OSPF external type 2, E - EGP
       i - IS-IS, L1 - IS-IS level-1, L2 - IS-IS level-2, ia - IS-IS inter area
       * - candidate default, U - per-user static route, o - ODR
       P - periodic downloaded static route

Gateway of last resort is 172.25.1.1 to network 0.0.0.0

S    192.168.10.0/24 [1/0] via 172.22.1.4
     172.16.0.0/24 is subnetted, 1 subnets
C       172.16.2.0 is directly connected, FastEthernet0/0.2
     172.20.0.0/16 is variably subnetted, 3 subnets, 3 masks
O       172.20.10.0/24 [110/74] via 172.20.1.2, 00:52:55, Serial0/0.2
C       172.20.1.0/30 is directly connected, Serial0/0.2
O       172.20.100.1/32 [110/65] via 172.20.1.2, 00:52:55, Serial0/0.2
     172.22.0.0/16 is variably subnetted, 2 subnets, 2 masks
D       172.22.0.0/16 is a summary, 20:31:03, Null0
C       172.22.1.0/24 is directly connected, FastEthernet0/1
Router1#
```

The key to choosing a good alias command name is to pick something that is short and easy to remember. Of course, it is critical to select an alias that does not conflict with an existing command. In our example, we choose rt as a short, easy-to-remember mnemonic for "Route Table" that didn't conflict with any existing IOS command.

You can also use a command alias as part of a longer command. For example, we could use our rt alias to shorten the command *show ip route 172.16.2.0*:

```
Router1#rt 172.16.2.0
Routing entry for 172.16.2.0/24
  Known via "connected", distance 0, metric 0 (connected, via interface)
  Routing Descriptor Blocks:
  * directly connected, via FastEthernet0/0.2
      Route metric is 0, traffic share count is 1
Router1#
```

Command aliases are most effective if you use them consistently among all the routers that you manage. Otherwise, you'll have to remember a different set of alias commands for each group of devices. If you want to use this feature, we recommend that the entire network management team work together to develop a standard set of aliases before implementing them. We also recommend keeping the aliases simple. Above all, resist the urge to alias every possible command. Instead, create aliases for only the most common commands.

Command aliases are also useful for scripting. You can build a script to perform a task on a router that might be slightly different on each router. For example, suppose you want to clear the counters of a particular access list on a weekly basis, but some of your routers use a different access list number. You can simply build an alias with the same name on each router, but make the actual commands represented by the alias appropriate to each individual router. Finally, you can build a script to issue the command alias and automate what would otherwise be an extremely onerous task.

The *show alias* command displays all the command aliases configured on the router:

```
Router1#show aliases
Exec mode aliases:
  h               help
  lo              logout
  p               ping
  r               resume
  s               show
  u               undebug
  un              undebug
  w               where
  rt              show ip route
  on              show ip ospf neighbor

Router1#
```

If you type this command on any router, you will see that Cisco implements several command aliases by default.

2.2 Managing the Router's ARP Cache

Problem

You want to adjust the ARP table timeout value.

Solution

To modify the ARP timeout value, use the *arp timeout* configuration command:

```
Router1#configure terminal
Enter configuration commands, one per line.  End with CNTL/Z.
Router1(config)#interface Ethernet0
Router1(config-if)#arp timeout 600
Router1(config-if)#end
Router1#
```

Discussion

Every LAN device has an Address Resolution Protocol (ARP) cache. This is a table that the device uses to map Layer 2 MAC addresses to Layer 3 IP addresses. Without this mapping, the device could build its IP packets, but couldn't build the Layer 2 frames to carry these packets.

Devices discover the information in the ARP cache dynamically. If a device needs to send a packet to an IP destination, and it doesn't have a corresponding MAC address, it sends out a broadcast ARP request packet. This packet reaches every device on the LAN segment, and the one that "owns" the IP address in question sends back an ARP response packet to complete the process.

Many LAN devices also automatically send a *gratuitous ARP* packet when they first connect to the network. A gratuitous ARP is a broadcast packet that is effectively an unsolicited ARP response. Every device on the LAN segment will receive this packet so it can update its ARP cache in case there is ever a need to talk to this new device.

The ARP request and response process obviously takes time to complete, introducing a delay in packet processing. Furthermore, because the ARP request packets are broadcasts, they go to every device on the LAN segment, where they interrupt whatever that device was doing. If there are too many of these packets on the segment, it can cause traffic congestion and CPU loading on the connected devices.

So to keep the ARP traffic down, all IP devices maintain a cache of these ARP entries. Old entries that are no longer valid need to be periodically removed. The router needs to flush out old ARP cache entries faster in environments where devices frequently change their address, such as when there are very short DHCP lease times. In some cases there are so many devices that the ARP cache table becomes unwieldy, taking up too much memory or too much CPU time to support. But you need to maintain a balance between removing old invalid entries and keeping the amount of ARP traffic down.

By default, Cisco routers use an ARP cache timeout period of four hours. This means that if the router hasn't sent or received any packets with a particular address for the last four hours, it will flush the ARP entry from its cache. This period usually works well on Ethernet networks. However, there are special situations when you can improve network performance by adjusting this period.

The example in this recipe reduces the ARP timeout period to 600 seconds (10 minutes):

```
Router1(config-if)#arp timeout 600
```

Of course, you could just as easily use this command to increase the default ARP timeout period. In general we don't recommend using an ARP timeout period of less than about five minutes because it tends to cause too much CPU and network loading.

The *show ip arp* command prints out the current contents of the router's ARP cache:

```
Router1#show ip arp
Protocol  Address          Age (min)  Hardware Addr   Type   Interface
Internet  172.25.1.5               8  0001.9670.b780  ARPA   Ethernet0
Internet  172.25.1.7               -  0000.0c92.bc6a  ARPA   Ethernet0
Internet  172.25.1.1               9  0010.4b09.5700  ARPA   Ethernet0
Internet  172.25.1.3               2  0010.4b09.5715  ARPA   Ethernet0
Router1#
```

Notice that this output includes the IP address, Age in minutes, MAC address, and the Interface information for each ARP entry. The router resets the ARP age counter to zero whenever it sees valid traffic from the corresponding device. This ensures that the addresses of active devices are never flushed out of the cache, no matter how long they have been known.

You can specify a particular IP address with the *show ip arp* command. This can be useful when you are only interested in particular entries in a large cache table. On a large LAN core router, there could be hundreds or even thousands of ARP entries in the cache, which is too many to scan by eye:

```
Router1#show ip arp 172.25.1.5
Protocol  Address          Age (min)  Hardware Addr   Type   Interface
Internet  172.25.1.5               2  0001.9670.b780  ARPA   Ethernet0
Router1#
```

The same command can also display the ARP information for a particular MAC address, as follows:

```
Router1#show ip arp 0010.4b09.5715
Protocol  Address          Age (min)  Hardware Addr   Type   Interface
Internet  172.25.1.3               3  0010.4b09.5715  ARPA   Ethernet0
Router1#
```

And you can even get a listing of ARP information for a particular router interface:

```
Router1#show ip arp Ethernet0
Protocol  Address          Age (min)  Hardware Addr   Type   Interface
Internet  172.25.1.5               4  0001.9670.b780  ARPA   Ethernet0
Internet  172.25.1.7               -  0000.0c92.bc6a  ARPA   Ethernet0
```

```
Internet   172.25.1.1              2    0010.4b09.5700   ARPA   Ethernet0
Internet   172.25.1.3              4    0010.4b09.5715   ARPA   Ethernet0
Router1#
```

When you are having an ARP problem, or when there are stale entries that you need to remove immediately, it can be useful to clear the entire cache. To manually clear the router's entire ARP cache, use the *clear arp* command:

```
Router1#clear arp
Router1#
```

Unfortunately, there is no way to remove a single ARP entry. If you need to manually clear an entry, you must erase the entire table. Doing this will cause a brief spike in ARP traffic as the router attempts to rebuild the ARP cache for the active device, so we recommend that you use this command very sparingly.

The *show interface* command includes information about the ARP timeout setting for a particular interface:

```
Router1#show interface Ethernet0
Ethernet0 is up, line protocol is up
  Hardware is Lance, address is 0000.0c92.bc6a (bia 0000.0c92.bc6a)
  Internet address is 172.25.1.7/24
  MTU 1500 bytes, BW 10000 Kbit, DLY 1000 usec, rely 255/255, load 1/255
  Encapsulation ARPA, loopback not set, keepalive set (10 sec)
  ARP type: ARPA, ARP Timeout 00:10:00
  <Removed for brevity>
```

2.3   Tuning Router Buffers

Problem

You want to change your default buffer allocations to improve router efficiency.

Solution

The router maintains two different sets of buffers: public buffers and interface buffers. The router uses these as temporary storage while processing packet data. You can tune the public buffer pools as follows:

```
Router1#configure terminal
Enter configuration commands, one per line.  End with CNTL/Z.
Router1(config)#buffers big initial 100
Router1(config)#buffers big max-free 200
Router1(config)#buffers big min-free 50
Router1(config)#buffers big permanent 50
Router1(config)#end
Router1#
```

And you can adjust the interface buffer pools by using a similar set of commands:

```
Router1#configure terminal
Enter configuration commands, one per line.  End with CNTL/Z.
```

```
Router1(config)#buffers Ethernet0 initial 200
Router1(config)#buffers Ethernet0 max-free 300
Router1(config)#buffers Ethernet0 min-free 50
Router1(config)#buffers Ethernet0 permanent 50
Router1(config)#end
Router1#
```

Discussion

Before we start this discussion, we need to offer three notes of caution on tuning buffers. First, adjusting your router's buffers is usually not necessary. Second, a poor set of buffer parameters can cause serious performance problems on your router and for traffic passing through the router. Third, if you do find that you need to adjust these parameters, the necessary adjustments will be unique to your network, and perhaps even to each router, so we unfortunately can only offer general guidance, but can't really recommend appropriate parameters.

The router maintains two different sets of buffers: public pools that the router can use for anything, and interface specific pools that it can use only for processing packets on that interface.

The public buffers fall into several different pools, according to their size. They are shown in Table 2-1.

Table 2-1. Public buffer pools

Buffer size	Buffer pool name
104 bytes	Small buffers
600 bytes	Middle buffers
1,536 bytes	Big buffers
4,520 bytes	VeryBig buffers
5,024 bytes	Large buffers
18,024 bytes (default)	Huge buffers

Note that the Huge buffers are 18,024 bytes by default. But unlike the other public buffer pools, you can actually change the size of the buffers in this pool as follows:

```
Router1(config)#buffers huge size 36048
```

You can configure any size between 18,024 and 100,000 bytes for your Huge buffers. However, we should mention that it is extremely rare to find that you need to change this buffer size. Since the router can use memory only in buffer-sized chunks, having extremely large buffers can be useful if you find that you need to manipulate extremely large packets for some reason. However, the default value of 18,024 should be large enough to handle the largest MTU values for all standard interface types. So it is extremely rare to find that you actually have to adjust this parameter. The remaining buffer sizes are all fixed and cannot be adjusted.

There are four different parameters that you can adjust on each of the public buffer pools:

```
Router1(config)#buffers big initial 100
Router1(config)#buffers big max-free 200
Router1(config)#buffers big min-free 50
Router1(config)#buffers big permanent 50
```

The first of these commands sets the number of buffers of this type that the router will allocate at boot time. If this router is in an extremely high traffic environment, it may take a while to allocate enough buffers to handle the load. So you may find that the router has a few buffer failures right after booting. You can resolve this problem by increasing the number of *initial* buffers.

The second command uses the keyword *max-free* to set the maximum number of free buffers of this type that the system should keep. In the router's normal functioning, it will see periodic bursts of activity that may force it to allocate more buffers. When the burst is over, setting a relatively low value for max-free will ensure that the router frees this extra memory to make it available for other purposes. But if you set it too low in an extremely bursty environment, the router may not be able to allocate new buffers quickly enough to meet the demand.

In the third command, we have applied the *min-free* keyword to take care of the opposite side of the same problem. In order to help ensure that the router is able to handle the rising demand for packets, as soon as the router finds that it has fewer than min-free more unused buffers of a particular type, it will start allocating more from system memory. If you specify a min-free value that is large enough, the router will be able to cope with any demands. But making the value too large will force the router to do additional work by allocating additional buffers that it will never need.

In the final command we set the minimum number of buffers of this type by using the keyword *permanent*. The router will allocate this many buffers at boot time, and it will not return their memory to the general pool of memory. A good value for this parameter is high enough to reduce the amount of work that the router has to do allocating and trimming buffers, but not so high as to waste precious memory resources.

As you can see from the second example, the parameters for tuning the interface buffer pools are exactly the same as the ones we have just described for the public pools:

```
Router1(config)#buffers Ethernet0 initial 200
Router1(config)#buffers Ethernet0 max-free 300
Router1(config)#buffers Ethernet0 min-free 50
Router1(config)#buffers Ethernet0 permanent 50
```

The best way to tell whether your buffers need adjusting is to look at the output of the *show buffers* command:

```
Router1>show buffers
Buffer elements:
     498 in free list (500 max allowed)
     760166 hits, 0 misses, 0 created
```

```
Public buffer pools:
Small buffers, 104 bytes (total 50, permanent 50):
     50 in free list (20 min, 150 max allowed)
     265016 hits, 0 misses, 0 trims, 0 created
     0 failures (0 no memory)
Middle buffers, 600 bytes (total 25, permanent 25, peak 49 @ 1d09h):
     23 in free list (10 min, 150 max allowed)
     40749 hits, 10 misses, 30 trims, 30 created
     0 failures (0 no memory)
Big buffers, 1536 bytes (total 50, permanent 50):
     50 in free list (5 min, 150 max allowed)
     33780 hits, 0 misses, 0 trims, 0 created
     0 failures (0 no memory)
VeryBig buffers, 4520 bytes (total 10, permanent 10):
     10 in free list (0 min, 100 max allowed)
     0 hits, 0 misses, 0 trims, 0 created
     0 failures (0 no memory)
Large buffers, 5024 bytes (total 0, permanent 0):
     0 in free list (0 min, 10 max allowed)
     0 hits, 0 misses, 0 trims, 0 created
     0 failures (0 no memory)
Huge buffers, 18024 bytes (total 0, permanent 0):
     0 in free list (0 min, 4 max allowed)
     0 hits, 0 misses, 0 trims, 0 created
     0 failures (0 no memory)

Interface buffer pools:
Ethernet0 buffers, 1524 bytes (total 32, permanent 32):
     8 in free list (0 min, 32 max allowed)
     24 hits, 0 fallbacks
     8 max cache size, 8 in cache
     30963 hits in cache, 0 misses in cache
Serial0 buffers, 1524 bytes (total 32, permanent 32):
     4 in free list (0 min, 32 max allowed)
     54 hits, 3 fallbacks
     8 max cache size, 7 in cache
     172593 hits in cache, 32 misses in cache
Serial1 buffers, 1524 bytes (total 32, permanent 32):
     7 in free list (0 min, 32 max allowed)
     25 hits, 0 fallbacks
     8 max cache size, 8 in cache
     0 hits in cache, 0 misses in cache


Router1>
```

First, let us zoom in on one of the public buffer pools to explain what the fields mean:

```
Small buffers, 104 bytes (total 50, permanent 50):
     50 in free list (20 min, 150 max allowed)
     265016 hits, 0 misses, 0 trims, 0 created
     0 failures (0 no memory)
```

This section looks at Small buffers, which are 104-byte chunks of memory. The router currently has allocated a total of 50 of these buffers; all 50 of them are permanent, meaning that the router will not attempt to return any of them to the pool of generally available memory.

In the second line, you can see that all 50 of these buffers are currently in the free list, meaning that they are all unused. The numbers 20 and 150 in this line are the minfree and max-free parameters that we discussed above.

In the third line, the number of hits indicates how many times the router has successfully allocated buffers from this pool. The number of misses indicates how many times the router successfully allocated a buffer from this pool, but in doing so had to allocate additional buffers. The field called trims counts the number of dynamically allocated buffers that the router has subsequently returned. And the created field shows how many buffers the router has actually created in response to miss events.

The last line shows serious problems, which are the only reason that you should alter your buffer parameters. The failures field counts the number of times that the router has attempted to allocate a buffer and failed, causing it to drop the packet. The last field is labeled "no memory." It counts the number of times a failure happened because the router had no memory from which to allocate additional buffers. This is clearly an extremely serious problem, which is usually best treated by adding memory to the router.

It is also important to remember that if the router tries and fails to allocate a buffer from one pool, it will request a buffer from the next largest pool. So, for example, if the router is unable to get a Big buffer to handle a 1,500 byte packet, it will use one from the *VeryBig* pool. This is why you can sometimes see buffer hits in the *VeryBig* pool, even if every interface on the router has an MTU of 1,500 bytes. So it is a good idea to allocate a few permanent buffers from the pool larger than your highest MTU.

Now let's look at the interface buffers:

```
Ethernet0 buffers, 1524 bytes (total 32, permanent 32):
     8 in free list (0 min, 32 max allowed)
     24 hits, 0 fallbacks
     8 max cache size, 8 in cache
     30963 hits in cache, 0 misses in cache
```

This shows a similar set of values to what we just discussed for the public buffer pools, but there are a few differences. The first difference is the fallbacks field. This counts the number of times that the router has needed additional buffers on this interface, and has allocated them from the corresponding public buffer pool of the appropriate size. In this case, the Ethernet buffers are 1,524 bytes, so the router would allocate additional buffers from the big buffer public pool.

The router keeps a cache of buffers on each interface that are effectively in use whether there is data or not. This field varies somewhat depending on the hardware type. But once again, you should watch out for misses. As long as the number of misses and fallbacks are low, there is no need to adjust the interface buffers.

We would like to offer one final warning about adjusting buffers. Always be sure to look at your router's free memory with the show memory before and after making any adjustment:

```
Router1#show memory
              Head    Total(b)    Used(b)    Free(b)   Lowest(b)  Largest(b)
Processor    17DA4C  13112756    2308632   10804124   10577100   10663072
      I/O    E00000   2097152     336980    1760172    1740988    1759812
```

Keep close track of how much the Free memory in particular changes when you adjust your router's buffers. Both the Processor and the I/O memory can be affected by these changes. If you inadvertently over allocate your buffers while trying to improve system performance, you may find that the router does not have enough memory to operate properly when the load increases.

2.4   Auto Tuning Buffers

Problem

You want the router to automatically tune the buffers, based on computed needs of the router.

Solution

Use the *buffers tune automatic* command to enable the router to auto tune the system buffers:

```
Router#configure terminal
Enter configuration commands, one per line.  End with CNTL/Z.
Router(config)#buffers tune automatic
Router(config)#end
Router#
```

This command was introduce in IOS Version 12.3(14)T, and the router computes the correct buffer parameters regardless if the command is entered or not. Once the buffers tune automatic command is entered, the router buffers will change to the computed values.

Discussion

As we discussed in Recipe 2.3, tuning the router's system buffers can be a tricky endeavor that can result in poor performance if not done correctly. What's more, Cisco recommends against the practice of tuning system buffers without assistance from their technical support representatives.

With the introduction of auto tuning of system buffers, the end user can enable the feature and allow the router to monitor and calculate the correct system parameters. Because the router continues to monitor the buffer parameters over time, you can be assured the buffer parameters will remain properly set, which means there's no need to revisit the settings.

As we mentioned in the Solution section, the router automatically begins calculating the correct buffer parameters based on system requirements, even if the feature isn't immediately enabled. Once enabled, the router will use the computed parameters.

To monitor the parameter changes to the system buffers, use the *show buffers tune* command:

```
Router# show buffers tune

Tuning happened for the pool Small
Tuning happened at 22:43:19
Oldvalues
permanent:50  minfree:20  maxfree:150
Newvalues
permanent:62  minfree:15  maxfree:78
Tuning happened for the pool Middle
Tuning happened at 22:43:19
Oldvalues
permanent:25  minfree:10  maxfree:150
Newvalues
permanent:36  minfree:9  maxfree:45
Router#
```

This example shows that the router automatically tuned the buffer settings at 22:43. It also shows that the router adjusted the Small and Middle buffers, and includes the old and new values.

The autotuning feature will override the manually set values if necessary. Be sure to remove all manual buffer change statements before enabling the auto tuning feature.

See Also

Recipe 2.3.

2.5   Using the Cisco Discovery Protocol

Problem

You want to see summary information about what is connected to your router's interfaces.

Solution

You can selectively enable or disable Cisco Discovery Protocol (CDP) on the entire router, or on individual interfaces:

```
Router1#configure terminal
Enter configuration commands, one per line.  End with CNTL/Z.
Router1(config)#cdp run
Router1(config)#interface Serial0/0
Router1(config-if)#cdp enable
Router1(config-if)#exit
Router1(config)#interface FastEthernet0/0
Router1(config-if)#no cdp enable
Router1(config-if)#exit
Router1(config)#interface FastEthernet1/0
Router1(config-if)#cdp enable
Router1(config-if)#end
Router1#
```

Discussion

CDP is enabled by default on the router, and on all interfaces. If you have previously disabled it, as discussed in Recipe 2.6, and you want to re-enable CDP on the router, you can issue the *cdp run* global configuration command:

```
Router1(config)#cdp run
```

This turns on CDP processing on all supported interfaces by default. If you don't want to run CDP on a particular interface, you can use the *no cdp enable* command, as we did for the serial interface in the example:

```
Router1(config)#interface Serial0/0
Router1(config-if)#no cdp enable
```

CDP is a Cisco proprietary protocol that allows Cisco devices to identify one another and exchange useful identifying information. The *show cdp neighbors* command gives a summary of information about adjacent devices that also happen to be running CDP:

```
Router1#show cdp neighbors
Capability Codes: R - Router, T - Trans Bridge, B - Source Route Bridge
                  S - Switch, H - Host, I - IGMP, r - Repeater

Device ID       Local Intrfce    Holdtme    Capability  Platform  Port ID
Router2         Ser 0/0          179           R        2621      Ser 0/1
Switch1         Fas 1/0          152           T S      WS-C2924  2/2
Router1#
```

As you can see, this output tells you the name and type of device of each neighbor, including the model number. It also includes both the interface on this router that connects to each neighbor and the corresponding interface on the neighbor device.

Notice that the last of the devices listed is actually a Cisco Catalyst Ethernet switch. This switch points out one of the most useful features of CDP. While other mechanisms such as the ARP cache, routing protocols, or even simple PING tests can tell you things about the Layer 3 neighbors, CDP gives you information about the Layer 2 neighbors. This is true even when the Layer 2 neighbor does not have an IP addresses configured.

You can see additional information about these neighboring devices by adding the *detail* keyword:

```
Router1#show cdp neighbors detail
-------------------------
Device ID: Router2
Entry address(es):
  IP address: 10.1.1.2
Platform: cisco 2621,  Capabilities: Router
Interface: Serial0/0,  Port ID (outgoing port): Serial0/1
Holdtime : 136 sec

Version :
Cisco Internetwork Operating System Software
IOS (tm) C2600 Software (C2600-IK903S-M), Version 12.2(13), RELEASE SOFTWARE (fc1)
Copyright (c) 1986-2002 by cisco Systems, Inc.
Compiled Tue 19-Nov-02 22:27 by pwade

advertisement version: 2


Device ID: Switch1
Entry address(es):
  IP address: 172.25.1.4
Platform: WS-C2924,  Capabilities: Trans-Bridge Switch
Interface: FastEthernet1/0,  Port ID (outgoing port): FastEthernet0/12
Holdtime : 116 sec

Version :
Cisco Internetwork Operating System Software
IOS (tm) C2900XL Software (C2900XL-C3H2S-M), Version 12.0(5)WC3b, RELEASE SOFTWARE
(fc1)
Copyright (c) 1986-2002 by cisco Systems, Inc.
Compiled Fri 15-Feb-02 10:14 by antonino

advertisement version: 2
Duplex: full

Router1#
```

There is a lot of information in this output. It tells you the IP addresses of the adjacent interfaces on the neighbor devices. It also gives details about the Cisco IOS or CatOS version.

Both of these neighbor devices support CDP Version 2. In IOS Version 12.0(3)T, Cisco introduced this new version of CDP, which includes three new fields that are quite useful on LANs: VTP Domain Name, 802.1Q Native VLAN, and duplex. As you can see in the above output, the router and switch agree that they are operating at full duplex. Please refer to Chapter 16 for discussions of both 802.1Q and Ethernet Duplex configuration.

This new duplex option in particular is extremely useful because the router and switch can now automatically detect duplex mismatches. We deliberately created a duplex problem by changing the switch's setting to half duplex for the port facing this router. The router was able to detect the problem through CDP and issue the following log message:

```
Feb  6 11:36:11: %CDP-4-DUPLEX_MISMATCH: duplex mismatch discovered on
FastEthernet1/0 (not half duplex), with 003541987 (switch) FastEthernet0/12 (half
duplex).
```

CDP Version 2 is enabled by default on all IOS versions 12.0(3)T and higher. You can globally disable Version 2 support on a router, allowing only Version 1, by issuing the following global configuration command:

```
Router1(config)#no cdp advertise-v2
```

However, it is not entirely clear what purpose this would serve. We know of no interoperability problems between CDP Version 1 and Version 2. And, while there are security problems, which we will discuss in Recipe 2.6, they are better addressed by disabling CDP altogether.

You can see global information about the router's CDP configuration with the *show cdp* command:

```
Router1#show cdp
Global CDP information:
        Sending CDP packets every 60 seconds
        Sending a holdtime value of 180 seconds
        Sending CDPv2 advertisements is  enabled
Router1#
```

Here you can see that this router sends out CDP advertisement packets every 60 seconds, which is the default. The *holdtime* parameter is the length of time the router will wait to hear the next CDP advertisement from one of its neighbors. If it doesn't receive this advertisement packet within this time period, the router will flush the corresponding entry from its CDP neighbor table.

You can adjust these parameters globally for the entire router as follows:

```
Router1(config)#cdp timer 30
Router1(config)#cdp holdtime 240
```

Both of these commands accept an argument in seconds. The advertisement timer can have any value between 5 and 254 seconds, while the hold timer must be between 10 and 255 seconds.

See Also

Recipe 2.6; Chapter 16

2.6   Disabling the Cisco Discovery Protocol

Problem

You don't want to allow adjacent devices to gain information about this router for security reasons.

Solution

You can disable CDP on a single interface by using the command *no cdp enable* interface configuration command:

```
Router1#configure terminal
Enter configuration commands, one per line.  End with CNTL/Z.
Router1(config)#cdp run
Router1(config)#interface FastEthernet0/0
Router1(config-if)#no cdp enable
Router1(config-if)#end
Router1#
```

And you can disable all CDP on the router with the global configuration command, *no cdp run*:

```
Router1#configure terminal
Enter configuration commands, one per line.  End with CNTL/Z.
Router1(config)#no cdp run
Router1(config)#end
Router1#
```

Discussion

CDP can be an extremely useful feature because it tells you so much information about all of your neighboring devices. However, this can also represent a serious security problem. CDP packets are not encrypted in any way, so if somebody can just capture the CDP packets from a network segment as they pass between the routers, they can easily deduce a lot about your network architecture. And if they can get access to the router either via Telnet or SNMP, they can use the CDP tables to discover the entire topology of your network at Layer 2 and 3, including all IOS levels, router and switch model types, and IP addressing. If somebody was armed with this information and a Cisco bug list, they could launch a very effective attack against your network.

For this reason, many network engineers choose to disable CDP throughout their networks. In general, if you need to disable CDP for security reasons, you should probably disable it globally on the whole router, rather than on individual interfaces. If you disable CDP on a single interface, you will only prevent people from intercepting the CDP advertisement packets. But the CDP table information is easily accessible through Telnet and SNMP, so valuable topology information is still vulnerable to probing.

We would like to clarify that the security risk is that somebody will launch a deliberate and focused attack against your network either from the inside or from a directly connected network. We strongly recommend disabling CDP on any routers that connect to external networks, particularly the public Internet. However, for purely internal networks, it is important to remember that you would be protecting yourself against people who are already physically connected to the network in some way. At this point, you must balance the obvious usefulness of CDP against the risk of attack from people who probably have legitimate access to the network. Whether you disable CDP or not in this situation depends on how much you can trust your legitimate users not to launch a deliberate internal attack.

See Also

Recipe 2.5

2.7 Using the Small Servers

Problem

You want to enable or disable router services like *finger*, *echo*, and *chargen*.

Solution

The *finger* application provides a remote way of seeing who is logged into the router. You can enable it with the *ip finger* global configuration command:

```
Router1#configure terminal
Enter configuration commands, one per line.  End with CNTL/Z.
Router1(config)#ip finger
Router1#
```

Every Cisco router also has a set of small TCP and UDP server applications that are sometimes useful for test purposes:

```
Router1#configure terminal
Enter configuration commands, one per line.  End with CNTL/Z.
Router1(config)#service tcp-small-servers
Router1(config)#service udp-small-servers
Router1(config)#end
Router1#
```

Discussion

The *finger* command is a simple utility that allows you to do the equivalent of a *show users* command on a remote router. Unix computers generally have a standard *finger* program that you can run as follows:

```
Freebsd% finger @Router1
[Router1]
```

```
      Line        User       Host(s)            Idle       Location
   66 vty 0    kdooley     idle         00:22:47 freebsd
   67 vty 1    ijbrown     idle            1d07h freebsd
 * 68 vty 2                idle         00:00:00 freebsd

    Interface    User       Mode               Idle    Peer Address

Freebsd%
```

But you can also use the *Telnet* program, and connect to TCP port 79 to access the *finger* server as well. You can do this from another router, for example:

```
Router2#telnet 10.1.1.2 finger
Trying 10.1.1.2, 79 ... Open

      Line        User       Host(s)            Idle       Location
   66 vty 0    kdooley     idle         00:24:14 freebsd
   67 vty 1    ijbrown     idle            1d07h freebsd
 * 67 vty 1                idle         00:00:00 10.2.2.2

    Interface    User       Mode               Idle    Peer Address


[Connection to 10.1.1.2 closed by foreign host]
Router2#
```

Notice that in both cases the output includes not only the active users, but also the finger process itself, which is indicated as the line with the asterisk.

The finger protocol is defined in RFC 1288. It is disabled by default on Cisco routers. While this can be convenient to see who is logged in to a remote router without having to log in to check, it also can represent a serious security problem. Not only does it display a set of valid login IDs, which can be used to focus an attack, but it consumes a VTY line on the router, which can prevent legitimate access if done persistently. The finger protocol also has a checkered history. A bug in the original finger implementation was one of the methods used by the first great viral attack to shut down large sections of the Internet (the infamous Morris Worm).

For all of these reasons, we strongly recommend you keep this protocol disabled on all of your routers. If it has been enabled for any reason, you can disable it as follows:

```
Router1(config)#no ip finger
```

We should also note in passing that the *ip finger* command replaces the earlier *service finger* command, which you will find in many references:

```
Router1(config)#service finger
```

If you use this deprecated version of the command, the router will automatically replace it with the newer command.

Cisco routers also support a set of simple TCP and UDP applications that are relatively common standards for IP devices. In IOS levels 12.0 and higher, the TCP and

UDP small servers are disabled by default, and you must enable them if you wish to use them. In earlier IOS levels, they are enabled by default.

In general, we find that the small servers are only marginally useful, and we recommend disabling them when you are not actively using them for testing purposes. These servers listen for incoming packets from any source. There have been network denial of service attacks based on these servers. Usually the attacks simply exploit the fact that the TCP servers in particular will accept a connection from any device that requests one. If a hostile user sends a stream of TCP SYN packets to one of these ports, the router will have to respond to it and devote internal resources to keeping the session active. This can use up router resources.

The UDP servers are also potentially dangerous because a hostile user can spoof the source address in the packet to force your router to send a barrage of response packets to a third party. A similar attack could potentially be launched using the TCP servers, because the router will respond to any TCP SYN packet with a SYN ACK. Another network device could find itself unable to cope with receiving a barrage of unsolicited SYN ACK packets.

Therefore, we recommend disabling these services except when you specifically need to use one of them:

```
Router1(config)#no service tcp-small-servers
Router1(config)#no service udp-small-servers
```

However, with these cautions, the small servers do have legitimate uses.

The TCP and UDP small servers are shown in Table 2-2. The router implements both TCP and UDP based versions of each of these server functions, on the same port numbers. These are all well-known ports and commonly implemented applications. They are usually used for testing purposes.

Table 2-2. TCP and UDP small servers

Port number	Common name	RFC	Description
7	Echo	RFC 862	The server process responds to any client input by sending back the identical input.
9	Discard	RFC 863	The server process discards any data sent by the client.
13	Daytime	RFC 867	The server responds with the current time and date, and then closes the session.
19	Chargen	RFC 864	The server sends a constant stream of ASCII characters to the client.

The easiest way to explain what these functions do is to simply try them. The TCP versions are easier to demonstrate because you can use the standard Telnet application, and just tell it to connect to a different TCP port number.

The *echo* function just responds to whatever you type by sending back the same data:

```
Freebsd% telnet Router1 echo
Trying 172.25.25.1...
```

```
Connected to Router1.
Escape character is '^]'.
It gives a very echo to the seat where love is thron'd
It gives a very echo to the seat where love is thron'd
^]
telnet> quit
Connection closed.
Freebsd%
```

In its UDP version, the *echo* function merely copies the data segment of the packet and returns it to the sender.

The *discard* function is considerably less useful. The TCP version allows the client to establish a TCP session with the server, and then ignores everything you send it:

```
Freebsd% telnet Router1 discard
Trying 172.25.25.1...
Connected to Router1.
Escape character is '^]'.
Go off; I discard you: let me enjoy my private; go off.
^]
telnet> quit
Connection closed.
Freebsd%
```

The UDP version of this application listens for packets on UDP port number 9 and ignores them. It doesn't respond in any way to these packets.

The TCP version of the *daytime* server accepts a connection request, then immediately sends a packet containing the current time and date in ASCII format, and disconnects the session:

```
Freebsd% telnet Router1 daytime
Trying 172.25.25.1...
Connected to Router1.
Escape character is '^]'.
Sunday, January 5, 2003 17:41:21-EST
Connection closed by foreign host.
Freebsd%
```

The UDP *daytime* server listens on UDP port number 13 and responds with a single packet containing the same ASCII time data as the TCP version. The daytime server is marginally useful for checking a clock, but other applications such as NTP are much more robust if you actually want to configure a reliable time service. We discuss NTP in Chapter 14.

The Character Generation (*chargen*) function is probably the most useful of the TCP small servers. As soon as you make a connection to this port number, the router will start sending a continuous stream of data back to the client. We have often used this feature as a sort of poor man's traffic generator to investigate network loading issues:

```
Freebsd% telnet Router1 chargen
Trying 172.25.25.1...
Connected to Router1.
Escape character is '^]'.
!"#$%&'( )*+,-./0123456789:;<=>?@ABCDEFGHIJKLMNOPQRSTUVWXYZ[\]^_`abcdefg
```

```
!"#$%&'()*+,-./0123456789:;<=>?@ABCDEFGHIJKLMNOPQRSTUVWXYZ[\]^_`abcdefgh
"#$%&'()*+,-./0123456789:;<=>?@ABCDEFGHIJKLMNOPQRSTUVWXYZ[\]^_`abcdefghi
#$%&'()*+,-./0123456789:;<=>?@ABCDEFGHIJKLMNOPQRSTUVWXYZ[\]^_`abcdefghij
$%&'()*+,-./0123456789:;<=>?@ABCDEFGHIJKLMNOPQRSTUVWXYZ[\]^_`abcdefghijk
%&'()*+,-./0123456789:;<=>?@ABCDEFGHIJKLMNOPQRSTUVWXYZ[\]^_`abcdefghijkl
<similar lines deleted>
^]
telnet> quit
Connection closed.
Freebsd%
```

The UDP version of the *chargen* server listens for a UDP packet on the well-known port number 19, and then generates a single response packet back to the sender. This response packet contains a random number between 0 and 512 bytes of arbitrary character data.

See Also

Chapter 14; RFC 1288, RFC 862, RFC 863, RFC 864, RFC 867; *Twelfth Night: Or, What You Will* by William Shakespeare

2.8   Enabling HTTP Access to a Router

Problem

You want to configure and monitor your router using a browser interface.

Solution

Cisco includes an HTTP server in the IOS. You can enable this feature on a router, and then use any standard web browser to access the router instead of Telnet:

```
Router1#configure terminal
Enter configuration commands, one per line.  End with CNTL/Z.
Router1(config)#access-list 75 permit 172.25.1.1
Router1(config)#access-list 75 deny any
Router1(config)#ip http server
Router1(config)#ip http access-class 75
Router1(config)#end
Router1#
```

Discussion

After configuring this feature on a router, you can then connect to the router from a standard web browser. For example, using the Lynx text-based web browser, the router's home page looks like this:

```
                                                  Router1 Home Page


                     Cisco Systems


      Accessing Cisco 2621 "Router1"
```

```
Telnet - to the router.

Show interfaces - display the status of the interfaces.
Show diagnostic log - display the diagnostic log.
Monitor the router - HTML access to the command line interface at
        level 0,1,2,3,4,5,6,7,8,9,10,11,12,13,14,15

Connectivity test - ping the nameserver.

Show tech-support - display information commonly needed by tech
        support.

QoS Device Manager - Configure and monitor QoS through the web
        interface.
```

Help resources

```
1. CCO at www.cisco.com - Cisco Connection Online, including the
   Technical Assistance Center (TAC).
2. tac@cisco.com - e-mail the TAC.
3. 1-800-553-2447 or +1-408-526-7209 - phone the TAC.
4. cs-html@cisco.com - e-mail the HTML interface development group.
```

The highlighted words are links that allow you to execute IOS EXEC commands. For example, the *Show interfaces* link will run the *show interfaces* command and display the result on your browser. You can even use this interface to configure the router. If you select one of the command-line interface level options, it will give you access to all of the EXEC commands at the corresponding authorization level. Please refer to Chapter 3 for more information about these user authorization levels.

This option for accessing a router has been available since IOS level 11.2. However, there was an extremely serious bug in the feature that was fixed in IOS level 12.1(5). This bug would cause the router to crash if the user issued a relatively simple typographical error. If a Telnet user types a question mark as part of a command, the router will respond with a list of valid options for this command. However, including a question mark in a URL would cause the router to crash. So since even a legitimate user could easily make this mistake, we strongly recommend against using the feature in any IOS levels before 12.1(5).

In more recent IOS versions, this web interface is no more or less secure than Telnet access to the router's EXEC command-line interface. You still need to supply the same valid user authentication information to connect using a browser that you would need to connect with Telnet. In Chapters 3 and 4 we will discuss different authentication methods, such as AAA, that you can use with Telnet. These methods are also all available with HTTP, and you can configure the one you want using the *authentication* keyword. For example, you can configure the HTTP server to use AAA authentication as follows:

```
Router1(config)#ip http authentication aaa
```

You can even restrict which devices are permitted to access the router's web interface using the *access-class* keyword. In the example, we have told the router to restrict access to the router's web server based on access-list number 75, which allows only one workstation IP address:

```
Router1(config)#access-list 75 permit 172.25.1.1
Router1(config)#access-list 75 deny any
Router1(config)#ip http access-class 75
```

If you are concerned about security of the HTTP protocol, but you still want the convenience of a web interface, you can opt instead for HTTPS. We discuss HTTPS in Recipe 2.9.

We find that the Telnet command-line interface is much easier to use than the web interface. The only really compelling use for this option that we have encountered is to allow first level technical staff access to basic commands, such as show interfaces.

See Also

Recipe 2.9; Chapter 3; Chapter 4

2.9   Enabling Secure HTTP (HTTPS) Access to a Router

Problem

You want to configure and monitor your router using an encrypted browser interface.

Solution

To enable secure HTTP (HTTPS) access to a router, use the *ip http secure-server* command:

```
Core#configure terminal
Enter configuration commands, one per line.  End with CNTL/Z.
Core(config)#ip http secure-server
Core(config)#end
Core#
```

Cisco introduced secure HTTP access feature in IOS Version 12.2(14)S.

Discussion

The Secure HTTP feature provides you with a secure and encrypted method to access the router via a web browser using Secure Sockets Layer and Transport Layer Security. This prevents HTTP sessions from being intercepted or attacked.

By default, the router creates a self-signed digital certificate that is required for secure access. The router adds the digital certificate to its configuration:

```
Router2#show running-config | section crypto
crypto pki trustpoint TP-self-signed-2618906780
```

```
 enrollment selfsigned
 subject-name cn=IOS-Self-Signed-Certificate-2618906780
 revocation-check none
 rsakeypair TP-self-signed-2618906780
crypto pki certificate chain TP-self-signed-2618906780
 certificate self-signed 01
  3082024B 308201B4 A0030201 02020101 300D0609 2A864886 F70D0101 04050030
  31312F30 2D060355 04031326 494F532D 53656C66 2D536967 6E65642D 43657274
  69666963 6174652D 32363138 39303637 3830301E 170D3036 30313235 31373031
  32345A17 0D323030 31303130 30303030 305A3031 312F302D 06035504 03132649
  4F532D53 656C662D 5369676E 65642D43 65727469 66696361 74652D32 36313839
  30363738 3030819F 300D0609 2A864886 F70D0101 01050003 818D0030 81890281
  8100E12C BF2F0F2D 3FA6AAEC 6538D47B FF4A4129 2BE28AFE F1880962 659D06DC
  82992F38 4DDBC544 A071D74F AF503DC7 14C0EF28 7D03D6BA 4AD3D122 184034FF
  FBDE5616 0246528A 83B8E0BA 70C2FC46 605DA522 BC85B1F3 AD47E133 6C2CE562
  669048DB 7378B44A 5999D087 CDA95F74 9E073880 975FEA58 8B0B75EA AA62F996
  CDEB0203 010001A3 73307130 0F060355 1D130101 FF040530 030101FF 301E0603
  551D1104 17301582 13526F75 74657232 2E696A62 726F776E 2E636F6D 301F0603
  551D2304 18301680 1475B543 CAC80FB1 63018DD7 4A81D46A 03DF023B 35301D06
  03551D0E 04160414 75B543CA C80FB163 018DD74A 81D46A03 DF023B35 300D0609
  2A864886 F70D0101 04050003 81810070 5D025E22 B4120D0A BD1D2E33 904B198F
  D9E57BB0 55C90C11 8882A727 9DC42D5F 86619446 1AF7BA53 5DDEDCB5 3B32B70D
  0AFCBCE0 77EC5A50 B0428E89 656C641B F2A6A0E9 CEA331EE 9404F527 40BD66FB
  D30791B9 92BAB053 465FB50C 8C7D8B74 9926ED58 5881A515 7199D397 B69D385F
  329EC47B 9850E063 B4AC318D 76DC9D
 quit
Router2#
```

If this command doesn't show any self-signed certificates, you can generate them using the command crypto key generate rsa. We disscuss this command in more detail in Recipe 3.20.

It is a good idea to explicitly disable the HTTP server to ensure that only encrypted HTTP sessions are permitted once secure HTTP is enabled. To do so, use the *no ip http server* command to disable the HTTP server:

```
Router2#configure terminal
Enter configuration commands, one per line.  End with CNTL/Z.
Router2(config)#ip http secure-server
Router2(config)#no ip http server
Router2(config)#end
Router2#
```

By default, the secure HTTP server uses port 443. To change the secure server port, use the following command:

```
Router2#configure terminal
Enter configuration commands, one per line.  End with CNTL/Z.
Router2(config)#ip http secure-port 8080
Router2(config)#end
Router2#
```

In this example, we changed the secure HTTP port from 443, the default, to port 8080. You can set the secure port to most any unused port number; however, the HTTP and secure HTTP servers cannot be configured to use the same port.

If you do change the secure HTTP port number, then you need to explicitly specify the new port number in the browser's URL. For example: *https://router1.oreilly.com:8080*, where 8080 is the new port number of the secure server.

To view the secure HTTP configuration status, use the *show ip server* command:

```
Router2#show ip http server secure status
HTTP secure server status: Enabled
HTTP secure server port: 8080
HTTP secure server ciphersuite: 3des-ede-cbc-sha des-cbc-sha rc4-128-md5 rc4-128-sha
HTTP secure server client authentication: Disabled
HTTP secure server trustpoint:
HTTP secure server active session modules: ALL
Router2#
```

As you can see from the output of the show command, the secure server is enabled and is configured to use port 8080. Also, notice that client authentication is currently disabled. Secure HTTP client authentication is enabled by using the same method as the HTTP server. See Recipe 2.8 for more information on enabling HTTP authentication.

See Also

Recipe 2.8; Recipe 3.20

2.10 Using Static Hostname Tables

Problem

You want to create a static host lookup table on the router.

Solution

The *ip host* command lets you configure static host entries in the router:

```
Router1#configure terminal
Enter configuration commands, one per line.  End with CNTL/Z.
Router1(config)#ip host freebsd 172.25.1.1
Router1(config)#ip host router2 10.1.1.1 172.22.1.4
Router1(config)#end
Router1#
```

Discussion

Many router commands will accept a hostname in place of an IP address. This helps make the configuration files more readable because it is much easier for humans to work with device names than IP addresses. However, the router still needs to have a way of translating these names into the IP addresses that it prefers to work with. Cisco supports two methods for resolving hostnames into IP addresses. You can either use static host entries, as we do in this recipe, or DNS, as we do in the next recipe.

Static host entries are strictly local to the router. The router does not share this information with other routers or other devices. And unlike DNS, static host entries are not dependent on any external services such as nameservers. If you have both DNS and static host definitions, the router will prefer the static entries. This allows you to override the normal DNS if you don't want to use it.

The biggest problem with static entries is, quite simply, that they are static. So they don't respond to IP address changes without manual intervention. The biggest advantage to static entries is that being static, they don't depend on the reliability of any external servers. If you tie some critical function to a hostname instead of an IP address, you don't want that function to go away just because the DNS server became temporarily unreachable.

For this reason, if you use hostnames in your router configuration instead of IP addresses, we strongly recommend using static host entries rather than DNS.

In the example, the host called router2 has more than one IP address:

```
Router1(config)#ip host router2 10.1.1.1 172.22.1.4
```

When you associate multiple addresses with a single hostname like this, the router will attempt to connect to each address in the specified order. When building a static host entry for a neighboring router, you may wish to start with the loopback IP address, followed by its other, reachable IP addresses.

The *ip host* command also accepts a port number, which is the TCP port that the router will connect to when you use Telnet to connect to the specified hostname. By default, the telnet command will initiate a connection to TCP port 23. In the following example, we will define a host named mail, and instruct the router to use port 25 (SMTP) when making connections to this device:

```
Router1#configure terminal
Enter configuration commands, one per line.  End with CNTL/Z.
Router1(config)#ip host mail 25 172.25.1.1
Router1(config)#end
Router1#
```

Then Telnet to this hostname connects to the SMTP process on the device:

```
Router1#telnet mail
Trying mail (172.25.1.1, 25)... Open
220 freebsd.oreilly.com ESMTP Postfix
```

```
quit
221 Bye

[Connection to mail closed by foreign host]
Router1#
```

Notice that the router connected directly to the host's mail port, port 25. You can override the defined host port at the command prompt by including the required port number at the end of the *telnet* command:

```
Router1#telnet mail 25
```

You can use the *show hosts* command to get a complete list of all of the static host definitions:

```
Router1#show hosts
Default domain is not set
Name/address lookup uses static mappings

Host                    Port Flags      Age Type  Address(es)
freebsd                 None (perm, OK)  0  IP    172.25.1.1
router2                 None (perm, OK)  0  IP    10.1.1.1
                                                  172.22.1.4
mail                    25   (perm, OK)  0  IP    172.25.1.1
Router1#
```

See Also

Recipe 2.11

2.11   Enabling Domain Name Services

Problem

You want to configure your router to use DNS to resolve hostnames.

Solution

To configure the router to use DNS to resolve hostnames, you need to specify a *domain name* and at least one nameserver:

```
Router1#configure terminal
Enter configuration commands, one per line.  End with CNTL/Z.
Router1(config)#ip domain-lookup
Router1(config)#ip domain-name oreilly.com
Router1(config)#ip name-server 172.25.1.1
Router1(config)#ip name-server 10.1.20.5
Router1(config)#end
Router1#
```

Starting in IOS Version 12.2, Cisco changed the command syntax from *ip domain-lookup* to *ip domain lookup*. They also changed the command syntax from *ip domain-name* to *ip domain name*. The new IOS software still accepts previous versions of the commands.

Discussion

As we mentioned in Recipe 2.10, you can configure your router to use Domain Name Service (DNS) to resolve hostnames. In fact, Cisco routers have DNS name resolution enabled by default. However, since there is no default nameserver, the router will attempt to use the local broadcast address, 255.255.255.255, until you explicitly configure a proper nameserver. This means that the *ip domain-lookup* configuration command in the example is necessary only if someone has explicitly disabled DNS on the router.

After you configure the router with a valid nameserver, you can access any hostname that is known by your DNS server. For example, our DNS server exchanges information with the public Internet, so we can ping the Cisco web page by name:

```
Router1#ping www.cisco.com
Translating "www.cisco.com"...domain server (172.25.1.1) [OK]

Type escape sequence to abort.
Sending 5, 100-byte ICMP Echos to 198.133.219.25, timeout is 2 seconds:
!!!!!
Success rate is 100 percent (5/5), round-trip min/avg/max = 80/91/104 ms
Router1#
```

You can see in this output that the router sent a DNS query to the nameserver, 172.25.1.1, and asked it to translate the hostname www.cisco.com. The server responded with an IP address of 198.133.219.25. The router then behaved as if we had simply asked it to *ping* this destination IP address instead of the hostname.

In this example, we configure multiple nameservers:

```
Router1(config)#ip name-server 172.25.1.1
Router1(config)#ip name-server 10.1.20.5
```

The router will send its queries to these servers in the order that we entered them. For example, suppose we tried to ping a factitious host, cookbook.oreilly.com:

```
Router1#ping cookbook.oreilly.com
Translating "cookbook.oreilly.com"...domain server (172.25.1.1)(10.1.20.5)
% Unrecognized host or address, or protocol not running.

Router1#
```

As you can see, the router sent this query first to the nameserver at 172.25.1.1. When this device was unable to resolve the name, the router resorted to the second nameserver, 10.1.20.5. Ultimately the query failed because the hostname doesn't exist.

You can view the DNS configuration parameters with the *show hosts* command:

```
Router1#show hosts
Default domain is oreilly.com
Name/address lookup uses domain service
Name servers are 172.25.1.1, 10.1.20.5

Host                  Port  Flags      Age Type  Address(es)
www.cisco.com         None  (temp, OK)  0  IP    198.133.219.25
Router1#
```

This command displays the domain name, the nameservers (in their order of preference), as well recently resolved hostnames. The router keeps a name cache of recently resolved names to prevent unnecessary DNS lookups on successive attempts to the same host. The difference between these dynamically learned hosts and the statically configured ones that we saw last chapter is that the router will automatically flush the dynamic entries from the cache after a period of time. This time period is actually specified by the DNS server separately for each hostname, so you cannot change it on the router.

The *ip domain-name* command allows you to specify your network's domain name:

```
Router1(config)#ip domain-name oreilly.com
```

When you configure a domain name like this, you can work with just the local hostname instead of the *Fully Qualified Domain Name* (FQDN). For example, you could type mail instead of mail.oreilly.com, and the router would resolve it correctly.

Some organization use more than one domain name. You can configure the router to use multiple domain names by including several *ip domain-list* commands in the configuration. For example, we can configure the router to use a second registered domain name, ora.com:

```
Router1#configure terminal
Enter configuration commands, one per line.  End with CNTL/Z.
Router1(config)#ip domain-list ora.com
Router1(config)#ip domain-list oreilly.com
Router1(config)#end
Router1#
```

If no domain list is present but you do have a domain name, the router will use the domain name. However, as soon as you configure a domain list, the router will ignore the domain name. This is why we had to include the original domain name, oreilly.com, in the domain-list example.

Again, the order of the domain-list entries is important because this is how the router will build the FQDN it uses for its queries. For example, if you sent a query for the host named mail, the router would correctly find it in either domain. But if there was a host named mail in both domains, then the router would connect to mail.ora.com instead of mail.oreilly.com because the domain list specifies ora.com before oreilly.com. This doesn't prevent you from connecting to mail.oreilly.com; but you would have to specify the full name, rather than just mail.

The *show hosts* command output includes the domain list:

```
Router1#show hosts
Default domain is oreilly.com
Domain list: ora.com, oreilly.com
Name/address lookup uses domain service
Name servers are 172.25.1.1, 172.25.1.3, 10.1.20.5


Host                    Port  Flags      Age Type  Address(es)
www.cisco.com           None  (temp, OK)  0   IP    198.133.219.25
freebsd                 None  (perm, OK)  0   IP    172.25.1.1
Router1#
```

See Also

Recipe 2.10

2.12 Disabling Domain Name Lookups

Problem

You want to prevent your router from trying to connect to your typing errors.

Solution

To prevent the router from attempting to resolve typing errors, use the *no ip domain-lookup* command:

```
Router1#configure terminal
Enter configuration commands, one per line.  End with CNTL/Z.
Router1(config)#no ip domain-lookup
Router1(config)#end
Router1#
```

You can also prevent the router from trying to resolve typing errors on routers that use DNS by changing the default EXEC behavior for unknown commands:

```
Router1#configure terminal
Enter configuration commands, one per line.  End with CNTL/Z.
Router1(config)#line vty 0 4
Router1(config-line)#transport preferred none
Router1(config-line)#end
Router1#
```

Discussion

As we mentioned in Recipe 2.11, routers attempts to resolve all hostnames by using DNS by default. Unfortunately, if you don't configure a valid DNS nameserver, the router sends these queries to the local broadcast IP address, 255.255.255.255.

Querying a nonexistent nameserver is not only unproductive, but it can also be quite time consuming if it happens in an interactive session, since the router will not return the EXEC prompt until the query times out. This can be quite frustrating because, by default, the router will interpret any unknown command as a hostname that you want to connect to. So it will attempt to resolve any typing mistakes you enter on the command line:

```
Router1#pnig
Translating "pnig"...domain server (255.255.255.255)

Translating "pnig"...domain server (255.255.255.255)
 (255.255.255.255)
Translating "pnig"...domain server (255.255.255.255)
% Unknown command or computer name, or unable to find computer address
Router1#
```

As you can see, we accidentally mistyped the command *ping*. The router did not know this command, so it assumed that it must be the name of a foreign host and attempted to resolve it. Everybody who has used a Cisco router for more than a few minutes is familiar with this problem, compounding the annoyance of a typing error with having to wait several seconds for the name query to time out.

One easy way to prevent this from happening is to disable DNS lookups, as we did in our first example:

```
Router1(config)#no ip domain-lookup
```

This is an effective solution if we don't need to use DNS services on the router. With name resolution disabled, the router will still interpret our typing mistakes as names of foreign hosts, but it will try to resolve these names only from the static host entries, which don't need to time out:

```
Router1#pnig
Translating "pnig"
% Unknown command or computer name, or unable to find computer address
Router1#
```

The net result is that the router will return your prompt immediately and allow you to enter the command you intended to type.

Routers that are properly configured to use DNS services, as in Recipe 2.11, also will attempt to resolve your typing errors by default. In this case, there is a real server to respond to the request and definitively state that there is no such host, so the delay is somewhat shorter. The router will attempt to query each of the configured nameservers in order until it receives a response or gives up trying:

```
Router1#pnig
Translating "pnig"...domain server (172.25.1.1) (10.1.20.5)
% Unrecognized host or address, or protocol not running.

Router1#
```

This is still an extremely inefficient way of handling typing errors, though. And if you need to use DNS, the solution in our first example is not practical. So we have to attack the problem from a different angle.

The router attempts to resolve typo errors because, by default, every VTY line has preferred transport method of Telnet. This means that you can initiate a Telnet session by typing a hostname at the prompt. You don't need to explicitly issue the *telnet* command. Therefore, when we type in "pnig", the router interprets it as "*telnet pnig*". However, we can instead set the preferred transport method to be "*none*" so the router won't try to connect to a remote device unless we explicitly issue the *Telnet* command:

```
Router1(config)#line vty 0 4
Router1(config-line)#transport preferred none
```

This avoids the problem by preventing the router from misinterpreting our typos as hostnames in the first place:

```
Router1#pnig
       ^
% Invalid input detected at '^' marker.

Router1#
```

As you can see, the router now interprets the typing error as an invalid command rather than a hostname. We recommend using this solution to the problem because it doesn't prevent you from using DNS.

See Also

Recipe 2.10; Recipe 2.11

2.13   Specifying a Router Reload Time

Problem

You want to set the router to automatically reload at a specified time.

Solution

You can set the router to reload after waiting a particular length of time with the *reload in* command:

```
Router1#reload in 20
Reload scheduled for 11:33:53 EST Sat Feb 1 2003 (in 20 minutes)
Proceed with reload? [confirm] <enter>
Router1#
```

The *reload at* command lets you specify a particular time and date when you want the router to reload:

```
Router1#reload at 14:00 Feb 2
Reload scheduled for 14:00:00 EST Sun Feb 2 2003 (in 26 hours and 44 minutes)
Proceed with reload? [confirm] <enter>
Router1#
```

If you set the router to reload at a specific time and date, then we highly recommend using an accurate time source to ensure that the router reloads when you think it will. For more information on time and time sources, please see Chapter 14.

Discussion

Usually, when you reload a router, you want it to do so immediately. However, it can also be quite useful to specify a particular time to reload. For instance, reloading is the only way to fix badly fragmented memory on a router. But you almost certainly don't want to reload during production hours. This feature thus allows you to instruct the router to reload at a safe low-traffic time, such as the middle of the night.

Another excellent reason for using this delayed reload feature is to avoid locking yourself out of a router while making possibly dangerous configuration changes. There are many types of configurations changes, such as changes to access lists or routing configuration in particular, that can isolate a router and prevent you from getting back in to fix the problem. But before you make the changes, you can instruct the router to reload itself in, say, 15 minutes. If you lock yourself out of the router, you won't be able to save the running configuration to NVRAM. So when the router reloads, it will come up with the previous configuration. The bad configuration change will be miraculously undone.

And if it turns out that the new configuration is good, you can simply save it to NVRAM and cancel the reload. We show how to cancel a scheduled reload in a moment.

The *reload in* command also allows you to specify a reason for the reload:

```
Router1#reload in 1:20 IOS Upgrade
Reload scheduled for 12:37:45 EST Sat Feb 1 2003 (in 1 hour and 20 minutes)
Reload reason: IOS Upgrade
Proceed with reload? [confirm] <enter>
Router1#
```

The command interprets any text that you enter after the reload time as the reason for reloading. Starting in IOS Version 12.2, the router records a log message whenever you issue the *reload* command. Included in this message are the time that the reload was requested, the reload time, the username of the person who requested it, and the reload reason:

```
Feb  1 11:17:47: %SYS-5-SCHEDULED_RELOAD: Reload requested for 12:37:45 EST Sat Feb 1
2003 at 11:17:45 EST Sat Feb 1 2003 by ijbrown on vty0 (172.25.1.1). Reload Reason:
IOS Upgrade.
```

You can also include a reason with the *reload at* command:

```
Router1#reload at 23:20 Feb 15 IOS Upgrade
Reload scheduled for 23:20:00 EST Sat Feb 15 2003 (in 124 hours and 48 minutes)
```

```
Reload reason: IOS Upgrade
Proceed with reload? [confirm] <enter>
Router1#
```

The *show reload* command displays information on any impending reloads:

```
Router1#show reload
Reload scheduled for 12:37:45 EST Sat Feb 1 2003 (in 1 hour and 19 minutes) by
ijbrown on vty0 (172.25.1.1)
Reload reason: IOS Upgrade
Router1#
```

You can cancel a scheduled reload with the *reload cancel* command:

```
Router1#reload cancel
Router1#

***
*** --- SHUTDOWN ABORTED ---
***
```

When you cancel a reload like this, the router will send a system broadcast message notifying any active users that the reload has been canceled. Starting with IOS Version 12.2, the router also creates a logging message indicating that someone has canceled a scheduled reload:

```
Feb  1 11:19:10: %SYS-5-SCHEDULED_RELOAD_CANCELLED:  Scheduled reload cancelled at
11:19:10 EST Sat Feb 1 2003
Router1#
```

If you have scheduled a reload, the router will periodically send broadcast notices to all active users as a reminder. By default, the router will send these messages 1 hour before reload, 30 minutes before, 5 minutes before, and 1 minute before reload. You can cancel the reload at any time, up until the router actually shuts itself down:

```
Router1#

***
*** --- SHUTDOWN in 1:00:00 ---
***


***
*** --- SHUTDOWN in 0:30:00 ---
***


***
*** --- SHUTDOWN in 0:05:00 ---
***
```

```
***
*** --- SHUTDOWN in 0:01:00 ---
***
Connection closed by foreign host.
```

See Also

Chapter 14

2.14 Scheduling of Router Commands

Problem

You want to issue a command for the router to execute at regularly scheduled times.

Solution

Use the router's *Kron* facility to execute commands at regularly scheduled intervals:

```
Router#configure terminal
Enter configuration commands, one per line.  End with CNTL/Z.
Router(config)#kron policy-list OREILLY
Router(config-kron-policy)#cli write memory
Router(config-kron-policy)#exit
Router(config)#kron occurrence DAILYat5 at 17:00 recurring
Router(config-kron-occurrence)#policy-list OREILLY
Router(config-kron-occurrence)#end
Router#
```

Cisco first introduced the Kron facility in IOS Version 12.3(1).

> It is highly recommended that you configure the router with an accurate time source such as NTP or SNTP before configuring the Kron facilities, as it requires an accurate clock to work correctly. See Chapter 14 for more information on NTP and SNTP.

Discussion

The Cisco Kron facility is similar to the Unix *Cron* facility in that it allows you to schedule commands to be executed at regular intervals. In essence, it allows you to automate certain administrative functions that the router administrator would otherwise have to perform manually. Of course the major advantage is that once configured correctly, the Kron facility issues the commands at the exact time required and without the chance of typos. In addition, it does not require the administrator be present when the commands are run, which is important, especially in organizations with large numbers of routers.

Let's take a closer look at the configuration of the Kron facility. In the example provided, we have configured the Kron facility to automatically save the configuration to

NVRAM each day at 17:00 (5:00PM). First, we configured the *kron policy-list* and named it "OREILLY" and included the single CLI command *"write memory."* We then configured the *kron occurrence* named "DAILYat5" and set the launch time to 17:00. The keyword *recurring* is required to ensure that the Kron occurrence launches each day as opposed to a single instance. Once the Kron occurrence was configured, then we defined which Kron policies where to be invoked. Note that you can launch more than one Kron policy per occurrence, as shown in the next example:

```
Router#configure terminal
Enter configuration commands, one per line.  End with CNTL/Z.
Router(config)#kron occurrence DAILYat5 at 17:00 recurring
Router(config-kron-occurrence)#policy-list OREILLY
Router(config-kron-occurrence)#policy-list TEST
Router(config-kron-occurrence)#end
Router#
```

In this example, we have configured two Kron policies to launch via the same Kron occurrence. This means that each day at 17:00 the router will launch both policies.

As with the Unix Cron facility, you can schedule Kron occurrences to run every minute of the hour, once a year, or anywhere in between. To schedule a Kron occurrence to launch every hour, use the *in* keyword in conjunction with the *recurring* keyword:

```
Router#configure terminal
Enter configuration commands, one per line.  End with CNTL/Z.
Router(config)#kron occurrence Hourly in 60 recurring
Router(config-kron-occurrence)#policy-list TEST
Router(config-kron-occurrence)#end
Router#
```

The Kron facility will now launch the Kron occurrence "Hourly" every 60 minutes. To launch a Kron facility once a year, use the following configuration:

```
Router#configure terminal
Enter configuration commands, one per line.  End with CNTL/Z.
Router(config)#kron occurrence Yearly at 00:00 Jan 1 recurring
Router(config-kron-occurrence)#policy-list TEST
Router(config-kron-occurrence)#end
Router#
```

Unfortunately, there are some rather annoying limitations to the Kron facility. First of all, only EXEC level commands can be issued by the Kron facility, meaning that no configuration-based commands can be issued. Second, the Kron facility won't work with interactive-based EXEC commands, meaning commands that prompt you to verify the command. For instance, in the initial example we issued the CLI command *write memory* instead of *copy running-config startup-config* because the *write* command does not prompt to verify the action whereas the *copy* command does.

Some potentially useful uses for the Kron facility are saving the configuration to NVRAM, disabling all debug commands, clearing a particular interface, issuing a *ping* command to keep up a tunnel, etc.

You can view the scheduled Kron occurrences by using the *show kron schedule* command:

```
Core#show kron schedule
Kron Occurrence Schedule
DAILYat5 inactive, will run again in 0 days 05:40:54 at 17:00 on

Core#
```

You can see that the router will launch the Kron occurrence "DAILYat5" in 5 hours and 40 minutes.

See Also

Chapter 14.

2.15 Displaying Historical CPU Values

Problem

You want to display the router's historical CPU utilization values.

Solution

To display the router's historical CPU values, use the *show processes cpu history* command:

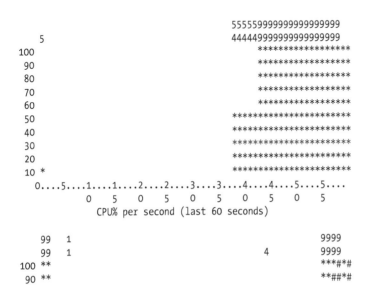

```
80 #*                                             *###*#
70 #*                                             *###*#
60 #*                                             *###*#
50 #*                                             *#####
40 #*                                             *#####
30 #*                                             ######
20 ##                                             ######
10 ##    *                                        ######
 0....5....1....1....2....2....3....3....4....4....5....5....
        0    5    0    5    0    5    0    5    0    5
             CPU% per minute (last 60 minutes)
           * = maximum CPU%   # = average CPU%
                     11
    9111 111 121 1 121 131009  111111 11 112  1111 12  21  1111 1 11 2221
    91137760973493622079940099902362467073149920257008802881014716059 00356
100 *                      ***
 90 *                      ***
 80 *                      ***
 70 *                      ***
 60 *                      ***
 50 *                      ***
 40 *                   *  ***
 30 *                   *  ***                                      *
 20 *    **  **     *  ** ***    *   *    *     *  *  *      * ****  *
 10 #**********************************************************************
  0....5....1....1....2....2....3....3....4....4....5....5....6....6....7.
         0    5    0    5    0    5    0    5    0    5    0    5    0
              CPU% per hour (last 72 hours)
            * = maximum CPU%   # = average CPU%
```

Router#

Cisco added the *history* keyword to the *show processes cpu* command in 12.2(2)T.
The *history* keyword displays the historical CPU values in graph form consisting of
three panes: one second, one minute, and one hour increments. In total, the router
keeps 72 hours worth of historical CPU values.

Discussion

Traditionally, the router would only display up to 5 minutes worth of CPU utilization history via the *show processes cpu* command. With the introduction of the
history keyword, the router maintains 72 hours worth of CPU utilization history.

Initially the graph output of this command can be confusing, but once you understand the layout and calculations behind the three graphs, you will find the output to
be quite efficient.

The top-most graph is the one second pane, which graphs the real-time CPU utilization once a second. As with all three graphs, the most recent statistics appear at the
left side of the graph and gradually move to the right as they age out. In all, the
router displays 60 one second snapshots of the router CPU utilization before moving
to the next graph down.

The middle graph displays the one-minute CPU utilization average as well as the peak CPU value reached during that minute. The average utilization is graphed using the "#" symbol and the peak utilization during the minute is graphed using the "*" symbol. More about the graphing symbols shortly. The number at the top of each column indicates the actual peak reached during the minute. It's important to point out that the peak value may have been reached once or multiple times during the minute.

The bottom graph displays the CPU average and peak utilization values reached during the hour. This graph maintains 72 values, or 3 days worth of data, before the router refreshes the data. Values older than this 72 hour limit are lost forever.

Let's take a closer look at the graphic representation of the CPU data and explain how the graphs are displayed:

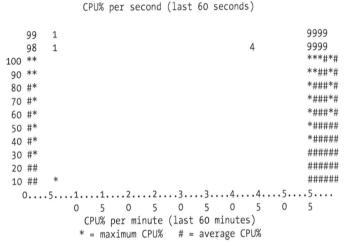

```
             CPU% per second (last 60 seconds)

     99   1                                    9999
     98   1                          4         9999
    100   **                                   ***#*#
     90   **                                   **##*#
     80   #*                                   *###*#
     70   #*                                   *###*#
     60   #*                                   *###*#
     50   #*                                   *#####
     40   #*                                   *#####
     30   #*                                   ######
     20   ##                                   ######
     10   ##        *                          ######
      0....5....1....1....2....2....3....3....4....4....5....5....
                0    5    0    5    0    5    0    5    0    5
                  CPU% per minute (last 60 minutes)
                  * = maximum CPU%   # = average CPU%
```

In this example, we've displayed only the middle graph, the one minute interval graph, for demonstration purposes. The numbers at the far left of the graph indicate CPU utilization and the numbers across the bottom of the graph indicate time, in minutes. As we mentioned earlier, the value at the left-most column is the most recent data, and it gradually moves to the right each minute.

At the top of the left-most column is a number written vertically, indicating the true peak value during the one minute interval. In this case, the peak CPU utilization was 99 percent. The text-based graph also represents the peak utilization using the "*" symbol.

On the same column, the average CPU utilization for the minute is graphed using the "#" symbol. Keep in mind that the graph is plus or minus 5 percent accurate, meaning in this example the average utilization for the minute was between 75 percent and 84 percent.

We would like to be able to offer useful rules of thumb about what CPU utilization values are acceptable and what values start to cause network perfomance problems. Unfortunately, this isn't really possible. How well your router copes with a high CPU utilization depends on many factors, including the specific hardware platform, the use of routing optimizations like CEF, and most importantly, on what specifically is causing the high CPU load. For example, high-end modular routers like the 7600 distribute most routine packet-forwarding fuctions to the media modules. So a high CPU load may not have an effect on real network performance. The best advice we can offer is to watch your routers and try to establish a rough baseline for what CPU load values are normal.

The *history* keyword allows you to quickly glance at the 3 graphs and get a good overall understanding of the CPU utilization over the past 72 hours. Sometimes a five-minute average just isn't sufficient to understand the health of the router's CPU. You will find this command very useful.

2.16   Creating Exception Dump Files

Problem

Your router is having serious problems and you need to create an *exception dump* to forward to Cisco's TAC.

Solution

To create an *exception dump* of a router's memory after a failure, you need to configure the *exception dump* command, as well as telling the router how automatically transfer this information to a server:

```
Router1#configure terminal
Enter configuration commands, one per line.  End with CNTL/Z.
Router1(config)#ip ftp source-interface Loopback0
Router1(config)#ip ftp username ijbrown
Router1(config)#ip ftp password ijpassword
Router1(config)#exception protocol ftp
Router1(config)#exception region-size 65536
Router1(config)#exception dump 172.25.1.3
Router1(config)#end
Router1#
```

Discussion

This is the one recipe in this book that we hope none of our readers ever need to use. The main reason for creating an exception dump of your router memory contents is to help Cisco's TAC in diagnosing catastrophic software problems with one of your routers. When you have these types of extreme problems, however, the TAC will often ask to do an *exception dump* on the router. So we have included this recipe so that you'll know what to do if it ever becomes necessary.

An exception dump is a snapshot of the router's memory contents taken just before a software error forces the router to reload. The router has to transfer this information to a server because it is too much information to store in nonvolatile storage.

The dump actually creates two files, one of the main system memory and one of the IO memory. The software engineers at Cisco can then use these two files to figure out what caused the software failure and hopefully create a fix for the next IOS release.

By default, the router will use TFTP to transfer the dump files. However, we strongly recommend using FTP instead. If your router has more than 16 MB of memory, most TFTP applications will fail, so FTP is the only option. FTP is much more reliable than TFTP, and you don't want to have to repeat the process if the TAC tells you that the file was corrupted during transfer. Our example shows how to configure a router to use FTP to transfer the exception dump files from the router to the server. For more information on configuring the router to use FTP, please see Recipe 1.14.

Exception dumps are prone to fail because the router doesn't attempt them until it has suffered a serious software failure. This software failure could corrupt your router's memory, making any further processing impossible, even creating the exception dump. You can greatly increase the chances of a successful exception dump by dedicating a small amount of memory to serve as a backup memory pool in case the main memory becomes corrupted:

```
Router1#configure terminal
Enter configuration commands, one per line.  End with CNTL/Z.
Router1(config)#exception region-size 65536
Router1(config)#end
Router1#
```

You can define how much memory the router should dedicate to creating exception dumps. The default is 16,384 bytes, but we recommend increasing this to the maximum value of 65,536 bytes. This will greatly increase the chances of a successful exception dump.

By default, the router creates two exception dump files named hostname-core and hostname-coreiomem. In our example, the router name is Router1, so the two files created will be called Router1-core and Router1-coreiomem. You can change the default naming convention of the core files with the *exception core-file* command:

```
Router1#configure terminal
Enter configuration commands, one per line.  End with CNTL/Z.
Router1(config)#exception core-file router5 compress
Router1(config)#end
Router1#
```

You will notice that we have included the optional keyword called *compress* in this command. This option instructs the router to compress the core files before transferring them to the server. You can then uncompress the files on the server with the Unix *uncompress* command. We actually don't recommend using this feature, though, because it adds an extra CPU and memory load to a router that is already in trouble. Furthermore, we have found that this option doesn't seem to shrink the files enough to be useful. In some cases, it even causes the main core file to grow larger.

On the server side, you need to ensure that you have enough disk space to hold the two dump files. The size of these files will vary from router to router, depending on the amount of memory they contain. Expect the dump files to equal the total amount of memory installed in the router.

You can force the router to perform a core dump of its normal memory with the *write core* command. This command provides an excellent way to test whether everything is configured correctly before a catastrophic failure forces the real dump:

```
Router1#write core
Remote host [172.25.1.3]? <enter>
Base name of core files to write [Router1-core]? <enter>
Writing Router1-coreiomem
!!!!!!!!!!!!!!!!!!!!!!!!!!!!!!!!!!!!!!!!!!!!!!!!!!!!!!!!!!!!!!!!!!!!!!!!!!!!!!!!!!!!!!!!!
!!!!!!!!!!!!!!!!!!!!!!!!!!!!!!!!!!!!!!!!!!!!!!!!!!!!!!!!!!!!!!!!!!!!!!!!!!!!!!!!!!!!!!!!!
!!!!!!!!!!!!!!!!!!!!!!!!!!!!!!!!!!!!!!!!!!!!!!!!!!!!!!!!!!
Writing Router1-core
!!!!!!!!!!!!!!!!!!!!!!!!!!!!!!!!!!!!!!!!!!!!!!!!!!!!!!!!!!!!!!!!!!!!!!!!!!!!!!!!!!!!!!!!!
!!!!!!!!!!!!!!!!!!!!!!!!!!!!!!!!!!!!!!!!!!!!!!!!!!!!!!!!!!!!!!!!!!!!!!!!!!!!!!!!!!!!!!!!!
!!!!!!!!!!!!!!!!!!!!!!!!!!!!!!!!!!!!!!!!!!!!!!!!!!!!!!!!!!
Router1#
```

When we display these files on the server, you can see that their combined sizes are 48 MB:

```
Freebsd% ls -la
drwxr-xr-x  3 ijbrown  ijbrown       512 Feb  1 13:50 ./
drwxr-xr-x  5 root     wheel         512 Feb  4  2002 ../
-rw-r--r--  1 ijbrown  ijbrown  46137344 Feb  1 13:54 Router1-core
-rw-r--r--  1 ijbrown  ijbrown   4194304 Feb  1 13:52 Router1-coreiomem
Freebsd%
```

To increase the chances of success, use a server that is as close as possible to the router. Time is of the essence during the creation of an exception dump, so forcing a router to write its core across a slow and congested WAN link decreases your chances of success.

See Also

Recipe 1.14

2.17 Generating a Report of Interface Information

Problem

You want to build a spreadsheet of active IP subnets for your network.

Solution

Keeping track of assigned IP subnets on a network is a vitally important, but often tedious, task. In large organizations, it can be extremely difficult to maintain accurate and up-to-date addressing information. The Perl script in Example 2-1 uses SNMP to automatically gather current IP subnet information directly from the routers themselves. The script creates an output file in CSV format so you can easily import the information into a spreadsheet.

Example 2-1. netstat.pl

```perl
#!/usr/local/bin/perl
#
#       netstat.pl -- a script to build a detailed IP interface
#                     listing directly from a list of routers.
#
#Set behavour
$workingdir="/home/cisco/net";
$snmpro="ORARO";
#
$rtrlist="$workingdir/RTR_LIST";
$snmpwalk="/usr/local/bin/snmpwalk -v 1 -c $snmpro";
$snmpget="/usr/local/bin/snmpget -v 1 -c $snmpro";
open (RTR, "$rtrlist") || die "Can't open $rtrlist file";
open (CSV, ">$workingdir/RESULT.csv") || die "Can't open RESULT.csv file";
while (<RTR>) {
    chomp($rtr="$_");
    @ifIndex=`$snmpwalk $rtr .1.3.6.1.2.1.4.20.1.2`;
    @ipAddress=`$snmpwalk $rtr .1.3.6.1.2.1.4.20.1.1`;
    @ipMask=`$snmpwalk $rtr .1.3.6.1.2.1.4.20.1.3`;
    $arraynum=0;
    print CSV "\n$rtr\n";
    print CSV "Interface, IP-Address, Mask, MTU, Speed, Admin, Operational\n";
    for $ifnumber (@ifIndex) {
        chomp(($foo, $ifnum) = split(/= /, $ifnumber));
        $ifDescription=`$snmpget $rtr ifDescr.$ifnum`;
        $ifMTU=`$snmpget $rtr ifMtu.$ifnum`;
        $ifSpeed=`$snmpget $rtr ifSpeed.$ifnum`;
        $ifAdminstatus=`$snmpget $rtr ifAdminStatus.$ifnum`;
        $ifOperstatus=`$snmpget $rtr ifOperStatus.$ifnum`;
        chomp(($foo, $ipaddr) = split(/: /, $ipAddress[$arraynum]));
        chomp(($foo, $mask) = split(/: /, $ipMask[$arraynum]));
        chomp(($foo, $ifdes, $foo) = split(/"/, $ifDescription));
        chomp(($foo, $mtu) = split (/= /, $ifMTU));
        chomp(($foo, $speed) = split (/: /, $ifSpeed));
        chomp(($foo, $admin) = split (/= /, $ifAdminstatus));
        chomp(($foo, $oper) = split (/= /, $ifOperstatus));
        if ( $speed > 3194967295 ) { $speed = 0 };
        $admin =~ s/\(.*\)//;
        $oper  =~ s/\(.*\)//;
        if ( $oper eq "dormant" ) { $oper = "up(spoofing)"};
        $speed = $speed/1000;
```

Example 2-1. netstat.pl (continued)

```
    if ( $speed > 1000) {
        $speed = $speed/1000;
        $speed =~ s/$/ Mb\/s/;
    }
    else {
    $speed =~ s/$/ Kb\/s/;
    }
    print CSV "$ifdes,$ipaddr,$mask,$mtu,$speed,$admin,$oper\n";
    $arraynum++;
    }
}
close(RTR);
close(CSV);
```

Discussion

The *netstat.pl* script uses SNMP to gather IP subnet information from a list of routers. This ensures that the information is accurate and current. The script gathers all of the pertinent information about each router's IP interfaces and outputs this information as a CSV file.

The *netstat.pl* script requires Perl and NET-SNMP and expects to find both in the */usr/local/bin* directory. For more information on Perl or NET-SNMP, please see Appendix A. If you keep these programs in a different location, you will need to modify the script appropriately.

Before using the script, you must define two variables, $workingdir and $snmpro. The $workingdir variable must contain the name of directory where you will store the script and its input and output files. The variable, $snmpro must contain the SNMP read-only community string for your routers. The script assumes that the same community string is valid on all devices.

The script systematically queries each router in a list, one after another. It expects to find this list in a file called RTR_LIST, located in the working directory. This router list should contain a single router name or IP address on each line with no comments or other information included. The results of the script will be stored in a file called RESULT.csv, also located in the working directory.

You can then import the RESULT.csv file into a spreadsheet. The results will look similar to the example report shown in Table 2-3.

Table 2-3. An example output of the netstat.pl script

Detroit

Interface	IP-Address	Mask	MTU	Speed	Admin	Oper
Serial0/0	10.1.1.1	255.255.255.252	1,500	768 Kb/s	up	up
Loopback0	10.2.2.2	255.255.255.252	1,514	0 Kb/s	up	up

Table 2-3. *An example output of the netstat.pl script (continued)*

Detroit						
FastEthernet1/0	172.22.1.4	255.255.255.0	1,500	100 Mb/s	up	up
Ethernet0/0	172.25.1.8	255.255.255.0	1500	10Mb/s	down	down
BRI0	10.1.99.55	255.255.255.0	1500	64 Kb/s	down	down
Ethernet0	172.25.1.7	255.255.255.0	1500	10 Mb/s	up	up
Loopback0	172.25.25.6	255.255.255.255	1514	0 Mb/s	up	up
Boston						
Interface	**IP-Address**	**Mask**	**MTU**	**Speed**	**Admin**	**Oper**
Serial0.1	172.20.1.2	255.255.255.252	0	28 Kb/s	up	up
Ethernet0	172.20.10.1	255.255.255.0	1500	10 Mb/s	up	up
Loopback0	172.20.100.1	255.255.255.255	1514	0 Mb/s	up	up

The script captures information about every interface that has been configured with an IP address. This includes interfaces that are administratively or operationally down, loopback interfaces, HSRP addresses, and IP unnumbered interfaces. The script will not display any interfaces or sub interfaces that are not configured for IP.

As a side benefit, this script uses only open standard SNMP MIBs. So you can use it to extract IP interface information from almost any SNMP-enabled device, including nonCisco equipment.

See Also

Appendix A

2.18 Generating a Report of Routing Table Information

Problem

You need to extract the IP routing table from one of your routers.

Solution

The script in Example 2-2, *rt.pl*, uses SNMP to extract the routing table from a specified router, and displays this information to standard output (STDOUT). The script expects to find a hostname or IP address of a router on the command line.

Example 2-2. rt.pl

```
#!/usr/bin/perl
#
#          rt.pl -- a script to extract the routing table
#                   from a router.
#
```

Example 2-2. rt.pl (continued)

```
#Set behavior
$snmpro="ORARO";
#
$x=0;
$snmpwalk="/usr/local/bin/snmpwalk -v 1 -c $snmpro";
$snmpget="/usr/local/bin/snmpget -v 1 -c $snmpro";
chomp ($rtr=$ARGV[0]);
if ( $rtr eq "" ) {die "$0: Must specify a router\n"};
print "Destination\tMask\t\tNexthop";
print "\t\t Proto\tInterface\n";
@iftable=`$snmpwalk $rtr ifDescr`;
for $ifnum (@iftable) {
    chomp (($intno, $intname) = split (/ = /, $ifnum));
    $intno=~s/.*ifDescr\.//;
    $intname=~s/"//gi;
    $int{$intno}=$intname;
}
@ipRouteDest=`$snmpwalk $rtr ipRouteDest`;
@ipRouteMask=`$snmpwalk $rtr ipRouteMask`;
@ipRouteNextHop=`$snmpwalk $rtr ipRouteNextHop`;
@ipRouteProto=`$snmpwalk $rtr ipRouteProto`;
@ipRouteIfIndex=`$snmpwalk $rtr ipRouteIfIndex`;
#@ipRouteMetric1=`$snmpwalk $rtr ipRouteMetric1`;
for $intnum (@ipRouteIfIndex) {
    chomp (($foo, $int) = split (/= /, $intnum));
    chomp (($foo, $dest) = split (/: /, @ipRouteDest[$x]));
    chomp (($foo, $mask) = split (/: /, @ipRouteMask[$x]));
    chomp (($foo, $nhop) = split (/: /, @ipRouteNextHop[$x]));
    chomp (($foo, $prot) = split (/= /, @ipRouteProto[$x]));
    #chomp (($foo, $metr) = split (/= /, @ipRouteMetric1[$x]));
    $int1 = $int{$int};
    if ($int1 eq '') {$int1="Local"};
    $prot=~s/\(.*//; $prot=~s/ciscoIgrp/\(e\)igrp/;
    printf ("%-15s %-15s %-15s %7s %-25s\n",$dest, $mask, $nhop, $prot, $int1);
    $x++
}
```

Discussion

The *rt.pl* script is written in Perl and uses NET-SNMP to extract the routing table information via SNMP. It expects to find both Perl and NET-SNMP in the /usr/local/ bin directory. For more information on Perl or NET-SNMP, please see Appendix A.

Before using the script, you must define the variable $snmpro to contain the SNMP read-only community string for the router:

```
Freebsd% ./rt.pl toronto
Destination    Mask            Nexthop      Proto  Interface
10.1.1.0       255.255.255.252 172.25.1.5    ospf  Ethernet0
10.2.2.2       255.255.255.255 172.25.1.5    ospf  Ethernet0
172.16.2.0     255.255.255.0   172.25.1.5    ospf  Ethernet0
```

```
172.20.0.0      255.255.0.0     172.25.1.5      local Local
172.20.1.0      255.255.255.252 172.25.1.5      ospf Ethernet0
172.20.10.0     255.255.255.0   172.25.1.5      ospf Ethernet0
172.20.100.1    255.255.255.255 172.25.1.5      ospf Ethernet0
172.22.0.0      255.255.0.0     172.25.1.5   (e)igrp Ethernet0
172.22.1.0      255.255.255.0   172.25.1.5      ospf Ethernet0
172.25.1.0      255.255.255.0   172.25.1.7      local Ethernet0
172.25.2.0      255.255.255.252 172.25.1.5   (e)igrp Ethernet0
172.25.25.1     255.255.255.255 172.25.1.5   (e)igrp Ethernet0
172.25.25.6     255.255.255.255 172.25.25.6     local Loopback0
172.25.26.4     255.255.255.252 172.25.1.5   (e)igrp Ethernet0
172.25.26.5     255.255.255.255 172.25.1.5      ospf Ethernet0
Freebsd%
```

The output from the script is relatively straightforward, except for static routes and directly connected routes, which require a little explanation.

For static routes, the output shows a value of local in the protocol field, and an interface name of Local. Directly connected routes also appear as local protocol information, but the interface name is the real interface associated with this route.

For example, the route 172.20.0.0 255.255.0.0 is a static route:

```
172.20.0.0      255.255.0.0     172.25.1.5      local Local
```

And 172.25.1.0 255.255.255.0 is a directly connected route:

```
172.25.1.0      255.255.255.0   172.25.1.7      local Ethernet0
```

Since this script queries only open standard SNMP MIB values, you can use it to extract IP route information from most any SNMP-enabled device, including non-Cisco equipment.

See Also

Appendix A

2.19   Generating a Report of ARP Table Information

Problem

You need to extract the ARP table from one of your routers to determine the MAC address associated with a particular IP address or the IP address for a particular MAC address.

Solution

The script in Example 2-3, *arpt.pl*, extracts the ARP table for a specified router or IP address and displays the results to standard output. The script expects to find a hostname or IP address of a router on the command line.

Example 2-3. arpt.pl

```perl
#!/usr/local/bin/perl
#
#          arpt.pl -- a script to extract the ARP cache from a router.
#
#Set behavour
$snmpro="ORARO";
#
$snmpwalk="/usr/local/bin/snmpwalk -v 1 -c $snmpro";
$snmpget="/usr/local/bin/snmpget -v 1 -c $snmpro";
chomp ($rtr=$ARGV[0]);
if ( $rtr eq "" ) {die "$0: Must specify a router \n"};
@iftable=`$snmpwalk $rtr ifDescr`;
for $ifnum (@iftable) {
    chomp (($intno, $intname) = split (/ = /, $ifnum));
    $intno=~s/.*ifDescr\.//;
    $intname=~s/"//gi;
    $arpint{$intno}=$intname;
}
printf ("%-22.22s %-10.10s  %-25.25s\n", Address, MAC, Interface);
@atTable=`$snmpwalk $rtr .1.3.6.1.2.1.3.1.1.1`;
for $atnum (@atTable) {
    chomp (($atip, $atint) = split (/ = /, $atnum));
    $atip =~ s/.*atIfIndex\.[0-9]+\.1\.//;
    $atphys=`$snmpget $rtr atPhysAddress.$atint.1.$atip`;
    chomp(($foo, $phys) = split(/: /, $atphys));
    $phys=~s/ /-/gi; chop ($phys);
    $phys=~tr/A-Z/a-z/;
    $int=$arpint{$atint};
    printf ("%-15.15s %17.17s  %-25.25s\n", $atip, $phys, $int);
}
```

Discussion

The *arpt.pl* script extracts the ARP table from a specific router using SNMP and displays it to standard output. The script requires Perl and NET-SNMP, and it expects to find both in the */usr/local/bin* directory. For more information on Perl or NET-SNMP, please see Appendix A.

Before using the script, you need to set the SNMP read-only community string, which is contained in the variable $snmpro:

```
Freebsd% ./arpt.pl toronto
Address                  MAC        Interface
172.22.1.1       00-01-96-70-b7-81  FastEthernet0/1
172.22.1.2       00-01-96-70-b7-81  FastEthernet0/1
172.22.1.3       00-01-96-70-b7-81  FastEthernet0/1
172.25.1.1       00-10-4b-09-57-00  FastEthernet0/0.1
172.25.1.5       00-01-96-70-b7-80  FastEthernet0/0.1
172.25.1.7       00-00-0c-92-bc-6a  FastEthernet0/0.1
172.25.1.254     00-00-0c-07-ac-01  FastEthernet0/0.1
172.16.2.1       00-01-96-70-b7-80  FastEthernet0/0.2
172.16.2.22      00-00-0c-07-ac-00  FastEthernet0/0.2
Freebsd%
```

The script creates a simple report, including the IP address, MAC address, and interface name of each ARP entry. You can then use a search utility of some kind to locate specific devices by its IP or MAC address. For example, on a Unix server, you could pipe the output to the *grep* command, as follows:

```
Freebsd% ./arpt.pl toronto | grep 172.25.1.5
172.25.1.5      00-01-96-70-b7-80  FastEthernet0/0.1
Freebsd%
```

The ARP tables on large routers can be quite large, which can make locating a single ARP entry difficult. This script allows you to track down a particular device remotely. You could also use the *grep* utility to find the IP address of a particular known MAC address:

```
Freebsd% ./arpt.pl toronto | grep 00-10-4b-09-57-15
172.25.1.3      00-10-4b-09-57-15  FastEthernet0/0.1
Freebsd%
```

This script only queries open standard SNMP MIBS, so you can use it to extract ARP table information from almost any SNMP enabled device, even nonCisco equipment.

See Also

Appendix A

2.20   Generating a Server Host Table File

Problem

You want to build a detailed host file containing the IP addresses and interface names of all of your routers.

Solution

The Perl script in Example 2-4, *host.pl*, builds a detailed host table that includes all of the IP addresses on each router in a list of devices. The script is written in Perl and requires NET-SNMP to extract data from the router list. No arguments are expected or required.

Example 2-4. host.pl

```
#!/usr/local/bin/perl
#
#        host.pl -- a script to build a detailed host file from
#                     information gathered from a router list.
#
#Set behavour
$workingdir="/home/cisco/net";
$snmpro="ORARO";
#
```

Example 2-4. host.pl (continued)

```
$rtrlist="$workingdir/RTR_LIST";
$snmpwalk="/usr/local/bin/snmpwalk -v 1 -c $snmpro";
$snmpget="/usr/local/bin/snmpget -v 1 -c $snmpro";
open (RTR, "$rtrlist") || die "Can't open $rtrlist file";
open (RESULT, ">$workingdir/RESULT") || die "Can't open RESULT file";
while (<RTR>) {
    chomp($rtr="$_");
    @ifIndex=`$snmpwalk $rtr ipAdEntIfIndex`;
    @ipAddress=`$snmpwalk $rtr ipAdEntAddr`;
    $rtr1=`$snmpget $rtr .1.3.6.1.4.1.9.2.1.3.0`;
    chomp(($foo, $RTR) = split (/"/, $rtr1));
    $arraynum=0;
    for $ifnumber (@ifIndex) {
        chomp(($foo, $ifnum) = split(/= /, $ifnumber));
        $ifDescription=`$snmpget $rtr ifName.$ifnum`;
        chomp(($foo, $ipaddr) = split(/: /, $ipAddress[$arraynum]));
        chomp(($foo, $ifdes) = split(/= /, $ifDescription));
        $name="$RTR-$ifdes";
        #$name=~s/\//-/;
        if ( $ifdes eq "Lo0" ) { $name=$RTR };
        print RESULT "$ipaddr\t\t$name\n";
        $arraynum++;
    }
}
close(RTR);
close(RESULT);
```

Discussion

Most organizations manually build a host table for their management server(s) with a single IP entry per router, usually the loopback IP address. This script automatically builds a host file that contains all known IP addresses for each router.

Here is an example of the output from the *host.pl* script:

```
10.1.1.1              miami-Se0/0
10.2.2.2              miami
172.20.6.8            miami-Se0/2
172.22.1.4            miami-Fa1/0
172.25.1.8            miami-Et0/0
10.1.1.2              toronto-Se0/1
172.20.1.1            toronto-Se0/0.2
172.22.1.1            toronto-Fa0/1
172.25.1.5            toronto-Fa0/0.1
172.25.2.1            toronto-Se0/0.1
172.25.25.1           toronto
172.25.26.5           toronto-Lo1
10.1.99.55            detroit-BR0
172.25.3.7            detroit-Et0
172.25.25.6           detroit
172.20.1.2            boston-Se0.1
172.20.10.1           boston-Et0
172.20.100.1          boston
```

This output is in the format required for a Unix */etc/hosts* file. The script extracts the IP address information via SNMP, and then associates each address with the related router name and interface. The script also automatically creates a primary host entry for each router using the address of the loopback0 interface, but with no interface information in the hostname. So, in this example, you can reach the router located in Boston with hostname boston rather than the less intuitive boston-Lo0.

Having a detailed host file is useful for many reasons. Sometimes the router will send a message to your server, either using SNMP or Syslog, and use the IP address of the interface instead of a main loopback interface. Also, having a detailed host file makes the output of a *traceroute* much easier to understand:

```
Freebsd% traceroute miami
traceroute to miami (10.2.2.2), 64 hops max, 52 byte packets
 1  detroit-Et0     (172.25.3.7)  2.263 ms  2.210 ms  2.178 ms
 2  toronto-Fa0/0.1 (172.25.1.5)  3.042 ms  3.060 ms  3.846 ms
 3  boston-Se0.1    (172.20.1.2)  8.234 ms  8.245 ms  8.145 ms
 4  miami-Se0/2     (172.20.6.8)  9.893 ms  9.893 ms  9.432 ms
Freebsd%
```

This makes it much easier to decipher the path between the management station and the Miami router. Not only can we tell which routers lie along the path, but we can also clearly see which interfaces a packet sent along this path will use.

The script does not update the */etc/hosts* file directly. You may need to manually import the script's output file into your system's */etc/hosts* file. However, you can make this task easier by building a master file containing your normal host information and concatenating this master file together with the script output. This way you could even use the *cron* utility to automatically run this script and create a new up-to-date host file on a nightly basis.

Before the script will work, you must modify two variables. The $workingdir variable must be set to the directory that you will launch the script from. The $snmpro variable must be set to your SNMP read-only community string. The script assumes that you use the same read-only community string on all of your routers.

The script reads through a router list, and queries each device in sequence. It expects to find this list in a file called RTR_LIST in the working directory. The list can contain router names or IP addresses, with one entry per router, and one router per line. The script will extract the hostname directly from the router, so you should also ensure that all of your routers are configured with unique hostnames. The results of the script are stored in a file called RESULT, contained in the working directory.

As a final note, we should mention that this script can generate hostnames that do not confirm to RFC 952, "DOD INTERNET HOST TABLE SPECIFICATION," which defines the official rules for hostnames. This is because the script can create hostnames with a "/" character in them, such as miami-Se0/2. This may cause problems for some applications, particularly if they use URL format addressing. For example, a query to *http://miami-Se0/2* will clearly cause problems because the last character, 2, will be interpreted as a filename. However, most common applications, such as ping and Telnet, will accept this hostname without any complaints.

If you are a purist, or if you have applications that complain about these hostnames, we've included a line in the script that you can use to convert all of the slashes, "/", to dashes, "-". This line is currently commented out, but you can invoke it by simply removing the comment character, "#", to change this line:

```
#$name=~s/\//-/;
```

to this:

```
$name=~s/\//-/;
```

See Also

RFC 952

## CHAPTER 3

User Access and Privilege Levels

3.0 Introduction

Many network administrators do only the minimum when it comes to setting up user access to their routers. In many cases, this is sufficient. In a lot of networks there are no serious security issues, and only a small number of people ever want to or need to access the router. But, unfortunately, not everybody can be quite so cavalier.

Most of the recipes in this chapter discuss methods for securing access to routers through important measures like usernames, passwords, controlling access line parameters, controlling remote access protocols, and affecting privileges of users and commands.

There are several important prerequisite concepts for this discussion. You should understand what VTYs and access lines are. You also need to understand a little bit about user and command privilege levels. These levels both are discussed in some detail in O'Reilly's *Cisco IOS in a Nutshell* in Chapters 4 and 13, respectively.

We discuss best practices, and provide a number of valuable recommendations in this chapter. In particularly, we refer to the National Security Agency (NSA) router security document throughout the chapter. The NSA has compiled an extremely useful set of recommendations for many different types of systems, including specifically Cisco routers. You can download a copy of this document from *http://www.nsa.gov/snac/*.

This chapter also contains three scripts written by the authors of this book. Two of these scripts are written in Perl, and the other in Expect. For more information on these languages, we encourage the reader to refer to the O'Reilly books, *Programming Perl* by Larry Wall, Tom Christiansen, and Jon Orwant, and *Exploring Expect* by Don Libes, respectively. Appendix A includes more information about how to obtain copies of these packages and where to find more documentation.

3.1   Setting Up User IDs

Problem

You want to assign individual (or group) user IDs and passwords to network staff.

Solution

To enable locally administered user IDs, use the following set of configuration commands:

```
Router1#configure terminal
Enter configuration commands, one per line.  End with CNTL/Z.
Router1(config)#username ijbrown password oreilly
Router1(config)#username kdooley password cookbook
Router1(config)#aaa new-model
Router1(config)#aaa authentication login local_auth local
Router1(config)#line vty 0 4
Router1(config-line)#login authentication local_auth
Router1(config-line)#exit
Router1(config)#end
Router1#
```

The *username* command also allows you to create usernames without passwords by specifying the *nopassword* keyword:

```
Router1#configure terminal
Enter configuration commands, one per line.  End with CNTL/Z.
Router1(config)#username weak nopassword
Router1(config)#aaa new-model
Router1(config)#aaa authentication login default local
Router1(config)#end
Router1#
```

However, we strongly recommend against doing this because it can severely weaken the router's security.

Discussion

Enabling locally administered usernames overrides the default VTY password-based authentication system. When you enable the *aaa new-model* command, as shown in this recipe, the router will immediately begin to prompt for usernames as well as passwords. Assigning unique usernames to individuals or groups provides account-ability, as we will show later. The following example shows the login prompt for a router using local authentication:

```
Freebsd%telnet Router1
Trying 172.25.1.5...
Connected to Router1.
Escape character is '^]'.

User Access Verification
```

```
Username: ijbrown
Password: <password>

Router1>
```

The router prompts for the username as well as the password. Compare this to how the router behaves when just a password is set on the VTY lines:

```
Freebsd%telnet Router2
Trying 172.25.1.6...
Connected to Router2.
Escape character is '^]'.

User Access Verification

Password: <password>

Router2>
```

When you configure locally administered usernames, the router will prompt for usernames on all lines, including the console and AUX ports, as well as the VTY ports used for Telnet sessions. To avoid locking yourself out of the router, you should always configure a *username* command before entering the AAA commands. It also is a good idea to use another session terminal to test the new authentication system before logging out of your original session. If you do accidentally lock yourself out of the router, you will need to follow the normal password-recovery procedures for your router type. We discuss AAA commands further in Chapter 4.

Locally administered usernames work well in a small environment with a limited number of administrators. However, this method does not scale well to a large network with many administrators. Keeping usernames synchronized across an entire network can become quite daunting. Fortunately, Cisco also supports an advanced authentication methodology called Authentication, Authorization, and Accounting (AAA), which we discuss in Chapter 4. AAA provides a centralized server that administers usernames and passwords (among other features).

Enabling username support causes the router to associate certain functions with usernames. This provides accountability for each username by showing exactly who is doing what. For instance, the output of the *show users* command will include active usernames:

```
Router1>show users
     Line        User       Host(s)           Idle      Location
   66 vty 0     ijbrown     idle          00:36:21 freebsd.oreilly.com
   67 vty 1     kdooley     idle          00:00:24 server1.oreilly.com
 * 68 vty 2     weak        idle          00:00:00 freebsd.oreilly.com

    Interface    User        Mode                      Idle    Peer Address

Router1>
```

More importantly, log messages will capture the username of the individual who invoked certain high-profile commands, such as configuration changes, the clearing of counters, and reloads. For example:

```
Jun 27 12:58:26: %SYS-5-CONFIG_I: Configured from console by ijbrown on vty2 (172.25.
1.1)
Jun 27 13:02:22: %CLEAR-5-COUNTERS: Clear counter on all interfaces by weak on vty2
(172.25.1.1)
Jun 27 14:00:14: %SYS-5-RELOAD: Reload requested by kdooley on vty0 (172.25.1.1).
```

Notice that these log messages now include the username associated with each action. So instead of just knowing that somebody changed the configuration or reloaded the router, you can see exactly who did it.

In addition, the router captures the username of the last person to modify its configuration or save the configuration to NVRAM, which is visible using the *show running-config*:

```
Router1#show running-config
Building configuration...

Current configuration : 4285 bytes
!
! Last configuration change at 12:58:26 EDT Fri Jun 27 2003 by ijbrown
! NVRAM config last updated at 13:01:45 EDT Fri Jun 27 2003 by kdooley
!
version 12.2
```

The *username* command also has an *autocommand* keyword, which you can use to assign an EXEC level command to a particular username. This is useful when you want to provide limited access to a particular command, while restricting access to everything else on the router. For example, you might want to set up a special username that anybody could use to run a single router command, and then terminate the session:

```
Router1#configure terminal
Enter configuration commands, one per line.  End with CNTL/Z.
Router1(config)#aaa new-model
Router1(config)#aaa authentication login default local
Router1(config)#aaa authorization exec default local
Router1(config)#username run nopassword noescape
Router1(config)#username run autocommand show ip interface brief
Router1(config)#end
Router1#
```

In this example, we defined the username run without a password and assigned it an *autocommand* of *show ip interface brief*. When you log in to the router with this username, the router will not prompt for a password. It will just automatically execute the command and then terminate the session:

```
Freebsd% telnet Router1
Trying 172.22.1.4...
Connected to Router1.
```

```
Escape character is '^]'.

User Access Verification

Username: run
Interface            IP-Address     OK? Method Status                 Protocol
BRIO/0               unassigned     YES NVRAM  administratively down down
Ethernet0/0          172.25.1.8     YES NVRAM  administratively down down
BRIO/0:1             unassigned     YES unset  administratively down down
BRIO/0:2             unassigned     YES unset  administratively down down
FastEthernet1/0      172.22.1.4     YES NVRAM  up                     up
Loopback0            192.168.20.1   YES NVRAM  up                     up
Connection closed by foreign host.
Freebsd%
```

Notice how the router issued the command and then terminated the session without providing the opportunity to issue another command.

The *noescape* keyword prevents the user from issuing an escape sequence to access the router EXEC. We strongly recommend using this keyword whenever you use autocommands.

See Also

Recipe 3.2; Recipe 3.3; Chapter 4

3.2   Encrypting Passwords

Problem

You want to encrypt passwords so that they do not appear in plain text in the router configuration file.

Solution

To enable password encryption on a router, use the *service password-encryption* configuration command:

```
Router1#configure terminal
Enter configuration commands, one per line.  End with CNTL/Z.
Router1(config)#enable password oreilly
Router1(config)#line vty 0 4
Router1(config-line)#password cookbook
Router1(config-line)#line con 0
Router1(config-line)#password cookbook
Router1(config-line)#line aux 0
Router1(config-line)#password cookbook
Router1(config-line)#exit
Router1(config)#service password-encryption
Router1(config)#end
Router1#
```

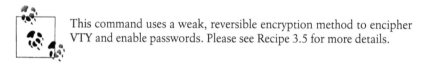

This command uses a weak, reversible encryption method to encipher VTY and enable passwords. Please see Recipe 3.5 for more details.

Discussion

By default, the router stores all passwords in clear text and presents them in a human-readable format when you look at the router's configuration. The *service password-encryption* command encrypts the passwords by using the *Vigenere* encryption algorithm. Unfortunately, the Vigenere encryption method is cryptographically weak and trivial to reverse, as we will illustrate in Recipe 3.5.

However, this functionality is still quite useful to prevent nosy neighbors from viewing passwords over your shoulder. As such, encrypting your passwords is still highly recommended in spite of the known weaknesses. You should be aware of the inherent weaknesses of this encryption scheme when storing or forwarding router configuration files, though. Recipe 3.4 provides a small utility to strip your router configuration files of all passwords (encrypted or not) to keep stored and forwarded configuration files safe from prying eyes.

The following example shows what a configuration file looks like with password encryption enabled:

```
Router1#show running-config
Building configuration...

Current configuration : 4385 bytes
!
! Last configuration change at 13:08:35 EDT Thu Jun 27 2002 by weak
! NVRAM config last updated at 13:01:45 EDT Thu Jun 27 2002 by kdooley
!
version 12.2
service password-encryption
!
!
hostname Router
!
enable password 7 06091D2445420500
!
username ijbrown password 7 045802150C2E
username kdooley password 7 070C285F4D06
!
line con 0
 password 7 0605002E474C06160E
line aux 0
 password 7 151104030F28242B23
line vty 0 4
 password 7 110A160A1C1004030F
 !
end
```

You will notice that the router now encrypts all of the passwords and no longer displays them in a human-readable format.

See Also

Recipe 3.3; Recipe 3.4; Recipe 3.5

3.3   Using Better Password-Encryption Techniques

Problem

You want to assign a privileged password with a stronger encryption standard than Cisco's trivial default encryption.

Solution

To enable strong, nonreversible encryption of the privileged password, use the *enable secret* configuration command:

```
Router1#configure terminal
Enter configuration commands, one per line.  End with CNTL/Z.
Router1(config)#enable secret ORAbooks
Router1(config)#end
Router1#
```

Beginning with IOS Version 12.2(8)T, Cisco introduced strong encryption for its *username* command as well. To enable strong encryption for router usernames, use the *username secret command*:

```
Router#configure terminal
Enter configuration commands, one per line.  End with CNTL/Z.
Router(config)#username ijbrown secret oreilly
Router(config)#end
Router#
```

Discussion

Cisco introduced the *enable secret* password to improve the security of the enable password command. This command uses the cryptographically strong MD5 algorithm to encrypt passwords. It it extremely difficult to crack this algorithm. In fact, there are no known ways to uniquely reverse MD5 encryptions, which is why it is called a *nonreversible* algorithm.

When you configure the router with an *enable secret* password, it will encrypt your *enable password* whether you have the *service password-encryption* command or not. The *service password-encryption* command has no effect on the enable secret password.

Configuring a nonreversible enable password provides greater security than the traditional *enable password* command. It is useful in environments that store or transfer configuration files across the network. The enable secret password takes precedence over the enable password. So if you have both types of enable passwords configured, the router will only use the secret version. We highly recommend using the enable secret password on all routers.

The following command shows what the enable secret command looks like when you look at the router's configuration file:

```
Router1#show running-config | include secret
enable secret 5 $1$Ahxf$4OivEQnOnOJneSObfRdSwO
Router1#
```

The following is a list of *enable secret* password restrictions:

- The password must contain between 1 and 25 alphanumeric characters (upper- or lowercase).

- Leading spaces are ignored while intermediate and trailing spaces are permitted and recognized.

- You can use a question mark, "?", in the password, but only if you precede the question mark with a "Control v" (the Ctrl key and the letter v key).

You should never use the same password for the enable password and enable secret commands. The router will warn you against doing this, but it will accept it:

```
Router1#configure terminal
Enter configuration commands, one per line.  End with CNTL/Z.
Router1(config)#enable password cisco
Router1(config)#enable secret cisco
The enable secret you have chosen is the same as your enable password.
This is not recommended.  Re-enter the enable secret.

Router1(config)#end
Router1#
```

Setting the same password for both commands defeats the purpose of using the enable secret command in the first place and renders its strong encryption useless. Avoid this problem by choosing a different password or removing the enable password altogether.

Cisco introduced the *username secret* command in Version 12.2(8)T to provide an added layer of security over the *username* password command. It provides greater security by using the same irreversible MD5 encryption as the *enable secret* command. However, because the password is not retrievable, some protocols that require clear test passwords, such as CHAP, will not work with the strong encryption.

Even strong encryption is vulnerable to dictionary and brute force attacks. To protect against such attacks, ensure that all of your passwords are difficult to guess and avoid using words found in the dictionary. For example, a common password-cracking program took less than a minute to find the password "cookbook11".

See Also

Recipe 3.5; Recipe 3.22

3.4 Removing Passwords from a Router Configuration File

Problem

You want to remove sensitive information from a router configuration file.

Solution

The following Perl script removes sensitive information like passwords and SNMP community strings from configuration files. The script takes the name of the file containing the router's configuration as its only command-line argument.

Here's some sample output:

```
Freebsd% strip.pl Router1-confg

version 12.2
service password-encryption
!
hostname Router1
!
aaa new-model
aaa authentication login default local
enable secret <removed>
enable password <removed>
!
username ijbrown password <removed>
username kdooley password <removed>
!
!Lines removed for brevity
!
!
snmp-server community <removed> RO
snmp-server community <removed> RW
!
line con 0
 password <removed>
line aux 0
 password <removed>
line vty 0 4
 password <removed>
 end
Freebsd%
```

The Perl code follows in Example 3-1.

Example 3-1. strip.pl

```perl
#!/usr/local/bin/perl
#
#       strip.pl    -- a script to remove sensitive information
#                      from a router configuration file.
#
#
my $configf;
undef $/;
#
$configf = shift(@ARGV);
if (open (CNFG, $configf ) ){
        $config=<CNFG>;
        close (CNFG);
        $config =~ s/password .*/password <removed>/gi;
        $config =~ s/secret .*/secret <removed>/gi;
        $config =~ s/community [^ ]+/community <removed>/gi;
        print $config;
} else {
        print STDERR "Failed to open config file \"$configf\"\n";
        }
```

Discussion

This script strips sensitive information from router configuration files. You can safely store or forward the resulting "stripped" configuration files to others, including vendors, partners, or colleagues. Recipe 3.5 shows how trivial the default password-encryption method is, which highlights why stripping a configuration file like this is so important.

This script should require no modifications to work in most environments. Because the script sends its output to the screen, if you want to save a copy of the "stripped" configuration file, you will have to direct the standard output into a file:

>   Freebsd% **strip.pl** *Router1-confg* > */Router1-stripped*

This example runs the script and sends the output to a file called Router1-stripped that is located in the directory /. Of course, you can direct the output of the script to any file you wish.

In earlier recipes, we mentioned that the *enable secret* password was encrypted using a strong method, MD5, which is extremely difficult to crack. However, there are brute force attacks in which an attacker systematically encrypts likely sequences of letters, numbers and characters in an attempt to find an encrypted match. Although these types of attacks are time consuming, there are a number of freely available software packages that offer efficient password cracking capabilities. In short, it is better to be safe than sorry.

You can easily modify the script to strip other sensitive configuration commands (such as TACACS keys, routing keys, etc.) simply by adding more substitution lines.

For instance, to strip TACACS keys, add the following line of code near the other lines that begin with $config =~:

```
$config =~ s/tacacs-server key .*/tacacs-server key <removed>/gi;
```

See Also

Recipe 3.2; Recipe 3.3; Recipe 3.5

3.5   Deciphering Cisco's Weak Password Encryption

Problem

You want to reverse the weak Cisco password encryption algorithm to recover forgotten passwords.

Solution

To recover a lost router password from a configuration file, use the following Perl script to decipher weakly encrypted passwords. This script expects to read router configuration commands via standard input (STDIN). It then prints the same commands to standard output (STDOUT) with the passwords decrypted.

Here is an example of the program's output:

```
Freebsd% cpwcrk.pl < Router1-confg

version 12.2

service password-encryption
!
hostname Router1
!
enable secret 5 $1$4y6Q$bcGReJ3kGgmlpfr7/lT64.
enable password 7 06150E2F4A5C0817 (decrypted: sanfran)
!
username ijbrown password 7 121A0C041104 (decrypted: cisco)
username kdooley password 7 1306181D000E0B2520 (decrypted: cookbook)
!
<Lines removed for brevity>
!
line con 0
 password 7 06120A22445E1E1D (decrypted: techpwd)
line aux 0
 password 7 0212015803161825 (decrypted: techpwd)
line vty 0 4
 password 7 070033494705151C (decrypted: oreilly)
 login
!
end
```

The program in Example 3-2 is written as a Perl script.

Example 3-2. cpwcrk.pl

```perl
#!/usr/local/bin/perl
#
#  cpwcrk.pl  -- a small script to crack Cisco's Type 7 password
#                  encryption
#
#
$k='dsfd;kfoA,.iyewrkldJKDHSUB';
for($i=0; $i<length($k); $i++) { $ks[$i] = ord(substr($k, $i, 1)); }

while (<STDIN>) {
    if(/ord 7 [01]/) {
        chop; $w=$_; s/.* //g; $C = $_;
        printf "$w (decrypted: ";

        $o=substr($C, 0, 2);
        for ($i=0; $i < (length($C)-1)/2; $i++) { $cs[$i]=hex(substr($C,2*$i,2)); }

        for ($j=1; $j < $i; $j++) { printf("%c", $ks[$o+$j-1] ^ $cs[$j]); }
        printf ")\n";
    } else {
        printf $_;
    }
}
```

 Note that this script will not decrypt *enable secret* passwords because they are encrypted by using strong MD5 encryption.

Discussion

This little Perl script is deliberately written to be small and fast, which unfortunately makes it somewhat difficult to read. We will give a brief explanation of how it works.

The first thing it does is to take the standard key string, $k, and translate it into an array of hexadecimal numbers, $ks, to make it easier to work with. Then it reads the input configuration file one line at a time, looking for any password 7 lines. To make the search slightly quicker, the script only looks for the string ord 7, followed by a space and either the number 0 or 1. It stores the encrypted password string in the variable $C.

The first two characters in the encrypted string are used for an offset, so the script stores them in the string, $o. It then goes through the crypt string, two characters at a time, and converts the result into hexadecimal, which it stores in the array, $cs.

The script then does all of the actual decryption work in a simple loop that calculates an XOR (exclusive OR) operation between the offset original key and the elements of the $cs array.

The encryption algorithm is nothing more than a bitwise XOR between the password string and a known key offset by a random amount. This random offset is encoded into the first two characters of the result, so it is easy to uniquely reverse the cipher.

Cisco chose to use such a simple algorithm because the router needs to be able to uniquely decrypt passwords for some applications, such as CHAP authentication. This is different from most password applications in which the device can take an incoming password string, encrypt it with a one-way algorithm, and compare the resulting encrypted version with the encrypted version of the locally stored password. In those applications it is sufficient to work only with the encrypted versions of the passwords.

See Also

Recipe 3.2; Recipe 3.3; Recipe 3.4

3.6   Displaying Active Users

Problem

You want to find out who else is logged in to a router.

Solution

To see which users are currently logged into the router and on which line, use the *show users* EXEC command:

```
Router1#show users
```

Use the keyword *all* to view all lines whether a user is currently active or not:

```
Router1#show users all
```

Use the EXEC command *who* to view the same output as the *show users* command:

```
Router1#who
```

To remotely view which users are logged into a router, use the *finger* command from your management server:

```
Freebsd% finger @Router1
```

This last command will work only if the *finger* service is enabled on the router.

Discussion

The router provides a number of different methods to view active users. The output from all of these commands is nearly identical. For security purposes, for operational reasons, or just for curiosity, many administrators like to know which users are accessing the router.

The format of the output is as follows: the absolute line number, the VTY line number, the username, listing of connected hosts, the inactivity timer, and the source address of the session. Also notice that one line of the output has an asterisk * in the left margin, indicating your current session.

The *show users* command displays the current active users and their associated line information:

```
Router1#show users
    Line       User       Host(s)           Idle        Location
  66 vty 0     ijbrown    idle              00:56:15 freebsd.oreilly.com
  67 vty 1     kdooley    idle              00:17:52 freebsd.oreilly.com
* 68 vty 2     weak       idle              00:00:00 freebsd.oreilly.com

    Interface   User        Mode                  Idle    Peer Address

Router1#
```

If you add the keyword *all* to this command, the router will display all of its lines, whether or not they have an active session:

```
Router1#show users all
    Line       User       Host(s)           Idle        Location
   0 con 0                                  00:00:00
  65 aux 0                                  00:00:00
  66 vty 0     ijbrown    idle              00:56:24 freebsd.oreilly.com
  67 vty 1     kdooley    idle              00:18:01 freebsd.oreilly.com
* 68 vty 2     weak       idle              00:00:00 freebsd.oreilly.com
  69 vty 3                                  00:00:00
  70 vty 4                                  00:00:00

    Interface   User        Mode                  Idle    Peer Address

Router1#
```

The *who* command is named after popular Unix program, which displays active users. The router's version of *who* displays exactly the same information as the *show users* command:

```
Router1#who
    Line       User       Host(s)           Idle        Location
  66 vty 0     ijbrown    idle              00:56:58 freebsd.oreilly.com
  67 vty 1     kdooley    idle              00:18:36 freebsd.oreilly.com
* 68 vty 2     weak       idle              00:00:00 freebsd.oreilly.com

    Interface   User        Mode                  Idle    Peer Address

Router1#
```

The *finger* command is another popular Unix program that displays the active users of a remote system by using a simple open IP based protocol. The router will respond to any finger request with output similar to that of the *show users* command. In the following example, we use *finger* from a Unix server to see which users are logged into a particular router:

```
Freebsd% finger @Router1
[Router1]

    Line      User     Host(s)           Idle      Location
 * 66 vty 0            idle              00:00:00 freebsd.oreilly.com
   67 vty 1   ijbrown  idle              00:01:48 freebsd.oreilly.com
   69 vty 3   ijbrown  idle              00:59:04 freebsd.oreilly.com

    Interface  User     Mode              Idle     Peer Address
 Freebsd%
```

Notice that we were able to remotely extract the active user list without even logging into the router. For security purposes, we recommend that you disable the finger service to prevent illegitimate use of protocol. For example, somebody could use this command to discover a valid username as well as a remote workstation that is allowed to log into the router. This can be a dangerous amount of information to give away freely.

You can disable the finger service on a router with the following configuration command:

```
Router1#configure terminal
Enter configuration commands, one per line.  End with CNTL/Z.
Router1(config)#no ip finger
Router1(config)#end
Router1#
```

For more information regarding the disabling of the finger service, see Recipe 2.7.

See Also

Recipe 2.7; Recipe 3.1; Recipe 3.7; Chapter 4

3.7   Sending Messages to Other Users

Problem

You want to send a message to another user logged into the same router.

Solution

To send a text message to all active users logged into a router, use the *send* EXEC command. You must have administrator privileges to use this command:

```
Router1#send *
```

To send a private message to a user logged onto a specific line, use the send command with the line number:

```
Router1#send 66
```

To send a private message to a user on the AUX port, use the following command:

```
Router1#send aux 0
```

To send a private message to a user on the console port, use the following command:

```
Router1#send console 0
```

To send a private message to a user on a specific VTY port, use the following command:

```
Router1#send vty 2
```

Discussion

Sending messages to other users on a router is quite useful. You might want to use it to warn other users that you are about to reload or make changes to the router. This is a particularly valuable feature when remote users are located in different geographical areas. You can exchange messages with other users immediately without having to track down individuals via phone, pager, or cell phone.

We often use this feature while troubleshooting network problems. It is particularly useful for communicating with an on-site technician connected to the router's Console, especially if you have no other means to reach them. When there is no telephone near the router, and cell phones won't work in an electrically noisy equipment room, this is a great way to coordinate everybody's efforts.

To view all of the active users on the router, use the *show users* EXEC command:

```
Router1#show users
    Line       User       Host(s)              Idle       Location
   66 vty 0    ijbrown    idle                 01:08:46 freebsd.oreilly.com
   67 vty 1    kdooley    idle                 00:05:34 freebsd.oreilly.com
 * 68 vty 2    weak       idle                 00:00:00 freebsd.oreilly.com

   Interface   User       Mode                     Idle     Peer Address

Router1#
```

In the next example, we send a message to user kdooley who is connected to VTY1:

```
Router1#send vty 1
Enter message, end with CTRL/Z; abort with CTRL/C:
Kev,

I need to reload this router to clear a fragmented memory problem.
Please save your work and log off, ASAP...  Thanks

IJ
^Z
Send message? [confirm] <enter>
Router1#
```

Notice that once you submit the *send* command, the router enters a text editor mode. At this point, you can enter any free-form text. To exit the text editor mode, type Control-Z. The router then prompts you for a confirmation, and if you confirm, sends the message.

An incoming message looks like the following:

```
Router1#

***
***
*** Message from tty68 to tty67:
***
Kev,

I need to reload this router to clear a fragmented memory problem.
Please save your work and log off, ASAP...

IJ
Router1#
```

See Also

Recipe 3.6

3.8   Changing the Number of VTYs

Problem

You want to increase or decrease the number of users who can Telnet to the router simultaneously.

Solution

If you want to increase the number of VTY ports available on the router for remote access, create a reference to the additional lines in the configuration as follows:

```
Router1#configure terminal
Enter configuration commands, one per line.  End with CNTL/Z.
Router1(config)#line vty 0 9
Router1(config-line)#exit
Router1(config)#end
Router1#
```

This command defines the characteristics for a range of VTY ports from 0 to 9. Since ports 0 to 4 exist by default, this has the effect of creating ports 5 through 9.

Discussion

By default, most Cisco routers provide five virtual terminals (VTYs) for remote access. Often the default number of VTYs is not sufficient and increasing the number can be quite useful. This is particularly true in lab or training environments that require a large number of concurrent sessions on a particular router. In addition, organizations that disable exec-timeouts, as in Recipe 3.9, often require a larger number of VTYs to prevent locking administrators out of their routers.

The router can support up to 181 virtual terminals. However, it is extremely rare to actually need more than about 20. Keep in mind that additional virtual terminals will utilize system resources, so don't go over board. You must explicitly configure all of the new VTY lines with *passwords*, *access-classes*, *exec-timeouts*, *transport* protocols, and so forth.

To view the newly created VTY terminals, use the *show users all* EXEC command:

```
Router1#show users all
    Line       User       Host(s)          Idle       Location
    0 con 0                                 00:00:00
   65 aux 0                                 00:00:00
   66 vty 0    ijbrown    idle             01:15:29 freebsd.oreilly.com
   67 vty 1    kdooley    idle             00:12:17 freebsd.oreilly.com
 * 68 vty 2    weak       idle             00:00:00 freebsd.oreilly.com
   69 vty 3                                 00:00:00
   70 vty 4                                 00:00:00
   71 vty 5                                 00:00:00
   72 vty 6                                 00:00:00
   73 vty 7                                 00:00:00
   74 vty 8                                 00:00:00
   75 vty 9                                 00:00:00

    Interface     User       Mode              Idle    Peer Address

Router1#
```

There are five new VTY lines available on this router (VTY 5–9).

To remove the newly created VTY lines, use the *no* version of the command:

```
Router1#configure terminal
Enter configuration commands, one per line.  End with CNTL/Z.
Router1(config)#no line vty 5
Router1(config)#end
Router1#show users all
    Line       User       Host(s)          Idle       Location
    0 con 0                                 00:00:00
   65 aux 0                                 00:00:00
 * 66 vty 0    ijbrown    idle             00:00:00 freebsd.oreilly.com
   67 vty 1                                 00:00:00
   68 vty 2                                 00:00:00
   69 vty 3                                 00:00:00
   70 vty 4                                 00:00:00

    Interface     User       Mode              Idle    Peer Address

Router1#
```

You cannot create or delete VTY lines out of order. Adding VTY line 20 will automatically create lines numbered from 5 to 20. Similarly, removing VTY line 5 will implicitly remove all lines above line 5 (as illustrated in the previous example).

The router will not allow you to remove the original five virtual terminals. If you do attempt to delete them, the router will produce the following warning message:

```
Router1#configure terminal
Enter configuration commands, one per line.  End with CNTL/Z.
Router1(config)#no line vty 4
% Can't delete last 5 VTY lines
Router1(config)#end
Router1#
```

See Also

Recipe 3.9; Recipe 3.10; Recipe 3.16

3.9   Changing VTY Timeouts

Problem

You want to prevent your Telnet session from timing out.

Solution

To prevent Telnet (or SSH) sessions from timing out, use the following command:

```
Router1#configure terminal
Enter configuration commands, one per line.  End with CNTL/Z.
Router1(config)#line vty 0 4
Router1(config-line)#exec-timeout 0 0
Router1(config-line)#exit
Router1(config)#end
Router1#
```

You can use this same command to simply increase the EXEC timeout to a large value, such as three hours, as follows:

```
Router1#configure terminal
Enter configuration commands, one per line.  End with CNTL/Z.
Router1(config)#line vty 0 4
Router1(config-line)#exec-timeout 240 0
Router1(config-line)#exit
Router1(config)#end
Router1#
```

Discussion

By default, the router will terminate an EXEC session after 10 minutes of inactivity. Often administrators find that 10 minute inactivity timers are a nuisance and dislike having to log in to a router several times throughout the day. So Cisco provides a way to modify or disable the inactivity timer. It is important to note that this affects only timeouts due to inactivity. In Recipe 3.11, we discuss a way to disconnect sessions after a specified length of time whether they are active or not.

The *exec-timeout* command has two arguments:

```
Router1(config-line)#exec-timeout 240 0
```

The first argument is the length of time in minutes, and the second argument is seconds. This allows you to specify a timeout period as short as one second or as long as 35,791 minutes, which is over 24 days.

The first example shows how to disable the inactivity timer altogether, by setting the timeout values to zero. There are a few drawbacks to disabling the EXEC timeout that you should bear in mind. First, since the router provides only five VTYs for remote access by default, forgotten sessions can easily block available VTYs until service is completely blocked. Second, sessions that do not terminate correctly, for example when a workstation crashes, can cause VTY sessions to remain active indefinitely.

To prevent dead sessions from needlessly occupying VTY ports, use the *service tcp-keepalives* configuration command:

```
Router1#configure terminal
Enter configuration commands, one per line.  End with CNTL/Z.
Router1(config)#service tcp-keepalives-in
Router1(config)#end
Router1#
```

TCP keepalives will ensure that the far end is up and active; otherwise, it will terminate the session regardless of the inactivity timer. If you choose to disable the inactivity timer, then we strongly recommend using the TCP *keepalive* command.

You can see your current session's inactivity timer with the *show terminal* EXEC command:

```
Router1#show terminal
Line 68, Location: "", Type: "VT100"
Length: 43 lines, Width: 95 columns
Baud rate (TX/RX) is 9600/9600
Status: PSI Enabled, Ready, Active, No Exit Banner, Automore On
Capabilities: none
Modem state: Ready
Group codes:    0
Special Chars: Escape  Hold  Stop  Start  Disconnect  Activation
               ^^x     none   -     -      none
Timeouts:      Idle EXEC    Idle Session   Modem Answer  Session   Dispatch
               never        never                        none      not set
```

The second example sets the inactivity timer to three hours. This tends to be safer than completely disabling the timer because it will eventually terminate all sessions. However, please check your local security policies to ensure that your inactivity timers are set within your organizational guidelines. Many organizations mandate a 15-minute inactivity timer for all types of electronic access to ensure that you do not leave authenticated sessions available to intruders. The NSA recommends an inactivity timer of no more than five minutes.

See Also

Recipe 3.11; Recipe 3.14

3.10   Restricting VTY Access by Protocol

Problem

You want to restrict what protocols can be used to access the router's VTY ports.

Solution

To restrict what protocols that you can use to access the routers VTY ports, use the *transport input* configuration command:

```
Router1#configure terminal
Enter configuration commands, one per line.  End with CNTL/Z.
Router1(config)#line vty 0 4
Router1(config-line)#transport input telnet
Router1(config-line)#exit
Router1(config)#end
Router1#
```

Discussion

Most administrators do not realize that, by default, Cisco routers will allow VTY access via other protocols besides Telnet. In some instances, intruders can bypass security measures that you have in place for Telnet and access your VTYs directly. To be safe, we recommend that you disable all unused protocols from accessing your VTYs. This will prevent anybody from gaining VTY access through one of these other protocols.

Our example shows how to restrict VTY access to Telnet only. Of course, your organization may require other protocols be included as well, such as Secure Shell (SSH). Recipe 3.20 discusses how to enable the SSH protocol and prevent all other forms of nonsecure access.

Table 3-1 lists the valid protocols that Cisco router VTYs support.

Table 3-1. VTY input transport protocols

Protocol	Description
all	Enables all protocols
lat	Enables Digital LAT protocol connections
mop	Enables Maintenance Operation Protocol (MOP) transport
nasi	Enables NetWare Access Servers Interface (NASI) transport
none	Disables all input protocols
pad	Enables X.3 PAD connections

Table 3-1. VTY input transport protocols (continued)

Protocol	Description
rlogin	Enables the Unix rlogin protocol
ssh	Enables the Secure Shell (SSHv1) protocol
telnet	Enables inbound Telnet connections
v120	Enables the V.120 protocol

Use the *show terminal* EXEC command to view the permitted protocol types for the active line. For a router with the default configuration, there is a long list of allowed protocols:

```
Router1#show terminal | include input
Allowed input transports are lat pad v120 lapb-ta telnet rlogin ssh.
Router1#
```

After we restrict the VTY access to Telnet only, the output looks like this:

```
Router1#show terminal | include input
Allowed input transports are telnet.
Router1#
```

See Also

Recipe 3.14; Recipe 3.16; Recipe 3.20

3.11   Enabling Absolute Timeouts on VTY Lines

Problem

You want to enable absolute timeouts on your VTY lines.

Solution

To enable absolute VTY timeouts, use the following set of configuration commands:

```
Router1#configure terminal
Enter configuration commands, one per line.  End with CNTL/Z.
Router1(config)#line vty 0 4
Router1(config-line)#absolute-timeout 5
Router1(config-line)#logout-warning 30
Router1(config-line)#exit
Router1(config)#end
Router1#
```

Discussion

To prevent users from indefinitely tying up valuable router VTY lines, you can implement absolute timers. Absolute timers differ from the inactivity timers discussed in Recipe 3.9 because they will terminate a session whether it is active or not. Although absolute timers are rarely used, there are times when they can be quite useful. For example, in classroom and lab situations, the absolute timeout can help to ensure that nobody uses more than their faire share of login time.

The prospect of having a session terminated in the middle of troubleshooting a problem in a production network is not appealing to most administrators. So, if you do choose to implement an absolute timer, we recommend setting the timer to a reasonable amount of time (no less than 10 minutes). In addition, you should enable a logout warning to ensure that the user has plenty of notice to save their work. The following is an example of a logout-warning banner:

```
Router1>
*
*
* Line timeout expired
*
*
Router1>Connection closed by foreign host.
Freebsd%
```

Note that the argument for the *absolute-timeout* command is a time value in minutes, whereas the *logout-warning* command uses seconds. In the example, we set the absolute timeout to 5 minutes and the warning message to 30 seconds. A 30-second warning may be too aggressive in a production environment.

See Also

Recipe 3.9

3.12   Implementing Banners

Problem

You want to implement a banner message to display a security warning.

Solution

The following commands configure various types of banners on a router:

```
Router1#configure terminal
Enter configuration commands, one per line.  End with CNTL/Z.
Router1(config)#banner exec # This is an exec banner #
Router1(config)#banner login # This is a login banner #
Router1(config)#banner motd $ This is a motd banner $
Router1(config)#end
Router1#
```

Notice that the router accept almost any delimiter character, as long as the start and end delimiter is identical. These delimiters allow you to make your banner message several lines long. Our first two examples use the pound symbol, #, while the last example uses the dollar sign, $, as a delimiter. You have to be slightly careful that you don't use the delimiter character within the banner message itself or the router will accept only part of the message.

Discussion

Cisco routers support three main types of banners and display them in strict order. First the *Message of the Day* (motd) and then the login banner appear before the login prompt, and the router prints the exec banner after successful authentication:

```
Freebsd% telnet Router1
Trying 172.22.1.4...
Connected to Router1.
Escape character is '^]'.
 This is a motd banner
 This is a login banner

User Access Verification

Username: ijbrown
Password: <xxxxxxxxx>
 This is an exec banner
Router1>
```

Login banners are mainly used to display a warning message for security purposes, which we will discuss in a moment. The *motd banner* derives from the Unix banner bearing the same name. The Cisco motd banner is of little use in production environments and is rarely used. The *EXEC banner*, on the other hand, is useful for displaying administrator messages, much like the Unix motd banner, since it is presented only to authenticated users.

Banners are an important and often overlooked part of a good security policy. Although a banner alone will not repel the crafty hacker, it will provide a certain level of legal protection. In fact, a well designed warning message may indeed repel a would-be hacker, since the mere threat of legal action can be a wonderful deterrent. If unauthorized users suspect that your organization is serious about legal action, then they are less likely to target your devices. So we highly recommend implementing login banners on all production routers.

A good login banner should meet the following objectives:

- It should notify people who attempt to access the router that unauthorized use is prohibited and only authorized users with official business are permitted.
- It should mention that users should have no expectation of privacy since all activities may be monitored and/or recorded without further notification.
- The banner should remind users that unauthorized access is unlawful and that recorded logs may be used in legal action.
- Most importantly, the banner shouldn't surrender sensitive information about the router, your organization, or any other piece of information that can aid a hacker.

Laws governing legal notification vary significantly between jurisdictions and situational purposes. We recommend that you clear all proposed banners with your legal department before implementation. In addition, we strongly suggest that you include a proper legal notification, in the form of a login banner, on all of the routers that you manage. Doing so can simplify the prosecution of hackers that unlawfully access your systems by explicitly notifying unauthorized users that their actions are indeed unauthorized. Think of the banner as the electronic equivalent of a sign saying, "trespassers will be prosecuted." Without this sign, somebody could theoretically claim that they didn't know it was a private system. It may not hold up in court, but why take the risk?

The following banner message shows a particularly well-written legal notice that meets all of requirements mentioned earlier. The FBI's Atlanta computer crime squad provided this sample banner. Again, please check with your local authorities before creating a warning banner to ensure that it meets you local legal requirements:

```
Router1#configure terminal
Enter configuration commands, one per line.  End with CNTL/Z.
Router1(config)#banner login #
Enter TEXT message.  End with the character '#'.

+--------------------------------------------------------------+
|                          WARNING                             |
|                          -------                             |
| This system is solely for the use of authorized users for official |
| purposes.  You have no expectation of privacy in its use and to    |
| ensure that the system is functioning properly, individuals using  |
| this computer system are subject to having all of their activities |
| monitored and recorded by system personnel. Use of this system     |
| evidences an express consent to such monitoring and agreement that |
| if such monitoring reveals evidence of possible abuse or criminal  |
| activity, system personnel may provide the results of such         |
| monitoring to appropriate officials.                         |
+--------------------------------------------------------------+
#
Router1(config)#end
Router1#
```

Starting with Version 12.0(3)T of IOS, Cisco routers began to support *banner token* functionality. Tokens are variables embedded within a banner message that substitute such things as hostname and domain name. You can find a complete list of tokens in Table 3-2.

Table 3-2. Supported banner tokens list

Token name	Substituted information
$(hostname)	Displays the router's hostname
$(domain)	Displays the configured domain name
$(line)	Displays the active line number
$(line-desc)	Displays a description of the active line

Tokens allow you to distribute a single banner message throughout your network using variable substitution to make it look slightly different on each device. This ensures that any local differences in the information are always accurate. The banner message can dynamically adapt to changes in hostname or line number, for instance.

Although all banner types support tokens, we recommend only using them in EXEC banners. Since tokens surrender information about the router, it is inappropriate to use them within login or motd banners, which are visible before the user supplies a valid username or password. EXEC banners, on the other hand, are only visible to authenticated users. The following example shows how to configure an EXEC banner with tokens:

```
Router1#configure terminal
Enter configuration commands, one per line.  End with CNTL/Z.
Router1(config)#banner exec #
Enter TEXT message.  End with the character '#'.
Welcome, you have connected to router $(hostname).$(domain):
on line $(line) ($(line-desc)).
#
Router1(config)#line vty 0 4
Router1(config-line)#location 999 Queen Street West
Router1(config)#end
Router1#exit
Connection closed by foreign host.
Freebsd% telnet Router1
Trying 172.25.1.7...
Connected to Router1.
Escape character is '^]'.


User Access Verification

Password: <vtypassword>
Welcome, you have connected to router Router1.oreilly.com:
on line 5 (999 Queen Street West).

Router1>
```

Notice that the router substitutes the appropriate router information where the tokens were. For example, it replaces the *hostname token*, $(hostname), with the hostname, Router1. The *domain token*, $(domain), is derived from the *ip domain-name* command. The *line token*, $(line), is replaced with the active line number. Finally, the *line description* token, $(line-desc), is derived from the line's configured location using the *location* command.

See Also

Recipe 3.13

3.13 Disabling Banners on a Port

Problem

You want to disable the banner on a particular port to prevent it from confusing an attached device such as a modem.

Solution

To disable banners on particular lines, use the following commands:

```
Router1#configure terminal
Enter configuration commands, one per line.  End with CNTL/Z.
Router1(config)#line aux 0
Router1(config-line)#no motd-banner
Router1(config-line)#no exec-banner
Router1(config-line)#exit
Router1(config)#end
Router1#
```

Discussion

By default, the router will display the configured banner messages on all of its lines. However, there are circumstances when these banner messages can confuse directly attached devices. For instance, modems connected to terminal servers or AUX lines can react erratically to banner messages. In these situations, you will need to disable the banner on the associated line.

Notice that you cannot disable the login banner on a line-by-line basis. So if you find that you need to do this, you should use the motd banner instead of the login banner to display the warning message. The *motd* and the *EXEC* banners are nearly identical, so this shouldn't cause any problems.

See Also

Recipe 3.12

3.14 Disabling Router Lines

Problem

You want to disable your router's AUX port to help prevent unauthorized access.

Solution

To completely disable access via the router's AUX port, use the following set of commands:

```
Router1#configure terminal
Enter configuration commands, one per line.  End with CNTL/Z.
```

```
Router1(config)#line aux 0
Router1(config-line)#transport input none
Router1(config-line)#no exec
Router1(config-line)#exec-timeout 0 1
Router1(config-line)#no password
Router1(config-line)#exit
Router1(config)#end
Router1#
```

You can disable access to the router through the VTY lines as follows:

```
Router1#configure terminal
Enter configuration commands, one per line.  End with CNTL/Z.
Router1(config)#access-list 98 deny any log
Router1(config)#line vty 0 4
Router1(config-line)#transport input none
Router1(config-line)#exec-timeout 0 1
Router1(config-line)#no exec
Router1(config-line)#access-class 98 in
Router1(config-line)#exit
Router1(config)#end
Router1#
```

Discussion

It is extremely important to secure access to your routers. The most effective way to secure router ports is to simply disable them if they aren't needed. Of course, it isn't always feasible to disable all router ports, but you can improve security by disabling any unused ones. For instance, network administrators rarely use the router's AUX port, so they should consider disabling it. If your routers are physically close to the administrators so that remote access is not necessary, you might want to disable the VTY ports as well to provide greater security.

Our first example shows a somewhat paranoid method of disabling a router's AUX port. We say paranoid because it involves using several different techniques, each of which should be sufficient alone, strung together for added protection. The *transport input none* command prevents *reverse TELNET* access from the network (see Recipe 3.10). The *no exec* command prevents the AUX port from running an EXEC session. Without an EXEC process, you will get no response when you connect a terminal to the port. Further, the *exec-timeout* command sets the EXEC timeout to one second (see Recipe 3.9). This effectively limits the ability to submit commands in case an attacker somehow manages to start an EXEC process. Finally, *no password* forces the router to clear its line password, so there is no way to authenticate if somebody is able to connect.

The example of disabling VTY ports is also paranoid but effective. This example also illustrates several different methods to disable connectivity in a single example. In reality, any one of these methods would work, but we recommend including at least one secondary method as a safety measure. It is important to note that these extra precautions don't cost anything. They don't increase the router's CPU load or memory consumption appreciably. So for the extra level of safety, you might as well string together several methods as we have shown.

To disable the VTY interfaces, we first set the *transport input* to none (see Recipe 3.10) to disable all inbound transport methods. We also set the *exec-timeout* to one second (see Recipe 3.9). Then we disable the EXEC process on this line, which renders the VTY port useless. Finally, we implement an input *access-class* that prevents all IP addresses from accessing the VTY ports (see Recipe 3.16).

If you try to connect to a VTY line that is disabled, as shown in this recipe, the router will refuse the connection:

```
Freebsd% telnet Router1
Trying 172.22.1.4...
telnet: connect to address 172.22.1.4: Connection refused
telnet: Unable to connect to remote host
Freebsd%
```

The console port is the most important access line your router has. It is the last place you can still connect to when everything else goes wrong, so we do not recommend disabling it. However, we do recommend increasing the security of your console port to provide maximum protection. By default, the console port will not prompt for a login or password. This means that unauthorized users can easily gain access to your router's EXEC without effort. Of course, the router is always vulnerable to console access via the password recovery process, which highlights why physical security is important. You should always house routers in restricted rooms or closets to ensure physical security.

To increase the security of a router's console port, use the following set of configuration commands:

```
Router1#configure terminal
Enter configuration commands, one per line.  End with CNTL/Z.
Router1(config)#line con 0
Router1(config-line)#exec-timeout 5 0
Router1(config-line)#password ora22bkz
Router1(config-line)#login
Router1(config-line)#exit
Router1(config)#end
Router1#
```

This example enables a login prompt by configuring the *login* and *password* commands, and reduces the *exec-timeout* to five minutes to ensure that console sessions will disconnect themselves if somebody walks away from the terminal. Note however, that *login* and *password* commands become unnecessary if you configure your router to use local authentication or AAA. The stronger authentication method overrides the configurations of all of the lines, including the console port.

See Also

Recipe 3.1; Recipe 3.9; Recipe 3.10; Recipe 3.16; Chapter 4

3.15 Reserving a VTY Port for Administrative Access

Problem

You want to prevent all of your VTY lines from being used up, effectively locking you out of the router.

Solution

You can ensure that at least one VTY port is available to you for access at all times with the following commands:

```
Router1#configure terminal
Enter configuration commands, one per line.  End with CNTL/Z.
Router1(config)#access-list 9 permit 172.25.1.1
Router1(config)#line vty 4
Router1(config-line)#access-class 9 in
Router1(config-line)#exit
Router1(config)#end
Router1#
```

You can also reserve a particular inbound *telnet* port for administrator access by assigning VTY(s) into a rotary group by using the *rotary* command:

```
Router1#configure terminal
Enter configuration commands, one per line.  End with CNTL/Z.
Router1(config)#access-list 9 permit 172.25.1.1
Router1(config)#line vty 5 7
Router1(config-line)#rotary 25
Router1(config-line)#access-class 9 in
Router1(config-line)#exit
Router1(config)#end
Router1#
```

Discussion

Receiving the dreaded "Connection Refused" message from one of your routers can be quite distressing, particularly if you're trying to troubleshoot a serious problem. Generally, it means that other sessions have control of all of your router's limited number of VTY lines. However, it can also mean that someone has launched a Denial of Service (DoS) attack. DoS attacks against router VTYs are simple to launch. Just sitting at a login prompt is enough to tie up a VTY line. This means that you don't need a username or a password to use up all of the VTY lines, locking out all of the legitimate administrators.

Whether the lockout is caused by legitimate sessions or not, this is what it looks like:

```
Freebsd% telnet Router1
Trying 172.22.1.4...
telnet: connect to address 172.22.1.4: Connection refused
telnet: Unable to connect to remote host
Freebsd%
```

You can implement a safeguard to ensure that this never happens. Enabling a restrictive *access-class* on the last accessible VTY ensures that the administrator will always retain access at all times. The key is to ensure that your access-list is as restrictive as possible (i.e., an administrator's IP address).

To view the VTY access statistics, use the *show line* command:

```
Router1#show line vty 0 4
    Tty Typ     Tx/Rx     A Modem  Roty AccO AccI   Uses   Noise  Overruns   Int
*   66 VTY                -     -      -    -    -    10      0     0/0        -
*   67 VTY                -     -      -    -    -    10      0     0/0        -
*   68 VTY                -     -      -    -    -     2      0     0/0        -
*   69 VTY                -     -      -    -    -     1      0     0/0        -
*   70 VTY                -     -      -    -    9     1      0     0/0        -

Router1#
```

Notice that access-class 9 was assigned to the last VTY session (the *AccI* column) and was only accessed once (the Uses column).

The *rotary* configuration command lets you dedicate a group of VTY ports to administrative access. In our example, we created three new VTY lines. By using the *rotary* command, we also changed the Telnet port of the group of VTY lines from the normal port 23 to Telnet port 3025. The only way to Telnet to this rotary group is to Telnet to port 3025 from your remote server (port 3000 + the rotary group number—in this case, 25):

```
Freebsd% telnet 172.25.1.101 3025
Trying 172.25.1.101...
Connected to 172.25.1.101.
Escape character is '^]'.

User Access Verification

Username: ijbrown
Password: **********
Router>
```

After Telneting to the router rotarty group, you can display the VTY you're connected to by issuing the *show line* command:

```
Router>show line vty 0 7
    Tty Typ     Tx/Rx     A Modem  Roty AccO AccI   Uses   Noise  Overruns   Int
   162 VTY                -     -      -    -    -     5      0     0/0        -
   163 VTY                -     -      -    -    -     2      0     0/0        -
   164 VTY                -     -      -    -    -     0      0     0/0        -
   165 VTY                -     -      -    -    -     0      0     0/0        -
   166 VTY                -     -      -    -    -     0      0     0/0        -
*  167 VTY                -     -     25    -    9     2      0     0/0        -
   168 VTY                -     -     25    -    9     0      0     0/0        -
   169 VTY                -     -     25    -    9     0      0     0/0        -

Router>
```

Notice that we are connected to TTY 167 (VTY 5) as indicated by the "*" on the left most column. Also, notice that column "Roty" in dicates the VTY 5, 6 and 7 are all part of rotary 25.

See Also

Recipe 3.16; Recipe 3.17

3.16   Restricting Inbound Telnet Access

Problem

You want to restrict Telnet access to the router to allow only particular workstations.

Solution

You can restrict which IP addresses can access the router as follows:

```
Router1#configure terminal
Enter configuration commands, one per line.  End with CNTL/Z.
Router1(config)#access-list 99 permit 172.25.1.0 0.0.0.255
Router1(config)#access-list 99 deny any log
Router1(config)#line vty 0 4
Router1(config-line)#access-class 99 in
Router1(config-line)#exit
Router1(config)#end
Router1#
```

This example uses a standard access-list. You can also use extended access-lists in an *access-class* statement. But because you already know the TCP port numbers, as well as the source and destination IP addresses, extended access-lists don't give much extra functionality.

Discussion

Telnet is an inherently insecure protocol because it sends passwords over the network in clear text. We highly recommend using *access-class* statements to help to ensure that only authorized users can access router VTYs. These access-class statements do not secure the Telnet protocol itself, but they will prevent unauthorized users from receiving a router login prompt. Even if someone manages to sniff your router passwords, this will make them virtually useless.

For increased security, limit the permitted hosts to a few network management servers. This will force legitimate users to follow a two-stage authentication process to access your routers. They will need to authenticate their session on some central device such as the network management server before they can log into the router. The logic is that it is much easier to secure a single server than a dozen workstations.

This feature provides a similar functionality to the Unix *TCPwrapper* tool set, which can restrict daemon access to a limited number of IP addresses. And, just like TCP-Wrapper, we can log the IP addresses of refused users by using the keyword log in the access-list definition. This will create a log message for every unauthorized Telnet attempt, such as the following:

```
Router1#show logging | include list 99
Jun 27 14:14:25: %SEC-6-IPACCESSLOGS: list 99 denied 172.22.1.3 1 packet
Router1#
```

In the example, we have added an explicit *deny any* command to allow the router to count refused sessions:

```
Router1#show access-lists 99
Standard IP access list 99
    permit 172.25.1.0, wildcard bits 0.0.0.255 (4 matches)
    deny   any log (1 match)
Router1#
```

This command shows you the running total of permitted and refused Telnet sessions. In this example, the access-list has denied a single Telnet session from accessing a router VTY. A large number of access attempts might indicate that someone is trying to access your routers. The log messages will capture the IP source address of each denied attempt, making it easy to investigate.

See Also

Recipe 3.15; Recipe 3.17

3.17 Logging Telnet Access

Problem

You want to log every Telnet session to the router.

Solution

To log every Telnet session to the router, use the followings set of commands:

```
Router1#configure terminal
Enter configuration commands, one per line.  End with CNTL/Z.
Router1(config)#access-list 90 permit any log
Router1(config)#line vty 0 4
Router1(config-line)#access-class 90 in
Router1(config-line)#exit
Router1(config)#end
Router1#
```

Discussion

Keeping detailed log records of every Telnet session that your router accepts can be useful for security purposes. By configuring an access-class ACL to log every session, the router will capture which IP source addresses attempt to access the Telnet port. Note, however, that this method will capture both successful and unsuccessful Telnet attempts, which is an invaluable capability.

Of course, you can combine this functionality with the other access-classes that we discussed in Recipes 3.15 and 3.16. This recipe doesn't introduce any new features, but rather a different way to use the same commands.

To view all captured Telnet attempts onto the router, use the following EXEC command:

```
Router1# show logging | include list 90
Jun 27 14:44:45: %SEC-6-IPACCESSLOGS: list 90 permitted 172.25.1.1 1 packet
Router1#
```

The logged messages will always show permitted, whether the session authentication was successful or not.

See Also

Recipe 3.15; Recipe 3.16

3.18 Setting the Source Address for Telnet

Problem

You want to force your router to use a particular IP source address when making outbound Telnet connections.

Solution

To configure a single common IP source address for all outbound Telnet session, use the following configuration command:

```
Router1#configure terminal
Enter configuration commands, one per line.  End with CNTL/Z.
Router1(config)#ip telnet source-interface loopback0
Router1(config)#end
Router1#
```

You can also set the IP source address for individual outbound Telnet sessions on the command line:

```
Router1#telnet 172.25.1.5 /source-interface loopback0
```

Discussion

By default, the router uses the IP address of the closest interface to the destination as the source address when it makes an outbound Telnet session. Network administrators frequently want to use an address other than the closest to the destination, however. For instance, access-lists or route filters may prevent the default source address from reaching its destination. Selecting a particular source IP address of a Telnet session can also help in troubleshooting network problems.

Cisco provides two methods for setting the source IP address of Telnet sessions, one global and one session specific. The global configuration example forces all Telnet sessions to use the IP address of the configured interface as its source address. However, if the configured interface has no IP address, or is operationally down, then the router will resort to its default behavior of using the closest interface IP address.

The session specific method allows the administrator to select an appropriate IP source address on a per session basis. Again, if the configured interface has no IP address or is operationally down, then the router will resort to its default behavior. Also, note that the individual method of setting the Telnet source address supercedes the global setting.

3.19   Automating the Login Sequence

Problem

You want to automate the process of logging into a router, typing usernames, passwords, and so forth.

Solution

The following script automates the process of logging into the router using a scripting language called *Expect*. Expect is a powerful scripting language that provides automation of interactive sessions (see Appendix A for more details). The script takes a router name or IP address as a command line argument. It then performs an automated login sequence before returning the session back to you for a normal interactive session.

Here is the sample output:

```
Freebsd% tel Router1
spawn telnet Router1
Trying 172.25.1.5...
Connected to Router1.
Escape character is '^]'.
```

```
User Access Verification

Username: ijbrown
Password:

Router1>
Router1 - vty login ok
enable
Password:
Router1#
Router1 - enable login ok

Router1#term mon
Router1#
```

The Expect code follows in Example 3-3.

Example 3-3. tel

```
#!/usr/local/bin/expect
#
#              tel -- a script to perform automated login onto a Cisco
#                     router using either a hostname or IP address.
#
#
# Set behaviour
set userid ijbrown
set vtypasswd oreilly
set enablepwd cookbook
#
#
set timeout 10
set rtr [lindex $argv 0]
spawn telnet $rtr
expect {
        {Username}   { send "$userid\r"
                        expect {
                                {*Password*} { send "$vtypasswd\r" }
                        }
                     }
        {telnet>}    { send_user "$rtr - telnet failed\n"
                       exit
                     }
        {Password}   { send "$vtypasswd\r" }
        }

expect {
        {Password}   { send_user "\n$rtr - vty login failed\n"
                       exit
                     }
        {Username}   { send_user "\n$rtr - vty login failed\n"
                       exit
                     }
        {>}          { send_user "\n$rtr - vty login ok\n" }
        }
```

Example 3-3. tel (continued)

```
send "enable\r"
expect "Password"
send "$enablepwd\r"
#
expect {
        {*#}         { send_user "\n$rtr - enable login ok\n" }

        {*>}         { send_user "\n$rtr - enable login failed\n"
                       exit
                     }
        {Password}   { send_user "\n$rtr - enable login failed\n"
                       exit
                     }

        }
#
send "\r"
expect "*#*"
send "term mon\r"
#
interact
```

Discussion

This script is intended to save you time when you have to repeatedly log into routers. The *tel* script will connect to the VTY and send the login sequence before returning the session back to you. The script can login to routers that use local usernames, AAA authentication, or the default VTY/enable passwords. You can also use it to submit router commands before returning control back to the end user. Since the script can respond immediately to the various router prompts, the entire login sequence is much faster than what a human can type.

This script also notifies the user when it experiences problems in the login sequence, and it displays the entire sequence so that you can follow its progress on the screen. Generally, if the script experiences a problem, it will terminate with an appropriate error message, if possible. It also includes a global timeout variable to ensure that problems do not hang the user session. The default global timeout is 10 seconds.

This script requires the scripting language Expect to be loaded on the server and located in the directory /usr/local/bin. You will also need to set a few variables. First, the userid variable must be set to your router username: either the local administered username or your AAA username. If your router does not prompt for usernames, then the script ignores this variable.

Second, the variable vtypasswd must be set to the password associated with your username, or if your router is not configured to use used usernames, it should be the VTY password.

Third, the variable enablepwd must be set to the router's enable password.

This script should be stored in your home directory with read, write, and execute privileges restricted to only yourself. This is to ensure that unauthorized users cannot view your ID and password, which are stored in clear text, or use the script to login to a device using your credentials:

Freebsd% **chmod 700 *tel***

 Many corporate security organizations frown on storing unencrypted passwords in flat files. Please check your security guidelines before using this script.

The final step in the script login sequence is to submit useful commands before returning the session back to the user. This is a time-saving step to automatically submit commands that you use regularly. By default, the script will send the *terminal monitor* command before terminating; however, you can easily add other commands with little effort. You can also easily modify it to send a standard set of commands and then exit from the router without needing to turn over control.

The *tel* script has proven to be an invaluable tool during the writing of this book. We have used it literally thousands of times, saving countless keystrokes in the process. Think of it as a preventative measure for Carpal Tunnel Syndrome.

See Also

Recipe 3.1; Chapter 4

3.20 Using SSH for Secure Access

Problem

You want to use SSH for secure encrypted remote access to your router.

Solution

You can configure your router to run an SSH Version 1 server for VTY access:

```
Router1#configure terminal
Enter configuration commands, one per line.  End with CNTL/Z.
Router1(config)#hostname Router1
Router1(config)#ip domain-name oreilly.com
Router1(config)#crypto key generate rsa
The name for the keys will be: Router1.oreilly.com
Choose the size of the key modulus in the range of 360 to 2048 for your
  General Purpose Keys. Choosing a key modulus greater than 512 may take
  a few minutes.

How many bits in the modulus [512]: 1024
Generating RSA keys ...
[OK]
```

```
Router1(config)#
Jun 27 15:04:15: %SSH-5-ENABLED: SSH 1.5 has been enabled
Router1(config)#ip ssh time-out 120
Router1(config)#ip ssh authentication-retries 4
Router1(config)#end
Router1#
```

SSH became available in Cisco's IOS, starting with release 12.1(1)T. However, only versions of IOS that support IPSec (DES or 3DES) encryption include SSH support. Note that there are severe restrictions on exporting any software that includes 3DES outside of United States and Canada.

Beginning with IOS Version 12.3(4)T, Cisco introduced support for SSH Version 2. The configuration is identical. However, only IOS versions that support 3DES encryption will support SSH Version 2. Also, the RSA key-pair size must be greater than or equal to 768.

Discussion

SSH provides a secure method of communication between network entities by the means of transparent encryption. It is a protocol that encrypts all traffic, including passwords, between a client and a server. This makes it an excellent replacement for Telnet and Rlogin protocols.

The main reason to consider replacing Telnet with SSH is security. The entire Telnet session, including passwords, is transmitted in clear-text. If anybody has a protocol analyzer in between the Telnet client and server, they can easily discover the username and password, as well as see all of the data sent by both ends of the conversation. SSH, on the other hand, uses strong encryption algorithms to ensure the entire session is unintelligible to anybody except for the intended party. This allows for secure communication, even through a public network such as the Internet.

The transparent encryption scheme used by SSH ensures that, except for initial configuration, SSH behaves much the same way as Telnet does. The SSH protocol hides the security functionality from the end user, leaving a session that operates like a native Telnet session would. The actual encryption algorithm used in a given SSH session is negotiated between the client and host devices, with the best available technique selected.

Configuring SSH Version 1 requires the following steps:

- Ensure that your router is running IOS Version 12.1(1)T or higher.
- Ensure that your IOS version contains the IPSec feature set (DES or 3DES). 3DES is preferred.
- Configure an authentication method that supports usernames and passwords, such as local authentication or AAA. SSH does not support the default VTY password-encryption method because it needs usernames as well as passwords. See Recipe 3.1 for information on local authentication and Chapter 4 for more information on AAA.

- Set the router's hostname to something other than the default "Router".

- Configure the *ip domain-name* on your router to match the organization's domain name.

- Generate the SSH host keys using the *crypto key generate rsa* configuration command. The router can accept a key length between 360 and 2048 bits. Larger keys provide greater security, but affect performance. We don't recommend using a key that is shorter than 1024 bits. Creating keys requires a large number of CPU cycles, usually a few minutes of high CPU utilization (depending on the router type and the key length). Once created, keys are stored in NVRAM and are inaccessible. You can delete a set of keys with the *crypto key zeroize rsa* configuration command.

Generating a set of SSH keys automatically enables the SSH protocol. As soon as you have created the keys, the router is able to start accepting SSH sessions. The first time you attempt to access an SSH enabled device, your SSH client software will prompt you store the device host key. This prevents other devices from masquerading as a legitimate device. As a general rule, you do not need to generate keys on the client device to use SSH:

```
Freebsd% ssh -l ijbrown Router1
The authenticity of host 'Router1 (172.25.1.5)' can't be established.
RSA1 key fingerprint is 7a:97:99:2a:ef:08:40:fb:c3:dd:c4:8c:29:fc:2f:4d.
Are you sure you want to continue connecting (yes/no)? yes
Warning: Permanently added 'Router1' (RSA1) to the list of known hosts.
ijbrown@Router's password: xxxxxxxxxx

Router1>exit
Connection to Router1 closed.
```

SSH will pass the current username to the SSH server, which in turn will prompt for the password of the current user. However, with the Unix version of SSH, you can override this behavior by specifying the -l option, followed by an alternate username. In the example above, we explicitly specified a particular username (ijbrown). The default behavior looks like this:

```
Freebsd% ssh Router1
ijbrown@Router1's password: xxxxxxxxxx

Router1>
```

No username was defined, yet the router prompted for the password for the username ijbrown, the current Unix username.

If you decide to use SSH as your transport protocol for administrative access to your routers, we recommend that you disable all other forms of VTY access using the *transport input* configuration command. Running nonsecure protocols defeats the purpose of implementing SSH in the first place. For more information on disabling transport protocols on virtual terminals, see Recipe 3.10. The following example illustrates how to disable all inbound protocols except SSH:

```
Router1#configure terminal
Enter configuration commands, one per line.  End with CNTL/Z.
Router1(config)#line vty 0 4
Router1(config-line)#transport input ssh
Router1(config-line)#exit
Router1(config)#end
Router1#
```

Starting with Version 12.1(3)T, Cisco's IOS began to support SSH client functionality as well. SSH clients allow you to access other SSH servers, including SSH enabled routers. In the following example we initiate a SSH session from our router to an SSH-enabled Unix server:

```
Router1#ssh -l ijbrown server
Trying server.oreilly.com (172.25.1.3)... Open

Password: xxxxxxxxxxx
FreeBSD 4.6-STABLE (IJB)

Welcome to FreeBSD!

You have new mail.
Freebsd%
```

Many SSH clients and servers are readily available for most popular operating systems. There are also several free SSH packages available on the Internet, including OpenSSH and PuTTY (see Appendix A for more details).

The *show ssh* EXEC command displays the active SSH sessions and their attributes, such as VTY number, SSH version, encryption type, session state, and username:

```
Router1#show ssh
Connection     Version Encryption     State               Username
0              1.5     3DES           Session started     ijbrown
3              1.5     3DES           Session started     morewood
```

The command *show ip ssh* displays the SSH server configuration status, including the SSH version, authentication timeout, and number of retries:

```
Router1#show ip ssh
SSH Enabled - version 1.5
Authentication timeout: 120 secs; Authentication retries: 4
Router1#
```

Configuring SSH Version 2 requires the following steps:

- Ensure that your router is running IOS Version 12.3(4)T or higher.

- Ensure that your IOS version contains support for 3DES.

- Configure an authentication method that supports usernames and passwords, such as local authentication or AAA. SSH does not support the default VTY password-encryption method because it needs usernames as well as passwords. See Recipe 3.1 for information on local authentication and Chapter 4 for more information on AAA.

- Set the router's hostname to something other than the default "Router".
- Configure the *ip domain-name* on your router to match the organization's domain name.
- Generate the SSH host keys using the *crypto key generate rsa* configuration command. The router can accept a key length between 360 and 2048 bits; however, SSH Version 2 requires a minimum 768 key-pair. Larger keys provide greater security, but affect performance. We don't recommend using a key that is shorter than 1024 bits. Creating keys requires a large number of CPU cycles, usually a few minutes of high CPU utilization (depending on the router type and the key length). Once created, keys are stored in NVRAM and are inaccessible. You can delete a set of keys with the *crypto key zeroize rsa* configuration command.

By default, the router will run in compatibility mode, meaning it will enable both versions of SSH. Since SSH Version 2 has significant security advantages over SSH Version 1 we highly suggest you disable SSH Version 1 whenever possible. To enable only SSH Version 2, use the *ip ssh version command*:

```
Router1#configure terminal
Enter configuration commands, one per line.  End with CNTL/Z.
Router1(config)#ip ssh version 2
Router1(config)#end
Router1#
```

See Also

Recipe 3.1; Chapter 4

3.21   Changing Privilege Level of IOS Commands

Problem

You want to change the privilege level of specific IOS commands

Solution

To reduce the privilege level of an enable command from 15 to 1, use the following command:

```
Router1#configure terminal
Enter configuration commands, one per line.  End with CNTL/Z.
Router1(config)#privilege exec level 1 show startup-config
Router1(config)#end
Router1#
```

You can also increase the privilege level of a level 1 command:

```
Router1#configure terminal
Enter configuration commands, one per line.  End with CNTL/Z.
Router1(config)#privilege exec level 15 show ip route
```

```
Router1(config)#privilege exec level 1 show ip
Router1(config)#privilege exec level 1 show
Router1(config)#end
Router1#
```

Notice that raising the privilege level of the *show ip route* command also increased the level of the *show ip* set of commands and all of the other *show* commands in the process. In this example, we lowered the *show ip* and *show* commands back to privilege 1 to ensure that all of the other *show* commands operated normally.

Discussion

Cisco routers support sixteen privilege levels, ranging from zero to fifteen. By default, Cisco assigns commands to only three of these privilege levels: zero, user, and enable. There are five commands with privilege level zero: disable, enable, exit, help, and logout. The user level (privilege level 1) has a wide variety of commands available that cannot alter the router's configuration. Enable mode (privilege level 15), by contrast, allows complete access to all router commands.

In practical terms, only levels 1 and 15 are normally used. When you first access the router using your VTY password (or local authentication), the router assigns privilege level 1 to your session. In order to access privilege level 15, you must use the *enable* EXEC command:

```
Router1>show privilege
Current privilege level is 1
Router1>enable 15
Password: <password>
Router1#show privilege
Current privilege level is 15
Router1#
```

You can specify any valid privilege level with the *enable* command, but the default is level 15. You can also reduce the privilege level of your current session with the *disable* command:

```
Router1#show privilege
Current privilege level is 15
Router1#disable 1
Router1>show privilege
Current privilege level is 1
Router1>
```

The *disable* command will default to privilege level 1, if you don't specify a target privilege level.

By default, Cisco assigns a subset of commands to privilege 1 and the full set of commands to privilege 15. However, sometimes the default commands for each privilege level are not sufficient in your organization. Many organizations find it useful to modify the default command privileges.

The first example in this recipe shows how to change the privilege level of the *show startup-config* from its default privilege value of 15, giving it a new value of 1. This allows normal unprivileged users to see the router's startup configuration without having to give them full enable access in the process. Usually people use this feature to reduce the privilege of certain key commands. By allowing normal users to access the few commands that they need, this feature allows you to keep tighter restrictions on the commands that change the router's configuration.

Although you can change the privilege mode of any router command, the *show running-config* command does not function correctly at levels below 15:

```
Router1#configure terminal
Enter configuration commands, one per line.  End with CNTL/Z.
Router1(config)#privilege exec level 1 show running-config
Router1(config)#end
Router1#disable
Router1>show running-config
Building configuration...

Current configuration : 85 bytes
!
! Last configuration change at 22:02:36 EDT Sun Jul 7 2002 by ijbrown
!
!
!
!
end

Router1>
```

Although the router permits the command to execute, the output is unusable.

The second recipe example shows how to increase the privilege level of a command, *show ip route*, from 1 to 15. This will prevent user level staff from viewing our routing table. The NSA guide to Cisco security recommends that administrators increase the privilege level of the following commands from 1 to 15: *connect, rlogin, telnet, show ip access-lists, show access-lists,* and *show logging*:

```
Router1#configure terminal
Enter configuration commands, one per line.  End with CNTL/Z.
Router1(config)#privilege exec level 15 connect
Router1(config)#privilege exec level 15 rlogin
Router1(config)#privilege exec level 15 telnet
Router1(config)#privilege exec level 15 show ip access-lists
Router1(config)#privilege exec level 15 show access-lists
Router1(config)#privilege exec level 15 show logging
Router1(config)#privilege exec level 1 show
Router1(config)#privilege exec level 1 show ip
Router1(config)#end
Router1#
```

Note that changing the privilege level of the *show ip route* command from one to fifteen also increases the privilege level of all *show ip* and *show* commands to 15. So in this example, we have explicitly reduced the privilege of these commands back to level 1 so that we don't lose access to all of the other *show* commands.

To reset the privilege level of a particular command back to its normal setting, you can use the *no* form of the *privilege* command or, starting in IOS Version 12.3(6)T, you can use the *reset* keyword:

```
Router1#configure terminal
Enter configuration commands, one per line.  End with CNTL/Z.
Router1(config)#no privilege exec level 1 show startup-config
Router1(config)#privilege exec reset show startup-config
Router1(config)#end
Router1#
```

See Also

Recipe 3.22; Recipe 3.23

3.22   Defining Per User Privileges

Problem

You want to set different privilege levels to different users.

Solution

To assign a particular privilege level to user, use the following set of commands:

```
Router1#configure terminal
Enter configuration commands, one per line.  End with CNTL/Z.
Router1(config)#aaa new-model
Router1(config)#aaa authentication login default local
Router1(config)#aaa authorization exec default local
Router1(config)#username slowell privilege 10 password maceng#1
Router1(config)#privilege exec level 10 show ip route
Router1(config)#privilege exec level 1 show ip
Router1(config)#privilege exec level 1 show
Router1(config)#end
Router1#
```

You can also create several global privilege levels, which any user can access with the appropriate password:

```
Router1#configure terminal
Enter configuration commands, one per line. End with CNTL/Z.
Router1(config)#enable secret level 10 lvl10passwd
Router1(config)#privilege exec level 10 show ip route
Router1(config)#privilege exec level 1 show ip
Router1(config)#privilege exec level 1 show
Router1(config)#end
Router1#
```

Discussion

Sometimes having two privilege level groups doesn't give fine enough granularity. For example, you might have three levels of administrators. The user-level staff members are not allowed to see the router's routing table. The mid-level staff can see the routing table, but they aren't allowed to make configuration changes. Only the highest-level engineers have access to everything.

You could accomplish this by using either of the two methods shown in the recipe example. For example, you could create user accounts for the staff members, assigning the appropriate privilege level to each user or group of users. Or you could create user accounts for all of the users, and then have a series of different global *enable* levels. Either approach would work.

Our first example uses the *username* command, discussed in Recipe 3.1, to assign a particular privilege level to a username. We have assigned user slowell the privilege level 10 and increased the privilege level of the command *show ip route* to 10. Without the *aaa authorization* command, you cannot change the default privilege level. Essentially, we have created a new privilege level, 10, and assigned it a single command. However, it also inherits the commands from all of the lower the privilege levels:

```
Freebsd% telnet Router1
Trying 172.22.1.4...
Connected to Router1.
Escape character is '^]'.


User Access Verification

Username: slowell
Password: <maneng#1>
Router1#show privilege
Current privilege level is 10
Router1#show ip route
Codes: C - connected, S - static, I - IGRP, R - RIP, M - mobile, B - BGP
       D - EIGRP, EX - EIGRP external, O - OSPF, IA - OSPF inter area
       N1 - OSPF NSSA external type 1, N2 - OSPF NSSA external type 2
       E1 - OSPF external type 1, E2 - OSPF external type 2, E - EGP
       i - IS-IS, L1 - IS-IS level-1, L2 - IS-IS level-2, ia - IS-IS inter area
       * - candidate default, U - per-user static route, o - ODR
       P - periodic downloaded static route

Gateway of last resort is 172.22.1.3 to network 0.0.0.0

     172.16.0.0/24 is subnetted, 1 subnets

C       172.22.1.0 is directly connected, FastEthernet1/0
O*E1 0.0.0.0/0 [110/3] via 172.22.1.3, 00:15:56, FastEthernet1/0
Router1#disable 1
Router1>show ip route
            ^
% Invalid input detected at '^' marker.
```

Notice that when this user logs in, he automatically gets the increased privilege level without having to issue an *enable* command. He then executes the *show ip route* command, which we have assigned to level 10, so it works normally. If he then reduces his level to 1 and tries the *show ip route* command again, it doesn't work.

You could assign a username to privilege level 15 (enable level), but we do not recommend doing this. The extra layer of password protection and the strong encryption that the enable secret commands uses outweighs the convenience of assigning a user privilege level 15.

The second example defines a new privilege level using the *enable secret* command. You can also use the *enable password* command to define per level usernames, but the *enable secret* command gives much better encryption, as we showed in Recipe 3.5.

The second method has two distinct advantages over the first example. First, the *enable secret* command uses strong MD5 encryption to store its passwords in the configuration. Second, it ensures that the new privilege level is available to all user-level staff, and not just the single username we assigned earlier.

You can then use the command *enable* 10, which has its own password, to reach this new level:

```
Router1>enable 10
Password: <lvl10passwd>
Router1#show ip route
Codes: C - connected, S - static, I - IGRP, R - RIP, M - mobile, B - BGP
       D - EIGRP, EX - EIGRP external, O - OSPF, IA - OSPF inter area
       N1 - OSPF NSSA external type 1, N2 - OSPF NSSA external type 2
       E1 - OSPF external type 1, E2 - OSPF external type 2, E - EGP
       i - IS-IS, L1 - IS-IS level-1, L2 - IS-IS level-2, ia - IS-IS inter area
       * - candidate default, U - per-user static route, o - ODR
       P - periodic downloaded static route

Gateway of last resort is 172.22.1.3 to network 0.0.0.0

C       172.22.1.0 is directly connected, FastEthernet1/0
O*E1 0.0.0.0/0 [110/3] via 172.22.1.3, 1w2d, FastEthernet1/0
Router1#disable 1
Router1>show ip route
                 ^
% Invalid input detected at '^' marker.

Router1>
```

To access the new privilege level, the user used the *enable* command with the optional privilege-level keyword, 10. The router prompted her for the level 10 password. Then she could use the *show ip route* command. Then she reduced her privilege level back to default user level (privilege level 1), where the *show ip route* command no longer works.

See Also

Recipe 3.1; Recipe 3.5; Recipe 3.21; Recipe 3.23

3.23   Defining Per Port Privileges

Problem

You want to set the privilege level according to which port you use to access the router.

Solution

To configure the privilege level of a particular line, use the following configuration command:

```
Router1#configure terminal
Enter configuration commands, one per line.  End with CNTL/Z.
Router1(config)#line aux 0
Router1(config-line)#privilege level 5
Router1(config-line)#exit
Router1(config)#privilege exec level 5 show ip route
Router1(config)#privilege exec level 1 show ip
Router1(config)#privilege exec level 1 show
Router1(config)#end
Router1#
```

Discussion

By default, every access line has a privilege level of 1. You can change the privilege level assigned to a particular line with the *privilege level* command. The following example shows what happens when we connect to the AUX port when it is configured with privilege level 5:

```
Press RETURN to get started.

Router1#show privilege
Current privilege level is 5
Router1#show ip route
Codes: C - connected, S - static, I - IGRP, R - RIP, M - mobile, B - BGP
       D - EIGRP, EX - EIGRP external, O - OSPF, IA - OSPF inter area
       N1 - OSPF NSSA external type 1, N2 - OSPF NSSA external type 2
       E1 - OSPF external type 1, E2 - OSPF external type 2, E - EGP
       i - IS-IS, L1 - IS-IS level-1, L2 - IS-IS level-2, ia - IS-IS inter area
       * - candidate default, U - per-user static route, o - ODR
       P - periodic downloaded static route

Gateway of last resort is 172.22.1.3 to network 0.0.0.0

C     172.22.1.0 is directly connected, FastEthernet1/0
O*E1 0.0.0.0/0 [110/3] via 172.22.1.3, 1w2d, FastEthernet1/0
```

```
Router1#disable
Router1>show ip route
              ^
% Invalid input detected at '^' marker.
Router1>
```

You will notice that no username or password is needed to log in, and the privilege level defaults to 5. This permits us to issue a *show ip route* command. We have raised the privilege of this command to the same level, so it works. When we use the *disable* command to set the privilege level back to 1 and attempt to issue the *show ip route* command again, it fails.

Although we have just shown how to increase the privilege level of a router port, this command is more commonly used to lower the level to 0. Lowering the privilege level provides greater security on insecure lines and provides greater flexibility in restricting commands. For instance, you can use this method to restrict the commands available to a user connected on a particular port down to just Telnet, preventing all other commands. You can accomplish this by configuring a port to privilege level 0 and lowering the privilege level of the Telnet command to the same level. This is useful when the router is acting as a terminal server.

See Also

Recipe 3.21; Recipe 3.22

CHAPTER 4

TACACS+

4.0   Introduction

The Terminal Access Controller Access Control System (TACACS) protocol dates back to an earlier era in networking when terminal servers were common. The terminal server was also called a Terminal Access Controller (TAC). So TACACS was the TAC Access Control System.

The TACACS protocol was developed in the early 1980s by a company called BBN, which played a key role in the early development of the Internet (parts of BBN were subsequently absorbed by companies such as Verizon and Cisco). The original protocol only included basic functionality to forward login credentials to a central server, and the ability for the server to respond with a pass or fail on those credentials.

Cisco implemented several extensions to the original TACACS protocol in 1990, and called the new version XTACACS (Extended TACACS), which is described in RFC 1492. However, the IETF considers this RFC to be purely informational, and not an official protocol specification.

More recently, Cisco has replaced both of these earlier versions of TACACS by a newer implementation called TACACS+. The three different versions are not compatible with one another. In fact, Cisco considers the two earlier versions to be obsolete and no longer supports them, although they are still included in the IOS for backward compatibility reasons. This chapter will focus on only the newest TACACS+ version. There is no RFC protocol specification for TACACS+.

It is important to remember that TACACS+ is a Cisco proprietary standard, unlike the competing Remote Authentication Dial In User Service (RADIUS), standard, which is documented in RFC 2865.

TACACS+ uses a TCP transport, on port 49, which makes it more reliable than RADIUS, which uses UDP. RFC 2865 includes a lengthy technical defense of the RADIUS UDP implementation. However, TACACS+ and RADIUS use different implementation models. TACACS+ prefers to get a reliable delivery of data between the client and server, while RADIUS prefers a stateless model that allows it to quickly switch to a backup server.

There are also more tangible benefits to using TACACS+. The biggest real advantage is that TACACS+ allows true command authorization. This means that you can create very clear usage policies with TACACS+, where different users have access to different commands with very fine administrative granularity. TACACS+ can do this because it separates Authentication and Authorization functions, while RADIUS combines them.

Another important advantage is that TACACS+ encrypts the entire payload of the client server exchange. This is important in highly secure environments. RADIUS, on the other hand, only encrypts the password. So intercepting packets can reveal important information.

The strongest point in favor of RADIUS is the fact that it is an open standard implemented by many vendors, including Cisco. Therefore, if you operate a multi-vendor network that already includes RADIUS, you may prefer to use RADIUS with your Cisco routers. This chapter does not specifically cover RADIUS, although many of the concepts discussed here are equally applicable to both TACACS+ and RADIUS.

TACACS+ is part of Cisco's Authentication, Authorization, and Accounting (AAA) framework and works with each of these three functions separately:

Authentication
> Authentication identifies users by challenging them to provide a username and password. This information can be encrypted if required, depending on the underlying protocol.

Authorization
> Authorization provides a method of authorizing commands and services on a per user profile basis.

Accounting
> Accounting functions collect detailed system and command information and store it on a central server, where it can be used for security and quality assurance purposes.

Throughout this chapter, we will discuss some of the most important benefits of using centralized AAA services with TACACS+. These include the ability to administer login IDs from a central server, as well as centrally defining login and command authorizations for each user centrally. This allows for easy grouping of users by their administrative functions. For example, you can give network operators access to one set of commands, web site administrators access to a different set, and still allow network engineers to have full access. In addition, you can define and modify these capabilities centrally so that a particular user has similar capabilities on all routers, without having to configure this separately on each router.

4.1   Authenticating Login IDs from a Central System

Problem

You want to administer login ID and password information centrally for all routers.

Solution

Cisco changed the AAA syntax slightly in Version 12.0(5)T. The following set of commands allows you to configure TACACS+ authentication in the older (pre-12.0(5)T) IOS versions:

```
Router1#configure terminal
Enter configuration commands, one per line.  End with CNTL/Z.
Router1(config)#aaa new-model
Router1(config)#aaa authentication login default tacacs+
Router1(config)#aaa authentication enable default tacacs+
Router1(config)#tacacs-server host 172.25.1.1
Router1(config)#tacacs-server key COOKBOOK
Router1(config)#end
Router1#
```

Newer IOS versions require the group keyword, which defines server groups. Therefore, you would now configure the same functionality as follows:

```
Router1#configure terminal
Enter configuration commands, one per line.  End with CNTL/Z.
Router1(config)#aaa new-model
Router1(config)#aaa authentication login default group tacacs+
Router1(config)#aaa authentication enable default group tacacs+
Router1(config)#tacacs-server host 172.25.1.1
Router1(config)#tacacs-server key COOKBOOK
Router1(config)#end
Router1#
```

Discussion

When you configure AAA authentication on a router, it starts to ignore the locally configured passwords in favor of those provided by the TACACS+ server. In this example, we have configured the router to consult TACACS+ for both the login and enable passwords. This is a great labor saver because it means that you don't have to reconfigure all of your routers just because you want to change passwords. Instead, because the passwords are stored on a central server, you can change them once, and the new passwords instantly propagate to all of your routers. If the router can't reach the TACACS+ server due to a failure of either the network or the server, then it will resort to using the locally configured passwords.

For audit and control reasons, most organizations that implement AAA supply a unique username and password for each individual user. While it is possible to store all of this information locally on the router, if you have a large number of routers, it is extremely time consuming to reconfigure all of the routers to reflect a password change, or simply to add a new user. One of the main advantages to using TACACS+ for AAA authentication is that none of the information is stored on the router. Instead, when a user tries to log in, the router automatically sends a query to the TACACS+ server to verify the login credentials. This minimizes the configuration on each router. And, because this query is done each time, the information is always up to date.

When TACACS+ is working correctly, the router will prompt for a login ID and password instead of the usual line password only:

```
freebsd% telnet toronto
Trying 172.25.1.5...
Connected to toronto.
Escape character is '^]'.


User Access Verification

Username: ijbrown
Password: xxxxxxxx

Router1>
```

The most obvious drawback to using a central server for authentication is that it represents a single point of failure. Therefore, TACACS+ allows you to configure several servers:

```
Router1#configure terminal
Enter configuration commands, one per line.  End with CNTL/Z.
Router1(config)#tacacs-server host 172.25.1.1 key COOKBOOK
Router1(config)#tacacs-server host 10.12.1.33 key OREILLY
Router1(config)#end
Router1#
```

Note that we have defined different encryption keys for each server. This is the key that TACACS+ will use to encrypt the session between the router and the central server. It is important to protect this encryption key. The ability to configure different keys for the different servers helps to improve your overall security by making sure that you can always switch quickly to the backup server if you suspect that the primary's encryption key has been compromised.

The order of these server commands is important because it reflects the order that the router will consult the servers. If the first server is unreachable, the router will resort to the next one, and so on. If no server responds, then the router will use locally configured passwords. This also allows you to easily set up a simple load sharing among multiple servers by making one group of routers use the first server as their primary, and making the second group of routers use the second server. Then you can configure both groups of routers to use the other server as a backup. In this way, you can have all of the benefits of fault tolerance as well as load balancing.

The examples in this recipe and many others throughout this chapter show two sets of syntaxes because Cisco changed the AAA commands in IOS Version 12.0(5)T. The big change is the addition of AAA server groups. In the recipe example, we have opted to use the default TACACS+ group, which consists of all of the servers defined using *tacacs-server host* commands:

```
Router1(config)#aaa authentication login default group tacacs+
Router1(config)#aaa authentication enable default group tacacs+
Router1(config)#tacacs-server host 172.25.1.1
```

However, some organizations are so large that they have to deploy many TACACS servers. In this case, it is convenient to create groups of servers, by either geography or some other logical grouping:

```
Router1(config)#aaa group server tacacs+ SERVERGROUP-A
Router1(config-sg-tacacs+)#server 172.25.1.1
Router1(config-sg-tacacs+)#server 10.12.1.33
Router1(config-sg-tacacs+)#exit
Router1(config)#aaa authentication login default group SERVERGROUP-A
```

You can also create groups of RADIUS servers, if required.

By default, the router will allow three login attempts before dropping a session. You can modify this limit using the TACACS+ command *tacacs-server attempts*. In the following example, we have configured the router to allow only failed one login attempt before dropping the session:

```
Router1#configure terminal
Enter configuration commands, one per line.  End with CNTL/Z.
Router1(config)#tacacs-server attempts 1
Router1(config)#end
Router1#
```

Once you implement this command, the router's login behavior will change:

```
freebsd% telnet toronto
Trying 172.25.1.5...
Connected to toronto.
Escape character is '^]'.

User Access Verification

Username: ijbrown
Password: <wrong password>
Connection closed by foreign host.
freebsd%
```

You can configure the maximum number of failed login attempts to be any number between 1 and 1,000. However, having a high number makes it considerably easier to launch a brute-force password-guessing attack. So in general it is better to keep the maximum number small.

Most large organizations have a security policy that dictates the maximum number of failed logins, with typical values being three or four attempts. Check with your local security department to see what policies you should be following.

See Also

Recipe 3.1; Recipe 4.3; Recipe 4.8

4.2   Restricting Command Access

Problem

You want to restrict permission so that specific users can use only certain commands.

Solution

You can enable TACACS+ command authorization in newer IOS versions with the following set of configuration commands:

```
Router1#configure terminal
Enter configuration commands, one per line.  End with CNTL/Z.
Router1(config)#aaa new-model
Router1(config)#aaa authorization exec default group tacacs+
Router1(config)#aaa authorization commands 15 default group tacacs+
Router1(config)#tacacs-server host 172.25.1.1
Router1(config)#tacacs-server key COOKBOOK
Router1(config)#end
Router1#
```

In any IOS version before 12.0(5)T, the AAA syntax was slightly different:

```
Router2#configure terminal
Enter configuration commands, one per line.  End with CNTL/Z.
Router2(config)#aaa new-model
Router2(config)#aaa authorization exec default tacacs+
Router2(config)#aaa authorization commands 15 default tacacs+
Router2(config)#end
Router2#
```

Discussion

After you configure AAA authorization, the router will query the TACACS+ server each time somebody enters a command to see if it is allowed. If the user is permitted to use this particular command, the TACACS+ server will respond with an "accept" message, and the router will proceed to execute the command. However, if the user is not permitted to issue the command, the TACACS+ server responds with a "reject" message, and the router will not execute the command. The router also shows a rejection status message on the screen:

```
Router1#configure terminal
Command authorization failed.

Router1#
```

In this case, the current user is unable to modify the router configuration because of an AAA authorization rejection.

Command authorization is useful in many situations. For example, you can use it to allow novice users to access some commands on the router, while preventing them from modifying the configuration. Or, in other cases, you might need to give special access to different groups of users according to their job functions. For example, the night operator might need to have access to look at the routing tables. But you may not want to give this person the same command set as your network engineers. In Recipe 4.8, we illustrate how to configure a TACACS+ server to permit and deny specific commands.

In the recipe examples, we have configured the router to authorize enable-level commands only, by specifying the number 15 as an argument:

```
Router1(config)#aaa authorization commands 15 default tacacs+
```

You may recall from Chapter 3 that the enable level commands are assigned level 15, whereas VTY level commands are at level 1. You can authorize all level 1 commands as well, depending on the level of security and control you wish to enforce. You could authorize all level 1 commands as follows:

```
Router1#configure terminal
Enter configuration commands, one per line.  End with CNTL/Z.
Router1(config)#aaa new-model
Router1(config)#aaa authorization commands 1 default tacacs+
Router1(config)#end
Router1#
```

See Also

Chapter 3; Recipe 4.3; Recipe 4.8

4.3   Losing Access to the TACACS+ Server

Problem

You want to ensure that your router can still authenticate user sessions even if it loses access to the TACACS+ server.

Solution

It is important to make sure that you can still enter commands on your router if your TACACS+ server becomes unreachable for any reason. The following set of commands ensures that you don't lose functionality just because you lose your server connection:

```
Router1#configure terminal
Enter configuration commands, one per line.  End with CNTL/Z.
Router1(config)#aaa new-model
Router1(config)#aaa authentication login default group tacacs+ enable
Router1(config)#aaa authentication enable default group tacacs+ enable
Router1(config)#aaa authorization commands 15 default group tacacs+ if-authenticated
Router1(config)#tacacs-server host 172.25.1.1
Router1(config)#tacacs-server key COOKBOOK
Router1(config)#end
Router1#
```

Discussion

One of the potential problems with using a central server to authenticate user access is the issue of what happens when you lose access to that server. It would not be terribly useful if you couldn't plug in a console device and reconfigure the router to fix the problem that caused the router to lose access in the first place. But, by default, a router that can't communicate with its AAA server can't authenticate or authorize users.

Fortunately, Cisco's AAA implementation also includes the ability to do authentication locally on the router in case it can't reach its TACACS+ server. Cisco documentation often refers to this authentication as the "password of last resort." The various authentication methods available within the AAA feature set are shown in Table 4-1.

Table 4-1. AAA Authentication methods

Keyword	Definition
tacacs+	TACACS+ authentication
radius	RADIUS authentication
line	Line-based authentication (password)
local	Local username authentication
local-case	Case-sensitive local authentication
enable	Enable password or enable secret
none	No authentication

The example in this recipe shows how to use the router's enable password as a redundant authentication method by adding the keyword *enable* to the *aaa authentication* command. As long as the primary authentication method is working, TACACS+ in this case, the router never uses this password of last resort. However, when the server connection is lost, users will be prompted for the enable password instead of the TACACS+ username and password. This ensures that you will never be locked out of your routers.

You can also implement other backup authentication methods such as local authentication, line-based passwords, and even RADIUS. However, we recommend using the combination of the enable password method shown in this recipe, along with an enable secret password, for two reasons. The first reason is that this password is local to the router, so it will never become unavailable. Second, when you use enable secret passwords, the router stores the password using MD5 encryption internally, which will help protect it from prying eyes. We should also mention in passing that it is possible to string together a few different methods of authentication, although it's usually not necessary.

This example assumes that we are doing command authorization as well as authentication. The same issues apply here. It doesn't do you any good to get into the router if the router can't verify which command you are authorized to use. This is why we have included the *if-authenticated* keyword in the *aaa authorization* command:

```
Router1(config)#aaa authorization commands 15 default group tacacs+ if-authenticated
```

We highly recommend using the *if-authenticated* option whenever you enable AAA authorization.

See Also

Recipe 4.1; Recipe 4.2

4.4   Disabling TACACS+ Authentication on a Particular Line

Problem

You want to disable TACACS+ authentication on your router's console interface.

Solution

You can disable TACACS+ authentication on the router's console port, while leaving it active on the rest of the router lines:

```
Router1#configure terminal
Enter configuration commands, one per line.  End with CNTL/Z.
Router1(config)#aaa new-model
Router1(config)#aaa authentication login default group tacacs+ local
Router1(config)#aaa authentication login OREILLY line
Router1(config)#line con 0
Router1(config-line)#login authentication OREILLY
Router1(config-line)#end
Router1#
```

Discussion

By default, when you configure a router to use AAA authentication, it automatically applies this authentication method to all lines. This means that you don't have to explicitly configure each line to use AAA authentication. Normally this default behavior is useful because it requires less configuration. But there are times when you may want to use different authentication methods on different lines. For instance, in our example we wanted to be able to access the router's console line with a simple password. But we didn't want this change to affect the AAA authentication on any of the VTY or AUX lines.

The first two lines in the example simply enable TACACS+ authentication for all login access to the router:

```
Router1(config)#aaa new-model
Router1(config)#aaa authentication login default group tacacs+ local
```

As soon as you enter these commands, every line on the router, including the console, will begin to use TACACS+ for authentication. The next command creates a new AAA authentication group called OREILLY that uses the local line password for authentication:

```
Router1(config)#aaa authentication login OREILLY line
```

This command doesn't do anything yet, though, because none of the router's lines belongs to this new authorization group. So we have to then configure the console line with the *login authentication* OREILLY command to associate this line with the authentication group:

```
Router1(config)#line con 0
Router1(config-line)#login authentication OREILLY
```

Now, when a user connects on the console, she uses the type of authentication specified for this group. In this case, if you look back at the group definition, you will see that the OREILLY group uses line authentication. However, because we have only associated the console line with this group, all of the other lines continue to use the TACACS+ authentication method.

If you wanted to, you could configure a different group for every line. But in general, we recommend using the default TACACS+ authentication method on all lines, even the console, unless there is a compelling reason to do otherwise. You don't need to worry about losing console access because of the central server, because you can always implement a password of last resort, as described in Recipe 4.3.

You can return the console to the default authentication group by simply changing the login authentication line again:

```
Router1#configure terminal
Enter configuration commands, one per line.  End with CNTL/Z.
Router1(config)#line con 0
Router1(config-line)#login authentication default
Router1(config-line)#end
Router1#
```

See Also

Recipe 4.1; Recipe 4.3

4.5   Capturing User Keystrokes

Problem

You want to capture and timestamp all keystrokes typed into a router and associate them with a particular user.

Solution

The AAA Accounting feature allows you to capture keystrokes and log them on the TACACS+ server:

```
Router1#configure terminal
Enter configuration commands, one per line.  End with CNTL/Z.
Router1(config)#aaa new-model
Router1(config)#aaa accounting commands 1 default stop-only group tacacs+
```

```
Router1(config)#aaa accounting commands 15 default stop-only group tacacs+
Router1(config)#end
Router1#
```

Discussion

The ability to capture every keystroke entered into a router is a powerful security and quality assurance feature that that is extremely useful. For instance, keystroke logging provides the ability to perform network forensic reconstruction of events. TACACS+ provides the ability to capture all keystrokes typed into your routers and log them for future reference. The TACACS+ log contains the command that was typed along with useful information, such as time and date, router name, username, originating IP address, and privilege level. Here is an example of a TACACS+ accounting record:

```
Fri Jan  3 11:08:47 2003        toronto ijbrown tty66   172.25.1.1      stop    task_
id=512 start_time=1041610127   timezone=EST    service=shell   priv-lvl=15
cmd=configure terminal <cr>
```

In this log entry, we can see that user ijbrown submitted the command *configure terminal* on router toronto at 11:08 on January 3, 2003. It also shows that this user accessed the router from IP address 172.25.1.1 using tty66.

To save disk space on your TACACS+ server, you may decide to log only level 15-based commands, which is done with this command:

```
Router1(config)#aaa accounting commands 15 default stop-only group tacacs+
```

Level 1 commands are generally relatively benign and pose little real threat to the security or health of the router. So logging them is less important than for level 15 commands. But we generally recommend logging all commands, if you're logging commands at all, because the level 1 commands might show useful patterns of information. Of course, you can log the commands issued at any user level by adding more *aaa accounting* lines and specifying the appropriate user level.

See Also

Recipe 4.6; Recipe 4.8

4.6   Logging System Events

Problem

You want to log various system events.

Solution

AAA Accounting includes the ability to log a variety of system events, including timestamps, along with associated usernames:

```
Router1#configure terminal
Enter configuration commands, one per line.  End with CNTL/Z.
Router1(config)#aaa new-model
Router1(config)#aaa accounting exec default start-stop group tacacs+
Router1(config)#aaa accounting connection default start-stop group tacacs+
Router1(config)#aaa accounting system default stop-only group tacacs+
Router1(config)#end
Router1#
```

Discussion

In addition to capturing keystroke logs, AAA accounting can gather other useful pieces of information, such as exec, connection, and system events:

exec
>   This feature captures and timestamps the beginning and ending of a user's Exec session on the router.

connection
>   This allows you to gather information about outgoing connections using an interactive protocol such as Telnet, SSH, or RSH.

system
>   When you enable this feature, AAA forwards information about system events such as router reboots or the disabling of AAA accounting.

Here is an example of an exec log entry:

```
Fri Jan  3 11:11:40 2003       toronto ijbrown tty67   172.25.1.1      start   task_
id=514 start_time=1041610300   timezone=EST    service=shell

Fri Jan  3 11:18:47 2003       toronto ijbrown tty67   172.25.1.1      stop    task_
id=514 start_time=1041610300   timezone=EST    service=shell  disc-cause=1   disc-
cause-ext=1020 connect-progress=101    elapsed_time=427         nas-rx-speed=0  nas-
tx-speed=0
```

These two records show that user ijbrown logged into router toronto at 11:11:40 AM on January 3rd, 2003, and stayed connected for 427 seconds. This information is useful for security auditing, and also can be used for billing purposes, if required. For example, if you are using this router to provide PAD or terminal server services to paying customers, this would be an ideal way to gather billing information.

Here is an example of a connection log event:

```
Fri Jan  3 11:30:19 2003       toronto ijbrown tty67   172.25.1.1      stop    task_
id=522start_time=1041611404   timezone=EST    service=connection     protocol=telnet
addr=10.2.2.2 cmd=telnet 10.2.2.2    pre-bytes-in=0  pre-bytes-out=0 pre-paks-in=0
pre-paks-out=0 bytes_in=1843   bytes_out=81    paks_in=43      paks_out=50
connect-progress=47    elapsed_time=15 nas-rx-speed=0  nas-tx-speed=0
```

In this record, you can see that user ijbrown initiated a Telnet session to IP address 10.2.2.2 and terminated it 15 seconds later. And you can even see the total number of bytes and packets both sent and received by the Telnet process.

The system event log entries look like this:

```
Fri Jan  3 11:35:19 2003       toronto unknown unknown unknown stop     task_id=265
start_time=1041611719  timezone=EST    service=system  event=sys_acct
reason=shutdown

Fri Jan  3 11:37:35 2003       toronto unknown unknown unknown start    task_id=1
timezone=EST    service=system  event=sys_acct  reason=reload
```

These records show that somebody reloaded the router called toronto at 11:35 on January 3, 2003. It came back up at 11:37, some 2 minutes later. Notice that the system event logging did not capture information on the user who submitted the *reload* command. That information could be captured using command logging.

Actually, this points out an interesting side benefit to capturing this information on a central server. If you were just using regular system logging in the router's log buffer, this information would be lost during the reboot. However, by storing system events on the TACACS+ server, you don't lose anything when the router reboots. For more information regarding logging, please see Chapter 18.

See Also

Recipe 4.5; Recipe 4.8; Chapter 18

4.7   Setting the IP Source Address for TACACS+ Messages

Problem

You want the router to use a particular source IP address when sending TACACS+ logging messages.

Solution

The *ip tacacs source-interface* configuration command allows you to specify a particular source IP address for TACACS logging messages:

```
Router1#configure terminal
Enter configuration commands, one per line.  End with CNTL/Z.
Router1(config)#ip tacacs source-interface Loopback0
Router1(config)#end
Router1#
```

Note that implementing this command will not only affect AAA accounting; it will also affect AAA authentication and AAA authorization.

Discussion

Normally, when you enable TACACS+ on a router, the source IP addresses on the messages that it sends to the TACACS+ server will be the address of the router's nearest interface. However, this is not always meaningful. If there are many different paths to the server, the router could wind up sending messages through different interfaces. On the server, then, these messages usually will look like they came from different routers, which can make it difficult to analyze the logs.

However, if you use a loopback address for the source, all messages from this router will look the same, regardless of which interface they were delivered through. In many networks, the DNS database only contains these loopback IP addresses, which helps make the logs more useful as well.

We strongly recommend using this command.

See Also

Recipe 4.5; Recipe 4.6

4.8 Sample Server Configuration Files

Problem

You want to configure a TACACS+ server to accept AAA requests from your network devices.

Solution

Here is an example of a TACACS+ server configuration file that accepts AAA requests from network devices to authenticate users. Use Example 4-1 as a template to help you build your own configuration files.

Example 4-1. tac.conf – sample TACACS server configuration file

```
key = "COOKBOOK"

accounting file = /var/log/tacacs

user = ijbrown {
    default service = permit
    member = staff
    login = cleartext cisco
}

user = kdooley {
    default service = permit
    member = staff
    login = des l5c2fHiF21uZ6
}

user = $enab15$ {
    login = cleartext happy
}
```

Example 4-1. tac.conf – sample TACACS server configuration file (continued)

```
group = staff {
    # Default Group
}
```

Discussion

In this recipe, we will look at how to configure Cisco's free TACACS+ server software because we want to show how the TACACS+ server works. Most of the configuration is done at the central server, so understanding a basic configuration helps with understanding AAA services in general. You can obtain a copy of this software via FTP from ftp-eng.cisco.com in the directory */pub/tacacs*. Please note that other TACACS+ servers use different configuration syntax; however, the basic concepts are the same.

The first thing you first need to configure is the TACACS+ encryption key. This key must be identical to the one configured on your router configuration with the tacacs-server key command. If the keys are not identical, none of the TACACS+ services will work. In the following example, we use the same encryption key as in Recipe 4.1, COOKBOOK:

```
key = "COOKBOOK"
```

To configure authentication for a single user, you need to define a username and password combination as follows:

```
user = ijbrown {
        login = cleartext cisco
}
```

In this example, we configured the username ijbrown and assigned it a password, cisco. If you prefer, you can encrypt the password using DES encryption and store only this encrypted form in the configuration file. However, for this example we chose to use a clear text password. The TACACS+ server is now ready to accept authentication requests for this user.

If you choose to use TACACS+ to authenticate your enable password as well, then you will need to define a special enable user called $enabl15$. The following example creates this enable account by using the password happy. After you define this username, the TACACS+ server will be able to handle authentication requests for the enable password:

```
user = $enab15$ {
    login = cleartext happy
}
```

To enable AAA authorization, you need to define command authorization by using a series of grep-style regular expressions. For more information on regular expressions, please see your *egrep* man page, or *Mastering Regular Expressions* by Jeffrey Friedl (O'Reilly).

By default, TACACS+ will implicitly deny all commands. So unless you explicitly allow a user to issue a command, it will be denied. Note also that the router will fully expand all commands before sending them to TACACS+ server. This means that if a user types in sh ip rou, as a short form for show ip route, the TACACS+ server will be asked to authorize the long form version of the command, show ip route. This is important to remember when you build your regular expression command statements.

The following example shows how to enable command authorization by using the *cmd* statement. This configuration example permits the user sarnott to issue all *show* commands, with the exception of *show running-config*:

```
user = sarnott {
    member = staff
    login = cleartext nssor
    cmd = show {
        deny running-config
        permit .*
    }
}
```

Notice that we have included two instructions in the *cmd = show* section. The first command, *deny running-config*, denies the user access to the *show running-config* command, while the *permit .** line enables access to all other *show* commands. This works because the regular expression .* matches everything.

We mentioned earlier that, by default, the TACACS+ server implicitly denies all commands. This is a fail-safe approach, but it does make things more difficult when you want to allow a large number of commands. Fortunately, you can use the *default service = permit* command to change this default behavior so TACACS+ will permit any commands that you don't explicitly deny. When you include this command in a user's configuration, users can issue any command they like. If there are certain commands that you don't want them to use, you can use a *deny* statement to prevent the specific commands, as follows:

```
user = ijbrown {
    default service = permit
    login = cleartext cisco
    cmd = debug {
        deny .*
    }
}
```

Here we have configured user ijbrown so he is permitted to access all commands by default. Then we have then specifically denied access to the *debug* commands by using the *cmd* statement. You can include several such *cmd* statements, if required. This illustrates one of TACACS+'s greatest strengths, which is the fine granularity of its command authorization.

TACACS+ also allows you to put users into TACACS+ groups for easier administration. You can define several different profile groups and assign users to them as required. For example, you might create a group for users who are only allowed to look at show commands, another group for users who can do everything except debugging, and an administration group with full access to everything. You simply define a group, build its attributes, and assign users to the group. These users will inherit the group attributes, which will keep administration to a minimum.

Our next example creates a group and assigns a user to the new group:

```
user = kdooley {
    default service = permit
    member = staff
    login = des 15c2fHiF21uZ6
}

group = staff {
    # Default Group
    cmd = debug {
        deny .*
    }
}
```

In this example, we have assigned the user kdooley to the group called staff using the *member* command. This new user will now inherit the group's attributes. In this example, like all other members of the staff group, user kdooley is allowed to use any command except the *debug* commands.

Finally, if you wish to enable AAA accounting, then you need to define the log file for TACACS+ to store these accounting messages. Interestingly enough, this is the only configuration command required to enable accounting on the server. As soon as you define this accounting file, the TACACS+ server is able to begin capturing these messages from any routers that are configured to send them.

AAA accounting logs can grow rather unruly, especially if you are using command logging. So we highly recommend cycling your accounting log on a daily basis, keeping at least a week's worth of logs in case of emergencies. Recipe 18.11 shows a script that will rotate your accounting log files:

```
accounting file = /var/log/tacacs
```

See Also

Recipe 4.1; Recipe 4.2; Recipe 4.5; Recipe 18.11; *Mastering Regular Expressions* by Jeffrey Friedl (O'Reilly)

## CHAPTER 5

IP Routing

5.0   Introduction

IP Routing works by comparing the destination addresses of IP packets to a list of possible destinations called the Routing Table. The destination address in a packet usually identifies a single host. It is also possible to use the multicast functions of the IP protocol to send packets to many hosts simultaneously, as we will discuss in Chapter 23. In this chapter, however, we will focus on routing to a specific single destination.

In a very large network such as the public Internet or a large corporate network, it is impractical keep track of every device individually. So the IP protocol groups devices into subnets. A subnet is, in effect, a summary address representing a group of adjacent hosts. Similarly, you can summarize adjacent groups of subnet addresses. The result is an extremely efficient hierarchical addressing system.

There are two different sets of rules for how groups of subnets can be summarized together. The older method uses a concept called *class*, while the newer method is *classless*, and is often referred to by the acronym Classless Interdomain Routing (CIDR). CIDR is described in detail in RFC's 1517, 1518, and 1519. Both methods are still in common use, although the public Internet makes extensive use of CIDR, and all new registered IP addressing follows the new rules.

You can turn on CIDR in Cisco routers with the global configuration command *ip classless*. Classless routing has been the default since IOS Version 11.3. If the older rules are required, you have to explicitly disable CIDR with the *no ip classless* command.

For small networks the distinction is often irrelevant, particularly if they don't use a dynamic routing protocol. However, using a mixture of classful and classless addressing and routing models in a network can cause some extremely strange and unexpected routing behavior. Many network administrators are unclear on the distinctions. So a brief review is in order.

The biggest difference between classful and classless addressing is that classful addressing assumes that the first few bits of the address can tell you how big the network is. Table 5-1 shows how address classes are defined. As you can see, a Class A address is any network from 0.0.0.0 to 127.0.0.0, and all of these networks are assumed to have a mask of 255.0.0.0 (/8).

Table 5-1. Classes of IP addresses

Class	Range of network addresses	Mask	Mask bits
A	0.0.0.0–127.0.0.0	255.0.0.0	8
B	128.0.0.0–191.255.0.0	255.255.0.0	16
C	192.0.0.0–223.255.255.0	255.255.255.0	24
D	224.0.0.1–239.255.255.255	255.255.255.255	32
E	240.0.0.1–255.255.255.255	255.255.255.255	32

You can create several subnets within a Class A, B, or C network. However, it is harder to work with structures that are larger than the network. For example, if you wanted to work with the networks 192.168.4.0/24, 192.168.5.0/24, 192.168.6.0/24, and 192.168.7.0/24, CIDR would allow you to address this entire group (called a *supernet*) as 192.168.4/22 (or 192.168.4.0 255.255.252.0 in netmask notation). However, with classful routing, the router would have to maintain routes to all of these ranges as separate Class C networks.

A router decides where to send a packet by comparing the destination address in the header of the IP packet with its routing table. The rule is that the router will always use the most specific match in the table. This will be the entry that has the most bits in its netmask, so it is often called the *longest* match. This longest match rule is required because the routing table will often contain several possible matches for a particular destination.

For example, suppose the destination address in a particular packet was 10.5.15.35. The router will look in its routing table for possible matches and the accompanying next hop information that will tell it where to send this packet. If there is a match for the specific host, 10.5.15.35/32, then it doesn't need to look any further. But, it is more likely that the router will find a more general route such as 10.5.15.0/24 or 10.5.0.0/16. And if it can't find any reasonable matches, there will usually be a *default route* or *gateway of last resort*, 0.0.0.0/0, that matches anything. If there is no match at all, then the router must drop the packet.

Classless routing can use a mask of any length when looking for the best route to a destination. But in classful routing this is not true. For example, CIDR would allow the four networks 192.168.4.0/24, 192.168.5.0/24, 192.168.6.0/24, and 192.168.7.0/24 to be written together as 192.168.4.0/22. But if a router uses classful routing, it would not consider the destination address 192.168.5.15 to be a part of 192.168.4.0/22 because it knows that anything beginning with 192 must be a Class C network. Instead, if there was no specific route for 192.168.5.0/24 or a subnet containing this destination, the router will skip straight to the default route. If you mix classless and classful routing, this could be the wrong path, and in the worst case, it could even cause a routing loop.

This is why it is so important to make sure that you are consistent about which type of routing and addressing you want to use. In general, it is better to use CIDR because of the improved flexibility. Also, since CIDR allows more levels of route summarization, you can often simplify your routing tables so that they take up less memory in the routers. This, in turn, can improve network performance.

Summary routes have another important benefit. The router will keep its summary route as long as any of its subnets exist. This means that the summary route is as stable as the most stable route in the summarized range. Without summarization, if there is one route that repeatedly flaps up and down, the routing protocol must propagate every transition throughout the network. But a summary route can hide this instability from the rest of the network. The routing protocol doesn't need to waste resources installing and removing the flapping route, which improves overall network stability.

Unregistered Addresses

Most of the IP addresses used in examples in this book are unregistered. The Internet Engineering Task Force (IETF) and the Internet Assigned Numbers Authority (IANA) have set aside several unregistered ranges of addresses for anybody to use at any time. The only stipulation is that because anybody and everybody is using these numbers, they cannot be allowed to leak onto any public sections of the Internet. The allowed ranges of unregistered IP addresses are defined in RFC 1918, and summarized in Table 5-2. It is a good practice to address all private networks using these address ranges.

Table 5-2. RFC 1918 allowed unregistered IP addresses

Class	Network	Mask	Comment
Class A	10.0.0.0	255.0.0.0	One large Class A network
Class B	172.16.0.0 through 172.31.0.0	255.255.0.0	16 Class B networks
Class C	192.168.0.0 through 192.168.255.0	255.255.255.0	256 Class C networks

Note that RFC 3330 defines a number of other special ranges, including a special TEST-NET range, 192.0.2.0/24, which is reserved for documentation purposes. We occasionally use this address range in this book. You should not use it in production networks, however.

5.1 Finding an IP Route

Problem

You want to find a particular route in your router's routing tables.

Solution

The EXEC level command to look at the entire IP routing table is:

```
Router>show ip route
Codes: C - connected, S - static, I - IGRP, R - RIP, M - mobile, B - BGP
       D - EIGRP, EX - EIGRP external, O - OSPF, IA - OSPF inter area
       N1 - OSPF NSSA external type 1, N2 - OSPF NSSA external type 2
       E1 - OSPF external type 1, E2 - OSPF external type 2, E - EGP
       i - IS-IS, L1 - IS-IS level-1, L2 - IS-IS level-2, * - candidate default
       U - per-user static route, o - ODR

Gateway of last resort is 172.25.1.1 to network 0.0.0.0

     192.168.17.0/27 is subnetted, 1 subnets
C       192.168.17.0 is directly connected, Loopback1
     172.16.0.0/30 is subnetted, 1 subnets
C       172.16.1.0 is directly connected, Async1
     172.25.0.0/16 is variably subnetted, 6 subnets, 3 masks
C       172.25.25.0/30 is directly connected, Tunnel0
C       172.25.1.0/24 is directly connected, Ethernet0
C       172.25.9.0/24 is directly connected, Ethernet1
C       172.25.10.1/32 is directly connected, Loopback0
O       172.25.100.1/32 [110/11] via 172.25.9.2, 4d09h, Ethernet1
O IA    172.25.100.0/24 [110/11] via 172.25.1.1, 2d11h, Ethernet0
     192.168.1.0/32 is subnetted, 1 subnets
S       192.168.1.1 [1/0] via 172.25.1.4
O*E1 0.0.0.0/0 [110/11] via 172.25.1.1, 1d07h, Ethernet0
```

You can also find the route to a particular device, such as 172.25.100.15:

```
Router>show ip route 172.25.100.15
Routing entry for 172.25.100.0/24
  Known via "ospf 55", distance 110, metric 11, type inter area
  Redistributing via ospf 55
  Last update from 172.25.1.1 on Ethernet0, 2d12h ago
  Routing Descriptor Blocks:
  * 172.25.1.1, from 172.25.1.1, 2d12h ago, via Ethernet0
      Route metric is 11, traffic share count is 1
```

Discussion

The output of first command contains a lot of useful information. At the top is an explanation of the different codes used in the information that follows. For example, every line that begins with a "C" refers to a route that is directly connected to one of the router's interfaces, "S" means a static route, and so forth.

Note it's possible to have more than one such code, as in the route for 172.25.100.0/24. In this case, the first letter, "O", indicates that this route was learned via the OSPF routing protocol. The next two letters, "IA," indicate that this is an OSPF interarea route. Similarly, the entry for 0.0.0.0/0 is an OSPF external route of Type 1. The "*" indicates that this route is a candidate for default route. There may be several such candidates, but the one that the router thinks is best is captured at the top of the table in the line beginning "Gateway of last resort."

In a large network, it is often not very useful to list the entire routing table like this. Instead, if you are looking for a particular route, you can search for it directly, as the second example in this recipe shows.

Notice that the router did not have a 32-bit match for this particular destination, so it shows instead its best match, 172.25.100.0/24. The result shows several useful pieces of information. It says exactly which match is being used. It tells you how the router knows about this route, via OSPF Process ID number 55, in this case. It also indicates that the next hop required to reach that destination is the device 172.25.1.1, and that it reaches this device through the interface *Ethernet0*.

If the desired route cannot be resolved except by means of the default gateway, the response is much shorter:

```
Router> show ip route 172.15.101.5
% Network not in table
```

This means that the router will use the default route when trying to reach this device. If there is no default route, it will drop the packets. Note that this assumes that we are using classless routing. If we had enabled classful routing on the router, then, if it has a route for any subnet of the classful network, it will also have an entry for the entire network. In this case the classful network would be 172.15.0.0/16.

5.2 Finding Types of IP Routes

Problem

You want to look for a particular type of route in your router's routing tables.

Solution

Often you are more interested in finding all of the directly connected networks, or all of the static routes, rather than in finding a specific route. This is found easily by specifying the type of route in the *show* command:

```
Router>show ip route connected
     192.168.17.0/27 is subnetted, 1 subnets
C       192.168.17.0 is directly connected, Loopback1
     172.16.0.0/30 is subnetted, 1 subnets
C       172.16.1.0 is directly connected, Async1
     172.25.0.0/16 is variably subnetted, 6 subnets, 3 masks
```

```
C       172.25.25.0/30 is directly connected, Tunnel0
C       172.25.1.0/24 is directly connected, Ethernet0
C       172.25.9.0/24 is directly connected, Ethernet1
C       172.25.10.1/32 is directly connected, Loopback0

Router>show ip route static
        192.168.1.0/32 is subnetted, 1 subnets
S       192.168.1.1 [1/0] via 172.25.1.4
```

And another useful variant of the *show ip route* command summarizes all of the different types of routes in the table:

```
Router>show ip route summary
IP routing table name is Default-IP-Routing-Table(0)
Route Source    Networks    Subnets     Overhead    Memory (bytes)
connected       0           3           328         432
static          1           0           64          144
ospf 55         1           3           256         576
   Intra-area: 1 Inter-area: 2 External-1: 1 External-2: 0
   NSSA External-1: 0 NSSA External-2: 0
internal        2                                   2328
Total           4           6           648         3480
```

Discussion

You can see the full list of possibilities by using a *?* on the command line:

```
Router>show ip route ?
Hostname or A.B.C.D  Network to display information about or hostname
  bgp                    Border Gateway Protocol (BGP)
  connected              Connected
  egp                    Exterior Gateway Protocol (EGP)
  eigrp                  Enhanced Interior Gateway Routing Protocol (EIGRP)
  igrp                   Interior Gateway Routing Protocol (IGRP)
  isis                   ISO IS-IS
  list                   IP Access list
  odr                    On Demand stub Routes
  ospf                   Open Shortest Path First (OSPF)
  profile                IP routing table profile
  rip                    Routing Information Protocol (RIP)
  static                 Static routes
  summary                Summary of all routes
  supernets-only         Show supernet entries only
  traffic-engineering    Traffic engineered routes
  <cr>
```

This is useful when you want to see all of the routes that the router has learned via a particular routing protocol, or all of the statically configured or directly connected routes. The output format with the different type keywords is exactly the same as for the general *show ip route*, but it presents only the routes of the required type.

The *show ip route summary* command gives useful information about the size of the routing table and how much memory the router has allocated to storing this information, conveniently broken down by routing protocol. The example also shows how many routes belong to each of the different OSPF area types.

This has several uses. First, it gives you a convenient way to estimate your routing table's memory requirements. In this case, the routing table is very small, so there is more memory used to store connected routes than OSPF routes. However, in a larger network, you will often want to know if one routing protocol is causing memory problems for your routers. This can help you to decide if you need route filtering or summarization mechanisms. Routers exchanging BGP routing information with the public Internet can have particularly serious memory utilization problems.

Second, because it shows how many routes are learned by each mechanism, you can easily check the stability of the routing table by seeing whether this number changes in time. If you look at the entire routing table, you may not notice that a handful of routes periodically disappear and reappear, but looking at this summary information makes it much easier to spot such problems.

And third, you can easily see whether your routing table is getting its information the way you expect. It can be a very quick and easy way to check if the router is installing floating static routes or external routes in its routing table.

5.3   Converting Different Mask Formats

Problem

You want to convert between the three different formats that Cisco routers use for presenting mask information: standard netmask, ACL wildcards, and CIDR bit number format.

Solution

The following Perl script converts from any of these formats—netmask, wildcard, or bit count—to any other. The usage syntax is mask-cvt {n|w|b} {n|w|b} {nnn.nnn.nnn. nnn|/bits}, where the first argument specifies what the input format is and the second argument specifies the output format. In both cases, "n" is for netmask format, "w" is for wildcard format, and "b" is for CIDR bit format (with or without the leading slash, as in /24).

For example:

```
$ mask-cvt.pl n w 255.255.248.0
0.0.7.255
$ mask-cvt.pl n b 255.255.248.0
/21
$ mask-cvt.pl w n 0.3.255.255
255.252.0.0
$ mask-cvt.pl w b 0.3.255.255
/14
```

```
$ mask-cvt.pl b n /21
255.255.248.0
$ mask-cvt.pl b w /21
0.0.7.255
```

The Perl code follows in Example 5-1.

Example 5-1. mask-cvt.pl

```perl
#!bin/perl
#
#   mask-cvt.pl -- a script to convert between the various
#                  methods of masking IP addresses
#

sub usage( ) {
   print "mask-cvt [nwb] [nwb] {nnn.nnn.nnn.nnn|bbb}\n";
   print "    where the first argument, [nwba], specifies the input \n";
   print "            format as one of netmask, wildcard or number of \n";
   print "            bits and the second argument, [nwb], specifies \n";
   print "            the output format\n";
   exit( );
}

if($#ARGV != 2) { usage( ); }

# get the input format style
$_ = @ARGV[0];

if(/[nN]/) {
     # incoming format netmask, what's the outgoing
     $_ = @ARGV[1];
     if(/[nN]/) {
         # no conversion
         $output = @ARGV[2];
        } elsif (/[wW]/) {
           # out is wildcard
           $output = do_subtract(@ARGV[2]);
        } elsif (/[bB]/) {
           # out is wildcard
           $output = do_bits(@ARGV[2]);
        } else {
           usage( );
        }
   } elsif (/[wW]/) {
     # incoming format wildcard, what's the outgoing
     $_ = @ARGV[1];
     if(/[wW]/) {
         # no conversion
         $output = @ARGV[2];
        } elsif (/[nN]/) {
           # out is wildcard
           $output = do_subtract(@ARGV[2]);
```

Example 5-1. mask-cvt.pl (continued)

```perl
        } elsif (/[bB]/) {
            # out is wildcard
            $output = do_bits(do_subtract(@ARGV[2]));
        } else {
            usage();
        }
    } elsif (/[bB]/) {
        # remove any leading "/" in the bit count
        $_ = @ARGV[2];
        s/[-\/]//;
        $bits = $_;

        # incoming format is bit count, what's the outgoing
        $_ = @ARGV[1];
        if(/[bB]/) {
            # no conversion
            $output = @ARGV[2];
            print "no conversion\n";
        } elsif (/[nN]/) {
                # out is netmask
                $output = cvt_bits_mask($bits);
        } elsif (/[wW]/) {
            # out is wildcard
            $output = do_subtract(cvt_bits_mask($bits));
        } else {
            usage();
        }
    } else {
        usage();
    }
}

print "$output\n";

sub do_subtract() {
    local($ip) = @_;

    # break up the bytes of the incoming IP address
    $_ = $ip;
    ($a, $b, $c, $d) = split(/\./);

    if ($a > 255 || $b > 255 || $c > 255 || $d > 255 || /[^0-9.]/) {
        print "invalid input mask or wildcard\n";
        exit();
    }

    $a = 255 - $a;
    $b = 255 - $b;
    $c = 255 - $c;
    $d = 255 - $d;

    return ($a . "." . $b . "." . $c . "." . $d);
}
```

Example 5-1. mask-cvt.pl (continued)

```perl
sub do_bits() {
  local($ip) = @_;

  # break up the bytes of the incoming IP address
  $_ = $ip;
  @ip_bytes = split(/\./);

  if ($ip_bytes[0] > 255 || $ip_bytes[1] > 255 || $ip_bytes[2] > 255
      || $ip_bytes[3] > 255 || /[^0-9.]/ || $#ip_bytes != 3) {
    print "invalid input mask or wildcard\n";
    exit();
  }

  $bits = 0;
  for ($i=0; $i < 4 ; $i++) {
    if ($ip_bytes[$i] > 0 && $bits < 8*$i) {
      print "invalid mask for bit count format\n";
      exit();
    }
    if ($ip_bytes[$i] == 255 ) { $bits += 8;
    } elsif ($ip_bytes[$i] == 254 ) { $bits += 7;
    } elsif ($ip_bytes[$i] == 252 ) { $bits += 6;
    } elsif ($ip_bytes[$i] == 248 ) { $bits += 5;
    } elsif ($ip_bytes[$i] == 240 ) { $bits += 4;
    } elsif ($ip_bytes[$i] == 224 ) { $bits += 3;
    } elsif ($ip_bytes[$i] == 192 ) { $bits += 2;
    } elsif ($ip_bytes[$i] == 128 ) { $bits += 1;
    } elsif ($ip_bytes[$i] != 0 ) {
      print "invalid mask for bit count format\n";
      exit();
    }
  }
  return("/" . $bits);
}
sub cvt_bits_mask() {
  local($bits) = @_;

  if ($bits <= 8 ) {
    $a = bits_to_dec($bits);
    $b=$c=$d=0;
  } else {
    $a=255;
    if ($bits <= 16 ) {
      $b = bits_to_dec($bits-8);
      $c=$d=0;
    } else {
      $b=255;
      if ($bits <= 24 ) {
        $c = bits_to_dec($bits-16);
        $d=0;
      } else {
        $c=255;
```

Example 5-1. mask-cvt.pl (continued)

```
        if ($bits <= 32 ) {
            $d = bits_to_dec($bits-24);
        } else {
            print "invalid bit count\n";
            exit( );
        }
      }
    }
  }
  return ($a . "." . $b . "." . $c . "." . $d);
}

sub bits_to_dec( ) {
  local($bits) = @_;

  if($bits == 0 ) { return 0; }
  if($bits == 1 ) { return 128; }
  if($bits == 2 ) { return 192; }
  if($bits == 3 ) { return 224; }
  if($bits == 4 ) { return 240; }
  if($bits == 5 ) { return 248; }
  if($bits == 6 ) { return 252; }
  if($bits == 7 ) { return 254; }
  if($bits == 8 ) { return 255; }
}
```

Discussion

This script performs several different functions. It converts from netmask format to either wildcard or bit count format, from wildcard to either netmask or bit count format, and from bit count to either netmask or wildcard format. Many experienced network engineers pride themselves on doing these conversions in their heads. But it is still relatively common to find router configurations in which the conversion has been done incorrectly.

The difference between netmask and wildcard formats is that netmask format uses ones in the bit pattern to represent bits that do not change, while wildcard format uses zeroes to represent these bits. So, for example, if you are constructing an access-list that looks at all of the devices in the subnet 192.168.1.0/24, the netmask would be 255.255.255.0, and the wildcard in the access-list would be 0.0.0.255.

The reason for the difference is that you will sometimes want to construct an access-list that doesn't care which subnet a device is on, but can be used to select a particular set of devices on that subnet. Access-lists don't look at subnets, they do pattern matching on addresses.

To convert from wildcard format to netmask format, or vice versa, the program simply subtracts each byte in the mask from the number 255, which is 8 bits of all ones.

It should be relatively easy to see that this converts all of the ones in a binary pattern to zeroes, and all of the zeroes to ones.

The conversion to or CIDR bit count format is slightly more complicated in the program, but easier in concept. If the input is a netmask, the CIDR bit count is simply the number of ones in the bit pattern, counting from the left. Similarly, if the source is a wildcard, then the bit count can be found by counting zeroes. The program actually only has one subroutine for counting bits. If it needs to convert a wildcard pattern to a bit count, it converts it to netmask format first.

It is important to notice that the CIDR bit count format only makes sense if all of the ones in a netmask are on the left, and all of the zeroes on the right. Then this number simply represents the location of the transition from ones to zeroes, which in turn represents the division point between the network and host portions of the address. So the program includes a check to ensure that the netmask pattern is valid, with no zeroes to the left of any ones in the pattern.

5.4   Using Static Routing

Problem

You want to configure a static route.

Solution

You can configure a static route with the *ip route* command, as follows:

```
Router#configure terminal
Enter configuration commands, one per line.  End with CNTL/Z.
Router(config)#ip route 10.35.15.5 255.255.255.255 Ethernet0
Router(config)#end
Router#
```

You can also configure a static route to point to a particular next hop router:

```
Router#configure terminal
Enter configuration commands, one per line.  End with CNTL/Z.
Router(config)#interface Serial0
Router(config-if)#ip address 10.35.6.2 255.255.255.0
Router(config-if)#exit
Router(config)#ip route 172.16.0.0 255.255.0.0 10.35.6.1 2
Router(config)#end
Router#
```

If you want to ensure a route remains in place even if the next-hop IP address becomes unreachable, or the interface goes down, you can use the *permanent* keyword:

```
Router#configure terminal
Enter configuration commands, one per line.  End with CNTL/Z.
Router(config)#ip route 10.35.15.5 255.255.255.255 Ethernet0 permanent
```

```
Router(config)#ip route 172.16.0.0 255.255.0.0 10.35.6.1 2 permanent
Router(config)#end
Router#
```

You can also manually configure routing tags that use static routes by using the *tag* keyword:

```
Router#configure terminal
Enter configuration commands, one per line.  End with CNTL/Z.
Router(config)#ip route 172.16.0.0 255.255.0.0 10.35.6.1 2 tag 36291
Router(config)#end
Router#
```

Discussion

The first version sends all packets destined to the single host 10.35.15.5 out through the Ethernet0 interface. In this case, the router will need to figure out which device on this segment to forward the packet to, because it must put the MAC address of the next hop router in the Layer 2 frame header. The standard mechanism for associating IP addresses with MAC addresses is the Address Resolution Protocol (ARP). The router will send out an ARP request onto the Ethernet segment. If the device that owns the packet's destination IP address happens to be on this segment, it will respond with its MAC address. Otherwise, a router that is configured for Proxy ARP will have to respond on its behalf. This is important because if you do not have Proxy ARP configured on the next hop router, this command will fail. So for multiple access media such as Ethernet segments, we recommend using specifying the IP address of the next hop router rather than the interface.

Please refer to Chapter 22 for more information about enabling and disabling Proxy ARP.

You can also specify a point-to-point media such as a Serial interface for the route destination:

```
Router#configure terminal
Enter configuration commands, one per line.  End with CNTL/Z.
Router(config)#ip route 10.35.15.5 255.255.255.255 Serial0 5
Router(config)#end
Router#
```

In this case there is no ambiguity. You can reach only one other device through this Serial interface, so the Proxy ARP issues that we just described do not apply.

The *ip route* command in the second example affects any packet whose destination address is in the range from 172.16.0.1 to 172.16.255.254, which will be forwarded to the next hop router, 10.35.6.1:

```
Router(config)#ip route 172.16.0.0 255.255.0.0 10.35.6.1 2
```

The last number in this *ip route* command, 2, is the administrative distance for this route. This specifies a distance value that indicates how good this route is. The router will use this distance value to help it to decide between routes to the same destination prefix from different sources. For example, if you have more than one static route to the same destination, or if the router has learned another route to this destination via RIP, it will compare this administrative distances and use the route with the lowest distance value.

If there is no administrative distance value, as in the first example, the router will use a default value of 1.

The syntax for static routes specifies both an IP address and a netmask. This follows the standard rules for netmasks. However, it is useful to remember that the static route statement only controls how packets should be handled on this router. For example, suppose the range 172.16.0.0/16 includes the networks 172.16.1.0/24, 172.16.2.0/24, 172.16.5.4/30, and 172.16.5.8/30. If all the paths to all of these networks go through the router whose address is 10.35.6.1, then they can all be taken together with the same single route statement, as follows:

```
Router(config)#ip route 172.16.0.0 255.255.0.0 10.35.6.1 2
```

It is interesting to see what happens when you need to break up a range of addresses. Carrying on with the same example, suppose there is another network, 172.16.3.0/24, that is connected through a different next-hop router, 10.35.7.2. In this case, you can configure the router as follows:

```
Router#configure terminal
Enter configuration commands, one per line.  End with CNTL/Z.
Router(config)#ip route 172.16.0.0 255.255.0.0 10.35.6.1 2
Router(config)#ip route 172.16.3.0 255.255.255.0 10.35.7.2 2
Router(config)#end
Router#
```

This may appear to have a conflict, because 172.16.3.0/24 is contained within the range 172.16.0.0/16, but there is in fact no conflict because of the longest match rule that we discussed earlier in this chapter. Also note that the router will use the more specific route, even if it has a higher administrative distance. The distance values are used only when selecting between routes with the same mask length. So for example, you could configure two static routes to the same destination:

```
Router#configure terminal
Enter configuration commands, one per line.  End with CNTL/Z.
Router(config)#ip route 172.16.3.0 255.255.255.0 10.35.6.1 2
Router(config)#ip route 172.16.3.0 255.255.255.0 10.35.7.3 5
Router(config)#end
Router#
```

In this case, as long as the router has a route for the better next hop, 10.35.6.1, it will use only this line. The router will install the other route with the higher distance only if it can't reach the better next-hop device.

Note that this is a cumbersome and unreliable way of achieving automatic rerouting because it works only when the route to the next hop disappears, not when the next hop itself becomes unavailable. So, for example, if these two next hop routers were connected through different physical interfaces, and one of those interfaces went down, the router could switch to the router with the higher distance. But if both devices were on the same directly connected Ethernet segment, this would not provide a fail-over. So while this method is useful for some limited applications, in general it is better to use a dynamic routing protocol such as RIP, EIGRP, or OSPF, which are described in later chapters.

By default, the router does this adjustment to evaluate the validity of the next-hop device once every 60 seconds. In 12.3(10), Cisco introduced a new command that allows you to change this time if you need a faster update period:

```
Router(config)#ip route static adjust-time 30
```

In this example, we have reduced the adjust-time interval for next-hop evaluation of static routes from 60 to 30 seconds. This has the obvious effect of improving convergence times for networks with static routes, but it also has some negative consequences. If you have a lot of static routes, setting the adjust-time interval too low can cause CPU overhead problems.

The third example in this recipe uses the *permanent* keyword:

```
Router(config)#ip route 10.35.15.5 255.255.255.255 Ethernet0 permanent
Router(config)#ip route 172.16.0.0 255.255.0.0 10.35.6.1 2 permanent
```

You would use this when you want to ensure that the static route always remains in the routing table, even if the next-hop interface is down. There is sometimes a danger that the dynamic routing protocol will install a route that you do not want to use, and it may be preferable to drop the packets than to use the dynamic route. For example, if you had a private link to another IP network, and this link went down, you might not want your routers to try to find a path via the public Internet, even if one were advertised. This is sort of the opposite of the floating static route of Recipe 5.5.

The last example in this recipe uses routing tags:

```
Router(config)#ip route 172.16.0.0 255.255.0.0 10.35.6.1 2 tag 36291
```

Route tags are used when redistributing from one routing protocol to another. They provide a convenient way to tell which routes came from what external protocols or networks. This concept will be discussed in more detail in the Chapters 6, 7, 8, and 9.

See Also

Recipe 5.5; Chapters 6, 7, 8, 9, and 22

5.5   Floating Static Routes

Problem

You want to use a static route only when the dynamic route is not available.

Solution

The router will use a floating static route for a particular network prefix only if that same route is not available from the dynamic routing protocol. You can accomplish this by setting the administrative distance of the static route to a value greater than the administrative distance of the dynamic routing protocol:

```
Router#configure terminal
Enter configuration commands, one per line.  End with CNTL/Z.
Router(config)#ip route 10.0.0.0 255.0.0.0 172.16.1.1 190
Router(config)#end
Router#
```

You can use the floating static to trigger a dialer interface as follows:

```
Router#configure terminal
Enter configuration commands, one per line.  End with CNTL/Z.
Router(config)#ip route 0.0.0.0 0.0.0.0 Dialer1 190
Router(config)#end
Router#
```

Discussion

The static routes that we discussed in the previous section all had relatively low administrative distance values. If the router has two routes to the same destination but with different distances, it will always choose the one with the lower distance value. This concept also includes the routes that come from other sources, such as dynamic routing protocols.

Every routing protocol has an *administrative distance* that indicates how much the router trusts the information it receives by this method. Table 5-3 shows the default values for these administrative distances. Recipe 5.7 demonstrates how to change these values when they are not appropriate for your network. However, for the current example the default values are sufficient.

Table 5-3. Cisco default administrative distances

Routing protocol or source	Administrative distance
Connected interface	0
Static route	1
EIGRP summary route	5
External BGP	20
Internal EIGRP	90
IGRP	100
OSPF	110

Table 5-3. Cisco default administrative distances (continued)

Routing protocol or source	Administrative distance
IS-IS	115
RIP	120
EGP	140
ODR	160
External EIGRP	170
Internal BGP	200
Unknown	255

A floating static route is simply one that has an administrative distance value greater than that of the dynamic routing protocol being used. For example, any route that is learned via OSPF will have an administrative distance value is 110 by default. This administrative distance applies to all routes learned by this method regardless of what metric they may have within that protocol.

In the case of static routes, you can directly set the administrative distance for any given static route when you define the route. If the static route's distance value is greater than 110, then any OSPF route that includes this destination is considered better. If OSPF has a route for this destination, the router will use it.

The router will install the floating static route if it doesn't have a similar route from the dynamic routing protocol. Bear in mind, though, that the router will always use the route that has the most precise (longest netmask) match. For example, if the router has learned a route for 10.35.15.0/24 from OSPF, and also has a static route for 10.35.15.0/27, it will use the static route even if it has a higher administrative distance. The administrative distance is used only to decide between competing routes of the same mask length.

Floating static routes are often used to trigger automated backup mechanisms when the routing protocol fails. In this case, you could configure a floating static default route, 0.0.0.0/0, which would point to the dialer interface:

```
Router(config)#ip route 0.0.0.0 0.0.0.0 Dialer1 190
```

If the router loses contact with the rest of the network because of a circuit failure, then all of the dynamic routes will drop out of the routing table. The router will then install the floating static route, which will trigger the dial backup connection. We discuss dial backup scenarios in more detail in Chapter 13.

See Also

Recipe 5.4; Recipe 5.7; Chapter 13

5.6 Using Policy-Based Routing to Route Based on Source Address

Problem

You want to use different network links depending on the source address.

Solution

Policy-based routing allows you to configure special routing rules beyond the normal IP routing table. One common application is to route packets based on the IP source address rather than the destination address:

```
Router#configure terminal
Enter configuration commands, one per line.  End with CNTL/Z.
Router(config)#access-list 1 permit 10.15.35.0 0.0.0.255
Router(config)#access-list 2 permit 10.15.36.0 0.0.0.255
Router(config)#interface Ethernet0
Router(config-if)#ip address 10.15.22.7 255.255.255.0
Router(config-if)#ip policy route-map Engineers
Router(config-if)#ip route-cache policy
Router(config-if)#exit
Router(config)#route-map Engineers permit 10
Router(config-route-map)#match ip address 1
Router(config-route-map)#set ip next-hop 10.15.27.1
Router(config-route-map)#exit
Router(config)#route-map Engineers permit 20
Router(config-route-map)#match ip address 2
Router(config-route-map)#set interface Ethernet1
Router(config-route-map)#end
Router#
```

Discussion

This configuration example defines a special routing policy for a group of users defined by the route map called "Engineers." This name is arbitrary, and we recommend that you choose names for your route maps that are meaningful in your organization. This example applies the route map to all of the packets received on the interface Ethernet0. This might be required because these users need to use a special higher capacity link, for example.

There are two clauses in this route-map. The numbers 10 and 20 at the end of each of the *route-map* command lines are used to specify the order that the router will apply these clauses when making routing decisions. It is a good practice to use widely spaced numbers like this to make it easier to insert new clauses between them. For example, if we needed to add a new clause that had to be executed after the first one, but before the last one, we could give it a value of 15.

It is also important to remember that every route map ends with an implicit *deny all*. This means that the packets that don't match either of the clauses in this route map will be unaffected, and will use the standard IP routing table.

The *permit* field is somewhat confusing in general because it governs whether the route map clause will permit or deny the *set* operation contained below it. There are very few cases when the *deny* option is used in practice.

The first route-map clause takes action based on the *match* command:

```
Router(config)#route-map Engineers permit 10
Router(config-route-map)#match ip address 1
Router(config-route-map)#set ip next-hop 10.15.27.1
Router(config-route-map)#exit
```

This command compares the contents of the IP header with what is defined in access-list number 1. Note that this is a standard access-list, which is used only to match the source address in the IP header. You can also use extended access-lists to match any of the header contents. With extended access lists, you can even match TCP or UDP port numbers. The term *address* in the route-map *match* clause is slightly misleading when extended access-lists are used because you can actually match just about anything in the IP header. However, in this case we do happen to be looking for an address.

Access-list 1 will match any packet with a source address in the range from 10.15.35.0 to 10.15.35.255:

```
Router(config)#access-list 1 permit 10.15.35.0 0.0.0.255
```

If the match is successful, the route-map will then apply the *set* command, which overrides any routing table information and sends the packet to the next-hop router, 10.15.27.1. Note that this next-hop router must be on a directly connected network because the router will bypass its routing table when it forwards these packets. If the next hop address is not part of a directly connected subnet, the router can't route the packet because it has already bypassed the routing table in its decision process.

The second clause works in a similar way, but matches with a different access-list and sets a different next-hop value:

```
Router(config)#route-map Engineers permit 20
Router(config-route-map)#match ip address 2
Router(config-route-map)#set interface Ethernet1
```

This clause also handles the routing differently. Instead of specifying a next-hop, it specifies that any packets matching this rule will be forwarded directly out the interface Ethernet1. This means that either the destination device must be on this segment, or there must be a router configured with Proxy ARP that can forward the packet to the ultimate destination.

Because the route map ends with an implicit *deny all*, any packets that don't match any clause are routed in the normal way using information in the routing table.

You can use the *set next-hop* command to set a series of possible next-hops:

```
Router(config-route-map)#set ip next-hop 10.15.27.1 10.15.37.1
```

And you can also specify several different possible interfaces:

```
Router(config-route-map)#set interface Ethernet1 Ethernet2
```

This allows you to define what to do if there is no way to route to one of these next-hop devices. If the first address, or the first interface, is not available, the router will use the second.

The router will consult its routing table to decide whether the specified next-hop router or interface is available. This is important because in many cases, such as Ethernet segments, it is possible to lose contact with the next-hop router, but not lose the routing table entry. In this case, the packet will simply be dropped.

In IOS version 12.0(3)T and later, there is a partial solution to this problem. You can specify the *set ip next-hop verify-availability* command to make the router use CDP to test whether the next-hop device is up:

```
Router(config)#route-map Engineers permit 10
Router(config-route-map)#match ip address 1
Router(config-route-map)#set ip next-hop 10.15.27.1
Router(config-route-map)#set ip next-hop verify-availability
```

Since this uses CDP, you have to ensure the CDP is enabled on the interface that leads to this next-hop device, and that device also has to be running CDP (meaning it must be another Cisco router). This is not a perfect solution because not all media types support CDP, and because it can cause performance problems. Furthermore, CDP uses a relatively long timeout period by default (180 seconds), so it is slow to respond to failures.

If none of the next-hops is available, the router will simply use its normal routing table. If the routing table does not have an entry for this route, you may want to specify a different default than the router's general default gateway:

```
Router(config)#route-map Engineers permit 10
Router(config-route-map)#set ip default next-hop 10.15.47.1
```

You can also specify a default interface in a similar way:

```
Router(config)#route-map Engineers permit 10
Router(config-route-map)#set default interface Null0
```

In this case, the default interface is the Null0 interface. Setting this will force the router to discard the packets rather than use the router's general default gateway.

There is one other extremely important command in the main recipe example, *ip route-cache policy*:

```
Router(config)#interface Ethernet0
Router(config-if)#ip route-cache policy
```

This command tells the router to use fast switching rather than process switching when processing policy commands on this interface. This command is new with IOS Version 12.0. Without it, all policy processing is handled by the router's CPU. This can cause serious performance problems in a slower router, or if the traffic load is heavy.

Note, however, that not all Policy-Based Routing commands can be fast-switched. In particular, the *set ip default next-hop* and *set default interface* commands are not supported. Furthermore, Fast Switching has only limited support for the *set interface* command. In particular, the destination interface must have route-caching enabled, or it must be a point-to-point link. And even if these conditions are true, the router still must check its routing table to ensure that the destination interface is valid, and this happens at the process level. Recipe 5.7 discusses these commands.

It is important to remember that because policy-based routing overrides the normal routing tables within the router, it can result in some interesting and confusing troubleshooting problems. In the example above, if the next-hop value, 10.15.27.1 suffers a failure but its subnet doesn't drop out of the routing table, then there is no dynamic routing protocol involved to find a new path. Worse still, when you try to diagnose the problem, normal procedures like trying to *ping* from the router to the required destination, will give unpredictable results because the ICMP packets originating on the router will not be subject to the routing policy. So you may find that you can ping, but that the application doesn't work for certain users.

For this reason, we recommend avoiding policy-based routing unless there is no other way to accomplish the required goals.

See Also

Recipe 5.7

5.7 Using Policy-Based Routing to Route Based on Application Type

Problem

You want different applications to use different network links.

Solution

This example is similar to the previous one, except that instead of looking at the source address of the incoming IP packet, it looks at other protocol information such as TCP or UDP port number. The example redirects HTTP traffic (TCP port 80) for certain source addresses.

```
Router#configure terminal
Enter configuration commands, one per line.  End with CNTL/Z.
Router(config)#access-list 101 deny tcp 10.15.25.0 0.0.0.255 any eq www
Router(config)#access-list 101 permit tcp any any eq www
Router(config)#interface Ethernet0
Router(config-if)#ip address 10.15.22.7 255.255.255.0
Router(config-if)#ip policy route-map Websurfers
Router(config-if)#ip route-cache policy
Router(config-if)#exit
Router(config)#route-map Websurfers permit 10
Router(config-route-map)#match ip address 101
Router(config-route-map)#set ip next-hop 10.15.27.1
Router(config-route-map)#exit
Router(config)#route-map Websurfers permit 20
Router(config-route-map)#set ip default next-hop 10.15.26.1
Router(config-route-map)#end
Router#
```

This second example looks instead at the IP TOS field:

```
Router#configure terminal
Enter configuration commands, one per line.  End with CNTL/Z.
Router(config)#access-list 102 permit ip any any tos 4
Router(config)#interface Serial0
Router(config-if)#ip address 10.15.23.6 255.255.255.252
Router(config-if)#ip policy route-map High-priority
Router(config-if)#ip route-cache policy
Router(config-if)#exit
Router(config)#route-map High-priority permit 10
Router(config-route-map)#match ip address 102
Router(config-route-map)#set ip next-hop 10.15.27.1
Router(config-route-map)#end
Router#
```

This third example shows how to use Policy-Based Routing for traffic that originates on the router itself:

```
Router#configure terminal
Enter configuration commands, one per line.  End with CNTL/Z.
Router(config)#ip local policy route-map dlswtraffic
Router(config)#access-list 103 permit tcp any any eq 2065
Router(config)#access-list 103 permit tcp any eq 2065 any
Router(config)#route-map dlswtraffic permit 10
Router(config-route-map)#match ip address 103
Router(config-route-map)#set ip next-hop 10.15.27.3
Router(config-route-map)#end
Router#
```

Discussion

These examples show how to route traffic based on protocol information rather than address information. The first example redirects HTTP packets that originate on any device in the range from 10.15.25.0 to 10.15.25.255. Access list 101 has two lines:

```
Router(config)#access-list 101 deny tcp 10.15.25.0 0.0.0.255 any eq www
Router(config)#access-list 101 permit tcp any any eq www
```

The second line matches any TCP packets with any source or destination IP address, and with a destination TCP port number of 80 (HTTP). The first line excludes from the match any packets with the specified range of address and with a destination TCP port number of 80.

When the client makes the initial TCP connection, it places a request to the target IP address by using a particular port number as the destination. The packet also contains the client's IP address as the source of the packet, and it specifies a source port number, which is usually a random number greater than 1023.

The first clause in the route map then redirects the traffic matched by this access list to the specified next hop router:

```
Router(config)#route-map Websurfers permit 10
Router(config-route-map)#match ip address 101
Router(config-route-map)#set ip next-hop 10.15.27.1
```

The second clause in this route-map shows how to handle a default next hop:

```
Router(config)#route-map Websurfers permit 20
Router(config-route-map)#set ip default next-hop 10.15.26.1
```

This is invoked as a catch-all in case the packet doesn't match the first clause, and it doesn't have an appropriate routing table entry to allow the router to direct it. This can be used to prevent the router from dropping packets with unknown destinations, in case you have some other use for them, such as sending them to a proxy server. Note that this *default next-hop* command specifies the route to be used only if there is no explicit route in the routing table. If there is a route, this clause will not be used.

As we mentioned in Recipe 5.5, using the *set ip default next-hop* command means that the processing of this clause must be done at the process level. So this type of command can be very CPU intensive if a large number of packets are involved. If you require this command, it is a good practice to put this clause at the end of the list of policy clauses, as we have done here. This way, hopefully most of the packets will be handled by one of the previous clauses where they can be fast switched.

The second example shows how to route based on the IP TOS field. Once again, the match is made based on an extended access-list:

```
Router(config)#access-list 102 permit ip any any tos 4
```

Please refer to Chapter 11 or Appendix B for a more detailed discussion of TOS, IP Precedence, and prioritization in general.

The third example shows how to use policy-based routing when traffic originates on the router itself. There are many types of traffic for which the router itself is the source. This includes several obvious applications such as SNMP network management traffic, telnet communication with the router's virtual TTY for configuration, and logging.

But there are also some less obvious cases in which the router is engaged in protocol translation, as in DLSw (Data Link Switching) and XOT (X.25 over TCP). So this example shows how to use policy-based routing to affect DLSw packets that originate with this router. We discuss DLSw in more detail in Chapter 15.

The only important difference between local policy-based routing and the earlier examples that were tied to particular interfaces is the global configuration command *ip local policy route-map*:

```
Router(config)#ip local policy route-map dlswtraffic
```

This command applies the policy called dlswtraffic to all locally generated traffic.

See Also

Recipe 5.5; Chapters 11 and 15; Appendix B

5.8   Examining Policy-Based Routing

Problem

You want to see information about how policy-based routing has been applied on a router.

Solution

The *show ip policy* command shows what routing policies have been applied on a router. Here is the output for a router that has all three of the policies from Recipe 5.7:

```
Router>show ip policy
Interface      Route map
local          dlswtraffic
Ethernet0      Websurfers
Serial0        High-priority
```

You can see more detail on what each of these policies do by looking at the route maps:

```
Router>show route-map
route-map High-priority, permit, sequence 10
  Match clauses:
    ip address (access-lists): 101
  Set clauses:
    ip next-hop 10.15.27.1
  Policy routing matches: 0 packets, 0 bytes
route-map Websurfers, permit, sequence 10
  Match clauses:
    ip address (access-lists): 102
  Set clauses:
    ip next-hop 10.15.27.1
  Policy routing matches: 0 packets, 0 bytes
```

```
route-map Websurfers, permit, sequence 20
  Match clauses:
  Set clauses:
    ip default next-hop 10.15.26.1
  Policy routing matches: 4 packets, 531 bytes
route-map dlswtraffic, permit, sequence 10
  Match clauses:
    ip address (access-lists): 103
  Set clauses:
    ip next-hop 10.15.27.3
  Policy routing matches: 5 packets, 500 bytes
```

Discussion

The first command, *show ip policy*, tells you about all of the routing policies that have been applied on the router. The second command, *show route-map*, shows all of the route maps. It is important to note that the first command only shows the routing policies that have actually been applied on the router, whether for local traffic or packets coming from an interface. It shows all applied routing policies, whether the interfaces involved are active or not. The second command shows all configured route-maps, whether or not they've been applied to anything.

The *show route-map* command also gives useful information about how the route-maps are being used. Notice that the second clause of the Websurfers route-map has matched 4 packets for a total of 531 bytes since it was applied, and the dlswtraffic route-map has similarly matched 5 packets for a total of 500 bytes. You can dig a little further by looking at the access-lists that these route maps use to match packets:

```
router>show access-list 103
Extended IP access list 103
    permit tcp any any eq 2065 (3 matches)
    permit tcp any eq 2065 any (2 matches)
```

This shows not only the details of how the access-list used in the route map works, but also precisely which lines are being used.

See Also

Recipe 5.7

5.9   Changing Administrative Distances

Problem

You want to change the administrative distance for an external network.

Solution

You use the *distance* command to adjust the administrative distance for a particular routing protocol. The precise syntax depends on the routing protocol. This example uses RIP:

```
Router#configure terminal
Enter configuration commands, one per line.  End with CNTL/Z.
Router(config)#router rip
Router(config-route)#network 192.168.15.0
Router(config-route)#distance 15 192.168.15.1 0.0.0.0
Router(config-route)#distance 200 192.168.15.0 0.0.0.255
Router(config-route)#distance 255
Router(config-route)#end
Router#
```

For EIGRP, you can specify the distance for routes learned from both internal and external neighbors:

```
Router#configure terminal
Enter configuration commands, one per line.  End with CNTL/Z.
Router(config)#router eigrp 111
Router(config-route)#network 192.168.16.0
Router(config-route)#distance eigrp 55 200
Router(config-route)#end
Router#
```

With OSPF, you can also control the distance, depending on whether the neighboring router is in the same area:

```
Router#configure terminal
Enter configuration commands, one per line.  End with CNTL/Z.
Router(config)#router ospf 66
Router(config-route)#distance ospf inter-area 115
Router(config-route)#distance ospf intra-area 105
Router(config-route)#distance ospf external 125
Router(config-route)#end
Router#
```

And you can configure BGP distances for internal, external, and local routes:

```
Router#configure terminal
Enter configuration commands, one per line.  End with CNTL/Z.
Router(config)#router bgp 65520
Router(config-route)#distance bgp 115 220 50
Router(config-route)#end
Router#
```

Discussion

When dealing with administrative distances, always bear in mind that they only affect route selection on this particular router. Administrative distances are not distributed by the routing protocols. However, they can affect the routing protocols.

Distance vector algorithms in particular only distribute the routes that are used locally. Adjusting the administrative distance could change which routes are used. So you should always be extremely careful when adjusting administrative distances.

In fact, the main place where it makes sense to consider changing the administrative distance for a routing protocol is when the same route is distributed by two different protocols. For example, suppose you have an OSPF network that uses EIGRP to distribute routes for dial backup links. When both the primary OSPF link and backup EIGRP link are active, the router will prefer the routes it learns via EIGRP by default because of the lower administrative distance values. This will cause performance problems, since the backup link most likely has lower bandwidth, and it will probably also interfere with dropping the dialup connection because it is actively passing traffic. Changing the administrative distance can be an effective way of resolving this kind of conflict.

However, we want to stress that this is a relatively unusual case.

The default values for administrative distances are mentioned in Table 5-3 and discussed in Recipe 5.4. You can adjust these values to force the router to prefer routes learned by one protocol over those learned from another. In Recipe 5.4, we gave high administrative distances to static routes so that the router would not use them unless the dynamic routing protocol was unavailable. And this recipe shows that it is also possible to modify the administrative distances for the routing protocols themselves to allow one protocol to dominate another.

In the RIP example, shown in the Solution section above, the last *distance* command overrides the default administrative distance for RIP routes and sets it to 255:

```
Router(config)#router rip
Router(config-route)#distance 255
```

This is the worst possible administrative distance value. Any route with an administrative distance of 255 is considered infinitely far away and will never be used. You could also configure a lower administrative distance value for this protocol. If we gave it a value of 105, for example, then by default RIP routes would be better than OSPF, but worse than IGRP.

The second *distance* command line overrides the new default value for routes received from one particular router, 192.168.15.1. These routes will have a distance value of 15:

```
Router(config-route)#distance 15 192.168.15.1 0.0.0.0
```

The last field in this line is an address wildcard pattern. In the binary representation of this number, the 0s represent values in the address that are important and 1s represent values that can be ignored. In this case, the wildcard is 0.0.0.0, which means that every bit is important. So this refers to a single specific device, which is a router whose RIP routes we want to treat differently.

The third *distance* command line in the RIP changes the administrative distance value to 200 for routes learned from devices in the 192.168.15.0 subnet:

```
Router(config-route)#distance 200 192.168.15.0 0.0.0.255
```

The last field, 0.0.0.255, includes every device in the subnet.

Note the router processes these commands sequentially and stops as soon as it gets a match. So although the device 192.168.15.1 is also a member of the 192.168.15.0 subnet, its routes receive an administrative distance of 15. However, if the two commands were set in the opposite order, the more specific one would never be invoked.

This example represents another interesting use for administrative distances. You can use them as we have in this RIP example to ensure that you favor routes learned from particular routers over other less reliable devices. Note that this is only possible with distance vector protocols. Please refer to Chapter 6 for more information about RIP.

The EIGRP and OSPF configurations are similar, except that they include different options. The EIGRP example uses the *distance eigrp* command:

```
Router(config)#router eigrp 111
Router(config-route)#distance eigrp 55 200
```

This sets the administrative distance for routes learned by EIGRP to 55 if they are from the same EIGRP network, or 200 if they are external routes that have been redistributed into EIGRP.

OSPF also allows you to set a different administrative distance for external routes. And for internal routes, you can specify different administrative distances, depending on whether the route destination is internal or external to the area. This might be useful in certain cases in which you want to connect to another area through an external network rather than through the OSPF core. However, in most cases you do not need to treat intra-area and inter-area OSPF routes differently.

When setting distances for use with BGP, the syntax is *distance bgp <external> <internal> <local>*:

```
Router(config-route)#distance bgp 115 220 50
```

The external and internal distances are used for routes learned through *eBGP* and *iBGP* protocols, respectively. Local routes in this context are routes to destinations inside of this Autonomous System. For more information on BGP, please refer to Chapter 9. Adjusting BGP administrative distances is relatively rare and frequently dangerous. The default value of 20 for eBGP and 200 for iBGP means that the router generally will prefer external BGP routes, but prefer any internal routing protocol to iBGP. This is almost always the required behavior. If you want to change the way the router handles BGP routes, we don't recommend using administrative distance. We discuss several options for manipulating BGP routes in Chapter 9.

See Also

Recipe 5.4; Chapters 6, 7, 8, and 9

5.10   Routing Over Multiple Paths with Equal Costs

Problem

You want to restrict how many paths your router can use simultaneously to reach a particular destination.

Solution

By default, the router will install up to four routes to the same destination for most routing protocols, except BGP where the default is one, and static routes that allow six. You can change this default to any value between one and sixteen by using the configuration command *maximum-paths*. In IOS versions before 12.3(2)T, the maximum number of paths was six:

```
Router#configure terminal
Enter configuration commands, one per line.  End with CNTL/Z.
Router(config)#router ospf 65510
Router(config-router)#maximum-paths 2
Router(config-router)#end
Router#
```

The same syntax works for other routing protocols:

```
Router#configure terminal
Enter configuration commands, one per line.  End with CNTL/Z.
Router(config)#router eigrp 99
Router(config-router)#maximum-paths 2
Router(config-router)#end
Router#
```

In IOS Version 12.2T, Cisco introduced a new command to allow you to configure the number iBGP paths separately from eBGP. You set the maximum number of eBGP paths using the standard *maximum-paths* command, and specify the number of paths for iBGP separately:

```
Router#configure terminal
Enter configuration commands, one per line.  End with CNTL/Z.
Router(config)#router bgp 65511
Router(config-router)#maximum-paths 2
Router(config-router)#maximum-paths ibgp 3
Router(config-router)#end
Router#
```

IOS releases prior to 12.2T only include a standard maximum-paths command. This command sets the maximum paths for both iBGP and eBGP.

Discussion

In large, highly redundant networks, it is common to have many possible paths between two points. By default, the router will install up to four routes to the same destination in the routing table for most routing protocols, provided that all of these routes have the same cost. But sometimes this is either too many or too few, so these commands offer a way to change the defaults.

For BGP, the default value is one path because of the sheer number of routes in the public Internet and the desire to simplify things when possible. However, BGP is not always used to connect to the Internet. Even when it is, there are times when you want to share the load between two Internet connections. With IOS Version 12.2T, Cisco has introduced the ability to control the number of iBGP paths separately from the number of eBGP paths using the command:

```
Router(config)#router bgp 65511
Router(config-router)#maximum-paths ibgp 2
```

This is useful in situations when there are several Autonomous System Boundary Routers (ASBR) sharing routing information within a complex multiply connected Autonomous System, but you still wish to keep your external routing tables as simple as possible.

Without the *ibgp* keyword, this command affects both iBGP and eBGP. So if you want two different values, you can specify them separately, as we have shown. Before IOS level 12.2T, you can only specify a single value for both iBGP and eBGP. Note that for BGP, the default value for this parameter is one. However, for all other protocols, the default is four.

When there are several paths available in the routing table, the router will generally alternate between the different possible paths. When you use process switching, the router will alternate packets among the different paths. With Fast Switching, however, it will alternate *flows* rather than individual packets. For TCP connections, this means that each separate connection will find one of the available paths and use this path exclusively. For UDP and ICMP, however, every packet is a separate flow, so successive packets will likely take different paths.

Alternating flows rather than packets results in slightly less efficient load sharing of TCP traffic. But it has the benefit that packets always arrive in the same order that they were sent. When packets take different paths through the network, they can arrive out of sequence. So in general it is better to use per-flow rather than per-packet load sharing.

By default, Cisco Express Forwarding (CEF) will also load balance by alternating flows rather than individual packets. You can configure CEF to load balance on a packet-by-packet basis by using the interface configuration command *ip load-sharing per-packet*:

```
Router#configure terminal
Enter configuration commands, one per line.  End with CNTL/Z.
```

```
Router(config)#ip cef
Router(config)#interface Ethernet0
Router(config-if)#ip load-sharing per-packet
Router(config-if)#end
Router#
```

We will discuss CEF in more detail in Chapter 11.

See Also

Chapter 9; Chapter 11

5.11 Static Routes That Track Interfaces or Other Routes

Problem

You want to install a static route only when an interface fails or a prefix drops out of the routing table.

Solution

One of the interesting new features in IOS Versions 12.3T and 12.4 is the ability to track things like interface status or routing table objects. This first example shows how to create a static route that tracks an interface:

```
Router#configure terminal
Enter configuration commands, one per line.  End with CNTL/Z.
Router(config)#track 10 interface Serial0/0 line-protocol
Router(config-track)#delay down 5 up 30
Router(config-track)#exit
Router(config)#ip route 192.168.10.0 255.255.255.0 10.3.12.26 track 10
Router(config)#end
Router#
```

This second example shows how to create a static route that tracks a prefix in the IP routing table:

```
Router#configure terminal
Enter configuration commands, one per line.  End with CNTL/Z.
Router(config)#track 11 ip route 10.2.95.0 255.255.255.0 reachability
Router(config-track)#delay down 5 up 5
Router(config-track)#exit
Router(config)#ip route 0.0.0.0 0.0.0.0 10.3.12.26 track 11
Router(config)#end
Router#
```

And the final example installs the static route when a combination of the previous conditions is met:

```
Router#configure terminal
Enter configuration commands, one per line.  End with CNTL/Z.
```

```
Router(config)#track 12 list boolean and
Router(config-track)#object 10 not
Router(config-track)#object 11
Router(config-track)#exit
Router(config)#ip route 192.168.13.0 255.255.255.0 10.3.12.26 track 12
Router(config)#end
Router#
```

Discussion

The idea of tracking objects should already be fairly familiar. In Recipe 5.5, we used a floating static route, which would be installed only if the dynamic routing protocol removed a similar routing prefix. In fact, you can use this method in conjunction with floating statics, as the *ip route track* command includes an optional administrative distance argument at the end of the line:

```
Router(config)#ip route 192.168.10.0 255.255.255.0 10.3.12.26 track 10 190
```

However, in most cases, this is probably not a good idea because it will make your routing more complicated and consequently more difficult to troubleshoot. Combining these two methods means that there are now two potentially complicated and interrelated decisions to be made in selecting which routes to install. So when you look at your routing table, you may not be able to immediately see why a given route is or is not present. Since this method does at least install the routes into the routing table, we prefer this complicated method to policy-based routing, which is always complicated to troubleshoot, but if you are tempted to use this feature, we recommend looking for a simpler solution first.

In Chapter 22, we will show how Hot Standby Routing Protocol (HSRP) can also track changes in interfaces, or how routing prefixes can affect which router is the default gateway for a subnet. The track feature offers a flexible and general method for doing this.

In each of the different examples, there are two steps. First, you define a tracked object:

```
Router(config)#track 10 interface Serial0/0 line-protocol
Router(config-track)#delay down 5 up 30
Router(config-track)#exit
```

In this case, we are tracking the line protocol state of interface Serial0/0. If the interface is in an up/up state, then this object will be considered "up" as well, and anything that is tracking this object will respond accordingly.

Note that we have also included a *delay* command in this example. By default the tracking object will change state as soon as the router notices that the line protocol has come up or gone down. However, this isn't always a good idea. If this interface is flapping up and down frequently, then it would be better to wait a while to ensure that it's really up. Also, some protocols, such as Frame Relay, can take a significant length of time to establish end-to-end connectivity. The *delay* command allows you to specify and appropriate delay. In this case, we have opted to wait 5 seconds after the interface goes down, and 30 seconds after it comes back up, before changing the state of the tracking object.

Once you have defined an object with the *track* command, you need to do something with that object. In this case, we have created a static route:

```
Router(config)#ip route 192.168.10.0 255.255.255.0 10.3.12.26 track 10
```

In Chapter 22, we will show how to use these tracked objects with Hot Standby Routing Protocol (HSRP) and Virtual Router Redundancy Protocol (VRRP), and introduce several other IOS features that can also respond to tracked objects.

To see the state of a tracking object, use the *show track* command:

```
Router#show track 10
Track 10
  Interface Serial0/0 line-protocol
  Line protocol is Up
    6 changes, last change 00:33:44
  Delay up 30 secs, down 5 secs
  Tracked by:
    STATIC-IP-ROUTING 0
Router#
```

And you can see the corresponding static route as follows:

```
Router#show ip route track-table
ip route 192.168.10.0 255.255.255.0 10.3.12.26 track 10 state is [up]
Router#
```

If the tracked interface goes down, the tracked object follows suit and the static route is removed:

```
Router#show track 10
Track 10
  Interface Serial0/0 line-protocol
  Line protocol is Down (hw down)
    7 changes, last change 00:00:03
  Delay up 30 secs, down 5 secs
  Tracked by:
    STATIC-IP-ROUTING 0
Router#show ip route track-table
ip route 192.168.10.0 255.255.255.0 10.3.12.26 track 10 state is [down]
Router#
```

Cisco offers a useful alternative to merely tracking the Layer 2 line protocol. You can opt instead to track the interface's Layer 3 IP protocol state with the *ip routing* keywords:

```
Router(config)#track 15 interface Serial0/0 ip routing
Router(config-track)#
```

In the second example from the Solution section of this recipe, we showed how to track a particular prefix from the IP routing table:

```
Router(config)#track 11 ip route 10.2.95.0 255.255.255.0 reachability
Router(config-track)#delay down 5 up 5
```

When you check the status of this object, it shows several useful pieces of information:

```
Router#show track 11
Track 11
  IP route 10.2.95.0 255.255.255.0 reachability
  Reachability is Up (EIGRP)
    2 changes, last change 00:00:09
  Delay up 5 secs, down 5 secs
  First-hop interface is FastEthernet0/0
  Tracked by:
    STATIC-IP-ROUTING 0
Router#
```

Here we can see that the tracked routing prefix is active in the routing table, that it was learned by EIGRP, when it last changed state, and even which interface the router uses to reach this destination.

In the example, we have configured a static default route to be installed whenever the dynamically learned one is also available:

```
Router(config)#ip route 0.0.0.0 0.0.0.0 10.3.12.26 track 11
```

The third example in the Solution section shows how you can combine several tracked objects into one:

```
Router(config)#track 12 list boolean and
Router(config-track)#object 10 not
Router(config-track)#object 11
Router(config-track)#exit
Router(config)#ip route 192.168.13.0 255.255.255.0 10.3.12.26 track 12
```

Here we have created a static route that is available only if the condition of object 10 is down and object 11 is up:

```
Router#show track 12
Track 12
  List boolean and
  Boolean AND is Up
    2 changes, last change 00:00:30
    object 10 not Down
    object 11 Up
  Tracked by:
    STATIC-IP-ROUTING 0
Router#show ip route track-table
 ip route 192.168.10.0 255.255.255.0 10.3.12.26 track 10 state is [down]
 ip route 0.0.0.0 0.0.0.0 10.3.12.26 track 11 state is [up]
 ip route 192.168.13.0 255.255.255.0 10.3.12.26 track 12 state is [up]
Router#
```

This allows you to construct some complex alternate routing rules that are much more flexible than simple floating static routes. When you get more complex rules that reference other rules like this, it can be useful to use the brief keyword:

```
Router#show track brief
Track   Object                          Parameter      Value
10      interface Serial0/0             line-protocol  Down (hw down)
11      ip route  10.2.95.0/24          reachability   Up (EIGRP)
12      list                            boolean        Up
Router#
```

We note in passing that there doesn't appear to be much error checking in this *list* feature. It is possible to construct an infinite loop of rules where, for example, tracked object 100 tracks object 101, which in turn tracks only the negated object 100. Doing this results in a constant flapping situation, which fortunately doesn't crash the router or run up the CPU, but isn't terribly constructive nonetheless, so we advise checking your logic carefully.

All of the examples we have discussed so far use straight binary up/down logic, but in fact the *track* feature allows for shades of grey by means of the *threshold* keyword. Here is an example of the syntax for this option:

```
Router#configure terminal
Enter configuration commands, one per line.  End with CNTL/Z.
Router(config)#track 15 ip route 10.4.4.4 255.255.255.4 metric threshold
Router(config-track)#threshold up 99 down 201
Router(config-track)#exit
Router(config)#ip route 0.0.0.0 0.0.0.0 10.3.12.26 track 11
Router(config)#end
Router#
```

The key to this command is the *threshold* command. The "up" and "down" threshold numbers that you specify on this line represent the routing protocol metric rescaled to a range from 0 to 255. What this actually corresponds to in practice depends on your routing protocol. Table 5-4 shows how to convert between routing protocol metrics and threshold numbers.

Table 5-4. Default conversion factors for scaled metrics

Routing protocol	Default conversion rule
RIP	Multiply by 17
EIGRP	Divide by 2,560
OSPF	Divide by 1

We haven't included BGP in this table because BGP metrics don't work in the same way, and consequently aren't supported with this feature.

As an aside, you can change these conversion values for EIGRP and OSPF (but not RIP) by specifying the new conversion rule value in the *track resolution* command:

```
Router(config)#track resolution ip route ospf 100
Router(config)#track resolution ip route eigrp 10000
```

This example will change the conversion factor from the default values shown in Table 5-4 to new values of 100 for OSPF and 10,000 for EIGRP.

In our example, we have configured an "up" threshold of 99 and a "down" threshold of 201, and we're using EIGRP for our routing protocol. This means that when the scaled metric value is less than or equal to 99 (EIGRP metric of 253,440, by default), the tracked object will be considered "up." Similarly, when the scaled metric is greater than or equal to 201 (EIGRP metric of 514,560, by default), it will be considered "down."

When the metric is in between these two values, the state of the tracked object depends on how it has changed. These are classic "rising" and "falling" thresholds, which we will discuss in more detail in Chapter 17. If the metric rises from a value below the "down" threshold value (201) to a higher value, then the tracked object changes state from "up" to "down." Conversely, if the metric falls from above to below the "up" threshold (99), then the tracked object changes state to "up."

The *track list* feature also allows you to work in logical shades of grey when you use the *threshold* option:

```
Router(config)#track 50 interface Serial0/0 line-protocol
Router(config)#track 51 interface Serial0/1 line-protocol
Router(config)#track 52 interface FastEthernet0/0 line-protocol
Router(config)#track 100 list threshold percentage
Router(config-track)#object 50
Router(config-track)#object 51
Router(config-track)#object 52
Router(config-track)#threshold percentage up 65 down 34
Router(config-track)#exit
Router(config)#ip route 192.168.13.0 255.255.255.0 10.3.12.26 track 100
```

In this example, we create a list of tracking objects that are associated with interfaces. Then we say that we want this list to be considered "up" if 65 percent or more of the objects in the list are "up" and "down" if 34 percent or less are "down." So, if any two of the three in this example are "up," the whole list is considered "up," and if two or more are "down," the whole list is "down."

You can see the state of the list as well as the individual objects very neatly with the *show track* command:

```
Router#show track 100
Track 100
  List threshold percentage
  Threshold Percentage is Up (66%)
    4 changes, last change 00:00:27
    object 50 Up (33%)
    object 51 Down (0%)
    object 52 Up (33%)
  Threshold percentage down 34% up 65%
  Tracked by:
    STATIC-IP-ROUTING 0
Router#
```

There is another way to construct such a list, using the *weight* keyword:

```
Router(config)#track 101 list threshold weight
Router(config-track)#object 50 weight 10
Router(config-track)#object 51 weight 15
Router(config-track)#object 52 weight 20
Router(config-track)#threshold weight down 15 up 30
Router(config-track)#exit
```

Using this method, you can assign different weighting values to each of the objects in the list to define their relative importance in your network. In this case, we have set the "up" threshold to a value of 30. This can be achieved if object 52 is up at the same time as either of 50 or 51. But it is not sufficient to have both 50 and 51 "up" if 52 is "down:"

```
Router#show track 101
Track 101
  List threshold weight
  Threshold Weight is Up (30/45)
    2 changes, last change 00:07:33
    object 50 Up (10/45)
    object 51 weight 15 Down (0/45)
    object 52 weight 20 Up (20/45)
  Threshold weight down 15 up 30
Router#
```

See Also

Recipe 5.5; Chapter 17; Chapter 22

5.12   Keeping Statistics on Routing Table Changes

Problem

You want to keep statistics on how stable your routing table is.

Solution

IOS Version 12.0 introduced a seldom-used feature that allows you to statistically monitor fluctuations in your routing tables:

```
Router#configure terminal
Enter configuration commands, one per line.  End with CNTL/Z.
Router(config)#ip route profile
Router(config)#end
Router#
```

Once this command is enabled, you can check the stability of your network:

```
Router#show ip route profile
IP routing table change statistics:
Frequency of changes in a 5 second sampling interval
```

```
-------------------------------------------------------------
Change/   Fwd-path  Prefix   Nexthop   Pathcount   Prefix
interval  change    add      change    change      refresh
-------------------------------------------------------------
0         327       327      335       335         331
1         4         4        0         0           1
2         2         2        0         0           1
3         0         0        0         0           0
4         1         1        0         0           1
5         1         1        0         0           1
10        0         0        0         0           0
15        0         0        0         0           0
20        0         0        0         0           0
25        0         0        0         0           0
30        0         0        0         0           0
55        0         0        0         0           0
80        0         0        0         0           0
105       0         0        0         0           0
130       0         0        0         0           0
155       0         0        0         0           0
280       0         0        0         0           0
405       0         0        0         0           0
530       0         0        0         0           0
655       0         0        0         0           0
780       0         0        0         0           0
1405      0         0        0         0           0
2030      0         0        0         0           0
2655      0         0        0         0           0
3280      0         0        0         0           0
3905      0         0        0         0           0
7030      0         0        0         0           0
10155     0         0        0         0           0
13280     0         0        0         0           0
Overflow  0         0        0         0           0
Router#
```

Discussion

It is often extremely difficult to tell when there are stability problems in your network. This command doesn't tell you much about what the problems are, but it can at least tell you how serious the problems are. However, to be useful, you must check these statistics periodically. Otherwise, it's difficult to know whether the issues highlighted occurred recently.

To explain what the output means, let's look at the first few lines in more detail:

```
Router#show ip route profile
IP routing table change statistics:
Frequency of changes in a 5 second sampling interval
-------------------------------------------------------------
Change/   Fwd-path  Prefix   Nexthop   Pathcount   Prefix
interval  change    add      change    change      refresh
```

```
----------------------------------------------------------
0          327        327        335        335        331
1          4          4          0          0          1
2          2          2          0          0          1
3          0          0          0          0          0
```

The first column indicates the number of changes per five-second interval. So, for example, you can see that the Fwd-path change column has a 4 in the 1 row and a 2 in the 2 row. This means that there were four 5-second intervals that saw one change and two 5-second intervals with two changes of this type. To put it another way, since this is a little confusing at first, the router is ticking along watching for routing table changes. It waits five seconds and notices that there was a single change of this type during this interval, so it increments the counter in the row labeled 1. In the next five-second interval, there may be two changes of this type, so it will increment the counter in the row labeled 2. After a while, this output shows that there have been 327 intervals with zero changes, 4 intervals with 1 change, 2 intervals with 2 changes, and no intervals with 3 changes.

As you go further down in the output of this command, you see more and more serious problems. Ideally, you want to see zeroes in every row except the first few rows. High numbers in the 0 row are normal.

Now let's look at the columns to explain what these numbers actually mean. The first column is labeled Fwd-path change. This represents changes in the forwarding path, and is essentially the total of the Prefix add, Nexthop change, and Pathcount change columns.

The Prefix add column counts the number of new IP route prefixes that have been added to the routing table. Note that the route profile feature does not keep track of deletions, only additions to the table.

Nexthop change shows how often the next hop parameter associated with an existing route changes. This most likely indicates that there has been a topology change. This is particularly useful for troubleshooting because you will only see numbers in this column on devices that are immediately adjacent to the trouble spot in your network.

In the Pathcount change column, you see information on routes with multiple paths. For example, if there are normally 4 redundant paths to a particular destination, and one or more of these paths is flapping up and down, you will see the numbers in this column increment. This is useful because in a highly redundant network, you might not be aware that there are problems, as the routing protocol may be covering them up for you.

Finally, the Prefix refresh column keeps track of how often the routing protocol has refreshed routes, without changing the actual routing information. Different routing protocols handle route refreshes differently, so you should watch this column to get an idea of what is normal for your network.

Although this command is a useful indicator of routing problems, it has several serious shortcomings that you should be aware of. First, it lacks a simple *clear* command to reset the table and eliminate old data. The only way to do this that we are aware of is to disable and re-enable the feature:

```
Router#configure terminal
Enter configuration commands, one per line.  End with CNTL/Z.
Router(config)#no ip route profile
Router(config)#ip route profile
Router(config)#end
Router#
```

A second problem with this feature is that there is no simple way to deduce what route prefixes, next-hops, or even what interfaces have been affected by instability. A final problem is that you can get very high numbers in some columns just from a few changes to every route in a large routing table. So it is difficult to tell from this command alone whether you have a small problem with a lot of routes or a big problem with a few routes.

Despite these shortcomings, this feature can be a helpful adjunct to other troubleshooting methods, as it does track some issues—particularly network layer issues, which can be much harder to spot.

## CHAPTER 6

RIP

6.0 Introduction

RIP Version 1 was the Internet's first widely used routing protocol. It was standardized in RFC 1058, although implementations of the protocol based on de facto standards existed much earlier. It is still useful in small simple networks, as well as at the edges or in small regions of larger networks. RIP Version 2 is documented in RFC 1723.

All Cisco routers support RIP Version 1. Version 2 support was integrated into IOS Version 11.1. A detailed discussion of RIP Version 1 and 2 is beyond the scope of this book. If you are unfamiliar with dynamic routing protocols in general or with RIP in particular, you can find theoretical descriptions of how the protocol works in *IP Routing* by Ravi Malhotra (O'Reilly) and *Designing Large-Scale LANs* by Kevin Dooley (O'Reilly), as well as from RFCs 1058 and 1723.

RIP is useful in some situations, but you have to remember its limitations. First, Version 1 of the protocol is a purely classful; it doesn't support variable length subnet masks. So you should not use this protocol if you do any complex subnetting. Second, both Versions 1 and 2 of RIP use the very small metric value of 16 to signify "infinity." The protocol considers any network that is more than 16 hops away to be unreachable. This becomes even more important if you adjust any metric values to make RIP favor a fast link over a slow one. In practice, it is quite easy to exceed the maximum metric, even in small networks.

However, RIP can be extremely useful over small parts of a network. For example, it is much easier to configure than BGP as a method for interconnecting two or more different OSPF or EIGRP Autonomous Systems. And because RIP has been around for so long, it is often useful when exchanging routing information with legacy equipment. Indeed, it is almost impossible to find a router of any age from any vendor that doesn't implement RIP.

In this book, we assume that you are familiar with RIP in general, and will focus on Cisco's implementation of it. We will also discuss some specific issues that we think are particularly important.

One of the central features of RIP is that it distributes the entire routing table every 30 seconds. The protocol requires that every device add a small random amount to this time period to prevent synchronized bursts of traffic throughout your network every 30 seconds. But the RFC doesn't specify the size of this offset, or whether it should be positive or negative. Cisco routers always reduce the period slightly by subtracting a random variable amount of time, up to 4.5 seconds.

If a particular route is not seen for 6 successive update cycles, or 180 seconds by default, then the routers will mark it as invalid. They will flush the invalid route from their routing tables if they don't see it for 8 cycles, or 240 seconds. So this implies that RIP will converge rather slowly after a failure. But this is actually just a worst case. The network will converge much more quickly by taking advantage of a protocol feature called *triggered updates*. This means that when a route's metric suddenly changes, for whatever reason, the router will not wait for the full update cycle before distributing information about the change to the other routers in the network.

This is different from the modification to RIP described in Recipe 6.12, which is also called a *triggered update*. This feature, which is a partial implementation of RFC 2091, allows the routers to send routing updates only when there are changes. Instead of sending the entire routing table at each update cycle, this makes it possible to configure the routers to just send incremental changes. A better term for this might be non-periodic updates, to avoid confusion with the other kind of triggered updates that we discussed in the previous paragraph. Using these non-periodic triggered updates drastically improves RIP performance, but it must be configured on all of the routers sharing the link, and it is often not supported by legacy equipment. Furthermore, Cisco routers only support this feature on point-to-point serial links.

Cisco routers implement a hold-down timer with RIP. This is a protocol feature that is not described in the standard protocol RFC's. When the router marks a route invalid, it starts the hold-down timer, which is 180 seconds by default, and ignores all updates for this route. This helps to make the network somewhat more stable.

RIP uses a distance vector algorithm rather than a link state protocol like OSPF. As a result, you can use Cisco's distribute lists to make a router advertise only certain routes to other routers. This allows you to prevent distribution of routing information that you don't want to be generally visible. And you can also reject incoming routing information that you don't want to use. This can be extremely useful when exchanging routing information between networks, or when connecting small network regions with legacy equipment.

6.1   Configuring RIP Version 1

Problem

You want to run RIP on a simple network.

Solution

The following commands show how to configure basic RIP functionality:

```
Router2#configure terminal
Enter configuration commands, one per line.  End with CNTL/Z.
Router2(config)#interface Ethernet0
Router2(config-if)#ip address 192.168.30.1 255.255.255.0
Router2(config-if)#interface Serial0.1
Router2(config-subif)#ip address 172.25.2.2 255.255.255.0
Router2(config-subif)#exit
Router2(config)#router rip
Router2(config-router)#network 172.25.0.0
Router2(config-router)#network 192.168.30.0
Router2(config-router)#exit
Router2(config)#end
Router2#
```

Discussion

You enable RIP for an interface by associating its IP address with a network. For example, the Serial0.1 subinterface in this example has an IP address of 172.25.2.2. So if you want this subinterface to take part in RIP route distribution, you just need to include a *network* statement that includes its address:

```
Router2(config)#router rip
Router2(config-router)#network 172.25.0.0
```

If you have other interfaces that are also part of 172.25.0.0/16 on this router, they will take part in RIP as well. It's important to note that RIP *network* statements work with classful network addresses. The *network* command may appear to accept subnets of classful addresses, but it will internally rewrite these subnet addresses with the classful network address:

```
Router2#configure terminal
Enter configuration commands, one per line.  End with CNTL/Z.
Router2(config)#router rip
Router2(config-router)#network 172.25.1.0
Router2(config-router)#end
Router2#show run | begin router rip
router rip
network 172.25.0.0
<lines deleted for brevity>
Router2#
```

Since 172.25.0.0 is a Class B network, the statement *network* 172.25.0.0 tells the router to include all interfaces with IP address in this range. Note, however, that the other address on this router, 192.168.30.1, is part of the Class C network, 192.168.30.0/24, which is why we need the second *network* command:

```
Router2(config)#router rip
Router2(config-router)#network 192.168.30.0
```

If your router has several addresses that belong to different network classes, as in, for example, 192.168.x.0/24, you have to specify them all separately:

```
Router2(config)#router rip
Router2(config-router)#network 192.168.1.0
Router2(config-router)#network 192.168.2.0
Router2(config-router)#network 192.168.3.0
```

It can sometimes be confusing to know which networks to specify. You use the *network* command to specify both the routes that RIP advertises and the interfaces that it uses.

If your router receives a route from another router, it will pass it along to other routers, whether you have specified a network statement for this address or not. So the network command selects only the routes that are local to this router, such as directly connected networks. However, the router will only distribute information about directly connected routes if there is a network statement for these routes. And the router will exchange RIP information only through interfaces specified by network statements.

The network command also selects the interfaces that will use RIP. By default, the router will run RIP on any interfaces whose IP addresses are contained within the range specified in the network statement. We discuss exceptions to this rule in Recipe 6.6.

The *show ip protocol* command gives a lot of useful information about what interfaces and address ranges are involved in the routing protocol:

```
Router2#show ip protocol
Routing Protocol is "rip"
  Sending updates every 30 seconds, next due in 7 seconds
  Invalid after 180 seconds, hold down 180, flushed after 240
  Outgoing update filter list for all interfaces is not set
  Incoming update filter list for all interfaces is not set
  Redistributing: rip
  Default version control: send version 1, receive any version
    Interface            Send  Recv  Triggered RIP  Key-chain
    Ethernet0             1      1 2
    Serial0.1             1      1 2
  Automatic network summarization is in effect
  Maximum path: 4
  Routing for Networks:
    172.25.0.0
    192.168.30.0
```

```
Routing Information Sources:
  Gateway          Distance     Last Update
  172.25.2.1            120      00:00:17
Distance: (default is 120)

Router2#
```

As you can see from the output of this command, the router will send RIP Version 1 on both interfaces Ethernet0 and Serial0.1, but it will listen for both Versions 1 and 2. You can force the router to use only Version 1 to send and receive routing information for all interfaces with the following command:

```
Router2#configure terminal
Enter configuration commands, one per line.  End with CNTL/Z.
Router2(config)#router rip
Router2(config-router)#version 1
Router2(config-router)#end
Router2#
```

However, it is usually better to restrict what you send rather than what you receive. That way, if another device is misconfigured to send the other version, it doesn't break the network. We will discuss how to configure different RIP version options in Recipe 6.14.

Once you have RIP running successfully between two or more routers, you can look at your routing table to see which routes the router is learning, and from where:

```
Router2#show ip route rip
R    172.22.0.0/16 [120/1] via 172.25.2.1, 00:00:00, Serial0.1
R    172.25.1.0/24 [120/1] via 172.25.2.1, 00:00:00, Serial0.1
R    192.168.20.0/24 [120/2] via 172.25.2.1, 00:00:00, Serial0.1
Router2#
```

This command just gives a subset of the output of the more general *show ip route* command, which we discussed in Chapter 5. The example output shows that the router has learned that it can get to the destination network 192.168.20.0/24 through the next-hop router, 172.25.2.1, which is on interface Serial0.1.

The two numbers in the square brackets, [120/2], are the administrative distance and the RIP metric respectively. Cisco routers give all RIP routes a default administrative distance of 120. The metric value of 2 indicates how far away this network is. By default, the metric is the same as the number of hops, but you can adjust metric values to break this rule. We will discuss how to change metric values in Recipes 6.3, 6.4, 6.5, and 6.9, and we talk about administrative distances in Chapter 5.

Another useful command for looking at RIP functions on your router is the *show ip rip database* command, introduced in IOS level 12.0(6)T:

```
Router2#show ip rip database
172.22.0.0/16     auto-summary
172.22.0.0/16
    [1] via 172.25.2.1, 00:00:13, Serial0.1
172.25.0.0/16     auto-summary
```

```
172.25.1.0/24
   [1] via 172.25.2.1, 00:00:13, Serial0.1
172.25.2.0/24    directly connected, Serial0.1
192.168.20.0/24    auto-summary
192.168.20.0/24
   [2] via 172.25.2.1, 00:00:13, Serial0.1
192.168.30.0/24    auto-summary
192.168.30.0/24    directly connected, Ethernet0
Router2#
```

This allows you to see more detailed information about each of the routes in the RIP database.

See Also

Recipe 6.3; Recipe 6.4; Recipe 6.5; Recipe 6.6; Recipe 6.9; Recipe 6.14; Chapter 5

6.2   Filtering Routes with RIP

Problem

You want to restrict what routing information is exchanged within RIP.

Solution

You can filter inbound RIP routes on a per interface basis with a *distribute-list*:

```
Router2#configure terminal
Enter configuration commands, one per line.  End with CNTL/Z.
Router2(config)#access-list 10 deny 192.168.20.0
Router2(config)#access-list 10 permit any
Router2(config)#router rip
Router2(config-router)#distribute-list 10 in Serial 0.1
Router2(config-router)#network 172.25.0.0
Router2(config-router)#network 192.168.30.0
Router2(config-router)#exit
Router2(config)#end
Router2#
```

This configuration example shows how to filter outbound RIP-based routes on a per interface basis:

```
Router1#configure terminal
Enter configuration commands, one per line.  End with CNTL/Z.
Router1(config)#access-list 20 permit 0.0.0.0
Router1(config)#access-list 20 deny any
Router1(config)#router rip
Router1(config-router)#distribute-list 20 out Serial0/0.2
Router1(config-router)#network 172.25.0.0
Router1(config-router)#exit
Router1(config)#end
Router1#
```

Discussion

The access list in the first configuration example of this recipe prevents this router from accepting any routing information about the network 192.168.20.0:

```
Router2(config)#access-list 10 deny 192.168.20.0
Router2(config)#access-list 10 permit any
```

You can see that this route, which was visible in Recipe 6.1, no longer appears in the routing table:

```
Router2#show ip route rip
R    172.22.0.0/16 [120/1] via 172.25.2.1, 00:00:21, Serial0.1
R    172.25.1.0/24 [120/1] via 172.25.2.1, 00:00:21, Serial0.1
Router2#
```

The *show ip protocol* command shows which interfaces have inbound or outbound distribute lists:

```
Router2#show ip protocol
Routing Protocol is "rip"
  Sending updates every 30 seconds, next due in 27 seconds
  Invalid after 180 seconds, hold down 180, flushed after 240
  Outgoing update filter list for all interfaces is not set
  Incoming update filter list for all interfaces is not set
    Serial0.1 filtered by 10 (per-user), default is 10
  Redistributing: rip
  Default version control: send version 1, receive any version
    Interface           Send  Recv  Triggered RIP  Key-chain
    Ethernet0           1     1 2
    Loopback0           1     1 2
    Serial0.1           1     1 2
  Automatic network summarization is in effect
  Maximum path: 4
  Routing for Networks:
    172.25.0.0
    192.168.30.0
  Routing Information Sources:
    Gateway         Distance      Last Update
    172.25.2.1           120      00:00:17
  Distance: (default is 120)

Router2#
```

This shows that the interface Serial0.1 uses access list number 10 to filter incoming routing information. You can then use the *show access-list* command to see what this affects.

Note that if you control both the sending and receiving routers, it is usually best to filter the routes before sending them instead of sending them across the network and then ignoring them. So inbound filtering is most common in situations when you are receiving routes from a device that you don't control. Since RIP frequently runs on end devices such as Unix servers, inbound filtering is fairly common.

You can use outbound filtering, on the other hand, for reducing the size of routing tables on access routers. For example, it is extremely useful in hub-and-spoke type WANs. In this case, each remote branch router cares only about its local segments and "everything else." It can reach all of the nonlocal routes via the hub router. So you can reduce unnecessary WAN bandwidth utilization as well as memory consumption on the branch router by configuring the hub router to send out only a single default route. In fact, when used in conjunction with the periodic updates discussed in Recipe 6.12, this makes a good WAN routing solution.

The second example in the Solution section of this recipe shows the configuration of the hub router so that it only sends the default route, 0.0.0.0/0. The routing table of the other router then becomes extremely simple:

```
Router2#show ip route rip
R*   0.0.0.0/0 [120/5] via 172.25.2.1, 00:00:02, Serial0.1
Router2#
```

The *show ip protocol* command shows the filter on the hub router:

```
Router1#show ip protocol
Routing Protocol is "rip"
  Sending updates every 30 seconds, next due in 9 seconds
  Invalid after 180 seconds, hold down 180, flushed after 240
  Outgoing update filter list for all interfaces is not set
    Serial0/0.2 filtered by 20 (per-user), default is 20
  Incoming update filter list for all interfaces is not set
  Redistributing: rip
  Default version control: send version 1, receive any version
    Interface           Send  Recv  Triggered RIP  Key-chain
    FastEthernet0/0.1     1    1 2
    Serial0/0.2           1    1 2
    FastEthernet0/1       1    1 2
   Automatic network summarization is in effect
  Maximum path: 4
  Routing for Networks:
    172.22.0.0
    172.25.0.0
  Routing Information Sources:
    Gateway         Distance      Last Update
    172.25.1.7          120       00:00:23
    172.25.2.2          120       00:00:07
    172.22.1.4          120       00:00:19
  Distance: (default is 120)

Router1#
```

You can also configure the router to filter all interfaces simultaneously with a single rule:

```
Router2#configure terminal
Enter configuration commands, one per line.  End with CNTL/Z.
Router2(config)#access-list 10 deny 192.168.20.0
Router2(config)#access-list 10 permit any
```

```
Router2(config)#router rip
Router2(config-router)#distribute-list 10 in
Router2(config-router)#end
Router2#
```

This feature is rarely used because you usually want apply different filters to different interfaces, depending on what other devices are connected. But when you want to explicitly eliminate certain unwanted routes from your network, regardless of the interface you might learn them through, this is the easiest way to do it. With the *show ip protocols* command, you can see that access list number 10 has been applied to traffic coming in from all interfaces:

```
Router2#show ip protocols
Routing Protocol is "rip"
  Sending updates every 30 seconds, next due in 0 seconds
  Invalid after 180 seconds, hold down 180, flushed after 240
  Outgoing update filter list for all interfaces is not set
  Incoming update filter list for all interfaces is 10
  Redistributing: rip
  Default version control: send version 1, receive any version
    Interface             Send  Recv  Triggered RIP  Key-chain
    Ethernet0             1     1 2
    Loopback0             1     1 2
    Serial0.1            1     1 2
  Automatic network summarization is in effect
  Maximum path: 4
  Routing for Networks:
    172.25.0.0
    192.168.30.0
  Routing Information Sources:
    Gateway         Distance      Last Update
    172.25.2.1            120      00:00:03
  Distance: (default is 120)

Router2#
```

You can use global distribute lists together with interface specific distribute lists. The result actually combines the effects of both. Suppose, for example, that you have a global distribute list that blocks a particular network. Then if you apply another list that blocks another address to a particular interface, this interface will block both addresses.

See Also

Recipe 6.12

6.3   Redistributing Static Routes into RIP

Problem

You want RIP to redistribute static routes that you have configured on your router.

Solution

The *redistribute static* command tells RIP to advertise static routes, as well as directly connected routes and the routes that have been learned from other RIP routers:

```
Router1#configure terminal
Enter configuration commands, one per line.  End with CNTL/Z.
Router1(config)#ip route 192.168.10.0 255.255.255.0 172.22.1.4
Router1(config)#router rip
Router1(config-router)#redistribute static
Router1(config-router)#end
Router1#
```

You can define how these routes look to other routers when they are redistributed:

```
Router1#configure terminal
Enter configuration commands, one per line.  End with CNTL/Z.
Router1(config)#ip route 192.168.10.0 255.255.255.0 172.22.1.4
Router1(config)#router rip
Router1(config-router)#redistribute static metric 5
Router1(config-router)#distribute-list 7 out static
Router1(config-router)#exit
Router1(config)#access-list 7 permit 192.168.10.0
Router1(config)#end
Router1#
```

Discussion

The biggest potential problem that you will encounter with redistributing routes into RIPv1 comes from breaking network class boundaries. This version of RIP is classful, so you have to be rather careful about how you distribute routing information from other sources that may be classless. In the example in this recipe, Router1 redistributes a static route for the Class C network 192.168.10.0. But if we tried instead to redistribute a larger range, such as 192.168.12.0/22, RIPv1 would not generate any errors; the router would just quietly refuse to forward this route. RIPv2, on the other hand, will redistribute this supernet route.

Looking at the RIP database on a router with IOS level 12.0(6)T or higher shows the redistributed static route:

```
Router1#show ip rip database 192.168.10.0 255.255.255.0
192.168.10.0/24     redistributed
    [5] via 0.0.0.0,
Router1#
```

After configuring the second example, the output of *show ip protocols* includes information about the filtering. This command also tells you what other protocols RIP is redistributing routes from:

```
Router1#show ip protocols
Routing Protocol is "rip"
  Sending updates every 30 seconds, next due in 5 seconds
  Invalid after 180 seconds, hold down 180, flushed after 240
```

```
   Outgoing update filter list for all interfaces is not set
     Redistributed static filtered by 7
   Incoming update filter list for all interfaces is not set
   Redistributing: static, rip
   Default version control: send version 1, receive any version
     Interface            Send  Recv  Triggered RIP  Key-chain
     FastEthernet0/0.1     1     1  2
     Serial0/0.2           1     1  2
     FastEthernet0/1       1     1  2
    Automatic network summarization is in effect
   Maximum path: 4
   Routing for Networks:
     172.22.0.0
     172.25.0.0
   Routing Information Sources:
     Gateway        Distance      Last Update
     172.25.1.7          120      00:00:03
     172.25.2.2          120      00:00:06
     172.22.1.4          120      00:00:08
   Distance: (default is 120)
 Router1#
```

In addition to static routes, you can distribute information from other dynamic routing protocols into RIP simply by specifying which protocol's routes you want RIP to use. For example, if you have an EIGRP network that uses process number 65530 on the same router, you would redistribute it into RIP like this:

```
Router1#configure terminal
Enter configuration commands, one per line.  End with CNTL/Z.
Router1(config)#router eigrp 65530
Router1(config-router)#network 192.168.1.0
Router1(config-router)#exit
Router1(config)#router rip
Router1(config-router)#redistribute eigrp 65530
Router1(config-router)#end
Router1#
```

If you look at the *show ip protocols* command now, you can see that RIP redistributes routes it learns from EIGRP, but EIGRP does not redistribute routes learned from RIP. If you also want EIGRP to redistribute RIP routes, you must explicitly configure it to do so. We discuss EIGRP configuration, including redistribution examples, in Chapter 7:

```
Router1#show ip protocols
Routing Protocol is "rip"
  Sending updates every 30 seconds, next due in 0 seconds
  Invalid after 180 seconds, hold down 180, flushed after 240
  Outgoing update filter list for all interfaces is
  Incoming update filter list for all interfaces is
  Redistributing: static, rip, eigrp 65530
  Default version control: send version 1, receive any version
    Interface         Send  Recv  Key-chain
    FastEthernet0/0.1   2     2
```

```
    Serial0/0.2          2    2
    FastEthernet0/1      2    2
 Automatic network summarization is in effect
 Maximum path: 4
 Routing for Networks:
   172.22.0.0
   172.25.0.0
 Routing Information Sources:
   Gateway        Distance      Last Update
   172.25.1.7          120      00:00:03
   172.25.2.2          120      00:00:06
   172.22.1.4          120      00:00:08
 Distance: (default is 120)

Routing Protocol is "eigrp 65530"
 Outgoing update filter list for all interfaces is
 Incoming update filter list for all interfaces is
 Default networks flagged in outgoing updates
 Default networks accepted from incoming updates
 EIGRP metric weight K1=1, K2=0, K3=1, K4=0, K5=0
 EIGRP maximum hopcount 100
 EIGRP maximum metric variance 1
 Redistributing: eigrp 65530
 Automatic network summarization is in effect
 Routing for Networks:
   192.168.1.0
 Routing Information Sources:
   Gateway        Distance      Last Update
 Distance: internal 90 external 170

Router1#
```

Table 6-1 shows a list of foreign protocols that RIP can redistribute.

Table 6-1. Protocols that RIP can redistribute

Type	Description
bgp	Border Gateway Protocol
connected	Directly connected interfaces
egp	Exterior Gateway Protocol
eigrp	Enhanced IGRP
igrp	Interior Gateway Routing Protocol
isis	ISO IS-IS Routing Protocol
mobile	IP Mobility routes
ospf	Open Shortest Path First
rip	Routing Information Protocol
static	Static routes

The second example shows how to set a particular metric when redistributing a route into RIP:

```
Router1(config)#router rip
Router1(config-router)#redistribute static metric 5
```

In this case, all static routes will appear with a RIP metric of 5. Because of the maximum metric value of 16, you need to be extremely careful with how you distribute routes into RIP. This example shows how to set a metric when redistributing static routes, but you can use the same technique when redistributing routes from any source:

```
Router1(config)#router rip
Router1(config-router)#redistribute eigrp 65530 metric 5
```

Finally, we will point out a slightly confusing irregularity with the *redistribute* command. Although this command seems to allow you to redistribute RIP into RIP, in fact it won't allow it:

```
Router1(config)#router rip
Router1(config-router)#redistribute rip
redistribution of "rip" via "rip" not allowed
dialhost(config-router)#
```

This is actually a good thing because RIP doesn't support process numbers, unlike other routing protocols available on Cisco routers. It makes sense to redistribute, for example, one EIGRP process into another EIGRP process; it doesn't make sense to redistribute within a process. If this were possible, it would be ambiguous which routes were internal and which were external.

See Also

Recipe 6.4; Chapter 7

6.4   Redistributing Routes Using Route Maps

Problem

You want to use route maps for more detailed control over how RIP redistributes routing information from other sources.

Solution

Route maps give you much better control over how RIP redistributes external routes. This example uses static routes, but the same principles apply when redistributing routes from other protocols:

```
Router1#configure terminal
Enter configuration commands, one per line.  End with CNTL/Z.
Router1(config)#ip route 192.168.10.0 255.255.255.0 172.22.1.4
Router1(config)#ip route 192.168.11.0 255.255.255.0 172.22.1.4
```

```
Router1(config)#ip route 192.168.12.0 255.255.255.0 172.22.1.4
Router1(config)#access-list 20 permit 192.168.10.0
Router1(config)#access-list 21 permit 192.168.11.0
Router1(config)#route-map STATIC permit 10
Router1(config-route-map)#match ip address 20
Router1(config-route-map)#set metric 2
Router1(config-route-map)#set tag 2
Router1(config-route-map)#exit
Router1(config)#route-map STATIC permit 20
Router1(config-route-map)#match ip address 21
Router1(config-route-map)#set metric 8
Router1(config-route-map)#route-map STATIC deny 30
Router1(config-route-map)#exit
Router1(config)#router rip
Router1(config-router)#redistribute static route-map STATIC
Router1(config-router)#exit
Router1(config)#end
Router1#
```

Discussion

In this example, we want RIP to distinguish among the different routes. There are two parameters that we can change, the metric and the route tag. We have already discussed metrics, which basically represent the distance or cost of the path to the remote network. A route tag is simply an arbitrary number that RIP will attach to a particular route. RIP doesn't actually use these tag values, but as we discuss in Recipe 6.17, RIP Version 2 will distribute them with the routing table so you can use this information when distributing these routes into other routing protocols.

The route map in this recipe has three clauses. The first assigns a metric of 2 and a tag of 2 to the network 192.168.10.0. Then it gives a metric of 8 to 192.168.11.0. The last clause discards all other routes. This is different from Recipe 6.3, in which all routes were redistributed with the same metric.

This kind of redistribution is useful when you want to control how traffic load is balanced between two links. For example, if you have two routers that both connect to the same set of remote networks, you could balance them so that one router has a better metric for half of the routes, and the other has a better metric for the rest of the routes. In this way, you can ensure that both links are used equally, and if one router fails, the other will take over for it.

It is often easier to understand route-maps by looking at the *show route-map* command rather than the configuration commands. In this case, for example, you can see exactly what access lists apply to each clause, along with all of the values that are set as a result. This output also shows how many times each policy has been applied:

```
Router1#show route-map STATIC
route-map STATIC, permit, sequence 10
  Match clauses:
    ip address (access-lists): 20
```

```
  Set clauses:
    metric 2
    tag 2
  Policy routing matches: 0 packets, 0 bytes
route-map STATIC, permit, sequence 20
  Match clauses:
    ip address (access-lists): 21
  Set clauses:
    metric 8
   Policy routing matches: 0 packets, 0 bytes
route-map STATIC, deny, sequence 30
  Match clauses:
  Set clauses:
  Policy routing matches: 0 packets, 0 bytes
Router1#
```

Looking at the RIP database, you can see the metrics that RIP uses for distributing each of these static routes:

```
Router1#show ip rip database
192.168.10.0/24    auto-summary
192.168.10.0/24    redistributed
    [2] via 0.0.0.0,
192.168.11.0/24    auto-summary
192.168.11.0/24    redistributed
    [8] via 0.0.0.0,
Router1#
```

You can also use the route map technique for distributing routes from dynamic routing protocols. For example, if you had another route map called EIGRPMAP that you wanted to use when redistributing routes learned through EIGRP process number 65530, you could configure the router like this:

```
Router1#configure terminal
Enter configuration commands, one per line.  End with CNTL/Z.
Router1(config)#router eigrp 65530
Router1(config-router)#network 192.168.1.0
Router1(config-router)#exit
Router1(config)#router rip
Router1(config-router)#redistribute eigrp 65530 route-map EIGRPMAP
Router1(config-router)#end
Router1#
```

See Also

Recipe 6.3; Recipe 6.17

6.5   Creating a Default Route in RIP

Problem

You want RIP to propagate a default route.

Solution

There are two ways to get RIP to propagate a default route. The preferred method is using the *default-information originate* command as follows:

```
Router1#configure terminal
Enter configuration commands, one per line.  End with CNTL/Z.
Router1(config)#ip route 0.0.0.0 0.0.0.0 172.25.1.1
Router1(config)#router rip
Router1(config-router)#default-information originate
Router1(config-router)#end
Router1#
```

In simple situations, you can accomplish the same thing by just redistributing a static route:

```
Router1#configure terminal
Enter configuration commands, one per line.  End with CNTL/Z.
Router1(config)#ip route 0.0.0.0 0.0.0.0 172.25.1.1
Router1(config)#access-list 7 permit 0.0.0.0
Router1(config)#router rip
Router1(config-router)#redistribute static
Router1(config-router)#distribute-list 7 out static
Router1(config-router)#end
Router1#
```

Discussion

There are two main advantages to using *default originate* instead of simply redistributing static routes. The first is that you may have other static routes on your router that you do not want to distribute, or that you want to distribute with a different default metric. In this case, if you just use *redistribute static*, you will need to filter out the unwanted routes using route maps, as shown in Recipe 6.4, or a *distribute-list*, as we use in this recipe.

The other important advantage is that the *default-information originate* option lets you create a conditional default route. This means that you can configure the router to create and distribute a default route only if some other route is present. Usually this other route is a distant network that indicates that the router is able to see enough of the outside world to be a reliable default router:

```
Router1#configure terminal
Enter configuration commands, one per line.  End with CNTL/Z.
Router1(config)#access-list 20 permit 192.168.55.0
Router1(config)#route-map DEFAULTROUTE permit 10
Router1(config-route-map)#match ip address 20
Router1(config-route-map)#exit
Router1(config)#router rip
Router1(config-router)#default-information originate route-map DEFAULTROUTE
Router1(config-router)#end
Router1#
```

In this example, if the distant network 192.168.55.0 is present in the routing table, RIP will generate and distribute a default route. Usually you would just do this on the RIP router that forms a gateway to another network.

You can see how RIP distributes the default route with the *show ip rip database* command:

```
Router1#show ip rip database 0.0.0.0 0.0.0.0
0.0.0.0/0    redistributed
    [1] via 0.0.0.0,
Router1#
```

See Also

Recipe 6.4

6.6   Disabling RIP on an Interface

Problem

You want to prevent an interface from participating in RIP.

Solution

You can prevent an interface from participating in RIP with the following set of commands:

```
Router1#configure terminal
Enter configuration commands, one per line.  End with CNTL/Z.
Router1(config)#access-list 12 deny any
Router1(config)#router rip
Router1(config-router)#passive-interface FastEthernet0/1
Router1(config-router)#distribute-list 12 in FastEthernet0/1
Router1(config-router)#end
Router1#
```

Discussion

As we discussed in Recipe 6.1, you enable RIP on an interface with a *network* command. But because RIP expects any networks you specify this way to follow address class rules, it is quite easy to inadvertently enable RIP on an interface that you don't want to use this protocol.

There are two important reasons that might lead you to disable RIP on a particular interface. First, if you are already running another protocol on a particular interface, then the additional RIP traffic could consume important bandwidth resources. Second, there may be devices on a particular network segment that you do not trust. In this case you want to make sure that you don't let them distribute routing information into your network. This is particularly important because some Unix workstations run RIP by default, but the administrators rarely devote much attention to making sure that any local static routes have the correct metric values. It is possible for one misconfigured workstation to completely disrupt routing for an entire network.

This recipe does two things to disable RIP. First, the *passive-interface* command tells RIP not to send any routing information out through the specified interface. But this does not prevent the router from listening for incoming routes. So we have also applied an inbound *distribute-list* command to the interface to prevent RIP from learning any routes this way.

To demonstrate this, in the following example, we have applied the passive interface command, but not the distribute list:

```
Router1#show ip route rip
R    192.168.30.0/24 [120/1] via 172.25.2.2, 00:00:09, Serial0/0.2
     172.25.0.0/16 is variably subnetted, 6 subnets, 3 masks
R       172.25.25.2/32 [120/1] via 172.25.2.2, 00:00:09, Serial0/0.2
R    192.168.20.0/24 [120/1] via 172.22.1.4, 00:00:08, FastEthernet0/1
Router1#
```

As you can see, the router is still learning routes through the *FastEthernet0/1* port. A debug trace proves that although the router doesn't send any routing information out through this interface, it does receive information this way:

```
Router1#debug ip rip
RIP protocol debugging is on
Aug 11 02:35:33.403: RIP: sending v1 flash update to 255.255.255.255 via
FastEthernet0/0
Aug 11 02:35:33.403: RIP: build flash update entries
Aug 11 02:35:33.403:    subnet 0.0.0.0 metric 16
Aug 11 02:35:33.403: RIP: sending v1 flash update to 255.255.255.255 via Serial0/0.2
Aug 11 02:35:33.403: RIP: build flash update entries
Aug 11 02:35:33.403:    subnet 0.0.0.0 metric 1
Aug 11 02:35:33.403:    network 172.21.0.0 metric 1
Aug 11 02:35:39.012: RIP: received v1 update from 172.22.1.4 on FastEthernet0/1
Aug 11 02:35:39.012:       192.168.20.0 in 1 hops
```

Then, when we add the *distribute-list* command inbound on the FastEthernet0/1 interface, the unwanted route disappears from the routing table:

```
Router1#show ip route rip
R    192.168.30.0/24 [120/1] via 172.25.2.2, 00:00:04, Serial0/0.2
     172.25.0.0/16 is variably subnetted, 5 subnets, 2 masks
R       172.25.25.2/32 [120/1] via 172.25.2.2, 00:00:04, Serial0/0.2
Router1#
```

You can see the effects of both commands in the output of the *show ip protocols* command:

```
Router1#show ip protocols
Routing Protocol is "rip"
```

```
Sending updates every 30 seconds, next due in 13 seconds
Invalid after 180 seconds, hold down 180, flushed after 240
Outgoing update filter list for all interfaces is not set
Incoming update filter list for all interfaces is not set
  FastEthernet0/1 filtered by 12 (per-user), default is 12
Redistributing: rip
Default version control: send version 1, receive any version
  Interface            Send  Recv  Triggered RIP  Key-chain
  FastEthernet0/0.1    1     1 2
  Serial0/0.2          1     1 2
 Automatic network summarization is in effect
Maximum path: 4
Routing for Networks:
   172.22.0.0
   172.25.0.0
Passive Interface(s):
   FastEthernet0/1
Routing Information Sources:
   Gateway         Distance      Last Update
   172.25.1.7           120      00:00:08
   172.25.2.2           120      00:00:00
Distance: (default is 120)

Router1#
```

Note that you could apply an inbound access list to an interface to prevent the router from receiving RIP updates from other devices. To do this, you would simply apply a filter to block UDP port 520. However, as we discuss in Chapter 19, you cannot use access control lists on an interface to filter outbound router packets. In any case, that method forces the router to look at every incoming packet. This can cause serious CPU problems on fast links. It is far more efficient to just let the RIP process do the filtering, as we have shown in this recipe.

Similarly, it is more efficient to use the *passive interface* command to prevent the router from sending routes out through an interface, rather than using an outbound distribute list that merely blocks all routes. This is because with the *passive interface* command, the router doesn't have to compare the routes it wants to send to an access list to decide whether to send them. Instead, it just knows not to send any routes.

See Also

Recipe 6.2

6.7 Default Passive Interface

Problem

You want to disable RIP on all of a router's interfaces, except for a few that you specify.

Solution

You can disable the sending of RIP updates on all interfaces with the *passive-interface default* command:

```
Router1#configure terminal
Enter configuration commands, one per line.  End with CNTL/Z.
Router1(config)#router rip
Router1(config-router)#passive-interface default
Router1(config-router)#no passive-interface FastEthernet0/0.1
Router1(config-router)#network 172.22.0.0
Router1(config-router)#network 172.25.0.0
Router1(config-router)#network 192.168.1.0
Router1(config-router)#exit
Router1(config)#end
Router1#
```

Discussion

The RIP *network* command has two functions. The first function tells RIP which routing prefixes to distribute. The second turns on RIP updates on all interfaces whose addresses are included in the range specified by the *network* command. Sometimes you want to send routing information for a subnet, but you don't want to actually run RIP on the corresponding interface, as we described in Recipe 6.6. If there are interfaces that you don't want to send RIP updates, you can individually disable them by using the *passive-interface* command, as we did in Recipe 6.6. But sometimes you don't want interfaces to take part in RIP unless you explicitly enable them, even if they happen to have addresses that are covered by a *network* command.

This is mostly used as a convenience on routers that have a lot of interfaces, particularly when only a few of those interfaces will be running RIP. You use this feature by entering the *passive-interface default* command, and then explicitly re-enabling RIP with the *no passive-interface* command on those interfaces where you do want it:

```
Router1(config)#router rip
Router1(config-router)#passive-interface default
Router1(config-router)#no passive-interface FastEthernet0/0.1
```

You can then use as many *network* commands as you like, but RIP updates will only be sent on the interfaces that you explicitly list.

Using the *passive-interface default* command can save time, while also making it simpler to troubleshoot problems because you don't have to carefully count all of the interfaces to figure out which ones should be running the routing protocol:

```
Router1#show ip protocols
Routing Protocol is "rip"
  Sending updates every 30 seconds, next due in 13 seconds
  Invalid after 180 seconds, hold down 180, flushed after 240
  Outgoing update filter list for all interfaces is not set
  Incoming update filter list for all interfaces is not set
```

```
Redistributing: rip
Default version control: send version 1, receive any version
  Interface          Send  Recv  Triggered RIP  Key-chain
  FastEthernet0/0.1   1     1 2
 Automatic network summarization is in effect
Maximum path: 4
Routing for Networks:
  172.22.0.0
  172.25.0.0
Passive Interface(s):
  FastEthernet0/1
  Serial0/0.2
Routing Information Sources:
  Gateway        Distance      Last Update
  172.25.1.7          120      00:00:09
  172.25.2.2          120      00:00:01
Distance: (default is 120)

Router1#
```

See Also

Recipe 6.6

6.8   Unicast Updates for RIP

Problem

You want to exchange routing information with one device on a network, but not
with any others.

Solution

You can configure RIP to send its updates to a neighboring router using unicast
instead of broadcast or multicast packets. This is useful in two situations. First, on
Nonbroadcast Multiple Access (NBMA) networks, you can't use the standard broadcast or multicast methods for distributing information because the media doesn't
support it. Second, sometimes you need to exchange routing information with one or
more specific devices on a segment, but you don't trust the rest to give you reliable
information. This feature is rarely used, but it can be extremely valuable in these
types of situations:

```
Router1#configure terminal
Enter configuration commands, one per line.  End with CNTL/Z.
Router1(config)#router rip
Router1(config-router)#passive-interface FastEthernet0/1
Router1(config-router)#neighbor 172.22.1.4
Router1(config-router)#end
Router1#
```

Discussion

This recipe uses the *passive-interface* command discussed in Recipes 6.6 and 6.7 to prevent the router from sending routing information to the interface in general. Note that it does not prevent the router from receiving routing information from other devices on the segment. We will discuss how to solve that problem in a moment.

A debug trace helps to show how the unicast update option works:

```
Router1#debug ip rip
RIP protocol debugging is on
Router1#
Aug 11 02:41:13.632: RIP: sending v1 update to 255.255.255.255 via FastEthernet0/0.1
(172.25.1.5)
Aug 11 02:41:13.636: RIP: sending v1 update to 255.255.255.255 via Serial0/0.2 (172.
25.2.1)
Aug 11 02:41:13.644: RIP: sending v1 update to 172.22.1.4 via FastEthernet0/1 (172.
22.1.3)
```

Here you can see that this router sends its updates to the general broadcast address, 255.255.255.255, for all of the other interfaces, but for FastEthernet0/1, the update goes directly to 172.22.1.4. We note in passing that this is RIP Version 1. If it were Version 2, it would send updates using the multicast address 224.0.0.9, instead of the general segment broadcast address by default. However, the unicast option for Version 2 would work exactly the same as shown here.

The output of the *show ip protocols* command includes information about any unicast neighbors:

```
Router1#show ip protocols
Routing Protocol is "rip"
  Sending updates every 30 seconds, next due in 21 seconds
  Invalid after 180 seconds, hold down 180, flushed after 240
  Outgoing update filter list for all interfaces is not set
  Incoming update filter list for all interfaces is not set
  Redistributing: rip
  Neighbor(s):
    172.22.1.4
  Default version control: send version 1, receive any version
    Interface          Send  Recv  Triggered RIP  Key-chain
    FastEthernet0/0.1   1    1 2
    Serial0/0.2         1    1 2
  Automatic network summarization is in effect
  Maximum path: 4
  Routing for Networks:
    172.22.0.0
    172.25.0.0
  Passive Interface(s):
    FastEthernet0/1
  Routing Information Sources:
    Gateway         Distance      Last Update
    172.25.1.7         120        00:00:26
    172.25.2.2         120        00:00:14
```

```
   172.22.1.4          120      00:00:07
 Distance: (default is 120)
```

```
Router1#
```

As we noted in Recipe 6.6, just making an interface passive does not prevent it from listening for updates. But one of the most common reasons for using unicast neighbors with RIP is to ensure that the router accepts routing information only from specific devices on a segment. So we need to configure the router to reject incoming RIP information from all other devices. This is most easily accomplished by using an access list, as follows:

```
Router1#configure terminal
Enter configuration commands, one per line.  End with CNTL/Z.
Router1(config)#access-list 101 permit udp host 172.22.1.4 any eq rip
Router1(config)#access-list 101 deny udp any any eq rip
Router1(config)#access-list 101 permit ip any any
Router1(config)#interface FastEthernet0/1
Router1(config-if)#ip access-group 101 in
Router1(config-if)#end
Router1#
```

See Also

Recipe 6.6; Recipe 6.7

6.9   Applying Offsets to Routes

Problem

You want to modify the routing metrics for routes learned from or sent out through a particular interface.

Solution

You can modify the RIP metrics for a list of routes learned through a particular interface with the *offset-list* configuration command:

```
Router2#configure terminal
Enter configuration commands, one per line.  End with CNTL/Z.
Router2(config)#access-list 22 permit 192.168.20.0
Router2(config)#router rip
Router2(config-router)#offset-list 22 in 5 Serial0.1
Router2(config-router)#exit
Router2(config)#end
Router2#
```

A similar command changes the metrics for a list of routes as they are sent out through a specified interface:

```
Router2#configure terminal
Enter configuration commands, one per line.  End with CNTL/Z.
```

```
Router2(config)#access-list 33 permit 192.168.30.0
Router2(config)#router rip
Router2(config-router)#offset-list 33 out 10 Serial0.1
Router2(config-router)#exit
Router2(config)#end
Router2#
```

Discussion

The *offset-list* command is most useful when you need RIP to take account of the costs of different links. By default, RIP only looks at the number of hops to the destination. But sometimes the longer path is significantly faster. For example, you might have a primary link that uses a T1 to get to a router in another building, and an Ethernet segment to get from there to another router that connects to a server. It's probably better to take this primary link than a backup 56Kbps circuit that happens to connect directly to the last hop router.

Other routing protocols, such as OSPF, address this problem by assigning a cost to each link and adding up the costs to find the best path. But RIP only has a simple hop count metric. So if you want to ensure that one path is preferred over another, shorter one, you have to modify the metrics so that slower links actually appear to be more than one hop long.

Cisco routers give considerable flexibility in changing metrics by adding an offset. This allows you to change each route independently as it is received or sent. You can even affect routes according to which interface the router receives them through. But you need to be extremely careful because you can only increase a metric; you can never decrease it, and the maximum metric value is only 16. When the metric reaches a value of 16, RIP considers the network to be unreachable.

Sometimes you want to ensure that a particular path is never used to reach a certain destination. In this case, you can apply an offset of 16, and the router will have to find a different path. The router also allows you to apply an offset of 0, but this has no effect.

The *show ip protocols* command lists all of the offsets that are configured, including information about the access-lists, interfaces, and the size of the offset that is applied:

```
Router2#show ip protocols
Routing Protocol is "rip"
  Sending updates every 30 seconds, next due in 25 seconds
  Invalid after 180 seconds, hold down 180, flushed after 240
  Outgoing update filter list for all interfaces is not set
  Incoming update filter list for all interfaces is not set
  Outgoing routes in Serial0.1 will have 10 added to metric if on list 33
  Incoming routes in Serial0.1 will have 5 added to metric if on list 22
  Redistributing: rip
  Default version control: send version 1, receive any version
    Interface          Send  Recv  Triggered RIP  Key-chain
    Ethernet0           1     1 2
```

```
    Loopback0               1     1 2
    Serial0.1               1     1 2
  Automatic network summarization is in effect
  Maximum path: 4
  Routing for Networks:
    172.25.0.0
    192.168.30.0
  Routing Information Sources:
    Gateway        Distance      Last Update
    172.25.2.1          120      00:00:12
  Distance: (default is 120)
Router2#
```

A debug trace shows the incoming and outgoing routes. Note that the trace always shows the metric values after applying the offset for both inbound and outbound updates:

```
Router2#debug ip rip
RIP protocol debugging is on
Aug 10 23:24:36: RIP: sending v1 update to 255.255.255.255 via Serial0.1
Aug 10 23:24:36: RIP: build update entries
Aug 10 23:24:36:        subnet 172.25.25.2 metric 1
Aug 10 23:24:36:        network 192.168.30.0 metric 11
Aug 10 23:24:48: RIP: received v1 update from 172.25.2.1 on Serial0.1
Aug 10 23:24:48:        0.0.0.0 in 1 hops
Aug 10 23:24:48:        172.22.0.0 in 1 hops
Aug 10 23:24:48:        172.25.1.0 in 1 hops
Aug 10 23:24:48:        192.168.20.0 in 7 hops
Router2#
```

6.10   Adjusting Timers

Problem

You wish to tune your routing protocol performance to improve the time that the network takes to converge after a topology change.

Solution

RIP has several timers that control things like how often it sends updates and how long it takes to remove a bad route. You can adjust these values with the *timers basic* configuration command:

```
Router2#configure terminal
Enter configuration commands, one per line.  End with CNTL/Z.
Router2(config)#router rip
Router2(config-router)#timers basic 20 80 80 120
Router2(config-router)#exit
Router2(config)#end
Router2#
```

Discussion

The *timers basic* command controls all of the adjustable timers for RIP:

```
Router2(config-router)#timers basic 20 80 80 120
```

The four arguments are, in order, the *update period*, the *invalid route timer*, the *holddown timer*, and the *flush timer*. All of these times are in seconds.

The *update period* controls how often the router sends updates to its neighbors. The default update period is 30 seconds. Reducing this period can help improve convergence times. However, you have to remember that RIP sends the entire routing table in each update cycle. So if the routing table is large, reducing this period too much can cause serious bandwidth loading problems on slower links.

The *invalid route timer* controls how long the router will wait before a particular route is declared invalid. If the route disappears from routing updates from neighboring routers for this length of time, the router will mark it invalid. The router will set the RIP metric for invalid routes to 16, or unreachable, when distributing them. This technique is often called "route poisoning." It is important to remember that the router doesn't remove invalid routes from its own routing table, and it will continue to distribute them to other routers.

The default invalid route timer value is 180 seconds. Most references advise making this value at least three times the update period. Shorter invalid route timers can cause instability problems. But if you make it too much longer, then the network doesn't respond well to topology changes.

The *holddown timer* for a particular route starts when the router gets a routing update that says that a particular route is inaccessible. This could happen, for example, if another router's invalid route timer for this route has expired. But it can also happen as a result of a triggered update, indicating that a particular interface pointing to this network has gone down.

The router will keep the unreachable route in its table, and will distribute it to other routers with an unreachable metric. After the holddown timer expires, the router will delete the unreachable route and start to accept other routing information for this route.

The default holddown period is 180 seconds. It is usually a good idea to keep the holddown time the same as the invalid route timer to help ensure network stability.

The final parameter is the *flush timer*. This controls how long the router will keep a route in its routing table before purging it. The default flush period is 240 seconds. It must be greater than the holddown time; otherwise, routes can be flushed before the holddown timer expires, which makes the holddown time meaningless.

We recommend using extreme caution when adjusting RIP timers. The timers on every router in a RIP network must be equal, or you will see terrible instability problems. Note that the RIP timers affect the entire RIP process, meaning that you can't

---

set the timer values separately for different neighbors, or different interfaces. So it isn't possible to slow down the update timers over a slow WAN link and make them shorter over a faster LAN link.

In this example, we wanted to make RIP converge faster after topology changes, so we decreased all of the timers:

```
Router2(config)#router rip
Router2(config-router)#timers basic 20 80 80 120
```

The net result is that we have reduced the time to flush a bad route to 2 minutes from the default value of 4. But it is important to notice that we had to decrease all of the timers to achieve this result without compromising overall network stability.

As we mentioned earlier, routers will send the entire routing table on every update cycle. So making the timers too short can cause congestion problems on slower links. However, you can get away with shorter update periods if you use route summarization or filtering, as shown in Recipe 6.16. You can also decrease bandwidth consumption while improving convergence times by configuring the routers to send updates only when there are changes, as in Recipe 6.12.

Usually people are interested in reducing these timers to improve convergence times. We don't recommend increasing them from the default values because it will make the network respond too slowly to topology changes. If you have a problem with older or slower routers that are unable to receive RIP updates as quickly as they are sent, a better solution is to adjust the interpacket delay, as shown in Recipe 6.10.

You can view the values for all of the configured RIP timers with the *show ip protocols* command:

```
Router2#show ip protocols
Routing Protocol is "rip"
  Sending updates every 20 seconds, next due in 8 seconds
  Invalid after 80 seconds, hold down 80, flushed after 120
  Outgoing update filter list for all interfaces is not set
  Incoming update filter list for all interfaces is not set
    Redistributing: rip
  Default version control: send version 1, receive any version
    Interface             Send  Recv  Triggered RIP  Key-chain
    Ethernet0             1     1 2
    Serial0.1            1     1 2
  Automatic network summarization is in effect
  Maximum path: 4
  Routing for Networks:
    172.25.0.0
    192.168.30.0
  Routing Information Sources:
    Gateway         Distance      Last Update
    172.25.2.1           120      00:00:14
  Distance: (default is 120)
Router2#
```

See Also

Recipe 6.10; Recipe 6.12; Recipe 6.16

6.11 Configuring Interpacket Delay

Problem

You want to slow down the rate that a router sends the packets in a single update to ensure that slower devices aren't so overwhelmed that they lose information.

Solution

Use the *output-delay* configuration command to adjust the inter-packet delay of the RIP protocol:

```
Router2#configure terminal
Enter configuration commands, one per line.  End with CNTL/Z.
Router2(config)#router rip
Router2(config-router)#output-delay 10
Router2(config-router)#exit
Router2(config)#end
Router2#
```

Discussion

If the routing table distributed in each update is small, it will fit into a single packet. But the maximum size for a RIP update packet is 512 bytes. Each packet has an 8-byte UDP header, and 4 bytes of general RIP information. The remaining 500 bytes of the packet carry the actual routes. Each individual route takes 20 bytes, so there can be at most 25 routes in one packet. If you have more than 25 routes in your routing table, RIP must send it as multiple packets.

The problem with this is that some devices can't process large amounts of incoming routing information quickly, and they wind up missing some of the routing information. This is particularly true for older legacy equipment, or routers with slow processors or insufficient memory. So if you find that one or more of the neighboring routers has a mysteriously incomplete routing table, it might help to increase the interpacket spacing. The other reason for increasing the *output-delay* is to prevent bursts of RIP traffic from causing network congestion.

For example, in Frame Relay networks, if you burst above the Committed Information Rate (CIR), the extra packets are marked as *Discard Eligible*, meaning that if there is congestion, these are the first packets that the network should drop. Dropping routing protocol packets can cause serious problems. Spreading out this burst of RIP traffic might be sufficient to prevent this sort of problem.

The *output-delay* command allows you to specify the interpacket delay in milliseconds. The default is 0, meaning that the router will send packets as fast as it can. You can specify any delay value between 8 and 50 milliseconds with this command. It is not necessary to specify a corresponding delay on neighboring routers.

The output of the *show ip protocols* command includes the output delay value if you specify any nondefault value:

```
Router2#show ip protocols
Routing Protocol is "rip"
  Sending updates every 60 seconds, next due in 17 seconds
  Invalid after 180 seconds, hold down 180, flushed after 240
  Output delay 10 milliseconds between packets
  Outgoing update filter list for all interfaces is not set
  Incoming update filter list for all interfaces is not set
  Redistributing: rip
  Default version control: send version 1, receive any version
    Interface           Send  Recv  Triggered RIP  Key-chain
    Ethernet0           1     1 2
    Serial0.1           1     1 2
  Automatic network summarization is in effect
  Maximum path: 4
  Routing for Networks:
    172.25.0.0
    192.168.30.0
  Routing Information Sources:
    Gateway         Distance      Last Update
    172.25.2.1          120       00:00:23
  Distance: (default is 120)
Router2#
```

See Also

Chapter 10

6.12   Enabling Nonperiodic Updates

Problem

You want to reduce RIP bandwidth requirements by configuring routers to forward changes only to the routing table instead of forwarding the entire routing table every 30 seconds.

Solution

The *ip rip triggered* interface configuration command tells the router to only send those parts of the RIP database that have changed, instead of sending the entire database on each RIP update cycle:

```
Router1#configure terminal
Enter configuration commands, one per line.  End with CNTL/Z.
```

```
Router1(config)#interface Serial0/0.2
Router1(config-subif)#ip rip triggered
Router1(config-subif)#end
Router1#
```

Be sure to enable these nonperiodic "triggered" updates on the adjacent router as well:

```
Router2#configure terminal
Enter configuration commands, one per line.  End with CNTL/Z.
Router2(config)#interface Serial0.1
Router2(config-subif)#ip rip triggered
Router2(config-subif)#end
Router2#
```

 You must enable this feature on both routers sharing the point-to-point link, or you risk losing all routing information.

Discussion

It is important to distinguish between this feature and the triggered updates that are part of the standard RIP protocol. What is normally called a *triggered update* in RIP simply means that the protocol sends out updated route information as soon as it notices a change, rather than waiting for the next update cycle. The triggered update feature in this recipe would be more accurately called a *nonperiodic update*; it simply means that the router generally refrains from sending any routing information unless there is a change.

This feature is based on RFC 2091, although it doesn't implement all of the features described in that RFC (in particular, RFC 2091 includes extensions to the Novell IPX RIP and SAP update process that Cisco does not implement). You can use it with both RIP Versions 1 and 2. It became available starting in IOS Version 12.0(1)T.

Triggered updates are available only for point-to-point serial interfaces. They are particularly useful for slower serial WAN links where bandwidth is an issue. This feature is also used with dial-on-demand interfaces, where it can save money by eliminating periodic RIP updates that would keep the link up unnecessarily.

When you enable this feature on an interface, the router sends routing updates only in a few well-defined situations. It sends a full copy of the database when it is first powered on to ensure that there is at least one full update. The router also sends a full copy of the database if the neighboring router requests it. If the triggered interface itself goes up or down, the router sends a partial database to update the neighboring router on the changes since it last connected. And, in a relatively stable network, it only sends updates indicating incremental changes to the RIP database.

In a stable network, if there are no changes to the routing table, there are no updates. You can see the time since the last update with the *show ip protocols* command. In this case, from a very stable network, over 12 hours have elapsed since the last update:

```
Router2#show ip protocols
Routing Protocol is "rip"
  Sending updates every 60 seconds, next due in 52 seconds
  Invalid after 180 seconds, hold down 180, flushed after 240
Outgoing update filter list for all interfaces is not set
  Incoming update filter list for all interfaces is not set
  Redistributing: rip
  Default version control: send version 1, receive any version
    Interface         Send  Recv  Triggered RIP  Key-chain
    Ethernet0          1    1 2
    Serial0.1          1    1 2         Yes
  Automatic network summarization is in effect
  Maximum path: 4
  Routing for Networks:
    172.25.0.0
    192.168.30.0
  Routing Information Sources:
    Gateway        Distance      Last Update
    172.25.2.1        120        12:08:06
  Distance: (default is 120)
Router2#
```

Note that we only enabled triggered updates on the Serial0.1 subinterface, but this is not the only interface taking part in RIP. In particular, the Ethernet0 interface uses the normal periodic updates, although it is using a 60-second cycle rather than the default 30-second update period.

If you combine this feature with route filtering and summarization as discussed in Recipes 6.2 and 6.16, you can hide any instability that might exist elsewhere in the network. This is particularly useful for dialup links when you don't want to dial just because of a topology change elsewhere in the network.

The *show ip rip database* command marks routes learned via triggered interfaces as *permanent*:

```
Router2#show ip rip database 192.168.20.0 255.255.255.0
192.168.20.0/24
    [7] via 172.25.2.1, 00:02:43 (permanent), Serial0.1
  * Triggered Routes:
    - [7] via 172.25.2.1, Serial0.1
Router2#
```

This terminology is slightly confusing because this route is clearly not permanent like a static route would be. But it is not like normal RIP database entries that are subject to the holddown and flush timers, which is why it is marked this way.

The following debug trace shows a triggered update for a route that became inaccessible. We ran this debug for 20 minutes, and this was the only event it recorded:

```
Aug 11 13:18:25: RIP: received v1 triggered update from 172.25.2.1 on Serial0.1
Aug 11 13:18:25: RIP: sending v1 ack to 172.25.2.1 via Serial0.1, seq# 15
Aug 11 13:18:25:     192.168.20.0 in 16 hops (inaccessible)
```

Note that RIP didn't send any packets, not even a Hello type packet to ensure that the next hop router was still accessible. This is why the feature is available only on point-to-point links. In any multiple access medium, such as an Ethernet segment, the router wouldn't be able to determine whether its neighbors had become unreachable.

See Also

Recipe 6.2; Recipe 6.16

6.13   Increasing the RIP Input Queue

Problem

You want to increase the size of the RIP input queue to prevent your low-speed router from losing routing information.

Solution

To increase the size of the shared RIP queue, use the *input-queue* configuration command:

```
Router2#configure terminal
Enter configuration commands, one per line.  End with CNTL/Z.
Router2(config)#router rip
Router2(config-router)#input-queue 200
Router2(config-router)#end
Router2#
```

Discussion

This command allows you to control how much incoming RIP update information the router can hold before it has can process the information and integrate it into its routing table. Sometimes a router simply can't keep up with all of the information that it receives. This is most likely to be the case with less powerful routers on a busy network with many routes.

Bear in mind that each RIP update packet can hold up to 25 routes, and the default queue size is more than adequate to hold this many routes. So the input-queue size is only likely to be a problem if you have many times this number of routes, or if you have many routers all sharing the same segment. If this is the case, and you find that a less powerful router is randomly losing routes from its table, then it is relatively safe and easy to increase this queue depth.

The default value is 50. In this recipe, we have increased the queue depth to 200. This is a good starting point if you think that you have a queue depth problem. You can set this value to anything from 0 to 1024, although it is not clear why you would want to decrease the queue depth.

Recipe 6.10 shows another, alternative solution to this same problem. Instead of increasing the queue size on the slower router, you may opt to change the inter-packet delay on the faster routers. And, in some cases, it may be necessary to combine both of these solutions.

See Also

Recipe 6.10

6.14 Configuring RIP Version 2

Problem

You want to use the more flexible features of RIP Version 2.

Solution

By default, Cisco routers will listen for both RIP Version 1 and 2 packets, but they will only send Version 1. If you want to configure the router to send and receive only Version 2 RIP packets, use the *version 2* configuration command:

```
Router2#configure terminal
Enter configuration commands, one per line.  End with CNTL/Z.
Router2(config)#router rip
Router2(config-router)#version 2
Router2(config-router)#network 172.25.0.0
Router2(config-router)#network 192.168.30.0
Router2(config-router)#end
Router2#
```

You can also enable RIP Version 2 by sending and receiving separately for individual interfaces:

```
Router1#configure terminal
Enter configuration commands, one per line.  End with CNTL/Z.
Router1(config)#interface Serial0/0.2
Router1(config-subif)#ip rip send version 2
Router1(config-subif)#ip rip receive version 2
Router1(config-subif)#end
Router1#
```

Discussion

By default, the router listens for Version 1 and 2 packets but it only sends Version 1. You can run both versions simultaneously on the same interface by simply specifying both versions as follows:

```
Router1(config)#interface Serial0/0.2
Router1(config-subif)#ip rip send version 1 2
```

However, the router will then have to transmit all updates by using both versions, which can cause an unnecessary burden both for the router and the network. In general, RIP Version 2 is preferred, particularly because of the support for modern IP features, such as variable length subnet masks:

```
Router2#show ip protocols
Routing Protocol is "rip"
  Sending updates every 60 seconds, next due in 19 seconds
  Invalid after 180 seconds, hold down 180, flushed after 240
  Output delay 10 milliseconds between packets
  Outgoing update filter list for all interfaces is not set
  Incoming update filter list for all interfaces is not set
    Redistributing: rip
  Default version control: send version 2, receive version 2
    Interface          Send  Recv  Triggered RIP  Key-chain
    Ethernet0           2     2
    Serial0.1           2     2             Yes
  Automatic network summarization is in effect
  Maximum path: 4
  Routing for Networks:
    172.25.0.0
    192.168.30.0
  Routing Information Sources:
    Gateway         Distance     Last Update
    172.25.2.1           120     01:04:31
  Distance: (default is 120)
Router2#
```

This command shows that the router is sending and receiving only Version 2 on both interfaces. In this case, the router will reject any incoming RIP Version 1 packets on either of these ports. So you need to make sure that the neighboring routers on these interfaces are also running Version 2.

The second configuration example leaves the default configuration for all of the interfaces except Serial0/0.2, which only sends and receives RIP Version 2:

```
Router1#show ip protocols
Routing Protocol is "rip"
  Sending updates every 30 seconds, next due in 11 seconds
  Invalid after 180 seconds, hold down 180, flushed after 240
  Outgoing update filter list for all interfaces is not set
  Incoming update filter list for all interfaces is not set
  Redistributing: static, rip
  Default version control: send version 1, receive any version
```

```
    Interface          Send  Recv  Triggered RIP  Key-chain
    Serial0/0.2         2     2           Yes
    FastEthernet0/1     1     1 2
  Automatic network summarization is in effect
  Maximum path: 4
  Routing for Networks:
    172.22.0.0
    172.25.0.0
  Routing Information Sources:
    Gateway        Distance       Last Update
    172.25.2.2          120       14:40:28
    172.22.1.4          120       01:06:11
  Distance: (default is 120)
Router1#
```

Debug traces show which version the router sends and receives for every update:

```
Router2#debug ip rip
RIP protocol debugging is on
Router2#
Aug 11 14:38:54: RIP: received v2 update from 172.25.2.1 on Serial0.1
Aug 11 14:38:54:      0.0.0.0/0 via 0.0.0.0 in 1 hops
Aug 11 14:38:54:      172.22.0.0/16 via 0.0.0.0 in 1 hops
Aug 11 14:38:54:      172.25.0.0/16 via 0.0.0.0 in 1 hops
Aug 11 14:38:54:      172.25.1.0/24 via 0.0.0.0 in 1 hops
Aug 11 14:38:54:      172.25.25.1/32 via 0.0.0.0 in 1 hops
Aug 11 14:38:57: RIP: sending v2 update to 224.0.0.9 via Serial0.1
Aug 11 14:38:57: RIP: build update entries
Aug 11 14:38:57:        172.25.25.2/32 via 0.0.0.0, metric 1, tag 0
Aug 11 14:38:57:        192.168.30.0/24 via 0.0.0.0, metric 11, tag 0
Router2#
```

If you configure a router to listen only for one version, however, it will just drop any packets of the other version that it receives:

```
Router2#debug ip rip
RIP protocol debugging is on
Router2#
Aug 11 14:43:11: RIP: ignored v1 packet from 172.25.2.1 (illegal version)
Aug 11 14:43:11: RIP: received v2 update from 172.25.2.1 on Serial0.1
```

6.15   Enabling RIP Authentication

Problem

You want to authenticate your RIP traffic to ensure that unauthorized equipment cannot affect how traffic is routed through your network.

Solution

The following set of commands enables plain-text RIP authentication:

```
Router1#configure terminal
Enter configuration commands, one per line.  End with CNTL/Z.
```

```
Router1(config)#key chain ORA
Router1(config-keychain)#key 1
Router1(config-keychain-key)#key-string oreilly
Router1(config-keychain-key)#exit
Router1(config)#interface FastEthernet0/0.1
Router1(config-subif)#ip rip authentication key-chain ORA
Router1(config-subif)#ip rip authentication mode text
Router1(config-subif)#exit
Router1(config)#end
Router1#
```

For greater security, Cisco routers can also use MD5-based authentication:

```
Router1#configure terminal
Enter configuration commands, one per line.  End with CNTL/Z.
Router1(config)#key chain ORA
Router1(config-keychain)#key 1
Router1(config-keychain-key)#key-string oreilly
Router1(config-keychain-key)#exit
Router1(config)#interface FastEthernet0/0.1
Router1(config-subif)#ip rip authentication key-chain ORA
Router1(config-subif)#ip rip authentication mode md5
Router1(config-subif)#end
Router1#
```

Discussion

RIP authentication is one of the protocol enhancements that appeared in Version 2. It is not available for Version 1.

The first configuration example in this recipe uses plain-text authentication. In general, we recommend using the MD5 authentication because the plain-text version is far too easy to break. If you want to set up authentication to ensure that you only receive updates from the appropriate devices, you should use the safer MD5 version. The only reason to consider the less secure plain-text version is if some of the RIP devices cannot support MD5. Because the RFC for RIP Version 2 only describes plain text authentication, some non-Cisco devices do not support MD5 authentication.

Both forms of RIP authentication help to ensure that only legitimate network equipment is allowed to take part in RIP updates. This is particularly important if you have network segments that contain foreign devices that may corrupt the routing tables. This could happen because of malice, but it's also relatively easy for a misconfigured Unix workstation running the *routed* program to cause serious routing problems.

When you enable plain text authentication, the first route field in each update packet contains the authentication string instead of a route. Note that this implies that each update packet can then hold a maximum of 24 route entries. Because the MD5 authentication scheme carries more information, it uses the first and last route fields in each update packet. So this leaves a maximum of 23 route entries per update packet.

In the example, you can see that the key is applied to an interface. This allows you to specify a different key for each network segment. However, there is nothing to stop you from using the same key on more than one interface, or even a single key throughout the network.

The following debug traces were taken with authentication enabled. The first trace shows plain-text authentication, and includes the password:

```
Router1#debug ip rip
RIP protocol debugging is on
Aug 12 02:08:03.386: RIP: received packet with text authentication oreilly
Aug 12 02:08:03.390: RIP: received v2 update from 172.25.1.7 on FastEthernet0/0.1
```

The second trace shows an update containing MD5 authentication. Note that in this case, the router is not able to decode the authentication string. Instead, it compares the encrypted password string with the encrypted version of its own password to see if they match. There are no known methods to uniquely invert MD5 encryption:

```
Router3#debug ip rip
RIP protocol debugging is on
Aug 11 22:14:50 EDT: RIP: received packet with MD5 authentication
Aug 11 22:14:50 EDT: RIP: received v2 update from 172.25.1.5 on Ethernet0
```

The *show ip protocols* command includes information about the authentication key chains:

```
Router3#show ip protocols
Routing Protocol is "rip"
  Sending updates every 30 seconds, next due in 16 seconds
  Invalid after 180 seconds, hold down 180, flushed after 240
  Outgoing update filter list for all interfaces is
  Incoming update filter list for all interfaces is
  Redistributing: rip
  Default version control: send version 2, receive version 2
    Interface        Send  Recv  Key-chain
    Ethernet0        2     2     ORA
  Routing for Networks:
    172.25.0.0
  Routing Information Sources:
    Gateway          Distance      Last Update
    172.25.1.5            120      00:00:01
  Distance: (default is 120)
Router3#
```

If the router receives a RIP update that has an incorrect key, or no key at all, it will discard the packet, as shown in the following debug trace:

```
Router3#debug ip rip
RIP protocol debugging is on
Aug 11 22:17:07 EDT: RIP: ignored v2 packet from 172.25.1.5 (invalid authentication)
```

We will discuss key management schemes, such as setting key lifetimes and using multiple keys when we look at EIGRP authentication. The key management systems are identical on both cases.

See Also

Chapter 7

6.16   RIP Route Summarization

Problem

You want to decrease the size of your routing tables to improve the stability and efficiency of the routing process.

Solution

You can manually configure address summarization on an individual interface with the *ip summary-address rip* configuration command:

```
Router1#configure terminal
Enter configuration commands, one per line.  End with CNTL/Z.
Router1(config)#interface Serial0/0.2
Router1(config-subif)#ip summary-address rip 172.25.0.0 255.255.0.0
Router1(config-subif)#exit
Router1(config)#end
Router1#
```

By default, RIP will summarize groups of subnets into classful network routes. You can disable this automatic summarization with the *no auto-summary* configuration command:

```
Router1#configure terminal
Enter configuration commands, one per line.  End with CNTL/Z.
Router1(config)#router rip
Router1(config-router)#no auto-summary
Router1(config-router)#exit
Router1(config)#end
Router1#
```

Discussion

RIP automatically summarizes along classful network boundaries. So if your router sees that several subnets of the same network all use the same path, and there are no subnets of this network using a different path, it will automatically summarize this information. The routes to the individual subnets are suppressed. Then any downstream devices from this router will see only a summary route, such as 172.25.0.0/16 instead of all of the individual subnets like 172.25.1.0/24, 172.25.2.16/28, and so forth.

The downstream devices don't need to know that they are seeing summary routes instead of the actual individual routes. So this works well even with legacy equipment.

Note, however, that the *auto-summary* feature works only along classful network boundaries. So, for example, it will not summarize a group of networks such as

192.168.16.0/24 through 192.168.31.0/24 into 192.168.16.0/20 because these are all separate Class C networks. RIP cannot advertise supernets like this.

The interface specific summarization command became available in IOS Version 12.0(6)T. Configuring a summary addresses on an interface tells the router to send this summary information out through this interface. Then all of the routers that are downstream from the configured interface will see only the summary route, and none of the constituent subnet routes. As long as any of these subnet routes is valid, the router will propagate the summary information. But when the last subnet that is part of the summarized range disappears, the router stops sending the summary route through this interface.

You cannot configure more than one summary address from the same classful network address on an interface. For example, the following code is invalid because both of the summary addresses are subnets of 172.25.0.0/16:

```
Router1#configure terminal
Enter configuration commands, one per line.  End with CNTL/Z.
Router1(config)#interface Serial0/0.2
Router1(config-subif)#ip summary-address rip 172.25.16.0 255.255.240.0
Router1(config-subif)#ip summary-address rip 172.25.35.0 255.255.255.0
IP-RIP:No summary for 172.25.35.0/24.Summary 172.25.16.0/20 already on interface
Router1(config-subif)#end
Router1#
```

However, note that either of these summarizations would be fine on its own. You can configure several different summary addresses as long as they are for different networks:

```
Router1#configure terminal
Enter configuration commands, one per line.  End with CNTL/Z.
Router1(config)#interface Serial0/0.2
Router1(config-subif)#ip summary-address rip 172.25.16.0 255.255.240.0
Router1(config-subif)#ip summary-address rip 172.26.35.0 255.255.255.0
Router1(config-subif)#ip summary-address rip 10.101.0.0 255.255.0.0
Router1(config-subif)#end
Router1#
```

Route summarization has two important advantages. First, it reduces the size and complexity of the routing table. This in turn reduces the amount of memory and processing required on the downstream routers. The second advantage is that because all information about the individual subnets is suppressed, the downstream routers will not know or care about flapping interfaces in another part of the network. These two factors combine to improve overall network stability.

Suppose you have a routing table that looks like this before summarization:

```
Router2#show ip route rip
R    172.21.0.0/16 [120/1] via 172.25.2.1, 00:00:01, Serial0.1
R    172.22.0.0/16 [120/1] via 172.25.2.1, 00:00:01, Serial0.1
     172.25.0.0/16 is variably subnetted, 6 subnets, 3 masks
R       172.25.25.6/32 [120/2] via 172.25.2.1, 00:00:01, Serial0.1
```

```
R       172.25.25.1/32 [120/1] via 172.25.2.1, 00:00:01, Serial0.1
R       172.25.1.0/24 [120/1] via 172.25.2.1, 00:00:01, Serial0.1
R       172.25.0.0/16 [120/1] via 172.25.2.1, 00:00:01, Serial0.1
R*   0.0.0.0/0 [120/1] via 172.25.2.1, 00:00:02, Serial0.1
Router2#
```

If you then enable autosummarization, the router will replace all of the highlighted subnets with a single summary for the entire classful network address:

```
Router2#show ip route rip
R    172.21.0.0/16 [120/1] via 172.25.2.1, 00:00:01, Serial0.1
R    172.22.0.0/16 [120/1] via 172.25.2.1, 00:00:01, Serial0.1
     172.25.0.0/16 is variably subnetted, 3 subnets, 3 masks
R       172.25.0.0/16 [120/1] via 172.25.2.1, 00:00:01, Serial0.1
R*   0.0.0.0/0 [120/1] via 172.25.2.1, 00:00:01, Serial0.1
Router2#
```

You can see if a router is doing any summarization by looking at the *show ip protocols* command. This command shows both automatic summarization that is enabled by default as well as any interface-specific manually configured summarization:

```
Router1#show ip protocols
Routing Protocol is "rip"
  Sending updates every 30 seconds, next due in 14 seconds
  Invalid after 180 seconds, hold down 180, flushed after 240
  Outgoing update filter list for all interfaces is not set
  Incoming update filter list for all interfaces is not set
  Redistributing: static, rip
  Default version control: send version 2, receive version 2
    Interface           Send  Recv  Triggered RIP  Key-chain
    FastEthernet0/0.1    2     2                    ORA
    Serial0/0.2          2     2
    FastEthernet0/1      2     2
  Automatic network summarization is in effect
  Address Summarization:
    172.25.0.0/16 for Serial0/0.2
  Maximum path: 4
  Routing for Networks:
    172.22.0.0
    172.25.0.0
  Routing Information Sources:
    Gateway         Distance      Last Update
    172.25.1.7           120      00:00:23
    172.25.2.2           120      00:00:00
    172.22.1.4           120      08:00:53
  Distance: (default is 120)
Router1#
```

The only thing you have to be careful of with summarization is when you have discontiguous network addressing. If you configure a router to advertise a summary route for downstream routers, then you have to ensure that no subnets in the summarized range exist in the downstream part of the network. The problem that can result from summarizing discontiguous networks is that any router in the middle of your network will see two or more identical summaries, pointing to two different RIP neighbors. Because the summary routes suppress the individual routes, there is no way to tell which way to send traffic for each individual subnet.

6.17   Route Tagging

Problem

You want RIP to include a tag when it distributes specific routes to prevent routing loops when redistributing between routing protocols.

Solution

RIP Version 2 allows you to tag external routes. For a static route, for example, the configuration looks like this:

```
Router1#configure terminal
Enter configuration commands, one per line.  End with CNTL/Z.
Router1(config)#ip route 0.0.0.0 0.0.0.0 172.25.1.1
Router1(config)#access-list 7 permit 0.0.0.0
Router1(config)#route-map TAGGING permit 10
Router1(config-route-map)# match ip address 7
Router1(config-route-map)# set tag 5
Router1(config-route-map)#exit
Router1(config)#router rip
Router1(config-router)#redistribute static route-map TAGGING
Router1(config-router)#exit
Router1(config)#end
Router1#
```

Discussion

You can only apply a route tag to external routes; that is, routes that are not learned from RIP. The example shows a static route, but you can apply a tag to routes learned from other routing protocols in exactly the same way. For example, the following code shows how to apply a tag to certain routes learned via EIGRP:

```
Router1#configure terminal
Enter configuration commands, one per line.  End with CNTL/Z.
Router1(config)#access-list 7 permit 192.168.1.0
Router1(config)#route-map TAGGING permit 10
Router1(config-route-map)#match ip address 7
Router1(config-route-map)#set tag 5
Router1(config-route-map)#exit
Router1(config)#router eigrp 65530
Router1(config-router)#network 192.168.1.0
Router1(config-router)#exit
Router1(config)#router rip
Router1(config-router)#redistribute eigrp 65530 route-map TAGGING
Router1(config-router)#exit
```

```
Router1(config)#end
Router1#
```

RIP does not make use of the tags directly; it only distributes them. Once a route has a tag associated with it, every RIP Version 2 router will propagate this tag with the route. Tags are useful when redistributing routes into another routing process. For instance, if our RIPv2 network were being used as a transit network between two other networks, we could tag routes learned from one of these external networks and redistribute only those routes into the other network. This way, the RIP network would allow the two networks to talk to one another, but neither of the external networks can use the internal resources of the RIP network itself.

A debug trace shows the tagging in action:

```
Router1#debug ip rip
RIP protocol debugging is on
Aug 13 03:27:23.870: RIP: sending v2 update to 224.0.0.9 via Serial0/0.2
Aug 13 03:27:23.870: RIP: build update entries
Aug 13 03:27:23.870:    0.0.0.0/0 via 0.0.0.0, metric 1, tag 5
Aug 13 03:27:23.870:    172.22.0.0/16 via 0.0.0.0, metric 1, tag 0
Aug 13 03:27:23.874:    172.25.1.0/24 via 0.0.0.0, metric 1, tag 0
Aug 13 03:27:23.874:    172.25.25.1/32 via 0.0.0.0, metric 1, tag 0
Aug 13 03:27:23.874:    172.25.25.6/32 via 0.0.0.0, metric 2, tag 0
```

And if we were to run a similar trace on a downstream router, we would see that while the metric increments at each hop, the tag remains the same.

Here is an example that redistributes only the tagged routes into an attached EIGRP network. Note that you could easily construct a network where different tag values have different meanings. For example, you could make the tags equal to the routing process numbers of the various external networks. This allows you to easily redistribute only the routes you want into other networks:

```
Router1#configure terminal
Enter configuration commands, one per line.  End with CNTL/Z.
Router1(config)#router eigrp 11
Router1(config-router)#redistribute rip route-map TAGOUT
Router1(config-router)#exit
Router1(config)#route-map TAGOUT permit 10
Router1(config-route-map)#match tag 5
Router1(config-route-map)#route-map TAGOUT deny 20
Router1(config-route-map)#exit
Router1(config)#end
Router1#
```

RIPv2 supports 16-bit tags, which gives a range of values between 0 and 65,535. As we discuss in Chapters 7 and 8, EIGRP and OSPF use 32-bit tags, for a range from 0 to 4,294,967,295. Of course, it is unlikely that you will need this many route tags.

See Also

Chapter 7; Chapter 8

EIGRP

7.0   Introduction

Enhanced Interior Gateway Routing Protocol (EIGRP) is a Cisco proprietary routing protocol. Because it is proprietary, you can use it only in an all-Cisco network. But EIGRP more than makes up for this deficiency by being easy to configure, fast, and reliable. A detailed discussion of the protocol's theory and operation is out of the scope of this book. So if you are unfamiliar with EIGRP in general, or if you need more detail on how the protocol works, we recommend reading the relevant sections from *IP Routing* by Ravi Malhotra (O'Reilly).

Like RIP, EIGRP is based on a distance vector algorithm to determine the best path to a destination. But EIGRP uses a more complex metric than RIP's simple hop count. The EIGRP metric, which is based on the minimum bandwidth and net delay along each possible path, means that EIGRP can accommodate larger networks than RIP. But it also means that EIGRP needs a different algorithm for loop removal. This is because in EIGRP it isn't possible to simply increment the hop count to infinity to eliminate a loop, as RIP does. EIGRP uses a more sophisticated algorithm is called Diffusing Update Algorithm (DUAL).

The DUAL algorithm ensures that every router can individually make sure that its routing table is always free from loops. It allows the router to take advantage of several different possible paths, if they all have the same metric. This facilitates load sharing among equal cost links. Further, the EIGRP topology database on each router keeps track of higher cost candidates for the same destinations. This helps routing tables throughout the network to reconverge quickly after a topology change, such as a link or router failure.

EIGRP operates very efficiently over large networks. It achieves this efficiency in part by sending non-periodic updates. This means that unlike RIP, EIGRP only distributes information about routes that have changed, and only when there is a change to report. The rest of the time, routers only exchange small "Hello" packets that are used to verify that routing peers are still available. So, in a relatively stable network, EIGRP uses very little bandwidth. This is especially useful in WAN configurations.

It is also extremely efficient over LAN portions of a network. On each network segment, routers exchange routing information by using multicast packets, which helps to limit bandwidth usage on segments that hold many routers. EIGRP uses a multicast address 224.0.0.10, sending packets as raw IP packets by using protocol number 88. These multicast packets are always sent with a TTL value of 1 to ensure that locally relevant routing information doesn't leak off the local segment and confuse routers elsewhere in the network.

EIGRP includes many of the features that are needed in larger networks, such as Classless Interdomain Routing (CIDR) and Variable Length Subnet Masks (VLSM). But we suspect that this protocol owes most of its popularity to the fact that it is considerably easier to configure in a medium-sized to large network than other protocols with similar capabilities, such as Open Shortest Path First (OSPF).

Much of this chapter will discuss special features that Cisco has built into this protocol to help improve scalability. A detailed discussion of design guidelines for building scalable and reliable EIGRP networks is out of the scope of this book. Please refer to *Designing Large-Scale LANs* by Kevin Dooley (O'Reilly) for information about efficient EIGRP architectures.

7.1   Configuring EIGRP

Problem

You want to run EIGRP on a simple network.

Solution

The following commands configure EIGRP on one router in a simple network:

```
Router1#configure terminal
Enter configuration commands, one per line.  End with CNTL/Z.
Router1(config)#interface Ethernet0
Router1(config-if)#ip address 192.168.20.1 255.255.255.0
Router1(config-if)#exit
Router1(config)#interface Serial0.1 point-to-point
Router1(config-subif)#ip address 172.25.2.2 255.255.255.252
Router1(config-subif)#exit
Router1(config)#router eigrp 55
Router1(config-router)#network 172.25.0.0
Router1(config-router)#network 192.168.20.0
Router1(config-router)#exit
Router1(config)#end
Router1#
```

Naturally you would need to configure the other routers in this network to also exchange routing information using EIGRP process number 55. For example:

```
Router2#configure terminal
Enter configuration commands, one per line.  End with CNTL/Z.
Router2(config)#interface Serial0.1 point-to-point
Router2(config-subif)#ip address 172.25.2.1 255.255.255.252
Router2(config-subif)#exit
Router2(config)#router eigrp 55
Router2(config-router)#network 172.25.0.0
Router2(config-router)#exit
Router2(config)#end
Router2#
```

Discussion

This example shows how simple the basic EIGRP configuration is. To get the standard default functionality, you only need to enable EIGRP and add at least one *network* statement. In the example, we have set the EIGRP process ID numbers on both routers to 55:

```
Router1(config)#router eigrp 55
```

This process ID number, which is sometimes referred to as an Autonomous System Number (ASN), is just an arbitrary number between 1 and 65535. The only restriction is that all of the routers that will be exchanging interior routing information via EIGRP must be configured with the same process number. You can configure multiple EIGRP instances on the same router by specifying different process ID numbers, but the router will keep them separate unless you configure it to redistribute routes from one into the other.

As we discuss in Chapter 9, BGP attaches much greater significance to an ASN, using it to label the networks that a path passes through. In BGP, the ASN must be globally unique. The EIGRP process ID number, on the other hand, has no significance outside of the AS.

The *network* statements in EIGRP serve a dual role, both defining which networks this router will distribute, and which interfaces will take part in the routing protocol. So the *network* 172.25.0.0 command in this example means that if this router has any interfaces that are directly connected to subnets of 172.25.0.0, then it will inject this information into the routing protocol. It also means that it will try to find EIGRP neighbor routers through these same interfaces.

It is important to remember that while EIGRP is a classless routing protocol, the argument of the *network* statement is classful by default. This isn't actually a problem, though, because you can separately prevent certain interfaces from taking part in the protocol, and you can define classless summarization of subnets along whatever boundaries you like. We will discuss these features in Recipes 7.5 and 7.9

respectively. There is also a classless version of the *network* command, which we will discuss later in this recipe.

The *show ip protocols* command allows you to look at the details of your EIGRP configuration:

```
Router1#show ip protocols
Routing Protocol is "eigrp 55"
  Outgoing update filter list for all interfaces is not set
  Incoming update filter list for all interfaces is not set
  Default networks flagged in outgoing updates
  Default networks accepted from incoming updates
  EIGRP metric weight K1=1, K2=0, K3=1, K4=0, K5=0
  EIGRP maximum hopcount 100
  EIGRP maximum metric variance 1
  Redistributing: eigrp 55
  Automatic network summarization is in effect
  Automatic address summarization:
    192.168.20.0/24 for Loopback0, Serial0.1
    172.25.0.0/16 for Ethernet0
      Summarizing with metric 128256
  Maximum path: 4
  Routing for Networks:
    172.25.0.0
    192.168.20.0
  Routing Information Sources:
    Gateway         Distance      Last Update
    172.25.2.1            90      00:01:49
  Distance: internal 90 external 170
Router2#
```

In this case, you can see that this router is using EIGRP process number 55 to redistribute routing information about 172.25.0.0 and 192.168.20.0. It also shows several other useful pieces of information, such as what filters this router applies when sending and receiving routes, what external information is redistributed into EIGRP, and what neighboring devices we exchange information with. Most of the parameters shown in this particular output reflect the default values for EIGRP, but throughout this chapter you will find other examples showing several different useful variations.

One of the most useful EIGRP commands is *show ip eigrp neighbors*:

```
Router1#show ip eigrp neighbors
IP-EIGRP neighbors for process 55
H   Address                 Interface    Hold Uptime   SRTT   RTO  Q  Seq Type
                                         (sec)         (ms)        Cnt Num
0   172.25.2.1              Se0.1          13 00:00:01     1  2000  2  296
Router1#
```

By default, the router attempts to find adjacent routers on all interfaces included in your *network* statements. In this case, we see only one EIGRP neighbor router. The router will exchange routing information only with the active neighbors listed in this command.

The *show ip route eigrp* command lists the routes that have been learned through EIGRP:

```
Router1#show ip route eigrp
D    172.22.0.0/16 [90/2172416] via 172.25.2.1, 00:00:35, Serial0.1
     172.25.0.0/16 is variably subnetted, 6 subnets, 4 masks
D        172.25.25.6/32 [90/2300416] via 172.25.2.1, 00:00:35, Serial0.1
D        172.25.25.1/32 [90/2297856] via 172.25.2.1, 00:00:35, Serial0.1
D        172.25.1.0/24 [90/2172416] via 172.25.2.1, 00:00:35, Serial0.1
D        172.25.0.0/16 is a summary, 00:03:10, Null0
D    10.0.0.0/8 [90/4357120] via 172.25.2.1, 00:00:35, Serial0.1
Router1#
```

This output shows, for example, that we can reach the destination subnet 172.25.1. 0/24 through the neighboring router at 172.25.2.1, which is connected through interface Serial0.1. This route has an EIGRP metric value of 2172416 and an administrative distance of 90. Please refer to Chapter 5 for a more detailed discussion of administrative distance.

Starting in IOS Version 12.0(4)T, Cisco added a *netmask* argument to the *network* command, following a similar syntax to the corresponding OSPF command. This gives greater control over which interfaces will take part in the protocol, as well as what networks will be distributed into EIGRP:

```
Router1#configure terminal
Enter configuration commands, one per line.  End with CNTL/Z.
Router1(config)#router eigrp 55
Router1(config-router)#network 172.25.2.2 0.0.0.0
Router1(config-router)#network 192.168.20.0 0.0.0.255
Router1(config-router)#end
Router1#
```

Note that this command uses a wildcard rather than a netmask. So the first command specifies only the single address 172.25.2.2/32, while the second command includes anything that is a subnet of 192.168.20.0/24.

The output of *show ip protocols* shows the change:

```
Router1#show ip protocols
Routing Protocol is "eigrp 55"
  Outgoing update filter list for all interfaces is not set
  Incoming update filter list for all interfaces is not set
    Serial0.1 filtered by (prefix-list) Inbound
  Default networks flagged in outgoing updates
  Default networks not accepted from incoming updates
  EIGRP metric weight K1=1, K2=0, K3=1, K4=0, K5=0
  EIGRP maximum hopcount 100
  EIGRP maximum metric variance 1
  Redistributing: static, eigrp 55
  Automatic network summarization is not in effect
```

```
     Maximum path: 4
     Routing for Networks:
        172.25.2.2/32
        192.168.20.0/24
     Routing Information Sources:
        Gateway          Distance      Last Update
        172.25.2.1             90      00:17:06
     Distance: internal 90 external 170
   Router1#
```

This configuration can be slightly confusing because, for example, we have config-ured an EIGRP *network* statement for just the one address, 172.25.2.2/32. Looking at the actual interface, you can see that while its IP address does match this, it belongs to a larger subnet, 172.25.2.0/30. So while we know that this will enable EIGRP for this interface, you might think that the router would advertise the host route, 172.25.2.2/32, instead of the whole subnet, 172.25.2.0/30. If you try it in practice, you will see that the router advertises the larger /30 subnet. This is usually the desired behavior. However, if you want something else, Recipe 7.2 shows how to filter routes with EIGRP.

See Also

Recipe 7.2; Recipe 7.5; Recipe 7.9; Chapter 5

7.2   Filtering Routes with EIGRP

Problem

You want restrict which routes EIGRP propagates through the network.

Solution

You can filter the routes that EIGRP receives on a particular interface (or subinter-face) using the *distribute-list in* command as follows:

```
Router2#configure terminal
Enter configuration commands, one per line.  End with CNTL/Z.
Router2(config)#access-list 34 deny 192.168.30.0
Router2(config)#access-list 34 permit any
Router2(config)#router eigrp 55
Router2(config-router)#distribute-list 34 in Serial0.1
Router2(config-router)#exit
Router2(config)#end
Router2#
```

EIGRP also provides a *distribute-list out* command that allows you to filter the routes that are sent out through a particular interface (or subinterface):

```
Router1#configure terminal
Enter configuration commands, one per line.  End with CNTL/Z.
Router1(config)#access-list 57 permit 172.25.1.0
```

```
Router1(config)#access-list 57 deny any
Router1(config)#router eigrp 55
Router1(config-router)#distribute-list 57 out Serial0/0.2
Router1(config-router)#exit
Router1(config)#end
Router1#
```

And, with the *gateway* keyword, you can apply different filters to different neighbors on the same multiple access network:

```
Router9#configure terminal
Enter configuration commands, one per line.  End with CNTL/Z.
Router9(config)#ip prefix-list ALLOWED-PREFIXES permit 10.0.0.0/8 le 32
Router9(config)#ip prefix-list ALLOWED-PREFIXES deny 0.0.0.0/0 le 32
Router9(config)#ip prefix-list ALLOWED-NEIGHBORS permit 172.18.19.1/32
Router9(config)#ip prefix-list ALLOWED-NEIGHBORS permit 172.18.19.4/32
Router9(config)#ip prefix-list ALLOWED-NEIGHBORS deny 0.0.0.0/0 le 32
Router9(config)#router eigrp 55
Router9(config-router)#distribute-list prefix ALLOWED-PREFIXES gateway ALLOWED-
NEIGHBORS in
Router9(config-router)#exit
Router9(config)#end
Router9#
```

Discussion

The best way to see the action of these *distribute-list* commands is to look at the routing tables both with and without the filters. In the example, this is how the routing table looked before we applied any distribute lists:

```
Router2#show ip route eigrp
D    192.168.30.0/24 [90/2300416] via 172.25.2.1, 00:00:06, Serial0.1
D    172.22.0.0/16 [90/2172416] via 172.25.2.1, 00:04:04, Serial0.1
     172.25.0.0/16 is variably subnetted, 6 subnets, 4 masks
D       172.25.25.6/32 [90/2300416] via 172.25.2.1, 00:04:04, Serial0.1
D       172.25.25.1/32 [90/2297856] via 172.25.2.1, 00:04:04, Serial0.1
D       172.25.1.0/24 [90/2172416] via 172.25.2.1, 00:04:04, Serial0.1
D       172.25.0.0/16 is a summary, 00:06:39, Null0
D    10.0.0.0/8 [90/4357120] via 172.25.2.1, 00:04:04, Serial0.1
Router2#
```

Then, after applying the inbound filter, you can see that network 192.168.30.0 is gone:

```
Router2#show ip route eigrp
D    172.22.0.0/16 [90/2172416] via 172.25.2.1, 00:00:08, Serial0.1
     172.25.0.0/16 is variably subnetted, 6 subnets, 4 masks
D       172.25.25.6/32 [90/2300416] via 172.25.2.1, 00:00:08, Serial0.1
D       172.25.25.1/32 [90/2297856] via 172.25.2.1, 00:00:08, Serial0.1
D       172.25.1.0/24 [90/2172416] via 172.25.2.1, 00:00:08, Serial0.1
D       172.25.0.0/16 is a summary, 00:08:42, Null0
D    10.0.0.0/8 [90/4357120] via 172.25.2.1, 00:00:08, Serial0.1
Router2#
```

The *show ip protocols* command shows what filters have been applied to which inter-faces, both inbound and outbound:

```
Router2#show ip protocols
Routing Protocol is "eigrp 55"
  Outgoing update filter list for all interfaces is not set
  Incoming update filter list for all interfaces is not set
    Serial0.1 filtered by 34 (per-user), default is 34
  Default networks flagged in outgoing updates
  Default networks accepted from incoming updates
  EIGRP metric weight K1=1, K2=0, K3=1, K4=0, K5=0
  EIGRP maximum hopcount 100
  EIGRP maximum metric variance 1
  Redistributing: eigrp 55
  Automatic network summarization is in effect
  Automatic address summarization:
    192.168.20.0/24 for Loopback0, Serial0.1
    172.25.0.0/16 for Ethernet0
      Summarizing with metric 128256
  Maximum path: 4
  Routing for Networks:
    172.25.0.0
    192.168.20.0
  Routing Information Sources:
    Gateway         Distance      Last Update
    172.25.2.1            90      00:02:10
  Distance: internal 90 external 170
Router2#
```

The second example in the Solution section of this recipe shows an outbound dis-tribute list. It is difficult to see the effect of an outbound filter from the router that has the filter. So we will apply this filter to the neighbor device.

Look back at the output of the previous *show ip route eigrp* command to remember what the routing table looked like before applying this filter. Then, after applying the outbound *distribute-list* command on the neighboring router, the routing table looks like this:

```
Router2#show ip route eigrp
     172.25.0.0/16 is variably subnetted, 4 subnets, 4 masks
D      172.25.1.0/24 [90/2172416] via 172.25.2.1, 00:03:56, Serial0.1
Router2#
```

In this case, you will notice that we have applied an extremely restrictive outbound route filter. This technique is often used in WAN situations in which there is only one path from the remote site to the rest of the network. In such cases, it is often possible to send only a few summary routes, perhaps even a single default route, 0.0.0.0/0.

Again, the *show ip protocols* command shows information about both the filters and the interfaces that they act on:

```
Router1#show ip protocols
Routing Protocol is "eigrp 55"
```

```
Outgoing update filter list for all interfaces is not set
  Serial0/0.2 filtered by 57 (per-user), default is 57
Incoming update filter list for all interfaces is not set
Default networks flagged in outgoing updates
Default networks accepted from incoming updates
EIGRP metric weight K1=1, K2=0, K3=1, K4=0, K5=0
EIGRP maximum hopcount 100
EIGRP maximum metric variance 1
Redistributing: eigrp 55
Automatic network summarization is in effect
Automatic address summarization:
  172.25.0.0/16 for FastEthernet0/1, Serial0/1
    Summarizing with metric 28160
  172.22.0.0/16 for FastEthernet0/0.1, Serial0/0.2, Loopback0
    Serial0/1
    Summarizing with metric 28160
  10.0.0.0/8 for FastEthernet0/0.1, Serial0/0.2, Loopback0
    FastEthernet0/1
    Summarizing with metric 3845120
Maximum path: 4
Routing for Networks:
  10.0.0.0
  172.22.0.0
  172.25.0.0
Routing Information Sources:
  Gateway         Distance      Last Update
  10.1.1.1              90      00:04:45
  172.25.1.7            90      00:04:45
  172.25.2.2            90      00:04:45
  172.22.1.4            90      00:04:45
Distance: internal 90 external 170
Router1#
```

You can also use *prefix lists* to filter routes with EIGRP. This technique is most commonly used for filtering routes with BGP. Prefix lists do essentially the same thing as the access lists that we have already discussed. But they give you a different way to approaching filtering that is in some ways more in tune with how we think about routing. And because of the highly granular control they offer, it is often much easier to configure a prefix list to do the same job as an access list. Further, in mixed BGP/EIGRP networks, it can be extremely convenient to be able to use the same method for both routing protocols:

```
Router2#configure terminal
Enter configuration commands, one per line.  End with CNTL/Z.
Router2(config)#ip prefix-list Inbound seq 10 permit 10.0.0.0/8
Router2(config)#ip prefix-list Inbound seq 20 deny 10.0.0.0/8 ge 9
Router2(config)#ip prefix-list Inbound seq 30 permit 0.0.0.0/0 le 32
Router2(config)#router eigrp 55
Router2(config-router)#distribute-list prefix Inbound in Serial0.1
Router2(config-router)#exit
Router2(config)#end
Router2#
```

There are three lines in the prefix list called Inbound in this example. The first line permits the 10.0.0.0/8 network. Then the second line denies any network belonging to 10.0.0.0 that happens to have a mask with nine or more bits. The final line permits all other routes.

Again, to see how this works, it is easiest to look at the routing table before and after applying the filter. So in this case, we start with a routing table that looks like this:

```
Router2#show ip route eigrp
D    192.168.30.0/24 [90/2300416] via 172.25.2.1, 00:00:16, Serial0.1
     10.0.0.0/8 is variably subnetted, 3 subnets, 3 masks
D EX    10.0.0.0/8 [170/4357120] via 172.25.2.1, 00:00:16, Serial0.1
D       10.2.2.0/24 [90/2300416] via 172.25.2.1, 00:00:16, Serial0.1
D       10.1.1.0/30 [90/4357120] via 172.25.2.1, 00:00:16, Serial0.1
D*EX 0.0.0.0/0 [170/2172416] via 172.25.2.1, 00:00:16, Serial0.1
Router2#
```

After applying this filter, this routing table is reduced to the following:

```
Router2#show ip route eigrp
D    192.168.30.0/24 [90/2300416] via 172.25.2.1, 00:00:22, Serial0.1
D EX 10.0.0.0/8 [170/4357120] via 172.25.2.1, 00:00:22, Serial0.1
D*EX 0.0.0.0/0 [170/2172416] via 172.25.2.1, 00:00:22, Serial0.1
Router2#
```

The *gateway* keyword is useful in some limited situations. This command is only allowed on inbound distribute lists. It then lets you filter which EIGRP neighbors to accept routing updates from. It does not allow you to filter one group of routes from one neighbor and a different group from a different neighbor, which makes the command less useful than it might initially appear.

 Although the command allows it, never specify an interface on the *distribute-list* command if you want to use the *gateway* keyword. The interface name overrides the gateway feature, causing the router to ignore it quietly.

The command tells the router to accept only routes that are in the list of allowed prefixes, and only if they are received from the allowed group of neighbors:

```
Router9(config-router)#distribute-list prefix ALLOWED-PREFIXES gateway ALLOWED-
NEIGHBORS in
```

This feature is most useful in situations in which you want to block all routing updates from some neighbors, but you still want these neighbors to receive all of the outbound routing updates.

See Also

Chapter 9

7.3   Redistributing Routes into EIGRP

Problem

You want to redistribute routes learned with another means into the EIGRP routing process.

Solution

The simplest way to redistribute routes into EIGRP uses the *redistribute* command, as follows:

```
Router1#configure terminal
Enter configuration commands, one per line.  End with CNTL/Z.
Router1(config)#ip route 192.168.10.0 255.255.255.0 192.168.20.5
Router1(config)#router eigrp 55
Router1(config-router)#redistribute static
Router1(config-router)#exit
Router1(config)#end
Router1#
```

You can set the properties of the routes that are redistributed from another routing protocol with the *default-metric* command:

```
Router1#configure terminal
Enter configuration commands, one per line.  End with CNTL/Z.
Router1(config)#router eigrp 55
Router1(config-router)#redistribute rip
Router1(config-router)#default-metric 1000 100 250 100 1500
Router1(config-router)#exit
Router1(config)#end
Router1#
```

Discussion

The *show ip protocols* command tells you about any route redistribution that the protocol is doing:

```
Router1#show ip protocols
Routing Protocol is "eigrp 55"
  Outgoing update filter list for all interfaces is not set
  Incoming update filter list for all interfaces is not set
    Serial0.1 filtered by 34 (per-user), default is 34
  Default networks flagged in outgoing updates
  Default networks accepted from incoming updates
  EIGRP metric weight K1=1, K2=0, K3=1, K4=0, K5=0
  EIGRP maximum hopcount 100
  EIGRP maximum metric variance 1
  Redistributing: static, eigrp 55
  Automatic network summarization is in effect
  Automatic address summarization:
    192.168.20.0/24 for Loopback0, Serial0.1
    172.25.0.0/16 for Ethernet0
```

```
       Summarizing with metric 128256
   Maximum path: 4
   Routing for Networks:
     172.25.0.0
     192.168.20.0
   Routing Information Sources:
     Gateway         Distance       Last Update
     (this router)        90         00:05:00
     172.25.2.1           90         00:01:57
   Distance: internal 90 external 170
Router1#
```

If you look at the routing table of a downstream router, you can see that EIGRP has forwarded information about this static route:

```
Router2#show ip route eigrp
D    192.168.30.0/24 [90/156160] via 172.22.1.4, 00:00:02, FastEthernet0/1
D EX 192.168.10.0/24 [170/2195456] via 172.25.2.2, 00:00:01, Serial0/0.2
Router2#
```

There are two extremely important things to note in this output. The first is that the redistributed route is tagged as external, which is signified by the EX near the start of the line. An external route is any route that didn't originate with this routing protocol. This makes the information inherently less reliable than any internal route. So EIGRP also sets a higher administrative distance to ensure that internal EIGRP routes are always preferred over redistributed routes. This becomes extremely important when you have two or more redistribution points in your network that might be injecting the same routing information.

In this case, you can see that the administrative distance for the redistributed static route is 170 instead of the default EIGRP distance of 90. Recall from Chapter 5 that the default administrative distance for static routes is 1.

The second example in this recipe shows how to redistribute routes from a foreign routing protocol, instead of just static routes. The key difference is the *default-metric* command:

```
Router1(config-router)#redistribute rip
Router1(config-router)#default-metric 1000 100 250 100 1500
```

With static routes, you don't need to configure a default metric—you can just use the *redistribute static* command. However, whenever you redistribute another routing protocol into EIGRP, you must configure the default metric. There is no default default-metric (strangely enough), so if you don't put it in, the router will not redistribute anything.

The parameters in the *default-metric* command allow EIGRP to construct an appropriate metric. Since none of this information is available from the foreign protocol, you have to specify it manually. The parameters are, in order:

Bandwidth

This value specifies the minimum bandwidth along the path in Kilobits per second. It can have any value between 1 and 4294967295.

Delay

This value defines the mean latency for the path in 10 microsecond units. It can be anything between 0 and 4294967295.

Reliability

The reliability parameter is a numerical estimate of how likely the route and the path are to be available at any given moment. You can specify any value between 0 and 255, where 255 represents perfect 100 percent reliability.

Effective bandwidth (loading)

This value is intended to provide a way of shifting traffic off heavily loaded network links. You can give it a value between 0 and 255, where 255 represents 100 percent utilization.

Maximum Transmission Unit (MTU)

You can use this value to specify a path MTU to reach the foreign routing protocol. The range of values for this metric is between 0 and 4294967295.

As it turns out, however, EIGRP doesn't use most of this information by default. If you look at the output of any show IP protocols command in this chapter, you will see a line that specifies the EIGRP metric weights:

```
EIGRP metric weight K1=1, K2=0, K3=1, K4=0, K5=0
```

EIGRP uses these K values as coefficients in an involved equation that specifies how to combine all of these different individual metrics into a single numerical value, the composite EIGRP metric. You will notice that only K1 and K3 are nonzero. The result is that, by default, EIGRP uses only bandwidth and delay when computing its metric. So, in fact, you can generally fill in just about anything for the other parameters in the default-metric command, and it won't make any difference.

We note as an aside that while you can change these different K values by using the *metric weights* command, we strongly advise against changing the defaults. These values were of some use in IGRP, and when Cisco introduced EIGRP, with its superior DUAL algorithm, they carried the parameters forward. However, it was discovered that in practice it was relatively easy to make routing extremely unstable by changing them. And it's almost impossible to make things any better by changing these weight values in EIGRP.

The *default-metric* command sets the metric values for all external routing protocols. If you need to specify different metrics for different protocols, you can put the same information on the redistribute command line as follows:

```
Router1(config-router)#redistribute rip metric 1000 100 250 100 1500
Router1(config-router)#redistribute ospf 99 metric 1500 10 255 10 1500
```

Table 7-1 shows all of the different protocols that you can redistribute into EIGRP by using this method. You must specify each redistributed protocol separately.

Table 7-1. Valid redistribution protocols for EIGRP

Type	Description
bgp	Border Gateway Protocol
connected	Directly connected routes
egp	Exterior Gateway Protocol
eigrp	Enhanced IGRP
igrp	Interior Gateway Routing Protocol
isis	ISO IS-IS Routing Protocol
mobile	Mobile routes
odr	On Demand stub routes
ospf	Open Shortest Path First
rip	Routing Information Protocol
static	Static routes

Actually, there is an important exception in this list. If a router has EIGRP and IGRP, both sharing the same process ID number, it will automatically redistribute between them. This is a convenient feature because it makes it relatively easy to migrate an IGRP network to EIGRP. However, if the EIGRP process number is not the same as the one used for IGRP, you need to explicitly configure the redistribution. However, as Cisco has dropped IGRP support from all IOS images starting in 12.2T and 12.3, this older protocol is no longer available. If you are still running IGRP in any parts of your network, we strongly recommend migrating to EIGRP.

Sometimes you don't want to redistribute all of the routes from a particular external routing protocol, just some of them. In this case, you can apply a *distribute-list* as in Recipe 7.2 to only the routes that are redistributed from a particular protocol. For example, you might have several static routes on your router, and you want to redistribute only some of them. In that case, you can apply a distribute-list to only the static routes as follows:

```
Router1(config)#router eigrp 55
Router1(config-router)#redistribute static
Router1(config-router)#distribute-list 7 out static
```

This will apply access list number 7 to all of the static routes before distributing them. You can also use this technique when redistributing routes learned from other routing protocols. For example, you might want to filter the routes learned from OSPF before redistributing them into EIGRP. You can do this as follows:

```
Router1(config)#router eigrp 55
Router1(config-router)#redistribute ospf 99
Router1(config-router)#distribute-list 7 out ospf 99
```

See Also

Recipe 7.2; Chapter 5

7.4   Redistributing Routes into EIGRP Using Route Maps

Problem

You require greater control over the routes that are redistributed and their associated metrics and route tags.

Solution

You can use route maps to do more sophisticated redistribution of routes into EIGRP:

```
Router1#configure terminal
Enter configuration commands, one per line.  End with CNTL/Z.
Router1(config)#ip route 192.168.10.0 255.255.255.0 172.22.1.4
Router1(config)#ip route 192.168.11.0 255.255.255.0 172.22.1.4
Router1(config)#ip route 192.168.12.0 255.255.255.0 172.22.1.4
Router1(config)#access-list 20 permit 192.168.10.0
Router1(config)#access-list 21 permit 192.168.11.0
Router1(config)#route-map STATIC permit 10
Router1(config-route-map)#match ip address 20
Router1(config-route-map)#set metric 56 100 255 1 1500
Router1(config-route-map)#set tag 2
Router1(config-route-map)#exit
Router1(config)#route-map STATIC permit 20
Router1(config-route-map)#match ip address 21
Router1(config-route-map)#set metric 128 200 255 1 1500
Router1(config-route-map)#exit
Router1(config)#route-map STATIC deny 30
Router1(config-route-map)#exit
Router1(config)#router eigrp 55
Router1(config-router)#redistribute static route-map STATIC
Router1(config-router)#exit
Router1(config)#end
Router1#
```

Discussion

This recipe is extremely similar to Recipe 6.4 in the RIP chapter of this book. And just as in that example, we use route maps to set not only metrics, but also route tags for redistributed static routes. Please refer to Recipe 6.4 for a detailed discussion of how route maps work.

The one thing that you need to be careful of with EIGRP is that, as we discussed in Recipe 7.3, there is no default default-metric. So if you don't define EIGRP metrics for foreign routing protocols, EIGRP will not redistribute anything. This is not necessary for the static routes shown in the example, though.

See Also

Recipe 6.4; Recipe 7.3

7.5   Disabling EIGRP on an Interface

Problem

You want to disable an interface from participating in EIGRP.

Solution

You can prevent an interface from participating in EIGRP by simply designating it as *passive*:

```
Router1#configure terminal
Enter configuration commands, one per line.  End with CNTL/Z.
Router1(config)#router eigrp 55
Router1(config-router)#passive-interface Serial0/1
Router1(config-router)#exit
Router1(config)#end
Router1#
```

Discussion

The *passive-interface* command in EIGRP prevents directly connected routers from establishing an EIGRP neighbor relationship. Since they can't become neighbors, they will never exchange routing information. This is critically different from the way RIP behaves, as we saw in Chapter 6. In RIP, making an interface passive means that it will still accept routes; it just won't send them. But with EIGRP, a passive interface will not send or receive any routing information.

Furthermore, configuring one router to be passive means that it can't form an EIGRP adjacency relationship with any other routers through this interface. So if there are only two routers on a link, you can disable EIGRP on that link by simply configuring one of the routers with a passive interface.

You can see the neighbor relationships with the following command:

```
Router1#show ip eigrp neighbors
IP-EIGRP neighbors for process 55
H   Address           Interface    Hold Uptime   SRTT   RTO  Q  Seq Type
                                   (sec)         (ms)       Cnt Num
0   172.25.2.2        Se0/0.2      11 00:07:03 1563  5000  0  81
3   172.25.1.7        Fa0/0.1      77 00:18:17   11   200  0  348
2   172.22.1.4        Fa0/1        12 00:18:42    4   200  0  197
1   10.1.1.1          Se0/1        14 00:18:43    7   200  0  196
Router1#
```

If we then implement the *passive-interface* command on this router, as shown above, you can see that the neighbor disappears from the table:

```
Router1#show ip eigrp neighbors
IP-EIGRP neighbors for process 55
H   Address            Interface   Hold Uptime   SRTT   RTO  Q  Seq Type
                                   (sec)         (ms)        Cnt Num
0   172.25.2.2         Se0/0.2     14 00:08:56 1563   5000  0  81
3   172.25.1.7         Fa0/0.1     69 00:20:10   11    200  0  348
2   172.22.1.4         Fa0/1       12 00:20:35    4    200  0  197
Router1#
```

The *show ip protocols* command lists all of the passive interfaces that are configured on this router:

```
Router1#show ip protocols
Routing Protocol is "eigrp 55"
  Outgoing update filter list for all interfaces is not set
    Redistributed static filtered by 7
  Incoming update filter list for all interfaces is not set
  Default networks flagged in outgoing updates
  Default networks accepted from incoming updates
  EIGRP metric weight K1=1, K2=0, K3=1, K4=0, K5=0
  EIGRP maximum hopcount 100
  EIGRP maximum metric variance 1
  Redistributing: static, eigrp 55
  Automatic network summarization is in effect
  Automatic address summarization:
    172.25.0.0/16 for FastEthernet0/1
      Summarizing with metric 28160
    172.22.0.0/16 for FastEthernet0/0.1, Serial0/0.2, Loopback0
      Summarizing with metric 28160
    10.0.0.0/8 for FastEthernet0/0.1, Serial0/0.2, Loopback0
      FastEthernet0/1
      Summarizing with metric 3845120
  Maximum path: 4
  Routing for Networks:
    10.0.0.0
    172.22.0.0
    172.25.0.0
  Passive Interface(s):
    Serial0/1
  Routing Information Sources:
    Gateway         Distance      Last Update
    172.25.1.7            90      00:09:57
    172.25.2.2            90      00:09:57
    172.22.1.4            90      00:09:57
  Distance: internal 90 external 170
Router1#
```

A useful variant of the *passive-interface* command is *passive-interface default*:

```
Router1#configure terminal
Enter configuration commands, one per line.  End with CNTL/Z.
Router1(config)#router eigrp 55
```

```
Router1(config-router)#passive-interface default
Router1(config-router)#no passive-interface Serial0/1
Router1(config-router)#exit
Router1(config)#end
Router1#
```

This command makes all of the router's interfaces passive by default so that they will not take part in EIGRP. Then you can specifically enable only those interfaces that you want to take part by using a *no passive-interface* command. This is particularly useful when there are a lot of interfaces on the router and only a few of them will be running the routing protocol.

See Also

Chapter 6

7.6   Adjusting EIGRP Metrics

Problem

You want to modify the routing metrics for routes learned via EIGRP.

Solution

You can use the *offset-list* configuration command to modify the metrics of routes that EIGRP learns through a particular interface:

```
Router1#configure terminal
Enter configuration commands, one per line.  End with CNTL/Z.
Router1(config)#access-list 22 permit 192.168.30.0
Router1(config)#router eigrp 55
Router1(config-router)#offset-list 22 in 10000 Serial0.1
Router1(config-router)#exit
Router1(config)#end
Router1#
```

This command can also modify the EIGRP metrics of routes as the router sends them out through an interface:

```
Router1#configure terminal
Enter configuration commands, one per line.  End with CNTL/Z.
Router1(config)#access-list 33 permit 192.168.30.0
Router1(config)#router eigrp 55
Router1(config-router)#offset-list 33 out 10000 Serial0.1
Router1(config-router)#exit
Router1(config-router)#end
Router1#
```

Discussion

The *offset-list* command simply adds a constant value to the metrics of all routes that are either sent or received through a particular interface. There are actually two other ways to modify metrics in EIGRP. Recall that the EIGRP metric is a combination of the aggregate delay and the minimum bandwidth along a path. So instead of adding an offset to the entire metric, you can modify the bandwidth and delay separately as follows:

```
Router1(config)#interface Serial0.1
Router1(config-if)#bandwidth 56
Router1(config-if)#delay 1000
```

The *bandwidth* command takes an argument in kilobits per second, and will accept a value between 1 and 10,000,000 kbps. The *delay* command is measured in tens of microseconds, and can be anywhere between 1 and 16,777,215. So, in this case, we have specified a value of 1000, meaning a delay of 10,000 microseconds (10 milliseconds). You can see the current values for both of these values with the *show interfaces* command:

```
Router1#show interfaces serial0.1
Serial0.1 is up, line protocol is up
  Hardware is HD64570
  Internet address is 172.25.2.2/30
  MTU 1500 bytes, BW 1544 Kbit, DLY 20000 usec,
     reliability 255/255, txload 1/255, rxload 1/255
  Encapsulation FRAME-RELAY
Router1#
```

In this example, subinterface Serial0.1 has the default values for a serial interface, a bandwidth of 1544 kbps (a T1), and a delay of 20,000 microseconds (20 milliseconds). It is always a good idea to check the current values before adjusting either the bandwidth or delay parameters, if only to make sure that you are moving them in the right direction.

However, we would offer one important caution on adjusting the *bandwidth* parameter, in particular. This same value also appears in the SNMP variable *ifSpeed* for this interface. This is often used by performance management software to define the total available bandwidth for the interface. So changing this number to fix an EIGRP issue might cause a problem for your performance management system.

One of the problems with adjusting the *delay* and *bandwidth* on the interface is that you can't use this to separately adjust inbound and outbound routing metrics. If you need this level of control, the *offset-list* method discussed above is the best way to achieve it.

You can see the effect of an offset list in the output of the *show ip protocols* command:

```
Router1#show ip protocols
Routing Protocol is "eigrp 55"
  Outgoing update filter list for all interfaces is not set
  Incoming update filter list for all interfaces is not set
```

```
    Serial0.1 filtered by (prefix-list) Inbound
    Incoming routes in Serial0.1 will have 10000 added to metric if on list 22
    Default networks flagged in outgoing updates
    Default networks not accepted from incoming updates
    EIGRP metric weight K1=1, K2=0, K3=1, K4=0, K5=0
    EIGRP maximum hopcount 100
    EIGRP maximum metric variance 1
    Redistributing: static, eigrp 55
    Automatic network summarization is in effect
    Automatic address summarization:
      192.168.20.0/24 for Loopback0, Serial0.1
      172.25.0.0/16 for Ethernet0
        Summarizing with metric 128256
    Maximum path: 4
    Routing for Networks:
      172.25.0.0
      192.168.20.0
    Routing Information Sources:
      Gateway         Distance      Last Update
      172.25.2.1            90      00:02:09
    Distance: internal 90 external 170
  Router1#
```

And you can also see the difference it makes by looking at the routing tables. In this case, the route looked like this before we applied the offset-list:

```
Router1#show ip route eigrp
D    192.168.30.0/24 [90/200416] via 172.25.2.1, 00:00:24, Serial0.1
```

And, as you can see, the metric has increased by 10,000 after applying the offset:

```
Router1#show ip route eigrp
D    192.168.30.0/24 [90/210416] via 172.25.2.1, 00:00:24, Serial0.1
```

7.7   Adjusting Timers

Problem

You wish to tune your EIGRP timers to improve network convergence.

Solution

There are two important EIGRP timers, the *hello interval* and the *hold time*. You can adjust both of these timers separately on each interface on a router as follows:

```
Router1#configure terminal
Enter configuration commands, one per line.  End with CNTL/Z.
Router1(config)#interface Serial0.1
Router1(config-subif)#ip hello-interval eigrp 55 3
Router1(config-subif)#ip hold-time eigrp 55 9
Router1(config-subif)#exit
Router1(config)#end
Router1#
```

Discussion

One of the unique features of EIGRP is that you can adjust its timers separately on each interface. Recall from Chapter 6 that RIP requires you to adjust every router participating in RIP. And in Chapter 8 you will see that while OSPF allows you to adjust the timers separately on each link, you have to make sure that it is the same on all routers on this link. But with EIGRP, you can adjust the timers on one router on a link independently of what you have configured on other interfaces on this router, or on other routers on this link.

EIGRP handles this by simply telling the other routers on the link what its parameters are. Therefore, if one router has a particular hello time of, say, five seconds, then all of the other routers on this link will expect to see a hello packet from this router every five seconds. This is true regardless of what the other routers have for their own parameters. The result is that when you adjust the timers on an interface on one router, you affect what its neighbors expect to see from it.

The default timer values for most interface types are 5 seconds for hellos and a 15-second hold timer. This means that the router will send out a hello packet to verify its neighbor relationships every five seconds. And if it doesn't hear from a neighbor device, it will wait 15 seconds before declaring that neighbor down.

On multipoint interfaces with sub-T1 speeds, the default hello time is 60 seconds, with a hold time of 180 seconds. Notice that the defaults always have the hold time equal to three times the hello time. It is a good rule of thumb to keep this three-to-one ratio if you choose to adjust your timers.

You can cause serious network stability problems if you don't adjust them together. In particular, if the hold time is less than the hello time, you will see frequent loss of neighbor status, causing instability. And if the hold time is too long, you will find that your network does not converge quickly after link failures.

In our example, we have attempted to speed up convergence by decreasing the timers. The new hello time is three seconds, and the hold time is nine seconds. Before applying this change, you can see that the hold time is 15 seconds:

```
Router1#show ip eigrp neighbors
IP-EIGRP neighbors for process 55
H   Address                 Interface   Hold Uptime   SRTT   RTO  Q  Seq Type
                                        (sec)         (ms)        Cnt Num
0   172.25.2.1              Se0.1        15 00:10:02    16    200  0  549
Router1#
```

This command actually shows the amount of time remaining in the hold time interval. Each time you look at the neighbor table, you will see that the router is counting down from the configured hold time. Each time this router receives a hello packet from the specified neighbor router, it resets its hold timer and begins counting down again. If it ever reaches zero, it will reset the neighbor relationship.

If we go to the neighbor router in the example, you can see that the hold time for Router2 counts down from 9 seconds, instead of the default 15:

```
Router2#show ip eigrp neighbors
IP-EIGRP neighbors for process 55
H   Address                Interface   Hold Uptime   SRTT   RTO  Q  Seq Type
                                       (sec)         (ms)        Cnt Num
1   172.25.2.2             Se0/0.2       9 00:10:50    16   200  0  114
2   172.25.1.7             Fa0/0.1      65 1d22h       15   200  0  377
0   172.22.1.4             Fa0/1        13 1d22h        2   200  0  230
Router2#
```

See Also

Chapter 6; Chapter 8

7.8   Enabling EIGRP Authentication

Problem

You want to authenticate your EIGRP traffic to ensure that no unauthorized equipment can affect your routing tables.

Solution

To enable MD5-based EIGRP packet authentication, you must first define a key chain for the encryption, and then apply the authentication commands to the interface as follows:

```
Router1#configure terminal
Enter configuration commands, one per line.  End with CNTL/Z.
Router1(config)#key chain ORA
Router1(config-keychain)#key 1
Router1(config-keychain-key)#key-string oreilly
Router1(config-keychain-key)#exit
Router1(config-keychain)#exit
Router1(config)#interface Serial0/1
Router1(config-if)#ip authentication mode eigrp 55 md5
Router1(config-if)#ip authentication key-chain eigrp 55 ORA
Router1(config-if)#exit
Router1(config)#end
Router1#
```

Discussion

As soon as we configure EIGRP authentication on this router, the neighbor relationship dropped because it failed to authenticate:

```
IP-EIGRP 55: Neighbor 172.25.2.2 (Serial0/0.2) is down: Auth failure
```

To bring this neighbor back up, you have to ensure that both routers use the same authentication keys.

It's important to remember that this is just an authentication system. The routers do not encrypt the routing update packets as they send them through the network. They just authenticate these packets using MD5. This prevents people from either accidentally or maliciously injecting routes into your network. This is often useful in environments where you don't control all of the routers.

You can see from the following debug trace that when the authentication fails, EIGRP simply ignores the routing updates:

```
Router1#debug eigrp packet
EIGRP Packets debugging is on
    (UPDATE, REQUEST, QUERY, REPLY, HELLO, IPXSAP, PROBE, ACK, STUB, SIAQUERY,
SIAREPLY)
Router1#
Oct  3 01:40:59.704: EIGRP: ignored packet from 172.25.2.2 opcode = 5
(invalid authentication)
```

One of the biggest problems with using this sort of authentication system is that changing the keys can break routing throughout your network. The following example shows a way around this problem. By configuring timed keys, you can roll out a new key throughout your network without disrupting service:

```
Router1#configure terminal
Enter configuration commands, one per line.  End with CNTL/Z.
Router1(config)#key chain Mars
Router1(config-keychain)#key 1
Router1(config-keychain-key)#key-string rocket
Router1(config-keychain-key)#accept-lifetime 00:00:00 Jan 1 1993 00:15:00 Nov 1 2006
Router1(config-keychain-key)#send-lifetime 00:00:00 Jan 1 1993 00:00:00 Nov 1 2006
Router1(config-keychain-key)#key 2
Router1(config-keychain-key)#key-string martian
Router1(config-keychain-key)#accept-lifetime 23:45:00 Oct 31 2006 infinite
Router1(config-keychain-key)#send-lifetime 00:00:00 Nov 1 2006 infinite
Router1(config-keychain-key)#end
Router1#
```

In this case, this router will accept the original key string, rocket, until 12:15 AM on November 1, 2006. It will send this same key string until 12:00 AM on the same date. And it will start accepting the new key string, martian, at 11:45 PM. on October 31, 2006. In this way, there is a safe 30-minute transition period that you can configure in advance throughout the network. Then, the next day or whenever it is convenient, you can remove the configuration for the old key string on all the affected routers.

The *show key chain* command includes information about all of the configured key chains and the corresponding key strings:

```
Router1#show key chain
Key-chain ORA:
    key 1 -- text "oreilly"
        accept lifetime (always valid) - (always valid) [valid now]
        send lifetime (always valid) - (always valid) [valid now]
```

```
Key-chain Mars:
    key 1 -- text "rocket"
        accept lifetime (00:00:00 Jan 1 1993) - (00:15:00 Nov 1 2006) [valid now]
        send lifetime (00:00:00 Jan 1 1993) - (00:00:00 Nov 1 2006) [valid now]
    key 2 -- text "martian"
        accept lifetime (23:45:00 Oct 31 2006) - (infinite)
        send lifetime (00:00:00 Nov 1 2006) - (infinite)
Router1#
```

See Also

Recipe 6.15

7.9   EIGRP Route Summarization

Problem

You want to reduce the size of your routing tables to improve the stability and efficiency of the routing process.

Solution

The *ip summary-address eigrp* configuration command allows you to configure manual summary addresses on a per-interface basis:

```
Router1#configure terminal
Enter configuration commands, one per line.  End with CNTL/Z.
Router1(config)#interface Serial0/0.2
Router1(config-subif)#ip summary-address eigrp 55 172.25.0.0 255.255.0.0
Router1(config-subif)#exit
Router1(config)#end
Router1#
```

EIGRP can automatically summarize subnet routes into classful network-level routes. You can enable this command with the *auto-summary* command or disable it with the *no auto-summary* configuration command:

```
Router1#configure terminal
Enter configuration commands, one per line.  End with CNTL/Z.
Router1(config)#router eigrp 55
Router1(config-router)#no auto-summary
Router1(config-router)#exit
Router1(config)#end
Router1#
```

A useful new feature allows you to configure a leak-map so that the router will advertise the summary route, as well as some subset of the summarized addresses:

```
Router9# configure terminal
Enter configuration commands, one per line.  End with CNTL/Z.
Router9(config)#ip prefix-list 10.5.5/24 permit 10.5.5.0/24
```

```
Router9(config)#route-map LEAK10-5-5 permit 10
Router9(config-route-map)#match ip address prefix-list 10.5.5/24
Router9(config-route-map)#exit
Router9(config)#interface Serial0/0
Router9(config-if)#ip summary-address eigrp 55 10.5.0.0 255.255.0.0 leak-map LEAK10-
5-5
Router9(config-if)#exit
Router9(config)#end
Router9#
```

Discussion

Summarization is one of the most powerful features of EIGRP, and one of the most
frequently overlooked methods for improving network efficiency. Unlike RIP, which
summarizes along classful network boundaries, EIGRP uses CIDR, allowing you to
summarize at any bit in the address, as well as allowing supernets. And while OSPF
also allows this sort of summarization, as we will discuss in Chapter 8, OSPF can
only summarize at the ABR. Conversely, EIGRP allows you to summarize at any
router in the network. This means that with EIGRP, you can have multiple hierarchical levels of address summarization, which can greatly improve the maximum size
and efficiency of a large network, but only if it is designed properly to allow it.

 The *auto-summary* command was enabled by default until IOS version 12.2(8)T, when it started to be disabled by default.

You can see all of the summarization information, including which interfaces will
send out summary addresses, using the *show ip protocols* command:

```
Router1#show ip protocols
Routing Protocol is "eigrp 55"
  Outgoing update filter list for all interfaces is not set
    Redistributed static filtered by 7
  Incoming update filter list for all interfaces is not set
  Default networks flagged in outgoing updates
  Default networks accepted from incoming updates
  EIGRP metric weight K1=1, K2=0, K3=1, K4=0, K5=0
  EIGRP maximum hopcount 100
  EIGRP maximum metric variance 1
  Redistributing: static, eigrp 55
  Automatic network summarization is not in effect
  Address Summarization:
    172.25.0.0/16 for Serial0/0.2
      Summarizing with metric 28160
  Maximum path: 4
  Routing for Networks:
    10.0.0.0
    172.22.0.0
    172.25.0.0
  Routing Information Sources:
```

```
    Gateway         Distance      Last Update
    10.1.1.1             90        1d23h
    172.25.1.7           90        00:00:57
    172.25.2.2           90        00:00:57
    172.22.1.4           90        00:00:57
  Distance: internal 90 external 170
Router1#
```

In this example, we have only summarized 172.25.0.0/16 on interface Serial0/0.2. However, it is important to remember that you can summarize several networks at the same time on a single interface by simply configuring all of the different summary addresses, as follows:

```
Router1#configure terminal
Enter configuration commands, one per line.  End with CNTL/Z.
Router1(config)#interface Serial0/0.2
Router1(config-subif)#ip summary-address eigrp 55 172.25.0.0 255.255.0.0
Router1(config-subif)#ip summary-address eigrp 55 10.0.0.0 255.0.0.0 80
Router1(config-subif)#end
Router1#
```

When it summarizes addresses, EIGRP will automatically suppress all of the routes that are included in the summary. Of course, if there are no routes to summarize, the router won't distribute the summary address.

The metric of this summary route will be equal to the best metric of the routes being summarized. It is important to remember this because if the route with the best metric goes away for any reason, EIGRP will change the metric of the summary. So if the route with the best metric is unstable, it will make the summary route unstable. If you want to ensure that this doesn't happen, you can configure a static route within the summarized range, and point it to a null interface. Then you must configure the router to redistribute this static route into EIGRP.

The following example shows a CIDR supernet summarization:

```
Router1#configure terminal
Enter configuration commands, one per line.  End with CNTL/Z.
Router1(config)#interface Serial0/0.2
Router1(config-subif)#ip summary-address eigrp 55 0.0.0.0 0.0.0.0
Router1(config-subif)#end
Router1#
```

In this case, if there are any routes to distribute at all, EIGRP will distribute only the default route 0.0.0.0/0 and suppress all of the individual routes. This is actually an extremely useful technique on low-speed WAN links, particularly when this link represents the only path to the rest of the network. In such cases, the remote site only needs to know that it can get to everything it needs through this link. Further, because routing is always done by taking the longest match first, if the remote site happens to have more specific routing information for a particular destination, it won't use this summary route.

You could accomplish the same thing by redistributing a single static default route by using the redistribution techniques discussed in Recipe 7.3 and filtering out everything except 0.0.0.0/0 using a distribute list as in Recipe 7.2. But this summary address technique does both of these actions in a single step. Furthermore, with this technique, the default route appears in the routing table as an internal route:

```
Router2#show ip route eigrp
D*   0.0.0.0/0 [90/2172416] via 172.25.2.1, 00:00:30, Serial0.1
Router2#
```

Leak-maps became available in IOS level 12.3(14)T. This feature allows you to configure a summary address, and also advertise some of the summarized networks. In the example shown in the Solutions section above, we have summarized all of the 10.5.0.0/16 range of addresses:

```
Router9(config)#interface Serial0/0
Router9(config-if)#ip summary-address eigrp 55 10.5.0.0 255.255.0.0 leak-map LEAK10-
5-5
```

This summary includes a *leak-map* called LEAK10-5-5, which is defined by using a route map:

```
Router9(config)#ip prefix-list 10.5.5/24 permit 10.5.5.0/24
Router9(config)#route-map LEAK10-5-5 permit 10
Router9(config-route-map)#match ip address prefix-list 10.5.5/24
```

This route map does nothing but match a particular prefix, 10.5.5.0/24, and exclude it from summarization. We can then look at the routing table on a neighboring router:

```
Router2#show ip route 10.0.0.0
Routing entry for 10.0.0.0/8, 9 known subnets
  Variably subnetted with 3 masks
  Redistributing via eigrp 55

D     10.1.2.1/32 [90/2300416] via 172.20.10.9, 00:20:34, Serial0/0
D     10.5.5.0/24 [90/2838016] via 172.20.10.9, 00:00:37, Serial0/0
D     10.1.1.0/24 [90/2300416] via 172.20.10.9, 00:20:34, Serial0/0
D     10.5.0.0/16 [90/2838016] via 172.20.10.9, 00:18:53, Serial0/0
Router2#
```

This router now receives both the summary address, 10.5.0.0/16, and the specific prefix 10.5.5.0/24. This can be quite useful in situations when you have imperfect summarization. That is, you might be able to reduce all of the routes for a particular part of your network to a single summary route, 10.5.0.0/17. But if the single network 10.5.5.0/24 resides in a different part of the network, you need to make sure that this specific prefix also appears in routing tables throughout the network. Recall that routers will always use the most specific route when forwarding packets.

Previously, if you couldn't summarize all of the prefixes in a network, you had to advertise all of the individual routes. So the *leak-map* feature allows you to reduce the size of your routing table without causing problems for a few exceptions.

Note that because the feature uses route maps to define the leaked routes, you could also match parameters such as the route type (internal, external, or local) tag, or the router's next-hop interface for that route. For example you could use the interface matching to leak individual routes only if the remote site is on dial backup.

See Also

Recipe 7.2; Recipe 7.3; Chapter 8

7.10   Logging EIGRP Neighbor State Changes

Problem

You want to log EIGRP neighbor state changes.

Solution

To enable the logging of EIGRP neighbor state changes, use the *eigrp log-neighbor-changes* configuration command:

```
Router1#configure terminal
Enter configuration commands, one per line.  End with CNTL/Z.
Router1(config)#router eigrp 55
Router1(config-router)#eigrp log-neighbor-changes
Router1(config-router)#exit
Router1(config)#end
Router1#
```

Another closely related feature is the *eigrp log-neighbor-warnings* configuration command:

```
Router1#configure terminal
Enter configuration commands, one per line.  End with CNTL/Z.
Router1(config)#router eigrp 55
Router1(config-router)#eigrp log-neighbor-warnings 300
Router1(config-router)#exit
Router1(config)#end
Router1#
```

Discussion

When a neighbor relationship is lost, you also lose all of the routing entries for that neighbor. And the effects of this lost routing information are often felt throughout the network. Therefore, it can be extremely useful to have a good log of neighbor change events for troubleshooting strange intermittent network problems. However, this feature also gives you a good way of looking for faults on links that don't have a way of telling you about loss of connectivity.

Two important examples of this are tunnels and LAN extensions. In many cases, when the network breaks, bringing down a tunnel, the two tunnel end points are unable to see the problem. Similarly, in a LAN extension service, the two end point routers are both connected to Layer 2 LAN switches that are then bridged to one another through some other medium such as ATM. The problem in this case is that the intermediate network between the switches can break, and neither router will see a problem because they are both connected to an active switch port. It's also important to note that EIGRP neighbor relationships can break just because of noisy or congested links.

Whatever the cause, one of the easiest ways to detect a connectivity problem in the hidden network is to configure EIGRP between the routers via this link. In some cases, this will be done on a separate EIGRP process ID number to make it easier to differentiate between normal network topology changes and these hidden network faults. If you log EIGRP neighbor changes and configure the routers to send their SYSLOG events to a central fault management server, as discussed in Chapter 18, you can get an instant alarm on these types of problems.

The log messages generated by the *eigrp log-neighbor-changes* command show not only that the neighbors have changed, but they also give you an indication of why they changed state. This command is enabled by default:

```
Oct  2 22:00:38: %DUAL-5-NBRCHANGE: IP-EIGRP 55: Neighbor 172.25.2.1 (Serial0.1) is
up: new adjacency
Oct  2 22:03:23: %DUAL-5-NBRCHANGE: IP-EIGRP 55: Neighbor 172.25.2.1 (Serial0.1) is
down: summary configured
Oct  2 22:03:23: %DUAL-5-NBRCHANGE: IP-EIGRP 55: Neighbor 172.25.2.1 (Serial0.1) is
up: new adjacency
Oct  2 22:04:14: %DUAL-5-NBRCHANGE: IP-EIGRP 55: Neighbor 172.25.2.1 (Serial0.1) is
down: manually cleared
Oct  2 22:04:19: %DUAL-5-NBRCHANGE: IP-EIGRP 55: Neighbor 172.25.2.1 (Serial0.1) is
up: new adjacency
Oct  2 22:07:26: %DUAL-5-NBRCHANGE: IP-EIGRP 55: Neighbor 172.25.2.1 (Serial0.1) is
down: peer restarted
Oct  2 22:07:27: %DUAL-5-NBRCHANGE: IP-EIGRP 55: Neighbor 172.25.2.1 (Serial0.1) is
up: new adjacency
Oct  2 22:30:06: %DUAL-5-NBRCHANGE: IP-EIGRP 55: Neighbor 172.25.2.1 (Serial0.1) is
down: holding time expired
Oct  2 22:30:38: %DUAL-5-NBRCHANGE: IP-EIGRP 55: Neighbor 172.25.2.1 (Serial0.1) is
up: new adjacency
```

In this example, we have shown four different reasons for EIGRP to reset its neighbor relationships. Of these, only the last one, an expired holding time, is likely to indicate a network fault. Because this command is enabled by default, if you don't want to see these messages, perhaps because you aren't interested in monitoring your neighbors, or because you have some other method of doing so, you must disable it as follows:

```
Router1(config)#router eigrp 55
Router1(config-router)#no eigrp log-neighbor-changes
```

The *log-neighbor-warnings* command is also enabled by default. This command causes the router to display warning information about problems with neighbors. The most common such warning is the "not on common subnet" message:

```
Oct  2 22:32:22: IP-EIGRP(Default-IP-Routing-Table:55): Neighbor 192.168.100
.112 not on common subnet for FastEthernet0/0
```

This command accepts a numerical argument, which specifies how often the router should repeat these warning messages in seconds. By default, the router will issue these warning messages roughly every 15 seconds. In many networks, this is unnecessarily frequent, though, and could result in losing more important messages from your router's logging buffer. In the example in the Solution section of this recipe, we have changed the frequency to once every five minutes:

```
Router1(config)#router eigrp 55
Router1(config-router)#eigrp log-neighbor-warnings 300
```

See Also

Chapter 18

7.11   Limiting EIGRP's Bandwidth Utilization

Problem

You want to limit the fraction of an interface's bandwidth available to EIGRP for routing updates.

Solution

To modify the amount of bandwidth percentage available to EIGRP, use the *ip bandwidth-percent* configuration command:

```
Router1#configure terminal
Enter configuration commands, one per line.  End with CNTL/Z.
Router1(config)#interface Serial0.1
Router1(config-subif)#ip bandwidth-percent eigrp 55 40
Router1(config-subif)#exit
Router1(config)#end
Router1#
```

Discussion

The example above shows how to restrict EIGRP to use at most 40 percent of the available capacity of this link. By default, EIGRP limits its own bandwidth utilization to ensure that it never takes more than 50 percent of a link's capacity. However, this default isn't always appropriate. Sometimes you need to reduce this fraction to reduce overall congestion. And sometimes the total bandwidth value specified on an interface is not accurate.

For example, in Recipe 7.6, we discussed how to change what the router thinks the interface's bandwidth is. If this value is significantly lower than the real physical bandwidth of the interface, you might want to increase the fraction that EIGRP can use. This can help to improve network convergence times when EIGRP needs to suddenly exchange a large amount of routing information.

In the following example, we have manually reduced bandwidth value on this 128 kbps interface to 32 kbps to affect the EIGRP metric. Since this is much less than the true value, we have then increased the fraction that EIGRP can use to 200 percent, bringing it up to a maximum of 56 kbps, which would be the default for a real 128 kbps circuit:

```
Router1#configure terminal
Enter configuration commands, one per line.  End with CNTL/Z.
Router1(config)#interface Serial0.1
Router1(config-subif)#bandwidth 32
Router1(config-subif)#ip bandwidth-percent eigrp 55 200
Router1(config-subif)#exit
Router1(config)#end
Router1#
```

See Also

Recipe 7.6

7.12   EIGRP Stub Routing

Problem

You want to stabilize your network by sending smaller routing tables out to stub branches and reducing the scope of EIGRP queries.

Solution

To enable stub routing, use the *eigrp stub* configuration command:

```
Router1#configure terminal
Enter configuration commands, one per line.  End with CNTL/Z.
Router1(config)#router eigrp 55
Router1(config-router)#eigrp stub
Router1(config-router)#exit
Router1(config)#end
Router1#
```

Discussion

This feature became available starting in IOS 12.0(15)S. It is most commonly used in hub-and-spoke network designs where a remote router connects to the rest of the network through only one or two central routers, and where the remote router is the only connection for a small number of LAN segments. In general, you would configure the central routers in this case to send only a default route, as discussed in Recipe 7.9.

In situations when a route suddenly goes away, by default, every router will ask all of its neighbors if they have a path to that remote network. However, it is never going to be fruitful to ask these remote branch routers if they can reach the missing network. If these stub routers are reachable at all, they will already be exchanging information about the few networks that they can access. No trick of topology will allow them to find the missing route if the central routers don't have it. So the EIGRP stub feature disables these queries. This should help to improve overall network stability. And, in particular, this feature could significantly improve the stability of hub-and-spoke WANs:

```
Router2#show ip eigrp neighbors detail
IP-EIGRP neighbors for process 55
H   Address                Interface   Hold Uptime   SRTT   RTO  Q  Seq Type
                                       (sec)         (ms)       Cnt Num
1   172.25.2.2             Se0/0.2       6 00:15:57  787   4722  0  148
    Version 12.2/1.2, Retrans: 0, Retries: 0
    Stub Peer Advertising ( CONNECTED SUMMARY ) Routes
2   172.25.1.7             Fa0/0.1      70 1w0d       12    200  0  405
    Version 12.0/1.0, Retrans: 1, Retries: 0
0   172.22.1.4             Fa0/1        12 1w0d        1    200  0  258
    Version 12.2/1.2, Retrans: 2, Retries: 0
Router2#
```

The *eigrp stub* command can take six different keywords:

Receive-only

The router becomes a *receive-only* neighbor. This router will not share its routing information with its neighbors.

Connected

This router will only advertise connected networks. Note that you must configure the appropriate *network* statements for these connected networks, or alternatively use the *redistribute connected* command.

Static

The router will advertise static routes. Note that with this option, you must also configure the *redistribute static* command

Summary

The router will advertise summary routes. This function is enabled by default. Please refer to Recipe 7.9 for details on route summarization.

Leak-map

The router will advertise summary routes, as well as certain specific route prefixes. Please refer to Recipe 7.9 for details on leak maps.

Redistributed

The router will advertise external routes that have been redistributed from other protocols. By default, the stub feature will not advertise external routes. Please refer to Recipe 7.3 for details on route redistribution.

See Also

Recipe 7.3; Recipe 7.9

7.13 Route Tagging

Problem

You want to tag specific routes to prevent routing loops while mutually redistributing routes between two routing protocols.

Solution

This example shows how to tag external routes in EIGRP:

```
Router1#configure terminal
Enter configuration commands, one per line.  End with CNTL/Z.
Router1(config)#ip route 0.0.0.0 0.0.0.0 172.25.1.1
Router1(config)#access-list 7 permit 0.0.0.0
Router1(config)#route-map TAGGING permit 10
Router1(config-route-map)#match ip address 7
Router1(config-route-map)#set tag 5
Router1(config-route-map)#exit
Router1(config)#router eigrp 55
Router1(config-router)#redistribute static route-map TAGGING
Router1(config-router)#exit
Router1(config)#end
Router1#
```

In this case, the external routes are static, but the same technique applies to routes learned through other routing protocols.

Discussion

You can only tag routes that EIGRP has learned from another routing protocol. As we saw when talking about route tags with RIP, EIGRP does not use these tags directly; it only distributes them. You would use these tags at network boundaries when redistributing routes into another routing process.

For instance, if our EIGRP network were being used as a transit network between two other routing protocols, we could tag routes learned from the first external network. We could then redistribute only the first network's routes into the second external network. Similarly, we could redistribute only the second network's routes into the first network. In this way, we could ensure that the external networks use only the EIGRP network for transit, and prevent them from reaching anything internal.

As we discussed in Chapter 6, RIP Version 2 supports 16-bit tags, which gives it a range from 0 to 65,535. EIGRP and OSPF use 32-bit tags for a range from 0 to 4,294,967,295. These tags are purely internal, of course, so there is no interoperability problem. It is unlikely that you will need 4 billion tags, but this expanded range can be useful because you can map the 32-bit tags to IP addresses as a mnemonic for the external network information:

```
Router1#show ip eigrp topology 0.0.0.0
IP-EIGRP (AS 55): Topology entry for 0.0.0.0/0
  State is Passive, Query origin flag is 1, 1 Successor(s), FD is 28160
  Routing Descriptor Blocks:
  0.0.0.0, from Rstatic, Send flag is 0x0
      Composite metric is (28160/0), Route is External
      Vector metric:
        Minimum bandwidth is 100000 Kbit
        Total delay is 100 microseconds
        Reliability is 255/255
        Load is 1/255
        Minimum MTU is 1500
        Hop count is 0
      External data:
        Originating router is 172.25.25.1 (this system)
        AS number of route is 0
        External protocol is Static, external metric is 0
        Administrator tag is 5 (0x00000005)
        Exterior flag is set
  0.0.0.0 (Null0), from 0.0.0.0, Send flag is 0x0
      Composite metric is (28160/0), Route is Internal
      Vector metric:
        Minimum bandwidth is 100000 Kbit
        Total delay is 100 microseconds
        Reliability is 255/255
        Load is 1/255
        Minimum MTU is 1500
        Hop count is 0
      Exterior flag is set
Router1#
```

The following is a simple example in which we redistribute from EIGRP into OSPF only those routes that have a route tag value of 5. Presumably, this tag was set at another network boundary:

```
Router1#configure terminal
Enter configuration commands, one per line.  End with CNTL/Z.
Router1(config)#route-map TAGOUT permit 10
Router1(config-route-map)#match tag 5
Router1(config-route-map)#route-map TAGOUT deny 20
Router1(config-route-map)#exit
Router1(config)#router ospf 11
Router1(config-router)#redistribute eigrp 55 route-map TAGOUT
Router1(config-router)#exit
Router1(config)#end
Router1#
```

See Also

Chapter 6

7.14 Viewing EIGRP Status

Problem

You want to check the status of EIGRP on the router.

Solution

There are several useful commands for looking at EIGRP status. As we have seen throughout this chapter, the *show ip protocols* command displays a wealth of useful information:

```
Router1#show ip protocols
```

You can look at a routing table of only those routes that were learned via EIGRP by adding the *eigrp* keyword as follows:

```
Router1#show ip route eigrp
```

Another extremely useful EIGRP command displays a table of all of the adjacent EIGRP routers:

```
Router1#show ip eigrp neighbors
```

You can see information about the interfaces that exchange routing information by using EIGRP with this command:

```
Router1#show ip eigrp interfaces
```

This information is nicely augmented with the new *show ip eigrp accounting* command:

```
Router9#show ip eigrp accounting
```

And finally, you can view the EIGRP topology database as follows:

```
Router1#show ip eigrp topology
```

Discussion

The precise output of the *show ip protocols* command varies, depending on what features are enabled. However, we have shown several examples of different output throughout this chapter:

```
Router1#show ip protocols
Routing Protocol is "eigrp 55"
  Outgoing update filter list for all interfaces is not set
  Incoming update filter list for all interfaces is not set
    Serial0.1 filtered by (prefix-list) Inbound
  Default networks flagged in outgoing updates
```

```
Default networks not accepted from incoming updates
EIGRP metric weight K1=1, K2=0, K3=1, K4=0, K5=0
EIGRP maximum hopcount 100
EIGRP maximum metric variance 1
Redistributing: static, eigrp 55
Automatic network summarization is not in effect
Maximum path: 4
Routing for Networks:
   172.25.2.2/32
   172.25.0.0
   192.168.20.0
Routing Information Sources:
   Gateway          Distance      Last Update
   (this router)          90      5d23h
   172.25.2.1             90      00:03:32
Distance: internal 90 external 170
Router1#
```

The standard command to view the IP routing table is *show ip route*. However, this will show you all of the IP routes, including static routes, connected routes, and routes learned through other protocols, as well as EIGRP routes. If you just want to see the EIGRP routes, you can add the keyword *eigrp* to this command:

```
Router1#show ip route eigrp
D*EX 0.0.0.0/0 [170/91942912] via 172.25.2.1, 00:04:29, Serial0.1
Router1#
```

One of the most useful commands when troubleshooting EIGRP problems looks at the neighbor table:

```
Router1#show ip eigrp neighbors
IP-EIGRP neighbors for process 55
H    Address              Interface    Hold Uptime   SRTT   RTO  Q  Seq Type
                                       (sec)         (ms)       Cnt Num
1    172.25.2.2           Se0/0.2        7 00:25:16  641   3846  0  148
2    172.25.1.7           Fa0/0.1       80 1w0d       17    200  0  406
0    172.22.1.4           Fa0/1         12 1w0d        3    200  0  259
Router1#
```

There are several important pieces of information in this list. Obviously, it's useful to look at the IP addresses and interfaces. But it can also be extremely useful to look at the uptime. In this case, you can see that two of these neighbors have been up and stable for a week, but the third one was reset 25 minutes ago. The router will sort this output so that the most recent neighbors are at the top. This gives you an immediate way of seeing which neighbors might have problems.

Also useful in this output is the Q column. This tells you how many EIGRP packets are currently queued for this neighbor. If the router is consistently queuing EIGRP packets, then there may be a congestion or queuing problem with this interface.

If you think you see EIGRP congestion or performance problems like this, it can be useful to look at the interfaces in more detail:

```
Router1#show ip eigrp interfaces
IP-EIGRP interfaces for process 55

                     Xmit Queue   Mean  Pacing Time  Multicast  Pending
  Interface   Peers  Un/Reliable  SRTT  Un/Reliable  Flow Timer Routes
  Fa0/0.1     1      0/0          17    0/10         50         0
  Lo0         0      0/0          0     0/10         0          0
  Fa0/1       1      0/0          3     0/10         50         0
  Se0/0.2     1      0/0          641   0/15         3163       0
Router1#
```

This command shows useful information, such as how many peers there are on each interface. It also tells you more about any possible queuing issues, breaking out exactly how many routes are still pending.

There is a useful new *show* command in IOS Version 12.3(14)T. The *show ip eigrp accounting* command gives you useful operational information about your EIGRP neighbors:

```
Router9#show ip eigrp accounting
IP-EIGRP accounting for AS(55)/ID(172.18.5.9)
Total Prefix Count: 50  States: A-Adjacency, P-Pending, D-Down
State Address/Source   Interface     Prefix   Restart  Restart/
                                     Count    Count    Reset(s)
  A   172.20.10.1      Se0/0         1        0        0
  A   172.18.19.1      Fa0/0         39       0        0
  A   172.18.19.4      Fa0/0         1        0        0
  A   172.18.19.6      Fa0/0         6        0        0

Router9#
```

In this case, the output shows that most of the prefixes in the EIGRP routing table come from a single neighbor router. In this case, you will notice that the total of the Prefix Count column doesn't add up to the Total Prefix Count on the second line. The difference is due to prefixes that originate with this router.

The final two columns in this display, Restart Count and Restart Reset, are only relevant to the new *maximum-prefix* command, which is not discussed in this book because it is not available in most IOS feature sets.

Another useful command when debugging EIGRP problems is the *show ip eigrp toplogy* command. This command gives a view of the EIGRP topology table. This is useful because it often includes information about routes that EIGRP has received, but that the router isn't using for whatever reason. For example, if there is a similar route with a better administrative distance, such as a static route, the *show ip route* command will indicate only the static route. So this command allows you to look through the whole EIGRP topology table to see exactly why the other route is better:

```
Router1#show ip eigrp topology
IP-EIGRP Topology Table for AS(55)/ID(172.25.25.1)
```

```
Codes: P - Passive, A - Active, U - Update, Q - Query, R - Reply,
       r - reply Status, s - sia Status

P 0.0.0.0/0, 1 successors, FD is 28160, tag is 5
        via Rstatic (28160/0)
        via Summary (28160/0), Null0
P 10.2.2.0/24, 1 successors, FD is 156160
        via 172.22.1.4 (156160/128256), FastEthernet0/1
P 10.1.1.0/30, 1 successors, FD is 3845120
        via Connected, Serial0/1
P 192.168.10.0/24, 1 successors, FD is 28160, tag is 5
        via Rstatic (28160/0)
P 192.168.30.0/24, 1 successors, FD is 156160
        via 172.22.1.4 (156160/128256), FastEthernet0/1
P 192.168.20.0/24, 1 successors, FD is 2195456
        via 172.25.2.2 (2195456/281600), Serial0/0.2
P 172.25.25.6/32, 1 successors, FD is 156160
        via 172.25.1.7 (156160/128256), FastEthernet0/0.1
P 172.25.25.1/32, 1 successors, FD is 128256
        via Connected, Loopback0
P 172.25.25.2/32, 1 successors, FD is 2297856
        via 172.25.2.2 (2297856/128256), Serial0/0.2
P 172.25.1.0/24, 1 successors, FD is 28160
        via Connected, FastEthernet0/0.1
P 172.25.2.0/30, 1 successors, FD is 2169856
        via Connected, Serial0/0.2
P 172.22.1.0/24, 1 successors, FD is 28160
        via Connected, FastEthernet0/1
Router1#
```

The EIGRP topology table also shows the successors for each route. The successor is the route that will be installed in case the better one goes away.

## CHAPTER 8

OSPF

8.0 Introduction

Open Shortest Path First (OSPF) is a popular routing protocol for IP networks for several key reasons. It is classless, offering full *CIDR* and *VLSM* support; it scales well; converges quickly; and guarantees loop-free routing. It also supports address summarization and the tagging of external routes, similar to EIGRP. For networks that require additional security, you can configure OSPF routers to authenticate with one another to ensure that unauthorized devices can't affect routing tables.

Perhaps the most important reasons for OSPF's popularity are that it is both an open standard and a mature protocol. Virtually every vendor of routing hardware and software supports it. This makes it the routing protocol of choice in multivendor enterprise networks. It is also frequently found in ISP networks for the same reasons.

But for all of these benefits, OSPF is also considerably more complicated to set up than EIGRP or RIP. Unlike EIGRP, which can be readily retrofitted into almost any existing network, your network has to be designed with OSPF in mind if you want it to scale well. For more information on OSPF network design, please refer to *Designing Large-Scale LANs* by Kevin Dooley (O'Reilly). And you can find more information about the protocol itself in *IP Routing* by Ravi Malhotra (O'Reilly). The remainder of this section is intended only to serve as a reminder to readers who are already familiar with OSPF.

OSPF is currently in its second version, which is documented in RFC 2328. It uses a large, dimensionless metric on every link (also equivalently called a "cost"), with a maximum value of 65535. But unlike RIP and EIGRP, which use a metric that reflects the cost of the entire path, OSPF's metric is just a per-link cost. The RFC does not specify a maximum total path cost. So, in fact, any given path through an OSPF network can include many high-cost links, but still be usable. This 16-bit OSPF metric, while significantly larger than the simple hop-count metric used in RIP, is much smaller than EIGRP's 32-bit metric. So many of the metric manipulation techniques we discussed for EIGRP in Chapter 7 do not work in OSPF. The smaller metric sometimes means that you have to exercise care in how you define the costs of each link. We will discuss this issue in more detail in Recipe 8.3.

Like EIGRP, OSPF routers only start to exchange routing information after they have established a neighbor relationship. However, unlike EIGRP, OSPF routers don't actually exchange routing tables directly. Instead, they exchange Link State Advertisements (LSA), which describe the states of different network links. Each router then obtains an accurate image of the current topology of the network, which it uses to build its routing tables. If you group the routers into Areas, as we will discuss in a moment, every router in each Area sees the same LSA information, which guarantees that all of the routing tables are compatible with one another.

The OSPF protocol operates directly at the IP layer by using IP protocol number 89, without an intervening transport layer protocol such as UDP or TCP. Devices exchange OSPF information using multicast packets that are confined to the local segment. OSPF actually uses two different multicast IP addresses. All OSPF routers use 224.0.0.5, and Designated Router (DR) routers use 224.0.0.6.

The DR is basically a master router for a network segment. This is only relevant when there are several OSPF routers on a multiple access medium such as an Ethernet segment. In this case, to avoid the scaling problems of establishing a mesh of neighbor relationships between all of the routers on the segment, one router becomes the DR for the segment. Then all of the other routers talk to the DR. Each segment also elects a Backup Designated Router (BDR) in case the DR fails.

One of the most important features of OSPF is the concept of an *Area*. This is also partly what makes OSPF more difficult to configure. An OSPF network can be broken up into areas that are connected by Area Border Routers (ABR). Routing information can then be summarized at the ABR before being passed along to the next area. This means that routers in one area don't need to worry about the LSA information from routers in other areas, which drastically improves network stability and convergence times, as well as reducing the amount of resources required to support OSPF on the routers.

For OSPF to work well, you need to allocate your IP addresses appropriately among the Areas. In particular, you want to be able to summarize the routes for an Area when you pass this information along to the next Area. The summarization doesn't need to reduce perfectly to a single route for each Area. But the fewer LSAs you need to pass between Areas, the better OSPF will scale.

Each Area has a 32-bit identifier number, which is often represented in dotted decimal notation, similar to IP addresses. Every OSPF network should have an Area 0 (or 0.0.0.0), and every ABR must be a member of Area 0. This enforces a hierarchical design model for OSPF networks. The one exception to this rule happens in a network with only one Area. In this case, you can actually give this Area any number. We recommend using an Area 0, even if it is the only area in your network to avoid some of the problems that will occur if you ever need to partition the network into Areas later. The only time this ability to run a single area network with no Area 0 relevant is when a network failure isolates one Area from the rest of the network. In this case, the isolated Area can continue working normally internally.

You can get around this strict design requirement of having all Areas connected only through Area 0 by using OSPF *virtual links*. These are essentially little more than IP tunnels. You can use virtual links to ensure that every ABR connects to Area 0, even if one or more of them are not physically connected to Area 0. However, we should stress that we do not recommend using virtual links, except as a temporary measure—perhaps while migrating your network to a new architecture or while merging two networks.

The OSPF protocol defines several different LSA types. We will briefly review these different types before discussing the area types, because it will help to understand what is going on in these different area types. The standard LSA types are summarized in Table 8-1.

Table 8-1. LSA types

LSA type	Name	Description
1	Router-LSA	A Router-LSA includes information about the link states of all of a router's interfaces. These LSAs are flooded throughout the area, but not into adjacent areas.
2	Network-LSA	On NBMA and broadcast capable network segments, the DR originates Network-LSAs. The Network-LSA describes the routers that are connected to this broadcast or NBMA segment. Network-LSAs are flooded throughout the area, but not into adjacent areas.
3	Summary-LSA	ABR routers originate Summary-LSAs to describe interarea routes to networks that are outside of the area but inside of the AS. They are flooded throughout an area. Type 3 LSAs are used for routes to networks.
4	Summary-LSA	Type 4 LSAs are similar to Type 3 LSAs, except that they are used for routes to ASBR routers.
5	AS-external-LSA	ASBR routers originate Type 5 LSAs to describe routes to networks that are external to the AS. Type 5 LSAs are flooded throughout the AS.
6	MOSPF-LSA	Type 6 LSAs are used for carrying multicast routing information with MOSPF. Cisco routers do not currently support Type 6 LSAs.
7	NSSA-External-LSA	Type 7 LSAs are originated by ASBRs in an NSSA area. They are similar to Type 5 LSAs, except that they are only flooded throughout the NSSA area. When Type 7 LSAs reach the ABR, it translates them into Type 5 LSAs and distributes them to the rest of the AS.

There are several different types of OSPF Areas. They are differentiated by how they summarize information into and out of the area. The other important difference between area types concerns whether or not they can be used for transit between other parts of the network. A transit Area allows packets to simply pass through the area on their way to another area or another network. Any router that connects OSPF to another network or a different routing protocol is called an Autonomous System Boundary Router (ASBR).

The first important type of Area is the *backbone area*, which is used by Area 0. This area is special because it can always act as a transit area, between other areas, between this OSPF autonomous system and external networks, or even between external networks.

The second Area type is called a *stub area*. Stub areas see detailed routing information on all other areas, but only summary information about networks outside of the AS. The ABR sends Type 3 LSA packets to summarize this information. The ABR connecting to a stub area summarizes routes to external networks, outside of the AS. All external routes are reduced to a single summary. This is important because it means that you cannot make connections to external networks via a stub area. It also means that if your network is essentially all one big AS, perhaps with a default route to the Internet, then there is no advantage to using a stub area. Stub areas are most useful when there are many external routes, so summarizing them saves router resources.

In terms of LSA types, the distinguishing factor for a stub area is that the ABR will not send any Type 5 LSAs into this area.

Third is the *totally stub area*. Totally stub areas, also called "stub no-summary," summarize not only external routes, but also routes from other areas (interarea routes). Routers in this type of area only see routing information local to their area, plus a default route pointing to the ABR, from which they can reach all other areas and all other networks. The ABR accomplishes this by preventing all Type 3, 4, and 5 LSA messages, except for the default summary route, which it transmits as a single Type 3 LSA message.

As with regular stub areas, you cannot make connections to external networks through totally stub areas by using redistribution into OSPF.

Totally stub areas are clearly useful in WAN situations where the overhead of maintaining and updating a large link state database is both onerous and unnecessary. The only problem with totally stub areas is that this is essentially a Cisco invention. Some other vendors have added support for this area type, but it is not universally supported, so you might have problems implementing it in a multivendor network. But as long as you use Cisco ABR routers, the other routers inside of a totally stub Area won't know that anything special has happened to their routing information, so the nonABR routers can be any non-Cisco devices.

Not So Stubby Areas (NSSA) are defined in RFC 1587. This is a variant of the stub area that is able to connect to external networks. It accomplishes this by introducing a new LSA type (LSA Type 7) that is used within the area to carry external routes that originate with ASBRs connected to this area. The ABR only summarizes those external routes that are received from other areas, and therefore reached through the ABR. External routes from ASBRs inside the area are not summarized. In order to pass the internally generated external routes to the rest of the network, the ABR translates these Type 7 LSAs into the more conventional Type 5 LSA before relaying this information into Area 0.

The result is that you can use NSSA areas to connect to external networks. This is extremely important to remember because even a simple redistributed static route is considered an external route. If you want external routes to be available for the rest of the network, then NSSA is a good way to handle them. NSSA is an open standard part of the OSPF protocol, so most of the router vendors who implement OSPF include NSSA support.

Finally, another useful Cisco adaptation is the *Totally Stubby Not So Stubby Area* type. This comical sounding name belies an extremely useful feature. This area type combines the best of NSSA and totally stub areas by summarizing information from all other areas, but handling external routes like NSSA. It allows you to summarize internal routes from other areas while still allowing you to put an ASBR happens inside of the area.

As with the totally stub area, the ABR connecting to a Totally Stubby NSSA area prevents all Type 3, 4, and 5 LSAs. And, like an NSSA, it uses Type 7 LSA messages to carry external routes from ASBR routers inside of the area. So the Totally Stubby NSSA Area can be used as a transit Area to an external network, but it can also benefit from summarization of interarea routes.

In many networks, the number of external routes is relatively small, while there are many internal (interarea) routes. So it is actually much more important to summarize the internal routes in these cases. But the stub and totally stub area types that allow this interarea route summarization don't allow you to connect to external networks. The Totally Stubby NSSA Area type is ideal when you need to connect to an external network through an area that you would really prefer to keep stubby for performance and scaling reasons.

Another important concept in OSPF involves how it exchanges routing information with external autonomous systems. Any router that advertises an external route to the rest of the network must be on the border with another network, so it is called an Autonomous System Border Router (ASBR).

OSPF defines two different types of external routes. The only difference between them is in the way that OSPF calculates their costs. The cost of a Type 1 external route is the sum of the external metric plus the internal cost to reach the ASBR. The cost of a Type 2 external route is just the external metric cost. For Type 2 external routes, OSPF does not add in the cost to reach the ASBR.

When making routing decisions, OSPF prefers Type 1 to Type 2 external routes. So, for example, you can use Type 1 external routes to ensure that every internal router selects the closest ASBR that connects to a particular external network. But you might want to also set up a backup ASBR that injects Type 2 routes. Then the internal routers will prefer the Type 1 routes, if they are present.

8.1   Configuring OSPF

Problem

You want to run OSPF on a simple network.

Solution

You can enable OSPF on router by defining an OSPF process and assigning an address range to an area as follows:

```
Router5#configure terminal
Enter configuration commands, one per line.  End with CNTL/Z.
Router5(config)#router ospf 87
Router5(config-router)#network 0.0.0.0 255.255.255.255 area 0
Router5(config-router)#exit
Router5(config)#end
Router5#
```

Discussion

The first line in this configuration example defines the OSPF process:

```
Router5(config)#router ospf 87
```

The OSPF process number (87) doesn't propagate outside of the router. So you can use a different value for every router in an AS. Note that this is different from EIGRP, where every router in the AS must have the same process number. The process number can take any value between 1 and 65,535.

The *network* statement in this example then takes the simplest possible approach to defining areas by putting every interface on the router into area 0:

```
Router5(config-router)#network 0.0.0.0 255.255.255.255 area 0
```

The first two arguments of the *network* statement are an IP address and a corresponding set of wildcard bits. In this case, 0.0.0.0 255.255.255.255 matches every possible IP address. So every interface on this router is assigned to area 0.

In this case, we have defined the area by using a single number. You can define area numbers to be anything between 0 and 4,294,967,295. You can also use dotted decimal notation for areas, in which case you would write area 0 as 0.0.0.0.

OSPF treats the area number internally as a 32-bit field regardless of whether you choose to represent it as a single number or by using dotted decimals. So you could mix and match if you wanted to. But we recommend picking whichever approach better suits your network and sticking to it. It is far too easy to get confused when translating between the two formats.

In general, for small networks it is easier to remember single numbers. But for larger networks, it is often easier to work with dotted decimal notation, perhaps developing some locally meaning mnemonic to help give the area numbers significance. For example, in an international WAN, you might want to make the first octet stand for the country, the second for state or province, the third for city, and the fourth defining the actual area. Or you might want to make the area numbers the same as the summary IP addresses for each area. The only special area number is area 0, which must be the routing backbone of the network and must connect to all other areas directly, as we discussed in the Introduction to this chapter.

If you have more than one *network* statement, the order becomes important. In the following example, the last line matches all IP addresses and assigns them to area 0. But because this line comes last, it only picks up any addresses that are not captured by either of the lines above it. However, if we had written this line first, then all of the interfaces would wind up in area 0:

```
Router1#configure terminal
Enter configuration commands, one per line.  End with CNTL/Z.
Router1(config)#router ospf 55
Router1(config-router)#network 10.0.0.0 0.255.255.255 area 2
Router1(config-router)#network 172.20.0.0 0.0.255.255 area 100
Router1(config-router)#network 0.0.0.0 255.255.255.255 area 0
Router1(config-router)#exit
Router1(config)#end
Router1#
```

The *show ip protocols* command lists useful information about the OSPF configuration:

```
Router1#show ip protocols
Routing Protocol is "ospf 55"
  Outgoing update filter list for all interfaces is not set
  Incoming update filter list for all interfaces is not set
  Router ID 172.25.25.1
  It is an area border and autonomous system boundary router
  Redistributing External Routes from,
  Number of areas in this router is 3. 3 normal 0 stub 0 nssa
  Maximum path: 4
  Routing for Networks:
    10.0.0.0 0.255.255.255 area 2
    172.20.0.0 0.0.255.255 area 100
    0.0.0.0 255.255.255.255 area 0
  Routing Information Sources:
    Gateway         Distance      Last Update
    192.168.30.1         110      00:01:30
    172.25.25.6          110      16:44:07
    172.25.25.1          110      00:01:30
    172.25.25.2          110      00:01:30
    172.25.1.7           110      00:01:30
    172.25.1.1           110      16:56:15
  Distance: (default is 110)
Router1#
```

If you want more control, you can specify individual interface IP addresses with a wildcard mask of 0.0.0.0 to match only one address at a time:

```
Router5#configure terminal
Enter configuration commands, one per line.  End with CNTL/Z.
```

```
Router5(config)#router ospf 87
Router5(config-router)#network 172.25.1.7 0.0.0.0 area 0
Router5(config-router)#network 172.25.25.6 0.0.0.0 area 0
Router5(config-router)#exit
Router5(config)#end
Router5#
```

This can be useful when your addresses don't summarize well, which can be the case when you are changing your network architecture or merging two networks.

In IOS level 12.3(11)T, Cisco introduced a new way to assign interfaces to OSPF areas, using the *ip ospf area* interface configuration command:

```
Router9#configure terminal
Enter configuration commands, one per line.  End with CNTL/Z.
Router9(config)#router ospf 87
Router9(config-router)#exit
Router9(config)#interface FastEthernet0/0
Router9(config-if)#ip address 172.18.5.9 255.255.255.0
Router9(config-if)#ip ospf 87 area 10
Router9(config-if)#exit
Router9(config)#end
Router9#
```

We like this new method, particularly on ABRs, because it makes it very easy to look at a router's configuration and understand the OSPF configuration. With a complicated set of *network* statements, on the other hand, it can be quite a time-consuming task to figure out which interfaces belong to which areas and which don't take part in the routing protocol at all.

8.2   Filtering Routes in OSPF

Problem

You want to apply a filter so that OSPF populates only certain routes into the routing table.

Solution

You can filter inbound routes to prevent the router from putting them in its routing table:

```
Router5#configure terminal
Enter configuration commands, one per line.  End with CNTL/Z.
Router5(config)#access-list 1 deny 172.20.10.0
Router5(config)#access-list 1 permit any
Router5(config)#router ospf 87
Router5(config-router)#distribute-list 1 in Ethernet0/0
Router5(config-router)#exit
Router5(config)#end
Router5#
```

The OSPF algorithm requires that every router in an area receives all of the LSAs for that area, so you cannot filter outbound routing information in the same way:

```
Router5#configure terminal
Enter configuration commands, one per line.  End with CNTL/Z.
Router5(config)#router ospf 87
Router5(config-router)#distribute-list 1 out Ethernet0/0
% Interface not allowed with OUT for OSPF
Router5(config-router)#exit
Router5(config)#end
Router5#
```

Filtering outbound LSAs is possible only if you filter out all of the LSAs. There are two ways to do this. For point-to-multipoint media, you can filter LSAs by going to a particular neighbor:

```
Router1#configure terminal
Enter configuration commands, one per line.  End with CNTL/Z.
Router1(config)#router ospf 87
Router1(config-router)#neighbor 192.168.1.3 database-filter all out
Router1(config-router)#exit
Router1(config)#end
Router1#
```

And on broadcast, nonbroadcast, and point-to-point media, you can prevent the router from sending any LSAs out a particular interface.

```
Router1#configure terminal
Enter configuration commands, one per line.  End with CNTL/Z.
Router1(config)#interface Serial0/0
Router1(config-if)#encapsulation frame-relay
Router1(config-if)#exit
Router1(config)#interface Serial0/0.10 multipoint
Router1(config-subif)#ip address 192.168.1.1 255.255.255.0
Router1(config-subif)#ip ospf network broadcast
Router1(config-subif)#ip ospf database-filter all out
Router1(config-subif)#frame-relay map ip 192.168.1.3 101 broadcast
Router1(config-subif)#frame-relay map ip 192.168.1.5 109 broadcast
Router1(config-subif)#exit
Router1(config)#router ospf 1
Router1(config-router)#network 0.0.0.0 255.255.255.255 area 10
Router1(config-router)#exit
Router1(config)#end
Router1#
```

Discussion

It's important to remember that unlike EIGRP and RIP, OSPF uses a link state rather than a distance vector algorithm. One place where this difference becomes clear is in route filtering. At a minimum, every router in an area must see the LSAs for every other router in the same area. Depending on the type of area, it may also see summary LSAs representing routing information from other areas or other autonomous systems. These LSA packets are flooded throughout the area, with each router forwarding LSA information on to any downstream devices. Every router then separately computes the best routing table based on this link state information.

If you prevented a router from forwarding some of the LSA information, its downstream routers would not have a full link state database, and consequently wouldn't be able to generate an accurate routing table. When you try to do this kind of outbound filtering, the router gives you an error message:

```
Router5(config) #router ospf 87
Router5(config-router) #distribute-list 1 out Ethernet0/0
% Interface not allowed with OUT for OSPF
```

So it is not possible to do the kind of route filtering that we discussed for RIP and EIGRP in Chapters 6 and 7, respectively. The only filtering we can do is to prevent a router from installing a route learned via OSPF into its routing table. This way the link state database remains intact on every router in the area. If you really want to break up the forwarding of LSA information, then you should subdivide the area.

You can see the effect of the inbound distribute list by looking at the routing table both before and after applying the filter. Before the inbound filter is enabled, you can see that the route is there:

```
Router5#show ip route 172.20.10.0
Routing entry for 172.20.10.0/24
  Known via "ospf 87", distance 110, metric 74, type inter area
  Last update from 172.18.5.3 on Ethernet0/0, 00:00:09 ago
  Routing Descriptor Blocks:
  * 172.18.5.3, from 172.19.2.1, 00:00:09 ago, via Ethernet0/0
      Route metric is 74, traffic share count is 1
Router5#
```

Then, after we apply the filter, the route is gone:

```
Router5#show ip route 172.20.10.0
% Subnet not in table
Router5#
```

However, the *show ip ospf database* command shows this LSA is still in the database:

```
Router5#show ip ospf database

            OSPF Router with ID (172.18.6.1) (Process ID 87)

                Router Link States (Area 10)

   Link ID         ADV Router      Age       Seq#       Checksum Link count
   172.18.6.1      172.18.6.1      108       0x80000005 0x008367 4
   172.19.2.1      172.19.2.1      144       0x80000004 0x00C25B 1
   192.168.2.3     192.168.2.3     109       0x80000006 0x001DDE 4
   192.168.2.5     192.168.2.5     109       0x80000006 0x007CFD 3

                Net Link States (Area 10)
```

```
Link ID        ADV Router      Age     Seq#        Checksum
172.18.5.3     172.19.2.1      144     0x80000003  0x001612
192.168.1.1    172.18.6.1      208     0x80000001  0x007CE5
192.168.2.1    172.18.6.1      208     0x80000001  0x0071EF

             Summary Net Link States (Area 10)

Link ID        ADV Router      Age     Seq#        Checksum
0.0.0.0        172.19.2.1      978     0x80000001  0x00F288
2.2.2.2        172.19.2.1      973     0x80000001  0x0096DC
2.2.2.3        172.19.2.1      973     0x80000001  0x008CE5
2.2.2.4        172.19.2.1      973     0x80000001  0x0082EE
172.19.2.1     172.19.2.1      973     0x80000001  0x00298F
172.20.10.0    172.19.2.1      397     0x80000001  0x00472A
Router5#
```

As you can see, the inbound *distribute-list* method doesn't filter LSAs; it just tells the router not to install certain routes in the routing table.

This router floods the LSA for this route normally through all of its OSPF interfaces. As a result, the route appears in the routing tables of any downstream routers:

```
Router3#show ip route 172.20.10.0
Routing entry for 172.20.10.0/24
  Known via "ospf 1", distance 110, metric 138, type inter area
  Last update from 192.168.1.1 on Serial0/0.1, 00:04:51 ago
  Routing Descriptor Blocks:
  * 192.168.2.1, from 172.19.2.1, 00:04:51 ago, via Serial0/0.2
      Route metric is 138, traffic share count is 1
    192.168.1.1, from 172.19.2.1, 00:04:51 ago, via Serial0/0.1
      Route metric is 138, traffic share count is 1

Router3#
```

The *database-filter* commands shown in the Solution section above have an entirely different result from the *distribute-list* commands because they actually do filter the LSAs, and therefore affect downstream routers. This can be rather confusing and have potentially dangerous results, so we should look at it in some detail. These commands both are intended for use in highly redundant meshed environments that are also relatively stable. And it is important to note what these commands do and do not block. They do not block OSPF Hello packets, so the routers will still form full and normal adjacencies. Also, they only block the sending of LSA packets. The router will receive routes normally.

The intent of these commands is to reduce traffic due to flooding, particularly over congested WAN links. The assumption is that if you are going to use these commands, the neighboring routers must have another way of receiving the required LSAs. To see how this works, suppose that you have a network with two redundant connections between two adjacent OSPF routers. We will construct a slightly artificial example network by using redundant Frame Relay PVCs so we can easily break individual neighbor relationships for demonstration purposes. For more information on Frame Relay, please refer to Chapter 10. And for more information on the *ip ospf network* command and its options, please refer to Recipe 8.14:

```
Router1(config)#interface Serial0/0.10 multipoint
Router1(config-if)#ip address 192.168.1.1 255.255.255.0
Router1(config-if)#ip ospf network broadcast
Router1(config-if)#ip ospf database-filter all out
Router1(config-if)#frame-relay map ip 192.168.1.3 101 broadcast
Router1(config-if)#frame-relay map ip 192.168.1.5 109 broadcast
Router1(config-if)#exit
Router1(config)#interface Serial0/0.11 multipoint
Router1(config-if)#ip address 192.168.2.1 255.255.255.0
Router1(config-if)#ip ospf network broadcast
Router1(config-if)#frame-relay map ip 192.168.2.3 201 broadcast
Router1(config-if)#frame-relay map ip 192.168.2.5 209 broadcast
Router1(config-if)#exit
Router1(config)#end
```

Now we want to verify that the LSA filtering is working. First we will list all of the neighbors:

```
Router1#show ip ospf neighbor

Neighbor ID     Pri   State          Dead Time   Address        Interface
192.168.2.3      0    FULL/DROTHER   00:00:34    192.168.1.3    Serial0/0.10
192.168.2.5      0    FULL/DROTHER   00:00:31    192.168.1.5    Serial0/0.10
192.168.2.3      0    FULL/DROTHER   00:00:33    192.168.2.3    Serial0/0.11
192.168.2.5      0    FULL/DROTHER   00:00:30    192.168.2.5    Serial0/0.11
172.19.2.1       1    FULL/DR        00:00:36    172.18.5.3     Ethernet0/0
```

Then we will look at one particular neighbor with the *show ip ospf neighbor detail* command:

```
Router1#show ip ospf neighbor detail 192.168.2.3
 Neighbor 192.168.2.3, interface address 192.168.1.3
    In the area 10 via interface Serial0/0.10
    Neighbor priority is 0, State is FULL, 6 state changes
    Database-filter all out
    DR is 192.168.1.1 BDR is 0.0.0.0
    Options is 0x40
    Dead timer due in 00:00:39
    Neighbor is up for 00:13:20
    Index 4/4, retransmission queue length 0, number of retransmission 0
    First 0x0(0)/0x0(0) Next 0x0(0)/0x0(0)
    Last retransmission scan length is 0, maximum is 0
    Last retransmission scan time is 0 msec, maximum is 0 msec
 Neighbor 192.168.2.3, interface address 192.168.2.3
    In the area 10 via interface Serial0/0.11
    Neighbor priority is 0, State is FULL, 6 state changes
    DR is 192.168.2.1 BDR is 0.0.0.0
    Options is 0x40
    Dead timer due in 00:00:39
    Neighbor is up for 00:05:52
    Index 2/2, retransmission queue length 0, number of retransmission 1
    First 0x0(0)/0x0(0) Next 0x0(0)/0x0(0)
```

```
        Last retransmission scan length is 1, maximum is 1
        Last retransmission scan time is 0 msec, maximum is 0 msec
    Router1#
```

If we then go to the neighboring router and look at the routing table, it looks normal. Notice in particular that both paths appear as valid in the routing table:

```
Router3#show ip route ospf
        2.0.0.0/32 is subnetted, 2 subnets
O IA    2.2.2.2 [110/75] via 192.168.1.1, 00:08:47, Serial0/0.1
                [110/75] via 192.168.2.1, 00:08:47, Serial0/0.2
O IA    2.2.2.3 [110/75] via 192.168.1.1, 00:08:47, Serial0/0.1
                [110/75] via 192.168.2.1, 00:08:47, Serial0/0.2
<deleted for brevity>
Router3#
```

If we then take down the Frame Relay PVC that does not have the database-filter command on it, we lose the corresponding neighbor relationship, but we keep the neighbor that is filtering LSAs:

```
Router1#show ip ospf neighbor detail 192.168.2.3
  Neighbor 192.168.2.3, interface address 192.168.1.3
    In the area 10 via interface Serial0/0.10
    Neighbor priority is 0, State is FULL, 6 state changes
    Database-filter all out
    DR is 192.168.1.1 BDR is 0.0.0.0
    Options is 0x40
    Dead timer due in 00:00:38
    Neighbor is up for 00:23:41
    Index 4/4, retransmission queue length 0, number of retransmission 0
    First 0x0(0)/0x0(0) Next 0x0(0)/0x0(0)
    Last retransmission scan length is 0, maximum is 0
    Last retransmission scan time is 0 msec, maximum is 0 msec
Router1#
```

On the neighboring router, the routing table has lost the corresponding routes:

```
Router3#show ip route ospf
        2.0.0.0/32 is subnetted, 2 subnets
O IA    2.2.2.2 [110/75] via 192.168.1.1, 00:02:31, Serial0/0.1
O IA    2.2.2.3 [110/75] via 192.168.1.1, 00:02:31, Serial0/0.1
<deleted for brevity>
Router3#
```

And this is where the *database-filter* feature becomes both visible and dangerous. Suppose we add another route for 2.2.2.4/32 on an upstream router. Router1 learns about the new route:

```
Router1#show ip route 2.0.0.0
Routing entry for 2.0.0.0/32, 3 known subnets

O IA    2.2.2.2 [110/11] via 172.18.5.3, 00:05:22, Ethernet0/0
O IA    2.2.2.3 [110/11] via 172.18.5.3, 00:05:22, Ethernet0/0
O IA    2.2.2.4 [110/11] via 172.18.5.3, 00:00:08, Ethernet0/0
Router1#
```

But, because Router1 is filtering LSAs for Router3, the downstream router is not notified of the change to the routing table:

```
Router3#show ip route 2.0.0.0
Routing entry for 2.0.0.0/32, 2 known subnets

O IA    2.2.2.2 [110/75] via 192.168.1.1, 00:08:25, Serial0/0.1
O IA    2.2.2.3 [110/75] via 192.168.1.1, 00:08:25, Serial0/0.1
Router3#
```

Then, as soon as the failed Frame-Relay PVC is restored, Router3 finally learns about all of the changes to the routing table:

```
Router3#show ip route 2.0.0.0
Routing entry for 2.0.0.0/32, 3 known subnets

O IA    2.2.2.2 [110/75] via 192.168.1.1, 00:00:08, Serial0/0.1
                [110/75] via 192.168.2.1, 00:00:08, Serial0/0.2
O IA    2.2.2.3 [110/75] via 192.168.1.1, 00:00:08, Serial0/0.1
                [110/75] via 192.168.2.1, 00:00:08, Serial0/0.2
O IA    2.2.2.4 [110/75] via 192.168.1.1, 00:00:08, Serial0/0.1
                [110/75] via 192.168.2.1, 00:00:08, Serial0/0.2

Router3#
```

Clearly, this is an extremely dangerous feature because it is possible for routing tables to get completely out of sync across your network. We don't recommend using it unless you are absolutely certain that you understand the consequences. However, this feature can be useful in situations where you have very low bandwidth links to isolated network regions, allowing you to create a sort of stub area within a larger area.

See Also

Chapters 6 and 7; Chapter 10; Recipe 8.14

8.3   Adjusting OSPF Costs

Problem

You want to change the OSPF link costs.

Solution

The *auto-cost reference-bandwidth* command allows you to change the reference bandwidth that OSPF uses to calculate its metrics:

```
Router5#configure terminal
Enter configuration commands, one per line.  End with CNTL/Z.
Router5(config)#router ospf 87
Router5(config-router)#auto-cost reference-bandwidth 1000
Router5(config-router)#exit
Router5(config)#end
Router5#
```

You can also adjust the OSPF cost of a single interface with the *ip ospf cost* configuration command:

```
Router5#configure terminal
Enter configuration commands, one per line.  End with CNTL/Z.
Router5(config)#interface Ethernet0
Router5(config-if)#ip ospf cost 31
Router5(config-if)# exit
Router5(config)#end
Router5#
```

Discussion

The custom in OSPF networks is to make the link cost inversely proportional to the bandwidth of a link. This isn't required, but it is common, and it is the default behavior for Cisco routers. The reference bandwidth defines the link speed that has an OSPF cost of 1. By default, the reference bandwidth is 100 Mbps.

However, if you have faster links in your network, such as gigabit Ethernet or OC-3 connections, OSPF can't give these links a better cost than 1. So you should set the reference bandwidth to at least as high as the fastest link in your network. In fact, you may want to set this value higher than the bandwidth of your fastest link to ensure that you don't have to reconfigure your whole network when you eventually upgrade some of your core links.

It is important to set the same reference bandwidth on all routers in an area, and preferably throughout the entire network. Recall that OSPF allows every router to calculate its own routing table based on the LSAs that they receive. So they must all agree on the relationship between costs and bandwidth. Suppose you set the reference bandwidth differently on two routers, so that they advertise different link costs for their Ethernet interfaces. This could cause seriously strange routing patterns as OSPF will try to avoid using the higher cost links. It may decide, for example, that a FastEthernet interface on one router is faster than a Gigabit Ethernet interface on the other router.

But there is another interesting problem with the way OSPF calculates its metrics. The problem is the OSPF metric is only 16 bits long, giving it a maximum per-link cost value of 65,535. So, if your fastest links use 10 Gbps Ethernet, and you set the cost of this link to 1, then a relatively common 56 kbps serial link would need to have a cost of 178,571, and a 128 kbps circuit would cost 78,125. Since this is not possible, OSPF would use the maximum link cost of 65,535 for both of these low-speed links. This could cause some very poor routing patterns.

We suggest using an alternate costing strategy to avoid this problem. The idea is that the cost of a link doesn't actually have to be 10 times as high just because the link is 1/10 as fast. In fact, this default behavior implies that it is better to go through a succession of 10 FastEthernet links rather than use a single Ethernet, which is probably not true in most cases. So a useful alternative strategy is to use the square root of the bandwidth instead of the bandwidth when calculating the link cost. The result of this strategy is shown in Table 8-2.

Table 8-2. Suggested OSPF costs for different media

Medium	Nominal bandwidth	Default cost	Changing reference bandwidth	Cost with 1/square root model
9.6 kbps line	9.6 kbps	10,416	1,041,666	1,020
56 kbps line	56 kbps	1,785	178,571	422
64 kbps line	64 kbps	1,562	156,250	395
T1 circuit	1.544 Mbps	64	6,476	80
E1 circuit	2.048 Mbps	48	4,882	69
T3 circuit	45 Mbps	2	222	14
Ethernet	10 Mbps	10	1,000	31
Fast Ethernet	100 Mbps	1	100	10
Gigabit Ethernet	1 Gbps	1	10	3
10 Gigabit Ethernet	10 Gbps	1	1	1
4 Mbps Token Ring	4 Mbps	25	2,500	50
16 Mbps Token Ring	16 Mbps	6	625	25

As you can see in Table 8-2, if you use the default costs, then the three fastest links all wind up with a cost of 1. Changing the reference bandwidth to 10Gbps, however, produces impossibly large metrics for the three slowest links (the router will assign them all a link cost of 65,535). So no matter what reference bandwidth you use, if you retain the default 1/bandwidth cost mode, you will need to manually adjust either the fastest or slowest several link costs.

The second example shows how to change the OSPF cost for a single interface:

```
Router5(config)#interface Ethernet0
Router5(config-if)#ip ospf cost 31
```

You could also achieve a similar effect by just adjusting the bandwidth statements on each interface. However, this will have other consequences as well. It will affect any other routing protocols that you might also be running. And it will mean that an SNMP query of the interface speed will give an incorrect value, which could confuse network management software. We recommend the direct approach of manually setting the OSPF cost because what you are doing and why is more clear, in case somebody else comes along and wants to change the router configuration.

8.4   Creating a Default Route in OSPF

Problem

You want to propagate a default route within an OSPF network.

Solution

To propagate a default route with OSPF, use the *default-information originate* configuration command:

```
Router1#configure terminal
Enter configuration commands, one per line.  End with CNTL/Z.
Router1(config)#ip route 0.0.0.0 0.0.0.0 172.25.1.1
Router1(config)#router ospf 55
Router1(config-router)#default-information originate metric 30 metric-type 1
Router1(config-router)#exit
Router1(config)#end
Router1#
```

Discussion

Unlike RIP and EIGRP, you cannot create a default route in OSPF by simply redistributing a static route. Even if there is a default route in the routing table, by default Cisco's OSPF implementation will not forward it to the rest of the network. This is because OSPF uses a link state algorithm that keeps track of links rather than routes. So summary routes are very special elements in OSPF, and it's important to be careful when distributing them. The default route, 0.0.0.0/0, is the ultimate summary of summaries, and it has the potential to cause serious confusion if it isn't handled properly.

So Cisco forces you to be sure that you really want to source a default route into OSPF by requiring you to specifically enable it with the *default-information originate* command. This command also allows you to specify precisely the metric of this default route and, since a default route is implicitly external to the AS, the type of external route. This has the added advantage of giving finer granularity of control over default route propagation.

You can look at the external routes in the OSPF database with the following command:

```
Router1#show ip ospf database external

            OSPF Router with ID (172.25.25.1) (Process ID 55)

            Type-5 AS External Link States

    LS age: 163
    Options: (No TOS-capability, DC)
    LS Type: AS External Link
    Link State ID: 0.0.0.0 (External Network Number )
    Advertising Router: 172.25.25.1
    LS Seq Number: 80000002
    Checksum: 0x18E6
    Length: 36
    Network Mask: /0
          Metric Type: 1 (Comparable directly to link state metric)
          TOS: 0
          Metric: 30
```

```
      Forward Address: 0.0.0.0
      External Route Tag: 55

  Router1#
```

In this example, you can see that the default route is advertised by the router 172.25.25.1 with a metric of 30 and a metric type of 1. The metric type in this case refers to whether this route is considered by OSPF to be a Type 1 or Type 2 external route. It is a Type 1 route because we configured it this way in the *default-information* command:

```
  Router1(config-router)#default-information originate metric 30 metric-type 1
```

As we mentioned in the Introduction to this chapter, the cost of a Type 1 external route is the cost shown by the external metric, which is 30 in this case, plus the internal cost to reach the router that advertises the external route (the ASBR).

Then, on another router in the same area, you can see that the default route's cost is 40, because the cost to reach the ASBR is 10. All of the internal routers can see that this is a Type 1 external route, as well as other important attributes, such as the administrative distance and the ASBR that originated this route:

```
  Router5#show ip route 0.0.0.0
  Routing entry for 0.0.0.0/0, supernet
    Known via "ospf 87", distance 110, metric 40, candidate default path
    Tag 55, type extern 1
    Redistributing via ospf 87
    Last update from 172.25.1.5 on Ethernet0, 00:01:24 ago
    Routing Descriptor Blocks:
    * 172.25.1.5, from 172.25.25.1, 00:01:24 ago, via Ethernet0
        Route metric is 40, traffic share count is 1

  Router5#
```

With default routes in particular, you sometimes want to ensure that that ASBR continues to advertise the external route, even if it disappears from its routing table. You can do this by adding the keyword *always* to the default-information command as follows:

```
  Router1#configure terminal
  Enter configuration commands, one per line.  End with CNTL/Z.
  Router1(config)#ip route 0.0.0.0 0.0.0.0 172.25.1.1
  Router1(config)#router ospf 55
  Router1(config-router)#default-information always metric-type 1
  Router1(config-router)#exit
  Router1(config)#end
  Router1#
```

You can also create a default route using a stub area. In this case, you can configure your ABR routers to advertise only a simple default route into the area. We will discuss stub areas in Recipe 8.10.

See Also

Recipe 8.5; Recipe 8.10

8.5 Redistributing Static Routes into OSPF

Problem

You want OSPF to propagate one or more static routes.

Solution

To redistribute static routes into an OSPF process, use the *redistribute static* configuration command:

```
Router1#configure terminal
Enter configuration commands, one per line.  End with CNTL/Z.
Router1(config)#ip route 192.168.10.0 255.255.255.0 172.22.1.4
Router1(config)#ip route 172.24.1.0 255.255.255.0 172.22.1.4
Router1(config)#ip route 10.100.1.0 255.255.255.0 172.22.1.4
Router1(config)#router ospf 55
Router1(config-router)#redistribute static
% Only classful networks will be redistributed
Router1(config-router)#exit
Router1(config)#end
Router1#
```

Discussion

As the warning message indicates, OSPF will only redistribute classful network routes by default. In the example, we included three static routes. Of these routes, only 192.168.10.0/24 is classful. If we then look at the routing table on a different router, we can see that the other two routes are not present:

```
Router5#show ip route ospf
O E2 192.168.10.0/24 [110/20] via 172.25.1.5, 00:02:49, Ethernet0
     172.16.0.0/24 is subnetted, 1 subnets
O        172.16.2.0 [110/20] via 172.25.1.5, 00:02:49, Ethernet0
     172.20.0.0/16 is variably subnetted, 3 subnets, 3 masks
O IA     172.20.10.0/24 [110/1582] via 172.25.1.5, 00:02:49, Ethernet0
O IA     172.20.1.0/30 [110/1572] via 172.25.1.5, 00:02:49, Ethernet0
O IA     172.20.100.1/32 [110/1573] via 172.25.1.5, 00:02:49, Ethernet0
     172.22.0.0/24 is subnetted, 1 subnets
O        172.22.1.0 [110/20] via 172.25.1.5, 00:02:49, Ethernet0
     172.25.0.0/16 is variably subnetted, 3 subnets, 2 masks
O        172.25.25.1/32 [110/11] via 172.25.1.5, 00:02:49, Ethernet0
     10.0.0.0/8 is variably subnetted, 2 subnets, 2 masks
O IA     10.2.2.2/32 [110/1573] via 172.25.1.5, 00:02:49, Ethernet0
O IA     10.1.1.0/30 [110/1572] via 172.25.1.5, 00:02:49, Ethernet0
Router5#
```

You can ensure that all routes are redistributed, regardless of whether they are classful or not, by including the *subnets* keyword:

```
Router1#configure terminal
Enter configuration commands, one per line.  End with CNTL/Z.
Router1(config)#router ospf 55
```

```
Router1(config-router)#redistribute static subnets
Router1(config-router)#exit
Router1(config)#end
Router1#
```

As you can see, all three static routes are advertised now:

```
Router5#show ip route ospf
O E2 192.168.10.0/24 [110/20] via 172.25.1.5, 00:04:23, Ethernet0
     172.16.0.0/24 is subnetted, 1 subnets
O       172.16.2.0 [110/20] via 172.25.1.5, 00:04:23, Ethernet0
     172.20.0.0/16 is variably subnetted, 3 subnets, 3 masks
O IA    172.20.10.0/24 [110/1582] via 172.25.1.5, 00:04:23, Ethernet0
O IA    172.20.1.0/30 [110/1572] via 172.25.1.5, 00:04:23, Ethernet0
O IA    172.20.100.1/32 [110/1573] via 172.25.1.5, 00:04:23, Ethernet0
     172.22.0.0/24 is subnetted, 1 subnets
O       172.22.1.0 [110/20] via 172.25.1.5, 00:04:23, Ethernet0
     172.25.0.0/16 is variably subnetted, 3 subnets, 2 masks
O       172.25.25.1/32 [110/11] via 172.25.1.5, 00:04:23, Ethernet0
     172.24.0.0/24 is subnetted, 1 subnets
O E2    172.24.1.0 [110/20] via 172.25.1.5, 00:00:24, Ethernet0
     10.0.0.0/8 is variably subnetted, 3 subnets, 3 masks
O IA    10.2.2.2/32 [110/1573] via 172.25.1.5, 00:04:23, Ethernet0
O IA    10.1.1.0/30 [110/1572] via 172.25.1.5, 00:04:23, Ethernet0
O E2    10.100.1.0/24 [110/20] via 172.25.1.5, 00:00:24, Ethernet0
Router5#
```

Another useful thing to notice about this output is the fact that all of these external static routes are marked as type E2, meaning that they are external routes of Type 2. As we discussed in the Introduction to this chapter, any time you distribute a foreign route into OSPF, it is always considered external. This helps OSPF to ensure that it doesn't create any loops through an external network when there are multiple connection points.

When OSPF distributes Type 2 External routes, it doesn't add the internal link cost to the net route cost. OSPF always prefers Type 1 to Type 2 External routes because Type 1 routes do include the internal path cost in the metric. If you want to distribute static routes as Type 1 instead of the default type 2, you need to include the *metric-type* keyword in the *redistribute static* command:

```
Router1#configure terminal
Enter configuration commands, one per line.  End with CNTL/Z.
Router1(config)#router ospf 55
Router1(config-router)#redistribute static subnets metric 40 metric-type 1
Router1(config-router)#exit
Router1(config)#end
Router1#
```

In this example, we have also set the default metric for these static routes to a value of 40. Notice that the next hop router now shows the total cost of the path as 60 because it now includes the internal link cost of 20:

```
Router5#show ip route 192.168.10.0
Routing entry for 192.168.10.0/24
```

```
Known via "ospf 87", distance 110, metric 60, type extern 1
Redistributing via ospf 87
Last update from 172.25.1.5 on Ethernet0, 00:01:20 ago
Routing Descriptor Blocks:
* 172.25.1.5, from 172.25.25.1, 00:01:20 ago, via Ethernet0
    Route metric is 60, traffic share count is 1
Router5#
```

8.6   Redistributing External Routes into OSPF

Problem

You want OSPF to distribute routes from another routing protocol.

Solution

The redistribute configuration command allows you to redistribute routes from
another dynamic routing protocol into an OSPF process:

```
Router1#configure terminal
Enter configuration commands, one per line.  End with CNTL/Z.
Router1(config)#router ospf 55
Router1(config-router)#redistribute eigrp 11 subnets
Router1(config-router)#exit
Router1(config)#end
Router1#
```

One of the dangers when redistributing between routing protocols is that you will accidentally import more information than your routers can handle. In Version 12.3(2)T,
Cisco added a feature to protect against this issue:

```
Router1#configure terminal
Enter configuration commands, one per line.  End with CNTL/Z.
Router1(config)#router ospf 55
Router1(config-router)#redistribute eigrp 11 subnets
Router1(config-router)#redistribute maximum-prefix 1000 80
Router1(config-router)#exit
Router1(config)#end
Router1#
```

Discussion

Redistributing external routes from another routing protocol is similar to redistributing static routes, as we did in Recipe 8.5. In the example above, all of the routes that
this router learns through EIGRP process number 11 will be propagated into OSPF
as Type 2 external routes. Also, as shown in the following output from the *show ip
protocols* command, because we also included the *subnets* keyword, every route will
be redistributed. If we had not included this keyword, OSPF would only redistribute
classful summary routes from EIGRP:

```
Router1#show ip protocols
Routing Protocol is "ospf 55"
```

```
Outgoing update filter list for all interfaces is not set
Incoming update filter list for all interfaces is not set
Router ID 172.25.25.1
It is an area border and autonomous system boundary router
Redistributing External Routes from,
  static with metric mapped to 40, includes subnets in redistribution
  eigrp 11, includes subnets in redistribution
Number of areas in this router is 3. 3 normal 0 stub 0 nssa
Maximum path: 4
Routing for Networks:
  10.0.0.0 0.255.255.255 area 2
  172.20.0.0 0.0.255.255 area 100
  0.0.0.0 255.255.255.255 area 0
Routing Information Sources:
  Gateway         Distance      Last Update
  172.25.1.7            110      00:06:24
  172.25.1.1            110      1d15h
  172.25.1.3            110      00:06:24
  Distance: (default is 110)
Router1#
```

If you prefer, you can redistribute routes from the foreign routing protocol as Type 1 external routes. To do this, you need to specify the *metric-type* keyword in the *redistribute* command:

```
Router1#configure terminal
Enter configuration commands, one per line.  End with CNTL/Z.
Router1(config)#router ospf 55
Router1(config-router)#redistribute eigrp 11 subnets metric 35 metric-type 1
Router1(config-router)#exit
Router1(config)#end
Router1#
```

You can also do some rather interesting things when redistributing OSPF routes into another protocol. For example, you might choose to only redistribute internal routes to the foreign routing protocol, like this:

```
Router1#configure terminal
Enter configuration commands, one per line.  End with CNTL/Z.
Router1(config)#router eigrp 11
Router1(config-router)#redistribute ospf 55 match internal
Router1(config-router)#exit
Router1(config)#end
Router1#
```

There are several other options for this *match* keyword. You could just as easily choose to match only External Type 1 routes as follows:

```
Router1(config-router)#redistribute ospf 55 match external type 1
```

You can also combine types to allow you to redistribute both internal and external Type 1 routes, but not external Type 2:

```
Router1(config-router)#redistribute ospf 55 match internal match external type 1
```

This *match* option on the *redistribute* command is much easier than configuring a route-map. But, if you require still greater control and flexibility, route-maps are the best choice. This is particularly true if you want to handle routing tags in a special way. For a discussion of using route-maps while redistributing routes between protocols, please refer to Recipe 8.15 on OSPF route tagging.

One of the potential dangers with route redistribution is the possibility of accepting too many routes from another network and overwhelming your network resources. This is a problem not only for router memory, but also for bandwidth because all of these external routes must be flooded throughout the OSPF network. To deal with this problem, Cisco introduced the *redistribute maximum-prefix* command in IOS Version 12.3(2)T.

In the Solution section of this recipe, we set the maximum number of redistributed routes to 1,000:

```
Router9(config)#router ospf 87
Router9(config-router)#redistribute eigrp 11 subnets
Router9(config-router)#redistribute maximum-prefix 1000 80
```

Now this router will redistribute a maximum of 1,000 prefixes from all protocols. If any additional routes match redistribution rules, they will simply be ignored.

The final argument on this command specifies a warning threshold percentage. In this case, the value is 80 percent, or 800 total prefixes. If the number of redistributed prefixes rises above this threshold, the router will issue a syslog warning message.

To demonstrate this, we can introduce a large number of routes and watch what happens. When there are less than 800 redistribute routes, all of the routes are distributed normally:

```
Router9#show ip route sum
IP routing table name is Default-IP-Routing-Table(0)
IP routing table maximum-paths is 16
Route Source    Networks    Subnets    Overhead    Memory (bytes)
connected       0           1          72          136
static          0           0          0           0
eigrp 11        0           791        56952       107576
ospf 87         3           2          360         680
   Intra-area: 5 Inter-area: 0 External-1: 0 External-2: 0
   NSSA External-1: 0 NSSA External-2: 0
internal        6                                  6936
Total           9           794        57384       115328
Router9#
```

If we then introduce a few more EIGRP prefixes to be redistributed to exceed the 80% warning threshold, the router produces this message:

```
*Mar  1 15:01:51.583: %IPRT-4-REDIST_THR_PFX: Redistribution prefix threshold ha
s been reached "ospf 87" - 800 prefixes
Router9#show ip route summary
IP routing table name is Default-IP-Routing-Table(0)
```

```
IP routing table maximum-paths is 16
Route Source    Networks    Subnets    Overhead    Memory (bytes)
connected       0           1          72          136
static          0           0          0           0
eigrp 11        0           800        57600       108800
ospf 87         3           2          360         680
  Intra-area: 5 Inter-area: 0 External-1: 0 External-2: 0
  NSSA External-1: 0 NSSA External-2: 0
internal        6                                  6936
Total           9           803        58032       116552
Router9#
```

If we then increase this number beyond the configured maximum of 1,000, the router gives another message and refuses to accept any further prefixes, although it will continue to redistribute all of the prefixes that it has already seen:

```
*Mar  1 15:04:12.659: %IPRT-4-REDIST_MAX_PFX: Redistribution prefix limit has be
en reached "ospf 87" - 1000 prefixes
```

This message appears whenever the threshold is crossed. If you continue to add routes past the threshold, it will not appear again. If the number of prefixes drops below the threshold and then rises above it again, you will see the message again:

```
Router9#show ip route summary
IP routing table name is Default-IP-Routing-Table(0)
IP routing table maximum-paths is 16
Route Source    Networks    Subnets    Overhead    Memory (bytes)
connected       0           1          72          136
static          0           0          0           0
eigrp 11        0           1085       78120       147560
ospf 87         3           2          360         680
  Intra-area: 5 Inter-area: 0 External-1: 0 External-2: 0
  NSSA External-1: 0 NSSA External-2: 0
internal        6                                  6936
Total           9           1088       78552       155312
Router9#
```

Any downstream router will only see 1,000 redistributed prefixes originating on Router9:

```
Router3#show ip route summary
IP routing table name is Default-IP-Routing-Table(0)
Route Source    Networks    Subnets    Overhead    Memory (bytes)
connected       3           1          528         576
static          0           0          0           0
ospf 1          0           1002       64128       144288
  Intra-area: 2 Inter-area: 0 External-1: 0 External-2: 1000
  NSSA External-1: 0 NSSA External-2: 0
internal        6                                  6984
Total           9           1003       64656       151848
Router3#
```

See Also

Recipe 8.5; Recipe 8.15

8.7 Manipulating DR Selection

Problem

You want to manipulate the Designated Router (DR) selection process on a particular subnet.

Solution

The *ip ospf priority* configuration command allows you to weight the Designated Router (DR) selection process on a network segment. The following configuration examples are for three different routers that all share the same Ethernet segment. Router5 has the highest OSPF priority, so it will become the DR. Router1 has the second highest priority because we want it to be the Backup Designated Router (BDR).

Router1 is connected to this network segment through a VLAN trunk:

```
Router1#configure terminal
Enter configuration commands, one per line.  End with CNTL/Z.
Router1(config)#interface FastEthernet0/0.1
Router1(config-subif)#ip ospf priority 2
Router1(config-subif)#exit
Router1(config)#end
Router1#
```

We will configure Router3 with a priority of 0. The default priority is 1. A router with priority 0 will never become the DR or BDR:

```
Router3#configure terminal
Enter configuration commands, one per line.  End with CNTL/Z.
Router3(config)#interface FastEthernet0/0.1
Router3(config-subif)#ip ospf priority 0
Router3(config-subif)#exit
Router3(config)#end
Router3#
```

Router5 has the highest priority, so it will become the DR for the segment:

```
Router5#configure terminal
Enter configuration commands, one per line.  End with CNTL/Z.
Router5(config)#interface Ethernet0
Router5(config-if)#ip ospf priority 10
Router5(config-if)#exit
Router5(config)#end
Router5#
```

Discussion

There are several reasons for rigging the DR election process, as we have done in this recipe. The most common reason is simply to ensure that the router closest to the network core is responsible for distributing routing information. This is actually a somewhat aesthetic requirement, because all of the routers in an area see all of the

LSAs for that area, so nobody's routing table is more accurate than anybody else's. But it can result in faster convergence in some network configurations.

But there are two times when it is critical to force a particular router to become the DR. The first is when you are using MOSPF to handle multicast routing. MOSPF uses the same DR as regular OSPF. So if you have a mix of MOSPF and regular OSPF on the same segment, it is critical that an MOSPF router be the DR, or no multicast routes will be distributed. Because Cisco routers do not support MOSPF, this means that you must set the priority to 0 for all Cisco routers on such a segment.

The second place where DR selection is critical is in Nonbroadcast Multiple Access (NBMA) networks. A typical example of this would be a Frame Relay WAN that uses multipoint subinterfaces, as described in Recipe 10.4. In this case, all of the routers are members of the same subnet, but only the central hub router can talk directly to the branch devices. A branch router should never act as DR because it can't talk directly to any of the other branches. The central router is the only device that can be the DR, or the routing updates will not work.

If you don't adjust the priorities to help force a particular winner to the DR election, the DR will be the router with the highest Router ID (RID) value. See Recipe 8.8 for a discussion of RID values.

It is important to note that setting a higher priority can help to rig the DR election process, but it doesn't guarantee that another lower priority router device won't become DR if it happens to be there first. And if a higher priority router comes up on a segment that already has a DR, it will not preempt either the DR or the BDR. If the higher priority router isn't available when a lower priority router joins the segment, then the lower priority router will become DR. Once a router is DR, it will remain DR until you either manually reset the neighbor relationships or until there is a network failure on the segment that forces the change.

The exception to this rule is when you configure a router with a priority of 0. In this case, the router will never become DR, even if it is the only router on the segment.

You can see the state of all of the neighboring routers on a segment with the *show ip ospf neighbor* command:

```
Router5#show ip ospf neighbor Ethernet0

Neighbor ID    Pri   State          Dead Time   Address       Interface
Router1        2     FULL/BDR       00:00:31    172.25.1.5    Ethernet0
Router3        0     FULL/DROTHER   00:00:31    172.25.1.3    Ethernet0
Router4        1     FULL/DROTHER   00:00:39    172.25.1.1    Ethernet0
Router5#
```

In this output, we have asked the router to only show the neighbors on the Ethernet0 interface. You can see that Router1 is the BDR, and the other two routers on the segment have a state of DROTHER. This means that they are neither DR nor BDR, but are neighbors. Notice that none of the routers listed is the DR. This is because the router we typed this on was the DR itself.

You can verify that this router is the DR, and that it has a priority of 10 with the *show ip ospf interface* command:

```
Router5#show ip ospf interface
Ethernet0 is up, line protocol is up
  Internet Address 172.25.1.7/24, Area 0
  Process ID 87, Router ID 172.25.1.7, Network Type BROADCAST, Cost: 10
  Transmit Delay is 1 sec, State DR, Priority 10
  Designated Router (ID) 172.25.25.6, Interface address 172.25.1.7
  Backup Designated router (ID) Router1, Interface address 172.25.1.3
  Timer intervals configured, Hello 10, Dead 40, Wait 40, Retransmit 5
    Hello due in 00:00:03
  Neighbor Count is 3, Adjacent neighbor count is 3
    Adjacent with neighbor Router3
    Adjacent with neighbor Router1  (Backup Designated Router)
    Adjacent with neighbor Router4
  Suppress hello for 0 neighbor(s)
Router5#
```

In the following example, we have increased the priority of Router4 to 10, as well. However, as you can see, not only does it not pre-empt the DR, it doesn't even pre-empt the BDR:

```
Router5#show ip ospf neighbor

Neighbor ID    Pri   State          Dead Time   Address      Interface
Router4        10    FULL/DROTHER   00:00:30    172.25.1.5   Ethernet0
Router1        2     FULL/BDR       00:00:38    172.25.1.3   Ethernet0
Router3        0     FULL/DROTHER   00:00:30    172.25.1.1   Ethernet0
Router5#
```

Because higher priority routers will not pre-empt existing DR and BDR routers, if there are routers that should not become DR for any reason, you should be careful to set their priorities to 0. Otherwise, you may find that the DR is simply the router that has been active for the longest time, instead of the one that you actually wanted.

See Also

Recipe 8.8; Recipe 10.4; Recipe 23.10

8.8   Setting the OSPF RID

Problem

You want to set the OSPF Router ID (RID) of a particular router.

Solution

There are several ways to set the OSPF Router ID (RID). The easiest is to create and configure a Loopback interface:

```
Router5#configure terminal
Enter configuration commands, one per line.  End with CNTL/Z.
```

```
Router5(config)#interface Loopback0
Router5(config-if)#ip address 172.25.25.6 255.255.255.255
Router5(config-if)#exit
Router5(config)#end
Router5#
```

If you don't want to use a Loopback interface, you can still force the router ID to use a particular IP address with the *router-id* configuration command:

```
Router5#configure terminal
Enter configuration commands, one per line.  End with CNTL/Z.
Router5(config)#router ospf 87
Router5(config-router)#router-id 172.25.1.7
Router5(config-if)#exit
Router5(config)#end
Router5#
```

Discussion

If you don't use either of these methods, the router will select the highest IP address from its interfaces and use this as the OSPF RID. The trouble with doing this is that you might add a new IP address to the router at some point. If this new address is higher than the previous RID, the router will change its RID the next time OSPF restarts. This could have strange consequences because if the interface priorities are the same, OSPF uses the highest RID to select the DR. Please refer to Recipe 8.7 for more information on DR selection.

We recommend using the Loopback interface method. Loopback interfaces ensure there is a single unique IP address for every router in the network, which is extremely useful for network management. Further, it is common to configure your loopback addresses in DNS, but not to necessarily include all of your interfaces. This is useful when if you enable domain name lookups on your router, as discussed in Recipe 8.20.

In IOS level 12.0, Cisco introduced a new way to select the RID by using the *router-id* command. This command allows you to set the RID to any IP address. You can even set the RID to be an address that is not configured on any of the router's interfaces, or even an address that is not in the routing tables. However, this is not a very wise thing to do because it makes troubleshooting much more difficult.

In some cases, you might have both a router ID and a loopback address set. The rule is that OSPF will use the *router-id* command first, if one exists. If there is no *router-id* command, then it uses the highest IP address on any of the loopback interfaces. Bear in mind that you can configure as many loopback interfaces as you like (although this is somewhat unusual in production networks, there are special situations when additional loopback interfaces can be useful). Finally, if there is no *router-id* command and no loopback interface, the OSPF process will use the highest IP address on the router for the RID.

You can see what the RID for your router is with the following command:

```
Router5#show ip ospf
 Routing Process "ospf 87" with ID 172.25.1.7
```

```
Supports only single TOS(TOS0) routes
SPF schedule delay 5 secs, Hold time between two SPFs 10 secs
Minimum LSA interval 5 secs. Minimum LSA arrival 1 secs
Number of external LSA 5. Checksum Sum 0x28868
Number of DCbitless external LSA 0
Number of DoNotAge external LSA 0
Number of areas in this router is 1. 1 normal 0 stub 0 nssa
    Area BACKBONE(0)
        Number of interfaces in this area is 2
        Area has no authentication
        SPF algorithm executed 47 times
        Area ranges are
        Number of LSA 36. Checksum Sum 0xEEAA1
        Number of DCbitless LSA 9
        Number of indication LSA 0
        Number of DoNotAge LSA 0
Router5#
```

The router continues to use the same RID address even if you subsequently add a *router-id* command or a loopback interface. To force OSPF to update the RID, either reload the router or restart the OSPF process using the *clear ip ospf process* command:

```
Router5#clear ip ospf process
Reset ALL OSPF processes? [no]: yes
Router5#
```

See Also

Recipe 8.7; Recipe 8.20

8.9   Enabling OSPF Authentication

Problem

You want to authenticate your OSPF neighbor relationships to ensure that no unauthorized equipment is allowed to affect routing.

Solution

To enable OSPF MD5 authentication, you need to define the encryption key, which is essentially just a password, on an interface. And you also must enable authentication for the entire area. For the first router, you could do this as follows:

```
Router1#configure terminal
Enter configuration commands, one per line.  End with CNTL/Z.
Router1(config)#interface Serial0/1
Router1(config-if)#ip ospf message-digest-key 1 md5 oreilly
Router1(config-if)#exit
Router1(config)#router ospf 55
Router1(config-router)#area 2 authentication message-digest
Router1(config-router)#exit
Router1(config)#end
Router1#
```

Similarly, you must enable OSPF authentication on other routers in the area, as well as making sure that the authentication keys match on all interfaces that share the same network segment:

```
Router2#configure terminal
Enter configuration commands, one per line.  End with CNTL/Z.
Router2(config)#interface Serial0/0
Router2(config-if)#ip ospf message-digest-key 1 md5 oreilly
Router2(config-if)#exit
Router2(config)#router ospf 12
Router2(config-router)#area 2 authentication message-digest
Router2(config-router)#exit
Router2(config)#end
Router2#
```

Discussion

RFC 2328, which defines OSPF Version 2, includes three different types of authentication for OSPF: null authentication, simple password authentication, and cryptographic authentication. Null authentication simply means that there is no authentication, which is the default on Cisco routers. In the simple password method of authentication, passwords are exchanged in clear text on the network. Even the RFC that specifies this method points out that it is easily compromised. Anybody who wants to deliberately corrupt your routing tables needs to have direct access to your network to do so anyway. Having that access means that it is relatively easy to capture these passwords. We recommend that you use the cryptographic authentication method if you require authentication with OSPF.

The cryptographic method uses the open standard MD5 (Message Digest type 5) encryption standard. MD5 is a one-way irreversible cipher. Two devices exchange only the MD5-encrypted versions of the password. Both devices know the same password. Each router is able to verify that the encrypted password that it receives is correct by using the same algorithm to encrypt the password that it already knows. To make sure that nobody can just intercept and use the encrypted version of the password directly, a time value that the receiving router also knows is added to the password before encrypting. Anybody else listening on the network is only able to see the encrypted version of the password, but they cannot deduce the original password.

Unfortunately, the RFC is not completely clear on how this time value should be added to the original pass phrase, nor does it mandate MD5 encryption. So there is a good chance that cryptographic authentication will not work well between routers from different vendors.

 If you need to exchange authenticated OSPF routes with nonCisco routers, you may be forced to use the less secure simple password method.

If you use authentication in an OSPF area, you must configure all of the routers in the area to support authentication. Every interface on a router doesn't have to be configured with authentication. But if you require authentication in any part of an area, you must include authentication support throughout the area. In the above example, this is done for area 2 with this command:

```
Router2(config-router)#area 2 authentication message-digest
```

The *show ip ospf interface* command shows that we have configured authentication on this interface:

```
Router2#show ip ospf interface Serial0/0
Serial0/0 is up, line protocol is up
  Internet Address 10.1.1.1/30, Area 2
  Process ID 12, Router ID 192.168.30.1, Network Type POINT_TO_POINT, Cost: 130
  Transmit Delay is 1 sec, State POINT_TO_POINT,
  Timer intervals configured, Hello 10, Dead 40, Wait 40, Retransmit 5
    Hello due in 00:00:06
  Index 1/1, flood queue length 0
  Next 0x0(0)/0x0(0)
  Last flood scan length is 1, maximum is 1
  Last flood scan time is 0 msec, maximum is 0 msec
  Neighbor Count is 1, Adjacent neighbor count is 1
    Adjacent with neighbor 172.25.25.1
  Suppress hello for 0 neighbor(s)
  Message digest authentication enabled
    Youngest key id is 1
Router2#
```

Notice that this also says that we are using specifically "Message digest authentication," meaning MD5, and it also indicates that key number 1 is currently active.

You can use a different key on each of a router's interfaces, or a single password throughout the entire network. All that matters is that the all of the routers on a single network segment use the same OSPF key for the interfaces that share this segment. The problem with using too many different keys is that it can become rather difficult to manage.

You can also configure several keys on a single interface. We recommend using this as a transition method while changing keys. The old keys should be removed quickly to prevent anybody from gaining access by using an old key:

```
Router2#configure terminal
Enter configuration commands, one per line.  End with CNTL/Z.
Router2(config)#interface Serial0/0
Router2(config-if)#ip ospf message-digest-key 1 md5 oreilly
Router2(config-if)#ip ospf message-digest-key 2 md5 cookbook
Router2(config-if)#exit
Router2(config)#end
Router2#
```

In this case, we have defined two keys, which have key numbers 1 and 2, respectively:

```
Router2#show ip ospf interface Serial0/0
Serial0/0 is up, line protocol is up
```

```
Internet Address 10.1.1.1/30, Area 2
Process ID 12, Router ID 192.168.30.1, Network Type POINT_TO_POINT, Cost: 130
Transmit Delay is 1 sec, State POINT_TO_POINT,
Timer intervals configured, Hello 10, Dead 40, Wait 40, Retransmit 5
  Hello due in 00:00:03
Index 1/1, flood queue length 0
Next 0x0(0)/0x0(0)
Last flood scan length is 1, maximum is 1
Last flood scan time is 0 msec, maximum is 0 msec
Neighbor Count is 1, Adjacent neighbor count is 1
  Adjacent with neighbor 172.25.25.1
Suppress hello for 0 neighbor(s)
Message digest authentication enabled
  Youngest key id is 2
  Rollover in progress, 1 neighbor(s) using the old key(s):
    key id 1
Router2#
```

This display indicates that key number 2 is the newest, and that one neighbor is still using the old key. This command is useful when you want to see if it is safe to remove the old key yet.

Looking at the router's configuration file, you can see that these keys are stored in plain text by default:

```
interface Serial0/0
  ip address 10.1.1.1 255.255.255.252
  ip ospf message-digest-key 1 md5 oreilly
  ip ospf message-digest-key 2 md5 cookbook
```

If you define the password encryption service on the router, it will store these keys using the weak Cisco Type 7 encryption method:

```
Router2#configure terminal
Enter configuration commands, one per line.  End with CNTL/Z.
Router2(config)#service password-encryption
Router2(config)#end
```

As we discussed in Chapter 2, this causes the router to store passwords in an encrypted form when you view the configuration file. However, this encryption method is easily broken if somebody gains access to the router. It is still useful, though, to prevent somebody from getting the passwords by looking over your shoulder.

If you want to use authentication, but the neighboring devices don't support MD5, then you need to use clear text authentication, which you can configure as follows:

```
Router1#configure terminal
Enter configuration commands, one per line.  End with CNTL/Z.
Router1(config)#interface Serial0/1
Router1(config-if)#ip ospf authentication-key oreilly
Router1(config-if)#exit
Router1(config)#router ospf 55
Router1(config-router)#area 2 authentication
Router1(config-router)#exit
Router1(config)#end
Router1#
```

As with MD5 authentication, if you configure clear text authentication on an interface, you must configure the same authentication method and the same key on all other routers that share this segment:

```
Router2#configure terminal
Enter configuration commands, one per line.  End with CNTL/Z.
Router2(config)#interface Serial0/0
Router2(config-if)#ip ospf authentication-key oreilly
Router2(config-if)#exit
Router2(config)#router ospf 12
Router2(config-router)#area 2 authentication
Router2(config-router)#exit
Router2(config)#end
Router2#
```

Now the output of the *show ip ospf interface* command indicates the alternative authentication method:

```
Router2#show ip ospf interface Serial0/0
Serial0/0 is up, line protocol is up
  Internet Address 10.1.1.1/30, Area 2
  Process ID 12, Router ID 192.168.30.1, Network Type POINT_TO_POINT, Cost: 130
  Transmit Delay is 1 sec, State POINT_TO_POINT,
  Timer intervals configured, Hello 10, Dead 40, Wait 40, Retransmit 5
    Hello due in 00:00:07
  Index 1/1, flood queue length 0
  Next 0x0(0)/0x0(0)
  Last flood scan length is 1, maximum is 1
  Last flood scan time is 0 msec, maximum is 0 msec
  Neighbor Count is 1, Adjacent neighbor count is 1
    Adjacent with neighbor 172.25.25.1
  Suppress hello for 0 neighbor(s)
  Simple password authentication enabled
Router2#
```

See Also

Chapter 2

8.10   Selecting the Appropriate Area Types

Problem

You want to limit the number of routes and entries in the Link State database to conserve router resources and ensure good convergence properties.

Solution

In the Introduction to this chapter, we talked about the various types of OSPF areas. You can configure these different types areas by using the appropriate keywords on the *area* command.

For a Stubby Area, use the *stub* keyword:

```
Router1#configure terminal
Enter configuration commands, one per line.  End with CNTL/Z.
Router1(config)#router ospf 55
Router1(config-router)#area 100 stub
Router1(config-router)#exit
Router1(config)#end
Router1#
```

To configure a Totally Stubby Area, combine the *stub* and *no-summary* keywords on the ABR router:

```
Router1#configure terminal
Enter configuration commands, one per line.  End with CNTL/Z.
Router1(config)#router ospf 55
Router1(config-router)#area 100 stub no-summary
Router1(config-router)#exit
Router1(config)#end
Router1#
```

Only the ABRs needs the *no-summary* keyword, because they are the only routers that will be doing the route summarization. The other routers in a Totally Stubby Area need only be configured using the *stub* keyword, as in the previous example.

For Not So Stubby Areas (NSSA), you need to specify the *nssa* keyword. In this case we have also included the *default-information-originate* option so that the router can summarize external routes to a single default route:

```
Router1#configure terminal
Enter configuration commands, one per line.  End with CNTL/Z.
Router1(config)#router ospf 55
Router1(config-router)#area 100 nssa default-information-originate
Router1(config-router)#exit
Router1(config)#end
Router1#
```

In the Introduction we also discussed an interesting variant, called the Totally Stubby, Not So Stubby Area. You can configure it as follows on the ABR:

```
Router1#configure terminal
Enter configuration commands, one per line.  End with CNTL/Z.
Router1(config)#router ospf 55
Router1(config-router)#area 100 nssa no-summary
Router1(config-router)#exit
Router1(config)#end
Router1#
```

Once again, you can simply configure the other routers in this area with the *nssa* keyword.

Discussion

In all of the configuration examples, we showed the configuration for just one router. It is important to remember that the routers in an area have to agree on the area type.

However, it is mostly the ABR that cares about the area type, because it has to decide what kinds of information to forward from other parts of the network. Every router in a stub area must be configured as stub, although only the ABR needs to worry about the difference between stub and totally stub. Every router in an NSSA area must be configured to support NSSA type 7 LSA messages. But, once again, only the ABR cares about the difference between NSSA and totally stub NSSA.

If you have any ASBR devices that inject routes from other autonomous systems in this area, then they also need to use the area type information. The other routers are only really concerned with forwarding the LSAs around the area.

When you look at the routing table, you can see there are several kinds of routes:

```
Router3#show ip route ospf
O E1 192.168.10.0/24 [110/3611] via 172.20.1.1, 00:00:20, Serial0.1
     172.16.0.0/24 is subnetted, 1 subnets
O IA    172.16.2.0 [110/3581] via 172.20.1.1, 00:00:20, Serial0.1
     172.20.0.0/16 is variably subnetted, 5 subnets, 3 masks
O       172.20.220.1/32 [110/11] via 172.20.10.2, 00:00:20, Ethernet0
O       172.20.200.1/32 [110/11] via 172.20.10.2, 00:00:20, Ethernet0
     172.22.0.0/24 is subnetted, 1 subnets
O IA    172.22.1.0 [110/3581] via 172.20.1.1, 00:00:20, Serial0.1
     172.25.0.0/16 is variably subnetted, 3 subnets, 2 masks
O IA    172.25.25.6/32 [110/3582] via 172.20.1.1, 00:00:20, Serial0.1
O IA    172.25.25.1/32 [110/3572] via 172.20.1.1, 00:00:20, Serial0.1
O IA    172.25.1.0/24 [110/3581] via 172.20.1.1, 00:00:20, Serial0.1
     172.24.0.0/24 is subnetted, 1 subnets
O E1    172.24.1.0 [110/3611] via 172.20.1.1, 00:00:20, Serial0.1
     10.0.0.0/8 is variably subnetted, 4 subnets, 3 masks
O IA    10.2.2.2/32 [110/5134] via 172.20.1.1, 00:00:20, Serial0.1
O E1    10.2.2.0/30 [110/3606] via 172.20.1.1, 00:00:20, Serial0.1
O IA    10.1.1.0/30 [110/5133] via 172.20.1.1, 00:00:20, Serial0.1
O E1    10.100.1.0/24 [110/3611] via 172.20.1.1, 00:00:20, Serial0.1
O E2 192.168.50.0/24 [110/20] via 172.20.1.1, 00:00:20, Serial0.1
Router3#
```

This output shows only routes that were learned via OSPF, which is indicated by the O at the start of each line. In this routing table, there are several external routes. Most of them are Type 1 externals, which are labeled E1. There is also one Type 2 external route, which is labeled E2 in the output. Some of the other routes have IA beside them, which indicates they are interarea routes, meaning that they did not originate in this area. The remaining routes, such as 172.20.220.1/32, represent networks in this area.

This routing table shows no summarization. For example, the 10.0.0.0/8 classful network has several distinct subnets, including both 10.2.2.0/30 and its subnet 10.2.2.2/32. It's also useful to look at the OSPF database on this router to see how different routes are categorized:

```
Router3#show ip ospf database

   OSPF Router with ID (172.25.25.2) (Process ID 44)
```

```
                Router Link States (Area 100)

Link ID         ADV Router      Age      Seq#         Checksum Link count
172.20.220.1    172.20.220.1    47       0x80000004 0xB352    3
172.25.25.1     172.25.25.1     89       0x80000067 0xE771    2
172.25.25.2     172.25.25.2     47       0x80000065 0x4C66    4

                Net Link States (Area 100)

Link ID         ADV Router      Age      Seq#         Checksum
172.20.10.1     172.25.25.2     42       0x80000002 0xF11B

                Summary Net Link States (Area 100)

Link ID         ADV Router      Age      Seq#         Checksum
10.1.1.0        172.25.25.1     173      0x80000002 0x86AC
10.2.2.2        172.25.25.1     173      0x80000002 0x77B3
172.16.2.0      172.25.25.1     173      0x80000002 0xBFD3
172.22.1.0      172.25.25.1     173      0x80000002 0x820C
172.25.1.0      172.25.25.1     173      0x80000002 0x5E2D
172.25.25.1     172.25.25.1     173      0x80000002 0xF08A
172.25.25.6     172.25.25.1     173      0x80000002 0x2349

                Summary ASB Link States (Area 100)

Link ID         ADV Router      Age      Seq#         Checksum
172.25.1.7      172.25.25.1     173      0x80000001 0xC78
172.25.25.1     172.25.25.1     173      0x80000001 0xBCDF

                Type-5 AS External Link States

Link ID         ADV Router      Age      Seq#         Checksum Tag
10.2.2.0        172.25.25.1     1138     0x8000000A 0x9588    0
10.100.1.0      172.25.25.1     1138     0x80000009 0x4A6B    0
172.24.1.0      172.25.25.1     1138     0x80000009 0x9BC3    0
192.168.10.0    172.25.25.1     1138     0x80000009 0x6C45    0
192.168.50.0    172.25.1.7      428      0x80000002 0xFF36    0
Router3#
```

This represents a relatively small OSPF network. But it's a useful example because there are some instances of each type of route.

When we configure this area to be a Stubby Area, the ABR prevents External routes from being propagated into the area and replaces them with a default route. ASBRs are not permitted in stubby areas:

```
Router3#show ip route ospf
     172.16.0.0/24 is subnetted, 1 subnets
O IA    172.16.2.0 [110/3581] via 172.20.1.1, 00:00:07, Serial0.1
     172.20.0.0/16 is variably subnetted, 5 subnets, 3 masks
O       172.20.220.1/32 [110/11] via 172.20.10.2, 00:00:20, Ethernet0
O       172.20.200.1/32 [110/11] via 172.20.10.2, 00:00:20, Ethernet0
     172.22.0.0/24 is subnetted, 1 subnets
O IA    172.22.1.0 [110/3581] via 172.20.1.1, 00:00:07, Serial0.1
```

```
         172.25.0.0/16 is variably subnetted, 3 subnets, 2 masks
O IA     172.25.25.6/32 [110/3582] via 172.20.1.1, 00:00:07, Serial0.1
O IA     172.25.25.1/32 [110/3572] via 172.20.1.1, 00:00:07, Serial0.1
O IA     172.25.1.0/24 [110/3581] via 172.20.1.1, 00:00:07, Serial0.1
         10.0.0.0/8 is variably subnetted, 2 subnets, 2 masks
O IA     10.2.2.2/32 [110/5134] via 172.20.1.1, 00:00:07, Serial0.1
O IA     10.1.1.0/30 [110/5133] via 172.20.1.1, 00:00:07, Serial0.1
O*IA 0.0.0.0/0 [110/3572] via 172.20.1.1, 00:00:07, Serial0.1
Router3#
```

As you can see, all of the external routes are gone, but the tnterarea routes remain. Looking at the OSPF database, you can see that there is considerably less information for the router to keep track of:

```
Router3#show ip ospf database

          OSPF Router with ID (172.25.25.2) (Process ID 44)

              Router Link States (Area 100)

Link ID         ADV Router      Age    Seq#       Checksum Link count
172.20.220.1    172.20.220.1    22     0x80000006 0xCD38   3
172.25.25.1     172.25.25.1     86     0x80000069 0xFB5F   2
172.25.25.2     172.25.25.2     22     0x80000068 0x644D   4

              Net Link States (Area 100)

Link ID         ADV Router      Age    Seq#       Checksum
172.20.10.1     172.25.25.2     17     0x80000003 0xEFF

              Summary Net Link States (Area 100)

Link ID         ADV Router      Age    Seq#       Checksum
0.0.0.0         172.25.25.1     92     0x80000001 0x213D
10.1.1.0        172.25.25.1     92     0x80000003 0xA291
10.2.2.2        172.25.25.1     92     0x80000003 0x9398
172.16.2.0      172.25.25.1     92     0x80000003 0xDBB8
172.22.1.0      172.25.25.1     92     0x80000003 0x9EF0
172.25.1.0      172.25.25.1     92     0x80000003 0x7A12
172.25.25.1     172.25.25.1     92     0x80000003 0xD6F
172.25.25.6     172.25.25.1     92     0x80000003 0x3F2E
Router3#
```

Totally stubby areas prevent external routes like ordinary stub areas. But the ABRs for totally stubby areas also prevent interarea routes from being propagated into the area, replacing them with a single default route instead. The default route is the only summary route allowed. ASBRs are not permitted in stub or Totally Stubby areas:

```
Router3#show ip route ospf
     172.20.0.0/16 is variably subnetted, 5 subnets, 3 masks
O        172.20.220.1/32 [110/11] via 172.20.10.2, 00:00:15, Ethernet0
O        172.20.200.1/32 [110/11] via 172.20.10.2, 00:00:15, Ethernet0
O*IA 0.0.0.0/0 [110/3572] via 172.20.1.1, 00:00:15, Serial0.1
Router3#
```

The Totally Stubby Area has radically reduced the size of the routing table, as well as the OSPF database:

```
Router3#show ip ospf database

        OSPF Router with ID (172.25.25.2) (Process ID 44)

            Router Link States (Area 100)

Link ID          ADV Router       Age        Seq#       Checksum Link count
172.20.220.1     172.20.220.1     104        0x80000006 0xCD38   3
172.25.25.1      172.25.25.1      22         0x8000006B 0xF761   2
172.25.25.2      172.25.25.2      104        0x80000068 0x644D   4

            Net Link States (Area 100)

Link ID          ADV Router       Age        Seq#       Checksum
172.20.10.1      172.25.25.2      99         0x80000003 0xEFF

            Summary Net Link States (Area 100)

Link ID          ADV Router       Age        Seq#       Checksum
0.0.0.0          172.25.25.1      23         0x80000002 0x1F3E
Router3#
```

There are two main differences between stubby and NSSA areas. The first is that the NSSA prevents the ABR from propagating external routes throughout the area, but does not replace them with a single default route. The second is that the NSSA may contain ASBRs, which use Type 7 LSAs to carry information about external routes. These Type 7 LSAs are flooded throughout the NSSA area. When they reach the ABR, they are translated into Type 5 LSAs and forwarded to the rest of the OSPF network:

```
Router3#configure terminal
Enter configuration commands, one per line.  End with CNTL/Z.
Router3(config)#ip route 192.168.88.0 255.255.255.0 172.20.10.2
Router3(config)#router ospf 44
Router3(config-router)#redistribute static subnet
Router3(config-router)#area 100 nssa default-information-originate
Router3(config-router)#exit
Router3(config)#end
Router3#
```

With the *default-information-originate* option, the ABR will forward a default route to summarize all external routes that originate outside of the area:

```
Router3#show ip route ospf
      172.16.0.0/24 is subnetted, 1 subnets
O IA    172.16.2.0 [110/3581] via 172.20.1.1, 00:07:43, Serial0.1
      172.20.0.0/16 is variably subnetted, 5 subnets, 3 masks
O       172.20.220.1/32 [110/11] via 172.20.10.2, 00:07:43, Ethernet0
O       172.20.200.1/32 [110/11] via 172.20.10.2, 00:07:43, Ethernet0
      172.22.0.0/24 is subnetted, 1 subnets
O IA    172.22.1.0 [110/3581] via 172.20.1.1, 00:07:43, Serial0.1
      172.25.0.0/16 is variably subnetted, 3 subnets, 2 masks
```

```
O IA     172.25.25.6/32 [110/3582] via 172.20.1.1, 00:07:43, Serial0.1
O IA     172.25.25.1/32 [110/3572] via 172.20.1.1, 00:07:43, Serial0.1
O IA     172.25.1.0/24 [110/3581] via 172.20.1.1, 00:07:43, Serial0.1
         10.0.0.0/8 is variably subnetted, 2 subnets, 2 masks
O IA     10.2.2.2/32 [110/5134] via 172.20.1.1, 00:07:43, Serial0.1
O IA     10.1.1.0/30 [110/5133] via 172.20.1.1, 00:07:43, Serial0.1
O*N2 0.0.0.0/0 [110/1] via 172.20.1.1, 00:07:43, Serial0.1
Router3#
```

The OSPF database for an NSSA area shows information about Type 7 LSAs:

```
Router3#show ip ospf database

              OSPF Router with ID (172.25.25.2) (Process ID 44)

              Router Link States (Area 100)

Link ID          ADV Router       Age       Seq#        Checksum Link count
172.20.220.1     172.20.220.1     973       0x80000008 0x51AA    3
172.25.25.1      172.25.25.1      502       0x80000072 0x77D0    2
172.25.25.2      172.25.25.2      968       0x8000006E 0xE5BB    4

              Net Link States (Area 100)

Link ID          ADV Router       Age       Seq#        Checksum
172.20.10.1      172.25.25.2      967       0x80000004 0x9371

              Summary Net Link States (Area 100)

Link ID          ADV Router       Age       Seq#        Checksum
10.1.1.0         172.25.25.1      1124      0x80000003 0x2A02
10.2.2.2         172.25.25.1      1124      0x80000003 0x1B09
172.16.2.0       172.25.25.1      1124      0x80000003 0x6329
172.22.1.0       172.25.25.1      1124      0x80000003 0x2661
172.25.1.0       172.25.25.1      1124      0x80000003 0x282
172.25.25.1      172.25.25.1      1124      0x80000003 0x94DF
172.25.25.6      172.25.25.1      1124      0x80000003 0xC69E

              Type-7 AS External Link States (Area 100)

Link ID          ADV Router       Age       Seq#        Checksum Tag
0.0.0.0          172.25.25.1      508       0x80000001 0xF31B    0
10.2.2.0         172.25.25.1      1123      0x80000001 0x2FE7    0
10.100.1.0       172.25.25.1      1123      0x80000001 0xE90B    0
172.24.1.0       172.25.25.1      1123      0x80000001 0x3B63    0
192.168.10.0     172.25.25.1      1123      0x80000001 0xCE4     0
192.168.88.0     172.25.25.2      974       0x80000001 0x3AEC    0
Router3#
```

It is also interesting to look at the routing table entry for one of these Type 7 routes on another router within the same area:

```
Router1#show ip route 192.168.88.0
Routing entry for 192.168.88.0/24
  Known via "ospf 55", metric 20, type NSSA extern 2, forward metric 1572
```

```
    Last update from 172.20.1.2 on Serial0/0.2, 00:08:56 ago
    Routing Descriptor Blocks:
    * 172.20.1.2, from 172.25.25.2, 00:08:56 ago, via Serial0/0.2
       Route metric is 20, traffic share count is 1
  Router1#
```

The aptly named Totally Stubby Not So Stubby Area is similar to an NSSA area, but it also acts like a Totally Stubby area in preventing the ABR from advertising Inter Area routes and replaces them with a single summary route, the default route. The ABR for a Totally Stubby NSSA will create a default route by default:

```
Router3#show ip route ospf
     172.20.0.0/16 is variably subnetted, 5 subnets, 3 masks
O       172.20.220.1/32 [110/11] via 172.20.10.2, 00:00:47, Ethernet0
O       172.20.200.1/32 [110/11] via 172.20.10.2, 00:00:47, Ethernet0
O*IA 0.0.0.0/0 [110/3572] via 172.20.1.1, 00:00:47, Serial0.1
Router3#
```

Despite the confusing name, this is an extremely useful type of area. In many large OSPF networks, most of the routes in the routing table are interarea routes. But you can also put an ASBR in this type of area and use it as a transit area to connect to external networks:

```
Router3#show ip ospf database

          OSPF Router with ID (172.25.25.2) (Process ID 44)

          Router Link States (Area 100)

Link ID         ADV Router      Age        Seq#        Checksum Link count
172.20.220.1    172.20.220.1    1209       0x80000008 0x51AA   3
172.25.25.1     172.25.25.1     91         0x80000074 0x73D2   2
172.25.25.2     172.25.25.2     1204       0x8000006E 0xE5BB   4

          Net Link States (Area 100)

Link ID         ADV Router      Age        Seq#        Checksum
172.20.10.1     172.25.25.2     1203       0x80000004 0x9371

          Summary Net Link States (Area 100)

Link ID         ADV Router      Age        Seq#        Checksum
0.0.0.0         172.25.25.1     92         0x80000001 0xA8AD

          Type-7 AS External Link States (Area 100)

Link ID         ADV Router      Age        Seq#        Checksum Tag
10.2.2.0        172.25.25.1     88         0x80000002 0x2DE8   0
10.100.1.0      172.25.25.1     82         0x80000003 0xE50D   0
172.24.1.0      172.25.25.1     88         0x80000002 0x3964   0
192.168.10.0    172.25.25.1     88         0x80000002 0xAE5    0
192.168.88.0    172.25.25.2     86         0x80000002 0x38ED   0
Router3#
```

Like an NSSA area, the ABR translates Type 7 to Type 5 LSAs:

```
Router1#show ip ospf
 Routing Process "ospf 55" with ID 172.25.25.1
 <lines removed for brevity>
    Area 100
        Number of interfaces in this area is 1
        It is a NSSA area
        Perform type-7/type-5 LSA translation
        Area has no authentication
        SPF algorithm executed 75 times
        Area ranges are
        Number of LSA 13. Checksum Sum 0x6B01B
        Number of opaque link LSA 0. Checksum Sum 0x0
        Number of DCbitless LSA 0
        Number of indication LSA 0
        Number of DoNotAge LSA 0
        Flood list length 0
Router1#
```

See Also

IP Routing by Ravi Malhotra (O'Reilly)

8.11   Using OSPF on Dial Interfaces

Problem

You want to use OSPF on a dial interface, but you don't want the protocol traffic to keep the link active unnecessarily.

Solution

In this example, Router4 will dial into Router1 by using an ISDN circuit:

```
Router4#configure terminal
Enter configuration commands, one per line.  End with CNTL/Z.
Router4(config)#username Router1 password 0 cisco
Router4(config)#interface BRI0
Router4(config-if)#ip address 192.168.15.4 255.255.255.0
Router4(config-if)#encapsulation ppp
Router4(config-if)#ip ospf demand-circuit
Router4(config-if)#dialer map ip 192.168.15.1 broadcast 4165550000
Router4(config-if)#dialer-group 1
Router4(config-if)#isdn switch-type basic-ni
Router4(config-if)#isdn spid1 416555001000 4165550010
Router4(config-if)#isdn spid2 416555001100 4165550011
Router4(config-if)#ppp authentication chap
Router4(config-if)#ppp multilink
Router4(config-if)#exit
Router4(config)#dialer-list 1 protocol ip permit
Router4(config)#router ospf 87
```

```
Router4(config-router)#network 192.168.15.0 0.0.0.255 area 10
Router4(config-router)#exit
Router4(config)#end
Router4#
```

The configuration of the other router is similar, although it does not require the *ip ospf demand-circuit* command:

```
Router1#configure terminal
Enter configuration commands, one per line.  End with CNTL/Z.
Router1(config)#username Router4 password 0 cisco
Router1(config)#interface BRI0/0
Router1(config-if)#ip address 192.168.15.1 255.255.255.0
Router1(config-if)#encapsulation ppp
Router1(config-if)#dialer-group 1
Router1(config-if)#isdn switch-type basic-ni
Router1(config-if)#isdn spid1 416555000000 4165550000
Router1(config-if)#isdn spid2 416555000100 4165550001
Router1(config-if)#ppp authentication chap
Router1(config-if)#ppp multilink
Router1(config-if)#exit
Router1(config)#dialer-list 1 protocol ip permit
Router1(config)#router ospf 87
Router1(config-router)#network 192.168.15.0 0.0.0.255 area 10
Router1(config-router)#exit
Router1(config)#end
Router1#
```

Discussion

In this example, we have used ISDN to provide a specific example for an OSPF Demand Circuit. In fact, you could use a similar configuration anywhere that you want to make the OSPF neighbor relationships and routing information remain, even when the link becomes unavailable. Most of the time, of course, this means some sort of dial link. For more information on the ISDN and dialup portions of this configuration, please refer to Chapter 13.

The critical command is the *ip ospf demand-circuit* command, which we have configured on the BRI interface of one of the routers:

```
Router4(config)#interface BRI0
Router4(config-if)#ip ospf demand-circuit
```

You can see the effect of this command with the *show ip ospf interface* command:

```
Router4#show ip ospf interface Bri0
BRI0 is up, line protocol is up (spoofing)
  Internet Address 192.168.15.4/24, Area 10
  Process ID 87, Router ID 172.18.6.4, Network Type POINT_TO_POINT, Cost: 1562
  Configured as demand circuit.
  Run as demand circuit.
  DoNotAge LSA allowed.
  Transmit Delay is 1 sec, State POINT_TO_POINT,
  Timer intervals configured, Hello 10, Dead 40, Wait 40, Retransmit 5
```

```
        Hello due in 00:00:03
      Index 1/1, flood queue length 0
      Next 0x0(0)/0x0(0)
      Last flood scan length is 1, maximum is 1
      Last flood scan time is 0 msec, maximum is 0 msec
      Neighbor Count is 1, Adjacent neighbor count is 1
        Adjacent with neighbor 172.18.6.1  (Hello suppressed)
      Suppress hello for 1 neighbor(s)
   Router4#
```

The other router also knows that this is a demand circuit, even though it is not explicitly configured as such:

```
   Router1#show ip ospf interface Bri0/0
   BRI0/0 is up, line protocol is up (spoofing)
      Internet Address 192.168.15.1/24, Area 10
      Process ID 87, Router ID 172.18.6.1, Network Type POINT_TO_POINT, Cost: 1562
      Run as demand circuit.
      DoNotAge LSA allowed.
      Transmit Delay is 1 sec, State POINT_TO_POINT,
      Timer intervals configured, Hello 10, Dead 40, Wait 40, Retransmit 5
        Hello due in 00:00:09
      Index 5/5, flood queue length 0
      Next 0x0(0)/0x0(0)
      Last flood scan length is 2, maximum is 2
      Last flood scan time is 0 msec, maximum is 0 msec
      Neighbor Count is 1, Adjacent neighbor count is 1
        Adjacent with neighbor 172.18.6.4  (Hello suppressed)
      Suppress hello for 1 neighbor(s)
   Router1#
```

The OSPF neighbor relationship and the routing table remain intact after the dialer interface has dropped due to inactivity:

```
   Router4#show dialer

   BRI0 - dialer type = ISDN

   Dial String      Successes   Failures    Last DNIS   Last status
   4165550000               6          2    00:05:48      successful
   0 incoming call(s) have been screened.
   0 incoming call(s) rejected for callback.

   BRI0:1 - dialer type = ISDN
   Idle timer (120 secs), Fast idle timer (20 secs)
   Wait for carrier (30 secs), Re-enable (15 secs)
   Dialer state is idle

   BRI0:2 - dialer type = ISDN
   Idle timer (120 secs), Fast idle timer (20 secs)
   Wait for carrier (30 secs), Re-enable (15 secs)
   Dialer state is idle
   Router4#
```

The *show ip ospf neighbor* command confirms that even though the dial connection has dropped, the neighbor relationship is still active:

```
Router4#show ip ospf neighbor

Neighbor ID    Pri  State       Dead Time   Address        Interface
172.18.6.1       1  FULL/  -        -        192.168.15.1   BRI0
Router4#
```

Notice in particular that the output of this command shows a dead time for this neighbor of "-", indicating that this neighbor will not time out due to the absence of OSPF Hello packets. Also, the routes that have been learned through this link are maintained in the routing table:

```
Router4#show ip route ospf
     10.0.0.0/32 is subnetted, 1 subnets
O       10.1.2.1 [110/1563] via 192.168.15.1, 00:02:41, BRI0
O       10.1.1.1 [110/1563] via 192.168.15.1, 00:02:41, BRI0
Router4#
```

And because the next hop router shown in each of the routing table entries is the one listed in the *dialer-map* statement, any traffic directed to one of these prefixes will automatically activate the interface again:

```
Router4#ping 10.1.1.1

Type escape sequence to abort.
Sending 5, 100-byte ICMP Echos to 10.1.1.1, timeout is 2 seconds:
.
01:05:14: %LINK-3-UPDOWN: Interface BRI0:1, changed state to up
01:05:15: %LINK-3-UPDOWN: Interface Virtual-Access1, changed state to up!!!!
Success rate is 80 percent (4/5), round-trip min/avg/max = 36/36/36 ms
Router4#
01:05:15: %LINEPROTO-5-UPDOWN: Line protocol on Interface BRI0:1, changed state
to up
01:05:16: %LINEPROTO-5-UPDOWN: Line protocol on Interface Virtual-Access1, chang
ed state to up
Router4#
```

There are a few cautions that you should be aware of when dealing with demand circuits. The first is that the configuration in the example will only allow Router4 to dial to Router1. If Router1 has traffic for Router4, it cannot be delivered. To address this change, you should configure a *dialer-map* statement on Router1, as well as Router4. The second and more serious potential issue is that, by its very nature, a demand-circuit will not keep an up-to-date routing table. If there are topology changes on the other side of the dial link, the router will not know until it eventually has a reason to dial and obtain the latest OSPF database.

See Also

Chapter 13

8.12 Summarizing Routes in OSPF

Problem

You want to reduce the size of your routing tables without losing any connectivity within your network.

Solution

Using the *area x range* configuration command on your ABRs allows you summarize routes between OSPF areas:

```
Router1#configure terminal
Enter configuration commands, one per line.  End with CNTL/Z.
Router1(config)#router ospf 55
Router1(config-router)#area 100 range 172.20.0.0 255.255.0.0
Router1(config-router)#area 0 range 172.25.0.0 255.255.0.0
Router1(config-router)#area 2 range 10.0.0.0 255.0.0.0
Router1(config-router)#exit
Router1(config)#end
Router1#
```

Discussion

The easiest way to see the effect of summarization is to look at the routing table before and after it is enabled. Here is a sample routing table before summarization. The ranges that we will be summarizing are 172.20.0.0/16 and 172.25.0.0/16. We have highlighted the route with the lowest metric in each of these ranges:

```
Router2#show ip route ospf
      172.16.0.0/24 is subnetted, 1 subnets
O IA    172.16.2.0 [110/140] via 10.1.1.2, 00:05:06, Serial0/0
      172.20.0.0/16 is variably subnetted, 3 subnets, 3 masks
O IA    172.20.10.0/24 [110/1702] via 10.1.1.2, 00:05:06, Serial0/0
O IA    172.20.1.0/30 [110/1692] via 10.1.1.2, 00:05:06, Serial0/0
O IA    172.20.100.1/32 [110/1693] via 10.1.1.2, 00:05:06, Serial0/0
      172.25.0.0/16 is variably subnetted, 3 subnets, 2 masks
O IA    172.25.25.6/32 [110/141] via 10.1.1.2, 00:05:06, Serial0/0
O IA    172.25.25.1/32 [110/131] via 10.1.1.2, 00:05:06, Serial0/0
O IA    172.25.1.0/24 [110/140] via 10.1.1.2, 00:00:25, Serial0/0
Router2#
```

Then, after enabling summarization, you can see that all of the individual routes in each of these ranges have been replaced with a single route for the entire range. Notice also that the cost for the summary is equal to the lowest cost of the individual routes that this summary replaces. This is an extremely important point because it means that a summary route will be only as stable as the lowest cost route being replaced. The summary could replace a hundred routes that are all rock stable, but if the one with the lowest cost happens to bounce up and down frequently, the cost of the summary will have to fluctuate with it. And this also means that it will have to be repeatedly distributed throughout the area, wasting bandwidth and using extra CPU cycles on all of the routers. Conversely, if the lowest cost route is stable, then the summary will be completely stable as well, even if all of the other summarized routes are unstable:

```
Router2#show ip route ospf
       172.16.0.0/24 is subnetted, 1 subnets
O IA    172.16.2.0 [110/140] via 10.1.1.2, 00:09:28, Serial0/0
O IA 172.20.0.0/16 [110/1692] via 10.1.1.2, 00:00:42, Serial0/0
O IA 172.25.0.0/16 [110/131] via 10.1.1.2, 00:00:25, Serial0/0
Router2#
```

In fact, the situation we just described, where the ABR adopts the lowest summarized cost for the summary route, is not the RFC standard method. This method was the standard in RFC 1583. But when OSPF was updated in RFC 2178 (and subsequently updated again in RFC 2328), the rule changed. In these newer versions of the OSPF standard, the rule is that the summary route should have the same cost as the highest cost summarized route.

Naturally, there is the potential to cause serious problems in OSPF networks if some routers use the RFC 1583 rule and others use the newer rule. So when the new standard came out, Cisco kept the old rule as the default, but included a command to allow you to easily change to the new standard:

```
Router1(config)#router ospf 55
Router1(config-router)#no compatible rfc1583
```

This command is available in IOS level 12.0 and higher. We recommend using caution when migrating a network from the old system of summarization to the new one. It is relatively common in OSPF networks to have several ABR routers to connect an area to area 0. If you changed one of these ABRs to use the new summarization method, it would automatically have a worse metric than any of the other ABRs. So all of the routers in the area would stop using the summary route pointing to this new style ABR in favor of the routes distributed by the remaining RFC 1583 ABRs. This has the potential to be extremely disruptive to a network, so you have to migrate all of the ABRs for an area at the same time.

You also have to remember that the issue we discussed earlier about the stability of the individual route with the best metric now switches to concern about the stability of the route with the worst metric.

It's interesting to look at these summary routes on the ABR, which is responsible for doing all of the summarization. The ABR also includes the summary routes, but they aren't real routes, so it simply points them to its Null0 interface. Cisco calls them *discard routes*. They help to prevent routing loops during summarization:

```
Router1#show ip route ospf
       172.20.0.0/16 is variably subnetted, 4 subnets, 4 masks
O        172.20.10.0/24 [110/1572] via 172.20.1.2, 00:07:42, Serial0/0.2
```

```
O        172.20.0.0/16 is a summary, 00:07:42, Null0
O          172.20.100.1/32 [110/1563] via 172.20.1.2, 00:07:42, Serial0/0.2
         172.25.0.0/16 is variably subnetted, 4 subnets, 3 masks
O          172.25.25.6/32 [110/11] via 172.25.1.7, 00:07:42, FastEthernet0/0.1
O        172.25.0.0/16 is a summary, 00:07:42, Null0
         10.0.0.0/8 is variably subnetted, 5 subnets, 4 masks
O          10.2.2.2/32 [110/1563] via 10.1.1.1, 00:07:42, Serial0/1
O        10.0.0.0/8 is a summary, 00:07:42, Null0
Router1#
```

Before IOS level 12.1(6), the only way to generate a discard route was to manually create a static route, such as:

```
Router1(config)#ip route 172.20.0.0 255.255.0.0 Null0
```

However, in IOS levels 12.1(6) and higher, this discard route is generated by default, and you don't need to create it. If you want to disable creation of the discard route, you can use the *no discard-route* command as follows:

```
Router1(config)#router ospf 55
Router1(config-router)#no discard-route internal
Router1(config-router)#no discard-route external
```

With the *internal* keyword, this command prevents the router from automatically generating discard routes for internal summary routes. And, similarly, the *external* keyword is for external routes. However, we urge caution with this command because the absence of a discard route can cause loops.

See Also

RFC 1583; RFC 2328

8.13   Disabling OSPF on Certain Interfaces

Problem

You want to prevent the some of a router's interfaces from taking part in OSPF.

Solution

The *passive-interface* configuration command effectively disables OSPF on an interface by preventing it from forming OSPF adjacencies:

```
Router3#configure terminal
Enter configuration commands, one per line.  End with CNTL/Z.
Router3(config)#router ospf 44
Router3(config-router)#network 0.0.0.0 255.255.255.255 area 100
Router3(config-router)#passive-interface Ethernet0
Router3(config-router)#exit
Router3(config)#end
Router3#
```

A useful variant of this command allows you to make all interfaces passive by default until you explicitly enable them:

```
Router3#configure terminal
Enter configuration commands, one per line.  End with CNTL/Z.
Router3(config)#router ospf 44
Router3(config-router)#network 0.0.0.0 255.255.255.255 area 100
Router3(config-router)#passive-interface default
Router3(config-router)#no passive-interface Ethernet0
Router3(config-router)#exit
Router3(config)#end
Router3#
```

Discussion

OSPF will not start to exchange any routing information until two routers on a segment have formed an adjacency and agreed on the various area parameters, including any authentication requirements. So simply preventing one router from taking part in this handshake is sufficient to prevent the exchange of OSPF information on the interface. Also, while you can use a *passive-interface* command as shown in the example, you can also prevent an interface from taking part in OSPF by just using more restrictive *network* commands. In the example, the *network* statement includes every possible route prefix, and consequently every IP-enabled interface. But you could just as easily use a network statement that restricts OSPF to a list of specific interfaces, as follows:

```
Router3#configure terminal
Enter configuration commands, one per line.  End with CNTL/Z.
Router3(config)#router ospf 44
Router3(config-router)#network 172.20.1.2 0.0.0.0 area 100
Router3(config-router)#network 172.20.10.1 0.0.0.0 area 100
Router3(config-router)#exit
Router3(config)#end
Router3#
```

Any interfaces that aren't explicitly included by a *network* statement will not take part in OSPF. On the other hand, sometimes a router can have a large number of interfaces, and you want all but one or two of them to take part in OSPF. In this case, it is more convenient to use *passive interface* commands.

To see the effect of this command, we'll look at a network both with and without the passive interface configured. Here is the neighbor list before configuring any passive interfaces:

```
Router3#show ip ospf neighbor

Neighbor ID     Pri  State      Dead Time   Address        Interface
172.20.220.1     1   FULL/BDR    00:00:39   172.20.10.2    Ethernet0
172.25.25.1      1   FULL/  -    00:00:37   172.20.1.1     Serial0.1
Router3#
```

Then, after making the Ethernet0 interface passive, the router drops all of the neighbor relationships on this interface. We are left with only one neighbor:

```
Router3#show ip ospf neighbor

Neighbor ID    Pri  State         Dead Time  Address      Interface
172.25.25.1      1  FULL/  -      00:00:38   172.20.1.1   Serial0.1
Router3#
```

Of course, this also affects any routes that point to neighboring routers through this interface. This is the routing table before configuring *Ethernet0* as passive:

```
Router3#show ip route ospf
     172.20.0.0/16 is variably subnetted, 5 subnets, 3 masks
O       172.20.220.1/32 [110/11] via 172.20.10.2, 00:00:02, Ethernet0
O       172.20.200.1/32 [110/11] via 172.20.10.2, 00:00:02, Ethernet0
O*IA 0.0.0.0/0 [110/3572] via 172.20.1.1, 00:00:02, Serial0.1
Router3#
```

With the passive interface configured, all of the corresponding routes are also gone:

```
Router3#show ip route ospf
O*IA 0.0.0.0/0 [110/3572] via 172.20.1.1, 00:01:53, Serial0.1
Router3#
```

In this case, the routes disappear completely because there is no other path through this network to reach these destination prefixes. If other paths did exist, then the routing table would still show the routes, but it would indicate that they are reachable through different interfaces.

The *passive-interface default* command has exactly the same effect as the *passive-interface* command, except that it forces you to explicitly enable any interfaces that you do want to send and receive OSPF packets by means of a *no passive-interface* command:

```
Router3(config)#router ospf 44
Router3(config-router)#network 0.0.0.0 255.255.255.255 area 100
Router3(config-router)#passive-interface default
Router3(config-router)#no passive-interface Ethernet0
Router3(config-router)#exit
Router3(config)#end
Router3#
```

The great advantage to this configuration is that, with a single *network* command, as we have shown here, you can force OSPF to exchange routing information about all of its interfaces, but only to send OSPF packets through a few interfaces. In many cases, this can greatly simplify your router configuration.

8.14   Changing the Network Type on an Interface

Problem

You want to change the default OSPF network type on an interface.

Solution

OSPF supports several different types of logical networks on interfaces. The default values are often exactly what you want, but it is sometimes useful to change them:

```
Router9#configure terminal
Enter configuration commands, one per line.  End with CNTL/Z.
Router9(config)#interface FastEthernet0/0
Router9(config-if)#ip ospf network ?
  broadcast            Specify OSPF broadcast multi-access network
  non-broadcast        Specify OSPF NBMA network
  point-to-multipoint  Specify OSPF point-to-multipoint network
  point-to-point       Specify OSPF point-to-point network

Router9(config-if)#
```

Discussion

Before altering the OSPF network type on an interface, it is useful to understand the differences between the different network types and what the defaults are. Table 8-3 shows the default OSPF network types for a variety of common media.

Table 8-3. OSPF default network types for several common media

Media type	Type or layer 2 encapsulation	Default OSPF network
Serial, ISDN, Async, Dialer	HDLC	Point-to-point
	PPP	Point-to-point
	LAPB	Point-to-point
	Frame Relay	Nonbroadcast
	ATM-DXI	Nonbroadcast
	X.25	Nonbroadcast
	SMDS	Nonbroadcast
ATM	N/A	Nonbroadcast
Point-to-point subinterface	Frame Relay, ATM, etc.	Point-to-point
Multipoint subinterface	Frame Relay, ATM, etc.	Nonbroadcast
Ethernet, FastEthernet, GigabitEthernet	N/A	Broadcast
Ethernet VLAN, Subinterface	ISL, dot1Q	Broadcast
Loopback	N/A	Loopback
Tunnel	N/A	Point-to-point

The configuration example in the Solutions section above shows the different available options that you can set on an interface:

```
Router9(config)#interface FastEthernet0/0
Router9(config-if)#ip ospf network ?
  broadcast            Specify OSPF broadcast multi-access network
  non-broadcast        Specify OSPF NBMA network
  point-to-multipoint  Specify OSPF point-to-multipoint network
  point-to-point       Specify OSPF point-to-point network
```

These four keywords control two main factors: whether or not the medium is capable of supporting broadcast or multicast packets, and whether it is necessary to elect a Designated Router (DR) for the network.

The *broadcast* keyword means that the network does support broadcasts, and that it requires a DR. In this case, because the routers can communicate by means of broadcasts (and implicitly also multicasts), they can make use of the well-known reserved OSPF multicast addresses 224.0.0.5 and 224.0.0.6. Traffic addressed to the first of these addresses is received by every OSPF router on the network segment. Traffic addressed to the latter address is received only by the DR and BDR.

Although the *broadcast* network type requires that all of the OSPF routers on the segment establish adjacencies with one another and that they elect a DR and BDR, they are able to do both of these actions automatically without further configuration.

The *nonbroadcast* keyword specifies that this network is Nonbroadcast Multiple Access (NBMA). This means that there could be several OSPF devices on the network, but that they cannot use the standard multicast addresses to communicate with one another. Because there are potentially several OSPF devices on the network, they must have a DR and a BDR for scalability reasons, but all OSPF packets between the routers must be unicast. As a result, with this network type, you will need to manually configure OSPF neighbors with the *neighbor* command.

To demonstrate the options, we will use a series of Frame Relay examples. For more information on Frame Relay, please refer to Chapter 10:

```
Router9#configure terminal
Enter configuration commands, one per line.  End with CNTL/Z.
Router9(config)#interface Serial0/0
Router9(config-if)#ip address 192.168.10.9 255.255.255.0
Router9(config-if)#encapsulation frame-relay
Router9(config-if)#frame-relay map ip 192.168.10.2 123 broadcast
Router9(config-if)#exit
Router9(config)#router ospf 1
Router9(config-router)#network 192.168.10.0 0.0.0.255 area 0
Router9(config-router)#neighbor 192.168.10.2
Router9(config-router)#exit
Router9(config)#end
Router9#
```

We also need to configure a corresponding neighbor command on the other router:

```
Router2(config)#router ospf 1
Router2(config-router)#network 192.168.10.0 0.0.0.255 area 0
Router2(config-router)#neighbor 192.168.10.9
```

Then these two routers are able to establish an OSPF adjacency:

```
Router9#show ip ospf neighbor

Neighbor ID     Pri   State       Dead Time   Address       Interface
192.168.15.3      1   FULL/BDR    00:01:43    192.168.10.2  Serial0/0
Router9#
```

In this case, because we have left the default OSPF network type for a Frame Relay interface, it is assumed to be nonbroadcast:

```
Router9#show ip ospf interface Serial0/0
Serial0/0 is up, line protocol is up
  Internet Address 192.168.10.9/24, Area 0
  Process ID 1, Router ID 172.19.2.1, Network Type NON_BROADCAST, Cost: 64
  Transmit Delay is 1 sec, State DR, Priority 1
  Designated Router (ID) 172.19.2.1, Interface address 192.168.10.9
  Backup Designated router (ID) 192.168.15.3, Interface address 192.168.10.2
  Timer intervals configured, Hello 30, Dead 120, Wait 120, Retransmit 5
    oob-resync timeout 120
    Hello due in 00:00:29
  Index 1/2, flood queue length 0
  Next 0x0(0)/0x0(0)
  Last flood scan length is 1, maximum is 1
  Last flood scan time is 0 msec, maximum is 0 msec
  Neighbor Count is 1, Adjacent neighbor count is 1
    Adjacent with neighbor 192.168.15.3  (Backup Designated Router)
  Suppress hello for 0 neighbor(s)
Router9#
```

If we change the OSPF network type to *point-to-multipoint*, the router will start to treat each Frame Relay PVC on the interface as a separate point-to-point link. In this case, there is no need for a DR or BDR, and we also don't need to manually configure the neighbors:

```
Router9(config)#interface Serial0/0
Router9(config-if)#ip address 192.168.10.9 255.255.255.0
Router9(config-if)#encapsulation frame-relay
Router9(config-if)#frame-relay map ip 192.168.10.2 123 broadcast
Router9(config-if)#ip ospf network point-to-multipoint
Router9(config-if)#exit
Router9(config)#router ospf 1
Router9(config-router)#network 192.168.10.0 0.0.0.255 area 0
Router9(config-router)#exit
```

Now the router is able to able to automatically find its neighbor:

```
Router9#show ip ospf neighbor

Neighbor ID     Pri   State       Dead Time   Address        Interface
192.168.15.3      0   FULL/  -    00:01:47    192.168.10.2   Serial0/0
Router9#
```

There is another option available for the point-to-multipoint network type. You will notice that we have deliberately configured the *broadcast* keyword on our *frame-relay map* command. This keyword tells the router to forward broadcast and multicast traffic across this PVC. This is necessary because the point-to-multipoint network type works like a collection of separate point-to-point networks, for which OSPF still uses the well known multicast address 224.0.0.5. If the individual PVCs were not capable of handling this multicast traffic, we would have to specify the additional *nonbroadcast* keyword on the *ip ospf network point-to-multipoint* command. If we do this, then we once again require the *neighbor* command because the neighboring routers are not able to discover one another without the multicast capability:

```
Router9(config)#interface Serial0/0
Router9(config-if)#ip address 192.168.10.9 255.255.255.0
Router9(config-if)#encapsulation frame-relay
Router9(config-if)#frame-relay map ip 192.168.10.2 123
Router9(config-if)#ip ospf network point-to-multipoint non-broadcast
Router9(config-if)#exit
Router9(config)#router ospf 1
Router9(config-router)#network 192.168.10.0 0.0.0.255 area 0
Router9(config-router)#neighbor 192.168.10.2
Router9(config-router)#exit
```

The only network type that we haven't yet discussed is the *point-to-point* option. This type of network doesn't require a DR or BDR, but it does require multicast packets to establish neighbor relationships. So, once again, if you have a medium that supports multicasts, the neighbors should find one another automatically; otherwise, you must manually configure OSPF *neighbor* commands on both routers.

Of the OSPF network types listed in Table 8-3, the Loopback interface stands out because it doesn't fit into any of the categories mentioned up until now. Cisco routers treat Loopback interfaces differently. By default, OSPF will advertise addresses on Loopback interfaces as /32 networks.

Naturally, there is never another OSPF device on the other end of a Loopback interface, so it doesn't matter whether or not it supports multicasts. And there will never be a requirement for a DR or BDR on this type of interface. But sometimes you want to use Loopback interfaces to advertise networks with longer prefixes. In this case, you can configure a point-to-point OSPF network type on the Loopback interface to force OSPF to advertise the network with the correct mask:

```
Router9(config)#interface Loopback0
Router9(config-if)#ip address 10.2.5.2 255.255.255.0
Router9(config-if)#ip ospf network point-to-point
Router9(config-if)#exit
Router9(config)#interface Loopback1
Router9(config-if)#ip address 10.2.6.2 255.255.255.0
Router9(config-if)#exit
```

Here you can see that the only difference between these two interfaces is that one of them has been configured with a point-to-point network type. And on another router, you can see the result:

```
Router3#show ip route ospf
     10.0.0.0/8 is variably subnetted, 2 subnets, 2 masks
O       10.2.6.2/32 [110/65] via 192.168.10.9, 00:00:02, Serial0/0.10
O       10.2.5.0/24 [110/65] via 192.168.10.9, 00:00:02, Serial0/0.10
Router3#
```

See Also

Chapter 10

8.15   OSPF Route Tagging

Problem

You want to tag specific routes to prevent routing loops during mutual redistributing between routing protocols.

Solution

You can tag external routes in OSPF by using the *redistribute* command with the *tag* keyword:

```
Router1#configure terminal
Enter configuration commands, one per line.  End with CNTL/Z.
Router1(config)#router ospf 55
Router1(config-router)#redistribute eigrp 11 metric-type 1 subnets tag 67
Router1(config-router)#exit
Router1(config)#end
Router1#
```

Discussion

Route tagging in OSPF is similar to route tagging in RIP Version 2 and EIGRP, which we discussed in Chapters 6 and 7, respectively. Just like those protocols, OSPF doesn't directly use the route tags. But they are useful when distributing routes into foreign routing protocols.

In the example configuration, this router, Router1, is an ASBR that connects to a network that uses EIGRP process number 11. We have configured this router so that it redistributes these EIGRP routes into OSPF as External Type 1 routes with a tag value of 67:

```
Router5#show ip route 10.2.2.0
Routing entry for 10.2.2.0/30
  Known via "ospf 87", distance 110, metric 45
  Tag 67, type extern 1
  Redistributing via ospf 87
  Last update from 172.25.1.5 on Ethernet0, 00:07:14 ago
  Routing Descriptor Blocks:
  * 172.25.1.5, from 172.25.25.1, 00:07:14 ago, via Ethernet0
      Route metric is 45, traffic share count is 1
Router5#
```

The tags become useful when you go to redistribute the tagged routes into another network. For example, the following configuration shows how we might redistribute this group of external routes into RIP, but no internal OSPF routes. This sort of configuration is useful if you want to allow the RIP and EIGRP external networks to talk to one another through your OSPF network, but prevent them from seeing your own routing tables:

```
Router1#configure terminal
Enter configuration commands, one per line.  End with CNTL/Z.
```

```
Router1(config)#router rip
Router1(config-router)#version 2
Router1(config-router)#redistribute ospf 87 route-map TAGGEDROUTES
Router1(config-router)#exit
Router1(config)#route-map TAGGEDROUTES permit 10
Router1(config-route-map)#match tag 67
Router1(config-route-map)#exit
Router1(config)#route-map TAGGEDROUTES deny 20
Router1(config-route-map)#exit
Router1(config)#end
Router1#
```

See Also

Chapter 6; Chapter 7

8.16 Logging OSPF Adjacency Changes

Problem

You want to monitor OSPF adjacency state changes to ensure network stability.

Solution

The *log-adjacency-changes* configuration command instructs the router to create a log message whenever two OSPF routers establish or break their adjacency relationship:

```
Router2#configure terminal
Enter configuration commands, one per line.  End with CNTL/Z.
Router2(config)#router ospf 12
Router2(config-router)#log-adjacency-changes
Router2(config-router)#exit
Router2(config)#end
Router2#
```

Discussion

No routes are exchanged between routers if they lose their adjacency relationship. Every time this relationship is lost, the corresponding routes are removed, and every router in the area must be updated with the new network topology. This can be quite disruptive to a network. So it can be extremely useful to log these changes for troubleshooting, as well as for reconstructing serious problems that occurred in the past. We recommend using this option.

Here are some example log messages. The first message shows that the adjacency has been lost due to an expired timer. This means that this router has not heard its neighbor's regularly scheduled "hello" messages recently, so it needs to delete its routes. A few minutes later, the neighbor has come back and reestablished its adjacency:

```
Oct 14 09:54:13: %OSPF-5-ADJCHG: Process 12, Nbr 172.25.25.1 on Serial0/0 from FULL
to DOWN, Neighbor Down: Dead timer expired
```

```
Oct 14 09:57:43: %OSPF-5-ADJCHG: Process 12, Nbr 172.25.25.1 on Serial0/0 from
LOADING to FULL, Loading Done
```

Starting in 12.1, Cisco added the keyword *detail*:

```
Router2#configure terminal
Enter configuration commands, one per line.  End with CNTL/Z.
Router2(config)#router ospf 12
Router2(config-router)#log-adjacency-changes detail
Router2(config-router)#exit
Router2(config)#end
Router2#
```

When you enable the detailed logging, you get considerably more information. It now shows all of the various stages that OSPF neighbors need to go through to establish their adjacencies:

```
%OSPF-5-ADJCHG: Process 12, Nbr 172.25.25.1 from FULL to DOWN, Neighbor Down: Dead
timer expired
%OSPF-5-ADJCHG: Process 12, Nbr 172.25.25.1 from DOWN to INIT, Received Hello
%OSPF-5-ADJCHG: Process 12, Nbr 172.25.25.1 from INIT to 2WAY, 2-Way Received
%OSPF-5-ADJCHG: Process 12, Nbr 172.25.25.1 from 2WAY to EXSTART, AdjOK?
%OSPF-5-ADJCHG: Process 12, Nbr 172.25.25.1 from EXSTART to EXCHANGE, Negotiation
Done
%OSPF-5-ADJCHG: Process 12, Nbr 172.25.25.1 from EXCHANGE to LOADING, Exchange Done
%OSPF-5-ADJCHG: Process 12, Nbr 172.25.25.1 from LOADING to FULL, Loading Done
```

This level of detail is rarely required unless you suspect that there is a problem with the handshake process between two routers. In that case, it might be more effective to use debugging as discussed in Recipe 8.21. We wouldn't normally recommend using the *detail* option in production networks because it just fills up the logs with extra messages. It is usually sufficient to know when two neighbors lost their adjacency and when they managed to reestablish it.

See Also

Recipe 8.21

8.17 Adjusting OSPF Timers

Problem

You want to change the default OSPF timers to improve stability or convergence behavior.

Solution

You can improve the convergence time of OSPF on a particular interface by reducing the hello and dead timers:

```
Router1#configure terminal
Enter configuration commands, one per line.  End with CNTL/Z.
```

```
Router1(config)#interface Serial0/1
Router1(config-if)#ip ospf hello-interval 5
Router1(config-if)#ip ospf dead-interval 20
Router1(config-if)#exit
Router1(config)#end
Router1#
```

If you make this change on one router, you must make it on all of the other routers sharing the same network segment:

```
Router2#configure terminal
Enter configuration commands, one per line.  End with CNTL/Z.
Router2(config)#interface Serial0/0
Router2(config-if)#ip ospf hello-interval 5
Router2(config-if)#ip ospf dead-interval 20
Router2(config-if)#exit
Router2(config)#end
Router2#
```

Discussion

OSPF uses two timers. The hello timer controls how often the router sends routine messages to its neighbors simply by indicating that it is still up. If the neighbors don't hear any hello messages for a length of time defined by the *dead-interval*, they assume that the router is no longer reachable and drop it from the adjacency table.

The default values are 10 seconds for the hello time, and 40 seconds for the dead time. The usual rule of thumb with OSPF is to keep the dead time value four times the hello interval. However, this is not a strict rule. EIGRP, for example, uses a dead time that is only three times its hello interval. So if you wanted OSPF to have convergence times that more closely matched those of EIGRP, you could set the OSPF hello time to 5 seconds, and the dead interval to 15 seconds. Bear in mind that shortening the hello timer will increase the amount of traffic on the link. And shortening the dead interval increases the chances of losing adjacency just because of network congestion or link errors.

It is important to adjust the timers on all routers on the network segment together. Unlike EIGRP, which allows every router to use a different set of timers, in OSPF, the routers cannot establish adjacencies if their timers do not match exactly. But you can adjust the timers separately on different interfaces on a router. So you can use slower timers on low bandwidth links, and faster timers on faster links. In general, we don't recommend increasing the timers from their default values, but it can be useful to decrease them to improve convergence on important high-speed segments.

You can see the new timers with the *show ip ospf interface* command:

```
Router2#show ip ospf interface Serial0/0
Serial0/0 is up, line protocol is up
  Internet Address 10.1.1.1/30, Area 2
  Process ID 12, Router ID 192.168.30.1, Network Type POINT_TO_POINT, Cost: 130
  Transmit Delay is 1 sec, State POINT_TO_POINT,
```

```
Timer intervals configured, Hello 5, Dead 20, Wait 20, Retransmit 5
  Hello due in 00:00:04
Index 1/1, flood queue length 0
Next 0x0(0)/0x0(0)
Last flood scan length is 1, maximum is 1
Last flood scan time is 0 msec, maximum is 0 msec
Neighbor Count is 1, Adjacent neighbor count is 1
  Adjacent with neighbor 172.25.25.1
Suppress hello for 0 neighbor(s)
Simple password authentication enabled
Router2#
```

Looking at the neighbor table, you can see that the dead time reflects the configuration change. Note that the time indicated in this output is the actual time remaining before OSPF declares this neighbor invalid. So if everything is working properly, this value show count down from the configured dead time value until the hello interval expires. Then another hello packet will be sent, and the dead timer will start over at its maximum value:

```
Router2#show ip ospf neighbor

Neighbor ID    Pri  State     Dead Time   Address     Interface
172.25.25.1      1  FULL/  -  00:00:19    10.1.1.2    Serial0/0
Router2#
```

See Also

Chapter 7

8.18 Reducing OSPF Traffic in Stable Networks

Problem

You have a stable network that doesn't require all of the overhead of LSA flooding.

Solution

You can reduce the overhead due to OSPF LSA flooding by applying the interface-level command *ip ospf flood-reduction*:

```
Router9#configure terminal
Enter configuration commands, one per line.  End with CNTL/Z.
Router9(config)#interface Serial0/0
Router9(config-if)#ip address 192.168.10.9 255.255.255.0
Router9(config-if)#ip ospf flood-reduction
Router9(config-if)#exit
Router9(config)#end
Router9#
```

Discussion

By default, OSPF will flood the area with all known LSAs every 3,600 seconds (1 hour). This is done as a sort of fail-safe to ensure that whatever else might happen to the LSA database, it will be corrected at least once an hour. In most networks this is unnecessary, as OSPF does a good job of forwarding LSA messages whenever there is a change in the network. But it is usually safe and may correct pathological conditions where one or more LSAs have been dropped in the network, which is why the designers of OSPF included the feature. However, if you are concerned about the bandwidth overhead on your network, and if your network is exceptionally stable, you can probably make do without this fail-safe feature. You can see the effect by looking at the *show ip ospf interface* command:

```
Router9#show ip ospf interface Serial0/0
Serial0/0 is up, line protocol is up
  Internet Address 192.168.10.9/24, Area 0
  Process ID 1, Router ID 172.19.2.1, Network Type POINT_TO_MULTIPOINT, Cost: 64

  Reduce LSA flooding.
  Transmit Delay is 1 sec, State POINT_TO_MULTIPOINT,
  Timer intervals configured, Hello 30, Dead 120, Wait 120, Retransmit 5
    oob-resync timeout 120
    Hello due in 00:00:17
  Index 1/2, flood queue length 0
  Next 0x0(0)/0x0(0)
  Last flood scan length is 1, maximum is 1
  Last flood scan time is 0 msec, maximum is 0 msec
  Neighbor Count is 1, Adjacent neighbor count is 1
    Adjacent with neighbor 192.168.15.3
  Suppress hello for 0 neighbor(s)
Router9#
```

This feature actually does two things. In addition to eliminating the standard, once-per-hour LSA flooding, it tells OSPF to send all LSAs with the DoNotAge bit set. This means that they will never be flushed out of the link state databases of downstream routers unless there is a topology change.

8.19 OSPF Virtual Links

Problem

You want to configure a virtual link between two routers to link up a fragmented Area.

Solution

Use the *area virtual-link* command to configure an OSPF virtual link between two routers:

```
Router9#configure terminal
Enter configuration commands, one per line.  End with CNTL/Z.
```

```
Router9(config)#router ospf 1
Router9(config-router)#area 10 virtual-link 10.54.0.1
Router9(config-router)#exit
Router9(config)#end
Router9#
```

Discussion

This feature is commonly used when an area has become fragmented and two routers need to tunnel their OSPF neighbor relationship across multiple links. This is usually not a problem if the two routers and the intervening networks are all in the same area. However, it can be a serious problem in particular if you have an ABR that is buried inside a nonbackbone area without a direct connection to area 0.

You can see the status of a virtual link with the *show ip ospf virtual-links* command:

```
Router9#show ip ospf virtual-links
Virtual Link OSPF_VL1 to router 10.54.0.1 is up
  Run as demand circuit
  DoNotAge LSA allowed.
  Transit area 10, via interface Serial0/0, Cost of using 74
  Transmit Delay is 1 sec, State POINT_TO_POINT,
  Timer intervals configured, Hello 10, Dead 40, Wait 40, Retransmit 5
    Hello due in 00:00:00
Router9#
```

There are a few tricks to this command. First, you must configure the virtual link command on both of the routers that you wish to connect. Second, the IP address that you configure in this command must be the OSPF router ID of the other router. This also means that you must make sure that you can *ping* this router ID address:

```
Router9(config)#router ospf 1
Router9(config-router)#area 10 virtual-link 10.54.0.1
```

And finally, the OSPF area indicated as the second field in the command is the area that the virtual link must pass through to reach the destination router. It needn't have anything to do with the fragmented area that you are trying to reconnect.

8.20   Viewing OSPF Status with Domain Names

Problem

You would prefer to view proper domain names rather than see the raw IP addresses in the output of your OSPF *show* commands.

Solution

You can configure OSPF to resolve IP addresses into router names with the following global configuration command:

```
Router3#configure terminal
Enter configuration commands, one per line.  End with CNTL/Z.
```

```
Router3(config)#ip ospf name-lookup
Router3(config)#end
Router3#
```

Discussion

When you configure OSPF name-lookup, the router will use its locally configured host table, if it has one, or DNS to resolve the names. If both are present, the router will check the local host table first. You can enable DNS on a router with the *ip domain-lookup* and *ip name-server* commands, as we discussed in Chapter 2.

Enabling name resolution can be useful when displaying information like OSPF neighbor tables. For example, if we look at the neighbor table without name-lookup enabled, we see IP addresses:

```
Router3#show ip ospf neighbor

Neighbor ID   Pri   State     Dead Time   Address       Interface
172.20.220.1   1    FULL/DR   00:00:34    172.20.10.2   Ethernet0
172.25.25.1    1    FULL/ -   00:00:31    172.20.1.1    Serial0.1
Router3#
```

But with name lookup, the router replaces the router IDs with names:

```
Router3#show ip ospf neighbor

Neighbor ID   Pri   State     Dead Time   Address       Interface
Router6        1    FULL/DR   00:00:37    172.20.10.2   Ethernet0
Router1        1    FULL/ -   00:00:36    172.20.1.1    Serial0.1
Router3#
```

The output will show an IP address rather than a name if the router can't resolve the address into a name, either because it can't reach the name server or because the name server doesn't include this address.

See Also

Recipe 8.8

8.21 Debugging OSPF

Problem

OSPF is not behaving properly, and you want to debug it to isolate and solve the problem.

Solution

There are several OSPF debugging options. But usually, if there is an OSPF problem, you will see it as instabilities in the neighbor relationships. So the most useful debugging option traces the formation of adjacencies.

```
Router3#debug ip ospf adj
OSPF adjacency events debugging is on
Router3#
```

Discussion

This particular debug output is particularly useful because it helps to diagnose problems when routers fail to form adjacencies with one another. For example, the following debug message indicates that there is an authentication problem. The neighbor router in this case is configured for MD5 authentication, while this router is configured for no authentication.

```
Dec 21 16:00:14.341: OSPF: Rcv pkt from 172.25.1.7, FastEthernet0/0.1 : Mismatch
Authentication type. Input packet specified type 2, we use type 0
```

## CHAPTER 9

BGP

9.0 Introduction

Border Gateway Protocol (BGP) Version 4 is the lifeblood of the Internet. It is responsible for exchanging routing information between all of the major Internet Service Providers (ISPs), as well between larger client sites and their respective ISPs. And in some large enterprise networks, BGP is used to interconnect different geographical or administrative regions.

Primarily to support the complexity of the public Internet, Cisco has added several clever and useful features to its BGP implementation. Because this book is focused on solutions to real-world problems, we will not try to describe all of these features. And it would take a whole book to describe how to operate BGP in a large ISP network, so we avoid discussing extremely large-scale BGP problems. Instead, we look at two main classes of BGP problems: connecting a network to the public Internet, and interconnecting two or more Interior Gateway Protocols (IGPs) in an Enterprise network.

A detailed discussion of the BGP protocol and its features is out of the scope of this book. For this type of information, we recommend referring instead to *IP Routing* by Ravi Malhotra (O'Reilly), or *BGP* by Iljitsch van Beijnum (O'Reilly). The current protocol definition is contained in RFC 4271 (January 2006), which provides several important updates from the original RFC 1771 (March 1995). We include a brief review of the most critical concepts.

BGP is an Exterior Gateway Protocol (EGP), which means that it exchanges routing information between Autonomous Systems (AS). This is different from pure IGPs, such as RIP, EIGRP, and OSPF, which we discussed in Chapters 6, 7, and 8, respectively. It also uses a different basic algorithm for building a loop-free topology than any of those protocols. RIP is a Distance Vector protocol, OSPF is a Link State protocol, and EIGRP is a Distance Vector protocol that incorporates many of the advantages of a Link State protocol. BGP, on the other hand, uses a Path Vector algorithm. This means that instead of reducing each route's relative importance in the routing table to a single metric or cost value, BGP keeps a list of every AS that the path passes through. It uses this list to eliminate loops because a router can check whether a route has already passed through a particular AS by simply looking at the path.

Basic Terminology

One of the most critical concepts in BGP is the Autonomous System (AS). RFC 1930 describes what the Internet Engineering Task Force (IETF), which is the official Internet standards organization, considers to be the Best Current Practices (BCP) for creating and numbering ASs. This document defines an AS as "a connected group of one or more IP prefixes run by one or more network operators which has a single and clearly defined routing policy." In practical terms, what appears on the Internet as a single AS may in fact represent an ISP as well as all of the customer networks of this ISP that aren't using BGP to advertise themselves as unique administrative domains.

A consistent routing policy in this context means that if a device on the edge of the AS advertises that it can handle routing for a particular set of prefixes, then all of the routers in the same AS can handle the same prefixes. It doesn't matter whether some of these prefixes refer to internal routes and others refer to external routes. What matters is that the routers inside the AS must agree with one another on how to handle each route, and which internal or external router is the best place to send traffic for this particular network. This is what it means for the AS to behave consistently.

It is important to note that this definition doesn't mean that there has to be one and only one IGP inside of an AS. In fact, there could be many IGPs, and there could even be no IGP. The interior routing inside of the AS could be handled entirely by a combination of BGP and static routes, for example.

BGP routers talk to one another over a permanent TCP connection on port 179. When BGP operates between two routers that are in the same AS, it is called Interior Border Gateway Protocol (iBGP). And when the peers are in different ASs, they use External Border Gateway Protocol (eBGP). Unless you are using one of the more complex features that were invented to improve scalability, all of the BGP routers in an AS must peer with one another in a complete mesh. This ensures that the AS behaves consistently when advertising routes to other ASs.

Synchronization is a concept that comes up frequently in BGP configurations. Because the AS needs to behave consistently, if you run an IGP and iBGP, they have to agree. Think of a network where the iBGP peers are several hops apart and the intervening network uses an IGP to communicate between them. Synchronization requires that for a BGP route to be useable, the IGP must also contain a route to the same prefix. This ensures that one of these BGP peer routers doesn't try to forward a packet to the other internal BGP peer unless the network connecting them knows what to do with this packet.

Cisco routers allow you to disable synchronization. This is actually necessary in any case when you don't redistribute the IGP routes into BGP. But then you have to make sure that your network design doesn't require the IGP to have access to the BGP routes in order to communicate between the iBGP peers.

Every discussion of BGP includes frequent references to IP *prefixes*. A prefix is a Classless Interdomain Routing (CIDR) block of addresses. We previously discussed CIDR in Chapter 5. CIDR is a set of rules for IP subnetting that allows you to summarize groups of IP addresses. For example, you might have four network segments that use the IP addresses 172.25.4.0/24, 172.25.5.0/24, 172.25.6.0/24, and 172.25.7.0/24. Each of these network addresses is a prefix. If, for example, you wanted to send a packet to the device 172.25.5.5/32, your router only needs to know how to route packets for 172.25.5.0/24. This route prefix includes the specific host address.

But you can go one step further than this. If the paths to all of these IP networks pass through the same router, it is often useful to summarize or aggregate the prefixes. The router that leads to all of these networks might simply advertise a single prefix, 172.25.4.0/22, which covers all of the individual networks.

Similarly, CIDR allows you to create *supernets* that summarize several *classful* networks. For example, you could summarize 172.24.0.0/16 through 172.31.0.0/16 as 172.24.0.0/13.

BGP requires that every AS must have a 16-bit Autonomous System Number (ASN). Because it is 16 bits long, the ASN can have any value between 0 and 65535.

The ASN is a globally unique identification number. BGP uses these ASNs to eliminate loops. Suppose two networks are using the same ASN. A router in the first AS will send out its routes normally, but the BGP router for the second network will drop these routes because they already appear to have passed through this AS. So it is important to ensure that you follow the standard rules for ASN selection, which are described in RFC 1930.

RFC 1930 originally divided up the range from 1 through 22,527 among the three major international Internet registry organizations (RIPE, ARIN, and APNIC) to allocate to networks connected to the public Internet. Since publication of that RFC, however, the IANA has distributed further blocks of numbers. Currently, as of the time of writing this book, over 35,000 ASNs have been assigned, with some 22,000 being advertised to the public Internet at any given time.

Just as RFC 1918 defines private unregistered ranges of IP addresses for networks that don't connect directly to the public Internet, RFC 1930 defines a series of private unregistered ASN values. You can use these private ASNs freely as long as they don't leak onto the public Internet. And, just as you can use NAT to hide your private IP addresses when you connect to the Internet, you can also hide private ASNs, as long as the AS that connects directly to the public Internet has a registered ASN and registered IP addresses.

All ASN values between 64,512 and 65,534 are designated for private use. This gives 1,023 ASN values that you can freely use in your internal network without registering, and without fear of conflict. If you use these private ASNs in an enterprise network, you must ensure that each private ASN is unique throughout the network. Enterprise networks that are large enough to require multiple ASs are generally managed by several different groups. So it is critical to coordinate the use of these private ASNs. If there is ever a conflict, with two ASs using the same ASN, it will disrupt routing to both of the conflicting ASs. And, if either of the conflicting ASs is used for transit, it could disrupt routing throughout the entire enterprise network, causing routing loops and unreachable networks. Each individual AS will continue to function normally internally, but traffic between ASs will behave unpredictably.

There are many situations when you can use unregistered ASNs. In fact, the only time you absolutely require a registered ASN is when you need to use BGP to exchange routing information with an ISP. Note that if you only have a single link to a single ISP, then you really don't require BGP at all. If you only have a single connection to the Internet, then you can get by with a single default route pointing to your ISP's router because everything passes through this one link. If the link goes down, there's nothing you can do anyway. So in this case, running BGP is overkill. A small router with a default route is more than adequate.

You should consult your ISP to discuss your options. They might also be willing to let you use BGP and a private ASN, which they will remove when passing your routes to the rest of the world. Or they may even be willing to let you run a simpler routing protocol such as RIPv2 to provide redundancy among two or more links that all use their network. In any case, your ISP will probably not pass your routes directly to the Internet anyway. It is more likely, and preferable, that they will allocate addresses to your network that are part of a range that they can summarize. Then the ISP will just pass a single routing entry to the rest of the Internet to represent many customer networks.

You can also do this kind of AS Path filtering internally. If you have several internal ASs, only one of which connects to the public Internet, then you can register the one directly connected ASN, and simply filter the private ASNs out of any path information that you pass to your ISPs. We show an example of this kind of filtering in Recipe 9.9.

Another special ASN value that bears mentioning is 65,535, which the IANA reserves for future requirements. RFC 1930, on the other hand, says that this ASN is part of the range that is freely available for unregistered use. We recommend avoiding this number because the IANA is the ultimate authority. Although there is currently no conflict with this number, the IANA may decide to give it some special significance later, which could break existing private networks that might use it.

 Throughout this chapter we will use private ASNs and private IP addresses in examples that are intended to represent the public Internet. This is purely for demonstration purposes. You must never allow these private values to reach the public Internet.

BGP Attributes

BGP associates several different basic attributes with each route prefix. These attributes include useful pieces of information about the route, where it came from, and how to reach it. *Well known attributes* must be supported by every BGP implementation. Some well known attributes are mandatory. All of the *mandatory attributes* must be included with every route entry. A BGP router will generate an error message if it receives a route that is missing one or more well known mandatory attributes.

There are also well known *discretionary attributes*, which every BGP router must recognize and support, but that don't have to be present with every route entry. Whenever a router passes along a route that it has learned via BGP to another BGP peer, it must include all of the well known attributes that came with this route, including any discretionary attributes. Of course, the router may need to update some of these attributes before passing them along, to include itself in the path, for example.

BGP routes can also include one or more *optional attributes*. These are not necessarily supported by all BGP implementations. Optional attributes can be either *transitive* or *nontransitive*, which is specified by a special flag in the attribute type field. If a router receives a route with a transitive optional attribute, it will pass this information along intact to other BGP routers, even if it doesn't understand the option. The router will mark the Partial bit in the attribute flags to indicate that it was unable to handle this attribute, however.

The router will quietly drop any unrecognized nontransitive optional attributes from the route information without taking any action.

We will now describe several of the most common BGP attributes.

ORIGIN—Well known, Mandatory
> This attribute can have one of three different values, reflecting how the BGP router that was responsible for originating the route first learned it. The possible values are:
> - 0—IGP: the route came from an IGP interior to the originating AS.
> - 1—EGP: the route came from an EGP other than BGP.
> - 2—Incomplete: any other method.

AS_PATH—Well known, Mandatory
> The AS_PATH is a list of ASNs, which show the path taken to reach the destination network. There are actually two types of AS_PATHs. An AS_SEQUENCE describes the literal path taken to reach the destination, while an AS_SET is an unordered list of ASNs along the path. Each time a BGP router passes a route update to an eBGP peer, it updates the AS_PATH variable to include its own ASN.

NEXT_HOP—Well known, Mandatory

This attribute carries the IP address of the first BGP router along the path to the destination network. When the router installs the route for the associated prefix in its routing table, it will use this attribute for the next hop router. This is where the router will forward its packets for this destination network.

By default, the NEXT_HOP router will be the router that announced this route to the AS. For routes learned from an external AS via eBGP, the NEXT_HOP router will be the first router in the neighboring AS. This information is passed intact throughout the AS by using iBGP, so all routers in the AS see the same NEXT_HOP router.

MULTI_EXIT_DISC—Optional, Nontransitive

The Multiple Exit Discriminatory (MED) option is also often called the BGP Metric. Because this 32-bit value is non-transitive, it is only propagated to adjacent ASs. Routers can use the MED to help differentiate between two or more equivalent paths between these ASs.

LOCAL_PREF—Well known, Discretionary

BGP only distributes Local Preference information with routes inside of an AS. Routers can use this number to allow the network to favor a particular exit point to reach a destination network. This information is not included with eBGP route updates.

ATOMIC_AGGREGATE—Well known, Discretionary

When a BGP router aggregates several route prefixes to simplify the routing tables that it passes to its peers, it usually sets the ATOMIC_AGGREGATE attribute to indicate that some information has been lost. It doesn't set this attribute, however, in cases in which it uses an AS_SET in its AS_PATH to show the ASNs of all of the different prefixes being summarized.

AGGREGATOR—Optional, Transitive

The AGGREGATOR attribute indicates that a router has summarized a range of prefixes. The router doing the route aggregation can include this attribute, which will include its own ASN and IP address or Router ID.

COMMUNITY—Optional, Transitive

A COMMUNITY is a logical grouping of networks. This attribute is defined in RFC 1997, and RFC 1998 describes a useful application of the concept to ISP networks.

MP_REACH_NLRI—Optional, Nontransitive

This attribute carries information about reachable multiprotocol destinations and next-hop routers. Multiprotocol in this context could refer to any foreign protocol, such as IPv6, although it is most commonly used with IP multicast, as we will discuss in Chapter 23. Multiprotocol Label Switching (MPLS) also uses MBGP for per-VPN routing tables.

Carrying foreign routing information this way ensures backward compatibility. Routers that don't support the extension can easily interoperate with routers that do.

MP_UNREACH_NLRI—Optional, Nontransitive

The MP_UNREACH_NLRI attribute is similar to the MP_REACH_NLRI, except that it carries information about unreachable multiprotocol destinations.

BGP has several other optional attributes as well, although we will not discuss them in this book. For more information, we suggest referring to *Internet Routing Architectures* by Sam Halabi and Danny McPherson (Cisco Press).

Route Selection

Unlike the various interior routing protocols that we discussed in the preceding chapters, BGP doesn't support *multipath* routing by default. So if there are two or more paths to a destination, BGP will go to great extremes to ensure that only one of them is actually used.

BGP decides which route to use by applying a series of tests in order. It is important to understand these tests and the order that the router looks at them, particularly when you are trying to influence which routes are used. Otherwise you might end up wasting a lot of time trying to adjust your routing tables by using one method, while the router is making the actual decision at some earlier step, and never seeing your adjustments.

Note that at each step, there may be several routes to the same destination prefix that all meet the requirement, or are equal after a particular test. In that case, BGP will proceed to the next test to attempt to break the tie.

We should point out that these are the route selection rules on Cisco routers. Several of these rules are not part of the BGP specification. So for nonCisco equipment, you should consult the vendor's BGP documentation to see what the differences are.

1. The first test is whether the next hop router is accessible. By default, routers do not update the next-hop attribute when exchanging routes by iBGP. So it is possible to receive a route whose next hop router is actually several hops away, and perhaps unreachable. BGP will not pass these routes to the main routing table, but it will keep them in its own route database.

2. If synchronization is enabled, the router will ignore any iBGP routes that are not synchronized.

3. The third test uses the Cisco proprietary *weight* parameter, selecting the route with the largest weight value. This parameter is not part of the routing protocol. Adjusting the weight of a particular route on a router will only affect route selection on this router. It is a purely local concept. The default weight value is zero,

except for locally sourced routes, which get a default weight of 32,768. The maximum possible weight is 65,535.

4. If the weights are the same, BGP then selects the route with the highest Local Preference value, from the LOCAL_PREF attribute. Routers only include this attribute when communicating within an AS (iBGP). For external routes, the router that receives a particular route via eBGP sets the Local Preference value. For internal routes, it is set by the router that introduced the route into BGP. This allows you to force every router in your AS to preferentially send traffic for a particular destination through a particular eBGP link.

5. Next, the router looks to see if any of the equivalent routes were originated locally on this router by either a *network* or an *aggregate* command, with those originated locally by a *network* command being preferred.

6. If two or more routes to the same destination network are still equal, the router moves on to look at the AS_PATH. This is the path vector that gives BGP its essential character. It is a set of AS numbers that describes the path to the destination network.

   A BGP router will prefer any routes that originate inside its own AS.

   For routes that originate outside of the AS, BGP will prefer the one with the shortest path (i.e., the one with the fewest ASNs). This is a simple indication of the most direct path.

7. BGP then looks at the ORIGIN attribute if the AS Path lengths are the same, and selects IGP routes in preference to EGP, and EGP in preference to INCOMPLETE routes. An INCOMPLETE route is one that is injected into BGP via redistribution, so BGP isn't able to vouch for its validity.

8. The next test looks at the Multiple Exit Discriminator (MED) and selects route with the lowest value. The MED is only used if both routes are received from the same AS, or if the command *bgp always-compare-med* has been enabled. With this command enabled, BGP will compare MED values even if they come from different ASs, although to reach this step the AS_PATHs must have the same length. Note that if you use this command at all, you should use it throughout the AS or you risk creating routing loops. MED values are only propagated to adjacent ASs, so routers that are further downstream don't see them at all.

9. BGP will prefer eBGP to iBGP paths. This helps to eliminate loops by ensuring that the route selected is the one that leads out of the AS most directly. Note that the iBGP routes don't include internal routes that are sourced from within your AS because they are selected at step number 5 above. So this test looks only at routes to external destinations.

10. The next test compares the IGP costs of the paths to the next hop routers and selects the closest one. This helps to ensure that faster links and shorter paths are used when possible.

11. Next, BGP will look at the ages of the routes and use the oldest route to a particular destination. This is an indication of stability. If two routes are otherwise equivalent, it is best to use the one that appears to be the most stable.

12. And finally, if the routes are still equivalent, BGP resorts to the router IDs of the next hop routers to break any ties, selecting the next hop router with the lowest router ID. Since router IDs are unique, this is guaranteed to eliminate any remaining duplicate route problems.

Note that there are subtle variations to these rules for special situations such as AS Confederations, and many individual rules can be disabled if you want the router to skip them.

Cisco has also implemented a *BGP Multipath* option that changes this route selection process somewhat. If you enable multiple path support, BGP will still perform the first seven tests, evaluating everything up to and including the MED values. But if two or more routes are still equivalent at this point, the router will install some or all of them, depending on how you implement this feature. Please refer to Recipe 9.8 for a discussion of this option.

9.1   Configuring BGP

Problem

You want to run BGP in a simple network.

Solution

In its simplest configuration, BGP exchanges routes between a router in one AS and another router in a different AS. The first router is in AS 65500:

```
Router1#configure terminal
Enter configuration commands, one per line.  End with CNTL/Z.
Router1(config)#interface Serial0
Router1(config-if)#ip address 192.168.55.6 255.255.255.252
Router1(config-if)#exit
Router1(config)#router bgp 65500
Router1(config-router)#network 192.168.1.0
Router1(config-router)#neighbor 192.168.55.5 remote-as 65501
Router1(config-router)#no synchronization
Router1(config-router)#exit
Router1(config)#end
Router1#
```

The second router is in AS 65501:

```
Router2#configure terminal
Enter configuration commands, one per line.  End with CNTL/Z.
Router2(config)#interface Serial0
Router2(config-if)#ip address 192.168.55.5 255.255.255.252
Router2(config-if)#exit
```

```
Router2(config)#router bgp 65501
Router2(config-router)#network 172.25.17.0 mask 255.255.255.0
Router2(config-router)#neighbor 192.168.55.6 remote-as 65500
Router2(config-router)#no synchronization
Router2(config-router)#exit
Router2(config)#end
Router2#
```

Discussion

This example shows two routers in different Autonomous Systems. Router1 is in AS 65500, and is configured to share routing information only for a single network using the command *network* 192.168.1.0. Because this is a classful network, we don't need to include a mask. However, you will notice that the syntax of the *network* command on Router2 is different:

```
Router2(config-router)#network 172.25.17.0 mask 255.255.255.0
```

This is because the routing information we want to share only includes 172.25.17.0/24, and not the entire classful network, 172.25.0.0/16.

The first thing you should do after configuring two routers for BGP is to ensure that they are able to establish a BGP connection. You can verify this with the command *show ip bgp summary*:

```
Router1#show ip bgp summary
BGP router identifier 192.168.99.5, local AS number 65500
BGP table version is 7, main routing table version 7
4 network entries and 4 paths using 484 bytes of memory
2 BGP path attribute entries using 196 bytes of memory
BGP activity 11/7 prefixes, 11/7 paths

Neighbor        V    AS MsgRcvd MsgSent   TblVer  InQ OutQ Up/Down  State/PfxRcd
192.168.55.5    4 65501      17      18        7    0    0 00:12:38            2
Router1#
```

Here you can see that Router1 has a BGP neighbor, 192.168.55.5, in AS 65501. The most critical detail here is the last column, State/PfxRcd. In this column, you will see either a word, indicating the state of the peer connection, or a number, indicating the number of routing prefixes (that is, the number of distinct subnets in the routing table) that have been received from this peer.

In this case, the router had a valid BGP session with the neighbor device, 192.168.55.5 for just over 12 minutes. If this session is broken for any reason, you will most likely see either the word "Active" or "Idle" in this field. The following output shows another peer device, 172.25.2.2, which is down:

```
Router1#show ip bgp summary
BGP router identifier 192.168.99.5, local AS number 65500
BGP table version is 7, main routing table version 7
4 network entries and 4 paths using 484 bytes of memory
2 BGP path attribute entries using 196 bytes of memory
BGP activity 11/7 prefixes, 11/7 paths
```

```
Neighbor          V    AS MsgRcvd MsgSent   TblVer  InQ OutQ Up/Down  State/PfxRcd
192.168.55.5      4 65501      17      18        7    0    0 00:12:38         2
172.25.2.2        4 65531     527     526        0    0    0 21:05:23 Active
Router1#
```

More than one engineer has seen the word "Active" (or "Connect") here and thought that the session was active. But, in fact it means that this peer relationship is currently down. The BGP connection is only up if you see a number in the last column. Note also that the word "Idle" in this column indicates that the router doesn't believe that a session is even possible with this peer device, or that it has not yet attempted to connect (the router will wait several seconds before attempting a connection). If the Idle condition persists, this usually indicates that the remote peer is unreachable. A persistent "Active" state, on the other hand, most likely indicates a configuration problem.

It often takes almost a minute to establish a BGP peer connection, so be patient if you don't see the peers immediately connect. If after this time they still have failed to connect, you should double check your "*neighbor*" configuration statements. Make sure that you have the right remote IP address and AS number, in particular. If these are correct, and you can ping the remote peer's IP address. Then you should make sure that the routers are using the interfaces that you think they are to reach the destination.

The example in the Solutions section of this recipe shows an eBGP peer relationship because we have configured different ASNs on the two routers:

```
Router1(config)#router bgp 65500
Router1(config-router)#neighbor 192.168.55.5 remote-as 65501
```

This shows that Router1 is in AS 65500, while Router2 is in AS 65501. You configure iBGP peers the same way, but the *neighbor* statement specifies the same ASN value as the *router bgp* statement. We can add a iBGP peer in AS 65500 as follows:

```
Router1#configure terminal
Enter configuration commands, one per line.  End with CNTL/Z.
Router1(config)#interface Ethernet0
Router1(config-if)#ip address 192.168.1.5 255.255.255.0
Router1(config-if)#exit
Router1(config)#router bgp 65500
Router1(config-router)#neighbor 192.168.1.6 remote-as 65500
Router1(config-router)#exit
Router1(config)#end
Router1#
```

And we would configure the other iBGP peer router like this:

```
Router3#configure terminal
Enter configuration commands, one per line.  End with CNTL/Z.
Router3(config)#interface Ethernet0
Router3(config-if)#ip address 192.168.1.6 255.255.255.0
Router3(config-if)#exit
Router3(config)#router bgp 65500
Router3(config-router)#neighbor 192.168.1.5 remote-as 65500
```

```
Router3(config-router)#exit
Router3(config)#end
Router3#
```

There is no need to establish a peer relationship between this new router and the eBGP peer, Router2. Router3 may connect to one or more other, completely different ASs, though. And there is nothing to prevent you from having an iBGP peer that doesn't connect to any eBGP peers. However, it is important to create a full mesh of iBGP relationships among all of the BGP routers inside any given AS.

BGP uses a permanent TCP connection between pairs of peer routers, and every peer relationship must be configured manually. This is actually one of the biggest strengths of BGP because it allows you to configure unique properties, such as unique filtering for each peer. With the various IGPs that we have already discussed, the routing peers generally discover one another dynamically by default.

However, the above examples only specify the destination IP address, not the source address. In this particular case, there is only one way to reach the destination, so there is no need to specify the source address, as the routers will simply use the IP address of the nearest interface. There are some cases where you do need to specify the source address, though.

For example, you might have two iBGP routers in your network, with several different possible paths between them. In this case, it would be better to configure the two routers to use their loopback addresses for the peer configuration, rather than the physical interfaces, which could go down. If you have redundant paths, you may as well use them. You could configure the router to use its loopback address for BGP as follows:

```
Router1#configure terminal
Enter configuration commands, one per line.  End with CNTL/Z.
Router1(config)#interface Ethernet0
Router1(config-if)#ip address 192.168.55.6 255.255.255.0
Router1(config-if)#exit
Router1(config)#interface Ethernet1
Router1(config-if)#ip address 192.168.56.10 255.255.255.0
Router1(config-if)#exit
Router1(config)#interface Loopback0
Router1(config-if)#ip address 172.21.19.1 255.255.255.255
Router1(config-if)#exit
Router1(config)#ip route 172.20.1.2 255.255.255.255 192.168.55.1
Router1(config)#ip route 172.20.1.2 255.255.255.255 192.168.56.1
Router1(config)#router bgp 65500
Router1(config-router)#neighbor 172.20.1.2 remote-as 65500
Router1(config-router)#neighbor 172.20.1.2 update-source Loopback0
Router1(config-router)#exit
Router1(config)#end
Router1#
```

Then, on the other router, you would have:

```
Router3#configure terminal
Enter configuration commands, one per line.  End with CNTL/Z.
```

```
Router3(config)#interface Ethernet0
Router3(config-if)#ip address 192.168.55.1 255.255.255.0
Router3(config-if)#exit
Router3(config)#interface Ethernet1
Router3(config-if)#ip address 192.168.56.1 255.255.255.0
Router3(config-if)#exit
Router3(config)#interface Loopback0
Router3(config-if)#ip address 172.20.1.2 255.255.255.255
Router3(config-if)#exit
Router3(config)#ip route 172.21.19.1 255.255.255.255 192.168.55.6
Router3(config)#ip route 172.21.19.1 255.255.255.255 192.168.56.10
Router3(config)#router bgp 65500
Router3(config-router)#neighbor 172.21.19.1 remote-as 65500
Router3(config-router)#neighbor 172.21.19.1 update-source Loopback0
Router3(config-router)#exit
Router3(config)#end
Router3#
```

Each of these routers uses the other's loopback IP address for its BGP *neighbor* statement. But to create a TCP session, you need the source address from one end to match the destination address of the other. So we have included commands to force each router to use their loopback interfaces for these source addresses:

```
Router1(config-router)#neighbor 172.20.1.2 update-source Loopback0
```

We strongly recommend using the **update-source** option, specifying a loopback interface on both routers, whenever you have redundant paths between iBGP peers.

So far, everything that we have discussed has to do with establishing the iBGP and eBGP peer relationships. We haven't exchanged any actual routing information yet. This brings us to the *network* commands in the example configuration files. On the first router, we used the classful version of the command to advertise an entire Class C network, 192.168.1.0/24:

```
Router1(config)#router bgp 65500
Router1(config-router)#network 192.168.1.0
```

The second router, however, uses the more general classless version of the *network* command:

```
Router2(config)#router bgp 65501
Router2(config-router)#network 172.25.17.0 mask 255.255.255.0
```

These commands allow the router to pick up routes out of its routing table and pass them along using BGP. BGP will not advertise anything that it doesn't have in its routing table. The first command will advertise the prefix 192.168.1.0/24 if it is in the routing table, while the second one will advertise 172.25.17.0/24. It is important to realize that these are literally the prefixes that BGP will advertise. If you have a route for 192.168.1.4/32, then the first *network* statement we mentioned will not cover it. Instead, you would have to explicitly include a *network* command for this prefix:

```
Router1(config)#router bgp 65500
Router1(config-router)#network 192.168.1.4 mask 255.255.255.255
```

You can also use redistribution to inject routes into BGP from either static routes or foreign routing protocols. As we discuss in Recipe 9.14, however, redistribution is messy and complicated. We strongly recommend against redistribution to introduce routes into BGP if it can be avoided.

Note that because BGP will only advertise a prefix if it is in the routing table, an unstable IGP route could introduce instability into BGP. You can ensure the route is always available, though, by using a floating static route pointing to the null interface:

```
Router1(config)#ip route 192.168.1.0 255.255.255.0 null0 250
```

Here we have specified an Administrative Distance of 250 for this route. This value is deliberately very high to ensure that it is worse than any IGP, as well as iBGP. Now when the dynamic route drops out of the IGP routing table, the router replaces it with this floating static route, and BGP continues to advertise the prefix. This is not always desirable, of course. You may want this BGP router to stop advertising routes that it cannot reach. But in most cases, stability is more important. See Recipe 5.5 for more information about floating static routes.

Looking back at the example in the Solutions section of this recipe, you will see that we disabled synchronization on both routers:

```
Router1(config)#router bgp 65500
Router1(config-router)#no synchronization
```

Synchronization is enabled by default. This feature is intended for situations in which your AS acts as a transit for packets from one AS to another, but where some of the routers in your AS do not run BGP. In this case, the routers that only run the IGP need to have the same routing table as the BGP routers, or the AS could become a black hole for the unsynchronized routes. If synchronization is enabled in this situation, BGP will only advertise routes that are present in both the IGP and BGP route tables.

In this example, we had no intention of carrying the BGP routing table through the IGP. We generally recommend disabling synchronization, unless you are running an IGP and redistributing routes between BGP and the IGP.

Take a close look at the examples in this recipe because they show how Cisco's BGP configuration syntax works. When you want to change the parameters for a particular peer, you must first define the neighbor and the AS that this peer resides in. Then you can start to define any nondefault behavior for this peer with further *neighbor* commands that specify the same peer IP address. There are literally dozens of different options you can adjust this way. We mention several of these options in this chapter.

See Also

Recipe 5.5; Recipe 9.2; Recipe 9.14

9.2   Using eBGP Multihop

Problem

You want to use BGP to exchange routes with an external peer router that is more than one hop away because the router at the edge of the network doesn't support BGP.

Solution

Cisco provides a useful option called eBGP Multihop, which allows you to establish eBGP peer relationships between routers that aren't directly connected to one another:

```
Router1#configure terminal
Enter configuration commands, one per line.  End with CNTL/Z.
Router1(config)#ip route 172.20.1.2 255.255.255.255 192.168.1.5 2
Router1(config)#router bgp 65500
Router1(config-router)#neighbor 172.20.1.2 remote-as 65530
Router1(config-router)#neighbor 172.20.1.2 update-source Loopback0
Router1(config-router)#neighbor 172.20.1.2 ebgp-multihop 3
Router1(config-router)#exit
Router1(config)#end
Router1#
```

Discussion

In this example, we have shown the configuration for only one of the routers, although you will need to configure the *ebgp-multihop* keyword for the corresponding peer device as well.

This feature isn't a standard part of the BGP protocol, but several router vendors implement it. The standard behavior requires eBGP routers to be adjacent to one another.

You might want to use this feature, for example, if the router at the edge of either your AS or the AS you are connecting to doesn't support BGP. The router will also need to have a route to the destination device because it is not directly connected. We have included a static route for this purpose.

The *ebgp-multihop* keyword takes an optional argument, which can be any integer between 1 and 255. This represents the maximum number of hops between this router and the neighbor, which is used in the TTL field of the IP packet when establishing the peer connection. If you don't specify *ebgp-multihop*, the router will assume that the peers are adjacent and use a TTL value of 1. However, if you specify this keyword without an argument, the router will default to a TTL value of 255.

Note that you can cause some seriously strange routing problems by using a high TTL value with this option. Suppose you have two ISPs, and your connection to one of them becomes unavailable. The routers could discover another path to one another, and re-establish their BGP peer relationship through the second ISP. This would cause extremely inefficient routing. You can avoid this problem by using static host routes, directing traffic for each peer router through the correct circuit.

In general, we recommend using the lowest possible value that still reaches the destination. However, RFC 3682 describes another extremely interesting way of using this feature to improve security. The idea is that the only way that a packet can reach its destination with a TTL value of 254 or 255 is if the source is adjacent to the destination. If a more distant device were to attempt a BGP spoofing attack, the packets would arrive with a lower TTL value unless the attacker was also on a physically adjacent network.

So this reference suggests deliberately configuring your routers to use the highest possible TTL value. Then the routers would check the TTL value and discard any BGP packets with a TTL of less than 254. Cisco implemented this feature in IOS Version 12.3(7)T:

```
Router1#configure terminal
Enter configuration commands, one per line.  End with CNTL/Z.
Router1(config)#router bgp 65500
Router1(config-router)#neighbor 192.168.55.5 remote-as 65501
Router1(config-router)#neighbor 192.168.55.5 ttl-security hops 1
Router1(config-router)#exit
Router1(config)#end
Router1#
```

If the peer device is running an older IOS that doesn't support this feature and is an eBGP peer, you can simply use the *ebgp-multihop* command to specify an initial TTL of 255:

```
Router2#configure terminal
Enter configuration commands, one per line.  End with CNTL/Z.
Router2(config)#router bgp 65501
Router2(config-router)#bgp log-neighbor-changes
Router2(config-router)#neighbor 192.168.55.6 remote-as 65500
Router2(config-router)#neighbor 192.168.55.6 ebgp-multihop 255
Router2(config-router)#exit
Router2(config)#end
Router2#
```

However, you cannot configure the *ttl-security* option for one peer and use the *ebgp-multihop* option for this same peer:

```
Router1(config)#router bgp 65500
Router1(config-router)#neighbor 192.168.100.1 ebgp-multihop 1
Remove ttl-security before configuring ebgp-multihop
Router1(config-router)#
```

You can also configure *ttl-security* for iBGP peers:

```
Router1(config)#router bgp 65500
Router1(config-router)#neighbor 192.168.100.2 remote-as 65500
Router1(config-router)#neighbor 192.168.100.2 ttl-security hops 1
```

However, while this is a useful feature, it is still not as secure as using MD5 authentication to secure your BGP peers. We discuss this method in Recipe 9.16.

See Also

Recipe 9.16; RFC 3682 by V. Gill et al., February 2004

9.3 Adjusting the Next-Hop Attribute

Problem

You want to change the next-hop attribute on routes while distributing them via iBGP so that the routes always point to a next-hop address that is inside your AS.

Solution

By default, the value of the next-hop attribute for an external route is the IP address of the external BGP router that announced this route to the AS. You can change this behavior so that the next-hop router is an internal router instead by using the *next-hop-self* command:

```
Router1#configure terminal
Enter configuration commands, one per line.  End with CNTL/Z.
Router1(config)#router bgp 65500
Router1(config-router)#neighbor 192.168.1.6 remote-as 65500
Router1(config-router)#neighbor 192.168.1.6 next-hop-self
Router1(config-router)#exit
Router1(config)#end
Router1#
```

Discussion

The next-hop attribute for a route depends on which router announces it. When a router passes route information to a peer in a different AS (using eBGP), it will generally update the next-hop attribute with its own IP address. However, by default iBGP peers will not change this attribute. For internal routes, the next-hop attribute will be the IP address of the router that sourced the internal route into BGP.

The result is that all of the routers inside of an AS will see the same external device as the next-hop BGP router, even if that router is actually several physical hops away. The following output shows the BGP table of one of the routers in our AS before we specified the *next-hop-self* command. All of the next-hop addresses correspond to routers in other ASs:

```
Router2#show ip bgp
BGP table version is 10, local router ID is 11.5.5.1
Status codes: s suppressed, d damped, h history, * valid, > best, i - internal
Origin codes: i - IGP, e - EGP, ? - incomplete
```

```
   Network          Next Hop        Metric LocPrf Weight Path
<routes delete for brevity>
*>i172.22.1.0/24    172.25.1.7           0    100      0 65510 ?
* i172.24.0.0        172.22.1.3           0    100      0 ?
* i172.25.0.0        172.22.1.3           0    100      0 i
*>i172.25.2.0/30    172.25.1.7           0    100      0 65510 ?
*>i172.20.0.0/14    172.20.1.2                100      0 65530 65501 ?
```

This can cause serious routing problems if this router doesn't know how to reach one of these next hop routers. And this is actually a distinct possibility because for all external routes, these next-hop IP addresses will be in a different AS. Unless you use static routes or take pains to ensure that the IGP distributes all of these addresses, the other iBGP routers will not have a route to the next hop.

As we mentioned in the Introduction to this chapter, the first thing that BGP checks when looking at BGP routes is whether the next hop router is reachable. Even if BGP didn't do this check, a route that has an unreachable next hop router clearly is not going to be very useful.

However, you can use the *next-hop-self* command to configure a router to insert its own IP address in the next-hop attribute when passing routes to another router via iBGP:

```
Router1(config)#router bgp 65500
Router1(config-router)#neighbor 192.168.1.6 remote-as 65500
Router1(config-router)#neighbor 192.168.1.6 next-hop-self
```

Then the next-hop of every route in the route table is guaranteed to be accessible:

```
Router2#show ip bgp
BGP table version is 10, local router ID is 11.5.5.1
Status codes: s suppressed, d damped, h history, * valid, > best, i - internal
Origin codes: i - IGP, e - EGP, ? - incomplete

   Network          Next Hop        Metric LocPrf Weight Path
<routes delete for brevity>
*>i172.22.1.0/24    192.168.1.6          0    100      0 65510 ?
* i172.24.0.0        192.168.1.6          0    100      0 ?
* i172.25.0.0        192.168.1.6          0    100      0 i
*>i172.25.2.0/30    192.168.1.6          0    100      0 65510 ?
*>i172.20.0.0/14    192.168.1.6               100      0 65530 65501 ?
```

You can also configure this keyword for an eBGP peer, but it has no effect.

Note that you can also construct a route map to manually set the *next-hop* attribute to any IP address that you like. However, we don't recommend doing this, as it too easy to make a mistake and forward routes with unreachable next-hop routers.

9.4   Connecting to Two ISPs

Problem

You want to set up BGP to support two redundant Internet connections.

Solution

The following configuration shows how to make the basic BGP connections, but it has serious problems that we will show how to fix in other recipes in this chapter:

```
Router1#configure terminal
Enter configuration commands, one per line.  End with CNTL/Z.
Router1(config)#interface Serial0
Router1(config-if)#description connection to ISP #1, ASN 65510
Router1(config-if)#ip address 192.168.1.6 255.255.255.252
Router1(config-if)#exit
Router1(config)#interface Serial1
Router1(config-if)#description connection to ISP #2, ASN 65520
Router1(config-if)#ip address 192.168.2.6 255.255.255.252
Router1(config-if)#exit
Router1(config)#interface Ethernet0
Router1(config-if)#description connection to internal network, ASN 65500
Router1(config-if)#ip address 172.18.5.2 255.255.255.0
Router1(config-if)#exit
Router1(config)#router bgp 65500
Router1(config-router)#network 172.18.5.0 mask 255.255.255.0
Router1(config-router)#neighbor 192.168.1.5 remote-as 65510
Router1(config-router)#neighbor 192.168.2.5 remote-as 65520
Router1(config-router)#no synchronization
Router1(config-router)#exit
Router1(config)#end
Router1#
```

 We do not recommend using this configuration as printed for a real Internet connection because it leaves out several key components. A more complete example is shown in Recipe 9.19.

Discussion

Perhaps the most common BGP application involves connecting a single router to two different ISPs to share information about a single /24 IP address range. A setup like this is the simplest way of building a redundant Internet connection. You can improve this redundancy by using two routers, one for each ISP connection, as shown in Recipe 9.5. Figure 9-1 shows the connections used in this recipe.

This example shows the configuration for the router at the customer site. The customer network uses ASN 65500, while the two ISPs use 65510 and 65520, respectively. Both of these connections are made through serial connections.

This configuration is a simple extension of the one shown in Recipe 9.1. The main difference is that we have set up two different peers, both in different ASs. This router is configured to distribute routing information for its 172.18.5.0/24 segment with both ISPs, and to receive their routing tables.

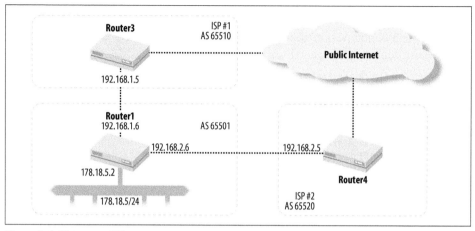

Figure 9-1. Using two ISPs

There are two critical problems with this simple configuration. First, the full Internet routing table is extremely large and consumes a vast amount of memory, so we will probably want to do some filtering. The second problem is that this configuration allows your network to act as a transit path between the two ISPs, which you probably don't want in practice.

The full Internet routing table has roughly 187,000 prefixes, a number that grows over time. Each BGP route entry consumes somewhere between 100 and 200 bytes of memory on the router, and you wouldn't use BGP unless there were at least two ISPs, each of which will likely supply a similar sized routing table, doubling the memory requirement. Then, if the router puts all of these prefixes into its main routing table, as well as the CEF table, you can wind up consuming as much as 1KB of router memory per route prefix. So we don't recommend using a router with less than 100 MB of memory when connecting to the Internet without significant filtering. In fact, Internet backbone routers frequently have hundreds of megabytes of memory.

Here is a typical routing summary taken from a BGP route server:

```
route-server>show ip route summary
IP routing table name is Default-IP-Routing-Table(0)
Route Source    Networks    Subnets    Overhead    Memory (bytes)
connected       0           3          272         480
static          2           9          704         1760
ospf 2          0           2          128         320
   Intra-area: 2 Inter-area: 0 External-1: 0 External-2: 0
   NSSA External-1: 0 NSSA External-2: 0
bgp 65000       115207      70435      11881088    29713940
   External: 185642 Internal: 0 Local: 0
internal        1808                               2133440
Total           117017      70449      11882192    31849940
route-server>
```

As you can see here, this router's routing table consumes most of the over 31 MB of system memory. The same device uses roughly 29 MB of memory just for its BGP table, as you can see from the following output:

```
route-server>show ip bgp summary
BGP router identifier 10.1.2.5, local AS number 65000
BGP table version is 283729, main routing table version 283729
185761 network entries using 18761861 bytes of memory
3529036 path entries using 169393728 bytes of memory
44183 BGP path attribute entries using 2474248 bytes of memory
40017 BGP AS-PATH entries using 1041908 bytes of memory
4 BGP community entries using 96 bytes of memory
0 BGP route-map cache entries using 0 bytes of memory
0 BGP filter-list cache entries using 0 bytes of memory
BGP using 191671841 total bytes of memory
Dampening enabled. 1637 history paths, 559 dampened paths
185644 received paths for inbound soft reconfiguration
BGP activity 186953/1192 prefixes, 3559638/30597 paths, scan interval 60 secs

<information deleted for brevity>

route-server>
```

This represents a 45 percent increase in memory requirements since we wrote the first edition of this book, just a few years ago!

We will discuss BGP route servers in more detail in Recipe 9.19.

Fixing the transit problem is somewhat easier than the route filtering that is necessary to reduce the size of the Internet route tables. To prevent the external networks from using your network for transit, you simply have to ensure that you never pass BGP routing information that you learn from one ISP over to the other ISP. This way neither ISP will know that it can reach the other through your network, so they won't send their traffic this way.

The easiest way to accomplish this is to put a filter on the AS Path. In the following example, we will apply the same filter to both BGP peers. This filter will force our router to advertise only local routes. Any route that already has an entry in its AS Path must have come from somewhere else, so we prevent the router from forwarding these routes. The router will add its own ASN to the AS Path only after doing this filter processing, so the local routes will still be sent out:

```
Router1#configure terminal
Enter configuration commands, one per line.  End with CNTL/Z.
Router1(config)#ip as-path access-list 15 permit ^$
Router1(config)#router bgp 65500
Router1(config-router)#network 172.18.5.0 mask 255.255.255.0
Router1(config-router)#neighbor 192.168.1.5 remote-as 65510
Router1(config-router)#neighbor 192.168.1.5 filter-list 15 out
Router1(config-router)#neighbor 192.168.2.5 remote-as 65520
Router1(config-router)#neighbor 192.168.2.5 filter-list 15 out
Router1(config-router)#exit
```

```
Router1(config)#end
Router1#
```

Please refer to Recipe 9.10 for more information about how to use AS filters.

Before you can solve the problem of the large size of the Internet routing tables, you have to make some decisions about how you want your Internet connections to work. Specifically, you might want one of these ISPs to be the primary and the other the backup for all traffic. Alternatively, you might want to just use the first ISP to handle traffic for its directly connected customers, while the second ISP handles everything else. Or you could opt to have load sharing between the two ISPs. These options are discussed in Recipes 9.7, 9.8, and 9.19.

You should also think about whether you want to control which path inbound traffic uses to reach you. If one of your ISP links has a large usage charge, you might prefer to force all of the inbound traffic through the other link. This can be slightly tricky because you don't directly control the ISP routers. But you can control how your routing information looks to the ISP. Techniques for doing this are discussed in Recipes 9.13 and 9.19.

See Also

Recipe 9.5; Recipe 9.7; Recipe 9.8; Recipe 9.10; Recipe 9.13; Recipe 9.19

9.5 Connecting to Two ISPs with Redundant Routers

Problem

You want to connect your network to two different ISPs using two routers to eliminate any single points of failure.

Solution

In this example, we have two routers in our AS, which has ASN 65500. The first router has a link to the first ISP, whose ASN is 65510:

```
Router1#configure terminal
Enter configuration commands, one per line.  End with CNTL/Z.
Router1(config)#interface Serial0
Router1(config-if)#description connection to ISP #1, ASN 65510
Router1(config-if)#ip address 192.168.1.6 255.255.255.252
Router1(config-if)#exit
Router1(config)#interface Ethernet0
Router1(config-if)#description connection to internal network, ASN 65500
Router1(config-if)#ip address 172.18.5.2 255.255.255.0
Router1(config-if)#exit
Router1(config)#ip as-path access-list 15 permit ^$
Router1(config)#router bgp 65500
Router1(config-router)#network 172.18.5.0 mask 255.255.255.0
Router1(config-router)#neighbor 172.18.5.3 remote-as 65500
```

```
Router1(config-router)#neighbor 172.18.5.3 next-hop-self
Router1(config-router)#neighbor 192.168.1.5 remote-as 65510
Router1(config-router)#neighbor 192.168.1.5 filter-list 15 out
Router1(config-router)#no synchronization
Router1(config-router)#exit
Router1(config)#end
Router1#
```

Then the second router connects to the second ISP, which uses ASN 65520. And because these two routers are both members of the same AS, they also must have an iBGP connection:

```
Router2#configure terminal
Enter configuration commands, one per line.  End with CNTL/Z.
Router2(config)#interface Serial1
Router2(config-if)#description connection to ISP #2, ASN 65520
Router2(config-if)#ip address 192.168.2.6 255.255.255.252
Router2(config-if)#exit
Router2(config)#interface Ethernet0
Router2(config-if)#description connection to internal network, ASN 65500
Router2(config-if)#ip address 172.18.5.3 255.255.255.0
Router2(config-if)#exit
Router2(config)#ip as-path access-list 15 permit ^$
Router2(config)#router bgp 65500
Router2(config-router)#network 172.18.5.0 mask 255.255.255.0
Router2(config-router)#neighbor 192.168.2.5 remote-as 65520
Router2(config-router)#neighbor 192.168.2.5 filter-list 15 out
Router2(config-router)#neighbor 172.18.5.2 remote-as 65500
Router2(config-router)#neighbor 172.18.5.2 next-hop-self
Router2(config-router)#no synchronization
Router2(config-router)#exit
Router2(config)#end
Router2#
```

Discussion

This recipe is similar to Recipe 9.4, but here we have split the functions across two routers to ensure that you can sustain a link failure or a router failure without losing your Internet connection. Figure 9-2 shows the new network topology.

The main difference is that we have had to configure an eBGP link from each router to its ISP, as well as an iBGP link between the two routers. Note that we have included the same AS Path filter on both routers to ensure that our network doesn't allow transit routing from one ISP to the other.

However, just as in the single router example, you have to decide how you want to deal with the problem of the excessive number of routes that you will receive from both of these ISPs.

Notice we have included the *next-hop-self* option for the iBGP peers on both routers:

```
Router1(config)#router bgp 65500
Router1(config-router)#neighbor 172.18.5.3 remote-as 65500
Router1(config-router)#neighbor 172.18.5.3 next-hop-self
```

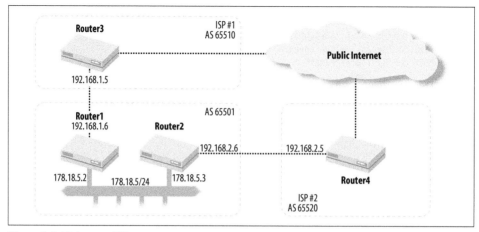

Figure 9-2. Using two ISPs

Without this option, the next hop IP address for prefixes learned through Router1 will be the ISP connected to Router1. But even in this simple network, Router2 will not have a route to this next hop address. We could also get around this problem by including static routes on both routers. We discuss the *next-hop-self* option in more detail in Recipe 9.3.

In this example, we only have two routers inside our AS. You could add more, using exactly the same configuration commands that we used here. However, you need to remember to create a full mesh of iBGP peer relationships between all of these routers. Every BGP router must have a *neighbor* statement connecting to every other BGP router in the same AS.

See Also

Recipe 9.3; Recipe 9.4

9.6 Restricting Networks Advertised to a BGP Peer

Problem

You want to restrict which routes your router advertises to another AS.

Solution

There are three ways to filter routes in BGP. The first one uses extended access lists and route maps, as follows:

```
Router1#configure terminal
Enter configuration commands, one per line.  End with CNTL/Z.
Router1(config)#access-list 105 deny ip host 172.25.0.0 host 255.255.0.0
Router1(config)#access-list 105 permit ip any any
```

```
Router1(config)#route-map ACL-RT-FILTER permit 10
Router1(config-route-map)#match ip address 105
Router1(config-route-map)#exit
Router1(config)#route-map ACL-RT-FILTER deny 20
Router1(config-route-map)#exit
Router1(config)#router bgp 65500
Router1(config-router)#neighbor 192.168.1.5 remote-as 65510
Router1(config-router)#neighbor 192.168.1.5 route-map ACL-RT-FILTER in
Router1(config-router)#exit
Router1(config)#end
Router1#
```

The second method uses a *distribute-list*:

```
Router1#configure terminal
Enter configuration commands, one per line.  End with CNTL/Z.
Router1(config)#access-list 106 deny ip host 172.25.0.0 host 255.255.0.0
Router1(config)#access-list 106 permit ip any any
Router1(config)#router bgp 65500
Router1(config-router)#neighbor 192.168.1.5 remote-as 65510
Router1(config-router)#neighbor 192.168.1.5 distribute-list 106 in
Router1(config-router)#exit
Router1(config)#end
Router1#
```

But the most common way to filter routes in BGP is to use prefix lists. The following example has a similar effect the preceding ones:

```
Router1#configure terminal
Enter configuration commands, one per line.  End with CNTL/Z.
Router1(config)#ip prefix-list PREFIX-FILTER seq 10 deny 172.25.0.0/16
Router1(config)#ip prefix-list PREFIX-FILTER seq 20 permit 0.0.0.0/0 le 32
Router1(config)#router bgp 65500
Router1(config-router)#neighbor 192.168.1.5 remote-as 65510
Router1(config-router)#neighbor 192.168.1.5 prefix-list PREFIX-FILTER in
Router1(config-router)#exit
Router1(config)#end
Router1#
```

Discussion

In all of these examples, the router will suppress the route 172.25.0.0/16 from its BGP route table if it is received from the eBGP peer, 192.168.1.5. The first example uses route maps, the second one uses a distribute list, and the third uses prefix lists. Examples of route maps and access lists appear throughout this book, so they should already be somewhat familiar to the reader. You can use them for a variety of different applications, such as adjusting route tags, Local Preference, and BGP Weight values. Here we just use the route map to look at the incoming routes from a peer device and reject certain routes.

The access list in the first example uses a "deny" clause to suppress the unwanted route, and ends with a "permit" command to allow all other routes to pass normally:

```
Router1(config)#access-list 105 deny ip host 172.25.0.0 host 255.255.0.0
Router1(config)#access-list 105 permit ip any any
```

Then the route map uses this access list to define which routes are permitted to pass:

```
Router1(config)#route-map ACL-RT-FILTER permit 10
Router1(config-route-map)#match ip address 105
```

Then we have added an explicit deny all clause to the route map that simply rejects anything that the first clause hasn't matched:

```
Router1(config-route-map)#route-map ACL-RT-FILTER deny 20
Router1(config-route-map)#exit
```

Note that every route map ends with an implicit deny all clause, so this was not strictly necessary. But it does make our intentions more clear to the next person who reads this router configuration.

For the distribute list example, we have created a normal access list that specifies the routes that are to be either included or excluded from the distribution. This is almost identical to the route map technique that we discussed for RIP and EIGRP in Chapters 6 and 7, respectively.

Note also the rather odd construction of the extended access lists in both the route map and the distribute list examples. As we discuss in Chapter 19, the first address and wildcard pair usually refers to the source, and the second set refers to the destination. But in this case, we are actually trying to match specific route prefixes, and not source and destination addresses, so the meanings are somewhat different. When filtering routes with extended ACLs, the first address defines the prefix, while the second part of the ACL defines the length of the prefix. This particular ACL matches the prefix 172.25.0.0/16:

```
Router1(config)#access-list 105 permit ip host 172.25.0.0 host 255.255.0.0
```

If we had wanted to match the prefix 172.25.0.0/24 instead, we could have used an ACL that looks like this:

```
Router1(config)#access-list 105 permit ip host 172.25.0.0 host 255.255.255.0
```

Note that you can also use standard ACLs for route filtering, but the results can be a little strange. Suppose we had used this ACL instead of the one we discussed above:

```
Router1(config)#access-list 5 permit 172.25.0.0
```

This will match 172.25.0.0/16. But it doesn't specify the length of the prefix. So it will also match, for example, 172.25.0.0/24, if it exists. But it doesn't include any of the other subnets of 172.25.0.0/16, such as 172.25.1.0/24. We don't recommend using standard ACLs for route filtering because of this strange behavior.

Because it is so easy to get confused when using ACLs for matching prefixes, most people now prefer to use prefix lists instead.

Prefix lists provide another way of doing the same kind of filtering. But it is often considerably easier to create useful filters with prefix lists because they were designed specifically for this purpose. Look at the prefix list in the example:

```
Router1(config)#ip prefix-list PREFIX-FILTER seq 10 deny 172.25.0.0/16
Router1(config)#ip prefix-list PREFIX-FILTER seq 20 permit 0.0.0.0/0 le 32
```

The first line of this list rejects the prefix 172.25.0.0/16. The second line explicitly allows all other prefixes. Notice that there is a sequence number in each line, specified by the argument of the *seq* keyword. This provides a convenient way of either inserting or removing new lines in the middle of a prefix list, as well as at the beginning or the end.

We suggest that you space these numbers in steps of 10, as we have done here, so that you can easily add lines. If you use a smaller step size between sequence numbers, you might find that there isn't enough room to add new rules. When this happens, you will have to delete the entire set of rules and re-enter the commands with new sequence numbers.

Prefix lists show their real power when you want to deal with subnets. For example, suppose what you actually wanted to do was reject all of the subnets of 172.25.0.0/16, while allowing a single summary route for the entire network. You could do this with the following prefix list:

```
Router1(config)#ip prefix-list PRE-RTFILTER seq 10 deny 172.25.0.0/16 ge 17
Router1(config)#ip prefix-list PRE-RTFILTER seq 20 permit 0.0.0.0/0 le 32
```

The first line rejects any subnets of 172.25.0.0/16 that have a prefix length of 17 bits or longer. So this would include, for example, 172.25.15.8/30, 172.25.100.0/24, and 172.25.252.0/22. But this rule does not suppress the summary route, 172.25.0.0/16, itself because it has a prefix length of only 16 bits. The rule only rejects prefixes that are 17 or more bits long.

This also helps to clarify the meaning of the second line of the prefix list. This line looks at any subnets of 0.0.0.0/0, which is the entire IPv4 address range, and matches anything with a prefix length of 32 bits or less, which is everything.

You can also combine the *ge* and *le* keywords to create useful lists. For a slightly artificial example, if you wanted to permit all routes with prefixes of 8 to 16 bits, but nothing longer and nothing shorter, you could use the following single line prefix list:

```
Router1(config)#ip prefix-list CLASS-A-B permit 0.0.0.0/0 ge 8 le 16
```

This also shows that you can match on prefix length independently of the actual network number. Notice also that we have omitted the sequence number in this example. By default, the router will rewrite this command and store it with a default sequence number of 5 as follows:

```
ip prefix-list CLASS-A-B seq 5 permit 0.0.0.0/0 ge 8 le 16
```

If we were to then add another line to this list, the router would automatically give it sequence number 10, always incrementing in steps of 5. But we recommend using explicit sequence numbers to ensure that things are in the order you expect.

Here is a similar example that selects only the subnets of 172.25.0.0/16 that are between 19 and 24 bits long:

```
Router1(config)#ip prefix-list BIG-SUBNETS permit 172.25.0.0/16 ge 19 le 24
```

Once you have created a prefix list, you need to apply it to a *neighbor* statement by using the *prefix-list* keyword as follows:

```
Router1(config)#router bgp 65500
Router1(config-router)#neighbor 192.168.1.5 remote-as 65510
Router1(config-router)#neighbor 192.168.1.5 prefix-list PREFIX-FILTER in
```

You have to define the peer with a *neighbor remote-as* command before you can apply any special options like prefix lists to it. Otherwise, the router will simply reject the command.

Notice the keyword *in* at the end of the *neighbor* command. As with route maps, you can assign a prefix list either inbound or outbound by using the keywords in or out, respectively, at the end of the line.

See Also

Chapter 6; Chapter 7; Chapter 19

9.7   Adjusting Local Preference Values

Problem

You want to change the Local Preference values to control which routes you use.

Solution

There are two ways to adjust Local Preference values on a router. The first method changes the Local Preference values for every route distributed into iBGP from this router:

```
Router1#configure terminal
Enter configuration commands, one per line.  End with CNTL/Z.
Router1(config)#router bgp 65500
Router1(config-router)#bgp default local-preference 200
Router1(config-router)#exit
Router1(config)#end
Router1#
```

The second method uses route maps to give finer granularity control over which routes get what Local Preference values:

```
Router1#configure terminal
Enter configuration commands, one per line.  End with CNTL/Z.
Router1(config)#ip prefix-list LOW_LP_PREFIXES seq 10 permit 172.22.0.0/16
Router1(config)#route-map LOCALPREF permit 10
Router1(config-route-map)#match ip address prefix-list LOW_LP_PREFIXES
Router1(config-route-map)#set local-preference 50
Router1(config-route-map)#exit
Router1(config)#route-map LOCALPREF permit 20
Router1(config-route-map)#exit
```

```
Router1(config)#router bgp 65500
Router1(config-router)#neighbor 192.168.1.5 remote-as 65510
Router1(config-router)#neighbor 192.168.1.5 route-map LOCALPREF in
Router1(config-router)#exit
Router1(config)#end
Router1#
```

Discussion

When BGP routers within an AS exchange information about a particular route using iBGP, they include the Local Preference value. All of the routers in the AS are then able to use this value to decide how to weight this route versus other BGP routes to the same destination. BGP consults the Local Preference value early in the route selection process, before even the AS Path attribute. So this provides an extremely useful and flexible way of forcing particular routes to use particular paths. Routers do not include Local Preference information when exchanging routes through eBGP connections.

A common example would be if you had two connections to an external network and you wanted to ensure that one was the primary path and the other was a backup. Suppose further that one of the routers in the AS handles the primary path and a second router handles the secondary path. The first example shows how to globally increase the Local Preference values of all routes received by one of these routers:

```
Router1(config)#router bgp 65500
Router1(config-router)#bgp default local-preference 200
```

Now all of the external routes that this router handles will have a Local Preference value of 200. If you can reach a particular prefix through more than one path, the other routers in this AS will prefer to use the one with the highest Local Preference value. The default Local Preference is 100.

To see how this works in practice, we will once again use the network shown in Figure 9-2. The following output shows two paths to the network 10.0.0.0/8. This router learned the first route through iBGP from another router. You can see from the LocPrf column that this route has the default Local Preference value of 100:

```
Router2#show ip bgp
BGP table version is 4, local router ID is 172.18.5.3
Status codes: s suppressed, d damped, h history, * valid, > best, i - internal
Origin codes: i - IGP, e - EGP, ? - incomplete

   Network          Next Hop            Metric LocPrf Weight Path
* i10.0.0.0         172.18.5.2                    100      0 65510 65531 i
*>                  192.168.2.5                            0 65520 65531 i
Router2#
```

This router learned the second route through eBGP, so it doesn't have a Local Preference value. The router treats any missing Local Preference values as if they had the default value of 100. Note that although BGP has a route selection rule that prefers eBGP routes to iBGP routes, this rule is consulted after the Local Preference is, but for now the Local Preference values are equal. So, all other things being equal, this router prefers to use the more direct route that it learned itself, which is indicated by the ">" character at the beginning of the line.

Now we will change the default Local Preference value on the other router to 200, using the *bgp default local-preference* command as shown above:

```
Router2#show ip bgp
BGP table version is 4, local router ID is 172.18.5.3
Status codes: s suppressed, d damped, h history, * valid, > best, i - internal
Origin codes: i - IGP, e - EGP, ? - incomplete

   Network          Next Hop           Metric LocPrf Weight Path
*>i10.0.0.0         172.18.5.2                   200      0 65510 65531 i
*                   192.168.2.5                           0 65520 65531 i
Router2#
```

As you can see, the Local Preference value has changed to 200 for the iBGP route. So this router now prefers the iBGP route. You can see more detail by specifying the prefix with this command:

```
Router2#show ip bgp 10.0.0.0/8
BGP routing table entry for 10.0.0.0/8, version 4
Paths: (2 available, best #1, table Default-IP-Routing-Table)
  Advertised to non peer-group peers:
  192.168.2.5
  65510 65531
    172.18.5.2 from 172.18.5.2 (172.18.5.2)
      Origin IGP, localpref 200, valid, internal, best
  65520 65531
    192.168.2.5 from 192.168.2.5 (172.21.1.1)
      Origin IGP, localpref 100, valid, external
Router2#
```

This clearly shows that the router interprets the missing Local Preference value as 100 on this router. If we now change the default value on this router to 75, you can see that it will use this new value instead when the value is missing:

```
Router2#configure terminal
Enter configuration commands, one per line.  End with CNTL/Z.
Router2(config)#router bgp 65500
Router2(config-router)#bgp default local-preference 75
Router2(config-router)#end
Router2#clear ip bgp *
<wait until the BGP peers reconnect>
Router2#show ip bgp 10.0.0.0/8
BGP routing table entry for 10.0.0.0/8, version 2
Paths: (2 available, best #2, table Default-IP-Routing-Table)
  Advertised to non peer-group peers:
  192.168.2.5
  65520 65531
    192.168.2.5 from 192.168.2.5 (172.21.1.1)
      Origin IGP, localpref 75, valid, external
```

```
     65510 65531
       172.18.5.2 from 172.18.5.2 (172.18.5.2)
         Origin IGP, localpref 200, valid, internal, best
     Router2#
```

Notice that we had to clear the BGP peers and wait until they reconnected for this change to take effect. Also notice that, by chance, the router displays the routes in the opposite order. There is no particular significance to this ordering. The route that entered the AS via eBGP on this router (Router2) now has a Local Preference value of 75, while the route that entered via Router1 has a Local Preference of 200, which we configured earlier in this recipe.

You can also use route maps to define different Local Preference values for different individual routes. This gives you a finer granularity, even allowing you to manually balance the load between these links by forcing some routes through one path and the rest through the other path.

The second example shows how to use a route map to adjust Local Preference values:

```
Router1(config)#ip prefix-list LOW_LP_PREFIXES seq 10 permit 172.22.0.0/16
Router1(config)#route-map LOCALPREF permit 10
Router1(config-route-map)#match ip address prefix-list LOW_LP_PREFIXES
Router1(config-route-map)#set local-preference 50
Router1(config-route-map)#exit
Router1(config)#route-map LOCALPREF permit 20
Router1(config-route-map)#exit
```

Here we have defined a prefix list that just matches the prefix 172.22.0.0/16. Whenever the route map sees a route that matches this prefix list, it sets the Local Preference value for this route to 50.

We have included an empty clause at the end of the route map, which simply passes all other routes unchanged. Every route map ends with an implicit deny all. So if we didn't include this, the router would simply drop any prefixes that didn't match the first clause.

Then we invoke this rule by using the standard *route-map* option to the *neighbor* command:

```
Router1(config)#router bgp 65500
Router1(config-router)#neighbor 192.168.1.5 remote-as 65510
Router1(config-router)#neighbor 192.168.1.5 route-map LOCALPREF in
```

Notice that we are applying this route map to all incoming routes received from this specific eBGP peer. Now you can see that this particular route has a local preference value of 50:

```
Router1#show ip bgp 172.22.0.0/16
BGP routing table entry for 172.22.0.0/16, version 5
Paths: (2 available, best #2, table Default-IP-Routing-Table)
Flag: 0x208
  Advertised to non peer-group peers:
  192.168.1.5
```

```
          65510 65531
            192.168.1.5 from 192.168.1.5 (172.25.26.55)
              Origin IGP, localpref 50, valid, external
          65520 65531
            172.18.5.3 from 172.18.5.3 (172.18.5.3)
              Origin IGP, localpref 75, valid, internal, best
       Router1#
```

Note also that the other iBGP router is still using the Local Preference value of 75 that we configured a moment ago.

Because this method used a route map, you can easily construct rules that would change the Local Preference values based on a large variety of different parameters. For example, you could match based on the AS Path, which is a technique that we will discuss in more detail in Recipe 9.10. You could do this to give a higher or lower Local Preference value, based on whether or not the route passes through a particular remote AS:

```
       Router1(config)#ip as-path access-list 17 permit _65531_
       Router1(config)#route-map LOCALPREF permit 25
       Router1(config-route-map)#match as-path 17
       Router1(config-route-map)#set local-preference 75
       Router1(config-route-map)#exit
```

See Also

Recipe 9.10

9.8   Load-Balancing

Problem

You want to load-balance traffic over two or more links, between two eBGP or iBGP neighbors.

Solution

Although BGP goes to great lengths to ensure that there is only one path for each route by default, Cisco routers also allow you to configure load-balancing for equal cost paths:

```
       Router1#configure terminal
       Enter configuration commands, one per line.  End with CNTL/Z.
       Router1(config)#router bgp 65500
       Router1(config-router)#maximum-paths 4
       Router1(config-router)#exit
       Router1(config)#end
       Router1#
```

Discussion

This option is useful when there are multiple paths to a particular adjacent AS. As you can see from the following BGP route table, there are three different options for these routes:

```
Router1#show ip bgp
BGP table version is 12, local router ID is 172.18.5.2
Status codes: s suppressed, d damped, h history, * valid, > best, i - internal
Origin codes: i - IGP, e - EGP, ? - incomplete

     Network          Next Hop         Metric LocPrf Weight Path
 *   10.0.0.0         192.168.1.5                        0 65510 65520 i
 *>                   192.168.2.5            0            0 65520 i
 *                    192.168.3.5                        0 65520 i
 *   172.25.0.0       192.168.1.5                        0 65510 65520 i
 *>                   192.168.2.5            0            0 65520 i
 *                    192.168.3.5                        0 65520 i
Router1#
```

But without the *maximum-paths* command enabled, there is only one route for each of these destinations in the IP routing table:

```
Router1#show ip route bgp
     172.25.0.0/16 is variably subnetted, 2 subnets, 2 masks
B       172.25.0.0/16 [20/0] via 192.168.2.5, 00:06:58
B    10.0.0.0/8 [20/0] via 192.168.2.5, 00:06:58
```

We then increase the maximum path value to 4 from the default of 1:

```
Router1(config)#router bgp 65500
Router1(config-router)#maximum-paths 4
```

The router now installs two routes in the IP routing table for each prefix:

```
Router1#show ip route bgp
     172.25.0.0/16 is variably subnetted, 2 subnets, 2 masks
B       172.25.0.0/16 [20/0] via 192.168.2.5, 00:00:02
                      [20/0] via 192.168.3.5, 00:00:02
B    10.0.0.0/8 [20/0] via 192.168.2.5, 00:00:02
                [20/0] via 192.168.3.5, 00:00:02
```

Note the router did not install all three of the available BGP routes. This is because the other routes, the ones that use 192.168.1.5 for the next-hop router, both have a longer AS Path. Similarly, if one of these routes had a smaller Local Preference value, it also would not be used. As we mentioned when discussing the BGP route selection rules in the introduction to this chapter, the router uses BGP Multipath feature only for routes that are equivalent after all tests up to and including the MED test.

This feature only works for routes that leave the AS. If you have multiple paths to a remote AS, but they depart through different routers, then they will not load balance.

Also note that for eBGP connections, this only balances the outbound traffic load. Incoming packets are subject to whatever routing policies your neighboring AS uses.

9.9   Removing Private ASNs from the AS Path

Problem

You want to prevent your internal private ASNs from reaching the public Internet.

Solution

You have to be extremely careful that any unregistered ASNs that you may be using don't propagate into the public Internet.

In this example, the router has a BGP connection to an ISP, which uses ASN 1. Our router uses ASN 2 and connects to another router with an unregistered ASN, 65500:

```
Router1#configure terminal
Enter configuration commands, one per line.  End with CNTL/Z.
Router1(config)#interface Serial0
Router1(config-if)#description connection to ISP #1, ASN 1
Router1(config-if)#ip address 192.168.1.6 255.255.255.252
Router1(config-if)#exit
Router1(config)#interface Serial1
Router1(config-if)#description connection to private network, ASN 65500
Router1(config-if)#ip address 192.168.5.1 255.255.255.252
Router1(config-if)#exit
Router1(config)#router bgp 2
Router1(config-router)#neighbor 192.168.5.2 remote-as 65500
Router1(config-router)#neighbor 192.168.1.5 remote-as 1
Router1(config-router)#neighbor 192.168.1.5 remove-private-AS
Router1(config-router)#no synchronization
Router1(config-router)#exit
Router1(config)#end
Router1#
```

Discussion

An unregistered ASN is a little bit like an unregistered IP address, in that anybody can use it. So if your routing prefixes have an unregistered ASN, this information is eventually passed to another router somewhere else in the Internet, and that router happens to be using the same unregistered ASN, then that router will assume that there is a routing loop, and drop your routes.

Having said this, if you look on an Internet backbone router at any given moment, there is a reasonably good chance of seeing several unregistered ASNs being propagated. This is a dangerous situation because the misbehaving networks could well be working perfectly well today. But tomorrow somebody else could start using the same unregistered ASN. Every route from the first network will look like a loop when received by the second network. So two ASs will not be able to communicate if they both use the same ASN.

All of the work in this example is done by the simple *remove-private-AS* command. Here is what the BGP route table looks like on this router:

```
Router1#show ip bgp
BGP table version is 6, local router ID is 192.168.55.1
Status codes: s suppressed, d damped, h history, * valid, > best, i - internal
Origin codes: i - IGP, e - EGP, ? - incomplete

   Network          Next Hop         Metric LocPrf Weight Path
*> 10.0.0.0         172.20.1.2            0             0 1 i
*> 172.21.0.0       172.25.1.7            0             0 65500 i
*> 172.25.1.0/24    172.25.1.7            0             0 65500 i
Router1#
```

As you can see, we are receiving information about network 10.0.0.0 from the ISP router in AS 1, and 172.21.0.0 from the router with ASN 65500. Looking at the routes on the ISP router before turning on the *remove-private-AS* feature, you can see that this private ASN is propagating into the Internet, which is not allowed:

```
Router3#show ip bgp
BGP table version is 8, local router ID is 172.20.100.1
Status codes: s suppressed, d damped, h history, * valid, > best, i - internal
Origin codes: i - IGP, e - EGP, ? - incomplete

   Network          Next Hop         Metric LocPrf Weight Path
*> 10.0.0.0         0.0.0.0               0         32768 i
*> 172.21.0.0       172.20.1.1                          0 2 65500 i
*> 172.25.1.0/24    172.20.1.1                          0 2 65500 i
Router3#
```

But after turning on the command, as shown above, all of the private ASNs are removed, while the routes are propagated normally:

```
Router3#show ip bgp
BGP table version is 8, local router ID is 172.20.100.1
Status codes: s suppressed, d damped, h history, * valid, > best, i - internal
Origin codes: i - IGP, e - EGP, ? - incomplete

   Network          Next Hop         Metric LocPrf Weight Path
*> 10.0.0.0         0.0.0.0               0         32768 i
*> 172.21.0.0       172.20.1.1                          0 2 i
*> 172.25.1.0/24    172.20.1.1                          0 2 i
Router3#
```

Be careful of this feature, though, because it can't remove private ASNs from the middle of an AS Path. If you have a topology where there is a public ASN behind a private one, it's not safe to remove the private ASN because you could cause routing loops. So the *remove-private-AS* feature completely gives up and passes on the entire path for routes that have a public ASN after a private ASN.

If this is the case, your only recourse is to suppress the route with the illegal path. Then, as long as you distribute a prefix that includes this route, everything will work.

9.10 Filtering BGP Routes Based on AS Paths

Problem

You want to filter the BGP routes that you either send or receive based on AS Path information.

Solution

You can use AS Path filters, either inbound or outbound, to filter either the routes you send or the routes you receive, respectively. You must apply these filters to each peer separately:

```
Router1#configure terminal
Enter configuration commands, one per line.  End with CNTL/Z.
Router1(config)#ip as-path access-list 15 permit ^65501$
Router1(config)#ip as-path access-list 25 permit _65530_
Router1(config)#ip as-path access-list 25 deny _65531$
Router1(config)#ip as-path access-list 25 permit .*
Router1(config)#router bgp 65500
Router1(config-router)#neighbor 192.168.1.5 remote-as 65510
Router1(config-router)#neighbor 192.168.1.5 filter-list 15 in
Router1(config-router)#neighbor 192.168.2.5 remote-as 65520
Router1(config-router)#neighbor 192.168.2.5 filter-list 25 out
Router1(config-router)#exit
Router1(config)#end
Router1#
```

Discussion

One of the most common reasons for filtering routes based on the AS Path is to prevent AS transit, as we showed in Recipes 9.4 and 9.5. However, there are some other useful applications for AS Path filters. The example shown above contains two distinct filters, one of which applies to routes received inbound from one neighbor, and the other works on outbound routes sent to a second neighbor.

AS Path filters are constructed by using a subset of UNIX regular expressions. Regular expressions provide an extremely powerful and general pattern matching syntax. Many scripting languages, such as Perl, Java, awk, sed, PHP, and Python, use regular expressions for string manipulation. A detailed description of the syntax is out of the scope of this book, but fortunately, BGP path filters don't require all of the magic of the regular expression syntax. This is because all AS Paths consist of simply numbers separated by whitespace. There are no other characters to worry about, and every AS Path has a similar construction. Only the specific ASNs and the number of whitespaces ever change. For more information on regular expressions in general, please refer to *Mastering Regular Expressions* by Jeffrey Friedl (O'Reilly).

In Recipe 9.4, we showed a simple AS Path filter, which used the pattern ^$. In a regular expression, the symbol ^ stands for the start, and $ for the end of the field. So the pattern ^$simply means that the field is empty because the start is immediately followed by the end. In the case of a BGP AS Path, that means that this route must originate inside this AS.

Looking at the example above, then, it should be clear that access-list number 15 looks for paths that contain only one ASN, which must be 65501:

```
Router1(config)#ip as-path access-list 15 permit ^65501$
```

Because there is both a ^ and a $ in the pattern, this filter will match routes whose AS Path consists of just a single ASN, which must have a value of 65501. This filter will remove any downstream routes that AS 65501 is merely passing along. Also, as with normal access lists, AS Path filters end with an implicit deny all clause. So the router will suppress any other routes that don't match this pattern.

The second AS Path filter in the example is somewhat more complicated:

```
Router1(config)#ip as-path access-list 25 permit _65530_
Router1(config)#ip as-path access-list 25 deny _65531$
Router1(config)#ip as-path access-list 25 permit .*
```

This shows that you can have filters that span multiple lines, although the example itself is a little bit artificial. The first line in this filter permits any routes that pass through AS 65530. The ASN in this line is surrounded by _ characters. The _ character stands for whitespace, although it is a little bit confusing because, for example, _65530_ seems to imply that it will match the ASN 65530 only if it appears in the middle of an AS Path. But, in fact, _65530_ will match any path containing the ASN, 65530, even if it is at the beginning or the end of the path. Conversely, _65531$ will only match AS Paths that end with AS 65531, meaning those routes that originate in AS 65531.

This little _ delimiter character is extremely important because AS Path filters use a literal text pattern matching. For example, consider the following filter, which doesn't include this character:

```
Router1(config)#ip as-path access-list 26 permit 55
```

This AS Path filter will match not only paths containing AS 55, but any other ASN that happens to contain the digits 55, such as 65530, 7553, or 255. But it is unlikely that you actually want to match on substrings within an ASN like this. So you should always remember to include these delimiter characters.

We included the following line in the recipe example because we needed to counter-act the implicit deny all at the end of any AS Path access list:

```
Router1(config)#ip as-path access-list 25 permit .*
```

This statement explicitly permits all other AS Paths that have not matched any of the earlier lines in the filter rule. The character "." in this filter matches any character, while the * indicates that there can be any number of characters. In fact, * literally means zero or more matches. In many cases, you actually need to match one or more times, for which you can use the + character.

There are many interesting uses for AS Path filters. For example, you might want to allow routes from an ISP and its immediate customers, but not from anything further away. This is easily accomplished with the following filter:

```
Router1(config)#ip as-path access-list 27 permit ^[0-9]+$
Router1(config)#ip as-path access-list 27 permit ^[0-9]+_[0-9]+$
```

This filter uses a couple of little tricks. The first trick is to specify a range, as in [0-9]. This means that the rule will match any character that falls in the range from 0 to 9, inclusive. Following this with the + character means that the rule matches one or more of these patterns. So the first line in this filter matches all paths that contain one and only one ASN, although it doesn't matter what this ASN actually is. The second line similarly matches all paths that contain exactly two ASNs. The net effect is to allow only routes from the directly attached ISP AS, and from any other AS that is directly connected to the ISP.

Another way to write the same thing is to match on the delimiters in the AS Path, instead of the actual ASN values. To do this, you might use a pattern like this:

```
Router1(config)#ip as-path access-list 28 deny _.+_.+_.+_
Router1(config)#ip as-path access-list 28 permit .*
```

In the first line of this access list, the "." character matches anything, including delimiters as well as digits. So this pattern will match an AS Path that includes at least four AS Path delimiters, with something in between them. Since the first and last delimiters could be the beginning and end of the AS Path, rather than actual whitespace, this access list causes the router to suppress any AS Path that includes three or more ASNs. It's slightly confusing because you have to think in terms of matching on delimiters rather than ASNs, but the net effect of AS Path access list number 28 is identical to 27 above. And, if you wanted to increase the maximum number of ASN values in the path from two to, say, five, this syntax is much more flexible:

```
Router1(config)#ip as-path access-list 29 deny _.+_.+_.+_.+_.+_.+_
Router1(config)#ip as-path access-list 29 permit .*
```

It's useful to remember that you can affect not only the routes you receive, but also the routes that you send using AS Path filters. In Recipe 9.4, we showed an extremely useful technique that uses AS Path filters to prevent an AS from being used for transit between external networks:

```
Router1(config)#ip as-path access-list 15 permit ^$
Router1(config)#router bgp 65500
Router1(config-router)#neighbor 192.168.1.5 remote-as 65520
Router1(config-router)#neighbor 192.168.1.5 filter-list 15 out
```

In this case, the filter permits only routes that have an empty AS Path, meaning that the routes must have originated locally within this AS. This filter suppresses any external routing information when forwarding its routing table. So the external networks don't know about any downstream networks that can be reached through this router.

You could use a slightly more complicated outbound filter if you wanted. This example allows only directly connected networks to use your AS for transit:

```
Router1(config)#ip as-path access-list 16 deny _.+_.+_
Router1(config)#ip as-path access-list 16 permit .*
Router1(config)#router bgp 65500
Router1(config-router)#neighbor 192.168.1.5 remote-as 65520
Router1(config-router)#neighbor 192.168.1.5 filter-list 16 out
```

The router applies this filter before it adds itself to the AS Path. So when we deny the pattern _.+_.+_, this suppresses all AS Paths with two or more ASNs, leaving only AS Paths that have a single ASN. Any path with one ASN must originate in a directly connected AS.

This AS Path filter might seem a little bit confusing because it denies paths that we don't want rather than permitting the ones we do. If you prefer, you could create a filter that has the identical effect by explicitly permitting only the paths that we want and implicitly denying the ones we don't want:

```
Router1(config)#ip as-path access-list 17 permit ^[0-9]+$
Router1(config)#ip as-path access-list 17 permit ^$
```

Both of these filters allow the router to forward routing information that originates in this AS, and in any networks that are directly connected to us. Bear in mind that this doesn't prevent a device that is fifteen hops away from reaching one of our neighbors through our network. But it does prevent them from reaching anything more distant than one of our direct neighbors through our AS.

See Also

Recipe 9.4; Recipe 9.5; *Mastering Regular Expressions* by Jeffrey Friedl (O'Reilly)

9.11   Reducing the Size of the Received Routing Table

Problem

You want to summarize the incoming routing information to reduce the size of your routing table.

Solution

One of the easiest ways to reduce your routing table size is to filter out most of the external routes and replace them with a default. To do this, you first create a static default route pointing to some known remote network. If this remote network is up, then you can safely assume that your ISP is working properly. Then you simply filter out all of the remaining uninteresting routes:

```
Router1#configure terminal
Enter configuration commands, one per line.  End with CNTL/Z.
```

```
Router1(config)#ip route 0.0.0.0 0.0.0.0 192.168.101.0 1
Router1(config)#ip route 0.0.0.0 0.0.0.0 192.168.102.0 2
Router1(config)#ip prefix-list CREATE-DEFAULT seq 10 permit 192.168.101.0/24
Router1(config)#ip prefix-list CREATE-DEFAULT seq 20 permit 192.168.102.0/24
Router1(config)#router bgp 65500
Router1(config-router)#neighbor 192.168.1.5 remote-as 65520
Router1(config-router)#neighbor 192.168.1.5 prefix-list CREATE-DEFAULT in
Router1(config-router)#exit
Router1(config)#end
Router1#
```

Discussion

For most typical Internet connections, you will need to drastically reduce the amount of routing information that you receive. A typical Internet backbone router needs to support BGP routes for well over 100,000 prefixes. So unless you are operating the ISP and need to support a large fraction of the public address space, it is a good idea to cut out as much as possible. It is important to remember that removing routing information means that some of your routing decisions will not be as good as they might otherwise be, however. There is always a tradeoff involved in filtering routing information.

This recipe shows a good way to drastically reduce the size of your Internet routing table. It looks for two different remote networks on the Internet, 192.168.101.0/24 and 192.168.102.0/24, and points a default route to each of them. This way, if either route happens to fail because of some normal (but hopefully rare) network problem, you will still have a default route. Then we created a prefix list that allows only these two routes, and applied it to all routes that we received from the peer router at our ISP. Please refer to Recipe 9.6 for more information on prefix lists.

The result is a very small Internet routing table that consists of only these two routes and a default route with two destinations. In practice, you will probably want to use more than two routes, however. Just to guard against the possibility that the remote networks you picked happen to be down at the same time for some reason, it is a good idea to pick a wide variety of different remote networks, some very far away and some relatively close. Avoid picking all of them in the same country, so you won't lose your default just because of a telecom disaster in that country. You could even pick a dozen or so remote routes like this, giving excellent fault tolerance, while still providing a tiny Internet routing table.

Notice the two static routes in the example have different administrative distances:

```
Router1(config)#ip route 0.0.0.0 0.0.0.0 192.168.101.0 1
Router1(config)#ip route 0.0.0.0 0.0.0.0 192.168.102.0 2
```

We did this to prevent load balancing between the default routes. If you have more than one ISP, it is quite likely that the best routes for these prefixes will be through different providers. You can allow load balancing, if you prefer, by simply giving all of these static routes the same administrative distance. But bear in mind that this will balance among routes, not among ISP connections.

If you have only one ISP, on the other hand, load balancing between these default routes accomplishes nothing useful.

If you then want to pass this default route information along to other routers by using BGP, the best way to do so is to use the *default-originate* option on the *neighbor* command, and include a route map to specify the prefixes that you want to associate with your default route:

```
Router1(config)#ip prefix-list CREATE-DEFAULT seq 10 permit 192.168.101.0/24
Router1(config)#ip prefix-list CREATE-DEFAULT seq 20 permit 192.168.102.0/24
Router1(config)#route-map DEFAULT-ROUTE permit 10
Router1(config-route-map)#match ip address prefix-list CREATE-DEFAULT
Router1(config-route-map)#exit
Router1(config)#router bgp 65500
Router1(config-router)#neighbor 172.18.5.3 default-origniate route-map DEFAULT-ROUTE
Router1(config-router)#exit
```

This is a dangerous thing to do, though, because BGP will now start to distribute default routing information to this peer, which may then start to distribute the default route out to the Internet. So it is a good idea to explicitly suppress the default route for any peers that should not receive it, and do this on all of your BGP routers:

```
Router1(config)#ip prefix-list BLOCK-DEFAULT permit 0.0.0.0/0 ge 1
Router1(config)#router bgp 65500
Router1(config-router)#neighbor 192.168.1.5 prefix-list BLOCK-DEFAULT out
```

Another popular way to reduce the size of the Internet routing table is to simply refuse to accept any routes /24 prefixes. Over 50 percent of the routes appearing on the Internet backbone are for /24 prefixes. So eliminating them will cut the memory requirements in half:

```
Router1(config)#ip prefix-list BLOCK-24 permit 0.0.0.0/0 le 23
Router1(config)#router bgp 65500
Router1(config-router)#neighbor 192.168.1.5 prefix-list BLOCK-24 in
```

However, if you do this, you should also use a default static route method discussed earlier. This is because some of the /24 prefixes in the Internet routing tables may not be included in other prefixes or summary routes.

We note in passing that the fraction of routes appearing on the backbone with a /24 prefix is steadily dropping over time. In early 2001, almost 59 percent of all prefixes were /24 networks, while over two years later in 2003, the number had dropped to roughly 55 percent. We expect this trend to continue over time, as ISPs improve their route summarization.

See Also

Recipe 9.4; Recipe 9.5; Recipe 9.6

9.12   Summarizing Outbound Routing Information

Problem

You want to summarize your routing table before forwarding it to another router.

Solution

BGP includes an automatic summarization feature that is on by default:

```
Router1#configure terminal
Enter configuration commands, one per line.  End with CNTL/Z.
Router1(config)#router bgp 65500
Router1(config-router)#neighbor 192.168.1.5 remote-as 65520
Router1(config-router)#auto-summary
Router1(config-router)#exit
Router1(config)#end
Router1#
```

Discussion

By default, BGP will try to summarize routes. This is not always desirable, though, which is why we have explicitly disabled this feature in many of the examples in this chapter. In fact, many engineers prefer to manually summarize their routing tables because they want to control what gets summarized and what doesn't.

The first problem with auto-summarization is that it is strictly classful. Your AS may not control all of the subnets in a classful network, and even if you do, this may not be the most useful prefix on which to summarize your networks. The second problem is that autosummarization only works on routes that are redistributed into BGP, and not on routes from BGP or routes injected via the *network* command. Please refer to Recipe 9.14 for more information on redistributing routes into BGP.

Suppose you wanted to summarize several routes to a single nonclassful route, or to summarize routes from several downstream BGP networks. You might be tempted to handle this by redistributing a static route for the summary and suppressing the individual routes with a filter. The problem with doing this is that the static route never goes away, even if all of the routes that you are trying to summarize become unreachable.

Cisco gets around this problem by implementing a special *aggregate-address* command that allows you to do the summarization without needing to manually create some routes and suppress others.

In the network shown in Figure 9-3, suppose the engineer responsible for AS 65530 wants to summarize the routes he receives from AS 65501 before passing this information along to another AS such as AS 65520. Router1 in AS 65501 advertises the prefixes 172.20.0.0/16 and 172.21.0.0/16, which it learned from Router2 in AS

65502, and adds to it the prefixes 172.22.0.0/16 and 172.23.0.0/16. All of these networks are covered by the aggregate address, 172.20.0.0/14:

```
Router3(config)#router bgp 65530
Router3(config-router)#aggregate-address 172.20.0.0 255.252.0.0 summary-only
```

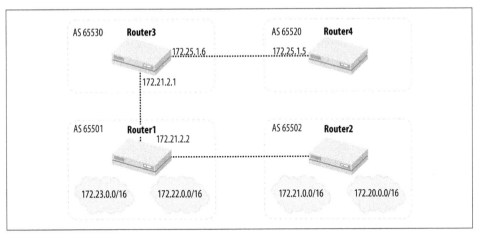

Figure 9-3. Route aggregation example

The *summary-only* keyword here means that BGP will suppress the individual subnets.
On the router doing the route aggregation, you can see which routes will be suppressed:

```
Router3#show ip bgp
BGP table version is 29, local router ID is 172.20.100.1
Status codes: s suppressed, d damped, h history, * valid, > best, i - internal
Origin codes: i - IGP, e - EGP, ? - incomplete

   Network          Next Hop          Metric LocPrf Weight Path
<routes deleted for brevity>
s> 172.20.0.0       172.21.2.2             0            0 65501 65502 ?
*> 172.20.0.0/14    0.0.0.0                         32768 i
s> 172.21.0.0       172.21.2.2             0            0 65501 65502 ?
s> 172.22.0.0       172.21.2.2             0            0 65501 ?
s> 172.23.0.0       172.21.2.2             0            0 65501 ?
Router3#
```

Then, in downstream ASs such as AS 65520, there is no indication of the summarized networks:

```
Router4#show ip bgp
BGP table version is 284, local router ID is 172.27.9.1
Status codes: s suppressed, d damped, h history, * valid, > best, i - internal
Origin codes: i - IGP, e - EGP, ? - incomplete

   Network          Next Hop          Metric LocPrf Weight Path
<routes deleted for brevity>
*> 172.20.0.0/14    172.25.1.6                          0 65530 i
Router4#
```

If you omit the *summary-only* keyword, BGP will advertise the summary address as well as the summarized subnets:

```
Router4#show ip bgp
BGP table version is 284, local router ID is 172.27.9.1
Status codes: s suppressed, d damped, h history, * valid, > best, i - internal
Origin codes: i - IGP, e - EGP, ? - incomplete

   Network          Next Hop         Metric LocPrf Weight Path
<routes deleted for brevity>
*> 172.20.0.0       172.25.1.6                         0 65530 65501 65502 ?
*> 172.20.0.0/14    172.25.1.6                         0 65530 i
*> 172.21.0.0       172.25.1.6                         0 65530 65501 65502 ?
*> 172.22.0.0       172.25.1.6                         0 65530 65501 ?
*> 172.23.0.0       172.25.1.6                         0 65530 65501 ?
Router4#
```

As long as the router doing the aggregation continues to see any routes that are within the summarized range, it will advertise the summary route. However, if all of the component routes disappear, it will stop advertising the summary. This is true whether or not you use the *summary-only* keyword:

```
Router4#show ip bgp 172.20.0.0
% Network not in table
Router4#
```

There is a problem with doing route summarization because it inherently discards information. To see why this can cause problems, suppose there was a link between Router1 and Router4. Router4 will advertise the summary route, which does not have Router1's ASN in the AS Path. So Router1 will accept this as a new, distinct route that passes through Router4. If Router1 then loses its route to one of the summarized addresses, say 172.23.0.0/16, it will try to use the summary route, and send packets for this prefix to Router4. Router4 will forward the packets to Router3. If Router3 still has the suppressed route in its BGP table, it will simply forward the packet back to Router1, completing a routing loop.

Eventually Router3 will purge the unreachable prefix from its routing table, but in more complex networks, it could take a while for this to happen.

To get around this problem, BGP includes the concept of an AS Set that can be used with route aggregation. An AS Set is a grouping of ASNs in an AS Path. It indicates that the route passed through one or more of the listed ASs, although it doesn't show their order. Because the AS Path now contains every ASN, you can again eliminate loops.

You can enable AS Sets with the *as-set* keyword in the *aggregate-address* command:

```
Router3(config)#router bgp 65530
Router3(config-router)#aggregate-address 172.20.0.0 255.255.252.0 as-set summary-only
```

Then, on a downstream router, the *show ip bgp* output includes the AS Set and represents it in curly braces:

```
Router4#show ip bgp
BGP table version is 36, local router ID is 172.25.26.5
Status codes: s suppressed, d damped, h history, * valid, > best, i - internal
Origin codes: i - IGP, e - EGP, ? - incomplete

   Network          Next Hop        Metric LocPrf Weight Path
<routes deleted for brevity>
*> 172.20.0.0/14    172.25.1.6                      0 65530 {65501,65502} ?
Router4#
```

And you can see more detail by specifying the route prefix with the *show ip bgp* command. Note that this output even tells you the BGP router ID of the router that did the aggregation as well as the ASN that this router resides in:

```
Router4#show ip bgp 172.20.0.0
BGP routing table entry for 172.20.0.0/14, version 36
Paths: (1 available, best #1, table Default-IP-Routing-Table)
  Not advertised to any peer
  65530 {65501,65502}, (aggregated by 65530 172.20.100.1)
    172.25.1.6 from 172.25.1.6 (172.27.9.1)
      Origin incomplete, localpref 100, valid, external, best
Router4#
```

You need to be careful with route summarization, particularly when you don't control all of the subnets in the range that you intend to summarize. In our example, suppose we advertised the summary for 172.20.0.0/14, but we didn't know how to route some part of this range, such as 172.21.15.0/24.

Ideally, this wouldn't actually matter because the real owner of 172.21.15.0/24 and its subnets would advertise a more precise route than our summary. But this is not a completely ideal world, and sometimes people might filter out the longer masks as a matter of course to reduce their routing tables (as we did in Recipe 9.11). So it is entirely possible that our router will be called upon to route packets for a device in 172.21.15.0/24. If our response to this is simply to toss the packet back to our default gateway, then we could easily wind up with a routing loop.

If you intend to summarize, make sure you can vouch for all the subnets you are summarizing. This is true regardless of the techniques you use.

See Also

Recipe 9.11; Recipe 9.14

9.13   Prepending ASNs to the AS Path

Problem

You want to increase the length of an AS Path so that one inbound path looks better than another.

Solution

In situations when you have multiple connections between ASs, you will often want to make remote networks prefer one inbound path when sending packets to your network. The easiest way to do this is to prepend your own ASN to the AS PATH several times, instead of just once, as it would do by default:

```
Router1#configure terminal
Enter configuration commands, one per line.  End with CNTL/Z.
Router1(config)#ip as-path access-list 15 permit ^$
Router1(config)#route-map PREPEND permit 10
Router1(config-route-map)#match as-path 15
Router1(config-route-map)#set as-path prepend 65500 65500 65500
Router1(config-route-map)#exit
Router1(config)#route-map PREPEND permit 20
Router1(config-route-map)#exit
Router1(config)#router bgp 65500
Router1(config-router)#neighbor 192.168.1.5 remote-as 65510
Router1(config-router)#neighbor 192.168.1.5 route-map PREPEND out
Router1(config-router)#exit
Router1(config)#end
Router1#
```

This example uses the same network shown in Figure 9-2, earlier in this chapter.

Discussion

We have already discussed methods for making your outbound traffic prefer one path over another in Recipe 9.7. But, as we mentioned in that recipe, that only affects your outbound path. If you also want to ensure that inbound traffic prefers one path over another, then you have to somehow trick the remote networks into believing that one path is better than the other.

As we mentioned in the Introduction to this chapter, if there are many options for different paths to a destination network, a BGP router will go through several steps to decide which one to use. You can adjust the attributes associated with each route to help force other BGP routers to select the paths that you want them to use. The easiest way to force routers outside of your AS to favor a particular route is to adjust the AS Path.

If you can simply make the path appear longer for routes that use one link, then remote networks will tend to prefer to reach you through whatever other links are available. There will always be situations when it is still closer to use the route with the artificially lengthened path. But these should be relatively rare, and the more times you prepend your ASN to the path, the less likely this will be.

Of course, it isn't safe or wise to put an arbitrary ASN into the AS Path. But you can insert your own ASN a few extra times without causing any problems, which is exactly what this recipe shows. Note that there is no hard limit to how long your AS

Path can be (although it would probably cause problems if the path were so long that the routing information couldn't fit into a single BGP packet), and some sites prepend their ASN 10 or 20 times to make absolutely certain that a particular path is used only in case of a failure of the primary path. However, the longest AS Paths in the public Internet rarely have more than a dozen ASNs. So you shouldn't need to prepend your ASN very many times to make one path look better than the other from anywhere in the Internet.

This recipe also takes the precaution of only lengthening the AS Paths of locally generated routes. It does this by including a match clause in the route map that only affects routes that have an empty AS Path. Clause number 20 in the route map is a catch-all that simply passes through all other routes unchanged:

```
Router1(config)#ip as-path access-list 15 permit ^$
Router1(config)#route-map PREPEND permit 10
Router1(config-route-map)#match as-path 15
Router1(config-route-map)#set as-path prepend 65500 65500 65500
Router1(config-route-map)#exit
Router1(config)#route-map PREPEND permit 20
Router1(config-route-map)#exit
```

But you might not want this restriction. You might prefer to rewrite all of the routes that you send. Or, you might use an outbound filter, such as the one discussed in Recipe 9.4, to suppress external routes. In both of these cases, you can make the route map considerably simpler:

```
Router1(config)#route-map PREPEND permit 10
Router1(config-route-map)#set as-path prepend 65500 65500 65500
Router1(config-route-map)#route-map PREPEND permit 20
Router1(config-route-map)#exit
```

The difference caused by prepending your ASN to the AS Path of a route is only visible on a remote router:

```
Router3#show ip bgp 172.18.5.0/24
BGP routing table entry for 172.18.5.0/24, version 26
Paths: (2 available, best #2)
  Advertised to non peer-group peers:
    192.168.1.6
  65500 65500 65500 65500
    192.168.1.6 from 192.168.1.6 (172.18.5.2)
      Origin IGP, metric 0, localpref 100, valid, external, ref 2
  65531 65520 65500
    192.168.99.6 from 192.168.99.6 (192.168.99.10)
      Origin IGP, localpref 100, valid, external, best, ref 2
Router3#
```

Here you can see that there are two routes for the prefix 172.18.5.0/24, one passes through AS 65500 and the other through ASs 65531 and 65520 to reach AS 65500. The path that goes directly to AS 65500 is actually shorter. But, because we have prepended the ASN three times on this route, this router prefers the other path.

You can also verify that everything is working properly by disabling the peer relationship with the preferred ISP and making sure that everything still works. You can temporarily disable a peer with the by using the *shutdown* keyword on the *neighbor* command:

```
Router1(config)#router bgp 65500
Router1(config-router)#neighbor 192.168.2.5 shutown
```

Be sure to re-enable this peer after you have finished testing:

```
Router1(config)#router bgp 65500
Router1(config-router)#no neighbor 192.168.2.5 shutown
```

See Also

Recipe 9.4; Recipe 9.7

9.14 Redistributing Routes with BGP

Problem

You want to redistribute routes between an IGP and BGP.

Solution

When connecting two or more IGPs using BGP, you sometimes need to configure redistribution between the IGP and BGP on both routers. To make the example more interesting, we will assume that we need to connect an EIGRP network to an OSPF network using a pair of BGP routers.

The first router redistributes routes from BGP into OSPF:

```
Router1#configure terminal
Enter configuration commands, one per line.  End with CNTL/Z.
Router1(config)#router ospf 100
Router1(config-router)#network 172.26.0.0 0.0.255.255 area 0
Router1(config-router)#redistribute bgp 65500 metric 500 subnets
Router1(config-router)#exit
Router1(config)#router bgp 65500
Router1(config-router)#neighbor 192.168.1.5 remote-as 65520
Router1(config-router)#network 172.26.0.0
Router1(config-router)#exit
Router1(config)#end
Router1#
```

And this is the configuration for the router that redistributes BGP routes into EIGRP:

```
Router2#configure terminal
Enter configuration commands, one per line.  End with CNTL/Z.
Router2(config)#router eigrp 99
Router2(config-router)#network 172.25.0.0
Router2(config-router)#redistribute bgp 65520 metric 500 10 255 1 1500
Router2(config-router)#exit
```

```
Router2(config)#router bgp 65520
Router2(config-router)#neighbor 192.168.1.6 remote-as 65500
Router2(config-router)#network 172.25.0.0
Router2(config-router)#exit
Router2(config)end
Router2#
```

Discussion

Before we say anything about this recipe, we need to stress that redistribution with BGP is often a very messy business. The example specifically shows using BGP to handle routing between two IGPs rather than redistribution into the public Internet, because this technique is only really relevant in a large enterprise network. Even here, it's easy to create routing loops, particularly when redistributing from BGP into an IGP and then back out into BGP. This is why we have actually chosen to distribute from BGP into the other protocols, rather than full two-way redistribution. We will discuss two-way redistribution in a moment.

For Internet connections, we strongly recommend against redistributing routes from BGP into the IGP. This is because it is too easy to inadvertently wind up distributing tens of thousands of Internet routing prefixes into your IGP. And, when passing IGP routing information to the Internet, it is better to pass a few summary routes using *network* statements, as we have done in the above example, than to directly redistribute IGP prefixes.

In addition, there is a huge danger when you redistribute BGP routes from the Internet, into an IGP, and then back into BGP and onto the Internet. Unless you carefully filter routes, or unless your ISP filters for you, you will wind up sending routes back into the Internet with very short AS Paths that originate in your network. This could reroute the entire Internet through your IGP, which would be a Bad Thing.

However, BGP isn't just used on the public Internet. Many large enterprise networks also use BGP for interconnecting IGPs. In this case, although you have to redistribute routes from BGP into the IGP, it may not be necessary to redistribute IGP routes into BGP. So, in the above example, we have actually only used one-way redistribution from the BGP into the IGP, but not the other way around. Instead, we have relied on *network* statements to summarize the IGP routes into BGP:

```
Router1(config)#router bgp 65500
Router1(config-router)#neighbor 192.168.1.5 remote-as 65520
Router1(config-router)#network 172.26.0.0
```

If you need BGP to advertise a large number of IGP routes, you can use as many *network* statements as are necessary to accomplish this. Note that before IOS Version 12.0, you could configure a maximum of 200 network statements. However, Cisco has now removed this restriction.

Having said all of this, it is possible to redistribute prefixes from the IGP into BGP. Two-way redistribution can be convenient when you want to use BGP to connect two IGPs that use overlapping address ranges. This might happen, for example, if a single IGP became too large and needed to be split for stability reasons.

We have already discussed how to redistribute foreign routing protocols into both EIGRP and OSPF in Chapters 7 and 8, respectively, so we will focus instead on the redistribution of these protocols into BGP here.

The work is all done by a simple *redistribute* command in the BGP configuration clause. For simple redistribution, all we need to do is specify the IGP protocol and its process ID number:

```
Router1(config)#router bgp 65500
Router1(config-router)#redistribute ospf 100
```

However, by default, when you do this, BGP takes the IGP metric and uses it as the BGP metric, also called the MED. BGP distributes this metric with the route. Routers use the lowest metric value to select the best route if two or more BGP routes have the same AS Path length.

This may provide exactly the right behavior, selecting the BGP router that is closest to the IGP destination network. But in some cases you might want to force a particular metric value to ensure that a particular BGP router or link is used when routing to IGP destinations. You can do this most easily by simply setting a default metric for all redistributed IGP routes:

```
Router2(config)#router bgp 65520
Router2(config-router)#redistribute eigrp 99 metric 500
```

Although we have only assigned a default metric to the EIGRP routes, you can use the same syntax to give a default metric to the routes redistributed from OSPF.

We also mentioned in Chapters 7 and 8 that you can assign a route tag to external routes in both OSPF and EIGRP. This can be extremely useful when you do lots of redistribution. In particular, suppose that the EIGRP and OSPF sides of this network have a back door connection to one another, redistributing part or all of their routing tables. In this case, we will need to restrict which routes we redistribute into BGP and suppress all of these back door routes, or we will have routing loop problems.

You can do this with a route map. The simplest case, which is useful for the back door example, is to suppress all external routes when redistributing from the IGP into BGP:

```
Router2(config)#route-map REDIST deny 10
Router2(config-route-map)#match route-type external
Router2(config-route-map)#exit
Router2(config)#route-map REDIST permit 20
Router2(config-route-map)#exit
Router2(config)#router bgp 65520
Router2(config-router)#redistribute eigrp 99 route-map REDIST metric 500
```

You would need to apply a similar route map at both redistribution points to prevent loops.

However, the route map we just created will match all external routes, not just the external routes due to the back door connection. You might have some redistributed static routes in your IGP, or perhaps some isolated part of your network uses RIP to support legacy equipment. This is where route tags become invaluable. If you have external routes you need to redistribute into BGP, and you know they have a particular tag value such as 123, you can use a slightly more complicated route map like this:

```
Router2(config)#route-map REDIST permit 5
Router2(config-route-map)#match tag 123
Router2(config-route-map)#exit
Router2(config)#route-map REDIST deny 10
Router2(config-route-map)#match route-type external
Router2(config-route-map)#exit
Router2(config)#route-map REDIST permit 20
Router2(config-route-map)#exit
Router2(config)#router bgp 65520
Router2(config-router)#redistribute eigrp 99 route-map REDIST metric 500
```

This route map now allows BGP to redistribute all local routes and all external routes that have the tag value 123. But it suppresses all other external routes. You might use a redistribution system like this if you were using BGP to act as a transit between two networks. The router that redistributes routes into BGP from the other network would mark them with this tag value. Then, at this router, we can use this tag to select only these particular external routes for distribution into this particular IGP.

See Also

Chapter 7; Chapter 8

9.15   Using Peer Groups

Problem

You want to apply the same options to several peers.

Solution

Peer groups allow you to apply the same BGP configuration to a number of neighbors at the same time:

```
Router1#configure terminal
Enter configuration commands, one per line.  End with CNTL/Z.
Router1(config)#router bgp 65500
Router1(config-router)#neighbor EBGP-PEERS peer-group
Router1(config-router)#neighbor EBGP-PEERS prefix-list PRE-RTFILTER in
Router1(config-router)#neighbor EBGP-PEERS filter-list 15 out
Router1(config-router)#neighbor 192.168.1.5 remote-as 65520
Router1(config-router)#neighbor 192.168.1.5 peer-group EBGP-PEERS
Router1(config-router)#neighbor 192.168.1.9 remote-as 65521
Router1(config-router)#neighbor 192.168.1.9 peer-group EBGP-PEERS
```

```
Router1(config-router)#neighbor 192.168.1.13 remote-as 65522
Router1(config-router)#neighbor 192.168.1.13 peer-group EBGP-PEERS
Router1(config-router)#neighbor 192.168.1.17 remote-as 65523
Router1(config-router)#neighbor 192.168.1.17 peer-group EBGP-PEERS
Router1(config-router)#exit
Router1(config)#end
Router1#
```

Discussion

Peer groups have been around since IOS Version 11.0, but they had several unfortunate restrictions that were eliminated in Version 12.0. The most important of these were that all eBGP members of the same peer group had to be members of the same IP subnet, and you couldn't act as a transit router to eBGP neighbors that were members of the same peer group. These restrictions have been removed now, but you will still sometimes see these problems discussed in older references.

Peer groups are most useful when you have several neighbors, all with nearly the same BGP parameters. In the above example, we have created a peer group called EBGP-PEERS that we then apply to several different neighbors. This allows you to set up common properties such as filter lists or route maps, and apply them identically to a large list of peers.

The biggest value for this feature is for ISPs who want to set up common properties for all of the other ISP routers at a large Internet exchange point. But peer groups can also be useful in enterprise networks that include several ASs that all connect with one another.

Suppose, for example, that you need to connect to four different ASs, and that each connection point used two BGP routers for redundancy. Then each router would have an eBGP connection to two routers in each of three different ASs, for a total of six eBGP connections.

If you need to do any special filtering that would be common to all of these routers, then you would have to configure six different eBGP neighbors with an identical set of filters. Or, if you use peer groups, you can set up the filters just once and reduce the typing as well as the chance of errors. Further, if you need to make any changes to your filters, you can make them once and they will instantly apply to all of the group members.

It's also important to remember that you can use the peer group as a basic template, but still add further options for one or more individual peers:

```
Router1(config)#router bgp 65500
Router1(config-router)#neighbor EBGP-PEERS peer-group
Router1(config-router)#neighbor EBGP-PEERS prefix-list PRE-RTFILTER in
Router1(config-router)#neighbor EBGP-PEERS filter-list 15 out
Router1(config-router)#neighbor 192.168.1.5 remote-as 65520
Router1(config-router)#neighbor 192.168.1.5 peer-group EBGP-PEERS
Router1(config-router)#neighbor 192.168.1.5 ebgp-multihop 5
```

The example in the "Solution" section of this recipe uses eBGP peers, but you can also use peer groups for iBGP peers. To be worthwile, however, there should be at least three common BGP neighbor commands that you want to sue with two or more peers:

```
Router1(config)#router bgp 6550
Router1(config-router)#neighbor IBGP-PEERS peer-group
Router1(config-router)#neighbor IBGP-PEERS update-source Loopback0
Router1(config-router)#neighbor IBGP-PEERS route-reflector-client
Router1(config-router)#neighbor 192.168.101.5 remote-as 65500
Router1(config-router)#neighbor 192.168.101.5 peer-group IBGP-PEERS
Router1(config-router)#neighbor 192.168.101.9 remote-as 65500
Router1(config-router)#neighbor 192.168.101.9 peer-group IBGP-PEERS
```

9.16 Authenticating BGP Peers

Problem

You want to authenticate your BGP peer relationships to help prevent tampering with your routing tables.

Solution

The BGP protocol includes an MD5-based authentication system for authenticating peers:

```
Router1#configure terminal
Enter configuration commands, one per line.  End with CNTL/Z.
Router1(config)#router bgp 65500
Router1(config-router)#neighbor 192.168.55.5 remote-as 65501
Router1(config-router)#neighbor 192.168.55.5 password password-1234
Router1(config-router)#exit
Router1(config)#end
Router1#
```

The same password must be configured on both routers:

```
Router2#configure terminal
Enter configuration commands, one per line.  End with CNTL/Z.
Router2(config)#router bgp 65501
Router2(config-router)#neighbor 192.168.55.6 remote-as 65500
Router2(config-router)#neighbor 192.168.55.6 password password-1234
Router2(config-router)#exit
Router2(config)#end
Router2#
```

Discussion

MD5 authentication is a standard part of BGP Version 4 that was introduced in RFC 2385. The IETF went further in RFC 3013 (which is also called BCP 46) to recommend that "BGP authentication should be used with routing peers" in the public Internet. This language "should be used" indicates a strong recommendation, but not a requirement.

BGP is different than the routing protocols that we discussed in Chapters 6, 7, and 8 because you must explicitly configure the peer relationships between routers. These peers then use point-to-point TCP connections to exchange information. So it is much more difficult for a malicious user to surreptitiously establish a peer relationship with one of your routers and corrupt your routing tables. But it is still possible to hijack an existing TCP connection between two BGP peers and inject bad routes. And if the attackers are on the same network segment as one of the peers, they can potentially hijack the IP address of the legitimate peer and set up a new BGP session.

With authentication, this type of attack is considerably more difficult. This is because the attacker must not only get the TCP sequence numbers right, but he must also insert the correct encrypted authentication key.

It is worth mentioning also that some sources have claimed that this MD5 authentication scheme is not sufficient for BGP because there are effective attacks that can break it. The Internet Draft document, "Security Requirements for Keys used with the TCP MD5 Signature Option," (*draft-ietf-idr-md5-keys-00.txt*), comments on this threat and makes the following recommendations:

- Make your keys between 12 and 24 bytes long.
- In situations with multiple BGP peers, avoid using the same keys with all peers.
- Change your keys at least every 90 days.

It is also important to note that introducing authentication can cause delays in BGP message passing, although it shouldn't seriously affect normal IP packet processing. It can also cause increased CPU overhead on the BGP peer routers.

Despite all of this, in a hostile network, authentication can be useful because it makes it significantly harder for somebody to disrupt your routing tables. If your ISP supports this service, it is probably a good idea to use it.

It is also worth mentioning that in your router's configuration file, the password will be stored in plain text unless you have enabled the *service password-encryption* global configuration command. When you turn on password encryption, the router will store the command using the Cisco proprietary Type 7 encryption:

```
!
router bgp 65500
neighbor 192.168.55.5 remote-as 65501
neighbor 192.168.55.5 password 7 15020A1F173D24362C7E64704053
!
```

As we mentioned in Chapter 3, it is quite easy to break this encryption algorithm. But as long as you maintain good control over your router configuration files, this at least prevents somebody from learning the encryption key by looking over your shoulder.

When there is an authentication mismatch between two BGP peers, they will not be able to establish a connection. You will also see the following error message on one or both routers:

```
Jan  7 10:01:48 EST: %TCP-6-BADAUTH: No MD5 digest from 192.168.55.6:13662 to 192.
168.55.5:179
```

See Also

Chapter 3; RFC 3013; "Security Requirements for Keys used with the TCP MD5 Signature Option," *draft-ietf-idr-md5-keys-00.txt*, February 2002.

9.17   Using BGP Communities

Problem

You want to configure BGP Communities to control routing and route propagation.

Solution

Configuring Cisco routers to use BGP Communities is a two-step process. You must specify the desired Community values by using a route map associated with a *neighbor* command:

```
Router3#configure terminal
Enter configuration commands, one per line.  End with CNTL/Z.
Router3(config)#ip prefix-list 10.101/16 seq 5 permit 10.101.0.0/16
Router3(config)#ip prefix-list 10.102/16 seq 5 permit 10.102.0.0/16
Router3(config)#ip prefix-list 10.103/16 seq 5 permit 10.103.0.0/16
Router3(config)#ip prefix-list 10.104/16 seq 5 permit 10.104.0.0/16
Router3(config)#ip prefix-list 10.105/16 seq 5 permit 10.105.0.0/16
Router3(config)#route-map APPLY_COMMUNITY_A permit 10
Router3(config-route-map)#match ip address prefix-list 10.101/16
Router3(config-route-map)#set community no-advertise
Router3(config-route-map)#exit
Router3(config)#route-map APPLY_COMMUNITY_A permit 20
Router3(config-route-map)#match ip address prefix-list 10.102/16
Router3(config-route-map)#set community no-export
Router3(config-route-map)#exit
Router3(config)#route-map APPLY_COMMUNITY_A permit 30
Router3(config-route-map)#match ip address prefix-list 10.103/16
Router3(config-route-map)#set community local-AS
Router3(config-route-map)#exit
Router3(config)#route-map APPLY_COMMUNITY_A permit 40
Router3(config-route-map)#match ip address prefix-list 10.104/16
Router3(config-route-map)#set community internet
Router3(config-route-map)#exit
Router3(config)#route-map APPLY_COMMUNITY_A permit 50
Router3(config-route-map)#match ip address prefix-list 10.105/16
Router3(config-route-map)#set community 4293328976
Router3(config-route-map)#exit
Router3(config)#route-map APPLY_COMMUNITY_A permit 100
Router3(config-route-map)#exit
Router3(config)#router bgp 65500
Router3(config-router)#no synchronization
```

```
Router3(config-router)#neighbor 172.18.5.3 remote-as 65500
Router3(config-router)#neighbor 172.18.5.3 next-hop-self
Router3(config-router)#neighbor 172.18.5.3 send-community both
Router3(config-router)#neighbor 172.18.5.10 remote-as 65500
Router3(config-router)#neighbor 172.18.5.10 next-hop-self
Router3(config-router)#neighbor 172.18.5.10 send-community both
Router3(config-router)#neighbor 192.168.1.9 remote-as 65520
Router3(config-router)#neighbor 192.168.1.9 send-community both
Router3(config-router)#neighbor 192.168.1.9 route-map APPLY_COMMUNITY_A in
Router3(config-router)#exit
Router3(config)#end
Router3#
```

Then, for all of the downstream routers that you want to use and/or propagate the Community values that you are setting, you must include the *neighbor send-community* command:

```
Router2#configure terminal
Enter configuration commands, one per line.  End with CNTL/Z.
Router2(config)#router bgp 65500
Router2(config-router)#no synchronization
Router2(config-router)#neighbor 172.18.5.4 remote-as 65500
Router2(config-router)#neighbor 172.18.5.4 send-community both
Router2(config-router)#neighbor 172.18.5.10 remote-as 65500
Router2(config-router)#neighbor 172.18.5.10 send-community both
Router2(config-router)#no auto-summary
Router2(config-router)#exit
Router2(config)#end
Router2#
```

Discussion

A standard BGP Community is simply a 32-bit number that BGP can attach to routing prefixes. This attribute is defined in RFC 1997, which also specifies that the values 0×00000000 through 0×0000FFFF and 0×FFFF0000 through 0×FFFFFFFF are reserved. It is classed as an Optional Transitive attribute, which means that Community values are passed along with routes, across both iBGP and eBGP links, and whether the receiving router understands what to do with them or not. RFC 4360 defines the Extended Community attribute, which is nearly identical, except that it uses a 64-bit field to help reduce the potential for overlapping uses.

There are two common uses for Communities. The first simply uses the few Well Known Community attributes:

local-AS (Well Known Community)
> This Community value indicates that the associated route should not be advertised outside of the AS. So it is distributed among iBGP peers, but not via eBGP.

no-advertise—do not advertise to any peer (Well Known Community)
> The no-advertise Community instructs routers not to advertise this route to any other BGP peers, not even iBGP peers.

no-export—do not export to next AS (Well Known Community)

Routes containing the no-export Community value are not advertised to any router outside of the Confederation or to any routers outside of the AS.

Internet (Well Known Community)

Routes tagged with the *internet* community are assumed to be associated with the Public Internet. There is no special action associated with this Community value.

Using these Well Known Community values allows you to exercise control over how routes are distributed throughout your AS and into neighboring ASs. For example, if you have a route in your BGP tables that you want to restrict to your own AS and not advertise it to any external peers, you would simply set the *local-AS* Community value. If you are using BGP Confederations, you can similarly restrict a route to within a given Confederation by tagging it with the *no-export* Community. If you are not using Confederations, then the *local-AS* and *no-export* Communities have an identical result.

The second use for Communities is a little bit more complicated and requires agreement between ISPs and their clients. The application suggested in RFC 1998 allows customers of an ISP to affect routing decisions for their own routes within their ISP's network. In this system, the customer can tag their routes with a community value containing an ASN and a Local Preference value. The ASN value defines the AS that the customer would like to affect, and is contained in the first 16 bits of the Community value. The remaining 16 bits then contain a Local Preference value. This allows the customer to affect inbound routing for their networks in real time on a prefix-by-prefix basis.

For example, suppose you have two ISPs with ASNs 65511 and 65512. If you want to specify that inbound traffic to your network for a particular prefix is to use the first ISP preferentially, you would include a Community value of 65511:100 (which is FFE7:0064 in hex or 4293328996 in decimal) to request that the ISP set a Local Preference of 100 for this route.

Conversely, if you wanted to make this ISP the backup link for this particular route prefix, you could request a lower Local Preference value such as 80 by including a Community value of 65511:80 (which is FFE7:0050 in hex or 4293328976 in decimal).

The reason why we include these different formats for Community values is because the router configuration file displays them as decimal numbers. However you can also configure them as colon-separated 16-bit decimal numbers to allow ASN:*nn* format:

```
Router3(config)#route-map APPLY_COMMUNITY_A permit 50
Router3(config-route-map)#match ip address prefix-list 10.105/16
Router3(config-route-map)#set community 65511:80
```

This *set community* command will be displayed as:

```
!
route-map APPLY_COMMUNITY_A permit 50
 match ip address prefix-list 10.105/16
```

```
    set community 4293328976
  !
```

And some IOS versions even get confused by the 32-bit number and incorrectly display it as a signed integer:

```
  !
  route-map APPLY_COMMUNITY_A permit 50
   match ip address prefix-list 10.105/16
   set community -1638320
  !
```

But however your router displays the values, they all function identically.

You use route maps to apply Communities to routes, exactly the same way that we handled Local Preference values in Recipe 9.7. For example, this part of the route map uses a prefix-list to select a particular route, and sets its Community value to *no-export*:

```
  Router3(config)#ip prefix-list 10.102/16 seq 5 permit 10.102.0.0/16
  Router3(config)#route-map APPLY_COMMUNITY_A permit 20
  Router3(config-route-map)#match ip address prefix-list 10.102/16
  Router3(config-route-map)#set community no-export
  Router3(config-route-map)#exit
```

You then need apply this route map to a *neighbor* command:

```
  Router3(config)#router bgp 65500
  Router3(config-router)#neighbor 192.168.1.9 remote-as 65520
  Router3(config-router)#neighbor 192.168.1.9 send-community both
  Router3(config-router)#neighbor 192.168.1.9 route-map APPLY_COMMUNITY_A in
```

In this case, we have applied the route map to incoming routes from this eBGP peer. As a general rule of thumb, to ensure consistency across your AS, you should attach any Community values to routes on the first router to handle the routes. In this case, the required routes are outside of the AS. However, if the routes originate within the AS, then we would have applied the route map outbound on the router that originates them. In that case, we would need to be careful to apply the route map to all of the iBGP peers.

The other important command in dealing with Communities is the *neighbor send-community* command:

```
  Router3(config-router)#neighbor 192.168.1.9 send-community both
```

By default, Cisco routers do not propagate Community values with BGP routes. So you must include this command for all of the peers that need to see this attribute. This is why, in the Solution section of this recipe, we have been careful to include this command on the other routers inside our AS, even if those routers don't update the Community attribute. The *both* keyword in this command indicates that this router should send both Standard 32-bit and Extended 64-bit Community values. You can configure the router to use just one or the other if you prefer, but in most cases, if you are using Communities, you will want to make sure that you a propagating all of the attributes, so we generally recommend forwarding both types.

There are three useful commands for looking at Community values on a router. The first is the common *show ip bgp summary* command:

```
Router2#show ip bgp summary
BGP router identifier 172.18.5.3, local AS number 65500
BGP table version is 37, main routing table version 37
12 network entries using 1212 bytes of memory
12 path entries using 576 bytes of memory
7 BGP path attribute entries using 420 bytes of memory
1 BGP rrinfo entries using 24 bytes of memory
3 BGP AS-PATH entries using 72 bytes of memory
5 BGP community entries using 120 bytes of memory
0 BGP route-map cache entries using 0 bytes of memory
0 BGP filter-list cache entries using 0 bytes of memory
BGP using 2424 total bytes of memory
BGP activity 46/34 prefixes, 54/42 paths, scan interval 60 secs

Neighbor        V    AS MsgRcvd MsgSent   TblVer  InQ OutQ Up/Down  State/PfxRcd

172.18.5.4      4 65500      54      45       37    0    0 00:00:31        4
172.18.5.10     4 65500      47      65       37    0    0 00:08:35        8
Router2#
```

This output shows that there are five BGP routes on this router that have Community values associated with them. We can see which routes they are with the command *show ip bgp community*:

```
Router2#show ip bgp community
BGP table version is 37, local router ID is 172.18.5.3
Status codes: s suppressed, d damped, h history, * valid, > best, i - internal,
              r RIB-failure, S Stale
Origin codes: i - IGP, e - EGP, ? - incomplete

   Network          Next Hop          Metric LocPrf Weight Path
*>i10.11.0.0/16     172.18.5.2             0    100      0 65510 i
*>i10.102.0.0/16    172.18.5.4             0    100      0 65520 i
*>i10.103.0.0/16    172.18.5.4             0    100      0 65520 i
*>i10.104.0.0/16    172.18.5.4             0    100      0 65520 i
*>i10.105.0.0/16    172.18.5.4             0    100      0 65520 i
Router2#
```

As you can see, the list includes four of the five routes that we tagged on Router3, plus another route that was tagged elsewhere in the network. It's worth pointing out that we don't see 10.101.0.0/16 in this table because it was tagged with the *no-advertise* community. Consequently, Router3 did not advertise this route to Router2. You can see exactly which communities are associated with these routes as follows:

```
Router3#show ip bgp 10.101.0.0/16
BGP routing table entry for 10.101.0.0/16, version 10
Paths: (1 available, best #1, table Default-IP-Routing-Table, not advertised to
any peer)
```

```
    Not advertised to any peer
    65520
      192.168.1.9 from 192.168.1.9 (10.104.0.1)
        Origin IGP, metric 0, localpref 100, valid, external, best
        Community: no-advertise
Router3#show ip bgp 10.102.0.0/16
BGP routing table entry for 10.102.0.0/16, version 11
Paths: (1 available, best #1, table Default-IP-Routing-Table, not advertised to
EBGP peer)
  Advertised to non peer-group peers:
  172.18.5.3 172.18.5.10
  65520
      192.168.1.9 from 192.168.1.9 (10.104.0.1)
        Origin IGP, metric 0, localpref 100, valid, external, best
        Community: no-export
Router3#
```

This shows that the route 10.101.0.0/16 has the *no-advertise* community, and consequently is not being advertised. The route 10.102.0.0/16 has a community value of *no-export*, and is being advertised to two BGP peer routers.

Of course, just being able to set arbitrary Community values is not of much use. Your routers also need to be able to read and react appropriately to these values. To do this, you use a special kind of ACL called a *community-list*, which specifies community values for use in route maps:

```
Router2#configure terminal
Enter configuration commands, one per line.  End with CNTL/Z.
Router2(config)#ip community-list 10 permit 65511:80
Router2(config)#route-map MATCH-COMMUNITY permit 10
Router2(config-route-map)#match community 10
Router2(config-route-map)#set local-preference 80
Router2(config-route-map)#exit
Router2(config)#route-map MATCH-COMMUNITY permit 100
Router2(config-route-map)#exit
Router2(config)#router bgp 65500
Router2(config-router)#no synchronization
Router2(config-router)#neighbor 172.18.5.4 remote-as 65500
Router2(config-router)#neighbor 172.18.5.4 route-map MATCH-COMMUNITY in
Router2(config-router)#exit
Router2(config)#end
Router2#
```

If we do a *show ip bgp community* now and compare to the output above, you can see that the Local Preference value has been changed for this route:

```
Router2#show ip bgp community
BGP table version is 21, local router ID is 172.18.5.3
Status codes: s suppressed, d damped, h history, * valid, > best, i - internal,
              r RIB-failure, S Stale
Origin codes: i - IGP, e - EGP, ? - incomplete

   Network          Next Hop            Metric LocPrf Weight Path
*>i10.11.0.0/16     172.18.5.2               0    100      0 65510 i
```

```
*>i10.102.0.0/16    172.18.5.4              0   100    0 65520 i
*>i10.103.0.0/16    172.18.5.4              0   100    0 65520 i
*>i10.104.0.0/16    172.18.5.4              0   100    0 65520 i
*>i10.105.0.0/16    172.18.5.4              0    80    0 65520 i
Router2#
```

As you can see, the Local Preference value for this route has now been changed appropriately.

See Also

Recipe 9.7

9.18   Using BGP Route Reflectors

Problem

You want to simplify your iBGP peer relationships by using route reflectors.

Solution

There are three types of configurations to consider when working with BGP Route Reflectors: the Route Reflector itself, the Client Peer, and the Nonclient Peer. In this example, which follows Figure 9-4, the Route Reflector is Router2, and it has two Client Peers—Router1 and Router3. It also has a Nonclient Peer, Router4.

The configurations for Client and Nonclient Peers contain no special commands. Router1 is the Client Peer:

```
Router1#configure terminal
Enter configuration commands, one per line.  End with CNTL/Z.
Router1(config)#interface Ethernet0/0
Router1(config-if)#ip address 172.18.5.2 255.255.255.0
Router1(config-if)#exit
Router1(config)#interface Serial0/0
Router1(config-if)#ip address 192.168.1.6 255.255.255.252
Router1(config-if)#exit
Router1(config)#interface Loopback0
Router1(config-if)#ip address 172.18.6.1 255.255.255.255
Router1(config-if)#exit
Router1(config)#router bgp 65500
Router1(config-router)#no synchronization
Router1(config-router)#neighbor 172.18.6.2 remote-as 65500
Router1(config-router)#neighbor 172.18.6.2 next-hop-self
Router1(config-router)#neighbor 172.18.6.2 update-source Loopback0
Router1(config-router)#neighbor 192.168.1.5 remote-as 65510
Router1(config-router)#exit
Router1(config)#ip route 172.18.6.2 255.255.255.255 172.18.5.3
Router1(config)#ip route 172.18.6.3 255.255.255.255 172.18.5.4
Router1(config)#ip route 172.18.6.4 255.255.255.255 172.18.5.10
Router1(config)#end
Router1#
```

Router4 is the Nonclient Peer:

```
Router4#configure terminal
Enter configuration commands, one per line.  End with CNTL/Z.
Router4(config)#interface Ethernet0
Router4(config-if)#ip address 172.18.5.10 255.255.255.0
Router4(config-if)#exit
Router4(config)#interface Loopback0
Router4(config-if)#ip address 172.18.6.4 255.255.255.255
Router4(config-if)#exit
Router4(config)#router bgp 65500
Router4(config-router)#no synchronization
Router4(config-router)#neighbor 172.18.6.2 remote-as 65500
Router4(config-router)#neighbor 172.18.6.2 update-source Loopback0
Router4(config-router)#exit
Router4(config)#ip route 172.18.6.1 255.255.255.255 172.18.5.2
Router4(config)#ip route 172.18.6.2 255.255.255.255 172.18.5.3
Router4(config)#ip route 172.18.6.3 255.255.255.255 172.18.5.4
Router4(config)#end
Router4#
```

The only special configuration required is on the Route Reflector itself:

```
Router2#configure terminal
Enter configuration commands, one per line.  End with CNTL/Z.
Router2(config)#interface FastEthernet0/0
Router2(config-if)#ip address 172.18.5.3 255.255.255.0
Router2(config-if)#exit
Router2(config)#interface Loopback0
Router2(config-if)#ip address 172.18.6.2 255.255.255.255
Router2(config-if)#exit
Router2(config)#router bgp 65500
Router2(config-router)#no synchronization
Router2(config-router)#neighbor 172.18.6.1 remote-as 65500
Router2(config-router)#neighbor 172.18.6.1 route-reflector-client
Router2(config-router)#neighbor 172.18.6.1 update-source Loopback0
Router2(config-router)#neighbor 172.18.6.3 remote-as 65500
Router2(config-router)#neighbor 172.18.6.3 route-reflector-client
Router2(config-router)#neighbor 172.18.6.3 update-source Loopback0
Router2(config-router)#neighbor 172.18.6.4 remote-as 65500
Router2(config-router)#neighbor 172.18.6.4 update-source Loopback0
Router2(config-router)#no auto-summary
Router2(config-router)#exit
Router2(config)#ip route 172.18.6.1 255.255.255.255 172.18.5.2
Router2(config)#ip route 172.18.6.3 255.255.255.255 172.18.5.4
Router2(config)#ip route 172.18.6.4 255.255.255.255 172.18.5.10
Router2(config)#end
Router2#
```

Discussion

In the standard BGP peering model that prevailed in every other recipe in this chapter, there is a strict rule that any external route learned by one of the BGP routers in an AS must be advertised to any other BGP routers in the same AS by the router that used the original route. To see what this means, consider Figure 9-4.

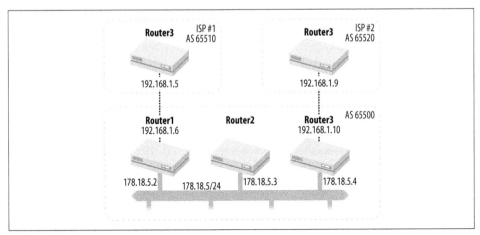

Figure 9-4. BGP route reflection

In this diagram, Router1 receives a routing update from external Router4. So Router1 must readvertise this information to Router2 and Router3, the other routers in the AS. When Router2 receives this update, it may pass the information along to external peers, but it must not relay it to another router in the same AS, such as Router3. The reason for this is simply to prevent routing loops.

This is a sensible rule, in most cases, but it means that every router in an AS must have an iBGP peer relationship with every other router in that AS. This full mesh of iBGP peers doesn't scale very well when you have a lot of BGP routers in one AS. So RFC 2796 provides a way to relax this rule. We can configure Router2 as a Route Reflector, and Router1 and Router3 as its *Client Peers*.

Note that there could be other routers in this AS as well, which may or may not also be client peers of the same route reflector. Router4 is a Nonclient Peer of Router2. The Nonclient Peers must have the usual full mesh peering relationship among one another, although they do not have to peer with any of the Client peers of the route reflector. They can get all of the information for all of the route reflector's client peers at once by simply peering with the route reflector.

You could have more complicated systems of route reflectors in an AS. For example, you might want to divide up your AS into several different regions, each represented by a pair of redundant route reflectors. The peers of each route reflector would then establish iBGP peering relationships with their own reflectors, but not with any other routers in the AS. The route reflectors would then peer with one another in a full mesh to ensure full connectivity within the AS.

It's also important to remember that the route reflectors do not have to pass all of the traffic for their respective clients. Their only special function is in making sure that all of their clients have good BGP routing information.

To configure one router as a Route Reflector, you simply configure a *neighbor* command with the *route-reflector-client* keyword for those neighbor devices that will be Client Peers:

```
Router2(config)#router bgp 65500
Router2(config)#router bgp 65500
Router2(config-router)#no synchronization
Router2(config-router)#neighbor 172.18.6.1 remote-as 65500
Router2(config-router)#neighbor 172.18.6.1 route-reflector-client
Router2(config-router)#neighbor 172.18.6.1 update-source Loopback0
Router2(config-router)#neighbor 172.18.6.3 remote-as 65500
Router2(config-router)#neighbor 172.18.6.3 route-reflector-client
Router2(config-router)#neighbor 172.18.6.3 update-source Loopback0
Router2(config-router)#neighbor 172.18.6.4 remote-as 65500
Router2(config-router)#neighbor 172.18.6.4 update-source Loopback0
Router2(config-router)#no auto-summary
Router2(config-router)#exit
```

This specifies that the two peers, 172.18.6.1 and 172.18.6.3, are Client Peers. We have not included a *neighbor route-reflector-client* command for the other neighbor, 172.18.6.4, making it a Nonclient Peer of this route reflector. There is no special configuration required on either Client or Nonclient Peer routers and, indeed, these devices don't even know or care about the difference. The only router that needs to do anything special is the Route Reflector itself.

When configuring two or more redundant BGP Route Reflectors, though, another little trick is required. In the current example, if we were to just turn on Route Reflection on Router4 with the same clients as Router2, this would cause some problems, as the two Route Reflectors hear about every reflected routing prefix both from the original source and from the other Route Reflector. This could cause strange behavior if the real source of the route becomes unavailable. The two Route Reflectors will both believe that the route is reachable through one another.

To prevent this problem, we need to specify a cluster ID on each Route Reflector to identify a particular group of Client Peers:

```
Router2#configure terminal
Enter configuration commands, one per line.  End with CNTL/Z.
Router2(config)#router bgp 65500
Router2(config-router)#bgp cluster-id 1234
```

And you need to configure the same cluster ID on the other Route Reflector:

```
Router4#configure terminal
Enter configuration commands, one per line.  End with CNTL/Z.
Router4(config)#router bgp 65500
Router4(config-router)#bgp cluster-id 1234
```

There is one important caveat about implementing cluster IDs, however. In a case like this one, where we had one router acting as a Route Reflector, and we wanted to either implement a new cluster ID, or to change an existing one, we had to manually remove the Client Peer configuration from the Route Reflector first. Then we configured the *cluster-id* command and replaced the Client Peer neighbor configuration statements.

When working with Route Reflectors, we strongly recommend implementing two or more redundant reflectors. If you have a single reflector for a large network, then this becomes a dangerous single point of failure for your entire BGP routing infrastructure.

See Also

RFC 2796

9.19 Putting It All Together

Problem

You want to combine all of best the elements in this chapter to create a good redundant ISP connection.

Solution

For simplicity, we will extend the single router dual ISP configuration of Recipe 9.4 rather than the dual router dual ISP example of Recipe 9.5. It should be clear from the discussion in Recipe 9.5 how to extend this example to the two-router case:

```
Router1#configure terminal
Enter configuration commands, one per line.  End with CNTL/Z.
Router1(config)#interface Serial0
Router1(config-if)#description connection to ISP #1, ASN 65510
Router1(config-if)#ip address 192.168.1.6 255.255.255.252
Router1(config-if)#exit
Router1(config)#interface Serial1
Router1(config-if)#description connection to ISP #2, ASN 65520
Router1(config-if)#ip address 192.168.2.6 255.255.255.252
Router1(config-if)#exit
Router1(config)#interface Ethernet0
Router1(config-if)#description connection to internal network, ASN 65500
Router1(config-if)#ip address 172.18.5.2 255.255.255.0
Router1(config-if)#exit
Router1(config)#ip as-path access-list 15 permit ^$
Router1(config)#ip route 0.0.0.0 0.0.0.0 192.168.101.0 1
Router1(config)#ip route 0.0.0.0 0.0.0.0 192.168.102.0 2
Router1(config)#ip prefix-list CREATE-DEFAULT seq 10 permit 192.168.101.0/24
Router1(config)#ip prefix-list CREATE-DEFAULT seq 20 permit 192.168.102.0/24
Router1(config)#ip prefix-list BLOCK-DEFAULT seq 10 permit 0.0.0.0/0 ge 1
Router1(config)#route-map PREPEND permit 10
Router1(config-route-map)#set as-path prepend 65500 65500
```

```
Router1(config-route-map)#exit
Router1(config)#route-map LOCALPREF permit 10
Router1(config-route-map)#set local-preference 75
Router1(config-route-map)#exit
Router1(config)#route-map DEFAULT-ROUTE permit 10
Router1(config-route-map)#match ip address prefix-list CREATE-DEFAULT
Router1(config-route-map)#exit
Router1(config)#router bgp 65500
Router1(config-router)#network 172.18.5.0 mask 255.255.255.0
Router1(config-router)#neighbor 172.18.5.3 remote-as 65500
Router1(config-router)#neighbor 172.18.5.3 password password_number1
Router1(config-router)#neighbor 172.18.5.3 default-origniate route-map DEFAULT-ROUTE
Router1(config-router)#neighbor 192.168.1.5 remote-as 65510
Router1(config-router)#neighbor 192.168.1.5 password password_number2
Router1(config-router)#neighbor 192.168.1.5 filter-list 15 out
Router1(config-router)#neighbor 192.168.1.5 prefix-list CREATE-DEFAULT in
Router1(config-router)#neighbor 192.168.1.5 prefix-list BLOCK-DEFAULT out
Router1(config-router)#neighbor 192.168.2.5 remote-as 65520
Router1(config-router)#neighbor 192.168.2.5 password password_number3
Router1(config-router)#neighbor 192.168.2.5 filter-list 15 out
Router1(config-router)#neighbor 192.168.2.5 prefix-list CREATE-DEFAULT in
Router1(config-router)#neighbor 192.168.2.5 prefix-list BLOCK-DEFAULT out
Router1(config-router)#neighbor 192.168.2.5 route-map PREPEND out
Router1(config-router)#neighbor 192.168.2.5 route-map LOCALPREF in
Router1(config-router)#no synchronization
Router1(config-router)#exit
Router1(config)#end
Router1#
```

Discussion

In this recipe, we put together several of the concepts discussed throughout the chapter. This router has three BGP peers, two of which are ISPs, and the other is an internal BGP router.

We have disabled synchronization. We aren't using an IGP on this router, so synchronization doesn't serve any purpose. We have used a *network* statement that covers only part of a classful network:

```
Router1(config)#router bgp 65500
Router1(config-router)#network 172.18.5.0 mask 255.255.255.0
Router1(config-router)#no synchronization
```

All of the peer relationships, including the internal peer, use MD5 authentication, which we have configured by using the *neighbor password* command, as discussed in Recipe 9.16:

```
Router1(config)#router bgp 65500
Router1(config-router)#neighbor 172.18.5.3 password password_number1
Router1(config-router)#neighbor 192.168.1.5 password password_number2
Router1(config-router)#neighbor 192.168.2.5 password password_number3
```

Note that we have configured different passwords on each peer, and each password is between 12 and 24 characters long, as we discussed in Recipe 9.16.

We have configured an AS Path filter to each of the ISP peers to prevent them from using our network for transit purposes:

```
Router1(config)#router bgp 65500
Router1(config)#ip as-path access-list 15 permit ^$
Router1(config-router)#neighbor 192.168.1.5 filter-list 15 out
Router1(config-router)#neighbor 192.168.2.5 filter-list 15 out
```

We have followed Recipe 9.11 to replace the entire Internet routing table with a default route. This router then passes its default route along to the internal BGP router, which forces us to be careful that we don't distribute the default back to the ISP routers:

```
Router1(config)#ip route 0.0.0.0 0.0.0.0 192.168.101.0 1
Router1(config)#ip route 0.0.0.0 0.0.0.0 192.168.102.0 2
Router1(config)#ip prefix-list CREATE-DEFAULT seq 10 permit 192.168.101.0/24
Router1(config)#ip prefix-list CREATE-DEFAULT seq 20 permit 192.168.102.0/24
Router1(config)#ip prefix-list BLOCK-DEFAULT permit 0.0.0.0/0 ge 1
Router1(config)#route-map DEFAULT-ROUTE permit 10
Router1(config-route-map)#match ip address prefix-list CREATE-DEFAULT
Router1(config-route-map)#exit
Router1(config)#router bgp 65500
Router1(config-router)#neighbor 172.18.5.3 remote-as 65500
Router1(config-router)#neighbor 172.18.5.3 default-origniate route-map DEFAULT-ROUTE
Router1(config-router)#neighbor 192.168.1.5 remote-as 65510
Router1(config-router)#neighbor 192.168.1.5 prefix-list CREATE-DEFAULT in
Router1(config-router)#neighbor 192.168.1.5 prefix-list BLOCK-DEFAULT out
Router1(config-router)#neighbor 192.168.2.5 remote-as 65520
Router1(config-router)#neighbor 192.168.2.5 prefix-list CREATE-DEFAULT in
Router1(config-router)#neighbor 192.168.2.5 prefix-list BLOCK-DEFAULT out
```

Next, we have used Recipe 9.7 to make ISP #2 less attractive for outbound traffic. This may be because this ISP has higher usage charges, or perhaps it is a lower bandwidth connection. Using Local Preference for this ensures that all of the BGP routers inside the AS can share this information about the best outbound path:

```
Router1(config)#route-map LOCALPREF permit 10
Router1(config-route-map)#set local-preference 75
Router1(config-route-map)#exit
Router1(config)#router bgp 65500
Router1(config-router)#neighbor 192.168.2.5 route-map LOCALPREF in
```

And, finally, we have followed Recipe 9.13 to make sure that inbound traffic from the public Internet also uses the link through ISP #1 preferentially:

```
Router1(config)#route-map PREPEND permit 10
Router1(config-route-map)#set as-path prepend 65500 65500
Router1(config-route-map)#exit
Router1(config)#router bgp 65500
Router1(config-router)#neighbor 192.168.2.5 route-map PREPEND out
```

You should feel free to mix and match these types of configuration elements to make your configuration match your requirements.

Many backbone ISPs have looking glass servers that allow you to see how your BGP routes look several hops away from your network. These are generally web pages that allow you to submit show BGP type queries for specific routes. You can find a list of looking glass servers around the world on *http://www.traceroute.org*. This site also lists a large number of traceroute servers, which will allow you to test which paths inbound connections will use to reach your network.

See Also

Recipe 9.4; Recipe 9.5; Recipe 9.7; Recipe 9.11; Recipe 9.13; Recipe 9.16

## CHAPTER 10

Frame Relay

10.0 Introduction

Frame Relay is a popular WAN protocol because it makes it easy to construct reliable and inexpensive networks. Its main advantage over simple point-to-point serial links is the ability to connect one site to many remote sites through a single physical circuit. Frame Relay uses *virtual circuits* to connect any physical circuit in a cloud to any other physical circuit. Many virtual circuits can coexist on a single physical interface.

This section will offer only a quick refresher of how Frame Relay works. If you are unfamiliar with Frame Relay, we recommend reading the more detailed description of the protocol and its features that are found in *T1: A Survival Guide* by Matthew Gast (O'Reilly).

The Frame Relay standard allows for both Switched (SVC) and Permanent (PVC) Virtual Circuits, although support for SVCs in Frame Relay switching equipment continues to be relatively rare. Most fixed Frame Relay WANs use PVCs rather than SVCs. This allows you to configure the routers to look like a set of point-to-point physical connections. SVCs, on the other hand, provide a mechanism for the network to dynamically make connections between any two physical circuits as they are needed. In general, SVCs are more complicated to configure and manage. Most network engineers prefer to use PVCs unless the carrier offers significant cost benefits for using SVCs. SVCs tend to be most practical when the site-to-site traffic is relatively light and intermittent.

Each virtual circuit is identified by a Data Link Connection Identifier (DLCI), which is simply a number between 0 and 1023. In fact, Cisco routers can only use DLCI numbers in the range 16 through 1007 to carry user data.

If the router at Site A wants to send a packet to Site B, it simply specifies the appropriate DLCI number for the virtual circuit that connects to Site B site in the Frame Relay header. Although a physical circuit can have many virtual circuits, each connecting to a different remote circuit, there is no ambiguity about where the network should send each individual packet.

It's important to remember, though, that the DLCI number only has local significance. That is, the DLCI number doesn't uniquely identify the whole virtual circuit, just the connection from the local physical circuit to the Frame Relay switch at the Telco central office. The DLCI number associated with this virtual circuit can change several times before it reaches the remote physical circuit.

We like to use this fact to our advantage when constructing a Frame Relay network. Instead of thinking of the DLCI number as a virtual circuit identifier, we use it to uniquely label each physical circuit. Suppose, for example, that Site A has virtual circuits to both Sites B and C. Then we would use the same DLCI number at both Sites B and C to label the virtual circuits that terminate at Site A. This is just one of many possible DLCI numbering schemes, but we prefer it because it makes troubleshooting easier. Unfortunately, while this scheme works well in hub-and-spoke network topologies, it tends to become unworkable in meshed or partially meshed networks.

Frame Relay QoS Features

Frame Relay has several built-in Quality of Service (QoS) features. Each virtual circuit has two important service level parameters, the Committed Information Rate (CIR) and the Excess Information Rate (EIR). The CIR is the contracted minimum throughput of a virtual circuit. As long as you send data a rate that is less than the CIR value, it should all arrive. The EIR is the available capacity above the CIR. The worst case is when the router is sending data through a single virtual circuit at the line speed of the physical circuit. The network will generally just drop all packets that exceed the EIR. So it is customary to have the sum of CIR+EIR for each virtual circuit equal to the line speed of the physical circuit. This makes it physically impossible to exceed the EIR for any PVC.

When the router sends packets faster than the CIR rate that you have contracted with your network provider, the carrier network may drop some or all of the excess packets if there is congestion in the cloud. To indicate which packets are in the excess region, the first switch to receive them will often mark the Discard Eligible (DE) bit in their Frame Relay headers. If there is no congestion, the packet will be delivered normally. But if the packet goes through a congested part of the carrier's network, the switches will know that they can drop this packet without violating the CIR commitments. So just by counting the packets that have their DE bit set on the receiving router, you get a useful measure of how often your network exceeds the CIR on each PVC, and in each direction.

By default, the router will send frames into the cloud without the DE bit set. What happens next is up to the carrier, but it is common for the first switch to monitor the incoming traffic rate using some variation of the following. During each sample period (typically a short period of time such as a second), the switch will count the incoming bytes on each PVC. If there is more data than the CIR for this PVC, the switch will mark the DE bit in all of the excess frames.

However, it is also possible to configure the router to set the DE bit on low-priority traffic in the hopes that the network will drop these low-priority packets in preference to the high-priority packets. This is something of a gamble, of course, and its success depends critically on the precise algorithm that your WAN vendor uses for handling congestion. You should consult with your vendor to understand these traffic shaping and policing mechanisms before attempting this type of configuration.

There are two other extremely useful flags in the Frame Relay header: the Forward Explicit Congestion Notification (FECN) and the Backward Explicit Congestion Notification (BECN). These simply indicate that the packet encountered congestion somewhere in the carrier's network. Congestion is most serious when you are sending at a rate higher than the CIR value. If your carrier marks the DE bit of these excess packets, then congestion in one of their switches could mean dropped packets.

If a packet encounters congestion in a carrier switch, that switch will often set the FECN flag in the packet's header. Then, when the other router finally receives this packet, it will know that it was delayed. But this is actually not all that useful because the receiving router is not able directly affect the rate that the sending router forwards packets along this virtual circuit. So the Frame Relay standard also includes the BECN flag.

When a switch encounters congestion and needs to set the FECN flag on a packet, it looks for another packet traversing the same PVC in the opposite direction, and marks it with a BECN flag. This way, the sending router immediately knows that the packets it is sending are encountering congestion.

Note, however, that not all Frame Relay switches implement these features in the same way. So just because you see no FECN or BECN frames doesn't mean you can safely assume that there is no congestion. Similarly, not seeing DE frames doesn't necessarily mean that you aren't exceeding the CIR for a PVC. In Recipe 10.6, for example, we show how to configure a router to act as a Frame Relay switch. But the router does not implement these congestion notification features by default. And the DE counter is also not a meaningful indicator of how often you exceed CIR if your devices are configured to send low priority frames with the DE bit set.

By default, the router will not react to FECN and BECN markings. Recipe 10.10 shows how you can look at statistics on FECN and BECN frames to get an idea of the network performance. However, in the next chapter, Recipe 11.14 shows how to configure a router to automatically adapt to congestion in the carrier network by reading and responding to the BECN flags, reducing the sending rate until the congestion disappears.

10.1 Setting Up Frame Relay with Point-to-Point Subinterfaces

Problem

You want to configure Frame Relay services so that each PVC is assigned to a separate subinterface.

Solution

Probably the cleanest way to set up a Frame Relay network is to use point-to-point subinterfaces. If you have a host site that connects to two or more branches through a Frame Relay WAN, you could configure the central host router like this:

```
Central#configure terminal
Enter configuration commands, one per line.  End with CNTL/Z.
Central(config)#interface Serial0
Central(config-if)#description Frame-Relay host circuit
Central(config-if)#no ip address
Central(config-if)#encapsulation frame-relay
Central(config-if)#exit
Central(config)#interface Serial0.1 point-to-point
Central(config-subif)#description PVC to first branch - DLCI 101
Central(config-subif)#ip address 192.168.1.5 255.255.255.252
Central(config-subif)#frame-relay interface-dlci 101
Central(config-fr-dlci)#exit
Central(config-subif)#exit
Central(config)#interface Serial0.2 point-to-point
Central(config-subif)#description PVC to second branch - DLCI 102
Central(config-subif)#ip address 192.168.1.9 255.255.255.252
Central(config-subif)#frame-relay interface-dlci 102
Central(config-fr-dlci)#exit
Central(config-subif)#exit
Central(config)#end
Central#
```

And all of the branches would follow the same basic configuration, but with different IP addresses and DLCI numbers:

```
Branch1#configure terminal
Enter configuration commands, one per line.  End with CNTL/Z.
Branch1(config)#interface Serial0
Branch1(config-if)#description Frame-Relay circuit
Branch1(config-if)#no ip address
Branch1(config-if)#encapsulation frame-relay
Branch1(config-if)#exit
Branch1(config)#interface Serial0.1 point-to-point
Branch1(config-subif)#description PVC to Central host - DLCI 50
Branch1(config-subif)#ip address 192.168.1.6 255.255.255.252
Branch1(config-subif)#frame-relay interface-dlci 50
```

```
Branch1(config-fr-dlci)#exit
Branch1(config-if)#exit
Branch1(config)#end
Branch1#
```

Discussion

In this example, we have assumed that all of the Frame Relay circuits connect to serial interfaces on the routers. This is normally the case, but there are other options. Frame Relay is usually delivered on low speed 56 or 64 Kbps circuits, or fractional or full T1 or E1 circuits. However, there are useful Frame Relay implementations all the way up to T3 speeds. The most common way to deliver Frame Relay service faster than T1 or E1 speeds is on either a coax T3 or a High Speed Serial Interface (HSSI) connection.

In all cases, the router is the Data Terminal Equipment (DTE) device, and the Frame Relay switch in the carrier's network is the Data Communications Equipment (DCE). Make sure that you have the right DTE type cable.

As an aside, while many carriers currently offer T3 Frame Relay service, very few Frame Relay switches are able to reliably switch packets along a single PVC much faster than T1 or E1 speeds. This means that a T3 or HSSI circuit makes an excellent aggregation point for a large number of branches with T1, E1, or slower circuits. However, you should talk it over very thoroughly with your WAN provider before attempting to build a Frame Relay network that requires CIR rates greater than a T1 or E1.

By default, the router will dynamically determine the encapsulation format for the data payload of each packet. If you have to connect to non-Cisco equipment, you may prefer to manually specify the open standard encapsulation format described in RFC 1490 instead. You can configure this either for each subinterface separately, or globally for the entire interface. To configure one subinterface to use RFC 1490 encapsulation, use the *ietf* keyword:

```
Central(config)#interface Serial0.1 point-to-point
Central(config-subif)#frame-relay interface-dlci 101 ietf
Central(config-fr-dlci)#end
```

You can make RFC 1490 encapsulation the default for all subinterfaces on an interface as follows:

```
Central(config)#interface Serial0
Central(config-if)#encapsulation frame-relay ietf
Central(config-if)#end
```

When you do this, you do not need to specify the *ietf* keyword on each subinterface. The other option for payload encapsulation is a Cisco proprietary standard. If you want to use to the Cisco encapsulation format on a particular PVC, you can do so with the *cisco* keyword:

```
Central(config)#interface Serial0.1 point-to-point
Central(config-subif)#frame-relay interface-dlci 101 cisco
Central(config-fr-dlci)#end
```

It is extremely important to specify the *point-to-point* keyword here. The problem is that you can't change a subinterface type. If you specify the wrong type of subinterface, you must delete the incorrect one, and then reboot the router before you can recreate it with the correct type. This was particularly serious in earlier IOS releases because the default was multipoint, rather than point-to-point. In Version 12.0 and higher, there is no default, and you must explicitly specify either point-to-point or multipoint. We will discuss multipoint subinterfaces in Recipe 10.4.

The *show frame-relay pvc* command shows the status and several useful statistics for each PVC:

```
Central#show frame-relay pvc

PVC Statistics for interface Serial0 (Frame Relay DTE)

DLCI = 101, DLCI USAGE = LOCAL, PVC STATUS = ACTIVE, INTERFACE = Serial0.1

    input pkts 4092         output pkts 1331        in bytes 573274
    out bytes 364868        dropped pkts 0          in FECN pkts 0
    in BECN pkts 0          out FECN pkts 0         out BECN pkts 0
    in DE pkts 0            out DE pkts 0
    out bcast pkts 1277        out bcast bytes 361391
    pvc create time 21:16:46, last time pvc status changed 21:16:46

DLCI = 102, DLCI USAGE = LOCAL, PVC STATUS = DELETED, INTERFACE = Serial0.2

    input pkts 0            output pkts 2           in bytes 0
    out bytes 566           dropped pkts 0          in FECN pkts 0
    in BECN pkts 0          out FECN pkts 0         out BECN pkts 0
    in DE pkts 0            out DE pkts 0
    out bcast pkts 2           out bcast bytes 566
    pvc create time 00:02:08, last time pvc status changed 00:01:15
Central#
```

In this case, two DLCIs are configured on the router. Only one of these is in an active state; the other shows as DELETED, which means that it is not configured on the switch. This command also shows you if there are other PVCs configured in the Frame Relay switch but not on the router. These DLCIs are easy to spot because the DLCI USAGE field is listed as UNUSED:

```
Central#show frame-relay pvc

PVC Statistics for interface Serial1 (Frame Relay DTE)

DLCI = 101, DLCI USAGE = LOCAL, PVC STATUS = ACTIVE, INTERFACE = Serial0.1

    input pkts 11           output pkts 14          in bytes 2218
    out bytes 1825          dropped pkts 3          in FECN pkts 0
    in BECN pkts 0          out FECN pkts 0         out BECN pkts 0
    in DE pkts 0            out DE pkts 0
    out bcast pkts 9           out bcast bytes 1305
    pvc create time 00:02:45, last time pvc status changed 00:02:24
```

```
DLCI = 102, DLCI USAGE = LOCAL, PVC STATUS = DELETED, INTERFACE = Serial0.2

  input pkts 0          output pkts 2         in bytes 0
  out bytes 566         dropped pkts 0        in FECN pkts 0
  in BECN pkts 0        out FECN pkts 0       out BECN pkts 0
  in DE pkts 0          out DE pkts 0
  out bcast pkts 2        out bcast bytes 566
  pvc create time 00:02:08, last time pvc status changed 00:01:15

DLCI = 103, DLCI USAGE = UNUSED, PVC STATUS = INACTIVE, INTERFACE = Serial0

  input pkts 0          output pkts 0         in bytes 0
  out bytes 0           dropped pkts 0        in FECN pkts 0
  in BECN pkts 0        out FECN pkts 0       out BECN pkts 0
  in DE pkts 0          out DE pkts 0
  out bcast pkts 0        out bcast bytes 0         Num Pkts Switched 0
  pvc create time 00:00:08, last time pvc status changed 00:00:08
Central#
```

In this case, you can see that a new PVC with DLCI 103 was created on the switch eight seconds ago on the circuit that connects to the router's *Serial0* interface. This new PVC is not associated with a subinterface, and it is not passing any traffic.

The *show interface* command gives other useful information, particularly about the Local Management Interface (LMI) protocol:

```
Router#show interface Serial0
Serial0 is up, line protocol is up
  Hardware is HD64570
  Description: Frame-Relay circuit
  MTU 1500 bytes, BW 1544 Kbit, DLY 20000 usec, rely 255/255, load 1/255
  Encapsulation FRAME-RELAY, loopback not set, keepalive set (10 sec)
  LMI enq sent  7932, LMI stat recvd 7932, LMI upd recvd 0, DTE LMI up
  LMI enq recvd 0, LMI stat sent  0, LMI upd sent  0
  LMI DLCI 1023  LMI type is CISCO  frame relay DTE
  Broadcast queue 0/64, broadcasts sent/dropped 1320/0, interface broadcasts 2
  Last input 00:00:00, output 00:00:00, output hang never
  Last clearing of "show interface" counters 22:01:52
  Input queue: 0/75/0 (size/max/drops); Total output drops: 0
  Queueing strategy: weighted fair
  Output queue: 0/1000/64/0 (size/max total/threshold/drops)
   Conversations  0/1/256 (active/max active/max total)
     Reserved Conversations 0/0 (allocated/max allocated)
  5 minute input rate 0 bits/sec, 0 packets/sec
  5 minute output rate 0 bits/sec, 0 packets/sec
     12481 packets input, 720402 bytes, 0 no buffer
     Received 0 broadcasts, 0 runts, 0 giants, 0 throttles
     0 input errors, 0 CRC, 0 frame, 0 overrun, 0 ignored, 0 abort
     9579 packets output, 500221 bytes, 0 underruns
     0 output errors, 0 collisions, 0 interface resets
     0 output buffer failures, 0 output buffers swapped out
     0 carrier transitions
     DCD=up  DSR=up  DTR=up  RTS=up  CTS=up
Branch1#
```

LMI provides many of Frame Relay's useful features, such as keepalives, that can tell a router when one or more PVCs become unavailable. This example shows CISCO type LMI, which uses DLCI number 1023. If we had specified the CCITT or ANSI LMI standards, the router would use DLCI number 0 for LMI. Recipe 10.2 shows how to configure these different LMI options.

When you enable Frame Relay on an interface, the router automatically activates the Inverse ARP protocol, which is described in RFC 1293. The router uses Inverse ARP to make a dynamic mapping between a Frame Relay DLCI number and a Layer 3 address. This Layer 3 address could be for any supported protocol such as IP, Appletalk, IPX, and so forth.

In this recipe, we built a static mapping between the DLCI number and the IP address, so we don't actually need Inverse ARP. Each subinterface always associates a particular DLCI number with a particular Layer 3 address. This means that we can safely disable Inverse ARP. You can do this for an individual protocol as follows:

```
Central(config)#interface Serial0
Central(config-if)#no frame-relay inverse-arp ip
```

Or you can disable Inverse ARP globally for all protocols:

```
Central(config)#interface Serial0
Central(config-if)#no frame-relay inverse-arp
```

In this case, if you want to reenable Inverse ARP just for a particular protocol you can do so like this:

```
Central(config)#interface Serial0
Central(config-if)#frame-relay inverse-arp ipx 100
```

This tells the router that it should use Inverse ARP to discover the IPX address of the device on the other end of the virtual circuit with DLCI number 100. If you don't need Inverse ARP, we generally recommend disabling it.

See Also

Recipe 10.2; Recipe 11.14

10.2 Adjusting LMI Options

Problem

You want to configure different LMI options on your Frame Relay circuit.

Solution

There are several different LMI options. The first specifies which version of LMI protocol you wish to use:

```
Branch1#configure terminal
Enter configuration commands, one per line.  End with CNTL/Z.
Branch1(config)#interface Serial0
Branch1(config-if)#encapsulation frame-relay
Branch1(config-if)#frame-relay lmi-type ansi
Branch1(config-if)#exit
Branch1(config)#end
Branch1#
```

By default, LMI sends keepalive packets through every PVC every 10 seconds to verify that the path is still available. You can adjust this value with the *keepalive* command:

```
Branch1#configure terminal
Enter configuration commands, one per line.  End with CNTL/Z.
Branch1(config)#interface Serial0
Branch1(config-if)#encapsulation frame-relay
Branch1(config-if)#keepalive 5
Branch1(config-if)#exit
Branch1(config)#end
Branch1#
```

LMI is not supported on all networks. If this is the case in your network, you must configure the router to announce its own DLCI number with the *local-dlci* command:

```
Branch1#configure terminal
Enter configuration commands, one per line.  End with CNTL/Z.
Branch1(config)#interface Serial0
Branch1(config-if)#encapsulation frame-relay
Branch1(config-if)#frame-relay local-dlci 50
Branch1(config-if)#exit
Branch1(config)#end
Branch1#
```

Discussion

The first example in this recipe sets an alternative LMI type. By default, Cisco routers will attempt to detect the LMI type. There are three options. The first is called *cisco* on the router, although this is slightly confusing because it is not a Cisco proprietary standard, but rather was developed jointly by Cisco and other vendors. In fact, this default setting is usually the one you want because it is the default setting in many Frame Relay switches. The second LMI-type option is called ANSI, and the third is Q933A.

The example shows how to set the ANSI standard LMI type:

```
Branch1(config-if)#frame-relay lmi-type ansi
```

Another LMI option, *q933a*, is also available. This option configures the router to use the Annex A of the ITU-T standard. This is sometimes called the CCITT LMI standard. The Q933A LMI type is most commonly used for SVCs, although it can also support Frame Relay PVCs:

```
Branch1(config-if)#frame-relay lmi-type q933a
```

You must ensure that the LMI type you use matches what your carrier uses. It is not even necessary that all routers in the network use the same LMI type, as long as each router matches the settings on its respective Frame Relay switch. In most cases, the router is able to successfully auto-detect the LMI type, so you would only use these commands if there is a problem with this process.

The second example sets the LMI keepalive time. Once again, this parameter depends on what is configured on the switch. In fact, as long as you use a keepalive setting that is less than the period on the switch, you should have no problems. In networks that do not use LMI, you should disable this polling as follows:

```
Branch1#configure terminal
Enter configuration commands, one per line.  End with CNTL/Z.
Branch1(config)#interface Serial0
Branch1(config-if)#encapsulation frame-relay
Branch1(config-if)#no keepalive
Branch1(config-if)#exit
Branch1(config)#end
Branch1#
```

The last option defines a local DLCI:

```
Branch1(config-if)#frame-relay local-dlci 50
```

Here we have set the router's serial interface to use DLCI number 50. This command is only required on networks that do not use LMI, but there is no harm in configuring it for networks that do use LMI. In fact, some network engineers opt to configure this statement on all of their Frame Relay circuits as a mnemonic to remind them of the DLCI numbers that other devices use to reach this circuit. However, if you use the local DLCI number for this purpose, you should not disable keepalives because LMI requires them.

10.3   Setting Up Frame Relay with Map Statements

Problem

You want to configure Frame Relay services so that every PVC appears to share the same interface.

Solution

In its simplest form, the Frame Relay map configuration involves considerably less typing than the subinterface version of the same configuration:

```
Central#configure terminal
Enter configuration commands, one per line.  End with CNTL/Z.
Central(config)#interface Serial0
Central(config)#description Frame Relay to branches
Central(config-if)#ip address 192.168.1.1 255.255.255.0
Central(config-if)#encapsulation frame-relay
```

```
Central(config-if)#frame-relay map ip 192.168.1.10 101
Central(config-if)#frame-relay map ip 192.168.1.11 102
Central(config-if)#frame-relay map ip 192.168.1.12 103
Central(config-if)#exit
Central(config)#end
Central#
```

Discussion

Instead of treating the Frame Relay WAN as a series of point-to-point logical connections as we did in Recipe 10.1, you can set configure it to look similar to a LAN segment with a contiguous block of IP addresses. There are two ways to do this—either by using *frame-relay map* statements, as in this recipe, or using multipoint subinterfaces, as in Recipe 10.4. In general, we prefer to use point-to-point subinterfaces for Frame Relay networks because it gives you more detailed controls over the routing protocol.

Furthermore, when you use point-to-point subinterfaces, the router can generate a trap when a DLCI becomes inactive, which makes network management much easier. With multipoint subinterfaces, the router will generate a trap only when all of the associated DLCIs become unavailable, but not for individual failures. And when you use frame-relay map statements, as in this recipe, the router will not provide any notification of DLCI failures. However, while the Frame Relay map method lacks some of the features of subinterfaces, it is still perfectly acceptable in less complicated networks.

The *frame-relay map* command has several useful options. In the example, we used the simplest version of the command:

```
Central(config-if)#frame-relay map ip 192.168.1.10 101
```

This associates the IP address 192.168.1.10 with DLCI number 101. If you have other protocols, such as IPX or Appletalk, you must configure them separately:

```
Central(config-if)#frame-relay map ipx 10AF.0.0.1 101
Central(config-if)#frame-relay map appletalk 1.15 101
```

The configuration of the router on the other end of this PVC can use either a similar map statement, or a subinterface, as in Recipe 10.1. If you use a *map* statement on the remote router, it should be configured with the IP address and DLCI number for the router on this end:

```
Branch1(config-if)#frame-relay map ip 192.168.1.1 50
```

Note that when you configure a Frame Relay map like this, you create a static mapping between a DLCI number and a Layer 3 protocol address, IP in this case. In Recipe 10.1 we mentioned that when you create a static map between these Layer 2 and Layer 3 parameters, you can disable Inverse ARP. If you don't need the router to make dynamic associations between Frame Relay DLCI numbers and Layer 3 addresses, we recommend disabling Inverse ARP:

```
Central(config)#interface Serial0
Central(config-if)#no frame-relay inverse-arp
```

When you set up a TCP/IP network using *map* statements, you have to bear in mind that the Frame Relay network does not handle broadcasts to the remote sites like a LAN segment. In fact, it is the classic example of a Nonbroadcast Multiple Access (NBMA) network. This can make OSPF configuration somewhat more complex, and it can cause serious problems for routing protocols that don't handle NBMA media well.

The default configuration for most routing protocols assumes that you can reach all of the adjacent routers through a particular interface with either a broadcast or a multicast advertisement packet. With some protocols you can configure the neighbors statically, and instruct them to use unicast packets to exchange routing information instead. However, if you leave this in the default configuration, the routing protocols will not work at all.

Cisco routers also allow you to cheat a little bit and treat the Frame Relay network as if it were a broadcast medium by simply adding the *broadcast* keyword to the map statement:

```
Central(config-if)#frame-relay map ip 192.168.1.10 101 broadcast
```

In this case, if you were to send a packet to the broadcast address, 192.168.1.255, the router would make copies of the broadcast packet and send it out to all of the remote sites configured on this interface. Please refer to Chapter 6 for more information on RIP, andChapter 8 for OSPF.

The *ietf* keyword is another useful option in some situations. This tells the router to use RFC 1490 encapsulation instead of the default Cisco proprietary encapsulation:

```
Central(config-if)#frame-relay map ip 192.168.1.10 101 ietf
```

The default encapsulation does not work well with equipment from some vendors. So if you have problems connecting to nonCisco equipment, this option might help. You can also enable RFC 1490 encapsulation globally on the whole interface as follows:

```
Central(config)#interface Serial0
Central(config-if)#encapsulation frame-relay ietf
Central(config-if)#end
```

In this case it is no longer necessary to specify the *ietf* keyword on each *map* statement. However, if you want to revert to the default Cisco encapsulation on a particular PVC, you can use the *cisco* keyword:

```
Central(config-if)#frame-relay map ip 192.168.1.10 101 cisco
```

We discuss some more options for the *frame-relay map* command in Recipe 10.9.

Finally, we note in passing that with Inverse ARP you can automatically discover the Frame Relay DLCIs and associated IP addresses. So a particularly simple and elegant way of creating a Frame Relay network is to allow the routers to automatically detect the LMI type, the encapsulation method and all DLCIs. To do this, you just configure an IP address and the default Frame Relay encapsulation on the physical interface as follows:

```
Central(config)#interface Serial0
Central(config-if)#ip address 192.168.1.1 255.255.255.0
Central(config-if)#encapsulation frame-relay
```

Then a *show frame-relay map* command shows that Inverse ARP has done all of the other work for you:

```
Central#show frame map
Serial0/0 (up): ip 172.19.1.6 dlci 201(0xC9,0x3090), dynamic,
               broadcast,, status defined, active
Serial0/0 (up): ip 192.168.1.10 dlci 101(0x65,0x18C0), dynamic,
               broadcast,, status defined, active
Serial0/0 (up): ip 192.168.1.11 dlci 102(0x66,0x18D0), dynamic,
               broadcast,, status defined, active
Serial0/0 (up): ip 192.168.1.12 dlci 103(0x67,0x1870), dynamic,
               broadcast,, status defined, active
R3#
```

Notice in this output that Inverse ARP has also discovered DLCI 201 connected to another router, which is on a different subnet. So this method can very quickly help with troubleshooting as well.

However, as simple and elegant as this configuration method is, we still prefer to use point-to-point subinterfaces wherever we can. This is because it gives us so much greater control. For example, we can specify different routing protocol costs for PVCs with different CIR values, and we avoid a lot of the complications involved in running routing protocols over the NBMA multipoint Frame Relay network. Further, as we mentioned earlier, point-to-point subinterfaces provide the only way to get SNMP alerts when the corresponding DLCI goes away in the Frame Relay cloud. And a final compelling reason to avoid simply relying on Inverse ARP is that it can take a considerable length of time for the router to discover all of the remote devices.

See Also

Recipe 10.1; Recipe 10.9; Chapter 6 for more on RIP; Chapter 8 for more on OSPF

10.4   Using Multipoint Subinterfaces

Problem

You want to configure Frame Relay so that many PVCs share the same subinterface.

Solution

You can connect several virtual circuits to a single subinterface as follows:

```
Central#configure terminal
Enter configuration commands, one per line.  End with CNTL/Z.
Central(config)#interface Serial0.1 multipoint
Central(config-subif)#description Frame Relay to branches
Central(config-subif)#ip address 192.168.1.1 255.255.255.0
```

```
Central(config-subif)#frame-relay interface-dlci 101
Central(config-subif)#frame-relay interface-dlci 102
Central(config-subif)#frame-relay interface-dlci 103
Central(config-subif)#frame-relay interface-dlci 104
Central(config-subif)#exit
Central(config)#end
Central#
```

Discussion

Recipe 10.1 showed how to create a separate subinterface for each Frame Relay DLCI. Recipe 10.3 showed how to configure all of the DLCIs to share the same interface and the same address range. This recipe shows a method that is somewhere in between these two extremes, with several virtual circuits sharing a common subinterface. You can even combine these multipoint subinterfaces with point-to-point subinterfaces on the same physical interface if you wish to create a hybrid of the two styles.

When you use multipoint configuration as in this recipe, the subinterface will appear to be active unless all of the DLCIs associated with it become unavailable. Then the subinterface will go into a down state and the router will send a trap. This is different from using frame-relay maps on the physical interface, as we discussed in Recipe 10.3. In that case, the interface will only change state if the signaling on the physical interface fails. For this reason, we recommend using multipoint configuration instead of *frame-relay maps*.

As an interesting aside, you can configure frame-relay maps on a multipoint subinterface. This could be useful if you need to mix point-to-point and multipoint interface types on a network that doesn't support inverse ARP.

Note that, as we mentioned in Recipe 10.1, it is not a simple matter to change the subinterface type between point-to-point and multipoint. If you have already defined a subinterface as one type and you want to change it to the other, you must delete the subinterface and reboot the router. Then you can add the subinterface configuration back to the router with the correct type.

The biggest difference between using multipoint subinterfaces and any of the previous examples is that here we do not configure a static mapping between a particular DLCI number and a remote IP address. So, to make this association, the router must use Inverse ARP. If you disable Inverse ARP here, as we did in the previous recipes, the network will not work.

You can see that Inverse ARP is correctly mapping IP addresses to DLCI numbers with the *show frame-relay map* command:

```
Central#show frame-relay map
Serial0.1 (up): ip 192.168.55.6 dlci 100(0x64,0x1840), dynamic,
              broadcast,, status defined, active
Central#
```

If we reconfigure the same DLCI to use a point-to-point subinterface instead (which requires rebooting the router, as we mentioned earlier), you see the output of the *show frame-relay map* command changes significantly to tell you about the static mapping:

```
Central#show frame-relay map
Serial0.1 (up): point-to-point dlci, dlci 100(0x64,0x1840), broadcast
        status defined, active
Central#
```

See Also

Recipe 10.1; Recipe 10.3

10.5   Configuring Frame Relay SVCs

Problem

You want to configure the router to support Frame Relay SVCs.

Solution

Frame Relay SVCs are not extremely common, but some carrier networks support them. The advantage to using SVCs is that the router can add and remove inactive virtual circuits dynamically in a lightly used network. Because of the extra complexity and the management problems associated with dynamic network topologies, most network engineers will use this feature only if it offers significant cost advantages.

You can configure SVCs to use subinterfaces, as in Recipe 10.1:

```
Central#configure terminal
Enter configuration commands, one per line.  End with CNTL/Z.
Central(config)#interface Serial0
Central(config-if)#encapsulation frame-relay
Central(config-if)#frame-relay lmi-type q933a
Central(config-if)#frame-relay svc
Central(config-if)#exit
Central(config)#interface Serial0.10 point-to-point
Central(config-subif)#ip address 192.168.1.129 255.255.255.252
Central(config-subif)#frame-relay interface-dlci 100
Central(config-subif)#map-group SVCMAP
Central(config-fr-dlci)#class SVCclass
Central(config-fr-dlci)#exit
Central(config-subif)# exit
Central(config)#map-list SVCMAP source-addr X121 1234 dest-addr X121 4321
Central(config-map-list)#ip 192.168.55.6 class SVCclass ietf
Central(config-map-list)#exit
Central(config)#map-class frame-relay SVCclass
Central(config-map-class)#frame-relay traffic-rate 56000 128000
Central(config-map-class)#exit
Central(config)#end
Central#
```

And you can also configure Frame Relay SVCs without subinterfaces, similar to the *map* configuration for PVCs, which we discussed in Recipe 10.3:

```
Central#configure terminal
Enter configuration commands, one per line.  End with CNTL/Z.
Central(config)#interface Serial0
Central(config-if)#ip address 192.168.55.1 255.255.255.0
Central(config-if)#encapsulation frame-relay
Central(config-if)#frame-relay lmi-type q933a
Central(config-if)#frame-relay svc
Central(config-if)#map-group SVCMAP
Central(config-if)#frame-relay interface-dlci 50
Central(config-fr-dlci)#class SVCclass
Central(config-fr-dlci)#exit
Central(config-if)#exit
Central(config)#map-list SVCMAP source-addr X121 1234 dest-addr X121 4321
Central(config-map-list)#ip 192.168.55.6 class SVCclass ietf
Central(config-map-list)#exit
Central(config)#map-class frame-relay SVCclass
Central(config-map-class)#frame-relay traffic-rate 56000 128000
Central(config-map-class)#exit
Central(config)#end
Central#
```

Discussion

You can enable Frame Relay SVCs on an interface simply by including the *frame-relay svc* command. This is required whether you use maps or subinterfaces:

```
Central(config-if)#frame-relay svc
```

However, this doesn't tell the network how to actually build the virtual circuits. To do that, you need to define a *map-list* and a *map-class* as follows:

```
Central(config)#map-list SVCMAP source-addr X121 1234 dest-addr X121 4321
Central(config-map-list)#ip 192.168.55.6 class SVCclass ietf
Central(config-map-list)#exit
Central(config)#map-class frame-relay SVCclass
Central(config-map-class)#frame-relay traffic-rate 56000 128000
Central(config-map-class)#end
```

The *map-list* associates an IP address with either X.121 or E.164 source and destination addresses. In the example, we have used X.121 addresses, but if your carrier's network uses E.164 addressing instead, you would simply replace the keyword *X121* with *E164*, and specify the appropriate E.164 addresses:

```
Central(config)#map-list SVCMAP source-addr E164 1234 dest-addr E164 4321
```

The *map-class* command tells the router about the actual SVC parameters such as CIR and EIR. In this example, we want the network to create SVCs with CIR of 56000 and total burst rate (CIR+EIR) of 128000 bits per second.

By default the router will keep an idle SVC for 120 seconds before tearing it down. You can change this period using the *frame-relay idle-timer* command. There are three ways to specify an idle time. You can have the router tear down an idle PVC if there is no traffic in either direction for a specified time period like this:

```
Central(config)#map-class frame-relay SVCclass
Central(config-map-class)#frame-relay idle-timer 60
```

Or you can specify the inbound and outbound directions separately:

```
Central(config)#map-class frame-relay SVCclass
Central(config-map-class)#frame-relay idle-timer in 20
Central(config-map-class)#frame-relay idle-timer out 30
```

In each case, the argument is the time period specified in seconds.

You can view the SVC map information on a router with the *show frame-relay svc* command:

```
Central#show frame-relay svc maplist SVCMAP
Map List : SVCMAP
Address : Source X121 1234 <----> Destination X121 4321

Protocol : ip 192.168.55.6                        Encapsulation : IETF

FMIF (Frame Mode Information Field Size), bytes
Configured : In = 1500, Out = 1500

CIR (Committed Information Rate), bits/sec
Configured : In = 56000,       Out = 56000,

Minimum Acceptable CIR, bits/sec
Configured : In = 56000,       Out = 56000,

Bc (Committed Burst Size), bits
Configured : In = 56000,       Out = 56000,

Be (Excess Burst Size), bits
Configured : In = 56000,       Out = 56000,

Central#
```

It is useful to remember that whether you use maps or subinterfaces, you can combine SVCs and PVCs on the same physical interface.

See Also

Recipe 10.1; Recipe 10.3

10.6   Simulating a Frame Relay Cloud

Problem

You want to use a router to simulate a Frame Relay cloud in the lab.

Solution

A Cisco router can function as a Frame Relay switch. This is mostly useful when you are trying to simulate a Frame Relay cloud in a lab to test your router configurations:

```
Cloud#configure terminal
Enter configuration commands, one per line.  End with CNTL/Z.
Cloud(config)#frame-relay switching
Cloud(config)#interface Serial0
Cloud(config-if)#description Frame-relay connection to Central - DLCI 50
Cloud(config-if)#encapsulation frame-relay
Cloud(config-if)#clock rate 125000
Cloud(config-if)#frame-relay lmi-type cisco
Cloud(config-if)#frame-relay intf-type dce
Cloud(config-if)#frame-relay route 101 interface Serial1 50
Cloud(config-if)#frame-relay route 102 interface Serial2 50
Cloud(config-if)#exit
Cloud(config)#interface Serial1
Cloud(config-if)#description Frame-relay connection to Branch1 - DLCI 101
Cloud(config-if)#encapsulation frame-relay
Cloud(config-if)#clock rate 125000
Cloud(config-if)#frame-relay lmi-type cisco
Cloud(config-if)#frame-relay intf-type dce
Cloud(config-if)#frame-relay route 50 interface Serial0 101
Cloud(config-if)#exit
Cloud(config)#interface Serial2
Cloud(config-if)#description Frame-relay connection to Branch2 - DLCI 102
Cloud(config-if)#encapsulation frame-relay
Cloud(config-if)#clock rate 125000
Cloud(config-if)#frame-relay lmi-type cisco
Cloud(config-if)#frame-relay intf-type dce
Cloud(config-if)#frame-relay route 50 interface Serial0 102
Cloud(config-if)#exit
Cloud(config)#end
Cloud#
```

Discussion

This type of configuration can be extremely useful when you need to test basic Frame Relay functionality in a lab, and you don't happen to have a real Frame Relay switch available. However it's extremely important to remember that a router is not a Frame Relay switch, and it doesn't emulate all of the functionality of the switch. In particular, the router will not support switching of SVCs. Also, although Cisco has introduced the *frame-relay congestion-management* command, you can still only generate FECN and BECN notifications on a limited set of router hardware and software configurations. So if you are using this type of configuration to test adaptive traffic shaping or any other feature that relies on BECN notifications, it will not give you a reliable simulation of a real cloud.

To use the router as a Frame Relay switch, you must first enable the *frame-relay switching* option. Then you must configure each interface as DCE with the *frame-relay intf-type* command, and supply a clock signal with the *clock rate* command. Cisco routers will not allow you to configure this command unless you use a DCE cable on the interface. And, finally, you need to map the PVCs. In this case, we have configured a central hub router and two branch routers, as in Recipe 10.1. The central router can see both of the branch routers, one with DLCI 101, and the other with DLCI 102. Both of the branch routers see the central router with DLCI 50. The two branch routers cannot see one another directly.

In this example, all three of the Frame Relay connections are to DTE devices such as routers, so all of the interfaces are configured for DCE signaling. However, you can also configure connections to other switching devices. This might be useful if you were interested in constructing your own private Frame Relay cloud. In this case, you would still need to designate one of the devices to be the physical DCE and supply the clock. Then you would configure the interface type on both devices as *nni*:

```
Cloud#configure terminal
Enter configuration commands, one per line.  End with CNTL/Z.
Cloud(config)#interface Serial2
Cloud(config-if)#description Frame-relay connection to next switch
Cloud(config-if)#encapsulation frame-relay
Cloud(config-if)#clock rate 125000
Cloud(config-if)#frame-relay lmi-type cisco
Cloud(config-if)#frame-relay intf-type nni
Cloud(config-if)#exit
Cloud(config)#end
Cloud#
```

You would also use *frame-relay route* statements to configure one or more PVCs to be served by this neighboring switch. The PVC routing commands in this case are identical to those for DCE interfaces.

You can look at the routing of the virtual circuits on a router that is configured for Frame Relay switching with the *show frame-relay route* command:

```
Cloud#show frame-relay route
Input Intf      Input Dlci      Output Intf     Output Dlci     Status
Serial0         101             Serial1         50              active
Serial0         102             Serial2         50              inactive
Serial0         103             Serial3         50              inactive
Serial1         50              Serial0         101             active
Serial1         102             Serial2         101             inactive
Serial1         103             Serial3         101             inactive
Serial2         50              Serial0         102             inactive
Serial2         101             Serial1         102             inactive
Serial2         103             Serial3         102             inactive
Serial3         50              Serial0         103             inactive
Serial3         101             Serial1         103             inactive
Serial3         102             Serial2         103             inactive
Cloud#
```

This output shows, for example, that traffic received on DLCI number 101 through interface *Serial0* is forwarded to DLCI number 50 on *Serial1*. And a few lines lower, you can see the reverse path as well. The status for both of these lines is active, so this virtual circuit is working properly.

Another extremely useful option for creating private Frame Relay networks is the ability to specify a GRE tunnel as the destination of a Frame Relay *route* command:

```
Cloud(config)#interface Loopback1
Cloud(config-if)#ip address 192.168.2.1 255.255.255.255
Cloud(config-if)#exit
Cloud(config)#interface Tunnel1
Cloud(config-if)#ip address 192.168.1.5 255.255.255.252
Cloud(config-if)#tunnel source 192.168.2.1
Cloud(config-if)#tunnel destination 192.168.2.2
Cloud(config-if)#exit
Cloud(config)#interface Serial1
Cloud(config-if)#frame-relay route 201 interface Tunnel1 101
Cloud(config-if)#exit
```

In this case, we have created a GRE tunnel interface called *Tunnel1*, which terminates on another router somewhere else in the network. Then we route Frame Relay DLCI 201 to this tunnel interface. On the other router, you would need to create a similar GRE tunnel interface. Then, on a *Serial* interface on that other router, you would put a matching *frame-relay route* statement:

```
Cloud9(config)#interface Loopback1
Cloud9(config-if)#ip address 192.168.2.2 255.255.255.255
Cloud9(config-if)#exit
Cloud9(config)#interface Tunnel1
Cloud9(config-if)#ip address 192.168.1.6 255.255.255.252
Cloud9(config-if)#tunnel source 192.168.2.2
Cloud9(config-if)#tunnel destination 192.168.2.1
Cloud9(config-if)#exit
Cloud9(config)#interface Serial1
Cloud9(config-if)#frame-relay route 301 interface Tunnel1 101
Cloud9(config-if)#exit
```

This is an extremely efficient way of creating a virtual Frame Relay cloud layered on top of an existing IP network.

See Also

Chapter 12; Recipe 10.1

10.7 Compressing Frame Relay Data on a Subinterface

Problem

You want to configure your router to do Frame Relay compression on a subinterface.

Solution

Cisco offers several different types of compression with Frame Relay. You can opt to compress only the TCP headers as follows:

```
Central#configure terminal
Enter configuration commands, one per line.  End with CNTL/Z.
Central(config)#interface Serial0
Central(config-if)#encapsulation frame-relay
Central(config-if)#frame-relay ip tcp header-compression passive
Central(config-if)#exit
Central(config)#end
Central#
```

This command also works at the subinterface level:

```
Central#configure terminal
Enter configuration commands, one per line.  End with CNTL/Z.
Central(config)#interface Serial0.1 point-to-point
Central(config-subif)#frame-relay ip tcp header-compression passive
Central(config-subif)#exit
Central(config)#end
Central#
```

There are also two different payload compression options. The first uses the FRF.9 Frame Relay compression standard:

```
Central#configure terminal
Enter configuration commands, one per line.  End with CNTL/Z.
Central(config)#interface Serial0.1 point-to-point
Central(config-if)#frame-relay payload-compression frf9 stac
Central(config-if)#exit
Central(config)#end
Central#
```

And the second uses Cisco's proprietary *packet-by-packet* compression:

```
Central#configure terminal
Enter configuration commands, one per line.  End with CNTL/Z.
Central(config)#interface Serial0.1 point-to-point
Central(config-if)#frame-relay payload-compression packet-by-packet
Central(config-if)#exit
Central(config)#end
Central#
```

Discussion

The nice thing about the first example in this recipe is that with the *passive* keyword, the router sends packets with compressed TCP headers only if it receives packets with compressed headers. So if you have a variety of remote sites, some of which have routers that don't support header compression, this can be a useful configuration option. You need to configure the device on at least one end without the *passive* keyword:

```
Branch1#configure terminal
Enter configuration commands, one per line.  End with CNTL/Z.
```

```
Branch1(config)#interface Serial0
Branch1(config-if)#encapsulation frame-relay
Branch1(config-if)#frame-relay ip tcp header-compression
Branch1(config-if)#exit
Branch1(config)#end
Branch1#
```

Note that Cisco recommends shutting down the interface before changing this feature. It is not dangerous, but with some routers you need to reset the interface to ensure that it picks up the new configuration. The cleanest way to do this is to shut it down before making the change, and then bring it back up when you are done.

For the payload compression examples, it is critical to configure the same compression on both ends. This is a subinterface level command, so you can configure each PVC to use compression or not, according to what the device on the other end supports.

In both cases, by default the router will do the compression in a Compression Service Adapter (CSA), if one exists. If the router doesn't have a CSA, then it will use a Versatile Interface Processor (VIP-2) card instead. And, if it doesn't have either of these hardware options, then it will do the compression in software using the router's CPU. Some external Frame Relay Access Devices (FRAD) also include FRF.9 compression, but it is unlikely that you will find a FRAD the supports Cisco's packet-by-packet compression.

The FRF.9 compression command can also take several different options that allow you to force different hardware options. For example, you can force the router to use a particular CSA as follows:

```
Central(config-if)#frame-relay payload-compression frf9 stac csa 1
```

Or, if you want to force the router to do the compression in its CPU, you can use the *software* keyword:

```
Central(config-if)#frame-relay payload-compression frf9 stac software
```

The *stac* keyword in all of these FRF.9 examples specifies the standard Stacker algorithm. In fact, this is the only option available for FRF.9 compression.

In general, we recommend using FRF.9 rather than packet-by-packet compression because it is an open standard, while packet-by-packet will only work with Cisco equipment. There is no noticeable performance difference between the two compression types. Cisco introduced its own packet-by-packet compression method before the FRF.9 standard was available, and continues to support it primarily for backward compatibility.

You can see statistics on the header compression with the following command:

```
Router#show frame-relay ip tcp header-compression
  DLCI 100      Link/Destination info:  point-to-point dlci
  Interface Serial1:
    Rcvd:    220 total, 219 compressed, 0 errors
             0 dropped, 0 buffer copies, 0 buffer failures
```

```
Sent:    482 total, 481 compressed,
         17001 bytes saved, 229749 bytes sent
         1.7 efficiency improvement factor
Connect: 16 rx slots, 16 tx slots, 1 long searches, 1 misses
         99% hit ratio, five minute miss rate 0 misses/sec, 0 max

Router#
```

See Also

Recipe 10.9

10.8 Compressing Frame Relay Data with Maps

Problem

You want to configure your router to do Frame Relay compression with map statements.

Solution

The same Frame Relay compression options that we discussed for subinterfaces are also available with *map* statements. You can turn on FRF.9 compression by simply adding a few additional keywords to the *frame-relay map* statement as follows:

```
Central#configure terminal
Enter configuration commands, one per line.  End with CNTL/Z.
Central(config)#interface Serial0
Central(config-if)#description Frame Relay to branches
Central(config-if)#ip address 192.168.1.1 255.255.255.0
Central(config-if)#encapsulation frame-relay
Central(config-if)#frame-relay map ip 192.168.1.10 101 payload-compression frf9 stac
Central(config-if)#exit
Central(config)#end
Central#
```

Or you can opt to use Cisco's proprietary packet-by-packet compression instead:

```
Central#configure terminal
Enter configuration commands, one per line.  End with CNTL/Z.
Central(config)#interface Serial0
Central(config-if)#description Frame Relay to branches
Central(config-if)#ip address 192.168.1.1 255.255.255.0
Central(config-if)#encapsulation frame-relay
Central(config-if)#frame-relay map ip 192.168.1.10 101 payload-compression packet-by-
packet
Central(config-if)#exit
Central(config)#end
Central#
```

The *map* configuration also supports TCP header compression:

```
Central#configure terminal
Enter configuration commands, one per line.  End with CNTL/Z.
```

```
Central(config)#interface Serial0
Central(config-if)#description Frame Relay to branches
Central(config-if)#ip address 192.168.1.1 255.255.255.0
Central(config-if)#encapsulation frame-relay
Central(config-if)#frame-relay map ip 192.168.1.10 101 compress
Central(config-if)#exit
Central(config)#end
Central#
```

Discussion

As we discussed in Recipe 10.7, Cisco routers are able to compress the data payload
of packets before sending them through Frame Relay circuits. This recipe simply
shows how to do the same thing using *map* statements instead of subinterfaces. Note
that the header compression example shown in Recipe 10.7 applies to the physical
interface. So the configuration for header compression is identical, whether you are
using maps or subinterfaces.

You can combine the payload compression option with the other options we discussed in Recipe 10.3 by specifying all of the required options on the same command line:

```
Central(config)#interface Serial0
Central(config-if)#encapsulation frame-relay
Central(config-if)#frame-relay map ip 192.168.1.10 101 ietf broadcast payload-
compression frf9 stac
Central(config-if)#end
```

Note that you can specify these keywords in any order, as long as the compression
options are last. However, you cannot combine the different compression options
with one another.

See Also

Recipe 10.3; Recipe 10.7

10.9   PPP over Frame Relay

Problem

You want to run use PPP encapsulation over a Frame Relay PVC.

Solution

To configure PPP over Frame Relay, you need to associate the DLCI with a Virtual
Template, which will carry the Layer 3 information. Because PPP fundamentally
involves a single connection between two devices, it is most natural to use this feature on point-to-point subinterfaces:

```
Router1#configure terminal
Enter configuration commands, one per line.  End with CNTL/Z.
```

```
Router1(config)#interface Loopback1
Router1(config-if)#ip address 10.1.200.5 255.255.255.252
Router1(config-if)#exit
Router1(config)#interface Virtual-Template1
Router1(config-if)#ip unnumbered Loopback1
Router1(config-if)#encapsulation ppp
Router1(config-if)#exit
Router1(config)#interface Serial0
Router1(config-if)#no ip address
Router1(config-if)#encapsulation frame-relay
Router1(config-if)#exit
Router1(config)#interface Serial0.1 point-to-point
Router1(config-subif)#frame-relay interface-dlci 104 ppp Virtual-Template1
Router1(config-fr-dlci)#exit
Router1(config-subif)#exit
Router1(config)#end
Router1#
```

You can also use this feature directly on a physical interface:

```
Router2#configure terminal
Enter configuration commands, one per line.  End with CNTL/Z.
Router2(config)#interface Loopback1
Router2(config-if)#ip address 10.1.200.6 255.255.255.252
Router2(config-if)#exit
Router2(config)#interface Virtual-Template1
Router2(config-if)#ip unnumbered Loopback1
Router2(config-if)#encapsulation ppp
Router2(config-if)#exit
Router2(config)#interface Serial0/0
Router2(config-if)#no ip address
Router2(config-if)#encapsulation frame-relay
Router2(config-if)#frame-relay interface-dlci 105 ppp Virtual-Template1
Router2(config-fr-dlci)#exit
Router2(config-if)#exit
Router2(config)#end
Router2#
```

Discussion

RFC 1973 defines the standard for running the Point-to-Point Protocol (PPP) standard over a Frame Relay PVC. Normally you wouldn't want to do this, as the default Frame Relay encapsulation standards discussed in Recipe 10.1 are more than adequate for most situations. However, a PVC that is delivered via a Frame Relay circuit at one location may be converted to an ATM VC inside the carrier's cloud, and could ultimately arrive at another location as a DSL circuit delivered through an Ethernet interface. The only Layer 2 frame format that supports all of these standards is PPP. It is for these types of situations that RFC 1973 was developed.

The router uses *Virtual-Template* interfaces in an interesting and unusual way. When trying to bring up the PPP link, the router will first *clone* the *Virtual-Template* interface to create a *Virtual-Access* interface. You can see all of these interfaces with the *show ip interface brief* command:

```
Router2#show ip interface brief
Interface              IP-Address      OK? Method Status                    Prot
ocol
FastEthernet0/0        141.200.5.5     YES NVRAM  up                            up
Serial0/0              unassigned      YES manual up                            up
BRI0/0                 unassigned      YES NVRAM  administratively down down
BRI0/0:1               unassigned      YES unset  administratively down down
BRI0/0:2               unassigned      YES unset  administratively down down
Virtual-Access1        10.1.200.6      YES TFTP   up                            up
Virtual-Template1      10.1.200.6      YES TFTP   down                          down
Loopback1              10.1.200.6      YES manual up                            up
Router2#
```

You can see here that the Frame Relay interface or subinterface (interface, in this case) has no IP address. The Layer 3 information representing this Frame Relay PVC is held on the interface Virtual-Access1, which the router dynamically created from the Virtual-Template1 interface:

```
Router2#show interfaces Virtual-Access1
Virtual-Access1 is up, line protocol is up
  Hardware is Virtual Access interface
  Interface is unnumbered. Using address of Loopback1 (10.1.200.6)
  MTU 1500 bytes, BW 100000 Kbit, DLY 100000 usec,
     reliability 255/255, txload 1/255, rxload 1/255
  Encapsulation PPP, loopback not set
  Keepalive set (10 sec)
  DTR is pulsed for 5 seconds on reset
  LCP Open
  Open: IPCP
  Bound to Serial0/0 DLCI 105, Cloned from Virtual-Template1
  Last input 00:00:01, output never, output hang never
  Last clearing of "show interface" counters 00:24:53
  Input queue: 0/75/0/0 (size/max/drops/flushes); Total output drops: 0
  Queueing strategy: fifo
  Output queue: 0/40 (size/max)
  5 minute input rate 0 bits/sec, 0 packets/sec
  5 minute output rate 0 bits/sec, 0 packets/sec
     370 packets input, 7372 bytes, 0 no buffer
     Received 0 broadcasts, 0 runts, 0 giants, 0 throttles
     0 input errors, 0 CRC, 0 frame, 0 overrun, 0 ignored, 0 abort
     401 packets output, 7240 bytes, 0 underruns
     0 output errors, 0 collisions, 0 interface resets
     0 output buffer failures, 0 output buffers swapped out
     0 carrier transitions
Router2#
```

One of the side benefits of using PPP encapsulation on a Frame Relay PVC like this is you can enforce an extra measure of security by requiring PPP CHAP authentication:

```
Router1(config)#username Router2 password cookbook
Router1(config)#interface Virtual-Template1
```

```
Router1(config-if)#ip unnumbered Loopback1
Router1(config-if)#encapsulation ppp
Router1(config-if)#ppp authentication chap
```

Naturally, the authentication method and password must match on the other router:

```
Router2(config)#username Router1 password cookbook
Router2(config)#interface Virtual-Template1
Router2(config-if)#ip unnumbered Loopback1
Router2(config-if)#encapsulation ppp
Router2(config-if)#ppp authentication chap
```

When you do this, the Virtual-Access interfaces remain in a down state until the routers pass PPP authentication. Since the IP address information is not exchanged until the PPP session is established, it is not possible to use Inverse ARP to deduce a good IP address and insert a rogue router into the network. We note, however, that this type of attack is only possible if you don't control the physical security of the router at the remote site.

Finally, we note in passing that we always create a Loopback interface to carry the IP addresses for Virtual-Template interfaces. In this particular example, because we must use separate IP addressing on every PVC, this is not actually necessary. We could have assigned the IP address directly to the Virtual-Template interface. However, we do it this way because Virtual-Template interfaces are also used for other purposes such as dial backup and PPP over ATM. In some cases, you may want to have more than one type of Virtual-Template configuration, but with the same IP addressing. So because of these situations, it is a good general practice to put the IP address on a Loopback interface, as we have done here.

See Also

RFC 1973; Recipe 10.1

10.10 Viewing Frame Relay Status Information

Problem

You want to check the status of a Frame Relay circuit or VC.

Solution

There are several useful show commands for looking at Frame Relay circuits and virtual circuits. It is usually best to start at the physical layer and work upward through the protocol layers. You can look at the physical interface with the *show interfaces* command:

```
Central#show interfaces Serial0
```

The *show frame-relay pvc* command allows you to see information about each of your Frame Relay PVCs:

```
Central#show frame-relay pvc
```

And sometimes it is also useful to look at the LMI status:

```
Central#show frame-relay lmi
```

Discussion

The *show interfaces* command has a lot of useful information. When the interface is configured for Frame Relay, this command shows the LMI configuration, whether the interface is configured for SVCs as well as PVCs, and it also shows you whether the interface is set up to be DCE or DTE. But the most important thing to look at is always the first line, where it shows the physical and the protocol status:

```
Central#show interfaces Serial0
Serial0 is up, line protocol is up
  Hardware is HD64570
  Description: Frame Relay connection
  MTU 1500 bytes, BW 1544 Kbit, DLY 20000 usec,
     reliability 255/255, txload 3/255, rxload 3/255
  Encapsulation FRAME-RELAY, loopback not set, keepalive set (10 sec)
  LMI enq sent  263, LMI stat recvd 263, LMI upd recvd 0, DTE LMI up
  LMI enq recvd 0, LMI stat sent  0, LMI upd sent  0
  LMI DLCI 0  LMI type is CCITT  frame relay DTE
  FR SVC enabled, LAPF state down
  Broadcast queue 0/64, broadcasts sent/dropped 44/0, interface broadcasts 0
  Last input 00:00:03, output 00:00:03, output hang never
  Last clearing of "show interface" counters never
  Input queue: 0/75/0 (size/max/drops); Total output drops: 0
  Queueing strategy: weighted fair
  Output queue: 0/1000/64/0 (size/max total/threshold/drops)
     Conversations  0/2/256 (active/max active/max total)
     Reserved Conversations 0/0 (allocated/max allocated)
  5 minute input rate 24000 bits/sec, 0 packets/sec
  5 minute output rate 23000 bits/sec, 0 packets/sec
     2838 packets input, 1604468 bytes, 0 no buffer
     Received 0 broadcasts, 0 runts, 0 giants, 0 throttles
     0 input errors, 0 CRC, 0 frame, 0 overrun, 0 ignored, 0 abort
     2951 packets output, 1623730 bytes, 0 underruns
     0 output errors, 0 collisions, 20 interface resets
     0 output buffer failures, 0 output buffers swapped out
     2 carrier transitions
     DCD=up  DSR=up  DTR=up  RTS=up  CTS=up
Central#
```

If the interface is up, you should be able to see useful PVC information:

```
Central#show frame-relay pvc

PVC Statistics for interface Serial1 (Frame Relay DTE)

DLCI = 100, DLCI USAGE = LOCAL, PVC STATUS = ACTIVE, INTERFACE = Serial0.1

  input pkts 1271        output pkts 1312       in bytes 843519
  out bytes 856138       dropped pkts 0         in FECN pkts 0
  in BECN pkts 0         out FECN pkts 0        out BECN pkts 0
  in DE pkts 0           out DE pkts 0
```

```
    out bcast pkts 40        out bcast bytes 11320
    pvc create time 01:08:11, last time pvc status changed 00:39:42
Central#
```

This output tells you, for example, that the PVC with DLCI 100 is active and configured on interface Serial0.1. None of the packets received on this interface have had their FECN, BECN, or DE bits set. This is the most useful place to check for congestion in the Frame Relay cloud. Note that the router is unlikely to ever set the FECN or BECN bits when sending packets, so the inbound counters are the most useful here.

The last line of this output for each PVC is particularly useful if you have a problem with flapping PVCs in the carrier cloud. In this case, you can see that the PVC has been active for just over an hour, but it had a status change 39 minutes ago. This doesn't tell you what caused the status change, though. In a stable network, you should not expect to see frequent PVC status changes. So this gives you a useful indication of problems either in the carrier cloud, or with your remote router.

Note that the *show frame-relay pvc* command will list all of the PVCs on a router, including any that are configured on the router but not in use, as well as any that are configured on the switch but not on the router. If you want to focus on a particular PVC, you can specify the one you want by its DLCI number:

```
Central#show frame-relay pvc 100
```

If you suspect an LMI problem, it is useful to look at the output of the *show frame-relay lmi* command:

```
Central#show frame-relay lmi

LMI Statistics for interface Serial1 (Frame Relay DTE) LMI TYPE = CCITT
  Invalid Unnumbered info 0        Invalid Prot Disc 0
  Invalid dummy Call Ref 0         Invalid Msg Type 0
  Invalid Status Message 0         Invalid Lock Shift 0
  Invalid Information ID 0         Invalid Report IE Len 0
  Invalid Report Request 0         Invalid Keep IE Len 0
  Num Status Enq. Sent 299         Num Status msgs Rcvd 299
  Num Update Status Rcvd 0         Num Status Timeouts 0
Central#
```

The first line of this output shows that the LMI type in this case is CCITT, which is configured with the *frame-relay lmi-type q933a* command. The other options are *cisco* and *ansi*, both of which use the same type field in the output of this command as in the configuration command.

Because LMI is the Frame Relay management protocol between the router and the switch, if you have an LMI problem, the usual symptom is that the physical interface is up, but the protocol is down and none of the PVCs will come up. If you repeatedly check the *show frame-relay lmi* command, you will see the Num Status Timeouts field incrementing. Because it can take several seconds for an interface to come up, it is sometimes hard to tell immediately if you have the right LMI type field, so this field gives you a relatively quick indication of when you have the right configuration.

## CHAPTER 11

Handling Queuing and Congestion

11.0 Introduction

Quality of Service (QoS) has been a part of the IP protocol since RFC 791 was released in 1981. However, it has not been extensively used until recently. The main reason for using QoS in an IP network is to protect sensitive traffic in congested links. In many cases, the best solution to the problem of congested links is simply to upgrade these links. All you can do with a QoS system is affect which packets are forwarded and which ones are dropped when congestion is encountered. This is only effective when the congestion is intermittent. If a link is just consistently over-utilized, QoS will at best offer a temporary stopgap measure until the link is upgraded or the network is redesigned.

There are several different traffic flow characteristics that you can set out to control with a QoS system. Some applications require a certain minimum bandwidth to operate; others require a minimum latency. Jitter, which is the difference in latency between consecutive packets, has to be carefully constrained for many real-time applications such as voice and video, in particular. Some applications do not tolerate dropped packets well. Others contain time-sensitive information that is better dropped than delayed.

There are essentially three steps to any traffic prioritization scheme. First, you have to know what your traffic patterns look like. This means you need to understand what traffic is mission critical, what can wait, and what traffic flows are sensitive to jitter, latency, or have minimum throughput requirements. Once you know this, the second step is to provide a way to identify the different types of traffic. Usually, in IP QoS you will use this information to tag the Type of Service (TOS) byte in the IP header. This byte contains a six-bit field called the Differentiated Services Control Point (DSCP) in newer literature, and is separated into a three-bit IP Precedence field and a TOS field (either three or four bits) in older literature. These fields are used for the same purpose, although there are differences in their precise meanings. We discuss these fields in more detail in Appendix B.

The third step is to configure the network devices to use this information to affect how the traffic is actually forwarded through the network. This is the step in which you actually have the most freedom, because you can decide precisely what you want to do with different traffic types. However, there are two main philosophies here: TOS-based routing and DSCP Per-Hop Behavior.

TOS-based routing basically means that the router selects different paths based on the contents of the TOS field in the IP header. However, the precise TOS behavior is left up to the network engineer, so the TOS values could affect other things such as queuing behavior. DSCP, on the other hand, generally looks at the same set of bits and uses them to decide how to handle the queuing when the links are congested. TOS-based routing is the older technique, and DSCP is newer.

You can easily implement TOS-based routing to select different network paths using Cisco's Policy Based Routing (PBR). For example, some networks use this technique of Frame Relay networks to funnel high-priority traffic into a different PVC than lower priority traffic. And many standard IP protocols, such as FTP and Telnet, have well-defined default TOS settings.

Most engineers prefer the DSCP approach because it is easier to implement and troubleshoot. If high-priority application packets take a different path than low-priority PING packets, as is possible in the TOS approach, it can be extremely confusing to manage the network. DSCP is also usually easier to implement and less demanding of the router's CPU and memory resources, as well as more consistent with the capabilities of modern routing protocols.

Note, however, that any time you stop a packet to examine it in more detail, you introduce latency and potentially increase the CPU load on the router. And the more fields you examine or change, the greater the impact. For this reason, we want to stress that the best network designs handle traffic prioritization by marking the packets as early as possible. Then other routers in the network only need to look at the DSCP field to handle the packet correctly. In general, you want to keep this marking function at the edges of the network where the traffic load is lowest, rather than in the core, where the routers are too busy forwarding packets to examine and classify packets.

We discuss the IP Precedence, TOS, and DSCP classification schemes in more detail in Appendix B.

Queuing Algorithms

The simplest type of queue transmits packets in the same order that it receives them. This is called a First In First Out (FIFO) queue. And although it sounds naively like it treats all traffic streams equally, it actually tends to favor resource-hungry, ill-behaved applications.

The problem is that if a single application sends a burst that fills a FIFO queue, the router will wind up transmitting most of the queued packets, but will have to drop incoming packets from other applications. If these other applications adapt to the decrease in available bandwidth by sending at a slower rate, then the ill-behaved application will greedily take up the slack and could gradually choke off all of the other applications.

Because FIFO queuing allows some data flows to take more than their share of the available bandwidth, it is called *unfair*. Fair Queuing (FQ) and Weighted Fair Queuing (WFQ) are two of the simpler algorithms that have been developed to deal with this problem. Both of these algorithms sort incoming packets into a series of *flows*.

We discuss Cisco's implementations of different Queuing algorithms in Appendix B.

When talking about queuing, it is easy to get wrapped up in relative priorities of data streams. However, it is just as important to think about how your packets should be dropped when there is congestion. Cisco routers allow you to even implement a congestion avoidance system called Random Early Detection (RED), which also has a weighted variant, Weighted Random Early Detection (WRED). These algorithms allow the router to start dropping packets before there is a serious congestion problem. This forces well-behaved TCP applications to back off and send their data more slowly, thereby avoiding congestion problems before they start. RED and WRED are also discussed in Appendix B.

Fast Switching and CEF

One of the most important performance limitations on a router depends on how the packets are processed internally. The worst case is where the router's CPU has to examine every packet to decide how to forward it. Packets that are handled in the CPU like this are said to use *Process Switching*. It is never possible to completely eliminate process switching in a router because the router has to react to some types of packets, particularly those containing network control information. And, as we will discuss in a moment, process switching is often used to bootstrap other more efficient methods.

For many years, Cisco has included more efficient methods for packet processing in routers. These often involve off-loading the routing decisions to special logic circuits, frequently associated with interface hardware. The actual details of how these circuits work is often not of much interest to the network engineer. The most important thing is to ensure that as many packets as possible use these more efficient methods.

Fast Switching is one of Cisco's earlier mechanisms for off-loading routing from the CPU. In Fast Switching, the router uses process switching to forward the first packet to a particular destination. The CPU looks up the appropriate forwarding information in the routing table, and then sends the packet accordingly. Then, when the router sees subsequent packets for the same destination, it is able to use the same forwarding information. Fast Switching records this forwarding information in an internal cache, and uses it to bypass the laborious route lookup process for all but the first packet in a flow. It works best when there is a relatively long stream of packets to the same destination. And, of course, it is necessary to periodically verify that the same forwarding information is still valid. So Fast Switching requires the router to process switch some packets just to check that the cached path is still the best path.

To allow for reliable load balancing, the Fast Switching cache includes only /32 addresses. This means that there is no network or subnet level summarization in this cache. Whenever the Fast Switching algorithm receives a packet for a destination that is not in its cache, or that it can't handle because of a special filtering feature that isn't supported by Fast Switching, it must *punt*. This means that the router passes the packet to a more general routing algorithm, usually process switching.

Fast switching only works with active traffic flows. A new flow will have a destination that is not in the fast-switching cache. Similarly, low-bandwidth applications that only send one packet at a time, with relatively long periods between packets, will not benefit from Fast Switching. In both of these cases, the router must punt and process-switch the packet. Another more serious example happens in busy Internet routers. These devices have to deal with so many flows that they are unable to cache them all.

Largely because of this last problem, Cisco developed a more sophisticated system called Cisco Express Forwarding (CEF) that improves on several of the shortcomings of Fast Switching. The main improvement is that instead of just caching active destinations, CEF caches the entire routing table. This increases the amount of memory required, but the routing information is stored in an efficient hashed structure.

The router keeps the cached table synchronized with the main routing table that is acquired through a dynamic routing protocol, such as OSPF or BGP. This means that CEF only needs to punt a packet when it requires features that don't work with CEF. For example, some Policy Based Routing rules do not work with CEF. So when you use them, CEF must still punt and process switch these packets.

In addition to caching the entire routing table, CEF maintains a table of information about all available next-hop devices. This allows the router to build the appropriate Layer 2 framing information for packets that need to be forwarded, without having to consult the system ARP table.

Because CEF rarely needs to punt a packet, even if it is the first packet of a new flow, it is able to operate much more efficiently than Fast Switching. And because it caches the entire routing table, it is even able to do packet-by-packet round-robin load sharing between equal cost paths. CEF shows its greatest advantage over Fast Switching in situations when there are many flows, each relatively short in duration. Another key advantage is that CEF has native support for QoS, while Fast Switching does not.

A Distributed CEF is available on routers that support Versatile Interface Processor (VIP) cards, such as the 7500 series. This allows each VIP card to run CEF individually to further improve scalability.

11.1   Fast Switching and CEF

Problem

You want to use the most efficient mechanism in the router to switch the packets.

Solution

As we discuss in Appendix B, one of the most important things you can do to improve router performance, and consequently network performance, is to ensure that you are using the best packet switching algorithm. All Cisco routers support Fast Switching, and it is enabled by default. However, some types of configurations require that it be disabled. The following example shows how to turn Fast Switching back on if it has been disabled:

```
Router#configure terminal
Enter configuration commands, one per line.  End with CNTL/Z.
Router(config)#interface FastEthernet0/0
Router(config-if)#ip route-cache
Router(config-if)#exit
Router(config)#end
Router#
```

If you are using policies, including policies for Class-based QoS, you also need to configure Fast Switching to handle them, using the *ip route-cache policy* command:

```
Router#configure terminal
Enter configuration commands, one per line.  End with CNTL/Z.
Router(config)#interface FastEthernet0/0
Router(config-if)#ip route-cache policy
Router(config-if)#exit
Router(config)#end
Router#
```

CEF, on the other hand, is not enabled by default. Unlike Fast Switching, which is enabled separately for each interface, you have to enable CEF globally for the entire router, as well as on each interface:

```
Router#configure terminal
Enter configuration commands, one per line.  End with CNTL/Z.
Router(config)#ip cef
Router(config)#interface FastEthernet0/0
Router(config-if)#ip route-cache cef
Router(config-if)#exit
Router(config)#end
Router#
```

Discussion

The *ip route-cache* command used to enable Fast Switching has a couple of useful options. The second example demonstrates one of these options, the *policy* keyword, which allows Fast Switching of policy-based routing:

```
Router(config-if)#ip route-cache policy
```

Another useful option is the *same-interface* keyword, which instructs the router to allow Fast Switching of packets that come in and go back out through the same physical interface:

```
Router(config)#interface Serial0/0
Router(config-if)#ip route-cache same-interface
```

You should use this option when the router frequently needs to switch packets between different networks that all connect to the same port. This could be the case for Frame Relay networks, as well as for LANs that use subinterfaces or secondary IP addresses.

Cisco supplies three useful commands to look at CEF performance. The first is *show cef interface*:

```
Router#show cef interface FastEthernet0/0
FastEthernet0/1 is up (if_number 4)
  Corresponding hwidb fast_if_number 4
  Corresponding hwidb firstsw->if_number 4
  Internet address is 172.22.1.3/24
  ICMP redirects are always sent
  Per packet load-sharing is disabled
  IP unicast RPF check is disabled
  Inbound access list is 120
  Outbound access list is not set
  IP policy routing is disabled
  Hardware idb is FastEthernet0/1
  Fast switching type 1, interface type 18
  IP CEF switching enabled
  IP CEF Feature Fast switching turbo vector
  Input fast flags 0x0, Output fast flags 0x0
  ifindex 4(4)
  Slot 0 Slot unit 1 VC -1
  Transmit limit accumulator 0x0 (0x0)
  IP MTU 1500
Router#
```

The output of this command shows that CEF is enabled on the interface *FastEthernet0/0*, as well as information about inbound and outbound ACL's and policies. In this example, you can see that the interface has an access-group configured to use access-list number 120 to filter inbound traffic.

You can use the *show cef drop* and *show cef not-cef-switched* commands to see more detailed CEF forwarding statistics:

```
Router#show cef drop
CEF Drop Statistics
Slot  Encap_fail  Unresolved Unsupported   No_route     No_adj  ChkSum_Err
RP            71           0           0        105          0           0
Router#show cef not-cef-switched
CEF Packets passed on to next switching layer
Slot  No_adj No_encap Unsupp'ted Redirect  Receive  Options   Access      Frag
RP         0        0          0        0      572        0        0         0
```

These commands show you details of CEF's operation on the router. The first command shows how many packets CEF has had to drop, and the reasons for the drops. The *Slot* column in the output of both commands refers to the VIP slot where the packets were received. In this case, the router didn't have any VIP cards because it was a Cisco 2600. So all packets are received by the Route Processor, which is indicated by the *RP* in the leftmost column.

The *Encap_fail* column in the *show cef drop* output shows the number of packets that CEF has dropped because they were incomplete and there was no adjacency route in the CEF table. *Unresolved* indicates the number of packets dropped because CEF could not resolve the destination address prefix. If there had been any packets that could not be switched by CEF because of unsupported features, they would appear in the *Unsupported* column. The *No_route* column shows the number of packets dropped because CEF didn't have a route to the destination. Similarly, *No_adj* shows the number of packets for which CEF did not have an entry in its adjacency table, so it had to send an ARP query. And, finally, *ChkSum_Err* shows the number of times that CEF had to drop packets because they were corrupted.

The *show cef not-cef-switched* command has similar output. *No_adj* is the same here as it was in the *show cef drop* command, while *Unsupp'ted* is the same as the *Unsupported* column. The *No_encap* column counts the number of packets that could not be switched because they were encapsulated in another protocol. *Redirect* means that CEF has had to send these packets to another algorithm, usually process switching, to handle. And *Receive* lists the number of packets that were received from another internal switching algorithm. The remaining columns are rarely of interest in practice.

You can display the CEF version of the routing table with the *show ip cef* command:

```
Router#show ip cef
Prefix              Next Hop          Interface
0.0.0.0/0           172.25.1.1        FastEthernet0/0.1
0.0.0.0/32          receive
172.16.2.0/24       attached          FastEthernet0/1
                    attached          FastEthernet1/1
172.22.1.0/24       attached          FastEthernet0/1
172.22.1.0/32       receive
172.22.1.3/32       receive
172.22.1.4/32       172.22.1.4        FastEthernet0/1
<many lines deleted>
Router#
```

Notice in this output that there are actually two equal-cost routes to 172.16.2.0/24. CEF supports load balancing between these two paths.

You can expand the detail on these entries with the *show ip cef detail* command:

```
Router#show ip cef detail
IP CEF with switching (Table Version 31), flags=0x0
  31 routes, 0 reresolve, 0 unresolved (0 old, 0 new), peak 1
```

```
31 leaves, 21 nodes, 25560 bytes, 62 inserts, 31 invalidations
0 load sharing elements, 0 bytes, 0 references
universal per-destination load sharing algorithm, id 0697166A
3(1) CEF resets, 0 revisions of existing leaves
Resolution Timer: Exponential (currently 1s, peak 1s)
0 in-place/0 aborted modifications
refcounts:  5672 leaf, 5632 node

Adjacency Table has 5 adjacencies
0.0.0.0/0, version 27, cached adjacency 172.25.1.1
0 packets, 0 bytes
  via 172.25.1.1, FastEthernet0/0.1, 0 dependencies
    next hop 172.25.1.1, FastEthernet0/0.1
    valid cached adjacency
0.0.0.0/32, version 0, receive
172.16.2.0/24, version 21, attached, connected
0 packets, 0 bytes
  via FastEthernet0/0.2, 0 dependencies
    valid glean adjacency
172.16.2.0/32, version 10, receive
172.16.2.1/32, version 9, receive
172.16.2.255/32, version 11, receive
172.22.1.0/24, version 22, attached, connected
0 packets, 0 bytes
  via FastEthernet0/1, 0 dependencies
    valid glean adjacency
172.22.1.0/32, version 16, receive
<many lines deleted>
Router#
```

See Also

Appendix B

11.2   Setting the DSCP or TOS Field

Problem

You want the router to mark the DSCP or TOS field of an IP packet to affect its priority through the network.

Solution

The solution to this problem depends on the sort of traffic distinctions you want to make, as well the version of IOS you are running in your routers.

There must be something that defines the different types of traffic that you wish to prioritize. In general, the simpler the distinctions are to make, the better. This is because all of the tests take router resources and introduce processing delays. The most common rules for distinguishing between traffic types use the packet's input interface and simple IP header information such as TCP port numbers. The following examples show how to set an IP Precedence value of immediate (2) for all FTP control traffic that arrives through the serial0/0 interface, and an IP Precedence of priority (1) for all FTP data traffic. This distinction is possible because FTP control traffic uses TCP port 21, and FTP data uses port 20.

The new method for configuring this uses class maps. Cisco first introduced this feature in IOS Version 12.0(5)T. This method first defines a *class-map* that specifies how the router will identify this type of traffic. It then defines a *policy-map* that actually makes the changes to the packet's TOS field:

```
Router#configure terminal
Enter configuration commands, one per line.  End with CNTL/Z.
Router(config)#access-list 101 permit any eq ftp any
Router(config)#access-list 101 permit any any eq ftp
Router(config)#access-list 102 permit any eq ftp-data any
Router(config)#access-list 102 permit any any eq ftp-data
Router(config)#class-map match-all ser00-ftpcontrol
Router(config-cmap)#description branch ftp control traffic
Router(config-cmap)#match input-interface serial0/0
Router(config-cmap)#match access-group 101
Router(config-cmap)#exit
Router(config)#class-map match-all ser00-ftpdata
Router(config-cmap)#description branch ftp data traffic
Router(config-cmap)#match input-interface serial0/0
Router(config-cmap)#match access-group 102
Router(config-cmap)#exit
Router(config)#policy-map serialftppolicy
Router(config-pmap)#description branch ftp traffic policy
Router(config-pmap)#class ser00-ftpcontrol
Router(config-pmap-c)#set ip precedence immediate
Router(config-pmap-c)#exit
Router(config-pmap)#class ser00-ftpdata
Router(config-pmap-c)#set ip precedence priority
Router(config-pmap-c)#exit
Router(config-pmap)#exit
Router(config)#interface serial0/0
Router(config-if)#ip route-cache policy
Router(config-if)#service-policy input serialftppolicy
Router(config-if)#exit
Router(config)#end
Router#
```

For earlier IOS versions, where class-maps were not available, you have to use policy-based routing to alter the TOS field in a packet. Applying this policy to the interface tells the router to use this policy to test all incoming packets on this interface and rewrite the ones that match the route map:

```
Router#configure terminal
Enter configuration commands, one per line.  End with CNTL/Z.
Router(config)#access-list 101 permit any eq ftp any
Router(config)#access-list 101 permit any any eq ftp
```

```
Router(config)#access-list 102 permit any eq ftp-data any
Router(config)#access-list 102 permit any any eq ftp-data
Router(config)#route-map serialftp-rtmap permit 10
Router(config-route-map)#match ip address 101
Router(config-route-map)#set ip precedence immediate
Router(config-route-map)#exit
Router(config)#route-map serialftp-rtmap permit 20
Router(config-route-map)#match ip address 102
Router(config-route-map)#set ip precedence priority
Router(config-route-map)#exit
Router(config)#interface serial0/0
Router(config-if)#ip policy route-map serialftp-rtmap
Router(config-if)#ip route-cache policy
Router(config-if)#exit
Router(config)#end
Router#
```

Discussion

Before you can tag a packet for special treatment, you have to have an extremely clear idea of what types of traffic need special treatment, as well as precisely what sort of special treatment they will need. In the example, we have decided to give a special priority to FTP traffic received on a specific serial interface. We show how to do this using both the old and new configuration techniques.

This may appear to be a somewhat artificial example. After all, why would you care about tagging inbound traffic that you have already received from a low-speed interface? Actually, one of the most important principles for implementing QoS in a network is that you should always tag the packet as early as possible, preferably at the edges of the network. Then, as it passes through the network, each router only needs to look at the tag, and doesn't need to do any additional classification. In this case, we would ensure that the FTP traffic returning in the other direction is tagged by the first router that receives it. So the outbound traffic has already been tagged, and it is a waste of router resources to reclassify the outbound packets.

Many organizations actually take this idea of marking at the edges one step further, and remark every received packet. This helps to ensure that users aren't requesting special QoS privileges that they aren't allowed to have. However, you should be careful of this because it can sometimes disrupt legitimate markings. For example, a real-time application might use RSVP to reserve bandwidth through the network. It is important that the packets for this application have the appropriate Expedited Forwarding (EF) DSCP marking or the network might not handle them properly. However, you also don't want to let other non-real-time applications from this same source have the same EF priority level. So, if you are going to configure your routers to remark all incoming packets at the edges, make sure you understand what incoming markings are legitimate.

Recipe 15.10 shows another interesting variation of this idea. In that case, the routers are running *DLSw* to bridge SNA traffic through an IP network. So the routers themselves actually create the IP packets. This creates an additional challenge because there is no incoming interface. So that recipe uses local policy-based routing. The fact that the router creates the packets also gives it an important advantage because it doesn't have to consider any *DLSw* packets that might just happen to pass through.

The advantages of the newer class-map method aren't obvious in this example, but one of the first big advantages appears if you want to use the more modern DSCP tagging scheme. Because the older policy-based routing method doesn't directly support DSCP, you have to fake it by setting both the IP Precedence and the TOS separately as follows.

```
Router(config)#route-map serialftp-rtmap permit 10
Router(config-route-map)#match ip address 115
Router(config-route-map)#set ip precedence immediate
Router(config-route-map)#set ip tos max-throughput
```

In this case, the packet will wind up with an IP Precedence value of immediate, or 2 (010 in binary), and TOS of max-throughput, or 4 (0100 in binary). Combining the bit patterns gives 0100100, but, as we discuss in Appendix B, DSCP only uses the first 6 bits, 010010. If you look up this bit combination in Table B-3 in Appendix B, you will see that it corresponds to a value of AF21, which is Class 2 and lowest drop precedence.

Doing the same thing with the class-map method is much more direct:

```
Router(config)#policy-map serialftppolicy
Router(config-pmap)#class serialftpclass
Router(config-pmap-c)#set ip dscp af21
```

Class-maps will also be useful later in this chapter when we talk about class-based weighted fair queuing and class-based traffic shaping.

It is important to note that throughout this entire example, we have only put a special value into the packet's TOS or DSCP field. This, by itself, doesn't affect how the packet is forwarded through the network. To do that, you must ensure that as each router in the network forwards these marked packets, the interface queues will react appropriately to this information.

Finally, we should note that while this recipe shows two useful ways of marking packets, Recipe 11.15 shows still another method, using Committed Access Rate (CAR) features. CAR tends to be more efficient on higher speed interfaces.

See Also

Recipe 11.3; Recipe 11.5; Recipe 11.6; Recipe 11.7; Recipe 11.10; Recipe 11.15; Recipe 11.16; Appendix B

11.3   Using Priority Queuing

Problem

You want to enable strict priority queues on an interface so that the router always handles high priority packets first.

Solution

To enable priority queuing on an interface, you must first define the priority list, and then you can apply it to the interface:

```
Router#configure terminal
Enter configuration commands, one per line.  End with CNTL/Z.
Router(config)#access-list 101 permit ip any any precedence 5 tos 12
Router(config)#access-list 102 permit ip any any precedence 4
Router(config)#access-list 103 permit ip any any precedence 3
Router(config)#priority-list 1 protocol ip high list 101
Router(config)#priority-list 1 protocol ip medium list 102
Router(config)#priority-list 1 protocol ip normal list 103
Router(config)#priority-list 1 default low
Router(config)#interface Ethernet0
Router(config-if)#priority-group 1
Router(config-if)#exit
Router(config)#end
Router#
```

Discussion

As we discuss in Appendix B, priority queues strictly ensure that high priority packets are always handled before lower priority packets. We stress that using pure priority queuing like this is usually a bad idea because the higher priority traffic can take all of the available bandwidth and completely starve all other network traffic. You only want to use this style of queuing when you can be absolutely certain that the aggregate bandwidth of all high priority traffic will never consume the available link bandwidth. This could be the case, for example, if the high priority traffic is shaped before reaching this router, or for applications like Voice over IP (VoIP) that use a relatively constant amount of bandwidth, and don't burst above this constant rate.

The *priority-list* command has a relatively flexible syntax for identifying what types of traffic will use which queues. However, we prefer the access-list method shown in the example. This is because it gives the greatest range of possibilities for identifying traffic types.

In the example, we use access-list 101 to decide which packets to send to the high priority queue:

```
Router(config)#access-list 101 permit ip any any precedence 5 tos 12
```

If you write out the bit patterns for an IP Precedence value of 5 and a TOS of 12, you get 101 and 1100. Combining these together and dropping the last bit gives 101110, which is identical to the Expedited Forwarding (EF) DSCP value. This is typically the DSCP value that is used to mark packets for real-time applications.

Cisco introduced a *dscp* keyword to the access-list command in IOS Version 12. 1(5)T. This allows you to accomplish the same thing with a slightly simpler access list. This access list should also process faster because it only makes one comparison instead of two:

```
Router(config)#access-list 101 permit ip any any dscp ef
```

The access-lists that define the other queues also select specific IP Precedence values. This is because we want to carefully limit the amount of processing that the router has to do. The less the access-list has to look at, the better.

Note also that the router will process the priority list in the order that it was entered. In general you will want to keep queuing latency for high priority packets as low as possible. This is why we define the higher priority queues first.

In the example, we also specifically included a command to put any unmatched packets into the low priority queue:

```
Router(config)#priority-list 1 default low
```

If we had not included this command, the router would have used the normal priority queue for any unmatched packets by default.

You can look at priority queuing information on an interface with the *show interface* command:

```
Router#show interface Ethernet0
Ethernet0 is up, line protocol is up
  Hardware is Lance, address is 0000.0cf0.8460 (bia 0000.0cf0.8460)
  Internet address is 192.168.1.201/24
  MTU 1500 bytes, BW 10000 Kbit, DLY 1000 usec,
     reliability 255/255, txload 1/255, rxload 1/255
  Encapsulation ARPA, loopback not set, keepalive set (10 sec)
  ARP type: ARPA, ARP Timeout 04:00:00
  Last input 00:00:00, output 00:00:00, output hang never
  Last clearing of "show interface" counters never
  Input queue: 0/75/0 (size/max/drops); Total output drops: 0
  Queuing strategy: priority-list 1
  Output queue (queue priority: size/max/drops):
     high: 0/20/0, medium: 0/40/0, normal 0/60/0, low 0/80/0
  5 minute input rate 1000 bits/sec, 2 packets/sec
  5 minute output rate 2000 bits/sec, 2 packets/sec
     7390 packets input, 655552 bytes, 0 no buffer
     Received 6687 broadcasts, 0 runts, 0 giants, 0 throttles
     0 input errors, 0 CRC, 0 frame, 0 overrun, 0 ignored, 0 abort
     0 input packets with dribble condition detected
     81097 packets output, 6240100 bytes, 0 underruns
     2 output errors, 0 collisions, 7 interface resets
```

```
                       0 babbles, 0 late collision, 0 deferred
                       2 lost carrier, 0 no carrier
                       0 output buffer failures, 0 output buffers swapped out
                 Router#
```

In this case, you can see that the high-priority queue has a maximum depth of 20 packets. The medium queue can hold 40 packets, normal holds 60, and the low-priority queue can hold 80 packets. This increasing queue depth pattern is necessary to help deal with queue starvation problems. You can modify these default values as follows:

```
        Router(config)#priority-list 1 queue-limit 10 15 25 35
```

This command sets the depths for all of the queues in increasing order. This particular example would set the high-priority queue to hold a maximum of 10 packets, 15 for the medium queue, 25 for the normal queue, and 35 for the low-priority queue.

Note that the router will automatically use the high-priority queue for critical network control information, such as routing updates and keepalives. If these packets are not sent in a timely fashion, it can disrupt how the network functions. If the router were to put this critical information into a lower priority queue, there would be a danger that higher priority application traffic could starve the lower priority queues, and disrupt routing or possibly even bring down parts of the network. CBWFQ and Cisco's new Low Latency Queuing (LLQ) algorithm offer all of the advantages of Priority Queuing discussed here, and fewer of the disadvantages. This feature is discussed in Recipe 11.16. We recommend using LLQ instead of Priority Queuing, if your router supports it. Cisco introduced LLQ in IOS level 12.0(6)T.

See Also

Recipe 11.16

11.4   Using Custom Queuing

Problem

You want to configure Custom Queuing on an interface to give different traffic streams a share of the bandwidth according to their IP Precedence levels.

Solution

Implementing Custom Queuing on a router is a two-step procedure. First, you must define the traffic types that will populate your queues. And then you apply the queuing method to an interface:

```
        Router#configure terminal
        Enter configuration commands, one per line.  End with CNTL/Z.
        Router(config)#access-list 103 permit ip any any precedence 5
        Router(config)#access-list 104 permit ip any any precedence 4
        Router(config)#access-list 105 permit ip any any precedence 3
```

```
Router(config)#access-list 106 permit ip any any precedence 2
Router(config)#access-list 107 permit ip any any precedence 1
Router(config)#queue-list 1 protocol ip 3 list 103
Router(config)#queue-list 1 protocol ip 4 list 104
Router(config)#queue-list 1 protocol ip 5 list 105
Router(config)#queue-list 1 queue 5 byte-count 3000 limit 55
Router(config)#queue-list 1 protocol ip 6 list 106
Router(config)#queue-list 1 protocol ip 7 list 107
Router(config)#queue-list 1 default 8
Router(config)#interface HSSI0/0
Router(config-if)#custom-queue-list 1
Router(config-if)#exit
Router(config)#end
Router#
```

Discussion

When you enable Custom Queuing, the router automatically creates 16 queues for application traffic plus one more for system requirements. You can look at the queues with a normal *show interface* command:

```
Router#show interface Ethernet0
Ethernet0 is up, line protocol is up
  Hardware is Lance, address is 0000.0cf0.8460 (bia 0000.0cf0.8460)
  Internet address is 192.168.1.201/24
  MTU 1500 bytes, BW 10000 Kbit, DLY 1000 usec,
     reliability 255/255, txload 2/255, rxload 1/255
  Encapsulation ARPA, loopback not set, keepalive set (10 sec)
  ARP type: ARPA, ARP Timeout 04:00:00
  Last input 00:00:00, output 00:00:00, output hang never
  Last clearing of "show interface" counters never
  Input queue: 2/75/0 (size/max/drops); Total output drops: 0
  Queuing strategy: custom-list 1
  Output queues: (queue #: size/max/drops)
     0: 0/20/0 1: 0/20/0 2: 0/20/0 3: 0/20/0 4: 0/20/0
     5: 0/55/3 6: 5/20/0 7: 0/20/0 8: 0/20/0 9: 0/20/0
     10: 0/20/0 11: 0/20/0 12: 0/20/0 13: 0/20/0 14: 0/20/0
     15: 0/20/0 16: 0/20/0
  5 minute input rate 5000 bits/sec, 12 packets/sec
  5 minute output rate 106000 bits/sec, 24 packets/sec
     132910 packets input, 14513345 bytes, 0 no buffer
     Received 109570 broadcasts, 0 runts, 0 giants, 0 throttles
     9 input errors, 0 CRC, 0 frame, 0 overrun, 9 ignored, 0 abort
     0 input packets with dribble condition detected
     1028116 packets output, 85603681 bytes, 0 underruns
     1 output errors, 42 collisions, 8 interface resets
     0 babbles, 0 late collision, 4 deferred
     1 lost carrier, 0 no carrier
     0 output buffer failures, 0 output buffers swapped out
Router#
```

In this output, you can see that queue number 6 currently has 5 packets queued and waiting for delivery (6: 5/20/0), while queue number 5 has had to drop 3 packets due to congestion (5: 0/55/3).

The example assigns queue number 3 for all packets with the highest application IP Precedence value of 5. Similarly, packets with Precedence 4 use queue number 4, Precedence 3 use queue 5, Precedence 2 use queue 6, Precedence 1 use queue 7, and everything else uses queue number 8.

Custom Queuing does not assign a default queue for unclassified traffic, so you must remember to do this. The command in the example defines the default as queue number 8:

```
Router(config)#queue-list 1 default 8
```

Note that if there is another nonIP protocol such as IPX configured on this interface, it will also use the default queue. If you prefer to give this other protocol its own set of queues, you can use define them using access lists for that protocol. The configuration is nearly identical to the IP example we have shown, except for the exact access list syntax, which naturally depends on the protocol.

By default, the Custom Queuing scheduler visits all queues in order and takes an average of 1,500 bytes from each, and each queue can hold up to 20 packets. In the example, we changed these default values for queue number 5:

```
Router(config)#queue-list 1 queue 5 byte-count 3000 limit 55
```

This tells the scheduler to take an average of 3000 bytes from this queue on each pass, and to store up to 55 packets in the queue. Increasing the number of bytes will effectively increase the share of the bandwidth that this queue receives. Increasing the queue depth decreases the probability of tail drops. But it also increases the amount of time that a packet could theoretically spend in the queue, which may increase latency and jitter.

In this example, all of the traffic types are selected by the IP Precedence value. It is also possible to select based on specific applications. You can do this either with an access-list or, in some cases, using keywords in the *queue-list* command. For example, if you wanted to select all DLSw traffic and send it to queue number 9, you could create an access-list:

```
Router(config)#access-list 117 permit ip any eq 2065 any
Router(config)#access-list 117 permit ip any any eq 2065
Router(config)#access-list 117 permit ip any eq 2067 any
Router(config)#access-list 117 permit ip any any eq 2067
Router(config)#queue-list 1 protocol ip 9 list 117
```

Or you could do it like this:

```
Router(config)#queue-list 1 protocol dlsw 9
```

This second method is clearly easier, but the number of protocol types that can be defined this way is unfortunately rather limited.

We have three important final notes on Custom Queuing that you should bear in mind. The first point is that if traffic from all of these streams is present, the router will share traffic between them. In this example, we have used six different queues: one for each of the five application precedence levels, plus a default. By default, each will receive a roughly equal share of the total bandwidth. So you may be surprised to find that despite imposing different queues for the different traffic types, the important traffic still doesn't get a large enough share of the bandwidth. You can affect this with the *byte-count* keyword, as we discussed earlier. Note that the queues are serviced by byte count rather than packet count. So suppose you have two queues, one of which supports an interactive session with many short packets, and another that contains a bulk transfer with a few large packets. If you configure the router to service these queues with the same byte-count, it will tend to forward a lot more of the small packets. But the net share of the bandwidth will be roughly equal on average.

Second, in Custom Queuing, the traffic within each queue competes directly with all other traffic in the same queue. So, for example, if one user sends a burst of application traffic that fills one of the queues, this will cause tail drops for other users whose traffic uses the same queue. This will cause a smaller version of the global problem of a FIFO queue that we discuss in Appendix B.

And the third point is that the more queues you define, the smaller the share of the total bandwidth each queue receives. Further, having more queues increases the amount of processing the router has to do to segregate the traffic.

The second and third points compete with one another. The second one tends to point toward increasing the number of queues to limit the competition within each queue. But the third point should convince you that there is a point of diminishing returns where more queues will not help the situation. In practice, the third rule tends to win out. It rarely turns out to be beneficial to have more than five or six Custom Queues, unless some of those queues are only used very lightly.

Custom Queuing is an older QoS mechanism on Cisco routers. In most cases, you will likely find that a newer algorithm such as CBWFQ will be more flexible and give better results.

11.5   Using Custom Queues with Priority Queues

Problem

You want to combine Custom Queuing with Priority Queuing on an interface so the highest priority packets are always handled first, and lower priority traffic streams share bandwidth with one another.

Solution

You can split the queues so that some use Priority Queuing and the remainder Custom Queuing:

```
Router#configure terminal
Enter configuration commands, one per line.  End with CNTL/Z.
Router(config)#access-list 101 permit ip any any precedence 7
Router(config)#access-list 102 permit ip any any precedence 6
Router(config)#access-list 103 permit ip any any precedence 5
Router(config)#access-list 104 permit ip any any precedence 4
Router(config)#access-list 105 permit ip any any precedence 3
Router(config)#access-list 106 permit ip any any precedence 2
Router(config)#access-list 107 permit ip any any precedence 1
Router(config)#queue-list 1 protocol ip 1 list 101
Router(config)#queue-list 1 protocol ip 2 list 102
Router(config)#queue-list 1 protocol ip 3 list 103
Router(config)#queue-list 1 protocol ip 4 list 104
Router(config)#queue-list 1 protocol ip 5 list 105
Router(config)#queue-list 1 protocol ip 6 list 106
Router(config)#queue-list 1 protocol ip 7 list 107
Router(config)#queue-list 1 lowest-custom 4
Router(config)#interface HSSI0/0
Router(config-if)#custom-queue-list 1
Router(config-if)#exit
Router(config)#end
Router#
```

Discussion

This example is similar to Recipe 11.4, which looked at a pure Custom Queuing example. In this case, however, we have added the command:

```
Router(config)#queue-list 1 lowest-custom 4
```

This command allows you to mix Custom and Priority Queue types. Note that this command only works with queue-list number 1. It is not available for any other queue-lists.

In this example, queue number 4 is the lowest numbered Custom Queue. So, in this example, queues 1, 2, and 3 are all Priority Queues. This means that the router will deliver all of the packets in queue number 1, then all of the packets in queue number, and then all of the packets in queue number 3. Then, if these high priority queues are all empty, it will use custom queuing to deliver the packets in the lower priority queues.

The main advantage to this sort of configuration is that it gives absolute priority to real-time applications. This is important not because of the bandwidth, but because priority queuing the real-time applications minimizes their queuing latency. However, as with the pure Priority Queuing example of Recipe 11.3, you have to be extremely careful to prevent the high-priority traffic from starving the other queues.

See Also

Recipe 11.3; Recipe 11.4; Recipe 11.16

11.6 Using Weighted Fair Queuing

Problem

You want your routers to use the TOS/DSCP fields when forwarding packets.

Solution

The simplest way to make your routers use DSCP or TOS information is to just make sure that Weighted Fair Queuing is enabled:

```
Router#configure terminal
Enter configuration commands, one per line.  End with CNTL/Z.
Router(config)#interface Serial0/0
Router(config-if)#fair-queue
Router(config-if)#exit
Router(config)#end
Router#
```

WFQ is enabled by default on all interfaces of E1 speeds (roughly 2 Mbps) or less. You can enable WFQ on higher speed interfaces as well, but we don't recommend it.

To configure more specific behavior, you can tell WFQ how to allocate its queues:

```
Router#configure terminal
Enter configuration commands, one per line.  End with CNTL/Z.
Router(config)#interface Serial0/0
Router(config-if)#fair-queue 64 512 10
Router(config-if)#exit
Router(config)#end
Router#
```

Discussion

Before we discuss these examples in any detail, we should mention that WFQ works well even if you don't use any TOS/DSCP marking. In this case, it simply gives the same default weighting to every flow, which is the same as conventional Fair Queuing (without the weights). As we discuss in Appendix B, Fair Queuing is much more effective than FIFO queuing. However, with TOS/DSCP marking, WFQ really shows its value, giving higher priority flows more of the bandwidth, and preventing high volume flows from starving low volume flows, regardless of their TOS markings.

The first example just enables WFQ on the interface. In fact, this is the default for all interfaces that operate slower than 2.048 Mbps (E1 speed), except for interfaces that use LAPB or SDLC. WFQ does not work with LAPB or SDLC.

The second example is a little bit more interesting, though, because it changes the default queues. The *fair-queue* command has three optional parameters. In the example, we specified:

```
Router(config-if)#fair-queue 64 512 10
```

The first number specifies the congestive discard threshold. This just means that if there are more than 64 packets in any given queue, the router will start to discard any new packets. The default threshold is 64.

The second number is the number of dynamic queues. The values must be a multiple of 16 to a maximum of 4,096 (i.e., one of the following values: 16, 32, 64, 128, 256, 512, 1,024, 2,048, and 4,096). The default value is 256. If this interface must support a large number of flows, then it is a good idea to choose a larger value.

The last number, 10 in this case, is the number of queues that the router will set aside for RSVP reservation requests. Please see Recipes 11.10, 11.11, and 11.12 for more information about RSVP.

In most cases, the default parameters are good enough. However, there are two times in particular when it is useful to modify them. First, if the interface must support an extremely large number of flows, you will get better performance by using a larger number of queues. However, you need to be careful doing this on faster interfaces because the router may start to have trouble processing the additional queues. In that case, you could actually get a performance improvement by decreasing the number of queues. In this case, each queue could wind up simultaneously handling a few distinct flows.

You will also need to change the default queue parameters if you are using RSVP to reserve queues. By default, this parameter is zero. So if you are using RSVP with WFQ, you must allocate some reserved queuing space.

See Also

Recipe 11.10; Recipe 11.11; Recipe 11.12

11.7 Using Class-Based Weighted Fair Queuing

Problem

You want to use Class-Based Weighted Fair Queuing on an interface.

Solution

There are three steps to configuring Class-Based Weighted Fair Queuing (CBWFQ) on a router. First, you have to create one or more class maps that describe the traffic types.

Then you create a policy map that tells the router what to do with these traffic types. Finally, you need to attach this policy map to one or more of the router's interfaces:

```
Router#configure terminal
Enter configuration commands, one per line.  End with CNTL/Z.
Router(config)#class-map highprec
Router(config-cmap)#description Highest priority Prec=5
Router(config-cmap)#match ip precedence 5
Router(config-cmap)#exit
Router(config)#class-map medhiprec
Router(config-cmap)#description Medium-high priority Prec=4
Router(config-cmap)#match ip precedence 4
Router(config-cmap)#exit
Router(config)#class-map medloprec
Router(config-cmap)#description Medium-low priority Prec=2,3
Router(config-cmap)#match ip precedence 2 3
Router(config-cmap)#exit
Router(config)#policy-map cbwfqpolicy
Router(config-pmap)#class highprec
Router(config-pmap-c)#bandwidth percent 25
Router(config-pmap-c)#exit
Router(config-pmap)#class medhiprec
Router(config-pmap-c)#bandwidth percent 25
Router(config-pmap-c)#exit
Router(config-pmap)#class medloprec
Router(config-pmap-c)#bandwidth percent 25
Router(config-pmap-c)#exit
Router(config-pmap)#class class-default
Router(config-pmap-c)#fair-queue 512
Router(config-pmap-c)#queue-limit 96
Router(config-pmap-c)#exit
Router(config-pmap)#exit
Router(config)#interface serial0/1
Router(config-if)#service-policy output cbwfqpolicy
Router(config-if)#exit
Router(config)#end
Router#
```

This feature is available in IOS levels 12.0(5)T and higher.

Discussion

CBWFQ need not be significantly different from regular WFQ. In the example we have defined all traffic with an IP Precedence value of critical (5) to have a special queue. We have also created a single queue for traffic with Precedence 4, and another one for traffic with Precedence values of 2 and 3. All other traffic, including traffic with Precedence 0 and 1, as well as all nonIP traffic uses regular WFQ. To make this fact slightly more clear, we have modified the default WFQ parameters with the following commands:

```
Router(config)#policy-map cbwfqpolicy
Router(config-pmap)#class class-default
Router(config-pmap-c)#fair-queue 512
Router(config-pmap-c)#queue-limit 96
```

This simply modifies the default WFQ behavior for all traffic that doesn't match one of the other defined classes. It sets the number of WFQ queues to 512, and sets the queue depth to a maximum of 96 packets. You could achieve the same effect by using the *fair-queue* interface command from Recipe 11.6:

```
Router(config-if)#fair-queue 96 512 0
```

But that example doesn't give you the ability to also have separate queues for special classes of traffic, as shown in this recipe. We note in passing that the final argument for this *fair-queue* interface command specifies the number of queues to set aside for RSVP. We are trying to duplicate the effect of the *cbwfqpolicy* policy map, which doesn't include any RSVP queues, so we have set the last argument to zero here. Please refer to Recipe 11.6 for more information on this command.

You can create up to 64 Class-based queues for use with CBWFQ. You can control the share of the bandwidth to each queue using the *bandwidth* keyword either by using an absolute value in kilobits per second, or a percentage of the total available bandwidth. The following example shows the syntax for using a percentage:

```
Router(config-pmap)#class highprec
Router(config-pmap-c)#bandwidth percent 25
Router(config-pmap-c)#exit
```

The *bandwidth percent* command is available in IOS levels 12.1(1) and higher. For earlier releases, you can only specify an absolute bandwidth:

```
Router(config-pmap-c)#bandwidth 5000
```

The argument for this version of the command is a value in kilobits per second between 8 and 2,000,000, which should be sufficient for most interface types. Note that the upper limit here is 2 Mbps, which is roughly the E1 speed mentioned earlier as the effective upper limit to using WFQ. Because CBWFQ generally uses fewer queues and doesn't need to sort based on flow, you can use it for higher speed interfaces as well. However, you should let your average CPU utilization be your guide here. If you do too many tests when classifying packets, you might find that the router can't keep up with high packet rates.

In both versions, you have to keep two important factors in mind. First, although this is essentially a Layer 3 feature, when configuring the bandwidth you have to include any Layer 2 framing overhead. If a given queue supports a streaming multimedia application with a known bit rate, it is often a good idea to slightly overestimate the requirements to include this Layer 2 overhead. If the application doesn't use the excess, CBWFQ allocates it to other queues.

The second important factor is that the total allocated bandwidth must not exceed a configurable maximum value. By default, this maximum is 75 percent. You can change it, for example, to 80 percent by using the following interface level command:

```
Router(config-if)#max-reserved-bandwidth 80
```

You would apply this command to the interface that runs CBWFQ and needs a little extra reserved capacity. It is usually best to leave this at its default value, however. The router uses the remainder for unclassified traffic and network control packets. In this case, we have configured WFQ for the unclassified traffic. It is vital, however, to reserve enough bandwidth for critical network functions such as Layer 2 keepalive frames and routing protocols.

Creating the policy map alone doesn't actually change the way the router behaves. To do that, you have to attach this policy to an interface as follows:

```
Router(config)#interface serial0/1
Router(config-if)#service-policy output cbwfqpolicy
```

One of the classes defined in this example is a high-priority class that we called *highpriority*. This class map simply looks for traffic that is tagged with an IP precedence value of 5. The policy map then tells the interface to give up to 25 percent of its bandwidth to this high priority traffic. If there is not enough high-priority traffic to use this, the router will allocate the excess to the remaining traffic.

We will expand on this concept in Recipe 11.16.

See Also

Recipe 11.2; Recipe 11.6; Recipe 11.16

11.8 Using NBAR Classification

Problem

You wish to use the Network Based Application Recognition (NBAR) feature to identify and classify traffic at the application layer.

Solution

The NBAR feature is used to identify traffic within a *class-map*. You can then use the class-map in a *policy-map* to define how the router should handle each application data stream:

```
Router1#configure terminal
Enter configuration commands, one per line.  End with CNTL/Z.
Router1(config)#ip cef
Router1(config)#class-map INTERACTIVE
Router1(config-cmap)#match protocol citrix
Router1(config-cmap)#match protocol telnet
Router1(config-cmap)#exit
Router1(config)#policy-map QoSPolicy
Router1(config-pmap)#class INTERACTIVE
Router1(config-pmap-c)#bandwidth percent 50
Router1(config-pmap-c)#set dscp ef
Router1(config-pmap-c)#exit
```

```
Router1(config-pmap)#class class-default
Router1(config-pmap-c)#bandwidth percent 20
Router1(config-pmap-c)#random-detect dscp-based
Router1(config-pmap-c)#exit
Router1(config-pmap)#exit
Router1(config)#interface FastEthernet0/0
Router1(config-fi)#service-policy inbound QoSPolicy
Router1(config-if)#exit
Router1(config)#end
Router1#
```

Cisco also offers the ability to download specialized Packet Description Language Module (PDLM) files onto the router's flash device, and then activate them for use with NBAR classification:

```
Router1#show flash

System flash directory:
File  Length    Name/status
  1   23169076  c2600-ipvoice-mz.124-10.bin
  2   3100      bittorrent.pdlm
[23172304 bytes used, 9857836 available, 33030140 total]
32768K bytes of processor board System flash (Read/Write)

Router1#Router1#configure terminal
Enter configuration commands, one per line.  End with CNTL/Z.
Router1(config)#ip nbar pdlm flash://bittorrent.pdlm
Router1(config)#class-map BITTORRENT
Router1(config-cmap)#match protocol bittorrent
Router1(config-cmap)#exit
Router1(config)#end
Router1#
```

And you can also use NBAR to automatically profile the protocols on a particular interface:

```
Router1#configure terminal
Enter configuration commands, one per line.  End with CNTL/Z.
Router1(config)#interface FastEthernet0/0
Router1(config-if)#ip nbar protocol-discovery
Router1(config-if)#exit
Router1(config)#end
Router1#
```

Discussion

Network Based Application Recognition (NBAR) is an extremely useful feature that first became available in IOS Version 12.0(5)XE2, and more generally in 12.1(5)T. Cisco continues to add new protocols to NBAR, allowing you to categorize more and more different traffic streams on your network. The one caveat to using NBAR is that it can introduce a heavy additional load on your router's CPU. We recommend monitoring the CPU utilization after implementing any NBAR-based filtering, at least until you are confident that the router is not straining under the additional load.

The basic syntax is to set up a *class-map*, and then use the *match protocol* command with the appropriate keyword:

```
Router1(config)#class-map INTERACTIVE
Router1(config-cmap)#match protocol citrix
Router1(config-cmap)#match protocol telnet
```

We used Citrix as an example protocol in this recipe because it is a classic example of the need for the NBAR feature. This is a proprietary protocol that is used in thin-client architectures. The end user's workstation is just a terminal that displays graphical information from the screen of a centrally located computer running a virtual desktop for the user. The protocol transmits graphical information and keystrokes. Because it is an interactive application, it needs to be given high priority through the network. However, it is notoriously difficult to reliably identify from Layer 3 and 4 information:

As the example shows, you can then use this class in a *policy-map*:

```
Router1(config)#policy-map QoSPolicy
Router1(config-pmap)#class INTERACTIVE
Router1(config-pmap-c)#bandwidth percent 50
Router1(config-pmap-c)#set dscp ef
Router1(config-pmap-c)#exit
```

NBAR classifies applications at the application layer, allowing you to differentiate between different streams of traffic that may actually use the same UDP or TCP port numbers, as well as streams of traffic that may use a variety of ports or even arbitrary port numbers.

Here is a list of supported protocols as of IOS Version 12.4(10):

```
Router1(config-cmap)#match protocol ?
  arp             IP ARP
  bgp             Border Gateway Protocol
  bridge          Bridging
  cdp             Cisco Discovery Protocol
  citrix          Citrix Systems ICA protocol
  clns            ISO CLNS
  clns_es         ISO CLNS End System
  clns_is         ISO CLNS Intermediate System
  cmns            ISO CMNS
  compressedtcp   Compressed TCP (VJ)
  cuseeme         CU-SeeMe desktop video conference
  dhcp            Dynamic Host Configuration
  dns             Domain Name Server lookup
  edonkey         eDonkey
  egp             Exterior Gateway Protocol
  eigrp           Enhanced Interior Gateway Routing Protocol
  exchange        MS-RPC for Exchange
  fasttrack       FastTrack Traffic - KaZaA, Morpheus, Grokster...
  finger          Finger
  ftp             File Transfer Protocol
  gnutella        Gnutella Version2 Traffic - BearShare, Shareeza, Morpheus ...
  gopher          Gopher
```

```
gre              Generic Routing Encapsulation
h323             H323 Protocol
http             World Wide Web traffic
icmp             Internet Control Message
imap             Internet Message Access Protocol
ip               IP
ipinip           IP in IP (encapsulation)
ipsec            IP Security Protocol (ESP/AH)
irc              Internet Relay Chat
kazaa2           Kazaa Version 2
kerberos         Kerberos
l2tp             L2F/L2TP tunnel
ldap             Lightweight Directory Access Protocol
llc2             llc2
mgcp             Media Gateway Control Protocol
napster          Napster Traffic
netbios          NetBIOS
netshow          Microsoft Netshow
nfs              Network File System
nntp             Network News Transfer Protocol
notes            Lotus Notes(R)
novadigm         Novadigm EDM
ntp              Network Time Protocol
ospf             Open Shortest Path First
pad              PAD links
pcanywhere       Symantec pcANYWHERE
pop3             Post Office Protocol
pppoe            PPP over Ethernet
pptp             Point-to-Point Tunneling Protocol
printer          print spooler/lpd
rcmd             BSD r-commands (rsh, rlogin, rexec)
rip              Routing Information Protocol
rsrb             Remote Source-Route Bridging
rsvp             Resource Reservation Protocol
rtcp             Real Time Control Protocol
rtp              Real Time Protocol
rtsp             Real Time Streaming Protocol
secure-ftp       FTP over TLS/SSL
secure-http      Secured HTTP
secure-imap      Internet Message Access Protocol over TLS/SSL
secure-irc       Internet Relay Chat over TLS/SSL
secure-ldap      Lightweight Directory Access Protocol over TLS/SSL
secure-nntp      Network News Transfer Protocol over TLS/SSL
secure-pop3      Post Office Protocol over TLS/SSL
secure-telnet    Telnet over TLS/SSL
sip              Session Initiation Protocol
skinny           Skinny Protocol
smtp             Simple Mail Transfer Protocol
snapshot         Snapshot routing support
snmp             Simple Network Management Protocol
socks            SOCKS
sqlnet           SQL*NET for Oracle
sqlserver        MS SQL Server
ssh              Secured Shell
```

```
streamwork      Xing Technology StreamWorks player
sunrpc          Sun RPC
syslog          System Logging Utility
telnet          Telnet
tftp            Trivial File Transfer Protocol
vdolive         VDOLive streaming video
vofr            voice over Frame Relay packets
winmx           WinMx file-sharing application
xwindows        X-Windows remote access

Router1(config-cmap)#
```

You can obtain and install new PDLM files from Cisco. In the example, we have downloaded a new PDLM file that can identify the BitTorrent protocol. Once we put this file on the router's Flash device, we need to tell NBAR to load the file to make it available:

```
Router1(config)#ip nbar pdlm flash://bittorrent.pdlm
```

In the past, Cisco has also made PDLM files available to help network administrators to use NBAR to help to identify hostile applications such as viruses and worms.

We are not aware of PDLM files originating from sources other than Cisco, but we strongly recommend that you use only files that you obtain directly from Cisco. Otherwise, you could potentially open your network to serious security vulnerabilities.

We note in passing that Cisco has also added the option to manually create your own NBAR rules using the *ip nbar custom* command. This feature should allow you to, for example, define a new protocol by specifying TCP or UDP port numbers, as well as any special rules that look for identifiable content at a particular bit offset in the packet payload. However, the syntax for this feature is confusing, and the parser is apparently unstable in some IOS versions, so we don't currently recommend using it.

The last feature discussed in the Solution section of this recipe is the NBAR Protocol-Discovery feature. This is a useful tool for figuring out what is going through your network, particularly if you are trying to define a QoS strategy. You can use the *show ip nbar protocol-discovery* command to get detailed statistics on the utilization for every type of protocol that NBAR understands. However, NBAR now supports so many protocols that this complete list is often not very useful for spotting trends. Instead, we suggest using the *top-n* keyword with a relatively small argument number, such as 5, or at most 10. This will allow you to immediately see statistics for the top protocols for each interface on which you enabled the feature:

```
Router1#show ip nbar protocol-discovery top-n 5

FastEthernet0/0
                         Input                    Output
                         -----                    ------
        Protocol         Packet Count             Packet Count
                         Byte Count               Byte Count
                         5min Bit Rate (bps)      5min Bit Rate (bps)
                         5min Max Bit Rate (bps)  5min Max Bit Rate (bps)
```

icmp	220	110
	25080	12540
	0	0
	4000	3000
http	55	104
	3763	60019
	0	0
	1000	4000
telnet	130	71
	19212	4269
	0	0
	3000	1000
eigrp	90	45
	6660	3330
	0	0
	0	0
secure-http	4	4
	248	216
	0	0
	0	0
unknown	2	2
	122	112
	0	0
	0	0
Total	501	336
	55085	80486
	0	0
	8000	8000

```
Router1#
```

11.9   Controlling Congestion with WRED

Problem

You want to control congestion on an interface before it becomes a problem.

Solution

The syntax for configuring WRED changed with the introduction of class-based QoS. The old method defined WRED across an entire interface:

```
Router#configure terminal
Enter configuration commands, one per line.  End with CNTL/Z.
Router(config)#interface HSSI0/0
Router(config-if)#random-detect
Router(config-if)#random-detect precedence 0 10 20 10
Router(config-if)#random-detect precedence 1 12 20 10
Router(config-if)#random-detect precedence 2 15 25 15
Router(config-if)#random-detect precedence 3 18 25 15
Router(config-if)#random-detect precedence 4 20 30 20
Router(config-if)#random-detect precedence 5 22 30 20
```

```
Router(config-if)#random-detect precedence 6 30 40 25
Router(config-if)#random-detect precedence 7 40 50 100
Router(config-if)#random-detect precedence RSVP 45 50 100
Router(config-if)#exit
Router(config)#end
Router#
```

The new configuration method uses the same syntax as CBWFQ:

```
Router#configure terminal
Enter configuration commands, one per line.  End with CNTL/Z.
Router(config)#class-map Prec5
Router(config-cmap)#description Critical
Router(config-cmap)#match ip precedence 5
Router(config-cmap)#exit
Router(config)#policy-map cb_wred
Router(config-pmap)#class Prec5
Router(config-pmap-c)#random-detect dscp-based
Router(config-pmap-c)#exit
Router(config-pmap)#class class-default
Router(config-pmap-c)#fair-queue 512
Router(config-pmap-c)#queue-limit 96
Router(config-pmap-c)#random-detect dscp-based
Router(config-pmap-c)#exit
Router(config-pmap)#exit
Router(config)#interface HSSI0/1
Router(config-if)#service-policy output cb_wred
Router(config-if)#exit
Router(config)#end
Router#
```

Discussion

For the older method, you can set up the drop probabilities according to IP Precedence values by using the following command:

```
Router(config-if)#random-detect precedence 7 40 50 100
```

The first argument after the *precedence* keyword here is the IP Precedence value. The options are any integer between 0 and 7, or the keyword *RSVP*. After this are the minimum threshold, maximum threshold, and the so-called *mark probability* denominator.

The minimum threshold is the number of packets that must be in the queue before the router starts to discard. The probability at the minimum threshold is essentially zero, but it rises linearly as the number of packets in the queue rises. The maximum probability occurs at the maximum threshold. You specify the actual value of the probability at this maximum by using the mark probability denominator. In this case we have set the value to 100, which means that, at the maximum, we will discard one packet in 100. This means that halfway between the maximum and minimum thresholds, the router will drop one packet in 200.

Note that as we discuss in Appendix B, the router doesn't necessarily drop packets when the queue depth reaches the minimum threshold. Rather, it uses a moving average so that temporary bursts of data are not dropped. This configured minimum is the lower limit of this moving average, which is reached only when the congestion continues for a longer period of time.

If you do not change these values, the defaults take IP Precedence values into account. The default mark probability denominator is 10, so the router will discard one packet in 10. The default maximum threshold depends on the speed of the interface and the router's capacity for buffering packets, but it is the same for all Precedence values. So, by default, the only differences between WRED's treatment of different IP Precedence levels is in the minimum threshold. The default minimum threshold for packets with an IP Precedence of 0 is 50 percent of the maximum threshold. This value rises linearly with Precedence so that the minimum threshold for Precedence 7 and packets with RSVP reserved bandwidth allocations are almost the same as the maximum threshold.

In the new-style example, we have created only one class-based queue to show the principle. In practice, of course, you would probably want to create more than this. All of the traffic that doesn't have an IP Precedence value of 5 uses the default queue, where we have configured both WFQ and WRED.

This example uses DSCP-based random detection. WRED has a built-in ability to discriminate based on DSCP value, so that traffic streams with higher drop precedence values are more likely to drop packets. The default WRED settings when using DSCP-based random detection are shown in Table 11-1.

Table 11-1. Default WRED settins

DSCP value	Minimum threshold queue depth	Maximum threshold queue depth	Drop probability at maximum
AFx1	32	40	1/10
AFx2	28	40	1/10
AFx3	24	40	1/10

As Table 11-1 shows, the default DSCP-based thresholds are the same for every class. So, for example, AF12, AF22, AF32, and AF42 all begin dropping packets in a sustained congestion situation when the queue depth reaches 28 packets. They reach their maximum drop probability when there are 40 packets in the queue. In all cases, the drop probability at the maximum threshold value is 1/10 (the mark probability), meaning that the router will randomly drop one packet in 10.

You can change these values in a policy map as follows:

```
Router(config-pmap)#class AF1x
Router(config-pmap-c)#bandwidth percent 20
Router(config-pmap-c)#random-detect dscp-based
```

```
Router(config-pmap-c)#random-detect dscp af13 10 20
Router(config-pmap-c)#random-detect dscp af12 20 50
Router(config-pmap-c)#random-detect dscp af11 50 100 50
Router(config-pmap-c)#exit
```

In each of the *random-detect dscp* commands, the first argument is the DSCP value, followed by the minimum threshold, the maximum threshold, and the denominator of the mark probability. In the case of the AF11 entry, the router will start dropping these packets when there are more than 50 packets in the queue, and increase the probability until the number reaches 100. At that point, the probability of dropping a packet of this type will be one in 50.

Note that these thresholds apply to all traffic in the queue, not just traffic with this particular DSCP value. So there may be 20 AF11 packets, 10 AF12, and 20 more marked with the AF13 DSCP value. Since this adds up to 50 packets, the router will start to drop the AF11 packets. However, because the maximum thresholds for AF12 and AF13 packets are 50 and 20, respectively, the router will already be dropping packets of these types at the full rate (1 packet in 10 by default) before it starts to drop any AF11 packets.

This example assumes that you want to use DSCP values to control the WRED thresholds. This is not necessary, however. You can also use an unweighted version of the command as follows:

```
Router(config)#class-map AF11
Router(config-cmap)#match ip dscp af11
Router(config-cmap)#exit
Router(config)#policy-map example
Router(config-pmap)#class AF11
Router(config-pmap-c)#bandwidth percent 10
Router(config-pmap-c)#random-detect
Router(config-pmap-c)#exit
```

This is particularly useful when your class definitions already take DSCP values into account, as this class map does. Since there is no variation of DSCP values among the class of packets that have a DSCP value of AF11, it isn't necessary for WRED to look at the DSCP value again.

See Also

Recipe 11.7

11.10 Using RSVP

Problem

You want to configure RSVP on your network.

Solution

Basic RSVP configuration is relatively simple. All you need to do is define how much bandwidth can be reserved on the interface:

```
Router#configure terminal
Enter configuration commands, one per line.  End with CNTL/Z.
Router(config)#interface FastEthernet0/0
Router(config-if)#ip rsvp bandwidth 128 56
Router(config-if)#exit
Router(config)#end
Router#
```

Some network administrators have to worry about unauthorized use of bandwidth reservation. You can control this by specifying an access-list of allowed neighbor devices:

```
Router#configure terminal
Enter configuration commands, one per line.  End with CNTL/Z.
Router(config)#access-list 15 permit ip 192.168.1.0 0.0.0.255
Router(config)#interface FastEthernet0/0
Router(config-if)#ip rsvp bandwidth 128 56
Router(config-if)#ip rsvp neighbor 15
Router(config-if)#exit
Router(config)#end
Router#
```

Discussion

Note that before you can configure RSVP on an interface, you must first configure the interface for WFQ, CBWFQ, or WRED. This step is not included in this example, to make it easier to focus on the RSVP configuration. For examples of WFQ, CBWFQ, and WRED, please refer to Recipes 11.6, 11.7, and 11.9, respectively.

The first example tells the router to pay attention to RSVP signaling, and defines how much bandwidth can be reserved in the following command:

```
Router(config-if)#ip rsvp bandwidth 128 56
```

The first numerical argument, 128, specifies that applications can reserve a maximum aggregate bandwidth of 128 Kbps. The last argument, 56, means that the largest amount that a single application can request is 56 Kbps.

When you use the *ip rsvp neighbor* command, as in the second example, it is important to remember that this router receives RSVP reservation requests from neighboring devices. If this is an access router, then the neighboring device on the local LAN port could be an end device. But for other routers and other interfaces, it is likely that the RSVP request will come from another router, not from the end device making the initial request. So, for router-to-router connections, it may not be useful to specify an access list because all RSVP requests, legitimate or not, will come from a neighboring router. The best place to control which devices are allowed to reserve bandwidth is on the access router.

There are several useful show commands to look at the RSVP configuration of your router, as well as the dynamic reservation requests. The first of these is the *show ip rsvp interface* command, which shows information on the reservations that have been made by interface:

```
Router#show ip rsvp interface
interfac allocate i/f max  flow max per/255 UDP  IP   UDP_IP  UDP M/C
Et0      0M       1M       100K     0 /255 0    2    0       0
Too      50K      1M       100K     12 /255 0   1    0       0
```

This command shows that there are two interfaces that are currently supporting RSVP reservations, Ethernet0 and TokenRing0. The *allocate* column shows the amount of bandwidth that has been allocated to active RSVP requests on each interface. In all of these fields, the letter K stands for Kbps and M stands for Mbps. The *i/f max* column shows the total amount that can be allocated on each of these interfaces, while the *flow max* shows the maximum that can be requested by any one flow. These are the parameters from the *ip rsvp bandwidth* interface configuration command.

The remaining columns show information about the actual allocated streams. The *per/255* column shows the fraction of the total interface bandwidth that is used by each of these allocations. This is measured as a fraction of 255, as is common for expressing loads on Cisco interfaces. The UDP column shows the number of UDP-encapsulated sessions, IP counts the TCP-encapsulated sessions, and UDP_IP shows the sessions that use both UDP and TCP. The UDP M/C column shows whether the interface is configured to allow UDP reservations.

You can look at individual reservations in detail with the following command:

```
Router#show ip rsvp installed
RSVP: Ethernet0 has no installed reservations
RSVP: TokenRing0
BPS   To           From           Protoc DPort Sport Weight Conversation
50K   192.168.5.5  192.168.1.10   TCP    888   999   4      520
Router#
```

This shows that the router is currently supporting a 50Kbps TCP session between the two IP addresses that are shown, with the source and destination port numbers, 999 and 888 respectively. The *Weight* column shows the weighting factor, and *Conversation* shows the conversation (or flow) number used by WFQ for this queue. If you don't run WFQ on this interface, then both of these values appear as 0.

There is considerable overlap between the information shown in the *show ip rsvp installed* command and the output with the *reservation* and *sender* keywords. However, there are some important additional pieces of information here:

```
Router#show ip rsvp reservation
To           From           Pro DPort Sport Next Hop     I/F   Fi Serv BPS Bytes
192.168.5.5  192.168.1.10   TCP 888   999   192.168.3.2  Too   FF LOAD 50K  50K
```

```
Router#show ip rsvp sender
To              From            Pro DPort Sport Prev Hop        I/F BPS  Bytes
192.168.5.5     192.168.1.10    TCP 888   999   192.168.1.201   Et0 50K  50K

Router#
```

With the *reservation* keyword, you see details about what type of reservation has been made. In this case, FF indicates that this is a *Fixed Filter* reservation, which means that it contains a single conversation between two end devices. However, RSVP also allows aggregation of flows. If this column says SE, which stands for *Shared Explicit Filter*, then it represents a shared reservation of unlimited scope. The other option is WF, which stands for *Wildcard Filter*, and indicates a shared reservation that can only include certain end devices or applications.

With the *sender* flag, you see the actual path information for the reservation. The *Prev Hop* and *I/F* columns here show the address and interface of the previous hop router. The *BPS* column shows the reserved bandwidth for this session in Kbps, and the *Bytes* column shows the maximum burst size in Kilobytes.

The *show ip rsvp neighbor* command simply lists all of the IP addresses of active RSVP neighbors on all interfaces. This command is useful if you want to figure out what devices are making RSVP requests. As we mentioned earlier, since all RSVP requests are made hop-to-hop, it is quite likely that you will see a lot of routers in this list. However, on access routers, this command will help you to see whether the right end devices are making RSVP requests. If there are unauthorized devices in the list, you may want to consider using the *ip rsvp neighbor* interface configuration command to restrict which devices are allowed to make requests:

```
Router#show ip rsvp neighbor
Interfac Neighbor        Encapsulation
Et0      192.168.1.10    RSVP
Et0      192.168.1.201   RSVP
To0      192.168.3.2     RSVP
```

See Also

Recipe 11.6; Recipe 11.7; Recipe 11.9

11.11 Manual RSVP Reservations

Problem

You want to manually reserve bandwidth through your network to support a real-time application that isn't able to dynamically create new reservations as required.

Solution

In this example, we will assume that we have a host device, acting as the sender, with IP address 192.168.100.202 and a second host, acting as the receiver, with IP address 192.168.9.100. The first host is connected to *FastEthernet0/0 Router1*:

```
Router1#configure terminal
Enter configuration commands, one per line.  End with CNTL/Z.
Router1(config)#interface FastEthernet0/0
Router1(config-if)#ip address 192.168.100.21 255.255.255.0
Router1(config-if)#ip rsvp bandwidth 128 56
Router1(config-if)#exit
Router1(config)#interface Serial0/0
Router1(config-if)#no ip address
Router1(config-if)#encapsulation frame-relay
Router1(config-if)#fair-queue 64 256 37
Router1(config-if)#ip rsvp bandwidth
Router1(config-if)#exit
Router1(config)#interface Serial0/0.1 point-to-point
Router1(config-subif)#ip address 192.168.55.9 255.255.255.252
Router1(config-subif)#frame-relay interface-dlci 904
Router1(config-fr-dlci)#ip rsvp bandwidth 128 56
Router1(config-subif)#exit
Router1(config)#ip rsvp sender 192.168.9.100 192.168.100.202 UDP 1300 1300 192.168.
100.202 FastEthernet0/0 55 1
Router1(config)#end
Router1#
```

The second host is connected to the *Ethernet0/0* interface on *Router4*, which is several hops away:

```
Router4# configure terminal
Router4(config)#interface Ethernet0/0
Router4(config-if)#ip address 192.168.9.3 255.255.255.0
Router4(config-if)#ip rsvp bandwidth 128 56
Router4(config-if)#exit
Router4(config)#interface Serial0/0
Router4(config-if)#no ip address
Router4(config-if)#encapsulation frame-relay
Router4(config-if)#fair-queue 64 256 37
Router4(config-if)#ip rsvp bandwidth
Router4(config-if)#exit
Router4(config)#interface Serial0/0.1 point-to-point
Router4(config-subif)#ip address 192.168.56.5 255.255.255.252
Router4(config-subif)#frame-relay interface-dlci 107
Router4(config-fr-dlci)#ip rsvp bandwidth 128 56
Router4(config-subif)#exit
Router4(config)#ip rsvp reservation 192.168.9.100 192.168.100.202 UDP 1300 1300 192.
168.9.100 Ethernet0/0 FF RATE 55 1
Router4(config)#end
Router4#
```

Discussion

It is worthwhile to review how RSVP works before looking at the mechanics of this recipe. A host that wants to send a data stream to a particular destination address or multicast group first makes an RSVP request to its first-hop router. This request asks for a particular set of QoS parameters, such as application bandwidth requirements, and specifies the destination IP address. Each router decides whether it can meet the requirement, accepting or rejecting the reservation. They then make the same request of the next hop router along the path to the destination. Once all of the routers between the source and destination have reserved the appropriate resources, the original host can begin transmitting application data, using the reserved resources along the entire data path.

The method is identical for unicast and multicast reservation requests, with each router relaying the request to a downstream peer until all of the destinations have been reached. Note that RSVP is inherently unidirectional. That is, it requests resources for sending data from a particular source to a particular destination or multicast group. If you want to reserve network resources to support a two-way unicast application, both the sender and the receiver must separately initiate requests.

RESV and PATH messages

There are two general message types in RSVP, PATH, and RESV. The initial request begins with a PATH message. The PATH message describes the specific flow that will use this reservation. So it includes the source and destination IP addresses, as well as the IP Protocol, such as TCP or UDP, and any port numbers. The PATH message also includes the requested average bit rate and burst size.

The PATH message is received by an upstream router, or perhaps the ultimate destination. If it is received by an intermediate router, this router must analyze the request and decide whether it can honor it. Ultimately, if the request is accepted, the router will create a new PATH message, requesting the same resource reservation from the next upstream router, but specifying itself as the source.

PATH messages always flow from the requester toward the destination.

RESV messages flow the opposite direction. The RESV CONFIRM messages describe the actual detailed bit rate and delay characteristics required to fulfill the PATH request. If an upstream router doesn't have the necessary resource to fulfill the request, it responds with an RESV ERROR message.

In Cisco router configuration, you can configure static PATH requests by using the *ip rsvp sender* and *sender-host* commands. And you can make static reservations, which will be described to upstream routers in RESV messages, using the *ip rsvp reserveration* and *reservation-host* commands. We will describe all of these commands below.

Two service types

There are two distinct types of service that a host can specify in an RSVP request. The first is called Controlled Load Service, which is specified in RFC 2211, and the second, called either Guaranteed Quality of Service or, more accurately, Guaranteed Bit Rate Service, is specified in RFC 2212.

Controlled Load Service, in a nutshell, means that the network behaves as if each segment were completely unloaded and therefore uncongested, but with bandwidth limited to the requested amount. Cisco routers implement this type of service by isolating the different flows and employing queuing mechanisms that mimic this type of response.

Guaranteed Bit Rate Service is somewhat more complicated. This service means that the network will mathematically guarantee the worst-case end-to-end queuing delay. There are two things to note about this description, however. First, it only guarantees the worst-case latency, not the average latency. The second is that, despite this, it is possible to make an estimate of the jitter, as this is governed by the worst-case latency. As long as the worst-case latency is small, then the jitter can be effectively minimized by employing small amounts of buffering on the end devices.

Controlled Load Service is well suited to many TCP applications, which tend to behave well until they encounter congestion and dropped packets. Conversely, Guaranteed Bit Rate Service tends to be a better choice for real-time voice and video applications.

The examples

Everything we have described so far implies that the source and destination host devices or applications are making the RSVP requests. However, this is not necessarily the case. In fact, many applications that require this type of QoS support do not have RSVP capabilities. So, in this recipe, we show how to configure the routers themselves to initiate requests on behalf of the hosts.

For a description of the interface configurations, please refer to Recipe 11.10. That recipe also contains information about the basic RSVP configurations used on the routers between *Router1* and *Router4* (which we have mysteriously decided to call *Router2* and *Router3*).

The *ip rsvp sender* command tells the router to act as if it is periodically receiving RSVP PATH requests from the specified source device:

```
Router1(config)#ip rsvp sender 192.168.9.100 192.168.100.202 UDP 1300 1300 192.168.
100.202 FastEthernet0/0 55 1
```

You use this command as a proxy for a real device that is unable to send real RSVP PATH requests. So it includes all of the information that appears in a PATH request packet.

The first several arguments of this command specify the IP flow that will be using this reservation. The first two arguments specify the source and destination IP addresses, respectively. Then we have stipulated that it will use the UDP protocol with source and destination ports both equal to 1300.

The next two arguments, `192.168.100.202` and `FastEthernet0/0`, specify the previous-hop IP address and interface, respectively. Because we put this command on the first hop router, they may seem redundant, but actually we could put this command anywhere in the network to simulate an upstream source device.

The last two arguments request an average bit rate of 55 kbps and a burst of 1 kbyte.

Then, on the other router, we have configured a corresponding command that simulates a device sending RSVP RESV messages back toward the source:

```
Router4(config)#ip rsvp reservation 192.168.9.100 192.168.100.202 UDP 1300 1300 192.
168.9.100 Ethernet0/0 FF RATE 55 1
```

Many of the arguments of this command are identical to what we saw a moment ago for the *sender* command. We specified the same IP addresses and UDP port numbers to define the flow. And the last two arguments just duplicate the average bit rate and burst size from the previous discussion.

The differences are where the *sender* command specified the previous-hop IP address and interface, here we specify the next-hop IP address and interface. Then we have two new keywords, *FF* and *RATE*.

The *FF* keyword indicates that this is a *Fixed Filter* style reservation. There are three available styles of reservation. Fixed Filter means that this reservation is for a particular flow specification only. No other applications or sessions are permitted to use it. We could have instead specified either SE or WF.

SE indicates that the router will use a *Shared Explicit* filter for the reservation. This means that the receiving device is specifying a list of source devices and indicating that they may all share the same reservation.

And *WF* means that the reservation can be shared by a Wildcard Filter. This effectively means that any source can take part in this reservation.

Finally, the *RATE* keyword in the *ip rsvp reservation* command tells the network to use Guaranteed Bit Rate service type. The other option here is *LOAD*, which indicates a Controlled Load service type. The receiver makes this service type request, which is why it only appears in the *ip rsvp reservation* command, and not in the *ip rsvp sender* command.

There are several useful commands for looking at the RSVP reservations. You can look at the current status of any PATH and RESV messages passing through your network with the *show ip rsvp sender* and *show ip rsvp reservation* commands. These commands give the full details on every such RSVP exchange, whether it originates with a static command on the router, as in this recipe, or a dynamically generate request from a real host:

```
Router1#show ip rsvp sender
To              From              Pro DPort Sport Prev Hop        I/F     BPS
192.168.9.100   192.168.100.202 UDP 1300  1300  192.168.100.202 Fa0/0   55K
Router1#show ip rsvp reservation
To             From          Pro DPort Sport Next Hop       I/F      Fi Serv BPS
192.168.9.100 192.168.100.202 UDP 1300  1300  192.168.55.10 Se0/0.1  FF RATE 55K

Router1#
```

So if we go to another router in the path and enter these commands again, we see the same information:

```
Router2#show ip rsvp sender
To              From              Pro DPort Sport Prev Hop        I/F     BPS
192.168.9.100   192.168.100.202 UDP 1300  1300  192.168.55.9    Se0/0.1  55K
Router2#show ip rsvp reservation
To             From          Pro DPort Sport Next Hop       I/F      Fi Serv BPS
192.168.9.100 192.168.100.202 UDP 1300  1300  192.168.101.7 Fa0/0   FF RATE 55K

Router2#
```

See Also

Recipe 11.10; Recipe 11.12

11.12 Aggregating RSVP Reservations

Problem

You want to aggregate several RSVP reservations so that the core of your network doesn't need to keep track of them all separately.

Solution

This feature requires the creation of a boundary between the edge region of the network, where RSVP runs normally, and the core of the network where packets are classified purely using DSCP:

```
Router2#configure terminal
Enter configuration commands, one per line.  End with CNTL/Z.
Router2(config)#interface FastEthernet0/0
Router2(config-if)#ip address 192.168.101.1 255.255.255.0
Router2(config-if)#ip rsvp bandwidth 128 56
Router2(config-if)#ip rsvp data-packet classification none
Router2(config-if)#ip rsvp resource-provider none
Router2(config-if)#exit
Router2(config)#interface Serial0/0.1 point-to-point
Router2(config-subif)#ip address 192.168.55.10 255.255.255.252
Router2(config-subif)#frame-relay interface-dlci 409
```

```
Router2(config-fr-dlci)#ip rsvp bandwidth 128 56
Router2(config-subif)#ip rsvp data-packet classification none
Router2(config-subif)#ip rsvp resource-provider none
Router2(config-subif)#exit
Router2(config)#end
Router2#
```

Discussion

The biggest problem with RSVP is that it doesn't scale well when you have a large number of reservations. This is a good model at the edge of the network, but in the middle of the network, where there could be a huge number of flows to keep track of, it would be preferable to use traditional DSCP-based packet marking and queuing.

However, it is not sufficient to just run RSVP at the edges of the network and use a pure DSCP model in the core. Consider a model in which traffic must cross from one RSVP network region through the traditional DSCP core to another RSVP region. A reservation request originating in the first RSVP region will not reach the second region if the core doesn't support RSVP. Consequently, it is not possible to guarantee end-to-end quality of service.

Cisco introduced a new feature to get around this problem in IOS Version 12.2(2)T. The key is to configure RSVP on the core routers so that they can relay RSVP requests back and forth between the edge regions, but to instruct them not to actually use the RSVP information when queuing packets.

There are two commands required to do this, and they must be configured on every interface that will be forwarding RSVP packets through the core network region:

```
Router2(config)#interface FastEthernet0/0
Router2(config-if)#ip rsvp data-packet classification none
Router2(config-if)#ip rsvp resource-provider none
```

For example, in an MPLS network, you might want to use this type of configuration on the PE routers. This would allow all of the routers on the customer premises to support traditional RSVP, while the MPLS network core would prioritize based on its own internal classes of service.

See Also

Recipe 11.10; Recipe 11.11

11.13 Using Generic Traffic Shaping

Problem

You want to do traffic shaping on an interface.

Solution

Generic Traffic Shaping works on an entire interface to limit the rate that it sends data. This first version restricts all outbound traffic to 500,000 bits per second:

```
Router#configure terminal
Enter configuration commands, one per line.  End with CNTL/Z.
Router(config)#interface FastEthernet0/0
Router(config-if)#traffic-shape rate 500000
Router(config-if)#exit
Router(config)#end
Router#
```

You can also specify traffic shaping for packets that match a particular access-list. This will buffer only the matching traffic, and leave all other traffic to use the default queuing mechanism for the interface:

```
Router#configure terminal
Enter configuration commands, one per line.  End with CNTL/Z.
Router(config)#access-list 101 permit tcp any eq www any
Router(config)#access-list 101 permit tcp any any eq www
Router(config)#access-list 102 permit tcp any eq ftp any
Router(config)#access-list 102 permit tcp any any eq ftp
Router(config)#interface FastEthernet0/0
Router(config-if)#traffic-shape group 101 100000
Router(config-if)#traffic-shape group 102 200000
Router(config-if)#exit
Router(config)#end
Router#
```

There is also a newer class-based method for configuring traffic shaping on an interface using CBWFQ. We discuss this technique in Recipe 11.16.

Discussion

The first example shows how to configure an interface to restrict the total amount of outbound information. This is extremely useful when there is something downstream that will not cope well with hard bursts of traffic.

A common example is the method of delivering ATM WAN services through an Ethernet interface, frequently called *LAN Extension*. In this type of network, the Ethernet port on your router connects to the carrier's switch, which bridges one or more remote Ethernet segments by using an ATM network. The problem with this is that the Ethernet interface is able to send data much faster than the ATM network is configured to accept it. So you run the risk of dropping large numbers of packets within the ATM network. Since the carrier networks usually don't support customer Layer 3 QoS features, the entire ATM network acts just like a big FIFO queue with a tail drop problem. As we discuss in Appendix B, this is extremely inefficient.

So this is why it can be extremely useful to restrict the total amount of traffic leaving an interface. It can also be useful to restrict only certain applications, as we demonstrated in the second example. However, we discuss more efficient Class-based methods for controlling the total amount of traffic of a particular type in Recipe 11.7. So this older group traffic-shaping method should only be used on routers that do not support CBWFQ.

See Also

Recipe 11.7; Recipe 11.15; Recipe 11.16

11.14 Using Frame-Relay Traffic Shaping

Problem

You want to separately control the amount of traffic sent along each of the PVCs in a Frame Relay network.

Solution

This first example shows how to configure frame relay traffic shaping by using point-to-point frame relay subinterfaces:

```
Router#configure terminal
Enter configuration commands, one per line.  End with CNTL/Z.
Router(config)#interface HSSI0/0
Router(config-if)#encapsulation frame-relay
Router(config-if)#exit
Router(config)#interface HSSI0/0.1 point-to-point
Router(config-subif)#traffic-shape rate 150000
Router(config-subif)#frame-relay interface-dlci 31
Router(config-subif)#exit
Router(config)#end
Router#
```

Most Frame Relay carrier networks are sufficiently over-provisioned that you can actually use much more capacity than your contractual Committed Information Rate (CIR). So you might want to apply traffic shaping only when you encounter Frame-Relay congestion problems, and then only to reduce the data rate until the congestion goes away:

```
Router#configure terminal
Enter configuration commands, one per line.  End with CNTL/Z.
Router(config)#interface HSSI0/0
Router(config-if)#encapsulation frame-relay
Router(config-if)#exit
Router(config)#interface HSSI0/0.1 point-to-point
Router(config-subif)#traffic-shape adaptive 10000
Router(config-subif)#frame-relay interface-dlci 31
Router(config-subif)#exit
Router(config)#end
Router#
```

Discussion

Thes examples are different from the one that we showed in Recipe 11.13. In this recipe, we don't want to control the entire aggregate traffic flow, and we don't care about the traffic based on application. Here we want to ensure that every Frame Relay PVC using this interface is shaped separately so that they don't overrun the amount of bandwidth purchased from the WAN carrier. If you have 20 PVCs on an interface, it is fine to send the maximum per-PVC bandwidth to all of them simultaneously, but you will suffer from terrible performance problems if you try to send all of that bandwidth through a single PVC.

Usually you will purchase a particular amount of Frame Relay bandwidth, or CIR, from the WAN carrier for each PVC. So the first example shows how you can force the router to only send 150 Kbps through the PVC with DLCI 31. It is important to remember that you can have different CIR values for some PVC's than others. So you may need to have a different Frame-Relay traffic-shaping rate on every PVC.

The second example assumes that a lot of the time there will actually be very little congestion in the carrier's network, so you should be able to safely use some of the excess capacity. The Frame Relay protocol includes the ability to tell devices when there is congestion in the network. There are two types of congestion notifications, which are just noted as flags in the header portion of regular user frames. If a router receives a frame with the Forward Explicit Congestion Notification (FECN) flag set, it knows that the frame encountered congestion on its way from the remote device to the router. If the router receives a frame with the Backward Explicit Congestion Notification (BECN) flag set, this means that a frame encountered congestion on its way from this router to the remote device. Please refer to Chapter 10 for a more detailed discussion of these Frame Relay protocol features.

The *traffic-shape adaptive* command tells the router that when it sees frames with a BECN flag, it should reduce the sending rate on this PVC. By default, this command will back off the sending rate all the way to zero. So in the example, we have specified a minimum rate of 10,000 bps, which would correspond to the CIR for this PVC:

```
Router(config-subif)#traffic-shape adaptive 10000
```

In general, this adaptive traffic shaping method is preferred over the static method because it will give you significantly better network performance when the carrier's network is not congested. However, it is important to remember that the precise implementation of FECN and BECN markings is up to the carrier. Some carriers disable these features altogether, while others use them inconsistently. Since most customers ignore these markings, there is often very little reason to ensure that they are accurate.

You should check with your network vendor before implementing adaptive frame-relay traffic shaping. And, in fact, we recommend monitoring your FECN and BECN statistics for a reasonable period of time before implementing, to verify that they are reliable.

See Also

Recipe 11.13; Recipe 11.15; Chapter 10

11.15 Using Committed Access Rate

Problem

You want to use Committed Access Rate to control the flow of traffic through an interface.

Solution

Committed Access Rate (CAR) provides a useful method for policing the traffic rate through an interface. The main features of CAR are functionally similar to traffic shaping, but it also allows several extremely useful extensions. This first example shows the simplest application. We have configured CAR here to do basic rate limiting. The interface will transmit packets at an average rate of 500,000 bps, allowing bursts of 4500 bytes. If there is a burst of longer than 9000 bytes, the router will drop the excess packets:

```
Router#configure terminal
Enter configuration commands, one per line.  End with CNTL/Z.
Router(config)#interface HSSI0/0
Router(config-if)#rate-limit output 500000 4500 9000 conform-action transmit exceed-action drop
Router(config-if)#exit
Router(config)#end
Router#
```

This next example defines three different traffic classifications using access-lists, and separately limits the rates of these applications:

```
Router#configure terminal
Enter configuration commands, one per line.  End with CNTL/Z.
Router(config)#access-list 101 permit tcp any eq www any
Router(config)#access-list 101 permit tcp any any eq www
Router(config)#access-list 102 permit tcp any eq ftp any
Router(config)#access-list 102 permit tcp any any eq ftp
Router(config)#access-list 102 permit tcp any eq ftp-data any
Router(config)#access-list 102 permit tcp any any eq ftp-data
Router(config)#access-list 103 permit ip any any
Router(config)#interface HSSI0/0
Router(config-if)#rate-limit output access-group 101 50000 4500 9000 conform-action transmit exceed-action drop
Router(config-if)#rate-limit output access-group 102 50000 4500 9000 conform-action transmit exceed-action drop
Router(config-if)#rate-limit output access-group 103 400000 4500 9000 conform-action transmit exceed-action drop
Router(config-if)#exit
Router(config)#end
Router#
```

CAR also includes a useful option to match DSCP in the rate-limit command without needing to resort to an access-group. In the following example, the DSCP values with the highest drop precedence values are rate limited. Note that unlike several other Cisco commands, here you must specify the decimal value of the DSCP field. Please refer to Table B-3 in Appendix B for a list of these values:

```
Router#configure terminal
Enter configuration commands, one per line.  End with CNTL/Z.
Router(config)#interface HSSI0/0
Router(config-if)#rate-limit output dscp 14 50000 4500 9000 conform-action transmit
exceed-action drop
Router(config-if)#rate-limit output dscp 22 50000 4500 9000 conform-action transmit
exceed-action drop
Router(config-if)#rate-limit output dscp 30 50000 4500 9000 conform-action transmit
exceed-action drop
Router(config-if)#exit
Router(config)#end
Router#
```

And, finally, CAR also allows you to define a new kind of access-list called a rate-limiting access-list:

```
Router#configure terminal
Enter configuration commands, one per line.  End with CNTL/Z.
Router(config)#access-list rate-limit 55 5
Router(config)#interface HSSI0/0
Router(config-if)#rate-limit output access-group rate-limit 55 50000 4500 9000
conform-action transmit exceed-action drop
Router(config-if)#exit
Router(config)#end
Router#
```

Discussion

People are often confused about the difference between CAR and traffic shaping because they appear to perform extremely similar functions. However, there is one very important difference. When a traffic shaping interface experiences a burst of data, it attempts to buffer the excess. But CAR just does whatever *exceed-action* you have specified:

```
Router(config-if)#rate-limit output 500000 4500 9000 conform-action transmit exceed-
action drop
```

In this example, the exceed-action is to simply drop the packet. Meanwhile, the *conform-action* in each example is to simply transmit the packet. Any traffic that falls below the configured rate is said to conform. CAR includes several other possibilities besides simply transmitting or dropping the packet:

drop
    CAR drops the packet.

transmit
    CAR transmits the packet unchanged.

set-prec-transmit

> CAR changes the IP Precedence of the packet and then transmits it.

continue

> CAR moves on to evaluate the next *rate-limit* command on this interface

set-prec-continue

> CAR changes the IP Precedence and then evaluates the next *rate-limit* command.

Cisco has added several additional options to IOS Versions 12.0(14)ST and higher:

set-dscp-continue

> CAR changes the DSCP field and then evaluates the next *rate-limit* command.

set-dscp-transmit

> CAR changes DSCP field and then transmits the packet.

set-qos-continue

> CAR sets the qos-group and then evaluates next command.

set-qos-transmit

> CAR sets the qos-group and then transmits the packet.

And two additional commands that you can use with MPLS to alter the MPLS Experimental field:

set-mpls-exp-continue

> This sets the experimental field and then continues.

set-mpls-exp-transmit

> This option sets the experimental field and transmits the packet.

The various *continue* options allow you to string together a series of CAR commands on an interface to do more sophisticated things:

```
Router#configure terminal
Enter configuration commands, one per line.  End with CNTL/Z.
Router(config)#access-list 101 permit tcp any eq www any
Router(config)#access-list 101 permit tcp any any eq www
Router(config)#access-list 103 permit ip any any
Router(config)#interface HSSI0/0
Router(config-if)#rate-limit output 50000 4500 4500 conform-action transmit exceed-
action continue
Router(config-if)#rate-limit output access-group 101 100000 4500 9000 conform-action
set-prec-transmit 3 exceed-action continue
Router(config-if)#rate-limit output access-group 103 100000 4500 9000 conform-action
set-prec-transmit 0 exceed-action drop
Router(config-if)#exit
Router(config)#end
Router#
```

In this example, the interface will transmit all packets when the rate is 50,000 bps or less. As soon as the traffic exceeds rate, however, the router starts to bump up the IP Precedence of all HTTP traffic to a value of 3, and all other traffic goes down to a precedence of 0. It will continue to transmit all of these packets until the average rate exceeds 100,000 bps. You can use this sort of technique to carefully tune how your network behaves in congestion situations.

You can also use CAR and the *exceed-action set-prec-transmit* command to lower the Precedence of high-priority IP traffic when it exceeds its allocated portion of the bandwidth. Simply transmitting it with a lower Precedence represents a nice and useful intermediate step to dropping high priority packets outright. However, with real-time packets, it is better to drop than buffer or remark, because those options would introduce unwanted latency and jitter:

The other useful thing you can do with CAR is to rate-limit inbound traffic:

```
Router(config-if)#rate-limit input 50000 4500 4500 conform-action transmit exceed-
action drop
```

Of course, it's never completely ideal to allow a remote device to send too many packets across the network, only to drop them as they are received. But it is sometimes useful when your network acts as a service provider to other networks. For example, you might have downstream customers who have subscribed to a sub-rate service. This would include things like selling access through an Ethernet port, but restricting the customer to some lower rate such as 100 Kbps.

Alternatively, you could use inbound rate-limit commands to ensure that your downstream customers are allowed to use your network for surfing the Web, but only if the rate is kept below some threshold:

```
Router(config)#access-list 101 permit tcp any eq www any
Router(config)#access-list 101 permit tcp any any eq www
Router(config)#access-list 103 permit ip any any
Router(config)#interface HSSI0/0
Router(config-if)#rate-limit input 50000 4500 4500 conform-action transmit exceed-
action continue
Router(config-if)#rate-limit input access-group 101 100000 4500 9000 conform-action
drop exceed-action continue
Router(config-if)#rate-limit input access-group 103 100000 4500 9000 conform-action
transmit exceed-action drop
Router(config-if)#exit
Router(config)#end
Router#
```

Or you could even use CAR to simply rewrite the IP Precedence values of all packets received from a customer:

```
Router(config)#interface HSSI0/0
Router(config-if)#rate-limit input 100000 4500 9000 conform-action set-prec-transmit
0 exceed-action set-prec-transmit 0
Router(config-if)#exit
Router(config)#end
Router#
```

This same technique is also helpful in combating Internet-based Denial of Service attacks. For example, if your network is being inundated with PING flood or SYN ACK attacks, you might want to look specifically for these types of packets, and make sure that they are restricted to a low but reasonable rate. This way, the legitimate uses of these packets will not suffer, but you will reduce the service denial problem.

The last example in the Solution section of this recipe needs a little bit of explanation because some of the properties can be confusing:

```
Router(config)#access-list rate-limit 55 5
Router(config)#interface HSSI0/0
Router(config-if)#rate-limit output access-group rate-limit 55 50000 4500 9000
conform-action transmit exceed-action drop
```

The *access-list rate-limit* command allows you to create a new and special variety of access-lists, especially for use with CAR. There are three ranges of rate-limiting access-list index numbers. You use access-lists with values between 0 and 99 to match IP Precedence values. If the index number is between 100 and 199, it will match MAC addresses, and if it is between 200 and 299, it matches MPLS experimental field values. Please refer to Chapter 26 for more information on MPLS.

In the example above, access-list number 55 simply matches all packets with IP Precedence values of 5. You can also use a precedence bit mask to match several values in an 8-bit Precedence field that Cisco invented especially for this task. In this field, Precedence value 0 is represented by the binary number 00000001, 1 is represented as 00000010, and so forth up to IP Precedence value 7, which is 10000000. The mask is found by adding these binary values for each of the Precedence values you wish to include. For example, to match Precedence values 0, 1, and 2, you could use a mask of 00000111, which is 0x07 in hex:

```
Router(config)#access-list rate-limit 56 mask 07
```

The MPLS access-lists work in a similar way, matching the value in the MPLS experimental field:

```
Router(config)#access-list rate-limit 255 6
Router(config)#access-list rate-limit 256 mask 42
```

And the MAC address access-lists work on standard Ethernet or Token Ring 48-bit MAC addresses:

```
Router(config)#access-list rate-limit 155 0000.0c07.ac01
```

You have to be careful about how you use these rate-limiting access-lists, because it's easy to get them confused with regular access-lists. You can have a regular access-list with the same number as a rate-limiting access-list. The only difference is that you apply rate-limiting access-lists with the rate-limit keyword on the rate-limit command as follows:

```
Router(config)#interface HSSI0/0
Router(config-if)#rate-limit output access-group rate-limit 55 50000 4500 9000
conform-action transmit exceed-action drop
```

See Also

Chapter 26

11.16 Implementing Standards-Based Per-Hop Behavior

Problem

You want to configure your router to follow the RFC-defined Per-Hop Behaviors defined for different DSCP values.

Solution

This recipe constructs an approximate implementation of both Expedited Forwarding and Assured Forwarding, while still ensuring that network control packets do not suffer from delays due to application traffic. With the QoS enhancements provided in IOS Version 12.1(5)T and higher, there is a straightforward way to accomplish this using a combination of WRED, CBWFQ, and Low Latency Queuing (LLQ):

```
Router#configure terminal
Enter configuration commands, one per line.  End with CNTL/Z.
Router(config)#class-map EF
Router(config-cmap)#description Real-time application traffic
Router(config-cmap)#match ip precedence 5
Router(config-cmap)#exit
Router(config)#class-map AF1x
Router(config-cmap)#description Priority Class 1
Router(config-cmap)#match ip precedence 1
Router(config-cmap)#exit
Router(config)#class-map AF2x
Router(config-cmap)#description Priority Class 2
Router(config-cmap)#match ip precedence 2
Router(config-cmap)#exit
Router(config)#class-map AF3x
Router(config-cmap)#description Priority Class 3
Router(config-cmap)#match ip precedence 3
Router(config-cmap)#exit
Router(config)#class-map AF4x
Router(config-cmap)#description Priority Class 4
Router(config-cmap)#match ip precedence 4
Router(config-cmap)#exit
Router(config)#policy-map cbwfq_pq
Router(config-pmap)#class EF
Router(config-pmap-c)#priority 58 800
Router(config-pmap-c)#exit
Router(config-pmap)#class AF1x
Router(config-pmap-c)#bandwidth percent 15
Router(config-pmap-c)#random-detect dscp-based
Router(config-pmap-c)#exit
Router(config-pmap)#class AF2x
Router(config-pmap-c)#bandwidth percent 15
Router(config-pmap-c)#random-detect dscp-based
Router(config-pmap-c)#exit
```

```
Router(config-pmap)#class AF3x
Router(config-pmap-c)#bandwidth percent 15
Router(config-pmap-c)#random-detect dscp-based
Router(config-pmap-c)#exit
Router(config-pmap)#class AF4x
Router(config-pmap-c)#bandwidth percent 15
Router(config-pmap-c)#random-detect dscp-based
Router(config-pmap-c)#exit
Router(config-pmap)#class class-default
Router(config-pmap-c)#fair-queue 512
Router(config-pmap-c)#queue-limit 96
Router(config-pmap-c)#exit
Router(config-pmap)#exit
Router(config)#interface HSSI0/1
Router(config-if)#service-policy output cbwfqpolicy
Router(config-if)#exit
Router(config)#end
Router#
```

If you are running older IOS versions, you can use Custom Queuing to create different levels of forwarding precedence, but you can't combine them with WRED to enforce the standard drop precedence rules.

Discussion

We have repeatedly said throughout this chapter that Priority Queues are dangerous because they allow high-priority traffic to starve all lower priority queues. However, strict prioritization does give excellent real-time behavior for the highest priority traffic because it ensures minimal queuing latency. This recipe uses Cisco's Low Latency Queuing (LLQ), which avoids most of the problems of pure Priority Queuing.

This example creates an approximation of the Differentiated Services model defined in RFCs 2597 and 2598. All real-time and network control traffic uses LLQ to ensure that it is always delivered with minimal delay. All other IP traffic falls into one of the Assured Forwarding classes shown in Table B-3 in Appendix B, with the exception of packets that do not have a DSCP tag value. Untagged traffic, including nonIP traffic, will use the default forwarding behavior.

Each column in Table B-3 represents a precedence class, which we have called AF1x, AF2x, AF3x, and AF4x, respectively. For each of these classes, we have reserved a share of the bandwidth, and we have configured DSCP-based WRED:

```
Router(config-pmap)#class AF4x
Router(config-pmap-c)#bandwidth percent 15
Router(config-pmap-c)#random-detect dscp-based
Router(config-pmap-c)#exit
```

In the discussion to Recipe 11.9, we showed how to modify the default WRED thresholds and drop probabilities.

The example also defines a class called EF, which matches all packets with an IP Precedence value of 5, which has a binary representation of 101. Note that technically, the EF DSCP value looks like 101110 in binary. So the example allows packets to join this queue if only the first three bits of the DSCP are correct. This is for backward compatibility and to ensure that we don't leave out any high-priority traffic. However, if you wanted to create a queue for a real EF DSCP value and a separate queue for packets with IP Precedence 5, you could do so like this:

```
Router(config)#class-map EF
Router(config-cmap)#description Real-time application traffic
Router(config-cmap)#match ip dscp ef
Router(config-cmap)#exit
Router(config)#class-map Prec5
Router(config-cmap)#description Critical application traffic
Router(config-cmap)#match ip precedence 5
Router(config-cmap)#exit
Router(config)#policy-map cbwfq_pq
Router(config-pmap)#class EF
Router(config-pmap-c)#priority 58 800
Router(config-pmap-c)#exit
Router(config-pmap)#class Prec5
Router(config-pmap-c)#bandwidth percent 15
Router(config-pmap-c)#exit
```

Note that you must define the classes in the policy map in this order because the router matches packets sequentially. If you specified the EF class-map after the Prec5 map, you would find that all of your EF traffic would wind up in the other queue, which is not what you want. Note also that, as we discussed in Recipe 11.7, you have to be careful of the total reserved bandwidth in CBWFQ. Simply adding these lines to the recipe example would give a total of 75 percent allocated bandwidth. This is the default maximum value. If you want to exceed this value, Recipe 11.7 shows how to modify the maximum.

We have already discussed most of the commands shown in the class definitions in other recipes. However, the EF queue contains a special command:

```
Router(config-pmap-c)#priority 58 800
```

This defines a strict priority queue for this class with a sustained throughput of 58 Kbps. This is based on the assumption that the EF application uses a standard stream of 56 Kbps, and we have added a small amount on top of this to allow for Layer 2 overhead. The last argument in the *priority* command is a burst length in bytes. This allows the application to temporarily exceed the defined sustain rate, just long enough to send this many bytes. In this case, we're assuming that the real-time application uses small packets, so allowing it to send a burst of 800 bytes when it has already reached the configured sustain rate of 58 Kbps should be more than sufficient.

Note that this does not imply that there is strict policing on this queue. If you also want to enforce a maximum rate of 65 Kbps on this queue, for example, you could also include a *police* statement, as follows:

```
Router(config-pmap)#class EF
Router(config-pmap-c)#priority 58 800
```

```
Router(config-pmap-c)#police 65000 1600
Router(config-pmap-c)#exit
```

In this command we have also been slightly more generous with the burst size, extending it to 1600 bytes. Enforcing an upper limit like this is a good idea on priority queues because it helps to prevent the highest priority traffic from starving the other queues. However, it is not necessary to enforce the upper limit this way just to avoid starving the lower queues. This is because the *priority* command stops giving strict priority to this queue when the bandwidth rises above the specified limit.

It should be clear from the ability to allocate both minimum and maximum bandwidth with the CBWFQ *priority* and *police* commands, LLQ is a much more sophisticated and flexible type of queuing than the simple Priority Queuing discussed in Recipe 11.3. So if your router is capable of supporting CBWFQ, we recommend using LLQ for any situation in which you want Priority Queuing. Cisco introduced the LLQ feature in IOS level 12.0(6)T.

See Also

Recipe 11.3; Recipe 11.5; Recipe 11.7

11.17 AutoQoS

Problem

You want the router to automatically generate the Quality of Service policy map for either VoIP or general IP traffic.

Solution

There are two versions of AutoQoS. The first is specific to VoIP traffic:

```
Router1#configure terminal
Enter configuration commands, one per line.  End with CNTL/Z.
Router1(config)#ip cef
Router1(config)#interface Serial0/0
Router1(config-if)#no ip address
Router1(config-if)#encapsulation frame-relay
Router1(config-if)#exit
Router1(config)#interface Serial0/0.1 point-to-point
Router1(config-subif)#ip address 192.168.55.9 255.255.255.252
Router1(config-subif)#frame-relay interface-dlci 904
Router1(config-fr-dlci)#auto qos voip
%Creating new map-class.
Router1(config-fr-dlci)#exit
Router1(config-subif)#exit
Router1(config)#end
Router1#
*Mar  1 01:32:55.031: %RMON-5-FALLINGTRAP: Falling trap is generated because the
 value of cbQosCMDropBitRate.1169.1171 has fallen below the falling-threshold va
 lue 0
Router1#
```

The other AutoQoS option is called AutoQoS for the Enterprise. This feature is useful for automatically generating policy maps for more general IP traffic. For this feature, the router must first monitor the traffic by using the interface to decide how best to set up the policy maps. To enable this data collection phase, you use the *auto discovery qos* command:

```
Router1#configure terminal
Enter configuration commands, one per line.  End with CNTL/Z.
Router1(config)#ip cef
Router1(config)#interface Serial0/0
Router1(config-if)#no ip address
Router1(config-if)#encapsulation frame-relay
Router1(config-if)#exit
Router1(config)#interface Serial0/0.1 point-to-point
Router1(config-subif)#ip address 192.168.55.9 255.255.255.252
Router1(config-subif)#frame-relay interface-dlci 904
Router1(config-fr-dlci)#auto discovery qos
Router1(config-fr-dlci)#exit
Router1(config-subif)#exit
Router1(config)#end
Router1#
```

After the router has learned about the traffic patterns, you disable the discovery mode and enable *auto qos* instead:

```
Router1#configure terminal
Enter configuration commands, one per line.  End with CNTL/Z.
Router1(config)#interface Serial0/0.1 point-to-point
Router1(config-subif)#frame-relay interface-dlci 904
Router1(config-fr-dlci)#auto qos
%Creating new map-class.
Router1(config-fr-dlci)#no auto discovery qos
Router1(config-fr-dlci)#exit
Router1(config-subif)#exit
Router1(config)#end
Router1#
```

Discussion

AutoQoS is an extremely useful feature that can take a lot of the mystery out of building a QoS policy. Unfortunately, there are several restrictions on this feature that you need to be aware of.

First, it is only available on point-to-point links between routers. This includes point-to-point subinterfaces on ATM and Frame Relay PVCs, as shown in the example. The feature is also available on PPP and HDLC Serial connections. It cannot be used on any multiple access media, including Ethernets, or multipoint subinterfaces.

Second, it can't be used with any virtual templates or *frame map* statements. It cannot be used with either Frame Relay or ATM SVCs.

Third, it must be enabled on both ends of each link or PVC. This doesn't necessarily mean that both routers must run the same IOS version, however, as long as the AutoQoS feature is available on both routers.

Fourth, you should disable any other service policies or access-groups on the router, even if they are associated with different interfaces.

And finally, you must ensure that CEF is enabled for this feature to work.

AutoQoS for VoIP was introduced in IOS Version 12.2(15)T. This command is actually a macro that adds a series of commands to your router's configuration. You can use the *show auto qos* command to see exactly what it has added:

```
Router1#show auto qos
 !
 policy-map AutoQoS-Policy-UnTrust
  class AutoQoS-VoIP-RTP-UnTrust
   priority percent 70
   set dscp ef
  class AutoQoS-VoIP-Control-UnTrust
   bandwidth percent 5
   set dscp af31
  class AutoQoS-VoIP-Remark
   set dscp default
  class class-default
   fair-queue
 !
 ip access-list extended AutoQoS-VoIP-RTCP
  permit udp any any range 16384 32767
 !
 ip access-list extended AutoQoS-VoIP-Control
  permit tcp any any eq 1720
  permit tcp any any range 11000 11999
  permit udp any any eq 2427
  permit tcp any any eq 2428
  permit tcp any any range 2000 2002
  permit udp any any eq 1719
  permit udp any any eq 5060
 !
 rmon event 33333 log trap AutoQoS description "AutoQoS SNMP traps for Voice Drops"
 owner AutoQoS
 rmon alarm 33333 cbQosCMDropBitRate.1169.1171 30 absolute rising-threshold 1 33333
 falling-threshold 0 owner AutoQoS

 Serial0/0.1: DLCI 904 -
  !
  interface Serial0/0
   frame-relay traffic-shaping
  !
  interface Serial0/0.1 point-to-point
   frame-relay interface-dlci 904
    class AutoQoS-FR-Se0/0-904
  !
```

```
map-class frame-relay AutoQoS-FR-Se0/0-904
  frame-relay cir 1544000
  frame-relay bc 15440
  frame-relay be 0
  frame-relay mincir 1544000
  service-policy output AutoQoS-Policy-UnTrust
Router1#
```

Clearly, this little macro has done a lot of work, and in fact this command output doesn't show the class-maps that were created at the same time! Let's examine what it did. First, it created a policy-map called AutoQoS-Policy-UnTrust, which allocates up to 70% of the bandwidth on this link to voice traffic and another 5% to VoIP control packets. It also sets the DSCP values for these traffic streams, overriding whatever values were previously in the packets. All other traffic is configured to use weighted fair-queuing (WFQ).

Then, skipping over the access-lists, whose purpose is fairly clear, the macro has created an RMON rule that will automatically send an SNMP trap every time the router is forced to drop a voice packet. You can then use these trap logs to determine if the queuing parameters are appropriate. If you find that you are dropping a lot of packets, then you may need to increase your bandwidth to reduce congestion.

And finally, it has implemented Frame Relay Traffic Shaping to ensure that the router doesn't attempt to overrun the CIR for the PVC. This is a critical consideration because, by default, the router will assume that it can transmit at wire speed on each PVC individually. So if you have several PVCs on a single physical circuit, it will allow any of them to burst to the full bandwidth capacity of the interface, possibly over-running the CIR of the PVC. As a result, even with the best queuing strategy on the router, you could find yourself dropping packets in the frame cloud. For more information on Frame Relay Traffic Shaping, please refer to Recipe 11.14 and Chapter 10.

The AutoQoS for the Enterprise feature was introduced in IOS Version 12.3(7)T. It classifies traffic into 10 categories, which are listed in Table 11-2. Note that if the discovery feature doesn't see any traffic of a particular type, then AutoQoS will not create a corresponding class on the router.

Table 11-2. AutoQos traffic classes

Class Name	DSCP	Description
IP Routing	CS6	Routing protocol and ICMP traffic
Interactive Voice	EF	RTP Voice traffic
Interactive Video	AF41	RTP Video traffic
Streaming Video	CS4	Various streaming audio and video protocols, such as CU-SeeMe, RealAudio, and Netshow
Telephony Signaling	CS3	RTP and H.323

Table 11-2. AutoQos traffic classes (continued)

Class Name	DSCP	Description
Transactional/Interactive	AF21	Database protocols, such as SAP, SQLNet, and SQLServer, as well as interactive protocols, including Citrix, Telnet, Notes, SSH, and X11
Network Management	CS2	Primarily SNMP
Bulk Data	AF11	Batch file transfer protocols such as FTP, Exchange, POP3, SMTP, NNTP, and network printing
Scavenger	CS1	Various peer-to-peer and entertainment protocols, including Napster, Fast-track, and Gnutella; this group is given a worse than best-efforts priority
Best Effort	0	Various miscellaneous protocols, including HTTP, NFS, SunRPC, NTP, and gopher, as well as any unidentified traffic

We enabled auto discovery QoS on both ends of a Frame-Relay PVC, ran some traffic through the link and then looked at the output of the *show auto discovery qos* command to see what the router suggested for a QoS policy:

```
Router1#show auto discovery qos
Serial0/0.1
 AutoQoS Discovery enabled for applications
 Discovery up time: 3 minutes, 41 seconds
 AutoQoS Class information:
 Class Voice:
  No data found.
 Class Interactive Video:
  No data found.
 Class Signaling:
  No data found.
 Class Streaming Video:
  No data found.
 Class Transactional:
  Recommended Minimum Bandwidth: 1 Kbps/<1% (AverageRate)
  Detected applications and data:
  Application/      AverageRate      PeakRate        Total
  Protocol          (kbps/%)         (kbps/%)        (bytes)
  -----------       -----------      --------        -----------
  telnet            1/<1             32/2            53404
 Class Bulk:
  No data found.
 Class Scavenger:
  No data found.
 Class Management:
  Recommended Minimum Bandwidth: 1 Kbps/<1% (AverageRate)
  Detected applications and data:
  Application/      AverageRate      PeakRate        Total
  Protocol          (kbps/%)         (kbps/%)        (bytes)
  -----------       -----------      --------        -----------
  snmp              1/<1             11/<1           50245
 Class Routing:
  Recommended Minimum Bandwidth: 0 Kbps/0% (AverageRate)
  Detected applications and data:
```

```
Application/          AverageRate        PeakRate           Total
Protocol              (kbps/%)           (kbps/%)           (bytes)
-----------           -----------        --------           ------------
icmp                  0/0                8/<1               11432
eigrp                 0/0                0/0                6016
Class Best Effort:
Current Bandwidth Estimation: 3 Kbps/<1% (AverageRate)
Detected applications and data:
Application/          AverageRate        PeakRate           Total
Protocol              (kbps/%)           (kbps/%)           (bytes)
-----------           -----------        --------           ------------
http                  3/<1               33/2               84777
unknowns              0/0                0/0                184

Suggested AutoQoS Policy for the current uptime:
!
class-map match-any AutoQoS-Transactional-Se0/0.1
 match protocol telnet
!
class-map match-any AutoQoS-Management-Se0/0.1
 match protocol snmp
!
policy-map AutoQoS-Policy-Se0/0.1
 class AutoQoS-Transactional-Se0/0.1
  bandwidth remaining percent 1
  random-detect dscp-based
  set dscp af21
 class AutoQoS-Management-Se0/0.1
  bandwidth remaining percent 1
  set dscp cs2
 class class-default
  fair-queue
Router1#
```

As you can see, we didn't let the discovery phase run for very long, and consequently did not discovery very many types of traffic. The router saw no traffic in the Voice, Interactive Video, Telephony Signaling, Streaming Video, Bulk, or Scavenger classes. But it did see some TELNET traffic in the Transactional class, some SNMP traffic in the Network Management class, as well as some Routing Protocol and Best Efforts traffic. Note that the command output includes average and peak rate traffic statistics, which the router will use to help determine queuing parameters:

```
Class Best Effort:
Current Bandwidth Estimation: 3 Kbps/<1% (AverageRate)
Detected applications and data:
Application/          AverageRate        PeakRate           Total
Protocol              (kbps/%)           (kbps/%)           (bytes)
-----------           -----------        --------           ------------
http                  3/<1               33/2               84777
unknowns              0/0                0/0                184
```

The output then ends with a suggestion for a QoS policy-map to be applied to this interface. This output shows that the AutoQoS feature uses the NBAR *match* command to identify protocols. NBAR is the basis of AutoQoS. Please refer to Recipe 11.8 for more information about NBAR.

Once we are satisfied that this is a good QoS policy, we enable it by using the *auto qos* command:

```
Router1(config)#interface Serial0/0.1 point-to-point
Router1(config-subif)#frame-relay interface-dlci 904
Router1(config-fr-dlci)#auto qos
%Creating new map-class.
Router1(config-fr-dlci)#no auto discovery qos
Router1(config-fr-dlci)#exit
Router1(config-subif)#exit
```

 It is critical to enable AutoQoS before disabling the discovery feature. Otherwise, the router will lose all of the traffic information that it has learned.

If you want to see the new configuration commands that AutoQoS has added to your router, use the *show auto qos* command:

```
Router1#show auto qos
 !
 policy-map AutoQoS-Policy-Se0/0.1
  class AutoQoS-Transactional-Se0/0.1
   bandwidth remaining percent 1
   random-detect dscp-based
   set dscp af21
  class AutoQoS-Routing-Se0/0.1
   bandwidth remaining percent 1
   set dscp cs6
  class class-default
   fair-queue
 !
 policy-map AutoQoS-Policy-Se0/0.1-Parent
  class class-default
   shape average 1544000
   service-policy AutoQoS-Policy-Se0/0.1
 !
 class-map match-any AutoQoS-Transactional-Se0/0.1
  match protocol telnet
 !
 class-map match-any AutoQoS-Routing-Se0/0.1
  match protocol icmp
  match protocol eigrp
  match protocol rip

 Serial0/0.1: DLCI 904 -
 !
 interface Serial0/0.1 point-to-point
  frame-relay interface-dlci 904
   class AutoQoS-FR-Se0/0-904
```

```
!
map-class frame-relay AutoQoS-FR-Se0/0-904
  frame-relay cir 1544000
  frame-relay bc 15440
  frame-relay be 0
  frame-relay mincir 1544000
  service-policy output AutoQoS-Policy-Se0/0.1-Parent
Router1#
```

Note that the actual policy map does not exactly match the version that we saw earlier during the data collection phase. The biggest difference is that the router saw some additional RIP traffic in the meantime and added this protocol to the class called AutoQoS-Routing-Se0/0.1. It has also created a Frame Relay map class that includes traffic shaping parameters for the PVC.

Because AutoQoS adds so many different commands to the router configuration, if you want to disable AutoQoS, it is not sufficient to just remove the *auto qos* command. You will need to remove all of the other commands separately. In fact, you should be careful about removing this command because if you do so, the *show auto qos* command will no longer function, making it much more difficult to figure out what commands are actually related to this feature. To make matters worse, once you have removed the *auto qos* command, you can't even put it back because the router needs to repeat the discovery phase first!

If you want to remove this feature after you have enabled it, we recommend capturing the output of the *show auto qos* command and using a text editor to create a configuration script that selectively eliminates all of the associated commands.

AutoQoS for the Enterprise can be a useful way of generating a detailed queuing strategy for your network. We do urge some caution in using this feature, however. In our experience, the discovery option can be unreliable. In particular, if you are using NBAR or have access-groups enabled on the router, this can interfere with the data collection. Furthermore, we have seen questionable results in the output that went away after disabling and re-enabling the discovery option.

We strongly recommend looking very closely at the recommendations made by this command before implementing them.

See Also

Chapter 10, Recipe 11.8, Recipe 11.14

11.18 Viewing Queue Parameters

Problem

You want to see how queuing is configured on an interface.

Solution

Cisco provides several useful commands for looking at an interface's queuing configuration and performance. The first of these is the *show queue* command:

```
Router#show queue FastEthernet0/0
  Input queue: 0/75/105/0 (size/max/drops/flushes); Total output drops: 0
  Queuing strategy: weighted fair
  Output queue: 0/1000/96/0 (size/max total/threshold/drops)
     Conversations  0/1/128 (active/max active/max total)
     Reserved Conversations 0/0 (allocated/max allocated)
     Available Bandwidth 75000 kilobits/sec



Router#
```

Use the *show queuing* command to look the router's queuing configuration in general:

```
Router#show queuing
Current fair queue configuration:

   Interface          Discard   Dynamic  Reserved  Link    Priority
                      threshold  queues   queues    queues  queues
   FastEthernet0/0    96         128      258       8       1
   Serial0/0          64         256      37        8       1
   Serial0/1          96         128      256       8       1


Current DLCI priority queue configuration:
Current priority queue configuration:

List   Queue  Args
1      high   protocol ip           tcp port 198
1      high   protocol pppoe-sessi
2      high   protocol ip           udp port 199
3      low    default
3      high   protocol ip           list 101
Current custom queue configuration:
Current random-detect configuration:
Router#
```

Discussion

The *show queue* and *show queuing* commands augment the *show interface* output, which also shows important queuing information:

```
Router#show interface FastEthernet0/0
FastEthernet0/0 is up, line protocol is up
  Hardware is AmdFE, address is 0001.9670.b780 (bia 0001.9670.b780)
  MTU 1500 bytes, BW 100000 Kbit, DLY 100 usec,
     reliability 255/255, txload 1/255, rxload 1/255
  Encapsulation ARPA, loopback not set
  Keepalive set (10 sec)
  Full-duplex, 100Mb/s, 100BaseTX/FX
  ARP type: ARPA, ARP Timeout 04:00:00
```

```
            Last input 00:00:00, output 00:00:00, output hang never
            Last clearing of "show interface" counters never
            Input queue: 0/75/105/0 (size/max/drops/flushes); Total output drops: 0
            Queuing strategy: weighted fair
            Output queue: 0/1000/96/0 (size/max total/threshold/drops)
               Conversations  0/1/128 (active/max active/max total)
               Reserved Conversations 0/0 (allocated/max allocated)
               Available Bandwidth 75000 kilobits/sec
          5 minute input rate 1000 bits/sec, 2 packets/sec
          5 minute output rate 2000 bits/sec, 2 packets/sec
             2495069 packets input, 181306312 bytes
             Received 2333309 broadcasts, 0 runts, 0 giants, 0 throttles
             0 input errors, 0 CRC, 0 frame, 0 overrun, 0 ignored
             0 watchdog
             0 input packets with dribble condition detected
             1927544 packets output, 197958017 bytes, 0 underruns
             0 output errors, 0 collisions, 21 interface resets
             0 babbles, 0 late collision, 0 deferred
             0 lost carrier, 0 no carrier
             0 output buffer failures, 0 output buffers swapped out
       Router#
```

The *show queue* command is a good starting point when looking at queuing issues. It tells you what queuing algorithm is used, as well as information about any drops:

```
       Router#show queue FastEthernet0/0
         Input queue: 0/75/105/0 (size/max/drops/flushes); Total output drops: 0
         Queuing strategy: weighted fair
         Output queue: 0/1000/96/0 (size/max total/threshold/drops)
            Conversations  0/1/128 (active/max active/max total)
            Reserved Conversations 0/0 (allocated/max allocated)
            Available Bandwidth 75000 kilobits/sec
```

In this case, you can see that the interface uses WFQ. This can be slightly deceptive because we actually configured this interface for CBWFQ. The Reserved Connections line indicates that no RSVP reservation queues have been allocated for this interface. So if you tried to use RSVP on this interface, it would not work right now.

The *show queue* command gives no output at all when you use Custom Queuing or Priority Queuing on an interface.

The first section of output from the *show queuing* command gives some useful summary information on fair queuing parameters:

```
       Router#show queuing
       Current fair queue configuration:

         Interface          Discard   Dynamic  Reserved  Link    Priority
                            threshold  queues   queues    queues  queues
         FastEthernet0/0    96         128      258       8       1
         Serial0/0          64         256      37        8       1
         Serial0/1          96         128      256       8       1
```

In this case, you can immediately see and compare the queue sizes between different interfaces.

## CHAPTER 12

Tunnels and VPNs

12.0 Introduction

A tunnel is essentially just a method for encapsulating one protocol in another. There are many reasons for doing this. In Chapter 15, we will discuss DLSw, which is commonly used to transmit SNA traffic through an IP network. The SNA protocol is not routable, so the tunnel allows you to send this traffic through a scalable routed network.

You can also use tunnels to transmit protocols that are routable, but not fully supported by the network. For example, some organizations find that they need to be able to send IPX through their networks to support legacy applications. But few network engineers are willing to invest the extra time or money required to build native IPX support into their routing core. So this is an ideal situation for using tunnels.

And we often see tunnels for carrying IP traffic through an IP network. The classic example of this is a Virtual Private Network (VPN) that connects two private networks through a public network such as the Internet. But there are other places where it can be useful to tunnel IP in IP.

One of the most common reasons for tunneling IP in IP is to get around architectural problems with dynamic routing protocols. For example, in Chapter 8 we discussed OSPF Virtual Links. These links are effectively just tunnels that let you put routers in different OSPF Areas than their physical connections allow.

Another example appears when you need to extend a routing protocol through regions of the network that don't support this protocol. Some WAN carriers provide IP connectivity between customer locations, similar to a public Internet. But the carrier network can't always support the customer's routing protocol, and it is often not desirable to mix the carrier and customer routing tables.

Tunnels are extremely useful in lab or test environments, where they allow you to emulate more complex network topologies. Further, in lab environments it is sometimes necessary to tunnel test data through a production network to ensure that the testing cannot interfere with the functioning of the production network. And we expect to see a lot of tunneling during the migration phases of any future large-scale conversions to IPv6.

Most of the examples in this chapter will look at Generic Routing Encapsulation (GRE) tunnels, sometimes with encryption support using IPSec. GRE is an open standard that is documented in RFCs 1701 and 1702, and updated in RFC 2784. These documents actually describe GRE Version 0, which is the standard version of GRE. There is also a GRE Version 1, which is more commonly called Point to Point Tunneling Protocol (PPTP), and is described in RFC 2637. The key different between GRE and PPTP is that PPTP includes a PPP intermediate layer, while GRE directly supports Layer 3 protocols such as IP and IPX. This chapter does not have the space to cover PPTP or its cousins L2TP (Layer 2 Tunneling Protocol) and L2F (Layer 2 Forwarding). These protocols are commonly used in situations when mobile users need to make VPN connections through the public Internet to an enterprise IP network. There are simply too many different variations to adequately cover even the most common configurations.

GRE doesn't use either TCP or UDP. Instead, this protocol works directly with the IP layer, using IP Protocol number 47. It includes its own features for verifying delivery and integrity. The GRE packet's payload includes a complete Layer 3 packet with its payload and headers intact. The routers that terminate the tunnel take packets and wrap them in a new IP packet with a GRE header. They forward this GRE packet through the IP network to the router that supports the other end of the tunnel. The receiving router then simply unwraps the encapsulated packet and sends it on its way. To the encapsulated packet, this entire process has taken a single routing hop, even though the GRE packet may have traversed many routers to reach its destination. This means that the payload packet has its TTL field decremented by one for using the tunnel. Conversely, the encapsulating GRE packet that holds this payload packet will have its TTL decremented once for each routing hop in the external network.

There are other common tunnel protocols, such as IP-in-IP, which uses IP protocol number 4. This protocol is an open standard that is documented in RFC 2003. In general we prefer GRE to IP-in-IP because it offers considerably greater flexibility, particularly on Cisco routers.

Tunnels can have packet fragmentation issues. The problem is simply that when you put a second IP header on an existing packet, you get a bigger packet. If the original packet is already at or close to the Maximum Transmission Unit (MTU) packet size that the network can support, then putting this packet in a tunnel forces the router to fragment it. Most of the time this is not a problem. But some applications do not cope well with packet fragmentation.

Normally, applications that can't accept packet fragmentation will set the Don't Fragment (DF) bit in the IP header. The router must drop oversized packets that it cannot fragment, but it sends an ICMP message back to the end device to tell it to use a smaller packet size.

The net result is that when you use tunnels, you reduce the effective MTU of your network. This doesn't necessarily cause problems, but it is important to be aware of this.

Internet Protocol Security (IPSec)) is a suite of security related protocols and algorithms that is documented in RFCs 2401 through 2412 and 2451. This is far more information than we can even summarize in a book like this, so we will only mention some of the most immediately relevant points and refer the reader to other references, such as the RFCs or books like *The Complete Cisco VPN Configuration Guide* by Richard Deal (Cisco Press) for more information.

The IPSec framework provides features for authenticating and encrypting traffic, as well as for securely exchanging encryption and authentication keys. It is designed to work with both IPv4 and IPv6, and can accommodate a variety of different basic encryption, authentication, and key exchange algorithms. This algorithmic independence is one of the essential design criteria of IPSec. It allows you to transparently substitute a new encryption algorithm, for example, if somebody discovers a critical flaw in the old one, or if a new algorithm is more efficient.

IPSec provides security only at the IP layer. This allows it to protect applications and data operating at higher layers of the protocol stack. This is important because it means that you can use IPSec in conjunction with other insecure protocols or applications and, if done properly, achieve a good level of overall security. Also, because IPSec works at the IP layer, you can readily use it with any of the higher layer IP-based protocols such as TCP, UDP, ICMP, multicast, and so forth.

Unfortunately, one of the most confusing things about IPSec is the proliferation of different protocols and algorithms that handle different parts of the key management, authentication, and encryption processes. Therefore, we will briefly explain some of the more common terms and concepts.

Internet Security Association Key Management Protocol (ISAKMP) is essentially a framework for key exchange, a generic set of procedures and packet formats that allow devices to reliably and securely pass encryption and authentication keys to one another. It includes such concepts as the key Security Association, which defines not only the keys themselves, but important parameters such as the specific algorithms to be used and the length of time that this key is valid for. This information is all negotiated by the IPSec end devices when they first establish a session, and periodically updated if the session remains active for a longer period of time.

Internet Key Exchange (IKE) is a specific protocol for securely exchanging keys using the ISAKMP framework. It uses the OAKLEY key determination protocol, which is defined in RFC 2412. OAKLEY distributes keys of arbitrary types for arbitrary algorithms to use. One of the methods that it can use is the Diffie-Hellman (DH) key exchange model.

Diffie-Hellman is a mathematical algorithm that uses properties of large prime numbers to allow users to exchange key information in encrypted form. Both devices authenticating a session can calculate a common key based on the encrypted information that they exchange. There are two issues with this algorithm.

The first is that it can be broken by a "man in the middle" attack. This essentially involves somebody intercepting the exchanged key information and rewriting it to create a new valid key with each of the end devices. The various key management protocols get around this problem by using a separate authentication system to validate the exchanged information.

The second problem is that even with authentication, if the prime numbers aren't large enough, it is possible to mathematically deduce the key. To resolve this problem, Cisco routers offer several different DH Groups. Group 1 uses 768-bit values to define the prime numbers, Group 2 uses 1024-bit primes. And, in IOS level 12.1T, Cisco introduced support for Group 5 DH, which uses a 1536 bit value for its prime numbers. With current computing power, if somebody really wants your data, 768 bit values are not very secure. So we recommend using Group 2 or higher.

OAKLEY also supports the Perfect Forward Secrecy (PFS) system. PFS is a system that ensures that even if somebody is able to break one of the keys, this will tell them nothing about any other keys. This is because the keys are not derived from one another. Many of the Cisco commands related to key exchange include a *pfs* keyword that you can enable, although you need to ensure that the same options are enabled on both peers.

One of the most effective ways of managing large numbers of keys is to implement a Public Key Infrastructure (PKI), which is a paradigm that uses digital certificates to verify the validity of public encryption and authentication keys. They generally use a Certification Authority (CA), which is a trusted server that knows the public encryption keys for a large number of devices.

IPSec uses two important security protocols, the Authenticating Header (AH) and the Encapsulating Security Payload (ESP). These do pretty much what their names suggest. AH includes a cryptographic authentication scheme in the header of the IP packet, which allows you to ensure that the data has not been tampered with in any way, and that it really does come from the right source device. ESP, on the other hand, encrypts the packet's payload for privacy. We recommend that if you are using IPSec, you should use both AH and ESP together. Authentication and encryption clearly serve entirely different but complementary functions. But we believe it is rare to have data that is important enough to warrant implementing either authentication or encryption, but not both.

One of the main authentication methods for IPSec makes use of a cryptographic hash function. Hash functions are actually more common than you might think. The simple cyclic redundancy checksum (CRC) field in a packet is essentially just a hash function. The general definition of a hash function is an algorithm that takes a message of arbitrary length and produces an output of fixed length. This output is often called a message digest.

To be useful for authentication, this hash function must make it extremely difficult to generate two distinct messages that have the same message digest. There are several of these hash functions in existence. The most popular for use with IPSec are Message Digest Version 5 (MD5) and Secure Hash Algorithm. We have already discussed MD5 in another setting, when we talked about how Cisco routers store passwords internally in Chapter 3. Cryptographic hash functions makes excellent password crypts because the result is always the same length and almost impossible to reverse. If the algorithm is strong, the only way to decrypt the original password is to encrypt a series of systematic guesses and see if any of them match the unknown encrypted string.

The National Institute of Standards and Technology (NIST) developed the Secure Hash Algorithm (SHA) as an improvement over MD5. It is generally believed that SHA is somewhat more secure than MD5, although it is a little bit more CPU intensive. Several cryptographers have recently demonstrated serious weaknesses in MD5. However, while there are no known algorithms for breaking SHA, it is based on earlier algorithms that have been compromised. So there is widespread concern that SHA will also need to be replaced.

As a result, the IPSec world is gradually shifting to a new algorithm called Advanced Encryption Standard (AES). This algorithm is the one currently preferred by the NSA for securing U.S. government information. Cisco added AES support in IOS level 12.2(13)T.

IPSec uses these hash functions to create Hashed Message Authentication Codes (HMAC). The HMAC is effectively an irreversible cryptographic hash function of an original message that has been combined in a nontrivial way with a password. So you need to not only break the hash algorithm, but also the password to reconstruct the original message.

For the actual data encryption, IPSec again offers several different options. Cisco routers implement 56-bit and 168-bit Data Encryption Standard (DES) encryption, as well as 128-, 192-, and 256-bit Advanced Encryption Standard (AES). The 56-bit version of DES is the default, while the 168-bit version is often called Triple DES, and both versions of AES are considered strong cryptography. Since cryptography has military uses, the United States Government imposes restrictions on exporting cryptographic software to most of the world, making exceptions for a handful of close allies like Canada. Please check the following Cisco web page, *http://www.cisco.com/wwl/export/crypto/ tool/stqrg.html*, or send an email to *export@cisco.com* to see if you require a special export license in your country.

In the spirit of the Internet, several individuals and groups have developed several other encryption algorithms for use with IPSec. One of the most popular is called Blowfish. This is an unpatented and freely distributable encryption algorithm that is faster than standard DES, and believed to be more secure as well. Other encryption algorithms include International Data Encryption Algorithm (IDEA), CAST-256, and Skipjack. However, Cisco does not implement any of these alternative algorithms.

IPSec has two main modes of operation, called Tunnel mode and Transport mode. In this chapter, we will discuss examples of both. Tunnel mode essentially means that IPSec is responsible for operating its own tunnel. IPSec tunnels are modeled on the IP-in-IP Tunnel Protocol, which we mentioned earlier. As a result, any IPSec exchanges that use transport mode must be purely between the two end devices, while tunnel mode can support routing from devices that are further downstream. In Recipe 12.3, we show an example in which transport mode is used to encrypt traffic in a GRE tunnel. In this case, the GRE traffic always begins and ends on the routers themselves, although the payload of the GRE packets may contain IP packets routed from other downstream devices.

Recipes 12.4 and 12.7 show examples of tunnel mode. In Recipe 12.4, we configure two routers to connect using an IPSec tunnel to bridge LAN traffic. In Recipe 12.7, a remote workstation initiates the IPSec connection to the router. But the packets that this workstation sends are destined for end devices on the other side of the router. So tunnel mode is appropriate here.

By default, Cisco routers will use IPSec in Tunnel mode. This is because IPSec needs a well-defined starting and ending point for the encryption. So, with Transport mode, the source and destination IP addresses must be fixed somehow. This effectively means that Transport mode needs to operate inside of another tunnel protocol such as GRE if it is to carry user traffic between routers.

12.1   Creating a Tunnel

Problem

You want to tunnel IP traffic through your network.

Solution

The basic GRE tunnel configuration is simply a matter of defining the source and destination addresses or interfaces on both devices. On the first router, you need to create the tunnel interface and define its source and destination:

```
Router1#configure terminal
Enter configuration commands, one per line.  End with CNTL/Z.
Router1(config)#interface Tunnel1
Router1(config-if)#ip address 192.168.35.6 255.255.255.252
Router1(config-if)#tunnel source 172.25.1.5
Router1(config-if)#tunnel destination 172.25.1.7
Router1(config-if)#exit
Router1(config)#end
Router1#
```

Then, on the other router you must create a tunnel interface with a matching source and destination:

```
Router5#configure terminal
Enter configuration commands, one per line.  End with CNTL/Z.
```

```
Router5(config)#interface Tunnel3
Router5(config-if)#ip address 192.168.35.5 255.255.255.252
Router5(config-if)#tunnel source 172.25.1.7
Router5(config-if)#tunnel destination 172.25.1.5
Router5(config-if)#exit
Router5(config)#end
Router5#
```

Discussion

Creating a basic tunnel is very simple—you just need to define a source and destination on each of two routers. When you do this, as with any other virtual interface such as subinterfaces and loopback interfaces, there is an additional memory requirement on the router. However, the CPU overhead is not as bad as you might initially think. This is because GRE tunnels do work well with Cisco Express Forwarding (CEF). So the main scaling issue in creating tunnels on routers is the memory required to support them.

The only tricky part of configuring a tunnel is making sure that the source of the tunnel on one router matches the destination on the other. In this case, *Router1* uses a source IP address of 172.25.1.5, which happens to be its Ethernet port. If you look at the *tunnel destination* command on the other router, you will see that it matches. Similarly, the destination on the first router is 172.25.1.7, and the source is 172.25.1.5.

You could also use an alternative syntax, specifying the interface name, rather than the IP address:

```
Router5(config)#interface Tunnel3
Router5(config-if)#tunnel source Ethernet0
```

This points the tunnel source to the primary IP address on a particular interface on this router. It is crucial that this IP address match the destination address configured on the other router.

If you then look at the new tunnel interface, you will see that it is up:

```
Router1#show interfaces Tunnel1
Tunnel1 is up, line protocol is up
  Hardware is Tunnel
  Internet address is 192.168.35.6/30
  MTU 1514 bytes, BW 9 Kbit, DLY 500000 usec,
     reliability 255/255, txload 1/255, rxload 1/255
  Encapsulation TUNNEL, loopback not set
  Keepalive not set
  Tunnel source 172.25.1.5 (FastEthernet0), destination 172.25.1.7
  Tunnel protocol/transport GRE/IP, key disabled, sequencing disabled
  Checksumming of packets disabled,  fast tunneling enabled
  Last input 00:11:08, output 00:00:08, output hang never
  Last clearing of "show interface" counters never
  Input queue: 0/75/0/0 (size/max/drops/flushes); Total output drops: 0
  Queueing strategy: fifo
  Output queue: 0/0 (size/max)
```

```
    5 minute input rate 0 bits/sec, 0 packets/sec
    5 minute output rate 0 bits/sec, 0 packets/sec
       5 packets input, 740 bytes, 0 no buffer
       Received 0 broadcasts, 0 runts, 0 giants, 0 throttles
       0 input errors, 0 CRC, 0 frame, 0 overrun, 0 ignored, 0 abort
       73 packets output, 6604 bytes, 0 underruns
       0 output errors, 0 collisions, 0 interface resets
       0 output buffer failures, 0 output buffers swapped out
Router1#
```

This is deceptive, though. Even if we remove the tunnel configuration from the other router, this interface will still appear to be up. Indeed, this tunnel interface will appear to be up even if you turn off the power on the far end router. In IOS Version 12.2(8)T, Cisco introduced a new *keepalive* option for GRE tunnels that overcomes this limitation. When you configure a tunnel with this new feature, the interface will go down if there are any connection problems:

```
Router1(config)#interface Tunnel1
Router1(config-if)#keepalive
```

By default, this *keepalive* command sends a packet through the tunnel to check its status once every 10 seconds. If there is no response to three successive polls, the router declares the tunnel interface to be down. So this will change the tunnel's status about 30 seconds after a failure.

You can adjust both the time interval and the number of retries. For example, to send a keepalive packet every 5 seconds, but to keep the default three retry limit, you could use the following command:

```
Router1(config)#interface Tunnel1
Router1(config-if)#keepalive 5
```

And if you want to change the number of retries, you can specify the new value after the time interval. The following example will send a keepalive packet every 3 seconds, and will declare the tunnel down if it doesn't hear a response back to two successive keepalive tests:

```
Router1(config)#interface Tunnel1
Router1(config-if)#keepalive 3 2
```

If you are concerned about the integrity of tunneled data, you can enable checksums on a GRE tunnel:

```
Router1(config)#interface Tunnel1
Router1(config-if)#tunnel checksum
```

When you turn on checksums, the router will verify the checksum of every GRE packet it receives and drop any packets that don't match. A similar feature checks to see if packets are received in the correct order:

```
Router1(config)#interface Tunnel1
Router1(config-if)#tunnel sequence-datagrams
```

When you enable the *sequence-datagrams* option, the router will drop any packets that it receives out of their correct order. These two options can be useful in

---

networks that have a tendency to damage packets, or when there are multiple paths between the tunnel routers. Remember that GRE doesn't use TCP, so these features can help to improve the reliability of a tunnel connection. However, even when you enable these features, the routers will not resend dropped packets as TCP does.

We do suggest using some caution when you enable either checksums or sequencing on a GRE tunnel, because these features do not work with CEF. So as soon as you enable either of them, the router will have to resort to process switching, which could drive up your CPU utilization.

The tunnel used so far in all of the examples in this recipe hasn't specified any particular tunnel protocol, so the routers will use the default GRE protocol. If you prefer to use a different tunnel protocol, change it using the tunnel mode command as follows:

```
Router1(config)#interface Tunnel1
Router1(config-if)#tunnel mode ipip
```

Here we have opted to use the IP-in-IP tunnel protocol that we discussed in the introduction to this chapter. There are several other options for tunnel protocols, which we list in Table 12-1.

Table 12-1. Available tunnel modes

Command	Description
Router1(config-if)#**tunnel mode dvmrp**	DVMRP multicast tunnel.
Router1(config-if)#**tunnel mode eon**	Allows tunneling of CLNP OSI based protocols through IP networks.
Router1(config-if)#**tunnel mode gre ip**	GRE encapsulation, the default.
Router1(config-if)#**tunnel mode gre ip**multipoint	GRE encapsulation, an option that automatically creates a mesh of tunnels among the participating routers.
Router1(config-if)#**tunnel mode gre ipv6**	GRE encapsulation using IPv6 transport.
Router1(config-if)#**tunnel mode ipip**	IP in IP encapsulation.
Router1(config-if)#**tunnel mode ipv6**	IP in IP encapsulation using IPv6 transport.
Router1(config-if)#**tunnel mode mpls**	MPLS tunnels, useful for traffic engineering purposes.
Router1(config-if)#**tunnel mode nos**	A version of IP in IP that supports the KA9Q protocol.
Router1(config-if)#**tunnel mode decapsulate-any**	In this mode, the router will automatically decapsulate any incoming IP-in-IP type tunnel packets. You can use this as a termination point for several remote tunnels. However, you cannot send packets from an interface with this option configured.
Router1(config-if)#**tunnel mode ipsec ipv4**	IPSec Tunnel Mode for IPv4 transport only.
** Router1(config-if)#**tunnel mode aurp**	AppleTalk "TunnelTalk" encapsulation (**Note that Cisco announced that they would no longer support AppleTalk as of 12.2T. Although it is currently still available in Versions 12.4 and 12.4T, it is unlikely to remain available in the future.)

Table 12-1. Available tunnel modes (continued)

Command	Description
** Router1(config-if)#**tunnel mode cayman**	Cayman AppleTalk tunnel encapsulation.
** Router1(config-if)#**tunnel mode iptalk**	AppleTalk IPTalk encapsulation.

In the recipe example, the two routers shared an Ethernet segment, so the routing was trivial. But in practice, routing between the tunnel endpoints is often the most difficult thing to get right. The problem, which we will discuss more in Recipe 12.3, is that the tunnel itself is only one routing hop for packets that travel through it, although it might be several physical hops. As a result, the routing protocol will often decide that the best way to get to the tunnel's destination IP address is through the tunnel itself. This is called *recursive routing*, and it makes the tunnel useless. So when a router notices that it is routing GRE packets for a tunnel destination address through the same tunnel, it will automatically disable the tunnel with the following error message:

```
Jan 16 12:05:04 EST: %TUN-5-RECURDOWN: Tunnel1 temporarily disabled due to recursive
routing
Jan 16 12:05:05 EST: %LINEPROTO-5-UPDOWN: Line protocol on Interface Tunnel1, changed
state to down
```

Cisco has attempted to reduce this problem by making the default bandwidth for all tunnel interfaces 9 Kbps. For most routing protocols, this means that you have to traverse several hops before the tunnel looks like a better path. But some protocols, most notably RIP, don't look at interface bandwidths. And it is important to bear in mind that no matter what protocol you use, at some point a single hop of 9 Kbps is going to look better than a large number of higher bandwidth hops.

The only way to avoid this problem is to ensure that there is always a good route to the tunnel destination that doesn't use the tunnel itself. This is most easily accomplished by using static routes, although we discuss other techniques in Recipe 12.3.

One of the inherent problems with tunnels is that the entire IP packet is stuffed inside of another IP packet, which effectively means that the maximum size for your packet payload is smaller. For example, a GRE packet has a 24-byte header. So if your network uses the standard 1,500 byte Ethernet MTU, the largest packet that you can put through the tunnel is 1,476 bytes. If the payload packet's Don't Fragment (DF) bit is not set, then the router will simply break up any larger packets before encapsulating the pieces into multiple (usually 2) GRE packets.

This is a problem because the extra overhead due to packet fragmentation and reassembly can cause extra delays. And if one of the fragments of a tunneled TCP packet is lost due to congestion in the network, all of the fragments constituting the original packet must be retransmitted, which makes the congestion problems worse.

For TCP connections you can use the *ip tcp path-mtu-discovery* global configuration command to tell the router to monitor for the ICMP "fragmentation needed but DF bit set" messages. These ICMP messages tell end devices to adjust their MTU values to match the maximum that the network can transmit end-to-end. However, GRE doesn't use TCP so this approach doesn't work. Fortunately, in 12.0(7)T3, Cisco introduced an equivalent Path MTU Discovery (PMTUD) command for use with GRE and IP-in-IP tunnels:

```
Router1(config)#interface Tunnel1
Router1(config-if)#tunnel path-mtu-discovery
```

This command tells the routers to set the DF bit in the headers of GRE and IP-in-IP tunnels, monitor for ICMP messages, and to adjust MTU values accordingly exactly the way it is done for TCP PMTUD.

Note that this is an ongoing process. The routers must check ever packet because there may be multiple paths through the network, each with different MTU restrictions. The larger the effective MTU, the greater the efficiency of the network, so it is important to make the MTU as large as the network can carry. So the PMTUD process allows the routers to periodically try larger packet sizes, just in case the network topology has changed, and the new path can support larger packets. You can adjust the length of time when the router will hold only a particular MTU value before resetting to the maximum by using the *age-timer* keyword:

```
Router1(config)#interface Tunnel1
Router1(config-if)#tunnel path-mtu-discovery age-timer 15
```

This keyword takes a time-out value expressed in minutes. The default is 10 minutes.

Starting in IOS Version 12.2(13)T, you can also specify a minimum MTU value that the tunnel will negotiate down to by using the *min-mtu* keyword. If the network wants packets smaller than this, then the routers will just fragment:

```
Router1(config)#interface Tunnel1
Router1(config-if)#tunnel path-mtu-discovery min-mtu 500
```

The default here is the minimum value of 92 bytes. This command was added because of a clever denial of service attack in which attackers sent repeated ICMP "fragmentation required but DF bit set" packets to routers running tunnel interfaces, compelling them to reduce their MTUs to unfeasibly small values.

See Also

Recipe 12.3

12.2 Tunneling Foreign Protocols in IP

Problem

You want to tunnel a foreign protocol such as IPX traffic through your IP network.

Solution

One of the most important applications of tunnels is for passing foreign protocols through a network that only supports IP. A typical example of this would be IPX, although the configuration is similar for other protocols such as Appletalk:

```
Router1#configure terminal
Enter configuration commands, one per line.  End with CNTL/Z.
Router1(config)#ipx routing AAAA.BBBB.0001
Router1(config)#interface Tunnel1
Router1(config-if)#ipx network AAA
Router1(config-if)#tunnel source 172.25.1.5
Router1(config-if)#tunnel destination 172.25.1.7
Router1(config-if)#exit
Router1(config)#end
Router1#
```

Then on the other router you must create a tunnel interface with a matching source and destination, as well as a matching IPX network number:

```
Router5#configure terminal
Enter configuration commands, one per line.  End with CNTL/Z.
Router2(config)#ipx routing AAAA.BBBB.0002
Router5(config)#interface Tunnel3
Router5(config-if)#ipx network AAA
Router5(config-if)#tunnel source 172.25.1.7
Router5(config-if)#tunnel destination 172.25.1.5
Router5(config-if)#exit
Router5(config)#end
Router5#
```

Discussion

This recipe is nearly identical to Recipe 12.1, but instead of tunneling IP traffic through an IP network, we use the same kind of tunnel to pass IPX traffic through the same network. Note that of all the supported tunnel modes mentioned in Table 12.1, only the default GRE will transport IPX, although there are several AppleTalk tunnel modes.

This book does not cover IPX, so we won't go into any detail on the IPX-specific commands here. This is merely intended as an example of how to use GRE tunnels for foreign protocols. For more information on IPX, please refer to *Designing Large-Scale LANs* by Kevin Dooley (O'Reilly).

To enable IPX on both of these routers, first you have to make sure that you are running an IOS release that supports IPX. The various "Desktop" IOS versions support this protocol, as do the "Enterprise" versions. Please consult the Cisco IOS feature matrices for more details. Assuming, then, that your router supports IPX, you can enable it with the *ipx routing* command, as shown. Naturally, you need to enable IPX routing on both routers. Then the only other important detail is to configure both ends of the GRE tunnel with matching IPX network numbers, as we have done in the example.

It's important to note that you can configure a GRE tunnel to support more than one protocol by simply specifying appropriate network numbers for each protocol using the tunnel. We could, for example, add IP to this IPX tunnel by simply configuring an IP address on both ends, as we did in Recipe 12.1. Then the tunnel will support both protocols simultaneously:

```
Router1(config)#interface Tunnel1
Router1(config-if)#ip address 192.168.35.6 255.255.255.252
Router1(config-if)#ipx network AAA
Router1(config-if)#tunnel source 172.25.1.5
Router1(config-if)#tunnel destination 172.25.1.7
Router1(config-if)#exit
Router1(config)#end
Router1#
```

See Also

Recipe 12.1; *Designing Large-Scale LANs* by Kevin Dooley (O'Reilly)

12.3 Tunneling with Dynamic Routing Protocols

Problem

You need to pass a dynamic routing protocol through your tunnels.

Solution

Dynamic routing and tunnels can be a dangerous combination. It is critical to ensure that the routers never get confused and think that the best path to the tunnel destination is through the tunnel itself. We offer three different ways of resolving this problem.

The first is to use static routes for the tunnel destination address:

```
Router1#configure terminal
Enter configuration commands, one per line.  End with CNTL/Z.
Router1(config)#interface Tunnel1
Router1(config-if)#ip address 192.168.35.6 255.255.255.252
Router1(config-if)#tunnel source 172.25.1.5
Router1(config-if)#tunnel destination 172.22.1.2
Router1(config-if)#exit
Router1(config)#ip route 172.22.1.2 255.255.255.255 172.25.1.1
Router1(config)#router eigrp 55
Router1(config-router)#network 192.168.35.0
Router1(config-router)#exit
Router1(config)#end
Router1#
```

The second method simply excludes the tunnel's IP address range from the routing protocol. You can then run a different routing protocol for the addresses that you want to pass through the tunnel:

```
Router1#configure terminal
Enter configuration commands, one per line.  End with CNTL/Z.
```

```
Router1(config)#interface Tunnel1
Router1(config-if)#ip address 192.168.35.6 255.255.255.252
Router1(config-if)#tunnel source 172.25.1.5
Router1(config-if)#tunnel destination 172.22.1.2
Router1(config-if)#exit
Router1(config)#router eigrp 55
Router1(config-router)#network 172.22.0.0
Router1(config-router)#network 172.25.0.0
Router1(config-router)#end
Router1(config)#router rip
Router1(config-router)#network 192.168.35.0
Router1(config-router)#exit
Router1(config)#end
Router1#
```

And the third solution is to filter the routes of the supporting network to prevent them from passing through the tunnel:

```
Router1#configure terminal
Enter configuration commands, one per line.  End with CNTL/Z.
Router1(config)#interface Tunnel1
Router1(config-if)#ip address 192.168.35.6 255.255.255.252
Router1(config-if)#tunnel source 172.25.1.5
Router1(config-if)#tunnel destination 172.22.1.2
Router1(config-if)#exit
Router11(config)#ip prefix-list TUNNELROUTES seq 10 permit 192.168.0.0/16 ge 17
Router1(config)#router eigrp 55
Router1(config-router)#network 172.22.0.0
Router1(config-router)#network 172.25.0.0
Router1(config-router)#network 192.168.35.0
Router1(config-router)#distribute-list prefix TUNNELROUTES out Tunnel1
Router1(config-router)#exit
Router1(config)#end
Router1#
```

Discussion

As we mentioned in Recipe 12.1, you have to be careful when using a dynamic routing protocol anywhere near a GRE tunnel to avoid the dreaded *recursive routing* error message, which brings down the tunnel. This happens because the routers need to have a good path through the network to carry the tunnel to its destination. In addition, this path cannot go through the tunnel itself. But the problem is that because the tunnel forms a virtual connection that directly connects two routers, the path through the tunnel is almost always shorter than any path that goes through the real physical network.

The other way to look at the problem of recursive routing is to think about what the router has to do to a packet that it wants to send through the tunnel. It wraps this packet in the payload of a GRE packet, and it puts the tunnel's destination address in the header of this GRE packet. Then it looks in its routing table to find out where to send this packet. If it finds that the best path is through the tunnel, then it must take this GRE packet and wrap it in the payload of a GRE packet whose destination address is the tunnel destination, and so on. This makes it difficult to deliver the original packet, so the router shuts down the tunnel interface to avoid having to stuff an infinite number of GRE headers onto the front of the packet.

There are two extremely simple solutions to this problem, but they aren't always applicable. You can use static routes to connect to the tunnel destination, which allows you to force the tunnel traffic to go the right way. Or you can prevent the routing protocol from passing through the tunnel either by using a separate IP address range or with access lists. These two options are the first two examples in the Solutions section of this recipe.

Note that we have used a specific host route for the destination IP address to ensure that it always uses the right path:

```
Router1(config)#ip route 172.22.1.2 255.255.255.255 172.25.1.1
```

The problem with this solution is that it might eliminate some of your network redundancy. For example, if there are several paths to the router that holds the tunnel's destination, using a static route like this might mean that your tunnel will fail if there is a topology change in the network affecting the manually selected path. In many cases, you can get around this problem by pointing the static route at a carefully selected downstream destination address. But then you run the risk that the router will learn about this downstream destination address through the tunnel, in which case we're back at square one.

The second simple solution is to simply exclude the tunnel from your routing protocol. In the example, we gave the tunnel an IP address that doesn't belong to the same address range as the source or destination addresses. This makes excluding the tunnel from the routing protocol relatively easy.

In the second example, by simply not including the 192.168.35.0/24 network in any of the EIGRP network commands, we prevent the tunnel from taking part in the routing protocol. We could also exclude the interface from the routing protocol using a distribute list. Please see Chapter 7 for more information about these EIGRP features.

However, sometimes these simple solutions are not appropriate. Some network topologies require that you use a routing protocol both inside and outside of the tunnel. For example, if you use VPNs to construct your WAN, either through a private or a public IP network, you will probably have to have both.

The best way to approach this type of situation is to start by ensuring that the ranges of IP addresses are distinct. For example, if the network that supports the tunnel uses public addressing, you could use private addressing for routes that need to be learned through the tunnel. Then you can apply a filter to prevent the routes for the supporting network from passing through the tunnel.

There are two ways to accomplish this. One is simply to use distinct routing protocols inside and outside of the tunnel, and not redistribute between the protocols. For example, the routing protocol outside of the tunnel could be BGP, while the tunneled network uses OSPF or EIGRP through the tunnel, or EIGRP and RIP, as in the example above.

But another method is necessary if the two sets of routes use the same routing protocol, or if you need to redistribute. With distance vector type interior routing protocols such as EIGRP and RIP, you can apply a route distribution filter to the tunnel interface to block the supporting network's routes. Note that EIGRP is much more sophisticated than a simple distance vector protocol like RIP. But this kind of route filtering is not possible with link state protocols such as OSPF, so this is one place where EIGRP's distance vector roots come in handy.

In the example, we have shown how to do this using a prefix list with EIGRP. This will permit only the 192.168.0.0/16 range of IP addresses to pass through the tunnel, while information about the 172.22.0.0/16 and 172.25.0.0/16 networks that form the support network is never learned through the tunnel. You should apply this type of filter to both ends of the tunnel:

```
Router11(config)#ip prefix-list TUNNELROUTES seq 10 permit 192.168.0.0/16 ge 17
Router1(config)#router eigrp 55
Router1(config-router)#network 172.22.0.0
Router1(config-router)#network 172.25.0.0
Router1(config-router)#distribute-list prefix TUNNELROUTES out Tunnel1
```

For more information on EIGRP route distribution filters, please see Chapter 7. And for more information on prefix lists, you can refer to either Chapter 7 or Chapter 9.

See Also

Recipe 12.1; Chapter 7; Chapter 9

12.4   Viewing Tunnel Status

Problem

You want to check the status of a tunnel.

Solution

You can look at the attributes for a tunnel with the *show interface* command.

```
Router1#show interface Tunnel5
```

And the easiest way to determine if a tunnel is operational is simply to use a PING test to either the send ICMP packets through the tunnel or to its destination address:

```
Router1#ping 192.168.66.6
Router1#ping 172.22.1.4
```

Discussion

You can use the standard show interface command on a tunnel interface to see a considerable amount of useful information about it:

```
Router1#show interface Tunnel5
Tunnel5 is up, line protocol is up
```

```
Hardware is Tunnel
Internet address is 192.168.66.5/30
MTU 1514 bytes, BW 9 Kbit, DLY 500000 usec,
    reliability 255/255, txload 1/255, rxload 1/255
Encapsulation TUNNEL, loopback not set
Keepalive not set
Tunnel source 172.22.1.3, destination 172.22.1.4
Tunnel protocol/transport GRE/IP, key disabled, sequencing disabled
Tunnel TTL 255
Checksumming of packets disabled,  fast tunneling enabled
Last input 1d19h, output 00:00:06, output hang never
Last clearing of "show interface" counters never
Input queue: 0/75/0/0 (size/max/drops/flushes); Total output drops: 79
Queueing strategy: fifo
Output queue: 0/0 (size/max)
5 minute input rate 0 bits/sec, 0 packets/sec
5 minute output rate 0 bits/sec, 0 packets/sec
    2536 packets input, 1386605 bytes, 0 no buffer
    Received 0 broadcasts, 0 runts, 0 giants, 0 throttles
    0 input errors, 0 CRC, 0 frame, 0 overrun, 0 ignored, 0 abort
    23235 packets output, 2036436 bytes, 0 underruns
    0 output errors, 0 collisions, 0 interface resets
    0 output buffer failures, 0 output buffers swapped out
Router1#
```

As you can see from this output, the *show interface* command tells you what the tunnel's source and destination IP addresses are. You can see the input and output rate, as well as the total number of packets and bytes both sent and received on this tunnel interface. The output also shows that we are using the default GRE tunnel protocol, and we have not enabled checksums or keepalives on this tunnel.

There is only one serious problem with this output. Because we have not enabled keepalives, as we discussed in Recipe 12.1, the *show interface* command will almost always show the tunnel interface as being in an *up* state. As we mentioned in Recipe 12.1, the router will temporarily bring the tunnel interface down in response to recursive routing situations, and you can also use the *shutdown* command to disable a tunnel as you would with any other interface. However, usually the tunnel interface will appear to be in an up state, even if the router can't reach the tunnel destination router.

If you are running an IOS level that supports keepalives on tunnels, you can enable that feature. Then the show interface command will give a more realistic view of the tunnel's status. But without that feature, the easiest way to see if a tunnel is working is to simply ping through it:

```
Router1#ping 192.168.66.6

Type escape sequence to abort.
Sending 5, 100-byte ICMP Echos to 192.168.66.6, timeout is 2 seconds:
!!!!!
Success rate is 100 percent (5/5), round-trip min/avg/max = 12/14/20 ms
Router1#
```

Or, alternatively, you can ping the destination IP address of the tunnel:

```
Router1#ping 172.22.1.4

Type escape sequence to abort.
Sending 5, 100-byte ICMP Echos to 192.168.66.6, timeout is 2 seconds:
!!!!!
Success rate is 100 percent (5/5), round-trip min/avg/max = 12/14/20 ms
Router1#
```

See Also

Recipe 12.1

12.5 Creating an Encrypted Router-to-Router VPN in a GRE Tunnel

Problem

You want to create an encrypted VPN through the Internet by connecting two routers using preshared keys.

Solution

In this example, we show how to use IPSec to encrypt traffic from router to another through a GRE tunnel. Here is the configuration of the first router:

```
Router1#configure terminal
Enter configuration commands, one per line.  End with CNTL/Z.
Router1(config)#crypto isakmp policy 10
Router1(config-isakmp)#encr aes 256
Router1(config-isakmp)#authentication pre-share
Router1(config-isakmp)#group 2
Router1(config-isakmp)#exit
Router1(config)#crypto isakmp key TUNNELKEY01 address 172.16.2.1 no-xauth
Router1(config)#crypto ipsec transform-set TUNNEL-TRANSFORM ah-sha-hmac esp-aes 256
Router1(cfg-crypto-trans)#mode transport
Router1(cfg-crypto-trans)#exit
Router1(config)#crypto map TUNNELMAP 10 ipsec-isakmp
% NOTE: This new crypto map will remain disabled until a peer
    and a valid access list have been configured.
Router1(config-crypto-map)#set peer 172.16.2.1
Router1(config-crypto-map)#set transform-set TUNNEL-TRANSFORM
Router1(config-crypto-map)#match address 102
Router1(config-crypto-map)#exit
Router1(config)#access-list 102 permit gre host 172.16.1.1 host 172.16.2.1
Router1(config)#interface Tunnel1
Router1(config-if)#ip address 192.168.1.1 255.255.255.252
Router1(config-if)#tunnel source 172.16.1.1
Router1(config-if)#tunnel destination 172.16.2.1
Router1(config-if)#exit
```

```
Router1(config)#interface FastEthernet0/0
Router1(config-if)#ip address 172.16.1.1 255.255.255.0
Router1(config-if)#ip access-group 101 in
Router1(config-if)#crypto map TUNNELMAP
Router1(config-if)#exit
Router1(config)#access-list 101 permit gre host 172.16.2.1 host 172.16.1.1
Router1(config)#access-list 101 permit esp host 172.16.2.1 host 172.16.1.1
Router1(config)#access-list 101 permit udp host 172.16.2.1 host 172.16.1.1 eq isakmp
Router1(config)#access-list 101 permit ahp host 172.16.2.1 host 172.16.1.1
Router1(config)#access-list 101 deny ip any any log
Router1(config)#interface Loopback0
Router1(config-if)#ip address 192.168.16.1 255.255.255.0
Router1(config-if)#exit
Router1(config)#ip route 0.0.0.0 0.0.0.0 172.16.1.2
Router1(config)#ip route 192.168.15.0 255.255.255.0 192.168.1.2
Router1(config)#end
Router1#
```

And here is the corresponding configuration for the other router:

```
Router2#configure terminal
Enter configuration commands, one per line.  End with CNTL/Z.
Router2(config)#crypto isakmp policy 10
Router2(config-isakmp)#encr aes 256
Router2(config-isakmp)#authentication pre-share
Router2(config-isakmp)#group 2
Router2(config-isakmp)#exit
Router2(config)#crypto isakmp key TUNNELKEY01 address 172.16.1.1
Router2(config)#crypto ipsec transform-set TUNNEL-TRANSFORM ah-sha-hmac esp-aes 256
Router2(cfg-crypto-trans)#mode transport
Router2(cfg-crypto-trans)#exit
Router2(config)#crypto map TUNNELMAP 10 ipsec-isakmp
% NOTE: This new crypto map will remain disabled until a peer
    and a valid access list have been configured.
Router2(config-crypto-map)#set peer 172.16.1.1
Router2(config-crypto-map)#set transform-set TUNNEL-TRANSFORM
Router2(config-crypto-map)#match address 102
Router2(config-crypto-map)#exit
Router2(config)#access-list 102 permit gre host 172.16.2.1 host 172.16.1.1
Router2(config)#interface Tunnel1
Router2(config-if)#ip address 192.168.1.2 255.255.255.252
Router2(config-if)#tunnel source 172.16.2.1
Router2(config-if)#tunnel destination 172.16.1.1
Router2(config-if)#exit
Router2(config)#interface FastEthernet0/0
Router2(config-if)#ip address 172.16.2.1 255.255.255.0
Router2(config-if)#ip access-group 101 in
Router2(config-if)#crypto map TUNNELMAP
Router2(config-if)#exit
Router2(config)#access-list 101 permit gre host 172.16.1.1 host 172.16.2.1
Router2(config)#access-list 101 permit esp host 172.16.1.1 host 172.16.2.1
Router2(config)#access-list 101 permit udp host 172.16.1.1 host 172.16.2.1 eq isakmp
Router2(config)#access-list 101 permit ahp host 172.16.1.1 host 172.16.2.1
Router2(config)#access-list 101 deny ip any any log
```

```
Router2(config)#interface Loopback0
Router2(config-if)#ip address 192.168.15.1 255.255.255.0
Router2(config-if)#exit
Router2(config)#ip route 0.0.0.0 0.0.0.0 172.16.2.2
Router2(config)#ip route 192.168.16.0 255.255.255.0 192.168.1.1
Router2(config)#end
Router2#
```

Discussion

There are several steps to these configurations, but they are the same on both routers. The first step is to create an appropriate key exchange policy using ISAKMP. The following set of commands defines the policy with priority 10. When ISAKMP negotiates the security association (SA) parameters, it starts with the lowest priority and goes to the highest. The highest possible priority value is 10,000:

```
Router1(config)#crypto isakmp policy 10
Router1(config-isakmp)#encr aes 256
Router1(config-isakmp)#authentication pre-share
Router1(config-isakmp)#group 2
```

This policy uses 256-bit AES encryption, preshared authentication keys, and group 2 (1024 bit) for Diffie-Hellman (DH) exchange. If we did not configure this, the routers would have to resort to the default parameters, which are 56-bit DES encryption, Rivest Shamir Adleman (RSA) signatures for authentication, and DH group 1 (768 bit). You can see the available policies on a router with the *show crypto isakmp policy* command:

```
Router1#show crypto isakmp policy

Global IKE policy
Protection suite of priority 10
        encryption algorithm:   AES - Advanced Encryption Standard (256 bit keys
).
        hash algorithm:         Secure Hash Standard
        authentication method:  Pre-Shared Key
        Diffie-Hellman group:   #2 (1024 bit)
        lifetime:               86400 seconds, no volume limit
Default protection suite
        encryption algorithm:   DES - Data Encryption Standard (56 bit keys).
        hash algorithm:         Secure Hash Standard
        authentication method:  Rivest-Shamir-Adleman Signature
        Diffie-Hellman group:   #1 (768 bit)
        lifetime:               86400 seconds, no volume limit
Router1#
```

We could have also adjusted the hash algorithm and the lifetime of a particular SA as follows:

```
Router1(config)#crypto isakmp policy 20
Router1(config-isakmp)#hash md5
Router1(config-isakmp)#lifetime 600
```

This policy uses the somewhat less secure but faster MD5 hash algorithm and reduces the SA lifetime to 600 seconds (10 minutes). The default hash algorithm is the standard IPSec Secure Hash Algorithm (SHA), and the default lifetime is 86400 seconds (24 hours). Reducing the lifetime forces the routers to renegotiate the various SA parameters, including encryption keys, more frequently. This frequent renegotiation improves security, but at the expense of higher router CPU utilization and possible delays during the renegotiation process.

Then, because we have configured the routers to use pre-shared keys in this policy, we need to define this initial key with the *crypto isakmp key* command:

```
Router1(config)#crypto isakmp key TUNNELKEY01 address 172.16.2.1 no-xauth
```

As you can see, this sets this key only for one IP address, which is the address of the other router. We have included the *no-xauth* option on the command line to explicitly disable IKE Extended Authentication (XAuth) on the routers, which is not necessary when the peer is another router. ISAKMP can work with either IP addresses or host names to identify devices. So we could have specified this command like this instead:

```
Router1(config)#crypto isakmp key TUNNELKEY01 hostname Router2.oreilly.com no-xauth
```

However, to do this, we would also have needed to ensure that the remote device used its hostname when declaring its ISAKMP identity:

```
Router2(config)#crypto isakmp identity hostname
```

We avoided this extra complication by simply using IP addresses, which is the default behavior. But you might want to consider using hostnames instead of IP addresses if the network topology means that there could be some ambiguity in which IP address will be used.

There are several useful commands for looking at the ISAKMP functions on your router. The first is *show crypto isakmp key*, which lists all of the available preshared keys:

```
Router1#show crypto isakmp key
Keyring             Hostname/Address              Preshared Key

default             172.16.2.1                    TUNNELKEY01
outer1#
```

Note that this doesn't mean that there is an active SA using this key, merely that the key is available if required. If you want to see information on active ISAKMP SAs, you should use the following command:

```
Router1#show crypto isakmp sa
dst           src           state       conn-id slot status
172.16.2.1    172.16.1.1    QM_IDLE           1    0 ACTIVE

Router1#
```

In this case, you can see that there is an active connection between the two routers shown in the example. The connection ID for this particular SA is shown in the *conn-id* column. You can use this ID number to clear the SA and force the routers to renegotiate as follows:

```
Router1#clear crypto isakmp 1
Router1#show crypto isakmp sa
```

```
dst            src            state        conn-id slot status
172.16.2.1     172.16.1.1     MM_NO_STATE        1    0 ACTIVE (deleted)

Router1#
```

This particular ISAKMP SA is now in a deleted state, as the routers begin to renegotiate their ISAKMP parameters. A short time later, they will re-establish a new SA. Note, however, that this is just the ISAKMP SA, which is only needed at call setup time. So the actual IPSec security association is actually still active:

```
Router1#show crypto ipsec sa

interface: FastEthernet0/0
    Crypto map tag: TUNNELMAP, local addr 172.16.1.1

    protected vrf: (none)
    local  ident (addr/mask/prot/port): (172.16.1.1/255.255.255.255/47/0)
    remote ident (addr/mask/prot/port): (172.16.2.1/255.255.255.255/47/0)
    current_peer 172.16.2.1 port 500
      PERMIT, flags={origin_is_acl,}
     #pkts encaps: 14, #pkts encrypt: 14, #pkts digest: 14
     #pkts decaps: 14, #pkts decrypt: 14, #pkts verify: 14
     #pkts compressed: 0, #pkts decompressed: 0
     #pkts not compressed: 0, #pkts compr. failed: 0
     #pkts not decompressed: 0, #pkts decompress failed: 0
     #send errors 1, #recv errors 0

      local crypto endpt.: 172.16.1.1, remote crypto endpt.: 172.16.2.1
      path mtu 1500, ip mtu 1500
      current outbound spi: 0xDBE0A93(230558355)

      inbound esp sas:
       spi: 0x33CEA934(869181748)
         transform: esp-256-aes ,

Router1#ping 192.168.1.2

Type escape sequence to abort.
Sending 5, 100-byte ICMP Echos to 192.168.1.2, timeout is 2 seconds:
!!!!!
Success rate is 100 percent (5/5), round-trip min/avg/max = 8/8/8 ms
Router1#
```

We can knock down the IPSec session with this command:

```
Router1#clear crypto session
```

The next part of the router configuration defines the IPSec *transform set*, and gives it the name TUNNEL-TRANSFORM to distinguish it from other transform sets that we might want to use for other purposes:

```
Router1(config)#crypto ipsec transform-set TUNNEL-TRANSFORM ah-sha-hmac esp-aes 256
Router1(cfg-crypto-trans)#mode transport
```

A transform is simply the operation that IPSec will perform on any matching data packets. There are several possible transforms, which are discussed in Table 12-2.

Table 12-2. IPSec transform set options

Transform type	Transform name	Description
Compression	comp-lzs	Compress using Lempel Ziv Stac algorithm
Authentication Header (AH)	ah-md5-hmac	Authenticate using MD5 algorithm
	ah-sha-hmac	Authenticate using SHA algorithm
Encapsulating Security Payload (ESP)	esp-des	Encrypt using 56-bit DES
	esp-3des	Encrypt using 168-bit DES
	esp-aes {128|192|256}	Encrypt using the 128-bit, 192-bit, or 256-bit AES algorithm
	esp-null	No encryption
ESP with authentication	esp-md5-hmac	Encrypt, and use MD5 for authentication
	esp-sha-hmac	Encrypt, and use SHA for authentication

In the above example, we chose to combine the more secure 256-bit AES encryption with the more reliable SHA authentication system for maximum security on both the AH and ESP portions of the packet. As we said earlier, many of the combinations are not possible (for example, you cannot combine 56-bit DES with 168-bit DES, as it doesn't make sense). The router prevents you from entering impossible combinations.

It's also worth mentioning that, as Table 12-2 mentions, you can use IPSec to do compression of the IP packet payload. This is not commonly done, though, because there are problems with combining encryption with compression.

We note in passing that while the authors of the IPSec RFCs argue eloquently for the separate usefulness of authentication and encryption, in practice we believe that most of the time if your traffic is sensitive enough for one, you should do both. There are rare exceptions. It may be worthwhile authenticating NTP traffic, for example, to ensure that your time sources are valid, while the actual time of day information in the packet payload is not a sensitive piece of information. However, the extra configuration required to do both at the same time on the router is minimal, and if your router's CPU can't easily handle the load of both encrypting and authenticating, it is probably not the right router for the job. So if you are going to either authenticate or encrypt your traffic, we recommend using both together for added security.

In this transform set, we have also instructed the router to use IPSec Transport mode:

```
Router1(cfg-crypto-trans)#mode transport
```

By default, IPSec connections will use Tunnel mode, which means that the two devices will set up their own tunnel for IPSec to use. This actually uses the IP-in-IP tunnel protocol that we mentioned in the introduction to this chapter. However, in this example we want to use a GRE tunnel between the routers instead, and simply authenticate and encrypt the GRE packets. This requires Transport mode.

The main reasons for using GRE tunnels instead of IPSec's native tunnel mode are simplicity and flexibility. Using a GRE tunnel between these routers allows us to take advantage of some of the useful GRE features, if we want them. For example, we can easily use a GRE tunnel to pass other protocols such as IPX or Appletalk, and we can use the techniques discussed in Recipe 12.3 to pass routing protocol traffic through the encrypted tunnel. And the GRE tunnel makes debugging much easier as we can simply disable the encryption and ping through the tunnel, or ping the tunnel destination addresses to verify connectivity without the complications of authentication and encryption. If the other end of this tunnel was a workstation instead of a router, however, as in Recipe 12.7, we would have to use Tunnel mode.

The next step is to define a crypto map that combines all of these elements. The following set of commands defines a map called TUNNELMAP. The number following this name is a sequence number, similar to the route map sequence numbers that we discussed in Chapters 6, 7, and 8. This allows you to associate many peers with a single router interface, by creating several different map clauses with different sequence numbers, all associated with the same map.

The keyword *ipsec-isakmp* on the end of the *crypto map* command tells the router that this map will apply to IPSec connections that use ISAKMP for key management. You could also specify *ipsec-manual* if you wanted to do the key management manually. But in general, we don't recommend manual key management because it is so much trouble to get right, while ISAKMP automates most of the work for you:

```
Router1(config)#crypto map TUNNELMAP 10 ipsec-isakmp
% NOTE: This new crypto map will remain disabled until a peer
    and a valid access list have been configured.
Router1(config-crypto-map)#set peer 172.16.2.1
Router1(config-crypto-map)#set transform-set TUNNEL-TRANSFORM
Router1(config-crypto-map)#match address 102
Router1(config-crypto-map)#exit
Router1(config)#access-list 102 permit gre host 172.16.1.1 host 172.16.2.1
```

The crypto map defines an IPSec peer device by its IP address. If you are using hostnames instead of IP addresses, as we discussed earlier in this recipe, you should specify the peer's hostname instead of an IP address here. The map also selects the appropriate transform set, and matches on a particular set of IP addresses, defined in this case by access-list 102.

The access list tells IPSec what packets it should apply this transform set to. In this case, we specify a source IP address of 172.16.1.1, which is the IP address of the tunnel source, and 172.16.2.1, which is the tunnel's destination address. And because of the *gre* keyword, this access list will only match on GRE tunnel packets with these source and destination addresses.

Note that on the other router, the peer address is 172.16.1.1, and the access-list reverses the source and destination addresses:

```
Router2(config)#access-list 102 permit gre host 172.16.2.1 host 172.16.1.1
```

Then, with all of the IPSec and ISAKMP configuration in place, we can finally create the tunnel and turn on the encryption. The tunnel configuration is similar to what we used in Recipe 12.1:

```
Router1(config)#interface Tunnel1
Router1(config-if)#ip address 192.168.1.1 255.255.255.252
Router1(config-if)#tunnel source 172.16.1.1
Router1(config-if)#tunnel destination 172.16.2.1
Router1(config-if)#exit
Router1(config)#interface FastEthernet0/0
Router1(config-if)#ip address 172.16.1.1 255.255.255.0
Router1(config-if)#ip access-group 101 in
Router1(config-if)#crypto map TUNNELMAP
Router1(config-if)#exit
Router1(config)#access-list 101 permit gre host 172.16.2.1 host 172.16.1.1
Router1(config)#access-list 101 permit esp host 172.16.2.1 host 172.16.1.1
Router1(config)#access-list 101 permit udp host 172.16.2.1 host 172.16.1.1 eq isakmp
Router1(config)#access-list 101 permit ahp host 172.16.2.1 host 172.16.1.1
Router1(config)#access-list 101 deny ip any any log
```

It's extremely important to notice that we have applied the crypto map to the interface that will be receiving the GRE packets, and not to the tunnel itself. This is because IPSec is encrypting the GRE tunnel packets rather than the payload of those packets. For one thing, the GRE tunnel's payload is not necessarily an IP packet. However, even when they are IP packets, the source and destination IP addresses of the GRE payload could be devices somewhere behind the router. This breaks the essential requirement for IPSec's Transport mode, which is that the source and destination IP addresses must be the devices themselves. So the only way you could successfully apply the crypto map to the tunnel interface would be by using an IPSec tunnel inside of the GRE tunnel, which would not be very efficient.

Also notice the access-list that we have applied to the external interface in this example.

We have done this to more accurately simulate the configuration for running encrypted site-to-site VPNs through the public Internet. In such situations you will need to have some sort of inbound traffic restrictions on your router to block unwanted traffic. This access-list shows the types of packets that you should allow your router to accept from the Internet to support the VPN. You will probably have other rules in practice as well.

The first line of access-list 101 permits the GRE packets themselves. Recall that we will be encrypting the GRE packets, so you are unlikely to see GRE packets in the steady state. However, we like to include a rule like this because it makes troubleshooting easier. As we mentioned above, you can simply remove the crypto map command from the external interfaces and verify connectivity between the tunnel interfaces:

```
Router1(config)#access-list 101 permit gre host 172.16.2.1 host 172.16.1.1
```

The second line permits the Encapsulation Security Protocol (ESP), which contains the encrypted packet payloads:

```
Router1(config)#access-list 101 permit esp host 172.16.2.1 host 172.16.1.1
```

The next line allows UDP Port 500, which is used by the ISAKMP protocol for establishing the IPSec connection:

```
Router1(config)#access-list 101 permit udp host 172.16.2.1 host 172.16.1.1 eq isakmp
```

We also allow Authentication Header Protocol (AHP):

```
Router1(config)#access-list 101 permit ahp host 172.16.2.1 host 172.16.1.1
```

You can see that the encryption is working properly by looking at the output of the following command on either router:

```
Router2#show crypto engine connections active

   ID Interface        IP-Address     State  Algorithm           Encrypt  Decrypt
    3 FastEthernet0/0   172.16.2.1     set    HMAC_SHA+AES_256_C        0    0
 2000 FastEthernet0/0   172.16.2.1     set    HMAC_SHA                  0    522
 2001 FastEthernet0/0   172.16.2.1     set    HMAC_SHA                859    0
 2002 FastEthernet0/0   172.16.2.1     set    AES_256_CBC               0    522
 2003 FastEthernet0/0   172.16.2.1     set    AES_256_CBC             859    0

Router2#
```

This shows that the router has received and decrypted 522 encrypted packets from the peer we defined, and it has sent 859. It also shows we are using the SHA hash algorithm for authentication and 256-byte AES for encryption in the Algorithm column.

See Also

Recipe 12.1; Recipe 12.3; Recipe 12.9

12.6 Creating an Encrypted VPN Between the LAN Interfaces of Two Routers

Problem

You want to create an encrypted VPN through the Internet by connecting the LAN interfaces of two routers using pre-shared keys.

Solution

In this example, we show how to use IPSec in tunnel mode to encrypt traffic between the LAN interfaces of two routers. Here is the configuration of the first router:

```
Router1#configure terminal
Enter configuration commands, one per line.  End with CNTL/Z.
Router1(config)#crypto isakmp policy 10
Router1(config-isakmp)#encr aes 256
```

```
Router1(config-isakmp)#authentication pre-share
Router1(config-isakmp)#group 2
Router1(config-isakmp)#exit
Router1(config)#crypto isakmp key TUNNELKEY01 address 172.16.2.1 no-xauth
Router1(config)#crypto ipsec transform-set LAN2LAN-TRANSFORM ah-sha-hmac esp-aes 256
Router1(cfg-crypto-trans)#exit
Router1(config)#access-list 102 permit gre host 172.16.1.1 host 172.16.2.1
Router1(config)#crypto map LAN2LANMAP 10 ipsec-isakmp
% NOTE: This new crypto map will remain disabled until a peer
    and a valid access list have been configured.
Router1(config-crypto-map)#set peer 172.16.2.1
Router1(config-crypto-map)#set transform-set LAN2LAN-TRANSFORM
Router1(config-crypto-map)#match address 103
Router1(config-crypto-map)#exit
Router1(config)#access-list 103 permit ip 192.168.16.0 0.0.0.255 192.168.15.0 0.0.0.255
Router1(config)#interface FastEthernet0/1
Router1(config-if)#ip address 192.168.16.1 255.255.255.0
Router1(config-if)#exit
Router1(config)#interface FastEthernet0/0
Router1(config-if)#ip address 172.16.1.1 255.255.255.0
Router1(config-if)#ip access-group 101 in
Router1(config-if)#crypto map LAN2LANMAP
Router1(config-if)#exit
Router1(config)#ip route 0.0.0.0 0.0.0.0 172.16.1.2
Router1(config)#access-list 101 permit esp host 172.16.2.1 host 172.16.1.1
Router1(config)#access-list 101 permit udp host 172.16.2.1 host 172.16.1.1 eq isakmp
Router1(config)#access-list 101 permit ahp host 172.16.2.1 host 172.16.1.1
Router1(config)#access-list 101 deny ip any any log
Router1(config)#end
Router1#
```

The configuration for the second router is similar:

```
Router2#configure terminal
Enter configuration commands, one per line.  End with CNTL/Z.
Router2(config)#crypto isakmp policy 10
Router2(config-isakmp)#encr aes 256
Router2(config-isakmp)#authentication pre-share
Router2(config-isakmp)#group 2
Router2(config-isakmp)#exit
Router2(config)#crypto isakmp key TUNNELKEY01 address 172.16.1.1
Router2(config)#crypto ipsec transform-set LAN2LAN-TRANSFORM ah-sha-hmac esp-aes 256
Router2(cfg-crypto-trans)#exit
Router2(config)#crypto map LAN2LANMAP 10 ipsec-isakmp
% NOTE: This new crypto map will remain disabled until a peer
    and a valid access list have been configured.
Router2(config-crypto-map)#set peer 172.16.1.1
Router2(config-crypto-map)#set transform-set LAN2LAN-TRANSFORM
Router2(config-crypto-map)#match address 103
Router2(config-crypto-map)#exit
Router2(config)#access-list 103 permit ip 192.168.15.0 0.0.0.255 192.168.16.0 0.0.0.255

Router2(config)#interface FastEthernet0/1
Router2(config-if)#description Internal LAN
```

```
Router2(config-if)#ip address 192.168.15.1 255.255.255.0
Router2(config-if)#exit
Router2(config)#interface FastEthernet0/0
Router2(config-if)#description Connection to Internet
Router2(config-if)#ip address 172.16.2.1 255.255.255.0
Router2(config-if)#crypto map LAN2LANMAP
Router2(config-if)#exit
Router2(config)#ip route 0.0.0.0 0.0.0.0 172.16.2.2
Router2(config)#access-list 101 permit esp host 172.16.1.1 host 172.16.2.1
Router2(config)#access-list 101 permit udp host 172.16.1.1 host 172.16.2.1 eq isakmp
Router2(config)#access-list 101 permit ahp host 172.16.1.1 host 172.16.2.1
Router2(config)#access-list 101 deny ip any any log
Router2(config)#end
Router2#
```

Discussion

The net effect of Recipe 12.5 was to create a routable encrypted VPN link between two routers. Another common way of handling site-to-site VPNs is to take advantage of the native IPSec tunnel capability to create a bridged connection between the inside LAN interfaces of the two routers, which is what we do in this recipe.

Much of this example is nearly identical to the one shown in Recipe 12.3, so we will just focus on the differences. The first difference is in the definition of the transform-set:

```
Router1(config)#crypto ipsec transform-set LAN2LAN-TRANSFORM ah-sha-hmac esp-aes 256
Router1(cfg-crypto-trans)#exit
```

The key difference between this transform-set and the one in the previous recipe is to look at what's not there. In Recipe 12.3, our transform-set looked like this:

```
Router1(config)#crypto ipsec transform-set TUNNEL-TRANSFORM ah-sha-hmac esp-aes 256
Router1(cfg-crypto-trans)#mode transport
Router1(cfg-crypto-trans)#exit
```

In this recipe, we want to use IPSec tunnel mode instead of transport mode. We could include a *mode tunnel* command in our transform set definition, but since that's the default, we have left it out to get the same effect.

The next difference comes in the crypto map configuration, and is also subtle:

```
Router1(config)#crypto map LAN2LANMAP 10 ipsec-isakmp
% NOTE: This new crypto map will remain disabled until a peer
    and a valid access list have been configured.
Router1(config-crypto-map)#set peer 172.16.2.1
Router1(config-crypto-map)#set transform-set LAN2LAN-TRANSFORM
Router1(config-crypto-map)#match address 103
Router1(config-crypto-map)#exit
Router1(config)#access-list 103 permit ip 192.168.16.0 0.0.0.255 192.168.15.0 0.0.0.255
```

The principle difference here is that our access-list doesn't match GRE packets on the external Internet-facing interfaces of the routers. Instead it matches all IP packets on the internal LAN interfaces.

The remainders of the configurations are essentially the same as in the previous recipe. But the effect is very different. In this case, we wind up with two routers that bridge their internal LAN interfaces. Any packet matching access-list 103 will be automatically picked up and bridged to the other router. Conversely, in the previous recipe, traffic between the LAN segments at the two different sites was routed across the tunnel.

Note that this is not a fully functional Layer 2 bridge. In particular, it only passes IP traffic that happens to match the defined access-list. If you look at this access-list, you will see that it specifies different IP subnets for the source and destination addresses, which is not how you would normally construct a Layer 2 bridge. But the nice thing about doing this is that it automatically makes bridging loops impossible, which in turn means that we don't need to run Spanning Tree.

In general, we prefer to route rather than bridge. The biggest reason for this is that it allows us to run a routing protocol across the encrypted GRE tunnel. This in turn leads to several benefits:

- The routing protocol Hello packets will ensure that the ISAKMP keys are always refreshed.
- The ability to log neighbor changes makes it possible to track exactly when a VPN goes down and comes back up, which is highly useful in troubleshooting.
- In cases when there are three or more sites interconnected by VPNs, you can configure a redundant partial mesh of VPNs for relaying packets between sites.

See Also

Recipe 12.3

12.7 Generating RSA Keys

Problem

You want to create a shareable RSA key for authentication or encryption.

Solution

First, you must create the keys on both devices. We recommend using at least 1024-bit keys in production networks:

```
Router1#configure terminal
Enter configuration commands, one per line.  End with CNTL/Z.
Router1(config)#crypto key generate rsa
The name for the keys will be: Router1.oreilly.com
Choose the size of the key modulus in the range of 360 to 2048 for your
  General Purpose Keys. Choosing a key modulus greater than 512 may take
  a few minutes.
```

```
How many bits in the modulus [512]: 1024
Generating RSA keys ...
[OK]

Router1(config)#end
Router1#show crypto key mypubkey rsa
% Key pair was generated at: 01:19:45 EST Mar 1 2003
Key name: Router1.oreilly.com
 Usage: General Purpose Key
 Key Data:
  30819F30 0D06092A 864886F7 0D010101 05000381 8D003081 89028181 00E68338
  D561B2D1 7B8B75D6 7B34F6AF 1710B00B 5B6E9E8D D7183BE6 F08A6342 054EADFC
  B764DF9C 4592B891 522727F2 14233B47 8F757134 24F03DB3 833C5988 312B11E9
  FB6E0E20 4579C0A4 F2062353 4F1C8CE4 410EE57B 9FCEE784 DA7E3852 408E9742
  2584DF56 67293F3F F76B6A96 C4D518FB 1A0114BF E2449838 BE5794E2 37020301 0001
% Key pair was generated at: 01:19:52 EST Mar 1 2003
Key name: Router1.oreilly.com.server
 Usage: Encryption Key
 Key Data:
  307C300D 06092A86 4886F70D 01010105 00036B00 30680261 00BD928A BD5637E6
  2265621C 3AC57138 911CA27D 11F40AA1 E657EA26 6EBF654C 952A3319 D421A33C
  E2ECA87E CD7E050C 8A8FE64D B73954EA BF2ED639 BC6A8F74 5B9550EA 4119E796
  A97430E2 4B1BF7D3 ED1469FF AEA83690 A0FEA871 BBFBE8AD 19020301 0001
Router1#
```

And then you can use cut and paste to copy this manually generated key into the other device:

```
Router2#configure terminal
Enter configuration commands, one per line.  End with CNTL/Z.
Router2(config)#crypto key pubkey-chain rsa
Router2(config-pubkey-chain)#addressed-key 192.168.99.1
Router2(config-pubkey-key)#address 192.168.99.1
Router2(config-pubkey-key)#key-string
Enter a public key as a hexidecimal number ....

Router2(config-pubkey)#30819F30 0D06092A 864886F7 0D010101 05000381 8D003081 89028181
00E68338
Router2(config-pubkey)#D561B2D1 7B8B75D6 7B34F6AF 1710B00B 5B6E9E8D D7183BE6 F08A6342
054EADFC
Router2(config-pubkey)#B764DF9C 4592B891 522727F2 14233B47 8F757134 24F03DB3 833C5988
312B11E9
Router2(config-pubkey)#FB6E0E20 4579C0A4 F2062353 4F1C8CE4 410EE57B 9FCEE784 DA7E3852
408E9742
Router2(config-pubkey)#2584DF56 67293F3F F76B6A96 C4D518FB 1A0114BF E2449838 BE5794E2
37020301 0001
Router2(config-pubkey)#quit
Router2(config-pubkey-key)#exit
Router2(config-pubkey-chain)#exit
Router2(config)#end
Router2#show crypto key pubkey-chain rsa address 192.168.99.1
Key address: 192.168.99.1
 Usage: General Purpose Key
 Source: Manually entered
 Data:
```

```
30819F30 0D06092A 864886F7 0D010101 05000381 8D003081 89028181 00E68338
D561B2D1 7B8B75D6 7B34F6AF 1710B00B 5B6E9E8D D7183BE6 F08A6342 054EADFC
B764DF9C 4592B891 522727F2 14233B47 8F757134 24F03DB3 833C5988 312B11E9
FB6E0E20 4579C0A4 F2062353 4F1C8CE4 410EE57B 9FCEE784 DA7E3852 408E9742
2584DF56 67293F3F F76B6A96 C4D518FB 1A0114BF E2449838 BE5794E2 37020301 0001
```

```
Router2#
```

Discussion

The first thing to notice is that the output includes the following line:

```
The name for the keys will be: Router1.oreilly.com
```

The router name and domain name are always included in the key. So it is critical to define these two values before generating the keys. If you generate the keys first and then change the router's name or domain, the keys may no longer work:

```
Router1(config)#hostname Router1
Router1(config)#ip domain-name oreilly.com
```

When you use the *crypto key generate* command to create new keys, the router must delete any existing keys:

```
Router1(config)#crypto key generate rsa
The name for the keys will be: Router1.oreilly.com
% You already have RSA keys defined for Router1.oreilly.com.
% Do you really want to replace them? [yes/no]: yes
Choose the size of the key modulus in the range of 360 to 2048 for your
   General Purpose Keys. Choosing a key modulus greater than 512 may take
   a few minutes.

How many bits in the modulus [512]: 1024
Generating RSA keys ...
[OK]

Router1(config)#
```

This has the side effect that, during key generation, any services on the router currently using these keys will be temporarily disabled. Key generation can take a considerable length of time, depending on the model of router and the size of the key modulus. We have seen a low-end access router take as long as an hour to generate a key with a very large modulus for greater security. During this time, the router's CPU load was extremely high. So we urge caution when using this command.

You can remove existing keys with the *crypto key zeroize* command:

```
Router1(config)#crypto key zeroize rsa
% Keys to be removed are named Router1.oreilly.com.
Do you really want to remove these keys? [yes/no]: yes
Router1(config)#
```

If the router has any services that are using the deleted keys, it will automatically disable them until you generate new keys.

You can also generate special usage keys as follows:

```
Router1(config)#crypto key generate rsa usage-keys
The name for the keys will be: Router1.oreilly.com
% You already have RSA keys defined for Router1.oreilly.com.
% Do you really want to replace them? [yes/no]: yes
Choose the size of the key modulus in the range of 360 to 2048 for your
  Signature Keys. Choosing a key modulus greater than 512 may take
  a few minutes.

How many bits in the modulus [512]: 1024
Generating RSA keys ...
[OK]
Choose the size of the key modulus in the range of 360 to 2048 for your
  Encryption Keys. Choosing a key modulus greater than 512 may take
  a few minutes.

How many bits in the modulus [512]: 1024
Generating RSA keys ...
[OK]

Router1(config)#
```

This command creates separate authentication signature and encryption keys. Note that we have created a 1024-bit key in this example. In general, longer keys are more secure, but also require considerably more computing time to generate. SSH Communications Security Corporation, the original developer of the SSH protocol, currently recommends a key length of 2048 bits for most applications.

You can look at the public keys with the *show crypto key* command:

```
Router1#show crypto key mypubkey rsa
% Key pair was generated at: 01:29:04 EST Mar 1 2003
Key name: Router1.oreilly.com
 Usage: Signature Key
 Key Data:
  30819F30 0D06092A 864886F7 0D010101 05000381 8D003081 89028181 00AAED98
  0E454C8F ED9DB93E 312B00BD FF561C49 5480344A 094F0EA8 0D994051 AC627CF2
  5FA7F802 DB0A1206 4EB8F8E5 122C9B2D 0F3A20D8 C0E90280 D4F6518A 9C6C2E48
  A570D05A AE2881CA B9366990 931C4A7E EDC6B352 13815B91 3A02B44E 4655DE6D
  1CB5AB35 058B60AA 4639B696 A8EE735E DA15B300 B8A0CE51 7C42B73A 53020301 0001
% Key pair was generated at: 01:29:11 EST Mar 1 2003
Key name: Router1.oreilly.com
 Usage: Encryption Key
 Key Data:
  30819F30 0D06092A 864886F7 0D010101 05000381 8D003081 89028181 00D18F99
  EC2A5754 C1FEF911 E16BFD80 6C3E9517 42716B78 99692618 B57B529B A9C19B23
  6D4BF3CE 39728DEF 2B3D10F9 3DABBDFD 8CAB09F7 0A56768C 053BB4AF 7F224E44
  FA341851 10152A86 28C2084F C13E0738 4C478BED 9960E229 CB112077 097F3DC9
  DD40D109 0A513D31 FF0FD51D B3515CEA F81738B6 5BB02FF6 812A01AC F7020301 0001
% Key pair was generated at: 01:29:14 EST Mar 1 2003
Key name: Router1.oreilly.com.server
 Usage: Encryption Key
 Key Data:
  307C300D 06092A86 4886F70D 01010105 00036B00 30680261 00B43311 D047EFBC
```

```
314C57DB 93F3E755 5CEBF4B5 D0258169 6DAC695B A0F5DA35 C6C7B106 C2BB7863
0201B68A 7C2F3313 47223065 BDF84692 BF974F2E E4037D5D C976DB3A 231D2603
6DE8CDCE 8EAD613E 5C984091 55A6B0F5 920E285B 6E4ED34E 31020301 0001
Router1#
```

As you can see, the router now has a signature key and an encryption key where it previously had only a general purpose key. However, it is important to remember that this is only the public key. There is also a corresponding private key that you cannot view on the router. The router keeps this key in its NVRAM storage and sets file permissions so nobody can read it. The private key is what the router uses to encrypt things that it sends. The public key can decrypt anything encrypted with the private key. Every device that this router shares encrypted information with will need a copy of the public key, but the private key is secret.

As a side effect of this, the public key provides an excellent authentication system. If a remote device's public key successfully decrypts a message from that device, then you know that this message must have been encrypted with that device's private key. And, consequently, if the private key is really private, the message must actually have been sent by that device.

When you use these keys on routers, we highly recommend using the cut-and-paste feature on your terminal rather than trying to type all of this in manually. A single typographical error in this sequence will make the key useless. Note, however, that there is an inherent security risk in copying and pasting a key like this over a network. If you are using an insecure protocol like Telnet, the packet can be intercepted, and the key information is easily extracted. So you should avoid doing this over untrusted networks, or you should use a more secure access method such as SSH to access the routers. We discuss using SSH for router access in Recipe 3.20.

In Recipe 12.6, we show an example of how to use RSA keys.

See Also

Recipe 3.20; Recipe 12.6

12.8   Creating a Router-to-Router VPN with RSA Keys

Problem

You want to create an encrypted VPN between two routers using RSA keys.

Solution

As in Recipe 12.3, we will use IPSec Transport mode and a GRE tunnel for this encrypted router-to-router connection:

```
Router1#configure terminal
Enter configuration commands, one per line.  End with CNTL/Z.
Router1(config)#crypto key pubkey-chain rsa
Router1(config-pubkey-chain)#addressed-key 172.16.2.1
Router1(config-pubkey-key)#address 172.16.2.1
```

```
Router1(config-pubkey-key)#key-string
Enter a public key as a hexidecimal number ....
Router1(config-pubkey)#30819F30 0D06092A 864886F7 0D010101 05000381 8D003081 89028181
00EB0AB2
Router1(config-pubkey)#EA33B519 0CD95EFF EDFD4723 BED73640 97981CC0 1FC83FBF 5C6DF97C
8CB8CE0A
Router1(config-pubkey)#C5FE959D 1E055002 83B92EF4 35B69545 C3217E5F E0C32A73 44FD2373
15979E77
Router1(config-pubkey)#75598BE0 B4A4E7B2 3C318C2D 3BF3B192 8B71D8C9 A1E0F929 0E84BDAD
EC909833
Router1(config-pubkey)#BC425170 400BD26A 319E632F 4E9649F5 BA7ADA40 5A94B09C 05F8414E
33020301 0001
Router1(config-pubkey)#quit
Router1(config-pubkey-key)#exit
Router1(config-pubkey-chain)#exit

Router1(config)#crypto isakmp policy 100
Router1(config-isakmp)#encryption aes 256
Router1(config-isakmp)#authentication rsa-encr
Router1(config-isakmp)#group 2
Router1(config-isakmp)#exit
Router1(config)#crypto ipsec transform-set TUNNEL-TRANSFORM ah-sha-hmac esp-aes 256
Router1(cfg-crypto-trans)#mode transport
Router1(cfg-crypto-trans)#exit
Router1(config)#crypto map TUNNEL-RSA 10 ipsec-isakmp
% NOTE: This new crypto map will remain disabled until a peer
    and a valid access list have been configured.
Router1(config-crypto-map)#set peer 172.16.2.1
Router1(config-crypto-map)#set transform-set TUNNEL-TRANSFORM
Router1(config-crypto-map)#match address 102
Router1(config-crypto-map)#exit
Router1(config)#access-list 102 permit gre host 172.16.1.1 host 172.16.2.1
Router1(config)#interface Tunnel1
Router1(config-if)#ip address 192.168.1.1 255.255.255.252
Router1(config-if)#tunnel source 172.16.1.1
Router1(config-if)#tunnel destination 172.16.2.1
Router1(config-if)#exit
Router1(config)#interface FastEthernet0/0
Router1(config-if)#ip address 172.16.1.1 255.255.255.0
Router1(config-if)#ip access-group 101 in
Router1(config-if)#crypto map TUNNEL-RSA
Router1(config-if)#exit
Router1(config)#access-list 101 permit gre host 172.16.2.1 host 172.16.1.1
Router1(config)#access-list 101 permit esp host 172.16.2.1 host 172.16.1.1
Router1(config)#access-list 101 permit udp host 172.16.2.1 host 172.16.1.1 eq isakmp
Router1(config)#access-list 101 permit ahp host 172.16.2.1 host 172.16.1.1
Router1(config)#access-list 101 deny ip any any log
Router1(config)#end
Router1#
```

And here is the corresponding configuration for the other router:

```
Router2#configure terminal
Enter configuration commands, one per line.  End with CNTL/Z.
Router2(config)#crypto key pubkey-chain rsa
```

```
Router2(config-pubkey-chain)#addressed-key 172.16.1.1
Router2(config-pubkey-key)#address 172.16.1.1
Router2(config-pubkey-key)#key-string
Enter a public key as a hexidecimal number ....

Router2(config-pubkey)#30819F30 0D06092A 864886F7 0D010101 05000381 8D003081 89028181
00A0830E
Router2(config-pubkey)#01E4B6E1 08823E41 8A98A7F4 DB0E6277 1E7AA500 F7B620CA 49BCBEBA
B0A0455A
Router2(config-pubkey)#114BA6B9 5ADE0D2E 7DC3EFC1 D7D07015 01C83E08 7305ED3C 71F04B44
31A1C574
Router2(config-pubkey)#C0E6ACA2 C191DB07 3D347F88 2D2884BF 99C2AF80 45BC1BE9 6D2BF684
B60C04E6
Router2(config-pubkey)#0F3D5C09 7C26694F 8FB75F90 2FA1DF46 94401D54 82ACA366 E621DD04
4B020301 0001
Router2(config-pubkey)#quit
Router2(config-pubkey-key)#exit
Router2(config-pubkey-chain)#exit
Router2(config)#crypto isakmp policy 100
Router2(config-isakmp)#encryption aes 256
Router2(config-isakmp)#authentication rsa-encr
Router2(config-isakmp)#group 2
Router2(config-isakmp)#exit
Router2(config)#crypto ipsec transform-set TUNNEL-TRANSFORM ah-sha-hmac esp-aes 256
Router2(cfg-crypto-trans)#mode transport
Router2(cfg-crypto-trans)#exit
Router2(config)#crypto map TUNNEL-RSA 10 ipsec-isakmp
Router2(config-crypto-map)#set peer 172.16.1.1
Router2(config-crypto-map)#set transform-set TUNNEL-TRANSFORM
Router2(config-crypto-map)#match address 102
Router2(config-crypto-map)#exit
Router2(config)#access-list 102 permit gre host 172.16.2.1 host 172.16.1.1
Router2(config)#interface Tunnel1
Router2(config-if)#ip address 192.168.1.2 255.255.255.252
Router2(config-if)#tunnel source 172.16.2.1
Router2(config-if)#tunnel destination 172.16.1.1
Router2(config-if)#exit
Router2(config)#interface FastEthernet0/0
Router2(config-if)#ip address 172.16.1.1 255.255.255.0
Router2(config-if)#ip access-group 101 in
Router2(config-if)#crypto map TUNNEL-RSA
Router2(config-if)#exit
Router2(config)#access-list 101 permit gre host 172.16.1.1 host 172.16.2.1
Router2(config)#access-list 101 permit esp host 172.16.1.1 host 172.16.2.1
Router2(config)#access-list 101 permit udp host 172.16.1.1 host 172.16.2.1 eq isakmp
Router2(config)#access-list 101 permit ahp host 172.16.1.1 host 172.16.2.1
Router2(config)#access-list 101 deny ip any any log
Router2(config)#end
Router2#
```

Discussion

This recipe is similar to 12.5, except that here we use RSA keys for authentication
and encryption instead of pre-shared keys. This technique is more secure but more
time-consuming to configure.

The first step is to create a set of RSA encryption keys using the methods discussed in Recipe 12.5. We took the keys that we generated in this way and entered them into the router configurations. So, for example, we created the key on *Router1* as follows:

```
Router1#configure terminal
Enter configuration commands, one per line.  End with CNTL/Z.
Router1(config)#crypto key generate rsa
% You already have RSA keys defined named Router1.oreilly.com.
% Do you really want to replace them? [yes/no]: yes
Choose the size of the key modulus in the range of 360 to 2048 for your
  General Purpose Keys. Choosing a key modulus greater than 512 may take
  a few minutes.

How many bits in the modulus [512]: 1024
% Generating 1024 bit RSA keys ...[OK]

Router1(config)#exit
Router1#show crypto key mypubkey rsa
% Key pair was generated at: 14:59:44 UTC Jul 20 2006
Key name: Router1.oreilly.com
 Usage: General Purpose Key
 Key is not exportable.
 Key Data:
  30819F30 0D06092A 864886F7 0D010101 05000381 8D003081 89028181 00A0830E
  01E4B6E1 08823E41 8A98A7F4 DB0E6277 1E7AA500 F7B620CA 49BCBEBA B0A0455A
  114BA6B9 5ADE0D2E 7DC3EFC1 D7D07015 01C83E08 7305ED3C 71F04B44 31A1C574
  C0E6ACA2 C191DB07 3D347F88 2D2884BF 99C2AF80 45BC1BE9 6D2BF684 B60C04E6
  0F3D5C09 7C26694F 8FB75F90 2FA1DF46 94401D54 82ACA366 E621DD04 4B020301 0001
% Key pair was generated at: 14:59:51 UTC Jul 20 2006
Key name: Router1.oreilly.com.server
 Usage: Encryption Key
 Key is not exportable.
 Key Data:
  307C300D 06092A86 4886F70D 01010105 00036B00 30680261 009ED5E0 43DAC50E
  6866A933 07690DB6 BA02B4E2 4CF331AA D1818C34 5B8482B1 8174A365 80EBC4CC
  E4C88354 261C2FE8 C20DC047 621DB954 9294FD68 6B2A3C16 250402ED EFFE2A48
  9FCDB94B 72AB8D1A A45CD06A D2495940 EB7FACE8 AFA3886F 3F020301 0001
Router1#
```

Note that in this example we used the default 512-bit key. However, in production networks, we recommend using 1024 or more bit keys.

Then we took the general purpose key from this output and entered it into the other router as follows:

```
Router2(config)#crypto key pubkey-chain rsa
Router2(config-pubkey-chain)#addressed-key 172.16.1.1
Router2(config-pubkey-key)#address 172.16.1.1
Router2(config-pubkey-key)#key-string
Enter a public key as a hexidecimal number ....

Router2(config-pubkey)#30819F30 0D06092A 864886F7 0D010101 05000381 8D003081 89028181
00A0830E
```

```
Router2(config-pubkey)#01E4B6E1 08823E41 8A98A7F4 DB0E6277 1E7AA500 F7B620CA 49BCBEBA
B0A0455A
Router2(config-pubkey)#114BA6B9 5ADE0D2E 7DC3EFC1 D7D07015 01C83E08 7305ED3C 71F04B44
31A1C574
Router2(config-pubkey)#C0E6ACA2 C191DB07 3D347F88 2D2884BF 99C2AF80 45BC1BE9 6D2BF684
B60C04E6
Router2(config-pubkey)#0F3D5C09 7C26694F 8FB75F90 2FA1DF46 94401D54 82ACA366 E621DD04
4B020301 0001
Router2(config-pubkey)#quit
Router2(config-pubkey-key)#exit
Router2(config-pubkey-chain)#exit
```

And then we repeated the procedure on the other router.

With the keys in place, we proceeded to tell the routers how to use these keys to create an IPSec connection. Even though we are using a manually entered key, the two routers still need to use ISAKMP. The important difference between this example and the one in Recipe 12.3 is that here we are using RSA authentication keys. So we need to tell the routers to use this key method in the ISAKMP policy:

```
Router1(config)#crypto isakmp policy 100
Router1(config-isakmp)#encryption aes 256
Router1(config-isakmp)#authentication rsa-encr
Router1(config-isakmp)#group 2
```

After that, the remainder of the configuration is essentially identical to what we showed in Recipe 12.3. So it is also relatively straightforward to combine this recipe with Recipe 12.4 to use RSA authentication keys for a LAN-to-LAN IPSec tunnel.

See Also

Recipe 12.3; Recipe 12.4; Recipe 12.5

12.9 Creating a VPN Between a Workstation and a Router

Problem

You want to make a VPN from a remote workstation to a router.

Solution

There are several steps to configuring a router to accept IPSec VPN connections from remote PCs. The following discussion doesn't include requirements for the PC's software configuration, just the router's configuration. You should refer the software vendor's documentation for information about configuring the workstation software:

```
Router1#configure terminal
Enter configuration commands, one per line.  End with CNTL/Z.
Router1(config)#aaa new-model
```

```
Router1(config)#aaa authentication login default group tacacs+
Router1(config)#aaa authentication enable default group tacacs+
Router1(config)#tacacs-server host 172.25.1.1
Router1(config)#tacacs-server key COOKBOOK
Router1(config)#crypto isakmp policy 10
Router1(config-isakmp)#encryption 3des
Router1(config-isakmp)#authentication pre-share
Router1(config-isakmp)#group 2
Router1(config-isakmp)#exit
Router1(config)#crypto ipsec transform-set VPN-TRANSFORMS ah-sha-hmac esp-sha-hmac
esp-3des
Router1(cfg-crypto-trans)#mode tunnel
Router1(cfg-crypto-trans)#exit
Router1(config)#crypto dynamic-map VPN-USER-MAP 50
Router1(config-crypto-map)#description A dynamic crypto map for VPN users
Router1(config-crypto-map)#match address 115
Router1(config-crypto-map)#set transform-set VPN-TRANSFORMS
Router1(config-crypto-map)#exit
Router1(config)#access-list 115 deny any 224.0.0.0 35.255.255.255
Router1(config)#access-list 115 deny any 172.25.1.255 0.0.0.0
Router1(config)#access-list 115 permit any any
Router1(config)#crypto map CRYPTOMAP 10 ipsec-isakmp dynamic VPN-USER-MAP
Router1(config)#interface FastEthernet0/1
Router1(config-if)#ip address 172.25.1.5 255.255.255.0
Router1(config-if)#crypto map CRYPTOMAP
Router1(config-if)#exit
Router1(config)#exit
Router1#
```

Discussion

The first few lines in this example are the *aaa* and *tacacs-server* commands, which are described in more detail in Chapter 4. This simply sets up username authentication for all incoming VPN connections, and allows you to get these authentication credentials from a central server running the TACACS+ protocol.

We are using AAA and TACACS+ in this configuration to supply the pre-shared keys that ISAKMP will use to set up its SA for this VPN. This is similar to the use of pre-shared keys in Recipe 12.3, but here we expect to have a large number of remote VPN users, so it is administratively easier if we manage them from the TACACS+ server instead of on the router.

Then we set up the ISAKMP policy as follows:

```
Router1(config)#crypto isakmp policy 10
Router1(config-isakmp)#encryption 3des
Router1(config-isakmp)#authentication pre-share
Router1(config-isakmp)#group 2
```

This defines the policy for authentication and encryption keys, and is identical to the ISAKMP policy we used in Recipe 12.3. We selected these particular policy parameters because they are required for the Cisco Easy VPN Remote software. If you are using different client software, you may need to use different settings. This policy is also identical to the one we used in Recipe 12.3.

After doing this, we need to define the IPSec VPN properties. We begin by defining the *transform set* that we want to use for these VPN connections. We will call this transform set VPN-TRANSFORMS:

```
Router1(config)#crypto ipsec transform-set VPN-TRANSFORMS ah-sha-hmac esp-sha-hmac
esp-3des
Router1(cfg-crypto-trans)#mode tunnel
```

The VPN will use the *esp-sha-hmac* and *esp-3des* transforms. This transform set is almost the same as the one in Recipe 12.3, but this time we have specified that this VPN should use tunnel mode with the *mode* command. In Recipe 12.3, IPSec was used to encrypt traffic in a GRE tunnel. However, here we are dealing with VPNs that terminate on a user workstation, so it is not possible to create a GRE tunnel before establishing the connection. So this example uses tunnel mode, which is actually the default.

Because the workstation could in principle be anywhere on the Internet, we can't even define an IP address for it. But to use IPSec on a Cisco router, we need to create a *crypto map*, which is a template for the Security Association (SA) that IPSec will use for this session. Fortunately, Cisco provides the ability to create dynamic crypto maps for precisely these types of situations:

```
Router1(config)#crypto dynamic-map VPN-USER-MAP 50
Router1(config-crypto-map)#description A dynamic crypto map for VPN users
Router1(config-crypto-map)#match address 115
Router1(config-crypto-map)#set transform-set VPN-TRANSFORMS
```

This creates a dynamic map called VPN-USER-MAP. The number, 50, on the end of the line is a sequence number, similar to the sequence numbers used in route map statements. The router will look at all map entries in sequence until it finds a match. In this case, the match is decided by the *match address* command, which compares the IP addresses of packets to access-list 115. If the access-list matches the addresses in the packet header, it will then apply the transform set that we created earlier.

The access-list here blocks any packets whose destination addresses are either multicasts or local broadcasts. Obviously, this type of traffic cannot possible be associated with a VPN:

```
Router1(config)#access-list 115 deny any 224.0.0.0 35.255.255.255
Router1(config)#access-list 115 deny any 172.25.1.255 0.0.0.0
Router1(config)#access-list 115 permit any any
```

In practice, you may want to use a more restrictive access-list.

We can then build the actual crypto map that references this dynamic map. In the following command, we create a crypto map called, appropriately enough, CRYPTOMAP. This command is sequence number 10 in the definition of the map. In fact, it's the only command in the map's definition, but there could easily be others, including static crypto maps similar to the ones we discussed in Recipes 12.3 and 12.6. Usually, you actually want to put any dynamic maps at the end of your crypto map. This is because dynamic maps work best as catch-all conditions for unknown IP addresses. So if there are any known IP addresses that require special attention, you need to configure them first before the dynamic map statements.

You apply the crypto map to the interface that will be receiving the VPN requests:

```
Router1(config)#crypto map CRYPTOMAP 10 ipsec-isakmp dynamic VPN-USER-MAP
Router1(config)#interface FastEthernet0/1
Router1(config-if)#crypto map CRYPTOMAP
```

See Also

Recipe 12.3; Recipe 12.6; Chapter 4

12.10 Creating an SSL VPN

Problem

You want to create an SSL VPN using Cisco's WebVPN services on an IOS router.

Solution

You can configure a simple SSL VPN on a router, essentially constructing an HTTPS portal that includes simple port forwarding:

```
Core#configure terminal
Enter configuration commands, one per line.  End with CNTL/Z.
Core(config)#hostname Core
Core(config)#ip domain-name oreilly.com
Core(config)#aaa new-model
Core(config)#aaa authentication login local_auth local
Core(config)#username ijbrown secret ianspassword
Core(config)#username kdooley secret kevinspassword
Core(config)#crypto pki trustpoint WEBVPN
Core(ca-trustpoint)#enrollment selfsigned
Core(ca-trustpoint)#rsakeypair WEBVPN 1024
Core(ca-trustpoint)#subject-name CN=WEBVPN OU=cookbooks O=oreilly
Core(ca-trustpoint)#exit
Core(config)#crypto pki enroll WEBVPN
The router has already generated a Self Signed Certificate for
trustpoint TP-self-signed-3299111097.
If you continue the existing trustpoint and Self Signed Certificate
will be deleted.

Do you want to continue generating a new Self Signed Certificate? [yes/no]:yes
% Include the router serial number in the subject name? [yes/no]: no
% Include an IP address in the subject name? [no]: no
Generate Self Signed Router Certificate? [yes/no]: yes
```

```
Router Self Signed Certificate successfully created

Core(config)#interface Loopback0
Core(config-if)#ip address 172.25.100.2 255.255.255.255
Core(config-if)#exit
Core(config)#webvpn enable gateway-addr 172.25.100.2
Core(config)# Core(config)#webvpn
Core(config-webvpn)#ssl trustpoint WEBVPN
Core(config-webvpn)#ssl encryption 3des-sha1
Core(config-webvpn)#title "Cisco Cookbook WebVPN Portal"
Core(config-webvpn)#url-list COOKBOOKURLS
Core(config-webvpn-url)#heading "Cookbook URLs"
Core(config-webvpn-url)#url-text "Cisco Cookbook" url-value "http://www.oreilly.com/
catalog/ciscockbk/"
Core(config-webvpn-url)#url-text "Perl Cookbook" url-value
"http://www.oreilly.com/catalog/perlckbk2/"
Core(config-webvpn-url)#heading "Cisco URLs"
Core(config-webvpn-url)#url-text "The Books" url-value
"http://www.oreilly.com/pub/topic/cisco"
Core(config-webvpn-url)#exit
Core(config-webvpn)#port-forward list SERVERLOGIN local-port 20003 remote-server 172.
25.1.1 remote-port 23
Core(config-webvpn)#exit
Core(config)#end
Core#
```

 Cisco introduced WebVPN functionality on IOS routers in Version 12.3(14)T. This feature is only available on Cisco 1800, 2800, 3700, 3800, and 7200 series routers, and on Cisco 7301 routers.

Discussion

We should start by stressing that the Secure Socket Layer (SSL) WebVPN options available on an IOS router are severely limited compared to those available on dedicated VPN concentrator devices, such as the Cisco VPN 3000 series devices. In particular, the IOS version of WebVPN only supports SSL Version 3, and not Transport Layer Security (TLS), it doesn't support Cisco Security Desktop (CSD) or Cisco SSL VPN Client software, and it doesn't support Macromedia Flash URLs.

On the client side, you can run essentially any SSL-enabled browser such as Mozilla, Firefox, Internet Explorer, or Netscape. For full functionality, you must also have Java enabled on the browser, as WebVPN uses Java to handle the application port forwarding through the browser.

We begin this recipe by specifying the router's name and the domain name. This is because, as we mentioned in Recipe 12.5, this information is required for the key generation process:

```
Core(config)#hostname Core
Core(config)#ip domain-name oreilly.com
```

We then enable AAA, configure local user authentication, and define the usernames and passwords. Note that you could also use a Radius or TACACS+ server for this purpose, as we discuss in Chapter 4. If you have a lot of users, it is much easier to manage them on a central server:

```
Core(config)#aaa new-model
Core(config)#aaa authentication login local_auth local
Core(config)#username ijbrown secret ianspassword
Core(config)#username kdooley secret kevinspassword
```

Next, we need to define the certificate that we will use for the SSL connection. For simplicity we will use a self-signed certificate. In general it is preferable to use a trusted certificate authority rather than self-signed certificates, but for a purely internal purpose like an SSL VPN portal for enterprise users, self-signed certificates should be fine.

First, we must define the properties of the certificate:

```
Core(config)#crypto pki trustpoint WEBVPN
Core(ca-trustpoint)#enrollment selfsigned
Core(ca-trustpoint)#rsakeypair WEBVPN 1024
Core(ca-trustpoint)#subject-name CN=WEBVPN OU=cookbooks O=oreilly
Core(ca-trustpoint)#exit
```

In this case, we have stipulated that the certificate is to be self-signed and that we want to use 1024-bit RSA keys. The *subject-name* command allows you to specify other options in the certificate. This example sets the Organization (O=) and Organizational Unit (OU=) fields.

Next we create the certificate:

```
Core(config)#crypto pki enroll WEBVPN
The router has already generated a Self Signed Certificate for
trustpoint TP-self-signed-3299111097.
If you continue the existing trustpoint and Self Signed Certificate
will be deleted.

Do you want to continue generating a new Self Signed Certificate? [yes/no]:yes
% Include the router serial number in the subject name? [yes/no]: no
% Include an IP address in the subject name? [no]: no
Generate Self Signed Router Certificate? [yes/no]: yes

Router Self Signed Certificate successfully created
```

As you can see, this router already had a self-signed certificate. You can only have one such certificate on a router at a time, so creating this new certificate has destroyed the old one.

This router happens to be running the HTTPS administrative access system, which is already listening on TCP port 443. Because the SSL VPN will also use this same port, we have to be careful to assign it to its own IP address. For this purpose, we have created a new Loopback interface. We then simultaneously enable the WebVPN feature and assign the address to the process by using the *webvpn enable* command:

```
Core(config)#interface Loopback0
Core(config-if)#ip address 172.25.100.2 255.255.255.255
Core(config-if)#exit
Core(config)#webvpn enable gateway-addr 172.25.100.2
```

Next, we configure the actual HTTPS portal that users will see when they point their web browsers to this address. First we associate the SSL trustpoint with the certificate that we just defined, and then we specify that we will use Triple DES encryption with an SHA1 hash over the connection:

```
Core(config)# Core(config)#webvpn
Core(config-webvpn)#ssl trustpoint WEBVPN
Core(config-webvpn)#ssl encryption 3des-sha1
```

Other encryption methods are available, including single DES with SHA1 hashing:

```
Core(config-webvpn)#ssl encryption des-sha1
```

Or you can opt for RC4 encryption with an MD5 hash:

```
Core(config-webvpn)#ssl encryption rc4-md5
```

In our example, we opted for the most secure of the three options.

Then, if necessary, we can set up some links on the web page using the URLs of web sites to make it useful as a portal:

```
Core(config-webvpn)#title "Cisco Cookbook WebVPN Portal"
Core(config-webvpn)#url-list COOKBOOKURLS
Core(config-webvpn-url)#heading "Cookbook URLs"
Core(config-webvpn-url)#url-text "Cisco Cookbook" url-value "http://www.oreilly.com/
catalog/ciscockbk/"
```

There are many additional options available to make this web portal function more aesthetically pleasing on the screen, including the ability to alter colors and even include GIF or JPEG images. We encourage the reader to simply play with the different options and find a scheme that suits their organization.

And, most usefully, we can define port-forwarding rules:

```
Core(config-webvpn)#port-forward list SERVERLOGIN local-port 20003 remote-server 172.
25.1.1 remote-port 23
```

In this example, we have configured only one very simple rule called SERVERLOGIN for *telnet* access to a particular server. Once the user has connected to this WebVPN screen, they can use their local *telnet* application and use it to connect to their own loopback address, 127.0.0.1, on the specified port—20003, in this case. This connection is then intercepted by a Java application on their local system and redirected through the SSL connection and over to the destination IP address.

In a similar way, you could configure an email application to connect to a particular local port and the same workstation loopback address. Java will then redirect this traffic to the router, which will use another port-forwarding rule that you have defined to send it to the email server. For example, here is a rule for forwarding POP services:

```
Core(config-webvpn)#port-forward list POPEMAIL local-port 20004 remote-server 172.25.
1.1 remote-port 110
```

In this case, your workstation's POP mail client would be directed to get its mail from the address 127.0.0.1 and TCP port 20004.

See Also

Chapter 4; Recipe 12.5

12.11 Checking IPSec Protocol Status

Problem

You want to check the status of a VPN.

Solution

There are several useful commands for displaying IPSec parameters.

The command *show crypto isakmp sa* shows all of the ISAKMP security associations.

```
Router1#show crypto isakmp sa
```

And you can look at the IPSec security associations with this command:

```
Router1#show crypto ipsec sa
```

Even if you aren't using a key management protocol such as ISAKMP, you can see information on all of the active IPSec connections with the following command:

```
Router1#show crypto engine connections active
```

And this closely related command will tell you about packet drops within the encryption engine:

```
Router1#show crypto engine connections dropped-packet
```

The *show crypto map* command gives information about all of the IPSec crypto maps that you have configured on your router, whether or not they are in use:

```
Router1#show crypto map
```

And you can specify a particular crypto map with the *tag* keyword:

```
Router1#show crypto map tag TUNNELMAP
```

For information about dynamic crypto maps, you can use the following command:

```
Router1#show crypto dynamic-map
```

Discussion

The *show crypto isakmp sa* command lets you see information about the current state of any ISAKMP key exchanges that the router is involved in:

```
Router1#show crypto isakmp sa
dst             src             state           conn-id   slot
172.22.1.4      172.22.1.3      QM_IDLE               1      0

Router1#
```

Table 12-3 shows all of the possible ISAKMP SA states.

Table 12-3. ISAKMP SA states

Mode	State name	Description
Main Mode	MM_NO_STATE	There is an ISAKMP SA, but none of the parameters have been negotiated yet.
	MM_SA_SETUP	The devices have negotiated a set of parameters for the SA, but have not yet exchanged any key information.
	MM_KEY_EXCH	The devices have used the Diffie-Hellman algorithm to create a common key, but they have not yet authenticated the session.
	MM_KEY_AUTH	The devices have authenticated the SA. They can now proceed to Quick Mode.
Aggressive Mode	AG_NO_STATE	There is an ISAKMP SA, but none of the parameters have been negotiated yet.
	AG_INIT_EXCH	The devices have initiated an Aggressive Mode exchange.
	AG_AUTH	The devices have completed an Aggressive Mode exchange and authenticated the SA. They can now proceed to Quick Mode.
Quick Mode	QM_IDLE	The SA is authenticated and ready for use.

We used Main Mode in all of the examples in this chapter. Aggressive Mode allows faster SA setup by combining SA parameter negotiation, key exchange, and authentication information into the same packet. This has the disadvantage of not hiding the identity information on the peer devices, however. In Main Mode exchanges, this identity information is exchanged separately in encrypted form. Main Mode is the default. Because the extra overhead is minimal, you generally don't need to resort to Aggressive Mode for ISAKMP.

Quick Mode is only possible after the initial ISAKMP exchange has happened at least once. The routers then use this mode when periodically renegotiating the SA information of an SA that has been active for a while. Quick Mode can take advantage of the existing SA to encrypt its exchange.

Use the following rather verbose command to look at IPSec Security Associations:

```
Router1#show crypto ipsec sa

interface: FastEthernet0/1
    Crypto map tag: TUNNELMAP, local addr. 172.22.1.3
```

```
local  ident (addr/mask/prot/port): (172.22.1.3/255.255.255.255/0/0)
remote ident (addr/mask/prot/port): (172.22.1.4/255.255.255.255/0/0)
current_peer: 172.22.1.4
  PERMIT, flags={transport_parent,}
 #pkts encaps: 0, #pkts encrypt: 0, #pkts digest 0
 #pkts decaps: 0, #pkts decrypt: 0, #pkts verify 0
 #pkts compressed: 0, #pkts decompressed: 0
 #pkts not compressed: 0, #pkts compr. failed: 0, #pkts decompress failed: 0
 #send errors 0, #recv errors 0

  local crypto endpt.: 172.22.1.3, remote crypto endpt.: 172.22.1.4
  path mtu 1500, media mtu 1500
  current outbound spi: 0

  inbound esp sas:

  inbound ah sas:

  inbound pcp sas:

  outbound esp sas:

  outbound ah sas:

  outbound pcp sas:


local  ident (addr/mask/prot/port): (172.22.1.3/255.255.255.255/47/0)
remote ident (addr/mask/prot/port): (172.22.1.4/255.255.255.255/47/0)
current_peer: 172.22.1.4
  PERMIT, flags={origin_is_acl,transport_parent,parent_is_transport,}
 #pkts encaps: 466, #pkts encrypt: 466, #pkts digest 466
 #pkts decaps: 1156, #pkts decrypt: 1156, #pkts verify 1156
 #pkts compressed: 0, #pkts decompressed: 0
 #pkts not compressed: 0, #pkts compr. failed: 0, #pkts decompress failed: 0
 #send errors 1, #recv errors 0

  local crypto endpt.: 172.22.1.3, remote crypto endpt.: 172.22.1.4
  path mtu 1500, media mtu 1500
  current outbound spi: EB99FB6C

  inbound esp sas:
   spi: 0x5A48ACC4(1514712260)
     transform: esp-3des esp-sha-hmac ,
     in use settings ={Transport, }
     slot: 0, conn id: 2000, flow_id: 1, crypto map: TUNNELMAP
     sa timing: remaining key lifetime (k/sec): (4606612/3392)
     IV size: 8 bytes
     replay detection support: Y

  inbound ah sas:

  inbound pcp sas:
```

```
      outbound esp sas:
       spi: 0xEB99FB6C(3952737132)
          transform: esp-3des esp-sha-hmac ,
          in use settings ={Transport, }
          slot: 0, conn id: 2001, flow_id: 2, crypto map: TUNNELMAP
          sa timing: remaining key lifetime (k/sec): (4607955/3392)
          IV size: 8 bytes
          replay detection support: Y

      outbound ah sas:

      outbound pcp sas:


   Router1#
```

There is clearly a lot of information in this output. It breaks out the inbound and outbound information, and shows what crypto maps have been applied to which interfaces. It also includes information about the number of packets that the router has been both sent and received, as well as how much time remains before the SA must be renegotiated.

The *show crypto engine* commands allow you to see some of this same information in a more compact form. With the *connections active* keywords, this command tells you what interfaces are involved in IPSec SA's, the peer IP addresses, the algorithms used, and the number of packets sent and received through the encryption engine:

```
   Router1#show crypto engine connections active

      ID Interface       IP-Address      State  Algorithm            Encrypt  Decrypt
       1 <none>          <none>          set    HMAC_SHA+3DES_56_C         0        0
    2088 FastEthernet0/1 172.22.1.3      set    HMAC_SHA+3DES_56_C         0        5
    2089 FastEthernet0/1 172.22.1.3      set    HMAC_SHA+3DES_56_C       202        0

   Router1#
```

With the *connections dropped-packet* keywords, you get some simple statistics on dropped packets. In the following example, the encryption engine was forced to drop five packets because the router tried to send them before it had a valid connection:

```
   Router1#show crypto engine connections dropped-packet

   Packets dropped because of connection not established:
   Interface        IP-Address       Drop Count
   FastEthernet0/1      172.22.1.3            5

   Router1#
```

The command *show crypto map* displays information about all of the configured crypto maps on the router, including which interfaces are currently using them. Note that just because a particular interface is using a particular crypto map, this does not imply that there are any active IPSec SAs. It only means that you have applied this map to this interface by using the *crypto map* interface configuration command:

```
Router1#show crypto map
        Interfaces using crypto map VPN-MAP:

Crypto Map "CRYPTOMAP" 10 ipsec-isakmp
        Dynamic map template tag: VPN-USER-MAP
        Interfaces using crypto map CRYPTOMAP:

Crypto Map "TUNNELMAP" 10 ipsec-isakmp
        Peer = 172.22.1.4
        Extended IP access list 116
            access-list 116 permit gre host 172.22.1.3 host 172.22.1.4
        Current peer: 172.22.1.4
        Security association lifetime: 4608000 kilobytes/3600 seconds
        PFS (Y/N): N
        Transform sets={ TUNNEL-TRANSFORM, }
        Interfaces using crypto map TUNNELMAP:
                FastEthernet0/1

Router1#
```

If you have several crypto maps configured on your router, you can look at a particular one with the *tag* keyword:

```
Router1#show crypto map tag TUNNELMAP
Crypto Map "TUNNELMAP" 10 ipsec-isakmp
        Peer = 172.22.1.4
        Extended IP access list 116
            access-list 116 permit gre host 172.22.1.3 host 172.22.1.4
        Current peer: 172.22.1.4
        Security association lifetime: 4608000 kilobytes/3600 seconds
        PFS (Y/N): N
        Transform sets={ TUNNEL-TRANSFORM, }
        Interfaces using crypto map TUNNELMAP:
                FastEthernet0/1

Router1#
```

And if there are any dynamic maps, you can see more information about them with the following command:

```
Router1#show crypto dynamic-map
Crypto Map Template"VPN-USER-MAP" 50
        Extended IP access list 115
            access-list 115 permit tcp any port = 80 any
            access-list 115 permit tcp any any port = 80
            access-list 115 deny ip any 224.0.0.0 31.255.255.255
        Current peer: 0.0.0.0
        Security association lifetime: 4608000 kilobytes/3600 seconds
        PFS (Y/N): N
        Transform sets={ VPN-TRANSFORMS, }
Router1#
```

## CHAPTER 13

Dial Backup

13.0 Introduction

Dial backup is an important feature in a reliable WAN design. If the primary link to a remote site fails, dial backup links can ensure that you don't lose all connectivity. Of course, in most cases the dial backup link will have significantly lower bandwidth than the primary link. However, the principle advantage of using a dialup connection for backup is that the link will connect only when required. The rest of the time the connection is down, which usually saves money because you only pay for the access and avoid the connection charges.

The examples in this chapter are also useful for WAN designs for which the dial links are used as the primary connections. There are two common examples of networks like this. The first are networks that only connect when there is data to send. For example, in many retail environments, the remote store-front sites only need to exchange data at the end of the day to update inventory and report the day's sales.

The other common type of network that uses only dialup connections involve sites that are in separate buildings, but within the same local dialing area. In this case, if the telephone company doesn't charge a usage fee, a pure dialup network can be a very cost effective way of delivering low-bandwidth WAN services.

Three technologies are commonly used for dialup links: standard analog telephone lines with asynchronous modems, switched 56 Kbps synchronous digital service (sometimes called Centrex), and ISDN.

Analog Modems

The first are standard analog telephone lines with asynchronous modems. This is a reasonably effective dial backup technology, which has the great advantage of being nearly ubiquitous: in regions where you can get no other network services, you can often get an analog telephone line. Further, most Cisco routers have an AUX port that supports an analog modem connection.

But it has some important drawbacks. The first is that there are no guarantees about how much bandwidth you will get. Many analog modems are rated to speeds up to 56 Kbps, but in practice you will rarely get this much throughput. It is more typical to see a practical bandwidth of between 9.6 Kbps and 44 Kbps with asynchronous modems.

The second important problem with voice grade telephone lines is that they are susceptible to electrical noise, which can cause dropped packets, and sometimes even dropped calls.

Switched 56 Kbps Digital Service

Switched 56 Kbps digital service, which also goes by the brand name Centrex in some areas, is a synchronous digital dialup technology. We recommend using this in regions that don't offer ISDN because it offers greater bandwidth and reliability than voice-grade analog service. However, the number of local telephone companies that can offer Switched 56 Kbps but not ISDN is rapidly decreasing.

To use this technology, you need a synchronous serial port on your router, and an external Data Unit (DU), or synchronous modem.

ISDN

Integrated Services Digital Network (ISDN) is usually the best way to go for dialup networking. It has the highest bandwidth, and the greatest reliability. And when using ISDN with Cisco routers, you have the distinct advantage of being able to use built-in ISDN terminal adapters and NT1 units, which reduces both the complexity and the costs of implementation and maintenance.

ISDN circuits come in two basic varieties called Basic Rate Interface (BRI) and hPrimary Rate Interface (PRI), respectively. A BRI circuit supports two 64 Kbps B channels and a 16 Kbps D channel that handles the signaling for the two B channels. A PRI circuit, on the other hand, uses a single 64 Kbps D channel to support the signaling for 23 (if delivered through a T1 circuit) or 30 (for an E1 circuit) B channels. And many network vendors will also sell PRI services on fraction T1 or E1 circuits, allowing smaller numbers of B channels, as well.

You normally don't use the D channel for user data, but Cisco routers do allow you to bind the two B channels together for a net 128 Kbps link using the PPP multilink feature. Unlike analog modems, each of these B and D channels operates at full duplex, so you can send and receive simultaneously at the full channel speed.

We note in passing that it is possible to use the D channel of a PRI circuit for user data, but only if the carrier has not configured this channel to manage the B channels. In situations when you have multiple PRI circuits, it is possible to control all of the B channels from the D channel of the first PRI circuit, leaving the D channels of the other circuits available for data. The advantages of doing this are slight, however.

Many organizations use BRI interfaces for remote branch devices, and PRI interfaces for central dialup circuits. This way you can save on physical ports by having many branches dial into a single central PRI circuit. By default, a PRI circuit can accept calls from remote ISDN circuits. ISDN circuits can also terminate calls from Centrex or switched 56 Kbps-type circuits without requiring any special hardware. Further, Cisco has analog modem cards for several routers such as the AS5×00 and 3600/3800 series. These allow you to terminate analog calls from remote devices on the same PRI circuit. This is an extremely useful option because you can then configure all of your remote devices to dial to the same central ISDN PRI telephone number.

BRI interfaces come in two main varieties, called "S/T" and "U." Usually, a BRI circuit is delivered and terminated on a U interface, which is a two-wire digital telephone line. The U interface connects to an Network Termination Type 1 (NT1), which converts the U interface signaling to S/T interface signaling. The S/T interface then connects to a Terminal Adapter device, which allows you to connect the ISDN circuit to your equipment. Both S/T and U interfaces use standard RJ-45 cables.

Cisco allows you to eliminate some or all of these pieces of equipment, though, by offering a variety of ISDN hardware options. Many access routers come with an optional on-board Terminal Adapter, or can take an ISDN module with this functionality. The BRI interface is labeled "S/T" to indicate when the router has an on-board Terminal Adapter. You would then connect this port to an external NT1 device, which in turn connects to the telephone company's circuit.

Cisco also has a variety of BRI modules that include an on-board NT1. These also use an RJ-45 connector, but they are labeled "U" to indicate that you should connect directly to the ISDN circuit. We generally prefer to implement ISDN on routers with on-board NT1 units because it simplifies implementation.

If you want to take full advantage of ISDN features such as channel bonding, the router must at least have an on-board Terminal Adapter.

Estimating How Many Dialup Lines You Need

Many network engineers make the mistake of either under or overestimating how many dial backup lines they need to provide at their central site. In a hub and spoke WAN, you can easily estimate how many dialup lines you will need at the central site based on the probability failure for a branch's primary circuit.

The most common failure mode in any WAN is the so-called "last mile" failure, which means that the local loop circuit between the remote site and the WAN provider's Central Office (CO) breaks for some reason. The break could be due to a fibre cut or a cross-connection problem or, sadly, more common than anybody would like, human error. The provider will usually keep statistics on these problems, which they will use to define their Service Level Agreement (SLA) for each type of circuit.

The SLA effectively reflects a probability of a circuit failure. If, for example, your remote sites have a 99.9 percent SLA, this means that there is a 0.1 percent probability of failure. So, if you have a network with N circuits, each of which has the same probability of failure, P, then you can use the following formula to calculate the probability of k simultaneous failures:

$$P(k, N) = \frac{N!P^k(1-P)^{(N-k)}}{k!(N-k)!}$$

The symbol "!" is a standard shorthand notation for the factorial function:

```
N! = N * (N-1) * (N-2) * ... * 2 * 1
```

So for a WAN SLA of 99.9 percent, which is on the poor side, but typical, P is 0.1 percent (100 – 99.9 percent). If you have a hub and spoke WAN with N=100 circuits, the probability of there being a single circuit down is:

```
P(1,100) ~ 0.1 = 10%
```

So roughly 10 percent of the time, you can expect to have one circuit down. Similarly, the probabilities of there being two or more simultaneous failures are given by:

```
P(2,100) ~ .5%
P(3,100) ~ .02%
P(4,100) ~ 0.00038%
P(10,100) ~ 1.7*10-15%
```

It's clear from this that the probability of 10 simultaneous failures is very small indeed. But just looking at probabilities can be deceptive because all of the numbers look small. So we recommend multiplying these probabilities by the number of minutes in a year to get a better idea of how likely these failure scenarios actually are.

The probability of there being a single circuit failure is 10 percent, or 36.5 days per year. The probability of two simultaneous failures is 0.5 percent, which is roughly 44 hours per year. The probability of three simultaneous failures is .02 percent, or 105 minutes per year. And the probability of four simultaneous failures is .00038 percent, which is about 2 minutes per year.

So these are all things that you can expect to see happen at least once in the expected several-year lifespan of this WAN. But the probability of 10 simultaneous failures is so small that you would expect it to happen roughly $5*10^{-10}$ seconds per year. Looking at this another way, if this failure condition lasted for one second, you would expect it to happen about once every billion years. Those are odds that most of us could live with.

By doing this sort of analysis, you can tell that having three dial backup circuits would probably come in handy at least once a year, and you might even need as many as four. But you're not likely to ever need 10.

However, it's important to bear in mind that this analysis assumes that these failures are not correlated. Depending on how your WAN provider implements your circuits, a single failure could affect several branches. So it is usually a good idea to apply a safety rule and double the number of circuits that this analysis suggests you will need. In this case, you probably need 4 circuits, but if you have 8 or 10, you should be more than safe.

13.1 Automating Dial Backup

Problem

You want automatic dial recovery in case a WAN link fails.

Solution

One of the most reliable ways of implementing dial backup on a Cisco router is to use a *floating static* default route, as follows:

```
Router1#configure terminal
Enter configuration commands, one per line.  End with CNTL/Z.
Router1(config)#interface BRI0/0
Router1(config-if)#ip address 10.1.99.55 255.255.255.0
Router1(config-if)#encapsulation ppp
Router1(config-if)#dialer idle-timeout 300
Router1(config-if)#dialer map ip 10.1.99.1 name dialhost broadcast 95551212
Router1(config-if)#dialer load-threshold 50 either
Router1(config-if)#dialer-group 1
Router1(config-if)#isdn switch-type basic-ni
Router1(config-if)#isdn spid1 800555123400 5551234
Router1(config-if)#isdn spid2 800555123500 5551235
Router1(config-if)#ppp authentication chap
Router1(config-if)#ppp multilink
Router1(config-if)#exit
Router1(config)#username dialhost password dialpassword
Router1(config)#ip route 0.0.0.0 0.0.0.0 10.1.99.1 180
Router1(config)#dialer-list 1 protocol ip list 101
Router1(config)#access-list 101 deny eigrp any any
Router1(config)#access-list 101 permit ip any any
Router1(config)#router eigrp 55
Router1(config-router)#network 10.0.0.0
Router1(config-router)#end
Router1#
```

Then the matching configuration of the other end is shown in Recipe 13.2.

Discussion

This recipe includes several important features. First, notice that we have configured dial backup using an ISDN BRI interface on this router. So we have to set up the ISDN configuration:

```
Router1(config)#interface BRI0/0
Router1(config-if)#isdn switch-type basic-ni
Router1(config-if)#isdn spid1 800555123400 5551234
Router1(config-if)#isdn spid2 800555123500 5551235
```

This site is connected to a National ISDN switch. So we have defined the switch type to be *basic-ni*. If this had been a PRI rather than a BRI, we would have used *primary-ni*. And because it is a National ISDN switch, we also have to include the ISDN Service Profile Identifier (SPID) values. These define the telephone numbers associated with each of the two B channels in the BRI. Note that the syntax includes essentially the same number twice:

```
Router1(config-if)#isdn spid1 800555123400 5551234
```

The first argument is the whole telephone number including area code with 00 tacked on the end. These extra two digits vary between different telephone companies. Sometimes this needs to be a different code, such as 0101. The telephone company can tell you the correct value to include.

The second number is not always required. This is essentially the phone number that you would need to call this B channel from the other B channel. In this example, the telephone company uses seven-digit local dialing, so we can eliminate the area code.

There are several different kinds of ISDN switches, and it's important to find out what your carrier uses to ensure that you configure the router properly.

For telephone companies that use AT&T switches:

```
Router1(config-if)#isdn switch-type basic-5ess
```

For telephone companies that use Nortel DMS100 switches:

```
Router1(config-if)#isdn switch-type basic-dms100
```

Telephone companies outside of North America often use different kinds of ISDN switches. In France you would use the following command:

```
Router1(config-if)#isdn switch-type vn3
```

In Australia, the telephone company uses TS013 ISDN switches:

```
Router1(config-if)#isdn switch-type basic-ts013
```

In Norway and New Zealand:

```
Router1(config-if)#isdn switch-type basic-net3
```

In Germany:

```
Router1(config-if)#isdn switch-type basic-1tr6
```

And, in Japan:

```
Router1(config-if)#isdn switch-type ntt
```

Please contact the local telephone company supplying the BRI circuit to ensure that you have the right switch type. And be sure to ask them whether you need to configure SPIDs on your router. Some switches require them; others don't.

You can verify that you have your ISDN configuration working correctly with the *show isdn status* command:

```
Router1#show isdn status
Global ISDN Switchtype = basic-ni
ISDN BRI1/0 interface
    dsl 8, interface ISDN Switchtype = basic-ni
```

```
    Layer 1 Status:
    ACTIVE
    Layer 2 Status:
    TEI = 85, Ces = 1, SAPI = 0, State = MULTIPLE_FRAME_ESTABLISHED
    TEI = 86, Ces = 2, SAPI = 0, State = MULTIPLE_FRAME_ESTABLISHED
    TEI 85, ces = 1, state = 8(established)
        spid1 configured, spid1 sent, spid1 valid
    TEI 86, ces = 2, state = 8(established)
        spid2 configured, spid2 sent, spid2 valid
    Layer 3 Status:
    0 Active Layer 3 Call(s)
    Activated dsl 8 CCBs = 0
    The Free Channel Mask:  0x80000003
Total Allocated ISDN CCBs = 2
Router1#
```

In this case, you can see you have an "active" status at Layer 1, and both of the Terminal Endpoint Identifiers (TEI) are in a "MULTIPLE_FRAME_ESTABLISHED" state. This means that the router is talking with the telephone company's ISDN switch, and that both of the B channels are ready to go. This display also says that there are currently no active calls at Layer 3. As an aside, we should point out that this refers to the ISDN circuit's Layer 3, and not the IP network layer. When the router places a call, it will establish a PPP connection, which will support IP.

The actual dialing is done by the *dialer map* command:

```
Router1(config)#dialer-list 1 protocol ip list 101
Router1(config)#access-list 101 deny eigrp any any
Router1(config)#access-list 101 permit ip any any
Router1(config)#interface BRI0/0
Router1(config-if)#dialer map ip 10.1.99.1 name dialhost broadcast 95551212
Router1(config-if)#dialer-group 1
```

In this case, the dialer map says that to reach the IP address 10.1.99.1, it should dial the phone number 95551212 to reach the router called dialhost. Note that we have included a "9" at the start of this phone number. Again, you will need to ask your local telephone company whether there is a special code digit. We have seen places where we needed a 9, an 8, or nothing at all.

The *broadcast* keyword in this command allows both multicast and broadcast traffic to use this dialup link. This is extremely important for routing protocols such as EIGRP, RIPv2, and OSPF, which use multicasts for sending their updates between routers. This example uses EIGRP, so we need to include this keyword.

With this type of dialer configuration, you also need to define a *dialer group*. In this case, we have assigned this interface to dialer group number 1. You configure the behavior of this dialer group with the *dialer-list* statement, which defines what an interesting packet is for this network.

An interesting packet is one that will bring up the dialer, or keep it active if it is already up. If the circuit is up, then the router will reset the idle timer every time it sees an interesting packet. The result is that as long as there are interesting packets to send, the router will keep the dial session active. Otherwise, it will disconnect the call when the idle timer expires. This is particularly important when you are calling long distance numbers. If the wrong packets are considered interesting, it could mean an expensive phone bill.

So we have associated the dialer list with an access list that specifies what is interesting. In this case, all IP packets except EIGRP are interesting. It's important to remember that EIGRP packets will still pass through the dial link normally. But if the link is not active, an EIGRP packet is not sufficient to bring it up. And if the link is active, the presence of EIGRP packets alone won't prevent the router from dropping it.

This is extremely important because, as we discussed in Chapter 7, the router will send an EIGRP HELLO packet every few seconds by default. But we don't want the link to remain active unless there is real user traffic to send. If you are using a different routing protocol, you should specify its update packets here instead.

However, sometimes you do want the link to remain active all the time. For example, the administrators of some small WANs like to keep ISDN sessions nailed up all the time (usually because they only pay an access charge, and not a usage or long distance charge). So if the session drops for any reasons, they want it to immediately dial up again. In this case, you could replace the access list with a new one that finds all traffic interesting:

```
Router1(config)#access-list 101 permit ip any any
```

It's easier still if you modify the *dialer-list* command to make all IP traffic interesting:

```
Router1(config)#dialer-list 1 protocol ip permit
```

When the router dials, it will use Point-to-Point Protocol (PPP) to carry Layer 3 protocols such as IP. So you need to define several PPP parameters:

```
Router1(config)#interface BRI0/0
Router1(config-if)#encapsulation ppp
Router1(config-if)#ppp authentication chap
Router1(config-if)#exit
Router1(config)#username dialhost password dialpassword
```

The encapsulation command simply tells the router to use PPP as its Layer 2 protocol. But because you don't want just anybody dialing into this *dialhost* router, it's a good idea to include some authentication. In this case, we have configured the router to use Challenge Handshake Authentication Protocol (CHAP) for authenticating PPP sessions. This basically means that both this router and the router it dials to will exchange usernames and passwords when they connect. The username for this router is the router's name. And we define the username and password for the other router with the *username* command.

We note in passing that Cisco supports another PPP authentication scheme called *Password Authentication Protocol* (PAP). CHAP is much more secure because it only passes passwords in encrypted form rather than clear text, as PAP does. CHAP is no more complex to set up, and presents no appreciable extra load on the router's resources. So we strongly recommend using CHAP rather than PAP.

Because this is an ISDN BRI interface, we would like to be able to use both of the B channels to increase the available bandwidth:

```
Router1(config)#interface BRI0/0
Router1(config-if)#dialer load-threshold 50 either
Router1(config-if)#ppp multilink
```

The command *ppp multilink* means that this PPP session can be split across several physical connections. This feature allows full load balancing and packet sequencing across all of the connections in the multilink bundle. In this case, we want to bond the two ISDN B channels into a single 128 Kbps PPP link. By default, the router will use only one of these channels, whichever one is available. The *dialer load-threshold* command specifies the rule that the router will use to bring up the second link. In this case, we have specified that if the traffic utilization in either direction (input or output) reaches ~20 percent (50/255 link utilization), then the router should bring up the second channel.

We have also modified the default idle timeout:

```
Router1(config)#interface BRI0/0
Router1(config-if)#dialer idle-timeout 300
```

By default, the router will drop the dial session if there have been no interesting packets for 120 seconds. We have increased this value to 300 seconds. Because ISDN dials so quickly, this is not vital. But with asynchronous modem dialup, it can take up to a full minute to establish a new session. You often need to increase the idle timer is to make sure that the primary connection is up and stable before disconnecting the backup circuit. It is a good idea to wait for the routing protocol to converge, and to ensure that the primary circuit isn't simply bouncing up and down. You also have to trade off between the time required to establish a new session and the cost of any long distance charges on this line. We generally recommend using an idle timeout period of 5 minutes, as shown in the example.

Finally, we come to one of the most important features of this configuration, the trigger condition. This router will dial whenever it has traffic to send to the IP address 10.1.99.1, which is the IP address of the dialhost router itself. User traffic will be directed to end devices such as servers, not to routers. The only way to bring up this dial interface is if this router needs to send an interesting packet to the dial router's IP address. This is where the floating static route comes in.

In Chapter 5, we discussed floating static routes. These are routes whose administrative distances are so high that any dynamically learned route to the same destination will be better. So the router will only install this static route if the dynamic routing protocol can't offer anything better:

```
Router1(config)#ip route 0.0.0.0 0.0.0.0 10.1.99.1 180
```

In this particular case the routing protocol is EIGRP, which has an administrative distance of 90 by default for all internal routes and 170 for external routes. So, by creating this static default route with a metric of 180, we ensure that the router will never use it if it has anything better.

The net result is that if the primary link fails, EIGRP will lose all of its routes. So the router will install the floating static route to handle any user data packets that it needs to transmit. Since this route points to the far end of the dial link, this forces the router to bring up the dial connection.

The nice thing about this way of triggering dial backup is that it is extremely robust. Anything that causes you to lose connectivity for any reason will trigger the dial backup. This is better than the backup interface solution described in Recipe 13.4, for example, because it doesn't require loss of physical connectivity to trigger the backup.

Also, as we will discuss in Recipe 13.4, which uses the *backup interface* method to trigger dial backup, with the floating static configuration, you have the advantage that the interface remains up but not connected when the primary circuit is working. In the case of ISDN, this means that you can use the *show isdn* commands that we discuss in Recipe 13.7 to ensure that your circuit is still working.

And one of the most useful features of this type of trigger mechanism is that you can test the dial backup easily. If you look at the dialer list, you will see that all the router needs to initiate a dial session is to have a packet to send to the far end that matches the dialer list. So, in this particular example, you could easily bring up a dial session for testing by just logging into the remote router and pinging the IP address of the dial backup router:

```
Router1#ping 10.1.99.1
```

See Also

Recipe 13.2; Recipe 13.4; Chapter 5; Chapter 7

13.2   Using Dialer Interfaces

Problem

You want to treat several physical interfaces as a single dialer.

Solution

If you have several physical interfaces on your router that you want to treat as a single dialer, particularly for PPP multilink channel bonding, you can create a logical dialer interface:

```
Router1#configure terminal
Enter configuration commands, one per line.  End with CNTL/Z.
Router1(config)#interface BRI0/0
```

```
Router1(config-if)#encapsulation ppp
Router1(config-if)#dialer pool-member 1
Router1(config-if)#isdn switch-type basic-ni
Router1(config-if)#isdn spid1 800555123400 5551234
Router1(config-if)#isdn spid2 800555123500 5551235
Router1(config-if)#ppp authentication chap
Router1(config-if)#exit
Router1(config)#interface BRI0/1
Router1(config-if)#encapsulation ppp
Router1(config-if)#dialer pool-member 1
Router1(config-if)#isdn switch-type basic-ni
Router1(config-if)#isdn spid1 800555123600 5551236
Router1(config-if)#isdn spid2 800555123700 5551237
Router1(config-if)#ppp authentication chap
Router1(config-if)#exit
Router1(config)#interface Dialer1
Router1(config-if)#ip address 10.1.99.55 255.255.255.0
Router1(config-if)#encapsulation ppp
Router1(config-if)#dialer remote-name dialhost
Router1(config-if)#dialer pool 1
Router1(config-if)#dialer idle-timeout 300
Router1(config-if)#dialer string 95551212
Router1(config-if)#dialer load-threshold 50 either
Router1(config-if)#dialer-group 1
Router1(config-if)#ppp authentication chap
Router1(config-if)#ppp multilink
Router1(config-if)#exit
Router1(config)#username dialhost password dialpassword
Router1(config)#ip route 0.0.0.0 0.0.0.0 10.1.99.1 180
Router1(config)#dialer-list 1 protocol ip list 101
Router1(config)#access-list 101 deny eigrp any any
Router1(config)#access-list 101 permit ip any any
Router1(config)#router eigrp 55
Router1(config-router)#network 10.0.0.0
Router1(config-router)#end
Router1#
```

Dialer interfaces are particularly useful for the server side, where you can use them to bond together several ISDN BRI or PRI circuits:

```
dialhost#configure terminal
Enter configuration commands, one per line.  End with CNTL/Z.
dialhost(config)#username Router1 password dialpassword
dialhost(config)#controller T1 0
dialhost(config-controller)#framing esf
dialhost(config-controller)#clock source line primary
dialhost(config-controller)#linecode b8zs
dialhost(config-controller)#pri-group timeslots 1-24
dialhost(config-controller)#exit
dialhost(config)#interface Serial0:23
dialhost(config-if)#encapsulation ppp
dialhost(config-if)#dialer rotary-group 1
dialhost(config-if)#dialer-group 1
dialhost(config-if)#isdn switch-type primary-dms100
dialhost(config-if)#isdn not-end-to-end 56
```

```
dialhost(config-if)#exit
dialhost(config)#interface Dialer1
dialhost(config-if)#ip address 10.1.99.1 255.255.255.0
dialhost(config-if)#encapsulation ppp
dialhost(config-if)#dialer in-band
dialhost(config-if)#dialer idle-timeout 300
dialhost(config-if)#dialer-group 1
dialhost(config-if)#no peer default ip address
dialhost(config-if)#ppp authentication chap
dialhost(config-if)#ppp multilink
dialhost(config-if)#exit
dialhost(config)#access-list 101 deny eigrp any any
dialhost(config)#access-list 101 permit ip any any
dialhost(config)#dialer-list 1 protocol ip list 101
dialhost(config)#router eigrp 55
dialhost(config-router)#network 10.0.0.0
dialhost(config-router)#exit
dialhost(config)#end
dialhost#
```

Discussion

This example is similar to Recipe 13.1, but this time we have created a logical Dialer1 interface instead of using a *dialer map* command. The effect is the same. But with *dialer interfaces*, you have the advantage of being able to bond several different physical links into a single PPP multilink bundle.

In the first example, we have included two ISDN BRI interfaces, which gives us an effective total bandwidth of 256 Kbps for the backup link. However, as in Recipe 13.1, we have included a *dialer load-threshold* command so the router will only bring up these additional B channels if it requires them.

There are a couple of important differences between the first example in this recipe and the one in Recipe 13.1. First, notice that we have not included any IP addresses or any of the dialer configuration information on the physical interfaces. Instead, we put all of this information in the configuration of the logical dialer interface.

Then, to associate these physical interfaces with this particular logical interface, we use the *dialer pool-member* command on the physical interfaces and the *dialer pool* command on the dialer interface. In this example, we have created *dialer pool number* 1 on the interface, Dialer1, and assigned the two BRI interfaces to this pool. The dialer interface number is arbitrary. The only thing that matters is that the dialer pool numbers match the dialer pool-member numbers.

Because there is no *dialer map* command to define the telephone number to call, the destination hostname and the destination IP address, we have to configure these separately. First, we set up the remote hostname and the dialer string (which defines the destination phone number) as follows:

```
Router1(config)#interface Dialer1
Router1(config-if)#dialer remote-name dialhost
Router1(config-if)#dialer string 95551212
```

And, as in Recipe 13.1, we include a floating static route to trigger the dial backup:

```
Router1(config)#ip route 0.0.0.0 0.0.0.0 10.1.99.1 180
```

The rest of the configuration is essentially the same as in Recipe 13.1.

The second example in this recipe shows a sample server-side configuration. In many ways, it is similar to the branch, but there also a few key differences. The first difference is that the server is configured to use a PRI rather than a BRI circuit. In this case, the router uses a built-in T1 CSU, so we need to define the framing, line coding, and how the T1 time slices work:

```
dialhost(config)#controller T1 0
dialhost(config-controller)#framing esf
dialhost(config-controller)#clock source line primary
dialhost(config-controller)#linecode b8zs
dialhost(config-controller)#pri-group timeslots 1-24
dialhost(config-controller)#exit
```

This represents the most common options, *Extended Super Frame* (ESF) framing with *Binary 8-Zero Substitution* (B8ZS) line coding. And we will draw the clock from the circuit, rather than generating it in the router. The most important part of this is the definition of the T1 time slots. In this case, we have grouped all of 23 B channels and the D channel into a single PRI group. This reflects the fact that we purchased this circuit as a whole T1. However, you could just as easily work with a fractional T1 PRI circuit that only includes some of the available time slots. Please see Chapter 16 for more information on the *controller* command.

Once we have defined the T1 time slots for the PRI circuit, we can then configure the circuit for dialup:

```
dialhost(config)#interface Serial0:23
dialhost(config-if)#encapsulation ppp
dialhost(config-if)#dialer rotary-group 1
dialhost(config-if)#dialer-group 1
dialhost(config-if)#isdn switch-type primary-dms100
dialhost(config-if)#isdn not-end-to-end 56
dialhost(config-if)#exit
```

The name of this interface, Serial0:23, means that we are working with the circuit attached to interface Serial0, and that it includes 23 time slices. In this example, the telephone company's ISDN switch is a Nortel DMS100, so we have to configure it with the *isdn switch-type* command. The *encapsulation ppp* and the *dialer-group* commands are familiar from previous examples, but there are a couple of other options here.

The first new feature is the *dialer rotary-group* command. This is a useful variation on some of the dialer commands that we discussed earlier. Because the argument of this command is the number 1, this assigns this physical interface to be a member of a rotary group that is associated with the virtual interface, Dialer1. A rotary group is similar to any other dialer group, but it allows multiple simultaneous connections to different remote routers. This wasn't necessary for the branch routers, because they only ever dial to the one central router. But the host router must be able to accept calls from many branches at once.

The primary router doesn't require *dialer map* statements to accept inbound calls. These are only necessary for outbound calls. When the router receives a new inbound connection, it will create a dynamic map to associate the IP address with the dial connection.

The last command in this configuration is often required when using ISDN calls between different telephone companies, and particularly for long distance calls:

```
dialhost(config-if)#isdn not-end-to-end 56
```

By default, the router will assume that all calls use 64 Kbps ISDN B channels. But some regions use 56 Kbps instead of 64. And, worse still, sometimes you have a long distance call that starts and ends at 64 Kbps, but has a hidden leg of 56 Kbps in the middle of the carrier's network. In all of these cases, the router will drop the call by default because of the speed mismatch. This command manually forces the router to use 56 Kbps for all calls to prevent these speed mismatch problems.

See Also

Recipe 13.1; Chapter 16

13.3   Using an Async Modem on the AUX Port

Problem

You want to connect a standard asynchronous modem to the router's AUX port and use it for dial backup.

Solution

Many Cisco routers include an AUX port that is a low-speed asynchronous serial interface that can connect to a standard modem and support PPP:

```
Router1#configure terminal
Enter configuration commands, one per line.  End with CNTL/Z.
Router2(config)#interface Async65
Router2(config-if)#encapsulation ppp
Router2(config-if)#dialer in-band
Router2(config-if)#dialer pool-member 1
Router2(config-if)#ppp authentication chap
Router2(config-if)#async default routing
Router2(config-if)#exit
Router2(config)#interface Dialer1
Router2(config-if)#ip address 10.1.99.56 255.255.255.0
Router2(config-if)#encapsulation ppp
Router2(config-if)#dialer remote-name dialhost
Router2(config-if)#dialer pool 1
Router2(config-if)#dialer idle-timeout 300
Router2(config-if)#dialer string 95551212
Router2(config-if)#dialer-group 1
```

```
Router2(config-if)#ppp authentication chap
Router2(config-if)#exit
Router2(config)#line aux 0
Router2(config-line)#modem inout
Router2(config-line)#transport input all
Router2(config-line)#no exec
Router2(config-line)#speed 115200
Router2(config-line)#exit
Router2(config)#username dialhost password dialpassword
Router2(config)#ip route 0.0.0.0 0.0.0.0 10.1.99.1 180
Router2(config)#dialer-list 1 protocol ip list 101
Router2(config)#access-list 101 deny eigrp any any
Router2(config)#access-list 101 permit ip any any
Router2(config)#router eigrp 55
Router2(config-router)#network 10.0.0.0
Router2(config-router)#exit
Router2(config)#end
Router2#
```

Discussion

Much of this configuration is similar to the ISDN configuration shown in Recipe 13.2. It uses a dialer interface in exactly the same way. But here, because there is only one async modem in this example, we can't benefit from PPP multilink.

The first part of this configuration example sets up the AUX port to run PPP and associates it with a dialer pool:

```
Router2(config)#interface Async65
Router2(config-if)#encapsulation ppp
Router2(config-if)#dialer in-band
Router2(config-if)#dialer pool-member 1
Router2(config-if)#ppp authentication chap
Router2(config-if)#async default routing
```

The only thing here that hasn't appeared in a previous example is the *async default routing* command. This command allows the async interface to support a routing protocol such as EIGRP. By default, routing protocols are disabled on async interfaces, so you need to enable it.

The number of this particular interface, Async65, wasn't selected at random. The router automatically assigns a line number to every interface that can be used for terminal access (including VTY lines, AUX lines, and Console lines), and it varies from router to router, depending on the hardware configuration. So we used the *show line* command to see which line number corresponded to the AUX port on this router:

```
Router1#show line
    Tty Typ     Tx/Rx     A Modem  Roty AccO AccI   Uses   Noise  Overruns  Int
      0 CTY                -    -     -    -    -       0      0    0/0       -
     65 AUX     9600/9600  -    -     -    -    -       0      0    0/0       -
  *  66 VTY                -    -     -    -    -      10      0    0/0       -
  *  67 VTY                -    -     -    -    -      19      0    0/0       -
     68 VTY                -    -     -    -    -       3      0    0/0       -
```

69 VTY	-	-	-	-	-	0	0	0/0	-
70 VTY	-	-	-	-	-	0	0	0/0	-
71 VTY	-	-	-	-	-	0	0	0/0	-
72 VTY	-	-	-	-	-	0	0	0/0	-
73 VTY	-	-	-	-	-	0	0	0/0	-
74 VTY	-	-	-	-	-	0	0	0/0	-
75 VTY	-	-	-	-	-	0	0	0/0	-

```
Line(s) not in async mode -or- with no hardware support:
1-64

Router1#
```

As you can see, the AUX port is on line 65 on this router. It's important to do this before you attempt any of the rest of the configuration, so you know what to configure.

When you use the AUX port for dial backup, you also need to configure the terminal line information for this physical port:

```
Router2(config)#line aux 0
Router2(config-line)#modem inout
Router2(config-line)#transport input none
Router2(config-line)#no exec
Router2(config-line)#speed 115200
```

The first command here is *modem inout*, which configures the router to allow access to the modem, as well as allowing the modem access to the router. Then we added the command *transport input none*. By default, the router will act as a terminal server and allow you to connect through protocols like *telnet* to the AUX port. In this case, though, we want the router to reserve this port for routed traffic, so we disable all remote terminal access to the interface.

The *no exec* command is extremely important when using async dial, and almost universally ignored in Cisco references. By default, the router will start an EXEC session on your AUX port. So if you plug a terminal into this port, you will get a login prompt. Unfortunately, your modem doesn't know what to do with a login prompt. At best, it will just ignore it, so disabling the EXEC session is simply good form. But, at worst, we have seen problems where the modem attempts to respond to the login prompt, the EXEC session interprets this as a bad login attempt, and puts up a new prompt, to which the modem again attempts to respond. The result can be high CPU utilization and, more importantly, this activity will prevent the router from dialing. We strongly recommend disabling the EXEC session on any async dial ports, as we have done here.

And the last command in this section sets the line speed. It's important to remember that this is the speed between the router and the modem. The actual dial session will have a much lower net speed, likely less than 56 Kbps. However, it's a good idea to make the line speed as fast as the modem can support. This will ensure that you get the best possible speed. Note that the default speed here is only 9.6 Kbps. So, if you don't increase this value, you will not be able to get the full advantage of the compression capabilities of modern modems.

See Also

Recipe 13.1; Recipe 13.2

13.4 Using Backup Interfaces

Problem

You want to configure a router to dial only if it sees a physical failure on the primary WAN interface.

Solution

Cisco routers can watch the physical signals on an interface and trigger a backup interface if the primary link fails. The router will automatically drop the call after the primary circuit comes back up:

```
Router1#configure terminal
Enter configuration commands, one per line.  End with CNTL/Z.
Router1(config)#interface Serial0/0
Router1(config-if)#backup delay 0 300
Router1(config-if)#backup interface BRI0/0
Router1(config-if)#encapsulation frame-relay
Router1(config-if)#down-when-looped
Router1(config-if)#exit
Router1(config)#interface Serial0/0.1 point-to-point
Router1(config-subif)#ip address 10.1.1.10 255.255.255.252
Router1(config-subif)#frame-relay interface-dlci 50
Router1(config-subif)#exit
Router1(config)#interface BRI0/0
Router1(config-if)#ip address 10.1.99.55 255.255.255.0
Router1(config-if)#encapsulation ppp
Router1(config-if)#dialer idle-timeout 300
Router1(config-if)#dialer map ip 10.1.99.1 name dialhost broadcast 95551212
Router1(config-if)#dialer load-threshold 50 either
Router1(config-if)#dialer-group 1
Router1(config-if)#isdn switch-type basic-ni
Router1(config-if)#isdn spid1 800555123400 5551234
Router1(config-if)#isdn spid2 800555123500 5551235
Router1(config-if)#ppp authentication chap
Router1(config-if)#ppp multilink
Router1(config-if)#exit
Router1(config)#dialer-list 1 protocol ip permit
Router1(config)#end
Router1#
```

Discussion

In this example, the primary WAN interface is a Frame Relay connection. Please see Chapter 10 for more information about Frame Relay configuration. However, this would work just as well on just about any kind of interface. The main reason why we used Frame Relay is to show that you have to put the backup commands on the physical interface, not on any subinterfaces or virtual interfaces. If this router loses physical signaling on the serial interface, it will automatically bring up the dial backup. The key to this configuration method is the *backup* command, which you associate with the primary interface:

```
Router1(config)#interface Serial0/0
Router1(config-if)#backup delay 0 300
Router1(config-if)#backup interface BRI0/0
```

In this case, you can see that the backup interface for this serial port is the ISDN interface, BRI0/0. We also included a *backup delay* command, which specifies two times. The first parameter tells the router how long it should wait before bringing up the backup after it loses signals on this primary interface. In this case, we don't want to wait. If there is a failure, we want the backup to activate immediately. However, in some cases, you might want to delay slightly to save money on backup charges in case the primary comes back again right away. So, if you wanted to wait 15 seconds before dialing, you could configure it like this:

```
Router1(config-if)#backup delay 15 300
```

The second number tells the router how long to wait after the primary recovers before dropping the dial connection. In Frame Relay in particular, it can take a minute or more after you see physical signals before there is end-to-end connectivity. So it is important to keep the backup link active until everything has stabilized. Also, sometimes a link will bounce up and down if there are electrical problems. Specifying a sensible delay before dropping the backup link ensures helps with link stability.

We have also included the *down-when-looped* command on the primary interface:

```
Router1(config)#interface Serial0/0
Router1(config-if)#down-when-looped
```

The dial backup will only trigger if this interface line protocol is in a down state. Normally, when you put a circuit into a *loopback* state for testing, the router considers the interface to be in an up state, but looped. However, in this diagnostic state the circuit will not pass any data. So, by configuring *down-when-looped*, we ensure that the backup will trigger if somebody runs a loopback test (perhaps unintentionally) on the primary circuit.

In general, we don't recommend using the backup interface method for dial backup. There are many types of WAN problems in which you will lose IP connectivity, but you don't lose physical signaling on the interface. For example, in the Frame Relay case again, there could be a problem in the cloud that causes you to lose your virtual circuit. Or you might be connected to a faulty network termination device that keeps signals active even though it doesn't have a real connection. The floating static method of Recipes 13.1 and 13.2 is much more robust than the backup interface method.

There is another important disadvantage to using the backup interface method. The router keeps backup interfaces disabled until it needs to dial. This causes two problems.

First, it means that you have to wait longer to dial because the router has to first establish physical connectivity with the backup network. In the case of ISDN, this can take 10–15 seconds.

The second problem is that, with ISDN interfaces, you lose the ability to see the state of the ISDN connection. Normally, if an ISDN interface is connected but not dialed, you can use the *show isdn status* command to verify that it is talking to the carrier's switch correctly, as we discussed in Recipe 13.1. However, since the backup interface is disabled with the method shown in the current recipe, you can't easily verify that your backup circuit is working without failing the primary circuit.

There is actually an interesting way to get around this last problem, though. Instead of making your backup interface be a physical interface like an ISDN port, as we did in this example, you could make the backup interface be a dialer interface, as we discussed in Recipe 13.2. In this case, the dialer interface will remain down when the primary is working, but the ISDN interface will still be up. And this means that you will be able to use the various *show isdn* commands, as you can with the other methods.

There is one interesting extra option to the backup interface configuration that can be useful in some situations. In addition to triggering the backup circuit when the primary circuit fails, you can configure the router to trigger the backup circuit when the load on the primary circuit gets heavy. This is a form of bandwidth on demand:

```
Router1(config)#interface Serial0/0
Router1(config-if)#backup load 75 25
```

This command trigger the dial backup when the load on the primary interface rises about 75 percent, and deactivates it when the load drops below 25 percent.

 Unlike the *dialer load-threshold* command discussed in Recipe 13.1, the arguments of *backup load* command are percentages and not fractions over 255.

Note, however, that to be really useful as additional bandwidth, you have to make sure that the routing over this new connection makes sense. In particular, it doesn't really help much unless the routing protocol sees the two paths as equal and shares the load between them. This will generally require some careful metric tuning in your routing protocol or use of the unequal cost load-sharing features available in some routing protocols. It also may require that the dial backup circuit terminates on the same router as the primary circuit to ensure that two-way load sharing works properly.

See Also

Chapter 10; Recipe 13.1

13.5   Using Dialer Watch

Problem

You want to use Cisco's Dialer Watch feature to trigger dial backup.

Solution

The Dialer Watch feature allows the router to track a particular destination IP address in its routing table. If all of the tracked IP addresses disappear from the routing table, the router automatically triggers the dial backup connection:

```
Router1#configure terminal
Enter configuration commands, one per line.  End with CNTL/Z.
Router1(config)#interface BRI0/0
Router1(config-if)#ip address 10.1.99.55 255.255.255.0
Router1(config-if)#encapsulation ppp
Router1(config-if)#dialer map ip 10.1.1.0 name dialhost broadcast 95551212
Router1(config-if)#dialer map ip 10.2.0.0 name dialhost broadcast 95551212
Router1(config-if)#dialer map ip 10.1.99.1 name dialhost broadcast 95551212
Router1(config-if)#dialer load-threshold 50 either
Router1(config-if)#dialer watch-group 1
Router1(config-if)#dialer-group 1
Router1(config-if)#isdn switch-type basic-ni
Router1(config-if)#isdn spid1 800555123400 5551234
Router1(config-if)#isdn spid2 800555123500 5551235
Router1(config-if)#ppp authentication chap
Router1(config-if)#ppp multilink
Router1(config-if)#exit
Router1(config)#router eigrp 55
Router1(config-router)#network 10.0.0.0
Router1(config-router)#exit
Router1(config)#username dialhost password cisco
Router1(config)#access-list 101 deny eigrp any any
Router1(config)#access-list 101 permit ip any any
Router1(config)#dialer-list 1 protocol ip list 101
Router1(config)#dialer watch-list 1 ip 10.2.0.0 255.255.0.0
Router1(config)#dialer watch-list 1 ip 10.1.1.0 255.255.255.0
Router1(config)#dialer watch-list 1 delay route-check initial 300
Router1(config)#dialer watch-list 1 delay disconnect 15
Router1(config)#end
Router1#
```

Discussion

This configuration is similar to that of Recipe 13.1, but this time the router uses the dialer watch feature to trigger the dial backup. The *dialer watch-group* command configures the backup interface to belong to a particular group. Usually you would only configure one such group on a router, but there is nothing to prevent you from having several different watch groups with different dial interfaces in each.

The watch group in this example looks for two prefixes in the routing tables, 10.1.1.0/24 and 10.2.0.0/16. If both of these routes drop out of the routing table, the router will automatically bring up the dial interface. Note that all of the watched routes must disappear before the router will dial.

We have configured several dialer map statements for this example. There is the same dialer map statement that we used in Recipe 13.1 to define the basic IP routing of the interface. And we have also included a *dialer watch-list* that specifies the two watched IP addresses.

We have also included the same dialer list configuration here, as we did in Recipe 13.1. This is because we still don't want routine EIGRP packets to bring up the dial interface or to keep the link up after the watched routes have returned to the routing table.

After it triggers the dial backup, the dialer watch configuration will keep track of the primary interface by periodically looking for the watched IP addresses in its routing table. The dialer watch feature will only consider the primary circuit active if the watched routes exist in the routing table, and if they do not point through the dial interface. We have configured two special timers that affect the dialer watch behavior:

```
Router1(config)#dialer watch-list 1 delay route-check initial 300
Router1(config)#dialer watch-list 1 delay disconnect 15
```

The first of these commands, with the *delay route-check initial* keywords, tells the router to wait for 300 seconds (5 minutes) after the router boots before starting to watch the routing table. This is useful because it often takes some time for all of the links to come up, and longer still before the routing tables have stabilized. By default, the router will begin checking the routing table immediately after booting. So setting a reasonable value like 300 seconds, as we have done, prevents unnecessary and potentially costly dialing.

The second command, with the *delay disconnect* keywords, tells the router to wait the specified number of seconds before disconnecting the dialup link.

Both of these commands are new to IOS Version 12.2(8)T. For earlier IOS versions, you can set the disconnect time by using the *dialer watch-disable* command:

```
Router1(config-if)#dialer watch-disable 15
```

However, prior to Version 12.2(8)T, there is no option for preventing unnecessary dialing immediately after booting.

Note that we also have defined a *dialer-group* command in the example:

```
Router1(config)#interface BRI0/0
Router1(config-if)#dialer-group 1
Router1(config-if)#exit
Router1(config)#dialer-list 1 protocol ip list 101
Router1(config)#access-list 101 deny eigrp any any
Router1(config)#access-list 101 permit ip any any
```

This specifies the interesting packets that will reset the dial *idle-timer*. This is not strictly necessary, but we believe that it is a good idea. The router will only check the status of the watched routes when the idle-timer reaches zero. If we did not include a *dialer-group* command on the interface, then no packets would be considered interesting and the idle-timer would count down from its maximum value (120 seconds by default) before rechecking the watch condition. If the missing routes have returned, the router will start the *watch-disable* timer and then disconnect the dialer.

The default *dialer watch-list delay disconnect* timer is zero, meaning that the router will immediately drop the connection. This could cause problems because it is possible that the routing protocol has not yet fully converged throughout the network. In this case, we have set a watch disconnect timer of 15 seconds to make sure that there is sufficient time to allow the routing protocol to fully recover before breaking the connection. And, because we are somewhat paranoid, we have also configured a *dialer-group* command to ensure that the router will never drop the dial connection if it is still in use.

In general, we still prefer to use floating static routes to trigger dial backup, as in Recipes 13.1 and 13.2. This is because they offer greater control and flexibility. The floating static method allows you to dial on the loss of *any* of a list of routing prefixes, while the *dialer watch* method won't trigger until you lose *all* of the list of prefixes. However, it is interesting to note that the *dialer-group* configuration in this recipe is the same as in the floating static route examples. So you could actually combine the two approaches by simply including a static route with a high administrative distance pointing to the dialer interface.

See Also

Recipe 13.1; Recipe 13.2

13.6   Using Virtual Templates

Problem

You want to configure dial backup by using virtual templates.

Solution

Virtual templates provide another way of configuring a central dialup host router:

```
dialhost#configure terminal
Enter configuration commands, one per line.  End with CNTL/Z.
dialhost(config)#username Router1 password dialpassword
dialhost(config)#interface BRI0/0
dialhost(config-if)#no ip address
dialhost(config-if)#encapsulation ppp
dialhost(config-if)#dialer pool-member 1
```

```
dialhost(config-if)#isdn switch-type basic-ni
dialhost(config-if)#isdn point-to-point-setup
dialhost(config-if)#isdn spid1 800555123400 5551234
dialhost(config-if)#isdn spid2 800555123500 5551235
dialhost(config-if)#ppp authentication chap
dialhost(config-if)#ppp multilink
dialhost(config-if)#exit
dialhost(config)#interface Dialer1
dialhost(config-if)#no ip address
dialhost(config-if)#encapsulation ppp
dialhost(config-if)#dialer idle-timeout 300
dialhost(config-if)#dialer-group 1
dialhost(config-if)#no peer default ip address
dialhost(config-if)#ppp authentication chap
dialhost(config-if)#ppp multilink
dialhost(config-if)#exit
dialhost(config)#access-list 101 deny    eigrp any any
dialhost(config)#access-list 101 permit ip any any
dialhost(config)#dialer-list 1 protocol ip list 101
dialhost(config)#router eigrp 55
dialhost(config-router)#network 10.0.0.0
dialhost(config-router)#exit
dialhost(config)#interface Loopback1
dialhost(config-if)#ip address 10.1.99.1 255.255.255.0
dialhost(config-if)#exit
dialhost(config)#interface Virtual-Template1
dialhost(config-if)#ip unnumbered Loopback1
dialhost(config-if)#encapsulation ppp
dialhost(config-if)#ppp authentication chap
dialhost(config-if)#ppp multilink
dialhost(config-if)#ppp multilink load-threshold 50 either
dialhost(config-if)#exit
dialhost(config)#virtual-profile virtual-template 1
dialhost(config)#end
dialhost#
```

Discussion

Virtual templates allow you to dynamically create virtual interfaces for dial purposes as they are required. This is only a benefit on routers that need to support several simultaneous connections, particularly when these connections are spread across several physical interfaces. So the ideal situation for using this configuration is a central dialup host router for a large enterprise WAN. Virtual templates are also useful in networks where large numbers of remote users dial in for access, such as in Internet Service Provider (ISP) networks.

Virtual templates are also useful in Frame Relay and ATM networks, where you can configure dynamic Switched Virtual Circuit (SVC) connections. And you can also use virtual templates for Permanent Virtual Circuit (PVC) connections when you need to use a nonstandard Layer 2 encapsulation such as PPP. We discuss these scenarios further in Chapters 10 and 16.

Compare this recipe to Recipe 13.2, where we first introduced the idea of a dialer interface to support multiple connections. In this case, our physical interface is an ISDN BRI, rather than a PRI, but in either case you could use one or several interfaces of any type that supports dialing. The first difference you should notice is that we have not configured an IP address on the *Dialer* interface:

```
dialhost(config)#interface Dialer1
dialhost(config-if)#no ip address
```

This is because we intend to dynamically generate virtual interfaces, which will hold the IP address information. In fact, we have created a new *Loopback* interface to carry the IP address for all of these virtual interfaces:

```
dialhost(config)#interface Loopback1
dialhost(config-if)#ip address 10.1.99.1 255.255.255.0
dialhost(config-if)#exit
dialhost(config)#interface Virtual-Template1
dialhost(config-if)#ip unnumbered Loopback1
dialhost(config-if)#encapsulation ppp
dialhost(config-if)#ppp authentication chap
dialhost(config-if)#ppp multilink
dialhost(config-if)#ppp multilink load-threshold 50 either
dialhost(config-if)#exit
```

The configuration of the *Virtual-Template* interface includes all of the relevant PPP and IP information, including configuration for PPP multilink. The router will clone this *Virtual-Template* to create new virtual access interfaces as it needs them. Some of these virtual accesses may use PPP multilink so span several physical interfaces, so we need to include this configuration here.

Then we need to use the *virtual-profile* command to allow the router to use this template whenever it needs to dynamically create interfaces:

```
dialhost(config)#virtual-profile virtual-template 1
```

The final argument to this command, 1, specifies the *Virtual-Template1* interface configuration.

This router can now dynamically create virtual access interfaces as it requires them. Look at the output of the *show ip interface brief* command when there are no calls connected:

```
dialhost#show ip interface brief
Interface          IP-Address      OK? Method Status                 Protocol
FastEthernet0/0    192.168.5.12    YES NVRAM  up                     up
Serial0/0          unassigned      YES NVRAM  administratively down  down
BRI0/0             unassigned      YES NVRAM  up                     up
BRI0/0:1           unassigned      YES unset  down                   down
BRI0/0:2           unassigned      YES unset  down                   down
Virtual-Access1    unassigned      YES unset  down                   down
Virtual-Template1  10.1.99.1       YES TFTP   down                   down
Dialer1            unassigned      YES NVRAM  up                     up
Loopback0          192.168.57.12   YES NVRAM  up                     up
Loopback1          10.1.99.1       YES NVRAM  up                     up
dialhost#
```

After we bring up remote dial connection, you can see that the router has dynamically generated a new interface called *Virtual-Access2*:

```
dialhost#show ip interface brief
Interface          IP-Address       OK? Method Status                 Protocol
FastEthernet0/0    192.168.5.12     YES NVRAM  up                     up
Serial0/0          unassigned       YES NVRAM  administratively down  down
BRI0/0             unassigned       YES NVRAM  up                     up
BRI0/0:1           unassigned       YES unset  up                     up
BRI0/0:2           unassigned       YES unset  down                   down
Virtual-Access1    unassigned       YES unset  down                   down
Virtual-Template1  10.1.99.1        YES TFTP   down                   down
Virtual-Access2    10.1.99.1        YES TFTP   up                     up
Dialer1            unassigned       YES NVRAM  up                     up
Loopback0          192.168.57.12    YES NVRAM  up                     up
Loopback1          10.1.99.1        YES NVRAM  up                     up
dialhost#
```

You can use the *show vtemplate* command to get additional information and statistics on your virtual templates:

```
dialhost#show vtemplate
Virtual access subinterface creation is globally enabled

        Active    Active     Subint  Pre-clone Pre-clone Interface
        Interface Subinterface Capable Available Limit    Type
        --------- ------------ ------- --------- --------- ---------
Vt1         1          0      Yes       --        --      Serial

Usage Summary
                            Interface   Subinterface
                            ---------   ------------
Current Serial  in use          2            0
Current Serial  free            1            1
Current Ether   in use          0            0
Current Ether   free            0            0
Current Tunnel  in use          0            0
Current Tunnel  free            0            0
Total                           3            1

Cumulative created              6            8
Cumulative freed                3            8

Base virtual access interfaces: 1
Total create or clone requests: 4
Cancelled create or clone requests: 0
Current request queue size: 0
Current free pending: 0
Current recycle pending: 0

Maximum request duration: 8 msec
Average request duration: 4 msec
Last request duration: 8 msec
```

```
Maximum processing duration: 8 msec
Average processing duration: 4 msec
Last processing duration: 8 msec

dialhost#
```

This output shows that there is currently one virtual template clone in use, and that the router has created such cloned interfaces four times since it last booted. The structure of this output varies drastically, depending on which IOS version and feature set you have installed in your router. The above example shows a Version 12.4 IP Base image.

See Also

Chapters 10 and 16; Recipe 13.2

13.7   Ensuring Proper Disconnection

Problem

You want to ensure that the dial backup line disconnects properly when the primary link recovers.

Solution

Sometimes funny things happen when the primary link comes back and the backup link has not yet disconnected. These problems are usually due to poor routing metrics, causing at least one of the routers to prefer the dial path, even if the primary is available. The easiest way to handle these problems is to use *bandwidth* commands to ensure that the primary is the better path:

```
Router1#configure terminal
Enter configuration commands, one per line.  End with CNTL/Z.
Router1(config)#interface Serial0/0.1 point-to-point
Router1(config-subif)#bandwidth 56
Router1(config-subif)#exit
Router1(config)#interface BRI0/0
Router1(config-subif)#bandwidth 54
Router1(config-subif)#end
Router1#
```

Discussion

This example assumes that you have a Frame Relay connection using a 56 Kbps primary link, and an ISDN dial backup connection. The problem is that the default ISDN interface bandwidth is 64 Kbps. So, if both the primary and the backup are active at the same time, the routing protocol will see the backup link as the preferred path. As a result, there will always be interesting traffic flowing through the backup link, and the router will fail to disconnect the dialup session properly.

To address this problem, we have configured a bogus bandwidth on the BRI interface. This will ensure that if both primary and backup are active simultaneously, the primary will be the better path. The only stipulation is that the value be lower for the backup path.

Actually, this change only affects the routing decisions for traffic going from this router to the dial router. It is not difficult to get a situation in which traffic from the branch to the hub site takes the primary path, while outbound packets to the branch take the backup path. So you have to be careful to adjust the values on both ends.

Dial backup situations can get more complicated in some networks. Perhaps the most insidious problems happen when the router responsible for the primary WAN link summarizes a large number of branch IP address ranges. This summarization is normally a good thing because it simplifies the global routing tables, and improves overall performance.

However, suppose the branch has a LAN segment that uses 10.11.100.0/24. And suppose the primary WAN router connects to many branches, offering the network core only a summary route that describes all of the branches as 10.11.0.0/16. When the primary WAN link for this branch breaks, the branch router dials to a dedicated dial backup router. The dynamic routing works because although the primary WAN router advertises a summary route that includes this branch's LAN address, the backup router advertises a more specific route. So other devices in the network core can route to the branch by using the more specific route from the backup router.

The problem appears when the primary link recovers. There are now two paths available. By adjusting bandwidths as shown in this recipe, the branch router knows that it should switch to using the primary link. But the rest of the network doesn't see any change. The primary router continues to present only a summary route for all of its branches, and the dial backup host still presents the more specific route for this particular branch. So all outbound traffic to the branch still uses the backup link.

We know of no simple solution to this problem except to ensure that the branch router is responsible for dropping the dial connection with an appropriate timeout. The alternatives are to avoid summarization or to have the dial backup router be the same physical device as the primary WAN router. You can help the branch router to switch to the primary by ensuring that the dial host router only sends a default route rather than a full routing table. This way, when the primary circuit recovers, the branch router will use the more specific routes that it learns through the primary circuit, thus quickly removing any interesting packets from the backup link.

13.8 View Dial Backup Status

Problem

You want to check on the dialer status of a router.

Solution

Here are some useful commands for looking at the status of a dial backup link. For dial backup that uses the floating static or dialer watch type configurations, you can use the *show dialer* command:

```
Router1#show dialer
```

For dial configurations that use the *backup interface* configuration, you can use the *show backup* command:

```
Router1#show backup
```

And, for backup configurations that use ISDN, you can get some additional information from the *show isdn status*, *show isdn active*, and *show isdn history* commands:

```
Router1#show isdn status
Router1#show isdn active
Router1#show isdn history
```

Discussion

The *show dialer* command provides a lot of useful information about existing dial sessions, as well as some historical statistics:

```
Router1#show dialer
BRI0 - dialer type = ISDN

Dial String      Successes   Failures    Last DNIS   Last status
0 incoming call(s) have been screened.
0 incoming call(s) rejected for callback.

BRI0:1 - dialer type = ISDN
Idle timer (300 secs), Fast idle timer (20 secs)
Wait for carrier (30 secs), Re-enable (15 secs)
Dialer state is data link layer up
Dial reason: ip (s=10.1.99.55, d=224.0.0.10)
Interface bound to profile Dialer1
Current call connected 00:03:18
Connected to 95551212 (dialhost)

BRI0:2 - dialer type = ISDN
Idle timer (120 secs), Fast idle timer (20 secs)
Wait for carrier (30 secs), Re-enable (15 secs)
Dialer state is idle

Dialer1 - dialer type = DIALER PROFILE
Load threshold for dialing additional calls is 100
Idle timer (300 secs), Fast idle timer (20 secs)
Wait for carrier (30 secs), Re-enable (15 secs)
Dialer state is data link layer up
Number of active calls = 1
Number of active circuit switched calls = 0
```

```
            Dial String      Successes   Failures   Last DNIS   Last status
            95551212             2           0       00:03:19    successful   Default
            Router1#
```

There is a lot of useful information in this output. First, notice that there is an active dial session on the first B channel of this ISDN BRI interface, *BRI0:1*. It has been connected for a little more than three minutes, and you can see the dial string that represents the remote telephone number. The second ISDN B channel, *BRI0:2*, is not connected, presumably because the router has yet not seen the minimum traffic threshold that we specified for bringing up the second channel, or perhaps it isn't configure for PPP multilink.

But there is another extremely important piece of information here. Notice the line marked "Dial reason." This shows the source and destination IP addresses of the packet that originally caused the router to start the dial session. In this case, the source IP address is 10.1.99.55, which is the IP address of the dial interface itself. The destination IP address is 224.0.0.10, which is extremely interesting because this is the multicast IP address that EIGRP uses to talk between routers. This is fine if we intended for this dial connection to remain up all the time. However, if this router was supposed to only dial when a primary link failed, then looking at this output should tell you that the dialer list configuration is wrong.

The bottom of the display includes some historical information about each of the configured dial strings, and how often the router has been able to connect success-fully using each string. In this case, there is only one dial string, but if there were sev-eral, they would all appear with their respective totals.

The *show backup* command is only useful when you use the backup interface config-uration, which is discussed in Recipe 13.4:

```
    Router1#show backup


    Primary Interface    Secondary Interface    Status
    -----------------    -------------------    ------
    Serial0/0            BRI0/0                 active backup
```

In this case, the interface *BRI0/0* is actively operating as a backup for the primary interface, *Serial0/0*, because it has become unavailable. If the primary interface is working properly, the Status column will say "normal operation." In this case, the backup interface will go into a standby mode:

```
    Router1#show interface bri0/0
    BRI0 is standby mode, line protocol is down
      Hardware is BRI
      Internet address is 10.1.99.55/24
      MTU 1500 bytes, BW 64 Kbit, DLY 20000 usec,
         reliability 255/255, txload 1/255, rxload 1/255
      Encapsulation PPP, loopback not set
      Last input never, output never, output hang never
      Last clearing of "show interface" counters never
```

```
    Input queue: 0/75/0/0 (size/max/drops/flushes); Total output drops: 0
    Queueing strategy: weighted fair
    Output queue: 0/1000/64/0 (size/max total/threshold/drops)
      Conversations  0/0/16 (active/max active/max total)
      Reserved Conversations 0/0 (allocated/max allocated)
      Available Bandwidth 48 kilobits/sec
    5 minute input rate 0 bits/sec, 0 packets/sec
    5 minute output rate 0 bits/sec, 0 packets/sec
      0 packets input, 0 bytes, 0 no buffer
      Received 0 broadcasts, 0 runts, 0 giants, 0 throttles
      0 input errors, 0 CRC, 0 frame, 0 overrun, 0 ignored, 0 abort
      0 packets output, 0 bytes, 0 underruns
      0 output errors, 0 collisions, 7 interface resets
      0 output buffer failures, 0 output buffers swapped out
      0 carrier transitions
  Router1#
```

If you are using ISDN for dial backup in any of the configurations discussed, you can get other useful information through the various *show isdn* commands:

```
Router1#show isdn status
Global ISDN Switchtype = basic-ni
ISDN BRI0/0 interface
    dsl 0, interface ISDN Switchtype = basic-ni
    Layer 1 Status:
    ACTIVE
    Layer 2 Status:
    TEI = 89, Ces = 1, SAPI = 0, State = MULTIPLE_FRAME_ESTABLISHED
    TEI = 90, Ces = 2, SAPI = 0, State = MULTIPLE_FRAME_ESTABLISHED
    TEI 89, ces = 1, state = 8(established)
        spid1 configured, spid1 sent, spid1 valid
        Endpoint ID Info: epsf = 0, usid = 70, tid = 1
    TEI 90, ces = 2, state = 8(established)
        spid2 configured, spid2 sent, spid2 valid
        Endpoint ID Info: epsf = 0, usid = 71, tid = 2
    Layer 3 Status:
    1 Active Layer 3 Call(s)
    Activated dsl 0 CCBs = 1
    CCB:callid=801A, sapi=0, ces=1, B-chan=1, calltype=DATA
    The Free Channel Mask:  0x80000002
  Total Allocated ISDN CCBs = 2
  Router1#
```

This example shows a single active call on one of the ISDN B channels. The lines that say that each SPID was configured, sent, and considered "valid" by the switch are also useful. In this case, we were connected to a *basic-ni* type switch, which requires us to manually configure SPIDs. It is important to check that the switch accepted these values.

If there are active calls, then the output of *show isdn active* can also be useful:

```
Router1#show isdn active
--------------------------------------------------------------------------------
                              ISDN ACTIVE CALLS
--------------------------------------------------------------------------------
```

```
History table has a maximum of 100 entries.
History table data is retained for a maximum of 15 Minutes.
--------------------------------------------------------------------------
Call    Calling      Called       Remote  Seconds Seconds Seconds Charges
Type    Number       Number       Name    Used    Left    Idle    Units/Currency
--------------------------------------------------------------------------
Out                  +95551212    dialhost  207                   0       0
--------------------------------------------------------------------------

Router1#
```

Here you can see that there is a single active call. This output also tells you exactly how long the call has been connected, and whether it was an in- or outbound connection. You can also get some potentially useful historical information about previous calls from the *show isdn history* command:

```
Router1#show isdn history
--------------------------------------------------------------------------
                         ISDN CALL HISTORY
--------------------------------------------------------------------------
History table has a maximum of 100 entries.
History table data is retained for a maximum of 15 Minutes.
--------------------------------------------------------------------------
Call    Calling      Called       Remote  Seconds Seconds Seconds Charges
Type    Number       Number       Name    Used    Left    Idle    Units/Currency
--------------------------------------------------------------------------
Out                                        Failed
Out                  +95551212    dialhost  20                            0
Out                  +95551212    dialhost  219                   0       0
--------------------------------------------------------------------------

Router1#
```

This router has attempted to make three outbound calls. The first call failed, the second lasted 20 seconds before disconnecting, and the third lasted 219 seconds. This command can be particularly useful if you think your router might be dialing too often, or that it might be frequently dialing and dropping calls. You can also look in the router's logging buffer for log messages. By default, every time the router dials, it generates at least one log message. Please refer to Chapter 18 for more information on logging.

See Also

Recipe 13.4; Chapter 18

13.9 Debugging Dial Backup

Problem

Your dial backup is not behaving properly and you want to debug it to isolate and resolve the problem.

Solution

The most common reasons for failed dial backup calls are incorrect dial strings and PPP authentication problems. You can easily diagnose both of these problems with this command:

```
Router1#debug ppp authentication
```

Here is another useful command for diagnosing problems with dialer configurations:

```
Router1#debug dialer
```

Discussion

When you use CHAP authentication with PPP, as we have done throughout this chapter, it is relatively easy to debug most common problems. We like to use the *debug ppp authentication* command because it pinpoints the most frequent problems:

```
Jun 28 14:04:05.211: BR0/0:1 PPP: Phase is AUTHENTICATING, by both
Jun 28 14:04:05.211: BR0/0:1 CHAP: O CHALLENGE id 1 len 33 from "Router1"
Jun 28 14:04:05.211: BR0/0:1 AUTH: Started process 0 pid 60
Jun 28 14:04:05.235: BR0/0:1 CHAP: I CHALLENGE id 35 len 33 from "dialhost"
Jun 28 14:04:05.235: BR0/0:1 CHAP: O RESPONSE id 35 len 33 from "Router1"
Jun 28 14:04:05.267: BR0/0:1 CHAP: I SUCCESS id 35 len 4
Jun 28 14:04:05.271: BR0/0:1 CHAP: I RESPONSE id 1 len 33 from "dialhost"
Jun 28 14:04:05.271: BR0/0:1 CHAP: O SUCCESS id 1 len 4
```

This output shows the PPP Authentication challenge and response handshake between two routers. This is one of the first places to look when you have dialup sessions that refuse to connect. In this particular trace, the router Router1 has dialed to dialhost. Upon connection, both routers present a password challenge. In this case, you can see that both routers responded correctly and authentication was successful. You should see a similar trace on both routers if everything is working properly.

If you enable this debug command and you see nothing, then you know that the routers are not reaching this point. So there is a problem at a lower layer. It would then be a good idea to start by making sure that you have the correct dial string, which you can verify by simply looking at the state of the dial interface on the receiving end to see if it picks up the phone when you call from the other end.

Another useful command to see if your router is dialing appropriately is *debug dialer*:

```
Jun 28 14:04:02.691: BR0/0 DDR: rotor dialout [priority]
Jun 28 14:04:02.691: BR0/0 DDR: Dialing cause ip (s=10.1.99.55, d=10.1.99.1)
Jun 28 14:04:02.691: BR0/0 DDR: Attempting to dial 95551212
Jun 28 14:04:05.311: Di1 DDR: dialer protocol up
```

Here you can see that the router is dialing because of an IP packet, and the output shows the source and destination IP addresses of this packet. It also shows the dial string, the interface, and the fact that it connected successfully.

## CHAPTER 14

NTP and Time

14.0 Introduction

Many engineers overlook the importance of accurate timekeeping on a router. It is often extremely useful to be able to accurately pinpoint when a particular event occurred. You may want to compare network event messages from various routers on your network for fault isolation, troubleshooting, and security purposes. This is impossible if their clocks are not set to a common source. In fact, the problem is even worse than merely setting the clocks to a single common standard because some clocks run a little bit fast and others run a little bit slow. So they need to be continuously adjusted and synchronized.

Network Time Protocol (NTP) is the *de facto* standard for Internet time synchronization. The current standard for NTP is Version 3, which is defined in RFC 1305. The IETF is currently developing a new version.

The protocol allows devices to communicate over UDP port 123 to obtain time from an authoritative time source such as a radio clock, atomic clock, or GPS-based time source. An NTP server connected directly to one of these known reliable time sources is called a *Stratum 1* timeserver. Stratum 2 timeservers receive their time via NTP from a Stratum 1 server, and so forth, up to a maximum of Stratum 16. Stratum numbers are analogous to hop counts from the authoritative time source. NTP generally prefers lower stratum servers to higher stratum servers unless the lower stratum server's time is significantly different.

The algorithm is able to detect when a time source is likely to be extremely inaccurate, or *insane*, and to prevent synchronization in these cases, even if the inaccurate clock is at a lower stratum level. And it will never synchronize a device to another server that is not synchronized itself.

The NTP protocol is extremely efficient and lightweight. It can synchronize a client device's clock with the server device's clock to within milliseconds while exchanging packets as rarely as once every 1,024 seconds (roughly 17 minutes). Even over WAN links, NTP is able to synchronize clocks to within tens of milliseconds. To achieve this, it has to have algorithms that estimate and reduce the effects of network jitter and latency. It is also able to use multiple time sources simultaneously for improved reliability and fault tolerance.

As the idea of multiple stratum levels suggests, NTP uses a hierarchical topology. However, this is only relevant to the relationships between NTP clients and servers, which do not need to be physically adjacent on the network. The protocol does not require any particular underlying network topology. Version 3 of the protocol has three different operational modes: master/slave (server/client), symmetric (peers), and a broadcast mode in which the clients passively listen for updates from a server. Some implementations also have a multicast mode that most likely foreshadows some of what will be in Version 4. Cisco has recently added multicast support, which we will discuss in Recipe 14.10.

In the master/slave mode, the client device periodically sends a message to one or more servers to request synchronization. Because the server is a master that is closer to the original time source, its clock is assumed to be more reliable. So the server will synchronize the client's time, but will not allow the client to change its own clock. The server passively listens for these requests.

In the symmetric peer-to-peer mode, both NTP devices synchronize one another. Peers can operate in active or passive mode. However, at least one of a pair of peers must be active, or nobody will ever start the conversation.

The broadcast and multicast modes of operation are used to synchronize a large number of passive client devices in a network. This has the advantage of saving bandwidth caused by multiple requests for synchronization. In most cases, this overhead is minimal, however. These modes have the disadvantage of being less precise than a poll-response model because there is no way for the client device to estimate network latency. The multicast mode is somewhat more useful than the broadcast mode because it allows you to synchronize devices on many network segments from a single source. However, multicast routing must be enabled on the network. We will discuss multicast routing in Chapter 23.

The NTP client and server software runs on most modern operating systems including Unix, Windows, and MacOS. You can find source code and binary executable NTP software for various operating systems at: *http://www.eecis.udel.edu/~ntp/software/index.html*. The general information web page for all things related to NTP and the ongoing protocol and software development is *http://www.ntp.org*.

Organizations can purchase their own authoritative time sources or obtain time services via the Internet. There are small, cost-effective Global Positioning Satellite (GPS) Stratum 1 servers on the market today, which you can use as an extremely accurate reference clock. These devices typically cost a few thousand dollars and can be easily rack mounted in a computer room in the core of your network. Alternatively, there are hundreds of public Stratum 1 and 2 timeservers available on the

Internet that allow peer devices to connect and synchronize with them free of charge. The extra complication of sending synchronization signals through the public Internet introduces some additional jitter that is somewhat more difficult to estimate. So this method is slightly less accurate than using your own time server, but the difference is rarely more than a few milliseconds, and you can reduce the impact of this problem by synchronizing with multiple servers. For most applications, the publicly available servers are more than adequate.

The web site *http://www.eecis.udel.edu/~mills/ntp/servers.htm* has useful information about public NTP servers available through the Internet.

14.1   Time-Stamping Router Logs

Problem

You want the router to record the time along with log and debug messages.

Solution

The *service timestamp* global configuration command enables timestamps on debug and logging messages. Use the *log* keyword to turn on time-stamping of log messages:

```
Router#configure terminal
Enter configuration commands, one per line.  End with CNTL/Z.
Router(config)#service timestamps log datetime localtime
Router(config)#end
Router#
```

The command to turn on timestamps for debug messages is similar, but uses the debug keyword:

```
Router#configure terminal
Enter configuration commands, one per line.  End with CNTL/Z.
Router(config)#service timestamps debug datetime localtime
Router(config)#end
Router#
```

Discussion

By default, Cisco routers create log and debug messages without any form of timestamp. These messages are useful if the administrator is watching them in real time. However, it impossible to look at the logs later and understand what exactly happened when. This example illustrates the problem:

```
%SYS-5-CONFIG_I: Configured from console on vty1 (172.25.1.1)
%CLEAR-5-COUNTERS: Clear counter on all interfaces on vty1 (172.25.1.1)
%OSPF-5-ADJCHG: Process 55, Nbr 172.25.25.6 on FastEthernet0/0.1 from FULL to DOWN
```

You can't tell when the router configuration was changed or when the OSPF neighbor state change. And, in particular, you can't tell if the configuration change caused the OSPF problem. Having accurately time-stamped log messages makes trouble-shooting and problem determination much easier.

The example below shows the same incident with timestamps enabled:

```
Mar  9 04:43:31: %SYS-5-CONFIG_I: Configured from console on vty1 (172.25.1.1)
Mar  9 04:44:17: %CLEAR-5-COUNTERS: Clear counter on all interfaces on vty1 (172.25.
1.1)
Mar 11 06:19:27: %OSPF-5-ADJCHG: Process 55, Nbr 172.25.25.6 on FastEthernet0/0.1
from FULL to DOWN
```

In the above example, it is clear that the router configuration changed on March 9 at 04:44:17, but that the OSPF problem happened two days later. Hopefully, this example makes it clear why we strongly advocate enabling this feature on all routers.

The same issues are generally true with debug messages, except for two things. First, most network administrators tend to turn on debug only when it is required for troubleshooting a particular problem, so the problem isn't what hour or day something happened, but rather what millisecond. The second problem is that when troubleshooting a complex connectivity problem, it is often necessary to have the clocks synchronized extremely closely. We will deal with this second problem in Recipe 14.5 when we talk about NTP. However, the first problem means that the router has to display debugging messages with more precise timestamps than log messages, usually to the millisecond.

You can enable millisecond timestamps for debug messages using the *msec* keyword as follows:

```
Router#configure terminal
Enter configuration commands, one per line.  End with CNTL/Z.
Router(config)#service timestamps debug datetime localtime show-timezone msec
Router(config)#end
Router#
```

The resulting timestamps on debugging messages look like this:

```
Mar  9 04:44:39.009: IP: s=172.25.1.5 (local), d=172.25.1.1 FastEthernet0/0.1), len
65, sending
Mar  9 04:44:39.177: IP: s=172.25.1.5 (local), d=172.25.1.3 (FastEthernet0/0.1), len
65, sending
Mar  9 04:44:39.341: IP: s=172.25.1.3 (FastEthernet0/0.1), d=172.25.1.5
(FastEthernet0/0.1), len 111, rcvd 3
```

The *msec* keyword is also available for log timestamps, although it tends not to be as useful.

For large Wide Area Networks that span several time zones, it is useful to enable local time zone information as part of the timestamp as well. This is done by using the *show-timezone* keyword as follows:

```
Router#configure terminal
Enter configuration commands, one per line.  End with CNTL/Z.
Router(config)#service timestamps log datetime localtime show-timezone
```

```
Router(config)#end
Router#
```

```
Mar  9 13:47:03 EST: %SYS-5-CONFIG_I: Configured from console on vty1 (172.25.1.1)
```

Instead of using absolute time, with the *date-time* keyword, you can use the *uptime* keyword to force the router to display log timestamps based on how long the router had been up when the event occurred:

```
Router#configure terminal
Enter configuration commands, one per line.  End with CNTL/Z.
Router(config)#service timestamps log uptime
Router(config)#end
Router#
```

This gives log messages that look like this:

```
2d04h: %CLEAR-5-COUNTERS: Clear counter on all interfaces on vty2 (172.25.1.1)
```

This message says that somebody cleared the router's counters when the router had been active for two days and four hours. If you want to correlate this to a real clock time, then you have to look at the router's current uptime and subtract to find out when the even occurred. This is rarely as useful as the absolute date timestamps because it requires too much effort to correlate log messages from different routers. It is also considerably less accurate because of the uncertainty in figuring out the precise time that the router restarted. This sort of time-stamping is really only useful if you don't intend to set the clock to an accurate absolute time.

See Also

Recipe 14.5

14.2   Setting the Time

Problem

You want to set the clock on the router.

Solution

You can set the internal system clock, using the clock set in Enable mode:

```
Router#clock set 14:27:22 January 29 2006
Router#
```

Some high-end routers, such as 4500 series, 7000 series, 7200 series, and 7500 series, have a battery protected *calendar* function that continues to keep time even if the router is temporarily powered off. You can set this calendar function by using the *calendar set* command in Enable mode:

```
Router#calendar set 14:34:39 January 29 2006
Router#
```

In both cases the router will accept either "hh:mm:ss day month year" or "hh:mm:ss month day year" notation.

Discussion

Every Cisco router has an internal system clock. When the router boots, the internal system clock starts to maintain the current date and time. If there is no battery-protected calendar in the router, the clock starts with a default initial value of Monday, March 1, 1993 at midnight. If you want accurate time, either you need to set it manually as shown above, or you need an automated method for setting it as in Recipe 14.5.

Most high-end routers have an internal battery-powered clock called a *calendar*. Router calendars are able to maintain accurate time and date information even during power interruptions. When the router initializes, it automatically synchronizes the internal system clock with the date stored with the calendar.

You can view the current calendar time by using the following command:

```
Router>show calendar
14:34:39 UTC Sun Jan 29 2006
Router>
```

If your router returns an error message when you issue this command then it does not contain a calendar:

```
Router#show calendar
        ^
% Invalid input detected at '^' marker.

Router#
```

Note, however, that the "clock" time and the "calendar" time are kept on different clocks that may differ at any given moment. After router initialization, these two clocks may drift apart or they may be set independent of one another. Fortunately, Cisco's IOS does provide methods of synchronizing the two time sources after initial power up.

To set the calendar to the internal clock time, use the following command in Enable mode:

```
Router#clock update-calendar
Router#
```

You can also set the internal clock to the calendar time using the command:

```
Router#clock read-calendar
Router#
```

Both the internal system clock and calendar use 24-hour time notation rather than 12-hour AM/PM notation.

See Also

Recipe 14.5

14.3 Setting the Time Zone

Problem

You want to change the time zone on the router.

Solution

To configure the router's local time zone, use the following configuration command:

```
Router#configure terminal
Enter configuration commands, one per line.  End with CNTL/Z.
Router(config)#clock timezone EST -5
Router(config)#end
Router#
```

The *clock timezone* configuration command accepts any freeform zone name (EST, PST, Eastern, etc.), followed by an offset from the UTC (–24 to 24 hours) and an optional offset from UTC in minutes for areas that require it.

Discussion

By default, the router uses UTC, also called Coordinated Universal Time. UTC, formerly known as Greenwich Mean Time (GMT), has become the worldwide standard for time and date. The principles for calculating local time zones from UTC are the same as for GMT. The only difference is that UTC is based on precise atomic clocks, shortwave radio signals, and satellites to ensure accuracy, which need not actually be located in Greenwich, England.

It is useful to set the router's internal system clock to display the time in the local time zone. North American clocks set to UTC, for example, display the time between five and eight hours ahead of the local time. This means that somebody reading the clock has to do some mental arithmetic to translate to local time, which is sometimes awkward and makes correlating the times of network problems more difficult than it needs to be.

You can view the current time zone information with the *show clock detail* command:

```
Router>show clock detail
14:27:31.415 EST Sun Jan 29 2006
Time source is NTP
Router>
```

Many organizations choose to configure all of their routers to the same time zone to ease problem correlation, regardless of router location. The network administrators will configure all of their routers to the same time zone, even if they are physically located in a different part of the world. We recommend doing this because it simplifies troubleshooting by eliminating the need to do a lot of mental arithmetic that can unnecessarily slow down an already difficult and stressful situation.

Table 14-1 shows the configuration for several of the most commonly used time zones in North America. A detailed list of worldwide time zones is located in Appendix B.

Table 14-1. North American time zones

Time zone	Abbr.	Offset from UTC	Configuration command
Hawaiian Standard Time	HST	UTC -10	`clock timezone HST -10`
Alaska Standard Time	AKST	UTC -9	`clock timezone AKST -9`
Pacific Standard Time	PST	UTC -8	`clock timezone PST -8`
Mountain Standard Time	MST	UTC -7	`clock timezone MST -7`
Central Standard Time	CST	UTC -6	`clock timezone CST -6`
Eastern Standard Time	EST	UTC -5	`clock timezone EST -5`
Atlantic Standard Time	AST	UTC -4	`clock timezone AST -4`
Newfoundland Standard Time	NST	UTC -3.5	`clock timezone NST -3 30`

See Also

Recipe 14.4; Recipe 14.5; Appendix B

14.4   Adjusting for Daylight Saving Time

Problem

You want the router to automatically adjust to Daylight Saving Time.

Solution

Some areas, such as most of North America and Europe, have consistent and common rules for when to switch between winter or Standard time and summer or Daylight Saving Time. The traditional North American rule, and the default for Cisco routers when they are configured for summer time, is to move an hour ahead at 2:00 AM on the first Sunday in April, and back an hour at 2:00 AM on the last Sunday in October. We note in passing that this rule will change starting in 2007, which we discuss in more detail in Recipe 14.19:

```
Router#configure terminal
Enter configuration commands, one per line.  End with CNTL/Z.
Router(config)#clock summer-time EDT recurring
Router(config)#end
Router#
```

You can also specify exact recurrence rules. You could use the following command to explicitly define the North American rules:

```
Router#configure terminal
Enter configuration commands, one per line.  End with CNTL/Z.
Router(config)#clock summer-time EDT recurring first sun apr 02:00 last sun oct 02:00
Router(config)#end
Router#
```

You can modify this line to represent other standard recurrence rules. For example, in the Southern Hemisphere, Daylight Saving Time commences towards the end of the year to match their summer season. To define the rules for Australian Eastern Daylight Time (AEDT), you could use the following command:

```
Router#configure terminal
Enter configuration commands, one per line.  End with CNTL/Z.
Router(config)#clock summer-time AEDT recurring last sun oct 02:00 last sun mar 02:00
Router(config)#end
Router#
```

Some areas do not have consistent daylight saving rules. In these areas, you must configure the start and end dates explicitly:

```
Router#configure terminal
Enter configuration commands, one per line.  End with CNTL/Z.
Router(config)#clock summer-time EDT date 26 oct 2003 02:00 6 apr 2003 02:00
Router(config)#end
Router#
```

Discussion

The router will not observe Daylight Saving Time by default. The *clock summer-time* command allows you to automatically reset the router's clock each fall and winter so that you don't have to do so manually, which can be a daunting task in a large network.

You can see how the router plans to implement the change to summertime with the show clock detail command:

```
Router>show clock detail
15:48:30.544 EST Sun Jan 29 2006
Time source is NTP
Summer time starts 02:00:00 EST Sun Apr 2 2006
Summer time ends 02:00:00 EDT Sun Oct 29 2006
Router>
```

In this case, the router is set to the default North American Daylight Saving Time start and end dates.

See Also

Recipe 14.3; Recipe 14.19

14.5 Synchronizing the Time on All Routers (NTP)

Problem

You want your routers to automatically learn the time and synchronize their clocks through the network.

Solution

Network Time Protocol (NTP) is an open standard protocol for time synchronization. You can implement NTP on a router to provide automatic and efficient time synchronization. To enable a basic NTP configuration, enter the following commands:

```
Router#configure terminal
Enter configuration commands, one per line.  End with CNTL/Z.
Router(config)#clock timezone EST -5
Router(config)#clock summer-time EDT recurring
Router(config)#ntp server 172.25.1.1
Router(config)#end
Router#
```

The *ntp server* command accepts either IP addresses or hostnames. To use a hostname, however, you will need to configure the router to either use a static host table or DNS for name resolution, as discussed in Chapter 2.

Some low-end routers such as Cisco 1000 series, Cisco 1600 series, Cisco 1720, and Cisco 1750 series do not support NTP. For these, Cisco provides support for the Simple Network Time Protocol (SNTP), which is a compatible subset of the NTP standard. The SNTP configuration is similar to NTP:

```
Router#configure terminal
Enter configuration commands, one per line.  End with CNTL/Z.
Router(config)#clock timezone EST -5
Router(config)#clock summer-time EDT recurring
Router(config)#sntp server 172.25.1.1
Router(config)#end
Router#
```

Discussion

When NTP is enabled on a router, it will start trying to synchronize with the configured peers or servers as soon as it boots. By default, the router's clock always displays the time in the UTC time zone. So we recommend configuring an appropriate local time zone, as in this example, and shown in more detail in Recipes 14.3 and 14.4.

Most Cisco routers fully support NTP Versions 1, 2, and 3, and also include some features such as multicast support that are not yet fully standard. There are actually no important protocol differences between the three versions, and they operate together well. The main differences between them are in things like the algorithms used for estimating latency, and in some additional modes of operation.

Version three of the NTP protocol has several different modes of operation. A device can be a client, server, peer, multicast, broadcast client, or a broadcast server. Once a router has built a NTP association and synchronized its clock, it automatically becomes a fully functional NTP server itself capable of providing NTP services to other NTP clients.

By default, the source IP address that a router uses for its NTP packets will be the address of the interface that sends them. This is usually not a problem. However, in networks with many redundant paths, it is possible to have a router suddenly change the interface that it uses to communicate with another NTP device simply because the routing tables changed. If the other device is configured to only accept a limited number of connections, or if it has rules allowing connections only from certain specified devices, then NTP might break.

To get around these sorts of problems, Cisco provides two methods for manually assigning the source address of NTP packets. The first is a global command that affects all NTP packets, and the second sets different source addresses for different NTP associations.

The global command assigns a source IP address for all associations, even the ones that the router passively accepts:

```
Router#configure terminal
Enter configuration commands, one per line.  End with CNTL/Z.
Router(config)#ntp source loopback0
Router(config)#end
Router#
```

This example tells NTP to use the IP address of the loopback0 interface as the source address for all NTP associations.

Sometimes you want the router to use different source addresses for different servers:

```
Router#configure terminal
Enter configuration commands, one per line.  End with CNTL/Z.
Router(config)#ntp server 172.25.1.1 source FastEthernet 0/0.1
Router(config)#ntp server 10.1.1.1 source Serial 0/0
Router(config)#end
Router#
```

Assigning a source address for one NTP association like this does not effect other NTP associations on the router. You can assign the global command and the per association command at the same time, and the router will use the global address for everything except the specifically defined associations.

In Recipe 14.2 we mentioned that many high-end routers contain battery-protected calendars that operate independently from the main system clock. By default, NTP will only set the system clock. But you can also synchronize the calendar with NTP by using the *ntp update-calendar* command:

```
Router#configure terminal
Enter configuration commands, one per line.  End with CNTL/Z.
Router(config)#ntp update-calendar
```

```
Router(config)#end
Router#
```

Two other useful timestamps are automatically enabled on routers that have their clocks synchronized with NTP. First, the *show version* command gives the exact time when the router last initialized:

```
Router#show version
Cisco Internetwork Operating System Software
IOS (tm) C2600 Software (C2600-JK9O3S-M), Version 12.2(7a), RELEASE SOFTWARE (fc2)
Copyright (c) 1986-2002 by cisco Systems, Inc.
Compiled Thu 21-Feb-02 03:48 by pwade
Image text-base: 0x80008088, data-base: 0x8153F5D0

ROM: System Bootstrap, Version 11.3(2)XA4, RELEASE SOFTWARE (fc1)

router uptime is 3 days, 2 hours, 7 minutes
System returned to ROM by power-on
System restarted at 20:56:01 EST Sun Jan 28 2006
System image file is "flash:c2600-jk9o3s-mz.122-7a.bin"
<removed>
```

Second, the *show running-config* command gives a timestamp of when the configuration last changed and when the running configuration was last saved to NVRAM:

```
Router#show running-config
Building configuration...

Current configuration : 3353 bytes
!
! Last configuration change at 00:06:20 EST Fri Jan 27 2006 by ijbrown
! NVRAM config last updated at 00:08:59 EST Fri Jan 27 2006 by ijbrown
!
version 12.2
service timestamps debug datetime msec
service timestamps log datetime localtime
service password-encryption
service compress-config
<removed>
```

SNTP is another UDP-based time synchronization protocol—essentially a simplified version of NTP that only supports client time synchronization. Several of Cisco's low-end routers support only SNTP and cannot synchronize the clocks of other devices.

Since SNTP is essentially a subset of NTP, it allows the router to synchronize to central NTP servers, and it can use NTP broadcast messages as well. SNTP is much less accurate than NTP, generally only allowing devices to synchronize their clocks to within 100 milliseconds (a tenth of a second). SNTP based routers can obtain time services from multiple NTP sources, but SNTP lacks the ability to make intelligent server decisions (unlike NTP). If the router is configured with several servers, SNTP will simply choose the one with the lowest NTP stratum number. If it knows about two servers that are both at the same stratum level, the router chooses the one that sends the first packet. SNTP will only select an NTP server with a higher stratum if a lower stratum server becomes unreachable.

There are only two SNTP configuration options. The router can communicate directly with a server, or you can configure it to listen for NTP broadcasts:

```
Router#configure terminal
Enter configuration commands, one per line.  End with CNTL/Z.
Router(config)#sntp ?
  broadcast  Configure SNTP broadcast services
  server     Configure SNTP server
Router(config)#end
Router#
```

You can view the SNTP status on the router with the *show sntp* command:

```
Router>show sntp
SNTP server    Stratum    Version    Last Receive
172.25.1.1        2          3        00:00:24    Synced
172.25.1.3        2          3        00:00:51
Router>
```

See Also

Recipe 14.2; Recipe 14.3; Recipe 14.4

14.6   Configuring NTP Redundancy

Problem

You want to configure more than one NTP server for redundancy.

Solution

You can improve NTP reliability by configuring several redundant servers. The reliability is better still if the router uses different paths to reach these servers:

```
Router#configure terminal
Enter configuration commands, one per line.  End with CNTL/Z.
Router(config)#clock timezone EST -5
Router(config)#clock summer-time EDT recurring
Router(config)#ntp server 172.25.1.1
Router(config)#ntp server 10.121.33.231
Router(config)#ntp peer 192.168.12.12
Router(config)#end
Router#
```

Discussion

The NTP algorithms have built-in sanity checks to help choose the best time source. The NTP client chooses the most accurate time source and synchronizes its internal clock to that server. The algorithm continuously performs sanity checks to ensure that it synchronizes to the best possible server. It is also common for a router to change its preferred NTP server many times during a day.

Configuring multiple time sources improves reliability as well as the accuracy of a router's clock. Although NTP is a remarkably stable protocol, device and link failures can disrupt timing services to your router. Providing the router with a choice of NTP servers ensures accurate time synchronization and provides resilience in case of failure. Be sure to choose redundant NTP servers that provide alternate network paths and hardware.

An NTP network is a hierarchy of servers and clients configured in a redundant topology. At the top level, Stratum 1 NTP servers establish peer relationships with other Stratum 1 servers and server relationships to Stratum 2 servers. In turn, Stratum 2 servers peer symmetrically with other Stratum 2 servers, receive time feeds one or more Stratum 1 servers, and act as servers for Stratum 3 devices. This pattern repeats to create an overall tree topology of Stratum levels.

Figure 14-1 shows a typical NTP hierarchal topology with fully redundant paths and devices. The goal is to design a NTP hierarchy that can withstand a failure of any single networking entity, path, or device. Designing a resilient NTP topology requires little time and effort once you plot your time sources on an existing network diagram. Large networks tend to require more thought and effort to design an overall NTP hierarchy, whereas small networks can often make do with two NTP servers.

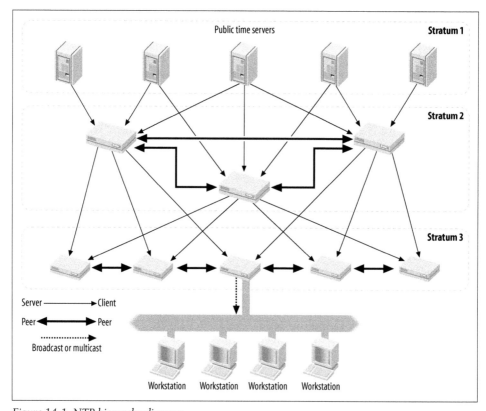

Figure 14-1. NTP hierarchy diagram

The important thing is to design the NTP topology to use its redundancy features. Once the NTP topology is defined, configuring the routers to participate in the hierarchy is straightforward. The example above demonstrates a typical NTP configuration that incorporates redundancy features. The router configuration includes two NTP servers and an NTP peer:

```
Router>show ntp associations

        address          ref clock     st  when  poll reach  delay  offset    disp
*~172.25.1.1         192.5.41.40       2    57    64  377   30.0   60.32    1.2
+~10.121.33.231      192.5.41.209      2    11    64  377   30.0  -54.85    1.1
 ~192.168.12.12      172.25.1.1        3  4588  1024    0    4.9   58.07  16000.
*master (synced), # master (unsynced), + selected, - candidate, ~ configured
*Router>
```

In this case, the router configuration includes multiple NTP time sources. The output indicates that one of the time sources, 192.168.12.12, is currently unreachable. Even though one of the configured time sources is unavailable, the router is unaffected because the other NTP associations remain up, and synchronized. This means that accurate time services are uninterrupted by losing a single NTP time feed.

If your organization receives its NTP feed from the Internet, then it is highly recommended that you use at least two such NTP servers. To provide maximum stability, configure each of your servers with multiple NTP Stratum 1 servers and build a peer relationship between them. This ensures that your organization's time source remains as stable as possible.

Routers that lose connectivity to their Stratum 1 servers will rely on their own internal clocks until service is restored. Similarly, routers that are isolated from their upstream Stratum servers also rely on their own internal clocks. However, in these situations, router internal clocks will not be synchronized to one another, meaning the network clocks will drift further apart until connectivity returns. NTP generally tolerates interruptions of less than an hour quite well.

See Also

Recipe 14.5; Recipe 14.6; Recipe 14.7

14.7 Setting the Router As the NTP Master for the Network

Problem

You want to use the router as an NTP server to act as the primary time source for the network.

Solution

There is no need for a dedicated NTP server; you can pick one or two routers to act as authoritative NTP servers for the whole network. (The router should have a calendar function):

```
Router#configure terminal
Enter configuration commands, one per line.  End with CNTL/Z.
Router(config)#clock timezone EST -5
Router(config)#clock summer-time EDT recurring
Router(config)#clock calendar-valid
Router(config)#ntp master 8
Router(config)#end
Router#
```

Discussion

When no authoritative time sources are available, and you still need to synchronize clocks throughout a network, you can configure a router to act as an NTP master server. Although this situation should be considered as a last resort, the router can become a "self-professed" NTP master, even if it is not actually synchronized from an accurate clock.

NTP provides two important services, accurate time setting and clock synchronization. Enabling a router to become a NTP master will not guarantee accurate time, but it will ensure that all network components' time remain synchronized. This distinction is important because routers acting as NTP masters can synchronize their entire network to an incorrect time. However, if the reliable time sources that your network uses become unreachable for any length of time, it is often useful to at least keep the clocks synchronized, even if they aren't completely accurate.

For this reason, we recommend that if your routers provide master NTP services, they should never advertise themselves as Stratum 1 servers. Timekeeping instability can occur on networks with both legitimate NTP time sources and router NTP masters. This is because NTP clients cannot distinguish between legitimate time sources and a router acting as a NTP master. So please use caution when configuring this feature.

 Setting a router to act as a NTP master can interrupt legitimate time sources.

In the example above the NTP master is set to the relatively safe Stratum level 8. In most cases, this will prevent the router from being preferred over valid time sources, since NTP clients tend to synchronize to the lowest available Stratum server, assuming their clock is sane.

For obvious reasons, only routers with battery-protected timers or calendars are good candidates to become NTP masters. Otherwise, a power failure or reload of a single router could cause the entire network to become unsynchronized. For increased resilience, the design should include a minimum of two NTP master routers with peering configured between them.

See Also

Recipe 14.3; Recipe 14.4; Recipe 14.5

14.8 Changing NTP Synchronization Periods

Problem

You want to adjust how often routers send NTP packets to verify clock synchronization.

Solution

NTP does not allow poll rates to be changed manually; however, there are algorithms that adaptively shape this parameter within the NTP protocol.

Discussion

NTP is an extremely efficient protocol that actively monitors all aspects of network timing to adjust its configuration accordingly. Upon initialization of NTP on a router, it sets its poll cycle to about once every 64 seconds. As the local clock becomes synchronized and stable, the router will adaptively back off the poll cycle to a maximum of 1,024 seconds (roughly 17 minutes):

```
Router>show ntp associations

        address         ref clock     st  when  poll reach delay offset   disp
*~172.25.1.1        130.207.244.240   2   440   1024  377   1.6   -3.23    5.6
+~172.25.1.3        204.152.184.72    2   829   1024  377   1.7    8.06    0.9
* master (synced), # master (unsynced), + selected, - candidate, ~ configured
Router>
```

Notice that the poll cycle for the two configured servers above has been throttled back to 1024 seconds. This indicates that the router is in a stable network and the time services are consistently accurate. This also illustrates NTP's remarkable efficiency.

See Also

Recipe 14.5

14.9   Using NTP to Send Periodic Broadcast Time Updates

Problem

You want to set up your router to use the NTP broadcast mode so that devices do not need to query periodically for the time.

Solution

Use the NTP broadcast interface configuration command to enable server-side NTP broadcasts:

```
Router1#configure terminal
Enter configuration commands, one per line.  End with CNTL/Z.
Router1(config)#clock timezone EST -5
Router1(config)#clock summer-time EDT recurring
Router1(config)#ntp server 172.25.1.1
Router1(config)#ntp server 172.25.1.2
Router1(config)#interface FastEthernet0/0
Router1(config-if)#ntp broadcast
Router1(config-if)#end
Router1#
```

To enable a NTP broadcast client on the router, enter the following:

```
Router2#configure terminal
Enter configuration commands, one per line.  End with CNTL/Z.
Router2(config)#clock timezone EST -5
Router2(config)#clock summer-time EDT recurring
Router2(config)#ntp broadcastdelay 4
Router2(config)#interface Ethernet0
Router2(config-if)#ntp broadcast client
Router2(config-if)#end
Router2#
```

Discussion

Usually NTP associations are configured in a master/slave relationship, but the server (router) can also send periodic time updates using broadcast messages. This is useful on LAN segments that contain a large number of devices requiring NTP synchronization. Instead of responding to a large number of *unicast* NTP packets through a single interface, the router can simply send a single broadcast packet at a regular interval.

NTP devices configured to accept NTP broadcast messages can synchronize their internal clocks without ever sending a single NTP request packet. However, this simplicity comes at the cost of reduced timing accuracy, since the traffic is one-way only. The accuracy improves slightly by configuring an estimated broadcast delay on the client side, using the *ntp broadcastdelay* configuration command, as in the client configuration example above.

Devices whose clocks are synchronized with NTP broadcasts are usually accurate to within a few hundreds of milliseconds. This is more than adequate for most client workstations. If some of the devices on the LAN require more accuracy, then you can configure these devices with regular NTP associations, as discussed in Recipes 14.5, 14.6, and 14.7. NTP broadcast mode does not prevent normal NTP client/server relationships from occurring as well, if required.

The example below shows a router configured as a NTP broadcast client that has synchronized its internal clock to a broadcast server:

```
Router2>show ntp associations detail
172.16.2.1 dynamic, our_master, sane, valid, stratum 3
ref ID 172.25.1.3, time C03A9BAB.5A1E7119 (22:46:51.352 EST Wed Mar 13 2003)
our mode bdcast client, peer mode bdcast, our poll intvl 64, peer poll intvl 64
root delay 116.56 msec, root disp 46.39, reach 376, sync dist 108.398
delay 5.19 msec, offset -0.3381 msec, dispersion 1.14
precision 2**16, version 3
org time C03A9C11.5A2376B6 (22:48:33.352 EST Wed Mar 13 2003)
rcv time C03A9C11.5B0B9E6E (22:48:33.355 EST Wed Mar 13 2003)
xmt time 00000000.00000000 (19:00:00.000 EST Thu Dec 31 1899)
filtdelay =    5.19    5.19    5.19    5.19    5.19    5.19    5.19    5.19
filtoffset =  -0.34   -0.53   -0.19   -0.18   -0.27   -0.32   -0.26   -0.34
filterror =    0.99    1.97    2.94    3.92    4.90    5.87    6.85    7.83
Router2>
```

Note that the *ntp broadcast* commands are interface configuration-level commands, configured on the interface that is sending or receiving the NTP broadcasts. However, the *ntp broadcastdelay* command is a global configuration command affecting all interfaces that use NTP broadcast features.

See Also

Recipe 14.10; Recipe 14.12

14.10 Using NTP to Send Periodic Multicast Time Updates

Problem

You want to set up your router to use the NTP multicast mode so that devices do not need to query periodically for the time.

Solution

Use the *ntp multicast* interface command to enable server-side NTP multicast packets:

```
Router1#configure terminal
Enter configuration commands, one per line.  End with CNTL/Z.
Router1(config)#clock timezone EST -5
```

```
Router1(config)#clock summer-time EDT recurring
Router1(config)#ntp server 172.25.1.1
Router1(config)#ntp server 172.25.1.3
Router1(config)#interface FastEthernet 0/0
Router1(config-if)#ntp multicast 224.0.1.1 ttl 1
Router1(config-if)#end
Router1#
```

To enable NTP multicast client functionality on the router, use the following commands:

```
Router2#configure terminal
Enter configuration commands, one per line.  End with CNTL/Z.
Router2(config)#clock timezone EST -5
Router2(config)#clock summer-time EDT recurring
Router2(config)#interface Ethernet0
Router2(config-if)#ntp multicast client 224.0.1.1
Router2(config-if)#ntp multicast version 3
Router2(config-if)#end
Router2#
```

NTP multicast support is available starting in IOS Version 12.1.

Discussion

On the surface, the ability to forward NTP broadcast packets and NTP Multicast packets on a LAN interface appear similar. However, there are some important differences. First, NTP sends broadcast packets to the 255.255.255.255 local broadcast address. This means that every device on the network must examine the NTP packet. If there are devices on the network that are not NTP broadcast clients, then they will waste valuable system resources reading and discarding these NTP broadcast packets.

On the other hand, NTP multicast packets are sent to the well-known NTP multicast address, 224.0.1.1 by default, and only participating NTP multicast clients will examine these packets. The decision of whether to look at a multicast packet is made by the client device's Network Interface Card (NIC), which makes multicast traffic more efficient.

Second, broadcast packets never leave the local LAN segment or broadcast domain. However, multicast packets can be forwarded beyond the local segment via multicast routing, as discussed in Chapter 23. In the above example, we have configured the server so that it sends these multicast packets with a Time-To-Live (TTL) value of one. This effectively limits the range of the NTP multicast packets to the local segment, so you do not have to enable multicast routing. But we could choose to route the packet further by increasing the TTL value and enabling multicast routing.

Third, upon initial startup, multicast clients will forward several unicast NTP queries in quick succession to accurately estimate delay and jitter to the server. This ensures that multicast NTP clients provide more accurate network time than broadcast NTP. Once the initial packet exchanges occur, the client becomes completely passive and listens for the regularly scheduled NTP multicast server packets.

The following example shows the output of a network analyzer configured to capture all NTP packets on the wire:

```
07:36:15 172.25.1.5.ntp > 224.0.1.1.ntp:v3 mcast strat 3  [ttl 1]
07:37:19 172.25.1.5.ntp > 224.0.1.1.ntp:v3 mcast strat 3  [ttl 1]
07:38:23 172.25.1.5.ntp > 224.0.1.1.ntp:v3 mcast strat 3  [ttl 1]
07:39:27 172.25.1.5.ntp > 224.0.1.1.ntp:v3 mcast strat 3  [ttl 1]
07:40:31 172.25.1.5.ntp > 224.0.1.1.ntp:v3 mcast strat 3  [ttl 1]
07:41:35 172.25.1.5.ntp > 224.0.1.1.ntp:v3 mcast strat 3  [ttl 1]
07:42:39 172.25.1.5.ntp > 224.0.1.1.ntp:v3 mcast strat 3  [ttl 1]
07:43:43 172.25.1.5.ntp > 224.0.1.1.ntp:v3 mcast strat 3  [ttl 1]
07:44:47 172.25.1.5.ntp > 224.0.1.1.ntp:v3 mcast strat 3  [ttl 1]
07:45:51 172.25.1.5.ntp > 224.0.1.1.ntp:v3 mcast strat 3  [ttl 1]
```

Notice that the NTP server enters into an active state by periodically forwarding NTP multicast messages. Also, notice that the clients on the local wire do not forward a single packet while in broadcast or multicast mode (after the initial setup). This effectively means the router can just send one packet every 64 seconds and synchronize a large number of clients.

The packet trace also displays some useful information about the server. First, the server's IP address is 172.25.1.5, and it is configured to send multicast NTP packets with the well-known NTP multicast address 224.0.1.1. It also shows that the server is running NTP Version 3 and is advertising itself as a stratum 3 NTP server. Finally, it shows that the server's TTL is one, which will contain its NTP packets to the local LAN segment.

Since multicast traffic is more efficient than broadcast traffic, it is the preferred method of providing NTP service via the local LAN. However, since not all NTP clients currently support NTP multicasting, you may have to also use NTP broadcast mode until all clients support multicasting. NTP broadcast services can safely co-exist on the same wire as NTP multicast traffic, which should assist network administrators in converting client software.

 For redundancy purposes, you can configure multiple NTP broadcast/multicast servers on a single subnet.

See Also

Chapter 23 on Multicast Routing; Recipe 14.9; Recipe 14.12

14.11 Enabling and Disabling NTP Per Interface

Problem

You want to control NTP services on a per-interface basis.

Solution

Depending on the level of access control required, you can use the *ntp disable* command to prevent the router from providing NTP services on a particular interface:

```
Router#configure terminal
Enter configuration commands, one per line.  End with CNTL/Z.
Router(config)#interface Serial0/1
Router(config-if)#ntp disable
Router(config-if)#end
Router#
```

You can also prevent the router from providing NTP services on an individual interface with access control lists:

```
Router#configure terminal
Enter configuration commands, one per line.  End with CNTL/Z.
Router(config)#access-list 107 deny udp any eq 123 any eq 123
Router(config)#access-list 107 permit ip any any
Router(config)#interface Serial0/1
Router(config-if)#ip access-group 107 in
Router(config-if)#end
Router#
```

Both examples above effectively disable the router from providing NTP services through the interface Serial0/1, although the inbound access-list provides more flexibility.

Discussion

By default, when you enable NTP services on a Cisco router, it automatically becomes an NTP server and provides time services on all interfaces. However, you may want to disable NTP services on one or more of the router's interfaces. For instance, you may want to prevent your router from providing NTP services to devices outside of your organization. You could accomplish this by disabling NTP on router interfaces that connect to these external networks. Further, some organizations insist that end devices should get their NTP services from a dedicated NTP server. In this case, you might want to prohibit routers from providing time services, although they would still take part in NTP for synchronizing their own clocks.

The *ntp disable* command in the example above prevents any NTP associations from using the Serial0/1 interface. This affects both inbound and outbound associations. However, it will not prevent the router from routing NTP traffic through this interface on its way to another NTP device. In contrast, the access-list example above prevents the router from passing any NTP packets received by this interface, regardless of the destination. And it will also prevent the router itself from using this interface for forming any NTP associations through this interface.

See Also

Recipe 14.14

14.12 NTP Authentication

Problem

You want to authenticate your NTP packets.

Solution

Use the *ntp authentication* command to authenticate NTP traffic between associations. To configure an NTP enabled router to require authentication when other devices connect to it, use the following commands:

```
Router1#configure terminal
Enter configuration commands, one per line.  End with CNTL/Z.
Router1(config)#ntp authentication-key 2 md5 oreilly
Router1(config)#ntp authenticate
Router1(config)#ntp trusted-key 2
Router1(config)#end
Router1#
```

Then you must configure the same authentication-key on the client router:

```
Router2#configure terminal
Enter configuration commands, one per line.  End with CNTL/Z.
Router2(config)#ntp authentication-key 2 md5 oreilly
Router2(config)#ntp authenticate
Router2(config)#ntp trusted-key 2
Router2(config)#ntp server 172.25.1.5 key 2
Router2(config)#end
Router2#
```

Discussion

People often confuse authentication with encryption. Authentication proves the authenticity of a packet's source, whereas encryption encodes or enciphers the packet contents. For the purposes of NTP, proving the authenticity of the packet is critical, whereas encrypting the contents of the packet is unnecessary, since it only contains time information, which isn't terribly sensitive in itself.

Cisco fully supports NTP authentication defined in RFC 1305. NTP authentication ensures that NTP associations synchronize time only to known and trusted NTP servers. This prevents servers from masquerading as legitimate timeservers either accidentally or intentionally.

Time services and the ability to manipulate time services are critical to organizations that may depend on accurate time for billing, business regulatory issues, fault isolation, or security purposes. In such organizations, there is at least a theoretical danger that somebody could put a false NTP server on the network to change the clocks, which could be useful in some larger nefarious scheme. To prevent such problems and enhance security, many organizations only allow authenticated NTP relationships within their corporate networks.

The NTP protocol uses the RSA Message Digest 5 (MD5) algorithm to provide cryptographic authentication of NTP packets. Although the NTP packet is not encrypted, a one-way hash, created using pre-shared keys, ensures the authenticity of the sender and packet. The contents of the NTP packet's time and date information do not warrant secrecy, so no encryption is required.

The example above shows a single client/server pair, enabling authentication between them. The NTP client and server pair must share the same key number and value ("oreilly," in this case) before authentication will work. Note that routers support multiple keys and can assign a different key for each association, if required. You can also configure the router to accept time updates from a mixture of authenticated and nonauthenticated servers. This example shows portions of a NTP debug trace:

```
Router1#debug ntp packet
NTP packets debugging is on
Router1#debug ntp authentication
NTP authentication debugging is on
Mar 18 22:39:12 EST: NTP: rcv packet from 172.16.2.2 to 172.25.1.7
Mar 18 22:39:12 EST:  leap 0, mode 3, version 3, stratum 4, ppoll 256
Mar 18 22:39:12 EST:  Authentication key 2

Mar 18 22:39:12 EST: NTP: stateless xmit packet to 172.16.2.2:
Mar 18 22:39:12 EST:  leap 0, mode 4, version 3, stratum 3, ppoll 256
Mar 18 22:39:12 EST:  Authentication key 2
```

Notice that the client polled the server with authentication key 2 and the server responded with its NTP response and authentication key 2 as well. Assuming that both key 2 strings are also equal, the client will form an association with the server and synchronize its internal clock with the server's.

Broadcast and multicast NTP associations also support NTP authentication:

```
Router3#configure terminal
Enter configuration commands, one per line.  End with CNTL/Z.
Router3(config)#clock timezone EST -5
Router3(config)#clock summer-time EDT recurring
Router3(config)#ntp authentication-key 2 md5 oreilly
Router3(config)#ntp trusted-key 2
Router3(config)#ntp server 172.25.1.1
Router3(config)#interface Ethernet0
Router3(config-if)#ntp multicast key 2
Router3(config-if)#end
Router3#
```

This example shows the configuration for an NTP multicast server that sends multicast packets by using the default NTP address 224.0.1.1 with authentication enabled. You can configure authentication for NTP broadcast mode similarly with the only difference being the command:

```
Router3(config-if)#ntp broadcast key 2
```

It is important to note that NTP broadcast and multicast modes use a single key for the entire multicast domain.

Organizations that receive NTP feeds from the Internet usually cannot rely on NTP authentication because few public servers support authentication functionality. This is not a major concern, since NTP algorithms ignore timeservers with outrageous dates and time. Reduce the risk of synchronizing to illegitimate NTP providers by configuring your NTP servers with multiple NTP Stratum 1 servers.

14.13 Limiting the Number of Peers

Problem

You want to limit the number of NTP peers the router will accept.

Solution

Use the *ntp max-associations* configuration command to limit the number of NTP associations the router will accept:

```
Router#configure terminal
Enter configuration commands, one per line.  End with CNTL/Z.
Router(config)#ntp max-associations 30
Router(config)#end
Router#
```

Discussion

To prevent oversubscribing valuable router resources by NTP associations, Cisco provides the ability to limit the number of associations that a router will accept. While the *ntp max-associations* command limits the number of inbound NTP associations, it does so without prejudice. The first 30 NTP associations, using the example above, will be permitted regardless of whom they are.

Other methods of controlling NTP associations mentioned in this chapter provide greater control and granularity than just limiting the number.

See Also

Recipe 14.14

14.14 Restricting Peers

Problem

You want to restrict whom your router will provide NTP services to.

Solution

You can use the *ntp access-group* command to restrict which devices you want your router to allow NTP associations with:

```
Router#configure terminal
Enter configuration commands, one per line.  End with CNTL/Z.
```

```
Router(config)#access-list 88 permit host 172.25.1.1
Router(config)#access-list 88 permit host 10.1.1.1
Router(config)#access-list 99 permit 172.25.0.0 0.0.255.255
Router(config)#access-list 99 permit 10.2.0.0 0.0.255.255
Router(config)#clock timezone EST -5
Router(config)#clock summer-time EDT recurring
Router(config)#ntp server 172.25.1.1 version 3
Router(config)#ntp server 10.1.1.1 version 3
Router(config)#ntp access-group peer 88
Router(config)#ntp access-group serve-only 99
Router(config)#end
Router#
```

Discussion

In this example, the router will allow the internal clock to be synchronized by the two NTP servers listed in access-list number 88, 172.25.1.1, and 10.1.1.1. The router also allows time requests only from the client devices permitted by access-list 99.

By default, NTP has no access controls, and it gives full access to all NTP devices. The *ntp access-group* command limits this access to various NTP services. In the example above, the *peer* keyword means that the router will only allow its internal clock to be changed by those remote servers and peers permitted by the access-list.

The *serve-only* keyword specifies the clients permitted to obtain time services from the router. In the above example, the serve-only access-list (99) permits two entire subnets, 172.2.0.0 255.255.0.0 and 10.2.0.0 255.255.0.0. This means that any NTP clients residing on either of these two subnets can obtain time services from the local router. Using the same method, you can limit the access-list to a single subnet, a group of hosts, or no one. Omitting the *ntp access-group serve-only* command completely prevents the router from providing time services.

NTP access-groups provide excellent granularity of access to time services on a global basis. Used in conjunction with the interface command *ntp disable*, NTP access-groups can form the basis of an effective access control strategy.

See Also

Recipe 14.11

14.15 Setting the Clock Period

Problem

You want to improve on the default value in the *ntp clock-period xxxxxx* command that automatically appears when you configure NTP on your router.

Solution

The router automatically generates a *ntp clock-period* line that it uses to help speed resynchronization after a reboot. Leave it alone:

```
Router#show running-config | include clock-period
ntp clock-period 17180200
Router#
```

Do not attempt to remove or modify the *ntp clock-period* command. The router automatically generates this command to compensate for internal timer inaccuracies.

Discussion

Do not modify or remove this statement from the router configuration. The router automatically adds this statement to the configuration when you enable NTP. After initialization of NTP, the router tunes the clock period to compensate for precision problems with the router's internal clock.

The router will actually constantly change the NTP clock period. For this reason, Cisco suggests that all routers have their configurations saved to NVRAM one week after enabling NTP. This ensures that the saved clock period is accurate for the next router initialization and allows for quicker NTP synchronization.

14.16 Checking the NTP Status

Problem

You want to verify the status of NTP on your router to make sure it's running properly.

Solution

Use the NTP and clock *show* commands to verify the status of NTP on your router. The best place to start is the *show clock detail* command, which provides information on the current time, time source, and time zone configuration:

```
Router>show clock detail
15:54:33.079 EST Sun Jan 29 2006
Time source is NTP
Summer time starts 02:00:00 EST Sun Apr 2 2006
Summer time ends 02:00:00 EDT Sun Oct 29 2006
Router>
```

To display the current NTP status of the local router, the command is:

```
Router>show ntp status
```

The command to display the current NTP associations is:

```
Router>show ntp associations
```

And you can display detailed information about the current NTP associations with the following command:

```
Router>show ntp associations detail
```

Discussion

You can view the current clock status by using the *show clock detail* command:

```
Router>show clock detail
.15:54:33.079 EST Sun Jan 29 2006
Time source is NTP
Summer time starts 02:00:00 EST Sun Apr 2 2006
Summer time ends 02:00:00 EDT Sun Oct 29 2006
Router>
```

In this example, the router's current date and time are correctly set, but notice the period or decimal appended to time (some routers display an asterisk instead of a period). This indicates that NTP is unsynchronized and will appear on show commands and log messages. Recognizing the significance of the period highlights problems with NTP even when you are not specifically looking for timing issues.

This command also provides valuable information on time zone and daylight savings time. The router above is set to Eastern Standard Time (EST) and observes daylight savings time.

To display detailed NTP status information, use the following *show* command:

```
Router>show ntp status
Clock is synchronized, stratum 4, reference is 172.16.2.1
nominal freq is 250.0000 Hz, actual freq is 249.9950 Hz, precision is 2**18
reference time is C787AA2F.FB9A0F44 (15:55:11.982 EST Sun Jan 29 2006)
clock offset is 7.0738 msec, root delay is 40.48 msec
root dispersion is 65.52 msec, peer dispersion is 8.15 msec
Router>
```

In this example, the router is synchronized to NTP server 172.16.2.1, and it is acting as a Stratum 4 NTP server. This means that this router is four NTP "hops" away from the authoritative clock, and that it is using the server 172.16.2.1 as its master time source. The command output also shows that the NTP client is currently synchronized, which is the desired state. Any other clock status indicates problems.

To display the status of all NTP associations, use the following command:

```
Router>show ntp associations

      address         ref clock     st  when  poll reach  delay  offset    disp
+~172.25.1.1       192.5.41.40      2   148  1024  377    30.0   33.66     8.0
*~172.25.1.3       192.5.41.40      2    42  1024  377    31.3  -69.53    10.8
+~172.25.1.5       172.25.1.3       3   780  1024  377    31.9  -107.7    26.1
 * master (synced), # master (unsynced), + selected, - candidate, ~ configured
Router>
```

This command gives a table of outbound NTP associations and their current status. However, it does not display the current inbound NTP associations that are receiving time from this router. This shows those NTP associations that have been explicitly configured as well as any broadcast and multicast servers that have been discovered.

There is a lot of useful information in this example. The most important is the NTP synchronization status for each destination. Notice the special characters situated at the left-most column of the table. These indicate the current status of the NTP associations. Table 14-2 shows what these symbols mean.

Table 14-2. NTP peer status codes

Character	Description
*	Synchronized to master
#	Close to synchronization
+	Selected for possible synchronization
-	Candidate for synchronization
~	Statically configured

The example above displays three synchronized NTP associations with one, 172.25.1.3, acting as master. The table also shows the reference clock for each neighbor, the NTP server they are synchronized to, and the current stratum number of each. Finally, the table displays polling information, availability statistics and clock offset timing. You can view detailed NTP association information by adding the keyword, *detail*:

```
Router>show ntp associations detail
172.25.1.1 configured, selected, sane, valid, stratum 2
ref ID 192.5.41.40, time C034F56D.49F8D2E5 (20:56:13.288 UTC Sat Mar 9 2003)
our mode client, peer mode server, our poll intvl 1024, peer poll intvl 1024
root delay 113.69 msec, root disp 67.46, reach 377, sync dist 148.895
delay 29.95 msec, offset 33.6585 msec, dispersion 8.00
precision 2**20, version 3
org time C034F86F.1132617C (21:09:03.067 UTC Sat Mar 9 2003)
rcv time C034F86F.0C6A77E0 (21:09:03.048 UTC Sat Mar 9 2003)
xmt time C034F86F.04B86272 (21:09:03.018 UTC Sat Mar 9 2003)
filtdelay =    29.95   29.77    4.24    5.19    5.20    5.08    5.22    5.26
filtoffset =   33.66   35.53   49.12   46.62   46.97   47.24   47.56   45.92
filterror =     0.02   15.64   31.27   46.91   62.53   78.16   93.78  109.41

172.25.1.3 configured, our_master, sane, valid, stratum 2
ref ID 192.5.41.40, time C034F647.75CB252C (20:59:51.460 UTC Sat Mar 9 2003)
our mode client, peer mode server, our poll intvl 1024, peer poll intvl 1024
root delay 135.13 msec, root disp 51.15, reach 377, sync dist 145.172
delay 31.30 msec, offset -69.5341 msec, dispersion 10.82
precision 2**20, version 3
org time C034F8D8.F76E503F (21:10:48.966 UTC Sat Mar 9 2003)
rcv time C034F8D9.0D3CCF79 (21:10:49.051 UTC Sat Mar 9 2003)
xmt time C034F8D9.0531A98E (21:10:49.020 UTC Sat Mar 9 2003)
filtdelay =    31.30   29.75    6.39    5.40    5.34    5.37    5.33    5.34
```

```
filtoffset = -69.53 -66.27 -51.98 -50.29 -50.13 -49.93 -46.16 -43.89
filterror =   0.02  15.64  31.27  46.91  62.53  78.16  93.78 109.41
Router>
```

This command displays much of the same information, but in greater detail, and it includes several pieces of timer information. The first line of each association is of particular interest. For example, server 172.25.1.3 is currently acting as this router's master, meaning that we are synchronized to him, and that he is acting as a Stratum 2 server with a valid and sane time.

14.17 Debugging NTP

Problem

You want to debug and isolate NTP problems.

Solution

Use the *show ntp association* command to view the status of the configured NTP associations:

```
Router>show ntp associations
```

Use the *ping* command to ensure connectivity to the NTP server exists:

```
Router>ping 172.25.1.1
```

Use the *debug ntp packet* command to view the NTP packets being generated by the router:

```
Router#debug ntp packets
```

NTP packets debugging is on.

Discussion

If the router's internal clock is incorrect and the router has NTP enabled, then the first step is check the status of the NTP associations:

```
Router>show ntp associations
       address          ref clock     st  when  poll reach  delay  offset    disp
   ~172.25.1.5        0.0.0.0          16    -    64    0    0.0    0.00   16000.
   ~10.1.1.1          192.168.15.32     2   60    64    0   27.6  -1100.   16000.
 * master (synced), # master (unsynced), + selected, - candidate, ~ configured
Router>
```

Notice that there are two NTP associations configured on this router, but neither is currently our synchronized master. The example also indicates that neither of the two NTP associations is currently reachable, since the "reach" statistic is zero.

The most obvious place to begin is to test connectivity. You can test connectivity from the router to its NTP association with the *ping* command. If the NTP

---

association does not respond to the ping request, then a network path may be obstructed or the peer may be down. Isolate and fix the connectivity issues, and hopefully this will rectify the NTP problem. Note that access control lists between the router and its NTP peer may prevent ping traffic from passing, but allow NTP, or vice versa:

```
Router>ping 172.25.1.5

Type escape sequence to abort.
Sending 5, 100-byte ICMP Echos to 172.25.1.5, timeout is 2 seconds:
!!!!!
Success rate is 100 percent (5/5), round-trip min/avg/max = 1/2/4 ms
Router>
```

This shows that at least one of the configured NTP associations is reachable, so the problem might be NTP specific, and it is unlikely to be a connectivity issue. Recall that earlier in the chapter we mentioned that an NTP client never synchronizes its clock to an unsynchronized server. To ensure that the NTP server is stable, you can either log in to the server device to check it or, if you do not have administrative access, you can use the router's debug facility:

```
Router#debug ntp packet
NTP packets debugging is on
.Mar 21 02:39:18: NTP: xmit packet to 172.25.1.5:
.Mar 21 02:39:18:  leap 3, mode 3, version 3, stratum 0, ppoll 64
.Mar 21 02:39:18:  rtdel 28C7 (159.286), rtdsp 2444 (141.663), refid AC190101
.Mar 21 02:39:18:  ref C043C43F.47A9CD5C (21:30:23.279 EST Wed Mar 20 2003)
.Mar 21 02:39:18:  org 00000000.00000000 (19:00:00.000 EST Thu Dec 31 1899)
.Mar 21 02:39:18:  rec 00000000.00000000 (19:00:00.000 EST Thu Dec 31 1899)
.Mar 21 02:39:18:  xmt C043C656.4DFC7394 (21:39:18.304 EST Wed Mar 20 2003)
.Mar 21 02:39:25: NTP: rcv packet from 172.25.1.5 to 172.16.2.2 on Fa0/0.1:
.Mar 21 02:39:25:  leap 3, mode 3, version 3, stratum 0, ppoll 64
.Mar 21 02:39:25:  rtdel 286E (157.928), rtdsp 0EC6 (57.709), refid AC190101
.Mar 21 02:39:25:  ref C043C4D7.1D633CDE (21:32:55.114 EST Wed Mar 20 2003)
.Mar 21 02:39:25:  org 00000000.00000000 (19:00:00.000 EST Thu Dec 31 1899)
.Mar 21 02:39:25:  rec 00000000.00000000 (19:00:00.000 EST Thu Dec 31 1899)
.Mar 21 02:39:25:  xmt C043C65D.1D0A6CBC (21:39:25.113 EST Wed Mar 20 2003)
.Mar 21 02:39:25:  inp C043C65D.1296E3C7 (21:39:25.072 EST Wed Mar 20 2003)
```

The output above shows a debug trace of NTP packets. The first packet captured is an active NTP poll from the local router to its NTP server, 172.25.1.5. The second packet captured is the passive response from the NTP server, and its current stratum level is set to zero. A zero Stratum level reported by the server means that it is currently not synchronized. If the server is not synchronized, then our router can't use it. The process of debugging the NTP problem can now shift to the NTP server.

NTP is remarkably stable. Typically, when there are problems, they are related to connectivity: a box has failed, a path has become unreachable or an access-list has prevented NTP from communicating. As we have discussed above, upstream problems affect downstream NTP associations, since nothing will synchronize to an unsynchronized server. This means that NTP issues must be isolated one hop at a time.

14.18 NTP Logging

Problem

You want to log significant NTP events.

Solution

Use the *ntp logging* command to enable the logging of NTP events:

```
Router2#configure terminal
Enter configuration commands, one per line.  End with CNTL/Z.
Router2(config)#ntp logging
Router2(config)#end
Router2#
```

Discussion

Starting in IOS Version 12.3(7)T, Cisco added the NTP logging feature. By implementing this feature, the router will log significant NTP events such as peer loss, peer reachability, and clock synchronization events.

To view the NTP logging events on the router, use the following command:

```
Router2#show logging | include NTP
000019: Jan 29 10:57:52.633 EST: %NTP-5-PEERSYNC: NTP synced to peer 172.25.1.5
000020: Jan 29 10:57:52.637 EST: %NTP-6-PEERREACH: Peer 172.25.1.5 is reachable
000023: Jan 29 10:57:53.635 EST: %NTP-6-PEERREACH: Peer 172.25.1.3 is reachable
000024: Jan 29 11:01:20.653 EST: %NTP-4-PEERUNREACH: Peer 172.25.1.5 is unreachable
000026: Jan 29 11:15:11.985 EST: %NTP-4-UNSYNC: NTP sync is lost
Router2#
```

In this example, we can see that the router initially synchronized its time to server 172.25.1.5 before the server became unreachable, causing the router to lose synchronization. This kind of forensic information can assist you in investigating NTP issues.

See Also

Recipe 14.16

14.19 Extended Daylight Saving Time

Problem

You want the router to automatically adjust to the Extended Daylight Saving Time which takes affect starting in March 2007.

Solution

To automatically adjust the router time to account for the new extended Daylight Saving Time, starting in March 2007, use the following commands:

```
Router2#configure terminal
Enter configuration commands, one per line.  End with CNTL/Z.
Router2(config)#clock timezone EST -5
Router2(config)#clock summer-time EDT recurring 2 Sun Mar 2:00 1 Sun Nov 2:00
Router2(config)#end
Router2#
```

Discussion

The U.S. Energy Policy Act of 2005 includes changes to extend Daylight Saving Time (DST) by one month each to conserve energy. Starting in 2007, DST will begin three weeks earlier, on the first Sunday in November.

In Recipe 14.4, we discussed how to configure the router to adjust the time for DST; however, starting in March 2007, the configuration for most U.S. time zones change, and we need to change the router configuration. Otherwise, the router will continue to abide by outdated and incorrect DST rules.

We can configure the router to follow the new rule using the command shown in the "Solution" section of this recipe:

```
Router2(config)#clock summer-time EDT recurring 2 Sun Mar 2:00 1 Sun Nov 2:00
```

This command says that DST begins on the second Sunday in March at 2:00 AM and ends on the first Sunday in November at 2:00 AM (exactly the new rule). Please refer to Recipe 14.14 for more options and information on this command.

Table 14-3 shows the new start and end dates for the extended DST.

Table 14-3. DST dates starting March 2007

Year	DST begins 2:00 AM (Second Sunday in March)	DST ends 2:00 AM (First Sunday in November)
2007	March 11	November 4
2008	March 9	November 2
2009	March 8	November 1
2010	March 14	November 7
2011	March 13	November 6
2012	March 11	November 4

To view the new the DST information, use the *show clock detail* command:

```
Router2#show clock detail
17:07:05.440 EST Sun Jan 28 2007
Time source is NTP
Summer time starts 02:00:00 EST Sun Mar 11 2007
Summer time ends 02:00:00 EDT Sun Nov 4 2007
Router2#
```

Notice the configured DST dates now conform to the new extended DST dates.

See Also

Recipe 14.4; Recipe 14.3

14.20 NTP Server Configuration

Problem

You want to configure the NTP server to provide time to your routers.

Solution

To configure an NTP server to provide time to your network, use the commands in Example 14-1.

Example 14-1. /etc/ntp.conf

```
#Define NTP Servers
#
server 10.1.1.1
server 10.2.2.2
server 10.3.3.3
#
#Define Access Control
restrict 10.1.1.1 nomodify notrap nopeer noquery
restrict 10.2.2.2 nomodify notrap nopeer noquery
restrict 10.3.3.3 nomodify notrap nopeer noquery
#
#Define NTP Drift File
driftfile /var/log/ntp.drift
```

 The NTP servers used in this example are fictitious. Please read the Discussion section to learn how to locate publicly available NTP servers.

Discussion

To find publicly available NTP servers to synchronize to, perform an *nslookup* on domain name *pool.ntp.org*. This DNS entry contains a number of Stratum 2 NTP servers that have agreed to participate in the DNS round robin group. Please be sure to perform the nslookup yourself to ensure you choose active and accurate NTP servers. The ones listed in the following example may have grown stale since the publication of this book:

```
Freebsd% nslookup pool.ntp.org
Server:  dns.oreilly.com
Address:  172.25.1.99
```

```
Non-authoritative answer:
Name:    pool.ntp.org
Addresses:  194.231.42.100, 216.52.237.151, 64.81.87.189, 65.111.164.224
            66.17.252.26, 66.180.134.50, 67.128.71.75, 72.21.46.202, 80.190.241.157,
84.16.227.201, 84.45.18.237, 139.140.181.133

Freebsd%
```

We strongly recommend that you use the IP addresses, since the *restrict* commands will not work with DNS names. The *restrict* commands define access control. For more information on access control commands, please see the manpages for *ntp.conf*.

Once configured and launched, you can monitor the current status of your NTP server by using the *ntpq* command. One of the most useful command options is *ntpq –p*, which shows you the current status of the server and its configured NTP servers:

```
Freebsd% ntpq -p
     remote           refid      st t when poll reach   delay   offset  jitter
==============================================================================
+10.1.1.1        .GPS.            1 u  479 1024  177   97.930   -0.552  13.109
*10.2.2.2        .USNO.           1 u  527 1024  377   41.933    1.565   2.462
+10.3.3.3        .WWV.            1 u  442 1024  377    0.956   -0.259   0.668
Freebsd%
```

As you can see, the three fictitious NTP servers are all active and reachable. We can also tell by the "*" that our server is synchronized to server 10.2.2.2, which is a Stratum 1 server, as listed in the "*st*" column. The other two servers are selected for possible synchronization, as denoted by the "+". For a complete listing of NTP status codes, please see Table 14-2 or the *ntpq* manpage.

To enable MD5 authentication on the server, so that your routers can access it securely, you must first create one or more keys in the NTP key file called */etc/ntp.keys* (Example 14-2).

Example 14-2. /etc/ntp.keys

```
2    M  oreilly
3    M  testing
```

In this example, we have created two MD5 keys, 2 and 3. Although the server will support other authentication methods, Cisco IOS only supports MD5 keys. The MD5 keys must be entered as clear text and must match the key(s) listed in your router configuration.

Once you have created your NTP keys, you must configure the server to enable authentication by modifying the *ntp.conf* file:

```
#Define NTP Servers
#
server 10.1.1.1
server 10.2.2.2
server 10.3.3.3
```

```
#
#Define Access Control
restrict 10.1.1.1 nomodify notrap nopeer noquery
restrict 10.2.2.2 nomodify notrap nopeer noquery
restrict 10.3.3.3 nomodify notrap nopeer noquery
#
#Define NTP Drift File
driftfile /var/log/ntp.drift
#
#Enable Authorization
enable auth
keys /etc/ntp.keys
trustedkey 2
```

In this example, we have highlighted the authentication portion of the *ntp.conf* file. As you can see, we have enabled authentication by using the *enable auth* command. We then defined where the NTP key file is located, and finally we enabled key number 2 as our trusted key. Once the NTP daemon is restarted, the server is ready to provide authenticated access to the routers.

The following example shows how to configure a router to securely access our server using NTP authentication. Please note that the authentication key number and password must be the same as the one configured in the server to work:

```
Router#configure terminal
Enter configuration commands, one per line.  End with CNTL/Z.
Router(config)#ntp authentication-key 2 md5 oreilly
Router(config)#ntp authenticate
Router(config)#ntp trusted-key 2
Router(config)#ntp server 172.25.1.1 key 2
Router(config)#end
Router#
```

For more information on configuring the router for NTP authentication, please see Recipe 14.12 or the *ntp.conf* manpage.

See Also

Recipe 14.12; Recipe 14.16

## CHAPTER 15

DLSw

15.0 Introduction

There are essentially two kinds of bridges. The first type is a Source Route Bridge, which allows end devices to request a particular path through the network, using a Routing Information Field (RIF) in the packet. In the default case, this type of bridge cannot forward any packet without a RIF. The second type is a Transparent Bridge, which hides all of that network detail from end devices. Transparent bridges have no concept of a RIF. Source Route Bridging is commonly used with Token Ring networks, while Transparent Bridging is popular with Ethernets, where it is used by Ethernet switches.

So bridging between Ethernet and Token Ring networks requires a special hybrid of these two that is able to translate between not only the media types, but also the bridging types. The Remote Source Route Bridging (RSRB) and Source Route Transparent (SRT) bridging protocols were invented to solve this problem, particularly over WANs.

Data Link Switching (DLSw) and DLSw+, which is Cisco's enhanced version of DLSw, also solve these problems and comply with the same bridging standards. These protocols are capable of connecting Token Rings to Ethernets, Synchronous Data Link Control (SDLC) serial connections, and even X.25 networks. So there is really very little reason to worry about the older bridging protocols and methods anymore. If you are considering building a new network involving the System Network Architecture (SNA) protocol, there is no particular reason to bother with either SRB or RSRB. If you have an existing network involving these protocols, it would be wise to consider moving to the more modern and flexible DLSw or DLSw+.

Because DLSw creates bridges that are able to connect different (or similar) layer 2 media together, it clearly has many applications beyond SNA, although that is the most common reason for deploying DLSw. It can also be used when bridging LAN segments for other nonroutable protocols, such as NetBIOS and Local Area Transport (LAT). And it can be used in conjunction with routing on the same interfaces so that some protocols are routed and others are bridged.

DLSw is an open standard protocol for bridging through TCP/IP networks. It was originally developed by IBM as a proprietary standard in 1992, and became an open standard with the publication of RFC 1434 the following year. Version 1 of the DLSw protocol was defined in detail in 1995 in RFC 1795, and updated to create Version 2 in 1997 in RFC 2166. This set of updates does not affect the underlying protocol, but rather extends its functionality. Meanwhile, Cisco independently implemented a distinct set of extensions to DLSw Version 1 and called the result DLSw+.

There are currently three different common versions of the protocol with different capabilities supported by different vendors, Version 1, Version 2, and DLSw+. Fortunately, all versions include a *capabilities* field that is used when two devices first attempt to make a DLSw connection. This allows them to agree on a set of common features. In most cases, this results in good transparency of operation among different vendors. However, it is useful to be aware of what features will not be supported when interconnecting in this way.

Most of the DLSw+ enhancements allow for greater scalability and variety of transport mechanisms. For example, DLSw+ allows the transport mechanism to be Fast-Sequenced Transport (FST), Frame Relay or High-Level Data Link Control (HDLC) protocols, as well as TCP/IP. This book will only cover the TCP/IP version, however. Other DLSw+ enhancements, such as peer groups and border peers, improve scalability and allow you to build a large bridged network out of smaller groups of devices that pass limited amounts of information between them as required.

Service Access Points (SAP and LSAP)

The Logical Link Control layer, IEEE 802.2, defines Service Access Points (SAP) and Link Service Access Points (LSAP). These are conceptually similar to TCP port numbers in many ways, although it is important to remember that they operate at the Logical Link Layer (Layer 2), not the Transport Layer (Layer 4), as TCP does. They are simply numbers that a device uses when it wants to establish a connection to another device to run a particular application. The number specifies a particular application protocol. The packets establishing a connection specify both a Source SAP number (SSAP) and a Destination SAP number (DSAP). These are, obviously enough, the SAP numbers of the source and destination applications. Table 15-1 lists several of the most common SAP numbers.

Table 15-1. Common SAP numbers

SAP number	Binary	Description
00	0000 0000	Null LSAP
02	0000 0010	Individual LLC Sublayer Management
03	0000 0011	Group LLC Sublayer Management
04	0000 0100	Individual SNA Path Control
05	0000 0101	Group SNA Path Control
06	0000 0110	IP

Table 15-1. Common SAP numbers (continued)

SAP number	Binary	Description
07	0000 0111	IP
08	0000 1000	SNA
09	0000 1001	SNA
0C	0000 1100	SNA
0D	0000 1101	SNA
0E	0000 1110	PROWAY Network Mgmt & Initialization
18	0001 1000	Texas Instruments
42	0100 0010	802.1 Spanning Tree Protocol
4E	0100 1110	EIA RS-511 Manufacturing Message Service
7E	0111 1110	X.25 over 802.2 LLC
80	1000 0000	Xerox Network Systems (XNS)
86	1000 0110	Nestar
8E	1000 1110	PROWAY Active Station List Maintenance
98	1001 1000	Address Resolution Protocol (ARP)
AA	1010 1010	Sub-Network Access Protocol (SNAP)
BC	1011 1100	Banyan Vines
E0	1110 0000	Netware
F0	1111 0000	NetBIOS
F4	1111 0100	Individual LAN Management
F5	1111 0101	Group LAN Management
F8	1111 1000	Remote Program Load (RPL)
FA	1111 1010	Ungermann-Bass
FE	1111 1110	ISO Network Layer Protocol
FF	1111 1111	Global LSAP

Cisco routers include the facility to filter based on LSAP numbers using access-lists in the range from 200 to 299. Here is an example of the syntax of an LSAP access-list:

```
access-list 201 permit 0x0000 0x0D0D
```

The first hexadecimal number after the *permit* keyword represents both the source and destination SAP numbers (SSAP and DSAP). The first two hex digits are the SSAP, and the second two are the DSAP. The next field is a wildcard bit pattern. Any place where the wildcard has a 0 bit, the corresponding bit in the SAP numbers must be exactly as it is in the given pattern, and any place where the wildcard has a 1 bit can have either a zero or a one.

The mask in this particular example is 0x0D0D. The hex number D has a bit pattern of 1101. So the access list as written will allow any packets with either SSAP or DSAP values, shown in Table 15-2.

Table 15-2. SAP values matched by the example ACL

Hex	Binary	SAP
0x00	0000 0000	Null LSAP
0x01	0000 0001	Unused
0x04	0000 0100	Individual SNA Path Control
0x05	0000 0101	Group SNA Path Control
0x08	0000 1000	SNA
0x09	0000 1001	SNA
0x0D	0000 1101	SNA

Such access-lists are usually used to block unwanted local ring traffic such as NetBIOS or Netware, while permitting the SNA traffic. If, on the other hand, you only wanted to permit NetBIOS traffic, blocking all other protocols, you could use an access-list like this:

```
access-list 202 permit 0xF0F0 0x0000
```

Explorers and RIFs

When a device wants to send a packet using Logical Link Control (LLC) protocols through a bridged network, it has the capability of Source-Routing this packet. This means that the end device is able to specify a particular network path. To do this, however, it first has to find an appropriate path. It does this by sending a packet called an *explorer* through the network. As this explorer packet passes through the network, each bridge adds information about itself to the packet and forwards it along. So when it finally arrives, it has a complete path description that the end device can use to build a RIF.

There are, in fact, two different kinds of explorers, called Spanning Tree Explorers and All Routes Explorers. They both perform the same basic function of trying to map the best path to the required destination. The difference, however, is that a Spanning Tree Explorer only follows one path, and the All Routes Explorer attempts all paths. When a bridge receives a Spanning Tree Explorer, it forwards the packet along a single path defined by the Spanning Tree Protocol (STP).

Spanning Tree is a protocol that eliminates loops from a bridged network. It is important to remember that running Spanning Tree is optional, and not every bridge is configured to run this protocol. It is frequently not used, in fact, in DLSw+ networks because the protocol has the ability to do useful things like load sharing between links. Spanning Tree inherently prevents load sharing among the many different possible paths through a network by shutting down all paths except for one.

Note that STP is required on transparently bridged networks, however, because there is no RIF to control path selection. If you have multiple connections between transparent bridges, such as Ethernet switches, you must use STP.

STP ensures that there is one and only one active path between any two points by first electing a Root Bridge. This device is the logical center of the bridged network. When a bridge receives a packet destined for a device that is not on one of its ports, it simply forwards that packet toward the center. The packet may take several hops to reach the Root Bridge. The Root Bridge has an exhaustive table of MAC addresses, and it knows how to forward every packet that it receives. If it doesn't know the destination, it will duplicate the packet and send it out every path except the one it was received on in the hopes of finding the destination.

A Spanning Tree Explorer packet is simply one that follows the STP path through the network to reach the required destination. An All Routes Explorer works similarly, but it follows all possible paths to reach the ultimate destination. At each bridge where there is a choice to be made between two or more possible paths, the bridge duplicates the packet and forwards it along all of them. So the destination device will probably receive several possible solutions. In general, it will pick the first one it receives on the assumption that this must represent the fastest path.

When the destination device receives an explorer packet, it turns it around and sends it back to the original source, retaining the routing information. Now both devices know how to request a path to each other through the network when they need to exchange information. When they send packets of application data, they will include a Routing Information Field (RIF) that specifies the desired path.

Obviously this process can get messy if there are a lot of devices, all trying to find one another at the same time. So DLSw+ includes some optimizations that allow routers to improve on the RIF discovery process. Every router contains a RIF cache of all of the remote devices that it knows how to reach. When a device on the local Token Ring sends an explorer looking for something the router already knows how to reach, DLSw doesn't need to bother forwarding this explorer through the network, and it responds directly without having to consume network resources forwarding the explorer.

Cisco IOS Code Sets

One common misunderstanding that people have about DLSw+ is that to implement Cisco routers in a network using IBM's Advanced Peer-to-Peer Networking (APPN) functionality, you have to use one of Cisco's APPN code sets. This is not the case. The core DLSw+ functionality is included in the default minimal *IP Only* IOS code set for all 12.x and most 11.x IOS levels. You only need to use the APPN code set if you intend for the router to take an active part in the higher layer protocols.

APPN is effectively the next generation version of SNA. Among many improvements, it makes the protocol routable for improved scalability. However, APPN still runs over the same lower layer protocols such as LLC2 on Token Rings and SDLC on serial interfaces. So, in most cases, the router doesn't need to know whether APPN or SNA is used at higher layers.

The APPN code set is required only if the router needs to provide native APPN routing. In most cases, even networks using APPN within the Mainframe and its Front End Processor (FEP), the bridging functions of DLSw+ are sufficient to provide all of the required connectivity.

We note in passing, though, that the most recent generations of mainframe computers from IBM are capable of supporting TCP/IP and Gigabit Ethernet directly. So we expect that the future of mainframe networking will use IP rather than APPN. In this case, SNA and DLSw will only be necessary to support legacy SNA equipment.

15.1   Simple Bridging

Problem

You wish to configure a router to bridge between two interfaces.

Solution

You can configure a router to bridge between two or more interfaces, as follows:

```
Router1#configure terminal
Enter configuration commands, one per line.  End with CNTL/Z.
Router1(config)#bridge 1 protocol ieee
Router1(config)#interface Ethernet0/0
Router1(config-if)#bridge-group 1
Router1(config-if)#exit
Router1(config)#interface Ethernet0/1
Router1(config-if)#bridge-group 1
Router1(config-if)#exit
Router1(config)#end
```

With Integrated Routing and Bridging (IRB), you can also create a Bridged Virtual Interface (BVI) for the bridge group:

```
Router1#configure terminal
Enter configuration commands, one per line.  End with CNTL/Z.
Router1(config)#bridge 1 protocol ieee
Router1(config)#bridge irb
Router1(config)#interface Ethernet0/0
Router1(config-if)#bridge-group 1
Router1(config-if)#exit
Router1(config)#interface Ethernet0/1
Router1(config-if)#bridge-group 1
Router1(config-if)#exit
Router1(config)#interface BVI1
Router1(config-if)#ip address 10.10.10.1 255.255.255.0
Router1(config-if)#exit
Router1(config)#end
```

Discussion

In the first example, we just want to configure simple bridging between two interfaces on this router. This example simply bridges all Ethernet traffic between the two interfaces. There are three key commands here. The first is the *bridge protocol* command:

```
Router1(config)#bridge 1 protocol ieee
```

In this case, we have associated bridge-group number 1 with the IEEE 802.1D Spanning Tree Protocol (STP). This is the most common standard for Spanning Tree, supported in particular by all popular brands of Ethernet switches. Spanning Tree is a Layer 2 protocol that automatically detects and eliminates loops.

The router also supports alternatives such as *dec*, which is the old Digital Equipment version of Spanning Tree. The only reason why you should ever configure this is if you need to connect to older Digital Equipment bridges.

Starting in IOS Version 12.0(1)T, the router also supports a Spanning Tree Protocol called *vlan-bridge*. This is intended to be used in situations when you have to connect to a switched Ethernet environment and interconnect two or more VLANs with a bridge. The trouble with doing this is that the switches use a per-VLAN 802.1D. However, if you are bridging VLANs together, it doesn't make sense to run a separate Spanning Tree for each VLAN. Instead, you want to run a single Spanning Tree that spans multiple VLANs. This is what the *vlan-bridge* feature gives you. And this is the only situation when you should use this feature.

IEEE Spanning Tree allows you to specify different bridge priorities and timers. By default, the router will send out "Hello" Bridge Protocol Data Unit (BPDU) packets once per second. You can set this to any value between 1 and 10 seconds with the *hello-time* keyword. The default is one second:

```
Router1(config)#bridge 1 hello-time 5
```

The second important timer in Spanning Tree deployments is the Forward Delay timer. This is the amount of time that the bridge will spend in Listening mode after an interface has been activated and before it starts forwarding packets. The default value is 30 seconds:

```
Router1(config)#bridge 1 forward-time 10
```

And the other key timer is the maximum age parameter. This defines how long a bridge will wait for a BPDU from the root bridge before deciding that a topology change must have occurred. You set this value by using the *max-age* keyword. The default max-age value is 15 seconds:

```
Router1(config)#bridge 1 max-age 10
```

The other critical Spanning Tree parameter is the bridge priority. This value is used when electing the root bridge for the network. The switch with the lowest priority value wins, with a series of tie-breaking rules that employ port numbers and MAC addresses. So setting a very high priority is a good idea if you want to ensure that the router will never become the root bridge. In a switched Ethernet environment, for example, you would usually want one of your backbone switches to be the root bridge. The default priority is 32768 for IEEE bridges, and 128 for DEC bridges.

```
Router1(config)#bridge 1 priority 65535
```

Once we have defined the appropriate Spanning Tree Protocol for the network and set the appropriate timers and priorities to match the other bridges on the network, you simply associate interfaces with the bridge group.

```
Router1(config)#interface Ethernet0/0
Router1(config-if)#bridge-group 1
```

One of the critical factors to consider when configuring bridging between two or more interfaces on a router is what protocols should be bridged and what should be routed. Cisco supports two feature sets to allow you to simultaneously bridge and route on an interface. These are called Integrated Routing and Bridging (IRB) and Concurrent Routing and Bridging (CRB). The main difference is that IRB allows you to associate a Bridged Virtual Interface (BVI) with the bridge group. This is useful because you can configure a BVI for a group of bridged ports and connect this virtual interface to a routing process. For this reason, we generally prefer IRB to CRB.

When you configure the bridge *irb* command, the router then allows you to specify which protocols you wish to bridge and which should be routed. For example, if you want to route IP but bridge all other protocols, you would use the following command:

```
Router1(config)#interface 1 route ip
```

To configure a Bridged Virtual Interface for a bridge group, you use the BVI interface type:

```
Router1(config)#interface BVI1
Router1(config-if)#ip address 10.10.10.1 255.255.255.0
```

You can think of the BVI as being similar to a VLAN interface on a Catalyst switch.

15.2   Configuring DLSw

Problem

You want to set up DLSw to allow Token Ring bridging through an IP network.

Solution

There are many different ways to configure two routers to allow Token Ring to Token Ring bridging through DLSw. The most common reason for doing this is to allow Token Ring SNA LLC2 devices to communicate with a mainframe Front End Processor (FEP) attached to another Token Ring. It is relatively common to have many remote rings connecting to a single central ring. In cases like this, it is often best to use one or more dedicated DLSw routers at the central location. The CPU overhead required for supporting a large number of DLSw connections can be relatively high, so it is useful to restrict this functionality to special purpose DLSw routers and keep it off of routers that also need to handle core routing functions.

Here is the DLSw configuration for central router, which is the one that connects directly to the ring that holds the FEP:

```
dlsw-central(config)#interface Loopback0
dlsw-central(config-if)#ip address 10.1.1.5 255.255.255.252
dlsw-central(config-if)#exit
dlsw-central(config)#access-list 701 permit 4000.3745.AAAA 8000.0000.0000
dlsw-central(config)#source-bridge ring-group 101
dlsw-central(config)#dlsw local-peer peer-id 10.1.1.5 promiscuous
dlsw-central(config)#dlsw timer explorer-wait-time 5
dlsw-central(config)#dlsw icanreach mac-exclusive
dlsw-central(config)#dlsw icanreach mac-address 4000.3745.AAAA mask ffff.ffff.ffff
dlsw-central(config)#dlsw cache-ignore-netbios-datagram
dlsw-central(config)#dlsw allroute-sna
dlsw-central(config)#interface TokenRing0
dlsw-central(config-if)#description Ring number 0x00A (10)
dlsw-central(config-if)#source-bridge 10 5 101
dlsw-central(config-if)#source-bridge spanning
dlsw-central(config-if)#source-bridge input-address-list 701
dlsw-central(config-if)#exit
dlsw-central(config)#end
dlsw-central#
```

And the remote routers are configured like this:

```
dlsw-branch#configure terminal
Enter configuration commands, one per line.  End with CNTL/Z.
dlsw-branch(config)#interface Loopback0
dlsw-branch(config-if)#ip address 10.1.2.5 255.255.255.252
dlsw-branch(config-if)#exit
dlsw-branch(config)#access-list 200 permit 0x0000 0x0D0D
dlsw-branch(config)#source-bridge ring-group 101
dlsw-branch(config)#dlsw local-peer peer-id 10.1.2.5
dlsw-branch(config)#dlsw timer explorer-wait-time 5
dlsw-branch(config)#dlsw remote-peer 0 tcp 10.1.1.5 lsap-output-list 200
dlsw-branch(config)#dlsw allroute-sna
dlsw-branch(config)#interface TokenRing0
dlsw-branch(config-if)#description branch Token Ring 0x047 (71)
dlsw-branch(config-if)#multiring all
dlsw-branch(config-if)#source-bridge 71 5 101
dlsw-branch(config-if)#source-bridge spanning
dlsw-branch(config-if)#exit
dlsw-branch(config)#end
dlsw-branch#
```

Discussion

These configurations will work well for situations when a large number of remote routers need to make DLSw connections to a central router. However, if you only need to connect two routers, you can still use the same pair of configurations. In that case, you simply need to decide which router will initiate the session. The initiating router will use the "dlsw-branch" configuration, and the receiving router will be "dlsw-central." The initiating router will start trying to establish the connection as soon as it boots, and will continue periodically until it succeeds. This is true whether or not there is any traffic to ready to send through this connection.

The peers

The first things to notice about these two configurations are the *dlsw local-peer* and *dlsw remote-peer* statements. These statements must match. In this case, the branch router uses the address 10.1.1.5 to specify the remote peer. This address corresponds to the *Loopback0* interface on the central router. So on the central router, it is critically important that the local-peer statement must also point to this same IP address.

The central router does not have a *dlsw remote-peer* statement. This is because the central router will not establish DLSw connections. The *promiscuous* keyword in the local-peer statement allows this router to simply accept incoming connections from other routers. In this example, we expect to have many remote branch routers connecting to the same central router. Configuring a separate remote-peer on the central router for every branch would be an onerous task, particularly if branch routers are added and deleted frequently. When building a many-to-one type bridge, it is generally preferable to configure the central router to simply accept all remote peers.

This means that the central router will accept a DLSw connection from anybody. Naturally, it doesn't make sense to configure *promiscuous* on both routers because one of them has to initiate the connection. So the branch router is configured with normal point-to-point *local-peer* and *remote-peer* commands.

When configuring the local and remote DLSw peers, you can specify the IP address for any interface on the router, as long as both routers agree on which address is to be used. In these configuration files, both local peers point to the respective *Loopback0* interfaces on each router. This is because the *Loopback0* interface is a purely internal software port that can never become unavailable due to an external failure. If the router is reachable at all through any path, then the *Loopback0* interface is reachable, and consequently the DLSw peer relationship will be kept alive. In the case of Token Ring to Token Ring bridging, it may make sense to bring down the peer relationship when one of the rings fails. In this case, you can configure the local-peers to point to an IP address on the Token Ring interface itself. However, if either router supports more than one SNA interface, such as a second Token Ring or an SDLC Serial port, then you will probably not want your SDLC traffic to fail just because of a Token Ring failure.

There are only two routers in this example. But it is relatively common to have a backup router on the central ring, for example. Each router can have many remote-peers, each configured with a separate *dlsw remote-peer* statement.

There are two other pieces of information in the *dlsw remote-peer* command on the branch router:

```
dlsw-branch(config)#dlsw remote-peer 0 tcp 10.1.1.5 lsap-output-list 200
```

The number 0 in the third field is a list number. The value of 0 is the default, and is sufficient for most applications. If any other value is specified, it tells DLSw that you want to set up ring lists or port lists. You would do this if you wanted to bridge traffic from one ring to one remote DLSw peer and traffic from another ring to a different peer. For example, if your router has four different rings, and you only want rings 1, 2, and 4, but not 3 to use this particular DLSw peer, you would configure a port-list as follows, arbitrarily calling this port-list number 5:

```
Router(config)#dlsw port-list 5 tokenring 1 tokenring 2 tokenring 4
Router(config)#dlsw remote-peer 5 tcp 10.1.1.5
```

An alternative way of doing this would be to use the ring numbers. If, for example, the ring number associated with these Token Ring interfaces were 70, 95, and 142 (all of these ring numbers are in decimal rather than the more conventional hexadecimal notation, which would be 46, 5F, and 8E, respectively), you could accomplish the same thing with a *dlsw ring-list* command:

```
Router(config)#dlsw ring-list 5 rings 70 95 142
Router(config)#dlsw remote-peer 5 tcp 10.1.1.5
```

Note that in general, if you are working with physical rings, there is usually less danger of confusion when using the port-list version of this command. It is easy to become confused by virtual ring numbers, bridge numbers, and so forth when constructing a ring-list, particularly because most devices will represent these values in hexadecimal notation, while the router uses decimal.

In both versions, if there are other Token Ring interfaces that do not appear in any ring-list, then they will not take part in any DLSw bridging. Alternatively, you could create more port-lists or ring-lists representing these other rings, and create more *dlsw remote-peer* statements for them, as follows:

```
Router(config)#dlsw port-list 5 tokenring 1 tokenring 2 tokenring 4
Router(config)#dlsw port-list 6 tokenring 3
Router(config)#dlsw remote-peer 5 tcp 10.1.1.5
Router(config)#dlsw remote-peer 6 tcp 10.1.1.9
```

These list numbers only have local significance to the router they are set on. So if you are sending port-list 5 to 10.1.1.5 and 6 to 10.1.1.9, as in this example, there is nothing special required to complete that relationship on the remote peer routers. The other router doesn't know or care that it isn't getting all of this router's DLSw traffic.

The last parts of the *remote-peer* command on the branch router define an *lsap-output-list*, and associate it with access-list 200. This is optional, but useful. To understand what it does, please refer to the discussion of Service Access Points in the "Introduction" section of this chapter.

Ring groups, ring numbers, and bridge numbers

Notice the ring groups on both routers. Each router has several different ring and bridge numbers that define what connects to what. Nothing will work if you don't get these right.

Both routers have the global configuration statement that looks like this:

```
Router(config)#source-bridge ring-group 101
```

This specifies a virtual ring number that can be easily compared to a VLAN number. This ring group number is also a ring number, so it appears in RIFs. If the router has interfaces in multiple different ring-groups, you can simply include several of them configuration lines, one for each ring-group that the router holds:

```
Router(config)#source-bridge ring-group 101
Router(config)#source-bridge ring-group 557
Router(config)#source-bridge ring-group 4031
```

This ring-group number appears in the configuration of each interface that takes part in the bridge. For example, the branch Token Ring port configuration includes the following statement:

```
dlsw-branch(config)#interface TokenRing0
dlsw-branch(config-if)#source-bridge 71 5 101
```

The first number in the *source-bridge* line is the local ring number, the second number is an internal bridge number, and the last number is the destination ring number. DLSw will bridge packets received on this interface to the other Token Rings around the network that are also members of this ring group.

In this case, the local ring number is 71, which would be 0x047 in the more conventional hexadecimal notation for Token Ring numbers. This local ring number is the value that appears in RIFs generated for this ring. It is essentially a network number for this ring, similar to the TCP/IP concept of a network number. The range of possible values is from 1–4,095, and each ring number must be globally unique. So no other ring in this ring-group, anywhere in the network, can have the same number. And remember also that the ring-group number is itself a ring number, so no ring can have the same number as the ring-group. It is important to note that if you configure a local ring number like this that is in conflict with a pre-existing ring number, the router will detect the error and shut down the port to prevent further communication problems on the ring.

The bridge-number is an integer value expressed as a decimal number between 1 and 15. In this case, the target ring number is the virtual ring number representing the entire DLSw ring-group. However, this same command could be used to simply bridge two rings on the same router as follows:

```
Router(config)#interface Tokenring0
Router(config-if)#source-bridge 70 5 71
Router(config-if)#exit
Router(config)#interface Tokenring1
```

```
Router(config-if)#source-bridge 71 5 70
Router(config-if)#exit
Router(config)#interface Tokenring2
Router(config-if)#source-bridge 72 6 73
Router(config-if)#exit
Router(config)#interface Tokenring3
Router(config-if)#source-bridge 73 6 72
Router(config-if)#exit
```

The bridge number is simply a locally unique identifier that the router uses to specify how it will connect these rings. In this little example, there are four rings. The first two rings are connected through bridge number 5, and the second pair connects via bridge number 6. In the larger DLSw example, the target ring is the ring-group number. The bridge number is unique only to the router it is configured on, and is particularly useful when you want to have different rings connected to different destinations.

Another important *source-bridge* feature shown in the example is the input-*address-list* keyword:

```
dlsw-central(config)#access-list 701 permit 4000.3745.AAAA 8000.0000.0000
dlsw-central(config)#interface TokenRing0
dlsw-central(config-if)#source-bridge input-address-list 701
```

This ensures that the bridge will only pick up packets from the ring if they have the source address shown in the access-list. Notice that this is the same MAC address that we used in the *dlsw icanreach* command, which we discuss in a moment:

```
dlsw-central(config)#dlsw icanreach mac-address 4000.3745.AAAA mask ffff.ffff.ffff
```

This is the MAC address of the FEP in our example. The reason for the input filter on the source-bridge command is simply to ensure that the router only forwards packets that originate with the FEP. Bear in mind that DLSw bridges a potentially large number of rings, so there could be a lot of strange and unexpected packets floating around on the FEP ring. In particular, we want to prevent our branch routers from talking directly to one another and wasting bandwidth.

Explorer options

As mentioned in the Introduction to this chapter, the Logical Link Control protocol (LLC) used in most Token Ring networks uses packets called *explorers* to build Routing Information Fields (RIF) for source-routing packets. DLSw+ includes several options for improving the efficiency of this process.

The first of these options appears in this line, which appears in both of the example router configurations:

```
dlsw-central(config)#dlsw allroute-sna
```

This command simply tells the router to use All Routes explorers rather than single route (or Spanning Tree) explorers when trying to find an SNA device. This command appears to be contradicted by the use of *source-bridge spanning* on the Token

Ring interfaces of both routers, but it isn't actually a contradiction. In fact, this provides an important advantage. The *source-bridge spanning* command simply prevents end devices on the Token Ring from using all-routes explorers. The routers themselves are still allowed to use all-routes explorers when communicating among themselves, however. In this way the routers maintain control over network routing, while at the same time preventing end devices from wasting network resources by sending out all route explorers unnecessarily.

The second important explorer configuration command also appears on both routers:

```
dlsw-central(config)#dlsw timer explorer-wait-time 5
```

This statement tells the routers to wait for five seconds after sending an explorer to ensure that it has received the results from all of the possible DLSw peers. This helps to ensure that it will always pick the best path. The default value if this command is not present is zero seconds, meaning that the router will always use the first path it sees. Clearly, this is only important when using all-routes explorers.

At the host router, we have configured two icanreach statements:

```
dlsw-central(config)#dlsw icanreach mac-exclusive
dlsw-central(config)#dlsw icanreach mac-address 4000.3745.AAAA mask ffff.ffff.ffff
```

This tells the router to restrict inbound traffic so the only MAC address that a remote device can reach through DLSw is the one that we have configured—4000.3745.AAAA, in this case. This would usually correspond to the mainframe's FEP address. You can easily include several MAC address definitions in the same way if there are other devices to which you want to allow access.

This helps to prevent unwanted traffic from being bridged across your WAN. In particular, it ensures nobody can use DLSw to bridge from one remote site to another.

It is important to note that the end devices on the Token Ring only need the RIF representing the local DLSw router. DLSw is said to "terminate the RIF," meaning that it effectively creates three regions of RIF tables, from end device A to Router A, from Router A to Router Z, and from Router Z to end device Z. This is different from RSRB, for example, which passes RIF information through the network so that end devices can specify their paths. In DLSw, however, the routers take over path selection. This allows the router to respond to local RIF requests without passing them through the network. It also drastically reduces the storage required for RIF tables on all devices.

Other features

There are a couple of other small commands in these examples that allow specific functionality or improve efficiency. On the central router you will see the command *dlsw cache-ignore-netbios-datagram*. This simply tells the router to ignore NetBIOS names that it receives through DLSw. This is useful in large networks because it allows the central router to avoid having to maintain a large NetBIOS name cache.

Because all connections are inbound anyway, the NetBIOS names of remote devices are never used in such a configuration, so this command allows you to ignore them.

And, finally, on the branch router, we have included the line *multiring all* in the configuration of the Token Ring interface. There are actually several different options besides *all* for this command. The most common one would be *multiring ip*. The *all* option allows all routable protocols, such as TCP/IP and IPX, to use the interface for routing, while purely bridged protocols like SNA are permitted to use it for bridging. Specifying *multiring ip* allow IP to use the interface, but not another routed protocol such as IPX.

15.3 Using DLSw to Bridge Between Ethernet and Token Ring

Problem

You want to set up DLSw to allow Token Ring to Ethernet bridging.

Solution

DLSw includes the capability to bridge different kinds of media. One common example of this is bridging an Ethernet segment to a Token Ring. In this example, we will suppose that we are connecting an Ethernet branch to the same central Token Ring DLSw router from Recipe 15.2:

```
dlsw-ether-branch#configure terminal
Enter configuration commands, one per line.  End with CNTL/Z.
dlsw-ether-branch(config)#interface Loopback0
dlsw-ether-branch(config-if)#ip address 10.1.3.5 255.255.255.252
dlsw-ether-branch(config-if)#exit
dlsw-ether-branch(config)#access-list 200 permit 0x0000 0x0D0D
dlsw-ether-branch(config)#source-bridge ring-group 101
dlsw-ether-branch(config)#dlsw local-peer peer-id 10.1.3.5
dlsw-ether-branch(config)#dlsw timer explorer-wait-time 5
dlsw-ether-branch(config)#dlsw remote-peer 0 tcp 10.1.1.5 lf 1470 lsap-output-list 200
dlsw-ether-branch(config)#dlsw bridge-group 1
dlsw-ether-branch(config)#dlsw transparent switch-support
dlsw-ether-branch(config)#dlsw allroute-sna
dlsw-ether-branch(config)#interface Ethernet0
dlsw-ether-branch(config-if)#description branch Ethernet
dlsw-ether-branch(config-if)#bridge-group 1
dlsw-ether-branch(config-if)#bridge 1 protocol ieee
dlsw-ether-branch(config-if)#exit
dlsw-ether-branch(config)#end
dlsw-ether-branch#
```

Discussion

Before looking at this in detail, we need to stress that routable protocols such as TCP/IP always behave better when they are routed. So you should only use bridging between different media, as in this example, when there are unroutable protocols that must communicate between them. Perhaps the most common example is when LLC2 SNA devices must be accessed from an Ethernet segment.

The important differences between this Ethernet branch example and the preceding Token Ring example are highlighted. The first difference is in the *remote-peer* command, where we added the flag *lf 1470*. This restricts the MTU of the bridged network to 1470 bytes so that the larger Token Ring frames cannot use the bridge. Token Ring supports much larger frames than Ethernet does. In a bridged network, there is no packet fragmentation facility as there is in routed networks. So if large Token Ring packets cross the bridge to an Ethernet segment, they must be dropped.

Ideally, this MTU restriction should be made on the *remote-peer* commands at both ends. If your central router must support both Ethernet and Token Ring branches, then it makes sense to configure two *remote-peer* commands on the central router, one for each type of remote medium. The command that the central router uses for bridging to Ethernet segments should then have the MTU restricted in the same way with the lf 1470 flag. If you like, you could also have a separate statement on the central router for remote Token Ring peers that can use the default value.

The next important difference between this Ethernet branch and the previous Token Ring branch is the presence of the command *dlsw transparent switch-support*. This is used in cases when the Ethernet segment that the router is connecting to the bridge is itself bridged. This would be the case if the local Ethernet segment contains an Ethernet switch. Remember from the Introduction of this chapter that all Ethernet switches are transparent bridges. This command is particularly important when there are two redundant DLSw routers on this Ethernet segment. In such a case, the switch will become confused by the fact that the same downstream MAC addresses appear from both routers. If you are using Ethernet hubs, this command is not necessary.

The interface configuration for Ethernet is completely different from the Token Ring example. There are three commands in this example that define the bridging characteristics of the Ethernet interface. The first is the *bridge-group* command, found in the Ethernet interface configuration block. This command tells the router to associate this interface with the first logical bridge group in the router. This number is purely local to the router. You could build a bridge between two Ethernet interfaces on the same router as follows:

```
Router(config)#interface Ethernet0
Router(config-if)#bridge-group 1
Router(config-if)#exit
Router(config)#interface Ethernet1
Router(config-if)#bridge-group 1
Router(config-if)#exit
```

But in the example, we want to connect this Ethernet port to a Token Ring on another router, so we have associated this bridge group instead with DLSw by using the *dlsw bridge-group* global configuration command:

```
dlsw-ether-branch(config)#dlsw bridge-group 1
dlsw-ether-branch(config)#interface Ethernet0
dlsw-ether-branch(config-if)#bridge-group 1
```

Then the bridging behaviour is defined with the following command:

```
dlsw-ether-branch(config-if)#bridge 1 protocol ieee
```

This command tells the router to use the IEEE 802.1d Spanning Tree Protocol for avoiding loops when creating the bridge, instead of the older and incompatible Digital Equipment Corporation (DEC) standard. Unless you are connecting to extremely old equipment that doesn't support the IEEE standard, you should always use this command.

Ethernet II or 802.3 framing

Bridging Ethernet frames to Token Ring frames actually introduces an important ambiguity. There are two different Ethernet framing standards: the older Ethernet II standard that is commonly used for TCP/IP, and the newer IEEE 802.3 standard that is used for many other protocols. The most immediately important difference between 802.3 and Ethernet standards is whether the header field immediately after the destination and source addresses is a length (less than 1500), as in 802.3, or a type (greater than 1500), as in Ethernet II.

The translation for 802.3 Ethernet frames is relatively clean because the Token Ring frames have a similar format, as they both share the same 802.2 header format. So this is the default, and this is what is shown in the example above. However, if you want to use Ethernet II framing for the bridged protocols on the Ethernet side, you have to configure the router to understand this frame type.

As an aside, you should bear in mind that you can run different Ethernet frame types for different protocols running on the same Ethernet segment. For example, it is relatively common to use 802.3 framing for IPX, while IP is always Ethernet II. There is no inherent conflict in running both of these frame types at the same time. It only becomes a problem if, for example, some of the IPX devices used one frame type and some used the other.

The Ethernet II frame type field has a value of 0x80d5 when bridging Ethernet II to Token Ring. This frame type technically refers to SNA traffic, although it applies equally to any traffic bridged from a Token Ring. To tell the router to use Ethernet II framing, you must apply this globally to all source-route bridging as follows:

```
dlsw-ether-branch(config)#source-bridge enable-80d5
```

Note this is a global command affecting all Ethernet interfaces on the router. You cannot have some interfaces using Ethernet II and others using 802.3 framing for bridging.

See Also

Recipe 15.2

15.4 Converting Ethernet and Token Ring MAC Addresses

Problem

You want to convert the bit ordering of MAC addresses to see how they will look after passing through an Ethernet-to-Token Ring bridge.

Solution

The Perl script in Example 15-1 converts Ethernet addresses to the way they will appear when connected through a bridge to a Token Ring. It also performs the reverse translation of Token Ring addresses to Ethernet, which is identical.

Example 15-1. eth-tok-mac.pl

```perl
#!/usr/local/bin/perl # # eth-tok-mac.pl -- a script to convert Ethernet to Token Ring MAC
#                   addresses when bridging with RSRB or DLSw
#
$convert[0] = "0";    $convert[1] = "8";
$convert[2] = "4";    $convert[3] = "C";
$convert[4] = "2";    $convert[5] = "A";
$convert[6] = "6";    $convert[7] = "E";
$convert[8] = "1";    $convert[9] = "9";
$convert[10] = "5";   $convert[11] = "D";
$convert[12] = "3";   $convert[13] = "B";
$convert[14] = "7";   $convert[15] = "F";


if($#ARGV != 0) {usage();}

$input_MAC = $ARGV[0];

# first split the incoming MAC into bytes
$_ = $input_MAC;
s/[.:-]//g;

for ($i=0; $i*2 < length($_); $i++) {
   @input_bytes[$i] = substr($_, $i*2, 2);
}

for ($i=0; $i <= $#input_bytes; $i++) {
   $_ = @input_bytes[$i];

   # first check that there aren't any illegal characters in this address
   if(/[^0-9a-fA-F]/) {
      usage();
   }
```

Example 15-1. eth-tok-mac.pl (continued)

```
   if (length( ) == 2 ) {
      @output_bytes[$i] = $convert[hex(substr($_, 1, 1))]
                       . $convert[hex(substr($_, 0, 1))];
   } else {
      usage( );
   }
}

print "the resulting MAC is: ";
for ($i=0; $i < $#input_bytes; $i++) {
   print "@output_bytes[$i]-";
}
print "@output_bytes[$#input_bytes]\n";

sub usage( ) {
  print "usage: eth-tok-mac.pl <MAC>\n";
  print "     where <MAC> is in the form HH:HH:HH:HH:HH:HH\n";
  print "     or HH-HH-HH-HH-HH-HH or HHHH.HHHH.HHHH";
  print "     (H is a hex number 0-F)\n";
  print "The output is the converted MAC address.\n";
  print "Note that this conversion is exactly the same whether converting\n";
  print "from Ethernet to Token Ring or Token Ring to Ethernet.\n";

  exit;
}
```

The program is run as follows:

```
$ eth-tok-mac.pl 00-00-0c-f0-84-60
the resulting MAC is: 00-00-30-0f-21-06
```

Discussion

Token Ring uses a convention of most significant bit first when writing a byte. Ethernet, on the other hand, puts the least significant bit first. So when a bridge connects these two media, the MAC addresses of devices on the Ethernet side will look unfamiliar when viewed from the Token Ring side, and vice versa. The rule for converting from one to the other is relatively simple, however, because it just reflects this reversing of the bit ordering.

Table 15-3 shows how the conversion algorithm works.

Table 15-3. Converting Token Ring to Ethernet MAC addresses

Token Ring	Ethernet				
Hex	Decimal	Binary	Binary	Decimal	Hex
0	0	0000	0000	0	0
1	1	0001	1000	8	8
2	2	0010	0100	4	4
3	3	0011	1100	12	C

Table 15-3. Converting Token Ring to Ethernet MAC addresses (continued)

Token Ring	Ethernet				
4	4	0100	0010	2	2
5	5	0101	1010	10	A
6	6	0110	0110	6	6
7	7	0111	1110	14	E
8	8	1000	0001	1	1
9	9	1001	1001	9	9
A	10	1010	0101	5	5
B	11	1011	1101	13	D
C	12	1100	0011	3	3
D	13	1101	1011	11	B
E	14	1110	0111	7	7
F	15	1111	1111	15	F

This table converts each individual hex character in a MAC address, but there is more to it than this because a byte is eight bits long, not four bits like a hex character.

Suppose the Ethernet address is 0000.0cf0.8460. The third byte of this address is 0c. To figure out how this byte will look on the Token Ring side of the bridge, you first switch the two hex characters to get c0. Then convert each of these characters by using Table 15-1. The c becomes 3 and the 0 stays the same, giving a final value of 30. So converting the entire address similarly gives 00-00-30-0f-21-06.

The script provides an automated way to do these translations. If the 8 bits in a byte are numbered from 1–8, this algorithm simply flips the order so that they appear from 8–1. This is clearly identical to the inverse translation where the bit order is converted from 8–1 to 1–8. So both the script and the above manual technique work identically when converting Ethernet addresses to Token Ring or Token Ring addresses to Ethernet.

See Also

Recipe 15.3

15.5 Configuring SDLC

Problem

You want to configure a serial port to connect to an SDLC device so that it can use DLSw to talk to a central mainframe.

Solution

The global configuration commands in this example are identical to those shown in Recipe 15.1 for using DLSw+ to connect two Token Rings. The central router's configuration is identical to what was used in Recipe 15.1, so the following only shows the remote branch configuration:

```
dlsw-branch#configure terminal
Enter configuration commands, one per line.  End with CNTL/Z.
dlsw-branch(config)#interface Loopback0
dlsw-branch(config-if)#ip address 10.1.2.5 255.255.255.252
dlsw-branch(config-if)#exit
dlsw-branch(config)#access-list 200 permit 0x0000 0x0D0D
dlsw-branch(config)#source-bridge ring-group 101
dlsw-branch(config)#dlsw local-peer peer-id 10.1.2.5
dlsw-branch(config)#dlsw timer explorer-wait-time 5
dlsw-branch(config)#dlsw remote-peer 0 tcp 10.1.1.5 lsap-output-list 200
dlsw-branch(config)#dlsw allroute-sna
dlsw-branch(config)#interface Serial1
dlsw-branch(config-if)#description Connection to one remote SDLC device
dlsw-branch(config-if)#encapsulation sdlc
dlsw-branch(config-if)#no keepalive
dlsw-branch(config-if)#nrzi-encoding
dlsw-branch(config-if)#clock rate 4800
dlsw-branch(config-if)#sdlc role primary
dlsw-branch(config-if)#sdlc vmac 4000.CCCC.0000
dlsw-branch(config-if)#sdlc poll-pause-timer 200
dlsw-branch(config-if)#sdlc address 20
dlsw-branch(config-if)#sdlc xid 20 017A0006
dlsw-branch(config-if)#sdlc partner 4000.3745.AAAA 20
dlsw-branch(config-if)#sdlc dlsw 20
dlsw-branch(config-if)#exit
dlsw-branch(config)#end
dlsw-branch#
```

Discussion

SDLC is a serial protocol that is commonly used for SNA devices. It is extremely popular in financial environments for devices such as banking machines, card readers, and account printers. Using SDLC in conjunction with DLSw is becoming increasingly common in these sorts of situations. This allows the remote SDLC devices to communicate with the Token Ring Interface Coupler (TIC) on a mainframe computer through an IP network. There is a huge advantage to this because it means that you don't have to have a separate serial port on your mainframe's Front End Processor (FEP) for every remote SDLC connection. Instead, you can have a single Token Ring interface supporting hundreds of remote devices that are connected through a reliable routed TCP/IP network.

Although it is essentially a synchronous serial protocol, there are several ways of constructing SDLC links. The simplest is a point-to-point connection from the router to an SDLC device, perhaps even another router. The SDLC link can also connect several devices in a long serial bus connection called a *multidrop*, and it can even be set up in a ring topology. To accomplish this SDLC requires that each device have a unique 8-bit address between 0x01 and 0xFF in hexadecimal (1-255 in decimal notation). Each device is configured to respond to one of these SDLC addresses. A primary SDLC device polls every known address in turn to ask the devices if they have data to send. So despite having many physical devices sharing a serial connection, there is no danger of collisions from two devices sending simultaneously. One of the advantages to DLSw is that it takes care of local acknowledgement of these SDLC polls. So if you connect two SDLC circuits by using DLSw, the polling traffic doesn't cross the WAN, which saves bandwidth.

The example above sets up the SDLC encapsulation on the port, provides the Data Communications Equipment (DCE) clock, and acts as the master device to a downstream SDLC device. The example also defines an artificial Token Ring MAC address for this device so that the FEP will be able to communicate with it through its Token Ring port. Let's look at these functions separately:

```
dlsw-branch(config)#interface Serial1
dlsw-branch(config-if)#encapsulation sdlc
dlsw-branch(config-if)#nrzi-encoding
dlsw-branch(config-if)#clock rate 4800
```

First, the command *encapsulation sdlc* sets up the interface to use SDLC framing. This is accompanied by the *nrzi-encoding* command that specifies the electrical characteristics of the signaling. Nonreturn to Zero Inverted (NRZI) is often required with IBM equipment. The default behavior for SDLC connections on Cisco routers is Nonreturn to Zero (NRZ), which you can set by just turning off NRZI encoding, *no nrzi-encoding*.

Next, this example assumes that the router is the DCE for this SDLC line, so it must supply the clock with the *clock rate* command. In the example, the clock rate is set to 4,800 bits per second. In general, you want the clock rate to be as high as the downstream devices can support to facilitate better data transfer rates. However, it is relatively common to see SDLC devices that work only intermittently at higher rates such as 19,200 bps. So a good practice when having problems with SDLC equipment is to turn the clock rate down somewhat and see if the problems go away.

Note also that anytime that you configure a router serial interface to be the DCE device, you must use a DCE cable. The router will not even accept the *clock rate* command if you have a DTE cable connected to the interface.

The command *sdlc role primary* is used with multidrop SDLC connections to define how the router's function in the multidrop network:

```
dlsw-branch(config-if)#sdlc role primary
```

A multidrop connection simply means that several devices are connected in series to the same serial port. You lose nothing by using this command with a single downstream device connected directly to the router, however. The different options for the *sdlc role* command are *primary*, *secondary*, and *prim-xid-poll*. Configuring the router to be the SDLC primary requires that all downstream devices are either PU 2.0, PU 2.1, or a mixture, and that the router will be the master. You should specify *prim-xid-poll* only if all downstream devices use PU 2.1 and you want the router to be the master device of the group.

In this example there is only one SDLC device connected to the router, and its SDLC address is specified as 0×20 in hex. This is specified by the *sdlc address* command. Recipe 15.6 shows how to configure the router for several downstream SDLC devices.

The SDLC address is purely local to this SDLC connection. So to uniquely identify a particular remote device anywhere in the network, the mainframe needs more information. Each device is identified in VTAM in a Switched Major Node definition using two parameters called IDBLK and IDNUM. Cisco concatenates these two identifiers together to form the Exchange of Identification (XID). The example shows how to associate a particular IDBLK/IDNUM with a particular SDLC address by using the following command:

```
dlsw-branch(config-if)#sdlc xid 20 017A0006
```

The IDBLK is contained in the first three digits of the XID field—017, in this case, and the IDNUM appears in the remaining five digits, A0006. Typographical errors in the XID string are some of the most common SDLC problems. Make sure that this 8-digit hexadecimal number precisely matches the IDBLK/IDNUM configured for this device in VTAM.

Next, look at the commands that work with DLSw to allow this particular device to communicate with the mainframe. First, there must be a virtual Token Ring MAC address, which is defined using the *sdlc vmac* command:

```
dlsw-branch(config-if)#sdlc vmac 4000.CCCC.0000
```

Recall that the mainframe thinks that this SDLC device is actually a Token Ring device. This command defines the fake Token Ring address that the mainframe will use to communicate with it. However, there could be several devices on this port, all of which must have unique MAC addresses. To solve this problem, the last two digits of this address are replaced by the SDLC address. So the last two hex characters in this configuration statement must be zero. In this particular case, the *sdlc vmac* command defines a MAC address of 4000.CCCC.0000 for the serial interface. The one configured downstream device has an SDLC address of 20 (in hex). So it will appear on the mainframe's ring with the MAC address 4000.CCCC.0020.

Just as the SDLC device must appear to be a Token Ring device to the mainframe, the mainframe must appear to be an SDLC device on this serial port. So your router must insert the FEP's MAC address into the LLC packet. This is configured with the *sdlc partner* command:

```
dlsw-branch(config-if)#sdlc partner 4000.3745.AAAA 20
```

Note that the SDLC address is specifically included in this command to allow the different devices on a multidrop SDLC circuit to communicate with different FEPs.

DLSw has to know to pick up this particular SDLC address and share it with its DLSw peer routers. You set this with the *sdlc dlsw* command:

```
dlsw-branch(config-if)#sdlc address 20
dlsw-branch(config-if)#sdlc dlsw 20
```

The router will reject this command if you have not previously defined this address with the *sdlc address* command.

In this example, we have modified one of the important SDLC timing parameters by using the *sdlc poll-pause-timer* command:

```
dlsw-branch(config-if)#sdlc poll-pause-timer 200
```

In SDLC, the primary device must poll the downstream devices to see if they have something to send. The example uses this command with an argument of 200, which instructs the router to wait a period of 200 milliseconds between these polls. The default value is 100 milliseconds. The reason for using a longer interval between polls is simply to allow the downstream devices more time to respond. In some cases, particularly if the SDLC line is long or involves modems or line drivers to reach a physically remote device, the default value is not sufficient to account for the natural latency of the line. Note, however, that this polling does not cross the DLSw bridge, only the SDLC side of the network. This ability to terminate the local polling saves bandwidth and makes the network more tolerant of WAN latency.

There is one important final note on SDLC to Token Ring bridging. In Example 15.3, when bridging Ethernet to Token Ring, we had to make a restriction on the MTU in the *dlsw remote-peer* command. This is not necessary for SDLC. The SDLC frame size is normally either 265 or 521 bytes, much smaller than even the Ethernet frame size. But the difference here is that DLSw can fragment the larger Token Ring packets when sending them out of the SDLC port. However, it cannot combine several smaller SDLC frames into a larger Token Ring frame. So these packets remain small.

See Also

Recipe 15.1; Recipe 15.3; Recipe 15.6

15.6 Configuring SDLC for Multidrop Connections

Problem

You want to configure a serial port for an SDLC multidrop line supporting several devices.

Solution

SDLC supports multidrop connections. These are serial links that connect to several downstream devices in series. Each device has its own SDLC address, which must be configured in the router. The global DLSw configuration for this example is omitted here because it is identical to the previous example:

```
dlsw-branch#configure terminal
Enter configuration commands, one per line.  End with CNTL/Z.
dlsw-branch(config)#interface Serial1
dlsw-branch(config-if)#description Connection to three remote SDLC devices
dlsw-branch(config-if)#encapsulation sdlc
dlsw-branch(config-if)#no keepalive
dlsw-branch(config-if)#nrzi-encoding
dlsw-branch(config-if)#clock rate 4800
dlsw-branch(config-if)#sdlc role primary
dlsw-branch(config-if)#sdlc vmac 4000.CCCC.0000
dlsw-branch(config-if)#sdlc poll-pause-timer 200
dlsw-branch(config-if)#sdlc address 20
dlsw-branch(config-if)#sdlc xid 20 017A0006
dlsw-branch(config-if)#sdlc partner 4000.3745.AAAA 20
dlsw-branch(config-if)#sdlc address 21
dlsw-branch(config-if)#sdlc xid 21 017A0007
dlsw-branch(config-if)#sdlc partner 4000.3745.AAAA 21
dlsw-branch(config-if)#sdlc address 22
dlsw-branch(config-if)#sdlc xid 22 017A0008
dlsw-branch(config-if)#sdlc partner 4000.3745.AAAB 22
dlsw-branch(config-if)#sdlc slow-poll 30
dlsw-branch(config-if)#sdlc dlsw 20 21 22
dlsw-branch(config-if)#end
dlsw-branch#
```

Discussion

The basic router configuration is the same here as it is for the single device shown in Recipe 15.5, with a few differences. The first difference you should notice is that all three of the SDLC addresses are configured, where the previous recipe had only one. Each SDLC address appears in four places, and you must ensure that all four are configured for all SDLC devices.

There must be an *sdlc address* command for each address. You must define the XID for each device with an *sdlc xid* command. And you must associate each SDLC address with a FEP Token Ring MAC address with the *sdlc partner* command. In this example, the *sdlc partner* command for the third SDLC address, 22, is associated with a different FEP MAC address than the other two, just to show how this can be done. In most cases, you would probably want to use the same FEP for all of the devices on a port, though.

Finally, you must associate each of these SDLC addresses with a DLSw bridge as follows:

```
dlsw-branch(config-if)#sdlc dlsw 20 21 22
```

This tells the router to share these three specific SDLC addresses with DLSw. The router will not accept this command unless there is a matching *sdlc address* command defining each of these addresses.

Besides defining the additional SDLC addresses for the multidrop operation, this example also includes the command *sdlc slow-poll* with an argument of 30. This tells the router only to poll each device to ask for its data every 30 seconds rather than the default 10 seconds. This is useful in multidrop configurations because it is often difficult to service all of the devices within the required time interval.

See Also

Recipe 15.5

15.7   Using STUN

Problem

You want to connect two serial devices through an IP network.

Solution

STUN provides the ability to emulate an SDLC circuit through an IP network. To simply connect two SDLC or two HDLC ports on different routers, you can use the following:

```
Stun-A#configure terminal
Enter configuration commands, one per line.  End with CNTL/Z.
Stun-A(config)#interface Loopback0
Stun-A(config-if)#ip address 10.1.15.5 255.255.255.252
Stun-A(config-if)#exit
Stun-A(config)#stun peer-name 10.1.15.5
Stun-A(config)#stun protocol-group 1 basic
Stun-A(config)#interface Serial1
Stun-A(config-if)#encapsulation stun
Stun-A(config-if)#nrzi-encoding
Stun-A(config-if)#clock rate 19200
Stun-A(config-if)#stun group 1
Stun-A(config-if)#stun route all tcp 10.1.15.9
Stun-A(config-if)#exit
Stun-A(config)#end
Stun-A#
```

And this router would connect this serial port to a port on a second router that is configured as follows:

```
Stun-B#configure terminal
Enter configuration commands, one per line.  End with CNTL/Z.
Stun-B(config)#interface Loopback0
Stun-B(config-if)#ip address 10.1.15.9 255.255.255.252
Stun-B(config-if)#exit
```

```
Stun-B(config)#stun peer-name 10.1.15.9
Stun-B(config)#stun protocol-group 1 basic
Stun-B(config)#interface Serial1
Stun-B(config-if)#encapsulation stun
Stun-B(config-if)#nrzi-encoding
Stun-B(config-if)#clock rate 19200
Stun-B(config-if)#stun group 1
Stun-B(config-if)#stun route all tcp 10.1.15.5
Stun-B(config-if)#exit
Stun-B(config)#end
Stun-B#
```

You can also do more interesting things with STUN. For example, if you wanted to create a virtual multidrop SDLC circuit, you could do something like this. The first router would connect to the controller, and the other two would hold the SDLC devices:

```
Stun-A#configure terminal
Enter configuration commands, one per line.  End with CNTL/Z.
Stun-A(config)#interface Loopback0
Stun-A(config-if)#ip address 10.1.15.5 255.255.255.252
Stun-A(config-if)#exit
Stun-A(config)#stun peer-name 10.1.15.5
Stun-A(config)#stun protocol-group 1 sdlc
Stun-A(config)#interface Serial1
Stun-A(config-if)#encapsulation stun
Stun-A(config-if)#nrzi-encoding
Stun-A(config-if)#clock rate 19200
Stun-A(config-if)#stun group 1
Stun-A(config-if)#stun sdlc role secondary
Stun-A(config-if)#sdlc address 20
Stun-A(config-if)#sdlc address 21
Stun-A(config-if)#stun route address 20 tcp 10.1.15.9 local-ack
Stun-A(config-if)#stun route address 21 tcp 10.1.15.13 local-ack
Stun-A(config-if)#exit
Stun-A(config)#end
Stun-A#
```

And you would configure the second router like this:

```
Stun-B#configure terminal
Enter configuration commands, one per line.  End with CNTL/Z.
Stun-B(config)#interface Loopback0
Stun-B(config-if)#ip address 10.1.15.9 255.255.255.252
Stun-B(config-if)#exit
Stun-B(config)#stun peer-name 10.1.15.9
Stun-B(config)#stun protocol-group 1 sdlc
Stun-B(config)#interface Serial1
Stun-B(config-if)#encapsulation stun
Stun-B(config-if)#nrzi-encoding
Stun-B(config-if)#clock rate 19200
Stun-B(config-if)#stun group 1
Stun-B(config-if)#stun sdlc role primary
Stun-B(config-if)#sdlc address 20
Stun-B(config-if)#stun route address 20 tcp 10.1.15.5 local-ack
Stun-B(config-if)#exit
```

```
Stun-B(config)#end
Stun-B#
```

And you would set up the third peer as follows:

```
Stun-C#configure terminal
Enter configuration commands, one per line.  End with CNTL/Z.
Stun-C(config)#interface Loopback0
Stun-C(config-if)#ip address 10.1.15.13 255.255.255.252
Stun-C(config-if)#exit
Stun-C(config)#stun peer-name 10.1.15.13
Stun-C(config)#stun protocol-group 1 sdlc
Stun-C(config)#interface Serial1
Stun-C(config-if)#encapsulation stun
Stun-C(config-if)#nrzi-encoding
Stun-C(config-if)#clock rate 19200
Stun-C(config-if)#stun group 1
Stun-C(config-if)#stun sdlc role primary
Stun-C(config-if)#sdlc address 21
Stun-C(config-if)#stun route address 21 tcp 10.1.15.5 local-ack
Stun-C(config-if)#exit
Stun-C(config)#end
Stun-C#
```

Discussion

In principle, you could configure DLSw to connect two SDLC ports across an IP network by using a slight variation of Recipe 15.6. But there is a simpler way to accomplish this. Cisco IOS includes two features called Serial Tunnel (STUN) and Block Serial Tunnel (BSTUN). STUN is useful for connecting things like SDLC ports, even to the extent of building virtual SDLC multidrop links. BSTUN, on the other hand, is most useful when connecting ports running the IBM Bisync protocol. BSTUN is discussed in Recipe 15.8.

The first example in this recipe shows how to simply connect two serial ports through an IP network by using an emulated serial line. This type of configuration can be useful when dealing with applications that use the serial data link protocols in a nonstandard way. It can also sometimes be useful if you have to provide a serial connection between two locations that are already in your IP network.

This example first defines a single STUN protocol group, as number 1 on each router. Then, in the interface configuration blocks, you reference this number to tell STUN how to interpret the data it receives on this interface. You could define several different protocol groups supporting different protocols if required. Note that the protocol group number is purely local to the router. So what appears as protocol group number 1 on the first router could be group number 5 on the second router.

The second example shows a somewhat more complicated configuration. In this case, STUN is used to emulate not a single circuit through an IP cloud, but rather a multidrop circuit for use with SDLC devices. In more complex situations like this, it is often better to use DLSw, but sometimes the SDLC devices need to see one another directly for one reason or another.

The only tricky part to this type of configuration is to understand which routers are *primary* and which are *secondary* for SDLC. It's a little bit easier to understand if you envision the primary as the top of the network. Everything feeds into the primary. So if a router interface connects to downstream SDLC devices, as in routers Stun-B and Stun-C, the serial port is configured as primary because it is controlling everything downstream. On Stun-A, however, the router is acting as the network for the real controller device, so this router's serial interface is configured as secondary.

This example also includes local acknowledgement to prevent SDLC polling from crossing the IP network:

```
Stun-C(config-if)#stun route address 21 tcp 10.1.15.5 local-ack
```

This means simply that the router will respond to polls on behalf of devices that are on the other end of the tunnel to save bandwidth and improve performance. Allowing acknowledgement frames to cross the IP network sometimes introduces large latencies to the SDLC network because the devices must wait longer before sending the next data frame.

See Also

Recipe 15.8

15.8 Using BSTUN

Problem

You want to connect two Bisync (BSC) devices through an IP network.

Solution

This pair of router configurations shows how to define a tunnel connecting two serial ports supporting Bisync (BSC or Binary Synchronous Communications) devices:

```
BSTUN-A#configure terminal
Enter configuration commands, one per line.  End with CNTL/Z.
BSTUN-A(config)#interface Loopback0
BSTUN-A(config-if)#ip address 10.1.16.5 255.255.255.252
BSTUN-A(config-if)#exit
BSTUN-A(config)#bstun peer-name 10.1.16.5
BSTUN-A(config)#bstun protocol-group 1 bsc
BSTUN-A(config)#interface Serial1
BSTUN-A(config-if)#encapsulation bstun
BSTUN-A(config-if)#clock rate 19200
BSTUN-A(config-if)#bstun group 1
BSTUN-A(config-if)#bsc char-set ebcdic
BSTUN-A(config-if)#bsc secondary
```

```
BSTUN-A(config-if)#bstun route all tcp 10.1.16.9
BSTUN-A(config-if)#exit
BSTUN-A(config)#end
BSTUN-A#
```

And the configuration of the second router is similar:

```
BSTUN-B#configure terminal
Enter configuration commands, one per line.  End with CNTL/Z.
BSTUN-B(config)#interface Loopback0
BSTUN-B(config-if)#ip address 10.1.16.9 255.255.255.252
BSTUN-B(config-if)#exit
BSTUN-B(config)#bstun peer-name 10.1.16.9
BSTUN-B(config)#bstun protocol-group 1 bsc
BSTUN-B(config)#interface Serial1
BSTUN-B(config-if)#encapsulation bstun
BSTUN-B(config-if)#clock rate 19200
BSTUN-B(config-if)#bstun group 1
BSTUN-B(config-if)#bsc char-set ebcdic
BSTUN-B(config-if)#bsc primary
BSTUN-B(config-if)#bstun route all tcp 10.1.16.5
BSTUN-B(config-if)#exit
BSTUN-B(config)#end
BSTUN-B#
```

Discussion

The configuration here is similar to the preceding STUN recipe. The main differences are in the protocols supported. The *bstun protocol-group* command in this case tells the router that BSTUN group number 1 will be passing BSC protocol data. There are several other options, including defaults for Diebold and MDI alarm systems, as well as a generic async option.

In this recipe, the *bsc char-set* command is set to IBM's EBCDIC character set. The other option here is ASCII. The choice depends on the type of traffic you are dealing with. Usually mainframe Bisync applications will use EBCDIC. At one time, Bisync was used as a popular way of connecting terminals and printers to a mainframe. But (thankfully) this ancient protocol inches closer to extinction with each passing year.

The only other important point to note is that the *bstun route* command can be used to different routing for different stations attached to the same Bisync line, depending on their addresses. Bisync allows many devices to be connected to the same controller, similar to an SDLC multidrop line. For example, if you wanted station C1 going to one destination and C2 to another, you could route them separately as follows:

```
BSTUN-A#configure terminal
Enter configuration commands, one per line.  End with CNTL/Z.
BSTUN-A(config)#interface Serial1
BSTUN-A(config-if)#bstun route address C1 tcp 10.1.16.9
BSTUN-A(config-if)#bstun route address C2 tcp 10.1.16.13
BSTUN-A(config-if)#exit
BSTUN-A(config)#end
BSTUN-A#
```

15.9 Controlling DLSw Packet Fragmentation

Problem

You want to control packet fragmentation in DLSw to improve throughput.

Solution

There are two methods for controlling packet fragmentation when using DLSw. The first is to set an MTU for the bridge, as mentioned above in the section on bridging Token Ring to Ethernet:

```
Router-A(config)#dlsw remote-peer 0 tcp 10.1.1.5 lf 1470 lsap-output-list 200
```

This is used primarily when connecting media with different MTU values. However, it is also common to connect two high MTU media such as Token Rings via an intervening network that has low MTU links. In this situation, you should take advantage of DLSw's TCP transport and the following command:

```
Router-A(config)#ip tcp path-mtu-discovery
```

Discussion

These two different commands work at different levels and accomplish different goals. The first one sets the MTU of packets that pass through the bridge. However the DLSw packets themselves need not have the same MTU. In fact, DLSw+ is able to break up a large Token Ring packet, carry it in a series of several DLSw packets, and then reassemble the large packet at the other end. So the first command above instructs DLSw not to accept any packets for bridging if they are larger than the specified size.

The most serious performance problems happen when the DLSw packets themselves must be fragmented in the network. In general, the DLSw routers will use the largest MTU that they can. This will usually wind up being the MTU of the first link into the IP network heading toward the router at the other end of the bridge. There could be a link along the path that can't transmit a packet this large, so some router in the middle of the network will fragment the packet according to standard TCP packet fragmentation rules. The receiving DLSw router reassembles the packet before de-encapsulating the payload packet.

This tends to be relatively inefficient, and it can cause serious throughput issues in some networks. So to avoid the problem, you can configure both DLSw peer routers to use a clever feature of TCP called Path MTU Discovery, which is described in RFC 1191. When the TCP connection is first made, in this case by forming a DLSw peer relationship between two routers, the routers start by figuring out the largest MTU that they can pass between them without fragmentation.

They do this by setting the Don't Fragment (DF) bit in the IP header and sending the largest packet that the interface can support. If a router somewhere in the network finds that it must fragment the packet to forward it, it will drop it instead and send back an informational ICMP "Datagram Too Big" packet to report the problem. The ICMP message includes the maximum size that it could have passed along. This allows the two end points to quickly deduce the largest packet size they can use.

TCP Path MTU Discovery is not enabled by default on Cisco routers. This command will affect all TCP sessions with this router, not just DLSw. In general, it is most effective if all of the DLSw routers have this feature enabled.

15.10 Tagging DLSw Packets for QoS

Problem

You want to set the Type of Service (TOS) field in DLSw packets to ensure that they get preferential treatment in the network.

Solution

In many organizations, the SNA traffic that is encapsulated in DLSw is considered both mission critical and time sensitive. So these organizations don't want lower priority traffic to interfere with it. The simplest way to accomplish this is to tag these high priority packets using the standard IP Precedence field:

```
Router-A#configure terminal
Enter configuration commands, one per line.  End with CNTL/Z.
Router-A(config)#ip local policy route-map dlswroutemap
Router-A(config)#ip route-cache policy
Router-A(config)#access-list 101 permit tcp any any eq 2065
Router-A(config)#access-list 101 permit tcp any eq 2065 any
Router-A(config)#access-list 101 permit tcp any any eq 2067
Router-A(config)#access-list 101 permit tcp any eq 2067 any
Router-A(config)#route-map dlswroutemap permit 10
Router-A(config-route-map)#match ip address 101
Router-A(config-route-map)#set ip precedence flash-override
Router-A(config-route-map)#exit
Router-A(config)#end
Router-A#
```

Discussion

The most important concept here is the idea that you should set the priority of a packet at the point where it enters the network. In this case, the DLSw packet is actually created by the router, so this is the perfect place to tag it. Then every other router in the network can simply react appropriately to this priority tag without having to look deeply into the packet to figure out how important it is.

This example just shows how to set the IP Precedence field—it doesn't actually affect the forwarding behavior. You have to ensure that the interfaces on routers that need to forward this packet are configured to deal with IP Precedence properly by using Weighted Fair Queuing or some other appropriate queuing mechanism. Techniques for doing this are shown in Chapter 11. The actual tagging of the packet is done by using policy-based routing, which is described in more detail in Chapter 5.

The IP Precedence value is set for every TCP packet with a source or destination port of 2065 or 2067. These are the two ports commonly used for DLSw traffic, 2065 is used by DLSw Version 1, and 2067 by Version 2. Cisco's DLSw+ primarily uses 2065, although Recipe 15.11 shows an exception to this.

Chapter 11 demonstrates some more sophisticated options for setting QoS tag values.

See Also

Recipe 15.11; Chapter 11

15.11 Supporting SNA Priorities

Problem

You want DLSw to preserve and support the SNA or APPN Class of Service definitions for forwarding packets through your IP network.

Solution

To configure DLSw to follow the SNA or APPN priorities defined in the traffic flow, you must configure the peer relationship to allow multiple distinct data streams:

```
Router-A#configure terminal
Enter configuration commands, one per line.  End with CNTL/Z.
Router-A(config)#dlsw remote-peer 0 tcp 10.1.1.5 lsap-output-list 200 priority
Router-A(config)#end
Router-A#
```

You can then go further and map the individual priority streams to specific IP Precedence values, as in the previous example. The default values are shown in Table 15-4:

```
Router-A#configure terminal
Enter configuration commands, one per line.  End with CNTL/Z.
Router-A(config)#dlsw tos map low 0 normal 1 medium 2 high 3
Router-A(config)#end
Router-A#
```

The TOS map does not need to match at both ends of a DLSw connection. But if you use the *priority* option on the *dlsw remote-peer* command on one router, you must also use it on the other.

Discussion

Recipe 15.10 showed how to configure the router to tag the IP Precedence field in all DLSw packets for preferential treatment through the network. This example allows for the creation of four separate DLSw priority levels that follow the SNA priorities. This is useful, for example, if the SNA traffic stream includes both bulk data transfers and interactive traffic.

As soon as you enable SNA prioritization in the *dlsw remote-peer* command, DLSw forms four TCP connections instead of just one. So it is critical you enable this option on both ends if it is required, or the remote router will simply reject the DLSw peer connection. DLSw then starts using the TCP Port numbers, as shown in Table 15-4.

Table 15-4. Default mapping of SNA priority to IP TOS and TCP ports

IP TOS	Value	SNA priority	DLSw TCP port
Routine	0		
Priority	1		
Immediate	2	Low	1983
Flash	3	Normal	1982
Flash Override	4	Medium	1981
Critical	5	High	2065
Internetwork Control	6		
Network Control	7		

Note that the highest priority SNA traffic has an IP TOS value of 5 (Critical) by default when SNA Priority is enabled. This is not a good choice in many networks. The routers need to reserve the top two Precedence values, Internetwork Control (6) and Network Control (7), for vital functions like routing protocols. Giving high priority SNA traffic a Precedence value of 5 means that there is no room for other high priority traffic such as voice. This is why we have included the *dlsw tos map* command in the recipe example. This command allows you to select more appropriate TOS values for the four SNA priorities.

Whether you use this method or the one in Recipe 15.10 to set up *DLSw* QoS is mostly a matter of whether you need to preserve the native SNA priority scheme. Opening 4 TCP connections, as in this recipe, causes the router to use more memory and CPU resources. This might become an issue on heavily loaded routers, particularly when many routers use a common central DLSw peer.

See Also

Recipe 15.10; Chapter 11

15.12 DLSw+ Redundancy and Fault Tolerance

Problem

You want to improve the fault tolerance of your DLSw network.

Solution

There are several things you can do to improve the reliability and fault tolerance of your network. Many of these solutions have the added benefit of improving performance. The first important thing to consider is having more than one DLSw peer router connected to the mainframe's Token Ring. In this case, you will want to make sure that you balance the load between the two peers as much as possible:

```
dlsw-branch#configure terminal
Enter configuration commands, one per line.  End with CNTL/Z.
dlsw-branch(config)#source-bridge ring-group 101
dlsw-branch(config)#dlsw local-peer peer-id 10.1.2.5
dlsw-branch(config)#dlsw timer explorer-wait-time 5
dlsw-branch(config)#dlsw load-balance circuit-count
dlsw-branch(config)#dlsw remote-peer 0 tcp 10.1.1.5 lsap-output-list 200
dlsw-branch(config)#dlsw remote-peer 0 tcp 10.1.1.9 lsap-output-list 200
dlsw-branch(config)#dlsw allroute-sna
dlsw-branch(config)#end
dlsw-branch#
```

Discussion

This example is extremely similar to the one shown in Recipe 15.2, so the interface parts of the configuration are left out for simplicity. The main difference is the presence of a second *dlsw remote-peer* command. This command points to the IP address of a second router that is on the same central Token Ring as the mainframe. So the same mainframe MAC address is visible on this branch router coming from both DLSw peers.

The command *dlsw load-balance circuit-count* tells the router to balance circuits between these two peers. For example, if several PCs are connected the branch Token Ring, and they all have SNA sessions to the mainframe, this feature will ensure that half of these sessions follow one path and half follow the other. If one of these peers fails, then the circuits will be re-established through the remaining path.

The routers will not tear down circuits to balance the load, but rather will look at the current number of circuits on each peer each time a new circuit is established. They will then use this information to decide where to put the new circuit.

The other option here is the default *round-robin* circuit balancing. Round robin has the disadvantage that it takes a very long time to rebalance the load after a failure. So we recommend using the *circuit-count* option for load balancing between two or more remote DLSw peers.

See Also

Recipe 15.2

15.13 Viewing DLSw Status Information

Problem

You want to check on DLSw status on your router.

Solution

This command shows the status of a DLSw peer relationship:

```
Router>show dlsw peers
Peers:                 state    pkts_rx  pkts_tx  type  drops ckts TCP    uptime
  TCP 10.1.1.5         CONNECT      350      350  conf     0    0   0 02:55:03
  TCP 10.1.1.9         CONNECT      124      124  conf     0    0   0 01:17:28
Total number of connected peers: 2
Total number of connections:     2
```

This command looks at the status of the SNA circuits carried within these peer connections:

```
Router>show dlsw circuits
Index          local addr(lsap)     remote addr(dsap)  state       uptime
1459617889     4000.5555.a820(04)   4000.3745.aaaa(04) CONNECTED    3d05h
2097152104     4000.5555.ac21(04)   4000.3745.aaaa(04) CONNECTED    2d18h
738197600      000c.2950.aa40(14)   4000.3745.aaaa(04) CONNECTED    3d06h
2214592610     4000.aaaa.3826(04)   4000.3745.aaaa(04) CONNECTED    3d05h
2785017948     4001.bbbb.6797(04)   4000.3745.aaaa(04) CONNECTED    3d06h
Total number of circuits connected: 5
```

Discussion

It is important to remember the difference between a peer and a circuit. A peer relationship exists between two DLSw routers. You can bring up a peer relationship between two routers and have no application information flowing between them. A circuit, on the other hand, is an SNA connection between a device connected to one of these routers to a device connected to the other.

The *show dlsw peers* command shows only information about the peer relationship. It indicates the state of each peer connection, how many packets have been sent and received along each path, how many circuits are active, and how long the peers have been up. The example shows two peer routers, as would be the case in Recipe 15.12. In this example, both peers are in a CONNECTED state, and neither has any active circuits passing through it (as shown in the ckts column).

The *show dlsw circuits* command looks at the status of the circuits. In this case, there are five active circuits. The output shows how long each of the circuits has been connected, and the MAC addresses involved. It also shows the SSAP and DSAP associated with each session. This can be helpful in determining which circuits apply to which applications.

The index number associated with each circuit is just an identifying number that you can use to manually disconnect a particular circuit. You can clear all of the circuits at once, as follows:

```
Router#clear dlsw circuits
```

Or, to clear only the second circuit listed in the example output, you would type the following:

```
Router#clear dlsw circuits 2097152104
```

15.14 Viewing SDLC Status Information

Problem

You want to check the status of an SDLC device on your router.

Solution

You can get a lot of useful SDLC information simply by looking at the interface:

```
Router>show int serial1
Serial1 is up, line protocol is up
  Hardware is HD64570
  Description: Connection to three remote SDLC devices
  MTU 1500 bytes, BW 1544 Kbit, DLY 20000 usec,
     reliability 255/255, txload 1/255, rxload 1/255
  Encapsulation SDLC, loopback not set
    Router link station role: PRIMARY (DCE)
    Router link station metrics:
      slow-poll 30 seconds
      T1 (reply time out) 3000 milliseconds
      N1 (max frame size) 12016 bits
      N2 (retry count) 20
      poll-pause-timer 200 milliseconds
      poll-limit-value 1
      k (windowsize) 7
      modulo 8
      sdlc vmac: 4000.CCCC.00--
  sdlc addr 20 state is CONNECT
      cls_state is CLS_IN_SESSION
      VS 0, VR 0, Remote VR 0, Current retransmit count 0
      Hold queue: 0/200 IFRAMEs 5025/618
      TESTs 0/0 XIDs 0/0, DMs 0/0 FRMRs 0/0
      RNRs 15/2 SNRMs 0/0 DISC/RDs 0/0 REJs 0/0
      Poll: clear, Poll count: 0, ready for poll, chain: 22/21
  sdlc addr 21 state is CONNECT
      cls_state is CLS_IN_SESSION
      VS 0, VR 0, Remote VR 0, Current retransmit count 0
      Hold queue: 0/200 IFRAMEs 127/15
      TESTs 0/0 XIDs 0/0, DMs 0/0 FRMRs 0/0
      RNRs 1/0 SNRMs 0/0 DISC/RDs 0/0 REJs 0/0
      Poll: clear, Poll count: 0, ready for poll, chain: 20/22
```

```
sdlc addr 22 state is SNRMSENT
    cls_state is CLS_CONNECT_RSP_PEND
    VS 0, VR 0, Remote VR 0, Current retransmit count 0
    Hold queue: 0/200 IFRAMEs 25/0
    TESTs 0/0 XIDs 0/0, DMs 0/0 FRMRs 0/0
    RNRs 0/0 SNRMs 0/0 DISC/RDs 0/0 REJs 0/0
    Poll: clear, Poll count: 0, ready for poll, chain: 21/20
  Last input 00:00:00, output 00:00:00, output hang never
  Last clearing of "show interface" counters 01:05:31
Input queue: 0/75/0/0 (size/max/drops/flushes); Total output drops: 0
  Queueing strategy: fifo
  Output queue :0/40 (size/max)
  5 minute input rate 6 bits/sec, 2 packets/sec
  5 minute output rate 3 bits/sec, 1 packets/sec
    157210 packets input, 315708 bytes, 0 no buffer
    Received 287021 broadcasts, 0 runts, 0 giants, 0 throttles
    0 input errors, 0 CRC, 0 frame, 0 overrun, 0 ignored, 0 abort
    156918 packets output, 307682 bytes, 0 underruns
    0 output errors, 0 collisions, 0 interface resets
    0 output buffer failures, 0 output buffers swapped out
    0 carrier transitions
    DCD=up  DSR=up  DTR=up   RTS=down  CTS=up
```

Discussion

This recipe shows the output of a *show interface* command for the multidrop configuration shown in Recipe 15.6. The first thing to look at is the first line, which reports that the interface is up and line protocol is also up. In general, these values are affected by physical issues such as whether the cabling is correctly connected, clocking, and the choice of NRZ or NRZI line coding. The other thing to look at if you have trouble bringing the line up is the duplex setting of the interface. On Cisco routers, SDLC uses full duplex by default. To change this to half duplex, use the *sdlc hdx* command:

```
Router-A#(config)#interface Serial1
Router-A#(config-if)#sdlc hdx
```

In the output of the *show interface* command above, you can immediately see that there are three SDLC addresses configured, with hexadecimal addresses 20, 21, and 22. In this particular case, only the first two stations are shown in a connected state, and the third is not responding. The router is trying to contact it, so it is listed in a SNRMSENT state. This means that the router has sent a Set Normal Response Mode (SNRM) request to initialize the Physical Unit (PU). Table 15-5 shows all of the possible states for SDLC devices.

Table 15-5. SDLC device states

State	Description
CONNECT	Circuit initialization has completed successfully for this device.
DISCONNECT	The router is not attempting to communicate with the device.

Table 15-5. SDLC device states (continued)

State	Description
DISCSENT	The router has sent a disconnection request to the device, but has not yet received a response.
SNRMSEEN	The router has received a connection request from the device (the router must be secondary, and the device must be primary).
SNRMSENT	The router has sent a connection request to the device, but has not yet received a response (the router must be primary to send a SNRM).
THEMBUSY	The device has sent an RNR frame.
USBUSY	The router has sent an RNR frame.
BOTHBUSY	The router and the device are both sending RNR frames.
XIDSENT	For PU2.1 devices, this means that the router has sent the XID to the device.
XIDSTOP	For PU2.1 devices, the device has sent its XID to the router.

In normal conditions, all of your devices should be in the CONNECT state, so this is a good thing to check when debugging an SDLC problem. If a device is connected, but you suspect that there is a problem with it, there is a useful EXEC command that is effectively an SDLC version of PING:

```
Router#sdlc test serial 1 20
SDLC Test for address C1 completed
Frames sent=10 Frames received=10
```

This command sends short SDLC frames out the specified interface (in this case Serial1) addressed to the desired destination address (in this case, 20). If the device is online and the circuit is configured correctly, then you should see the same number of frames received as sent. By default, it sends 10 frames. You can change the number and content of these frames, but usually this simple form is sufficient to see if there are problems reaching the device.

The most common problems with an SDLC connection are mismatched XID or SDLC addresses. Sometimes you will encounter physical problems caused by either a bad cable or electrical noise. And the other most common issues are caused by clock rate problems (either too fast or too slow for the attached devices), or an incorrect choice of NRZ or NRZI line coding. It is usually best to start with the physical layer and see if the interface is coming up at all. If the interface won't come up, or comes up but won't stay up, then look for physical problems such as these. If the interface comes up but you can't communicate with the devices, look for problems with XID values and SDLC addresses.

See Also

Recipe 15.6

15.15 Debugging DSLw

Problem

You want to debug and isolate DLSw problems.

Solution

The first thing to do with any DLSw issue is verify that the peers are working correctly, as in Recipe 15.13. If the peers are not established, then test IP connectivity with PING packets. If you can PING but the peers won't come up, then verify your configuration, as in Recipe 15.2. Ensure in particular that the remote-peer of each router precisely matches the local-peer of the other end.

If the DLSw peers are active, check the circuits, as in Recipe 15.13.

For failed circuits involving SDLC devices, check the interface, as in Recipe 15.14.

For Token Ring or Ethernet devices, verify that the interface is functioning properly as in Chapter 16.

If the peers are active and the interfaces look good, then there are three main things that could still be wrong. There could be a loop problem within the DLSw network. There could be a MAC address problem or a MAC or LSAP filtering issue. Or there could be a network congestion or performance problem.

There are several useful debug commands for use with DLSw. For looking at the router-to-router DLSw transport, you can use the *debug dlsw* command:

```
dlsw-branch#debug dlsw
```

You can get other useful information about SNA and LLC2 connection problems with these debug commands:

```
dlsw-branch#debug sna state
dlsw-branch#debug llc2 state
```

Discussion

If your routers will not establish a DLSw peer relationship, the most common problem is simple IP connectivity. Verify that you can PING the address in the remote-peer statement. Note also that at most, one end can use the *promiscuous* keyword to avoid configuring a *remote-peer* statement. This feature allows the router to sit and quietly wait for other routers to initiate connections. Somebody has to start the conversation.

Another common reason for failing to connect is simply a configuration mismatch between the local-peer and remote-peer definitions. Make sure that if you have a remote-peer statement, then the IP address exactly matches the address in the local-peer statement of the other router. It is not enough just to target any address on the remote-peer router; it must be exactly the same address.

If this is correct and you can PING, but still cannot connect, then there are two remaining possibilities. One is that there are port-specific filters or routing rules that permit PING but do something different with DLSw packets. This is particularly possible when using Policy-Based Routing to attempt to give DLSw packets a preferred path through the network. The preferred path may have serious congestion problems, for example.

The other possibility is that there is a complete incompatibility between the versions of DLSw running at the two ends. If both are Cisco routers, then this is not going to happen. But there are still some pre-RFC 1795 DLSw implementations out there, and Cisco's DLSw+ cannot negotiate a connection with noncompliant versions.

If you are trying to debug a DLSw problem, check first that the peers are connected:

```
dlsw-branch#show dlsw peers
Peers:            state    pkts_rx  pkts_tx  type  drops ckts TCP   uptime
  TCP 10.1.1.5    CONNECT  1348082   547505  conf      0    3   0    4w6d
  TCP 10.1.1.9    CONNECT   167013   200235  conf      0    3   0    4w5d
  TCP 10.2.1.5    DISCONN        0        0  conf      0    0   -      -
  TCP 10.2.1.9    DISCONN        0        0  conf      0    0   -      -
Total number of connected peers: 2
Total number of connections:     2
```

In this example, four peers have been configured, but only two of them are connected. A simple PING test would reveal in this case that the two disconnected peers are currently unreachable because of a network problem.

This command output also shows that there are three currently connected circuits to both of the active for a total of six active circuits. You can look at information on the individual circuits with the *show dlsw circuits* command:

```
dlsw-branch#show dlsw circuits
Index         local addr(lsap)     remote addr(dsap)   state       uptime
2164260933    4000.53aa.2440(04)   4000.3745.aaaa(04)  CONNECTED    5d00h
1627390033    4000.53aa.8420(04)   4000.3745.aaaa(04)  CONNECTED    2d01h
2684354644    4000.53aa.7023(04)   4000.3745.aaaa(04)  CONNECTED   09:41:36
2013265928    000c.29d0.bb41(14)   4000.3745.aaab(04)  CONNECTED    4w5d
654311497     4001.001b.a1f3(04)   4000.3745.aaab(04)  CONNECTED    3d18h
1342177367    4000.53aa.e3a1(04)   4000.3745.aaab(04)  CONNECTED   06:09:14
Total number of circuits connected: 6
```

Here you can see that these six circuits connect to two different FEP MAC addresses. All of the DSAP values are 0×04, and one of the circuits has an LSAP value of 0×14. This is useful in making sure that you have an appropriate SAP filters in place.

The following shows the output of a debug trace on this same router:

```
dlsw-branch#debug dlsw
DLSw reachability debugging is on at event level for all protocol traffic
DLSw peer debugging is on
DLSw local circuit debugging is on
DLSw core message debugging is on
DLSw core state debugging is on
```

```
DLSw core flow control debugging is on
DLSw core xid debugging is on
dlsw-branch#
May 15 22:18:35.320:  DLSW Received-ctlQ : CLSI Msg : TEST_STN.Ind   dlen: 40
May 15 22:18:35.320: CSM: Received CLSI Msg : TEST_STN.Ind   dlen: 40 from
TokenRing0/0
May 15 22:18:35.320: CSM:   smac c001.001b.21aa, dmac 0020.353f.ab4a, ssap 4 , dsap 0
May 15 22:18:35.320: broadcast filter failed mac check
May 15 22:18:35.320: broadcast filter failed mac check
May 15 22:18:35.320: CSM: Write to all peers not ok - PEER_NO_CONNECTIONS
May 15 22:18:35.556:  DISP Sent : CLSI Msg : TEST_STN.Req   dlen: 46
May 15 22:18:35.556:  DISP Sent : CLSI Msg : TEST_STN.Req   dlen: 46
May 15 22:18:35.556:  DISP Sent : CLSI Msg : TEST_STN.Req   dlen: 46
May 15 22:18:35.556:  DISP Sent : CLSI Msg : TEST_STN.Req   dlen: 46
May 15 22:18:35.556:  DISP Sent : CLSI Msg : TEST_STN.Req   dlen: 46
May 15 22:18:35.556:  DISP Sent : CLSI Msg : TEST_STN.Req   dlen: 46
May 15 22:18:36.240:  DLSW Received-ctlQ : CLSI Msg : TEST_STN.Ind   dlen: 40
May 15 22:18:36.244: CSM: Received CLSI Msg : TEST_STN.Ind   dlen: 40 from
TokenRing0/0
May 15 22:18:36.244: CSM:   smac c001.001b.21aa, dmac 0060.9442.7cf3, ssap 4 , dsap 0
May 15 22:18:36.244: broadcast filter failed mac check
May 15 22:18:36.244: broadcast filter failed mac check
May 15 22:18:36.244: CSM: Write to all peers not ok - PEER_NO_CONNECTIONS
```

Notice that one device, with a Token Ring MAC address of c001.001b.21aa, is attempting to make a connection to two different destination MAC addresses. These connections are being rejected with the message "broadcast filter failed mac check." This message appears because of the *dlsw icanreach mac-exclusive* command that filters out all MAC addresses from crossing the network unless they are explicitly configured on the router.

Watching this same debug trace for a little while longer reveals more interesting entries:

```
May 15 22:18:46.852: DLSw: 654311497 decr s - s:58 so:0 r:89 ro:0
May 15 22:18:46.852: DLSW Received-disp : CLSI Msg : DATA.Ind   dlen: 336
May 15 22:18:46.852: DLSw: START-FSM (654311497): event:DLC-Data.Ind state:CONNECTED
May 15 22:18:46.852: DLSw: core: dlsw_action_l( )
May 15 22:18:46: %DLSWC-3-SENDSSP: SSP OP = 10( INFO ) to peer 10.1.1.5(2065) success
May 15 22:18:46.852: DLSw: END-FSM (654311497): state:CONNECTED->CONNECTED
May 15 22:18:46: %DLSWC-3-RECVSSP: SSP OP = 10( INFO ) from peer 10.1.1.5(2065)
May 15 22:18:46.920: DLSw: 654311497 decr r - s:58 so:0 r:88 ro:0
May 15 22:18:46.920: DLSw: START-FSM (654311497): event:WAN-INFO state:CONNECTED
May 15 22:18:46.924: DLSw: core: dlsw_action_m( )
May 15 22:18:46.924:  DISP Sent : CLSI Msg : DATA.Req   dlen: 308
May 15 22:18:46.924: DLSw: END-FSM (654311497): state:CONNECTED->CONNECTED
May 15 22:18:48.612: DLSw: Keepalive Request sent to peer 10.1.1.9(2065))
May 15 22:18:48.628: DLSw: Keepalive Response from peer 10.1.1.9(2065)
```

In this section of the trace you can see that one of the circuits (with the identifier 654311497) actually sends and receives a piece of information. You can see that it uses the first of the active peers, 10.1.1.5, and that the conversation happens on TCP port number 2065. A short time later, you can see the router exchange keep-alive messages with the other peer to ensure that the peer relationship remains active.

The following shows what happens when a particular circuit disconnects suddenly. In this case, we have deliberately cleared on of the circuits:

```
dlsw-branch#clear dlsw circuit 2013265928
May 15 22:18:55.412: DLSw: START-FSM (2013265928): event:ADMIN-STOP state:CONNECTED
May 15 22:18:55.412: DLSw: core: dlsw_action_r( )
May 15 22:18:55: %DLSWC-3-SENDSSP: SSP OP = 25( HLTN )  to peer 10.1.1.5(2065)
success
May 15 22:18:55.412:  DISP Sent : CLSI Msg : DISCONNECT.Req   dlen: 4
May 15 22:18:55.412: DLSw: END-FSM (2013265928): state:CONNECTED->HALT_NOACK_PEND
May 15 22:18:55.424: SNA: Connection to Focal Point SSCP lost
May 15 22:18:55.424:  DLSW Received-ctlQ : CLSI Msg : DISCONNECT.Cfm CLS_OK dlen: 8
May 15 22:18:55.424: DLSw: START-FSM (2013265928): event:DLC-Disc.Cnf  state:HALT_
NOACK_PEND
May 15 22:18:55.424: DLSw: core: dlsw_action_z( )
May 15 22:18:55.424:  DISP Sent : CLSI Msg : CLOSE_STN.Req   dlen: 4
May 15 22:18:55.424: DLSw: END-FSM (2013265928): state:HALT_NOACK_PEND->CLOSE_PEND
May 15 22:18:55.424:  DLSW Received-ctlQ : CLSI Msg : DISCONNECT.Ind   dlen: 8
May 15 22:18:55.424: DLSw: START-FSM (2013265928): event:DLC-Disc.Ind state:CLOSE_
PEND
May 15 22:18:55.424: DLSw: END-FSM (2013265928): state:CLOSE_PEND->CLOSE_PEND
May 15 22:18:55.424:  DLSW Received-ctlQ : CLSI Msg : CLOSE_STN.Cfm CLS_OK dlen: 8
May 15 22:18:55.424: DLSw: START-FSM (2013265928): event:DLC-CloseStn.Cnf state:
CLOSE_PEND
May 15 22:18:55.428: DLSw: core: dlsw_action_y( )
May 15 22:18:55.428: DLSw: 2013265928 to dead queue
May 15 22:18:55.428: DLSw: START-TPFSM (peer 10.1.1.5(2065)): event:CORE-DELETE
CIRCUIT state:CONNECT
May 15 22:18:55.428: DLSw: dtp_action_v( ), peer delete circuit for peer 10.1.1.
5(2065)
May 15 22:18:55.428: DLSw: END-TPFSM (peer 10.1.1.5(2065)): state:CONNECT->CONNECT
May 15 22:18:55.428: DLSw: END-FSM (2013265928): state:CLOSE_PEND->DISCONNECTED
```

As you can see, there are several stages that the connection must go through to complete the disconnection request. First it goes into a HALT_NOACK_PEND state, meaning that both ends have not yet acknowledged the halt order. From there it goes into a CLOSE_PEND state, and finally DISCONNECTED, as the two DLSw peer routers finally agree that the connection has been terminated.

And, for one final example, here is what the *debug sna state* trace looks like for a similar disconnection and reconnection:

```
dlsw-branch#debug sna state
   SNA state change debugging is on for all PUs

dlsw-branch#clear dlsw circuit 2130706520
dlsw-branch#
May 15 22:22:57.399: SNA: LS VDLCTEST: input=Disc.Ind, Connected -> PendClose
May 15 22:22:57.403: SNA: PU VDLCTEST: input=T2ResetPu, Active -> Reset
May 15 22:22:57.403: SNA: LS VDLCTEST: input=Close.Cnf, PendClose -> Reset
```

```
May 15 22:22:57.403: SNA: Connection to Focal Point SSCP lost
May 15 22:23:27.035: SNA: LS VDLCTEST: input=StartLs, Reset -> PendConOut
May 15 22:23:33.035: SNA: LS VDLCTEST: input=ReqOpn.Cnf, PendConOut -> Xid
May 15 22:23:33.303: SNA: LS VDLCTEST: input=Connect.Ind, Xid -> ConnIn
May 15 22:23:33.303: SNA: LS VDLCTEST: input=Connected.Ind, ConnIn -> Connected
May 15 22:23:33.427: SNA: PU VDLCTEST: input=Actpu, Reset -> Active
May 15 22:23:33.427: SNA: Connection to Focal Point SSCP established
```

In this trace, you can see the exchange of XID information and the final activation of the circuit takes less than a second here. The main time lag occurs as the end devices wait a few seconds after disconnection before trying to reconnect their SNA sessions.

See Also

Recipe 15.2; Recipe 15.13; Recipe 15.14; Chapter 16

Router Interfaces and Media

16.0 Introduction

Cisco supports a huge variety of different media types. There are over 50 different types of interface adapters available for the 7200 series routers alone. Of course, many of these are closely related variants, such as the same OC3 card with multi-mode or single mode fibre. But the sheer variety of different media types makes it impossible for us to cover them all in any detail. So this chapter will focus instead on some of the most popular interface types. We will also look at a few interface types that have particularly interesting features or are tricky to set up properly.

We also encourage the reader to look at some of the other chapters in this book where we have covered interface specific material. For example, there is useful information on serial interfaces in the discussion of Frame Relay in Chapter 10. Similarly, we covered a lot of ISDN information while discussing Dial Backup in Chapter 13. And there is some discussion of both SDLC serial configuration and Token Ring features in Chapter 15, which looks at DLSw. Further, the HSRP discussion in Chapter 22 includes several useful Ethernet and Token Ring features.

Whole books have been written on each of the different media types discussed in this chapter, so we clearly can't offer a very comprehensive summary here. For information about the various serial media, we encourage the reader to refer to *T1: A Survival Guide* by Matthew Gast (O'Reilly). Charles Spurgeon's excellent book, *Ethernet: The Definitive Guide* (O'Reilly), includes a vast amount of useful and interesting information about how Ethernet works. And *Designing Large-Scale LANs* by Kevin Dooley (O'Reilly) includes information about other LAN protocols, including Token Ring and ATM, as well as information about VLAN trunking protocols.

16.1   Viewing Interface Status

Problem

You want to look at the status of your router's interfaces.

Solution

You can look at the current status of any interface using the *show interfaces* EXEC command. With no arguments, this command shows the status of all interfaces on the router:

```
Router1#show interfaces
```

You can also look at a particular interface by including its name with the command:

```
Router1#show interfaces FastEthernet0/1
```

It is also often useful to look specifically at the IP configuration of one or all of your interfaces by using the *show ip interface* command:

```
Router1#show ip interface brief
Router1#show ip interface FastEthernet0/1
```

Discussion

There is a huge amount of information in the output of the *show interfaces* command, and the actual content varies from one interface type to another:

```
Router1#show interfaces FastEthernet0/1
FastEthernet0/1 is up, line protocol is up
  Hardware is AmdFE, address is 0001.9670.b781 (bia 0001.9670.b781)
  Internet address is 172.22.1.3/24
  MTU 1500 bytes, BW 100000 Kbit, DLY 100 usec,
     reliability 255/255, txload 1/255, rxload 1/255
  Encapsulation ARPA, loopback not set
  Keepalive set (10 sec)
  Full-duplex, 100Mb/s, 100BaseTX/FX
  ARP type: ARPA, ARP Timeout 04:00:00
  Last input 00:00:04, output 00:00:00, output hang never
  Last clearing of "show interface" counters never
  Input queue: 0/75/0/0 (size/max/drops/flushes); Total output drops: 0
  Queueing strategy: fifo
  Output queue: 0/40 (size/max)
  5 minute input rate 0 bits/sec, 0 packets/sec
  5 minute output rate 1000 bits/sec, 1 packets/sec
     265295 packets input, 21235441 bytes
     Received 105678 broadcasts, 0 runts, 0 giants, 0 throttles
     0 input errors, 0 CRC, 0 frame, 0 overrun, 0 ignored
     0 watchdog
     0 input packets with dribble condition detected
     1337306 packets output, 125379250 bytes, 0 underruns
     0 output errors, 0 collisions, 8 interface resets
     0 babbles, 0 late collision, 0 deferred
```

```
      0 lost carrier, 0 no carrier
      0 output buffer failures, 0 output buffers swapped out
Router1#show interfaces Serial0/0
Serial0/0 is up, line protocol is up
  Hardware is PowerQUICC Serial
  MTU 1500 bytes, BW 1544 Kbit, DLY 20000 usec,
     reliability 255/255, txload 1/255, rxload 1/255
  Encapsulation FRAME-RELAY, loopback not set
  Keepalive set (10 sec)
  LMI enq sent  108260, LMI stat recvd 108252, LMI upd recvd 0, DTE LMI up
  LMI enq recvd 0, LMI stat sent  0, LMI upd sent  0
  LMI DLCI 0  LMI type is ANSI Annex D  frame relay DTE
  Broadcast queue 0/64, broadcasts sent/dropped 306266/2, interface broadcasts 306266
  Last input 00:00:04, output 00:00:02, output hang never
  Last clearing of "show interface" counters 1w5d
  Input queue: 0/75/0/0 (size/max/drops/flushes); Total output drops: 0
  Queueing strategy: weighted fair
  Output queue: 0/1000/64/0 (size/max total/threshold/drops)
     Conversations  0/3/256 (active/max active/max total)
     Reserved Conversations 0/0 (allocated/max allocated)
     Available Bandwidth 1158 kilobits/sec
  5 minute input rate 0 bits/sec, 1 packets/sec
  5 minute output rate 0 bits/sec, 0 packets/sec
     934269 packets input, 83226465 bytes, 0 no buffer
     Received 0 broadcasts, 0 runts, 0 giants, 0 throttles
     1 input errors, 0 CRC, 1 frame, 0 overrun, 0 ignored, 0 abort
     879200 packets output, 60483145 bytes, 0 underruns
     0 output errors, 0 collisions, 4 interface resets
     0 output buffer failures, 0 output buffers swapped out
     16 carrier transitions
     DCD=up  DSR=up  DTR=up  RTS=up  CTS=up

Router1#
```

The first line is one of the most important:

```
FastEthernet0/1 is up, line protocol is up
Serial0/0 is up, line protocol is up
```

This tells you that the interface is operational. There are four main possibilities here. The interface and line protocol can both be up, or they can both be down, or the interface can be up, with the line protocol down. A fourth option is that the interface can be Administratively down, which means that somebody has deliberately disabled it with a *shutdown* command. There are other options, such as standby and spoofing states, as well.

If the interface is up, this means that the router is receiving the correct Layer 1 physical signaling. For the line protocol to also be up, the router must also see correct Layer 2 information. Clearly, this varies for different media types. In some cases, such as virtual software interfaces, there is no physical carrier. So you will never see a loopback interface in an up/down state. But for other types of interfaces, this can be extremely useful information for debugging problems.

The next line tells you about the interface hardware:

```
Hardware is AmdFE, address is 0001.9670.b781 (bia 0001.9670.b781)
Hardware is PowerQUICC Serial
```

The interface in the first case is a *FastEthernet* interface that uses a *FastEthernet* ASIC made by AMD. This information tends to be useful only when there is a known hardware bug and you want to see if your router is affected. The rest of this line is extremely useful, however, because it tells you the Ethernet MAC address. Note that it lists both the address that the router is using as well as the Burned-In Address (BIA). Most of the time these will be the same, but in Recipe 16.10 we will show how you can make your router use a different Ethernet MAC address. The second interface is a Serial interface, which doesn't have a MAC address, so none is listed.

Next is the IP address, if one is configured:

```
Internet address is 172.22.1.3/24
```

In the *Serial* interface example above, the interface doesn't have any Layer 3 protocol addresses, so nothing is listed here. Note, however, that this command will also display IPX or AppleTalk addresses if they are configured.

Then come two lines that tell you a series of useful pieces of information about the interface's configuration and utilization. Here is the *FastEthernet* interface:

```
MTU 1500 bytes, BW 100000 Kbit, DLY 100 usec,
   reliability 255/255, txload 1/255, rxload 1/255
```

And here is the corresponding information for the *Serial* interface:

```
MTU 1500 bytes, BW 1544 Kbit, DLY 20000 usec,
   reliability 255/255, txload 1/255, rxload 1/255
```

The first field here is the Maximum Transmission Unit (MTU), which is 1,500 bytes for both interfaces. This 1,500-byte MTU size is typical for IP networks, although you can change it relatively easily using the *mtu* interface configuration command, as we show in Recipe 16.2. Using a variety of different MTU values in your network can cause performance problems due to fragmentation, however.

It is important to remember that this Layer 2 MTU affects all protocols that use the interface, and not just IP. This is the size of the largest Layer 2 packet that the router can send through this interface. Some media can support very large packets; others are more tightly constrained.

The BW field shows the configured bandwidth of the interface. It is important to note that sometimes this is not the actual throughput of the interface. On *Serial* interfaces, the router will always show the default value here. Even for Data Communications Equipment (DCE) serial interfaces that supply the clock signal and therefore have a good way of estimating the theoretical maximum throughput, this bandwidth value stays at its default value unless you change it manually by using the *bandwidth* interface configuration command. This parameter is used for calculating routing protocol metrics, as well as for converting raw bit transmission rates into utilization statistics. It has nothing to do with how fast the router will transmit packets.

The reliability field in the next line is no longer commonly used. It was part of the optional metric calculation for IGRP, so it is included for historical reasons. However, the other two values, *txload* and *rxload,* are very useful. These represent the traffic utilization for the interface outbound and inbound, respectively. Both of these values are expressed as fractions of 255 rather than percentages. This may seem like an odd value, but a range from 0–255 can be conveniently represented by using an 8-bit variable, which is why Cisco does it this way. Each of these values represents a fraction of the total available bandwidth shown in the *BW* field.

Because these *txload* and *rxload* values are rates, the router has to measure them by counting the number of bits sent and received over some finite period of time. By default, this interval is five minutes. However, you can adjust the measurement period with the *load-interval* interface configuration command:

```
Router1(config-if)#load-interval 60
```

This command takes a value in seconds as an argument. The number must be a multiple of 30 seconds, with a maximum value of 600.

The next set of lines describes the Layer 2 encapsulation on the interface. For the FastEthernet interface example, there are four lines:

```
Encapsulation ARPA, loopback not set
Keepalive set (10 sec)
Full-duplex, 100Mb/s, 100BaseTX/FX
ARP type: ARPA, ARP Timeout 04:00:00
```

In this case, you can see that this interface uses 100 Mbps full-duplex Ethernet on a 100BaseTX or 100BaseFX interface. At Layer 2, it uses ARPA (which stands for the Advanced Research Projects Agency of the U.S. government, the agency that sponsored the initial development of the TCP/IP protocol suite) encapsulation. There are two Layer 2 encapsulation types. The older ARPA encapsulation standard for IP packets is described in RFCs 894 and 895. This standard dates to a time when Ethernet was still an experimental protocol, and there was not yet an IEEE standard.

Some time later, the IEEE officially documented the Ethernet protocol and encapsulation standards. But the IEEE standards differed from the existing ARPA standard, which was already enjoying considerable popularity in IP networks. So, rather than changing, IP continues to use the old standard, while other Layer 3 protocols such as IPX offer a choice of encapsulation types.

The interface shown in this example is only configured for IP, which is why it shows ARPA encapsulation here.

The *Serial* interface in the example is using the Frame Relay protocol, so the show interface output includes different relevant information:

```
Encapsulation FRAME-RELAY, loopback not set
Keepalive set (10 sec)
```

```
LMI enq sent  108260, LMI stat recvd 108252, LMI upd recvd 0, DTE LMI up
LMI enq recvd 0, LMI stat sent  0, LMI upd sent  0
LMI DLCI 0  LMI type is ANSI Annex D  frame relay DTE
Broadcast queue 0/64, broadcasts sent/dropped 306266/2, interface broadcasts 306266
```

In both cases, you can see that these interfaces use the default *keepalive* value of 10 seconds. This means that these interfaces will send out a small packet every 10 seconds just to see if the interface is still working properly. If the keepalive test fails, the router will declare the interface's line protocol to be down.

Both of these examples also include the phrase "loopback not set." If you were to apply an external loopback test to this interface, so that the router gets back all the data that it transmits, this text would change to say "loopback set." And you would also see at the top of the show interface output that the line protocol is up but looped:

```
Serial0/0 is up, line protocol is up (looped)
```

Then the next few lines show how long it has been since the router has sent or received a packet on this interface, and how long it has been since you last cleared the statistical counters on this interface:

```
Last input 00:00:04, output 00:00:02, output hang never
Last clearing of "show interface" counters 1w5d
```

The queue parameters are extremely important. The *Serial* interface in the example is using weighted fair queueing, while the *Ethernet* uses First In First Out (FIFO). Please refer to Chapter 11 for more information on different queueing strategies:

```
Input queue: 0/75/0/0 (size/max/drops/flushes); Total output drops: 0
Queueing strategy: weighted fair
Output queue: 0/1000/64/0 (size/max total/threshold/drops)
   Conversations  0/3/256 (active/max active/max total)
   Reserved Conversations 0/0 (allocated/max allocated)
   Available Bandwidth 1158 kilobits/sec
```

The show interface output also shows the number of packets currently in each queue (size), the maximum number of packets that the queue can hold (max), and other parameters such as drop thresholds and the number of tail drops, which vary for different queueing strategies.

Next is a large and extremely useful block of performance related information:

```
5 minute input rate 0 bits/sec, 0 packets/sec
5 minute output rate 1000 bits/sec, 1 packets/sec
   265295 packets input, 21235441 bytes
   Received 105678 broadcasts, 0 runts, 0 giants, 0 throttles
   0 input errors, 0 CRC, 0 frame, 0 overrun, 0 ignored
   0 watchdog
   0 input packets with dribble condition detected
   1337306 packets output, 125379250 bytes, 0 underruns
   0 output errors, 0 collisions, 8 interface resets
   0 babbles, 0 late collision, 0 deferred
   0 lost carrier, 0 no carrier
   0 output buffer failures, 0 output buffers swapped out
```

The first two lines of this block show the rates for both sending and receiving data through this interface, measured in both bits per second and packets per second, and averaged over a five-minute period. This is an excellent way of quickly checking to see how much data this interface is handling. You can also get more detailed information from the exact counters that follow.

And, finally, the serial interface output ends with two lines that show you information about its physical state:

```
16 carrier transitions
DCD=up  DSR=up  DTR=up  RTS=up  CTS=up
```

In this case, the interface has gone up and down 16 times since the last time the interface counters were cleared. The last line shows current state of all of the Serial signals. The DCE device raises a voltage on the Data Carrier Detect (DCD) pin to indicate that the link is ready for transmitting data. For other types of media, this line may contain other relevant Layer 1 information.

The DCE device on a Serial medium sends the Data Set Ready (DSR) signal when it is ready to send or receive data. When the Data Terminal Ready (DTR) signal is high, it means that the DTE device is ready to send or receive data. By default, the DTE device will wait until it sees the DSR signal, and the DCE device will wait for the DTR signal by default before sending any packets.

The Request To Send (RTS) signal indicates that the DTE device would like to send data and is checking to make sure that the link and the far end are ready to receive it. If everything is ready, the DCE device responds by raising the Clear To Send (CTS) signal.

So, in the above example, all of the serial signals are high, which tells you immediately that everything is working properly. Sometimes the show interface output will show one or more of these signals in a down state. This may indicate a cabling problem, or it may simply indicate that the far end device is simply busy right now and can't accept packets.

The *show ip interface* command shows a different set of information about the interfaces. With the keyword *brief*, this command gives you an extremely useful listing of all of your interfaces:

```
Router1#show ip interface brief
Interface           IP-Address      OK? Method Status  Protocol
Async65             unassigned      YES NVRAM  down    down
FastEthernet0/0     unassigned      YES NVRAM  up      up
FastEthernet0/0.1   172.25.1.5      YES NVRAM  up      up
FastEthernet0/0.2   172.16.2.1      YES NVRAM  up      up
Serial0/0           unassigned      YES NVRAM  up      up
Serial0/0.1         172.25.2.1      YES NVRAM  up      up
Serial0/0.2         172.20.1.1      YES manual up      up
FastEthernet0/1     172.22.1.3      YES NVRAM  up      up
Serial0/1           10.1.1.2        YES NVRAM  up      up
Loopback0           172.25.25.1     YES NVRAM  up      up
Router1#
```

This output shows you all of your interfaces, their IP addresses, and both the interface and protocol status. The other two columns here are labeled "OK?" and "Method." "OK?" simply refers to whether the router thinks that interface is operating correctly, while "Method" indicates how the interface acquired its IP address.

Notice that the IP addresses of almost all of these interfaces were configured by NVRAM. This simply means that they have not changed since the last reboot. However, one of the interfaces, *Serial0/0.2*, was manually configured since the last reboot.

You can include a specific interface name in place of the *brief* keyword to get details on the IP configuration of this interface:

```
Router1#show ip interface FastEthernet0/1
FastEthernet0/1 is up, line protocol is up
  Internet address is 172.22.1.3/24
  Broadcast address is 255.255.255.255
  Address determined by non-volatile memory
  MTU is 1500 bytes
  Helper address is not set
  Directed broadcast forwarding is disabled
  Multicast reserved groups joined: 224.0.0.1 224.0.0.2 224.0.0.10 224.0.0.5
      224.0.0.6
  Outgoing access list is not set
  Inbound  access list is not set
  Proxy ARP is enabled
  Security level is default
  Split horizon is enabled
  ICMP redirects are always sent
  ICMP unreachables are always sent
  ICMP mask replies are never sent
  IP fast switching is enabled
  IP fast switching on the same interface is disabled
  IP Flow switching is disabled
  IP CEF switching is enabled
  IP CEF Fast switching turbo vector
  IP multicast fast switching is enabled
  IP multicast distributed fast switching is disabled
  IP route-cache flags are Fast, CEF
  Router Discovery is enabled
  IP output packet accounting is disabled
  IP access violation accounting is disabled
  TCP/IP header compression is disabled
  RTP/IP header compression is disabled
  Probe proxy name replies are disabled
  Policy routing is disabled
  Network address translation is disabled
  WCCP Redirect outbound is disabled
  WCCP Redirect inbound is disabled
  WCCP Redirect exclude is disabled
  BGP Policy Mapping is disabled
Router1#
```

In addition to these commands, there are two hidden commands that we find very useful. The first is simply to add the keyword *stats* to the *show interfaces* command:

```
Router1#show interfaces FastEthernet0/1 stats
FastEthernet0/1
          Switching path    Pkts In   Chars In   Pkts Out  Chars Out
              Processor      294567   18704930     239526   22219870
             Route cache       7758     681257      48303    6129834
                 Total       302325   19386187     287829   28349704
Router1#
```

This output displays packet switching statistics for this interface. The *Processor* line shows both how many packets and how many characters the router has switched using process switching, and the *Route* cache line shows the values for Fast Switching. The *Pkts In* and *Chars In* columns show the values for incoming packets, while the other two columns show values for packets transmitted out through this interface.

You can get a more detailed breakdown of this switching information by adding the *switching* keyword to the show interfaces command:

```
Router1#show interfaces FastEthernet0/1 switching
FastEthernet0/1
          Throttle count             0
  Drops          RP         0        SP          0
SPD Flushes     Fast        0        SSE         0
SPD Aggress     Fast        0
SPD Priority   Inputs    40510      Drops        0

     Protocol      Path    Pkts In   Chars In   Pkts Out  Chars Out
       Other     Process    11562    1022965      18730    1123800
            Cache misses        0
                    Fast        0          0          0          0
              Auton/SSE         0          0          0          0
        IP      Process   102271    8491851     220342   21066444
            Cache misses        0
                    Fast     7758     681257      48304    6129962
              Auton/SSE         0          0          0          0
       ARP      Process     1819     109140        467      31756
            Cache misses        0
                    Fast        0          0          0          0
              Auton/SSE         0          0          0          0
Router1#
```

For more information on Fast Switching and Process Switching, please see Chapter 11.

See Also

Chapter 11; Recipe 16.2; Recipe 16.10

16.2   Configuring Serial Interfaces

Problem

You want to configure a serial interface for a WAN connection.

Solution

When you configure a router's serial interface, you need to specify the encapsulation, the IP address, and whether the interface will be the DCE or DTE:

```
Router3#configure terminal
Enter configuration commands, one per line.  End with CNTL/Z.
Router3(config)#interface Serial1
Router3(config-if)#description WAN Connection to Chicago
Router3(config-if)#ip address 192.168.99.5 255.255.255.252
Router3(config-if)#encapsulation hdlc
Router3(config-if)#clock rate 56000
Router3(config-if)#no shutdown
Router3(config-if)#exit
Router3(config)#end
Router3#
```

Discussion

There are a couple of extremely important commands in this sample configuration. The first sets the serial encapsulation protocol. In this case, we have used the High-Level Data Link Control (HDLC) protocol, which is a standard Layer 2 protocol for synchronous serial connections:

```
Router3(config-if)#encapsulation hdlc
```

In fact, HDLC is the default encapsulation type for synchronous serial interfaces on Cisco routers, so we could have omitted this command. Because it is the default, this command does not show up in the configuration when we show the configuration:

```
Router3#show running-config interface Serial1
Building configuration...

Current configuration : 123 bytes
!
interface Serial1
 description WAN Connection to Chicago
 ip address 192.168.99.5 255.255.255.252
 clock rate 56000
end

Router3#
```

If you prefer to use a different encapsulation type, there are several other options that are appropriate in different situations. They are all set using the interface configuration command encapsulation, followed by one of the keywords shown in Table 16-1.

Table 16-1. Synchronous serial encapsulation types

Command	Description
`Router3(config-if)#`**`encapsulation hdlc`**	The default synchronous serial encapsulation type for Cisco routers.
`Router3(config-if)#`**`encapsulation sdlc`**	Sets SDLC encapsulation for use with SNA related protocols. Please refer to Chapter 15 for more information.
`Router3(config-if)#`**`encapsulation frame-relay`**	Sets Frame-Relay encapsulation. Please refer to Chapter 10 for more information.
`Router3(config-if)#`**`encapsulation ppp`**	Sets the standard PPP encapsulation.
`Router3(config-if)#`**`encapsulation x25`**	Sets X.25 encapsulation.
`Router3(config-if)#`**`encapsulation lapb`**	Sets LAPB encapsulation, which is commonly used with X.25 circuits.
`Router3(config-if)#`**`encapsulation atm-dxi`**	Sets ATM encapsulation for a serial interface.
`Router3(config-if)#`**`encapsulation smds`**	Sets SMDS encapsulation.

The last two of these options allow you to do things that are somewhat unusual. For example, the *atm-dxi* keyword sets up the serial interface to use an HDLC-like protocol called Data Exchange Interface (DXI) to carry ATM cells. This requires a special external ATM Data Service Unit (ADSU) that you connect to the router via a standard serial cable.

The last option in Table 16.1 uses the *smds* keyword to enable the Switched Multimegabit Data Service (SMDS) protocol. This is a high-speed WAN protocol used by some WAN service providers. If you use SMDS, you will require SMDS address information from your WAN vendor. SMDS is a relatively rare protocol, which makes it unfortunately beyond the scope of this book.

The second extremely important part of the example configuration is the *clock rate* command:

```
Router3(config-if)#clock rate 56000
```

This command sets the interface's line speed to 56 Kbps. Most Cisco synchronous serial interfaces can support line speeds between 1.2 Kbps and 4 Mbps, although they generally only accept specific round number values rather than arbitrary values: 1,200, 2,400, 4,800, 9,600, 14,400, 19,200, 28,800, 32,000, 38,400, 56,000, 57,600, 64,000, 72,000, 115,200, 125,000, 128,000, 148,000, 192,000, 250,000, 256,000, 384,000, 500,000, 512,000, 768,000, 800,000, 1,000,000, 1,300,000, 2,000,000, 4,000,000, and, on interfaces that support higher speeds, 8,000,000. Note, in particular, that there is no conventional T1 setting at 1,544 Kbps, the closest substitutes for a T1 being 1,300 Kbps or 2,000 Kbps. This is usually not an issue, however, because in real carrier-provided T1 circuits, the carrier's equipment generally supplies the clock.

But this *clock rate* command has another important effect. Because only Data Communication Equipment (DCE) interfaces can supply the clock signal on synchronous serial connections, configuring this command on an interface implies that this interface is the DCE device. If you want the router to be a Data Terminal Equipment (DTE) device, you must omit the *clock rate* command.

Note also that with serial cables, DTE has a male connector, while DCE is female on the equipment end. On the router end, all Cisco high density serial connectors look alike, regardless of whether the equipment end uses a V.35, RS 232, or any other standard serial connector. We should mention in passing that even though the router end of these cables uses a trapezoidal shaped connector to help ensure that the right pins go into the right holes, it is remarkably easy to inadvertently connect these cables to your router upside down. If you can't get the interface to come up, even though you're sure it is configured properly, try removing the cable and rotating the connector 180 degrees. You can also use the *show controller* command to see what kind of cable the router thinks you have connected:

```
Router3#show controller serial 0
HD unit 0, idb = 0x1BC830, driver structure at 0x1C1CC0
buffer size 1524  HD unit 0, V.35 DCE cable, clockrate 1300000
cpb = 0x2, eda = 0x40B4, cda = 0x40C8
RX ring with 16 entries at 0x4024000
00 bd_ptr=0x4000 pak=0x1C3D38 ds=0x402AEE8 status=80 pak_size=92
01 bd_ptr=0x4014 pak=0x1C4D58 ds=0x402E4C8 status=80 pak_size=14
02 bd_ptr=0x4028 pak=0x1C4344 ds=0x402C31C status=80 pak_size=80
<lines deleted for brevity>
Router3#
```

Unfortunately, the exact syntax and the output structure of this command varies somewhat from router to router, depending on the specific serial hardware. Note that you generally have to put a space between the interface type and the interface number, as we did. If the output says something like "No DCE cable," it is likely that you have not connected the cable correctly.

If you configure a serial interface with a *clock rate* command, and then connect a DTE cable, the router will ignore the *clock rate* command. And, if you already have a DTE cable connected to the interface, the router will reject this command. Furthermore, just using a null modem connector will not fool the router into thinking a DTE cable is DCE, you must use the right cable.

This particular feature confuses many people who are used to equipment that supports non-standard DTE clocking. Cisco routers strictly enforce the relationship between cable type and clocking.

There are a few other useful commands in the configuration example, as well:

```
Router3(config-if)#description WAN Connection to Chicago
```

The *description* command accepts an arbitrary text string that you can use for any purpose that will help you to manage your network. The comment in the example says where this particular circuit connects to, but you might also put other useful information, such as circuit numbers or emergency contact information.

Next is the IP address. This command takes as an argument the IP address of this particular interface, and the corresponding netmask:

```
Router3(config-if)#ip address 192.168.99.5 255.255.255.252
```

In this case, because we are dealing with a simple point-to-point link that can only have two devices on it, we have used a netmask of 255.255.255.252, or /30 in slash notation. There is nothing to prevent you from using a larger subnet on such a link, but we recommend using a more conservative approach to help ensure that you won't run out of addresses.

And, finally, we have included a *no shutdown* command:

```
Router3(config-if)#no shutdown
```

This is necessary because, by default, the router will keep all of its interfaces in an administratively disabled state until you configure them.

You can see the current state of this interface with the *show interfaces* command:

```
Router3#show interfaces Serial1
Serial1 is down, line protocol is down
  Hardware is HD64570
  Description: WAN Connection to Chicago
  Internet address is 192.168.99.5/30
  MTU 1500 bytes, BW 1544 Kbit, DLY 20000 usec,
     reliability 255/255, txload 1/255, rxload 1/255
  Encapsulation HDLC, loopback not set
  Keepalive set (10 sec)
  Last input never, output never, output hang never
  Last clearing of "show interface" counters never
  Input queue: 0/75/0/0 (size/max/drops/flushes); Total output drops: 0
  Queueing strategy: weighted fair
  Output queue: 0/1000/64/0 (size/max total/threshold/drops)
     Conversations  0/0/256 (active/max active/max total)
     Reserved Conversations 0/0 (allocated/max allocated)
     Available Bandwidth 1158 kilobits/sec
  5 minute input rate 0 bits/sec, 0 packets/sec
  5 minute output rate 0 bits/sec, 0 packets/sec
     0 packets input, 0 bytes, 0 no buffer
     Received 0 broadcasts, 0 runts, 0 giants, 0 throttles
     0 input errors, 0 CRC, 0 frame, 0 overrun, 0 ignored, 0 abort
     0 packets output, 0 bytes, 0 underruns
     0 output errors, 0 collisions, 2 interface resets
     0 output buffer failures, 0 output buffers swapped out
     0 carrier transitions
     DCD=down  DSR=down  DTR=down  RTS=down  CTS=down
Router3#
```

Note that this interface is configured, but it is not yet active because the circuit is not yet connected. It is also interesting to note that the router thinks that this interface has a bandwidth of 1,544 Kbps, which is indicated by the BW field above. This is in spite of the fact that we have explicitly configured this interface to be the DCE and to supply a much lower clock speed. This bandwidth number affects two things: routing protocol metrics and utilization statistics. If you want to configure a more realistic value here, you can do so with the *bandwidth* interface configuration command:

```
Router3(config)#interface Serial1
Router3(config-if)#bandwidth 56
```

Note that the argument of this command must be in Kilobits per second, rather than the bits per second format used for the *clock rate* command.

Change the MTU of an interface using the *mtu* interface configuration command:

```
Router3(config)#interface Serial1
Router3(config-if)#shutdown
Router3(config-if)#mtu 18000
Router3(config-if)#no shutdown
```

Changing the MTU will reset the interface. So it is usually a good idea to issue a *shutdown* command to disable the interface before making the change, as we have done here. Bear in mind that having a larger MTU on an interface does not necessarily mean that the router will be able to take advantage of this larger frame size. If this interface never originates packets, but just acts as a link to send IP packets between two routers, then the routers will not attempt to join smaller packets to accommodate the larger MTU. The only time this is really useful is when this interface connects directly to serial equipment that generates larger frames.

Note also that the serial interface *mtu* command is subtly different from the *ip mtu* command. The command we used here sets the Layer 2 MTU, which applies to all protocols, while the *ip mtu* command only affects IP packets.

See Also

Chapter 10; Chapter 15

16.3   Using an Internal T1 CSU/DSU

Problem

You want to configure an internal CSU/DSU for a WAN connection.

Solution

Cisco has a variety of different types of internal CSU/DSU devices that you can install in a router. In the following example, we have configured the internal CSU to support a fractional T1 circuit:

```
Router1#configure terminal
Enter configuration commands, one per line.  End with CNTL/Z.
Router1(config)#interface Serial0/1
Router1(config-if)#ip address 192.168.99.9 255.255.255.252
Router1(config-if)#no shutdown
```

```
Router1(config-if)#service-module t1 timeslots 1-12
Router1(config-if)#exit
Router1(config)#end
Router1#
```

Discussion

All of the work here is done with the *service-module* command:

```
Router1(config-if)#service-module t1 timeslots 1-12
```

This example tells the internal CSU/DSU to use the first 12 time slots of the T1 circuit. The dash character, "-", tells the router to use a range of values. If you have a more complicated list of time slots, you can configure the list by using a list of ranges separated by commas. For example:

```
Router1(config-if)#service-module t1 timeslots 1-3,5-19,21
```

Or, you could even configure all of the odd-numbered time slots, as follows:

```
Router1(config-if)#service-module t1 timeslots 1,3,5,7,9,11,13,15,17,19,21,23
```

If you want to use all of the time slots, you can just use the keyword *all*.:

```
Router1(config-if)#service-module t1 timeslots all
```

By default, the CSU will assume that all of these time slots are 64 Kbps DS0 channels. But if the circuit actually uses 56 Kbps channels, you can configure this by adding the *speed* keyword:

```
Router1(config-if)#service-module t1 timeslots 1-12 speed 56
```

Usually, in a production environment, the WAN carrier will provide the clock signal for a T1 circuit. But in some cases, particularly test and lab networks, you will need the internal CSU/DSU to act as the DCE device and supply the clock signal. You can configure the module to do this with the *clock source internal* keywords:

```
Router1(config-if)#service-module t1 clock source internal
```

By default, the router will use Binary 8 Zeroes Substitution (B8ZS) line coding. While B8ZS tends to be the most common way that T1 circuits are delivered, some service provides use Alternate Mark Inversion (AMI) instead. You can configure the internal CSU to use AMI line coding as follows:

```
Router1(config-if)#service-module t1 linecode ami
```

When you use AMI line coding, you have to either set the speed of each channel to 56 Kbps, as we did above, or use inverted data coding:

```
Router1(config-if)#service-module t1 data-coding inverted
```

And the other T1 option that you sometimes see is the use of Super Frame (SF) instead of the default Extended Super Frame (ESF). If your WAN vendor uses SF framing, you can configure this on your router with the following command:

```
Router1(config-if)#service-module t1 framing sf
```

Some network vendors require a special Facilities Data Link (FDL) configuration. There are three options. FDL can be disabled, it can be implemented according to the ANSI T1.403 standard, or it can use the AT&T standard. To enable the ANSI standard, you use the keyword *ansi*, as follows:

```
Router1(config-if)#service-module t1 fdl ansi
```

And you can turn on the AT&T option like this:

```
Router1(config-if)#service-module t1 fdl att
```

If you are using a WIC-1DSU-T1 module, FDL is disabled by default. However, on Cisco 2524 and 2525 routers, the built-in T1 CSU/DSU uses both ANSI and AT&T options simultaneously by default, and you can't disable FDL.

It is usually a good idea to enable the *remote-alarm-enable* option:

```
Router1(config-if)#service-module t1 remote-alarm-enable
```

This option allows the CSU to send remote alarms, also called yellow alarms, to the CSU on the other end of the circuit. It does this to let the other device know that it has encountered an alarm condition, such as a framing error or loss of signal on the circuit. You should only use this option with ESF framing because it conflicts with SF framing.

The following is a real-world configuration taken from a router installed in a remote area that only supported AMI line coding, SF framing, and ANSI standard FDL:

```
Router6(config)#interface Serial0/0
Router6(config-if)#service-module t1 framing sf
Router6(config-if)#service-module t1 linecode ami
Router6(config-if)#service-module t1 timeslots all speed 56
Router6(config-if)#service-module t1 fdl ansi
```

See Also

T1: A Survival Guide, by Matthew Gast (O'Reilly)

16.4   Using an Internal ISDN PRI Module

Problem

You want to configure an internal ISDN PRI module.

Solution

You can configure an ISDN PRI controller module by using the *controller T1* command set as follows:

```
Router8#configure terminal
Enter configuration commands, one per line.  End with CNTL/Z.
Router8(config)#isdn switch-type primary-dms100
Router8(config)#controller T1 0
```

```
Router8(config-controlle)#framing esf
Router8(config-controlle)#clock source line primary
Router8(config-controlle)#linecode b8zs
Router8(config-controlle)#pri-group timeslots 1-24
Router8(config-controlle)#exit
Router8(config)#end
Router8#
```

Discussion

The configuration for an ISDN PRI controller module is different from the configuration for a regular internal T1 module that we discussed in Recipe 16.3. But the basic parameters such as defining the framing, line coding, and so forth are similar.

In this example, we have also defined two ISDN-specific options. The first is to set the ISDN switch type to be a Nortel DMS 100 device:

```
Router8(config)#isdn switch-type primary-dms100
```

There are several other primary rate ISDN switch types available. If your ISDN vendor uses National ISDN switches, you would replace this command with the following:

```
Router8(config)#isdn switch-type primary-ni
```

Cisco has made a concerted effort to make the *primary-ni* option effectively switch independent in newer IOS releases. There are still some problems with some of the less common switch types, but, for the most part, you should be able to use *primary-ni* with PRI circuits from most ISDN vendors.

Note that it is often necessary to reboot the router after changing the ISDN switch type to ensure that the change takes effect.

The other ISDN-specific command in this configuration example is the *pri-group* command:

```
Router8(config-controlle)#pri-group timeslots 1-24
```

In this case, we have simply defined the available ISDN B channels to be on channels 1 through 24, inclusive.

See Also

Recipe 16.3

16.5 Using an Internal 56 Kbps CSU/DSU

Problem

You want to configure an internal 56 Kbps CSU/DSU.

Solution

The configuration for an internal 56 Kbps CSU/DSU is similar to that of an internal T1 CSU/DSU:

```
Router2#configure terminal
Enter configuration commands, one per line.  End with CNTL/Z.
Router2(config)#interface Serial0/1
Router2(config-if)#ip address 192.168.99.25 255.255.255.252
Router2(config-if)#no shutdown
Router2(config-if)#service-module 56k clock rate 9.6
Router2(config-if)#exit
Router2(config)#end
Router2#
```

Discussion

There are several options available for configuring internal 56 Kbps CSU/DSU cards in a router, and they all use the *service-module* command, similar to the T1 module. The above example shows how to set the CSU/DSU to a line speed of 9,600 bps using the *clock rate* option. This option takes as an argument the line speed in Kilobits per second, with valid options being 2.4, 4.8, 9.6, 19.2, 38.4, 56, or 64. The default line speed is 56 Kbps. You can also configure the module to automatically adapt to whatever the line speed might be using this *auto* keyword:

```
Router2(config-if)#service-module 56k clock rate auto
```

This is particularly useful if the line speed frequently changes for some reason.

Note, however, that this *clock rate* option does not imply that the internal CSU/DSU is the clock source for the circuit. By default, the CSU/DSU will assume that the clock signal comes from the network. If you want your router to supply the clock signal instead, you must configure it to do so as follows:

```
Router2(config-if)#service-module 56k clock source internal
```

Another important option for 56 Kbps modules sets the network type to be either a dial-up switched-56 (also sometimes called Centrex) or a leased line. Please refer to Chapter 13 for a brief discussion of switched-56 circuits. To configure the CSU/DSU to support a leased line, you use the keyword *dds*, which stands for Digital Data Service:

```
Router2(config-if)#service-module 56k network-type dds
```

And you can configure the module for switched-56 using the *switched* keyword:

```
Router2(config-if)#service-module 56k network-type switched
```

However, it is important to remember that some modules are designed only to support one network type. In particular, switched-56 uses two-wire signaling, while DDS uses four wires. All of Cisco's four-wire CSU/DSU modules such as the WIC-1DSU-56K4 can support both *switched* or *dds* options, although the default is *dds*.

However, the less common two-wire modules can only support the *switched* network type, and do not let you change this option.

Unfortunately, not all switched networks are created equal. Just about everybody has encountered the problem in which sometimes you hear an echo of your own voice when talking on the telephone, particularly on long distance calls. This is annoying for voice communications, but it can be devastating for digital data transmission. In the United States, AT&T's switched 56 Kbps network doesn't require echo canceling, while Sprint's does. You can specify that your carrier behaves like the AT&T network as follows:

```
Router2(config-if)#service-module 56k network-type switched
Router2(config-if)#service-module 56k switched-carrier att
```

Or, for networks like Sprint's, use the argument *sprint* instead:

```
Router2(config-if)#service-module 56k network-type switched
Router2(config-if)#service-module 56k switched-carrier sprint
```

You can also specify *other* as the argument, which behaves exactly the same as the *att* option, but presumably makes other network vendors feel better. It is important to note that enabling the echo-canceling feature will increase call setup times noticeably.

An interesting problem can occur on 64 Kbps DDS circuits. The problem is that these types of circuits often use in-band signaling for error conditions. This in particular means that there is a sequence of bits that the carrier's equipment will interpret as the control code to take the circuit out of service. It is only a matter of time in this type of situation before a series of data bits in a packet duplicates this pattern and causes problems.

You can use a simple algorithm called data scrambling to overcome this problem. This algorithm just jumbles up the bit patterns to ensure the control codes never appear on the line accidentally. You can enable this feature with the *data-coding scrambled* command:

```
Router2(config-if)#service-module 56k network-type dds
Router2(config-if)#service-module 56k clock rate 64
Router2(config-if)#service-module 56k data-coding scrambled
```

We included both the network type and clock rate commands with the command that does the data scrambling to remind you that this option is only useful on 64 Kbps DDS circuits. Also, always bear in mind that this feature does jumble user data, so you must use the same option on both ends of the circuit.

See Also

Recipe 16.3

16.6   Configuring an Async Serial Interface

Problem

You want to configure a sync/async interface in asynchronous mode.

Solution

Cisco has a class of serial modules that can support either synchronous or asynchronous communications, as required. You can use the *physical-layer async* command to change the interface from the default synchronous to asynchronous mode:

```
Router3#configure terminal
Enter configuration commands, one per line.  End with CNTL/Z.
Router3(config)#interface Serial1/7
Router3(config-if)#physical-layer async
Router3(config-if)#encapsulation ppp
Router3(config-if)#exit
Router3(config)#line 40
Router3(config-line)#speed 115200
Router3(config-line)#exit
Router3(config)#end
Router3#
```

Discussion

As soon as you configure the *physical-layer async* command, the router will wipe out any configuration that you previously might have had on this interface for synchronous communications.

The only real trick in this configuration is that you need to apply many of the important configuration commands to a terminal line rather than the interface itself. In this example, the only command we have included in the line section is the *speed* command, but there could be others. We discuss the line configuration commands for connecting to asynchronous modems in Chapter 13.

The line number in this configuration is not arbitrary. In fact, after you enable the *physical-layer async* command on the serial interface, you should break out of configuration mode and use the *show line* command to see which line the router has decided to associate with this serial interface:

```
Router3#show line
   Tty Typ    Tx/Rx     A Modem Roty AccO AccI  Uses  Noise  Overruns  Int
     0 CTY               -   -    -    -    -      0     0      0/0       -
    40 TTY  9600/9600    -   -    -    -    -      0     0      0/0     Se1/7
    65 AUX  2400/2400    F   -    -    -    -      0     0      0/0       -
*   66 VTY               -   -    -    -    -      5     0      0/0       -
    67 VTY               -   -    -    -    -      0     0      0/0       -
    68 VTY               -   -    -    -    -      0     0      0/0       -
    69 VTY               -   -    -    -    -      0     0      0/0       -
    70 VTY               -   -    -    -    -      0     0      0/0       -
```

```
Line(s) not in async mode -or- with no hardware support:
1-39,41-64

Router3#
```

Here you can see that the router has assigned our interface, *Serial1/7*, with line number 40. Note also that it has set it to the default speed of 9600 baud. So we have increased this speed in the example.

```
Router3(config)#line 40
Router3(config-line)#speed 115200
```

See Also

Recipe 16.2; Chapter 13

16.7 Configuring ATM Subinterfaces

Problem

You want to configure an ATM link with PVCs that connect to several other routers.

Solution

Our preferred way of handling ATM PVCs is to use ATM subinterfaces. We also recommend using the IOS feature that sends ATM OAM cells periodically to test the VC. Cisco provides two different syntaxes for configuring ATM PVCs. Here is an example of the older method:

```
Router2#configure terminal
Enter configuration commands, one per line.  End with CNTL/Z.
Router2(config)#interface ATM0/0
Router2(config-if)#no ip address
Router2(config-if)#exit
Router2(config)#interface ATM0/0.1 point-to-point
Router2(config-subif)#description PVC to New York
Router2(config-subif)#ip address 192.168.250.146 255.255.255.252
Router2(config-subif)#atm pvc 1 0 60 aal5snap 10000 5000 3 oam 5
Router2(config-subif)#exit
Router2(config)#end
Router2#
```

In IOS 11.3, Cisco introduced a new configuration method for ATM PVCs:

```
Router2#configure terminal
Enter configuration commands, one per line.  End with CNTL/Z.
Router2(config)#interface ATM0/0
Router2(config-if)#no ip address
Router2(config-if)#exit
Router2(config)#interface ATM0/0.1 point-to-point
Router2(config-subif)#description PVC to New York
Router2(config-subif)#ip address 192.168.250.146 255.255.255.252
```

```
Router2(config-subif)#pvc 0/60
Router2(config-if-atm-vc)#vbr-nrt 10000 5000 30
Router2(config-if-atm-vc)#oam-pvc manage 5
Router2(config-if-atm-vc)#exit
Router2(config)#end
Router2#
```

Discussion

These two configuration examples do exactly the same thing. The older syntax is considerably shorter, but the new version is a little easier to read. Let's look at the old version first:

```
Router2(config-subif)#atm pvc 1 0 60 aal5snap 10000 5000 30 oam 5
```

The first numerical argument is called the Virtual Circuit Descriptor (VCD). This is simply a unique number that you can use to distinguish this ATM VC from any others on the same router. The VCD value is strictly local to the router, so you can choose any value that you like, as long as it is unique.

The next two numbers, 0 and 60 in this case, are the Virtual Path Identifier (VPI) and Virtual Circuit Identifier (VCI), respectively. These are the numbers that the ATM switch uses to identify this particular ATM VC, so you have to make sure that these match the values that the switch uses.

Then we defined the encapsulation to be ATM Adaptation Layer 5 Logical Link Control/Subnetwork Access Protocol (AAL5 SNAP). This is a standard method for encapsulating higher layer protocols into ATM cells for data networks. There are other options here. We could have configured the *aal5ciscoppp* option, which is a Cisco proprietary ATM data encapsulation format that allows you to use standard PPP authentication for a VC if required. The *aal5mux* option is similar to aal5snap, but it only supports a single higher layer protocol on each VC. And the last option is aal5nlpid, which stands for Network Layer Protocol Identification. This option is required if you want to interoperate with an ADSU device, as we discussed in Recipe 16.2.

We generally recommend using AAL5 SNAP, unless you specifically need to support PPP authentication or interoperate with ADSU devices.

The next three fields in the *atm pvc* command configure traffic shaping for this VC. In this case, we have a maximum throughput of 10,000 Kbps, and an average rate of 5,000 Kbps. The maximum burst length is 30 ATM cells. These parameters are optional, but if we had not included them, the router would try to send at the full line rate for this ATM circuit.

The last part of the command tells the router to send ATM Operations Administration and Management (OAM) cells through this VC periodically to test that it is working properly. There are actually several different types of OAM cells, but one type, called the F5 or Loopback test cell, works like an IP PING. When the device that terminates this VC (such as the router on the far end) receives an F5 cell, it turns around and sends it back to the source. In this case, we have configured the router to send one of these OAM cells every five seconds. You can then use the *show atm pvc* command to ensure that you receive the same number of F5 cells that you send:

```
Router2#show atm pvc 0/60
ATMO/0.1: VCD: 1, VPI: 0, VCI: 60, etype:0x0, AAL5 - LLC/SNAP, Flags: 0x830
PeakRate: 10000, Average Rate: 5000, Burst Cells: 96, VCmode: 0xE000
OAM frequency: 5 second(s), InARP frequency: 15 minute(s)
InPkts: 1292959637, OutPkts: 3327374998, InBytes: 2196038015, OutBytes: 813592646
InPRoc: 19959239, OutPRoc: 24660, Broadcasts: 19481389
InFast: 1212924649, OutFast: 3297025318, InAS: 60075750, OutAS: 10843631
OAM F5 cells sent: 6804133, OAM cells received: 6740056
Status: ACTIVE
```

As you can see here, this VC has been active for a considerable length of time, and has sent and received a large number of F5 OAM cells. The numbers are nearly the same, but clearly some F5 cells have been lost at some point. If you suspect a problem, it is often useful to issue this command repeatedly and watch the OAM counters increment.

You can also use the *show atm pvc* command without an argument to see all of the PVC's on the router:

```
Router2>show atm pvc
                                 AAL /          Peak  Avg.  Burst
   Interface  VCD  VPI  VCI Type Encapsulation  Kbps  Kbps  Cells Status
   ATMO/0.1    1    0    60  PVC  AAL5-SNAP      10000 5000    30  ACTIVE
   ATMO/0.42  42    1    42  PVC  AAL5-SNAP      10000 5000    30  ACTIVE
Router2>
```

The second example uses the newer syntax to configure exactly the same parameters:

```
Router2(config-subif)#pvc 0/60
Router2(config-if-atm-vc)#vbr-nrt 10000 5000 30
Router2(config-if-atm-vc)#oam-pvc manage 5
```

The *pvc* command defines the VPI and VCI exactly as before. Note that there is no VCD value in this example. If you like, you can configure a unique name for this VC by adding up to 16 characters before the VPI/VCI values:

```
Router2(config-subif)#pvc NEWYORK 0/60
```

The *vbr-nrt* command lets you configure the traffic shaping parameters. This assumes, of course, that this is a Variable Bit Rate Nonreal Time (VBR-NRT) PVC. If it had been an Unspecified Bit Rate (UBR) PVC, you would simply leave out the *vbr-nrt* line because UBR is the default. For a Committed Bit Rate (CBR) PVC, the configuration specifies only the committed rate for the PVC:

```
Router2(config-if-atm-vc)#cbr 10000
```

But perhaps the biggest advantage to the new syntax is that Cisco routers can now mark ATM subinterfaces as being in a down state if the router sends out three OAM cells in a row without receiving a response. You can verify this using the *show interface* command:

```
Router2#show interfaces ATM0/0.1
ATM0/0.1 is down, line protocol is down
  Hardware is cyBus ATM
  Internet address is 172.25.25.5/30
  MTU 4470 bytes, BW 2000 Kbit, DLY 100 usec, rely 255/255, load 9/255
  Encapsulation ATM
```

Without this feature, you could power off one of the routers, and the other would still think that the PVC was still active. You can go one step further than this as well, by configuring the router to send an SNMP trap when it sees a PVC failure with the following command:

```
Router2(config)#snmp-server enable traps atm pvc extension oam failure loopback
```

This new feature was introduced in IOS Version 12.2(4)T.

See Also

Recipe 16.2

16.8   Setting Payload Scrambling on an ATM Circuit

Problem

You want to enable payload scrambling on your ATM circuit to prevent user data from being interpreted as an in-band control sequence.

Solution

The command to enable scrambling varies depending on the type of circuit. For a T3 ATM circuit, you must use the command *atm ds3-scramble*, as follows:

```
Router2#configure terminal
Enter configuration commands, one per line.  End with CNTL/Z.
Router2(config)#interface ATM0/0
Router2(config-if)#atm ds3-scramble
Router2(config-if)#exit
Router2(config)#end
Router2#
```

For E3 circuits, scrambling is actually enabled by default, but you can disable it with the *no* form of the command *atm e3-scramble*:

```
Router3#configure terminal
Enter configuration commands, one per line.  End with CNTL/Z.
Router3(config)#interface ATM0/0
Router3(config-if)#no atm e3-scramble
Router3(config-if)#exit
Router3(config)#end
Router3#
```

Both of the preceding commands will scramble the ATM cells at the Physical Layer Interface Module (PLIM) on the ATM interface. You can also opt to scramble only the ATM cell's payload as follows:

```
Router4#configure terminal
Enter configuration commands, one per line.  End with CNTL/Z.
Router4(config)#interface ATM0/0
Router4(config-if)#atm scrambling cell-payload
Router4(config-if)#exit
Router4(config)#end
Router4#
```

Discussion

In Recipe 16.5, we mentioned that some types of network devices use in-band signaling to indicate that there are errors on the circuit. This can cause network problems if a switch responds to a sequence of bits in a legitimate packet. In ATM networks, the problem is slightly different, however. Here the issue is not with in-band signaling, but rather with clocking.

Some ATM equipment relies on the cell contents to maintain its clocking. If it sees a long sequence of "1"s or "0"s, it runs the risk of losing track of where the bit boundaries are. You can avoid these types of problems by enabling scrambling on ATM cells.

However, there are two basically different ways to scramble an ATM cell. On physical circuits, such as DS3 and E3 circuits that support ATM services, you will often need to enable bit scrambling across the whole cell, including the ATM header. But with other equipment, such as OC3 circuits, it is sufficient to scramble only the payload. Most Cisco ATM interfaces support payload scrambling.

Note that if you intend to use payload scrambling, you must enable it on all of your ATM devices. And for physical layer scrambling on DS3 or E3 circuits, you should consult your ATM vendor to find out whether scrambling is required.

See Also

Recipe 16.5

16.9 Classical IP Over ATM

Problem

You want to configure your router to support ATM SVCs and Classical IP over ATM.

Solution

For Classical IP over ATM, you must define at least one ATMARP server:

```
Router1#configure terminal
Enter configuration commands, one per line.  End with CNTL/Z.
```

```
Router1(config)#interface ATM1/0
Router1(config-if)#no ip address
Router1(config-if)#atm ilmi-keepalive
Router1(config-if)#pvc 0/5 qsaal
Router1(config-if-atm-vc)#exit
Router1(config-if)#pvc 0/16 ilmi
Router1(config-if-atm-vc)#exit
Router1(config-if)#exit
Router1(config)#interface ATM1/0.1 multipoint
Router1(config-subif)#ip address 192.168.123.1 255.255.255.0
Router1(config-subif)#atm esi-address A000C0A87B01.01
Router1(config-subif)#atm arp-server self
Router1(config-subif)#exit
Router1(config)#end
Router1#
```

The remaining ATM devices in the network can be clients of this server:

```
Router2#configure terminal
Enter configuration commands, one per line.  End with CNTL/Z.
Router2(config)#interface ATM1/0
Router2(config-if)#no ip address
Router2(config-if)#atm ilmi-keepalive
Router2(config-if)#pvc 0/5 qsaal
Router2(config-if-atm-vc)#exit
Router2(config-if)#pvc 0/16 ilmi
Router2(config-if-atm-vc)#exit
Router2(config-if)#exit
Router2(config)#interface ATM1/0.1 multipoint
Router2(config-subif)#ip address 192.168.123.2 255.255.255.0
Router2(config-subif)#atm esi-address A000C0A87B02.01
Router2(config-subif)#atm arp-server nsap 47.00918100000000e014cd0001.A000C0A87B01.01
Router2(config-subif)#exit
Router2(config)#end
Router2#
```

Discussion

The previous ATM recipes in this chapter all used ATM PVCs. Because ATM has become primarily a WAN protocol, as opposed to a LAN protocol, and because WANs tend to have relatively fewer nodes and more static configurations, Permanent Virtual Circuit (PVC) configurations are much more common than Switched Virtual Circuit (SVC) configurations. However, there are several different ways to work with SVCs in an ATM network.

This recipe uses the Classical IP over ATM model for ATM SVCs, which is discussed in RFCs 1577 and updated in 2225. It's important to note that there are other models for using ATM SVCs, most notably Local Area Network Emulation (LANE) and Multiple Protocols over ATM (MPOA), but they all have a few things in common.

First, there must be some mechanism to allow end nodes to request an ATM connection to a particular ATM destination. This is handled using the Quasi Signaling

Application Adaptation Layer (QSAAL) protocol. And they need a way to map an ATM Layer 2 address to Layer 3 protocol address. In LANE and MPOA, a specialized server, called the LAN Emulation Server (LES), manages a list of every device connected to a particular Emulated LAN (ELAN), and can map the Layer 2 to Layer 3 addresses. These protocols also have a server called the Broadcast and Unknown Server (BUS), which can handle broadcasts, multicasts, and other packet flooding operations.

In Classical IP over ATM, there is no BUS. The mapping of Layer 2 to Layer 3 addresses is handled by the ATMARP server, and this server must also handle whatever broadcasts and multicasts are to be supported. We note in passing that the key difference between the Classical IP protocol discussed in RFC 1577 and the updated version in RFC 2225 is the ability to define multiple redundant ATMARP servers. Cisco does provide support for multiple ATMARP servers, as we discuss in a moment.

Another important element that is common to all of these methods for handling ATM SVCs is the use of Interim Local Management Interface (ILMI) to dynamically communicate addressing information between the ATM end devices and the switch. Technically, this step is optional, however, as the information can be configured statically.

Each device must have a configured VC for QSAAL and, optionally, for ILMI. There are well-known VC numbers for these services. QSAAL service is generally provided on VPI/VCI 0/5, while ILMI is usually on 0/16. You can change these values, although we have never seen a compelling reason to do so in practice, and it is far easier to troubleshoot problems later when you adhere to standard practices:

```
Router1(config)#interface ATM1/0
Router1(config-if)#pvc 0/5 qsaal
Router1(config-if-atm-vc)#exit
Router1(config-if)#pvc 0/16 ilmi
Router1(config-if-atm-vc)#exit
```

In Classical IP over ATM, each end device must have a static ATM address configured for the ATMARP server. Each time it wants to connect to an ATM device on the network, it will connect first to the ATMARP server and query for the ATM address of the destination device. Then it will set up a call to the end device using the information provided.

There are two example configurations in the Solution section of this recipe. The first shows the ATMARP server, and the second shows a client device. In general, you could have an arbitrary number of clients, but we show only one here.

We have put the IP address and ATM mapping information on a multipoint subinterface:

```
Router1(config)#interface ATM1/0.1 multipoint
Router1(config-subif)#ip address 192.168.123.1 255.255.255.0
Router1(config-subif)#atm esi-address A000C0A87B01.01
Router1(config-subif)#atm arp-server self
```

The ESI address noted here is an arbitrary 12-digit hex value, followed by a two-digit interface selector code. In this example, we have decided to encode the IP address in the ESI address. If you convert C0A87B01 to decimal, you will get 192.168.123.1. Then we have padded the ESI address with the hex number A000, just to get the right length. We recommend using logical and locally meaningful mnemonics like this.

As this is the ATMARP server, the interface must know that it should answer ARP queries and keep a local ARP cache for the ATM network. This is done by using the *atm arp-server self* command:

The configuration of the client device is similar, except that it must include the full ATM address of the ATMARP server:

```
Router2(config)#interface ATM1/0.1 multipoint
Router2(config-subif)#ip address 192.168.123.2 255.255.255.0
Router2(config-subif)#atm esi-address A000C0A87B02.01
Router2(config-subif)#atm arp-server nsap 47.00918100000000e014cd0001.A000C0A87B01.01
```

You should immediately notice that the ATM NSAP address for the ATMARP server in the *atm arp-server* command is much longer than the ESI address that we actually configured on our ATMARP server router. This is because the ATM NSAP address includes a long prefix that denotes the ATM switch to which this device is connected. In our case, this is a Cisco Lightstream 1010 switch. On this device, you can determine the prefix address by using the command *show atm address*, as follows:

```
ATM_switch#show atm address

Switch Address(es):
  47.0091.8100.0000.00e0.14cd.0001.00e0.14cd.0001.00 active
  NOTE: Switch addresses with selector bytes 01 through 7F
        are reserved for use by PNNI routing

PNNI Local Node Address(es):
  47.0091.8100.0000.00e0.14cd.0001.00e0.14cd.0001.01 Node 1

Soft VC Address(es):
  47.0091.8100.0000.00e0.14cd.0001.4000.0c80.1000.00 ATM0/1/0
  47.0091.8100.0000.00e0.14cd.0001.4000.0c80.1010.00 ATM0/1/1
  47.0091.8100.0000.00e0.14cd.0001.4000.0c80.1020.00 ATM0/1/2
  47.0091.8100.0000.00e0.14cd.0001.4000.0c80.1030.00 ATM0/1/3

Soft VC Address(es) for Frame Relay Interfaces :

ILMI Switch Prefix(es):
  47.0091.8100.0000.00e0.14cd.0001

ILMI Configured Interface Prefix(es):

LECS Address(es):
ATM_switch#
```

Here we have highlighted prefix portion of the switch's NSAP address. The ATMARP server's full NSAP address is this prefix concatenated to the ATMARP server's ESI address: 47.00918100000000e014cd0001.A000C0A87B01.01.

The ATM network is now ready to handle IP traffic:

```
Router2#ping 192.168.123.1

Type escape sequence to abort.
Sending 5, 100-byte ICMP Echos to 192.168.123.1, timeout is 2 seconds:
!!!!!
Success rate is 100 percent (5/5), round-trip min/avg/max = 4/5/8 ms
Router2#
```

If we look at the client router's ARP cache, we can see that it has added an entry for 192.168.123.1, associating it with the new SVC on VPI/VCI 0/35:

```
Router2#show arp
Protocol  Address          Age (min)  Hardware Addr   Type  Interface
Internet  192.168.1.104        -      00e0.1e7f.9e41  ARPA  Ethernet0/0
Internet  192.168.123.1        4      0 / 35          ATM   ATM1/0.1
Internet  192.168.132.3        -      00e0.1e7f.9e42  ARPA  Ethernet0/1
Router2#
```

You can see further information about this ATM SVC, including NSAP addresses and status by using the *show atm map* command:

```
Router2#show atm map
Map list ATM1/0.1_ATM_ARP : DYNAMIC
arp maps to NSAP 47.00918100000000E014CD0001.A000C0A87B01.01
        , connection up, VC 3, VPI 0, VCI 35, ATM1/0.1
ip 192.168.123.1 maps to NSAP 47.00918100000000E014CD0001.A000C0A87B01.01
        , broadcast, connection up, VC 3, VPI 0, VCI 35, ATM1/0.1

Router2#
```

You can configure additional ATMARP servers on a Cisco router. However, as this is not supported by the original RFC, you have to first enable protocol extensions with the command atm classic-ip-extensions BFI. We note in passing that there is no consensus on what the acronym BFI actually stands for. Cisco says that the acronym is "undefined." Other sources suggest "Bad Frame Indicator," despite the absence of anything resembling a bad frame indicator, while others more plausibly claim it stands for "Brute Force and Ignorance." In any case, once you have enabled this command, you can freely implement additional ATMARP servers:

```
Router2(config)#interface ATM1/0.1 multipoint
Router2(config-subif)#atm classic-ip-extensions BFI
Router2(config-subif)#atm arp-server nsap 47.00918100000000e14cd0001.A000C0A87B01.01
Router2(config-subif)#atm arp-server nsap 47.00918100000000e14cd0001.A000C0A140A0.01
Router2(config-subif)#exit
```

See Also

RFCs 1577 and 2225

16.10 Configuring Ethernet Interface Features

Problem

You want to force a particular Ethernet speed or duplex setting.

Solution

Cisco routers allow you to adjust several different Layer 1 and 2 parameters on Ethernet interfaces, depending on the specific hardware. On interfaces that support more than one medium, you can specify which media type you want to use with the media-type command:

```
Router1#configure terminal
Enter configuration commands, one per line.  End with CNTL/Z.
Router1(config)#interface FastEthernet0/0
Router1(config-if)#media-type 100BaseX
Router1(config-if)#duplex full
Router1(config-if)#speed 100
Router1(config-if)#exit
Router1(config)#end
Router1#
```

You can also adjust parameters such as the ARP timeout interval, the MAC address, and the keepalive timer on the interface:

```
Router1#configure terminal
Enter configuration commands, one per line.  End with CNTL/Z.
Router1(config)#interface FastEthernet0/0
Router1(config-if)#mac-address 0AAA.ABCD.0101
Router1(config-if)#arp timeout 60
Router1(config-if)#keepalive 5
Router1(config-if)#exit
Router1(config)#end
Router1#
```

Discussion

Most of the time, you will just want to use the default options when setting up Ethernet interfaces. By default, most Ethernet modules will automatically sense which media type is in use, as well as the duplex and speed settings. In this example, we have explicitly forced the router to use its 100BaseX medium, full duplex, and 100Mbps speed settings:

```
Router1(config)#interface FastEthernet0/0
Router1(config-if)#media-type 100BaseX
Router1(config-if)#duplex full
Router1(config-if)#speed 100
```

The options for the media-type command depend on the module. Fast Ethernet modules often include a Media Independent Interface (MII), for example. By default, the router will usually select the appropriate one by sensing the Ethernet carrier signal when you connect it to another device. But sometimes there are problems with this auto sense, and you want to force the router to use a particular one. Alternatively, you may want to ensure that nobody can come along and confuse the router by plugging the other unused media interface into another device.

By default, the router will also attempt to detect both duplex and speed on Fast Ethernet modules. Naturally, these options are not available on most conventional 10 Mbps Ethernet modules, although Cisco does make full-duplex capable 10 Mbps modules for some router models. The options for the duplex command are full, half, and auto. Interestingly, you can also set the duplex options with these alternative commands:

```
Router1(config-if)#full-duplex
Router1(config-if)#half-duplex
```

There are often problems with auto negotiation. When the duplex auto negotiation process fails to work properly, the interface will still work, but you will see poor performance with a large number of errors. Because the router is generally the most important device on a LAN segment, we strongly recommend deliberately setting both the speed and duplex on routers to ensure that there is no possibility for confusion between the router and the LAN switch or hub.

The parameters that we modified in the second example in this recipe rarely need to be changed in practice:

```
Router1(config)#interface FastEthernet0/0
Router1(config-if)#mac-address 0AAA.ABCD.0101
Router1(config-if)#arp timeout 60
Router1(config-if)#keepalive 5
```

The default MAC address is the burned-in address (BIA) that we discussed in Recipe 16.1. There are a few reasons why you might want to change the MAC address. For example, sometimes a piece of legacy equipment expects to see a particular MAC address, or there might be an access-list that filters traffic based on this address. In this case, it can be awkward to deal with hardware problems that force you to replace or upgrade either a router or a module. So you can use the *mac-address* command to give this router the same address as the previous router had.

Always be careful when changing MAC addresses. If two devices on the same network wind up with the same MAC address, it can disrupt traffic for both devices as the switches try to figure out which one is which. And, if one of these devices is a router, it can disrupt all off-segment traffic. MAC addresses must be unique.

The router uses its ARP cache table to map IP addresses to MAC addresses for devices on the local LAN segment. By default, if the router has not seen any traffic from a particular MAC address within 14,400 seconds (four hours), it will flush the entry out of its ARP cache.

Sometimes this is not appropriate, however. For example, in many bridged environments, the bridges will remove MAC table entries after a shorter period such as 10 minutes. In this case, if a station has been idle for more than 10 minutes but less than 4 hours, the router will send the packet normally, but the bridge will have to flood all segments with the traffic to find the destination device. It may be more efficient if the router simply sends out a fresh ARP query for the destination. So you will probably want to reduce your ARP timeout if this is the case.

You may also want to change the ARP timeout in environments where the MAC address associated with a particular IP address changes frequently. This could happen because of DHCP, for example. Or, you will get a similar effect if there are so many ARP entries that the ARP cache frequently fills up and the router has to drop entries. In these cases, you might want to reduce the ARP timeout period using the *arp timeout* command:

```
Router1(config-if)#arp timeout 60
```

The argument to this command is a time in seconds.

Finally, the *keepalive* command allows you to control how often the router sends out a keepalive packet on the interface. This allows the router to test whether the interface is still active. By default, the router will send a keepalive packet every 10 seconds, and consider the interface to be down if it fails to see three packets in a row. If you need the router to respond more quickly to failures, you can reduce this interval by using the *keepalive* command:

```
Router1(config-if)#keepalive 5
```

This command takes a single argument, which is the time interval in seconds. Giving this command an argument of 0 is the same as disabling keepalives on the interface. If you do this, the router will simply stop sending keepalive packets, and will always think that the interface is available no matter what happens.

16.11 Configuring Token Ring Interface Features

Problem

You want to configure a Token Ring interface.

Solution

The main thing that you need to take care to set properly for Token Ring interfaces is the ring speed:

```
Router2#configure terminal
Enter configuration commands, one per line.  End with CNTL/Z.
Router2(config)#interface TokenRing0
Router2(config-if)#ring-speed 4
Router2(config-if)#exit
```

```
Router2(config)#end
Router2#
```

You can also set the MAC address on a Token Ring interface:

```
Router2#configure terminal
Enter configuration commands, one per line.  End with CNTL/Z.
Router2(config)#interface TokenRing0
Router2(config-if)#mac-address 0006.1111.aaaa
Router2(config-if)#exit
Router2(config)#end
Router2#
```

And some routers can optionally support full-duplex Token Ring:

```
Router8#configure terminal
Enter configuration commands, one per line.  End with CNTL/Z.
Router8(config)#interface TokenRing0/8
Router8(config-if)#full-duplex
Router8(config-if)#exit
Router8(config)#end
Router8#
```

Discussion

You can set the Token Ring's ring speed with the *ring-speed* command:

```
Router2(config)#interface TokenRing0
Router2(config-if)#ring-speed 4
```

The default for Token Ring interfaces is 16 Mbps. In this example, we have reduced the speed to support the older 4 Mbps standard. You need to be very careful when doing this, however, because ring speed mismatches can cause serious problems on Token Ring networks. Inserting a device with the wrong ring speed not only means that the new device can't use the ring, but it will disrupt communications among all of the other devices as well:

Changing MAC addresses is actually considerably more common than it is for Ethernet. However, just as we mentioned in Recipe 16.10, you need to be careful to ensure that MAC addresses are unique:

```
Router2(config-if)#mac-address 0006.1111.aaaa
```

Full duplex support on Token Ring interfaces is not actually part of the IEEE standard, but many vendors have started to support it. In fact, only a few of Cisco's Token Ring modules, which are designed specifically for full-duplex, support this command. However, if you have a router with this feature, and a Token Ring switch that also supports it, this can significantly improve your network performance.

You can enable full-duplex support, where available, with the full-duplex command:

```
Router8(config-if)#full-duplex
```

The default is half duplex.

See Also

Recipe 16.10

16.12 Connecting VLAN Trunks with ISL

Problem

You want to connect an InterSwitch Link (ISL) VLAN trunk to your router.

Solution

The following set of commands allows you to connect an ISL trunk to your router:

```
Router1#configure terminal
Enter configuration commands, one per line.  End with CNTL/Z.
Router1(config)#interface FastEthernet0/0
Router1(config-if)#no ip address
Router1(config-if)#speed 100
Router1(config-if)#full-duplex
Router1(config-if)#exit
Router1(config)#interface FastEthernet0/0.1
Router1(config-subif)#encapsulation isl 1
Router1(config-subif)#ip address 172.25.1.5 255.255.255.0
Router1(config-subif)#exit
Router1(config)#interface FastEthernet0/0.2
Router1(config-subif)#encapsulation isl 2
Router1(config-subif)#ip address 172.16.2.1 255.255.255.0
Router1(config-subif)#exit
Router1(config)#interface FastEthernet0/0.3
Router1(config-subif)#encapsulation isl 574
Router1(config-subif)#ip address 10.22.1.2 255.255.255.0
Router1(config-subif)#exit
Router1(config)#end
Router1#
```

Discussion

A *trunk* is a point-to-point link containing one ore more Virtual LANs (VLANs). The main purpose of a trunk is to save physical interfaces. Without VLANs, if you wanted to connect two LAN segments into a router, you would need two Ethernet interfaces. Unfortunately, this does not scale well. It is relatively common for a switch to support many VLANs. So there is a clear advantage to using trunks to bundle the VLANs together into a single link.

While trunks carry traffic for many different VLANs, they are able to keep them separate by tagging each frame with the unique identification number for the appropriate VLAN. This allows traffic from multiple LAN segments to share the same physical link without any danger of frames leaking onto the wrong segment. When a network device receives a tagged frame from a trunk link, it removes the tag, and then forwards the frame to the appropriate LAN segment as a normal frame.

When you connect a router to a trunk, it can route Layer 3 packets between the various VLANs on the trunk. Because of the VLAN tagging scheme, Layer 2 frames cannot pass from one VLAN to another. So, without a router device of some kind, there is no way to interconnect the VLANs. The configuration where a router is connected to a trunk, to allow routing between the different VLANs, is often called a "router on a stick" because the router routes its packets back out onto the same physical interface that it received them through.

Cisco routers support two main trunking protocols, ISL and 802.1Q. ISL is a Cisco proprietary protocol, so you can only use it between Cisco devices. Conversely, 802.1Q is an IEEE open standard that is supported by most manufacturers of network hardware. Recipe 16.13 shows how to configure an 802.1Q trunk interface on a router.

Unfortunately, the 802.1Q open standard reached the market some time after the initial demand for trunking protocols. So most manufacturers of Layer 2 switching equipment developed their own proprietary standards to fill the void. Cisco developed ISL. All newer Cisco equipment now supports 802.1Q, but there are still many older Catalyst switches that cannot support the open standard, so ISL is your only choice with this equipment. In any case, Cisco's ISL support is generally more mature and stable than its 802.1Q implementations. So while we generally recommend working with open standards where possible, ISL is still clearly the more viable option in some networks.

The first step when configuring a trunk on a router is to select a physical LAN interface to connect the trunk to. In general, we don't recommend using anything slower than a Fast Ethernet interface for this purpose:

```
Router1(config)#interface FastEthernet0/0
Router1(config-if)#no ip address
Router1(config-if)#speed 100
Router1(config-if)#full-duplex
```

As you can see, there is no special configuration necessary on the physical interface.

Then you need to create one subinterface on this physical interface for each different VLAN. Because each VLAN represents a different Layer 3 network, you need to give each of the subinterfaces IP addresses from the corresponding IP subnets:

```
Router1(config)#interface FastEthernet0/0.1
Router1(config-subif)#encapsulation isl 1
Router1(config-subif)#ip address 172.25.1.5 255.255.255.0
```

The *encapsulation* command associates this subinterface with a particular ISL VLAN number. ISL VLAN numbers can have any value between 1 and 1,000. With this subinterface configured, the router is now able to route packets for any devices on this VLAN, exactly as if it were directly connected to the physical LAN segment.

The *show vlans* command displays information about all of the VLANs configured on the router:

```
Router1#show vlans

Virtual LAN ID:  1 (Inter Switch Link Encapsulation)

   vLAN Trunk Interface:    FastEthernet0/0.1

   Protocols Configured:    Address:           Received:        Transmitted:
            IP              172.25.1.5          203626            342261

Virtual LAN ID:  2 (Inter Switch Link Encapsulation)

   vLAN Trunk Interface:    FastEthernet0/0.2

   Protocols Configured:    Address:           Received:        Transmitted:
            IP              172.16.2.1              0             153807

Virtual LAN ID:  574 (Inter Switch Link Encapsulation)

   vLAN Trunk Interface:    FastEthernet0/0.3

   Protocols Configured:    Address:           Received:        Transmitted:
            IP              10.22.1.2               0                  6

Router1#
```

We have configured this router to support three different VLANs, each with its own subinterface and its own IP address. The subinterface number does not necessarily need to correspond to the VLAN ID, as we have assigned VLAN number 574 to sub-interface *FastEthernet0/0.3*. But if you make it a general rule to always keep the sub-interface number the same as the VLAN number, it will make maintenance and troubleshooting considerably simpler in a large network.

It is useful to remember that you don't need to create a distinct subinterface for every VLAN on the switch. There may be some VLANs on this switch that you don't wish to terminate on the router. In this case, the router will simply ignore any frames that are tagged with VLAN numbers that it doesn't support.

You can use the *show interfaces* command to see information about the trunking configuration of a particular subinterface:

```
Router1#show interfaces FastEthernet0/0.3
FastEthernet0/0.3 is up, line protocol is up
  Hardware is AmdFE, address is 0001.9670.b780 (bia 0001.9670.b780)
  Internet address is 10.22.1.2/24
  MTU 1500 bytes, BW 100000 Kbit, DLY 100 usec,
     reliability 255/255, txload 1/255, rxload 1/255
  Encapsulation ISL Virtual LAN, Color 574.
  ARP type: ARPA, ARP Timeout 04:00:00
Router1#
```

This shows the encapsulation type (ISL) and the VLAN number (574), along with the interface's IP address information.

Cisco added support for IP unnumbered addressing of VLAN subinterfaces in Version 12.2(4)T:

```
Router1(config)#interface FastEthernet0/0.1
Router1(config-if)#ip unnumbered Loopback0
```

See Also

Recipe 16.13

16.13 Connecting VLAN Trunks with 802.1Q

Problem

You want to connect an 802.1Q VLAN trunk directly to your router.

Solution

To connect an 802.1Q trunk to your router, use the following set of commands:

```
Router2#configure terminal
Enter configuration commands, one per line.  End with CNTL/Z.
Router2(config)#interface FastEthernet1/0
Router2(config-if)#no ip address
Router2(config-if)#speed 100
Router2(config-if)#full-duplex
Router2(config-if)#exit
Router2(config)#interface FastEthernet1/0.1
Router2(config-subif)#encapsulation dot1Q 1 native
Router2(config-subif)#ip address 172.25.1.47 255.255.255.0
Router2(config-subif)#exit
Router2(config)#interface FastEthernet1/0.2
Router2(config-subif)#encapsulation dot1Q 2
Router2(config-subif)#ip address 172.25.22.4 255.255.255.0
Router2(config-subif)#exit
Router2(config)#interface FastEthernet1/0.3
Router2(config-subif)#encapsulation dot1Q 548
Router2(config-subif)#ip address 172.20.1.1 255.255.255.0
Router2(config-subif)#exit
Router2(config)#end
Router2#
```

Please note that to support 802.1Q features, your router must have an IOS level of at least 12.0(5)T, with the IP Plus feature set.

Discussion

The configuration for 802.1Q trunks is almost identically to the ISL configuration we discussed in Recipe 16.12. Please refer to that recipe for a more detailed discussion of trunking in general.

The most important difference between ISL and 802.1Q trunks is that 802.1Q is an IEEE open standard. If all of your switches and routers were manufactured by Cisco, you can easily use ISL without fear of conflict. However, if you ever need to connect a trunk link to a piece of equipment from a different vendor, you may find that 802.1Q is the only option. Further, many organizations prefer to use open standard protocols as a matter of policy, even if all of their equipment happens to come from the same vendor.

One of the important but subtle differences between ISL and 802.1Q is the number of VLANs supported. ISL supports VLAN ID numbers 1 through 1000, while 802.1Q allows values from 1 through 4095. While it is unlikely that you will ever run out of VLAN numbers with either scheme, some early IOS versions, and many early switch versions, implemented 802.1Q as if it were ISL under the covers. The result is that some older devices may only support 802.1Q VLAN ID numbers between 1 and 1000. So you may find that you are not able to use any of the higher range of values. This limitation does not exist on newer versions of Cisco equipment, but we recommend being careful to avoid interoperability problems.

You configure 802.1Q by creating subinterfaces and using the encapsulation command with the *dot1Q* keyword to assign the subinterface to a particular VLAN:

```
Router2(config)#interface FastEthernet1/0.2
Router2(config-subif)#encapsulation dot1Q 2
Router2(config-subif)#ip address 172.25.22.4 255.255.255.0
```

The number after the *dot1Q* keyword is the VLAN number that you wish to associate with this subinterface.

The only tricky part of configuring 802.1Q is defining the *native* VLAN. This often causes problems for network administrators. The native VLAN is the master VLAN assigned to the interface, and it must match the native VLAN configured on the switch. The native VLAN is the only VLAN whose frames do not contain an 802.1Q VLAN tag in their Layer 2 frame headers. So if you connect two devices through an 802.1Q trunk, and they don't agree on which is the native VLAN, you will effectively merge the two native VLANs together, which is almost certainly not what you want to do.

In our example, VLAN 1 is the native VLAN, which we define using the *native* keyword, as follows:

```
Router2(config)#interface FastEthernet1/0.1
Router2(config-subif)#encapsulation dot1Q 1 native
```

The default native VLAN on many switches is VLAN number 1. But, you can easily configure a different native VLAN. For example, we could use the following set of commands to reconfigure VLAN number 2 as the native VLAN:

```
Router2(config)#interface FastEthernet1/0.1
Router2(config-subif)#encapsulation dot1Q 1
Router2(config-subif)#exit
```

```
Router2(config)#interface FastEthernet1/0.2
Router2(config-subif)#encapsulation dot1Q 2 native
Router2(config-subif)#exit
```

It's important to remember that there can only be one native VLAN at a time, and that whatever you configure on the router must match what is configured on the switch. It is not safe to simply assume that VLAN number 1 will always be the native VLAN.

You can use the *show vlans* command to see information about all VLANs configured on your router:

```
Router2#show vlans

Virtual LAN ID:  1 (IEEE 802.1Q Encapsulation)

   vLAN Trunk Interface:    FastEthernet1/0.1

  This is configured as native Vlan for the following interface(s) :
FastEthernet1/0

     Protocols Configured:   Address:            Received:       Transmitted:
            IP              172.25.1.47            4974             3149

Virtual LAN ID:  2 (IEEE 802.1Q Encapsulation)

   vLAN Trunk Interface:    FastEthernet1/0.2

     Protocols Configured:   Address:            Received:       Transmitted:
            IP              172.25.22.4            548              617

Virtual LAN ID:  548 (IEEE 802.1Q Encapsulation)

   vLAN Trunk Interface:    FastEthernet1/0.3

     Protocols Configured:   Address:            Received:       Transmitted:
            IP              172.20.1.1              0               613

Router2#
```

This command output shows the configured VLANs and identifies which VLAN is defined as native. To view a specific 802.1Q subinterface, use the *show interface* command:

```
Router2#show interface FastEthernet1/0.1
FastEthernet1/0.1 is up, line protocol is up
  Hardware is AmdFE, address is 00e0.1e84.5131 (bia 00e0.1e84.5131)
  Internet address is 172.25.1.47/24
  MTU 1500 bytes, BW 100000 Kbit, DLY 100 usec,
     reliability 255/255, txload 1/255, rxload 1/255
  Encapsulation 802.1Q Virtual LAN, Vlan ID  1.
  ARP type: ARPA, ARP Timeout 04:00:00
Router2#
```

Recipe 16.12

16.14 LPD Printer Support

Problem

You want to connect a printer to your router to use from the Berkeley Unix LPD print program.

Solution

You can connect a printer to any asynchronous interface on a router. This typically means your AUX port, but as we discussed in Recipe 16.6, there are several other options for asynchronous serial ports on routers:

```
Router1#configure terminal
Enter configuration commands, one per line.  End with CNTL/Z.
Router1(config)#printer rtlpr1 line 161
Router1(config)#end
Router1#
```

Discussion

The Berkeley Unix Line Printer Daemon (LPD) protocol is defined in RFC 1179. It is a relatively simple TCP protocol in which a device supporting a printer listens on TCP port 515 for inbound connections and accepts commands to do things like print a file or delete a job from the queue.

There are several prerequisites to making this deceptively simple recipe work properly. First, you must have a computer that supports the Berkeley Unix LPD print program. Second, you must correctly configure the */etc/printcap* file on this computer so that it will spool print jobs to the router. Third, you must have a printer that can take a serial input instead of the more customary parallel or USB connections. And fourth, you have to figure out the line number associated with this printer connection.

We assume you have the first point under control. Any standard Linux or FreeBSD system, as well as any commercial Unix implementation such as Solaris, HPUX, or AIX, will definitely have LPD support. Microsoft has also included LPD support in Windows XP. Please refer to this Microsoft web page (*http://support.microsoft.com/kb/324078/en-us*) for an excellent detailed step-by-step guide to configuring LPD print services on a Windows XP system.

For the second point, this depends somewhat on your system. The standard Berkeley printcap file format has many options, and we strongly recommend that you refer to your local documentation to determine the best settings. However, here is a simple example printcap entry for use with a printer connected to a router:

```
routerptr1|Printer connected to office WAN router:\
    :rm=router1:\
    :rp=rtlpr1:\
    :if=/usr/local/libexec/lpfilter:\
    :sd=/usr/spool/lpd/router1ptr:\
    :lf=/var/log/lpd-errs:
```

In this example, there are two key lines and a few others that you may need to play with. The printcap file format includes a list of variables that are generically called "capabilities," separated by colons ":". The "rm" capability defines the "remote machine," in this case the router, router1. Note that you must have this hostname defined either in DNS or on the hosts file on the local system.

Next is the "rp" capability, which lists the printer by the name by which it is known on the remote system. In our example, the *printer* command on the router defined the printer to be called rtlpr1, so that is the string that we must use here.

The remaining entries define filters, spool directories, and the location of the error file, where details of any problems printing to this device will be recorded.

Finally, getting back to the configuration of the router itself, we have to be careful about specifying the line number of the asynchronous serial port that connects to the printer. In this case, we are using the AUX port on the router. So we have to use the *show line* command to determine the line number associated with this port:

```
Router1#show line
    Tty Typ     Tx/Rx     A Modem  Roty AccO AccI   Uses   Noise  Overruns   Int
      0 CTY                -    -     -    -    -      0      0      0/0       -
    161 AUX     9600/9600  -    -     -    -    -      0      0      0/0       -
*   162 VTY                -    -     -    -    -      8      0      0/0       -
    163 VTY                -    -     -    -    -      1      0      0/0       -
    164 VTY                -    -     -    -    -      1      0      0/0       -
    165 VTY                -    -     -    -    -      0      0      0/0       -
    166 VTY                -    -     -    -    -      0      0      0/0       -
    167 VTY                -    -    25    -    9      0      0      0/0       -
    168 VTY                -    -    25    -    9      0      0      0/0       -
    169 VTY                -    -    25    -    9      0      0      0/0       -

Line(s) not in async mode -or- with no hardware support:
1-160

Router1#
```

In this case, you can see that the AUX port is line number 161. So this is the value that we must use in the *printer* command:

```
Router1(config)#printer rtlpr1 line 161
```

You will also notice that this line is configured with the default baud rate of 9600. It may be useful to alter the default settings. In particular, we recommend disabling logins on this interface. Otherwise a random bit of electrical noise from the printer might be interpreted as a carriage return by the router, which will respond by putting

up a login prompt. The printer will then print this prompt, causing great annoyance
and waste of paper:

```
Router1(config)#line aux 0
Router1(config-line)#no exec
Router1(config-line)#no login
Router1(config-line)#no password
Router1(config-line)#transport input none
Router1(config-line)#speed 115200
Router1(config-line)#exit
```

In this example, we have somewhat arbitrarily set the baud rate to 115,200 bps. You
should use the maximum speed your printer will reliably support.

To look at the status of a printer on the router, use the *show printer* command:

```
Router1#show printer
Printer  Line  Rotary  Errors Connections Datafiles Controlfiles   Bytes
rtlpr1   161    0        0         0          0          0            0
Router1#
```

See Also

Recipe 16.6; RFC 1179

## CHAPTER 17

Simple Network Management Protocol

17.0 Introduction

Since its introduction in 1988, the Simple Network Management Protocol (SNMP) has become the de facto network management protocol on TCP/IP-based networks. The IETF created SNMP to allow remote management of IP-based devices using a standardized set of operations. It is now widely supported by servers, printers, hubs, switches, modems, UPS systems, and, of course, Cisco routers.

The SNMP set of standards defines much more than a communication protocol used for management traffic. The standards also define how management data should be accessed and stored, as well as the entire distributed framework of SNMP agents and servers. The IETF has officially recognized SNMP as a fully standard part of the IP protocol suite. The original SNMP definition is documented in RFC 1157.

In 1993, SNMP Version 2 (SNMPv2) was created to address a number of functional deficiencies that were apparent in the original protocol. The added and improved features included better error handling, larger data counters (64-bit), improved efficiency (get-bulk transfers), confirmed event notifications (informs), and, most notably, security enhancements. Unfortunately, SNMPv2 did not become widely accepted because the IETF was unable to come to a consensus on the SNMP security features.

So a revised edition of SNMPv2 was released in 1996. It is discussed in RFCs 1905, 1906, and 1907 and included all of the proposed enhancements, except for the security facility. The IETF refers to this new version as SNMPv2c, and it uses the same insecure security model as SNMPv1. This model relies on passwords called *community strings* that are sent over the network as clear text. SNMPv2c never enjoyed widespread success throughout the IP community. Consequently, most organizations continue to use SNMPv1. The IETF recently announced that SNMPv3 would be the new standard, with SNMPv1, SNMPv2, and SNMPv2c being considered purely historical.

We should note in passing that Cisco's IOS supported SNMPv2 until Version 11.2(6)F, when Cisco began supporting SNMPv2c. Cisco continues to support SNMPv2c in every IOS version beginning with 11.2(6)F. In addition, every version of IOS has supported SNMPv1 since the earliest releases.

The compromise that became SNMPv2c left the management protocol without satisfactory security features. So, in 1998, the IETF began working on SNMPv3, which is defined in RFCs 2571–2575. Essentially, SNMPv3 is a set of security enhancements to be used in conjunction with SNMPv2c. This means that SNMPv3 is not a standalone management protocol and does not replace SNMPv2c or SNMPv1.

SNMPv3 provides a secure method for accessing devices using authentication, message integrity, and encryption of SNMP packets throughout the network. We have included a recipe describing how to use the SNMPv3 security enhancements (see Recipe 17.22). Table 17-1 lists the three supported versions of SNMP and highlights their security capabilities.

Table 17-1. SNMP versions supported by Cisco

Version	Authentication	Encryption	Description
v1	Community strings	None	Trivial authentication. Packets sent in clear text.
v2c	Community strings	None	Trivial authentication. Packets sent in clear text.
v3(noAuthNoPriv)	Username	None	Trivial authentication. Packets sent in clear text.
v3(authNoPriv)	SHA or MD5-encrypted passphrase	None	Strong authentication. Packets sent in clear text.
v3(authPriv)	SHA or MD5-encrypted passphrase	DES, 3DES, or AES	Strong authentication. Packets are encrypted.

SNMP Management Model

SNMP defines two main types of entities, *managers* and *agents*. A manager is a server that runs network management software that is responsible for a particular network. These servers are commonly referred to as Network Management Stations (*NMS*). There are several excellent commercial NMS platforms on the market. Throughout this book, we refer to the freely distributed NET-SNMP system as a reference NMS.

An agent is an embedded piece of software that resides on a remote device that you wish to manage. In fact, almost every IP capable device provides some sort of built-in SNMP agent. The agent has two main functions. First, the agent must listen for incoming SNMP requests from the NMS and respond appropriately. And second, the agent must monitor internal events and create SNMP traps to alert the NMS that something has happened. This book will focus mainly on how to configure the router's agent.

Usually, the NMS is configured to poll all of the key devices in the network periodically using *SNMP Get* requests. This is a UDP packet sent to the agent on the well-known SNMP port 161. The SNMP Get request prompts the remote device to respond with one or more pieces of relevant operating information.

However, because there could be hundreds or thousands of remote devices, it is often not practical to poll a particular remote device more often than once every few minutes (and in many networks, you are lucky if you can poll each device more than a few times per hour). On a schedule like this, it is possible for a remote device to suffer a serious problem, and possibly even crash and reboot in between polls from the NMS. So, on the next poll, the NMS will see everything operating normally and never know that it completely missed a catastrophe.

Therefore, an SNMP agent also has the ability to send information using an *SNMP Trap* without having to wait for a poll. A trap is an unsolicited piece of information, usually representing a problem situation (although some traps are more informational in nature). Traps are UDP packets sent from the agent to the NMS on the other well-known SNMP port number, 162. There are many different types of traps that an agent can send, depending on what type of equipment it manages. Some traps represent noncritical issues. It is often up to the network administrator to decide which types of traps will be useful.

It is important to remember the NMS does not acknowledge traps. Since traps are often sent to report network problems, it is not uncommon to for trap reports to get lost and never make it to the NMS. In many cases, this is acceptable because the trap represents a transient problem that the NMS discovers by other means if this trap is not delivered. However, critical information can be lost when a trap is not delivered.

To address this shortcoming, SNMPv2c and SNMPv3 include another type of packet called an *SNMP Inform*. This is nearly identical to a standard trap, except that the SNMP agent will wait for an acknowledgement. If the agent does not receive an acknowledgement within a certain amount of time, it will attempt to retransmit the inform. Informs also use UDP port 162.

SNMP informs not common today because SNMP Version 2c was never widely adopted. However, SNMP Version 3 also includes informs. Because SNMPv3 promises to become the mainstream SNMP protocol, it seems inevitable that enhancements like SNMP Informs will start to be more common.

MIBs and OIDs

SNMP uses a special tree structure called a Management Information Base (MIB) to organize the management data. People will often talk about different MIBs, such as the T1 MIB or an ATM MIB. In fact, these are all really just branches or extensions of the same global MIB tree structure. However, the relative independence of these different branches makes it convenient to talk this way.

A particular SNMP agent will only care about those few MIB branches that are relevant to the particular remote device this agent run on. If the device doesn't have any T1 interfaces, then the agent doesn't need to know anything about the T1 branch of the global MIB tree. Similarly, the NMS for a network that contains no ATM doesn't need to be able to resolve any of the variables in the ATM branches of the MIB tree.

The MIB tree structure is defined by a long sequence of numbers separated by dots, such as `.1.3.6.1.2.1.1.4.0`. This number is called an Object Identifier (OID). Since we will be working with OID strings throughout this chapter, it is worthwhile to take a brief review of how they work and what they mean.

The OID is a numerical representation of the MIB tree structure. Each digit represents a node in this tree structure. The trunk of the tree is on the left and the leaves are on the right. In the example string, .1.3.6.1.2.1.1.4.0, the first digit, .1, signifies that this variable is part of the MIB that is administered by the International Standards Organization (ISO). There are other nodes at this top level of the tree. The International Telephone and Telegraph Consultative Committee (CCITT) administers the .0 tree structure. And the ISO and CCITT jointly administer .2.

The first node under the ISO MIB tree of this example is .3. The ISO has allocated this node for all other organizations. The U.S. Department of Defense (DOD) is designated by the branch number .6. The DOD, in turn, has allocated branch number .1 for the Internet Activities Board (IAB). So just about every SNMP MIB variable you will ever see will begin with .1.3.6.1.

There are four commonly used subbranches under the IAB (also called simply "internet") node. These are designated directory (1), mgmt (2), experimental (3), and private (4). The directory node is seldom used in practice. The mgmt node is used for all IETF standard MIB extensions, which are documented in RFCs. This would include, for example, the T1 and ATM MIB structures mentioned earlier. However, it would not include any vendor-specific variables, such as the CPU utilization on a Cisco router. SNMP protocol and application developers use the experimental subtree to hold data that is not yet standard. This allows you to use experimental MIBs in a production network without fear of causing conflicts. And, finally, the private subtree contains vendor-specific MIB variables.

Before returning to the example, we want to take a brief detour down the private tree, because a lot of our examples in this book will include Cisco-specific MIB variables. A good example of a Cisco MIB variable is .1.3.6.1.4.1.9.2.1.8.0, which gives the amount of free memory in a Cisco router. There is only one subtree under the private node, and it is called enterprises, .1.3.6.1.4.1. Of the hundreds of registered owners of private MIB trees, Cisco is number 9, so all Cisco-specific MIB extensions begin with .1.3.6.1.4.1.9.

Referring again to the previous example string, .1.3.6.1.2.1.1.4.0, you can see that this represents a variable in the *mgmt* subtree, .1.3.6.1.2. The next digit is .1 here, which represents an SNMP MIB variable.

The following digit, .1, refers to a specific group of variables, which in the case of mgmt variables would be defined by an RFC. In this particular case, the value .1 refers to the *system* MIB, which is detailed in RFC 1450.

From this level down, a special naming convention is adopted to help you to remember which MIB you are looking at. The names of every variable under the *system* node begin with "sys". They are sysDescr (1), sysObjectID (2), sysUpTime (3), sysContact (4), sysName (5), sysLocation (6), sysServices (7), sysORLastChange (8), and sysORTable (9). You can find detailed descriptions of what all of these mean in RFC 1450. In fact, reading through MIB descriptions is an excellent way of understanding not only the hierarchical structure of the MIB, but also extremely useful when you are trying to decide what information you can and should be extracting from your equipment.

In the example string, `.1.3.6.1.2.1.1.4.0`, the value is `.4`, for `sysContact`. The following `.0` just tells the agent to send the contents of this node, rather than treating it as the root of further subtrees. So the OID string uniquely identifies a single piece of information, which in this case is the contact information for the device.

17.1 Configuring SNMP

Problem

You want to set up basic SNMP services on a router.

Solution

To enable read-only SNMP services, use the following configuration command:

```
Router#configure terminal
Enter configuration commands, one per line.  End with CNTL/Z.
Router(config)#snmp-server community ORARO ro
Router(config)#end
Router#
```

To enable read-write SNMP services, use the following command:

```
Router#configure terminal
Enter configuration commands, one per line.  End with CNTL/Z.
Router(config)#snmp-server community ORARW rw
Router(config)#end
Router#
```

 It is extremely risky to enable read-write SNMP services without the appropriate security controls. Please read the following discussion section before implementing this recipe.

Starting with IOS Version 12.0(3)T, Cisco introduced a new system for configuring SNMP services by using the *snmp-server group* and *snmp-server user* configuration commands. Use the following commands to enable read-only SNMP services with this new method:

```
Router#configure terminal
Enter configuration commands, one per line.  End with CNTL/Z.
Router(config)#snmp-server group COOKRO v1
Router(config)#snmp-server user TESTRO1 COOKRO v1
Router(config)#snmp-server group BOOKRO v2c
Router(config)#snmp-server user TESTRO2 BOOKRO v2c
Router(config)#end
```

Discussion

SNMP services are disabled by default on all Cisco routers. The examples highlighted in the solutions section show only how to configure the router to allow inbound SNMP services so that it will respond to SNMP Get and Set requests. These configuration examples do not enable SNMP traps or informs, which we discuss in Recipe 17.14.

When inbound SNMP services are enabled, the router starts to listen for incoming SNMP requests on UDP port 161. It is important to note that these methods enable SNMP Version 1 and SNMP Version 2c only (SNMPv3 is covered in Recipe 17.23).

The first example shows the older method of enabling SNMP services. It uses the *snmp community* command to enable both SNMPv1 and SNMPv2c simultaneously:

```
Router(config)#snmp-server community ORARO ro
```

Cisco documentation often refers to this as bilingual SNMP support because it allows the router to speak both SNMP languages (or versions).

The *show snmp group* command gives details on exactly what SNMP versions are enabled, as well as the security models they use. Running this command after implementing the first two configuration examples gives the following output:

```
Router#show snmp group
groupname: ORARO                          security model:v1
readview :v1default                       writeview: <no writeview specified>
notifyview: <no notifyview specified>
row status: active

groupname: ORARO                          security model:v2c
readview :v1default                       writeview: <no writeview specified>
notifyview: <no notifyview specified>
row status: active

groupname: ORARW                          security model:v1
readview :v1default                       writeview: v1default
notifyview: <no notifyview specified>
row status: active

groupname: ORARW                          security model:v2c
readview :v1default                       writeview: v1default
notifyview: <no notifyview specified>
row status: active
```

This shows that the groups we have configured each created two entries, one for SNMPv1 and the other for SNMPv2c support. This is possible because SNMPv1 and SNMPv2c use the same community string authorization model. Therefore, the router is capable of responding to either version of SNMP.

With the new method for enabling SNMP services, using the *snmp-server group* command, you can create an SNMP group entry that belongs to a single SNMP security model (SNMPv1 or SNMPv2c). Cisco added this command to support SNMPv3 services, and it may eventually replace the legacy method.

Both methods for enabling SNMP services assign a community string that acts as a password of sorts to protect access. SNMP services run on a well-known UDP port, so the router needs this password to help prevent unauthorized access. The router will simply discard any SNMP requests that contain incorrect SNMP community strings. It is important to note that in both Versions 1 and 2c, SNMP transmits these community strings through the network in clear text, making it relatively insecure.

You can configure the router for either read-only or read-write SNMP service. Read-only access means that users can view the router's MIB tree. This is relatively benign, although information about the router's configuration could be useful when planning an attack on your network. Read-write access, on the other hand, permits users to change some of the values in the MIB tree. A user with read-write access could potentially wreak havoc by disabling IP routing, disabling interfaces, erasing router flash, downloading router configurations, uploading configuration commands, or making a variety of other dangerous changes.

Be extremely careful when providing SNMP write access. If SNMP write access is not absolutely required, we recommend disabling it. Far too many organizations automatically enable full SNMP write access without regard for the dangers of possible unauthorized changes.

If write access is required, then consider using SNMPv3 (discussed in Recipe 17.23). SNMPv3 offers advanced authentication and encryption services that ensure safe delivery over insecure networks. Unfortunately, SNMPv3 is still a relatively young standard, and many NMS systems don't support it yet.

So, in those cases where SNMP Version 1 or 2c write access is an absolute requirement, we recommend using the security features described in Recipes 17.6, 17.7, and 17.8. These describe how to implement SNMP ACLs, limit SNMP views, and restrict SNMP TFTP access to help to reduce the risk.

See Also

Recipe 17.6; Recipe 17.7; Recipe 17.8; Recipe 17.14; Recipe 17.23

17.2   Extracting Router Information via SNMP Tools

Problem

You wish to extract or change router information via SNMP.

Solution

To extract router information via SNMP, we will use the suite of SNMP tools provided with the NET-SNMP toolkit (see Appendix A for more details).

Use *snmpget* to extract a single MIB object from the router's MIB tree. This example uses *snmpget* to extract the router's system contact information:

```
freebsd% snmpget -v1 -c ORARO Router .1.3.6.1.2.1.1.4.0
system.sysContact.0 = Helpdesk  800-555-2992
```

Use *snmpset* to alter MIB objects within the router's MIB tree. The next example demonstrates how to modify MIB variables, using *snmpset* to change the system contact information:

```
freebsd% snmpset -v1 -c ORARW Router .1.3.6.1.2.1.1.4.0 s "Ian Brown 555-1221"
system.sysContact.0 = Ian Brown 555-1221
freebsd% snmpget -v1 -c ORARO Router sysContact.0
system.sysContact.0 = Ian Brown 555-1221
```

The *snmpwalk* utility extracts a series of MIB objects from the router's MIB tree. This example uses *snmpwalk* to extract all of the router's interface descriptions:

```
freebsd% snmpwalk -v1 -c ORARO Router ifDescr
interfaces.ifTable.ifEntry.ifDescr.1 = "Ethernet0"
interfaces.ifTable.ifEntry.ifDescr.2 = "Serial0"
interfaces.ifTable.ifEntry.ifDescr.3 = "Serial1"
interfaces.ifTable.ifEntry.ifDescr.4 = "Null0"
interfaces.ifTable.ifEntry.ifDescr.5 = "Loopback0"
interfaces.ifTable.ifEntry.ifDescr.6 = "Serial0.1"
freebsd%
```

Discussion

For this recipe, we chose to demonstrate basic SNMP functionality by using the suite of SNMP tools provided by the NET-SNMP project (formerly UCD-SNMP). NET-SNMP provides a variety of useful SNMP tools that you can run from the command line interface of any Unix or Windows workstation. This software is freely distributed and available on a variety of platforms, which makes it extremely popular for scripts of all shapes and sizes. We consider NET-SNMP to be a sort of Swiss Army knife of SNMP that wonderfully illustrates the usefulness of SNMP for working with Cisco routers. Of course, many commercial software vendors also provide SNMP tools that are equally effective, frequently including a graphical user interface. The underlying concepts remain the same, even if the command syntax differs. In some cases, it is easier to do the types of SNMP commands shown in this recipe using a graphical user interface rather than a command line utility.

NET-SNMP provides a set of SNMP utilities for performing various useful SNMP functions. This recipe used three of the most basic tools:

snmpget

Gets a single MIB object and displays its contents. To do this, it sends the router an SNMP "get" request for a particular MIB object. The router responds with the value of the MIB object, if present. The command syntax for SNMPv1 and SNMPv2c queries is:

```
snmpget [options] {-c <community-string>} <hostname> [<MIB Object or OID>]
```

snmpwalk

Asks the router for a group of related MIB objects and displays their contents. It does this by sending the router a series of SNMP "get-next" commands to list all available MIB objects under the specified node in a MIB tree. The router will continue to respond to the server's "get-next" requests until it reaches the end of the MIB subtree. The command syntax is as follows:

```
snmpwalk [options] {-c <community-string>} <hostname> [<MIB Object or OID>]
```

Note that leaving out the MIB object or OID causes *snmpwalk* to walk the entire MIB tree. This can cause CPU overload problems on the router as well as congestion problems on low-speed links.

snmpset

Modifies the contents of a MIB object and displays the changed variable, if successful. It works by sending the router an SNMP "set" request for the specified MIB object. If the requested change is legal, the router will change the value of the corresponding MIB variable and respond back.

Not all MIB entries can be changed by an SNMP set. For example, it doesn't make sense to change the physical media type of an interface. And, of course, the router has to be configured to allow SNMP read-write access. The command syntax is as follows:

```
snmpset [options] {-c <community>} <hostname> [<objectID> <type> <value>]
```

Most NMS systems have similar commands that you can access from the command line and use in scripts. See your software documentation for details.

Table 17-2 shows a number of useful MIB entries and their associated OID numbers. Several of these variables are Cisco-specific, and will not make sense if used on equipment from other vendors.

Table 17-2. Common Cisco router SNMP MIB entries

Description	MIB name	OID
Hostname	sysName	.1.3.6.1.2.1.1.5.0
Uptime	sysUpTime	.1.3.6.1.2.1.1.3.0
System Description	sysDescr	.1.3.6.1.2.1.1.1.0
System Contact	sysContact	.1.3.6.1.2.1.1.4.0
System Location	sysLocation	.1.3.6.1.2.1.1.6.0
IOS Version	ciscoImageString.5	.1.3.6.1.4.1.9.9.25.1.1.1.2.5
1 Minute CPU Util.	avgBusy1	.1.3.6.1.4.1.9.2.1.57.0
5 Minute CPU Util.	avgBusy5	.1.3.6.1.4.1.9.2.1.58.0
Free Memory	freeMem	.1.3.6.1.4.1.9.2.1.8.0
IOS Feature Set	ciscoImageString.4	.1.3.6.1.4.1.9.9.25.1.1.1.2.4
Reload Reason	whyReload	.1.3.6.1.4.1.9.2.1.2.0

A complete listing of Cisco supported MIBs are located at the following URL: *http://www.cisco.com/public/sw-center/netmgmt/cmtk/mibs.shtml*. Note that this includes a huge amount of information. However, with a little time and effort you should be able to find a way to extract exactly the information you need.

You can extract the same MIB objects by using SNMPv2c:

```
freebsd% snmpget -v 2c -c ORARO Router sysContact.0
system.sysContact.0 = Ian Brown 416-555-2943
freebsd%
```

The only difference in this example is that we specified the SNMP version number as part of the *snmpget* command syntax. This is useful because SNMPv2c introduced 64-bit counters. Cisco supports a small number of MIB objects that can only be accessed using SNMPv2c (or SNMPv3). One such MIB object is *ifHCInOctets*:

```
Freebsd% snmpwalk -v 2c -c ORARO Router ifHCInOctets
ifHCInOctets.7 = Counter64: 145362298
ifHCInOctets.8 = Counter64: 85311547
Freebsd%
```

This MIB object counts the number of inbound bytes (octets) received by an interface. The older SNMPv1 *ifInOctets* MIB object counts exactly the same thing, but uses a 32-bit variable to hold the number. So the newer object does not roll over to zero as often, making it more useful for high-speed interfaces. If you attempt to get one of these 64-bit counter objects by using SNMPv1, the query will fail.

See Also

Recipe 17.1; Recipe 17.22; Appendix A

17.3   Recording Important Router Information for SNMP Access

Problem

You want to record important information, such as physical locations, contact names, and serial numbers for later SNMP access.

Solution

To record important physical information regarding the router, use the following commands:

```
Router#configure terminal
Enter configuration commands, one per line.  End with CNTL/Z.
Router(config)#snmp-server contact Ian Brown 416-555-2943
Router(config)#snmp-server location 999 Queen St. W., Toronto, Ont.
Router(config)#snmp-server chassis-id JAX123456789
Router(config)#end
Router#
```

Discussion

It is an extremely good network management practice to add useful information such as contact names, router locations, and serial numbers directly into the router configuration. This information can be extracted later using *snmpget* requests, either directly or invoked from scripts that make output easier to understand. This is true not only for Cisco routers, of course. Any time you have to manage remote equipment, you should configure important information like serial numbers and locations so that you can read it with SNMP. When a field technician swaps or moves a piece of equipment, they can update this information. So this way you can easily verify the information you store in your central equipment inventory database.

When you save the contact name, router location, and serial number in the router configuration like this, it is also easy to extract from the command line and configuration files as well:

```
Router#show snmp
Chassis: JAX123456789
Contact: Ian Brown 416-555-2943
Location: 999 Queen St. W., Toronto, Ontario
417 SNMP packets input
    0 Bad SNMP version errors
    141 Unknown community name
    3 Illegal operation for community name supplied
    0 Encoding errors
    224 Number of requested variables
    49 Number of altered variables
    224 Get-request PDUs
    0 Get-next PDUs
    52 Set-request PDUs
299 SNMP packets output
    0 Too big errors (Maximum packet size 1500)
    3 No such name errors
    0 Bad values errors
    0 General errors
    276 Response PDUs
    23 Trap PDUs

SNMP logging: enabled
    Logging to 172.25.1.1.162, 0/10, 21 sent, 2 dropped.
Router#
```

You can also extract individual pieces of information by using the following commands:

```
Router#show snmp contact
Ian Brown 416-555-2943
Router#show snmp location
999 Queen St. W., Toronto, Ontario
Router#show snmp chassis
JAX123456789
Router#
```

It is also useful to extract this information from a backup of the router's configuration file. It is a good network management practice to keep a backup copy of every router's configuration on a central server such as the NMS. Then you can extract vital information like the router's serial number. You will often need this information for service and support when a device fails. Of course, when a device fails, you can't reach it through SNMP, so it can be invaluable to be able to get this information from the backup configuration file. On a Unix server, you can use the *grep* utility to easily extract the required information:

```
Freebsd% grep snmp-server Router.confg
snmp-server community ORARO RO
snmp-server community ORARW RW
snmp-server location 999 Queen St. W., Toronto, Ontario
snmp-server contact Ian Brown 416-555-2943
snmp-server chassis-id JAX123456789
snmp-server host 172.25.1.1 ORATRAP
Freebsd%
```

If the router is reachable, you can also extract this information via SNMP:

```
Freebsd% snmpget -v1 -c ORARO Router .1.3.6.1.2.1.1.6.0
system.sysLocation.0 = 999 Queen St. W., Toronto, Ontario
Freebsd% snmpget -v1 -c ORARO Router .1.3.6.1.2.1.1.4.0
system.sysContact.0 = Ian Brown 416-555-2943
Freebsd% snmpget -v1 -c ORARO Router .1.3.6.1.4.1.9.3.6.3.0
enterprises.9.3.6.3.0 = "JAX123456789"
Freebsd%
```

Recipe 17.5 uses this information to construct a summary inventory report for all of the routers in a network.

17.4   Using SNMP to Extract Inventory Information from a List of Routers

Problem

You want to build a report of important router information for all of your managed routers.

Solution

The following Perl script extracts important router information—such as router name, physical location, contact name, and serial number from a list of routers—and creates a report of this information. The script is intended to be run manually, and no arguments are required or expected.

Here's some example output:

```
Freebsd% ./inventory.pl
   Router          Location                Contact            Serial
   Router     999 Queen St. W., Toronto, Ont  Ian Brown 416-555-2943   JAX123456
   Boston     1273 Main Street, Boston, MA    Bob Irwin 800-555-1221   JAX231567
```

```
Denver      24 Sussex Drive, Denver, CO      Helpdesk  800-555-2992    JAX928362
Frame       999 Queen St. W., Toronto, Ont   Ian Brown 416-555-2943    JAX212321
Toronto     999 Queen St. W., Toronto, Ont   Ian Brown 416-555-2943    JAX283291
Boston2     1273 Main Street, Boston, MA     Bob Irwin 800-555-1221    JAX292228
Denver2     24 Sussex Drive, Denver, CO      Helpdesk  800-555-2992    JAX219115
Freebsd%
```

The Perl code follows in Example 17-1.

Example 17-1. inventory.pl

```perl
#!/usr/bin/perl
#
#    inventory.pl -- a script to extract valuable information
#                    from a Router.  (Name, Location, Contact, S/N)
#
#
# Set behavior
$workingdir="/home/nms";
$snmpro="ORARO";
$rtrlist="$workingdir/RTR_LIST";
#
#
open (RTR, "$rtrlist") || die "Can't open $rtrlist file";
open (LOG, ">$workingdir/RESULT") || die "Can't open $workingdir/RESULT file";
printf "  Router\t\t Location\t\t\tContact\t\t  Serial\n";
printf LOG "  Router\t\t; Location\t\t\t;Contact\t\t ;Serial\n";
while (<RTR>) {
  chomp($rtr="$_");
  $snmpget="/usr/local/bin/snmpget -v1 -c $snmpro $rtr ";
  $rtr=`$snmpget .1.3.6.1.4.1.9.2.1.3.0`;
  $loc=`$snmpget .1.3.6.1.2.1.1.6.0`;
  $con=`$snmpget .1.3.6.1.2.1.1.4.0`;
  $sin=`$snmpget .1.3.6.1.4.1.9.3.6.3.0`;
  chomp(($foo, $RTR) = split (/"/, $rtr));
  chomp(($foo, $LOC) = split (/= /, $loc));
  chomp(($foo, $CON) = split (/= /, $con));
  chomp(($foo, $SIN) = split (/"/, $sin));
  printf ("%-12.12s  %-30.30s  %-25.25s  %-12.12s\n", $RTR, $LOC, $CON, $SIN);
  printf LOG ("%-12.12s; %-30.30s; %-25.25s; %-12.12s\n", $RTR, $LOC, $CON, $SIN);
}
```

Discussion

This script extracts important router information from a list of routers and presents that list in a semicolon-delimited file, as well as displaying it on the screen. It is a very simple script that just extracts MIB variables from a list of routers using *snmpget*, illustrating the value and versatility of SNMP.

This Perl script works by cycling through a list of routers. For each router, it uses SNMP get requests to extract the value of four variables: router name, location, contact, and serial number, as we did manually in Recipe 17.3. The core of this script is NET-SNMP's *snmpget* utility, which extracts SNMP data from the list of routers.

NET-SNMP must be present on the server, and *snmpget* must reside in the */usr/local/ bin* directory before this script will function.

This script contains three important variables that you have to set correctly before it will run properly. First, the variable *$workingdir* contains the directory in which the script resides. Next is the read-only SNMP community string, which is stored in the script's *$snmpro* variable. Substitute your organization's SNMP read-only community string for the example value shown, ORARO. Note that this script assumes that you use the same SNMP read-only community string on all routers.

The third variable, *$rtrlist*, contains the location of the router list. The example script uses a file called RTR_LIST, located in the working directory. You will need to change this variable to point to a file containing a list of routers on your network. The script expects this file to have a single router name per line.

The script produces two types of output. It displays the results on your screen while the script is executing. And the script also logs all results to a file called RESULT that resides in the working directory. The script automatically creates this file the first time you run it, and it overwrites the contents on each subsequent execution.

See Also

Recipe 17.3

17.5   Using Access Lists to Protect SNMP Access

Problem

You want to provide extra security to SNMP using access lists.

Solution

You can use the following commands to restrict which IP source addresses are allowed to access SNMP functions on the router. This is the legacy method:

```
Router#configure terminal
Enter configuration commands, one per line.  End with CNTL/Z.
Router(config)#access-list 99 permit 172.25.1.0 0.0.0.255
Router(config)#access-list 99 permit host 10.1.1.1
Router(config)#access-list 99 deny any
Router(config)#snmp-server community ORARO ro 99
Router(config)#access-list 98 permit 172.25.1.0 0.0.0.255
Router(config)#snmp-server community ORARW rw 98
Router(config)#end
Router#
```

Here is a newer method to do the same thing using SNMP server groups:

```
Router#configure terminal
Enter configuration commands, one per line.  End with CNTL/Z.
```

```
Router(config)#access-list 99 permit 172.25.1.0 0.0.0.255
Router(config)#access-list 99 permit host 10.1.1.1
Router(config)#access-list 99 deny any
Router(config)#snmp-server group COOKRO v1 access 99
Router(config)#snmp-server user TESTRO1 COOKRO v1
Router(config)#end
Router#
```

Beginning with IOS Version 12.3(2)T, support for standard named access lists was added:

```
Router2#configure terminal
Enter configuration commands, one per line.  End with CNTL/Z.
Router2(config)#ip access-list standard SNMPACL
Router2(config-std-nacl)#permit 172.25.1.0 0.0.0.255
Router2(config-std-nacl)#permit host 10.1.1.1
Router2(config-std-nacl)#deny any
Router2(config-std-nacl)#snmp-server community ORARO1 ro SNMPACL
Router2(config)#end
Router2#
```

Discussion

By default, when you enable inbound SNMP services, the router will permit all IP addresses to access the SNMP agent on the standard well-known UDP port number 161. We highly recommend using SNMP ACLs to restrict SNMP access to a few trusted hosts or subnets. This will help to protect sensitive data.

You could restrict SNMP access by simply applying an interface ACL to block incoming SNMP packets that don't come from trusted servers. However, this would not be as effective as using the global SNMP commands shown in this recipe. Because you can apply this method once for the whole router, it is much simpler than applying ACLs to block SNMP on all interfaces separately. Also, using interface ACLs would block not only SNMP packets intended for this router, but also may stop SNMP packets that just happened to be passing through on their way to some other destination device.

Despite the different syntax, all of the examples shown in this recipe work the same way. First, you define a standard access-list. Then you apply this access-list to your SNMP community string. You can assign each SNMP community a separate and unique access-list to restrict access. This can be useful when there are several different people or NMS systems that need to access information on different groups of routers. You can also assign an access-list to a read-write community string to block SNMP set commands from unauthorized IP source addresses.

SNMP access-lists alone are not an effective way of protecting read-write access to your routers. Because SNMP is a UDP protocol, a rogue device with access to your network can spoof the IP source address so that it matches the IP address of your management server. This means that somebody who knows your community string and the IP address of your management server can submit potentially dangerous

SNMP set commands to your router. This information is relatively easy to discover with a protocol analyzer on a well-chosen network segment because SNMP sends packets in clear text.

 Applying a nonexistent access-list to your SNMP configuration commands implicitly allows all IP source addresses to access your router's SNMP services. Always ensure that the access-list exists before applying it to an SNMP community string.

The following command shows the status of a particular access-list:

```
Router#show access-list 99
Standard IP access list 99
    permit 10.1.1.1 (1745 matches)
    permit 172.25.1.0, wildcard bits 0.0.0.255 (477 matches)
    deny    any (7 matches)
Router#
```

Notice that the router has denied seven requests. This means that the router received and discarded seven SNMP requests because source addresses were not allowed. Although the router automatically appends an implicit "deny all" to the end of every access-list, we recommend that you explicitly include a "deny all" statement at the end of each access-list to let you keep track of denied packets like this. It is an easy way of telling how often your routers receive SNMP requests from bad source addresses.

The *show snmp group* command shows you which access-lists are assigned to which SNMP community strings:

```
Router>show snmp group
groupname: ORARO                        security model:v1
readview :v1default                     writeview: <no writeview specified>
notifyview: <no notifyview specified>
row status: active      access-list: 99

groupname: ORARW                        security model:v1
readview :v1default                     writeview: v1default
notifyview: <no notifyview specified>
row status: active      access-list: 98

groupname: ORARO1                          security model:v1
readview : v1default                       writeview: <no writeview specified>
notifyview: <no notifyview specified>
row status: active      access-list: SNMPACL

Router>
```

In this example, the SNMP community string *ORARO* is protected by access-list 99, the SNMP community string *ORARW* is protected by access-list 98, and the SNMP community *ORARO1* is protected by the named access-list *SNMPACL*. Note that the *show snmp group* command is available only in 12.0(3)T and above.

See Also

Recipe 17.1; Recipe 17.7; Chapter 19

17.6 Logging Unauthorized SNMP Attempts

Problem

You want to log unauthorized SNMP attempts.

Solution

Use the following commands to configure your router to log unauthorized SNMP requests:

```
Router#configure terminal
Enter configuration commands, one per line.  End with CNTL/Z.
Router(config)#access-list 99 permit 172.25.1.0 0.0.0.255
Router(config)#access-list 99 permit host 10.1.1.1
Router(config)#access-list 99 deny any log
Router(config)#snmp-server community ORARO ro 99
Router(config)#snmp-server community ORARW rw 99
Router(config)#end
Router#
```

Discussion

If you are concerned about unauthorized access to SNMP services on your router, it can be quite useful to configure the router to maintain detailed records of every failed request. These verbose log messages can provide information on incorrectly configured management servers as well as malicious (or just plain nosy) users.

Simply adding the keyword *log* to the *deny any* line in your access-list instructs the router to log all unauthorized SNMP attempts.

The following command will display the status of your SNMP access-list:

```
Router#show access-list 99
Standard IP access list 99
    permit 10.1.1.1  (1293 matches)
    permit 172.25.1.0, wildcard bits 0.0.0.255 (630 matches)
    deny   any log (17 matches)
Router#
```

Unlike the example shown in Recipe 17.6, the *show access-list* output now includes the *log* keyword on the *deny any* line. The router will now send information on every unauthorized SNMP request to the logging facility (see Chapter 18 for more information on logging). Use the *show logging* EXEC command to view the router's internal logging buffer:

```
Router#show logging
Syslog logging: enabled (0 messages dropped, 0 flushes, 0 overruns)
```

```
      Console logging: disabled
      Monitor logging: level debugging, 26 messages logged
            Logging to: vty2(0)
      Buffer logging: level debugging, 49 messages logged
      Trap logging: level informational, 53 message lines logged
            Logging to 172.25.1.1, 53 message lines logged
            Logging to 172.25.1.3, 53 message lines logged

   Log Buffer (4096 bytes):
   Apr 15 22:33:21: %SEC-6-IPACCESSLOGS: list 99 denied 192.168.22.13 1 packet
   Apr 15 22:39:18: %SEC-6-IPACCESSLOGS: list 99 denied 10.121.212.11 3 packets
   Router#
```

This example shows that access-list 99, our SNMP access-list, has denied access attempts by two IP source addresses, 192.168.22.13 and 10.121.212.11, respectively. You can see that the final logging entry shows that the ACL denied three packets from source address 10.121.212.11. Note that every packet received doesn't result in a separate log entry. If you are building a custom script to extract failed SNMP attempts, you will need to keep this in mind.

See Also

Recipe 17.1; Recipe 17.6; Chapter 19

17.7   Limiting MIB Access

Problem

You want to limit which MIB variables can be remotely accessed with SNMP.

Solution

You can use the following commands to restrict SNMP access to portions of the MIB tree. This example shows the legacy configuration method:

```
   Router#configure terminal
   Enter configuration commands, one per line.  End with CNTL/Z.
   Router(config)#access-list 99 permit 172.25.1.0 0.0.0.255
   Router(config)#access-list 99 deny any log
   Router(config)#snmp-server view ORAVIEW mib-2 included
   Router(config)#snmp-server view ORAVIEW at excluded
   Router(config)#snmp-server view ORAVIEW cisco included
   Router(config)#snmp-server community ORARO view ORAVIEW ro 99
   Router(config)#snmp-server view RESTRICTED lsystem.55 included
   Router(config)#snmp-server community ORARW view RESTRICTED rw 99
   Router(config)#end
   Router#
```

Cisco also has a new method for restricting MIB access, which uses the *snmp-server group* command:

```
   Router#configure terminal
   Enter configuration commands, one per line.  End with CNTL/Z.
```

```
Router(config)#snmp-server view ORAVIEW mib-2 included
Router(config)#snmp-server view ORAVIEW at excluded
Router(config)#snmp-server view ORAVIEW cisco included
Router(config)#snmp-server group TEST v1 read ORAVIEW
Router(config)#snmp-server user ORARO TEST v1
Router(config)#snmp-server view RESTRICTED lsystem.55 included
Router(config)#snmp-server group TEST2 v1 write RESTRICTED
Router(config)#snmp-server user ORARW TEST2 v1
Router(config)#end
Router#
```

Discussion

By default, enabling SNMP services on your router allows SNMP servers to access the entire SNMP MIB tree. However, sometimes you want to limit which MIB variables can be remotely retrieved or changed, usually for security reasons. We strongly recommend that you limit SNMP write access to only those MIB objects that you absolutely need to change remotely. Remember that it is very easy for a malicious user to cause serious network problems by modifying MIB variables that control the router's configuration.

You can assign an SNMP MIB view to an individual community string or share a view among several community strings including both read-only and read-write access strings. Assigning a MIB view to a read-only community string restricts which MIB variables can be displayed. Similarly, assigning an SNMP MIB view to a read-write community string restricts which MIB variables you can view or alter.

A MIB view can restrict access to a single MIB object; it can allow access to all but one MIB object, or anything in between. For instance, in both examples, we created a view named RESTRICTED to the read-write community string ORARW. This view restricts access to a single MIB entry, lsystem.55, which is the MIB object that triggers the router to send its configuration file to a TFTP server (for nightly configuration backups). The router will prevent any other access to the MIB tree.

We also create an SNMP view named ORAVIEW, which is less restrictive. In this case, we want to allow access to the MIB-2 variables, but prevent access to the ARP table (AT) tree, which we can do using the *exclude* keyword. We also allow access to the entire Cisco proprietary MIB tree by including the cisco MIB.

To illustrate the functionality of SNMP MIB views, we can first run an SNMP walk of a router's default MIB tree:

```
Freebsd% snmpwalk -v1 -c ORARO Router
system.sysDescr.0 = Cisco Internetwork Operating System Software
IOS (tm) C2600 Software (C2600-JK9O3S-M), Version 12.2(7a), RELEASE SOFTWARE (fc2)
Copyright (c) 1986-2002 by cisco Systems, Inc.
Compiled Thu 21-Feb-02 03:48 by pwade
system.sysObjectID.0 = OID: enterprises.9.1.209
system.sysUpTime.0 = Timeticks: (26809590) 3 days, 2:28:15.90
system.sysContact.0 = Ian Brown 416-555-2943
system.sysName.0 = Router.oreilly.com
```

```
system.sysLocation.0 = 999 Queen St. W., Toronto, Ont.
system.sysServices.0 = 78
system.sysORLastChange.0 = Timeticks: (0) 0:00:00.00
interfaces.ifNumber.0 = 10
interfaces.ifTable.ifEntry.ifIndex.1 = 1
interfaces.ifTable.ifEntry.ifIndex.2 = 2
interfaces.ifTable.ifEntry.ifIndex.3 = 3
interfaces.ifTable.ifEntry.ifIndex.4 = 4
interfaces.ifTable.ifEntry.ifIndex.5 = 5
interfaces.ifTable.ifEntry.ifIndex.6 = 6
interfaces.ifTable.ifEntry.ifIndex.7 = 7
interfaces.ifTable.ifEntry.ifIndex.8 = 8
interfaces.ifTable.ifEntry.ifIndex.9 = 9
<8000+ lines Removed>
End of MIB
Freebsd%
```

Walking the full MIB Tree of a Cisco router can take a great deal of time. This router's MIB Tree consisted of more than 8,000 entries. However, if we implement a simple SNMP MIB view, the result is quite different:

```
Router#configure terminal
Enter configuration commands, one per line.  End with CNTL/Z.
Router(config)#snmp-server view TEST system.5 included
Router(config)#snmp-server community COOKBOOK view TEST ro
Router(config)#end
Router#
```

In this example, the router restricts access to a single MIB entry, *sysName* (system.5). Now when we attempt to walk the entire MIB Tree again, the router sends only this single variable:

```
Freebsd% snmpwalk -v1 -c COOKBOOK Router
system.sysName.0 = Router.oreilly.com
End of MIB
Freebsd%
```

Notice that the router displays a single entry, *sysName*, and reports that it has reached the "End of MIB," effectively preventing more than 8,000 MIB objects from being accessed via this particular community string.

You can use the *show snmp group* EXEC command to see which views are assigned to which community string:

```
Router>show snmp group
groupname: ORARO                        security model:v1
readview :v1default                     writeview: <no writeview specified>
notifyview: <no notifyview specified>
row status: active

groupname: COOKBOOK                      security model:v1
readview :TEST                          writeview: <no writeview specified>
notifyview: <no notifyview specified>
row status: active

Router>
```

In this example, the community string ORARO has the default SNMP view, v1default. This means the entire MIB tree is accessible.

To see which MIB entries are assigned to which SNMP MIB view, use the following (hidden) command:

```
Router#show snmp view
ORAVIEW mib-2 - included nonvolatile active
ORAVIEW at - excluded nonvolatile active
ORAVIEW cisco - included nonvolatile active
v1default internet - included volatile active
v1default internet.6.3.15 - excluded volatile active
v1default internet.6.3.16 - excluded volatile active
v1default internet.6.3.18 - excluded volatile active
RESTRICTED cisco - included nonvolatile active
RESTRICTED lsystem.55 - included nonvolatile active
Router#
```

Table 17-3 lists a number of valid MIB trees that the router will accept within a SNMP view. Keep in mind that this is not an exhaustive list, and that the router will also accept OIDs in their numerical format.

Table 17-3. Valid OID-trees for use with SNMP views

Keyword	Description
internet	Entire MIB tree
mib-2	Entire MIB-II tree
system	System branch of the MIB-II tree
interfaces	Interface branch of the MIB-II tree
at	ARP table branch of the MIB-II tree
ip	IP routing table branch of the MIB-II tree
icmp	ICMP statistics branch of the MIB-II tree
tcp	TCP statistics branch of the MIB-II tree
udp	UDP statistics branch of the MIB-II tree
transmission	Transmission statistics of the MIB-II tree
snmp	SNMP statistics branch of the MIB-II tree
ospf	OSPF MIB
bgp	BGP MIB
rmon	RMON MIB
cisco	Cisco's enterprise MIB tree
x25	X.25 MIB
ifEntry	Interface statistics of MIB objects
lsystem	Cisco's system MIB

See Also

Recipe 17.1; Recipe 17.2

17.8   Using SNMP to Modify a Router's Running Configuration

Problem

You want to use SNMP to either download or modify a router's configuration.

Solution

To upload or download a current copy of your router's configuration file to a TFTP server via SNMP, you have to first configure the router for read-write SNMP access:

```
Router#configure terminal
Enter configuration commands, one per line.  End with CNTL/Z.
Router(config)#snmp-server community ORARW rw
Router(config)#end
```

To download the current configuration file, you will need to create an empty file on your TFTP server. In this case, we assume a Unix server, although TFTP server software is available for essentially every popular operating system. Then you can send an SNMP command to the router to trigger the TFTP download:

```
Freebsd% touch /tftpboot/router.cfg
Freebsd% chmod 666 /tftpboot/router.cfg
Freebsd% snmpset -v1 -c ORARW Router .1.3.6.1.4.1.9.2.1.55.172.25.1.1 s router.cfg
enterprises.9.2.1.55.172.25.1.1 = "router.cfg"
Freebsd%
```

You can use SNMP to trigger the router to upload a configuration file from your TFTP server via SNMP as follows:

```
Freebsd% echo "no ip source-route" > /tftpboot/new.cfg
Freebsd% echo "end" >> /tftpboot/new.cfg
Freebsd% chmod 666 /tftpboot/new.cfg
Freebsd% snmpset -v1 -c ORARW Router .1.3.6.1.4.1.9.2.1.53.172.25.1.1 s new.cfg
enterprises.9.2.1.53.172.25.1.1 = "new.cfg"
Freebsd% snmpset -v1 -c ORARW Router .1.3.6.1.4.1.9.2.1.54.0 i 1
enterprises.9.2.1.54.0 = 1
Freebsd%
```

Discussion

The ability to extract or modify your router's configuration via SNMP is powerful yet scary. These examples illustrate the power of SNMP read-write access and the main reason we advocate SNMP security features. We highly recommend that you read recipe 17.11 before allowing open SNMP write access on your routers. That recipe demonstrates an effective way to mitigate unauthorized tampering with your router's configuration files.

This first example illustrates how to extract your router's running configuration file to a TFTP server using SNMP. Before a typical TFTP server will accept a file transfer, a world-writable file must exist. On a Unix platform, the *touch* command creates this file, and the *chmod* command ensures that it has the proper file attributes.

The *snmpset* command instructs the router to send its running configuration file to a particular file on a particular TFTP server:

```
Freebsd% snmpset -v1 -c ORARW Router .1.3.6.1.4.1.9.2.1.55.172.25.1.1 s router.cfg
```

In this command, *Router* is the name (or IP address) of the router. The read-write SNMP community string is *ORARW*. The MIB OID value is actually in two parts. The first part, .1.3.6.1.4.1.9.2.1.55, is the OID value in the Cisco MIB extension that instructs the router to send its configuration file. The second part, 172.25.1.1 in this case, is the IP address of your TFTP server. And *router.cfg* is the name of the file as it will appear on the TFTP server. In the other argument, the single letter "s" before the filename designates that the argument that follows will be a character string.

It is extremely useful to be able to extract a router's configuration file like this. The Bourne shell script in Example 17-2 uses this method to extract and store the current configuration file from a Cisco router. The script just automates the commands listed in the solution section to simplify the extraction of router configuration files.

The script takes a single argument, the router name or IP address, and it stores the router configuration file in the /tftpboot directory. The file will be the name of the router, with ".auto" appended to it (e.g., router.auto).

Example 17-2. conf

```
#!/bin/sh
#
#    conf -- A compact script to extract router configs to a
#            tftp server.
#
#
#  set behavior
snmprw="ORARW"
tftp="172.25.1.1"
#
#
router=$1
if [ "$router" = "" ]; then
echo "Usage: `basename $0` <hostname | ip address>" >&2 && exit 1
else
rm /tftpboot/$router-auto
touch /tftpboot/$router-auto
chmod 666 /tftpboot/$router-auto
snmpset="snmpset -v1 -c $snmprw $router "
$snmpset .1.3.6.1.4.1.9.2.1.55.$tftp s $router-auto
if [ -w /tftpboot/$router-auto -a -s /tftpboot/$router-auto ]; then
echo "Completed Successfully"
else
echo "Operation Failed"
fi
fi
```

You would run this script as follows:

```
Freebsd% ./conf router
Completed Successfully
Freebsd%
```

This script assumes NET-SNMP is on the server, and requires two variables to be set, *snmprw* and *tftp*. The *snmprw* variable contains the SNMP read-write community string of your organization, and the *tftp* variable contains the IP address of your TFTP server.

The second example in the Solution loads new configuration commands into a router. You must have a world readable file containing these router configuration commands in your TFTP directory before you can upload anything. So in the example, we have created a simple configuration file. In the example, we used Unix *echo* commands to create the file, although in practice you should probably use a text editor to help limit the number of typing errors in your router's configuration. The last line in the configuration file should have the *end* command. This prevents the router from complaining about an unexpected end to the configuration file.

Note that when you upload a configuration file like this, the router merges the commands into its existing configuration, just as it does when you type the commands at the router's console.

There are two important differences between *snmpset* commands to upload or download a configuration file. The first is the different OID values. Be very careful that you get the right value here because you don't want to accidentally upload an old configuration when you're trying to download. The second difference is that, after uploading the configuration file, we issued another different *snmpset* command. This second command saves the configuration changes to NVRAM. This is the same as logging into the router and typing *write memory* or *copy running-config startup-config*.

See Also

Recipe 17.2; Recipe 17.6; Recipe 17.8; Appendix A

17.9   Using SNMP to Copy a New IOS Image

Problem

You want use SNMP to remotely upgrade a router's IOS.

Solution

Before you can upload or download the router's IOS image to a TFTP server, you have to set up a valid read-write SNMP community string:

```
Router#configure terminal
Enter configuration commands, one per line.  End with CNTL/Z.
```

```
Router(config)#snmp-server community ORARW rw
Router(config)#end
```

Then you can download a copy of your router's current IOS file to your TFTP server with the following Unix commands:

```
Freebsd% touch /tftpboot/c2600-jk9o3s-mz.122-7a.bin
Freebsd% chmod 666 /tftpboot/c2600-jk9o3s-mz.122-7a.bin
Freebsd% snmpset -v1 -c ORARW Router .1.3.6.1.4.1.9.2.10.9.172.25.1.1 s c2600-jk9o3s-
mz.122-7a.bin
enterprises.9.2.10.9.172.25.1.1 = "c2600-jk9o3s-mz.122-7a.bin"
Freebsd%
```

Use the following commands to upload an IOS file from your TFTP server to the router's flash memory:

```
Freebsd% chmod 666 /tftpboot/c2600-jk9o3s-mz.122-7a.bin
Freebsd% snmpset -v1 -c ORARW Router .1.3.6.1.4.1.9.2.10.6.0 i 1
enterprises.9.2.10.6.0 = 1
Freebsd% snmpset -v1 -c ORARW Router.1.3.6.1.4.1.9.2.10.12.172.25.1.1 s c2600-jk9o3s-
mz.122-7a.bin
enterprises.9.2.10.12.172.25.1.1 = "c2600-jk9o3s-mz.122-7a.bin"
Freebsd%
```

Discussion

The first example demonstrates how to use SNMP to force a router to download its IOS file to a TFTP server. Most TFTP servers will not accept an incoming transfer unless the destination file is world writable. On Unix computers, the *touch* command creates a file, and the *chmod* command gives it the proper file attributes.

This *snmpset* command instructs the router to use TFTP to copy its IOS file to a particular file on the specified server:

```
Freebsd% snmpset -v1 -c ORARW Router .1.3.6.1.4.1.9.2.10.9.172.25.1.1 s c2600-jk9o3s-
mz.122-7a.bin
```

In this case, Router is the router's name or IP address, and we use ORARW for the read-write SNMP community string. The OID value of the Cisco MIB variable that instructs the router to transfer its IOS image is .1.3.6.1.4.1.9.2.10.9. You concatenate the server's IP address, which is 172.25.1.1 in this example, to the end of the OID value. The last argument, c2600-jk9o3s-mz.122-7a.bin, is the name of the file as it will appear on the TFTP server.

This command is useful because it allows you to easily build a central library of all running IOS versions on your network. Then, if you have problems with a router and need to replace it, you can easily make sure that the new device is running the same IOS version as the old one. It is also useful if you discover that a particular IOS version behaves better, and you want to copy that version into other routers.

The second example shows how to use SNMP to start a TFTP upload of a new IOS version. This is useful because it makes it easy to build a script to automate changing the IOS versions on a large number of similar routers. You should be careful when doing this, however. It is safe to copy a new IOS image into the router's flash memory on most Cisco routers. The router will continue running the old version until it reboots. So a good procedure for doing a large number of upgrades like this would be to run a script to copy the new images to the routers, and then you should check each router to ensure that the upload completed successfully before rebooting.

The method shown for uploading a new IOS file to a router is similar to the method for downloading an IOS file. The one important difference is the step that erases the flash before the uploading commences. In our example, the first *snmpset* command erases the flash:

```
Freebsd% snmpset -v1 -c ORARW Router .1.3.6.1.4.1.9.2.10.6.0 i 1
enterprises.9.2.10.6.0 = 1
```

This step is only necessary if there is not enough flash space available to load the new IOS file. Then the second command actually copies the image into the router's flash memory:

```
Freebsd% snmpset -v1 -c ORARW Router.1.3.6.1.4.1.9.2.10.12.172.25.1.1 s c2600-jk9o3s-
mz.122-7a.bin
```

Note that some types of Cisco routers do not support this method for uploading IOS images. In particular, Cisco 2500 series routers actually run directly from the IOS image in flash instead of copying an image of the IOS into processor memory at boot time. Changing the IOS version in flash would cause serious problems, so the router will not allow you to do it.

See Also

Recipe 17.2; Recipe 17.6; Recipe 17.8; Appendix A

17.10 Using SNMP to Perform Mass Configuration Changes

Problem

You want to automate the distribution of a set of configuration commands to a large number of routers.

Solution

The following Perl script will distribute configuration commands to a large number of routers. It works by using SNMP to trigger TFTP file transfers into the routers. In effect, this script lets you automatically distribute a series configuration commands to a list of routers. Automating routine changes like this saves time and effort, but more importantly, it virtually eliminates typographical mistakes.

Here's some example output:

```
Freebsd% ./snmpcfg.pl
===================================
toronto - Update Successful
toronto - Wr Mem Successful
===================================
boston  - Update Successful
boston  - Wr Mem Successful
===================================
denver  - Update Successful
denver  - Wr Mem Successful
===================================
newyork - Update Successful
newyork - Wr Mem Successful
===================================
detroit - Update Failed
===================================
chicago - Update Successful
chicago - Wr Mem Successful
===================================
sanfran - Update Successful
sanfran - Wr Mem Successful
===================================
seattle - Update Successful
seattle - Wr Mem Successful
===================================
Freebsd%
```

The Perl code follows in Example 17-3.

Example 17-3. snmpcfg.pl

```perl
#!/usr/bin/perl -w
#
#     snmpcfg.pl -- a script to perform mass configuration changes to
#                   a list of routers using SNMP.
#
#
# Set behavior
$workingdir="/home/nms";
$snmprw="ORARW";
$tftpsrv="172.25.1.1";
#
#
$rtrlist="$workingdir/RTR_LIST";
open (RTR, "$rtrlist") || die "Can't open $rtrlist file";
open (LOG, ">$workingdir/RESULT") || die "Can't open $workingdir/RESULT file";
#
while (<RTR>) {
  chomp($rtr="$_");
  print LOG "=================================== \n";
  print "=================================== \n";
  $snmpset="/usr/local/bin/snmpset -t 20 -r 2 -v1 -c $snmprw $rtr ";
  chomp($result=`$snmpset .1.3.6.1.4.1.9.2.1.50.$tftpsrv s SNMPCFG`);
```

Example 17-3. snmpcfg.pl

```
  if ($result=~/.+ = "(.+)"$/ ) {
          if( $1 eq SNMPCFG ) {
              print LOG "$rtr - Update Successful\n";
              print "$rtr - Update Successful\n";
              chomp($result=`$snmpset .1.3.6.1.4.1.9.2.1.54.0 i 1`);
              if ($result=~/.+ = (.+)$/ ) {
                      if( $1 == 1 ) {
                          print LOG "$rtr - Wr Mem Successful\n";
                          print "$rtr - Wr Mem Successful\n";
                      }
                      else {
                          print LOG "$rtr - Wr Mem Failed\n";
                          print "$rtr - Wr Mem Failed\n";
                      }
              }
              else {
                  print LOG "$rtr - Wr Mem Failed\n";
                  print "$rtr - Wr Mem Failed\n";
              }
          }
          else {
              print LOG "$rtr - Update Failed\n";
              print "$rtr - Update Failed\n";
          }
  }
  else {
    print LOG "$rtr - Update Failed\n";
    print "$rtr - Update Failed\n";
  }
}
```

Discussion

This script distributes a set of configuration commands to a list of routers using SNMP to trigger TFTP transfers, as we did manually in Recipe 17.9. The script goes through a list of routers in sequence, performing an *snmpset* command on each one to force the router to upload a pre-defined configuration file. If the file transfer completes successfully, then the script will issue another *snmpset* command that permanently saves the running configuration file to NVRAM. The script displays a status report to the terminal screen and sends the same messages to a flat log file.

This script requires the NET-SNMP toolset. The script looks for the executable *snmpset* in the default location, */usr/local/bin*. If your system has *snmpset* in another location, then you have to change the variable *$snmpset*.

Before running the script, change the variable *$workingdir* to point to the directory where the script resides. Also set the variable *$snmprw* to your organization's SNMP read-write community string. This script will not work with a read-only community string. And you will need to set the value of *$tftpsrv* to the IP address of the TFTP server where the configuration file resides.

The script expects to find the router list located in the working directory in a file called *RTR_LIST*. This file should have a single router name per line. You can change the default name and location of this file by modifying the variable *$rtrlist*.

By default, the script will copy the configuration file SNMPCFG residing in the /tftpboot directory to every router in the list. The configuration file must be world readable. This file should include a list of Cisco configuration commands as you would type them from a command prompt on the router. We recommended inserting the keyword *end* at the end of the configuration file to prevent spurious error messages. If you want to change the filename, you will need to change both occurrences of the default filename SNMPCFG to the name of the new file.

The script creates a status report in a file called RESULT in the working directory. The script will automatically create this file the first time you execute it and will clear its contents each time the script is run. The status file allows you to run the script unattended and check for failures later. The easiest way to check for failures is to use the Unix *grep* utility to search the status report file for the keyword Fail.

See Also

Recipe 17.2; Recipe 17.6; Recipe 17.8; Recipe 17.9; Appendix A

17.11 Preventing Unauthorized Configuration Modifications

Problem

You want to ensure that only authorized devices can use SNMP and TFTP to send or receive configuration information.

Solution

You can use the *snmp-server tftp-server-list* **configuration command** to restrict which TFTP servers the router can use in response to an SNMP trigger to upload or download configuration information:

```
Router#configure terminal
Enter configuration commands, one per line.  End with CNTL/Z.
Router(config)#access-list 92 permit 172.25.1.1
Router(config)#access-list 92 deny any log
Router(config)#snmp-server tftp-server-list 92
Router(config)#snmp-server community ORARW rw
Router(config)#end
Router#
```

Begin with IOS Version 12.3(2)T; support for standard named access lists was added:

```
Router2#configure terminal
Enter configuration commands, one per line.  End with CNTL/Z.
```

```
Router2(config)#ip access-list standard TFTPACL
Router2(config-std-nacl)#permit 172.25.1.1
Router2(config-std-nacl)#deny any log
Router2(config-std-nacl)#exit
Router2(config)#snmp-server tftp-server-list TFTPACL
Router2(config)#snmp-server community ORARW rw
Router2(config)#end
Router2#
```

Discussion

By default, the router will send or receive configuration information to any TFTP
server. But this can be dangerous because the SNMP request that triggers these transfers cannot be 100 percent protected. Recipe 17.6 showed how you can restrict
SNMP access to a specified list of devices. But because SNMP uses UDP, it is not difficult for a malicious user to put the IP address of one of these allowed devices in the
source of an SNMP packet, which means that the router will execute the request.
This packet could instruct the router to upload or download configuration information to or from any TFTP server. The attacker could then easily compromise the
security of the entire network.

Therefore, we strongly recommend that you use the *tftp-server-list* command to
restrict which TFTP servers your router will forward its configuration file to and
which TFTP servers your router will accept configuration changes from.

It is important to note that this command only restricts TFTP sessions that the router
initiates via SNMP. You can still use other TFTP servers for file transfers initiated
from the router's command prompt.

> If the access-list assigned to the tftp-server-list does not exist, then the
> router implicitly allows access for all TFTP servers.

The example authorizes the router to access only a single TFTP server. Notice that
the access-list is designed to log all unauthorized attempts:

```
Router(config)#access-list 92 permit 172.25.1.1
Router(config)#access-list 92 deny any log
```

We highly recommend doing this because it not only prevents unauthorized access,
but it also gives you information about what devices have been involved in the
attempts. If there are malicious users with access to you network, this can help you
figure out who they are.

Note that this is a global command that affects all SNMP read-write community
strings. There is no way to specify a different *tftp-server-list* for each community string.

See Also

Recipe 17.1; Recipe 17.6

17.12 Making Interface Table Numbers Permanent

Problem

You want to ensure that your router uses the same SNMP interface numbers every time it reboots.

Solution

To ensure that SNMP interface numbers remain permanent after a router power cycle, use the following command. This is a global command that affects all interfaces:

```
Router#configure terminal
Enter configuration commands, one per line.  End with CNTL/Z.
Router(config)#snmp-server ifindex persist
Router(config)#end
Router#
```

You can also fix the SNMP interface number of a single interface as follows:

```
Router#configure terminal
Enter configuration commands, one per line.  End with CNTL/Z.
Router(config)#interface Serial0/0
Router(config-if)#snmp ifindex persist
Router(config-if)#exit
Router(config)#end
Router#
```

This command is available in IOS Versions 12.1(5)T and above.

Discussion

Most engineers do not understand that the internal SNMP interface numbers assigned by the router are not stable. That is, the SNMP interface numbers are prone to change after router reboot, especially if you add or remove logical interfaces (i.e., subinterfaces) or physical modules.

This issue has plagued many administrators and software vendors for years. The problem is that most network performance software packages poll for interface data by using the unique interface number assigned by the router. However, if these numbers change after a router reboots, then the performance data becomes meaningless, since there is no guarantee that you are still polling the same interface. Most high-end SNMP performance software companies have built "fixes" to circumvent this exact issue.

Changing interface numbers particularly affects the router's built-in RMON monitoring. With RMON, you can configure the router to monitor its own MIB values and assign threshold values in which to send notifications. Unfortunately, before the new functionality shown in this recipe came along, RMON polling was not reliable for interface specific statistics. RMON services are discussed in detail in Recipe 17.23.

There are some minor costs to using this feature. First, each interface number requires 25 bytes of NVRAM to store. Second, some administrators have reported slightly slower boot times on routers that employ this feature. Otherwise, this new functionality is mostly transparent to the network administrator.

To illustrate the *ifindex* stability problem, consider the interface numbers on a typical router:

```
Freebsd% snmpwalk -v1 -c ORARO Router ifDescr
interfaces.ifTable.ifEntry.ifDescr.1 = "BRI0/0"
interfaces.ifTable.ifEntry.ifDescr.2 = "Ethernet0/0"
interfaces.ifTable.ifEntry.ifDescr.3 = "BRI0/0:1"
interfaces.ifTable.ifEntry.ifDescr.4 = "BRI0/0:2"
interfaces.ifTable.ifEntry.ifDescr.5 = "FastEthernet1/0"
interfaces.ifTable.ifEntry.ifDescr.6 = "Null0"
interfaces.ifTable.ifEntry.ifDescr.7 = "Loopback0"
```

Notice that the router assigns a unique number to each interface, starting with one. In this example, the interface FastEthernet1/0 has an *ifindex* value of 5. This is the number you would use in SNMP polls for various interface level performance statistics. Next, we will power-down the router and remove the BRI module before restoring power:

```
Freebsd% snmpwalk -v1 -c ORARO Router ifDescr
interfaces.ifTable.ifEntry.ifDescr.1 = "Ethernet0/0"
interfaces.ifTable.ifEntry.ifDescr.2 = "FastEthernet1/0"
interfaces.ifTable.ifEntry.ifDescr.3 = "Null0"
interfaces.ifTable.ifEntry.ifDescr.4 = "Loopback0"
```

Notice that the BRI interface entries are gone and the remaining interface numbers have completely changed. The *FastEthernet1/0* interface now appears as interface number two. And, worse still, there is no interface number 5 at all. So if you had been doing performance analysis on this port, it would suddenly stop working.

Returning the router to its original state restores the original interface numbers:

```
Freebsd% snmpwalk -v1 -c ORARO Router ifDescr
interfaces.ifTable.ifEntry.ifDescr.1 = "BRI0/0"
interfaces.ifTable.ifEntry.ifDescr.2 = "Ethernet0/0"
interfaces.ifTable.ifEntry.ifDescr.3 = "BRI0/0:1"
interfaces.ifTable.ifEntry.ifDescr.4 = "BRI0/0:2"
interfaces.ifTable.ifEntry.ifDescr.5 = "FastEthernet1/0"
interfaces.ifTable.ifEntry.ifDescr.6 = "Null0"
interfaces.ifTable.ifEntry.ifDescr.7 = "Loopback0"
```

However, if we enable the *snmp ifindex persist* command before powering down the router and removing the BRI module, the only difference is that the three entries associated with the BRI interface are removed:

```
Freebsd% snmpwalk -v1 -c ORARO 172.25.1.8 ifDescr
interfaces.ifTable.ifEntry.ifDescr.2 = "Ethernet0/0"
interfaces.ifTable.ifEntry.ifDescr.5 = "FastEthernet1/0"
interfaces.ifTable.ifEntry.ifDescr.6 = "Null0"
interfaces.ifTable.ifEntry.ifDescr.7 = "Loopback0"
```

The remaining interfaces have retained their original interface numbers after the router reboot. In particular, the FastEthernet1/0 interface is once again interface number 5, which means that all polled data will still be useful.

See Also

Recipe 17.23

17.13 Enabling SNMP Traps and Informs

Problem

You want the router to generate SNMP traps or informs in response to various network events.

Solution

The following configuration commands will enable your router to send unsolicited SNMP traps to a network management server:

```
Router#configure terminal
Enter configuration commands, one per line.  End with CNTL/Z.
Router(config)#snmp-server enable traps
Router(config)#snmp-server host 172.25.1.1 ORATRAP config entity envmon hsrp
Router(config)#snmp-server host nms.oreilly.com ORATRAP bgp snmp envmon
Router(config)#end
Router#
```

Notice that the *snmp-server host* command will accept either an IP address or a hostname.

Beginning with SNMP Version 2c, Cisco routers also support SNMP informs. To enable SNMP informs, use the following commands:

```
Router#configure terminal
Enter configuration commands, one per line.  End with CNTL/Z.
Router(config)#snmp-server enable informs
Router(config)#snmp-server host 172.25.1.1 informs version 2c ORATRAP snmp envmon
Router(config)#end
Router#
```

Discussion

SNMP Traps originate from the router's agent and are sent via UDP (port 162) to the network management station (NMS). Unlike the information that the router sends to the NMS in response to an SNMP poll, a trap is unsolicited. The router's agent decides that something important has happened, and that it needs to tell the NMS about it. Before the router agent can send traps, you must enable global trap support (see Table 17-4) and configure the trap host.

SNMP traps are one of the basic elements of fault management. In fact, Requirements for IP Version 4 Routers (RFC 1812) states that all routers must be capable of sending SNMP traps.

Cisco routers can send a large variety of different SNMP traps, including both standard traps, described in RFCs, and Cisco specific traps. The first step in configuring trap support is to enable the particular trap types you wish to use. In our examples, we choose to enable all SNMP trap types by using the configuration command *snmp-server enable traps*. The fact that we didn't specify individual trap types implicitly enables all trap types. However, you can restrict the router to send only certain types of traps that you are interested in receiving. The various trap-type keywords are shown in Table 17-4. Note that this is a global command that affects all SNMP trap receivers.

Table 17-4. Cisco SNMP trap types

Keyword	Description
bgp	Allow BGP state change traps
calltracker	Send Call Tracker cal start/end notifications
config	Allow SNMP configuration traps
cpu	Send cpu related notifications
director	Allow Distributed Director notifications
dspu	Allow dspu event traps
eigrp	Enable EGIRP SIA and neighbor auth failure traps
entity	Allow SNMP entity traps
envmon	Allow environmental monitor traps
flash	Send flash insertion and removal traps
frame-relay	Allow SNMP frame-relay traps
hsrp	Allow SNMP HSRP traps
iplocalpool	Allow IP local pool traps
ipmobile	Allow mobile IP notifications
Ipsec	Send IPsec notifications
isdn	Allow SNMP ISDN traps
l2tun-pseudowire-status	Send pseudowire state change notifications
l2tun-session	Send Layer 2 tunnel session traps
llc2	Sends logical link control type-2 notifications
memory	Allow memory pool and buffer pool notifications
mpls-ldp	Send MPLS ldp status change traps
mpls-traffic-eng	Send MPLS TE tunnel status change notifications
mpls-vpn	Send MPLS VPN notifications
ospf	Send OSPF sham link notifications
pim	Allow PIM notificaitons

Table 17-4. Cisco SNMP trap types (continued)

Keyword	Description
repeater	Send standard repeater notifications
rsrb	Allow rsrb event traps
rsvp	Allow RSVP flow change traps
rtr	Allow SNMP Response Time Reporter traps
sdlc	Allow SDLC event traps
sdllc	Allow SDLLC event traps
snmp	Allow SNMP-type notifications
srp	Send SRP notifications
stun	Allow stun event traps
syslog	Allow SNMP syslog traps
tty	Allow TCP connection traps
udp-port	The server host's UDP port number
voice	Allow SNMP voice traps
vrrp	Send VRRP notifications
vsimaster	Send VSI master notifications
X25	Allow x25 event traps

For example, you would use the following commands to tell the router to send only BGP and environmental-type traps:

```
Router#configure terminal
Enter configuration commands, one per line.  End with CNTL/Z.
Router(config)#snmp-server enable traps bgp
Router(config)#snmp-server enable traps envmon
Router(config)#end
Router#
```

You can also disable a particular type of SNMP trap by using the following command:

```
Router#configure terminal
Enter configuration commands, one per line.  End with CNTL/Z.
Router(config)#no snmp-server enable traps envmon
Router(config)#end
Router#
```

The following command displays which SNMP trap-types are enabled on a router:

```
Router#show running-config | include snmp-server enable
snmp-server enable traps snmp authentication linkdown linkup coldstart warmstart
snmp-server enable traps hsrp
snmp-server enable traps config
snmp-server enable traps entity
snmp-server enable traps envmon
snmp-server enable traps bgp
snmp-server enable traps ipmulticast
snmp-server enable traps msdp
```

```
snmp-server enable traps rsvp
snmp-server enable traps frame-relay
snmp-server enable traps syslog
snmp-server enable traps rtr
snmp-server enable traps dlsw
snmp-server enable traps dial
snmp-server enable traps dsp card-status
snmp-server enable traps voice poor-qov
Router#
```

The second step in configuring SNMP traps is to define the trap recipient by using the *snmp-server host* command. This command has the following attributes:

snmp-server host *host-addr* [**traps** | **informs**] [**version** {**1** | **2c**}] *community-string*
[**udp-port** *port*] [*trap-type*]

The *host-addr* argument is the name or IP address of the NMS server that will receive the traps. You can define whether the router will send SNMP traps or informs to this host by specifying either the *traps* or *informs* keyword. If neither is specified, the default is to send traps. Also, you can specify which version of SNMP traps the router will send by including either *version 1* or *version 2c*. If neither version is specified, the router will default to Version 1. Note that informs don't exist in SNMP Version 1, so you must specify Version 2c (or version 3) if you want to enable this feature.

The *community string* argument specifies the community string that the router will send within the SNMP trap or inform. This doesn't need to match either the read-only or read-write community strings on the router.

You can change the default SNMP trap port from 162 (the default) to another value with the optional *udp-port* keyword. This keyword must be followed by the alternative UDP port number that you want to use.

Finally, if the *trap-type* keyword is present, it allows you to configure the types of types that the router will send to this server. There is a list of valid trap types in Table 17-4. The command can accept one or more types. However, if no trap types are included, the router will default to sending every enabled trap type.

There are two important things to note about this command. First, you must enable trap-types via the global command before you can specify them for a particular host. Second, this command will allow you to send different sets of traps to different servers. This can sometimes be useful if you have multiple NMS servers that handle different management functions.

The configuration for SNMP informs is almost the same as SNMP traps. The main difference is that you can't enable individual inform types by using the global *snmp-server enable informs* command. The global inform command lacks the granularity of the same trap-based command. However, you can still enable specific inform types on the host-level command. This can mean more typing if there are several inform recipients. But there is no loss of functionality.

See Also

Recipe 17.22

17.14 Sending Syslog Messages As SNMP Traps and Informs

Problem

You want to send syslog messages as SNMP traps or informs.

Solution

You can configure the router to forward syslog messages to your network management server as SNMP traps instead of syslog packets with the following configuration commands:

```
Router#configure terminal
Enter configuration commands, one per line.  End with CNTL/Z.
Router(config)#logging history informational
Router(config)#snmp-server enable traps syslog
Router(config)#snmp-server host 172.25.1.1 ORATRAP syslog
Router(config)#end
Router#
```

To forward syslog messages as SNMP informs, use the following configuration commands:

```
Router#configure terminal
Enter configuration commands, one per line.  End with CNTL/Z.
Router(config)#logging history informational
Router(config)#snmp-server enable informs
Router(config)#snmp-server host 172.25.1.1 informs version 2c ORATRAP syslog
Router(config)#end
Router#
```

Discussion

Cisco routers normally forward *syslog* messages via the syslog facility by using UDP port 514. However, in networks that support SNMP traffic only, Cisco routers can encapsulate their syslog messages into SNMP traps before sending them.

This feature is most useful if your network management software doesn't support the syslog protocol. However, since routers can produce many more syslog messages than SNMP traps, we recommend using syslog when possible. Further, the fact that all of the syslog messages sent as SNMP traps use the same OID number can make parsing for particular log messages quite difficult.

Here is an example log message as it appears in the router's log:

```
Router#clear counters
Clear "show interface" counters on all interfaces [confirm]
```

```
Router#
May 28 10:07:04: %CLEAR-5-COUNTERS: Clear counter on all interfaces by ijbrown on
vty0 (172.25.1.1)
```

The router sends this message as a trap to the network management server, which records it in its trap log:

```
Freebsd% tail snmptrapd.log
May 28 10:07:04 freebsd snmptrapd[77759]: 172.25.25.1: Enterprise Specific Trap (1)
Uptime: 18 days, 22:35:26.99, enterprises.9.9.41.1.2.3.1.2.118 = "CLEAR",
enterprises.9.9.41.1.2.3.1.3.118 = 6, enterprises.9.9.41.1.2.3.1.4.118 = "COUNTERS",
enterprises.9.9.41.1.2.3.1.5.118 = "Clear counter on all interfaces by ijbrown on
vty0 (172.25.1.1)", enterprises.9.9.41.1.2.3.1.6.118 = Timeticks: (163652698) 18
days, 22:35:26.98
Freebsd%
```

In this example, we forced the router to create a log message by clearing the interface counters. The router displayed the raw syslog message to the vty session. The same information appears in the server's *snmptrapd.log* file. This is a flat file that contains all SNMP traps forwarded to the server. This assumes that the network management system uses the NET-SNMP package. Other network management systems store trap information in different formats and different filenames.

You can also configure the router to forward syslog messages as SNMP informs. The result is the same as for traps. For more information on syslog and logging in general, please refer to Chapter 18.

See Also

Recipe 17.14; Chapter 18

17.15 Setting SNMP Packet Size

Problem

You want to change the default SNMP packet size.

Solution

The following configuration command adjusts the default packet size for all SNMP packets leaving the router:

```
Router#configure terminal
Enter configuration commands, one per line.  End with CNTL/Z.
Router(config)#snmp-server packetsize 1480
Router(config)#end
Router#
```

Discussion

By default, Cisco routers limit their SNMP packet size to 1,500 bytes. It is usually not necessary to change this parameter. However, it may be useful to reduce it if your network has an MTU of less than 1,500 bytes to prevent unnecessary fragmentation.

Conversely, if your network media can accepts a larger MTU than 1,500 bytes, then increasing your SNMP packet size can improve performance, particularly when transferring large MIB tables.

Note that adjusting the maximum SNMP packet size will affect all types of SNMP packets, including responses to SNMP get or set requests, as well as SNMP traps and SNMP informs. You can set the SNMP packet size to any integer between 484 and 8,192 bytes.

17.16 Setting SNMP Queue Size

Problem

You want to increase the size of a router's SNMP trap queue.

Solution

The following command increases the size of a router's SNMP trap queue:

```
Router#configure terminal
Enter configuration commands, one per line.  End with CNTL/Z.
Router(config)#snmp-server queue-length 25
Router(config)#end
Router#
```

To increase the size of the router's SNMP inform queue, use the following configuration command:

```
Router#configure terminal
Enter configuration commands, one per line.  End with CNTL/Z.
Router(config)#snmp-server inform pending 40
Router(config)#end
Router#
```

Discussion

By default, the router can hold 10 trap messages in its queue. The queue holds traps until the router can forward them to the NMS. The queue fills when the router generates traps faster than it can forward them. If it generates additional traps when the queue is already full, these new trap messages are dropped. The router has only one SNMP message queue for all trap recipients.

Regardless of the network's capacity, the router will never send SNMP messages faster than four traps per second. This rate is hardcoded into the router and is not configurable. So if you have several NMS systems, or if your router creates a particularly large number of traps, you might want to increase the size of this queue to help prevent inadvertent discarding of traps.

The *snmp-server queue-length* command will accept any integer between 1 and 1,000, representing the maximum number of packets that can be held at a time.

To show the current number of SNMP messages in the queue, and the maximum queue size, use the *show snmp* EXEC command:

```
Router#show snmp
Chassis: JAX123456789
Contact: Ian Brown 416-555-2943
Location: 999 Queen St. W., Toronto, Ontario
270 SNMP packets input
    0 Bad SNMP version errors
    12 Unknown community name
    0 Illegal operation for community name supplied
    0 Encoding errors
    231 Number of requested variables
    25 Number of altered variables
    11 Get-request PDUs
    222 Get-next PDUs
    25 Set-request PDUs
584 SNMP packets output
    0 Too big errors (Maximum packet size 1480)
    2 No such name errors
    0 Bad values errors
    0 General errors
    258 Response PDUs
    326 Trap PDUs

SNMP logging: enabled
    Logging to 172.25.1.1.162, 0/25, 309 sent, 17 dropped.
Router#
```

In this example, the 0/25 in the last line means that no SNMP traps are currently queued for transmission, and the queue can accept up to 25 messages at once. You can use the number of dropped SNMP traps to verify whether your queue is too small by seeing if this number grows rapidly over time. In this case, the Trap PDUs line tells you that the router has tried to send 326 traps. Of these, the last line tells you that it has successfully sent 309 and dropped 17. This is a five percent drop rate, which suggests that the queue depth should probably be increased.

SNMP informs maintain a queue for messages pending acknowledgement. Each inform is held in the pending queue until an acknowledgement is received. Consequently, the inform queue must be considerably larger than the corresponding trap queue.

If you choose to implement SNMP informs, we highly recommend that you increase the size of the pending queue from the default value of 25:

```
Router(config)#snmp-server inform pending 40
```

The router will accept any integer between 1 and 4,294,967,295, representing the number of unacknowledged informs to hold. If the size of the pending queue is too small, then there is very little benefit to using informs, because the router will not be able to hold new messages.

17.17 Setting SNMP Timeout Values

Problem

You want to adjust the SNMP trap timeout value.

Solution

You can use the following configuration command to adjust a router's SNMP trap timeout value:

```
Router#configure terminal
Enter configuration commands, one per line.  End with CNTL/Z.
Router(config)#snmp-server trap-timeout 60
Router(config)#end
Router#
```

To adjust a router's SNMP inform timeout value, use the follow configuration commands:

```
Router#configure terminal
Enter configuration commands, one per line.  End with CNTL/Z.
Router(config)#snmp-server inform timeout 120
Router(config)#end
Router#
```

Discussion

Before a router can send an SNMP trap, it must have a route to the destination address of the trap. If a route to the SNMP server does not exist, the router will store the trap in the retransmission queue. By default, the router will hold a trap in the retransmission queue for 30 seconds before attempting to deliver it again. Sometimes it is useful to modify the default wait time to improve the chances of successful delivery.

For instance, if the router has to send the trap over a low-speed dial backup interface, 30 seconds may not be enough time for it to trigger a call, establish connectivity, and stabilize a routing table. In a situation like this, you should consider increasing the trap timeout. The value is specified as an integer number of seconds between 1 and 1,000.

SNMP informs use timeouts differently. The inform timeout is the number of seconds that the router waits for an acknowledgement before resending. The default value is 30 seconds, but the router will accept any value between 0 and 4,294,967,295 seconds.

Note that increasing the timeout values for traps and informs means that the router will tend to hold these messages for longer. And this, in turn, generally means that you will have to increase the queue size in order to hold them.

17.18 Disabling Link Up/Down Traps per Interface

Problem

You want to disable link up/down traps for specific interfaces.

Solution

To disable SNMP link-status change traps for a particular interface, use the following configuration command:

```
Router#configure terminal
Enter configuration commands, one per line.  End with CNTL/Z.
Router(config)#interface Serial0/0
Router(config-if)#no snmp trap link-status
Router(config-if)#exit
Router(config)#end
Router#
```

Discussion

By default, the router forwards SNMP link up or down traps whenever an interface changes states. Normally, you want to receive traps when an interface changes states because that could indicate a serious problem. But there are times when it is useful to disable these types of traps. For instance, dial interfaces may cycle up and down throughout the day without cause for concern. In these cases, you will probably want to suppress these types of traps to prevent network management staff from needlessly chasing meaningless failure reports.

It is also useful to disable SNMP traps for link up and down messages when you are troubleshooting, testing, or enabling interfaces to prevent extraneous failure reports.

This command will only work on physical interfaces and loopback interfaces. It will not allow you to disable link status traps on subinterfaces.

See Also

Recipe 17.14

17.19 Setting the IP Source Address for SNMP Traps

Problem

You want to set the source IP address for all SNMP traps leaving a router.

Solution

To set the default IP source address for all traps leaving a router, use the following configuration command:

```
Router#configure terminal
Enter configuration commands, one per line.  End with CNTL/Z.
Router(config)#snmp-server host 172.25.1.1 ORATRAP
Router(config)#snmp-server trap-source loopback0
Router(config)#end
Router#
```

Discussion

Normally, when you enable SNMP traps to a remote server, that server will see the source IP address of the router's closest interface. However, this is not always meaningful. For instance, it is a relatively common practice to populate your DNS with only the router's loopback interfaces. In this case, the server will not be able to resolve the originator of the trap.

Further, it can be difficult to correlate traps from the same router delivered through different interfaces. This could happen as a result of a network failure, for example. It can be confusing to see a link-down message coming from one IP address and the corresponding link-up message from a different one.

By enabling the *snmp-server trap-source* command, you can force the router to always use the same IP source address for all of the SNMP traps it sends. Industry best practices dictate that a loopback interface is usually the best choice for this because it is a virtual interface that is always available. Physical interfaces such as Ethernet or Serial interfaces can become unavailable and affect the effectiveness of this command. However, if you set the source interface to an unreachable interface, then the router will resort to using the closest interface as the source address.

Note that Cisco's IOS will even allow you to assign a trap-source interface that does not have an IP assigned address to it. However, the router will forward a syslog message highlighting the issue, and will resort to the default method of using the closest interface address for sending traps. Here is example of the log message that appears in this case:

```
Jun 12 00:22:00 EDT: %IP_SNMP-4-NOTRAPIP: SNMP trap source Loopback1 has no ip
address
```

17.20 Using RMON to Send Traps

Problem

You want the router to send a trap when the CPU rises above a threshold, or during other important events.

Solution

You can configure a router to monitor its own CPU utilization and trigger an SNMP trap when the value exceeds a defined threshold with the following set of configuration commands (Example 1):

```
Router#configure terminal
Enter configuration commands, one per line.  End with CNTL/Z.
Router(config)#rmon event 1 log trap ORATRAP description "CPU on Router has exceeded
threshold" owner ijbrown
Router(config)#rmon event 2 log description "CPU on Router has normalized" owner
ijbrown
Router(config)#rmon alarm 1 lsystem.57.0 60 absolute rising-threshold 70 1 falling-
threshold 40 2 owner ijbrown
Router(config)#end
Router#
```

The following commands will configure the router to monitor its own buffer failures and send an SNMP trap when the number of failures exceeded a threshold (Example 2):

```
Router#configure terminal
Enter configuration commands, one per line.  End with CNTL/Z.
Router(config)#rmon event 3 log trap ORATRAP description "Excessive buffer failures
on Router" owner ijbrown
Router(config)#rmon alarm 2 lsystem.46.0 300 delta rising-threshold 5 3 falling-
threshold -1 3 owner ijbrown
Router(config)#end
Router#
```

To configure a router to monitor its own memory utilization and trigger an SNMP trap when it exceeded its threshold, use the following set of configuration commands (Example 3):

```
Router#configure terminal
Enter configuration commands, one per line.  End with CNTL/Z.
Router(config)#rmon event 4 log trap ORATRAP description "Low memory condition on
Router" owner ijbrown
Router(config)#rmon event 5 log trap ORATRAP description "Low Memory condition
cleared on Router" owner ijbrown
Router(config)#rmon alarm 3 lsystem.8.0 60 absolute rising-threshold 1500000 5
falling-threshold 1000000 4 owner ijbrown
Router(config)#end
Router#
```

In this example, the router is configured to monitor the link utilization of a single interface and trigger an SNMP trap when it exceeds its threshold (Example 4):

```
Router#configure terminal
Enter configuration commands, one per line.  End with CNTL/Z.
Router(config)#rmon event 6 log trap ORATRAP description "Bandwidth utilization has
exceeded threshold on Router interface Serial 0/0" owner ijbrown
Router(config)#rmon event 7 log trap ORATRAP description "Bandwidth utilization has
normalized on Router interface Serial 0/0" owner ijbrown
Router(config)#! Configure inbound alarm on Serial0/0 (ifNumber 3)
```

```
Router(config)#rmon alarm 4 lifEntry.6.3 300 absolute rising-threshold 1000000 6
falling-threshold 800000 7 owner ijbrown
Router(config)#! Configure outbound alarm on Serial0/0 (ifNumber 3)
Router(config)#rmon alarm 5 lifEntry.8.3 300 absolute rising-threshold 1000000 6
falling-threshold 800000 7 owner ijbrown
Router(config)#end
Router#
```

To configure a router to monitor the number of interface errors on a particular interface, use the following set of commands (Example 5):

```
Router#configure terminal
Enter configuration commands, one per line.  End with CNTL/Z.
Router(config)#rmon event 7 log trap ORATRAP description "ifErrors have exceeded
threshold" owner ijbrown
Router(config)#rmon alarm 6 ifEntry.14.3 300 delta rising-threshold 5 7 falling-
threshold -1 7 owner ijbrown
Router(config)#rmon alarm 7 ifEntry.20.3 300 delta rising-threshold 5 7 falling-
threshold -1 7 owner ijbrown
Router(config)#end
Router#
```

If you choose to monitor interface specific MIBS, such as utilization or errors, then we strongly suggest that you implement Cisco's interface *persist* command, which we discuss in Recipe 17.13.

Discussion

IOS includes some extremely helpful but seldom-used remote monitoring (RMON) functionality. The main advantages to configuring the router to monitor its own performance are resource savings and flexibility.

The more conventional alternative is to have a centralized performance server that periodically polls routers for SNMP-based health statistics. On a large network, this can consume a lot of bandwidth. However, if you move the polling functionality into the router itself, you can get the same benefits without the same bandwidth requirements.

The second major advantage of having the router monitor its own health statistic is flexibility. You can configure each router to monitor itself by using the thresholds and parameters that are most meaningful to that router. Because most performance monitoring packages on the market today limit the amount of flexibility in assigning thresholds, this built-in monitoring technique can give more reliable results.

Of course, the biggest advantage of using RMON is that it is readily available in Cisco's IOS and requires no extra software. If your management software is capable of accepting SNMP traps, then no further tools are required. For the money, conscious administrator, RMON provides detailed performance threshold management without the added cost of performance software.

Cisco's RMON module comes standard in Cisco IOS, and is included in the base feature set. The purpose of RMON is to monitor a certain MIB object on the router and notify the system administrator if the object's value leaves a defined range. It does this by polling itself internally for the values of these MIB objects. You can configure the internal polling interval.

To prevent unnecessary trouble notifications, Cisco RMON alarms use a concept of rising and falling thresholds. An RMON event fires when a value of an SNMP object exceeds the value assigned to the "rising-threshold." However, subsequent polls that exceed the rising-threshold will not trigger an event firing until a polled value drops below the "falling-threshold" value. This concept of rising and falling thresholds prevents the agent from flooding the server with redundant events.

Our examples show how to configure RMON to monitor CPU utilization, low memory situations, buffer failures, link utilization and interface error counts. This is far from an exhaustive list of the RMON capabilities. Because the router's RMON capabilities rely on the polling of SNMP MIB objects, you can configure it to monitor any variable that has a MIB variable. The potential number of statistics you can configure the router to watch is enormous.

The first step in configuring RMON on a router is to define the RMON event(s) that you wish to monitor. In our first RMON example, we configured the router to monitor CPU utilization. The follow two commands tell the router what to do when the CPU load rises above the threshold, and what to do when it falls back into the normal range:

```
Router(config)#rmon event 1 log trap ORATRAP description "CPU on Router has exceeded
threshold" owner ijbrown
Router(config)#rmon event 2 log description "CPU on Router has normalized" owner
ijbrown
```

The following IOS command defines an RMON event:

```
rmon event number [log] [trap community] [description string] [owner string]
```

This *number* keyword assigns a unique identification number for the RMON event. RMON event numbers range between 1 and 65,535. The optional *log* keyword tells the agent to create a log entry as well as an SNMP trap when event is triggered.

The optional *trap* keyword is accompanied by a community string. This configures the agent to send an SNMP trap when the event is fired, and assigns the SNMP community string for the trap.

You can specify an optional description for an RMON event using the *description* keyword. The text that follows this keyword is sent with the trap.

This *owner* keyword specifies the owner of an event. In our examples, the owner is ijbrown. But if you do not have AAA usernames configured on your router, you should use the default admin user ID.

In this example, RMON event 1 creates a log entry and an SNMP trap when the CPU utilization on the router exceeds a certain threshold. RMON event 2 creates a log entry, but doesn't send a trap when the CPU utilization returns to normal.

To view the configured RMON events, use the following command:

```
Router>show rmon events
Event 1 is active, owned by ijbrown
 Description is CPU on Router has exceeded threshold
 Event firing causes log and trap to community ORATRAP, last fired 00:00:00
Event 2 is active, owned by ijbrown
 Description is CPU on Router has normalized
 Event firing causes log, last fired 2w2d
 Current log entries:
       index     time    description
          1      2w2d    CPU on Router has normalized
Router>
```

To make the RMON events meaningful, you also must create a corresponding RMON alarm that defines the conditions for each of the event conditions that we just discussed:

```
Router(config)#rmon alarm 1 lsystem.57.0 60 absolute rising-threshold 70 1 falling-
threshold 40 2 owner ijbrown
```

The syntax of this command is as follows:

```
rmon alarm number variable interval {absolute | delta}
                rising-threshold value [event-number]
                falling-threshold value [event-number] [owner string]
```

The *number* in this command is simply a value between 1 and 65,535 that uniquely identifies this alarm.

You can specify a particular MIB object that you want the router to monitor with the *variable* field. In this example, we are polling the CPU utilization MIB entry, lsystem.57.0.

The next value, *interval*, tells the router how often you want it to poll the MIB object. The value can be between 1 and 4,294,967,295 seconds. This example tells the router to poll on a 60-second cycle.

Once the data has been polled, you have the option of treating the value as an *absolute* or *delta*. In this example, we are interested in the actual value of the MIB variable, so we specified the *absolute* keyword. The keyword *delta* tells the router to take the numerical difference between the current sample and the previous one. This feature is most useful for determining when a variable's rate of change is too fast or too slow.

You set a rising-threshold value by using the *rising-threshold* keyword, which takes an argument between −2,147,483,648 and 2,147,483,647. In this example, the rising-threshold is 70 percent, meaning that the router will trigger an event when the CPU utilization rises through 70 percent. When this happens, you want the router to trigger a particular event. This association with a particular event is made with the *event-number* argument. In this example, if the rising-threshold is exceeded, then RMON event 1 will be triggered.

You configure a falling threshold by using the *falling-threshold* keyword. In this example, the falling-threshold is 40 percent, meaning that if the CPU utilization dips below 40 percent, it will trigger an event. As with rising thresholds, you can associate this alarm with a particular event number. In this example, the falling-threshold triggers event number 2.

And, finally, you can specify an owner for an alarm, just the same as for an event using the *owner* keyword.

So the example configures RMON alarm 1 to poll the MIB entry for CPU utilization, every minute. If the utilization exceeds 70 percent, the router will send a trap and create a log message. And when the utilization dips back below 40 percent, it will just create a lot message.

To view the configured RMON alarms, use the following command:

```
Router>show rmon alarms
Alarm 1 is active, owned by ijbrown
 Monitors lsystem.57.0 every 60 second(s)
 Taking absolute samples, last value was 0
 Rising threshold is 70, assigned to event 1
 Falling threshold is 40, assigned to event 2
 On startup enable rising or falling alarm
Router>
```

 Currently Cisco's RMON functionality only supports traps, and not SNMP informs.

See Also

Recipe 17.14

17.21 Enabling SNMPv3

Problem

You want to enable SNMPv3 on your router for security purposes.

Solution

SNMPv3 supports three modes of operation, each with different security features. These modes are summarized in Table 17-1. The following configuration commands enable SNMPv3 with no authentication and no encryption services (*noAuthNoPriv*):

```
Router#configure terminal
Enter configuration commands, one per line.  End with CNTL/Z.
Router(config)#snmp-server view TESTV3 mib-2 include
Router(config)#snmp-server group NOTSAFE v3 noauth read TESTV3
```

```
Router(config)#snmp-server user WEAK NOTSAFE v3
Router(config)#end
Router#
```

Use the following configuration commands to enable SNMPv3 with MD5 authentication and no encryption services (*authNoPriv*):

```
Router#configure terminal
Enter configuration commands, one per line.  End with CNTL/Z.
Router(config)#snmp-server view TESTV3 mib-2 include
Router(config)#snmp-server group ORAROV3 v3 auth read TESTV3
Router(config)#snmp-server user cking ORAROV3 v3 auth md5 daytona19y
Router(config)#end
Router#
```

And you can enable SNMPv3 with MD5 authentication and DES encryption services (*authPriv*) as follows:

```
Router#configure terminal
Enter configuration commands, one per line.  End with CNTL/Z.
Router(config)#snmp-server view TESTV3 mib-2 include
Router(config)#snmp-server group ORAROV3 v3 auth read TESTV3
Router(config)#snmp-server user bpugsley ORAROV3 v3 auth md5 hockeyrules priv des56
shortguy
Router(config)#end
Router#
```

Discussion

At the time of writing this book, the IETF had approved SNMP Version 3, SNMPv3, as a full standard and moved SNMPv1 and SNMPv2 to historic status. Essentially, SNMPv3 just acts like a set of security extensions to SNMPv2c, without providing much new core management functionality. All MIB objects and their associated OIDs remain the same from Versions 1 to 3 (with the small exception of 64 bits counters that were introduced in Version 2). So we will focus our attention on the new security features in Version 3.

Security has traditionally been the Achilles tendon of the legacy SNMP versions. The security model for Version 1 and 2c was little more than a simple password sent through the network as clear text. SNMP required a security facelift to continue to be useful into the future.

SNMPv3 is standards-based network management protocol that is interoperable between vendors. It provides a secure access to devices by providing authentication and encryption of SNMP packets throughout the network. To do this, SNMPv3 requires the following security features: authentication, message integrity, and encryption:

- Authentication ensures that the messages originated from a valid source. It proves the authenticity of the packet's source.

- Message Integrity ensures that a packet has not been tampered with during transmission.

- Encryption encodes the contents of the packet to prevent unauthorized people from viewing them.

SNMPv3 provides three security levels: *noAuthNoPriv*, *authNoPriv*, and *authPriv*:

noAuthNoPriv

Uses a username for authentication and most closely emulates the SNMPv1 and SNMPv2c authentication scheme of transmitting credentials in clear text. We do not recommend this level of SNMPv3 because it provides no significant advantage over SNMPv2c. If the advanced security features of SNMPv3 are not required for your implementation, it would probably be easier to use SNMPv1 or SNMPv2c instead.

authNoPriv

Provides authentication based on the MD5 or SHA algorithms. This level of SNMPv3 provides packet authentication and message integrity, but no encryption services. Since SNMP packets are authenticated and cannot be altered in transit, this level of security is sufficient for most organizations.

authPriv

Provides the same MD5 or SHA authentication as *authNoPriv*. In addition, *authPriv* allows you to encrypt SNMP packets by using 56-bit DES; 168-bit 3DES; or AES 128-, 192-, or 256-bit encryption algorithms so packet contents cannot be viewed without authorization. This provides the maximum security available by combining authentication, messages integrity, and encryption. The *authPriv* level of security is suitable for implementations that need to send SNMP packets through the public Internet, for instance.

All three SNMPv3 security models require the same three-step process to configure them. First, you must define an SNMP view. Second, you must create an SNMP group. And third, you need to create an SNMP user profile and assign it to an existing group.

Defining an SNMP view for SNMPv3 is no different than creating a view for SNMPv1 or SNMPv2c. In fact, if there are existing SNMP views on the router that were created for SNMPv1 or SNMPv2c, you can use them with SNMPv3 as well. For more information on creating SNMP views, please see Recipe 17.8.

For example, here is a simple SNMP view that allows full access to the MIB-2 tree:

```
Router#configure terminal
Enter configuration commands, one per line.  End with CNTL/Z.
Router(config)#snmp-server view TESTV3 mib-2 include
Router(config)#end
Router#
```

To define an SNMPv3 group, use the following command:

```
Router#configure terminal
Enter configuration commands, one per line.  End with CNTL/Z.
Router(config)#snmp-server group ORAROV3 v3 auth read TESTV3
Router(config)#end
Router#
```

In this example, we have created a group named ORAROV3 that we have configured as an SNMPv3 group (hence the "v3"). We have configured this group to require authentication and assigned it to SNMP view TESTV3. Notice that we have not assigned a write view to this group, which means that all users assigned to this group will be limited to read-only access. However, the *snmp-server group* command will also allow you to define a read and a write view at the same time. For example:

```
Router#configure terminal
Enter configuration commands, one per line.  End with CNTL/Z.
Router(config)#snmp-server view TESTRO mib-2 include
Router(config)#snmp-server view TESTRW system include
Router(config)#snmp-server group TESTGRP v3 auth read TESTRO write TESTRW
Router(config)#end
Router#
```

In this example, we defined two separate SNMP views, TESTRO and TESTRW, respectively, and assigned them to our group. Note, however, that you can assign the same SNMP view to both the read-only access and read-write.

To define an SNMPv3 user, use the following command:

```
Router#configure terminal
Enter configuration commands, one per line.  End with CNTL/Z.
Router(config)#snmp-server user bpugsley ORAROV3 v3 auth md5 hockeyrules priv des56
shortguy
Router(config)#end
Router#
```

In this example, we have created a user named bpugsley, and assigned that user to our group named ORAROV3. This user will inherit the qualities that we have configured for that group. We have also defined that our user will use the MD5 algorithm for authentication purposes and assigned an authentication password of hockeyrules. We have also configured our user to use the optional DES56 packet encryption with the password shortguy to provide maximum security. Note that this command, once entered, will not be viewable using the *show running-config* command. We suspect that this is for security purposes.

To view existing SNMP groups, use the *show snmp group* command:

```
Router#show snmp group

groupname: ORAROV3                      security model:v3 auth
readview :TESTV3                        writeview: <no writeview specified>
notifyview: <no notifyview specified>
row status: active

Router#
```

Notice that the group ORAROV3 is assigned to the security model *v3 auth*. Also notice that the read-only view is TESTV3, and that no read-write view exists.

To view the configured SNMPv3 users, use the following command:

```
Router#show snmp user
User name: bpugsley
```

```
Engine ID: 8000000090300000019670B770
storage-type: nonvolatile        active

Router#
```

Unfortunately, this command provides very little useful information. Apart from confirming if a user exists or not, the output does not display to which group the user belongs or if the user is configured to use authentication or encryption. When you consider that Cisco's IOS also hides the user SNMP commands from the running configuration, it becomes clear that managing SNMPv3 users is a difficult task. We hope that Cisco will change the output of this command in upcoming releases as SNMPv3 becomes more popular.

Starting with IOS Version 12.3(2)T, Cisco did enhance the output of the *show snmp user* command to include the authentication protocol, the privacy protocol, and the SNMP group name:

```
Router2#show snmp user

User name: bpugsley
Engine ID: 800000090300000DBCEFF638
storage-type: nonvolatile        active
Authentication Protocol: MD5
Privacy Protocol: DES
Group-name: ORAROV3

Router2
```

Using the SNMPv3 security levels

We will now demonstrate how to extract SNMP information from the router using each of the three SNMPv3 security levels. We will use NET-SNMP's *snmpget* command, which has full SNMPv3 support.

In our first example (*noAuthNoPriv*), we will poll the router for its system name by using a standard MIB-II object, *sysName*:

```
Freebsd% snmpget -v3 -u WEAK -l noAuthNoPriv  Router  sysName.0
system.sysName.0 = Router.oreilly.com
Freebsd%
```

Notice no user password was supplied, so the router simply accepted the user ID WEAK for authentication purposes. This userid was sent through the network in clear text. This command has also introduced two new attributes for the *snmpget* command, *-u* and *-l*. The *-u* attribute allows you to specify the security name, and the *-l* defines the security level.

The next example uses the *authNoPriv* security model. We will poll the exact same MIB object using MD5 authentication:

```
Freebsd% snmpget -v3 -u cking -l authNoPriv -a MD5 -A daytona19y Router sysName.0
system.sysName.0 = Router.oreilly.com
Freebsd%
```

Notice in this example we specify a user password daytona19y using the -A option, and an authentication protocol *MD5* using the -a option. SNMPv3 uses the authentication protocol to authenticate users without sending the password in clear text. It is important to notice that the result of this SNMP Get is the same as our first example. However, we gathered the information in a much more secure manner. In fact, the same MIB object, *sysName*, can be retrieved using SNMPv1 if the router were configured to accept the request. But this would be considerably less secure.

The final example illustrates how to poll a MIB object by using the authentication and encryption services of the *authPriv* security model:

```
Freebsd% snmpget -v3 -u bpugsley -l authPriv -a MD5 -A hockeyrules -x DES -X shortguy
Router sysName.0
system.sysName.0 = Router.oreilly.com
Freebsd%
```

In this example, we added two new variables, privacy protocol type DES using -x DES and a privacy protocol pass phrase with -x shortguy. These variables enable SNMPv3 packet encryption and specify the pass phrase to use. This ensures that prying eyes cannot view the packet contents in transit. To illustrate the effectiveness of SNMPv3's encryption service, we provide a captured SNMPv3 packet. The packet was captured using the Ethereal protocol analyzer (for more information on Ethereal, please see Appendix A):

```
Simple Network Management Protocol
    Version: 3
    Message Global Header
        Message Global Header Length: 16
        Message ID: 1608369049
        Message Max Size: 1480
        Flags: 0x03
            .... .0.. = Reportable: Not set
            .... ..1. = Encrypted: Set
            .... ...1 = Authenticated: Set
        Message Security Model: USM
    Message Security Parameters
        Message Security Parameters Length: 58
        Authoritative Engine ID: 80000009030000019670B780
        Engine Boots: 2
        Engine Time: 1469970
        User Name: bpugsley
        Authentication Parameter: B53EFA21230735541B207A39
        Privacy Parameter: 00000002C483B016
    Encrypted PDU (74 bytes)
```

Notice that the packet response from the router contains some useful SNMP information, such as current version, encryption enabled, authentication enabled, and username (bpugsley), but is unable to decipher the payload (Encrypted PDU). This is significant, since the other versions of SNMP, including the other security models within SNMPv3, transport payload information in clear text. At last, SNMP has evolved into a secure protocol.

Of course, SNMPv3 also provides full support for traps and informs, including authentication, messages integrity, and encryption. SNMPv3 traps and informs support the same three models of security as inbound services do. However, the *noAuthNoPriv* model provides no tangible advantage over SNMPv1 or SNMPv2c, and the *authPriv* model tends to be overkill, since few networks will require encrypted traps.

To enable SNMPv3 trap support using authentication and message integrity, use the following command:

```
Router#configure terminal
Enter configuration commands, one per line.  End with CNTL/Z.
Router(config)#snmp-server host 172.25.1.1 version 3 auth ijbrown snmp envmon
Router(config)#end
Router#
```

The process of enabling SNMPv3 traps, or informs, is similar to the SNMPv2c process, but with a few minor twists. First, you must define a SNMPv3 group and user, as in the previous examples. Second, you must include the keyword auth, which enables authentication. And third, you must include a valid SNMPv3 user (ijbrown, in this case). The router is then capable of forwarding SNMv3 traps with full SNMPv3 authentication and message integrity enabled. For more information on enabling SNMP traps in general, please see Recipe 17.14.

See Also

Recipe 17.1; Recipe 17.8; Recipe 17.14

17.22 Strong SNMPv3 Encryption

Problem

You want to increase the strength of SNMPv3 encryption.

Solution

Starting with IOS Version 12.4(2)T, Cisco introduced support for stronger encryption capabilities. To enable 3DES use the following command:

```
Router1#configure terminal
Enter configuration commands, one per line.  End with CNTL/Z.
Router1(config)#snmp-server user wbrejniak ORAROV3 v3 auth md5 authpass priv 3des
privpass
Router1(config)#end
Router1#
```

To enable AES encryption of SNMPv3 traffic, use the following command:

```
Router1#configure terminal
Enter configuration commands, one per line.  End with CNTL/Z.
Router1(config)#snmp-server user wbrejniak ORAROV3 v3 auth md5 authpass priv aes 128
privpass
```

```
Router1(config)#end
Router1#
```

Discussion

Beginning with IOS Version 12.4(2)T, Cisco enhanced the encryption capabilities of SNMPv3 by adding support for 3DES and Advanced Encryption Standard (AES). The addition of AES 128-bit encryption meets the RFC 3826 standard. In addition, Cisco has also added support for 168-bit 3DES, and 192-bit and 256-bit AES encryption, which is currently not part of the RFC standard.

 AES and 3DES encryption are only supported in IOS images that support encryption services.

To display the user encryption method to confirm configuration, use the *show snmp user* command:

```
Router1#show snmp user wbrejniak

User name: wbrejniak
Engine ID: 800000090300000E84244E70
storage-type: nonvolatile        active
Authentication Protocol: MD5
Privacy Protocol: 3DES
Group-name: ORAROV3

Router1#
```

Notice that user *wbrejniak* is currently configured to use 3DES encryption, as highlighted in our previous example:

```
Router1#show snmp user wbrejniak

User name: wbrejniak
Engine ID: 800000090300000E84244E70
storage-type: nonvolatile        active
Authentication Protocol: MD5
Privacy Protocol: AES128
Group-name: ORAROV3

Router1#
```

Now notice that we've changed the configuration of user *wbrejniak* to support AES 128-bit encryption.

In our next example, we'll use Net-SNMP to extract the hostname using strong encryption. Please note that Net-SNMP currently only supports DES 56-bit and AES 128-bit encryption because they are standards based:

```
Freebsd% snmpget -v 3 -u wbrejniak -l authPriv -a md5 -A authpass -x aes -X privpass
172.25.1.101 sysName.0
```

```
SNMPv2-MIB::sysName.0 = STRING: Router1.oreilly.com
Freebsd%
```

See Also

Recipe 17.22

17.23 Using SAA

Problem

You want to configure the routers to automatically poll one another to collect performance statistics.

Solution

Cisco supplies a feature called the Service Assurance Agent (SAA) in IOS Version 12.0(5)T and higher, which allows the routers to automatically poll one another to collect end-to-end performance statistics:

```
Router1#configure terminal
Enter configuration commands, one per line.  End with CNTL/Z.
Router1(config)#rtr responder
Router1(config)#rtr 10
Router1(config-rtr)#type echo protocol ipIcmpEcho 10.1.2.3
Router1(config-rtr)#tag ECHO_TEST
Router1(config-rtr)#threshold 1000
Router1(config-rtr)#frequency 300
Router1(config-rtr)#exit
Router1(config)#rtr schedule 10 life 2147483647 start-time now
Router1(config)#rtr 20
Router1(config-rtr)#type jitter dest-ipaddr 10.1.2.3 dest-port 99 num-packets 100
Router1(config-rtr)#tag JITTER_TEST
Router1(config-rtr)#frequency 300
Router1(config-rtr)#exit
Router1(config)#rtr schedule 20 life 100000 start-time now ageout 3600
Router1(config)#exit
Router1#
```

The target router, which is specified as the destination in both of these tests, 10.1.2.3, must be configured to respond to SAA tests as follows:

```
Router2#configure terminal
Enter configuration commands, one per line.  End with CNTL/Z.
Router2(config)#rtr responder
Router2(config)#exit
Router2#
```

Discussion

The SAA feature includes replaces the earlier Round Trip Reporter (RTR) and Route Trip Time Monitor (RTTMON) facilities, which were available in IOS Version 11.3, and uses the same basic syntax. However, where RTR only includes some simple round-trip PING and SNA tests, SAA includes several more interesting and useful features.

The first line in the example is the *rtr responder* command. This is required on all routers that will be taking part in SAA, including the targets of these tests. You will notice, for example, that both of the tests use a target IP address of 10.1.2.3. This destination must be another Cisco router that is also configured with the *rtr responder* command.

In this example, we have configured two tests. We have given the first test the arbitrary number, 10, and a name ECHO_TEST. The second test is number 20, and is called JITTER_TEST. Note that you don't actually need to give your SAA tests names, but it is a good idea if you have several of them. This name, or tag, is included in the SAA SNMP MIB table for this test. So, if you intend to download the test data via SNMP for performance management purposes, it can be extremely useful to name your tests.

Let's look at both of these example tests in more detail.

The first test does an ICMP echo (PING) to the destination device, 10.1.2.3:

```
Router1(config)#rtr 10
Router1(config-rtr)#type echo protocol ipIcmpEcho 10.1.2.3
Router1(config-rtr)#tag ECHO_TEST
Router1(config-rtr)#threshold 1000
Router1(config-rtr)#frequency 300
Router1(config-rtr)#exit
```

The *threshold* command defines a minimum interesting threshold, which in this case is set to 1,000 milliseconds. This allows you to count the number of ping tests where the round-trip time was greater than one second, in addition to keeping track of the PING times and number of PING failures, which we will show in a moment.

Next is the *frequency* command, which defines how often this test will be run in seconds. In this case, we want the test to run every five minutes (300 seconds).

Then, once you have defined the test in the *rtr* configuration block, you have to tell the router when to run it. This is done with the *rtr schedule* command:

```
Router1(config)#rtr schedule 10 life 2147483647 start-time now
```

This command defines the schedule for running test number 10. It sets a lifetime for this test of 2,147,483,647 seconds (a very long time), which is the maximum value. This effectively means that this test will continue to run indefinitely. It is scheduled to start immediately.

Note that when we scheduled the second test, we used slightly different parameters:

```
Router1(config)#rtr schedule 20 life 100000 start-time now ageout 3600
```

In this case, the test is scheduled to run only for 100,000 seconds, which is about 27 hours. We have also configured an *ageout* value of 3,600 seconds for this test. This says that the router will keep this test rule in memory for this length of time after it expires. This allows you to restart the test if you want to, without needing to reconfigure it.

You can view the data for the first test as follows:

```
Router1#show rtr operational-state 10
        Current Operational State
Entry Number: 10
Modification Time: 18:51:53.000 EST Tue Dec 17 2002
Diagnostics Text:
Last Time this Entry was Reset: Never
Number of Octets in use by this Entry: 1910
Connection Loss Occurred: FALSE
Timeout Occurred: FALSE
Over Thresholds Occurred: FALSE
Number of Operations Attempted: 203
Current Seconds Left in Life: 2147483647
Operational State of Entry: active
Latest Completion Time (milliseconds): 54
Latest Operation Start Time: 11:41:53.000 EST Wed Dec 18 2002
Latest Operation Return Code: ok
Latest 10.1.2.3
```

In this output, you can see that it has run this test 203 times, and the last test took 54 milliseconds, and completed successfully. Note that it doesn't give a running average PING time. However, one of the nicest features of SAA is that you can configure a network management station to download this data using SNMP, provided you have the SAA MIB loaded on your server.

The second test is considerably more interesting. This test measures jitter between the routers by sending a series of UDP packets and looking at the time differences between consecutive packets at both ends:

```
Router1(config)#rtr 20
Router1(config-rtr)#type jitter dest-ipaddr 10.1.2.3 dest-port 99 num-packets 100
Router1(config-rtr)#tag JITTER_TEST
Router1(config-rtr)#frequency 300
Router1(config-rtr)#exit
Router1(config)#rtr schedule 20 life 100000 start-time now ageout 3600
```

The *type* command defines a jitter test to the same destination IP address as the previous test. In this case, we have decided to use UDP port 99 for our test, and each test run will consist of 100 packets. The *frequency* command tells the router to run this test every five minutes. Here is some sample output from this test:

```
Router1#show rtr operational-state 20
        Current Operational State
Entry Number: 20
Modification Time: 10:25:36.000 EST Wed Dec 18 2002
Diagnostics Text:
Last Time this Entry was Reset: Never
Number of Octets in use by this Entry: 1742
Number of Operations Attempted: 22
```

```
Current Seconds Left in Life: 93400
Operational State of Entry: active
Latest Operation Start Time: 12:10:36.000 EST Wed Dec 18 2002
RTT Values:
NumOfRTT: 98      RTTSum: 6063      RTTSum2: 384317
Packet Loss Values:
PacketLossSD: 0 PacketLossDS: 2
PacketOutOfSequence: 2  PacketMIA: 0      PacketLateArrival: 0
InternalError: 0        Busies: 0
Jitter Values:
MinOfPositivesSD: 4       MaxOfPositivesSD: 14
NumOfPositivesSD: 32      SumOfPositivesSD: 175      Sum2PositivesSD: 1111
MinOfNegativesSD: 1       MaxOfNegativesSD: 5
NumOfNegativesSD: 60      SumOfNegativesSD: 175      Sum2NegativesSD: 547
MinOfPositivesDS: 1       MaxOfPositivesDS: 45
NumOfPositivesDS: 20      SumOfPositivesDS: 78       Sum2PositivesDS: 2166
MinOfNegativesDS: 1       MaxOfNegativesDS: 16
NumOfNegativesDS: 21      SumOfNegativesDS: 69       Sum2NegativesDS: 693
```

There is a clearly a lot more information in this test output. This is because measuring jitter is not a simple single variable test. What you want from a jitter measurement is to characterize the statistical distribution of packet-by-packet variation in latency in the forward and backward directions, as well as for the round trip. All of this information is here. Note that as with the SAA PING test we discussed earlier, the router only records the results of the most recent test. If you want to keep historical records, you need to poll and download the SAA MIB tables once per poll cycle.

The first set of numbers includes the Round Trip Time (RTT) values. You can see that this sample included 98 packets. The total of all of the round trip times of all of these packets was 6,063 milliseconds, and the sum of the squares of all of these times was 384,317 milliseconds. These values are not extremely meaningful in themselves, but if you divide the RTTSum value by the number of measurements, you get the average latency for this set of packets, roughly 61 milliseconds.

Applying some simple statistics, you can use the square value to understand how the actual values are spread around this average. The mean of the squares of the round-trip times is 3,922 milliseconds2 (just dividing the sum of the squares by the total number of samples). If you subtract the square of the average from this value, and take the square root, you get a statistical estimate of the variation in milliseconds. The higher this value, the greater the spread. In this case, you can calculate that this spread is roughly 10 milliseconds. This means that half of the time, the round trip latency is within the range 61 ± 10ms. Note that the ± symbol is a standard mathematical notation that, in this case, indicates a range from 51 ms (61 − 10) to 71 ms (61 + 10).

The next set of data records dropped packets. Recall that the sample size is 100 packets, but the NumOfRTT value is only 98. So the network must have dropped two of our test packets. SAA separately keeps track of packets lost in both directions, source to destination (PacketLossSD) and destination to source (PacketLossDS). This router is the source; the other router is the destination. So in this example, both of the lost packets happened on the way back. Notice also that the output claims that there were two out-of-sequence packets during this test, which is consistent with the number of dropped packets.

The next group of numbers includes the actual jitter measurements. There are two groups of numbers here. The variables that end with "SD" are measured from the source to the destination, and "DS" are for the return path. Within each of these groups there are two subgroups, one for "positives" and the other for "negatives." Positives are events where the spacing between two packets has increased since the last pair of successive packets. The "Negatives" counters record all of the times that the interpacket spacing decreased. Now let's look a little bit more closely at one set of values:

```
MinOfPositivesSD: 4      MaxOfPositivesSD: 14
NumOfPositivesSD: 32     SumOfPositivesSD: 175    Sum2PositivesSD: 1111
```

This says that of the 100 packets the router sent in this polling interval, there were 32 cases when the jitter in the forward direction had a positive value. Of these, the largest value was 14 milliseconds, and the smallest was 4 milliseconds. Then we can use the sum and the sum of the squares to calculate the average and spread of values in precisely the same way as we did to calculate the average latency a moment ago. The result here is that half the time the positive jitter in this direction was within the range 5.5 ± 2.2 ms.

Applying this same technique to the other jitter measurements gives the following statistics. The negative jitter from source to destination was 2.9 ± 0.8 ms, with a maximum of 5 ms and a minimum value of 1 ms. In the other direction, the positive jitter was 3.9 ± 9.6 ms, and the negative jitter was 3.3 ± 4.7 ms. These last two values might look a little bit funny because the spread is larger than the mean. This is actually not bad, though, because the output also shows that the maximum positive jitter in this direction was 45 ms, and 16 ms for negative jitter. So clearly, the spread is very large, but the mean jitter values are relatively small. This is a fairly typical result.

## CHAPTER 18

Logging

18.0 Introduction

Many network administrators overlook the importance of router logs. Logging is critical for fault notification, network forensics, and security auditing.

Cisco routers handle log messages in five ways:

- By default, the router sends all log messages to its console port. Only users that are physically connected to the router console port may view these messages, though. This is called *console logging*.

- *Terminal logging* is similar to console logging, but it displays log messages to the router's VTY lines instead. This type of logging is not enabled by default, so if you want to use it, you need to need activate it for each required line.

- *Buffered logging* creates a circular buffer within the router's RAM for storing log messages. This circular buffer has a fixed size to ensure that the log will not deplete valuable system memory. The router accomplishes this by deleting old messages from the buffer as new messages are added.

- The router can use *syslog* to forward log messages to external *syslog* servers for centralized storage. This type of logging is not enabled by default. Much of this chapter is devoted to configuring remote *syslog* features. The router sends syslog messages to the server on UDP port 514. The server does not acknowledge these messages.

- With *SNMP trap logging*, the router is able to use SNMP traps to send log messages to an external SNMP server. This is an effective method of handling log messages in a SNMP-based environment, but it has certain limitations. We will discuss this logging method in Chapter 17, which deals with SNMP configuration.

Cisco log messages are categorized by severity level, following the structure and format of the 4.3BSD Unix syslog framework. In particular, router log messages follow the syslog's severity levels, as shown in Table 18-1. Note that the lower the severity level, the more critical the log message is.

Table 18-1. Cisco logging severity levels

Level	Level name	Description	Syslog definition
0	Emergencies	Router unusable	LOG_EMERG
1	Alerts	Immediate action needed	LOG_ALERT
2	Critical	Critical conditions	LOG_CRIT
3	Errors	Error conditions	LOG_ERR
4	Warnings	Warning conditions	LOG_WARNING
5	Notifications	Normal but important conditions	LOG_NOTICE
6	Informational	Informational messages	LOG_INFO
7	Debugging	Debugging messages	LOG_DEBUG

Here is an example of a log message that shows the typical format of Cisco router log messages:

```
Apr 12 14:01:16: %CLEAR-5-COUNTERS: Clear counter on all interfaces by ijbrown on
vty0 (172.25.1.1)
```

As you can see, the log message is broken into three sections that are delimited by colons. The first section is the optional date and time section that is enabled by using the *service timestamp* configuration command. A detailed discussion of timestamps can be found in Chapter 14.

The second part of the log message, %CLEAR-5-COUNTERS, gives the message code and severity level. In the example log message above, the message code family is CLEAR, the priority level is -5-, which indicates a *Notifications* severity-level message, and a family type of COUNTERS. All Cisco log messages are arranged in this manner. There are many different message codes, such as FRAME for frame relay messages, SYS for system messages, and LINK for interface messages. Within each message code, log messages are categorized by severity type: 7 is the least severe to 0 is the most critical, following the syslog model. Finally, each specific message type is assigned a unique message code, such as COUNTERS, in this case, or UPDOWN for LINK messages, and so forth.

The final section of a log is the message body, which contains human readable text. The example message above contains the message body "Clear counter on all interfaces by *ijbrown* on *vty0* (172.25.1.1)". The message body generally contains easy to understand text as well as some custom variables, such as *ijbrown* and *vty0*, in this case, which help to make log messages more meaningful.

Table 18-2 shows a typical log message for each of the eight severity levels.

Table 18-2. Sample router log messages

Level	Level name	Sample router messages
0	Emergencies	System shutting down due to missing fan tray
1	Alerts	Core CRITICAL Temperature limit exceeded

Table 18-2. Sample router log messages (continued)

Level	Level name	Sample router messages
2	Critical	Memory allocation failures
3	Errors	Interface Up/Down messages
4	Warnings	Configuration file written to server, via SNMP request
5	Notifications	Line protocol Up/Down
6	Informational	Access-list violation logging
7	Debugging	Debug messages

You will rarely see log messages with severity levels of Alert or Emergency because any problems this severe generally mean the router is inoperable.

18.1   Enabling Local Router Logging

Problem

You want your router to record log messages, instead of just displaying them on the console.

Solution

Use the *logging buffered* configuration command to enable the local storage of router log messages:

```
Router#configure terminal
Enter configuration commands, one per line.  End with CNTL/Z.
Router(config)#logging buffered informational
Router(config)#end
Router#
```

Discussion

This feature causes the router to store all log messages to a revolving buffer called the logging buffer. Many network administrators find it convenient and useful to keep detailed router logs on the router itself. The router discards its oldest messages to make room for new ones. This ensures that the logging buffer contains the most recent messages without depleting the router's RAM. You can use the *show logging* command to view this buffer:

```
Router>show logging
Syslog logging: enabled (0 messages dropped, 0 messages rate-limited, 0 flushes, 0
overruns)
    Console logging: level debugging, 653 messages logged
    Monitor logging: level debugging, 65 messages logged
    Buffer logging: level informational, 1 messages logged
```

```
            Logging Exception size (4096 bytes)
            Trap logging: level informational, 657 message lines logged

      Log Buffer (4096 bytes):
      Mar 26 09:02:25: %SEC-6-IPACCESSLOGS: list 99 denied 172.16.2.2 5 packets
      Mar 26 09:04:56: %CLEAR-5-COUNTERS: Clear counter on all interfaces on vty1
      Mar 26 09:05:13: %SYS-5-CONFIG_I: Configured from console by ijbrown on vty1
      Router>
```

Note that the default severity logging level is set to debugging. You can adjust the severity level of the buffered log with the severity level keyword. In the example in the Solution section, we configured the router with the keyword *informational*. This will cause it to ignore debugging messages, but retain all other system log messages.

The log messages appear in order from oldest to most recent. By default, the *show logging* command displays all messages contained in the log buffer. However, you can display specific message types by using *output modifiers*:

```
      Router>show log | include denied
      Apr  7 21:16:12 EDT: %SEC-6-IPACCESSLOGS: list 98 denied 172.25.25.1 19 packets
      Apr  7 21:21:12 EDT: %SEC-6-IPACCESSLOGS: list 98 denied 172.25.1.5 1 packet
      Apr  7 21:26:12 EDT: %SEC-6-IPACCESSLOGS: list 98 denied 172.25.25.1 19 packets
      Apr  7 21:31:13 EDT: %SEC-6-IPACCESSLOGS: list 98 denied 172.25.25.1 5 packets
      Apr  7 21:33:13 EDT: %SEC-6-IPACCESSLOGS: list 98 denied 172.25.1.5 16 packets
      Apr  7 21:36:13 EDT: %SEC-6-IPACCESSLOGS: list 98 denied 172.25.25.1 5 packets
      Router>
```

By using output modifiers, you can display a single type of message based on a *regular expression*, similar to the *grep* command in Unix.

We discussed the importance of accurate time keeping and log time stamping in Chapter 14, where we highly recommended enabling log time stamps to help make the log messages more meaningful.

To disable the router's logging buffer, use the following command:

```
      Router#configure terminal
      Enter configuration commands, one per line.  End with CNTL/Z.
      Router(config)#no logging buffered
      Router(config)#end
      Router#
```

See Also

Recipe 18.2; Recipe 18.3; Chapter 14

18.2   Setting the Log Size

Problem

You want to change the size of the router's log.

Solution

You can use the optional size attribute with the *logging buffered* configuration command to change the size of your router's internal log buffer:

```
Router#configure terminal
Enter configuration commands, one per line.  End with CNTL/Z.
Router(config)#logging buffered 16000
Router(config)#end
Router#
```

Be careful, though, because adjusting the size of the router's logging buffer wipes out all of the current contents of the buffer.

Discussion

The typical default size of a router's logging buffer is 4,096 bytes (although some high-end routers will default to a higher value). A buffer of this size can hold approximately 50 log messages before overwriting occurs. Fifty messages, although better than no logging, is relatively small, and most engineers will want increase their buffer size to store more messages. To check the size of your router's logging buffer, use the *show buffer* command:

```
Router>show logging
Syslog logging: enabled (0 messages dropped, 0 messages rate-limited, 0 flushes, 0
overruns)
    Console logging: level debugging, 653 messages logged
    Monitor logging: level debugging, 65 messages logged
    Buffer logging: level debugging, 1 messages logged
    Logging Exception size (4096 bytes)
    Trap logging: level informational, 657 message lines logged

Log Buffer (16000 bytes):
Router>
```

As you can see, this router's buffer size is currently set to 16,000 bytes (roughly 16 KB).

The router will theoretically accept a wide range of buffer sizes ranging from 4,096 bytes (nothing smaller) to an astronomical 2,147,483,647 bytes (about 2 GB). Exercise caution when choosing the size of your logging buffer because it comes out of the router's system memory. A good rule is to set your logging buffer to 16 KB for smaller routers. Routers with more than 32 MB of memory can safely dedicate 32 KB, or even 64 KB, without problems. To be safe, always check the amount of free memory on your router with the *show memory* command before increasing your buffer size.

We note in passing that you can combine the keywords in Recipe 18.1 and 18.2 into a single router command:

```
Router#configure terminal
Enter configuration commands, one per line.  End with CNTL/Z.
Router(config)#logging buffered 16000 informational
Router(config)#end
Router#
```

In this case, we set the buffer size to 16,000 bytes, and the severity level to informational, by using a single configuration command.

See Also

Recipe 18.1

18.3 Clearing the Router's Log

Problem

You want to clear the router's log buffer.

Solution

Use the *clear logging* command to clear the router's internal log buffer:

```
Router#clear logging
Clear logging buffer [confirm]<enter>
Router#
```

Discussion

There are times when it is useful to be able to clear your router's internal buffer log. For instance, while debugging a network problem, old debug messages can cause unnecessary confusion during stressful moments. This will clear the router log:

```
Router#clear logging
Clear logging buffer [confirm]<enter>
Router>show logging
Syslog logging: enabled (0 messages dropped, 0 messages rate-limited, 0 flushes, 0
overruns)
    Console logging: level debugging, 64201 messages logged
    Monitor logging: level debugging, 64820 messages logged
    Buffer logging: level debugging, 9 messages logged
    Logging Exception size (4096 bytes)
    Trap logging: level debugging, 2253 message lines logged
        Logging to 172.25.1.1, 2253 message lines logged

Log Buffer (4096 bytes):
Router>
```

Note that this command has no effect on the other forms of logging.

18.4 Sending Log Messages to Your Screen

Problem

You want the router to display log messages to your VTY session in real time.

Solution

Use the *terminal monitor* command to enable the displaying of log messages to your VTY:

```
Router#terminal monitor
Router#
```

To disable logging to your VTY session, use the following command:

```
Router#terminal no monitor
Router#
```

Discussion

Routers forward all logging messages to their console ports by default, but not to their VTY lines. When you are troubleshooting a network problem on a remote router, it is often quite useful to instruct the router to send log messages to your VTY so that you can view them in real time. Here is an example showing how to configure the router to display messages with informational severity level and greater (see Table 18-1 for more information about logging severity levels) to VTY lines:

```
Router#configure terminal
Enter configuration commands, one per line.  End with CNTL/Z.
Router(config)#logging monitor informational
Router(config)#exit
Router#terminal monitor
Router#configure terminal
Enter configuration commands, one per line.  End with CNTL/Z.
Router(config)#interface Fastethernet0/0
Router(config-subif)#shutdown
Router(config-subif)#exit
Router(config)#end
Router#
Mar 26 09:36:43: %LINK-5-CHANGED: Interface Fastethernet0/0, changed state to
administratively down
```

This example changes the logging monitor level to *informational*, enables terminal monitoring and then changes the state of an interface to trigger a sample log message. By default, when you enable VTY displaying of log messages, the terminal monitor severity level is set to *debugging*, so you will see all messages. Notice that in this example, we have changed the severity level to *informational*. This will suppress the printing of debug messages, while continuing to display messages with all other severity levels. Keep in mind that setting the severity level for VTY logging is a configuration-based command whereas the command to enable VTY logging, *terminal monitor*, is a privileged-level command that must be set per session.

Enabling this type of logging makes a Telnet session to a router's VTY port look similar to connecting directly to the router's console port. You can use the show logging command to view the current monitor-logging configuration as follows:

```
Router>show logging
Syslog logging: enabled (0 messages dropped, 101 messages rate-limited, 0 flushes, 0
overruns)
    Console logging: level debugging, 66712 messages logged
    Monitor logging: level informational, 65263 messages logged
        Logging to: vty66(0)
    Buffer logging: level debugging, 644 messages logged
    Logging Exception size (4096 bytes)
    Trap logging: level debugging, 3805 message lines logged
        Logging to 172.25.1.1, 3805 message lines logged

Log Buffer (8000 bytes):
```

The highlighted section of the output shows that the monitor logging facility has been set to a severity level of *informational,* and that one session is currently in use, with the messages being displayed on vty66(0):

```
Router>show users
    Line      User      Host(s)           Idle      Location
*  66 vty 0   ijbrown   idle              00:00:00 freebsd.oreilly.com
   67 vty 1   kdooley   idle              00:00:26 solaris.oreilly.com
Router>
```

You can easily determine which user is currently using the monitor logging facility by issuing the show users command. This output indicates that the user *ijbrown* is currently using the monitor logging facility.

 Use caution when enabling VTY logging in conjunction with debugging, as it can overwhelm your session.

This feature is so useful that enabling it will soon become second nature.

18.5   Using a Remote Log Server

Problem

You want to send log messages to a remote syslog server.

Solution

Use the following command to send router log messages to a remote syslog server:

```
Router#configure terminal
Enter configuration commands, one per line.  End with CNTL/Z.
Router(config)#logging 172.25.1.1
Router(config)#end
Router#
```

Although configuring the router with a static IP address like this is the preferred method of configuring a syslog server, you can also specify a hostname to be resolved:

```
Router#configure terminal
Enter configuration commands, one per line.  End with CNTL/Z.
Router(config)#ip host nms.oreilly.com 172.25.1.1
Router(config)#logging nms.oreilly.com
Router(config)#end
Router#
```

With this configuration, the router will attempt to resolve the server name that is
provided. If the router cannot resolve the server name via DNS or static host lookup,
then the entry will fail. For more information about DNS and static host names,
please see Chapter 2.

Beginning with IOS Version 12.2(15)T, *logging host* replaced the *logging* command;
however, both methods are still supported:

```
Router2#configure terminal
Enter configuration commands, one per line.  End with CNTL/Z.
Router2(config)#logging host 172.25.1.1
Router2(config)#end
Router2#
```

Discussion

Forwarding log messages to a remote syslog server has several advantages over just
retaining log messages locally on the router. The primary advantage is that messages
sent to the server are stored to disk. All other forms of router logging are lost upon
router reload, including vital log messages that occurred just before a router crashes
due to error.

Another advantage of using a remote syslog server is storage capacity. A router stores
logging messages in internal system memory, which severely limits the number of
logs messages that can be stored. A syslog server, on the other hand, can store days,
weeks, or even months worth of log messages. It is not uncommon for an organization to retain a month or more of archived log messages for examination later.

Finally, being able to view log messages from all of your routers in a single location
can be quite useful. Forwarding all router log messages to a common logfile can
assist fault isolation, problem resolution, network forensics, and security investiga-
tions. In addition, parsing router logfiles by using custom scripts can provide an
excellent understanding of network health. In addition, many network management
software vendors now include tools to handle syslog messages.

The example below illustrates a router configured with two remote syslog servers:

```
Router>show logging
Syslog logging: enabled (0 messages dropped, 0 messages rate-limited, 0 flushes, 0
overruns)
    Console logging: level debugging, 654 messages logged
    Monitor logging: level debugging, 65 messages logged
    Buffer logging: level debugging, 2 messages logged
    Logging Exception size (4096 bytes)
    Trap logging: level informational, 658 message lines logged
```

```
Logging to 172.25.1.1, 1 message lines logged
Logging to 172.25.1.3, 1 message lines logged
```

```
Log Buffer (4096 bytes):
Router>
```

The syslog protocol resides on UDP port 514, and messages are forwarded asynchronously without acknowledgements from the server. In other words, communications between the router and server flow in a single direction, with the server acting as a passive receiver.

By default, the router sends its log messages tagged with only its IP address. In some instances, it is useful to tag the log messages with the router hostname as well. This is especially true if the syslog packets pass through a NAT device. The ability to tag syslog messages was introduced in IOS Version 12.2(15)T:

```
Router2#configure terminal
Enter configuration commands, one per line.  End with CNTL/Z.
Router2(config)#logging origin-id hostname
Router2(config)#end
Router2#
```

Before hostname tagging is enabled, the syslog server captures an example log message by only its IP address. Note that if the router IP address could be resolved by the syslog server, then the IP address would be converted to the resolved hostname. Here's an example of a normal syslog message:

```
Jul 15 20:35:07 172.25.1.100: Jul 15 20:35:07.499 EDT: %SYS-5-CONFIG_I: Configured
from console by ijbrown on vty0 (172.25.1.1)
```

After hostname tagging is enabled, the router's hostname is embedded within the log message. We've highlighted the embedded hostname:

```
Jul 15 20:37:05 172.25.1.100: Router2: Jul 15 20:37:05.173 EDT: %SYS-5-CONFIG_I:
Configured from console by ijbrown on vty0 (172.25.1.1)
```

See Also

Chapter 2; Recipe 18.6; Recipe 18.9; Recipe 18.14

18.6   Enabling Syslog on a Unix Server

Problem

You want to configure a Unix server to accept syslog messages from routers.

Solution

For most flavors of Unix and Linux, you simply need to modify the */etc/syslog.conf* file on your Unix server to include the following entry (basic configuration):

```
local7.info                                /var/log/rtrlog
```

This example stores all router messages using the default logging facility for Cisco routers, *local7*. It also stipulates that router log messages with a severity level of *informational* or greater (refer to Table 18-1) will be directed to the file */var/log/rtrlog*. The syntax of the *syslog.conf* file is log *facility.priority* notation, followed by a filename.

 Note that the *syslog.conf* file needs tabs, and not spaces, between the various fields.

Discussion

By default, your syslog server may not be equipped to handle router log messages. The above configuration entry will caused the syslog daemon to store all router messages, of *informational* severity level and higher, to a file called */var/log/rtrlog*. Before the server will begin forwarding messages to this file, it must exist and have the proper file attributes:

```
Freebsd# cd /var/log
/var/log
Freebsd# touch rtrlog
Freebsd# chmod 644 rtrlog
Freebsd#
```

Then you should reload or *HUP* the syslog daemon to force it to read your new configuration file and begin storing router log messages. On System V-based Unix servers, use the following commands:

```
Solaris# ps -ef | grep syslogd
    root   142    1  0   Nov 12 ?        1:21 /usr/sbin/syslogd -m 30
Solaris# kill -HUP 142
Solaris#
```

On BSD-based Unix and Linux servers, use the following commands:

```
Freebsd# ps -aux | grep syslogd
root      66  0.0  0.2   960  624  ??  Ss    3Mar02   0:28.66 syslogd -m 30
Freebsd# kill -HUP 66
Freebsd#
```

For more information on your syslog daemon and its configuration options, check your system's manual pages by using the Unix commands *man syslog* and *man syslog.conf*.

Note that some Unix flavors, including most Linux distributions, require the syslog daemon be initialized with the -r switch before they will accept remote syslog messages. See your manual pages for more information (*man syslogd*).

See Also

Recipe 18.7; Recipe 18.11; Recipe 18.12

18.7   Changing the Default Log Facility

Problem

You want to change the default logging facility.

Solution

Use the *logging facility* configuration command to change the syslog facility that the router sends error messages to:

```
Router#configure terminal
Enter configuration commands, one per line.  End with CNTL/Z.
Router(config)#logging host 172.25.1.1
Router(config)#logging facility local6
Router(config)#end
Router#
```

The default syslog facility setting is *local7*.

Discussion

By default, the router will forward all syslog messages to the server's *local7* log facility. You can modify this behavior and forward all of your router's syslog messages to another facility by utilizing the *logging facility* configuration command. Table 18-3 illustrates the possible logging facilities that a router will accept.

Table 18-3. Cisco logging facility types

Facility	Description
Auth	Authorization system
Cron	Cron/at facility
Daemon	System daemons
Kern	Kernel
local0	Local use
local1	Local use
local2	Local use
local3	Local use
local4	Local use
local5	Local use
local6	Local use
local7	Local use (Default facility for Cisco routers)
Lpr	Line printer system
Mail	Mail system
News	USENET news

Table 18-3. Cisco logging facility types (continued)

Facility	Description
sys9	System use
sys10	System use
sys11	System use
sys12	System use
sys13	System use
sys14	System use
Syslog	Syslog itself
User	User process
Uucp	Unix-to-Unix copy system

 We generally recommend that you choose one of the "local" facilities, as these are intended specifically for this type of use.

There are a number of reasons why it can be quite useful to choose a facility other than the default. First, another application on the syslog server itself may already be using the logging facility *local7*. Although most applications provide a means by which to change the default logging facility, some, regrettably, do not.

Second, you might want to separate log messages from routers and switches, or other types of network equipment. This makes parsing through the logfiles much easier. For example, you could configure your switches to forward all log messages to *local7*, and your routers to *local6*.

Third, it can often be important for security auditing reasons to be able to separate perimeter router logs from those of internal company routers. Perimeter routers protect the organization from outsiders and require more diligent attention. Sending their log messages to a separate file so that they are not lumped in with the rest of the organization's router messages makes it easier to give them this extra attention. For instance, perimeter router logs may require different archive periods, or might have specialized scripts to parse through them. Assigning a different log facility to them is generally a good idea.

The example below shows a sample portion of a *syslog.conf* file that forwards log messages from all perimeter routers to facility *local5*, all other router logs to facility *local6*, and all switch logs to facility *local7*:

```
local5.info              /var/log/seclog
local6.info              /var/log/rtrlog
local7.info              /var/log/switchlog
```

The sample router configuration in the solution section forwards router log messages to log facility *local6*. The next example illustrates how to configure the perimeter routers to forward their log messages to log facility *local5*:

```
Router#configure terminal
Enter configuration commands, one per line.  End with CNTL/Z.
Router(config)#logging host 172.25.1.1
Router(config)#logging facility local5
Router(config)#end
Router#
```

One final useful thing to do with your syslog configuration is to send high severity log messages to a separate file to make parsing easier. The following example shows a sample *syslog.conf* configuration that logs all router log messages to a single file called */var/ log/rtrlog*, and all high severity log messages to a file called */var/log/rtrpriority*:

```
local7.info                      /var/log/rtrlog
local7.err                       /var/log/rtrpriority
```

See Also

Recipe 18.8

18.8   Restricting What Log Messages Are Sent to the Server

Problem

You want to limit which logging levels the router will send to the syslog server.

Solution

Use the *logging trap* configuration command to limit the severity level of syslog messages:

```
Router#configure terminal
Enter configuration commands, one per line.  End with CNTL/Z.
Router(config)#logging host 172.25.1.1
Router(config)#logging trap notifications
Router(config)#end
Router#
```

Discussion

By default, when you enable remote logging on a router, it will forward only those messages with a severity level *informational* or higher (see Table 18-1). This means that the router forwards everything but debugging messages to the syslog server. Raising the severity of the log messages forwarded to the syslog server can help to reduce bandwidth utilization across the network, as well as the disk space required for storing the log messages on the server. This example shows the output of the *show logging* exec command:

```
Router>show logging
Syslog logging: enabled (0 messages dropped, 0 messages rate-limited, 0 flushes, 0
overruns)
    Console logging: level debugging, 658 messages logged
    Monitor logging: level debugging, 65 messages logged
    Buffer logging: level debugging, 6 messages logged
    Logging Exception size (4096 bytes)
    Trap logging: level notifications, 662 message lines logged
        Logging to 172.25.1.1, 5 message lines logged
        Logging to 172.25.1.3, 5 message lines logged

Log Buffer (4096 bytes):
Router>
```

Notice that the logging severity level is set to *notifications* and that both outbound servers are limited to the same level. It is important to note that the *logging trap* command sets the severity level for all syslog servers.

Another important use for the logging trap command is allowing the router to send debug level messages to a syslog server. The default severity level for syslog is *informational*, so the router will not forward any debug messages. Having the ability to store debug messages can often be useful in fault isolation and trouble resolution. The following commands show how to enable the forwarding of *debugging* severity-level messages:

```
Router#configure terminal
Enter configuration commands, one per line.  End with CNTL/Z.
Router(config)#logging host 172.25.1.1
Router(config)#logging trap debugging
Router(config)#end
Router#
```

You must also configure the syslog server to handle debug level messages. You can accomplish this in one of two ways—by creating a dedicated file to handle debug messages or by forwarding debug messages to the normal router logfile. The following two examples will demonstrate how to modify your *syslog.conf* file to handle both situations:

```
local7.debug                    /var/log/debug
```

Or:

```
local7.=debug                   /var/log/debug
```

The difference between these two methods is that while the first sends all messages with a severity greater than or equal to debug severity to the indicated file, the second directs only debug level messages to this file. The first example is a more traditional method to assign debug level messages to a particular file, but the second example is preferred since it allows you to separate debug messages from the normal router log messages. Most modern syslog facilities will handle the second example command syntax, but please check your manpages to ensure compatibility by issuing a *man syslog.conf*.

To simply forward all debug level messages to the default router log, change your *syslog.conf* files to include the following:

```
local7.debug                    /var/log/rtrlog
```

Use caution when enabling the remote storing of debug messages. Debug messages can quickly overwhelm your server if not properly enabled on the router.

18.9 Setting the IP Source Address for Syslog Messages

Problem

You want the router to use a particular source IP address for syslog messages.

Solution

Use the *logging source-interface* configuration command to specify a particular IP address for syslog messages:

```
Router#configure terminal
Enter configuration commands, one per line.  End with CNTL/Z.
Router(config)#logging host 172.25.1.1
Router(config)#logging source-interface Loopback0
Router(config)#end
Router#
```

Discussion

Normally, when you enable logging to a remote server, that server will see the source of the message as being the router's nearest interface. However, this is not always meaningful. Sometimes you want it to be a *loopback* address so that all messages from this router look the same. For example, it is a common practice to populate DNS with only the *loopback* IP addresses to facilitate router access. This means that none of the other router interfaces can be resolved by using DNS:

```
Apr  2 20:27:01 172.25.2.6 94: %SYS-5-CONFIG_I: Configured from on vty0
Apr  2 20:27:48 Boston 95: %SYS-5-CONFIG_I: Configured from on vty0
```

The above example shows two identical log messages originating from the same router, as they appear on the syslog server. The first message uses the IP address of a serial interface that the syslog server is unable to resolve. Notice that the server still stores the message, although it uses the IP address to identify the source.

The second log message occurs after configuring the router to use the *loopback* interface as the source address. Notice that the syslog server is now able to resolve the source IP address and identifies the source as the router *Boston*. This makes parsing the logfile for all syslog messages that belong to Boston straightforward and simple.

See Also

Recipe 18.5

18.10 Logging Router Syslog Messages in Different Files

Problem

You want the Unix server to send router log messages to a different logfile than the local system messages.

Solution

To disable router syslog messages from inundating your local system logfiles, use the following commands:

```
local7.info                                    /var/log/rtrlog
*.err;kern.debug;auth.notice;mail.crit;local7.none    /var/log/syslog
*.notice;kern.debug;auth.info;mail.crit;local7.none    /var/adm/messages
```

Discussion

Most common syslog facilities will, by default, log all messages of a certain severity and higher (see Table 18-1) to their generic local system logfiles. However, once you configure your *syslog.conf* file to store all router log messages to a specific file, */var/log/rtrlog*, in this case, you want to suppress this from occurring. Suppressing router log messages from being stored in your local system logfiles prevents cluttering, separates unrelated logfiles, and prevents the storing of redundant data.

The first line of the example above causes the syslog facility to store all router logs to a certain file. However, syslog will continue to archive router messages into the general system logfiles, as well. Notice that lines 2 and 3 above include a wildcard option (*.err* and *.info*, respectively). These wildcards match the *local7* logging facility and all others as well, causing all log messages of a certain severity level and higher, to be stored. To prevent the router logs from being stored in the general system logfiles, use the *local7.none*, which will override the wildcard setting.

See Also

Recipe 18.6

18.11 Maintaining Syslog Files on the Server

Problem

You want to automatically rotate and archive router logfiles on a Unix server.

Solution

The Bourne shell script in Example 18-1 automatically rotates router logfiles to ensure that these files don't become too big and cumbersome to navigate. The script is intended to be invoked via a *cron* job on a daily basis, but you can also run it manually. By default, the script retains seven days worth of archived logfiles and compresses files older than two days. No arguments are required or expected.

Example 18-1. rotatelog.sh

```
#!/bin/sh
#
#   rotatelog.sh -- a script to rotate logfiles and
#                   compress archived files
#
# Set behavior
SYSLOGPID=/etc/syslog.pid
LOGDIR=/var/log
LOG=rtrlog
DAYS=7
COMPRESS="/usr/bin/compress -f"
#
# Program body
[ -f $SYSLOGPID ] || echo "Syslog PID file doesn't exist"
if [ -d $LOGDIR ]; then
  cd $LOGDIR
  [ -f $LOG.1 ] && `$COMPRESS $LOG.1` && sleep 1
  while [ $DAYS -gt 1 ]
  do
        LOW=`expr $DAYS - 1`
        [ -f $LOG.$LOW.Z ] && mv $LOG.$LOW.Z $LOG.$DAYS.Z
        DAYS=$LOW
  done
[ -f $LOG ] || echo "Log file $LOG doesn't exist"
[ -f $LOG ] && mv $LOG $LOG.1
touch $LOG
chmod 644 $LOG
sleep 10
kill -HUP `cat $SYSLOGPID`
#
else
echo "Log directory $LOGDIR is not valid"
fi
```

Discussion

If left unchecked, the router logfiles grow until your disk space runs out. This script is designed to rotate router logfiles on a daily basis to ensure they don't grow too large.

This script will rotate logs on a daily basis and retain seven days worth of archived logfiles, and overwrite files that are older than this. To reduce the required disk space of the archived logfiles, the script will retain the previous day's log, in a normal format, and compress the remaining days. The number of archived days stored by the script is completely configurable. For instance, to change the number of archived days to 30, change the *DAYS* variable:

```
DAYS=30
```

The script is initially configured to rotate a file called */var/log/rtrlog*, but it can easily be configured to rotate any logfile by changing the two variables, *LOGDIR* and *LOG*. The variable named *LOGDIR* contains the directory that the logfiles reside in, and the variable *LOG* contains the name of the logfile itself. For instance, if you want to change the script to rotate a file called */var/adm/nmslog*, then you would modify the following lines in the script:

```
LOGDIR=/var/adm
LOG=nmslog
```

The final variable that may require modification is the *SYSLOGPID* variable. This variable contains the location of your system's *syslog.pid* file. The script assumes that the process ID number (PID), which is carried by the *SYSLOGPID* variable, can be found in the file */etc/syslog.pid*, which is a common location for Solaris-based machines (another common location is */var/run/syslog.pid*). Configuring the script with the correct *syslog.pid* location is vitally important; otherwise, your logfiles will not rotate correctly. To find the location of your *syslog.pid* file on your system, use the following command, which can take several minutes to run:

```
server% find / -name syslog.pid -print
/etc/syslog.pid
server%
```

As mentioned earlier, the script is intended to be launched from *cron* on a nightly basis. Since it will likely require root privileges to create the necessary files, launch the script from root's *crontab*. Below is an example of the *crontab* entry required to launch the script each day at midnight (assuming it is located in */usr/local/bin*):

```
0 0 * * *          /usr/local/bin/rotatelog.sh
```

Finally, since archived files older then one day, are compressed, we should mention some methods of working with compressed files. First, to view a compressed file, use the *zcat* command or *uncompress –c* command. To permanently uncompress a compressed file, use the *uncompress* command (without any switches).

18.12 Testing the Syslog Sever Configuration

Problem

You want to test the configuration of your syslog server to ensure that the log messages are stored in their correct location.

Solution

The Bourne shell script in Example 18-2 emulates syslog messages at various severity levels to ensure that your server routes them to the correct location. By default, the script will emulate syslog messages to the *local7* syslog facility, since Cisco routers default to *local7*, but the logging facility is completely configurable. No arguments are required or expected.

Example 18-2. testlog.sh

```
#!/bin/sh
#
#    testlog.sh -- a script to test the syslog facility to ensure that
#                  messages, at various levels, are being forwarded
#                  to the correct file(s)
#
# Set Behavior
FACILITY=local7
LOGGER="/usr/bin/logger"
#
$LOGGER -p $FACILITY.emerg   "This meassage was sent to $FACILITY.emerg (0)"
$LOGGER -p $FACILITY.alert   "This meassage was sent to $FACILITY.alert (1)"
$LOGGER -p $FACILITY.crit    "This meassage was sent to $FACILITY.crit (2)"
$LOGGER -p $FACILITY.err     "This meassage was sent to $FACILITY.err (3)"
$LOGGER -p $FACILITY.warning "This meassage was sent to $FACILITY.warning (4)"
$LOGGER -p $FACILITY.notice  "This meassage was sent to $FACILITY.notice (5)"
$LOGGER -p $FACILITY.info    "This meassage was sent to $FACILITY.info (6)"
$LOGGER -p $FACILITY.debug   "This meassage was sent to $FACILITY.debug (7)"
```

Discussion

This script is designed to test the syslog server configuration to ensure that router log messages forward to the correct file(s). Basically, the script emulates router log messages at the various severity levels to verify how the syslog daemon handles them.

We use the Unix *logger* command to generate log messages and forward them to the syslog daemon. The server should route these log messages to same location as the router log messages. If the test log messages either do not show up in the expected file or show up in undesirable locations, then there must be configuration problems in your *syslog.conf* file.

As noted above, the script's default syslog facility is set to *local7*, but this is completely configurable. For instance, if your routers are set to use *local6*, then the variable *FACILITY* needs to be *local6*:

```
FACILITY=local6
```

If your *syslog.conf* file includes an entry to forward *local7.info* log messages to a file called */var/log/rtrlog*, then the output from the script would look like the following:

```
Freebsd# ./testsyslog.sh

Message from syslogd@localhost at Sun Mar 31 22:44:09 2002 ...
localhost This message was sent to local7.emerg (0)
Freebsd# tail /var/log/rtrlog
Mar 31 22:44:09 localhost This message was sent to local7.emerg (0)
Mar 31 22:44:09 localhost This message was sent to local7.alert (1)
Mar 31 22:44:09 localhost This message was sent to local7.crit (2)
Mar 31 22:44:09 localhost This message was sent to local7.err (3)
Mar 31 22:44:09 localhost This message was sent to local7.warning (4)
Mar 31 22:44:09 localhost This message was sent to local7.notice (5)
Mar 31 22:44:09 localhost This message was sent to local7.info (6)
Freebsd#
```

Notice that one of the messages produced by the script was sent directly to the screen. This is because the test server's *syslog.conf* file is configured to forward all *emergency* level syslog messages to all TTY terminals, as is a commonly done on Unix machines. Although this message will not cause any system problems, it can strike fear into other active users, so be aware.

The second part of the output shows the contents of the */var/log/rtrlog* file. You will notice that the output shows seven lines of progressively decreasing priority log messages, but it does not display a severity 7 (debugging) message. This is because the *syslog.conf* configuration included a line for *local7.info*, which does not include debug level messages.

Finally, with a minor modification to your *syslog.conf* file, you can utilize this script to test remote syslog servers:

```
local7.info                 @nms.oreilly.com
```

This example would forward all *local7* log messages to a remote syslog server called *nms.oreilly.com*. Notice the syntax of this line introduces the @ sign to signify that a server name follows. Running the script again would forward *local7* log messages to the remote server, which would effectively emulate router log messages and test the server's syslog configuration. When testing is completed, make sure to remove or comment out the above configuration line; otherwise, incoming *local7* log messages will also be forwarded to the remote syslog server.

18.13 Preventing the Most Common Messages from Being Logged

Problem

You want to disable the router from creating link up/down syslog messages on unimportant router interfaces.

Solution

Use the *no logging event* configuration commands to disable the logging of common interface level messages:

```
Router#configure terminal
Enter configuration commands, one per line.  End with CNTL/Z.
Router(config)#interface Serial0/0
Router(config-if)#no logging event link-status
Router(config-if)#no logging event dlci-status-change
Router(config-if)#no logging event subif-link-status
Router(config-if)#exit
Router(config)#end
Router#
```

Discussion

By default, log messages are sent whenever a router interface status changes states. Generally, you want to see log messages that indicate that an interface status has changed, but there are times when it can be useful to disable these types of messages. For instance, dial interfaces may cycle up and down many times throughout the course of a normal day without being cause for concern. Having the capability to suppress these messages helps keep logs uncluttered and can prevent network management staff from wasting time responding to unnecessary trouble reports:

```
%LINK-3-UPDOWN: Interface Serial0, changed state to down
%LINEPROTO-5-UPDOWN: Line protocol on Interface Serial0, changed state to down
%LINK-3-UPDOWN: Interface Serial0, changed state to up
%LINEPROTO-5-UPDOWN: Line protocol on Interface Serial0, changed state to up
```

The example above shows the log messages that are sent when a router interface changes states from up to down and back to up. You can use the *no logging event link-status* command to suppress these messages.

On frame-relay interfaces, DLCI state changes trigger the router to create log messages. In large Frame Relay-based networks, many DLCI changes can occur daily, which can clutter logs and open duplicate trouble reports. Using the *no logging event dlci-status-change* configuration command will prevent these log messages from being created:

```
%FR-5-DLCICHANGE: Interface Serial0 - DLCI 50 state changed to INACTIVE
%LINEPROTO-5-UPDOWN: Line protocol on Interface Serial0.1, changed state to down
```

```
%FR-5-DLCICHANGE: Interface Serial0 - DLCI 50 state changed to ACTIVE
%LINEPROTO-5-UPDOWN: Line protocol on Interface Serial0.1, changed state to up
```

Finally, subinterface link up or down messages can be suppressed by using the *no logging event subif-link-status* configuration command. The example below demonstrates a typical frame-relay interface failure. Notice that the router sends a "line protocol down" log message for the main interface, as well as each of the subinterfaces. Although this example only shows one subinterface, it is not uncommon to see dozens of subinterfaces on a single physical interface. In these cases, it can be useful to suppress subinterface messages:

```
%LINK-3-UPDOWN: Interface Serial0, changed state to down
%FR-5-DLCICHANGE: Interface Serial0 - DLCI 50 state changed to DELETED
%FR-5-DLCICHANGE: Interface Serial0 - DLCI 102 state changed to DELETED
%FR-5-DLCICHANGE: Interface Serial0 - DLCI 103 state changed to DELETED
%LINEPROTO-5-UPDOWN: Line protocol on Interface Serial0.1, changed state to down
%LINEPROTO-5-UPDOWN: Line protocol on Interface Serial0, changed state to down
```

18.14 Rate-Limiting Syslog Traffic

Problem

You wish to rate-limit the syslog traffic to your server.

Solution

Use the *logging rate-limit* configuration command to limit the number of syslog packets sent to your server:

```
Router#configure terminal
Enter configuration commands, one per line.  End with CNTL/Z.
Router(config)#logging host 172.25.1.1
Router(config)#logging rate-limit 30 except warnings
Router(config)#end
Router#
```

To rate limit the number of log messages sent to the console port, use the following command:

```
Router#configure terminal
Enter configuration commands, one per line.  End with CNTL/Z.
Router(config)#logging rate-limit console 25 except warnings
Router(config)#end
Router#
```

This feature became available starting in IOS Version 12.1(3)T.

Discussion

By default, a router that is configured for remote logging will forward all log messages to the syslog server as they are created, regardless of how many there are. The *rate-limit* command will throttle the number of packets to ensure that router won't flood the network or syslog server. It is particularly useful to throttle syslog messages when forwarding debug traces or if the network is congested.

Cisco provides the option to throttle log messages sent to the console port, as well. This feature is important, since all messages written to the console port cause CPU interrupts. If a large number of log messages are being sent to the console port, then the router can suffer noticeable service degradation. Being able to rate-limit messages is an effective alternative to completely disabling them.

The syntax for rate limiting includes several options. The examples above limit the rate of syslog messages to 30 messages per second. The valid limits for this option are 1 to 10,000 messages per second. Since log messages vary in length, it is difficult to calculate a meaningful number in terms of bytes per second. However, a typical average size for a log message is between 150 and 170 bytes. So we can roughly estimate that 30 messages per second will correspond to 36,000 to 40,800 bits per second, which is a good limit for serial lines.

Both examples in this section use the optional keyword *except*. Use this keyword to ensure that only non-critical messages become rate-limited. For example, to rate-limit all messages at a warning severity level or lower, and to allow all other severity messages to be sent, use the *except warning* keywords. The examples in this section rate-limit only those messages set at a warning severity level or below. Note that the keyword *all* is equivalent to setting the *except* option at the debug level, meaning all messages are rate-limited.

18.15 Enabling Error Log Counting

Problem

You wish to see the number and type of log messages created by the router.

Solution

Use the *logging count* command to enable error log counting:

```
Router2#configure terminal
Enter configuration commands, one per line.  End with CNTL/Z.
Router2(config)#logging count
Router2(config)#end
Router2#
```

Discussion

The *logging count* command causes the router to maintain a count and timestamp of each recorded log type. To view the results of the log counting, use the *show logging count* command:

```
Router2#show logging count
Facility          Message Name                 Sev Occur      Last Time
========================================================================
NTP               PEERREACH                     6   3 Jul 13 20:31:34.441
NTP               PEERSYNC                      5   1 Jul 13 20:23:03.571
NTP               PEERUNREACH                   4   3 Jul 13 20:22:00.435
NTP               RESTART                       6   1 Jan 31 14:13:33.769
-------------     -----------------------------     -------------------------------
NTP TOTAL                                           8

SYS               ESMSHUTDOWN                   7   7 Jul 15 19:18:07.476
SYS               PRIV_AUTH_PASS                5   7 Jul 15 19:32:50.735
SYS               LOGGINGHOST_STARTSTOP         6   4 Jul 15 19:56:31.203
SYS               RESTART                       5   1 Jan 31 14:13:33.697
SYS               CONFIG_I                      5  23 Jul 15 20:11:14.943
SYS               CLOCKUPDATE                   6   4 Jul 13 20:21:59.574
-------------     -----------------------------     -------------------------------
SYS TOTAL                                           46

LINEPROTO         UPDOWN                        5   4 Jan 31 14:13:33.260
-------------     -----------------------------     -------------------------------
LINEPROTO TOTAL                                     4

LINK              CHANGED                       5   2 Jan 31 14:13:34.390
-------------     -----------------------------     -------------------------------
LINK TOTAL                                          2

CLEAR             COUNTERS                      5   4 Jul 15 20:09:00.005
-------------     -----------------------------     -------------------------------
CLEAR TOTAL                                         4

Router2#
```

Notice that the router displays a nice overview of error log messages that have occurred and a timestamp of the most recent occurrence. The router also groups log messages by type, keeping all NTP-related messages together, for instance.

On the highlighted output line, notice that the router's configuration has been modified 23 times since log counting was enabled. Also notice the last recorded message was July 15 at 20:11. Note that the "Sev" column indicates the log message's severity level.

Unfortunately, Cisco doesn't provide an easy way to clear these statistics. The only way to reset the logging count values is to reload the router.

18.16 XML-Formatted Log Messages

Problem

You wish to send your syslog messages in XML format.

Solution

To enable XML-formatted syslog messages, use the following commands:

```
Router2# configure terminal
Enter configuration commands, one per line.  End with CNTL/Z.
Router2(config)#logging console xml
Router2(config)#logging monitor xml
Router2(config)#logging buffered xml
Router2(config)#logging host 172.25.1.1 xml
Router2(config)#end
Router2#
```

Discussion

Beginning with IOS Version 12.2(15)T, Cisco introduced Extensible Markup Language (XML) formatted logging of system events and errors. XML provides a method of standardizing and consistently formatting messages, which can easily be utilized by third-party applications to extract data. When XML logging is enabled, system log messages are tagged using a standardized format. Detailed information regarding the message tagging is contained in Table 18-4.

XML tagging can be enabled on all logging facilities, including console, monitor, buffer, or remote syslog servers. However, XML tagged system messages are not as easily read or understood by humans, which means XML tagged messages are most likely sent to a remote syslog server for processing. For example, here is a typical system message created by a router in normal syslog format:

```
Jul 15 20:37:17.277 EDT: %SYS-5-CONFIG_I: Configured from console by ijbrown on vty0
(172.25.1.1)
```

The following is the same system message with XML tagging enabled:

```
<ios-log-msg><facility>SYS</facility><severity>5</severity><msg-id>CONFIG_I</msg-id>
<time>Jul 15 20:37:17.277 EDT</time><args><arg id="0">console</arg><arg id="1">
ijbrown on vty0 (172.25.1.1)</arg></args></ios-log-msg>
```

As you can see, the XML tagged system message is difficult to decipher for us humans; however, the consistent tagging structure is perfectly suited for external monitoring programs to extract data. The following table breaks down the various XML tags used by Cisco to encode system messages.

Table 18-4. XML Tags used for syslog messages

Tag applied	Item delimited
<ios-log-msg></ios-log-message>	Entire syslog message.
<facility></facility>	The facility name of the log message (e.g., SYS).
<severity></severity>	The severity level of the message from 0 to 7, with 0 the most severe (e.g., 5).
<msg-id></msg-id>	The error or event message type (e.g., CONFIG_I).
<seq></seq>	The message sequence number.

Table 18-4. XML Tags used for syslog messages (continued)

Tag applied	Item delimited
`<time></time>`	The timestamp of the message, including the time and date (e.g., Jul 15 20:37:27.277 EDT).
`<args></args>`	The variables contained within the human readable test. Note that the full human readable is not kept. Only the individual arguments are formatted and retained. See the next section.
`<arg id="x"></arg>`	The specific arguments that are embedded within the human readable test. These arguments are sequentially numbered starting from 0 (e.g., Arg0 = console Arg1= ijbrown on vty0 (172.25.1.1)).

If you are unfamiliar with XML, we recommend *XML Pocket Reference* by Simon St. Laurent and Michael Fitzgerald (O'Reilly). A simple description of XML is that it uses special tags that define objects. One tag defines the start of an object, and a second tag defines the end of that object. For example, in Table 18-4, we indicated that the entire log message begins with the tag `<ios-log-msg>` and ends with the same tag, but with a slash in it (`</ios-log-msg>`). You can then nest other objects inside this object, with each object surrounded by a similar pair of tags. However, as we mentioned earlier, XML is not really intended to be human-readable.

It's possible to enable both normal system log buffering and XML tagged log buffering concurrently. To view the XML buffered log on a router, use the *show log xml* command:

```
Router2#show logging xml
<syslog-logging status="enabled" msg-dropped="1" msg-rate-limited="1" flushes="0"
overruns="0"><xml>enabled</xml><filter>enabled</filter></syslog-logging>
    <console-logging level="debugging" messages-logged="131"><xml>enabled</xml>
<filter>disabled</filter></console-logging>
    <monitor-logging level="debugging" messages-logged="45"><xml>disabled</xml>
<filter>disabled</filter></monitor-logging>
        <logging-to><dest id="0">vty6(35)<dest></logging-to>
    <buffer-logging level="debugging" messages-logged="119"><xml messages-logged="7">
enabled</xml><filter>disabled</filter></buffer-logging>
    <logging-exception size="4096 bytes"></logging-exception>
    <count-and-timestamp-logging status="enabled"></count-and-timestamp-logging>
    <trap-logging level="informational" messages-lines-logged="91"></trap-logging>
        <logging-to><dest id="0" ipaddr="172.25.1.1" transport="udp" port="514"
audit="disabled" link="up" message-lines-logged="74"><xml>enabled</xml><filter>
disabled</filter><stream ="1"</stream><dest></logging-to>
        <logging-to><dest id="1" ipaddr="172.25.1.3" transport="udp" port="514"
audit="disabled" link="up" message-lines-logged="91"><xml>disabled</xml><filter>
disabled</filter><stream ="0"</stream><dest></logging-to>

<log-xml-buffer size="4096 bytes"></log-xml-buffer>

<ios-log-msg><facility>CLEAR</facility><severity>5</severity><msg-id>COUNTERS</msg-
id><time>Jul 16 10:09:43.832 EDT</time><args><arg id="0">all</arg><arg id="1">
interfaces</arg><arg id="2">ijbrown on vty0 (172.25.1.1)</arg></args></ios-log-msg>
Router2#
```

It is also possible to send standard system log messages to one host and XML-tagged log messages to another host; however you must specify a different IP address. You cannot send both standard and XML system messages to the same host concurrently:

```
Router2#configure terminal
Enter configuration commands, one per line.  End with CNTL/Z.
Router2(config)#logging host 172.25.1.1 xml
Router2(config)#logging host 172.25.1.3
Router2(config)#end
Router2#
```

In this example, the router is configured to send XML-tagged system messages to host 172.25.1.1, and standard system log messages to host 172.25.1.3.

See Also

Recipe 18.5; *XML Pocket Reference* by Simon St.Laurent and Michael Fitzgerald (O'Reilly)

18.17 Modifying Log Messages

Problem

You wish to change the default attributes of particular system-generated log messages.

Solution

In order to modify system log messages, you must configure the Embedded Syslog Manager (ESM) by using a combination of configuration commands and TCL scripts. First you must write a TCL script to perform a certain task and make it available via TFTP. In this simple example, the TCL script in Example 18-3 filters out a particular system log message (clear counters) and permits all other messages to be forwarded as normal.

Example 18-3. delcounters.tcl

```
# delcounters.tcl - This script deletes all log messages that
#                   have the mnemonic "COUNTERS".
if { [string compare -nocase COUNTERS $::mnemonic ] == 0 } {
return ""
} else {
return $::orig_msg
}
```

Now we must configure the router to retrieve the TCL script we've just created and implement it:

```
Router2#configure terminal
Enter configuration commands, one per line.  End with CNTL/Z.
Router2(config)#logging filter tftp://172.25.1.1/delcounters.tcl
```

```
Router2(config)#logging host 172.25.1.1 filtered
Router2(config)#end
Router2#
```

Discussion

The ESM was introduced in IOS Version 12.3(2)T, and it provides a programmable interface that allows you to filter, escalate, correlate, route, and customize system logging messages. The ESM allows you full control of system log messages via Tool Command Language-based (TCL) scripts, which can be stored locally or remotely.

In our example, we configured the router to delete all "clear counters" log messages while leaving all other system log messages to pass untouched. This is the most simple and practical example of the ESM in use. If we wanted to delete multiple system message types, we could modify the TCL script or load multiple TCL scripts into the router:

```
Router2#configure terminal
Enter configuration commands, one per line.  End with CNTL/Z.
Router2(config)#logging filter tftp://172.25.1.1/delcounters.tcl
Router2(config)#logging filter flash:test.tcl
Router2(config)#logging host 172.25.1.1 filtered
Router2(config)#end
Router2#
```

TCL filter scripts can be loaded by a wide variety of methods, both locally and remotely. For instance, scripts can be loaded remotely via TFTP, SCP, FTP, HTTP, etc., and TCL scripts can be locally stored in system flash or nvram. We recommend loading scripts locally whenever possible; however, it sometimes makes sense to keep scripts stored remotely. For instance, if a large number of routers utilize the same script, then keeping it centrally located makes administration and modification easier.

To view the ESM configuration on a router, use the *show logging* command:

```
Router2#show logging
Syslog logging: enabled (1 messages dropped, 1 messages rate-limited,
                0 flushes, 0 overruns, xml enabled, filtering enabled)
    Console logging: level debugging, 166 messages logged, xml enabled,
                    filtering disabled
    Monitor logging: level debugging, 64 messages logged, xml disabled,
                    filtering enabled
    Buffer logging: level debugging, 119 messages logged, xml disabled,
                    filtering disabled
    Logging Exception size (4096 bytes)
    Count and timestamp logging messages: enabled

Filter modules:
    tftp://172.25.1.1/delcounters.tcl
    flash:test.tcl

    Trap logging: level informational, 129 message lines logged
        Logging to 172.25.1.1 (udp port 514, audit disabled, link up), 107 message
lines logged, xml disabled,
```

```
                    filtering enabled
          Logging to 172.25.1.3 (udp port 514, audit disabled, link up), 129 message
      lines logged, xml disabled,
                    filtering disabled
```

Router2#

Notice that a new section has been added to the output of the show logging command called "Filter modules". Below this heading is a list of currently configured TCL filters. Please be aware that the order in which the filters are configured can affect the results of the filters. Also notice that filtering has been enabled on remote host 172.25.1.1, as we configured it earlier. ESM log filtering can be enabled on all logging facilities by using the keyword *filtered*:

```
Router2#configure terminal
Enter configuration commands, one per line.  End with CNTL/Z.
Router2(config)#logging buffered filtered
Router2(config)#logging monitor filtered
Router2(config)#logging console filtered
Router2(config)#logging host 172.25.1.1 filtered
Router2(config)#end
Router2#
```

In our first eample we demonstrated how to filter out a specific system log message "clear counters." In the next example, we will filter out an entire group of messages. Before we proceed, let's take a look at sample log messge and examine its standard format. The following is a sample line protocol log message:

```
%LINEPROTO-5-UPDOWN: Line protocol on Interface Serial0, changed state to up
```

All system log messages take the basic standard format of the following:

```
%<facility>-<severity>-<mnemonic>: <message-text>
```

In this example, then, the facility would be "LINEPROTO", severity would be "5", the mnemonic would be "UPDOWN", and the message-text would be "Line protocol on Interface Serial0, changed state to up."

Looking back at our first TCL script, you'll see that we filtered on the mnemonic and deleted all log messages that had the mnemonic of "COUNTERS". The script in Example 18-4 filters out all log messages with the facility equal to "LINEPROTO".

Example 18-4. facilitydel.tcl

```
# facilitydel.tcl - This script deletes all log messages that begin
#                   with the facility named "LINEPROTO".
if { [string compare -nocase LINEPROTO $::facility ] == 0 } {
return ""
} else {
return $::orig_msg
}
```

So far, we've looked at two pretty simple TCL scripts. Now let's look at a more sophisticated TCL script that Cisco has created to change the severity level of a given system log message. It's particularly interesting because the script also accepts command-line arguments, which the router must pass to it.

As we mentioned earlier, ESM filters can perform a number of tasks, including the modification of system hardcoded severity levels. Example 18-5 modifies whatever log message you specify to the new severity level you provide.

Example 18-5. sevrtyincr.tcl

```
# severityincr.tcl - Increases the severity level of a syslog message.
#                    Requires two arguments, first the mnemonic and
#                    second the new severity level.
#                    E.g., STATECHANGE 3
if { [string length $::orig_msg] == 0} {
   return ""
}

if { [info exists ::cli_args] } {
    set args [split $::cli_args]
    if { [ string compare -nocase [lindex $args 0] $::mnemonic ] == 0 } {
        set ::severity [lindex $args 1]
        set sev_index [ string first [lindex $args 0] $::orig_msg ]
        if { $sev_index >= 2 } {
           incr sev_index -2
           return [string replace $::orig_msg $sev_index $sev_index [lindex $args 1]]
        }
    }
}

return $::orig_msg
```

Before we implement this ESM script, let's apply it to a real world situation. One particularly important system log message that we feel has been assigned a low severity level is the HSRP change of state log message. By default, the HSRP change of state log message is assigned a rather low severity level of 6 (informational). For this example, we're going to assign it a new severity level of 3 (Errors):

```
Router2#configure terminal
Enter configuration commands, one per line.  End with CNTL/Z.
Router2(config)#logging filter tftp://172.25.1.1/sevrtyincr.tcl args STATECHANGE 3
Router2(config)#logging host 172.25.1.1 filtered
Router2(config)#end
Router2#
```

Notice that in this example we passed two arguments to the TCL script, "STATECHANGE" and "3". The first argument indicates the mnemonic of the log message we wish to modify, and the second argument indicates the new severity level. The nice thing about writing your TCL script to accept arguments is that you can use the same script to modify multiple system messages simply by changing the arguments supplied.

Now if we look at the output of the ESM filter, notice that the severity level has been increased from 6 to 3:

```
%HSRP-3-STATECHANGE: FastEthernet0/0 Grp 1 state Standby -> Active
```

We have only looked at a few simple applications for the ESM. It is capable of doing so much more, and is only limited by the capabilities of TCL.

See Also

Tcl/Tk in a Nutshell by Paul Raines and Jeff Tranter (O'Reilly)

## CHAPTER 19

Access-Lists

19.0 Introduction

An Access Control List (ACL) is generically a method for doing pattern matching on protocol information. There are many reasons for doing this type of pattern matching, such as restricting access for security reasons, as well as restricting routing tables for performance reasons.

Cisco has several different general kinds of access-lists. The most common are the *numbered ACLs*, which we summarize in Table 19-1. But there are also *named access-lists*, *reflexive access-lists*, *timed access-lists*, *context-based access-lists*, and *rate-limit access-lists*. Within each of these general categories, there are many different types of ACLs that match on different protocol information. When working with route filtering, it is often easiest to work with *prefix lists*, which are another type of ACL that we discuss in more detail in Chapters 6, 7, 8, and 9.

You can apply an ACL in many different ways. Applied to an interface, you can use it to accept or reject incoming or outgoing packets, based on protocol information such as source or destination address, port number, protocol number, and so forth. Applied to a routing protocol, this same ACL might prevent the router from sharing information about this particular route. And applied to a route-map, the ACL could just identify packets that need to be tagged or treated differently.

Table 19-1 shows all of the current ranges for *numbered access-lists*. Cisco periodically adds new ranges to this list, so earlier IOS levels may not support all of these ACL types. Also bear in mind that if your IOS feature set doesn't support a particular protocol such as IPX, XNS, or AppleTalk, then the corresponding ACL type will also not be available.

Table 19-1. Numbered access-list types

Numeric range	Access list type
1–99	Standard IP ACL
100–199	Extended IP ACL

Table 19-1. Numbered access-list types (continued)

Numeric range	Access list type
200–299	Ethernet Type Code ACL
700–799	48-bit MAC Address ACL
1,100–1,199	Extended 48-bit MAC Address ACL
1,300–1,999	Standard IP ACL, expanded range
2,000–2,699	Extended IP ACL, expanded range
2,700–2,999	SS7 (Voice) ACL

Some of these ranges deal with protocols or technologies that are beyond the scope of this book. This book's primary focus is on IP based technologies, so this chapter will not discuss ACL types that are intended for use with other protocols.

A named ACL is really just another way of writing either a Standard or Extended IP ACL. Named ACLs can make your configuration files considerably easier to read. Some commands that use an ACL for pattern matching will not accept named ACLs, but for the most part, *named ACLs* are interchangeable with normal IP ACLs. Their chief advantage is that you can nest other ACLs inside of a named ACL for greater flexibility.

Reflexive ACLs are more sophisticated objects that can contain temporary entries. Reflexive ACLs need to be nested inside of named ACLs. A reflexive ACL has two parts that are generally nested in two different named ACLs. One part watches for packets of a particular type by using normal extended IP ACL syntax. As soon as the router sees this packet, it activates a matching rule in another ACL. This allows you to do things like permitting inbound traffic of a particular type only after the router sees an initial outbound packet of the matching type.

However, reflexive ACLs are somewhat limited in their scope because they are not able to read into the IP packets. Many applications have more complicated behavior, such as using dynamically generated port numbers. To handle this type of situation, Cisco has developed another type of ACL called Context-Based Access Control (CBAC), which we discuss in Chapter 27.

Like reflexive ACLs, CBAC works by turning on and off temporary access-list rules. However, CBAC actively monitors applications using a stateful inspection algorithm that allows the router to react to the application and dynamically create new ACL rules. It can also watch for unusual application behavior and dynamically disable the corresponding temporary ACL rules.

You should always remember that every ACL ends with an implicit *deny all* clause. This means that if you are matching items (packets, for example) with an ACL, and the item fails to match any of the explicitly listed clauses of the ACL and falls off the end, it is the same as if the item matched an explicit *deny* clause. For this reason, if you are trying to block certain unwanted packets, for example, but you want to allow all others to pass, you must remember to include a *permit all* statement at the end of the ACL.

For more information on ACLs in general, we encourage the reader to refer to *Cisco IOS Access Lists* by Jeff Sedayao (O'Reilly).

19.1 Filtering by Source or Destination IP Address

Problem

You want to block packets to or from certain IP addresses.

Solution

You can use standard access-lists to block packets from specified IP source addresses:

```
Router1#configure terminal
Enter configuration commands, one per line.  End with CNTL/Z.
Router1(config)#access-list 50 deny host 10.2.2.2
Router1(config)#access-list 50 permit any
Router1(config)#interface Serial0/1
Router1(config-if)#ip access-group 50 in
Router1(config-if)#exit
Router1(config)#end
Router1#
```

You can filter packets based on both the source and destination addresses with an extended access-list:

```
Router1#configure terminal
Enter configuration commands, one per line.  End with CNTL/Z.
Router1(config)#access-list 150 deny ip host 10.2.2.2 host 172.25.25.1
Router1(config)#access-list 150 permit ip any any
Router1(config)#interface Serial0/1
Router1(config-if)#ip access-group 150 in
Router1(config-if)#exit
Router1(config)#end
Router1#
```

Discussion

The most obvious use for access-lists is traffic filtering. The two examples in this recipe both show how to use access control lists for filtering inbound packets. The first example uses the following access-list:

```
Router1(config)#access-list 50 deny host 10.2.2.2
Router1(config)#access-list 50 permit any
```

This is a numbered ACL with a value between 1 and 99, making it a *standard access-list*. Using a standard access like this allows you to filter only based on the source IP address. In the example, we have chosen to deny a single host address, 10.2.2.2, to prevent the router from accepting packets from this device. All other packets are permitted. This is a somewhat artificial thing to do, of course. It is more likely that you would want to allow only a limited group of devices and block all of the others. For example, you might want to allow all of the devices on 10.2.2.0/24, except the host 10.2.2.2, and drop packets from any other devices. You could do this with the following standard ACL:

```
Router1(config)#access-list 50 deny host 10.2.2.2
Router1(config)#access-list 50 permit 10.2.2.0 0.0.0.255
Router1(config)#access-list 50 deny any
```

The order of the statements in an access-list is critical. Consider what would have happened if we had put line that permitted 10.2.2.0/24 before the line that denied the specific host 10.2.2.2. Each time the router received a packet from the forbidden host, it would compare it to the ACL. Because this host is part of the permitted range, the router would accept the packet and not look any further.

Also, because the router will stop processing an ACL as soon as it finds a match, you can save the processor a lot of work by putting the most common rules near the top. You want the router to find a match as early as possible while parsing the ACL most of the time it uses this ACL. All of the examples in this chapter are relatively short, but if you have an ACL that is several hundred lines long, a good ordering can make a significant improvement in processing time. This will affect router CPU load, and could also improve jitter and latency issues.

The other important thing to look out for when constructing an ACL like this is the fact that they use wildcard bits rather than netmask format when defining ranges of addresses. In this example, we wanted to specify the range 10.2.2.0/24. This means that we want to fix all of the bits in the first three octets of the address, and allow any pattern of bits in the last octet. We can achieve this with a wildcard pattern of 0.0.0.255. Please refer to Recipe 5.3 for a more detailed discussion of the differences between wildcards and netmasks.

The basic notation is an IP address followed by a wildcard pattern. But there are two special cases. Suppose you want to match on a single IP address for particular devices, such as 10.2.2.2. You can write this as follows:

```
Router1(config)#access-list 50 deny 10.2.2.2 0.0.0.0
```

This wildcard pattern means that there are no free bits in the address, so we are looking for an exact match. Alternatively, you can use the more intuitive version that we used earlier in this recipe, with the *host* keyword:

```
Router1(config)#access-list 50 deny host 10.2.2.2
```

The two forms have an identical effect. And, in fact, for Standard IP ACLs like this one, the router will replace both of these with the following:

```
Router1(config)#access-list 50 deny 10.2.2.2
```

The *host* keyword is not redundant, however, for Extended IP ACLs, which we discuss below.

Alternatively, if you want to match any device, you could write this as follows:

```
Router1(config)#access-list 50 deny 0.0.0.0 255.255.255.255
```

Because all of the wildcard bits in this pattern are set, it means that any bit may have a value of either 0 or 1. So this pattern will match any IP address. The router will rewrite this ACL with the following simpler form:

```
Router1(config)#access-list 50 deny any
```

As we mentioned in the Introduction to this chapter, there are many different ways to apply an ACL. In this case, we want to apply this ACL to filter IP packets received on a particular router interface. To do this, we use the *ip access-group* command on the interface that will receive the data stream that we want to filter:

```
Router1(config)#interface Serial0/1
Router1(config-if)#ip access-group 50 in
```

In this command, the keyword *in* tells the router to apply the filter to inbound packets that is, packets received by this interface. In some cases, you might want to filter outbound packets instead. The router will even let you apply a different ACL to inbound and outbound packets:

```
Router1(config)#interface Serial0/1
Router1(config-if)#ip access-group 50 in
Router1(config-if)#ip access-group 51 out
```

The outbound access-group command has an interesting quirk that you should be aware of. This command will not filter packets that originate on the router itself. This is important because if you apply an outbound filter and then try to test it with a PING or Telnet from the router, your rule will appear not to work. Make sure to do these tests from a downstream device.

It's also important to remember that the router originates packets in several less obvious situations. For example, if you are using tunnels, then even if the router is encapsulating IP packets from downstream devices, the tunnel packets themselves originate on the router. The same is true when the router acts as a gateway for other protocols, such as SNA or X.25.

This also has security implications because it means that if somebody can convince the router to originate packets for them, they will bypass the rule. So, while the outbound access-group command is extremely useful, you need to be careful about how you use it, or it might be less effective than you expect.

The second example in the Solution section of this recipe does a similar kind of filtering, except that this time we have used an extended ACL:

```
Router1(config)#access-list 150 deny ip host 10.2.2.2 host 172.25.25.1
Router1(config)#access-list 150 permit ip any any
```

The syntax of the extended IP ACL is somewhat more involved than that of the standard ACL. It includes the same *permit* or *deny* keywords as the standard IP ACL. The next keyword in this example selects the IP protocol. Please refer to Recipe 19.3 for a discussion of other options.

Extended IP ACLs always include two IP addresses. The first is the source address, and the second is the destination. In the first line of the example, we have specified two host addresses for the source and destination, while the second line matches any address in either the source or the destination fields of the IP packet.

You can use the same wildcard matching system for IP addresses here, as we discussed above for the Standard IP ACL. Suppose, for example, that we want to allow any device on the 10.2.2.0/24 segment to access any destination device, but we wanted to specifically prevent the host, 10.2.2.2 from reaching 172.25.25.1, and we want to drop all packets from any other devices. We could do this with the following Extended IP ACL:

```
Router1(config)#access-list 150 deny ip host 10.2.2.2 host 172.25.25.1
Router1(config)#access-list 150 permit ip 10.2.2.0 0.0.0.255 any
Router1(config)#access-list 150 deny ip any any
```

Note that the last line of both the Standard and Extended ACL examples in this recipe explicitly denies everything that wasn't matched in one of the previous lines. This is actually not necessary because every ACL implicitly ends with a *deny all*, whether you include it or not. However, including an explicit *permit all* or *deny all* clause at the end of an ACL is generally a good practice because it makes things more clear. Also, when you look at an ACL with the *show access-list* command, it gives you a breakdown of how many times each rule found a match:

```
Router1#show access-list 150
Extended IP access list 150
    deny ip host 10.2.2.2 host 172.25.25.1 (422 matches)
    permit ip 10.2.2.0 0.0.0.255 any (743 matches)
    deny ip any any (387 matches)
Router1#
```

As you can see here, by including an explicit *deny all* rule at the end of this ACL, we can tell exactly how many packets were affected.

And, as we will discuss in Recipe 19.8, you can configure this line to log exactly which packets reach all the way to the end of the ACL without matching one of the earlier rules.

Finally, we need to mention one of the most annoying problems involved in managing large ACLs up until IOS Version 12.3(2)T (see Recipe 19.15 for more information). If you add a new rule to an ACL, it will always go at the very end of the list. This is not always what you want. Further, there is no way to remove individual lines from an ACL without removing the entire list.

We have found that the easiest way to get around this problem is to use the *show running-config* command to get a complete listing of the ACL you want to edit. Copy this into a text editor of some kind on your local workstation. Then you can use any common text editor to create the modified ACL. Delete the old ACL and copy in the new one. As we mentioned in Chapter 1, if you use TFTP to transfer the new commands into the router, it will not make the change until the transfer is complete. This is particularly important for ACLs, where you could enter the first line, and then find yourself locked out of the router by the implicit *deny all* that follows it. However, Recipe 19.15 shows another solution to this problem.

See Also

Recipe 5.3; Recipe 19.3; Recipe 19.8; Recipe 19.15

19.2   Adding a Comment to an ACL

Problem

You want to add a human readable comment to an ACL to help other engineers understand what you have done.

Solution

You can add a comment to any standard or extended IP ACL by using the *remark* keyword:

```
Router1#configure terminal
Enter configuration commands, one per line.  End with CNTL/Z.
Router1(config)#access-list 50 remark Authorizing thy trespass with compare
Router1(config)#access-list 50 deny host 10.2.2.2
Router1(config)#access-list 50 permit 10.2.2.0 0.0.0.255
Router1(config)#access-list 50 permit any
Router1(config)#end
Router1#
```

In addition, you can add a comment to a named ACL, as well:

```
Router2#configure terminal
Enter configuration commands, one per line.  End with CNTL/Z.
Router2(config)#ip access-list standard TESTACL
Router2(config-std-nacl)#remark Authorizing thy trespass with compare
Router2(config-std-nacl)#deny host 10.2.2.2
Router2(config-std-nacl)#permit 10.2.2.0 0.0.0.255
Router2(config-std-nacl)#permit any
Router2(config-std-nacl)#end
Router2#
```

Discussion

This command can be quite useful when you have to keep track of many different ACLs on a router, particularly when several of them look similar. The comment field can be up to 100 characters long. But if you require more space, you can simply add more remark lines to the ACL:

```
Router1(config)#access-list 50 remark Authorizing thy trespass with compare
Router1(config)#access-list 50 remark My self corrupting salving thy amiss,
Router1(config)#access-list 50 remark Excusing thy sins more than thy sins are
Router1(config)#access-list 50 remark Shakespeare, Sonnet 35
```

When you display this ACL by using the show access-list command, it will not show the remark lines:

```
Router1#show access-list 50
Standard IP access list 50
```

```
            deny    10.2.2.2
            permit 10.2.2.0, wildcard bits 0.0.0.255
            permit any
      Router1#
```

The only way to see these comments is to look at the router's configuration file:

```
      Router1#show running-config | include access-list 50
      access-list 50 remark Authorizing thy trespass with compare
      access-list 50 remark My self corrupting salving thy amiss,
      access-list 50 remark Excusing thy sins more than thy sins are
      access-list 50 remark Shakespeare, Sonnet 35
      access-list 50 deny    10.2.2.2
      access-list 50 permit 10.2.2.0 0.0.0.255
      access-list 50 permit any
      access-list 50 remark
      Router1#
```

Note that the router does not re-order the remark lines in the ACL. So you can use this feature to explain line-by-line what each command does:

```
      Router1(config)#access-list 50 remark loathsome canker
      Router1(config)#access-list 50 deny host 10.2.2.2
      Router1(config)#access-list 50 remark sweetest bud
      Router1(config)#access-list 50 permit 10.2.2.0 0.0.0.255
      Router1(config)#access-list 50 permit any
```

See Also

Complete Sonnets by William Shakespeare (Dover)

19.3   Filtering by Application

Problem

You want to filter access to certain applications.

Solution

Extended IP access-lists can also filter based on application information, such as protocol and port numbers:

```
      Router1#configure terminal
      Enter configuration commands, one per line.  End with CNTL/Z.
      Router1(config)#access-list 151 permit tcp any any eq www
      Router1(config)#access-list 151 deny tcp any any gt 1023
      Router1(config)#access-list 151 permit icmp any any
      Router1(config)#access-list 151 permit udp any any eq ntp
      Router1(config)#access-list 151 deny ip any any
      Router1(config)#interface Serial0/1
      Router1(config-if)#ip access-group 151 in
      Router1(config-if)#exit
      Router1(config)#end
      Router1#
```

Discussion

This example shows how to construct an Extended IP ACL to filter traffic based on application. In Recipe 19.1, we showed how to use Extended IP ACLs to match on any combination of source and/or destination IP addresses. But the Extended IP ACL also allows you to match on just about anything in the IP packet header.

The first argument after the *permit* or *deny* keyword represents the IP protocol number:

```
Router1(config)#access-list 151 permit tcp any any eq www
```

In this case, we want to match a TCP-based application, so we have used the keyword *tcp* in this position. This field represents the IP protocol number, which is an 8-bit value. TCP is protocol number 6, UDP is 17, and ICMP uses protocol number 1. The IANA has registered 134 different protocol numbers. You can find the complete list of registered IP protocols online at *http://www.iana.org/assignments/protocol-numbers*. Cisco supplies helpful mnemonics for several of these protocols, such as the *tcp*, *udp*, and *icmp* keywords used in the example, so you don't have to remember the protocol numbers. Table 19-2 shows all of the IP protocols for which Cisco supplies mnemonic keywords. You can always use the protocol number in decimal form if you prefer, but the router will replace it with the mnemonic in its configuration file.

Table 19-2. IP protocol numbers and their Extended ACL keywords

Protocol number	Keyword	Description
1	icmp	Internet Control Message Protocol
2	igmp	Internet Gateway Message Protocol
4	ipinip	IP in IP tunnel protocol
6	tcp	Transmission Control Protocol
9	igrp	Interior Gateway Routing Protocol
17	udp	User Datagram Protocol
21	nos	KA9Q tunnel protocol
47	gre	Generic Routing Encapsulation tunnel protocol
50	esp	IPSec Encapsulation Security Payload
51	ahp	IPSec Authenticating Header Protocol
88	eigrp	Enhanced Interior Gateway Routing Protocol
89	ospf	Open Shortest Path First routing protocol
103	pim	Protocol Independent Multicast protocol
108	pcp	IP Payload Compression Protocol

And, as we showed in Recipe 19.1, you can match on any IP protocol number by simply using the keyword *ip*.

After the IP protocol number or keyword are the source and destination IP addresses. We described how to use these fields in Recipe 19.1. Recall that the address keyword *any* is a shorthand that stands for an address of 0.0.0.0 with a wildcard pattern of 255.255.255.255.

Following each address is an optional field where you can specify particular protocol information such as port numbers. In the following example, we match on TCP port 80, which is used by the HTTP protocol. The router has a set of mnemonics for TCP and UDP port numbers, which we list below. These are similar to the protocol number mnemonics mentioned in Table 19-2. In this case, the mnemonic for port 80 is *www*:

```
Router1(config)#access-list 151 permit tcp any any eq www
```

Notice that the keywords *eq www* appear after the destination IP address, rather than the source IP address. This is because we are looking for the destination TCP port number. If you need to match on a source port number instead, you could simply move these keywords to follow the source IP address:

```
Router1(config)#access-list 151 permit tcp any eq www any
```

And, of course, you can always match on both:

```
Router1(config)#access-list 151 permit tcp any eq www any eq www
```

Note, however, that this ACL will only score a correct match if both source and destination TCP port numbers match. If you wanted to match HTTP traffic between any two devices, and you didn't know which device had initiated the TCP session, you would need to include two separate lines like this:

```
Router1(config)#access-list 151 permit tcp any any eq www
Router1(config)#access-list 151 permit tcp any eq www any
```

You can see all of the possible mnemonic keywords simply by using the online help facility:

```
Router1(config)#access-list 151 permit tcp any eq ?
  <0-65535>    Port number
  bgp          Border Gateway Protocol (179)
  chargen      Character generator (19)
  cmd          Remote commands (rcmd, 514)
  daytime      Daytime (13)
  discard      Discard (9)
  domain       Domain Name Service (53)
  echo         Echo (7)
  exec         Exec (rsh, 512)
  finger       Finger (79)
  ftp          File Transfer Protocol (21)
  ftp-data     FTP data connections (20)
  gopher       Gopher (70)
  hostname     NIC hostname server (101)
  ident        Ident Protocol (113)
  irc          Internet Relay Chat (194)
  klogin       Kerberos login (543)
  kshell       Kerberos shell (544)
  login        Login (rlogin, 513)
  lpd          Printer service (515)
  nntp         Network News Transport Protocol (119)
  pim-auto-rp  PIM Auto-RP (496)
```

```
pop2        Post Office Protocol v2 (109)
pop3        Post Office Protocol v3 (110)
smtp        Simple Mail Transport Protocol (25)
sunrpc      Sun Remote Procedure Call (111)
syslog      Syslog (514)
tacacs      TAC Access Control System (49)
talk        Talk (517)
telnet      Telnet (23)
time        Time (37)
uucp        Unix-to-Unix Copy Program (540)
whois       Nicname (43)
www         World Wide Web (HTTP, 80)

Router1#
```

As with the IP protocol numbers listed in Table 19-2, you can substitute the decimal numerical value for any of these keywords, and the router will replace it with the keyword.

The IANA reserves the TCP port numbers 1024 and above for local and temporary applications. Many TCP implementations use these high numbered ports for source port numbers, and for temporary or ephemeral purposes. It is relatively common to see ACLs that restrict the use of these ports. We included a sample ACL rule in this recipe:

```
Router1(config)#access-list 151 deny tcp any any gt 1023
```

This command blocks all packets that have a destination port number greater than 1023 (that is, ports 1024 through 65535). Remember that TCP applications often use these high port numbers for source ports. So you need to be careful about traffic direction when you apply such an ACL.

There is a similar set of port numbers for UDP applications:

```
Router2(config)#access-list 151 permit udp any eq ?
  <0-65535>     Port number
  biff          Biff (mail notification, comsat, 512)
  bootpc        Bootstrap Protocol (BOOTP) client (68)
  bootps        Bootstrap Protocol (BOOTP) server (67)
  discard       Discard (9)
  dnsix         DNSIX security protocol auditing (195)
  domain        Domain Name Service (DNS, 53)
  echo          Echo (7)
  isakmp        Internet Security Association and Key Management Protocol
                (500)
  mobile-ip     Mobile IP registration (434)
  nameserver    IEN116 name service (obsolete, 42)
  netbios-dgm   NetBios datagram service (138)
  netbios-ns    NetBios name service (137)
  netbios-ss    NetBios session service (139)
  non500-isakmp Internet Security Association and Key Management Protocol
                (4500)
  ntp           Network Time Protocol (123)
  pim-auto-rp   PIM Auto-RP (496)
  rip           Routing Information Protocol (router, in.routed, 520)
```

```
snmp            Simple Network Management Protocol (161)
snmptrap        SNMP Traps (162)
sunrpc          Sun Remote Procedure Call (111)
syslog          System Logger (514)
tacacs          TAC Access Control System (49)
talk            Talk (517)
tftp            Trivial File Transfer Protocol (69)
time            Time (37)
who             Who service (rwho, 513)
xdmcp           X Display Manager Control Protocol (177)

Router2(config)#
```

So, for example, you could block all Sun RPC traffic, which includes important but chatty applications such as Network File System (NFS) as follows:

```
Router1(config)#access-list 151 deny udp any eq sunrpc any
Router1(config)#access-list 151 deny udp any any eq sunrpc
```

Because we applied the UDP port number file separately to the source and destination ports, this will block RPC traffic going in either direction.

Once again, with UDP port numbers, as with TCP port numbers, the values from 1024 through 65535 are often used for temporary purposes such as source port numbers. So you can control the use of these port numbers with a similar ACL rule to the one we discussed above for high TCP port numbers:

```
Router1(config)#access-list 151 deny udp any any gt 1023
```

See Also

Recipe 19.1; Recipe 19.6

19.4   Filtering Based on TCP Header Flags

Problem

You want to filter on the flag bits in the TCP header.

Solution

The following ACL blocks several illegal combinations of TCP header flags:

```
Router1#configure terminal
Enter configuration commands, one per line.  End with CNTL/Z.
Router1(config)#access-list 161 deny tcp any any ack fin psh rst syn urg
Router1(config)#access-list 161 deny tcp any any rst syn
Router1(config)#access-list 161 deny tcp any any rst syn fin
Router1(config)#access-list 161 deny tcp any any rst syn fin ack
Router1(config)#access-list 161 deny tcp any any syn fin
Router1(config)#access-list 161 deny tcp any any syn fin ack
Router1(config)#end
Router1#
```

Beginning with IOS Version 12.3(4)T, Cisco changed the format of TCP flag filtering, while still maintaining support for the legacy method. The following is the same example as above using the new TCP flag filtering method:

```
Router2#configure terminal
Enter configuration commands, one per line.  End with CNTL/Z.
Router2(config)#ip access-list extended TCPFLAGFILTER
Router2(config-ext-nacl)#deny tcp any any match-all +ack +fin +psh +rst +syn +urg
Router2(config-ext-nacl)#deny tcp any any match-all +rst +syn
Router2(config-ext-nacl)#deny tcp any any match-all +rst +syn +fin
Router2(config-ext-nacl)#deny tcp any any match-all +rst +syn +fin +ack
Router2(config-ext-nacl)#deny tcp any any match-all +syn +fin
Router2(config-ext-nacl)#deny tcp any any match-all +syn +fin +ack
Router2(config-ext-nacl)#end
Router2#
```

Discussion

There are six flag bits in the TCP header that the devices use to control the session:

ACK
Acknowledgment.

SYN
Synchronize sequence numbers at the start of the session.

FIN
Terminate the session.

RST
Reset the session.

PSH
Push this data to the application immediately; this usually means that all of the data has been sent.

URG
Look at the Urgent pointer later in the packet.

TCP uses a so-called three-way handshake to set up sessions. To start a session, the client device sends a packet with the SYN bit, which is an instruction to synchronize sequence numbers. The server device responds with a packet that has both SYN and ACK bits set, which the first device then acknowledges with an ACK to complete the handshake process.

The session teardown procedure is similar, but it actually uses four packets instead of three. One device sends the other a packet with the FIN bit set. The second device then responds to this with an ACK. Then, in a separate packet, the second device sends its own FIN, which the first device responds to with an ACK to terminate the session.

Devices use the RST flag for a couple of different reasons, but one of the most common is the so-called *abortive close*. This happens when one device can't wait around for the other device to acknowledge the end of the session by using the normal FIN and ACK pattern. So it simply sends a packet that has both the RST and ACK bits set to end the session. There is no need for the other device to respond to this packet.

Obviously, some combinations of these bits are not valid, however. For example, it makes no sense to have a single packet with both the SYN and FIN bits set. And, in defining test cases for TCP implementations, RFC 1025 defines a packet with all six bits set as a *nastygram* (or a kamikaze packet, Christmas tree packet, or lamp test segment). The first line in the example ACL blocks *nastygrams*:

```
Router1(config)#access-list 161 deny tcp any any ack fin psh rst syn urg
```

The remaining lines block other illegal combinations of flags.

As mentioned in the Solution section, Cisco introduced a new method of filtering based on TCP flags that provides far greater control over the legacy method. Users can now match on TCP flags that are set, as well as TCP flags that are not set. In addition, you can now filter on any combination of TCP flags.

Cisco has introduced two new keywords: *match-any* and *match-all*. The match-any keyword matches the specified TCP flag(s), regardless of whether other TCP flags are set or not. In contrast, the match-all keyword only matches the exact specified TCP flags, and if others are set, then no match is made.

Let's take a look at an example:

```
Router2(config-ext-nacl)#permit tcp any any match-all +syn
Router2(config-ext-nacl)#permit tcp any any match-any +syn
```

Even though the two commands look nearly identical, their filtering behavior is quite different. The match-all command only permits TCP packets with the SYN bit set. If any other TCP flag is enabled, then it won't match this ACL entry. On the other hand, the match-any command will match all TCP packets that have the SYN bit set regardless of whether any other TCP flag is enabled. The match-any command emulates the legacy TCP flag filtering behavior.

As we mentioned earlier, the new method also permits us to filter on TCP flags that are not set. Instead of using a "+" sign, we use a "-" to identify which unset TCP flags to filter on. For example:

```
Router2(config-ext-nacl)#permit tcp any any match-any -syn
```

In this example, only TCP packets that don't have the SYN bit enabled will be permitted. There was no way of matching unset flags using the legacy method of TCP flag filtering.

See Also

RFC 1025

19.5 Restricting TCP Session Direction

Problem

You want to filter TCP sessions so that only the client device may initiate the application.

Solution

You can use the *established* keyword to restrict which device is allowed to initiate the session. In the following example, we want to allow the client device to telnet to the server, but not the other way around:

```
Router1#configure terminal
Enter configuration commands, one per line.  End with CNTL/Z.
Router1(config)#access-list 148 permit tcp any eq telnet any established
Router1(config)#access-list 148 deny ip any any
Router1(config)#interface FastEthernet0/0
Router1(config-if)#ip access-group 148 in
Router1(config-if)#exit
Router1(config)#end
Router1#
```

Discussion

In this example, the interface will accept incoming TCP packets only if they have a TCP source port number of 23 (Telnet), and only if this TCP session is already established. It does not restrict the destination port number, because this would be whatever random high-numbered port the initiating device had originally selected for its source port when it started the session.

The router considers an established TCP connection to be one that has either the RST or ACK bits set. We discuss these TCP header flags in more detail in Recipe 19.4. Because this does not include the SYN bit in particular, it is impossible to create a new TCP connection.

Note that you could actually write the same thing explicitly as two rules:

```
Router1(config)#access-list 148 permit tcp any eq telnet any ack
Router1(config)#access-list 148 permit tcp any eq telnet any rst
```

The combination of these two rules is identical to the version in the example:

```
Router1(config)#access-list 148 permit tcp any eq telnet any established
```

But the version with the *established* keyword executes more efficiently. Note that putting both RST and ACK in the same rule would match packets with both RST and ACK set, not one or the other.

To see why the *established* keyword is sometimes necessary, imagine what would happen if it were not present. The interface would accept any inbound TCP packets that happened to have a source port of 23. But this could be literally anything. A moderately clever hacker who knew how to set the source port on his Telnet application could easily initiate a connection to any device on the other side of the router.

So if you are using ACLs for to control TCP applications security reasons, you should consider using the *established* keyword.

19.6   Filtering Multiport Applications

Problem

You want to filter an application that uses more than one TCP or UDP port.

Solution

This example shows how to filter both FTP control and data sessions:

```
Router1#configure terminal
Enter configuration commands, one per line.  End with CNTL/Z.
Router1(config)#access-list 152 permit tcp any any eq ftp
Router1(config)#access-list 152 permit tcp any any eq ftp-data established
Router1(config)#interface FastEthernet0/0
Router1(config-if)#ip access-group 152 in
Router1(config-if)#exit
Router1(config)#end
Router1#
```

Discussion

Some protocols use multiple ports. A classic example is FTP, which is shown in the example. It is worthwhile reviewing how the FTP protocol works. For more details, please consult RFC 959.

When a client device wants to connect to a server to either upload or download files, it makes a TCP connection on port 21. This port 21 connection carries all of the interactive user traffic, such as usernames and passwords, as well as commands to move around to different directories. It also uses this control session to tell the server what port number it wants to use for transferring data. This will typically be a high-numbered temporary TCP port.

When the user then wants to transfer a file, he traditionally types a *put* or *get* command on the server. We say traditionally because this is not quite how things work when your FTP client software is driven through a web browser, as we discuss in Recipe 19.12.

The server then makes a new TCP connection to the high-numbered port on the client device that it previously learned about through the control session. The source port for this connection is the well known FTP data port number, 20. This is backwards from most TCP connections, by which the client device connects to the server using a well known destination port number. Here the server connects to the client by using a well known source port number.

The client and server exchange the file, and then disconnect this FTP data connection, leaving the FTP control connection on port 21 active. The server will actually use the FTP data connection to transfer any bulk data, including directory listings as well as files. This recipe shows how you can easily match both the control and data traffic streams using an ACL.

In this example, we will assume that the client device is connected to the router's FastEthernet0/0 interface, perhaps through other downstream routers. And, for the sake of the example, we will assume that this is the only data that we want to allow.

So the router will receive a TCP packet from client device as it initiates the FTP session with destination port 21. We match this connection with the following Extended IP ACL:

```
Router1(config)#access-list 152 permit tcp any any eq ftp
```

Note that we have used the keyword *ftp* in this ACL to mean TCP port 21.

Then, when there is data to exchange, the server will make a connection back to the client device on port number 20. The ACL keyword for this port is *ftp-data*:

```
Router1(config)#access-list 152 permit tcp any any eq ftp-data established
```

Now, it's important to note that the access group is applied inbound to packets received on the client Fast Ethernet port. So this ACL will not apply to any of the packets sent from the server to the client device, but only those sent from the client to the server. However, this is sufficient because the devices cannot establish a TCP session unless they can both send packets.

For a more generic multi-port TCP application, you can specify a range of ports in the ACL with the *range* keyword, as follows:

```
Router1(config)#access-list 153 permit tcp any any range 6000 6063
```

This example matches any packets whose destination port is between 6000 and 6063, inclusive, which is the range commonly used by the X Window system. You can also specify open-ended ranges. For example, to match any TCP port number greater than 1023, you can use the *gt* keyword:

```
Router1(config)#access-list 153 permit tcp any any gt 1023
```

And there are, similarly, "less than" and "not equal to" operators for port numbers:

```
Router1(config)#access-list 153 permit tcp any any lt 1024
Router1(config)#access-list 153 permit tcp any any neq 666
```

As an aside, TCP port number 666 is used by the Doom interactive network game, making it an excellent candidate for filtering.

These same operations also apply identically for UDP port numbers:

```
Router1(config)#access-list 154 permit udp any any range 6000 6063
Router1(config)#access-list 155 deny udp any any gt 1023
Router1(config)#access-list 156 permit udp any any lt 1024
Router1(config)#access-list 157 permit udp any any neq 666
```

See Also

Recipe 19.3; Recipe 19.12; RFC 959

19.7   Filtering Based on DSCP and TOS

Problem

You want to filter based on IP Quality of Service information.

Solution

You can filter packets based on the contents of the Differentiated Services Control Point (DSCP) field by using the *dscp* keyword:

```
Router1#configure terminal
Enter configuration commands, one per line.  End with CNTL/Z.
Router1(config)#access-list 162 permit ip any any dscp af11
Router1(config)#end
```

Similarly, to filter based on TOS, you can use the *tos* keyword:

```
Router1#configure terminal
Enter configuration commands, one per line.  End with CNTL/Z.
Router1(config)#access-list 162 permit ip any any tos max-reliability
Router1(config)#end
```

Discussion

In Chapter 11 and Appendix B, we discuss both the DSCP and IP TOS fields in more detail. Chapter 11 also includes several examples of ACLs that filter based on this information. Please refer to these sections for more information.

The first example looks for packets that have a DSCP field value of AF11, which has a bit pattern of 001010, or a decimal value of 10. The second example matches packets with a TOS value of maximum reliability, which has a decimal value of 2.

Note that you can use the decimal numerical values for any TOS or DSCP field, and the router will simply replace it with the mnemonic keyword, if one exists. For example, we could have written the second example as follows:

```
Router1(config)#access-list 162 permit ip any any tos 2
```

In this case, the router would have replaced the number 2 with the *max-reliability* keyword. However, there is no mnemonic keyword corresponding to the TOS value, 3. The router will accept values that do not have well-known names like this, but it will leave them as numerical values in the configuration file.

See Also

Chapter 11; Appendix B

19.8   Logging When an Access-List Is Used

Problem

You want to know when the router invokes an access-list.

Solution

Access-lists can generate log messages. The following example allows all packets to pass, and records them:

```
Router1#configure terminal
Enter configuration commands, one per line.  End with CNTL/Z.
Router1(config)#access-list 150 permit ip any any log
Router1(config)#interface Serial0/1
Router1(config-if)#ip access-group 150 in
Router1(config-if)#exit
Router1(config)#end
Router1#
```

And in this example, we use the *log-input* keyword to include additional information about where the packets came from:

```
Router1#configure terminal
Enter configuration commands, one per line.  End with CNTL/Z.
Router1(config)#access-list 150 permit tcp any any log-input
Router1(config)#access-list 150 permit ip any any
Router1(config)#interface Serial0/1
Router1(config-if)#ip access-group 150 in
Router1(config-if)#exit
Router1(config)#end
Router1#
```

Discussion

The first example uses the log keyword to record a log message every time the ACL makes a match. Here are some log messages generated by this command:

```
Feb  6 13:01:19: %SEC-6-IPACCESSLOGRP: list 150 permitted ospf 10.1.1.1 -> 224.0.0.5,
9 packets
Feb  6 13:01:19: %SEC-6-IPACCESSLOGDP: list 150 permitted icmp 10.1.1.1 -> 10.1.1.2
(0/0), 4 packets
```

You can also get a breakdown of how many matches each line in the ACL has recorded with the *show access-list* command:

```
Router1#show access-list 150
Extended IP access list 150
    permit ip any any log (15 matches)
Router1#
```

The second form, with the *log-input* keyword, causes the router to include other useful data in the log messages. With this option, the log messages will include the port where the packet was received:

```
Feb  6 13:08:31: %SEC-6-IPACCESSLOGP: list 150 permitted tcp 10.1.1.1(0) (Serial0/1 )
-> 10.1.1.2(0), 80 packets
```

```
Feb  6 13:08:38: %SEC-6-IPACCESSLOGP: list 150 permitted tcp 10.2.2.2(0) (Serial0/1 )
-> 172.25.26.5(0), 1 packet
Feb  6 13:10:29: %SEC-6-IPACCESSLOGP: list 150 permitted tcp 10.2.2.2(0) (Serial0/1 )
-> 172.20.100.1(0), 1 packet
```

If we apply this ACL on an Ethernet or Token Ring port, the log messages will also include MAC address information:

```
Feb  6 14:56:34: %SEC-6-IPACCESSLOGP: list 150 permitted tcp 172.25.1.1(0)
(FastEthernet0/0.1 0010.4b09.5700) -> 172.25.25.1(0), 1 packet
Router1#
Feb  6 14:58:20: %SEC-6-IPACCESSLOGP: list 150 permitted tcp 172.25.1.7(0)
(FastEthernet0/0.1 0000.0c92.bc6a) -> 172.25.1.5(0), 1 packet
```

The only problem with these commands is that they tend to produce huge numbers of log messages. To be really useful, we recommend using this feature in conjunction with a remote log server, as described in Chapter 18. Then you can store and analyze all of the messages without worrying that you will lose information when the router's internal log buffer overwrites itself. In Recipe 19.10, we offer a useful script for analyzing the messages to look for important patterns.

In general, we recommend logging all denied packets because they tend to represent the rejected traffic, which is not part of the normal functioning of the network. These are the log messages that the script in Recipe 19.10 looks for in particular.

Also note that while all of the examples in this recipe used extended ACLs, the *log* keyword is also available with standard ACLs:

```
Router1(config)#access-list 77 permit any log
```

The *log-input* option is only available for extended ACLs, however.

See Also

Recipe 19.10

19.9   Logging TCP Sessions

Problem

You want to log the total number of TCP sessions.

Solution

You can configure the router to log the total number of TCP sessions, rather than just the number of packets, with the following set of commands:

```
Router1#configure terminal
Enter configuration commands, one per line.  End with CNTL/Z.
Router1(config)#access-list 122 permit tcp any any eq telnet established
Router1(config)#access-list 122 permit tcp any any eq telnet
Router1(config)#access-list 122 permit ip any any
```

```
Router1(config)#interface Serial0/0
Router1(config-if)#ip access-group 122 in
Router1(config-if)#exit
Router1(config)#end
Router1#
```

Here is an alternative method that will also work:

```
Router1#configure terminal
Enter configuration commands, one per line.  End with CNTL/Z.
Router1(config)#access-list 121 permit tcp any any eq telnet syn
Router1(config)#access-list 121 permit tcp any any eq telnet
Router1(config)#access-list 121 permit ip any any
Router1(config)#interface Serial0/0
Router1(config-if)#ip access-group 121 in
Router1(config-if)#exit
Router1(config)#end
Router1#
```

Discussion

When you configure an access-list, the router counts the total number of times it finds something that matches each line in the ACL. While this information is often useful, it does not tell you whether these counters are recording a thousand packets on a single session, or a single packet from each of a thousand sessions. The ACLs in this recipe count the number of TCP sessions as well as the total number of packets.

In the first example, the first line in the ACL permits all established telnet packets to pass through the access-list, as we did in Recipe 19.5. The second line then matches all of the Telnet packets that the first one does not, which mainly means the initial SYN packet that starts the TCP session. As we mentioned in Recipe 19.4, the first packet of a TCP session contains the SYN bit. And, as we discussed in Recipe 19.5, an ACL that includes the *established* keyword will not match any packets that have the SYN bit set.

So the second line will catch the initial session establishment, while the first line matches all of the other packets in the session. Therefore, the second line will give us a way to count the total number of TCP sessions that pass through the router. Note that these sessions can be between any two devices; as long as they communicate through this router, we can count them. Of course, the ACL in the example only counts Telnet sessions, that is sessions on TCP port number 23. But it is easy enough to change the port number in the ACL to monitor other TCP-based applications.

After applying this ACL to an interface for a while, the *show access-list* command starts to show a running count of the number of Telnet sessions that have occurred:

```
Router1#show access-list 122
Extended IP access list 122
    permit tcp any any eq telnet established (3843 matches)
    permit tcp any any eq telnet (6 matches)
    permit ip any any (31937 matches)
Router1#
```

As you can see, six separate Telnet sessions have passed through the interface where we applied this ACL. If you want to know the total number of Telnet packets, you can simply add the first two line together: 3,843 + 6 = 3,849 packets.

The second example uses a slightly different method for counting the number of sessions. In this case, the first line of the access-list matches only Telnet packets with the SYN bit set, as we discussed in Recipe 19.4:

```
Router1(config)#access-list 121 permit tcp any any eq telnet syn
```

The only packets that have this bit set are the packets from the initial TCP three-phase handshake that establishes the session. So this also gives us a way of counting the total number of Telnet sessions. The second line of this ACL captures the remaining Telnet packets:

```
Router1#show access-list 121
Extended IP access list 121
    permit tcp any any eq telnet syn (7 matches)
    permit tcp any any eq telnet (3057 matches)
    permit ip any any (9404 matches)
Router1#
```

So this ACL has counted seven separate Telnet sessions and 7 + 3057 = 3064 total Telnet packets.

We can take the counting functionality of these ACLs a step further by adding the *log* keyword to the ACL lines that count the sessions:

```
Router1#configure terminal
Enter configuration commands, one per line.  End with CNTL/Z.
Router1(config)#access-list 121 permit tcp any any eq telnet syn log
Router1(config)#access-list 121 permit tcp any any eq telnet
Router1(config)#access-list 121 permit ip any any
Router1(config)#end
Router1#
```

Including the *log* keyword like this allows us to keep a log of every TCP session, without needing to log all of the packets in these sessions. This can be useful for security records and audits:

```
Router1#show logging | include list 121
Feb  7 15:36:13: %SEC-6-IPACCESSLOGP: list 121 permitted tcp 172.25.1.1(3886) -> 10.
2.2.2(23), 1 packet
Feb  7 15:36:39: %SEC-6-IPACCESSLOGP: list 121 permitted tcp 172.25.1.1(3887) -> 10.
2.2.2(23), 1 packet
Feb  7 15:38:32: %SEC-6-IPACCESSLOGP: list 121 permitted tcp 172.25.1.1(3888) -> 10.
2.2.2(23), 1 packet
Feb  8 07:48:20: %SEC-6-IPACCESSLOGP: list 121 permitted tcp 172.25.1.1(4332) -> 10.
2.2.2(23), 1 packet
Feb  8 07:49:35: %SEC-6-IPACCESSLOGP: list 121 permitted tcp 172.25.1.1(4333) -> 10.
2.2.2(23), 1 packet
Feb  8 08:08:57: %SEC-6-IPACCESSLOGP: list 121 permitted tcp 172.25.1.1(4339) -> 10.
2.2.2(23), 1 packet
Router1#
```

For more information about logging, please see Chapter 18.

See Also

Recipe 19.4; Recipe 19.5; Chapter 18

19.10 Analyzing ACL Log Entries

Problem

You want to analyze the log entries created by logging ACLs.

Solution

The Perl script in Example 19-1 parses a router syslog file and builds a detailed report of packets that were denied by logging ACLs. By default, the script will parse every ACL log message that it finds in the syslog file on a server. You can also look for messages associated with a particular ACL by specifying the ACL number or name as a command-line argument.

Example 19-1. logscan.pl

```perl
#!/usr/local/bin/perl
#
#        logscan.pl -- a script to extract ACL logs from a syslog file.
#
# Set behavior
$log="/var/log/cisco.log";
$ntop=10;
#
chomp ($acl=$ARGV[0]);
if ($acl == "") { $acl=".*"};

open(LOG , "<$log") or die;
while (<LOG>) {
 if (/IPACCESSLOGP: list $acl denied ([tcpud]+) ([0-9.]+)\(([0-9]+)\) -> ([0-9.]+)\(([0-
9]+)\), ([0-9]+) /) {
    $x=$6;
    $srca{$2}+=$x;
    $foo=sprintf("%16s  -> %16s  %3s port %-6s",$2,$4,$1,$5);
    $moo=sprintf("%3s port %-6s",$1,$5);
    $quad{$foo}+=$x;
    $port{$moo}+=$x;
 }
}
$n=0;
printf ("Connection Summary:\n");
foreach $i (sort { $quad{$b} <=> $quad{$a} } keys %quad) {
   if ($n++ >= $ntop) { last };
   printf ("%6s:%s\n", $quad{$i},$i);
}
$n=0;
printf ("\nDestination Port Summary:\n");
```

Example 19-1. logscan.pl

```
foreach $i ( sort { $port{$b} <=> $port{$a} } keys %port) {
    if ($n++ >= $ntop) { last };
    printf ("%6s: %s\n", $port{$i},$i);
}
$n=0;
printf ("\nSource Address Summary:\n");
foreach $i ( sort { $srca{$b} <=> $srca{$a} } keys %srca) {
    if ($n++ >= $ntop) { last };
    printf ("%6s: %s\n", $srca{$i},$i);
}
```

 Note that we have had to split the line that begins "if (/IPACCESS-LOGP: list" across two lines so that it will fit on the page. If you decide to use this script, please type it as a single line.

Discussion

It's a good idea configure your access-lists so that they log all of the packets that they deny. This is particularly true for security-related ACLs. You can then use these log messages for security or audit purposes. Unfortunately, this level of logging can create a large number of messages, which makes analysis difficult. This Perl script automates the most difficult part of this analysis by parsing through a large file of ACL log messages and building a report that can help to identify potential problems.

The report produced by the script has three sections that summarize connections, destination ports, and source IP addresses. The connection report displays the top 10 most common connection denied attempts, including the source address, destination source, and destination port number. The destination port summary displays the top 10 most frequently denied destination ports. And the source address summary displays the 10 hosts whose connection attempts were most frequently denied. In each case, the script looks at both TCP and UDP ports.

The following is a sample report:

```
Freebsd%./logscan.pl
Connection Summary:
   195:     172.25.1.1   ->   172.20.100.1  tcp port 23
    13:     172.25.1.1   ->   172.20.100.1  tcp port 22
     8:     172.20.1.2   ->     172.25.1.3  udp port 53
     6:     172.20.1.2   ->     172.25.1.1  udp port 123
     6:     172.25.1.1   ->       10.2.2.2  tcp port 23
     4:     172.20.1.2   ->     172.25.1.1  udp port 162
     4:     172.25.1.1   ->   172.20.100.1  tcp port 21
     4:     172.20.1.2   ->     172.25.1.1  udp port 53
     3:     172.25.1.1   ->   172.20.100.1  tcp port 80
     2:     172.20.1.2   ->     172.25.1.3  udp port 123

Destination Port Summary:
   206: tcp port 23
    14: tcp port 22
```

```
   12: udp port 53
    8: udp port 123
    4: tcp port 80
    4: udp port 162
    4: tcp port 21
    2: tcp port 443
    1: tcp port 6000
    1: tcp port 79

Source Address Summary:
  222: 172.25.1.1
   24: 172.20.1.2
    3: 172.25.1.6
    1: 192.168.4.217
    1: 172.25.1.9
    1: 10.2.3.134
    1: 172.25.1.4
    1: 172.22.1.9
    1: 10.23.55.121
    1: 172.25.1.3
Freebsd%
```

This report should help to identify troubling behavior that warrants further investigation. For instance, you will notice that address 172.25.1.1 has attempted to Telnet to 172.20.100.1 195 times. This may not have been evident by scanning the log file by hand.

The script can also build a report based on the messages from a particular ACL number or name:

```
Freebsd%./logscan.pl 122
Connection Summary:
    2:      172.25.1.6  ->      10.2.2.2  tcp port 443
    1:  192.168.4.217  ->      10.2.2.2  tcp port 23
    1:      172.22.1.9  ->      10.2.2.2  tcp port 6000
    1:    10.2.3.134  ->      10.2.2.2  tcp port 23
    1:      172.25.1.9  ->      10.2.2.2  tcp port 23
    1:   10.23.55.121  ->      10.2.2.2  tcp port 79
    1:      172.25.1.1  ->      10.2.2.2  tcp port 22
    1:      172.25.1.6  ->      10.2.2.2  tcp port 23

Destination Port Summary:
    4: tcp port 23
    2: tcp port 443
    1: tcp port 22
    1: tcp port 6000
    1: tcp port 79

Source Address Summary:
    3: 172.25.1.6
    1: 10.2.3.134
    1: 172.22.1.9
    1: 192.168.4.217
    1: 172.25.1.1
```

```
        1: 172.25.1.9
        1: 10.23.55.121
Freebsd%
```

Before you can use this script you must modify the variable *$log*. This variable must contain the full directory and filename of the syslog file that you wish to scan. The script is then ready to launch. The only other variable you may want to modify is the *$ntop* variable. This variable defines how long each section of the report will be. By default, the script is set to display the top 10 matches in each category. However, you can set this number to any number you prefer. Also note that, as you can see in the above example, if there are fewer than *$ntop* matches in any category, the script will show only the matches that it actually finds.

For more information on logging and remote logging to a Syslog server, please see Chapter 18.

See Also

Recipe 19.8; Recipe 19.9; Chapter 18

19.11 Using Named and Reflexive Access-Lists

Problem

You want to use a reflexive ACL, embedded in a named ACL.

Solution

A basic named ACL is similar to the numbered ACLs that we discussed earlier in this chapter. They can work like either Standard or Extended IP ACLs:

```
Router1#configure terminal
Enter configuration commands, one per line.  End with CNTL/Z.
Router1(config)#ip access-list standard STANDARD-ACL
Router1(config-std-nacl)#remark This is a standard ACL
Router1(config-std-nacl)#permit any log
Router1(config-std-nacl)#exit
Router1(config)#ip access-list extended EXTENDED-ACL
Router1(config-ext-nacl)#remark This is an extended ACL
Router1(config-ext-nacl)#deny tcp any any eq www
Router1(config-ext-nacl)#permit ip any any log
Router1(config-ext-nacl)#exit
Router1(config)#interface Serial0/1
Router1(config-if)#ip access-group STANDARD-ACL in
Router1(config-if)#exit
Router1(config)#end
Router1#
```

You can embed a reflexive ACL inside of a named Extended IP ACL. The *reflect* keyword defines the reflexive ACL rule, and the *evaluate* command executes it. The following example filters ICMP packets so that you can initiate a PING test from one side of the network, but not the other:

```
Router1#configure terminal
Enter configuration commands, one per line.  End with CNTL/Z.
Router1(config)#ip access-list extended PING-OUT
Router1(config-ext-nacl)#permit icmp any any reflect ICMP-REFLECT timeout 15
Router1(config-ext-nacl)#permit ip any any
Router1(config-ext-nacl)#exit
Router1(config)#ip access-list extended PING-IN
Router1(config-ext-nacl)#evaluate ICMP-REFLECT
Router1(config-ext-nacl)#deny icmp any any log
Router1(config-ext-nacl)#permit ip any any
Router1(config-ext-nacl)#exit
Router1(config)#interface Serial0/1
Router1(config-if)#ip access-group PING-OUT out
Router1(config-if)#ip access-group PING-IN in
Router1(config-if)#end
Router1#
```

Discussion

The first example in this recipe just demonstrates how to use named ACLs. There is very little difference between this example and the one shown in Recipe 19.1, except that here we have used a different type of ACL to accomplish the same thing. One useful difference between the two versions is that you can delete an individual rule from a named ACL:

```
Router1#show access-list EXTENDED-ACL
Extended IP access list EXTENDED-ACL
    deny tcp any any eq www
    permit ip any any log
Router1#configure terminal
Enter configuration commands, one per line.  End with CNTL/Z.
Router1(config)#ip access-list extended EXTENDED-ACL
Router1(config-ext-nacl)#no deny tcp any any eq www
Router1(config-ext-nacl)#end
Router1#show access-list EXTENDED-ACL
Extended IP access list EXTENDED-ACL
    permit ip any any log
Router1#
```

Just as with numbered ACLs, however, you cannot add individual rules to the middle of a named ACL.

Named ACLs start to show their real value, though, when you need to use more advanced features, such as *reflexive* ACLs, as we did in the second example. This example is similar in spirit to what we did to restrict TCP sessions in Recipe 19.5. In that case, we wanted to ensure that users on the trusted side of the network could initiate TCP connections to the untrusted side, but any incoming connection attempts would be rejected. Here we do the same thing with ICMP packets.

Of course, because TCP is a connection-oriented protocol, it is not quite so difficult to determine which side initiated the session. But ICMP doesn't have the concept of a session. So what we have to do is wait until somebody on the inside sends an ICMP packet to somebody on the outside. When this happens, we tell the router that it can expect to see an appropriate ICMP response from the same IP address, so it should let that packet through.

Let's look at the outbound ACL first:

```
Router1(config)#ip access-list extended PING-OUT
Router1(config-ext-nacl)#permit icmp any any reflect ICMP-REFLECT timeout 15
Router1(config-ext-nacl)#permit ip any any
```

The first *permit* command includes the keyword *reflect* and defines the reflection rule name as ICMP-REFLECT. We have applied this ACL to watch for outbound packets on the interface. As soon as we send out an ICMP packet, such as a PING query, the router starts looking for the reflected version of this packet—in this case, a PING response.

In this example, we have gone further than this by including the timeout keyword at the end of the line with an argument of 15. This tells the router that it should not wait more than 15 seconds after the last outbound packet for additional inbound packets.

The inbound rule uses the *evaluate* keyword to dynamically enable the reflection rule:

```
Router1(config)#ip access-list extended PING-IN
Router1(config-ext-nacl)#evaluate ICMP-REFLECT
Router1(config-ext-nacl)#deny icmp any any log
Router1(config-ext-nacl)#permit ip any any
```

Notice that this is the same rule name, ICMP-REFLECT, as we previously defined in the outbound ACL. If the incoming packet looks like a reflected version of whatever was defined when we created this rule, the ACL will *permit* the packet. If the packet doesn't match this rule, then it will continue checking the rest of the ACL normally. In this case, we have followed the evaluate command with a command that will explicitly deny all other ICMP packets that don't match the reflection rule.

Note that the router will check the reflected packet to ensure that it has the correct source and destination addresses, based on the outbound packet. If you use reflexive ACLs to match a UDP application, for example, the router will also check port numbers to ensure that the inbound packet is legitimate.

See Also

Recipe 19.1; Recipe 19.5

19.12 Dealing with Passive Mode FTP

Problem

You want to construct an ACL that can identify passive mode FTP sessions.

Solution

This example shows how to filter a Passive FTP control and data sessions:

```
Router1#configure terminal
Enter configuration commands, one per line.  End with CNTL/Z.
Router1(config)#access-list 144 permit tcp any gt 1023 any eq ftp
Router1(config)#access-list 144 permit tcp any gt 1023 any gt 1023
Router1(config)#access-list 144 deny ip any any
Router1(config)#interface Serial0/0.1
Router1(config-subif)#ip access-group 144 in
Router1(config-subif)#exit
Router1(config)#end
Router1#
```

Discussion

In Recipe 19.6, we briefly reviewed the traditional way that FTP works. However, there is another subtle variation on this process, which is commonly called Passive FTP. The user connects to the server on port 21, exactly as before. But in the Passive FTP case, the client software issues the command PASV, which instructs the server to listen on a new non-default data port, and wait for a connection. The server selects a new port, which it tells to the client. The server then opens this port and waits for a connection. The client device initiates a new TCP connection to this temporary port number, and uses this connection to transfer its data.

This may sound like an unusual way of doing things, and it probably is. However, this is actually the default mode for many web browsers, including Internet Explorer and Netscape when they do FTP file transfers. This makes passive FTP the most common FTP mode for many networks. The problem is that if you want to control this traffic using an ACL of any kind, you no longer know either the source or destination TCP port numbers. For example, if you need to restrict some traffic, but ensure that passive FTP is allowed, you will need an ACL that can somehow permit the temporary port numbers. In Chapter 27, we will demonstrate a filtering method in which the router uses CBAC to learn about the new port by watching the control session of the FTP session.

This example takes a simpler approach and uses an extended ACL to deal with passive FTP. The trouble with this ACL is that it opens all TCP ports from 1024 and above. Clearly, this is not desirable on a router facing the Internet, or some other unfriendly network. The problem is that passive FTP can pick a different source and destination port each time a web browser connects to it.

Although our example permits passive FTP to pass through, it opens up over 64,000 TCP ports in the process. Obviously, this is not preferred method of permitting passive FTP. In Chapter 27, we discuss a much more secure method of allowing passive FTP through your router.

See Also

Recipe 19.6; Chapter 27

19.13 Using Time-Based Access-Lists

Problem

You want to filter application data based on the time of day.

Solution

To filter application data based on the time of day, use the following commands:

```
Router1#configure terminal
Enter configuration commands, one per line.  End with CNTL/Z.
Router1(config)#time-range NOSURF
Router1(config-time-range)# periodic weekdays 9:00 to 17:00
Router1(config-time-range)#exit
Router1(config)#ip access-list extended NOSURFING
Router1(config-ext-nacl)# deny   tcp any any eq www time-range NOSURF
Router1(config-ext-nacl)# permit ip any any
Router1(config-ext-nacl)#exit
Router1(config)#interface FastEthernet0/1
Router1(config-if)#ip access-group NOSURFING in
Router1(config-if)#end
Router1#
```

 This feature relies on an accurate system clock to function properly. It is highly recommended that you use NTP to synchronize the router's clock. See Chapter 14 for more information regarding NTP.

Discussion

Timed-based access-lists allow you to filter application data based on the time of day. In our example, we've built an access-list that denies HTTP traffic during the work hours, Monday to Friday, from 9:00 to 17:00. Timed-based access-lists also allows control over other router features, based on the time of day, such as policy-based routing, CAR statements, ACL logging, on-demand link activation, or security policies, to name a few.

To configure a timed-based access-list, you must first configure a time-range:

```
Router2#configure terminal
Enter configuration commands, one per line.  End with CNTL/Z.
Router2(config)#time-range MONDAYONLY
Router2(config-time-range)#periodic monday 9:00 to 17:00
Router2(config-time-range)#end
Router2#
```

In this example, we've named the time-range *MONDAYONLY*, and assigned it a time range from Monday at 9:00 to 17:00. The *periodic* keyword is one way to define a time range. The other method is assign an absolute time by using the *absolute* keyword. Using the absolute method assigns a specific date in time to begin. The following is an example of a time range that uses the *absolute* keyword:

```
Router2#configure terminal
Enter configuration commands, one per line.  End with CNTL/Z.
Router2(config)#time-range SAMPLE
Router2(config-time-range)#absolute start 9:00 1 October 2006 end 18:00 31 December
2006
Router2(config-time-range)#end
Router2#
```

Notice that we have set an exact date and time to start and end on using the *absolute* keyword. In this example, the start time is 9:00 on October 1, 2006, and the end time is 18:00 on December 31, 2006.

You can combine periodic and absolute statements within a single time range; however, keep in mind that the absolute statements are given priority:

```
Router2#configure terminal
Enter configuration commands, one per line.  End with CNTL/Z.
Router2(config)#time-range SAMPLE
Router2(config-time-range)#absolute start 9:00 1 October 2006 end 18:00 31 December
2006
Router2(config-time-range)#periodic monday 9:00 to 17:00
Router2(config-time-range)#end
Router2#
```

Notice in this example that we've included a periodic and absolute statement within the same time range. In this case, the periodic statement is ignored until the absolute start time is reached, and then each Monday the time range will become active. The same holds true for the absolute end time. Once we reach the absolute end time of 18:00 on December 31, then the periodic statements will again be ignored.

You can configure multiple *periodic* statements within a time range but only one *absolute* statement.

Once you configure the time range, then you can assign it to an ACL entry:

```
Router1#configure terminal
Enter configuration commands, one per line.  End with CNTL/Z.
Router1(config)#ip access-list extended NOSURFING
Router1(config-ext-nacl)# deny   tcp any any eq www time-range NOSURF
Router1(config-ext-nacl)# permit ip any any
Router1(config-ext-nacl)#end
Router1#
```

Notice that we've assigned the time range *NOSURF* to the first ACL entry. This ACL entry will become active when the time range becomes true. Once active, the ACL entry acts like a normal entry, and will start denying traffic that matches its criteria. In this case, during work hours, our ACL will deny all HTTP traffic.

If we look at the timed access-list during the evening hours, we will see the timed ACL entry is inactive:

```
Router1#show clock
20:10:50.985 EDT Tue Aug 22 2006
Router1#
Router1#show ip access-list
Extended IP access list NOSURFING
    10 deny tcp any any eq www time-range NOSURF (inactive)
    20 permit ip any any
Router1#
```

During this period, the timed ACL entry is marked inactive and HTTP-based traffic is allowed to pass. During normal workday hours, however, the timed ACL entry is changed to active and HTTP traffic is now blocked:

```
Router1#show clock
09:39:22.279 EDT Wed Aug 23 2006
Router1#
Router1#show ip access-list
Extended IP access list NOSURFING
    10 deny tcp any any eq www time-range NOSURF (active)
    20 permit ip any any
Router1#
```

You can also construct more complicated examples where different lines in the same ACL have different time-range rules. In the following example, we have defined two time ranges: one is called *NOSURF*, and is valid every day between 9:00 AM and 5:00 PM; the other is *NOTELNET*, and is valid between 5:00 PM and 9:00 AM:

```
Router1#configure terminal
Enter configuration commands, one per line. End with CNTL/Z.
Router1(config)#time-range NOSURF
Router(config-time-range)# periodic weekdays 9:00 to 17:00
Router1(config-time-range #exit
Router1(config)#time-range NOTELNET
Router1(config-time-range)# periodic weekdays 17:00 to 9:00
Router1(config-time-range)#exit
Router1(config)#ip access-list extended NOSURFING
Router1(config-ext-nacl)# deny tcp any any eq www time-range
NOSURF
Router1(config-ext-nacl)# deny tcp any any eq telnet time-range
NOTELNET
Router1(config-ext-nacl)# permit ip any any
Router1(config-ext-nacl)#end
Router1#
```

Then, when you look at this ACL with the *show ip accesslist* command, the output shows which timed lines are currently being used (active) and which are not (inactive):

```
Router1#show ip access-list NOSURFING
Extended IP access list NOSURFING
    10 deny tcp any any eq www time-range NOSURF (inactive)
    20 deny tcp any any eq telnet time-range NOTELNET (active)
    20 permit ip any any
Router1#
```

See Also

Chapter 14

19.14 Filtering Based on Noncontiguous Ports

Problem

You want to filter noncontiguous ports efficiently.

Solution

To filter noncontiguous ports, use the following commands:

```
Router2#configure terminal
Enter configuration commands, one per line.  End with CNTL/Z.
Router2(config)#ip access-list extended OREILLY
Router2(config-ext-nacl)#permit tcp any host 172.25.100.100 eq 80 23 25 110 514 21
Router2(config-ext-nacl)#end
Router2#
```

 Cisco introduced the ability to filter noncontiguous ports in IOS Version 12.3(7)T.

Discussion

Historically, Cisco's IOS has only supported the filtering of contiguous port numbers that use the *range* keyword:

```
Router2#configure terminal
Enter configuration commands, one per line.  End with CNTL/Z.
Router2(config)#ip access-list extended PORTRANGE
Router2(config-ext-nacl)#permit tcp any any range 20 25
Router2(config-ext-nacl)#end
Router2#
```

In this example, we permit traffic by using TCP ports 20-25 to pass the ACL, which reduces the number of ACL entries and processing required. However, the ability to filter on contiguous port numbers was generally of little use because the required ports were rarely contiguous.

If you needed to filter based on noncontiguous ports, then you had no choice but to add an ACL line for each port. The following example demonstrates how you would normally filter six noncontiguous ports:

```
Router2#configure terminal
Enter configuration commands, one per line.  End with CNTL/Z.
Router2(config)#ip access-list extended OREILLY
Router2(config-ext-nacl)#permit tcp any host 172.25.100.100 eq 80
Router2(config-ext-nacl)#permit tcp any host 172.25.100.100 eq 23
Router2(config-ext-nacl)#permit tcp any host 172.25.100.100 eq 25
Router2(config-ext-nacl)#permit tcp any host 172.25.100.100 eq 110
Router2(config-ext-nacl)#permit tcp any host 172.25.100.100 eq 514
Router2(config-ext-nacl)#permit tcp any host 172.25.100.100 eq 21
Router2(config-ext-nacl)#end
Router2#
```

Notice that the example in our Solution section replaces six ACL entries with a single ACL entry. Both solutions achieve the desired result; however, being able to match more than one port per ACL entry greatly reduces ACL size and complexity.

See Also

Recipe 19.6

19.15 Advanced Access-List Editing

Problem

You want to edit an existing ACL directly on the router itself.

Solution

You can insert a single entry into an existing ACL by specifying a sequence number, as follows:

```
Router2#configure terminal
Enter configuration commands, one per line.  End with CNTL/Z.
Router2(config)#ip access-list extended OREILLY
Router2(config-ext-nacl)#12 permit tcp any host 172.25.100.100 eq 20
Router2(config-ext-nacl)#end
Router2#
```

The following commands show how to tell the router to automatically readjust the sequence numbers:

```
Router2#configure terminal
Enter configuration commands, one per line.  End with CNTL/Z.
Router2(config)#ip access-list resequence OREILLY 10 10
Router2(config)#end
Router2#
```

And you can remove an individual entry from an existing ACL by just using the keyword *no* and the sequence number of the line you wish to delete:

```
Router2#configure terminal
Enter configuration commands, one per line.  End with CNTL/Z.
Router2(config)#ip access-list extended OREILLY
Router2(config-ext-nacl)#no 60
Router2(config-ext-nacl)#end
Router2#
```

Discussion

Beginning with IOS Version 12.3(2)T, Cisco introduced the ability to edit ACLs using ACL entry sequence numbering. By default, the router will automatically add a sequence number to each ACL entry starting with 10, using increments of 10. The following is the sample ACL. Notice the sequence numbers on the far left of each line:

```
Router2#show ip access-lists OREILLY
Extended IP access list OREILLY
    10 permit tcp any host 172.25.100.100 eq www
    20 permit tcp any host 172.25.100.100 eq telnet
    30 permit tcp any host 172.25.100.100 eq smtp
    40 permit tcp any host 172.25.100.100 eq pop3
    50 permit tcp any host 172.25.100.100 eq cmd
    60 permit tcp any host 172.25.100.100 eq ftp
    70 deny ip any host 172.25.100.100
    80 permit ip any any
Router2#
```

The introduction of sequence numbering means you can now remove, edit, or add ACL entries in any sequence. This is an extremely useful and long overdue feature.

By default, if you don't specify a sequence number, then new ACL entries will be added to the bottom of the ACL, as it always has. However, if you specify a particular sequence number, then you can insert a new ACL entry in any position. In the next example, let's add a new ACL entry and assign it sequence number 12:

```
Router2#configure terminal
Enter configuration commands, one per line.  End with CNTL/Z.
Router2(config)#ip access-list extended OREILLY
Router2(config-ext-nacl)#12 permit tcp any host 172.25.100.100 eq 20
Router2(config-ext-nacl)#end
Router2#
```

Now, let's look at the ACL:

```
Router2#show ip access-lists OREILLY
Extended IP access list OREILLY
    10 permit tcp any host 172.25.100.100 eq www
    12 permit tcp any host 172.25.100.100 eq ftp-data
    20 permit tcp any host 172.25.100.100 eq telnet
    30 permit tcp any host 172.25.100.100 eq smtp
    40 permit tcp any host 172.25.100.100 eq pop3
    50 permit tcp any host 172.25.100.100 eq cmd
    60 permit tcp any host 172.25.100.100 eq ftp
```

```
    70 deny ip any host 172.25.100.100
    80 permit ip any any
Router2#
```

Notice that our new ACL entry inserted itself into the existing ACL. To accomplish this feat in the past, you would have had to delete the entire ACL, modified the ACL using a remote text editor of some sort, and then added the new ACL back into the router configuration.

The default numbering scheme allows you to add up to nine new ACL entries between existing ACL entries, but what happens if you want to add more? Cisco has added the ability to resequence the ACL numbering scheme, which provides you room to expand. Let's resequence the ACL to start with sequence number 10, the first number of the command, and let's use increments of 10, the second number provided:

```
Router2#configure terminal
Enter configuration commands, one per line.  End with CNTL/Z.
Router2(config)#ip access-list resequence OREILLY 10 10
Router2(config)#end
Router2(config)#
```

Let's view the ACL again:

```
Router2#show ip access-lists OREILLY
Extended IP access list OREILLY
    10 permit tcp any host 172.25.100.100 eq www
    20 permit tcp any host 172.25.100.100 eq ftp-data
    30 permit tcp any host 172.25.100.100 eq telnet
    40 permit tcp any host 172.25.100.100 eq smtp
    50 permit tcp any host 172.25.100.100 eq pop3
    60 permit tcp any host 172.25.100.100 eq cmd
    70 permit tcp any host 172.25.100.100 eq ftp
    80 deny ip any host 172.25.100.100
    90 permit ip any any
Router2#
```

Notice that ACL entry 12 has changed to sequence number 20, and all the other entries after that go up in increments of 10. We note in passing that sequence numbers are not stored in the configuration file, which provides for backward compatibility. It also means that the router assigns default sequence numbers after reboot. The router does ensure that ACLs are stored in the correct order within the configuration file.

To remove a particular ACL entry, use the following command:

```
Router2#configure terminal
Enter configuration commands, one per line.  End with CNTL/Z.
Router2(config)#ip access-list extended OREILLY
Router2(config-ext-nacl)#no 60
Router2(config-ext-nacl)#end
Router2#
```

Notice that you don't need to specify the entire ACL line—just the sequence number you wish to delete. Now if we view the ACL again, we'll see that ACL entry 60 is gone:

```
Router2#show ip access-lists OREILLY
Extended IP access list OREILLY
```

```
   10 permit tcp any host 172.25.100.100 eq www
   20 permit tcp any host 172.25.100.100 eq ftp-data
   30 permit tcp any host 172.25.100.100 eq telnet
   40 permit tcp any host 172.25.100.100 eq smtp
   50 permit tcp any host 172.25.100.100 eq pop3
   70 permit tcp any host 172.25.100.100 eq ftp
   80 deny ip any host 172.25.100.100
   90 permit ip any any
Router2#
```

See Also

Recipe 19.1

19.16 Filtering IPv6

Problem

You want to filter IPv6 traffic using access-lists.

Solution

Cisco supports named access-lists for IPv6:

```
Router1#configure terminal
Enter configuration commands, one per line.  End with CNTL/Z.
Router1(config)#ipv6 access-list EXAMPLES
Router1(config-ipv6-acl)#permit ipv6 AAAA:5::/64 any
Router1(config-ipv6-acl)#permit ipv6 host AAAA:5::FE:1 any
Router1(config-ipv6-acl)#permit tcp any any eq telnet established
Router1(config-ipv6-acl)#deny tcp any any eq telnet syn
Router1(config-ipv6-acl)#sequence 55 permit udp any any eq snmp
Router1(config-ipv6-acl)#remark this is a comment
Router1(config-ipv6-acl)#sequence 66 remark this comment has a sequence number
Router1(config-ipv6-acl)#permit icmp any any reflect ICMP-REFLECT
Router1(config-ipv6-acl)#deny ipv6 any host AAAA:6::1 log
Router1(config-ipv6-acl)#deny ipv6 any any log-input
Router1(config-ipv6-acl)#exit
Router1(config)#interface FastEthernet0/0
Router1(config-if)#ipv6 traffic-filter EXAMPLES in
Router1(config-if)#exit
Router1(config)#end
Router1#
```

Discussion

The ACL shown in this example isn't particularly useful, but it does show many of the features available with IPv6 access-lists. There are only named IPv6 access-lists, as numbered lists do not exist. However, as we previously saw in Recipes 19.11 and 19.15, this is not a drawback. Anything you can do with numbered access-lists, you can do with named access-lists, and several features such as reflexive access-lists and the ability to edit individual lines within an access-list are available only with named lists.

The first entry in the access-list shown in the Solution section shows how to filter traffic based on IPv6 addresses:

```
Router1(config)#ipv6 access-list EXAMPLES
Router1(config-ipv6-acl)#permit ipv6 AAAA:5::/64 any
```

This command allows any IPv6 packets with a source address in the specified range of IPv6 addresses to communicate with any destination device. IPv6 access-lists work exactly the same way as IPv4 named access-lists, listing the source address first, followed by the destination address. The *any* and *host* keywords are also available with IPv6 and work in exactly the same way that we have seen previously in this chapter:

```
Router1(config-ipv6-acl)#permit ipv6 host AAAA:5::FE:1 any
```

These access-lists offer the same facilities for filtering on IP protocols as the IPv4 access-lists do, and in a familiar syntax. The number of protocols directly supported with keywords is considerably less than for IPv4 access-lists, however you can specify other protocols by number:

```
Router1(config-ipv6-acl)#permit ?
  <0-255>              An IPv6 protocol number
  X:X:X:X::X/<0-128>   IPv6 source prefix x:x::y/<z>
  ahp                  Authentication Header Protocol
  any                  Any source prefix
  esp                  Encapsulation Security Payload
  host                 A single source host
  icmp                 Internet Control Message Protocol
  ipv6                 Any IPv6
  pcp                  Payload Compression Protocol
  sctp                 Streams Control Transmission Protocol
  tcp                  Transmission Control Protocol
  udp                  User Datagram Protocol

Router1(config-ipv6-acl)#
```

For TCP and UDP protocols, you can specify source and destination ports, either by number or keyword, with the same list of keywords available, as we saw in Recipe 19.3 for IPv4 access-lists:

```
Router1(config-ipv6-acl)#permit tcp any any eq ?
  <0-65535>   Port number
  bgp         Border Gateway Protocol (179)
  chargen     Character generator (19)
  cmd         Remote commands (rcmd, 514)
  daytime     Daytime (13)
  discard     Discard (9)
  domain      Domain Name Service (53)
  echo        Echo (7)
  exec        Exec (rsh, 512)
  finger      Finger (79)
  ftp         File Transfer Protocol (21)
```

```
ftp-data      FTP data connections (20)
gopher        Gopher (70)
hostname      NIC hostname server (101)
ident         Ident Protocol (113)
irc           Internet Relay Chat (194)
klogin        Kerberos login (543)
kshell        Kerberos shell (544)
login         Login (rlogin, 513)
lpd           Printer service (515)
nntp          Network News Transport Protocol (119)
pim-auto-rp   PIM Auto-RP (496)
pop2          Post Office Protocol v2 (109)
pop3          Post Office Protocol v3 (110)
smtp          Simple Mail Transport Protocol (25)
sunrpc        Sun Remote Procedure Call (111)
syslog        Syslog (514)
tacacs        TAC Access Control System (49)
talk          Talk (517)
telnet        Telnet (23)
time          Time (37)
uucp          Unix-to-Unix Copy Program (540)
whois         Nicname (43)
www           World Wide Web (HTTP, 80)

RouterHome1(config-ipv6-acl)#
```

As with IPv4 access-lists for TCP and UDP protocols, you specify the source port immediately after the source address and the destination port directly after the destination port.

You can also use the *established* keyword that we previously discussed in Recipe 19.5:

```
Router1(config-ipv6-acl)#permit tcp any any eq telnet established
```

You can also specify the content of the TCP flags, as we previously saw in Recipe 19.4:

```
Router1(config-ipv6-acl)#deny tcp any any eq telnet syn
```

All of the TCP flags are available via the keywords, *ack*, *fin*, *psh*, *rst*, *syn*, and *urg*. Please refer to Recipe 19.4 for a description of these flags and their meanings. Unfortunately, the new *match-all* and *match-any* keywords that we saw for IPv4 in Recipe 19.4 are not yet available for IPv6, as of Version 12.4T.

The new methods for editing access-lists that we saw in Recipe 19.15 are available for IPv6. So, for example, you can specify a sequence number for any line in an access-list:

```
Router1(config-ipv6-acl)#sequence 55 permit udp any any eq snmp
```

You can also specify sequence numbers at the end of the line:

```
Router1(config-ipv6-acl)#permit udp any any eq snmp sequence 55
```

These sequence numbers appear in the output of the *show ipv6 access-list* command:

```
Router1#show ipv6 access-list EXAMPLES
```

```
IPv6 access list EXAMPLES
    permit ipv6 AAAA:5::/64 any sequence 10
    permit ipv6 host AAAA:5::FE:1 any sequence 20
    permit tcp any any eq telnet established sequence 30
    deny tcp any any eq telnet syn sequence 40
    permit udp any any eq snmp sequence 55
    permit icmp any any reflect ICMP-REFLECT sequence 76
    permit ipv6 any any log sequence 86
    deny ipv6 any host AAAA:6::1 log sequence 106
    deny ipv6 any any log-input sequence 116
Router1#
```

Unlike the IPv4 sequence numbers, which we discussed in Recipe 19.15, this command shows these sequence numbers at the right-hand side of each line.

You can also specify comments to help internally document an access-list using the *remark* keyword, either with or without a sequence number:

```
Router1(config-ipv6-acl)#remark this is a comment
Router1(config-ipv6-acl)#sequence 66 remark this comment has a sequence number
```

Note that neither of these comments appears in the output of the *show ipv6 access-list* command above.

Unfortunately, there is no command to renumber the sequence numbers for an IPv6 access-list as we previously saw for IPv4 in Recipe 19.15.

The IPv6 access-list feature includes the ability to create reflexive access-lists:

```
Router1(config-ipv6-acl)#permit icmp any any reflect ICMP-REFLECT
```

This works exactly the same way as the IPv4 reflexive access-list discussed in Recipe 19.11. You specify a reflection rule with the *reflect* keyword, defining a name for the rule, generally applied to outbound traffic. Then you create a second access-list for the other direction of traffic looking for the expected returning traffic, which you specify using the *evaluate* keyword:

```
Router1(config)#ipv6 access-list RETURN-TRAFFIC
Router1(config-ipv6-acl)#evaluate ICMP-REFLECT
```

And, finally, you can use the *log* and *log-input* keywords that we discussed in Recipe 19.8 with the same results:

```
Router1(config-ipv6-acl)#deny ipv6 any host AAAA:6::1 log
Router1(config-ipv6-acl)#deny ipv6 any any log
```

The command to apply an access-list to filter traffic on an interface is *ipv6 traffic-filter*. Access-lists can be applied either inbound or outbound, as required:

```
Router1(config)#interface FastEthernet0/0
Router1(config-if)#ipv6 traffic-filter EXAMPLES in
```

See Also

Recipe 19.4; Recipe 19.5; Recipe 19.11; Recipe 19.15; Chapter 25

## CHAPTER 20

DHCP

20.0 Introduction

Dynamic Host Configuration Protocol (DHCP) is often used on networks to allow end devices to automatically retrieve their network configuration when they first connect to the network. It basically expands on the earlier Bootstrap Protocol (BOOTP), and uses the same UDP ports, numbers 67 and 68. The protocol itself is defined in RFC 2131, and the configuration options are in RFC 2132.

The most common application for DHCP is to automatically set up IP addresses, netmasks, and default gateways for end devices. However, the protocol can also configure many other options, such as DNS servers, domain names, time zones, NTP servers, and many others. Some software vendors have even added their own configuration options to automatically set up key applications on end devices.

DHCP makes it possible to give a minimal common configuration to all user workstations. Then anybody can simply plug the device into the network at any point, and DHCP will take care of getting an IP address that will work at that location. This minimizes errors due to manual configuration, centralizes control over configuration information, and greatly reduces technician costs, because anybody can connect a device to the network.

There are three distinct element types in a DHCP network. There must be a client and a server, and if these two elements are not on the same Layer 2 network, then there also must be a proxy, which usually runs on the router. The proxy is needed because the client device initially doesn't know its own IP address, so it must send out a Layer 2 broadcast to find a server that has this information. The router must relay these broadcasts to the DHCP server, and forward the responses back to the correct Layer 2 address so that the right end device gets the right configuration information.

Historically, the router's only role in BOOTP or DHCP was this proxy function. However Cisco routers have recently added both DHCP client and server functionality. This chapter will show configuration examples for all three of these functions, although the server configuration is most complex, so more of the recipes will focus on this.

A DHCP exchange starts with a client device, such as an end user workstation. Typically, this device will boot and connect to the network with no preconfigured network information. It doesn't know its IP address, the address of its router, or its subnet or netmask, and it doesn't even know the address of the server that will provide these pieces of information. So it does the only thing it can do, and it sends out a UDP broadcast packet looking for a server.

Most DHCP networks of any size include two or more DHCP servers for redundancy. The end devices typically just need this server at startup time, but they will not work at all without it. So redundancy is important. This also means that it is not unusual for an end device to see several responses to a DHCP request. It will generally just use the first response. However, this also underscores the importance of ensuring that all of the DHCP servers distribute the same information. Their databases of end device configuration parameters must be synchronized.

The end device then requests configuration information from one of the servers. It must specify exactly what options it requires. The server does not need to respond to all of the requested options, but it cannot offer additional unrequested information to the client even if it has additional information in its database. This is an important little detail to remember because it can be very confusing when an end device has some manually configured options that are not replaced by the information on the server.

Since duplicate IP addresses can cause serious problems on a network, most DHCP servers track address conflicts. They do this by attempting to PING each IP address before telling an end device that it is safe to use it. And many DHCP clients will also double check that the address is not already in use by sending an ARP request before using it. However, neither of these checks is mandatory, and some DHCP clients and servers do not check before using an address.

One of the important features of DHCP is the ability to allocate IP addresses only for a configurable period of time, called the *lease* period. If a client device wants to keep its IP address for longer than this period, it must renew the lease before it expires. Clients are free to renew their leases as often as they like.

The server can allocate IP addresses from a pool on a first-come, first-served basis, or it can associate IP addresses with the end device MAC addresses to ensure that a particular client always receives the same address.

20.1 Using IP Helper Addresses for DHCP

Problem

You want to configure your router to pass DHCP requests from local clients to a centralized DHCP server.

Solution

The *ip helper-address* configuration command allows the router to forward local DHCP requests to one or more centralized DHCP servers:

```
Router1#configure terminal
Enter configuration commands, one per line.  End with CNTL/Z.
Router1(config)#interface Ethernet0
Router1(config-if)#ip helper-address 172.25.1.1
Router1(config-if)#ip helper-address 172.25.10.7
Router1(config-if)#exit
Router1(config)#end
Router1#
```

Discussion

The traditional role of routers in DHCP has been simply to act as a proxy device, forwarding information between the client and server. Since IOS level 12.0(1)T, Cisco routers also have DHCP server and client features. But the DHCP proxy function is still the most common for routers.

Because the initial DHCP request comes from a client that typically doesn't have an IP address, it must find the server using a Layer 2 broadcast. So, if the router was not able to function as a proxy for these broadcasts, it would be necessary to put a DHCP server on every network segment.

The DHCP server needs two critical pieces of information before it can allocate an IP address to the client. It must know the subnet that the client is connected to, and it needs the client device's MAC address. The subnet information is needed to ensure that the address that the server allocates will actually work on client's network segment. And the MAC address is necessary so that the server can find any information that is unique to this workstation. This is particularly true if you need to ensure that the end device always gets the same IP address every time it connects to the network.

So the DHCP proxy, which is the router itself, must convert the local broadcast from the client to a unicast packet and forward it to the server. This is what the *ip helper-address* command does.

When the DHCP client sends the DHCP request packet, it doesn't have an IP address. So it uses the all-zeroes address, 0.0.0.0, as the IP source address. And it doesn't know how to reach the DHCP server, so it uses a general broadcast address, 255.255.255.255, for the destination.

So the router must replace the source address with its own IP address, for the interface that received the request. And it replaces the destination address with the address specified in the *ip helper-address* command. The client device's MAC address is included in the payload of the original DHCP request packet, so the router doesn't need to do anything to ensure that the server receives this information.

The DHCP server now has enough information to assign an address from the correct address pool, since it now knows what the originating subnet was for the DHCP request. The server then sends a unicast response back to the proxy router, which in turn sends the request back to the correct MAC address.

The example shows two *ip helper-address* commands. You should include one of these commands for each of your DHCP servers. The router will forward the DHCP broadcasts to all of these addresses. Most organizations use at least two DHCP servers because although the utilization is light, the functionality is critical. In the very likely event that the client device receives several responses to a DHCP request, it will usually just select the one it received first.

It is important to note that the *ip helper-address* command does not just forward DHCP requests. In fact, although you can configure it to forward any UDP broadcast you want, by default it will forward UDP broadcast packets for several different UDP ports to the specified address. In some cases, this unwanted traffic can cause problems on the network or DHCP server. Recipe 20.2 will focus on this issue.

The *show ip interface* command includes information about the helper addresses configured on an interface:

```
Router1#show ip interface Ethernet0
Ethernet0 is up, line protocol is up
  Internet address is 192.168.30.1/24
  Broadcast address is 255.255.255.255
  Address determined by setup command
  MTU is 1500 bytes
  Helper addresses are 172.25.1.3
                       172.25.1.1
  Directed broadcast forwarding is disabled
  <removed for brevity>
Router1#
```

See Also

Recipe 20.2

20.2   Limiting the Impact of IP Helper Addresses

Problem

After configuring your router to use IP helper addresses, you suffer from high link utilization or high CPU utilization on the DHCP server.

Solution

The *ip* helper-address command implicitly enables forwarding several different kinds of UDP broadcasts. You can prevent the router from forwarding the unwanted types of broadcasts with the *no ip forward-protocol udp* configuration command:

```
Router1#configure terminal
Enter configuration commands, one per line.  End with CNTL/Z.
Router1(config)#no ip forward-protocol udp tftp
Router1(config)#no ip forward-protocol udp nameserver
Router1(config)#no ip forward-protocol udp domain
Router1(config)#no ip forward-protocol udp time
Router1(config)#no ip forward-protocol udp netbios-ns
Router1(config)#no ip forward-protocol udp netbios-dgm
Router1(config)#no ip forward-protocol udp tacacs
Router1(config)#end
Router1#
```

Discussion

As mentioned in Recipe 20.1, if the DHCP client and server are on different network segments, the router on the client's segment must be configured with a helper address for DHCP to work. However, the helper address configuration forwards a variety of different UDP broadcasts, not just DHCP packets. This can cause network loading problems, as well as CPU loading problems on the DHCP server.

By default, when you configure the *ip helper-address* command on an interface, the router will automatically forward UDP broadcasts for all of the protocols shown in Table 20-1.

Table 20-1. Default UDP protocols for helper addresses

Type	Description	UDP port
bootpc	Bootstrap or DHCP client	68
bootps	Bootstrap or DHCP server	67
domain	Domain Name Service (DNS)	53
nameserver	IEN-116 name service (obsolete)	42
netbios-dgm	NetBios datagram service	138
netbios-ns	NetBios name service	137
tacacs	TAC Access Control System	49
time	Time	37
tftp	Trivial File Transfer Protocol	69

Note in particular that networks that include Microsoft Windows networking features use a lot of NetBIOS packets. The DHCP server receives broadcasts from many end-device segments throughout the network. It is possible to have enough traffic aggregating on this point to cause serious problems.

This recipe disables each unnecessary protocol, one at a time, using the *no ip forward-protocol* configuration command. Some organizations choose to disable only the NetBios protocols because this is the one that most frequently causes problems.

We strongly recommend using the *no ip forward-protocol* command to ensure that only the required protocols are being forwarded to your DHCP server. Note, however, that this command cannot forward different protocols to different helper addresses. If you have two different servers handling different UDP broadcast protocols, they will both receive all of the local broadcasts that the router accepts. So if you need more detailed control over these types of applications, you may find that the broadcast to multicast conversion features discussed in Chapter 23 will be more effective.

See Also

Recipe 20.1; Chapter 23

20.3 Using DHCP to Dynamically Configure Router IP Addresses

Problem

You want the router to obtain its IP addressing information dynamically.

Solution

The *ip address dhcp* configuration command allows the router to obtain the address information for an interface dynamically:

```
Router1#configure terminal
Enter configuration commands, one per line.  End with CNTL/Z.
Router1(config)#interface FastEthernet0/1
Router1(config-if)#ip address dhcp
Router1(config-if)#end
Router1#
Interface FastEthernet0/1 assigned DHCP address 172.25.1.57, mask 255.255.255.0
Router1#
```

 Prior to Release 12.2(8)T, the *ip address dhcp* command was only supported on Ethernet interfaces.

Discussion

Cisco started to include DHCP client functionality in IOS Version 12.1(2)T. This allows routers to obtain interface IP address information via DHCP. While we don't recommend using dynamic addressing for routers in an internal network, this can be extremely useful for routers that connect to the Internet through an ISP. It is increasingly common for service providers to use DHCP to give address information to allocate information to client devices.

When an interface on the router is configured as a DHCP client like this, it is able to dynamically learn its IP address, and netmask, via DHCP. In addition, the router also learns its TFTP server address, NETBIOS nameserver, vendor-specific information, static routes, domain name, DNS servers, and default router information.

Beginning with IOS Version 12.3(8)T, you can control which options are requested using the *ip dhcp client request* command. By default, all options are requested unless you explicitly disable them:

```
Router1#configure terminal
Enter configuration commands, one per line.  End with CNTL/Z.
Router1(config)#interface FastEthernet0/1
Router1(config-if)#no ip dhcp client request dns-nameserver
Router1(config-if)#end
Router1#
```

In this example, we've disabled the router from requesting DNS servers from the DHCP server. All other options will be requested as normal. The following keywords can be manually disabled using the *no ip dhcp client request* command: *tftp-server-address*, *netbios-nameserver*, *vendor-specific*, *static-route*, *domain-name*, *dns-nameserver*, or *router*.

In the following screen capture, the router has learned its default route via DHCP. Notice that the router displays this DHCP route as a static route and assigns it an administrative distance of 254. This ensures that the DHCP-learned default address is the absolute last possible route, and any other static or dynamic routes will take precedence:

```
Router1#show ip route
Codes: C - connected, S - static, I - IGRP, R - RIP, M - mobile, B - BGP
       D - EIGRP, EX - EIGRP external, O - OSPF, IA - OSPF inter area
       N1 - OSPF NSSA external type 1, N2 - OSPF NSSA external type 2
       E1 - OSPF external type 1, E2 - OSPF external type 2, E - EGP
       i - IS-IS, L1 - IS-IS level-1, L2 - IS-IS level-2, ia - IS-IS inter area
       * - candidate default, U - per-user static route, o - ODR
       P - periodic downloaded static route

Gateway of last resort is 172.25.1.1 to network 0.0.0.0

     172.25.0.0/24 is subnetted, 1 subnets
C       172.25.1.0 is directly connected, FastEthernet0/1
S*   0.0.0.0/0 [254/0] via 172.25.1.1
Router1#
```

In the ISP situation, the end devices will also need domain name and DNS server information. You can see this information with the *show host* command. This example shows a domain name and DNS server information learned via DHCP:

```
Router1#show host
Default domain is oreilly.com
Name/address lookup uses domain service
Name servers are 255.255.255.255, 172.25.1.1
```

```
Host                    Port  Flags       Age Type  Address(es)
www.oreilly.com         None  (temp, OK)  0   IP    192.168.22.57
Router1#
```

Notice that the router dynamically learned about the domain name and name server information via DHCP. DHCP-learned information will not overwrite statically configured information. For example, if you manually configure the router with a domain name, the router will quietly ignore the one it learns through DHCP. The router will simply add any name servers that it learns through DHCP to the static list of manually configured name servers.

The *show ip interface* command tells you that the router learned IP address from DHCP:

```
Router1#show ip interface
FastEthernet0/1 is up, line protocol is up
  Internet address is 172.25.1.57/24
  Broadcast address is 255.255.255.255
  Address determined by DHCP
  MTU is 1500 bytes
  <removed for brevity>
```

Beginning with IOS Version 12.3(4)T, Cisco added the ability to release and renew DHCP leases via the privilege command prompt. To release a DHCP-obtained IP address using the *release dhcp* command:

```
Router1#release dhcp FastEthernet0/1
Router1#
```

To renew a DHCP lease and retain an IP address, use the *renew dhcp* command:

```
Router1#renew dhcp FastEthernet0/1
Router1#
```

To view the DHCP lease information, use the *show dhcp lease* command:

```
Router1#show dhcp lease
Temp IP addr: 172.25.1.57  for peer on Interface: FastEthernet0/1
Temp  sub net mask: 255.255.255.0
   DHCP Lease server: 10.1.1.1, state: 3 Bound
   DHCP transaction id: B69
   Lease: 432000 secs,  Renewal: 216000 secs,  Rebind: 378000 secs
Temp default-gateway addr: 172.25.1.1
   Next timer fires after: 2d11h
   Retry count: 0    Client-ID: cisco-000e.8424.4e71-Fa0/1
   Client-ID hex dump: 636973636F2D303030652E383432342E
                       346537312D4661302F31
   Hostname: Router1
Router1#
```

Notice that the output shows the assigned IP address, net mask, DHCP server, lease duration/renewal/rebind times, the assigned default gateway, and the duration until the next lease renewal (next timer fires after).

Although controlling your router addresses from a centralized DHCP server might seem like a good idea, in general we don't recommend it. Routers are the core architecture of a network and should never rely on an external server to obtain IP addressing. Unless a DHCP server is available on every segment, the router needs a DHCP proxy, which is usually another router with a hardcoded IP address. In disaster scenarios when many routers fail simultaneously, it can be extremely difficult to bootstrap the network back into operation.

So, except for specific circumstances, like connecting to an ISP, where the router is at the edge of the network, we strongly discourage using this DHCP client functionality.

20.4 Dynamically Allocating Client IP Addresses via DHCP

Problem

You want to configure your router to be a DHCP server and allocate dynamic IP addresses to client workstations.

Solution

The following set of configuration commands allows the router to dynamically allocate IP addresses to client workstations:

```
Router1#configure terminal
Enter configuration commands, one per line.  End with CNTL/Z.
Router1(config)#service dhcp
Router1(config)#ip dhcp pool 172.25.1.0/24
Router1(dhcp-config)#network 172.25.1.0 255.255.255.0
Router1(dhcp-config)#default-router 172.25.1.1
Router1(dhcp-config)#exit
Router1(config)#ip dhcp excluded-address 172.25.1.1 172.25.1.50
Router1(config)#ip dhcp excluded-address 172.25.1.200 172.25.1.255
Router1(config)#end
Router1#
```

Discussion

Cisco incorporated DHCP server functionality starting in IOS Version 12.0(1)T. This allows routers to dynamically allocate IP addresses to client workstations without needing a centralized DHCP server.

Providing DHCP services from a router has some interesting advantages over using a central server. First, distributing the DHCP functionality into the access routers of a large network reduces the risk of a server configuration problem affecting the entire corporate network. Second, maintaining DHCP services within each remote branch router reduces the utilization over expensive WAN links. Third, when a WAN link fails, workstations are still able to function on the local segment. And fourth, the router based DHCP services can easily be administered by your network engineers via one common interface, the IOS prompt.

In our example, we have configured the router to dynamically allocate IP addresses for the subnet 172.25.1.0/24. First, we define a range of IP addresses using the *network* command. Then we need to exclude some addresses from the dynamic range with the *ip dhcp exclude-address* command. If you do not exclude a range of addresses, then the router will assign IP addresses from the entire subnet (254 addresses in total). But in most networks, at least some of the addresses are reserved for other purposes, such as servers or network equipment.

At a minimum, you should exclude the router's own IP address to prevent the DHCP service from trying to assign it elsewhere, causing a conflict. Many network engineers allocate the lower portion of the subnet to static devices such as routers, servers, printers, and other devices that do not support DHCP. In our example we reserved the first 50 addresses for statically addressed devices (172.25.1.1 – 172.25.1.50). We also chose to reserve addresses from 172.25.1.200 to 172.25.1.255 for future use, and to show that you can reserve multiple blocks of addresses.

When DHCP is enabled, the router will allocate IP addresses dynamically by binding them to device MAC addresses in the configured pool. IP addresses are allocated for a defined period of time called a *lease*, which we will discuss further in Recipe 20.6. You can view the address bindings with the *show ip dhcp binding* command as follows:

```
Router1#show ip dhcp binding
IP address        Hardware address        Lease expiration        Type
172.25.1.51       0100.0103.85e9.87       Apr 10 2003 08:55 PM    Automatic
172.25.1.52       0100.50da.2a5e.a2       Apr 10 2003 09:00 PM    Automatic
172.25.1.53       0100.0103.ea1b.ed       Apr 10 2003 08:58 PM    Automatic
Router1#
```

You will notice in this output that the MAC addresses look a little bit funny, because they have two extra hex digits (one extra octet) at the start. We will explain this in Recipe 20.7.

The router maintains an internal database of assigned IP addresses and their associated MAC addresses. In Recipe 20.8, we will show how to write this database to a remote server for backup purposes.

Note also that the example dynamically configures DCHP clients with the default router setting using the *default-router* command. We will discuss these DHCP options in detail in Recipe 20.5.

See Also

Recipe 20.5; Recipe 20.6; Recipe 20.7; Recipe 20.8; Recipe 20.9

20.5 Defining DHCP Configuration Options

Problem

You want to dynamically deliver configuration parameters to client workstations.

Solution

You can configure a wide variety of DHCP parameters for configuring client workstations:

```
Router1#configure terminal
Enter configuration commands, one per line.  End with CNTL/Z.
Router1(config)#ip dhcp pool ORAserver
Router1(dhcp-config)#host 172.25.1.34 255.255.255.0
Router1(dhcp-config)#client-name bigserver
Router1(dhcp-config)#default-router 172.25.1.1 172.25.1.3
Router1(dhcp-config)#domain-name oreilly.com
Router1(dhcp-config)#dns-server 172.25.1.1 10.1.2.3
Router1(dhcp-config)#netbios-name-server 172.25.1.1
Router1(dhcp-config)#netbios-node-type h-node
Router1(dhcp-config)#option 66 ip 10.1.1.1
Router1(dhcp-config)#option 33 ip 192.0.2.1 172.25.1.3
Router1(dhcp-config)#option 31 hex 01
Router1(dhcp-config)#lease 2
Router1(dhcp-config)#exit
Router1(config)#end
Router1#
```

Discussion

The strength of DHCP is its ability to configure client workstations from a centralized location using DHCP options. It greatly reduces costs if workstations can dynamically learn all of their configuration options instead of having to send a technician to every desk.

DHCP can assign default routes, domain names, name server addresses, and WINS server addresses, to name just a few. RFC 2132 defines a large number of standard configurable options, and includes provisions for further vendor-specific options. However, in reality most networks only use a small subset of these options. To make configuration easier, Cisco provides human-readable names for several of the most common options, as shown in Table 20-2.

Table 20-2. The RFC 2132 equivalent option numbers to Cisco's DHCP commands

Custom name	RFC 2132 Option #	Description
client-name	Option 12	Hostname (static map only)
default-router	Option 3	Default router(s)
domain-name	Option 15	Domain name

Table 20-2. The RFC 2132 equivalent option numbers to Cisco's DHCP commands (continued)

Custom name	RFC 2132 Option #	Description
dns-server	Option 6	Name server(s)
netbios-name-server	Option 44	WINS server(s)
netbios-node-type	Option 46	Netbios node type
lease	Option 58	Half of the lease time
host	Option 1	Subnet mask (plus IP address)

However, since it would be impossible to create user-friendly name for every possible DHCP option, Cisco allows you to manually configure any option by its number, using the *option* command.

You can also use the *option* command instead of the custom name. For example, Option 6 in RFC 2132 is reserved for name server addresses. Instead of using the Cisco provided user-friendly command *dns-server*, as we did in the recipe example, we can define it manually:

```
Router1#configure terminal
Enter configuration commands, one per line.  End with CNTL/Z.
Router1(config)#ip dhcp pool 172.25.2.0/24
Router1(dhcp-config)#option 6 ip 172.25.1.1
Router1(dhcp-config)#exit
Router1(config)#end
Router1#
```

The router will then translate the manual entry to its user-friendly equivalent in its running configuration file. This can sometimes be a little bit confusing when you are looking at the router configuration, and it isn't what you typed. But both forms are completely equivalent.

We note in passing that some options will accept multiple entries. For example, the default router option and the *dns-server* option will both accept up to eight IP addresses, in order of preference. However, you will rarely require that many possible entries for a single option. For the *default-router* option in particular, we recommend using defining a single default-router address. If there are several routers on a segment, the default-router would be the HSRP address. You would only use multiple default routers if you have many routers, but are not running HSRP, which is not a design that we would generally endorse. For more information about HSRP, please see Chapter 22.

To make configuration easier, you can create a hierarchy of DHCP pools. Parent DHCP pools are determined by IP address ranges. For instance, in the following example we configure a parent DHCP pool called ROOT, which is used to assign options to the entire classful network range, 172.25.0.0/16. We then configure two other DHCP pools for specific subnets of 172.25.1.0/24 and 172.25.2.0/24. These two child pools will automatically inherit the options defined within the ROOT pool. You can then over-write some of the inherited options within the child pools, if necessary:

```
Router1#configure terminal
Enter configuration commands, one per line.  End with CNTL/Z.
Router1(config)#ip dhcp pool ROOT
Router1(dhcp-config)#network 172.25.0.0 255.255.0.0
Router1(dhcp-config)#domain-name oreilly.com
Router1(dhcp-config)#dns-server 172.25.1.1 10.1.2.3
Router1(dhcp-config)#lease 2
Router1(dhcp-config)#exit
Router1(dhcp)#ip dhcp pool 172.25.1.0/24
Router1(dhcp-config)#network 172.25.1.0 255.255.255.0
Router1(dhcp-config)#default-router 172.25.1.1
Router1(dhcp-config)#exit
Router1(dhcp)#ip dhcp pool 172.25.2.0/24
Router1(dhcp-config)#network 172.25.2.0 255.255.255.0
Router1(dhcp-config)#default-router 172.25.2.1
Router1(dhcp-config)#lease 0 0 10
Router1(dhcp-config)#exit
Router1(config)#end
Router1#
```

The DHCP lease period is the only option that cannot be inherited from parent DHCP pools. This means that you must explicitly define a lease period for each pool. The router will use the default lease period of one day for any pool that doesn't have its own value.

The example in the Solution section of this recipe also includes several *option* statements to define parameters that don't have convenient mnemonics:

```
Router1(dhcp-config)#option 66 ip 10.1.1.1
Router1(dhcp-config)#option 33 ip 192.0.2.1 172.25.1.3
Router1(dhcp-config)#option 31 hex 01
```

These option codes are defined in RFC 2132. In this case, Option 66 identifies a TFTP server; Option 33 specifies static routes; and Option 31 tells the client to use ICMP Router Discovery Protocol (IRDP).

The static route statement tells the end device to send all traffic destined to the host, 192.0.2.1/32 to the router at 172.25.1.3.

IRDP allows the client workstation to listen for periodic updates from local routers to determine its default gateway. IRDP is discussed in the introduction to Chapter 22. IRDP is also used in IP Mobility, so we include some configuration examples in Chapter 24.

See Also

Recipe 20.4; Chapter 22; Chapter 24

20.6 Defining DHCP Lease Periods

Problem

You want to change the default lease time.

Solution

To modify the default DHCP lease time for a pool of IP addresses, use the *lease* configuration command:

```
Router1#configure terminal
Enter configuration commands, one per line.  End with CNTL/Z.
Router1(config)#ip dhcp pool 172.25.2.0/24
Router1(dhcp-config)#lease 2 12 30
Router1(dhcp-config)#exit
Router1(config)#end
Router1#
```

Discussion

The lease command takes up to three options: *lease days [hours] [minutes]*, with hours and minutes being optional. You can specify a maximum period of 365 days, 23 hours and 59 minutes, and a minimum of 1 second. The default is one day.

The shorter the lease period, the faster you can reconfigure DHCP options that may need to change. Short lease periods also permit IP addresses to be returned to the address pool for reallocation more quickly. This can be useful in environments where a large number of end devices connect and disconnect frequently, as in public wireless networks, such as at an airport. A short lease period of say 30 minutes might be useful to ensure that IP addresses are returned quickly to the shared pool. However, short lease periods also mean that workstations must renew their leases more often, which puts an extra strain on the network and DHCP server.

Conversely, a small office with a stable workforce may choose to increase their lease periods. Long lease periods can also reduce the impact of DHCP server failures. Unless a workstation reboots or needs to disconnect and reconnect to the network, most clients will wait until the lease is half expired before needing to talk to the server to renew it. If the server is unavailable, the client device will periodically retry the lease renewal until it succeeds. But most organizations have redundant DHCP servers, so there are few real benefits to extremely long lease periods.

In most situations, the default lease period of one day is sufficient. It allows the administrators to change global options in a timely fashion without putting an unnecessary burden on the network or server.

You can also configure the router to assign addresses with infinite lease periods by using the *infinite* keyword:

```
Router1#configure terminal
Enter configuration commands, one per line.  End with CNTL/Z.
```

```
Router1(config)#ip dhcp pool COOKBOOK
Router1(dhcp-config)#lease infinite
Router1(dhcp-config)#exit
Router1(config)#end
Router1#
```

Assigning an infinite lease period removes one of the major advantages of using DHCP. It can be extremely useful to be able to use DHCP to make wholesale configuration changes, but this means that the end devices have to check in periodically to renew their leases. Providing an indefinite lease period largely circumvents this advantage, since it forces you to wait until the end device disconnects and reconnects to the network before you can give it new information. Use the *infinite* keyword with caution.

You can view the lease expiration times of your active clients with the *show ip dhcp binding* command:

```
Router1#show ip dhcp binding
IP address       Hardware address      Lease expiration        Type
172.25.1.33      0100.0103.85e9.87     Infinite                Manual
172.25.1.53      0100.0103.ea1b.ed     Apr 11 2006 08:58 PM    Automatic
172.25.1.57      0100.6047.6c41.a4     Apr 11 2006 09:17 PM    Automatic
Router1#
```

Please refer to Recipe 20.7 for an explanation of the MAC address in this output.

See Also

Recipe 20.4; Recipe 20.7

20.7 Allocating Static IP Addresses with DHCP

Problem

You want to ensure that your router assigns the same IP address to a particular device every time it connects.

Solution

The following commands ensure that the router assigns the same IP address to a device each time it requests one:

```
Router1#configure terminal
Enter configuration commands, one per line.  End with CNTL/Z.
Router1(config)#ip dhcp pool IAN
Router1(dhcp-config)#host 172.25.1.33 255.255.255.0
Router1(dhcp-config)#client-identifier 0100.0103.85e9.87
Router1(dhcp-config)#client-name win2k
Router1(dhcp-config)#default-router 172.25.1.1
Router1(dhcp-config)#domain-name oreilly.com
Router1(dhcp-config)#dns-server 172.25.1.1
```

```
Router1(dhcp-config)#exit
Router1(config)#end
Router1#
```

Discussion

The router allows you to statically bind an IP address to a MAC address to ensure that a particular device always receives the same IP address. This is particularly useful for devices such as servers that must be available for access via a well-known IP address or DNS entry. Any device that accepts inbound sessions will probably require a static address. Being able to allocate these addresses via DHCP provides network administrator with greater control.

The configuration for a static DHCP mapping is slightly different than a dynamic pool. In particular, you must assign a separate *dhcp pool* for each static server. In our example, we created a pool named IAN to allocate a static IP address to user Ian. Also, instead of defining a network range of IP addresses, you assign a specific IP address using the *host* command. To avoid address conflicts, make sure that the static address you assign is not part of a dynamic pool already configured, using the *excluded-address* command if necessary.

You must configure the static pool with the device's MAC address using the *client-identifier* command. The client identifier is made up of two parts; the media type and the MAC address. The media type numbers can be found in RFC 3232 (assigned numbers) under the heading "Number Hardware Type." For 10/100/1000 Mb Ethernet, the media type number is 01. The router will combine the media type and MAC address into one large address. The router will automatically add the dots if you don't type them.

From this point on, the router will accept the same options as the dynamic pool options. Options can be inherited from dynamic pools as well. To view the configured static binding, use the show *ip dhcp binding* command as follows:

```
Router1#show ip dhcp binding
IP address         Hardware address        Lease expiration       Type
172.25.1.33        0100.0103.85e9.87       Infinite               Manual
172.25.1.52        0100.50da.2a5e.a2       Apr 11 2006 09:00 PM   Automatic
172.25.1.53        0100.0103.ea1b.ed       Apr 11 2006 08:58 PM   Automatic
Router1#
```

This display shows that we have successfully mapped a static IP address of 172.25.1. 33 to MAC address 0001-0385-e987. DHCP has put the code 01 at the start of this address to indicate that it is an Ethernet MAC.

Also, notice that the router marks the static clients as Manual clients to differentiate them. We should mention in passing that although the output indicates that the static lease is indefinite, in reality, it is not. The static *dhcp pool* can be assigned any lease period you desire, however, the router will only ever allocate the single static address. This can be useful if you want to change other DHCP options for this end device.

See Also

Recipe 20.5

20.8 Configuring a DHCP Database Client

Problem

You want to back up your DHCP database of address assignments to another device so that you won't lose it if the router reloads.

Solution

You can ensure your DHCP address assignments are not lost when a router reloads by configuring the router to periodically copy its DHCP database to a remote server.

The first example configures a router to use FTP to copy the DHCP database to a remote server:

```
Router1#configure terminal
Enter configuration commands, one per line.  End with CNTL/Z.
Router1(config)#ip dhcp database ftp://dhcp:bindsave@172.25.1.1/dhcp-leases
Router1(config)#end
Router1#
```

The second example uses TFTP as the transport protocol:

```
Router1#configure terminal
Enter configuration commands, one per line.  End with CNTL/Z.
Router1(config)#ip dhcp database tftp://172.25.1.1/dhcp-leases
Router1(config)#end
Router1#
```

And the third configures RCP as the transport protocol:

```
Router1#configure terminal
Enter configuration commands, one per line.  End with CNTL/Z.
Router1(config)#ip dhcp database rcp://dhcp@172.25.1.1/dhcp-leases
Router1(config)#end
Router1#
```

Discussion

By default, the router stores its DHCP binding database in memory. So when the router reloads, all DHCP database information is lost. You can configure the router to periodically send a copy this database to a remote server to avoid losing this important information. If the router reloads for any reason, it will automatically load the last version of the database file from the remote server and proceed from where it left off.

In our example, we have configured our test router to store its DHCP database to the server at 172.25.1.1 via FTP. FTP uses a simple username and password authentication system, so we have included the userid *dhcp* and password *bindsave* in the command. After authenticating, the router will store its database in a file called *dhcp-leases* in the default directory for this userid. If you have multiple routers storing their databases to the same server, make sure to use a unique filename that includes the router name. This will assist in troubleshooting later.

To view the status of the DHCP database, use the *show ip dhcp database* command:

```
Router1#show ip dhcp database
URL      : ftp://dhcp:bindsave@172.25.1.1/dhcp-leases
Read     : Never
Written  : Apr 09 2006 10:24 PM
Status   : Last write succeeded. Agent information is up-to-date.
Delay    : 300 seconds
Timeout  : 300 seconds
Failures : 1
Successes: 30

Router1#
```

Notice that the router is storing the database to the URL we specified, and that its last write was successful. The output also tells us that the router has successfully written its database to the server 30 times and only experienced a single failure. All of this indicates that the DHCP backup is working well. If we log on the server and view the contents of the database file, we will see the current DCHP bindings:

```
Freebsd% cat dhcp-leases
*time* Apr 09 2003 10:24 PM

!IP address      Type  Hardware address    Lease expiration
172.25.1.52      id    0100.50da.2a5e.a2   Apr 10 2006 09:00 PM
172.25.1.53      id    0100.0103.ea1b.ed   Apr 10 2006 08:58 PM

!IP address      Interface-index  Lease expiration      Vrf
*end*
Freebsd%
```

Fortunately, the file is a human-readable form and lets us see the latest DHCP bindings. Note that static address bindings are not sent to the remote database server, because they never change.

We will simulate a power failure by reloading the router:

```
Router1#show ip dhcp database
URL      : ftp://dhcp:bindsave@172.25.1.1/dhcp-leases
Read     : Apr 10 2006 10:35 PM
Written  : Never
Status   : Last read succeeded. Bindings have been loaded in RAM.
Delay    : 300 seconds
Timeout  : 300 seconds
Failures : 0
Successes: 1

Router1#
```

Now when we display the database information, we see that the router successfully read the database from the server and loaded the bindings into memory. Viewing the router bindings now, you can see that the database has been recovered:

```
Router1#show ip dhcp binding
IP address       Hardware address      Lease expiration        Type
172.25.1.33      0100.0103.85e9.87     Infinite                Manual
172.25.1.52      0100.50da.2a5e.a2     Apr 10 2006 09:00 PM    Automatic
172.25.1.53      0100.0103.ea1b.ed     Apr 10 2006 08:58 PM    Automatic
Router1#
```

See Also

Recipe 20.4; Recipe 20.12

20.9   Configuring Multiple DHCP Servers per Subnet

Problem

You want to configure multiple routers to act as DHCP servers for the same subnet to ensure availability.

Solution

You can configure multiple routers to act as DHCP servers for a single subnet, by ensuring that they don't use the same pool of addresses.

Here's Router1:

```
Router1#configure terminal
Enter configuration commands, one per line.  End with CNTL/Z.
Router1(config)#ip dhcp pool 172.22.1.0/24
Router1(dhcp-config)#network 172.22.1.0 255.255.255.0
Router1(dhcp-config)#default-router 172.22.1.1
Router1(dhcp-config)#domain-name oreilly.com
Router1(dhcp-config)#dns-server 172.25.1.1 10.1.2.3
Router1(dhcp-config)#exit
Router1(config)#ip dhcp excluded-address 172.22.1.1 172.22.1.49
Router1(config)#ip dhcp excluded-address 172.22.1.150 172.22.1.254
Router1(config)#ip dhcp database ftp://dhcp:bindsave@172.25.1.1/dhcp-leases-rtr1
Router1(config)#end
Router1#
```

And here's Router2:

```
Router2#configure terminal
Enter configuration commands, one per line.  End with CNTL/Z.
Router2(config)#ip dhcp pool 172.22.1.0/24
Router2(dhcp-config)#network 172.22.1.0 255.255.255.0
Router2(dhcp-config)#default-router 172.22.1.1
Router2(dhcp-config)#domain-name oreilly.com
Router2(dhcp-config)#dns-server 172.25.1.1 10.1.2.3
```

```
Router2(dhcp-config)#exit
Router2(config)#ip dhcp excluded-address 172.22.1.1 172.22.1.149
Router2(config)#ip dhcp database ftp://dhcp:bindsave@172.25.1.1/dhcp-leases-rtr2
Router2(config)#end
Router2#
```

Discussion

You can configure multiple DHCP servers to service the same subnet; in fact, we recommend it. However, you must take care to ensure that the two servers do not share the same dynamic pool of IP addresses.

In our example, we chose to let Router1 allocate the addresses between 172.25.1.50 and 172.25.1.149, Router2 allocates the pool from 172.25.1.150 to 172.25.1.254, and we reserve the range from 172.25.1.1 to 172.25.1.50 for static IP addresses.

You need to map out the allocated address space ahead of time and use the *ip dhcp excluded-address* configuration command to ensure that there is no overlap. The most critical thing about this type of configuration is to ensure that the allocated pool of DHCP addresses on a single router is sufficiently large to handle all of the DHCP clients on the segment if the other router fails. This way, although the two routers do not allocate addresses from the same pool, which would cause problems for the DHCP databases, you still have complete redundancy.

We have also configured the routers to store their DHCP binding databases to separate files on the same server. For added protection, you could opt to store the individual database files to different servers.

The rest of the option settings are identical, although they don't necessarily have to be. You might want to change the name server order, for instance, to help balance the load between DNS servers.

See Also

Recipe 20.4; Recipe 20.5

20.10 DHCP Static Mapping

Problem

You want to enable the assignment of static IP addresses from a text file.

Solution

To enable the assignment of static IP addresses from a text file, first you must create a static DHCP mapping file on your TFTP server:

```
Freebsd% cat /tftpboot/dhcp.static
*time* Aug 17 2006 03:52 PM
```

```
*version* 2

!IP address        Type      Hardware address           Lease expiration

10.1.1.16 /24      id        0100.104b.33da.74              Infinite
10.1.1.17 /24      id        0100.0dbc.eff6.38              Infinite
10.1.1.18 /24      id        0100.0a5e.4001.27              Infinite
10.1.1.19 /24      id        0100.0331.327e.41              Infinite
10.1.1.20 /24      id        0100.0d60.b21a.4c              Infinite

*end*
Freebsd%
```

To enable the router to read the static text file from the TFTP server, use the *origin file* command:

```
Router1#configure terminal
Enter configuration commands, one per line.  End with CNTL/Z.
Router1(config)#ip dhcp pool OREILLY
Router1(dhcp-config)#origin file tftp://172.25.1.1/dhcp.static
Router1(dhcp-config)#default-router 10.1.1.1
Router1(dhcp-config)#dns-server 172.25.1.1 172.25.1.3
Router1(dhcp-config)#domain-name oreilly.com
Router1(dhcp-config)#lease 3
Router1(dhcp-config)#end
Router1#
```

Discussion

As demonstrated in Recipe 20.7, we can statically bind IP addresses to hardware addresses; however, doing so requires a dedicated DHCP pool, and more importantly, many lines of configuration. For instance, the following is a sample configuration for a single statically mapped IP address:

```
Router1#configure terminal
Enter configuration commands, one per line.  End with CNTL/Z.
Router1(config)#ip dhcp pool IAN
Router1(dhcp-config)#host 172.25.1.33 255.255.255.0
Router1(dhcp-config)#client-identifier 0100.0103.85e9.87
Router1(dhcp-config)#default-router 172.25.1.1
Router1(dhcp-config)#domain-name oreilly.com
Router1(dhcp-config)#dns-server 172.25.1.1
Router1(dhcp-config)#end
Router1#
```

While this method of assigning static IP addresses is useful for sites with a few required static addresses, it doesn't scale well when you need to assign a large number of them. Building a new DHCP pool per static address not only consumes NVRAM space, but also clutters the router configuration file.

Beginning with IOS Version 12.3(11)T, Cisco supports the ability to assign static IP address via text files. To begin, you must first create the static mapping text file on your

TFTP server. There is no limit to the number of static entries you can add to the file; however, the file must follow a certain format. The following is an example text file:

```
Freebsd% cat /tftpboot/dhcp.static
*time* Aug 17 2006 03:52 PM

*version* 2

!IP address      Type      Hardware address          Lease expiration

10.1.1.16 /24    id        0100.104b.33da.74          Infinite
10.1.1.17 /24    id        0100.0dbc.eff6.38          Infinite
10.1.1.18 /24    id        0100.0a5e.4001.27          Infinite
10.1.1.19 /24    id        0100.0331.327e.41          Infinite
10.1.1.20 /24    id        0100.0d60.b21a.4c          Infinite

*end*
Freebsd%
```

The file must contain the following elements:

- Time the file was created
- Database version number
- IP address, including mask (must have a space before the mask)
- Hardware type
- Hardware address
- Lease expiration
- End of file designator

For more information regarding the elements of this file, see the Discussion section of Recipe 20.7.

Once you've created the static mapping text file, you can configure the router to read the file by using the *origin file* command:

```
Router1#configure terminal
Enter configuration commands, one per line.  End with CNTL/Z.
Router1(config)#ip dhcp pool OREILLY
Router1(dhcp-config)#origin file tftp://172.25.1.1/dhcp.static
Router1(dhcp-config)#end
Router1#
```

Use the *show ip dhcp binding* command to ensure that the static mapping text file loaded correctly:

```
Router1#show ip dhcp binding
Bindings from all pools not associated with VRF:
IP address           Client-ID/             Lease expiration       Type
                     Hardware address/
                     User name
10.1.1.16/24         0100.104b.33da.74      Infinite               Static
10.1.1.17/24         0100.0dbc.eff6.38      Infinite               Static
```

```
10.1.1.18/24      0100.0a5e.4001.27    Infinite         Static
10.1.1.19/24      0100.0331.327e.41    Infinite         Static
10.1.1.20/24      0100.0d60.b21a.4c    Infinite         Static
Router1#
```

You will notice that the static mapping have been loaded from the text file and the router is now ready to assign IP addresses based on the static mapping. If you modify the static mapping text file to add, change, or remove entries, then you need to disabled the DHCP server and start it again by removing the DHCP service. By doing so, the router will TFTP the new static mapping file:

```
Router1#configure terminal
Enter configuration commands, one per line.  End with CNTL/Z.
Router1(config)#no service dhcp
Router1(config)#service dhcp
Router1(config)#end
Router1#
```

See Also

Recipe 20.7

20.11 DHCP-Secured IP Address Assignment

Problem

You wish to synchronize the ARP entries to the DHCP bindings to prevent IP address spoofing.

Solution

To enable secured IP address assignment, use the *update arp* command:

```
Router1#configure terminal
Enter configuration commands, one per line.  End with CNTL/Z.
Router1(config)#ip dhcp pool OREILLY
Router1(dhcp-config)#update arp
Router1(dhcp-config)#end
Router1#
```

Discussion

Beginning with IOS Version 12.2(15)T, Cisco introduced the concept of DHCP secured IP address assignment. This feature synchronizes the ARP entry to the DHCP binding to ensure that IP addresses assign via DHCP can't be spoofed. By default, ARP tables dynamically map MAC addresses to IP addresses to facilitate communication. Unfortunately, it's rather easy for someone to spoof a DHCP assigned IP address and overwrite the router's ARP cache with his own MAC address.

Once the DHCP-secured IP address assignment is enabled, the router adds a secured ARP entry for each DHCP binding. This ensures that the ARP entry cannot be dynamically, or even manually, erased or overwritten. In fact, the only way to clear a secured ARP entry is by releasing the DHCP lease.

The following is an example configuration of DHCP-secured IP address assignment:

```
Router1#configure terminal
Enter configuration commands, one per line.  End with CNTL/Z.
Router1(config)#ip dhcp pool OREILLY
Router1(dhcp-config)#network 172.25.1.0 255.255.255.0
Router1(dhcp-config)#default-router 172.25.1.1
Router1(dhcp-config)#dns-server 172.25.1.1 172.25.1.3
Router1(dhcp-config)#domain-name oreilly.com
Router1(dhcp-config)#lease 3
Router1(dhcp-config)#update arp
Router1(dhcp-config)#end
Router1#
```

Once configured, the router will provide DHCP leases as normal; however, for each new binding, the router will also add a secured ARP entry. All of this is completely transparent to the end users. The next example shows three newly assigned DHCP leases:

```
Router1#show ip dhcp binding
Bindings from all pools not associated with VRF:
IP address           Client-ID/              Lease expiration      Type
                     Hardware address/
                     User name
172.25.1.51          0100.0d60.b21a.4c       Aug 24 2006 04:20 PM  Automatic
172.25.1.52          0100.104b.33da.73       Aug 24 2006 04:22 PM  Automatic
172.25.1.53          0100.0475.839d.3f       Aug 24 2006 04:48 PM  Automatic
Router1#
```

To confirm that the router has indeed created secured ARP entries, use the following command:

```
Router1#show ip dhcp server statistics
Memory usage         108579
Address pools        1
Database agents      0
Automatic bindings   3
Manual bindings      0
Expired bindings     0
Malformed messages   0
Secure arp entries   3

Message              Received
BOOTREQUEST          0
DHCPDISCOVER         135
DHCPREQUEST          18
DHCPDECLINE          0
DHCPRELEASE          13
DHCPINFORM           0
```

```
Message            Sent
BOOTREPLY          0
DHCPOFFER          24
DHCPACK            13
DHCPNAK            1
Router1#
```

Notice that the router has three new secured ARP entries, as highlighted in the previous example.

> You can add the *update arp* command to existing DHCP pools; however, the router will only create secured ARP entries once existing leases are renewed. Once leases are renewed, the router will automatically create secured ARP entries for the renewed DHCP bindings.

As we mentioned earlier, secured ARP entries cannot be erased manually. For instance, clearing the router's ARP cache does not erase the secured ARP entries:

```
Router1#clear arp-cache

Router1#show arp
Protocol  Address        Age (min)  Hardware Addr   Type  Interface
Internet  10.1.1.1           -      000e.8424.4e71  ARPA  FastEthernet0/1
Internet  10.1.1.17          0      000d.bcef.f638  ARPA  FastEthernet0/1
Internet  172.25.1.52        31     0010.4b33.da73  ARPA  FastEthernet0/0
Internet  172.25.1.53        25     0004.7583.9d3f  ARPA  FastEthernet0/0
Internet  172.25.1.51        33     000d.60b2.1a4c  ARPA  FastEthernet0/0
Internet  172.25.1.5         0      0001.9670.b780  ARPA  FastEthernet0/0
Internet  172.25.1.1         0      0010.4b09.5700  ARPA  FastEthernet0/0
Internet  172.25.1.3         0      000a.5e40.0126  ARPA  FastEthernet0/0
Internet  172.25.1.101       -      000e.8424.4e70  ARPA  FastEthernet0/0
Router1#
```

Notice that the age of the secured ARP entries remained the same even after we cleared the ARP cache. The secured ARP entries will remain in the ARP cache until the associated DHCP lease is terminated by either the client or DHCP server.

> The router can only secure directly connected clients on LAN interfaces.

20.12 Showing DHCP Status

Problem

You want to display the status of the DHCP server functions on the router.

Solution

To display the IP address bindings and their associated leases, use the following command:

    Router1#**show ip dhcp binding**

The following command displays any IP address conflicts that the router has detected in the DHCP address pool:

    Router1#**show ip dhcp conflict**

You can view the status of remote database backups with this command:

    Router1#**show ip dhcp database**

And you can see the global DHCP server statistics like this:

    Router1#**show ip dhcp server statistics**

Discussion

To display the status of the DHCP service, use the *show ip dhcp* EXEC command. If you add the keyword *binding*, this command displays the current DHCP bindings, which include the assigned IP addresses, the associated client MAC addresses, and the lease expiration time:

```
Router1#show ip dhcp binding
IP address         Hardware address      Lease expiration       Type
172.25.1.51        0100.0103.85e9.87     Apr 10 2006 08:55 PM   Automatic
172.25.1.52        0100.50da.2a5e.a2     Apr 10 2006 09:00 PM   Automatic
172.25.1.53        0100.0103.ea1b.ed     Apr 10 2006 08:58 PM   Automatic
Router1#
```

To view the IP addresses that are currently in conflict, use the *conflict* keyword. This command displays all of the IP addresses that the router has discovered conflicts for, and how the conflict was discovered:

```
Router1#show ip dhcp conflict
IP address         Detection method    Detection time
172.25.1.51        Ping                Apr 09 2006 09:08 PM
172.25.1.54        Gratuitous ARP      Apr 09 2006 10:00 PM
Router1#
```

With the *database* keyword, you can view the database configuration and status. This command shows all of the configured remote database servers and the current read and write status reports:

```
Router1#show ip dhcp database
URL     : ftp://dhcp:bindsave@172.25.1.1/dhcp-leases
Read    : Never
Written : Apr 09 2006 10:24 PM
Status  : Last write succeeded. Agent information is up-to-date.
Delay   : 300 seconds
Timeout : 300 seconds
```

```
       Failures : 1
       Successes: 30

       Router1#
```

Finally, the *statistics* keyword lets you view the overall DHCP statistics:

```
       Router1#show ip dhcp server statistics
       Memory usage         17996
       Address pools        4
       Database agents      1
       Automatic bindings   2
       Manual bindings      1
       Expired bindings     3
       Malformed messages   0

       Message              Received
       BOOTREQUEST          0
       DHCPDISCOVER         63
       DHCPREQUEST          203
       DHCPDECLINE          1
       DHCPRELEASE          27
       DHCPINFORM           19

       Message              Sent
       BOOTREPLY            0
       DHCPOFFER            63
       DHCPACK              139
       DHCPNAK              2
       Router1#
```

This command displays the high-level DHCP statistics, including the number of bindings, address pools, as well as the number of sent and received messages.

See Also

Recipe 20.4

20.13 Debugging DHCP

Problem

You want to debug a DHCP problem.

Solution

To debug the server events, use the following EXEC command:

```
       Router1#debug ip dhcp server events
```

The following command will allow you to monitor the actual DHCP-related packets being transmitted and received by the router:

```
       Router1#debug ip dhcp server packet
```

Discussion

The following debug capture shows a router performing normal housekeeping duties, such as updating its address pools, checking for expired leases, assigning new leases, and revoking expired leases:

```
Router1#debug ip dhcp server events
Sep 15 00:58:17.218: DHCPD: returned 172.25.1.51 to address pool COOKBOOK
Sep 15 00:58:22.566: DHCPD: assigned IP address 172.25.1.51 to client 0100.0103.85e9.
87.
Sep 15 01:01:15.056: DHCPD: writing bindings to ftp://dhcp:bindsave@172.25.1.1/dhcp-
leases-rtr1.
Sep 15 01:01:15.132: DHCPD: writing address 172.25.1.51.
Sep 15 01:01:15.148: DHCPD: wrote automatic bindings to ftp://dhcp:bindsave@172.25.1.
1/dhcp-leases-rtr1.
Sep 15 01:01:58.816: DHCPD: checking for expired leases.
Sep 15 01:03:58.841: DHCPD: checking for expired leases.
Sep 15 01:05:58.859: DHCPD: checking for expired leases.
Sep 15 01:07:58.874: DHCPD: checking for expired leases.
Sep 15 01:09:58.885: DHCPD: checking for expired leases.
Sep 15 01:09:58.885: DHCPD: the lease for address 172.25.1.51 has expired.
Sep 15 01:09:58.885: DHCPD: returned 172.25.1.51 to address pool COOKBOOK.
```

The next debug capture shows a typical DHCP client transaction between the client and router. The net result is that the router assigns IP address 172.25.1.51 to MAC address 00.0103.85e9.87:

```
Router1#debug ip dhcp server packet
Sep 15 01:19:41.211: DHCPD: DHCPDISCOVER received from client 0100.0103.85e9.87 on
interface FastEthernet0/0.1.
Sep 15 01:19:43.212: DHCPD: Sending DHCPOFFER to client 0100.0103.85e9.87 (172.25.1.
51).
Sep 15 01:19:43.212: DHCPD: creating ARP entry (172.25.1.51, 0001.0385.e987).
Sep 15 01:19:43.212: DHCPD: unicasting BOOTREPLY to client 0001.0385.e987 (172.25.1.
51).
Sep 15 01:19:43.216: DHCPD: DHCPREQUEST received from client 0100.0103.85e9.87.
Sep 15 01:19:43.216: DHCPD: Sending DHCPACK to client 0100.0103.85e9.87 (172.25.1.
51).
Sep 15 01:19:43.216: DHCPD: creating ARP entry (172.25.1.51, 0001.0385.e987).
Sep 15 01:19:43.216: DHCPD: unicasting BOOTREPLY to client 0001.0385.e987 (172.25.1.
51).
Router1#
```

## CHAPTER 21

NAT

21.0 Introduction

Network Address Translation, sometimes called Network Address Translator (NAT), was first described in RFC 1631 in 1994. The authors of that document were trying to solve the then imminent problem of running out of IPv4 addresses. They proposed a simple but brilliant solution. Their idea was to allow devices on the inside of a network to use the standard pool of unregistered IP addresses that are currently defined in RFC 1918. Then the router or firewall at the boundary between the internal private network and the external public network would have software that rewrites the internal IP addresses in every packet, replacing them with valid registered addresses.

There are four kinds of addresses: *inside local*, *inside global*, *outside local*, and *outside global*. Inside and outside pretty much depend on where you're standing, if you're just connecting two private networks. But if you are connecting a private network to the public Internet, then the Internet is outside. A *local* address is generally the private address, while the *global* address is the globally unique public address.

To help make these terms more clear, suppose you are connecting a network that uses RFC 1918 private addresses to the public Internet. Inside your network you have private addresses, such as 192.168.1.0/24. These are the *inside local* addresses. NAT will translate these addresses to globally unique registered addresses. These are the *inside global* addresses. The addresses on the public Internet are *outside global*. These external network addresses are all registered in this case, so there is no need to translate them, but if you did need to, you would translate an *outside global* to an *outside local* address.

To put this another way, the address that internal devices uses to communicate with other internal devices is the *inside local* address. The address that an internal device uses to communicate with external devices is the *outside local* address. The address that external devices use to communicate with internal devices is the *inside global* address. And external devices communicate with one another using *outside global* addresses.

NAT makes it possible to have a huge internal network with thousands of local addresses represented by a handful of global addresses or perhaps a single global address. This is why NAT is often credited with alleviating the address shortage problem. But it only really solves this problem if most people who use it have more local than global addresses.

In practice, there is a huge range of possibilities. You can map local addresses uniquely to individual global addresses. You can share one global address among several local addresses. You can allocate global addresses from a pool as they are requested. Or you can have a single global address and map all local addresses to this one address. And you can even define a combination of these different alternatives.

When a device sends a packet out from the private to the public network, the translator replaces the local source address with a registered address, and then routes the packet. For an inbound packet, the translator replaces the global address with the local address and routes the packet into the internal network. The translator has a much more difficult job with inbound packets than outbound. This is because it has to figure out which internal device to send the packet to. Since many internal devices could be using the same global address, the translator has to keep a state table of all of the devices that send or receive packets to or from the external network.

Suppose, for example, that two internal users are both using HTTP to view information on the public network. The translator has to be able to separate out which packets are intended for which internal device. It isn't sufficient to just look at the external device's IP address because both of these users could be looking at the same web page. They would both wind up with severely scrambled screens, if the translator couldn't tell which packets to send to which internal user.

This particular example is made somewhat easier by the fact that HTTP uses TCP. Since it is a connection-based protocol, there is a well-defined session initiation and termination that helps the translator to sort out the inbound flows, since these two users will have different TCP source ports. However, for UDP and ICMP packets, it can be more difficult. For example, if two internal users both PING the same external site at the same time, the translator has to assume that it will receive the responses in the same order that they were sent. Fortunately, this rarely presents real problems in production networks. But it is worth remembering that running NAT requires the router to keep track of a lot of state information that routers don't usually care about. Further, because IP addresses are included in both IP and TCP checksums, the translator must recalculate these checksum values. So NAT always consumes more CPU and memory resources on the router or firewall that it runs on, and this amount increases rapidly with both the number of packets and the number of different flows.

The other important thing to remember about NAT is that some protocols include IP address information in the payload of the packet as well as in the IP header. For example, the ubiquitous FTP protocol has a PORT command that contains an IP address encoded in ASCII. In this case, the FTP protocol is well understood and

NAT implementations can look out for this. But it is relatively easy to see that in other less popular protocols, there can be strange problems. And, if a server happens to run FTP on a nonstandard TCP port, you must tell NAT about the change so that it can rewrite the payload addresses appropriately.

SNMP also includes IP addresses in packet payloads. For example, IP address information is part of the standard interface MIB because it is an important piece of information about the interface. However, rewriting addresses in the payloads of SNMP packets is a much more difficult problem than for FTP because the address could be anywhere in the payload. Further, it is possible for the addresses in the payload to refer to different interfaces than the address in the header. And, to make the problem more difficult still, there is no common standard format for IP addresses in SNMP packets. They are sometimes transmitted as dotted decimal ASCII strings, as packed hex bytes, or a variety of other formats, depending on the specific MIB. Consequently, Cisco routers do not attempt to rewrite IP addresses in the payloads of SNMP packets.

We have also seen custom built applications that make life very hard for NAT by encoding IP addresses and port numbers in the data segment of a packet, and then using this information to attempt to open new connections. It can be difficult to get NAT to work in cases like this. Often the only workaround is to encapsulate the ill-behaved application in a tunnel.

21.1   Configuring Basic NAT Functionality

Problem

You want to set up Network Address Translation on your router.

Solution

In the simplest NAT configuration, all of your internal devices use the same external global address as the router's external interface:

```
Router#configure terminal
Enter configuration commands, one per line.  End with CNTL/Z.
Router(config)#access-list 15 permit 192.168.0.0 0.0.255.255
Router(config)#ip nat inside source list 15 interface FastEthernet0/0 overload
Router(config)#interface FastEthernet0/2
Router(config-if)#ip address 192.168.1.1 255.255.255.0
Router(config-if)#ip nat inside
Router(config-if)#exit
Router(config)#interface FastEthernet0/1
Router(config-if)#ip address 192.168.2.1 255.255.255.0
Router(config-if)#ip nat inside
Router(config-if)#exit
Router(config)#interface Ethernet0/0
Router(config-if)#ip address 172.16.1.5 255.255.255.252
Router(config-if)#ip nat outside
```

```
Router(config-if)#exit
Router(config)#end
Router#
```

Discussion

In this example, the router will rewrite that address of all of the internal devices whose IP addresses are in the range 192.168.0.0/16. When these internal devices connect to devices on the outside of the network, they will all appear to have the same source address as the external interface of the router, 172.16.1.5.

This example actually includes two internal interfaces and one external. You designate the internal interfaces with the *ip nat inside* command. You can have as many inside interfaces as you like:

```
Router(config)#interface FastEthernet0/1
Router(config-if)#ip nat inside
```

You also need to designate at least one outside interface using the command *ip nat outside*. There can be several outside interfaces, but this can be very difficult to control, so it is usually not recommended:

```
Router(config-if)#interface Ethernet0/0
Router(config-if)#ip nat outside
```

You configure the actual translation action with the line:

```
Router(config)#ip nat inside source list 15 interface FastEthernet0/0 overload
```

This tells the router to translate the source addresses of any internal devices that match access-list number 15. The router will translate the source addresses of all of these devices to the address that is configured on the interface FastEthernet0/0, which is the outside interface.

The *overload* keyword is actually assumed here, so if you leave it off, the router will automatically put it in. This option tells the router that many internal devices can use the same global address simultaneously. Since the router itself uses this address, if even a single internal address translates to this address, it is already overloaded. We will explain this option in more detail in Recipe 21.2.

To help explain what the access-list on this command does, we will change it so that it includes every address in the range except one:

```
Router(config)#access-list 15 deny 192.168.1.101
Router(config)#access-list 15 permit 192.168.0.0 0.0.255.255
```

Now if you make a connection from the excluded address, 192.168.1.101, the only difference is that the router will not rewrite this internal address. Instead, this address will appear unchanged on the outside.

NAT can be quite confusing because people usually think that there is some firewall function associated with it. There is not. If you exclude one device from your NAT access-list, as we just discussed, anybody on the outside of the network will be able to connect to this internal device by its real address. But there is nothing to prevent an inbound packet from reaching a particular internal device if the person on the outside knows the real internal address and can route to it. Further, NAT by itself doesn't do any firewall functions, such as UDP or TCP port filtering.

21.2 Allocating External Addresses Dynamically

Problem

You want to dynamically select addresses from a pool.

Solution

You can configure the router to automatically select global addresses from a pool as they are required:

```
Router#configure terminal
Enter configuration commands, one per line.  End with CNTL/Z.
Router(config)#access-list 15 permit 192.168.0.0 0.0.255.255
Router(config)#ip nat pool NATPOOL 172.16.1.100 172.16.1.150 netmask 255.255.255.0
Router(config)#ip nat inside source list 15 pool NATPOOL
Router(config)#interface FastEthernet 0/0
Router(config-if)#ip address 192.168.1.1 255.255.255.0
Router(config-if)#ip nat inside
Router(config-if)#exit
Router(config)#interface FastEthernet 0/1
Router(config-if)#ip address 192.168.2.1 255.255.255.0
Router(config-if)#ip nat inside
Router(config-if)#exit
Router(config)#interface Ethernet1/0
Router(config-if)#ip address 172.16.1.2 255.255.255.0
Router(config-if)#ip nat outside
Router(config-if)#exit
Router(config)#end
Router#
```

Discussion

This example is similar to Recipe 21.1. The important functional difference is that the internal devices will appear on the outside with different global addresses. The first internal device that makes an outbound connection will get the first address in the range, 172.16.1.100, the next one will get the next address, 172.16.1.101, and so forth.

You configure the range with the *ip nat pool* command:

```
Router(config)#ip nat pool NATPOOL 172.16.1.100 172.16.1.150 netmask 255.255.255.0
Router(config)#ip nat inside source list 15 pool NATPOOL
```

In this case, the *ip nat inside* command does not have the *overload* keyword. Without this keyword, when the pool of addresses is used up, the router will respond to any additional requests with an ICMP host unreachable message. So once all of the addresses in the poll are in use, any additional devices that try to make any connections through this router will simply fail. But if you include the *overload* keyword, the router will simply start over at the beginning of the range and allocate multiple interior addresses for each external one:

```
Router(config)#ip nat inside source list 15 pool NATPOOL overload
```

Once again, as in Recipe 21.1, any devices that are excluded by the access-list will simply not use this NAT rule. So the excluded devices will appear on the outside with their real (inside local) IP addresses.

Note that in this example, the IP address of the external interface is 172.16.1.2/24, and the pool of translation external addresses for use in translation is 172.16.1.100 through 172.16.1.150. So the pool of NAT addresses is part of the same IP subnet as the external IP address of the NAT router. This is a common practice for Internet connections where the ISP assigns a range of global addresses. But it is not necessary.

Your NAT pool can be anything, as long as the external network knows that this router can route to the NAT addresses. This is particularly useful in cases when you need a larger pool than what is available in that one subnet. For an extreme example, we could easily have made our NAT pool span the entire range 10.0.0.0/8 to give us access to a huge number of external addresses. Of course, this range is not globally unique, so it can't be used on the public Internet:

```
Router(config)#ip nat pool NATPOOL 10.0.0.1 10.255.255.254 netmask 255.0.0.0
```

See Also

Recipe 21.1

21.3   Allocating External Addresses Statically

Problem

You want to translate specific internal IP addresses to specific external addresses.

Solution

For some applications, you need each internal (inside local) address to always translate to the same external (inside global) address. This is particularly true if you need inbound connections from the outside network to always reach a particular internal device, such as a web or email server:

```
Router#configure terminal
Enter configuration commands, one per line.  End with CNTL/Z.
Router(config)#ip nat inside source static 192.168.1.15 172.16.1.10
Router(config)#ip nat inside source static 192.168.1.16 172.16.1.11
Router(config)#interface FastEthernet 0/0
Router(config-if)#ip address 192.168.1.1 255.255.255.0
Router(config-if)#ip nat inside
```

```
Router(config-if)#exit
Router(config)#interface FastEthernet 0/1
Router(config-if)#ip address 192.168.2.1 255.255.255.0
Router(config-if)#ip nat inside
Router(config-if)#exit
Router(config)#interface Ethernet1/0
Router(config-if)#ip address 172.16.1.2 255.255.255.0
Router(config-if)#ip nat outside
Router(config-if)#exit
Router(config)#end
Router#
```

Discussion

This recipe includes static translations for two internal devices. The internal address 192.168.1.15 will always appear on the outside as 172.16.1.10, and 192.168.1.16 will always appear as 172.16.1.11. Note that because these translations are static, they will work in either direction. So any packets sent to the NAT address from the external network will reach the internal device. External devices can even initiate TCP sessions.

This example only does NAT translation for these two specific addresses. The router will route all other addresses normally without any address translation.

See Also

Recipe 21.4

21.4 Translating Some Addresses Statically and Others Dynamically

Problem

You want certain hosts to have static address translation properties and all others to use dynamic translation.

Solution

In some cases you might need to use a combination of the two approaches. Some internal devices will always translate to specific external addresses, but others will use a dynamic pool. This is often the case when you have a few internal servers that need to be accessed from outside of the network, but other devices that will only make outbound connections:

```
Router#configure terminal
Enter configuration commands, one per line.  End with CNTL/Z.
Router(config)#access-list 15 deny 192.168.1.15 0.0.0.0
Router(config)#access-list 15 deny 192.168.1.16 0.0.0.0
Router(config)#access-list 15 permit 192.168.0.0 0.0.255.255
Router(config)#ip nat inside source static 192.168.1.15 172.16.1.10
```

```
Router(config)#ip nat inside source static 192.168.1.16 172.16.1.11
Router(config)#ip nat pool NATPOOL 172.16.1.100 172.16.1.150 netmask 255.255.255.0
Router(config)#ip nat inside source list 15 pool NATPOOL overload
Router(config)#interface FastEthernet0/0
Router(config-if)#ip address 192.168.1.1 255.255.255.0
Router(config-if)#ip nat inside
Router(config-if)#exit
Router(config)#interface FastEthernet0/1
Router(config-if)#ip address 192.168.2.1 255.255.255.0
Router(config-if)#ip nat inside
Router(config-if)#exit
Router(config)#interface Ethernet0/0
Router(config-if)#ip address 172.16.1.2 255.255.255.0
Router(config-if)#ip nat outside
Router(config-if)#exit
Router(config)#end
Router#
```

Discussion

In this recipe, we have the same pool of dynamic addresses as in Recipe 21.2, combined with the same two static translations from Recipe 21.3. It is often useful to combine NAT techniques like this, particularly when you use the connection between these networks for several different applications. Some applications might need to work with well-known IP addresses, while others could work well from a dynamic pool.

The access-list in this example specifically excludes the two addresses that will use static rather than dynamic NAT. This is not strictly necessary because the static NAT commands appear to have precedence over dynamic NAT in the router. However, this is still a good practice because it is absolutely clear to anybody looking at the router configuration what you intended to do.

The other important thing to notice in this example is that we have explicitly removed the static NAT addresses from the dynamic NAT pool. The dynamic pool is from 172.16.1.100 to 172.16.1.150, and the static addresses are 172.16.1.10 and 172.16.1.11. This is critically important because the dynamic NAT allocation does not check each address in the pool to make sure that is not configured for static NAT translation. So you could get serious address conflicts if you do not explicitly separate the static from the dynamic NAT addresses.

See Also

Recipe 21.2; Recipe 21.3

21.5 Using Route Maps to Refine Static Translation Rules

Problem

You want to use route maps to give finer control over your static NAT translation rules.

Solution

One of the best uses of this feature appears when you have two Internet Provider connections and you want to use distinct NAT rules for each:

```
Router1#configure terminal
Enter configuration commands, one per line.  End with CNTL/Z.
Router(config)#interface FastEthernet0/0
Router(config-if)#ip address 172.16.1.5 255.255.255.252
Router(config-if)#ip nat outside
Router(config-if)#exit
Router(config)#interface FastEthernet0/1
Router(config-if)#ip address 172.16.2.5 255.255.255.252
Router(config-if)#ip nat outside
Router(config-if)#exit
Router(config)#interface FastEthernet0/2
Router(config-if)#ip address 192.168.1.1 255.255.255.0
Router(config-if)#ip nat inside
Router(config-if)#exit
Router(config)#ip nat inside source route-map ISP-1 interface FastEthernet0/0
overload
Router(config)#ip nat inside source route-map ISP-2 interface FastEthernet0/1
overload
Router(config)#route-map ISP-1 permit 10
Router(config-route-map)#match interface FastEthernet0/0
Router(config-route-map)#exit
Router(config)#route-map ISP-2 permit 10
Router(config-route-map)#match interface FastEthernet0/1
Router(config-route-map)#exit
Router(config)#end
Router#
```

Discussion

This example shows a relatively common situation in which a network has two Internet connections for redundancy. Note that we don't show the redundancy mechanism here, but it could be handled by BGP, for example. There are three Fast Ethernet interfaces on this router, one for each of the two Internet Service Providers, and one for the internal network.

To understand the problem that we are looking at here, consider the standard *ip nat inside source* command that we used in Recipe 21.1:

```
Router(config)#access-list 15 permit 192.168.0.0 0.0.255.255
Router(config)#ip nat inside source list 15 interface FastEthernet0/0 overload
```

This rule translates the source address in all outbound packets to the address on one of the two external connections. As long as all of the traffic uses this particular interface, there is no problem, but then there's not much point in paying for the second connection. So consider what happens to any packets that are transmitted through the second connection when this rule is used. There are two possible consequences. The Internet Service Provider might accept the source address for the wrong network and forward the packet normally, and the return path from the destination might try to use the first Internet connection, which is bad because it might be down. Or, more likely, the second Internet provider will simply drop the packet because it appears to have a spoofed source address.

Instead, by using route maps in our *ip nat* command, we can specify two different rules, one for each of the two service providers:

```
Router(config)#ip nat inside source route-map ISP-1 interface FastEthernet0/0
overload
Router(config)#ip nat inside source route-map ISP-2 interface FastEthernet0/1
overload
```

The first line specifies that any packets matching the route map ISP-1 should have their source addresses changed to match the address on FastEthernet0/0. The second line specifies that packets matching the second route map should translate to the second interface's address.

The corresponding route maps simply match on the interfaces that interfaces that the router wants to forward these packets through:

```
Router(config)#route-map ISP-1 permit 10
Router(config-route-map)#match interface FastEthernet0/0
Router(config-route-map)#exit
Router(config)#route-map ISP-2 permit 10
Router(config-route-map)#match interface FastEthernet0/1
Router(config-route-map)#exit
```

See Also

Recipe 21.1

21.6   Translating in Both Directions Simultaneously

Problem

You want to translate both internal and external addresses.

Solution

In some cases, you might need to translate IP addresses on both sides of your router:

```
Router#configure terminal
Enter configuration commands, one per line.  End with CNTL/Z.
Router(config)#access-list 15 deny 192.168.1.15
Router(config)#access-list 15 permit 192.168.0.0 0.0.255.255
Router(config)#access-list 16 deny 172.16.5.25
Router(config)#access-list 16 permit 172.16.0.0 0.0.255.255
Router(config)#ip nat pool NATPOOL 172.16.1.100 172.16.1.150 netmask 255.255.255.0
Router(config)#ip nat pool INBOUNDNAT 192.168.15.100 192.168.15.200 netmask 255.255.255.0
Router(config)#ip nat inside source list 15 pool NATPOOL overload
Router(config)#ip nat inside source list 16 pool INBOUNDNAT overload
Router(config)#ip nat inside source static 192.168.1.15 172.16.1.10
Router(config)#ip nat outside source static 172.16.5.25 192.168.15.5
Router(config)#ip route 192.168.15.0 255.255.255.0 Ethernet0/0
Router(config)#interface FastEthernet 0/0
Router(config-if)#ip address 192.168.1.1 255.255.255.0
Router(config-if)#ip nat inside
Router(config-if)#exit
Router(config)#interface FastEthernet 0/1
Router(config-if)#ip address 192.168.2.1 255.255.255.0
Router(config-if)#ip nat inside
Router(config-if)#interface Ethernet0/0
Router(config-if)#ip address 172.16.1.2 255.255.255.0
Router(config-if)#ip nat outside
Router(config-if)#exit
Router(config)#end
Router#
```

Discussion

Sometimes you need to translate IP addresses on both the inside and the outside interfaces. This might happen, for example, when you need to connect to another network that uses an overlapping range of unregistered addresses. Cisco routers can do NAT translations of address on both the external and internal interfaces at the same time.

In this case, the router rewrites external addresses that are in the range 172.16.0.0/16 so that they appear to be on the 192.168.15.0/24 subnet in the range specified by the INBOUNDNAT pool. And, at the same time, it rewrites internal addresses that are part of the 192.168.0.0/16 subnet so that they appear on the outside to be part of 172.16.1.0/24 in the range specified by the NATPOOL pool.

Note that the access-lists that define which addresses should use the dynamic address pool both refer to the real addresses (inside local and outside global). So, for internal devices, the access-list should refer to the real internal addresses, while the list for external devices refers to the real external addresses.

The most significant reason for using this feature is to remove a conflict due to over-lapping address ranges. The following example shows how to remove an address conflict at the router between two networks that are both using the ubiquitous 10.0.0.0/8 address range. We will map the outside network to 11.0.0.0/8 and the inside to 12.0.0.0/8. Note that these two address ranges are both registered network numbers, so doing this will cause some problems for Internet access. We would only recommend doing this as a temporary measure to resolve an IP address conflict caused by merging two networks with overlapping IP address ranges:

```
Router#configure terminal
Enter configuration commands, one per line.  End with CNTL/Z.
Router(config)#access-list 17 permit 10.0.0.0 0.255.255.255
Router(config)#access-list 18 permit 10.0.0.0 0.255.255.255
Router(config)#ip nat pool OUTPOOL 11.0.0.1 11.255.255.254 netmask 255.0.0.0 type
match-host
Router(config)#ip nat pool INPOOL 12.0.0.1 12.255.255.254 netmask 255.0.0.0 type
match-host
Router(config)#ip nat inside source list 17 pool INPOOL
Router(config)#ip nat outside source list 18 pool OUTPOOL
Router(config)#ip route 11.0.0.0 255.0.0.0 Ethernet0/0
Router(config)#ip route 12.0.0.0 255.0.0.0 FastEthernet1/0
Router(config)#interface FastEthernet1/0
Router(config-if)#ip address 10.1.1.1 255.255.255.0
Router(config-if)#ip nat inside
Router(config-if)#exit
Router(config)#interface Ethernet0/0
Router(config-if)#ip address 10.2.1.2 255.255.255.0
Router(config-if)#ip nat outside
Router(config-if)#exit
Router(config)#end
Router#
```

Notice that we have used the *match-host* keyword in the NAT pool definitions:

```
Router(config)#ip nat pool OUTPOOL 11.0.0.1 11.255.255.254 netmask 255.0.0.0 type
match-host
```

When you use this option, the router will translate the network prefixes and leave the host portions of the address intact. So, in this example, an arbitrary IP address 10.1.2.3 would become 11.1.2.3, changing only the first byte. This has the advantage that the translations are always the same, so you can reliably make connections between any internal and external devices in either direction. You cannot do this with the ordinary dynamic address pools that we have discussed so far in this chapter. Note also that the *overload* option makes no sense in this configuration.

There are a few important things to watch out for when using NAT in both directions. First, the router must have routing table entries for the fictitious IP addresses. It is quite likely that the translated addresses used for external devices will not be part of a physical IP network that the router knows how to reach. This is why we have configured a static route directing traffic for this range out through the external interface:

```
Router(config)#ip route 192.168.15.0 255.255.255.0 Ethernet0/0
```

The second important thing to remember is that with dynamic NAT, the router does not create a translation for each device until it needs to. So if you want to connect through the router to a particular translated address, you have to make sure that the router retains the translation table information. This means that if you want any-to-any connections in either direction, you must either use static mappings or the *match-host* keyword. Dynamic NAT will not allow access in both directions.

And the third important thing to remember is that all of the other routers must know how to reach the translated addresses. So, if the external network is translated from 10.0.0.0/8 to 11.0.0.0/8, then you need to make sure that the internal routers all know that they can reach this fictitious 11.0.0.0/8 network through the NAT router. The best way to do this is to simply redistribute the static routes for the fictitious networks through your dynamic routing protocol.

Recipe 21.7 shows a somewhat better way to solve this overlapping address problem. Instead of doing simultaneous translation in both directions on the same router, it is better to do it on two routers with a different, nonconflicting address range in the middle. One router will simply translate the prefix for one of these networks from 10.0.0.0/8 to 11.0.0.0/8. The other router will translate the addresses on the other network from 10.0.0.0/8 to 12.0.0.0/8. This is a much more stable solution, and it does not suffer from the problems of dynamic NAT that we mentioned above.

See Also

Recipe 21.1; Recipe 21.2; Recipe 21.3; Recipe 21.4; Recipe 21.7

21.7 Rewriting the Network Prefix

Problem

You want to rewrite all of the addresses in a particular range by simply replacing the prefix with one of equal length.

Solution

Sometimes you need to connect your network to another network that uses an unregistered range, such as 172.16.0.0/16. However, if you already use this range in your network, the easiest thing to do is to simply replace this prefix with another one that doesn't have a conflict, such as 172.17.0.0/16:

```
Router#configure terminal
Enter configuration commands, one per line.  End with CNTL/Z.
Router(config)#ip nat outside source static network 172.16.0.0 172.17.0.0 /16 no-
alias
Router(config)#ip route 172.16.0.0 255.255.0.0 Ethernet1/0
Router(config)#ip route 172.17.0.0 255.255.0.0 Ethernet1/0
Router(config)#interface FastEthernet 0/0
```

```
Router(config-if)#ip address 10.1.1.1 255.255.255.0
Router(config-if)#ip nat inside
Router(config-if)#exit
Router(config)#interface Ethernet1/0
Router(config-if)#ip address 172.16.1.6 255.255.255.252
Router(config-if)#ip nat outside
Router(config-if)#exit
Router(config)#end
Router#
```

Discussion

Unlike the previous examples, this recipe shows a very simple static form of NAT that translates addresses by simply replacing one prefix with another. So, for example, the remote host, 172.16.55.19, gets its address rewritten simply as 172.17.55.19.

The router can accomplish this with the following command:

```
Router(config)#ip nat outside source static network 172.16.0.0 172.17.0.0 /16 no-alias
```

This defines a static mapping of one network prefix to another, as required.

Note that we have included the *no-alias* keyword in this command. If we didn't include this keyword, the router would try to generate aliases for the translated addresses to allow it to answer ARP requests for them. This keyword is necessary because one of the router's own interfaces belongs to the translated range.

21.8   Using NAT for Server Load Distribution

Problem

You have several application servers and you want to use NAT so that users can connect to them by a single IP address, distributing the load across all of the servers.

Solution

The *rotary* keyword allows you to do simple NAT-based load balancing of servers:

```
Router#configure terminal
Enter configuration commands, one per line.  End with CNTL/Z.
Router(config)#interface FastEthernet0/0
Router(config-if)#ip address 192.168.1.1 255.255.255.0
Router(config-if)#ip nat inside
Router(config-if)#exit
Router(config)#interface FastEthernet0/1
Router(config-if)#ip address 192.168.2.1 255.255.255.0
Router(config-if)#ip nat outside
Router(config-if)#exit
Router(config)#ip nat pool WEBSERVERS 192.168.1.101 192.168.1.105 netmask 255.255.
255.0 type rotary
Router(config)#access-list 20 permit host 192.168.1.100
Router(config)#ip nat inside destination list 20 pool WEBSERVERS
```

```
Router(config)#end
Router#
```

Discussion

This example is more applicable to an Intranet than to the public Internet. It shows a simple way of doing load balancing among a group of application servers that all perform the same function. We would like to stress that this load balancing is extremely limited, and if you want a fully featured load-balancing device, you would be much better off with one of Cisco's Content Services Switches, such as the CSS 11500 series. However, we understand that these devices are expensive, so if your requirements are fairly basic, this recipe provides a simpler and more cost effective solution.

We have a set of servers located on the LAN segment attached to the router's FastEthernet0/0 interface. In the example, we define a pool of servers on this segment called WEBSERVERS, which includes the addresses 192.168.1.101 through 192.168.1.105. These are the real physical addresses, the inside local addresses of the servers:

```
Router(config)#ip nat pool WEBSERVERS 192.168.1.101 192.168.1.105 netmask 255.255.
255.0 type rotary
```

Then we create the actual NAT rule, and use a standard ACL to define the virtual IP address that devices can use to access this group of servers:

```
Router(config)#access-list 20 permit host 192.168.1.100
Router(config)#ip nat inside destination list 20 pool WEBSERVERS
```

This NAT rule has a key difference from others that we have looked at so far in this chapter because it is a *destination* rather than a *source* rule. All of the previous examples have assumed that the inside device starts the conversation with the outside device, so we have needed to rewrite the source address of the inside device on this essentially outbound conversation. In that scenario, it is appropriate to use an *inside source* NAT rule. Here, however, the outside device will initiate the conversation with the inside device. So we must use an *inside destination* NAT rule.

Now we can verify that this configuration behaves as expected by repeatedly connecting to the virtual IP address on the HTTP TCP port (80) several times:

```
Router#show ip nat translations
Pro Inside global      Inside local      Outside local       Outside global
tcp 192.168.1.100:80   192.168.1.101:80  192.168.2.27:11012  192.168.2.27:11012
tcp 192.168.1.100:80   192.168.1.102:80  192.168.2.27:11013  192.168.2.27:11013
tcp 192.168.1.100:80   192.168.1.103:80  192.168.2.27:11014  192.168.2.27:11014
tcp 192.168.1.100:80   192.168.1.104:80  192.168.2.27:11015  192.168.2.27:11015
tcp 192.168.1.100:80   192.168.1.105:80  192.168.2.27:11016  192.168.2.27:11016
tcp 192.168.1.100:80   192.168.1.101:80  192.168.2.27:11017  192.168.2.27:11017
tcp 192.168.1.100:80   192.168.1.102:80  192.168.2.27:11018  192.168.2.27:11018
Router#
```

As you can see from the NAT translation table, each successive connection goes to the next address in the pool. It does this on a strict rotation, restarting at the first address in the range once it reaches the end.

Note that although this example uses a common TCP port, there is nothing in the configuration to restrict you to using this method for load balancing web servers. The technique would work equally well for sharing load among nonTCP application servers, such as the UDP-based DNS application.

This recipe shows a simple but effective load-balancer, but it does have several limitations compared to a fully featured load-balancer like the CSS 11500 series. These purpose-built devices are able to monitor all of the devices in the pool and remove any that become unavailable, for example. They also use more sophisticated load balancing algorithms that ensure that no one device in the pool winds up taking an overly large share of the load. Another alternative is the Server Load-Balancing (SLB) IOS feature set, which is currently available only on the 3640, 3660, 7200, and 7301 router platforms.

The method shown in this recipe has neither of these advantages. If any device in the pool becomes temporarily unreachable, or the application stops working, the NAT rule will continue to attempt sending new connections to it each time it comes up in the rotation. The end device will typically have to wait for a TCP connection time-out and reconnect, hopefully getting a different server from the pool.

Then, when the device comes back on line, it will again only receive new connections each time it comes up in the rotation. In most applications, this means that it will take a very long time to rebalance the load.

21.9   Stateful NAT Failover

Problem

You want to use NAT in a high availability configuration, allowing a second router to take over NAT functionality if the first fails.

Solution

Stateful NAT allows you to combine NAT functionality with HSRP using two routers in a high availability configuration:

```
Router-A#configure terminal
Enter configuration commands, one per line.  End with CNTL/Z.
Router-A(config)#access-list 11 permit any
Router-A(config)#ip nat pool NATPOOL 172.17.100.100 172.17.100.150 netmask 255.255.
255.0
Router-A(config)#ip nat inside source list 11 pool NATPOOL mapping-id 1
Router-A(config)#interface FastEthernet0/0
Router-A(config-if)#ip address 192.168.1.3 255.255.255.0
Router-A(config-if)#ip nat inside
Router-A(config-if)#standby 1 ip 192.168.1.1
Router-A(config-if)#standby 1 preempt
Router-A(config-if)#standby 1 name SNATGROUP
```

```
Router-A(config-if)#exit
Router-A(config)#interface Serial0/0
Router-A(config-if)#ip address 172.17.55.2 255.255.255.252
Router-A(config-if)#ip nat outside
Router-A(config-if)#exit
Router-A(config)#ip nat Stateful id 1
Router-A(config-ipnat-snat)#redundancy SNATGROUP
Router(config-ipnat-snat-red)#mapping-id 1
Router(config-ipnat-snat-red)#exit
Router-A(config)#end
Router-A#
```

The second router's configuration is nearly identical:

```
Router-B#configure terminal
Enter configuration commands, one per line.  End with CNTL/Z.
Router-B(config)#access-list 11 permit any
Router-B(config)#ip nat pool NATPOOL 172.17.100.100 172.17.100.150 netmask 255.255.
255.0
Router-B(config)#ip nat inside source list 11 pool NATPOOL mapping-id 1
Router-B(config)#interface FastEthernet0/0
Router-B(config-if)#ip address 192.168.1.2 255.255.255.0
Router-B(config-if)#ip nat inside
Router-B(config-if)#standby 1 ip 192.168.1.1
Router-B(config-if)#standby 1 priority 90
Router-B(config-if)#standby 1 preempt
Router-B(config-if)#standby 1 name SNATGROUP
Router-B(config-if)#exit
Router-B(config)#interface Serial0/0
Router-B(config-if)#ip address 172.17.55.6 255.255.255.252
Router-B(config-if)#ip nat outside
Router-B(config-if)#exit
Router-B(config)#ip nat Stateful id 1
Router-B(config-ipnat-snat)#redundancy SNATGROUP
Router(config-ipnat-snat-red)#mapping-id 1
Router(config-ipnat-snat-red)#exit
Router-B(config)#end
Router-B#
```

Discussion

When you use NAT with a router failover protocol such as HSRP, the backup router must be able to take over NAT functionality as well as the IP address of the primary router. The problem is that this necessarily includes the entire dynamic NAT translation table. Simply running NAT and HSRP on a pair of routers is not sufficient because any existing NAT session information will be lost when the backup router takes over.

Stateful Network Address Translation (SNAT) solves this problem. The key command, which must be present on both routers is the *ip nat Stateful* command, which became available in IOS Version 12.2(13)T:

```
Router-A(config)#ip nat Stateful id 1
Router-A(config-ipnat-snat)#redundancy SNATGROUP
Router(config-ipnat-snat-red)#mapping-id 1
Router(config-ipnat-snat-red)#exit
```

There are a couple of things to notice here. First, the keyword *Stateful* will appear in your configuration capitalized like this. When you enter the command, it is case insensitive, however it can be slightly confusing because one usually expects IOS configuration keywords to be all lowercase. We often take advantage of this fact by deliberately capitalizing user-defined strings like SNATGROUP in this example, making the distinction from keywords obvious.

Entering the *ip nat Stateful* command puts you into a new configuration mode that allows you to associate a particular SNAT mapping ID with an HSRP group name. You can give the HSRP group a name with the *standby name* command as follows:

```
Router-A(config)#interface FastEthernet0/0
Router-A(config-if)#ip address 192.168.1.3 255.255.255.0
Router-A(config-if)#ip nat inside
Router-A(config-if)#standby 1 ip 192.168.1.1
Router-A(config-if)#standby 1 preempt
Router-A(config-if)#standby 1 name SNATGROUP
```

For more information on HSRP, please refer to Chapter 22.

In this example we have used a simple dynamic NAT configuration by using a pool called NATPOOL:

```
Router-A(config)#access-list 11 permit any
Router-A(config)#ip nat pool NATPOOL 172.17.100.100 172.17.100.150 netmask 255.255.
255.0
Router-A(config)#ip nat inside source list 11 pool NATPOOL mapping-id 1
```

We could have just as easily used other NAT configuration methods such as static NAT, or PAT address overloading, as described elsewhere in this chapter.

With this configuration, one of the routers will take the virtual IP address, 192.168.1.1, acting as the default gateway for the interior network. The second router will operate in a passive backup mode, waiting to take over this virtual IP address in case the first router fails. The first router will maintain the NAT table for all connections. This means that you have to be very careful to ensure that inbound traffic uses the same path as outbound traffic, or the NAT table may not be able to rewrite the inside global IP address to the correct inside local address.

When the primary router fails, HSRP allows the backup router to transparently take over the virtual IP address. At the same time, SNAT ensures that the NAT translation table is also up to date, allowing the backup router to take over all NAT functions.

You can also use SNAT to create a dual redundancy active/active configuration in which both routers are passing HSRP and NAT traffic. We discuss the HSRP side of this technique in more detail in Chapter 22. The key is to create two HSRP groups, each representing a different virtual IP address. We then assign different priorities to each group so that during normal operation, the first router is active for the first virtual IP address and the second is active for the other address. However, in case of a failure of either router, the other one can take over functionality for both:

```
Router-A#configure terminal
Enter configuration commands, one per line.  End with CNTL/Z.
Router-A(config)#interface FastEthernet0/0
Router-A(config-if)#ip address 192.168.1.3 255.255.255.0
Router-A(config-if)#ip nat inside
Router-A(config-if)#standby 1 ip 192.168.1.1
Router-A(config-if)#standby 1 preempt
Router-A(config-if)#standby 1 name SNAT1
Router-A(config-if)#standby 2 ip 192.168.1.2
Router-A(config-if)#standby 2 priority 90
Router-A(config-if)#standby 2 preempt
Router-A(config-if)#standby 2 name SNAT2
Router-A(config-if)#exit
Router-A(config)#interface Serial0/0
Router-A(config-if)#ip address 172.17.55.2 255.255.255.252
Router-A(config-if)#ip nat outside
Router-A(config-if)#exit
Router-A(config)#ip nat Stateful id 1
Router-A(config-ipnat-snat)#redundancy SNAT1
Router(config-ipnat-snat-red)#mapping-id 1
Router(config-ipnat-snat-red)#redundancy SNAT2
Router(config-ipnat-snat-red)#mapping-id 2
Router(config-ipnat-snat-red)#exit
Router-A(config)#access-list 11 permit any
Router-A(config)#access-list 12 permit any
Router-A(config)#ip nat pool NATPOOL1 172.17.100.100 172.17.100.150 netmask 255.255.
255.0
Router-A(config)#ip nat inside source list 11 pool NATPOOL mapping-id 1
Router-A(config)#ip nat pool NATPOOL2 172.17.100.151 172.17.100.200 netmask 255.255.
255.0
Router-A(config)#ip nat inside source list 12 pool NATPOOL mapping-id 2
Router-A(config)#end
Router-A#
```

And the second router's configuration is similar:

```
Router-B#configure terminal
Enter configuration commands, one per line.  End with CNTL/Z.
Router-B(config)#interface FastEthernet0/0
Router-B(config-if)#ip address 192.168.1.4 255.255.255.0
Router-B(config-if)#ip nat inside
Router-B(config-if)#standby 1 ip 192.168.1.1
Router-B(config-if)#standby 1 preempt
Router-B(config-if)#standby 1 name SNAT1
Router-B(config-if)#standby 1 priority 90
Router-B(config-if)#standby 2 ip 192.168.1.2
Router-B(config-if)#standby 2 preempt
Router-B(config-if)#standby 2 name SNAT2
Router-B(config-if)#exit
Router-B(config)#interface Serial0/0
Router-B(config-if)#ip address 172.17.55.6 255.255.255.252
Router-B(config-if)#ip nat outside
Router-B(config-if)#exit
Router-B(config)#ip nat Stateful id 1
```

```
Router-B(config-ipnat-snat)#redundancy SNAT1
Router(config-ipnat-snat-red)#mapping-id 1
Router(config-ipnat-snat-red)#redundancy SNAT2
Router(config-ipnat-snat-red)#mapping-id 1
Router(config-ipnat-snat-red)#exit
Router-B(config)#access-list 11 permit any
Router-B(config)#ip nat pool NATPOOL 172.17.100.100 172.17.100.150 netmask 255.255.
255.0
Router-B(config)#ip nat inside source list 11 pool NATPOOL mapping-id 1
Router-B(config)#end
Router-B#
```

Here we have mapped both HSRP groups to the same NAT mapping-id on both routers. Now they can freely allocate addresses from the same pool, and update one another
in case either fails. Note that HSRP is the only high-availability protocol that works with
SNAT. Other protocols such as VRRP and GLBP are not currently supported.

See Also

Chapter 22

21.10 Adjusting NAT Timers

Problem

You want to change the length of time that NAT entries remain active.

Solution

The router will keep NAT entries in the translation table for a configurable length of
time. For TCP connections, the default timeout period is 86,400 seconds, or 24
hours. Because UDP is not connection based, the default timeout period is much
shorter—only 300 seconds, or 5 minutes. The router will remove translation table
entries for DNS queries after only 60 seconds.

You can adjust these parameters using the *ip nat translation* command, which
accepts arguments in seconds:

```
Router#configure terminal
Enter configuration commands, one per line.  End with CNTL/Z.
Router(config)#ip nat translation tcp-timeout 500
Router(config)#ip nat translation udp-timeout 30
Router(config)#ip nat translation dns-timeout 30
Router(config)#ip nat translation icmp-timeout 30
Router(config)#ip nat translation finrst-timeout 30
Router(config)#ip nat translation syn-timeout 30
Router(config)#end
Router#
```

To save router memory, you can also define a maximum number of NAT translation table entries:

```
Router#configure terminal
Enter configuration commands, one per line.  End with CNTL/Z.
Router(config)#ip nat translation max-entries 1000
Router(config)#end
Router#
```

Discussion

There are many reasons for adjusting these various timeout parameters; most are related to router performance. If sessions are generally short-lived, it is a waste of memory to maintain the NAT entries for a long time. The *finrst-timeout* and *syn-timeout* parameters are also useful when the router is connected to the public Internet because they can help to prevent denial of service attacks that are based on sending TCP control packet such as SYN, ACK, and FIN. If the router only keeps the NAT entries associated with these packets for a brief period of time, you can help to limit the impact of such attacks.

We recommend using extreme caution with the *max-entries* command:

```
Router(config)#ip nat translation max-entries 1000
```

When you set a limit like this, the router rejects any additional attempts to use NAT. So, in this example, if you already had 1,000 NAT table entries, the router would simply drop any new connection attempts. This can be useful to prevent excessive NAT processing from overloading the router, but it can also block legitimate access.

It is difficult to select a useful upper limit to the size of the NAT table in general. In most cases, it is best to use the default, which does not enforce any upper limit. You should use this command only if you start to run into serious memory or CPU utilization problems. Because it tells the router to refuse any further requests, however, restricting the table size like this should be a last resort. In most cases, it is more effective to decrease the various timeout values as shown in this recipe.

Start by looking at your NAT translation table, as shown in Recipe 21.12, and see what most of the entries look like. If you are using the *overload* option, you may find that there are several different entries for each internal host, each for different port numbers or protocols. The relatively long 24-hour timeout period for TCP sessions is probably the best place to start. You can usually reduce this drastically without causing application problems, and it could give a significant improvement to the size of the NAT table.

See Also

Recipe 21.12

21.11 Changing TCP Ports for FTP

Problem

You have an FTP server that uses a nonstandard TCP port number.

Solution

The FTP protocol includes IP address information in the packet payload. Normally, Cisco's NAT implementation rewrites IP address information in the payloads of FTP packets by looking in every packet sent on TCP port 21, which is the port that FTP uses to pass session control information by default. So when an FTP server uses a nonstandard TCP port number for session control, you have to configure the NAT router to expect FTP packets on this new port number:

```
Router#configure terminal
Enter configuration commands, one per line.  End with CNTL/Z.
Router(config)#access-list 19 permit 192.168.55.5
Router(config)#ip nat service list 19 ftp tcp port 8021
Router(config)#ip nat service list 19 ftp tcp port 21
Router(config)#end
Router#
```

Discussion

As we mentioned in the Introduction to this chapter, the common FTP protocol includes IP address information in the packet payload. Cisco routers expect this, and rewrite the information appropriately. But some FTP servers use a nonstandard TCP port number, which means that NAT will break the protocol. So in IOS Version 11.3, Cisco introduced the ability to look for FTP payload information on alternate TCP port numbers.

The example configures the router to expect FTP packets for the server 192.168.55.5 on both the default port number 21 and the nonstandard port number 8021. You can easily configure similar commands for other servers as well, or expand the access-list to include several servers that all use the same nonstandard FTP port number.

In IOS Version 12.2(4)T, Cisco introduced the *no-payload* keyword, which prevents NAT from modifying any addresses in the packet payload:

```
Router#configure terminal
Enter configuration commands, one per line.  End with CNTL/Z.
Router(config)#interface FastEthernet0/0
Router(config-if)#ip address 172.16.1.5 255.255.255.252
Router(config-if)#ip nat outside
Router(config-if)#exit
Router(config)#interface FastEthernet0/1
Router(config-if)#ip address 192.168.1.1 255.255.255.0
Router(config-if)#ip nat inside
Router(config-if)#exit
```

```
Router(config)#ip nat inside source static 192.168.1.10 172.16.1.5 no-payload
Router(config)#end
Router#
```

Here we have used the *no-payload* option to configure a static NAT entry. Any translations that use this rule will have the addresses in the IP header translated normally. But any IP addresses in the packet payload will remain untouched.

This command is useful in cases when translating the addresses inside the packet interferes with the functioning of the application.

21.12 Checking NAT Status

Problem

You want to see the current NAT information.

Solution

There are several useful EXEC commands for checking the status of NAT on a router. You can view the NAT translation table by using the following command:

```
Router#show ip nat translation
```

You can clear all or part of the NAT translation table by specifying either a * or a particular address. To clear a specific entry, you must specify either the global address for a device that is inside, or a local address for a device that is outside:

```
Router#clear ip nat translation *
Router#clear ip nat translation inside 172.18.3.2
Router#clear ip nat translation outside 192.168.1.10
```

You will often want to look at NAT statistics, including information on which interfaces use NAT, how many entries are in the NAT table, how often they have been used, and, most importantly, how often packets have bypassed NAT. The command to see this is *show ip nat statistics*:

```
Router#show ip nat statistics
```

And you can clear these statistics as follows:

```
Router#clear ip nat statistics
```

Discussion

The NAT translation table contains information about every translation that the router is currently tracking. In this example, you can see that there have been two connections between the interior device 192.168.1.10 and the exterior device 172.18.3.2. The first of these connections is shown as ICMP:

```
Router#show ip nat translation
Pro Inside global     Inside local      Outside local     Outside global
```

```
icmp 172.16.1.100:21776 192.168.1.10:21776 172.18.3.2:21776  172.18.3.2:21776
tcp 172.16.1.100:1029  192.168.1.10:1029   172.18.3.2:23      172.18.3.2:23
--- 172.16.1.10         192.168.1.15        ---               ---
--- 172.16.1.11         192.168.1.16        ---               ---
Router#
```

This command shows only the currently active NAT table entries. You can see, for example, that it translates the inside local address 192.168.1.10 to the inside global address 172.16.1.100. But this router isn't configured to translate outside addresses, so the outside local address is the same as the outside global addresses. As we discussed in Recipe 21.10, the router removes dynamic NAT entries after a defined period of time. For example, by default the router will delete NAT entries for TCP connections after 24 hours.

The output has five columns. The first is the protocol. This column is blank unless you use the *overload* option in your NAT configuration. The "Inside global" address column is the translated address of an internal device. The "Inside local" column, on the other hand, shows the real internal address for the same device. The "Outside local" column shows the translated addresses of external devices, while "Outside global" shows their real addresses.

This can be a little bit confusing at first sight. The real address on the inside is "local," and the translated address is "global," while the real address on the outside is "global," and it is translated to a "local" address. You can resolve this confusion by remembering that global addresses are always on the outside, and local addresses are on the inside.

The last two rows represent simple static NAT entries. It shows, for example, that the internal device whose real address is 192.168.1.15 is translated to 172.16.1.10 when its packets pass through this router. There are no external addresses listed for this entry. Because it is a static entry, this translation is the same for any external device. However, the row immediately above this one shows all four entries:

```
tcp 172.16.1.100:1029  192.168.1.10:1029  172.18.3.2:23      172.18.3.2:23
```

This line includes a lot of useful information. The first column indicates that this row represents a TCP connection, and that the translation is a dynamic entry. On the inside, the source address is 192.168.1.10, and the source TCP port it 1029, while the destination is 172.18.3.2, and the destination port is 23. On the outside, the destination address and port are the same, but the source address is rewritten as 172.16.1.100, and the source port is 1029.

The *verbose* keyword makes this command show age information about each table entry:

```
Router#show ip nat translation verbose
Pro Inside global     Inside local     Outside local     Outside global
icmp 172.16.1.100:21776 192.168.1.10:21776 172.18.3.2:21776  172.18.3.2:21776
192.168.3.2:4235
    create 00:00:36, use 00:00:36, left 00:00:23, flags: extended
```

```
tcp 172.16.1.100:1029  192.168.1.10:1029  172.18.3.2:23     172.18.3.2:23
    create 00:00:15, use 00:00:13, left 00:00:46, flags: extended, timing-out
--- 172.16.1.10         192.168.1.15     ---               ---
    create 1d00h, use 00:23:08, flags: static
--- 172.16.1.11         192.168.1.16     ---               ---
    create 1d00h, use 00:15:28, flags: static
Router#
```

This level of detail is most useful when you are trying to diagnose NAT table time-out issues.

The *show ip nat statistics* command includes useful information about the translation configuration. The following example shows one external and two internal interfaces, with a dynamic NAT pool that runs from 172.16.1.100 to 172.16.1.150:

```
Router#show ip nat statistics
Total active translations: 3 (2 static, 1 dynamic; 1 extended)
Outside interfaces:
  Ethernet0/0
Inside interfaces:
  FastEthernet0/0, FastEthernet0/1
Hits: 2628  Misses: 44
Expired translations: 37
Dynamic mappings:
-- Inside Source
access-list 15 pool NATPOOL refcount 1
 pool NATPOOL: netmask 255.255.255.0
       start 172.16.1.100 end 172.16.1.150
       type generic, total addresses 2, allocated 1 (50%), misses 9
Router#
```

The *Hits* field shows the total number of times that the router has had to create new translation table entries. The *Misses* field counts the exceptions. In this case, there is an access-list that excludes certain internal IP addresses.

21.13 Debugging NAT

Problem

You want to debug a NAT problem.

Solution

Cisco routers include a simple but useful debug facility for NAT. The basic form of the command is *debug ip nat*:

```
Router#debug ip nat
```

You can also add the *detailed* keyword to this command to get more information on each NAT event:

```
Router#debug ip nat detailed
```

It is often useful to use an access-list with the debug command. You can do this by simply specifying the number of the access-list. This will allow you to just look at NAT events for particular IP addresses that are permitted by the access-list:

```
Router#debug ip nat 15
```

You can also combine an access-list with the *detailed* keyword for more focused debugging:

```
Router#debug ip nat 15 detailed
```

Discussion

The following shows some typical log entries:

```
Router#terminal monitor
Router#debug ip nat
Sep  8 19:51:08.396 EDT: NAT: s=192.168.3.1->192.168.19.1, d=192.168.3.2 [0]
Sep  8 19:51:11.560 EDT: NAT*: s=192.168.1.10->192.168.19.55, d=192.168.3.2 [490
9]
Sep  8 19:51:11.568 EDT: NAT*: s=192.168.3.2, d=192.168.19.55->192.168.1.10 [490
9]
Sep  8 19:51:11.572 EDT: NAT: s=192.168.3.2, d=192.168.19.55->192.168.1.10 [4909
]
Sep  8 19:51:12.552 EDT: NAT*: s=192.168.1.10->192.168.19.55, d=192.168.3.2 [491
1]
Sep  8 19:51:12.564 EDT: NAT*: s=192.168.3.2, d=192.168.19.55->192.168.1.10 [491
1]
```

This particular trace follows a simple series of PING packets. The interior device 192.168.1.10 sends ICMP PING packets to the external destination 192.168.3.2. The router rewrites the internal address as 192.168.19.55 and forwards the packet to the external destination.

You can also see the PING responses coming back from the destination device. The router rewrites the internal address back to its true value and forwards the packet appropriately.

First Hop Redundancy Protocols

22.0   Introduction

First Hop Redundancy Protocol (FHRP) are a group of protocols that allow a router on a LAN segment to automatically take over if another one fails. They were developed to solve a common problem in shared networks such as Ethernet or Token Ring. The devices on this shared network segment are usually configured with a single default gateway address that points to the router that connects to the rest of the network. The problem is that even if there is a second router on the segment that is also capable of being the default gateway, the end devices don't know about it. Therefore, if the first default gateway router fails, the network stops working. The three main First Hop Redundancy Protocols discussed in this chapter are HSRP Versions 1 and 2, VRRP and GLBP.

Many methods for addressing this problem have come and gone over the years. The most obvious and seriously flawed solution is to have the end users reconfigure the default gateway address in their workstations. This is a terrible solution for several reasons. There is a large chance of typographical errors. The conversion is slow and laborious, and often requires a reboot of the workstation. It relies on users noticing the problem in a timely manner, and it is unlikely that anybody will bother to change the address back when the original router recovers. And it also requires that there is a human handy to make the change, which is not always the case because many devices such as printers and servers don't usually have somebody sitting beside them when problems appear.

A slightly better solution that many organizations have used is to run a dynamic routing protocol such as RIP or OSPF directly on the servers and workstations. Unix-based operating systems have access to good routing protocol implementations, such as the *routed* and *gated* programs. However, many popular desktop and server operating systems do not support these protocols. Even if every device in the network could run a routing protocol, this is not a very good solution to the problem for several reasons. Routing protocols tend not to converge well when the number of devices gets too large. So this technique would, at the very least, require a major network redesign. It is also generally a bad idea to let end devices affect the global routing tables throughout the network. If one of these devices is not configured properly, it could cause serious routing problems. And, more philosophically, it is a good principle of network design to keep network functions on network devices. Workstations and servers have enough to do already without having to worry about doing a router's job as well.

ICMP Router Discovery Protocol (IRDP), which is described in RFC 1256, represents still another interesting idea for allowing end devices to find a new router when their default gateway fails. This protocol requires routers to periodically send multicast "hello" messages to the LAN segment. End devices listen for these messages and use them to build their internal routing tables. If an end device doesn't hear these hello messages for a while, it assumes that the router must have failed. The end device then sends a multicast query looking for a new router to take over. Again, this method requires special software on the end devices. Few devices support IRDP, and it has never enjoyed particularly wide acceptance.

Cisco routers do support IRDP. If you want to use it, you can enable it by simply using the interface command *ip irdp* as follows:

```
Router#configure terminal
Enter configuration commands, one per line.  End with CNTL/Z.
Router(config)#interface FastEthernet 0/1
Router(config-if)#ip irdp
Router(config-if)#exit
Router(config)#end
Router#
```

We do not recommend using IRDP, however, because it is unlikely that all of the devices on a segment will be able to use and react to it appropriately. HSRP, which we will turn to in a moment, provides a much more robust and flexible router redundancy mechanism. The one exception is clients running IP Mobility require IRDP to work properly. For more information on IP Mobility, see Chapter 24.

As an aside, there is another protocol, also called Interdomain Routing Protocol (IDRP), which is part of the OSI protocol suite that provides similar functionality to BGP. The similarity of the names is just an accident. There is no relation between these protocols, although it is easy to get the acronyms confused.

One of the more popular solutions to the problem of router redundancy uses Proxy ARP, which is enabled by default on Cisco routers. In this configuration, the end devices are not configured with a default gateway at all. Instead, they discover the path to remote devices the same way that they find devices on the local LAN segment, using Address Resolution Protocol (ARP). You would then configure the routers to run *Proxy ARP*, which means that they respond to ARP requests on behalf of the remote device. Then the originating device simply sends a packet to the remote destination IP address using the MAC address of the local router, which is exactly the desired behavior.

The problem with the Proxy ARP solution, is that it doesn't switch to a backup router very quickly when the primary router fails. End devices don't tend to change their MAC addresses very often. The whole ARP cache procedure assumes that if an entry was once valid, it will remain valid unless it is explicitly changed by means of a *gratuitous ARP* from the other device declaring a new address. Most devices will remove a stale ARP entry if the device fails to respond for several minutes, but this is clearly not fast enough for a reliable fail-over mechanism. The only ways to speed this procedure up are to reboot or manually clear the ARP cache on the end device. Proxy ARP is also a rather messy solution because it requires a potentially large number of ARP requests on the local segment. Since ARP requests are broadcasts, this can cause serious problems on a busy segment.

Cisco developed Hot Standby Router Protocol (HSRP) to address the problem of router redundancy in a more reliable way. It provides a nondisruptive automatic failover method that doesn't require end devices to run any special software. HSRP is documented in RFC 2281, although it is a Cisco proprietary standard.

It works by allowing two routers to share the same virtual IP and MAC addresses. End devices simply send their off-segment packets to these addresses, as a standard default gateway. One of the routers will receive and forward the packets, so either can fail without disrupting traffic flow. One router is always active, and the other acts as a standby, in case the first one should fail. In fact, you can configure many standby routers for extreme high-availability situations. The HSRP routers that share a virtual IP address send multicast packets back and forth periodically. If the primary router ever stops sending these packets for any reason, one of the standby routers immediately takes over both the IP and MAC addresses, and continues to forward packets.

Figure 22-1 shows a simple example of an HSRP network that will make a good reference point for many of the examples in this chapter. If Host A uses Router1 as its default gateway, then it will lose access to the network if Router1 fails. This is true even if there is a second router, Router2, on the same segment.

In the HSRP configuration shown in this diagram, Router1 and Router2 share the virtual IP address 172.22.1.1. These two routers also have their own IP addresses, 172.22.1.3 and 172.22.1.2, respectively. We note in passing that this is a relatively common and useful way of allocating IP addresses in a /24 network. All end devices use the .1 address for their default gateway, which is the virtual router. The two physical routers then use the .2 and .3 addresses for their real addresses.

HSRP sends multicast packets between routers on the common LAN segment using multicast address 224.0.0.2 and UDP port 1985. By default, these packets are exchanged every 3 seconds, and if they are not seen for 10 seconds, the standby

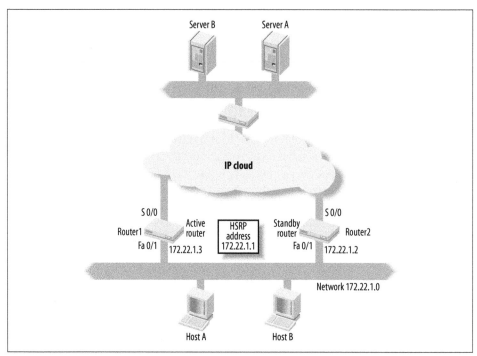

Figure 22-1. An HSRP-enabled network segment

router takes over. Each router in a group has a priority that defines whether it is active or standby. Both the timers and the priority values are configurable.

You can use up to 256 HSRP groups, numbered 0 through 255, on Ethernet and FDDI type networks. This can be useful in network designs in which a central backbone connects many distinct network segments carrying different subnets. For Token Ring LANs, however, you can only configure three distinct HSRP groups, numbered 0 through 2. For Token Rings, you can configure additional groups if you use the Burned In Address (BIA) on the router's Token Ring port, as we discuss in Recipe 22.7. The limitation of three HSRP groups applies to the default configuration mode, which uses a common MAC address for the virtual IP address on both routers.

It is important to note that the HSRP group number is only significant on the local LAN segment. You can use the same group number on different interfaces on the same router if the segments do not connect. However, many network administrators find that it helps to avoid confusion if they use different group numbers on different interfaces. Recipe 22.4 shows a good example of a case in which having multiple HSRP groups on a single LAN segment is extremely useful.

For Ethernet LANs, HSRP uses a standard set of MAC addresses from the range allocated to Cisco. The virtual Ethernet MAC addresses are 00-00-0C-07-AC-XX, where the

XX represents the HSRP group number in hex (00–FF). The following output shows an HSRP packet captured by using the popular Ethereal packet analyzer package:

```
Ethernet II
    Destination: 01:00:5e:00:00:02
    Source: 00:00:0c:07:ac:01
    Type: IP (0x0800)
Internet Protocol
    Version: 4
    Header length: 20 bytes
        Total Length: 48
        Protocol: UDP (0x11)
    Source: 172.22.1.3
    Destination: ALL-ROUTERS.MCAST.NET (224.0.0.2)
User Datagram Protocol
    Source port: 1985 (1985)
    Destination port: 1985 (1985)
    Length: 28
Cisco Hot Standby Router Protocol
    Version: 0
    Op Code: Hello (0)
    State: Active (16)
    Hellotime: Default (3)
    Holdtime: Default (10)
    Priority: 120
    Group: 1
    Reserved: 0
    Authentication Data: Non-Default (OREILLY)
    Virtual IP Address: 172.22.1.1
```

For Token Ring LANs, however, HSRP uses so-called Functional MAC addresses, which are reserved for special purpose applications. HSRP uses C0-00-00-01-00-00, C0-00-00-02-00-00, and C0-00-00-04-00-00 for groups 0, 1, and 2 respectively. However, as we will discuss in Recipe 22.7, many organizations actually use the BIA of the Token Ring interface card with HSRP instead of these functional addresses. As we mentioned a moment ago, when you use the BIA, you can configure additional groups. But it's important to remember that they will all use the same MAC address. This is only really useful, however, when you want to configure several IP subnets on the same physical ring, and use HSRP on all of them.

HSRP is only used for IP networking. However, the fact that it allows two devices to use the same MAC address can cause serious problems for some other protocols. In particular, if you use DECNet or XNS on the same segment, you must use the BIA to avoid bad protocol interactions. The command for this is *use-bia*, which we discuss in Recipe 22.7.

Cisco introduced HSRP Version 2, beginning with IOS Version 12.3(4)T. According to Cisco, HSRP Version 2 was introduced to prepare for further enhancements and to expand the capabilities beyond that of HSRP Version 1. Specifically, HSRP Version 2 provides the following enhancements: expanding of the HSRP group number from 256 to 4096 to match VLAN numbers on subinterfaces, improved management and troubleshooting, and introduces a new multicast IP address.

HSRP Version 1 uses multicast IP address 224.0.0.2. This conflicts with Cisco Group Management Protocol (CGMP) leave processing. HSRP Version 2 uses a new multicast IP address 224.0.0.102, which allows CGMP to be enabled at the same time as HSRP Version 2.

To allow for the expanded number of HSRP group numbers, HSRP Version 2 also uses a new range of MAC addresses, ranging from 0000.0C9F.F000 to 0000.0C9F.FFFF, respectively. The last three hex characters map directly to the newly expanded HSRP group numbers, 0 to 4,095 (000 – FFF).

Another similar solution to the same problem is the open standard Virtual Router Redundancy Protocol (VRRP), which is defined in RFC 2338. VRRP is currently supported by many vendors, but has not yet become an official IETF standard. Cisco added support for VRRP, beginning with IOS Version 12.2(15)T.

VRRP uses multicast IP address 224.0.0.18 to communicate between peers, and is assigned IP protocol number 112 by the IANA. Each VRRP packet must be sent with its TTL set to 255. Any VRRP packet received with a TTL not equal to 255 must be discarded according to the RFC.

VRRP supports up to 255 groups, from 1 to 255. For Ethernet LANs, VRRP uses a standard set of MAC addresses allocated to VRRP. The virtual Ethernet MAC addresses are 0000.5E00.01XX, where the XX represents the VRRP group number in hex (01 – FF).

Although HSRP represents a useful alternative to Proxy ARP, as we have already mentioned, you can use them together. This is particularly useful when you are migrating from an old Proxy ARP configuration to HSRP. In this case, the router uses the HSRP virtual MAC address when it responds to ARP requests.

It is also worth noting that the router will disable ICMP redirects by default when you enable HSRP on routers running IOS versions earlier than 12.1(3)T. Normally when you have two routers on the same segments, ICMP redirection allows you to send a packet to either one. If the other router has a better path to the destination, the receiving router will forward the packet to the other router and send a special ICMP redirect packet back to the source device. The source device receives this packet and updates its internal routing table accordingly so that all future packets to this destination use the better router.

Normally you don't want to use ICMP redirection with HSRP because it would it would allow the end devices to learn the real physical MAC addresses for the routers. Since the end devices update their internal routing tables with this information, if one of the routers failed, it would prevent the other from taking over all routing functions.

However, in Recipe 22.5 we will show how to configure HSRP routers to use ICMP redirection so that they only use the HSRP virtual MAC address instead of any physical addresses.

Cisco introduced another interesting first hop router redundancy protocol in IOS version 12.2(15)T, Gateway Load Balancing Protocol (GLBP). This is another proprietary Cisco standard, and in many ways it is quite similar to HSRP. The main difference from HSRP is that with GLBP, all of the routers in a redundancy group are active and able to share the traffic load.

GLBP accomplishes this by electing a master router, called the Active Virtual Gateway (AVG) for the group. This election is weighted by a priority, like HSRP. The routers in the group are called Active Virtual Forwarders (AVF), and the AVG is itself an AVF.

The AVG distributes virtual MAC addresses to all of the AVF routers in the group. Then, when any end device on the network segment sends an ARP packet looking for the default gateway virtual IP address, the AVG responds, specifying the MAC address of one of the AVF routers. In this way, individual devices on the network segment will all use the same default gateway address, but different physical routers.

The GLBP routers communicate among themselves by using multicast group 224.0. 0.102 with UDP source and destination ports both set to 3222. Note that this is the same multicast group number as HSRP Version 2.

22.1   Configuring Basic HSRP Functionality

Problem

You want a backup router to take over the MAC and IP addresses of a primary router if the primary fails.

Solution

Figure 22.1 represents a typical network design for use with HSRP on an Ethernet type LAN segment (including Fast Ethernet, Gigabit Ethernet, and 10 Gigabit Ethernet). There are two routers, called Router1 and Router2. They have IP addresses 172.22.1.3 and 172.22.1.2, respectively. When both routers are available, we want Router1 to handle all of the traffic, using the virtual IP address 172.22.1.1.

Configure the first router as follows:

```
Router1#configure terminal
Enter configuration commands, one per line.  End with CNTL/Z.
Router1(config)#interface FastEthernet 0/1
Router1(config-if)#ip address 172.22.1.3 255.255.255.0
Router1(config-if)#standby 1 ip 172.22.1.1
Router1(config-if)#standby 1 priority 120
Router1(config-if)#exit
Router1(config)#end
Router1#
```

The second router's configuration is similar, except that the interface has a different real IP address and a lower HSRP priority level:

```
Router2#configure terminal
Enter configuration commands, one per line.  End with CNTL/Z.
Router2(config)#interface FastEthernet 1/0
Router2(config-if)#ip address 172.22.1.2 255.255.255.0
Router2(config-if)#standby 1 ip 172.22.1.1
Router2(config-if)#standby 1 priority 110
Router2(config-if)#exit
Router2(config)#end
Router2#
```

Discussion

In this example, we use the first address of the subnet, 172.22.1.1, as the virtual HSRP address, and consequently the default gateway for the segment. This is a relatively common practice and a good rule of thumb because it makes troubleshooting easier. Whatever segment you are looking at, you always know that the first address in the range is the default gateway.

For HSRP configurations, we recommend using the next two addresses as the physical addresses 172.22.1.2 and 172.22.1.3, in the example. This way, when you are looking at a problem, you always know exactly what the physical router addresses should be, so you can PING them, or log in and check their configurations.

In fact, you can use physical addresses that are from a different IP subnet than the virtual address. However, we don't recommend this because, once again, it can make troubleshooting problems extremely difficult, particularly if the HSRP configuration is broken so that neither router has the right virtual address.

You can also use HSRP with secondary IP addresses. However, we don't recommend using secondary IP addresses unless it is unavoidable. With modern VLAN-based network designs, secondary IP addresses on a LAN segment should be used only for temporary measures like when you are making addressing changes on your network. To configure a secondary HSRP address, use the *secondary* keyword:

```
Router2(config-if)#standby 1 ip 172.22.2.1 secondary
```

The number 1 following all of the *standby* commands in this recipe is a group number. You can leave this out, in which case the router will assume group 0. The group number is necessary if you have more than one pair of HSRP routers on the same segment. However, if a router runs HSRP on more than one interface, many administrators also find that it helps with troubleshooting if they configure different group numbers for each interface. This is particularly true if the different segments appear as different VLANs in the same switch. Since the default virtual MAC address depends only on group number, it can cause problems for some switches to see the same MAC address on two different VLANs.

You must configure all of the routers that share the same virtual IP address with the same group number. For Ethernet type interfaces, group numbers can have any value between 0 and 255, while for Token Ring interfaces you can use group numbers 0, 1, or 2 unless you include the *use-bia* command, which we discuss in Recipe 22.7.

The *standby priority* command, which appears in both routers, is optional. Priority values can be any value between 0 and 255. If you don't configure a priority, the router will use a default value of 100. We changed the priority on both routers for clarity. However, we highly recommend giving at least one of the routers a nondefault priority. If both routers have the same priority, they must elect an active router. RFC 2281, which documents the HSRP protocol, stipulates that the interface with the higher physical IP address will win this election if two routers become active simultaneously. However, in practice, one router almost always comes up first and wins.

Usually you will want to give one of the routers a higher priority so that it is active by default. This way, you force a particular router to be active, which can help with troubleshooting.

When a router becomes active, it broadcasts a gratuitous ARP packet with the HSRP virtual MAC address to the affected LAN segment. If the segment uses an Ethernet switch, this allows the switch to change the location of the virtual MAC address so that packets go to the new router instead of the one that is no longer active. End devices don't actually need this gratuitous ARP if the routers use the default HSRP MAC address. However, if the routers use the Burned-In Address (BIA), as in Recipe 22.7, the gratuitous ARP is critical for updating the ARP caches of end devices to point to the new router.

By default, the router will send gratuitous ARP packets every 10 seconds. You can adjust this interval with the *standby mac-refresh* command, which takes an argument between 0 and 255 seconds. Many switches will remove an entry from their MAC tables if they don't see at least one packet every 5 minutes (300 seconds). However, sometimes random errors mean that a packet is not received properly. So we don't recommend using a value greater than 150 seconds here:

```
Router2(config-if)#standby mac-refresh 30
```

If you don't want the router to send these packets at all, you can specify a value of 0. Note that this command does not specify a group. If you change this value, it changes for all groups on the interface.

You can use the *show standby* command to see the status of HSRP on a router:

```
Router1#show standby
FastEthernet0/1 - Group 1
  Local state is Active, priority 120
  Hellotime 3 sec, holdtime 10 sec
  Next hello sent in 0.424
  Virtual IP address is 172.22.1.1 configured
  Active router is local
```

```
Standby router is 172.22.1.2 expires in 7.456
Virtual mac address is 0000.0c07.ac01
5 state changes, last state change 12:40:42
Router1#
```

In this example, you can see that this router is the active router, so the other must either be in a standby or an unavailable state. If this router were in the standby state, the line that currently says "Active router is local" would show the physical IP address of the active router. In this case, the following line shows the IP address of the standby router. The fact that the standby router is listed with an expiry time means that it is available. If the other router became unavailable for any reason, this line would be replaced by one saying "Standby router is unknown expired." This makes it very easy to see the state of both routers at once.

This command also shows other useful information, such as how frequently the router sends HSRP Hello packets (every three seconds). The "holdtime" shows how long the routers will wait before switching states—10 seconds, in this case. The output also shows the virtual MAC address that HSRP is using, and that this router has an HSRP priority of 120.

You can also configure a particular shared MAC address if you don't want to use the default or the BIA:

```
Router1(config-if)#standby 1 mac-address 0000.0c07.ad01
```

When you use this option, you should configure the same MAC address on both routers. By default, when you configure a particular standby group, the router will always select the same MAC address. This is useful because it means that two routers will always agree on the MAC address that they will be sharing. But it can also cause confusion for a LAN switch that sees the same MAC address on two different VLANs. This could happen, for example, if you have two routers using HSRP group number 1 on one VLAN and two different routers using the same group number on a different VLAN. If you encounter problems, you can use the *standby mac-address* command to ensure that the HSRP MAC addresses are globally unique.

The recipe example shows two routers for simplicity. You could add more routers to the same HSRP group by simply specifying another unique real IP address and a lower HSRP priority, as follows:

```
Router3#configure terminal
Enter configuration commands, one per line.  End with CNTL/Z.
Router3(config)#interface FastEthernet 1/0
Router3(config-if)#ip address 172.22.1.4 255.255.255.0
Router3(config-if)#standby 1 ip 172.22.1.1
Router3(config-if)#standby 1 priority 100
Router3(config-if)#exit
Router3(config)#end
Router3#
```

However, we stress that there is questionable benefit to using more than two routers in a full redundancy configuration. The reason has to do with simple probability. The probability of one router failing is relatively small, but it can happen. Cisco quotes typical Mean Time Between Failure (MTBF) values for its routers between 15 and 20 years. Assuming that it takes a full day to repair a broken router, this means that you should expect to need a backup about 0.018 percent of the time. This is a very small number, but if you have a lot of routers, the probability of having a critical failure somewhere in your network can become rather large.

Now if you have a backup router that uses HSRP to automatically and transparently take over all routing functions for this segment, then you will only have a critical outage if both routers fail simultaneously. The probability of this happening is the square of the probability of one router failing, or roughly 3×10^{-6} percent. The effective aggregate MTBF has gone from 15 years to about 80 thousand years.

So the advantage to using a backup router should be obvious. If you then added another backup router to this network segment, the probability of failure becomes about 6×10^{-10} percent, for an effective MTBF of over 400 million years. Very few networks actually need that sort of reliability.

In fact, all of these statistical arguments assume that the failure of one router is completely uncorrelated with the failure of the backup. This is not the case if both devices run from the same circuit breaker, for example. So, if you do find that you frequently suffer from multiple simultaneous failures, you should probably figure out why the failures are correlated. Simply adding another router might not help the situation at all.

And, of course, there are other reasons why routers become unavailable. In many networks, the most compelling reason for using HSRP is that it makes routine maintenance possible without disrupting production traffic. This is particularly important in networks that must be available at all times. You might even decide to use three HSRP routers on a segment to ensure that you still have full redundancy even when you take one of the routers down for maintenance.

See Also

Recipe 22.7

22.2 Using HSRP Preempt

Problem

You want to ensure that a particular router is always selected as the "active" HSRP router, whenever it is up and functioning.

Solution

You can ensure that a particular router is always selected as the HSRP active router if it is available. On the router that you wish to make your primary active HSRP router, you need to set a higher priority level and use the *standby preempt* command:

```
Router1#configure terminal
Enter configuration commands, one per line.  End with CNTL/Z.
Router1(config)#interface FastEthernet 0/1
Router1(config-if)#standby 1 ip 172.22.1.1
Router1(config-if)#standby 1 priority 120
Router1(config-if)#standby 1 preempt
Router1(config-if)#exit
Router1(config)#end
Router1#
```

The only difference on the second router is the HSRP priority level. The lower priority in conjunction with the *standby preempt* command forces the second HSRP router to remain in a standby state unless the primary router becomes unreachable. Then, when the primary router becomes available again, the secondary router will relinquish its role and allow the primary router to take over as the active HSRP router:

```
Router2#configure terminal
Enter configuration commands, one per line.  End with CNTL/Z.
Router2(config)#interface FastEthernet 1/0
Router2(config-if)#standby 1 ip 172.22.1.1
Router2(config-if)#standby 1 priority 110
Router2(config-if)#standby 1 preempt
Router2(config-if)#exit
Router2(config)#end
Router2#
```

You can also configure this feature by specifying the *preempt* keyword on the *standby priority* configuration command. Both methods produce exactly the same results:

```
Router2#configure terminal
Enter configuration commands, one per line.  End with CNTL/Z.
Router2(config)#interface FastEthernet 1/0
Router2(config-if)#standby 1 ip 172.22.1.1
Router2(config-if)#standby 1 priority 110 preempt
Router2(config-if)#exit
Router2(config)#end
Router2#
```

Discussion

The *standby preempt* feature means that the router with the higher priority is always the active router if it is available. If two routers have the same priority, then the interface with the highest physical IP address becomes active. However, as we mentioned in Recipe 22.1, it is a good practice to always set the priorities so that one router is the clear winner. This avoids any confusion.

In Recipe 22.3 we will describe another extremely useful HSRP feature, called interface tracking, which allows HSRP to react to problems on other interfaces on the router. In this case, it becomes much more important to ensure that the right router carries traffic in the default situation. We strongly advocate using the *standby preempt* feature whenever you use HSRP.

The protocol handles this feature by allowing routers to send HSRP Coup packets. If another router receives a coup message or even an HSRP Hello message from a router with higher priority, it will immediately send an HSRP Resign message in return, and give up its active state. Because one router will always have either higher priority or a higher IP address than any of the others, there is always one router that can unambiguously claim precedence, ensuring that all HSRP coups are bloodless.

In IOS 12.0(9) and higher, you can alter this behavior slightly, making the active router wait before relinquishing its active state. This is sometimes helpful when the newly active router needs a little bit of time to bring up slow WAN interfaces and populate routing tables. Frame Relay interfaces in particular can take as long as a minute to synchronize LMI (see Chapter 10 for more discussion of Frame Relay). However, by default, HSRP preempt will make the router become the active default gateway for the LAN within seconds of bringing up the LAN interface.

The following command will make a router wait 60 seconds before becoming the active HSRP router:

```
Router2(config-if)#standby 1 preempt delay 60
```

You can set this delay to any value between 0 and 3,600 seconds. You can also combine this command with the *priority* command:

```
Router2(config-if)#standby 1 priority 110 preempt delay 60
```

The *show standby* command shows additional information when the preempt option is configured:

```
Router1#show standby
FastEthernet0/1 - Group 1
  Local state is Active, priority 120, may preempt
  Preemption delayed for at least 60 secs
  Hellotime 3 sec, holdtime 10 sec
  Next hello sent in 2.236
  Virtual IP address is 172.22.1.1 configured
  Active router is local
  Standby router is 172.22.1.2 expires in 9.304
  Virtual mac address is 0000.0c07.ac01
  5 state changes, last state change 12:41:53
Router1#
```

In this case, the router is configured to wait 60 seconds before preempting. If you don't define a delay, the router omits this line from the output.

See Also

Recipe 22.1; Recipe 22.3; Chapter 10

22.3 Making HSRP React to Problems on Other Interfaces

Problem

You want HSRP to switch to the backup router when another port on the primary router becomes unavailable.

Solution

The *standby track* configuration command reduces the priority of an active HSRP router into a standby mode when one of its interfaces becomes unavailable. If the priority drops far enough, another router will take over:

```
Router1#configure terminal
Enter configuration commands, one per line.  End with CNTL/Z.
Router1(config)#interface FastEthernet0/1
Router1(config-if)#standby 1 ip 172.22.1.1
Router1(config-if)#standby 1 priority 120
Router1(config-if)#standby 1 preempt
Router1(config-if)#standby 1 track Serial0/0 20
Router1(config-if)#exit
Router1(config)#end
Router1#
```

Beginning with IOS Version 12.2(15)T, Cisco enhanced functionality by allowing you to track objects other than line-protocol state:

```
Router1#configure terminal
Enter configuration commands, one per line.  End with CNTL/Z.
Router1(config)#track 11 interface Serial1/1 ip routing
Router1(config-track)#exit
Router1(config)#interface FastEthernet0/0
Router1(config-if)#standby 1 ip 172.22.1.1
Router1(config-if)#standby 1 priority 120
Router1(config-if)#standby 1 preempt
Router1(config-if)#standby 1 track 11 decrement 50
Router1(config-if)#end
Router1#
```

Discussion

This configuration option is particularly useful when you have two identically configured WAN access routers using HSRP on their LAN ports. In this case, if you are using a dynamic routing protocol, then losing the WAN connection to one of the routers isn't actually a disaster. The routing protocol will tell the active router to forward all of its outbound traffic to the standby router, which will still have a good connection. However, this is obviously inefficient. It would be better if the active router simply resigned its active status and let the standby router take over.

HSRP does this by decreasing the priority for this router. By default, it decreases the priority by 10 points. But you can configure this amount. In the example, the router drops its HSRP priority by 20 points when the interface *Serial0/0* becomes unavailable:

```
Router1(config-if)#standby 1 track Serial0/0 20
```

In all of our examples so far, we have configured the priorities of the two HSRP routers to have a difference of 10 priority points. So if we used the default priority drop in this *standby track* command, a failure of the tracked interface would give the two routers equal priority. So the router with the higher IP address will become the active router when this interface fails. This might not be the right choice. We have specified a value of 20 priority points in this command to ensure that the other router will take over appropriately.

You can use the *standby track* command to track any router interface, or even multiple interfaces. To track several interfaces, you just specify all of the interfaces in separate *standby track* commands:

```
Router1#configure terminal
Enter configuration commands, one per line.  End with CNTL/Z.
Router1(config)#interface FastEthernet0/1
Router1(config-if)#standby 1 ip 172.22.1.1
Router1(config-if)#standby 1 priority 120
Router1(config-if)#standby 1 preempt
Router1(config-if)#standby 1 track Serial0/0 20
Router1(config-if)#standby 1 track Serial0/1 20
Router1(config-if)#exit
Router1(config)#end
Router1#
```

In this example, we have explicitly configured HSRP to decrement the priority by 20 if either of the tracked interfaces fails. So, if both interfaces fail, the priority will drop by 40 points.

For the *standby track* command to work properly, you must also configure *standby preempt*, as in Recipe 22.2. This is because you want to allow the router that now has the higher priority to send an HSRP Coup message and take over control.

When you use tracking like this, the *show standby* command includes information about the interface that is being tracked, as well as what will happen to the priority when that interface goes down:

```
Router1#show standby
FastEthernet0/1 - Group 1
  Local state is Active, priority 120, may preempt
  Hellotime 3 sec, holdtime 10 sec
  Next hello sent in 0.564
  Virtual IP address is 172.22.1.1 configured
```

```
        Active router is local
        Standby router is 172.22.1.2 expires in 9.848
        Virtual mac address is 0000.0c07.ac01
        5 state changes, last state change 12:47:08
        Priority tracking 1 interface, 1 up:
          Interface                    Decrement  State
          Serial0/0                        20     Up
    Router1#
```

When this interface goes down, causing an HSRP priority change, the router will send several messages to the log buffer:

```
Jun 24 23:24:58: %STANDBY-6-STATECHANGE: FastEthernet0/1 Group 1 state Active ->
Speak
Jun 24 23:25:00: %LINK-3-UPDOWN: Interface Serial0/0, changed state to down
Jun 24 23:25:01: %LINEPROTO-5-UPDOWN: Line protocol on Interface Serial0/0, changed
state to down
```

Notice that the HSRP change happens so quickly that the message actually precedes the *Serial* interface change. This is because the *Serial* interface doesn't send its message immediately when it loses control signals, but the HSRP change does react immediately. Upon repairing the *Serial* interface problem, the router will send several more messages to the log:

```
Jun 24 23:25:07: %STANDBY-6-STATECHANGE: FastEthernet0/1 Group 1 state Standby ->
Active
Jun 24 23:25:08: %LINK-3-UPDOWN: Interface Serial0/0, changed state to up
Jun 24 23:25:09: %LINEPROTO-5-UPDOWN: Line protocol on Interface Serial0/0, changed
state to up
```

Again, the *Serial* interface takes a few seconds to react, but the HSRP change is immediate. This underscores the need for the *preempt delay* command discussed in Recipe 22.2.

The *standby track* command has one other interesting application on routers that run IOS level 12.2(8)T and higher. In these versions you can use the *keepalive* command with GRE tunnels, as discussed in Chapter 12. With this option, GRE tunnels will mimic the behavior of physical interfaces, going into a *down* state if the far end of the tunnel becomes unavailable. This means that you can use *standby track* on a tunnel interface, which in turn means that you can now make your HSRP priority change in response to problems elsewhere in the network.

There were two important bugs with HSRP interface tracking prior to IOS level 12.1. The first happens when you track multiple interfaces. If you do not explicitly configure the priority decrement, the router will only drop the priority by a total of 10 points, no matter how many tracked interfaces fail. And the second is that if the tracked interface is down at boot time, and remains down, HSRP treats it as if it were up. Both of these bugs were fixed in IOS level 12.1.

The following example shows three different methods to track objects using the new method of object tracking. Object 11 tracks the IP routing protocol on interface

---

Serial1/1, object 12 tracks the line-protocol on Serial1/1 and object 13 tracks the reachability of route 172.26.1.0/24:

```
Router1#configure terminal
Enter configuration commands, one per line.  End with CNTL/Z.
Router1(config)#track 11 interface Serial1/1 ip routing
Router1(config-track)#exit
Router1(config)#track 12 interface Serial1/1 line-protocol
Router1(config-track)#exit
Router1(config)#track 13 ip route 172.26.1.0/24 reachability
Router1(config-track)#exit
Router1(config)#interface FastEthernet0/0
Router1(config-if)#standby 1 ip 172.22.1.1
Router1(config-if)#standby 1 priority 120
Router1(config-if)#standby 1 preempt
Router1(config-if)#standby 1 track 11 decrement 50
Router1(config-if)#standby 1 track 12 decrement 50
Router1(config-if)#standby 1 track 13 decrement 50
Router1(config-if)#end
Router1#
```

By tracking the IP routing protocol on an interface, you react to situations in which line-protocol remains up, but you lose routing neighbors or adjacencies. This can be useful on interfaces that may never go into a down/down state, such as ATM sub-interfaces or LAN Extension type interfaces.

Tracking a particular IP route within the router is another useful way of reacting to situations that may occur away from the router itself. This gives you the flexibility to make HSRP react locally to remote problems and to provide optimal routing even in some rather complex failure scenarios.

To view the current status of your tracked objects, use the *show track* command:

```
Router1#show track
Track 11
  Interface Serial1/1 ip routing
  IP routing is Down (hw admin-down, ip disabled)
    1 change, last change 00:12:48
  Tracked by:
    HSRP FastEthernet0/0 1
Track 12
  Interface Serial1/1 line-protocol
  Line protocol is Down (hw admin-down)
    1 change, last change 00:10:12
  Tracked by:
    HSRP FastEthernet0/0 1
Track 13
  IP route 172.26.1.0 255.255.255.0 reachability
  Reachability is Up (static)
    2 changes, last change 00:09:05
  First-hop interface is Serial1/0
  Tracked by:
    HSRP FastEthernet0/0 1
Router1#
```

Notice that object 11 is currently down because IP routing has been disabled. Also, notice that object 12 is down because the tracked interface is in an administrative down state. Finally, object 13 is currently up because the tracked route is currently reachable.

To view the effect of the track objects on HSRP, use the *show standby* command:

```
Router1#show standby
FastEthernet0/0 - Group 1
  State is Active
    2 state changes, last state change 01:28:50
  Virtual IP address is 172.22.1.1
  Active virtual MAC address is 0000.0c07.ac01
    Local virtual MAC address is 0000.0c07.ac01 (v1 default)
  Hello time 3 sec, hold time 10 sec
    Next hello sent in 0.936 secs
  Authentication MD5, key-string "OREILLY"
  Preemption enabled
  Active router is local
  Standby router is unknown
  Priority 20 (configured 120)
    Track object 11 state Down decrement 50
    Track object 12 state Down decrement 50
    Track object 13 state Up decrement 50
  IP redundancy name is "hsrp-Fa0/0-1" (default)
Router1#
```

Notice the currently priority of this HSRP instance is 20. The initial priority level was set to 120. However, because tracked objects 11 and 12 are down, they have each decreased the priority level by 50. You will also notice that, if all three of the tracked objects go down, the total decrement will be 150, which is greater than the initial priority of 120. In this case, the HSRP priority bec omes zero and will not drop any further.

See Also

Recipe 22.2; Chapter 12

22.4   Load-Balancing with HSRP

Problem

You want to load-balance your traffic between two (or more) HSRP routers.

Solution

You can configure HSRP so that both routers are always in use if they are available. This allows you to use your network resources more efficiently, but it is slightly more complicated to configure.

Configure the first router as follows, with two HSRP groups:

```
Router1#configure terminal
Enter configuration commands, one per line.  End with CNTL/Z.
```

```
Router1(config)#interface FastEthernet0/1
Router1(config-if)#ip address 172.22.1.3 255.255.255.0
Router1(config-if)#standby 1 ip 172.22.1.1
Router1(config-if)#standby 1 priority 120
Router1(config-if)#standby 1 preempt
Router1(config-if)#standby 2 ip 172.22.1.2
Router1(config-if)#standby 2 priority 110
Router1(config-if)#standby 2 preempt
Router1(config-if)#exit
Router1(config)#end
Router1#
```

Then, on the second router, you create the same two HSRP groups, but change the priority levels from those of the first router so that Router1 is active for group 1 and Router2 is active for group 2:

```
Router2#configure terminal
Enter configuration commands, one per line.  End with CNTL/Z.
Router2(config)#interface FastEthernet1/0
Router2(config-if)#ip address 172.22.1.4 255.255.255.0
Router2(config-if)#standby 1 ip 172.22.1.1
Router2(config-if)#standby 1 priority 110
Router2(config-if)#standby 1 preempt
Router2(config-if)#standby 2 ip 172.22.1.2
Router2(config-if)#standby 2 priority 120
Router2(config-if)#standby 2 preempt
Router2(config-if)#exit
Router2(config)#end
Router2#
```

This ensures that both router back up one another simultaneously. You must then configure half of your end devices on this segment to use the address 172.22.1.1 for their default gateway, and the other half to use 172.22.1.2.

Discussion

By default, when you use HSRP on a LAN segment, all of the traffic goes through whichever router is currently active. This means that the second router and its links are generally idle. If this is a remote site, and both routers have WAN links, then you will need to pay for an expensive WAN connection that is almost always unused. So this recipe shows you a way to use both routers.

This method only affects the outgoing traffic from the workstations to the routers and out to the WAN. If you want to balance the traffic going from the WAN to the LAN as well, you will need to look at your routing protocol, which determines which WAN connection is the best path to this LAN segment.

The recipe is actually very simple. It just creates two separate HSRP groups on the same segment. When everything is working normally, Router1 is the active router for one of the groups and Router2 is active for the other. Then, if either of these routers fails, the other takes over and becomes the active router for both groups.

This feature uses Multigroup HSRP (MHSRP). Not all routers support MHSRP. In particular, it does not work on Cisco 1600, 2500, 4000, or 5200/5300 devices. For Token Ring LANs, you can use MHSRP, but there are only three available HSRP groups for Token Rings. Other LAN media, such as Ethernet, FDDI, ATM, and various VLAN encapsulations (including LANE, ISL, 802.10, 802.1Q, and EtherChannel) will support 256 groups. Note that you can actually configure more HSRP groups for Token Ring if you use the *use-bia* option. But this means that every group will use the same MAC address. We will discuss this option and its benefits and restrictions in Recipe 22.7.

Once you have configured the routers this way so that they both back one another up, you need to configure the end devices. Half of these devices need to have a default gateway address of 172.22.1.1, and the other half must use 172.22.1.2. Deciding which devices use which address is the key to balancing the load between your routers. If you configure all of your busiest devices to use the same address, and consequently the same router, then you won't have a very well-balanced network load. This is also where the administration starts to become a little bit more complicated because you must decide which gateway each new device will use.

Of course, in a situation where both routers support two or more LAN segments, you could simply make one router primary for one segment and the other one primary for the other segment, instead of configuring two HSRP groups on the same interface. This is considerably simpler to administer, and it works well in larger networks.

The *show standby* command output includes information about both groups. For the first router in the example, you get the following output:

```
Router1#show standby
FastEthernet0/1 - Group 1
  Local state is Active, priority 120, may preempt
  Hellotime 3 sec, holdtime 10 sec
  Next hello sent in 1.184
  Virtual IP address is 172.22.1.1 configured
  Active router is local
  Standby router is 172.22.1.4 expires in 9.164
  Virtual mac address is 0000.0c07.ac01
  17 state changes, last state change 01:14:06
FastEthernet0/1 - Group 2
  Local state is Standby, priority 110, may preempt
  Hellotime 3 sec, holdtime 10 sec
  Next hello sent in 2.394
  Virtual IP address is 172.22.1.2 configured
  Active router is 172.22.1.4, priority 120 expires in 8.892
  Standby router is local
  4 state changes, last state change 00:32:22
Router1#
```

You can see that this router is active for group 1 and in standby for group 2. The same command on the second router shows the converse:

```
Router2#show standby
FastEthernet1/0 - Group 1
```

```
   Local state is Standby, priority 110, may preempt
   Hellotime 3 sec, holdtime 10 sec
   Next hello sent in 0.274
   Virtual IP address is 172.22.1.1 configured
   Active router is 172.22.1.3, priority 120 expires in 9.312
   Standby router is local
   4 state changes, last state change 01:23:46
   IP redundancy name is "hsrp-Fa1/0-1" (default)
FastEthernet1/0 - Group 2
   Local state is Active, priority 120, may preempt
   Hellotime 3 sec, holdtime 10 sec
   Next hello sent in 2.536
   Virtual IP address is 172.22.1.2 configured
   Active router is local
   Standby router is 172.22.1.3 expires in 8.936
   Virtual mac address is 0000.0c07.ac02
   1 state changes, last state change 01:21:49
Router2#
```

Cisco has recently developed a new solution to this same problem, called Gateway Load-Balancing Protocol (GLBP), which allows you to load-balance between several HSRP routers without having to reconfigure the end devieces. Please refer to Recipe 22.14 for more information on this technique.

See Also

Recipe 22.1; Recipe 22.2; Recipe 22.14

22.5   Redirecting ICMP with HSRP

Problem

You want to enable ICMP redirects with HSRP.

Solution

In older IOS releases, when you enable HSRP on an interface, the router will automatically disable ICMP redirection. However, starting with IOS Version 12.1(3)T, Cisco has changed how ICMP redirection works with HSRP, and it is now enabled by default.

You can explicitly enable ICMP redirects on HSRP-enabled interfaces with the following commands:

```
Router2#configure terminal
Enter configuration commands, one per line.   End with CNTL/Z.
Router2(config)#interface FastEthernet 1/0
Router2(config-if)#standby redirects enable
Router2(config-if)#exit
Router2(config)#end
Router2#
```

The following commands prevent the router from the sending ICMP redirects on HSRP-enabled interfaces:

```
Router2#configure terminal
Enter configuration commands, one per line.  End with CNTL/Z.
Router2(config)#interface FastEthernet 1/0
Router2(config-if)#no ip redirects
Router2(config-if)#standby redirects disable
Router2(config-if)#exit
Router2(config)#end
Router2#
```

The *unknown* keyword allows you to use ICMP redirection to nonHSRP routers:

```
Router2#configure terminal
Enter configuration commands, one per line.  End with CNTL/Z.
Router2(config)#interface FastEthernet 1/0
Router2(config-if)#standby redirects unknown
Router2(config-if)#exit
Router2(config)#end
Router2#
```

Discussion

When a router receives a packet from a LAN interface, but the route to the destination points to another router on the same LAN segment, the router will send an ICMP Redirect message. This is a single packet that includes information about the better route for this destination. The router will also forward the original packet over to the other router. When the end device receives the ICMP Redirect packet, it updates its own internal routing table so that all future packets for this destination use the better router.

But ICMP redirection is not usually a good idea with HSRP because it will cause the end device to update its internal routing table to use the real IP address and MAC address of one of the routers when it tries to communicate with a particular remote segment. If this router were to fail, all communication to this remote segment would stop. However, the new functionality resolves this problem by using only the virtual IP and MAC addresses if the other router is running HSRP. If the other router doesn't run HSRP, then it must use the physical addresses, of course.

This also implies that you will never see an ICMP redirect to an HSRP router that is not in the active state, because the standby router doesn't have a virtual MAC address.

22.6   Manipulating HSRP Timers

Problem

You want to decrease the amount of time it takes for the backup router to take over after the primary router fails.

Solution

You can configure HSRP-enabled routers to recover more quickly after the primary HRSP router becomes unavailable with the *standby timers* configuration command:

```
Router1#configure terminal
Enter configuration commands, one per line.  End with CNTL/Z.
Router1(config)#interface FastEthernet0/1
Router1(config-if)#standby 1 ip 172.22.1.1
Router1(config-if)#standby 1 priority 120
Router1(config-if)#standby 1 preempt
Router1(config-if)#standby 1 timers 1 3
Router1(config-if)#exit
Router1(config)#end
Router1#
```

If you change the HSRP timers on one router, then you must change the timers on all of the other routers in the same group:

```
Router2#configure terminal
Enter configuration commands, one per line.  End with CNTL/Z.
Router2(config)#interface FastEthernet1/0
Router2(config-if)#standby 1 ip 172.22.1.1
Router2(config-if)#standby 1 priority 110
Router2(config-if)#standby 1 preempt
Router2(config-if)#standby 1 timers 1 3
Router2(config-if)#exit
Router2(config)#end
Router2#
```

Discussion

By default, a router will send HSRP Hello packets every 3 seconds, and a standby router will declare itself active if it doesn't hear any Hello packets from the active router for 10 seconds. The command in the example changes the timers from these default values to a one-second Hello period and three-second failover:

```
Router1(config-if)#standby 1 timers 1 3
```

With this command, the standby router can reduce the amount of outage time by seven seconds. This might be useful in some highly mission critical networks.

The *show standby* command output includes the timer settings so you can easily see what values the router is using:

```
Router1#show standby
FastEthernet0/1 - Group 1
  Local state is Active, priority 120, may preempt
  Hellotime 1 sec, holdtime 3 sec
  Next hello sent in 0.420
  Virtual IP address is 172.22.1.1 configured
  Active router is local
  Standby router is 172.22.1.2 expires in 2.968
  Virtual mac address is 0000.0c07.ac01
```

```
    5 state changes, last state change 12:50:25
Router1#
```

Decreasing the HSRP Hello interval also increases the amount of background chatter on the network segment. But since HSRP routers exchange these packets using IP multicast, it is relatively efficient. Even if there are many routers in the same group, each packet only appears on the network once. And, unlike broadcasts, these packets shouldn't cause problems for other devices on the segment. So it is unlikely that anybody would want to increase these timers from their default values.

If you need the timers to be faster still, you can configure millisecond intervals:

```
    Router1(config-if)#standby 1 timers msec 100 msec 300
```

With the *msec* keyword, Cisco routers will accept a range of 15 to 999 msec for the Hello interval, and 50 to 3,000 for the hold timer. Without this keyword, the hello interval must be between 1 and 254 seconds, and the hold timer between 2 and 255 seconds.

We caution the reader to be extremely careful with these millisecond timings. They can cause two potential problems. If the timers are too short, for example, if you set the Hello timer to 15 milliseconds on a busy 4 Mbps Token Ring, you could cause congestion problems on the ring. The second problem to watch out for is using a timer that is too short for the network to reliably deliver. For example, if your LAN includes any bridges (including ATM LAN extensions) to remote sites, you may get spurious transitions just caused by random variation in latencies (jitter).

The HSRP RFC states that the hold time should be at least three times the value of the hello time and MUST be greater then the hello time. Setting your hold time to three times the hello time is a good rule of thumb. This allows the router to miss two packets due to congestion or random noise without disrupting the way the network functions.

22.7   Using HSRP on Token Ring

Problem

You want to configure HSRP on a Token Ring.

Solution

You can use HSRP on a Token Ring LAN exactly the same as in Recipe 22.1 if the only protocol on the segment is IP. However, if you have any other protocols, and particularly if the ring uses any source-route bridging, you must use a slightly different configuration:

```
Router1#configure terminal
Enter configuration commands, one per line.  End with CNTL/Z.
Router1(config)#interface Tokenring0
Router1(config-if)#ip address 172.22.1.3
```

```
Router1(config-if)#standby ip 172.22.1.1
Router1(config-if)#standby use-bia
Router1(config-if)#standby priority 120
Router1(config-if)#standby preempt
Router1(config-if)#exit
Router1(config)#end
Router1#
```

The second router is configured similarly:

```
Router2#configure terminal
Enter configuration commands, one per line.  End with CNTL/Z.
Router2(config)#interface Tokenring0
Router2(config-if)#ip address 172.22.1.2
Router2(config-if)#standby ip 172.22.1.1
Router2(config-if)#standby use-bia
Router2(config-if)#standby priority 110
Router2(config-if)#standby preempt
Router2(config-if)#exit
Router2(config)#end
Router2#
```

Discussion

The biggest functional difference between a Token Ring LAN and an Ethernet LAN is that Token Ring bridging is usually *source-routed*, while Ethernet almost always uses *transparent bridging*. Consequently, Token Ring devices use a Routing Information Field (RIF), which contains MAC address information.

This is particularly important when the two HSRP routers reside on different physical rings connected by a bridge, as in a switched Token Ring environment, for example. In this case, when HSRP changes the active router, the bridges will see the virtual MAC address suddenly jump from one ring to another, which will disrupt the RIF tables in every bridge.

So, when using HSRP in Token Ring environments, it is usually best to just use the router's burned-in address (BIA) instead of a virtual MAC address. Then HSRP will rely on gratuitous ARP packets to update the ARP cache of every device on the ring, and tell it that the default gateway router has changed.

The key command in this configuration is the *use-bia* command, which appears on both routers:

```
Router1(config-if)#standby use-bia
```

In this case, we are using standby group 0 because we didn't specify a group number, so the virtual MAC address would have been C0-00-00-01-00-00 if we had not changed it to the BIA. The output of a show standby command shows the address that the router is actually using:

```
Router1#show standby
TokenRing0 - Group 0
  Local state is Active, priority 120, may preempt, use bia
```

```
        Hellotime 3 holdtime 10
        Next hello sent in 00:00:02.338
        Hot standby IP address is 172.22.1.1 configured
        Active router is local
        Standby router is 172.22.1.3 expires in 00:00:09
        Standby virtual mac address is 0000.300f.2186
    Router1#
```

We chose to use standby group 0 in this example because, prior to IOS level 12.0(3.4)T, you could only use this feature with group 0. In newer IOS levels, however, this feature is available for all Token Ring HSRP groups. Without this option, there are only three HSRP groups available. With it, you can configure up to 255 groups, all of which will use the same BIA MAC address.

The *use-bia* option can also be useful in nonToken-Ring environments. Networks that use DECnet or Xerox Network Services (XNS) frequently encounter MAC address problems as well, even on Ethernet LANs. This is because devices that run both protocols will see two different MAC addresses for the same destination device, which causes confusion. So in these types of environments, we recommend using the burned-in address as well.

You should be aware of two important limitations to this command. First, and most importantly, when you use this option, HSRP must rely on gratuitous ARP to tell end devices that the MAC address of the default gateway has changed. However, some devices do not handle gratuitous ARP packets well. In some implementations, a device will only update its ARP cache if it receives an ARP packet in response to a specific ARP request.

The second limitation is that this option completely breaks Proxy ARP. This is because the end devices believe that the remote IP address is associated with the MAC address of the primary HSRP router. However, the backup router has no way of knowing which remote IP addresses the primary router has sent out Proxy ARP messages for. So it can't update these entries to tell the end devices to use the new MAC address instead.

We know of no workarounds for either of these problems. So please use caution when implementing this feature.

See Also

Recipe 22.1; Recipe 22.2

22.8   HSRP SNMP Support

Problem

You want to enable HSRP SNMP traps.

Solution

Cisco has developed an HSRP SNMP MIB to help manage routers using this feature. You can configure your router to send an SNMP trap every time the routers make an HSRP state change:

```
Router1#configure terminal
Enter configuration commands, one per line.  End with CNTL/Z.
Router1(config)#snmp-server enable traps hsrp
Router1(config)#snmp-server host 172.25.1.1 ORATRAP
Router1(config)#end
Router1#
```

Discussion

Usually when a router changes its HSRP state, this indicates that some sort of network problem has occurred. If you are tracking interfaces as in Recipe 22.3, then the problem may be that the WAN interface on the primary router has failed. In this case, you will almost certainly also receive a Link-Down trap from the primary router, as well as a trap indicating that the primary has become inactive and the secondary router has become active.

In some cases, it can be extremely useful to receive these traps. For example, the primary router's power supplies may have suddenly failed. In this case, the first indication you may get that there has been a problem will be the next time your network management system tries to poll the primary router. Clearly, there are cases when you want to know about the change sooner than that. So having the secondary router to send a trap to indicate the change of HSRP state may be the fastest way to get this information.

These traps can also be useful if there is something wrong with your HSRP setup, so that the two routers are continually flipping back and forth between active and standby states. As long as the traffic continues to flow, you may not otherwise know that there is a problem. This could happen, for example, if you set the HSRP timers improperly.

Cisco's HSRP MIB also allows you to use SNMP to query the routers for their current HSRP state information. Please refer to Chapter 17 for more information about using SNMP.

See Also

Recipe 22.3; Recipe 22.6; Chapter 17

22.9   Increasing HSRP Security

Problem

You want to increase the Security of HSRP between two (or more) routers.

Solution

You can configure HSRP to use password authentication with the following commands:

```
Router1#configure terminal
Enter configuration commands, one per line.  End with CNTL/Z.
Router1(config)#interface FastEthernet 0/1
Router1(config-if)#standby 1 ip 172.22.1.1
Router1(config-if)#standby 1 priority 120
Router1(config-if)#standby 1 authentication OREILLY
Router1(config-if)#exit
Router1(config)#end
Router1#
```

You must configure the same authentication password on all routers within the same HSRP group or the conflicts will prevent HSRP from working:

```
Router2#configure terminal
Enter configuration commands, one per line.  End with CNTL/Z.
Router2(config)#interface FastEthernet 1/0
Router2(config-if)#standby 1 ip 172.22.1.1
Router2(config-if)#standby 1 priority 110
Router2(config-if)#standby 1 authentication OREILLY
Router2(config-if)#exit
Router2(config)#end
Router2#
```

Beginning with IOS Version 12.3(2)T, Cisco introduced support for MD5-encrypted passwords. To configure strong MD5-encrypted passwords, use the following commands:

```
Router1#configure terminal
Enter configuration commands, one per line.  End with CNTL/Z.
Router1(config)#interface FastEthernet0/1
Router1(config-if)#standby 1 ip 10.1.1.1
Router1(config-if)#standby 1 priority 200
Router1(config-if)#standby 1 authentication md5 key-string OREILLY
Router1(config-if)#end
Router1#
```

You must also configure the same password and encryption type on all routers within the same HSRP group, or conflicts will prevent them from working:

```
Router2#configure terminal
Enter configuration commands, one per line.  End with CNTL/Z.
Router2(config)#interface FastEthernet0/0
Router2(config-if)#standby 1 ip 10.1.1.1
Router2(config-if)#standby 1 priority 150
Router2(config-if)#standby 1 authentication md5 key-string OREILLY
Router2(config-if)#end
Router2#
```

To prevent any other routers from becoming active, set the primary router's priority to the highest possible value, 255:

```
Router1#configure terminal
Enter configuration commands, one per line.  End with CNTL/Z.
Router1(config)#interface FastEthernet 0/1
Router1(config-if)#standby 1 ip 172.22.1.1
Router1(config-if)#standby 1 priority 255
Router1(config-if)#exit
Router1(config)#end
Router1#
```

Then you can configure the standby router to use a slightly lower priority number:

```
Router2#configure terminal
Enter configuration commands, one per line.  End with CNTL/Z.
Router2(config)#interface FastEthernet 1/0
Router2(config-if)#standby 1 ip 172.22.1.1
Router2(config-if)#standby 1 priority 254
Router2(config-if)#exit
Router2(config)#end
Router2#
```

This will help to ensure that no other routers that might be on this segment can take over because of an HSRP Coup.

Discussion

HSRP is not a terribly secure protocol, even with the precautions shown in this recipe. This is usually not a problem, however, because most network engineers only use it on internal trusted LAN segments.

HSRP has two main security-related problems. The first is simply caused by incorrect router configuration. It is possible to cause serious routing problems if more than one router is active, if no routers are active on a segment, or if the wrong router becomes active. The second potential security problem is that a hostile user can configure a device, such as another Cisco router, to take over as the HSRP active router. They might use this to capture and examine packets that they would not otherwise see in a switched LAN, to route packets to a different network, or they might just want to cause a simple denial of service. However, because HSRP uses the locally scoped multicast address 224.0.0.2, with a TTL of 1, it is extremely unlikely that anybody could launch an effective HSRP attack if they were not physically connected to this LAN segment.

You can use HSRP authentication to help prevent misconfigured routers from becoming active on a production LAN. The routers send the authentication password through the network in clear text (that is, not encrypted), using IP multicast, so it is relatively easy for any device on the LAN segment to determine this password.

The following is an HSRP hello packet that was captured using Ethereal:

```
Cisco Hot Standby Router Protocol
    Version: 0
    Op Code: Hello (0)
    State: Active (16)
```

```
Hellotime: Default (3)
Holdtime: Default (10)
Priority: 120
Group: 1
Reserved: 0
Authentication Data: Non-Default (OREILLY)
Virtual IP Address: 172.22.1.1
```

Notice that all of the important HSRP information, including timers, priorities, the group number, and even the virtual IP address, are readily available to anybody who captures HSRP packets on their local LAN segment. This illustrates both how insecure HSRP is by default and how easy it would be to create a false HSRP device to maliciously disrupt LAN communication.

The biggest problem with HSRP authentication, and the reason why you may decide not to use it, appears when the passwords on two routers in the same group do not agree. The two routers have no particular way of knowing which password is correct, so they both assume that the other is wrong. This can cause both routers to become active, which is not at all desirable. So this feature is not a very good way of preventing a malicious user from taking over control of the gateway.

If HSRP routers in the same group are configured with different authentication passwords, you will see the following messages in their logs:

```
Jun 25 11:00:15: %STANDBY-3-BADAUTH: Bad authentication from 172.22.1.4, group 1,
remote state Standby
```

Cisco intends for this feature to be used to prevent other routers from learning HSRP parameters, such as the virtual IP address and timer information. However we don't generally advise using it to address real security requirements.

You can use the *show standby* command to verify your HSRP authentication information:

```
Router1#show standby
FastEthernet0/1 - Group 1
  Local state is Active, priority 120, may preempt
  Hellotime 1 sec, holdtime 3 sec
  Next hello sent in 0.754
  Virtual IP address is 172.22.1.1 configured
  Active router is local
  Standby router is 172.22.1.2 expires in 2.824
  Virtual mac address is 0000.0c07.ac01
  Authentication text "OREILLY"
  5 state changes, last state change 12:56:36
Router1#
```

The use of the MD5-encrypted passwords prevents people from snooping your HSRP password and offers a greater level of security. We highly recommend using MD5 password authentication over the traditional clear text passwords whenever possible. Keep in mind that all routers participating in the same HSRP group must support MD5 password encryption in order to work. What's more, a mixture of MD5 and clear text passwords will not work either, even if the participating routers use the same password.

To show which password authentication method is currently configured; use the *show standby* command to view the current status:

```
Router1#show standby
FastEthernet0/1 - Group 1
  State is Active
    2 state changes, last state change 00:00:03
  Virtual IP address is 10.1.1.1
  Active virtual MAC address is 0000.0c07.ac01
    Local virtual MAC address is 0000.0c07.ac01 (v1 default)
  Hello time 3 sec, hold time 10 sec
    Next hello sent in 2.372 secs
  Authentication MD5, key-string "OREILLY"
  Preemption disabled
  Active router is local
  Standby router is unknown
  Priority 100 (default 100)
  IP redundancy name is "hsrp-Fa0/1-1" (default)
Router1#
```

Notice that Router1 has been configured to use MD5 authentication and the password has been set to "OREILLY".

The last example in the Solution section to this recipe shows how to configure your router to avoid another type of attack. A rogue user could configure a router with a higher priority than the current active router. This would cause an HSRP Coup, and the rogue router would be able to take over as the active router. This illegitimate router could then freely manipulate routing for this segment.

You can partially guard against this scenario by setting your primary router to the highest possible priority level. This should prevent a rogue router from forcing a priority election. However, recall that when two routers have the same HSRP priority, the one with the higher physical IP address will win the election. So, if you have good reason to be concerned about this type of attack, we recommend using the highest possible IP addresses on the segment for your physical IP addresses, as well as the highest possible priorities.

The output of this *show standby* command highlights the priority value:

```
Router1#show standby
FastEthernet0/1 - Group 1
  Local state is Active, priority 255, may preempt
  Hellotime 1 sec, holdtime 3 sec
  Next hello sent in 0.436
  Virtual IP address is 172.22.1.1 configured
  Active router is local
  Standby router is 172.22.1.2 expires in 2.508
  Virtual mac address is 0000.0c07.ac01
  Authentication text "OREILLY"
```

```
    5 state changes, last state change 13:00:48
  Router1#
```

See Also

Recipe 22.1; Chapter 12

22.10 Showing HSRP State Information

Problem

You want to see current HSRP information, such as which router is primary.

Solution

To view the HSRP information, use the following EXEC command:

```
Router2#show standby
```

You can view the HSRP information for a specific interface with the following EXEC command:

```
Router2#show standby FastEthernet 1/0
```

Use the keyword *brief* to show an overview of HSRP information:

```
Router2#show standby brief
```

Discussion

The basic *show standby* command without any additional keywords displays all of the HSRP information for all groups and interfaces on the router:

```
Router2#show standby
FastEthernet1/0 - Group 1
  Local state is Standby, priority 110, may preempt
  Hellotime 1 sec, holdtime 3 sec
  Next hello sent in 0.536
  Virtual IP address is 172.22.1.1 configured
  Active router is 172.22.1.3, priority 255 expires in 2.380
  Standby router is local
  Authentication text "OREILLY"
  1 state changes, last state change 15:43:34
  IP redundancy name is "hsrp-Fa1/0-1" (default)
Router2#
```

If your router runs HSRP on several interfaces, you might want to just look at the HSRP status for a particular interface:

```
Router2#show standby FastEthernet 1/0
FastEthernet1/0 - Group 1
  Local state is Standby, priority 110, may preempt
  Hellotime 1 sec, holdtime 3 sec
  Next hello sent in 0.036
```

```
        Virtual IP address is 172.22.1.1 configured
        Active router is 172.22.1.3, priority 255 expires in 2.796
        Standby router is local
        Authentication text "OREILLY"
        1 state changes, last state change 15:47:44
        IP redundancy name is "hsrp-Fa1/0-1" (default)
Router2#
```

The *show standby brief* command is particularly useful when you have many HSRP interfaces or groups. This command presents all of the most important information for each group on a single line:

```
Router2#show standby brief
                     P indicates configured to preempt.
                     |
Interface  Grp Prio P State   Active addr   Standby addr   Group addr
Fa1/0      1   110  P Standby 172.22.1.3    local          172.22.1.1
Fa1/0      2   120  P Active  local         172.22.1.3     172.22.1.2
Router2#
```

22.11 Debugging HSRP

Problem

You want to debug an HSRP problem.

Solution

To debug all HSRP error events, use the following command:

```
Router2#debug standby errors
```

The *events* keyword will display information about HSRP events:

```
Router2#debug standby events
```

With the *packets* keyword, you can look at the contents of all HSRP packets:

```
Router2#debug standby packets
```

You can use the *terse* keyword to see a short form of all HSRP errors, events, and packets:

```
Router2#debug standby terse
```

Discussion

HSRP is not a very complex protocol, and it is relatively simple to configure, so network engineers generally don't find that they need sophisticated debugging tools that are available with other protocols. Consequently, HSRP debugging facilities were relatively limited until IOS level 12.1(0.2), when the enhanced debugging described here was introduced. However, these features can be useful when you are faced with strange HSRP problems, such as general instability or multiple active routers.

We don't recommend starting with a packet level debug for anything because it can easily overwhelm the router. In the case of HSRP, which should only send a Hello packet every three seconds by default, this shouldn't be quite as dangerous as for many other protocols.

The *debug standby terse* command is probably the most useful option because it gives a short form output of all HSRP errors, events, and packets:

```
Router1#debug standby terse
HSRP:
  HSRP Errors debugging is on
  HSRP Events debugging is on
    (protocol, redundancy, track)
  HSRP Packets debugging is on
    (Coup, Resign)
Router1#
```

From here, if you see a Coup problem, for example, you might want to turn off the *terse* option and replace it with a full packet-level debug. Conversely, if you see that there is an issue with interface tracking, you might want to replace the *terse* option with the *event* option to get greater detail.

22.12 HSRP Version 2

Problem

You want to implement HSRP Version 2.

Solution

To enable HSRP Version 2, use the *standby version 2* configuration command:

```
Router1#configure terminal
Enter configuration commands, one per line.  End with CNTL/Z.
Router1(config)#interface FastEthernet0/1
Router1(config-if)#standby version 2
Router1(config-if)#standby 4095 ip 10.1.1.1
Router1(config-if)#standby 4095 timers msec 15 msec 50
Router1(config-if)#standby 4095 priority 200
Router1(config-if)#standby 4095 preempt
Router1(config-if)#end
Router1#
```

You must also configure every router that participates in the same HSRP group with the same version number:

```
Router2#configure terminal
Enter configuration commands, one per line.  End with CNTL/Z.
Router2(config)#interface FastEthernet0/0
Router2(config-if)#standby version 2
Router2(config-if)#standby 4095 ip 10.1.1.1
Router2(config-if)#standby 4095 timers msec 15 msec 50
```

```
Router2(config-if)#standby 4095 priority 150
Router2(config-if)#standby 4095 preempt
Router2(config-if)#end
Router2#
```

 Cisco added support for HSRP Version 2, beginning with IOS Version 12.3(4)T.

Discussion

Fortunately, all of the HSRP commands remain the same from Version 1, with one noticeable difference, the expanded HSRP group numbering range. As you recall from Recipe 22.1, HSRP Version 1 only supported 256 groups ranging from 0 to 255. One of the enhancements of HSRP Version 2 is the expanded group numbering, which ranges from 0 to 4,095. This enhancement allows you to match HSRP group numbers to VLAN numbers on Subinterfaces.

With the exception of the expanded HSRP group numbering, all of the previous HSRP commands remain valid. In fact, the router will default to HSRP Version 1 unless you explicitly configure the router to use Version 2. To upgrade to HSRP Version 2 you need only implement a single command, *standby version 2*.

 HSRP Version 1 and Version 2 are not interoperable. You cannot run both HSRP versions on a single interface; however, you can run different versions on different physical interfaces within the same router.

Also, since HSRP Version 1 and Version 2 use completely different virtual MAC addresses and IP multicast addresses, they will not communicate with one another, even if configured to use the same HSRP group number on the same network segment.

To view the current HSRP configuration, use the *show standby* command:

```
Router1#show standby
FastEthernet0/1 - Group 4095 (version 2)
  State is Active
    2 state changes, last state change 00:11:47
  Virtual IP address is 10.1.1.1
  Active virtual MAC address is 0000.0c9f.ffff
    Local virtual MAC address is 0000.0c9f.ffff (v2 default)
  Hello time 15 msec, hold time 50 msec
    Next hello sent in 0.007 secs
  Preemption enabled
  Active router is local
  Standby router is 10.1.1.3, priority 150 (expires in 0.030 sec)
  Priority 200 (configured 200)
  IP redundancy name is "hsrp-Fa0/1-4095" (default)
Router1#
```

Notice that Router1 is configured to use HSRP Version 2 as highlighted, and also notice the HSRP Version 2 virtual MAC address of 0000.0c9f.ffff.

We note in passing that although you can readily change from Version 1 to Version 2, you won't be permitted to change from Version 2 to Version 1 if you use one of the expanded group numbers. Since Version 1 only supports up to group number 255, the router will not permit you to change the version number if the group number exceeds 255. In the following example, we attempt to change back to Version 1; however, the router has been configured to use group 4,095:

```
Router1#configure terminal
Enter configuration commands, one per line.  End with CNTL/Z.
Router1(config)#standby version 1
                             ^
% Invalid input detected at '^' marker.

Router1(config)#end
Router1#
```

See the introduction of this chapter for more information about HSRP Version 2.

See Also

Introduction; Recipe 22.3

22.13 VRRP

Problem

You want to implement VRRP on your Cisco router.

Solution

To configure Router1 to be the Master VRRP router, use the following set of commands and assign a higher priority level:

```
Router1#configure terminal
Enter configuration commands, one per line.  End with CNTL/Z.
Router1(config)#interface FastEthernet0/1
Router1(config-if)#ip address 10.1.1.2 255.255.255.0
Router1(config-if)#vrrp 1 ip 10.1.1.1
Router1(config-if)#vrrp 1 preempt
Router1(config-if)#vrrp 1 priority 200
Router1(config-if)#end
Router1#
```

The configuration of the Backup VRRP router is identical, except the priority is set to a lower level:

```
Router2#configure terminal
Enter configuration commands, one per line.  End with CNTL/Z.
Router2(config)#interface FastEthernet0/0
Router2(config-if)#ip address 10.1.1.3 255.255.255.0
Router2(config-if)#vrrp 1 ip 10.1.1.1
Router2(config-if)#vrrp 1 preempt
```

```
Router2(config-if)#vrrp 1 priority 150
Router2(config-if)#end
Router2#
```

Discussion

The VRRP configuration commands are very similar to the HSRP commands, which makes configuring VRRP quite easy if you're already familiar with HSRP. One noticeable difference is that the VRRP group numbers range from 1 to 255, instead of 0 to 255 (or 0 to 4,095 for HSRP Version 2), and you must supply a group number.

Another interesting difference is the way you modify the timers for VRRP. You are only allowed to modify the hello timer. The hold timer is calculated automatically:

```
Router1(config-if)#vrrp 1 timers advertise 2
```

By default, the hello timer is set to one second, and all routers within a particular VRRP group must use the same timer values. If not, then the VRRP routers within the group will not communicate with one another. The valid timer range is from 1 second to 255 seconds unless the *msec* keyword is used—then the valid timer range is between 50 to 999 milliseconds:

```
Router1(config-if)#vrrp 1 timers advertise msec 50
```

One cool little VRRP feature is the ability to learn the configured timer interval from the master virtual router. By using the *learn* keyword, the backup virtual router will calculate its hello timer from its master advertisements:

```
Router1(config-if)#vrrp 1 timers learn
```

VRRP also supports authentication in the form of clear text passwords or MD5-encrypted passwords. The following is an example of how to configure clear text-based authentication:

```
Router1(config-if)#vrrp 1 authentication OREILLY
```

Even though MD5-encrypted passwords offer a much greater level of security, not all implementations support this feature because the RFC does not include MD5-encrypted authentication:

```
Router1(config-if)#vrrp 1 authentication md5 key-string OREILLY
```

One nice feature is the ability to add a description of each VRRP group. It allows you to add useful information about the VRRP group directly within the configuration and show commands.

```
Router1(config-if)#vrrp 1 description VRRP example for Cisco Cookbook
```

VRRP also allows you to track other objects and adjust VRRP priority levels according to tracked objects. In the following example, we track the presence of IP routing on interface *Serial1/0* and the line-protocol status on interface *Serial1/1*:

```
Router1#configure terminal
Enter configuration commands, one per line.  End with CNTL/Z.
```

```
Router1(config)#track 77 interface Serial1/0 ip routing
Router1(config-track)#exit
Router1(config)#track 88 interface Serial1/1 line-protocol
Router1(config-track)#exit
Router1(config)#interface FastEthernet0/1
Router1(config-if)#vrrp 1 track 77 decrement 100
Router1(config-if)#vrrp 1 track 88 decrement 100
Router1(config-if)#end
Router1#
```

For more information on object tracking, see Recipe 22.3.

To view the status of your VRRP configuration, use the *show vrrp* command:

```
Router1#show vrrp
FastEthernet0/1 - Group 1
  State is Backup
  Virtual IP address is 10.1.1.1
  Virtual MAC address is 0000.5e00.0101
  Advertisement interval is 2.000 sec
  Preemption enabled
  Priority is 0   (cfgd 200)
    Track object 77 state Down decrement 100
    Track object 88 state Down decrement 100
  Authentication MD5, key-string "oreilly"
  Master Router is 10.1.1.3, priority is 75
  Master Advertisement interval is 2.000 sec
  Master Down interval is 6.218 sec (expires in 6.166 sec) Learning

Router1#
```

VRRP is an open standard that is implemented by many vendors. So at least in theory, you can use VRRP to share a virtual IP address with a nonCisco device. However, we urge some caution in doing this. In particular, the authentication features implemented by Cisco may not interoperate well with nonCisco equipment.

See Also

Recipe 22.3

22.14 Gateway Load-Balancing Protocol

Problem

You want to use a first hop redundancy protocol that automatically load-balances among the participating routers.

Solution

You configure GLBP on an interface using the *glbp* command:

```
Router1#configure terminal
Enter configuration commands, one per line.  End with CNTL/Z.
```

```
Router1(config)#interface FastEthernet0/0
Router1(config-if)#ip address 172.22.1.3 255.255.255.0
Router1(config-if)#glbp 1 ip 172.22.1.1
Router1(config-if)#exit
Router1(config)#end
Router1#
```

As with HSRP and VRRP, you must configure other members of the same GLBP group to use the same virtual IP address:

```
Router2#configure terminal
Enter configuration commands, one per line.  End with CNTL/Z.
Router2(config)#interface FastEthernet0/0
Router2(config-if)#ip address 172.22.1.2 255.255.255.0
Router2(config-if)#glbp 1 ip 172.22.1.1
Router2(config-if)#exit
Router2(config)#end
Router2#
```

Discussion

In Recipe 22.4, we showed a way of using HSRP to load-balance between two active redundant routers on a LAN segment. There are two reasons why this solution was somewhat less than ideal, though. First, it required configuring different default gateway addresses on half of the end devices on a LAN segment. And second, the load balancing must be done by hand and is completely static. GLBP provides a much more elegant solution to the same problem that doesn't have these shortcomings.

In the examples, we have enabled GLBP with a single command, simply defining the group number and virtual IP address:

```
Router1(config-if)#glbp 1 ip 172.22.1.1
```

This makes the router into an Active Virtual Forwarder (AVF) for group number 1. The AVF routers will elect an Active Virtual Gateway (AVG), which will manage the functioning of the group. The AVG distributes MAC address to AVFs. The AVG also responds to ARP requests for the virtual IP address, including one of the AVF MAC addresses in the response. In this way, every ARP request gets a single unique response, but different devices on the network segment still wind up using different routers.

GLBP has 1,024 possible group numbers, ranging from 0 through 1,023. Unlike HSRP, though, you cannot leave out the group number to accept a default value.

You can look at GLBP status on a router by using the *show glbp* command:

```
Router1#show glbp
  State is Active
    4 state changes, last state change 01:55:47
  Virtual IP address is 172.22.1.1
  Hello time 3 sec, hold time 10 sec
    Next hello sent in 2.912 secs
  Redirect time 600 sec, forwarder time-out 14400 sec
  Preemption disabled
```

```
        Active is local
        Standby is 172.22.1.2, priority 100 (expires in 7.912 sec)
        Priority 100 (default)
        Weighting 100 (default 100), thresholds: lower 1, upper 100
        Load balancing: round-robin
        There are 2 forwarders (1 active)
        Forwarder 1
          State is Listen
            6 state changes, last state change 00:00:42
          MAC address is 0007.b400.0101 (learnt)
          Owner ID is 000e.d7d6.4d80
          Redirection enabled, 597.908 sec remaining (maximum 600 sec)
          Time to live: 14397.908 sec (maximum 14400 sec)
          Preemption enabled, min delay 30 sec
          Active is 172.22.1.2 (primary), weighting 100 (expires in 7.908 sec)
          Arp replies sent: 6
        Forwarder 2
          State is Active
            3 state changes, last state change 01:56:18
          MAC address is 0007.b400.0102 (default)
          Owner ID is 000e.d7d6.1060
          Redirection enabled
          Preemption enabled, min delay 30 sec
          Active is local, weighting 100
          Arp replies sent: 5
      Router1#
```

There is a lot of information in this output, but you rarely need all of it. Most of the time you just want to know about which routers are active and what MAC addresses they are using. Fortunately, you can add the *brief* keyword to see only these details:

```
Router1#show glbp brief
Interface   Grp  Fwd Pri State    Address          Active router   Standby router

Fa0/0       1    -   100 Active   172.22.1.1       local           172.22.1.2

Fa0/0       1    1   7   Listen   0007.b400.0101   172.22.1.2      -
Fa0/0       1    2   7   Active   0007.b400.0102   local           -
Router1#
```

The first line in this output, after the column header information, describes the AVG for the group. In the example, this router is the AVG (local), and the router whose physical IP address is 172.22.1.2 is the backup AVG, should this one fail.

The other two lines show the AVFs for the group. We see that the other router, the one with physical IP address 172.22.1.2, is using the MAC address 0007.b400.0101, and that this router is in an active state and is using a MAC address of 0007.b400.0102.

The word in the second line, Listen, is potentially confusing because it doesn't mean that the other router is in a Listen state. It actually means that this router is in a Listen state for this MAC address. If the other router becomes unavailable, this one will take over its MAC address, in addition to the one that it is already using.

You can configure priorities and preemption with GLBP in exactly the same way as HSRP:

```
Router2(config)#interface FastEthernet0/0
Router2(config-if)#ip address 172.22.1.2 255.255.255.0
Router2(config-if)#glbp 1 ip 172.22.1.1
Router2(config-if)#glbp 1 priority 120
Router2(config-if)#glbp 1 preempt
```

These commands only affect AVG election, though, so they are less critical than we previously saw for HSRP or VRRP. It usually doesn't matter so much which router is the AVG, because all of the routers are forwarding.

More importantly, though, you can configure authentication. Until IOS Version 12.3(2)T, only text authentication was available:

```
Router1(config)#interface FastEthernet0/0
Router1(config-if)#glbp 1 authentication text COOKBOOK
```

Starting in 12.3(2)T, you can use the considerably more secure MD5 algorithm to encrypt your GLBP authentication keys:

```
Router1(config)#interface FastEthernet0/0
Router1(config-if)#glbp 1 authentication md5 key-string 0 OREILLY
```

Cisco offers three different load-balancing algorithms for use with GLBP:

```
Router1(config)#interface FastEthernet0/0
Router1(config-if)#glbp 1 load-balancing ?
  host-dependent  Load balance equally, source MAC determines forwarder choice
  round-robin     Load balance equally using each forwarder in turn
  weighted        Load balance in proportion to forwarder weighting
  <cr>

Router1(config-if)#
```

The default load-balancing method is *round-robin*, which means that the AVG will simply alternate among the AVF MACs. Each time it receives an ARP request for the virtual IP address, the AVG will respond with the MAC of the next AVF.

The *host-dependent* keyword means that the AVG will base the selection of AVF on the MAC address of the device sending the ARP request. In this way, as long as the number of AVF devices in the group remains constant, each end device will always see the same MAC address in response to its ARP request. This is useful if you have problems with updating ARP tables properly on some of the devices on a segment.

Finally, the *weighted* keyword means that the AVG will respond to ARP requests according to a weighting factor. So if one of the routers in the GLBP group is connected to a faster link than the others, you could give it a higher weighting. This will cause the AVG to use the corresponding MAC address in ARP responses more often, allowing you to utilize the faster link more effectively.

You can adjust the weight factors for different AVF routers by using the *weighting* keyword. This allows you to set a static weight value as follows:

```
Router1(config)#interface FastEthernet0/0
Router1(config-if)#glbp 1 weight 150
```

The default weighting is 100, and you can specify any value between 1 and 254. Suppose, for example, that you have two AVFs, one with the default weighting of 100 and the other with a weight of 150. Then the AVG will give out the MAC address of the AVF with the higher weight three times for every two times it uses the one with the default weight.

Alternatively, you can make the weighting factor track other objects or interfaces by using the track command:

```
Router1(config)#interface FastEthernet0/0
Router1(config-if)#glbp 1 weight 10 decrement 25
Router1(config-if)#exit
Router1(config)#track 10 interface Serial0/0 ip routing
Router1(config-track)#exit
```

By default, the weighting factor will decrement by 10 when the tracked object changes state. In this example, however, we have changed this default decrement value to 25.

Please refer to Recipe 22.3 for more information on the *track* command.

See Also

Recipe 22.3; Recipe 22.4

## CHAPTER 23

IP Multicast

23.0 Introduction

Multicast routing differs from unicast routing in several ways. The most important differences are in the ways that multicast routers use source and destination addresses. A multicast packet is addressed to a special IP address representing a group of devices that can be scattered anywhere throughout a network. Since the destinations can be anywhere, the only reliable way to eliminate loops in multicast routing is to look at the reverse path back to the source. So, while unicast routing cares where the packet is going, multicast routing also needs to know where it came from.

For this reason, multicast routing protocols such as Protocol Independent Multicast (PIM) always work with the source address and destination group simultaneously. The usual notation for a multicast route is *(Source, Group)*, as opposed to the unicast case in which routes are defined by the destination address alone. We have already mentioned that this is necessary for avoiding loops, but the router also needs to keep track of both source and group addresses in each multicast routing table entry because there could be several sources for the same group.

For example, in the NTP chapter, we discussed how a central device can be configured to send time synchronization information as a multicast. In that chapter, we also explained why it was important to have more than one NTP server. So even in a simple multicast example like this, it is quite likely that the routers will need to forward packets to the same set of end devices from two sources that may be on different network segments. The group address alone doesn't tell you enough about how to forward packets belonging to this group.

When you look at the multicast routing table with the *show ip mroute* command, you will see not only *(Source, Group)* pairs like (192.168.15.35, 239.5.5.55), but also pairs that look like (*, 239.5.5.55). This means that the source is unspecified. Cisco routers organize their multicast routing tables with a parent *(*, Group)* for each group, and any number of *(Source, Group)* pairs under it. If there is a *(*, Group)* but no *(Source, Group)* entries for a group, then that just means that the router knows of group members but doesn't yet know where to expect this multicast traffic from.

Each of these *(Source, Group)* entries represents a Shortest Path Tree (SPT) that leads to the source of the multicast traffic. In sparse mode multicast routing, the root of the tree could actually be a central Rendezvous Point (RP) router rather than the actual traffic source. Because each router must know about the path back to the source or RP, the term Reverse Path Forwarding (RPF) is often used to describe the process of building the SPT.

Two important elements are required for a multicast network to work. The first we've already mentioned: you need a way to route multicast packets from the source to all of the various destinations in the group. The other critical element is that the multicast network has to provide a way for end devices to subscribe to a multicast group so that they can receive the data. The network uses the Internet Group Management Protocol (IGMP) to manage group subscriptions.

IGMP and CGMP

Internet Group Management Protocol (IGMP) functions mainly at Layer 3. Individual end devices use IGMP to announce that they wish to join a particular multicast group. The IGMP request is picked up by a router that then attempts to fulfill the request by forwarding the multicast data stream to the network containing this device. The IGMP protocol is in its third version, which is defined in RFC 3376. However, many devices still use IGMP Version 2 (RFC 2236), and some only support Version 1 (RFC 1112).

What IGMP does is relatively simple in concept. It provides a method for end devices to join and leave multicast groups. Here is the output of *tcpdump* showing the device 192.168.1.104 joining the group 239.5.5.55:

```
17:10:16.397055 192.168.1.104 > 239.5.5.55: igmp nreport 239.5.5.55 (DF) [ttl 1]
17:10:19.276998 192.168.1.104 > 239.5.5.55: igmp nreport 239.5.5.55 (DF) [ttl 1]
17:10:21.027002 192.168.1.104 > 239.5.5.55: igmp nreport 239.5.5.55 (DF) [ttl 1]
```

Note that the device sends three IGMP packets, stating its membership to make sure that it is heard. The router receives the request to join this group and sets a timer to count down for three minutes. As long as some device reasserts its membership with IGMP within this period, the group will remain in the router's multicast routing table. If all of the group members leave, or if they all simply stop sending IGMP updates for more than three minutes, then the router will remove this group from its tables to save memory.

When the device wants to stop receiving a multicast group, it sends a single IGMP Leave packet. The router immediately reacts by sending a query to this segment to find out if there are still any other members left in this group. It tries twice before deciding to stop sending traffic for this group to this network segment:

```
17:16:17.934667 192.168.1.104 > ALL-ROUTERS.MCAST.NET: igmp leave 239.5.5.55 (DF)
[ttl 1]
17:16:17.937715 192.168.1.1 > 239.5.5.55: igmp query [gaddr 239.5.5.55] [tos 0xc0]
[ttl 1]
17:16:19.050430 192.168.1.1 > 239.5.5.55: igmp query [gaddr 239.5.5.55] [tos 0xc0]
[ttl 1]
```

The important changes to the protocol between Versions 1 and 2 of IGMP have to do with determining when all of the members of a group in a particular network have left. The most important addition to Version 3 is the ability to specify and filter multicast sources. So a device may specify that it is interested in receiving multicast messages from one source, but not from another, even though both sources may be sending to the same group.

IGMP Version 3 is the new current standard, but many devices do not support the new extensions. However, Cisco provides a fully compliant IGMPv3 implementation. And, in fact, you lose nothing by using IGMPv3 because the protocol is backward-compatible.

In a switched Ethernet LAN (including 100 Mbps, 1,000 Mbps, and higher speed variants), there is an additional benefit to multicast transmission. If the switches are multicast aware, they can forward packets with a particular group address to only those devices that are members of this group. So it is not necessary to "flood" the entire VLAN with multicast packets just because one device is a multicast group member. Naturally, this means that the switch must be able to read and use Layer 3 information, so this sort of functionality is not available on all Ethernet switches.

Many multicast aware switches use *IGMP snooping* to read IGMP packets from devices as they join and leave particular groups. On the surface, this sounds like a perfect and simple solution, but in practice it can be very complex to implement in the switch. The first problem is that there are several special cases that are difficult to manage. For example, things become quite complex when you have several multicast routers on a segment, or when there are complicated trunk topologies or connections to workgroup hubs. Another important problem with IGMP snooping is that the switch must read the contents of all multicast packets passing through it so that it won't miss any IGMP *Join* or *Leave* messages. In effect, the switch acts as if it were a member of every multicast group. If there is a heavy multicast application such as a multimedia application, this can cause serious CPU overhead on the switch.

Cisco has developed a proprietary protocol called Cisco Group Management Protocol (CGMP) to deal with these problems. CGMP is implemented on all Cisco routers and most new switches, even those without Layer 3 capabilities. It is a relatively simple protocol that allows the router to do most of the hard work for the switch. When a device on the LAN segment joins a multicast group by sending an IGMP *Join* message, the switch simply passes the IGMP packet through to the router as it would with any other packet. The router then sends a CGMP packet to the switch to let it know the MAC addresses of the device and the group. Similarly, when a device leaves a group, the router uses CGMP to tell the switch to stop forwarding this particular multicast group to this device. In this way, the router, which has to keep track of this information anyway, can simply tell the switch what to do.

Unfortunately, CGMP doesn't solve all of the problems inherent in the IGMP model. Specifically, a device doesn't need to send an IGMP *Leave* message when it is no longer interested in receiving packets for that group. If the last group member leaves without sending the appropriate IGMP *Leave* message, the router will still think that there are devices in the group. It will continue to forward multicast packets to the segment until a timer expires. The router will eventually poll the LAN segment to see if any devices are still interested in receiving this group. If it gets no response, it will finally stop sending the multicast data stream. However, most implementations of IGMP Version 2 do send explicit *Leave* messages, unless the end devices crash or terminate improperly. In any case, it is usually better to have a device receive multicast data it didn't subscribe to than to lose the data. The only time when this isn't true is when the multicast data stream consumes too much bandwidth and starts to cause congestion for normal unicast traffic, or when processing the unnecessary multicast traffic causes CPU problems on the end devices.

Switches running newer versions of CGMP include a particularly nice feature called Local Leave Processing. They are able to intercept IGMP Leave messages from devices and process them internally. If there are other group members elsewhere on the switch, it can simply stop sending data from this group to the device that no longer wishes to be a member. Then, when the last group member leaves the group, the switch will send a global IGMP *Leave* packet to the router to tell it to stop sending this multicast group.

Multicast Routing Protocols

There are two general types multicast routing protocols, called *dense* and *sparse* mode. Dense mode means that every multicast router receives every multicast packet unless and until it explicitly says that it doesn't want it. As we will discuss shortly, this applies to each group and each interface separately. Sparse mode, on the other hand, means (loosely) that no router will receive a multicast group unless it explicitly requests it. It is important to note that end devices, whether multicast servers or group members, are completely unaware of which mode their network uses, or even which multicast routing protocol. Indeed it is possible to run a network where the routers use a combination of these modes.

There are many examples of dense-mode protocols, such as Protocol Independent Multicast-Dense Mode (PIM-DM), Distance Vector Multicast Routing Protocol (DVMRP), and Multicast Open Shortest Path First (MOSPF). There are fewer sparse-mode protocols, with the best examples being Protocol Independent Multicast–Sparse Mode (PIM-SM) and Core-Based Trees (CBT).

Not all of these protocols are available in Cisco routers. Like most vendors, Cisco implements PIM-DM and PIM-SM as well as MBGP. But Cisco does not implement MOSPF or CBT, and has a limited version of DVMRP.

There are two other general categories of multicast routing protocols: protocol dependent and protocol independent. The difference has to do with the interaction with an underlying routing protocol, and not with the ability to handle nonIP multicast traffic. All of the multicast protocols mentioned in this book are specific to IP multicast communications.

For example, MOSPF is protocol-dependent because it relies on OSPF and uses a special OSPF LSA type to carry information about multicast routing. PIM and CBT, on the other hand, both use the multicast traffic itself, along with the standard unicast IP routing table and IGMP requests to build the multicast forwarding trees. Since they don't care how the router got its unicast IP routing table, they are called *protocol independent*.

For the network engineer, these distinctions are quite important, since they affect flexibility, reliability, and network performance. In general, if you have a large network, particularly with bandwidth constrained WAN links, and the multicast sources and destinations can be more or less anywhere through your network, you should use a protocol independent sparse mode multicast routing protocol. If you're not sure if this really describes your network, it is generally safer and easier to lean in this direction anyway.

The PIM protocols, and, in particular, PIM-SM, are generally the best choices for implementing new multicast networks. In the past there were problems with interoperability in multi-vendor networks, as different router manufacturers implemented different sets of multicast routing protocols. Since DVMRP was the first widely implemented multicast routing protocol, the rule of thumb used to be that DVMRP was the best way to allow communication between groups of routers from different vendors. However, a quick survey of protocols supported by major router vendors shows that almost all of them now support PIM as well as DVMRP.

PIM-DM, PIM-SM, and Bidirectional PIM

There are three different flavors of PIM. The most current version of the Dense Mode protocol, PIM-DM, is defined in RFC 3973. The Sparse Mode PIM-SM protocol is specified in RFC 4601. At the time of this book's writing, Bidirectional PIM was still in the draft specification phase. You can obtain a copy of the draft specification from the IETF web site in the PIM Working Group's directory: *http://www.ietf.org/ids.by.wg/pim.html*.

Let's look schematically at how each builds and maintains its multicast forwarding trees to explain how they work. We note from the outset that this is not intended to be a rigorous explanation of the protocols. Instead, we just want to give you a good, basic understanding of what they do and how they do it. For more detailed information, please refer to the standards documents mentioned above, as well as RFC 2715, which details interoperability rules for multicast routing protocols.

When a device wants to join a group, G, the first thing it does is to send an IGMP Join message to its local router. If this is the first group member (and if the IGMP Join message doesn't specify a particular multicast source device, an option that we will discuss later), the router creates an entry in its multicast forwarding table for (*,G). This says that the router will forward to this interface all multicast packets addressed to group G from any source. At this point, if the router receives any packets for this group, it knows at least one place to forward them to.

In PIM-DM, the router will create the group and wait for packets. It will also send a PIM *Join* request to each of its PIM neighbors to find out if they have this group. If it receives multicast packets for a group that it doesn't care about, then the router will send *Prune* messages back to where they came from, to ask to be removed from the forwarding tree for this group. This is commonly called a "flood and prune" model, which is common to all dense mode multicast protocols.

If this router uses PIM-SM, however, it will attempt to join a multicast tree rooted at the Rendezvous Point (RP). An RP is a router somewhere in the network that acts as a central distribution point for one or more multicast groups. Later we will discuss how the other routers come to know about the RP, but for now we'll assume that they know how to find it. When the last-hop router receives an IGMP message from a device asking to join a group, it has to go looking for that group. The best place to start looking is the RP.

So the last-hop router looks at its unicast routing table to figure out which of its neighboring routers is the best path to the RP, and it sends it an explicit PIM-SM Join message for this group. If the neighboring router is already receiving this group, then the problem is solved and the data starts to flow. Otherwise, this neighbor must send another Join to the next hop router in the direction of the RP, and so on until a multicast-forwarding tree is created with its root at the RP.

The upstream router will automatically prune the branches of this multicast tree if they don't receive another explicit join within the three-minute timeout period. So, by default, the routers all refresh the tree with a new Join for every active group, once per minute. This creates and maintains a stable tree rooted at the RP and extending to all group members in the network that remains active, even if there is no multicast traffic being forwarded.

The only remaining piece of the puzzle is how the packets get from the sender to the RP. When the source device sends its first packet, the first-hop router receives it normally, as it would any other packet. This first-hop router has already learned where the RP is. When it receives a multicast packet from a new source, the router must register this source with the RP. The router encapsulates the multicast packet in a PIM-SM Registration packet, which it sends by unicast to the RP. The RP then removes the encapsulation and forwards the packet down the tree. The RP also sends an explicit PIM-SM Join message toward the source. The Join message links up a tree from the RP upstream to the source and downstream to the group members. Once the tree is built, there is no need for the first-hop router to continue encapsulating multicast packets to send them to the RP. So the first-hop router can revert to normal multicast forwarding instead, knowing that the RP is somewhere downstream on the SPT.

This process is shown schematically in Figure 23-1. The multicast source device sends out the packet (Step 1). The first hop router encapsulates this packet and sends it by unicast to the RP (Step 2). The RP sends the packet by multicast down the tree to the recipient devices (Step 3), who finally receive it from their own local routers (Step 4).

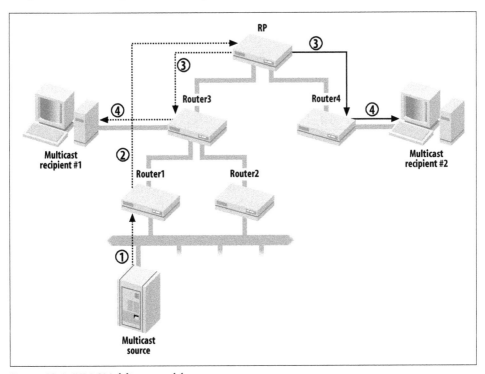

Figure 23-1. PIM-SM delivery model

Finally, once there is a tree connecting the ultimate source with all of the group members, there is no more need for the RP. So the last-hop routers start to send PIM-SM Join messages to create a new tree that is centered on the source rather than the RP. This is actually controlled by a minimum traffic flow threshold value, which is equal to zero by default in Cisco routers. PIM-SM starts to build the new tree rooted at the source only if the amount of traffic coming down the tree for this group exceeds this threshold.

Bidirectional PIM offers many of the advantages of PIM-SM, but with a considerably simpler method for setting up the multicast forwarding tree and less operational overhead. From the RP to the destination, Bidirectional PIM functions exactly the same as PIM-SM. The differences are in the way that the source devices forward packets to the RP.

The key to Bidirectional PIM is to remember that the first hop router, the one that is adjacent to the source device, can quickly establish a forwarding path from the RP by using normal PIM-SM methods. In Bidirectional PIM, the routers exploit this same path in reverse to reach the RP. As a result, there is no need for the complicated encapsulation method used to forward the first few packets of the multicast stream to the RP. As a tradeoff, Bidirectional PIM does not have the capability to create a source-rooted forwarding tree, as PIM-SM does.

To allow packets to traverse the multicast forwarding tree backwards to the RP, Bidirectional PIM needs a few additional tricks to help eliminate potential routing loops. The main trick is the use of a Designated Forwarder (DF) router on each network segment that is more than one hop away from the RP. The DF routers natively forward multicast packets to the RP. This has the added advantage that, if there are recipient devices along the path to the RP, they can receive the multicast packets immediately instead of waiting for the packets to reach the RP and come back. Figure 23-2 shows an example of how this works. As in the PIM-SM example, the source device sends the multicast packet to its local network segment where it is received by the first hop router (Step 1). In this case, because there are two routers on the segment, one of them (Router1) must be the DF, which handles the forwarding of this packet up the multicast tree toward the RP (Step 2). Along the way, because this is a native multicast packet, Router3 realizes that it supports a member of this group, and delivers the packet normally (Step 3), as well as continuing to forward it to the RP (Step 4). The RP then delivers the multicast packet normally, as it did with PIM-SM (Step 5).

DVMRP

Distance Vector Multicast Routing Protocol (DVMRP) is defined in RFC 1075, and was the first widely implemented multicast routing protocol. This protocol is similar to RIP in many ways. There are a few important differences, though. The maximum diameter of a RIP network is 16 hops, as we mentioned in Chapter 6. DVMRP has a maximum metric of 32, which drastically improves its flexibility. It's not hard to find a network with a diameter greater than 16 hops, but a 32-hop diameter is sufficient for most real-world corporate networks. It is not sufficient for the public Internet, but that is why multiprotocol extensions to the Border Gateway Protocol, sometimes also called Multicast Border Gateway Protocol (MBGP) was invented.

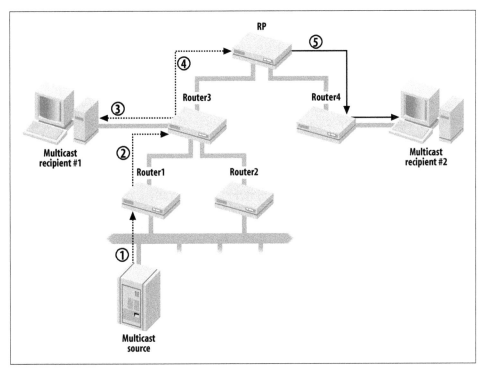

Figure 23-2. Bidirectional PIM delivery model

DVMRP is often a good choice for allowing routers from different manufacturers to exchange multicast routing information. It is a dense mode protocol, however, so it is generally less efficient with network resources. We recommend using DVMRP primarily as a mechanism for exchanging multicast routing information with older non-Cisco devices. In recent years, PIM has become the popular choice for multicast routing among most large router vendors, though, so DVMRP's niche is now mostly in interconnecting with existing nonCisco multicast networks.

In many ways, DVMRP functions in a similar way to PIM-DM. It uses a dense-mode strategy that forces all routers to prune themselves from any multicast trees that they don't require. And it also uses the unicast routing table to determine the shortest path back to the source device. The main difference, however, is that DVMRP includes its own internal unicast routing protocol that it uses to help make decisions about the best SPT.

DVMRP uses an algorithm called Truncated Reverse Path Broadcasting (TRPB) to allow every router in the network to determine where it is relative to the multicast source, and to calculate the optimal SPT back to the source. Because DVMRP uses its own internal unicast routing protocol, it is not considered protocol-independent.

You must take special measures to force DVMRP to follow the standard unicast routing table and make it protocol independent. Of course, this would break one of the main reasons for using DVMRP in the first place. Because it maintains its own routing tables, DVMRP is able to work in networks where the multicast and unicast topologies are different. This is not uncommon in cases where parts of the unicast network don't support multicast routing, or where traffic engineering leads you to put multicast traffic through different network links.

In fact, Cisco routers do not provide a full DVMRP implementation. They can take part in discovering and exchanging routing information with DVMRP neighbors. But the actual multicast routing is done using PIM while referring to the DVMRP routing tables.

MOSPF

Multicast Open Shortest Path First (MSOPF) is not really a separate protocol, but rather is a set of extensions to the popular Open Shortest Path First (OSPF) unicast routing protocol. OSPF is described in more detail in Chapter 8. To allow OSPF to carry multicast routing information, RFC 1584 added a new Link State Advertisement (LSA) type, called Type 6, or simply the MOSPF LSA.

Cisco routers do not support MOSPF, so we will not discuss this protocol in any detail except to point out that Cisco routers will generate log error messages whenever they encounter Type 6 OSPF LSAs. So Recipe 23.10 shows how to configure the router to ignore these packets.

The biggest advantage to MOSPF is that it is tightly integrated with OSPF, which can simplify network administration. Furthermore, because it uses the same Link State algorithm as OSPF, every router in the network can independently deduce the best path back to the source.

However, it is a dense-mode protocol, and is consequently less efficient with network resources, and it requires OSPF to work. This is almost certainly why Cisco has chosen not to implement it.

MBGP

MBGP is based on a small set of extensions to BGP defined in RFC 2858 to allow exchange of any routable protocol information between Autonomous Systems. It does this by simply introducing two new attributes to the BGP protocol: Multiprotocol Reachable Network Layer Routing Information (MP_REACH_NLRI) and Multiprotocol Unreachable Network Layer Routing Information (MP_UNREACH_NLRI), which are used to carry information about reachable and unreachable networks.

It's important to understand that MBGP is not really a multicast routing protocol in the same sense as PIM or DVMRP. It doesn't understand or have the ability to *Join* or *Prune* SPT's. It doesn't include any functionality for dealing with Rendezvous Points. All it does is forward information about multicast groups and sources, and make this information available to other multicast routing protocols. It needs another protocol to do all of the other work of joining and pruning multicast distribution trees. The two protocols most commonly used for this are PIM and DVMRP.

23.1 Configuring Basic Multicast Functionality with PIM-DM

Problem

You want to pass multicast traffic through the router.

Solution

In a small network with few routers and relatively light multicast application bandwidth requirements, the easiest way to implement multicast routing is to use PIM-DM. This example shows the configurations for two routers that are connected through a Serial connection, both with *FastEthernet* interfaces to represent the LAN connections. It is important to enable multicast routing on all interfaces that connect to other multicast-enabled routers or to multicast user or server segments.

The first router looks like this:

```
Router1#configure terminal
Enter configuration commands, one per line.  End with CNTL/Z.
Router1(config)#ip multicast-routing
Router1(config)#interface FastEthernet0/0
Router1(config-if)#ip address 192.168.1.1 255.255.255.0
Router1(config-if)#ip pim dense-mode
Router1(config-if)#exit
Router1(config)#interface Serial1/0
Router1(config-if)#ip address 192.168.2.5 255.255.255.252
Router1(config-if)#ip pim dense-mode
Router1(config-if)#end
Router1#
```

And the second router looks remarkably similar:

```
Router2#configure terminal
Enter configuration commands, one per line.  End with CNTL/Z.
Router2(config)#ip multicast-routing
Router2(config)#interface FastEthernet0/0
Router2(config-if)#ip address 192.168.3.1 255.255.255.0
Router2(config-if)#ip pim dense-mode
Router2(config-if)#exit
Router2(config)#interface Serial1/0
Router2(config-if)#ip address 192.168.2.6 255.255.255.252
Router2(config-if)#ip pim dense-mode
Router2(config-if)#end
Router2#
```

Discussion

With this simple configuration, you get all of the basic multicast functionality. The routers will distribute multicast packets properly, they will listen for end devices to join and leave groups with IGMP (Version 1, 2, or 3), and they will update one another with information about what multicast groups are currently in use as well as where the servers and group members are. For many types of multicast applications, this is all you need. But it is important to remember that the PIM-DM protocol is only appropriate for certain types of networks with relatively specific multicast routing requirements.

First, PIM-DM works best in relatively small networks with no more than a few hops between the sender and the most remote receiver. Second, the number of multicast servers should be small, and the receivers should be scattered throughout the network in relatively large numbers. And third, because PIM-DM uses the multicast traffic itself to gather information about where the servers are, it needs a steady flow of traffic. In particular, it's a bad idea to use PIM-DM with multicast applications that can pause more than three minutes between packets because the routers will flush the routing information out of their tables and have to rebuild these tables when the next packet is received.

If one or more of these conditions is not true for any of your multicast applications then you should probably consider one of the other routing protocols, particularly PIM-SM.

One final point to consider in any sort of routing is how the router will switch the packets. As we discussed in Chapter 11, you want to avoid process switching anything unless it's absolutely necessary. Fortunately, multicast packets are fast switched by default. However, in many configurations, it is customary to disable multicast fast switching. So it is a good idea to look at your router configurations and make sure that you don't have any multicast interfaces that include the statement *no ip mroute-cache*. If any interfaces do have this command, then you should re-enable the preferred default fast switching behavior by using the interface level command *ip mroute-cache*. This is true regardless of which multicast routing protocol you use.

23.2   Routing Multicast Traffic with PIM-SM and BSR

Problem

You want to enable routing of multicasts using Sparse Mode for better efficiency and use BSR for distributing RP information.

Solution

We've already discussed how PIM-SM requires a Rendezvous Point (RP) router. The most reliable way to achieve this is to have the network automatically discover the

RP. This way, if the RP fails, another can automatically take over for it. We recommend using the Bootstrap Router (BSR) mechanism to dynamically distribute RP information.

There are two different types of router configurations for this type of network. Most of the routers will support end devices, both group members and servers. But a small number are configured to act as candidate RP's and candidate Bootstrap Routers (BSR). In the example, we show the RP and BSR configuration in the same router. This isn't actually necessary, but it is convenient.

Router1 is an example of a "normal" multicast router. It forwards multicasts, takes part in PIM-SM, and may support group members or multicast servers as required:

```
Router1#configure terminal
Enter configuration commands, one per line.  End with CNTL/Z.
Router1(config)#ip multicast-routing
Router1(config)#ip pim rp-address 192.168.15.5
Router1(config)#interface FastEthernet0/0
Router1(config-if)#ip address 192.168.1.1 255.255.255.0
Router1(config-if)#ip pim sparse-mode
Router1(config-if)#interface Serial1/0
Router1(config-if)#ip address 192.168.2.5 255.255.255.252
Router1(config-if)#ip pim sparse-mode
Router1(config-if)#end
Router1#
```

Router RP1 is one of the candidate RP's, and it is also configured as a candidate BSR. It may also support multicast group members or servers, if required. It is a good idea to configure two or more routers as RPs and BSRs in each multicast domain like this to provide redundancy:

```
Router-RP1#configure terminal
Enter configuration commands, one per line.  End with CNTL/Z.
Router-RP1(config)#ip multicast-routing
Router-RP1(config)#interface Loopback0
Router-RP1(config-if)#ip address 192.168.12.1 255.255.255.255
Router-RP1(config-if)# ip pim sparse-mode
Router-RP1(config-if)#exit
Router-RP1(config)#interface FastEthernet0/0
Router-RP1(config-if)#ip address 192.168.1.1 255.255.255.0
Router-RP1(config-if)#ip pim sparse-mode
Router-RP1(config-if)#exit
Router-RP1(config)#interface Serial1/0
Router-RP1(config-if)#ip address 192.168.2.5 255.255.255.252
Router-RP1(config-if)#ip pim sparse-mode
Router-RP1(config-if)#exit
Router-RP1(config)#ip pim rp-address 192.168.12.1 15
Router-RP1(config)#ip pim rp-candidate loopback0 group-list 15
Router-RP1(config)#ip pim bsr-candidate loopback0 1
Router-RP1(config)#access-list 15 permit 239.5.5.0 0.0.0.255
Router-RP1(config)#access-list 15 deny any
Router-RP1(config)#end
Router-RP1#
```

Discussion

In larger networks, particularly networks with WAN links, the PIM-DM approach of forwarding all multicasts to all routers until they explicitly opt out of the group tends to be inefficient with network resources. So it is useful to configure a Sparse Mode multicast routing protocol such as PIM-SM. The basic configuration for most of the routers is similar to what we did in Recipe 23.1. The difference is that PIM-SM allows you to set up a Rendezvous Point (RP) router to act as the root of the multi-cast Shortest Path Trees (SPT).

There are two ways to configure the routers to use an RP. The conceptually simpler method is to explicitly define the RP in the other routers, using the *ip pim rp-address* command, as shown in the configuration for Router1 above:

```
Router1(config)#ip pim rp-address 192.168.15.5
```

This method has two important administrative problems. If you ever want to change the RP to another router, you have to change it separately in every router, and it lacks the ability to automatically switch to a backup RP in case of failure. However, it is statically configured in the example for a different reason, which we will explain in a moment.

The alternative is to configure the network to discover the RP dynamically, which is also shown in the Solution. This is preferable in most cases. In fact, there are two ways to accomplish this. One uses a Cisco proprietary method called Auto-RP, and the other called the Bootstrap Router method, which is part of the open PIM-SM standard defined in RFC 4601. This recipe shows the Bootstrap Router method, which we generally prefer for interoperability reasons. The Auto-RP, which will only work in an all-Cisco network, is discussed in Recipe 23.3.

In Router-RP1, there are two important commands that define how it will advertise itself. The first is *ip pim rp-candidate*, which allows the router to advertise itself as a possible RP:

```
Router-RP1(config)#ip pim rp-candidate loopback0 group-list 15
```

There are two modifiers on this command. The first, loopback0, tells the network to use the loopback interface as the RP address. If there are several candidate RP rout-ers, the PIM-SM algorithm prefers the one with the highest IP address. So be careful if you want a particular router to be the default.

This command also includes the *group-list* tag. In this case, it associates the RP func-tions for this router with access-list number 15, which specifies that this router will be RP for any multicast group between 239.5.5.0 and 239.5.5.255. You can specify that the RP router can support any set of multicast group addresses. If you want it to support all multicast groups, then simply eliminate the *group-list* keyword as follows:

```
Router-RP1(config)#ip pim rp-candidate loopback0
```

Using the group-list option is most useful if you have an extremely large number of multicast groups to distribute and the load is too heavy for one router. Some network administrators may also decide to use a different RP for a few specific local groups for ease of management as well. But in most networks there is relatively little benefit to breaking up the RP functions by group this way. We have just included the option here to show how it works in case you do need it. If you decide to break up the RP responsibilities among many routers, be careful to ensure that all possible groups have an RP available.

The next important command in Router-RP1 is *ip pim bsr-candidate*:

```
Router-RP1(config)#ip pim bsr-candidate loopback0 1
```

This allows the router to act as a Bootstrap Router (BSR). BSRs are responsible for distributing information about all of the known candidate RPs throughout the network. In this example, we use the loopback interface to define the IP address that this router will use when advertising itself as a BSR candidate. The protocol uses this address in the election process to select the BSR from all of the possible candidates. This command also accepts a *priority* keyword that you can use to help bias the election process to prefer one BSR candidate.

The last number in the example's *bsr-candidate* command, 1, is a hash value that helps to select different RP's for different ranges of multicast group addresses. Because the example uses a range of addresses from 239.5.5.0 to 239.5.5.255, we could have configured the candidate BSR to allow RPs to control a similar range of multicast addresses. There are 8 bits of freedom in this range, which would give a hash value of 8. If you're not sure what to use here, it is safest to just use a value of 1 bit. This will allow the network to select the best RPs on a group-by-group basis. In fact this option is really only useful when you have several RPs, each supporting different ranges of multicast group addresses. When in doubt, it is safe to use a value of 1. There is a slight performance advantage to using larger hash values, however.

We note in passing that the RP router's configuration in our example also includes a static *rp-address* configuration command, pointing to itself and including the same access-list defining the multicast groups served by this RP:

```
Router-RP1(config)#ip pim rp-address 192.168.12.1 15
```

This command is completely redundant in most IOS releases, but appears to have suddenly become necessary in IOS Version 12.3, as it ensures that the RP router is aware that it is the RP for these groups. We don't understand why this change was made, as the *ip pim rp-candidate* command would appear to perform the same function. In any case, it doesn't hurt anything to include this command, so we recommend including it.

We have one final comment on the configuration of the candidate RP/BSR router. Since we are using the loopback interface as the source for both RP and BSR functions, it is important that this interface be configured for PIM-SM. This seems counter-intuitive because a loopback interface can't have any neighbors by definition. But the BSR function in particular will not work properly without this configuration, because we use the loopback interface to define this router as a BSR candidate.

We use the loopback interface for this purpose because it can't go down. If there is any path to this router, it will retain the RP role. This may not always be desirable, of course. If this is a WAN router, for example, we certainly wouldn't want all multicast traffic to have to cross the WAN twice just because an Ethernet interface went down. In such cases, it would be better to use the Ethernet port for the BSR and RP addresses.

In general, it is a good practice to set up several BSR's to spread the word about several RPs with overlapping group ranges for redundancy. This gives a much more reliable network. And, if it ever happens that no RPs are available, the router will revert to the statically configured RP address, which we have configured using the following command:

```
Router1(config)#ip pim rp-address 192.168.15.5
```

Note that the address specified is not the same as *RouterRP1*. The static RP value is only needed when none of the usual RPs is available. So a good choice for this last resort RP would be one of your central core routers. Naturally, you must make sure that the router you specify is configured to act as an RP.

If you are going to use this BSR method for RP discovery, you need to take certain network design precautions. Sometimes you will want an RP to serve a particular section of the network. In smaller networks, you may have RPs serve the entire physical expanse of the network, but with different RPs serving different multicast groups. However, in larger networks, or when two or more networks adjoin, it is necessary to limit the region of the network served by any RP.

The BSR works by sending out information to all of the adjacent PIM routers. These routers record all of the information, and then relay the same information to all of the adjacent routers, except the one where this information came from in the first place. Because this process is repeated at each hop, it could expand indefinitely. In fact, the process is not even bounded by the usual IP TTL limit of 255 hops because a new packet is created at each hop. So it is possible to have the network choose an RP that some devices cannot reach, particularly if you use TTL to control multicast scope, as in Recipe 23.14.

To define distinct regions of a network served by different groups of RPs, first you need to decide where the boundaries of these regions will be, and then you configure the routers along the boundary so that they will neither transmit nor receive any BSR information on those interfaces:

```
Router-Border1#configure terminal
Enter configuration commands, one per line.  End with CNTL/Z.
Router-Border1(config)#ip multicast-routing
Router-Border1(config-if)#interface FastEthernet0/0
Router-Border1(config-if)#ip pim sparse-mode
```

```
Router-Border1(config-if)#ip pim border
Router-Border1(config-if)#end
Router-Border1#
```

Note that the *ip pim border* command affects only the exchange of BSR information. Multicast traffic can still flow across the interface, and PIM will still form SPT trees that cross the interface.

23.3 Routing Multicast Traffic with PIM-SM and Auto-RP

Problem

You want to allow routing of multicasts by using Sparse Mode, and use Auto-RP for distributing RP information.

Solution

This recipe accomplishes the same basic tasks as Recipe 23.2, but using a different method. If you are unfamiliar with PIM-SM, please read that recipe first. There are two different types of router configurations for Auto-RP configuration, just as there are for BSR. Router1 represents a regular multicast-enabled router anywhere in the network. This router supports end devices as group members or servers, as well as routing multicast traffic for other routers:

```
Router1#configure terminal
Enter configuration commands, one per line.  End with CNTL/Z.
Router1(config)#ip multicast-routing
Router1(config)#ip pim rp-address 192.168.15.5
Router1(config)#interface FastEthernet0/0
Router1(config-if)#ip address 192.168.1.1 255.255.255.0
Router1(config-if)#ip pim sparse-dense-mode
Router1(config-if)#exit
Router1(config)#interface Serial1/0
Router1(config-if)#ip address 192.168.2.5 255.255.255.252
Router1(config-if)#ip pim sparse-dense-mode
Router1(config-if)#end
Router1#
```

The second type of configuration is for a candidate RP router, called Router RP1. This router may also support group members or servers. As in the previous recipe, it is a good idea to configure two or more routers in each multicast domain like this to provide redundancy:

```
Router-RP1#configure terminal
Enter configuration commands, one per line.  End with CNTL/Z.
Router-RP1(config)#ip multicast-routing
Router-RP1(config)#interface Loopback0
Router-RP1(config-if)#ip address 192.168.12.1 255.255.255.255
Router-RP1(config-if)#ip pim sparse-dense-mode
```

```
Router-RP1(config-if)#exit
Router-RP1(config)#interface FastEthernet0/0
Router-RP1(config-if)#ip address 192.168.1.1 255.255.255.0
Router-RP1(config-if)#ip pim sparse-dense-mode
Router-RP1(config-if)#exit
Router-RP1(config)#interface Serial1/0
Router-RP1(config-if)#ip address 192.168.2.5 255.255.255.252
Router-RP1(config-if)#ip pim sparse-dense-mode
Router-RP1(config-if)#exit
Router-RP1(config)#ip pim send-rp-announce loopback0 scope 16 group-list 15
Router-RP1(config)#ip pim send-rp-discovery scope 16
Router-RP1(config)#access-list 15 permit 239.5.5.0 0.0.0.255
Router-RP1(config)#access-list 15 deny any
Router-RP1(config)#end
Router-RP1#
```

Discussion

Recipe 23.2 discussed one way of discovering the RPs in a PIM-SM network using the Bootstrap Router (BSR) method. This recipe shows an alternative method. The BSR method requires Version 2 of the PIM-SM protocol. Cisco started supporting this in IOS 11.3T. So if you have earlier IOS versions in your multicast network, you will need Auto-RP, perhaps used in parallel with BSR. As long as both systems select the same RPs, there should be no problems with running both methods simultaneously. If you do run into interoperability problems, however, you can disable the Version 2 functionality on newer routers using the following command:

```
Router1#configure terminal
Enter configuration commands, one per line.  End with CNTL/Z.
Router1(config)#ip pim version 1
Router1(config)#end
Router1#
```

Auto-RP distributes information about the multicast Rendezvous Points using the globally registered multicast group addresses 224.0.1.39 and 224.0.1.40. This is an elegant solution to the problem of how to tell the network where the RPs are. But it presents a bit of a paradox to the routers: how can they distribute multicast information using PIM-SM if they don't yet have an RP? Cisco solved this problem by creating a new hybrid PIM mode called sparse-dense mode. This means that the routers should use sparse mode if there is a known RP, and dense mode if there isn't. So the only difference in Router1's configuration between this recipe and the previous one is that all of the interfaces are configured with the command: *ip pim sparse-dense-mode*:

```
Router1(config-if)#ip pim sparse-dense-mode
```

There are two important differences between Router RP1's configuration in this recipe and Recipe 23.2. To advertise its willingness to become an RP using Auto-RP, this router includes the global configuration command *ip pim send-rp-announce*:

```
Router-RP1(config)#ip pim send-rp-announce loopback0 scope 16 group-list 15
```

The interface specified in this command, loopback0, has the address that other routers will use for all of their interactions with the RP. We have used a loopback interface to ensure as long as there is an active path to this router, it can continue to act as the RP.

As mentioned in the Recipe 23.2, however, this may not always be desirable. For example, if this router has a LAN interface and a WAN interface, you certainly don't want all of your multicast traffic to have to loop through the WAN if the LAN interface goes down. In such failure modes, you would probably want to stop using this RP and switch to a different candidate RP. You can do this by simply specifying the LAN interface in the *send-rp-announce* command.

The second difference in Router RP1's configuration is the command *ip pim send-rp-discovery*:

```
Router-RP1(config)#ip pim send-rp-discovery scope 16
```

This instructs the router to act not only as a candidate RP, but also as an RP Mapping Agent. The mapping agent function is similar to the BSR function that we discussed in Recipe 23.2. This is the router that is responsible for distributing information about all of the RPs throughout the network. Although you could make the mapping agent a different router, we have combined the functions on the candidate RP router for the same reasons as in the BSR case.

Note that for both the *send-rp-announce* and *send-rp-discovery* commands there is a *scope* keyword that sets the TTL scope for these functions to 16. Because Auto-RP uses multicasts to distribute its information, you can specify a particular initial TTL value. This controls the network area that will be able to use this particular RP. Recipe 23.14 includes a detailed discussion of how to use TTL for controlling multicast scope.

Finally, in the *send-rp-announce* command we have specified a *group-list* keyword. This is identical to the group-list in the BSR configuration of Recipe 23.2. It defines which groups this particular router is willing to act as RP for. As we mentioned in Recipe 23.2, most networks can easily support all of their multicast traffic on a single active RP. Having different RP's for different multicast groups is primarily useful for administrative reasons, and for rare networks that have too many multicast groups for one RP to support.

If you want one RP for all groups, simply leave out the *group-list* keyword and its arguments:

```
Router-RP1#configure terminal
Enter configuration commands, one per line.  End with CNTL/Z.
Router-RP1(config)#ip pim send-rp-announce loopback0 scope 16
Router-RP1(config)#ip pim send-rp-discovery scope 16
Router-RP1(config)#end
Router-RP1#
```

See Also

Recipe 23.2; Recipe 23.14

23.4   Filtering PIM Neighbors

Problem

You want to prevent your router from accepting PIM packets from another device.

Solution

In this example, we will configure a neighbor filter on Router1's FastEthernet interface, which it uses to connect to a foreign router called Router2:

```
Router1#configure terminal
Enter configuration commands, one per line.  End with CNTL/Z.
Router1(config)#ip multicast-routing
Router1(config)#interface FastEthernet0/0
Router1(config-if)#ip address 192.168.1.1 255.255.255.0
Router1(config-if)#ip pim sparse-mode
Router1(config-if)#ip pim neighbor-filter 18
Router1(config-if)#exit
Router1(config)#access-list 18 deny any
Router1(config)#end
Router1#
```

Then, on the foreign router, we must configure an *igmp helper-address*:

```
Router2#configure terminal
Enter configuration commands, one per line.  End with CNTL/Z.
Router2(config)#ip multicast-routing
Router2(config)#interface FastEthernet0/0
Router2(config-if)#ip address 192.168.1.2 255.255.255.0
Router2(config-if)#ip pim dense-mode
Router2(config-if)#ip igmp helper-address 192.168.1.1
Router2(config-if)#end
Router2#
```

Discussion

There are two main reasons for configuring a PIM neighbor filter. The first and most obvious reason is security. If you don't control all of the routers on a network segment, but you want to maintain administrative control over your multicast routing trees, you might want to prevent the foreign devices from taking part in PIM. In particular, since PIM elects a Designated Router (DR) to handle multicast forwarding for each network segment, you can use neighbor filtering to ensure that you control the DR. Furthermore, preventing foreign routers from joining your PIM domain also prevents these routers from discovering and using your RPs, and it also prevents those foreign routers from advertising their own RPs into your domain.

The second reason for using this feature is to create the multicast equivalent of "stub routing." In stub routing, the foreign routers are still able to take part in the forwarding of multicast packets, but they must do so by exchanging IGMP Join and Leave packets with your routers.

Multicast stub routing conserves resources by allowing routers to keep track of fewer PIM neighbors. And because the stub region uses PIM-DM, it conserves resources on your RPs.

There are two parts to the configuration. On our edge router, you configure the neighbor-filter command by using an access-list:

```
Router1(config)#interface FastEthernet0/0
Router1(config-if)#ip pim sparse-mode
Router1(config-if)#ip pim neighbor-filter 18
Router1(config-if)#exit
Router1(config)#access-list 18 deny any
```

If there are some routers on this segment that you do want to include in your PIM domain, you can simply define a more precise access-list, such as:

```
Router1(config)#access-list 18 deny 192.168.1.2
Router1(config)#access-list 18 permit any
```

In this example, we allow any PIM neighbors except for Router2. You could similarly construct a more complicated filter to have a more complicated mixture of allowed and denied neighbors.

The second part of the configuration is the *igmp-helper* configuration on the foreign router:

```
Router2(config-if)#ip igmp helper-address 192.168.1.1
```

This command is important, as it ensures that Router2 will forward all of the appropriate IGMP Join and Leave messages to the internal PIM router. Without this command, Router2 doesn't know that there is an adjoining multicast network that might be able to service these IGMP requests.

Finally, we would like to point out that the stub domain, Router2 in our example, runs PIM-DM. This is necessary because this router doesn't have access to the usual PIM-SM mechanisms for joining a multicast tree. Instead, it must rely on the simpler PIM-DM flood and prune mechanism. Router1, on the other hand, can run PIM-SM, PIM-DM, or even Bidirectional PIM, as required.

23.5   Configuring Routing for a Low-Frequency Multicast Application

Problem

You have a multicast application where the servers send packets less frequently than the standard PIM timeout intervals.

Solution

PIM-SM is best suited to this type of application. The configurations of the RP and BSR or Auto-RP routers for this example are identical to those shown in Recipes 23.2 and 23.3. The differences appear on the other routers in the network. So this recipe shows only the configurations for these other routers:

```
Router1#configure terminal
Enter configuration commands, one per line.  End with CNTL/Z.
Router1(config)#ip multicast-routing
Router1(config)#ip pim spt-threshold 10 group-list 15
Router1(config)#access-list 15 permit 239.5.5.55
Router1(config)#access-list 15 deny any
Router1(config)#interface FastEthernet0/0
Router1(config-if)#ip address 192.168.1.1 255.255.255.0
Router1(config-if)#ip pim sparse-dense-mode
Router1(config-if)#exit
Router1(config)#interface Serial1/0
Router1(config-if)#ip address 192.168.2.5 255.255.255.252
Router1(config-if)#ip pim sparse-mode
Router1(config-if)#end
Router1#
```

Discussion

Discussion of multicast applications usually focuses on high-bandwidth applications. But some multicast applications have the opposite behavior. For example, some news broadcast type applications allow message servers to send short messages to a large group of users. This sort of service might be used for administrative purposes ("the server is going down in five minutes") or for business purposes ("stop selling widgets, the warehouse is empty," or "buy more Cisco stock"). In either case, all of the users in the group need to receive the message.

But there are three problems. First, in this sort of application you can't afford to waste the first packet while setting up your multicast distribution trees because it may be the only packet sent. Second, you don't want to worry about finding a more optimal tree after you've delivered the first packet because there isn't going to be another packet for a long time. And third, by the time the next packet comes along, all of the routing that the network set up for the first packet may have timed out.

There are many possible solutions to this problem. You could statically configure the entire multicast network using static multicast routes and group memberships, and not use a multicast routing protocol at all. But this is clearly an administrative nightmare to keep updated, and it would make it difficult to use the same network for other multicast applications. So the recipe shows a better solution.

It is useful to step through the network from group member to sender and back to see all of the places where a low-frequency multicast application can cause problems. A router will assume that there are no group members on a network segment if it doesn't receive any IGMP messages for a defined period of time. However, the devices on the segment are responsible for sending periodic IGMP reports to ensure that this doesn't happen unless there really aren't any more members for a given group on the segment. So unless the timers are not configured properly on the end devices, the low-frequency multicast application should not represent a problem here. In particular, it should not be necessary to configure a static IGMP statement on the router interface. If it turns out that IGMP timeouts are a problem for an application, refer to Recipe 23.9 for information about setting up static IGMP statements on a router.

At this point, it is useful to think about whether you should use a dense mode or sparse mode multicast routing protocol. Recall that the difference between these modes is that a dense mode protocol forwards all multicast packets to all neighboring routers until they announce that they don't want to be members. In sparse mode, on the other hand, routers must explicitly join a group before they can receive it.

If you were to use PIM-DM in this network, the multicast packets themselves would help to establish the multicast tree structure. If a router didn't receive any packets for a group within a standard timeout period of three minutes, it would tear down this tree structure. So this is the first important place where the low-frequency application can cause problems. The network either has to be constructed so that it can build and tear down this forwarding tree for every individual multicast packet, or it has to keep the tree up.

All of the end devices in the low-frequency application pre-join the group, so before the first packet is sent, it is already clear where it should be delivered. If you used dense mode, the routers that did not have members would respond to the first packet with a round of Prune messages asking to be removed from the tree. Since we don't expect another packet anytime soon, these Prune messages are really just a waste of network resources. The entire tree structure will have been removed before the next packet arrives. So, all things considered, it is better to use PIM-SM than PIM-DM for this type of application. Note that the example actually uses "sparse-dense" mode so that it can function in dense mode if an RP is not available. This is discussed in Recipe 23.3.

As discussed in the introduction to this chapter, every PIM-SM router sends a fresh Join up the tree toward the RP once per minute. This ensures that the tree to the RP stays up even if there is no traffic. When the source device is finally ready to send a packet, it sends this packet to its first-hop router. The first-hop router encapsulates the multicast packet in a unicast Registration packet that it sends to the RP. The RP pulls the multicast packet back out of the encapsulation and forwards it down the multicast tree to all of the group members. It then extends the tree for this group over to the source so that it can use multicast all the way on subsequent packets.

The only impact of the low-frequency nature of the application here is that the extension of the tree from the RP over to the source will eventually be torn down because of lack of data. But we do need to be careful that the last-hop routers don't try to build a new multicast-forwarding tree rooted at the source. To prevent this, the recipe example shows how to set the SPT threshold value so that only high-traffic multicast streams will rebuild the tree like this.

This threshold is set by the command *ip pim spt-threshold*:

```
Router1(config)#ip pim spt-threshold 10 group-list 15
```

In the example, we set the threshold to 10 Kbps for the groups defined by access-list 15. All other groups will continue to use the default threshold of zero. If you instead wanted to have this command affect all multicast groups, you could simply leave out the group-list:

```
Router1(config)#ip pim spt-threshold 10
```

You can also use this command to tell the routers to always use the RP, and never switch over to the source-based SPT by using the keyword *infinity* for the threshold value:

```
Router1(config)#ip pim spt-threshold infinity
```

Or, you could use this option with a group-list statement to prevent the router from building a source-based STP just for a specific set of groups:

```
Router1(config)#ip pim spt-threshold infinity group-list 15
```

See Also

Recipe 23.2; Recipe 23.3; Recipe 23.9

23.6 Multicast over Frame Relay or ATM WANs

Problem

You want to use sparse-mode PIM to multicast over an NBMA network.

Solution

When using PIM-SM on an nonbroadcast multiple access (NBMA) network, such as a Frame Relay or ATM WAN, you must configure the *ip pim nbma-mode* interface command:

```
Router1#configure terminal
Enter configuration commands, one per line.  End with CNTL/Z.
Router1(config)#ip multicast-routing
Router1(config)#interface Serial0/0
Router1(config-if)#encapsulation frame-relay
Router1(config-if)#ip pim sparse-mode
Router1(config-if)#ip pim nbma-mode
Router1(config-if)#end
Router1#
```

Discussion

PIM-SM can suffer from some very interesting and difficult to troubleshoot problems on an NBMA network such as a Frame Relay WAN. Specifically, consider the case where Router1 connects to two downstream PIM-SM neighbors, Router2 and Router3, through a single nonbroadcast interface. If both of the neighboring routers are members of the same group, and Router2 issues a *prune* command to leave a group, then Router1 will prune the interface, causing Router3 to stop receiving the multicast group as well.

Also, if any of the downstream neighbors on an NBMA interface joins a group, all of the other downstream neighbors will start to receive this group. This is a less serious problem, as everybody who wants the group receives it, but since all of these multicast packets are unicast separately to each downstream neighbor, it can cause bandwidth problems on busy networks.

The solution to both of these problems is to configure the *ip pim nbma-mode* command on the multicast interface. This instructs the router to track all PIM-SM joins and prunes by neighbor. It will then send the appropriate multicast groups to the appropriate neighbors via unicast packets.

Note that this is only relevant on PIM-SM networks and on NBMA networks. If your Frame Relay or ATM network is configured to emulate broadcasts using the *frame-relay map broadcast* interface command, or if you use point-to-point subinterfaces, then multicasts will work correctly without this command. This command should not be used on networks that have native multicast capabilities, such as Ethernet, for example, because it will increase the processing and memory overhead on the router unnecessarily.

See Also

Recipe 23.2; Recipe 23.3; Chapter 10

23.7   Configuring CGMP

Problem

You want the router to use CGMP to communicate with a Catalyst switch.

Solution

When you enable multicast routing and turn on PIM on an interface, IGMP is enabled by default. However, you must explicitly enable CGMP on the router if you want your Catalyst switch to take advantage of this efficient way of handling group membership:

```
Router1#configure terminal
Enter configuration commands, one per line.  End with CNTL/Z.
```

```
Router1(config)#ip multicast-routing
Router1(config)#interface FastEthernet0/0
Router1(config-if)#ip pim sparse-dense-mode
Router1(config-if)#ip cgmp
Router1(config-if)#end
Router1#
```

Discussion

The introduction to this chapter discusses the reasons for CGMP and roughly how it works. It is important to remember that CGMP is a Cisco proprietary protocol, so it will only work with Catalyst switches. Table 23-1 shows the minimum switch software revision level required for CGMP for several types of switches. If in doubt, please check your switch's documentation.

Table 23-1. Catalyst switches that support CGMP

Catalyst model	Minimum software version
1900	6.0
2820	6.0
2900XL	11.2(8)SA
2901, 2902, 2926T/F/G	2.3
2940	Not supported
2948G	All
2950/2955	Not supported
2970	Not supported
3500XL	11.2(8)SA
3550, 3560, 3750	Not supported
4000 series (CatOS)	All
4000 series (IOS)	Not supported
4912	All
5000	2.3
6000	Not supported

The syntax for enabling CGMP on these devices varies. Also, on some of the supported switches, CGMP is enabled by default while it is disabled by default on others. So you should double check that the feature is enabled on your switch. On many of these switch types, you enable CGMP by simply typing the command "cgmp" in global configuration mode. For example, on a Catalyst 1900:

```
Switch-1900#configure terminal
Enter configuration commands, one per line.  End with CNTL/Z
Switch-1900(config)#cgmp
Switch-1900(config)#exit
Switch-1900#show cgmp
```

```
CGMP Status : Enabled
CGMP Fast Leave Status : Disabled
CGMP Holdtime (secs) : 600
Allow Reserved Address to Join : Enabled

VLAN    Address              Destination
-------------------------------------------------------------------
1       0100.5E7F.FFFA       Et0/22, Et0/24
1       0100.5E00.0128       Et0/22


VLAN    Router Address       Expiration    Interface
-------------------------------------------------------------------
1       0010.7B3B.27E5       595 sec       Et0/22
Switch-1900#
```

Similarly, on a 3500XL, the commands are the same, although the output is slightly different:

```
Switch-3500XL#configure terminal
Enter configuration commands, one per line.  End with CNTL/Z
Switch-3500XL(config)#cgmp
Switch-3500XL(config)#exit
Switch-3500XL#show cgmp
CGMP is running.
CGMP Fast Leave is not running.
CGMP Allow reserved address to join GDA .
Default router timeout is 300 sec.


vLAN    IGMP MAC Address    Interfaces
------  -----------------   -----------
   1    0100.5e00.0128        Fa0/1


vLAN    IGMP Router         Expire    Interface
------  -----------------   --------  ----------
   1    0009.7cb7.c9e2      288 sec   Fa0/1
Switch-3500XL#
```

23.8   Using IGMP Version 3

Problem

You want to take advantage of the new features in IGMP Version 3.

Solution

Cisco routers use IGMP Version 2 by default. If you want to use IGMP Version 3, and if the end devices on your network support this version, you can enable native v3 support as follows:

```
Router1#configure terminal
Enter configuration commands, one per line.  End with CNTL/Z.
```

```
Router1(config)#ip multicast-routing
Router1(config)#ip pim ssm default
Router1(config)#interface FastEthernet0/0
Router1(config-if)#ip pim sparse-dense-mode
Router1(config-if)#ip igmp version 3
Router1(config-if)#end
Router1#
```

Alternatively, if you want to take advantage of Source-Specific Multicast(SSM) features, but your end devices don't support IGMP Version 3, you can use Cisco's proprietary IGMP v3lite:

```
Router1#configure terminal
Enter configuration commands, one per line.  End with CNTL/Z.
Router1(config)#ip multicast-routing
Router1(config)#ip pim ssm default
Router1(config)#interface FastEthernet0/0
Router1(config-if)#ip pim sparse-dense-mode
Router1(config-if)#ip igmp v3lite
Router1(config-if)#end
Router1#
```

Discussion

The most useful single feature of IGMP Version 3 is SSM. This allows an end device to specify not only the multicast group that it wishes to receive, but also the multicast source. The range of multicast addresses that may use specific sources is defined in the *ip pim ssm global* configuration command:

```
Router1(config)#ip pim ssm default
```

In this form, the router allows SSM for multicast addresses in the range 232.0.0.0/8. This is the default range set aside for SSM multicasting by RFC 3569. However, you can define a different range of SSM multicast group addresses as follows:

```
Router1(config)#ip pim ssm range 19
Router1(config)#access-list 19 permit 239.0.0.0 0.255.255.255
```

It is important to note that all of the routers on the segment must use IGMP Version 3 for this feature to work. Furthermore, although an IGMPv3 router can support a mixture of client IGMP versions, you should always configure all of the routers on a given LAN segment to support the same IGMP version. This is because one of these routers will be elected the Designated Router (DR) for the segment, handling all multicast forwarding. If the routers do not agree on the IGMP version that they will support, this DR functionality will not switch gracefully between routers. In some earlier versions of IOS, the routers will automatically detect that other routers are using IGMP Version 1 and revert to that. However, this is no longer true: you must manually configure all of the routers to the same version.

The individual hosts on a segment need not agree on IGMP version. The routers will make note of the IGMP version numbers in packets received from each host and respond appropriately in the same version.

See Also

RFC 3569

23.9   Static Multicast Routes and Group Memberships

Problem

You want to override the dynamic multicast routing and group membership with static entries.

Solution

By default, PIM will use the same dynamic routing table learned by the unicast routing protocol. However, in some cases you don't want to use these routes. For example, you might have to send multicast traffic through a tunnel to bypass a section of network that doesn't support multicast routing. In this case, the unicast routing table is clearly the wrong path for multicast traffic. So you need to specify a different route for multicast traffic to use:

```
Router1#configure terminal
Enter configuration commands, one per line.  End with CNTL/Z.
Router1(config)#ip multicast-routing
Router1(config)#ip mroute 192.168.15.0 255.255.255.0 192.168.98.6
Router1(config)#interface Tunnel0
Router1(config-if)#ip address 192.168.98.5 255.255.255.252
Router1(config-if)#ip pim sparse-dense-mode
Router1(config-if)#tunnel mode gre ip
Router1(config-if)#end
Router1#
```

You can specify a static IGMP join to ensure that the router always thinks that there are group members on an interface:

```
Router1#configure terminal
Enter configuration commands, one per line.  End with CNTL/Z.
Router1(config)#ip multicast-routing
Router1(config)#interface FastEthernet0/0
Router1(config-if)#ip pim sparse-dense-mode
Router1(config-if)#ip igmp join-group 239.5.5.55
Router1(config-if)#end
Router1#
```

Discussion

The static *mroute* command is used only to describe the Reverse Path Forwarding (RPF) path the multicast traffic should take. PIM doesn't redistribute this information, but all devices on the internal network need to know that this router is the gateway to this particular external network so that they can also build their SPT trees

---

appropriately. So it is likely that other routers will also need static *mroutes*, if you are using tunnels like this.

Static multicast routes are most frequently used when the unicast network doesn't have the same topology as the multicast network. There are two main reasons why this might be the case. The recipe example suggests one of these reasons: there may be tunnels that bypass nonmulticast sections of the network.

The other common reason for using a static multicast route is to force multicast traffic to take a different path than unicast traffic. For example, you might have a separate network link for multicast traffic. As with all static routing, doing this creates administrative problems because it is very difficult to construct static routes that adapt to network failures.

The static IGMP Join example is most useful when there are devices on the segment that may have poor IGMP implementations or when they join and leave extremely rapidly. Alternatively, as in Recipe 23.19, the receiving devices may not know that this is a multicast application. A static IGMP statement ensures that the router always thinks that there are group members on this interface.

You should be careful about using this command on any links that contain other routers because it may lead to multicast routing loops. This is because the router will always forward packets for this group out this interface, even if PIM would normally prune this link from the tree. So this command should be used with extreme caution.

IOS levels 12.3(2)T and higher include the *ip igmp static-group* command as an alternative to the *ip igmp join-group* command. This command can specify an IGMP group, similar to the *join-group* command:

```
Router1(config-if)#ip igmp static-group 239.5.5.55
```

Or, if you are using source-specific multicasts, as allowed in IGMP Version 3, this command allows you to specify a particular source:

```
Router1(config-if)#ip igmp static-group 239.5.5.55 source 192.168.15.5
```

The other important difference between the *join-group* and *static-group* commands is that *join-group* forces the router to process switch multicast packets sent through this interface, while the new *static-group* variant employs the more efficient fast switching.

23.10 Routing Multicast Traffic with MOSPF

Problem

You want to distribute your multicast routing tables with MOSPF.

Solution

Unfortunately, Cisco does not support MOSPF. As mentioned in the Introduction to this chapter, MOSPF is a set of multicast extensions to OSPF that uses LSA Type 6. By default, when a Cisco router receives a Type 6 LSA packet it will generate a %OSPF-4-BADLSATYPE error message. To avoid this error message, you can configure your routers to ignore Type 6 LSA packets:

```
Router#configure terminal
Enter configuration commands, one per line.  End with CNTL/Z.
Router(config)#router ospf 65530
Router(config-router)#ospf ignore lsa mospf
Router(config-router)#end
Router#
```

Discussion

MOSPF has not enjoyed a particularly wide acceptance for several reasons, mostly related to the fact that it uses a dense-mode multicast-forwarding scheme, and because it is protocol dependant. It turns out to be most useful in networks that meet several key requirements:

- They should use a relatively small number of multicast applications.
- These applications should have few servers and many group members, with the group members scattered throughout the network.
- The network must use OSPF as its unicast protocol.
- The applications should deliver a flow of multicast traffic that is neither heavy enough to cause congestion problems on the slowest links in the network, nor so light that relationships time out in the routers.

Few router vendors have implemented MOSPF. Increasingly, the multicast routing protocol of choice appears to be PIM-SM.

However, it is important to note that the normal default behavior for PIM is to use the standard IP unicast routing table. If you happen to be using OSPF for your standard IP routing tables, PIM will use the same OSPF routing tables to construct its Reverse Path Forwarding (RPF) trees back to the multicast source or Rendezvous Point (RP) by default. So you can use OSPF with PIM, without needing any additional configuration.

The only thing that you miss by not being able to use MOSPF is the ability to dynamically distribute a multicast routing table that reflects a different topology than the unicast routing table.

23.11 Routing Multicast Traffic with DVMRP

Problem

You want to route multicast traffic by using the DVMRP protocol.

Solution

Cisco routers support DVMRP only as a gateway to PIM. So the configuration is remarkably similar to the PIM configuration. The key difference is in the *ip dvmrp unicast-routing* command, which tells the router to use the DVMRP multicast routing table instead of the usual PIM choice of the unicast routing table:

```
Router1#configure terminal
Enter configuration commands, one per line.  End with CNTL/Z.
Router1(config)#ip multicast-routing
Router1(config)#interface FastEthernet0/0
Router1(config-if)#ip pim sparse-dense-mode
Router1(config-if)#ip dvmrp unicast-routing
Router1(config-if)#ip dvmrp summary-address 192.168.0.0 255.255.0.0
Router1(config-if)#end
Router1#
```

Discussion

Before saying anything else, we will stress once again that DVMRP is not our first choice for a multicast routing protocol. PIM-DM is simpler to implement and more efficient with router resources if you want a dense-mode protocol. And PIM-SM scales much better in larger networks or when there are many groups. In fact, Cisco routers do not provide a full implementation of DVMRP. They can take part in DVMRP neighbor discovery and route exchange, but internally the multicast processing is done using PIM. However, you can configure PIM to use the DVMRP routing table, which is what this recipe actually does.

DVMRP is defined in RFC 1075, and was the first widely implemented multicast routing protocol, forming the core of the Internet's original Multicast Backbone (MBONE). So the main reasons for implementing it today are to give compatibility with an existing DVMRP network. It is unlikely that anybody would want to implement a new production DVMRP network today, just as few people would want to implement any other routing protocol that hasn't been significantly updated since 1988 (the original publication date for RFC 1075).

The DVMRP protocol differs from PIM-DM in a fundamental way. Where PIM-DM uses the router's existing unicast routing table to determine the shortest path back to the source, DVMRP distributes and maintains its own internal routing table. This was needed because early multicast networks tended to use a lot of tunnels to allow multicast traffic to cross large network regions that supported only unicast routing.

So the multicast network topology could be quite different from the unicast topology, necessitating a separate routing table.

DVMRP distributes routing information between adjacent routers by means of multicast packets sent on the globally defined well-known multicast address, 224.0.0.4. This process begins by exchanging neighbor information. Every router needs to know about all of its neighbors so that it can always determine the best path back to the source, which is the only way it can eliminate loops. This neighbor information is updated every 60 seconds by default. If a neighbor misses four consecutive updates, the router considers it dead and removes it from the routing tables.

These periodic updates also contain all of the multicast routing information for the network. If a route is not seen in two consecutive updates, then it is considered invalid if no longer used. It is removed from the tables if it remains invalid for two additional minutes. So when there are network problems, it is possible to have interruptions of up to two minutes.

Cisco does not offer a full DVMRP implementation. Instead, it gives the ability to make a gateway between DVMRP and PIM. This allows a Cisco router to perform many of the standard DVMRP functions, but it makes it impossible to use Cisco routers to build a pure DVMRP network. In particular, Cisco routers do not send any DVMRP Probe messages to establish new neighbor relationships.

However, when you enable PIM routing on an interface, the router also starts to listen for DVMRP announcements addressed to group 224.0.0.4. The Cisco router responds to these announcements by exchanging its routing tables with the DVMRP neighbors. However, by default, it does not use the DVMRP routing table it receives unless the interface has the command *ip dvmrp unicast-routing* enabled. This is particularly important in cases when the multicast topology is different than the unicast network topology, as in the DVMRP tunnel example in Recipe 23.12, for example.

Since DVMRP functionality on Cisco routers generally represents a gateway between pockets of PIM and DVMRP functionality, we have included another useful command in the recipe example. The command *ip dvmrp summary-address* tells the router to advertise only a summary route into the DVMRP network:

```
Router1(config-if)#ip dvmrp summary-address 192.168.0.0 255.255.0.0
```

This helps to simplify the multicast routing tables to save memory and improve overall efficiency.

In some cases, you might have a router connected to a segment with several DVMRP devices like Unix servers running *mrouted*. There are two ways that you can restrict what your router accepts from DVMRP devices, both are variants of the interface configuration command, *ip dvmrp accept-filter*:

```
Router1#configure terminal
Enter configuration commands, one per line.  End with CNTL/Z.
Router1(config)#ip multicast-routing
```

```
Router1(config)#access-list 11 permit 192.168.1.17 0.0.0.0
Router1(config)#access-list 11 permit 192.168.1.18 0.0.0.0
Router1(config)#access-list 11 deny any
Router1(config)#interface FastEthernet0/0
Router1(config-if)#ip pim sparse-dense-mode
Router1(config-if)#ip dvmrp unicast-routing
Router1(config-if)#ip dvmrp accept-filter 0 neighbor-list 11
Router1(config-if)#end
Router1#
```

This version of the *ip dvmrp accept-filter* command restricts the allowed DVMRP neighbors. If this router receives DVMRP updates from any devices not in the specified access-list, it will simply ignore them. Note that we have used an access-list number of 0 in this command, indicating that all sources should be accepted.

The other version of this command specifies what ranges of multicast source address ranges this router will accept:

```
Router1#configure terminal
Enter configuration commands, one per line.  End with CNTL/Z.
Router1(config)#ip multicast-routing
Router1(config)#access-list 12 permit 192.168.10.0 0.0.0.255
Router1(config)#access-list 12 deny any
Router1(config)#interface FastEthernet0/0
Router1(config-if)#ip pim sparse-dense-mode
Router1(config-if)#ip dvmrp unicast-routing
Router1(config-if)#ip dvmrp accept-filter 12 95
Router1(config-if)#end
Router1#
```

In this case, the router is only willing to listen to information about sources on the 192.168.10.0/24 network. And we have gone slightly further by specifying an administrative distance of 95 for these routes. When it hears about these multicast routes, this router will automatically give them a distance of 95. This will ensure that, if these same routes are learned by another method that has a better administrative distance, the router will not use them. For example, in Chapter 5 we saw that EIGRP has a default administrative distance value of 90 while OSPF has a value of 110. So this command will tell the router to use the DVMRP routes for constructing source-rooted multicast trees if the unicast route it has for the source is from OSPF. But if it has an EIGRP unicast route, it will use that route instead.

Note that the router will never use the DVMRP route for forwarding unicast traffic. It only uses this information for constructing loop-free trees back to the multicast source, which in turn tells the router which ports it can forward multicast traffic through.

See Also

Recipe 23.1; Recipe 23.12; Chapter 5; Chapter 6; RFC 1075

23.12 DVMRP Tunnels

Problem

You want to create a DVMRP tunnel to bypass a section of network that doesn't support multicast.

Solution

You can create a DVMRP tunnel from a Cisco router to a nonCisco DVMRP device by using the special DVMRP tunnel mode. This allows you to pass multicast traffic through a section of network that doesn't support multicast routing:

```
Router1#configure terminal
Enter configuration commands, one per line.  End with CNTL/Z.
Router1(config)#ip multicast-routing
Router1(config)#interface Tunnel0
Router1(config-if)#ip unnumbered FastEthernet0/0
Router1(config-if)#ip pim sparse-dense-mode
Router1(config-if)#ip dvmrp unicast-routing
Router1(config-if)#tunnel source FastEthernet0/0
Router1(config-if)#tunnel destination 192.168.99.15
Router1(config-if)#tunnel mode dvmrp
Router1(config-if)#exit
Router1(config)#interface FastEthernet0/0
Router1(config-if)#ip address 192.168.1.1 255.255.255.0
Router1(config-if)#ip pim sparse-dense-mode
Router1(config-if)#end
Router1#
```

Discussion

There are several important things to remember about DVMRP tunnels. First, you cannot create a DVMRP tunnel between two Cisco routers because neither router will send DVMRP Probe messages. So this feature is only used to create tunnels between Cisco routers and native DVMRP devices such as nonCisco routers or Unix servers running *mrouted*.

Second, a DVMRP tunnel is essentially just a standard IP-in-IP tunnel. However, it is just used to transmit multicast traffic. Unicast traffic follows the normal network path. This is markedly different from several of the examples of GRE tunneling (a more flexible variant of IP-in-IP tunneling) discussed in Chapter 12, where the tunnel was used to carry unicast traffic.

Third, the device on the other end of this tunnel must also be explicitly configured for this tunnel. The IP address it specifies for the tunnel destination must match the tunnel source address specified on the Cisco router. In this case, the source is the interface *FastEthernet0/0*, so the device on the other end must specify a tunnel destination address of 192.168.1.1, which is this interface's IP address. Similarly, the address specified as the tunnel source on the other device must match the tunnel destination address on the Cisco end.

Fourth, it is important to notice that both the Tunnel interface and the source interface have PIM enabled. We have used sparse-dense mode for PIM, which is just to cover all of the possibilities. But the router will not route multicast traffic correctly without some form of PIM enabled on these interfaces.

And, finally, if you want to create a PIM tunnel to another Cisco device, the easiest way to do so is to create a GRE tunnel and use a static *mroute*, as we did in Recipe 23.9. This will ensure that multicast traffic uses the tunnel rather than trying to use the unicast path. A DVMRP tunnel can only connect a Cisco router to a nonCisco native DVMRP device.

See Also

Recipe 23.9; Recipe 23.11; Chapter 12

23.13 Configuring Bidirectional PIM

Problem

You want to use Bidirectional PIM to improve efficiency of your sparse-mode multicast network.

Solution

To use Bidirectional PIM, you must configure all of the routers in your network to support this method of building multicast forwarding trees. The RP configuration looks like this:

```
Router-RP1#configure terminal
Enter configuration commands, one per line.  End with CNTL/Z.
Router-RP1(config)#ip multicast-routing
Router-RP1(config)#ip pim bidir-enable
Router-RP1(config)#ip pim rp-address 192.168.12.1 bidir
Router-RP1(config)#ip pim rp-candidate Loopback0 group-list 15 bidir
Router-RP1(config)#ip pim bsr-candidate Loopback0 1
Router-RP1(config)#access-list 15 permit 239.5.5.0 0.0.0.255
Router-RP1(config)#access-list 15 deny any
Router-RP1(config)#interface Loopback0
Router-RP1(config-if)#ip address 192.168.12.1 255.255.255.255
Router-RP1(config-if)# ip pim sparse-mode
Router-RP1(config-if)#exit
Router-RP1(config)#interface FastEthernet0/0
Router-RP1(config-if)#ip address 192.168.1.1 255.255.255.0
Router-RP1(config-if)#ip pim sparse-mode
Router-RP1(config-if)#exit
Router-RP1(config)#interface Serial1/0
Router-RP1(config-if)#ip address 192.168.2.5 255.255.255.252
```

```
Router-RP1(config-if)#ip pim sparse-mode
Router-RP1(config-if)#exit
Router-RP1(config)#end
Router-RP1#
```

And the other multicast routers in this network will be configured to use Bidirectional PIM for this RP, as follows:

```
Router1#configure terminal
Enter configuration commands, one per line.  End with CNTL/Z.
Router1(config)#ip multicast-routing
Router1(config)#ip pim bidir-enable
Router1(config)#ip pim rp-address 192.168.12.1 bidir
Router1(config)#interface FastEthernet0/0
Router1(config-if)#ip address 192.168.1.2 255.255.255.0
Router1(config-if)#ip pim sparse-mode
Router1(config-if)#interface Serial1/0
Router1(config-if)#ip address 192.168.3.5 255.255.255.252
Router1(config-if)#ip pim sparse-mode
Router1(config-if)#end
Router1#
```

Discussion

As we mentioned in the Introduction to this chapter, Bidirectional PIM is closely related to PIM-SM, but with a different method for building the multicast forwarding path from the source to the RP. In most cases, the actual path used by Bidirectional PIM will be identical to the path used by PIM-SM.

However, there are two key practical differences between PIM-SM and Bidirectional PIM. First, where PIM-SM must use unicast Registration packets to introduce a new multicast stream to the RP, Bidirectional PIM uses native multicasts and pre-builds the multicast tree to the RP. And second, PIM-SM can, after a multicast source has been sending packets for a predetermined period of time, revert to a source-rooted tree, eliminating the RP function. Bidirectional PIM does not have this capability, and barring changes in the network topology, will keep the same multicast forwarding tree for as long as the source continues to send packets.

If you plan to use this feature, it is important to remember that all of the routers in the network, including the RP, must be configured to support Bidirectional PIM. You do this by first enabling Bidirectional PIM mode, and specifying any statically configured RPs using the *bidir* option. These are global configuration commands:

```
Router1(config)#ip pim bidir-enable
Router1(config)#ip pim rp-address 192.168.12.1 bidir
```

On the RP you must also enable Bidirectional PIM by using the same *bidir-enable* command, and you must specify the *bidir* option on the *rp-candidate* command:

```
Router-RP1(config)#ip pim bidir-enable
Router-RP1(config)#ip pim rp-address 192.168.12.1 bidir
Router-RP1(config)#ip pim rp-candidate Loopback0 group-list 15 bidir
```

You will get very odd behavior if you configure some of your routers for Bidirectional PIM support and others for PIM-SM (regardless of whether you use AutoRP or BSR for locating the RP). If a Bidirectional PIM router initiates a new multicast source, it will attempt to reach the RP using multicast packets. Unfortunately, any upstream routers that are not running Bidirectional PIM will not have a pre-built Bidirectional tree rooted at the RP, and the multicast packets will not arrive.

 Since Bidirectional PIM became available in IOS level 12.2, if you have a mixture of IOS levels that includes earlier releases, you cannot use this feature in your network.

Note that in these examples we have used BSR to locate the RP, as in Recipe 23.2. We did this because it is somewhat simpler conceptually to see the interfaces configured in sparse mode. However, we could just as easily have used AutoRP for RP discovery, as in Recipe 23.3. In this case, the key is to configure the RP to advertise itself as bidirectional when it sends RP announcement packets:

```
Router-RP1(config)#ip pim send-rp-announce loopback0 scope 16 group-list 15 bidir
Router-RP1(config)#ip pim send-rp-discovery scope 16
```

And you must also configure all of the interfaces in sparse-dense mode, as we did in Recipe 23.3.

It is important to remember that Bidirectional PIM creates an RP rooted multicast tree for each RP. If you have more than one RP, then the protocol creates a separate forwarding tree for each RP (not one for each group). This also implies that you can configure a mixture of Bidirectional PIM and PIM-SM RPs, with different multicast groups using different tree construction protocols depending on which RP they use. Furthermore, if you use AutoRP and sparse-dense mode, the routers will resort to dense mode by default for any multicast groups that do not have an RP. So it is actually possible to mix all three flavors of PIM in a single network, although we don't generally recommend this approach, as it will make troubleshooting more complicated.

See Also

Recipe 23.2; Recipe 23.3

23.14 Controlling Multicast Scope with TTL

Problem

You want to ensure that your multicast traffic remains confined to a small part of the network.

Solution

You can define a TTL threshold value for each interface on a router. The *ttl-threshold* command instructs the router to drop any multicast packets that have a TTL value less than or equal to the specified value. The router will receive packets on this interface normally. This command only affects transmission of multicast packets:

```
Router1#configure terminal
Enter configuration commands, one per line.  End with CNTL/Z.
Router1(config)#ip multicast-routing
Router1(config)#interface FastEthernet0/0
Router1(config-if)#ip multicast ttl-threshold 16
Router1(config-if)#end
Router1#
```

This technique works for all multicast routing protocols.

Discussion

The first popular method for controlling the scope of multicast transmissions made use of the standard IP TTL header variable. This is an 8-bit variable that each router decrements by one as it forwards the packet. If a router receives a packet with a TTL value of 1, it won't forward it any further. The main use of TTL in unicast IP networking is to help to kill loops. In a loop situation, a packet may go around a few times, but the TTL value keeps decrementing and will eventually reach 1, when the network will drop it.

In multicast networking, TTL has a more subtle use. Most multicast applications include the ability to define an initial TTL value other than the default 255. This leads to a common method for keeping multicast traffic within a certain well-defined part of the network. The customary technique is to configure the multicast applications with an initial TTL value that defines the scope, as shown in Table 23-2.

Table 23-2. Commonly used TTL values for controlling multicast scope

Scope	Initial TTL value
Local segment	1
Site, department, or division	16
Enterprise	64
World	128

You would configure these values on your multicast server to define how far you want the application to reach. Then you must enforce these limits with your routers. For multicast traffic that is purely local to the server's network segment there is no need to do anything special on the routers. When a router receives a packet with a TTL value of 1, it decrements this value to get 0, and drops the packet without forwarding it any further.

The example above shows how you would configure the routers along the boundary between two departments. If a department has a multicast application that is intended to serve only this department, they would configure the routers that connect to other departments or to the network backbone to drop any multicast packets with a TTL value less than or equal to 16, as shown in the example:

```
Router1(config-if)#ip multicast ttl-threshold 16
```

It doesn't matter where in the internal departmental network this server is located, the boundary routers will always prevent these packets from reaching the rest of the network. This way another department in the same enterprise can have an application using the same multicast group address without conflict.

Similarly, if a multicast application serves an entire enterprise network, you would configure the server to use an initial TTL value of 64. Then you would configure the border around the edges of your enterprise network to drop any multicast packets with a TTL value greater than or equal to 64.

The reason for suggesting an initial TTL value of 128 for worldwide applications is simply to allow for future implementation of new multicast domains.

The TTL values shown in Table 23-2 are just suggestions based on common usage. There is no mandated standard, nor is there an IETF Best Current Practices document on this subject.

There are a couple of important problems with using TTL thresholds to control multicast scope. The most critical is that you must rely on the server configuration. If a new server is turned on to offer multicast services within a network, you have to cross your fingers and hope that the systems administrators have configured the initial TTL values properly to prevent leakage. The worst case is when two or more departments use applications the same multicast group numbers. If the traffic from one manages to leak to the other, it can cause serious confusion to the application. It is also relatively easy to have conflicts between global and local multicast applications using the same group addresses.

TTL scoping can also cause serious problems for multicast routing protocols at the network boundaries. The routers at these boundaries will have trouble pruning themselves from unwanted SPT trees in dense-mode routing because they effectively act as a sink for all multicast traffic. This can cause CPU problems on the border routers as they handle extra multicast traffic, only to drop it.

For these reasons, it is generally better to use Administratively Scoped Addressing for controlling multicast scope, as shown in Recipe 23.15.

Note that when a router needs to drop a unicast packet because of a TTL limitation, it sends an ICMP TTL Exceeded error message back to the source. However, according to RFC 1812, such messages are not generated for multicast packets. This is good because it would otherwise cause a continuous barrage of ICMP errors from the perimeter of the network that could potentially cause network congestion and CPU problems on the multicast source device.

See Also

Recipe 23.15

23.15 Controlling Multicast Scope with Administratively Scoped Addressing

Problem

You want to use RFC 2365 administratively scoped multicast addressing to control how multicast traffic is distributed through your network.

Solution

To configure regions of multicast scope using addressing rather than TTL, using the *ip multicast boundary* interface command:

```
Router1#configure terminal
Enter configuration commands, one per line.  End with CNTL/Z.
Router1(config)#ip multicast-routing
Router1(config)#access-list 15 deny 239.255.0.0 0.0.255.255
Router1(config)#access-list 15 permit any
Router1(config)#interface FastEthernet0/0
Router1(config-if)#ip multicast boundary 15
Router1(config-if)#end
Router1#
```

Note that the access-list uses a *deny* statement to specify which groups are to be dropped. Because access-lists have an implicit deny on all addresses not explicitly matched, you must include a *permit ip any* at the end of the access-list to allow all other multicast groups to pass normally.

Discussion

RFC 2365 defined a new way of handling the problem of controlling the scope of multicast applications. The IETF realized that you can't count on applications to have the right initial TTL value. The other important reason that they give for avoiding TTL scoping has to do with pruning in dense mode multicast protocols such as PIM-DM or DVMRP.

The problem is that the router at the boundary is dropping all multicast packets, but it can't tell its upstream neighbors that it no longer wants to be a member of this SPT. And it isn't sufficient to simply discover the problem and prune the tree at the previous node because of the possibility that the packets will still reach the destination by another path. The result is that the routers at the TTL boundary become "sinks" that receive all multicast traffic but cannot process it. If there is a lot of multicast traffic, this can cause performance problems.

Another problem is caused by misconfigured multicast servers causing multicast applications to leak out of their domains. This problem can occur either accidentally or deliberately, and in either case the result is that multicast applications in neighboring network regions will not work properly. And a similar problem occurs when the routers at the boundary are not configured properly, allowing even well-behaved multicast applications to leak out of their domains. Clearly a better solution is required.

The alternative proposed in RFC 2365 is to set aside particular ranges of multicast group addresses for unregistered use, similar to the RFC 1918 system of unregistered IP addresses. The RFC takes the range from 239.0.0.0 to 239.255.255.255 for this purpose. It defines how to use particular ranges of these addresses for multicast applications with different scopes. These ranges are summarized in Table 23-3.

We note in passing that the IANA has registered several other multicast addresses for specific applications. The range from 224.0.0.0 through 224.0.0.255 is reserved for routing protocols and other network maintenance applications that are confined to the local network segment. The multicast addresses between 224.0.1.0 and 224.0.1.255 have been designated for Internetwork control applications such as Cisco's RP discovery protocol. And the range from 224.0.2.0 through 224.0.255.255 is set aside for miscellaneous well-known registered application purposes. Refer to the IANA web site, *http://www.iana.org/assignments/multicast-addresses*, for specific well-known addresses.

Table 23-3. Multicast group address ranges

Scope	Address range	Access list
Site local	239.255.0.0/16	access-list 15 deny 239.255.0.0 0.0.255.255
Expanding site local	239.254.0.0/16, 239.253.0.0/16, etc.	access-list 15 deny 239.254.0.0 0.0.255.255, access-list 15 deny 239.253.0.0 0.0.255.255, etc.
Organization local	239.192.0.0/14	access-list 15 deny 239.192.0.0 0.3.255.255
Expanding organization local	239.128.0.0/10, 239.64.0.0/10, 239.0.0.0/10	access-list 15 deny 239.128.0.0 0.63.255.255, access-list 15 deny 239.64.0.0 0.63.255.255, access-list 15 deny 239.0.0.0 0.63.255.255

The configuration example shows a Site Local boundary. The *ip multicast boundary* command affects the packets sent and received on this interface. So you would configure this command on all interfaces that connect to other sites. For interfaces that connect to other organizations, the only difference is in the access-list, as shown in Table 23-3.

If you needed more multicast address space, you would add 239.254.0.0 first, then 239.253.0.0, and so forth.

In many organizations you will see both TTL (see Recipe 23.14) and Administratively Scoped Addressing used simultaneously to control the reach of multicast applications. The two methods work well together, which makes it relatively easy to accomplish a transition from one method to the other.

One final point is worth noting here. The *ip multicast boundary* command is not the same as simply putting an access list on the interface to block the exchange of packets. The actual multicast packets are not the only thing that you want to prevent from crossing this boundary. You also want to prevent PIM from joining any of these multicast distribution trees across the boundary. That is what this command does for you.

23.16 Exchanging Multicast Routing Information with MBGP

Problem

You want to exchange multicast routing information between two networks using MBGP.

Solution

Before setting up MBGP, you should set up multicast-routing on the Autonomous System Boundary Router (ASBR) and configure it to block multicast traffic that you know is only intended for the local network:

```
Router-ASBR1#configure terminal
Enter configuration commands, one per line.  End with CNTL/Z.
Router-ASBR1(config)#ip multicast-routing
Router-ASBR1(config)#access-list 15 deny 239.0.0.0 0.255.255.255
Router-ASBR1(config)#access-list 15 deny 224.0.1.39
Router-ASBR1(config)#access-list 15 deny 224.0.1.40
Router-ASBR1(config)#access-list 15 permit any
Router-ASBR1(config)#interface Serial0/0
Router-ASBR1(config-if)#ip multicast boundary 15
Router-ASBR1(config-if)#ip multicast ttl-threshold 64
Router-ASBR1(config-if)#ip pim dense-mode
Router-ASBR1(config-if)#end
Router-ASBR1#
```

Then you need to set up the MBGP configuration:

```
Router-ASBR1#configure terminal
Enter configuration commands, one per line.  End with CNTL/Z.
Router-ASBR1(config)#router bgp 65530
Router-ASBR1(config-router)#network 10.0.0.0 mask 255.0.0.0
Router-ASBR1(config-router)#neighbor 10.15.32.1 remote-as 65531
Router-ASBR1(config-router)#address-family ipv4 multicast
Router-ASBR1(config-router-af)#neighbor 10.15.32.1 activate
Router-ASBR1(config-router-af)#end
Router-ASBR1#
```

Discussion

Usually when people talk about using BGP, they immediately think of the public Internet. Since most of the Internet is not capable of transmitting multicast traffic (yet), MBGP may not seem immediately useful. However, BGP has many other uses besides connecting to the Internet. For example, many large networks use it for interconnecting larger corporate divisions for stability, scalability, or administrative reasons. And BGP is often used for interconnecting private networks belonging to separate companies that share information in large volume. In any case, where you use BGP for interconnecting two networks, it is natural to consider MBGP for sharing any required multicast routing information. And there is more and more interest and experimentation in multicast functionality in the public Internet.

However, it's important to remember that MBGP is not actually a multicast routing protocol in the same sense as PIM or DVMRP. It does not do *Join* or *Prune* operations to create SPTs, nor does it have a mechanism to find Rendezvous Points. It merely allows you to transmit routing information that the router can use in calculating the best path back to the source. This is why we have configured PIM-DM on the external interface in the example.

The reason why we have not specified PIM-SM in particular is because doing so implies that there must be an RP external to the Autonomous System. This is possible, and increasingly common. But it means that you need a way to discover it. The best way to do this is to use the Multicast Source Discovery Protocol (MSDP), which is described in Recipe 23.17.

The example configuration does several things. First, it uses the same principles demonstrated in Recipes 23.14 and 23.15 for controlling scope. The external interfaces drop any packets with a TTL value less than or equal to 64, to help prevent internal applications from reaching the adjacent network. And these interfaces are also configured to block all groups with addresses between 239.0.0.0 and 239.255. 255.255, to enforce administratively scoped addressing.

You will also notice that the same access list that enforces this address restriction also blocks two other groups: 224.0.1.39 and 224.0.1.40. These are used by Cisco's proprietary Auto-RP for discovering Rendezvous Points within a network. It is a good idea to prevent these groups from crossing network boundaries, whether you are using Auto-RP or not. Otherwise you risk leaking inappropriate RP information from one network into the other. It can cause serious confusion if your network tries to use the RP from an adjacent network for its internal traffic.

In the BGP configuration section, both multicast and unicast traffic use the same network paths. You can also break these up so that you send multicast traffic by a different path than unicast traffic. This is done by simply defining one of the BGP peers for multicast traffic, and leaving the other unmodified so that the router will use it for unicast traffic:

```
Router-ASBR1#configure terminal
Enter configuration commands, one per line.  End with CNTL/Z.
Router-ASBR1(config)#router bgp 65530
Router-ASBR1(config-router)#network 10.0.0.0 mask 255.0.0.0
Router-ASBR1(config-router)#neighbor 10.15.32.1 remote-as 65531
Router-ASBR1(config-router)#neighbor 10.15.32.2 remote-as 65531
Router-ASBR1(config-router)#address-family ipv4 multicast
Router-ASBR1(config-router-af)#neighbor 10.15.32.1 activate
Router-ASBR1(config-router-af)#end
Router-ASBR1#
```

Whether you route unicast and multicast traffic through the same or different paths, MBGP allows you to apply AS filtering separately to both kinds of traffic. There is a new route-map match clause that you can use specifically to identify multicast routing information:

```
Router-ASBR1(config)#route-map mbgp-test permit 10
Router-ASBR1(config-routemap)#match nlri multicast
```

See Also

Recipe 23.14; Recipe 23.15; Recipe 23.17

23.17 Using MSDP to Discover External Sources

Problem

You want to use MSDP to discover information about multicast sources in other Autonomous Systems.

Solution

The typical way to configure Multicast Source Discovery Protocol (MSDP) involves first selecting one of your MBGP routers as the RP for your internal network. Then you set up an MSDP peer relationship with the RP in another Autonomous System, which is usually an MBGP peer router in the next domain. The following configuration includes commands required to configure the router as an RP for the internal network using BSR, as discussed in Recipe 23.2, although you could just as easily use Auto-RP. It also includes configuration to prevent local multicast traffic from leaking into the neighboring network, as discussed in Recipes 23.14 and 23.15. And it includes MBGP configuration as in Recipe 23.16:

```
Router-ASBR1#configure terminal
Enter configuration commands, one per line.  End with CNTL/Z.
Router-ASBR1(config)#ip multicast-routing
Router-ASBR1(config)#interface Loopback0
Router-ASBR1(config-if)#ip address 192.168.12.1 255.255.255.255
Router-ASBR1(config-if)# ip pim sparse-mode
Router-ASBR1(config-if)#interface FastEthernet0/0
Router-ASBR1(config-if)#ip address 192.168.1.1 255.255.255.0
```

```
Router-ASBR1(config-if)#ip pim sparse-mode
Router-ASBR1(config-if)#exit
Router-ASBR1(config)#interface Serial1/0
Router-ASBR1(config-if)#ip address 192.168.2.5 255.255.255.252
Router-ASBR1(config-if)#ip multicast boundary 15
Router-ASBR1(config-if)#ip multicast ttl-threshold 64
Router-ASBR1(config-if)#ip pim sparse-mode
Router-ASBR1(config-if)#exit
Router-ASBR1(config)#ip pim rp-candidate loopback0
Router-ASBR1(config)#ip pim bsr-candidate loopback0 1
Router-ASBR1(config-if)#router bgp 65530
Router-ASBR1(config-router)#network 10.0.0.0 mask 255.0.0.0
Router-ASBR1(config-router)#neighbor 192.168.2.6 remote-as 65531
Router-ASBR1(config-router)#address-family ipv4 multicast
Router-ASBR1(config-router-af)#neighbor 192.168.2.6 activate
Router-ASBR1(config-router-af)#exit
Router-ASBR1(config-router)#exit
Router-ASBR1(config)#ip msdp peer 192.168.2.6
Router-ASBR1(config)#ip msdp sa-request 192.168.2.6
Router-ASBR1(config)#access-list 15 deny 239.0.0.0 0.255.255.255
Router-ASBR1(config)#access-list 15 deny 224.0.1.39
Router-ASBR1(config)#access-list 15 deny 224.0.1.40
Router-ASBR1(config)#access-list 15 permit any
Router-ASBR1(config)#end
Router-ASBR1#
```

Discussion

This is a rather long example, but most of the information here is discussed in earlier recipes. The important lines are just the two *ip msdp* commands:

```
Router-ASBR1(config)#ip msdp peer 192.168.2.6
Router-ASBR1(config)#ip msdp sa-request 192.168.2.6
```

This tells the router that it is to send Source Active (SA) messages to this peer device whenever it sees new multicast sources, and requests that the peer device do the same. The peer must also be configured with similar commands to ensure that it exchanges information about its multicast sources with this router.

You can configure several MSDP peers, but if you do, one of them should be configured as the default as follows:

```
Router-ASBR1#configure terminal
Enter configuration commands, one per line.  End with CNTL/Z.
Router-ASBR1(config)#ip msdp peer 192.168.2.6 connect-source Loopback0
Router-ASBR1(config)#ip msdp sa-request 192.168.2.6
Router-ASBR1(config)#ip msdp default-peer 192.168.3.6 connect-source Loopback0
Router-ASBR1(config)#ip msdp sa-request 192.168.3.6
Router-ASBR1(config)#end
Router-ASBR1#
```

Even though MSDP will allow the routers to exchange information about active sources and groups, it does not include the ability to *Join* and *Prune* SPTs for different multicast groups. So, for this reason, we have also configured PIM-SM on the connection to the peer router. As an alternative, if you don't want to exchange PIM information with the neighboring network, you could treat it as a stub network and use PIM neighbor filters, as shown in Recipe 23.4.

This multi-peer example shows how to specify a particular source address for this router. In this case, MSDP will use the address of the *Loopback0* interface.

You can also apply filters to both the sources and groups that you want to receive or distribute to another network with the *ip msdp sa-filter* command:

```
Router-ASBR1#configure terminal
Enter configuration commands, one per line.  End with CNTL/Z.
Router-ASBR1(config)#ip msdp sa-filter in 192.168.2.6 list 101
Router-ASBR1(config)#ip msdp sa-filter out 192.168.2.6 list 102
Router-ASBR1(config)#access-list 101 permit any 225.0.0.0 0.255.255.255
Router-ASBR1(config)#access-list 101 permit 10.0.0.0 0.255.255.255 any
Router-ASBR1(config)#access-list 101 deny any any
Router-ASBR1(config)#end
Router-ASBR1#
```

For more information on MSDP, please refer to the RFC 3618.

See Also

Recipe 23.2; Recipe 23.3; Recipe 23.4; Recipe 23.14; Recipe 23.15; Recipe 23.16; RFC 3618

23.18 Configuring Anycast RP

Problem

You want to configure two or more RPs and have your routers simply use whichever one is closest.

Solution

One of the most significant shortcomings of PIM-SM is that within any given multicast network boundaries, there can be only one RP for any multicast group. This has several potential problems including slow convergence after an active RP failure and potentially extra hops required to reach a distant RP. Anycast RP solves these problems.

The first RP configuration looks like this:

```
Router-RP1#configure terminal
Enter configuration commands, one per line.  End with CNTL/Z.
Router-RP1(config)#ip multicast-routing
Router-RP1(config)#interface Loopback0
Router-RP1(config-if)# ip address 10.4.4.4 255.255.255.255
Router-RP1(config-if)#exit
Router-RP1(config)#interface Loopback1
Router-RP1(config-if)# ip address 192.168.99.1 255.255.255.255
```

```
Router-RP1(config-if)# ip pim sparse-dense-mode
Router-RP1(config-if)#exit
Router-RP1(config)#ip pim send-rp-announce Loopback1 scope 16 group-list 22
Router-RP1(config)#ip pim send-rp-discovery Loopback1 scope 16
Router-RP1(config)#ip msdp peer 10.5.5.5 connect-source Loopback0
Router-RP1(config)#access-list 22 permit 239.0.0.0 0.255.255.255.255
Router-RP1(config)#end
Router-RP1#
```

The configuration for the second RP router is almost identical:

```
Router-RP2#configure terminal
Enter configuration commands, one per line.  End with CNTL/Z.
Router-RP2(config)#ip multicast-routing
Router-RP2(config)#interface Loopback0
Router-RP2(config-if)# ip address 10.5.5.5 255.255.255.255
Router-RP2(config-if)#exit
Router-RP2(config)#interface Loopback1
Router-RP2(config-if)# ip address 192.168.99.1 255.255.255.255
Router-RP2(config-if)# ip pim sparse-dense-mode
Router-RP2(config-if)#exit
Router-RP2(config)#ip pim send-rp-announce Loopback1 scope 16 group-list 22
Router-RP2(config)#ip pim send-rp-discovery Loopback1 scope 16
Router-RP2(config)#ip msdp peer 10.4.4.4 connect-source Loopback0
Router-RP2(config)#access-list 22 permit 239.0.0.0 0.255.255.255.255
Router-RP2(config)#end
Router-RP2#
```

Discussion

RFC 3446 describes this simple but clever idea for use with PIM-SM. The key is to configure the same IP address on the Loopback interfaces of two different RP routers and to distribute this address through a dynamic routing protocol. Then the routing protocol will ensure that the "closest" RP is selected.

The only tricky part is that a source may prefer to use one RP, while a destination may be closer to the other one. In this case, since the source is not registered with the RP selected by the recipient device, the RPs must have a mechanism for knowing about the groups supported by one other. Fortunately, there already exists such a mechanism, MSDP, which we discussed in Recipe 23.17.

In Recipe 23.17 we used MSDP between two BGP Autonomous Systems, but MSDP can also function within a single AS. In fact, the MSDP configuration for Anycast RP operation just involves defining a peer relationship between the RP routers.

Notice that in this recipe we have used an Anycast RP IP address of 192.168.99.1, which we have assigned to interface Loopback1 on both RP routers. This address will be distributed through the unicast routing protocol. While it is preferable for stability to do the MSDP peering between loopback interfaces, it is critical that it be a different interface from the one containing the Anycast RP address. This is because the

MSDP peer addresses must be unique, while the Anycast RP addresses must be the same on both RPs.

In the example, we have used AutoRP to distribute the RP information. However, you could just as easily use static RP definitions with the *ip pim rp-address* command or the Bootstrap Router method.

 Unfortunately, because the Anycast RP method requires routers to be able to select the appropriate RP on the fly for each group, it does not work with Bidirectional PIM, which pre-builds its RP rooted RPF trees.

One final note on the Anycast RP technique is worth bearing in mind. Each individual multicast router will use its unicast routing table to determine which RP is the closest. Exactly the same route selection rules are used for building multicast routing trees as for unicast routing. Specifically, the router will take the longest prefix match first, and use the Administrative Distance and then the route metric to break any ties.

This means that there are three cases when your routers may select a different RP than the one you expect. First, if you have two or more routing protocols in operation, you will need to watch your Administrative Distances. Second, if the two RPs turn out to have exactly the same metric, the router will alternate between them. Third, if you have unequal cost load balancing enabled, the router will select the RP in a more complicated weighted round robin fashion.

The good news is that in each of these cases, MSDP will always direct *Join* requests to the appropriate RP. But troubleshooting can become somewhat complicated if you don't know which RP you are using.

In the future, the MSDP part of this configuration may become unnecessary. Cisco has been working on an extension to PIM-SM that will allow a group of RP routers sharing a Loopback IP address to automatically forward Source Active Registration messages to one another. This method is documented in RFC 4610, although the feature has not been added to the main line 12.4 IOS version yet.

See Also

Recipe 23.2; Recipe 23.3; Recipe 23.17; RFC 4610

23.19 Converting Broadcasts to Multicasts

Problem

You have a broadcast-based application that you want to treat as multicast so that it can cross the network.

Solution

Cisco has a special feature called an IP Multicast Helper, which you can use to convert broadcast packets to multicast packets. Then you can use PIM to send these packets throughout the network. At the last-hop routers you can then convert the multicast packets back to broadcast. This is useful for older broadcast-based applications that do not support multicast transmission.

Router1 is the first-hop router, or the one closest to the broadcast source, which is on the interface *FastEthernet0/0*. It converts broadcast packets with UDP port 3535 received on this interface into multicast packets in group 239.3.5.35:

```
Router1#configure terminal
Enter configuration commands, one per line.  End with CNTL/Z.
Router1(config)#ip multicast-routing
Router1(config)#access-list 115 permit any any udp 3535
Router1(config)#access-list 115 deny any any udp
Router1(config)#interface FastEthernet0/0
Router1(config-if)#ip directed broadcast
Router1(config-if)#ip multicast helper-map broadcast 239.3.5.35 115
Router1(config-if)#exit
Router1(config)#ip pim sparse-dense-mode
Router1(config)#ip forward-protocol udp 3535
Router1(config)#end
Router1#
```

The last-hop router's configuration is similar, except that it must be configured to turn multicast packets for this group back into broadcasts:

```
Router2#configure terminal
Enter configuration commands, one per line.  End with CNTL/Z.
Router2(config)#ip multicast-routing
Router2(config)#access-list 115 permit any any udp 3535
Router2(config)#access-list 115 deny any any udp
Router2(config)#interface Ethernet0
Router2(config-if)#ip address 192.168.9.1 255.255.255.0
Router2(config-if)#ip directed broadcast
Router2(config-if)#ip multicast helper-map 239.3.5.35 192.168.9.255 115
Router2(config-if)#ip pim sparse-dense-mode
Router2(config-if)#exit
Router2(config)#ip igmp join-group 239.3.5.35
Router2(config)#ip forward-protocol udp 3535
Router2(config)#end
Router2#
```

Discussion

Before explaining this recipe in any detail, we would like to stress that the multicast helper feature should be used only as a temporary measure until a proper multicast application can be found. It tends to consume a lot of the router's CPU resources. And it can be difficult to troubleshoot application problems if the router is rewriting all of the packets. It is always preferable to use a native multicast application if possible.

The most important lines in this example are the *ip multicast helper-map* commands that are applied on the two routers. The command on Router A converts broadcast to multicasts with a group address of 239.3.5.35:

```
Router1(config-if)#ip multicast helper-map broadcast 239.3.5.35 115
```

Then Router B converts this group to the network broadcast address 192.168.9.255 of the destination network:

```
Router2(config-if)#ip multicast helper-map 239.3.5.35 192.168.9.255 115
```

End devices on the destination network can now receive the broadcast as if a device on this same segment had sent it.

This example doesn't convert all broadcasts received on the Fast Ethernet port of Router1 to multicasts. It first applies the access-list number 115 to broadcasts that it receives. This picks out a single UDP port, number 3535, for conversion. If you wanted to convert other broadcasts received on this port as well, it is simply a matter of opening up this access-list.

There are three additional commands in these configuration examples that are critical to the broadcast multicast conversion working properly. First is the *ip forward-protocol* command. The multicast conversion process is done in the router's CPU, so it cannot be fast switched. By default, the router will ignore all broadcasts except for a few important UDP ports such as NetBIOS. So this command forces the routers to see the broadcast packets so that it can decide whether to process them.

Second, and related to this, is the *ip directed-broadcast* command. A directed broadcast is one that is sent to a particular network or group of networks. So, for example, Router2 in the recipe turns the multicast packet into the directed broadcast with an address of 192.168.9.255. By default, a Cisco router will drop all incoming directed broadcasts. So this needs to be enabled on both routers. We note in passing, however, that this command can be dangerous on public network segments. There are several well-known denial of service attacks, most notably the *smurf* and *fraggle* attacks, that take advantage of directed broadcasts.

And, finally, we have included a static IGMP Join on the destination interface. Recall that in Recipe 23.9 we used this command when the devices on this interface require a group but don't implement IGMP properly. In this case, the devices on the segment don't even know that there is a multicast group to join. So we can use this command to ensure that this router receives the group. Otherwise, the multicast packets will never reach Router2.

You should be careful when using multicast helper commands in a network that uses TTL scoping. Cisco doesn't provide a way to adjust the initial TTL setting on these multicast packets. So you may need to set up address-based boundaries as in Recipe 23.15 to prevent these artificial multicasts from leaking out of the network.

One last point on the subject of broadcast to multicast conversion might be useful in some rare cases. If you have an application that is capable of sending multicasts but end devices that can only receive broadcasts, you might be able to use only the last-hop (Router2) configuration to get the packets to the receiving devices. Similarly, if you had a server that can only broadcast but end devices that understand multicasts, you could conceivably use just the first-hop (Router1) configuration. However, it is unlikely that you will encounter such strange applications in any production network.

See also

Recipe 23.9

23.20 Showing Multicast Status

Problem

You want to view the current status of multicast protocols on your router.

Solution

There are several useful commands for checking the status of multicast configuration and protocols. You can see what multicast routes pass through a router with the EXEC command:

```
Router#show ip mroute
```

There are two useful variants of this command. The first reports on forwarding statistics for each multicast group:

```
Router#show ip mroute count
```

And the second reports only on the groups that are currently active:

```
Router#show ip mroute active
```

You can look at statistics on group membership using the command:

```
Router#show ip igmp groups
```

Use the *interface* keyword to look at the IGMP information in more detail:

```
Router#show ip igmp interface
```

There are four useful commands for viewing PIM information. The first shows information about PIM neighbor relationships:

```
Router#show ip pim neighbor
```

The second command shows information about the PIM configuration on different interfaces:

```
Router#show ip pim interface
```

This command shows information about PIM-SM Rendezvous Points (RP):

```
Router#show ip pim rp
```

And, finally, if you are using the Bootstrap Router (PIM Version 2) technique for distributing RP information, you will want to use this command:

```
Router#show ip pim bsr-router
PIMv2 Bootstrap information
This system is the Bootstrap Router (BSR)
  BSR address: 172.17.254.5 (?)
  Uptime:      00:06:37, BSR Priority: 0, Hash mask length: 1
  Next bootstrap message in 00:00:22

Next Cand_RP_advertisement in 00:00:15
  RP: 172.17.254.5(Loopback0)
Router#
```

There are several commands that allow you to look at MSDP functions:

```
Router#show ip msdp count
```

```
Router#show ip msdp peer 192.168.201.15
```

```
Router#show ip msdp summary
```

You can look at details of the Reverse Path Forwarding trees by using two useful commands, *show ip rpf* and *mstat*:

```
Router#show ip rpf 192.168.3.2
```

```
Router#mstat 192.168.3.2 239.5.5.55
```

Discussion

The *show ip mroute* command gives information on multicast routing. It shows which interfaces the router will use to forward packets belonging to different groups, and it also shows where the sources or Rendezvous Points for these groups are:

```
Router#show ip mroute
IP Multicast Routing Table
Flags: D - Dense, S - Sparse, C - Connected, L - Local, P - Pruned
       R - RP-bit set, F - Register flag, T - SPT-bit set, J - Join SPT
Timers: Uptime/Expires
Interface state: Interface, Next-Hop or VCD, State/Mode

(*, 224.0.1.40), 03:29:10/00:00:00, RP 0.0.0.0, flags: DJCL
  Incoming interface: Null, RPF nbr 0.0.0.0
  Outgoing interface list:
    Ethernet1, Forward/Sparse-Dense, 03:29:10/00:00:00

(*, 239.5.5.55), 5d06h/00:02:59, RP 0.0.0.0, flags: DJC
  Incoming interface: Null, RPF nbr 0.0.0.0
  Outgoing interface list:
    Ethernet0, Forward/Sparse-Dense, 00:04:23/00:00:00
    Ethernet1, Forward/Sparse-Dense, 03:29:08/00:00:00
```

```
(192.168.5.2/32, 239.5.5.55), 00:00:50/00:02:09, flags: CT
    Incoming interface: Ethernet1, RPF nbr 0.0.0.0
    Outgoing interface list:
      Ethernet0, Forward/Sparse-Dense, 00:00:50/00:00:00
```

In this example, the router belongs to multicast trees for two groups, 224.0.1.40 and 239.5.5.55. The first of these groups is what Cisco routers use for the Auto-RP procedure to locate a Rendezvous Point. In this case, there is no source for this group, but there is a member on the segment *Ethernet1*. This group member is another router that is also looking for the RP.

The second group has two entries. The first is the general (*,G) entry. The second is a specific (S,G) entry that shows the only known source for this multicast group, 192.168.5.2. This specific entry indicates that this source is on the interface *Ethernet1*, and that there are members on interface Ethernet0.

The flags at the end of each group entry give useful information about the forwarding. Both of the general (*,G) entries include the flags, "D" and "J", which indicate that the router is using Dense-mode forwarding, and that it has joined a Shortest Path Tree. This is important because it says that although this router is configured for Sparse-Dense mode forwarding, it has not yet found an RP, so it is using Dense-mode forwarding.

The "C" flag, which you can see in all of the multicast routing entries, is for connected networks. This is most useful in the last entry because it shows that the multicast source, 192.168.5.2, is on a directly connected network segment. Since both the source and all of the group members are on interfaces on the same router, there is no need for it to try to join a tree connecting it to other routers.

The other interesting flag in this example is the "L" flag, which indicates that the router itself is a member of this group. This is true for the 224.0.1.40 group, because the router is hoping to discover the RP by listening to this group.

With the *count* keyword, this command gives statistics on multicast usage:

```
Router#show ip mroute count
IP Multicast Statistics
3 routes using 1776 bytes of memory
2 groups, 0.5 average sources per group
Forwarding Counts: Pkt Count/Pkts per second/Avg Pkt Size/Kilobits per second
Other counts: Total/RPF failed/Other drops(OIF-null, rate-limit etc)

Group: 224.0.1.40, Source count: 0, Group pkt count: 0

Group: 239.5.5.55, Source count: 1, Group pkt count: 1
    Source: 192.168.5.2/32, Forwarding: 1/0/100/0, Other: 1/0/0
```

The entry for 239.5.5.55 shows that there is only one source. It also shows that there has only been one packet associated with this group for all sources. The detail below this line breaks out the packet statistics for each source. The fields work as follows:

```
Source: 192.168.5.2/32, Forwarding: 1/0/100/0, Other: 1/0/0
```

There are four fields separated by slashes following the word "Forwarding." These represent the total number of packets that have been forwarded, the current forwarding rate in packets per second, followed by the average packet size, and, finally, the forwarding rate in kilobits per second. The three fields after the word "Other" are the total number of packets received, followed by the number of packets that had to be dropped for Reverse Path Forwarding failures, and the number of drops for all other reasons. Note that the total number of forwarded packets, from the first number after *Fowarding*, plus the last two fields after *Other*, should add up to the first field after *Other*. These last two fields simply give an indication of when packets are dropped and why.

The *active* keyword shows only those sources that are currently sending multicast traffic at a rate greater than 4 Kbps:

```
Router#show ip mroute active
Active IP Multicast Sources - sending >= 4 kbps

Group: 239.5.5.55, (?)
   Source: 192.168.5.2 (?)
     Rate: 6 pps/41 kbps(1sec), 14 kbps(last 15 secs), 1 kbps(life avg)
   Source: 192.168.254.5 (?)
     Rate: 2 pps/24 kbps(1sec), 12 kbps(last 15 secs), 1 kbps(life avg)
Router#
```

This command can be deceptive because many multicast applications operate significantly slower than the minimum 4-Kbps rate. The sources for those slower applications do not appear. However, this can be useful for higher bandwidth multimedia type applications. The output shows the rates in both packets per second (pps) and kilobits per second (Kbps) averaged over the last second, as well as the rates in Kbps for the last 15 seconds and averaged over the entire life of this source.

In this particular case, there are actually three sources for this multicast application, but one is below the threshold. You can see them all by using the following command:

```
Router#show ip mroute 239.5.5.55 count
IP Multicast Statistics
12 routes using 4908 bytes of memory
5 groups, 1.40 average sources per group
Forwarding Counts: Pkt Count/Pkts per second/Avg Pkt Size/Kilobits per second
Other counts: Total/RPF failed/Other drops(OIF-null, rate-limit etc)

Group: 239.5.5.55, Source count: 3, Group pkt count: 2319
  RP-tree: Forwarding: 0/0/0/0, Other: 0/0/0
  Source: 192.168.3.2/32, Forwarding: 65/0/76/0, Other: 65/0/0
  Source: 192.168.5.2/32, Forwarding: 1127/0/564/0, Other: 1128/1/0
  Source: 192.168.254.5/32, Forwarding: 1127/0/564/0, Other: 1127/0/0
Router#
```

To look at multicast group membership on the router, use the command:

```
Router# show ip igmp groups
Group Address   Interface       Uptime     Expires    Last Reporter
224.0.1.39      TokenRing0      01:17:44   00:02:59   192.168.3.2
224.0.1.40      Ethernet1       16:02:35   never      192.168.5.1
```

```
239.5.5.55      Ethernet0          00:22:07  00:02:50  192.168.1.104
239.5.5.55      TokenRing0         16:02:26  00:02:53  192.168.3.2
224.0.1.1       TokenRing0         16:02:26  00:02:51  192.168.3.2
Router#
```

This tells you where there are members for each of the active groups. The *Last Reporter* column tells you the last known group member for this group. The router will periodically query the segment to make sure that there are still active members. The *Uptime* column indicates how long this group has had members on this segment, and the *Expires* column shows when this group will be removed if there are no further membership reports. Note that one of the entries, 224.0.1.40, will never expire. This is because the router itself is a member of this group, as it is used for the Auto-RP process.

With the *interface* keyword, the *show ip igmp* command gives details on how IGMP is implemented on this particular interface. It tells you information about IGMP query periods and what router is the PIM Designated Router (DR) for the segment. In the following example, this router is the DR for the segment. When there is more than one router on a segment, one of them must claim the role of DR or every multicast packet will appear twice. So this is a useful way of figuring out which router is DR:

```
Router# show ip igmp interface Ethernet0
Ethernet0 is up, line protocol is up
  Internet address is 192.168.1.201/24
  IGMP is enabled on interface
  Current IGMP version is 2
  CGMP is disabled on interface
  IGMP query interval is 60 seconds
  IGMP querier timeout is 120 seconds
  IGMP max query response time is 10 seconds
  Inbound IGMP access group is not set
  IGMP activity: 2 joins, 0 leaves
  Multicast routing is enabled on interface
  Multicast TTL threshold is 15
  Multicast designated router (DR) is 192.168.1.201 (this system)
  IGMP querying router is 192.168.1.201 (this system)
  No multicast groups joined
```

Another useful piece of information in this example is the *Multicast TTL threshold* indicator. A TTL threshold of 15 has been set on this interface to prevent local multicast traffic from reaching this segment. One of the most common problems with multicast networks comes from incorrectly setting multicast TTL thresholds. This can either allow multicast traffic to leak out of the appropriate network region or cause a router to drop it prematurely.

You can look at a router's PIM neighbor table as follows, for IOS Version 11.x:

```
Router#show ip pim neighbor
PIM Neighbor Table
Neighbor Address  Interface      Uptime     Expires    Mode
192.168.5.2       Ethernet1      16:22:46   00:01:23   Sparse-Dense (DR)
192.168.3.2       TokenRing0     16:22:16   00:01:05   Sparse-Dense (DR)
Router#
```

This shows not only what the PIM neighbor routers are, but also what PIM mode they are using (Sparse-Dense for both of the routers in this example), how long the neighbor relationship has existed, and when the router will delete this neighbor from its table if it doesn't hear from it again. The very last field in both lines indicates that this router is the DR for both of these network segments. If you look at the same information on either of these neighbor routers, you will see that neither of them have this DR indication.

The format of this output changed slightly between IOS Versions 11.x and 12.x. It now includes PIM version information:

```
Router#show ip pim neighbor
PIM Neighbor Table
Neighbor Address  Interface      Uptime    Expires   Ver  Mode
192.168.5.1       Ethernet0      16:33:41  00:01:02  v1   Dense
192.168.254.6     Serial0        16:34:23  00:01:38  v2
Router#
```

As you can see, one of the neighbors is using PIM Version 1. This actually highlights the interoperability of the different PIM versions. You can easily build a hybrid network using both old and new routers.

The *show ip pim interface* command looks like this:

```
Router#show ip pim interface

Address          Interface      Version/Mode      Nbr   Query   DR
                                                  Count Intvl
192.168.5.2      Ethernet0      v2/Sparse-Dense   1     30      192.168.5.2
192.168.254.5    Serial0        v2/Sparse-Dense   1     30      0.0.0.0
Router#
```

Notice that there are slight differences between the output of this command and the previous one. In particular, the *interface* command indicates that the *Ethernet0* port is configured for PIM Version 2 (the default), using Sparse-Dense mode. However, the previous *neighbor* command shows that this port is actually using Dense mode and PIM Version 1 for compatibility with the older router.

When using PIM-SM, you can see information about the RPs using this command:

```
Router#show ip pim rp
Group: 239.255.255.250, RP: 192.168.3.2, v2, v1, uptime 00:00:43, expires 00:02:16
Group: 239.5.5.55, RP: 192.168.3.2, v2, v1, uptime 00:00:42, expires 00:02:17
Group: 224.0.1.1, RP: 192.168.3.2, v2, v1, uptime 00:00:42, expires 00:02:17
Router#
```

Note that you can have different RPs for different groups. So the output of this command shows the RP separately for each group. Of course, in this example there is only one RP for the entire network.

If you are using a BSR to distribute RP information, as in Recipe 23.2, you can look at the BSR status by using the *bsr-router* keyword:

```
Router#show ip pim bsr-router
PIMv2 Bootstrap information
```

```
This system is the Bootstrap Router (BSR)
  BSR address: 172.17.254.5 (?)
  Uptime:      00:06:37, BSR Priority: 0, Hash mask length: 1
  Next bootstrap message in 00:00:22

Next Cand_RP_advertisement in 00:00:15
  RP: 172.17.254.5(Loopback0)
Router#
```

In this example, the router itself claims to be the BSR for the network. This means simply that it is responsible for distributing RP information to the network. This command also shows what the next RP that this router intends to advertise will be, and when it will send out the next advertisement.

If you are running MSDP to distribute multicast source and RP information between networks, you will want to use the various *show ip msdp* commands. The *count* keyword allows you to see gross statistics for all of the configured MSDP peers:

```
Router#show ip msdp count
SA State per Peer Counters, <Peer>: <# SA learned>
    192.168.199.15: 0
    192.168.201.15: 0

SA State per ASN Counters, <asn>: <# sources>/<# groups>
    Total entries: 0
```

In this case, the peers are configured, but no sources or groups have been learned.

You can look at one peer in more detail with the *peer* keyword:

```
Router#show ip msdp peer 192.168.201.15
MSDP Peer 192.168.201.15 (?), AS ?
Description:
  Connection status:
    State: Down, Resets: 0, Connection source: none configured
    Uptime(Downtime): 00:13:28, Messages sent/received: 0/0
    Output messages discarded: 0
    Connection and counters cleared 00:13:28 ago
  SA Filtering:
    Input (S,G) filter: none, route-map: none
    Input RP filter: none, route-map: none
    Output (S,G) filter: none, route-map: none
    Output RP filter: none, route-map: none
  SA-Requests:
    Input filter: none
    Sending SA-Requests to peer: disabled
  Peer ttl threshold: 0
  SAs learned from this peer: 0
  Input queue size: 0, Output queue size: 0
```

And the *summary* keyword shows general information about all of the MSDP peers:

```
Router#show ip msdp summary
MSDP Peer Status Summary
Peer Address      AS    State    Uptime/  Reset SA    Peer Name
                                 Downtime Count Count
```

```
192.168.199.15   65531 Down       00:15:41 0    0   ?
192.168.201.15   ?     Down       00:15:30 0    0   ?
Router#
```

The last version shows a critical piece of information. These MSDP peers are currently unreachable, so no routing information is being exchanged. In this case, the peers have been down for over 15 minutes, allowing you to isolate exactly when the problem occurred.

The last two commands show details on the actual multicast trees. The first, *show ip rpf*, shows information about how the router would build an RPF tree for a specified source. Note that this does not actually require that this source must exist, or that it be currently sending multicast packets. It does require that the interface that leads to this source must be configured for multicast forwarding, however:

```
Router#show ip rpf 192.168.3.2
RPF information for ? (192.168.3.2)
  RPF interface: Ethernet0
  RPF neighbor: ? (192.168.5.1)
  RPF route/mask: 192.168.3.0/255.255.255.0
  RPF type: unicast
Router#
```

If there are two or more equal cost paths to the same destination, the router simply selects the one with the highest IP address:

```
Router#show ip route 192.168.4.29
Routing entry for 192.168.4.28/30
  Known via "eigrp 65530", distance 90, metric 297372416, type internal
  Redistributing via eigrp 65530
  Last update from 192.168.4.26 on Tunnel6, 00:07:25 ago
  Routing Descriptor Blocks:
  * 192.168.4.22, from 192.168.4.22, 00:07:25 ago, via Tunnel5
      Route metric is 297372416, traffic share count is 1
      Total delay is 505000 microseconds, minimum bandwidth is 9 Kbit
      Reliability 255/255, minimum MTU 1514 bytes
      Loading 1/255, Hops 1
    192.168.4.26, from 192.168.4.26, 00:07:25 ago, via Tunnel6
      Route metric is 297372416, traffic share count is 1
      Total delay is 505000 microseconds, minimum bandwidth is 9 Kbit
      Reliability 255/255, minimum MTU 1514 bytes
      Loading 1/255, Hops 1

Router#show ip rpf 192.168.4.29
RPF information for ? (192.168.4.29)
  RPF interface: Tunnel6
  RPF neighbor: ? (192.168.4.26)
  RPF route/mask: 192.168.4.28/255.255.255.252
  RPF type: unicast
Router#
```

This is helpful when debugging multicast routing issues because it tells you, for example, that this route uses the unicast routing table. If you had intended for this

routing information to come from some other source such as DVMRP or MBGP, it
tells you that there is probably an Administrative Distance problem. Here is how the
output looks for another source that has a static multicast route:

```
Router#show ip rpf 192.168.55.5
RPF information for ? (192.168.55.5)
  RPF interface: Serial0
  RPF neighbor: ? (192.168.254.6)
  RPF route/mask: 192.168.55.5/255.255.255.0
  RPF type: static mroute
Router#
```

For tracing the multicast trees for real sources, you can use the *mstat* command to
get much more detail:

```
Router>mstat 192.168.3.2 239.5.5.55
Type escape sequence to abort.
Mtrace from 192.168.3.2 to 192.168.5.2 via group 239.5.5.55
From source (?) to destination (?)
Waiting to accumulate statistics......
Results after 10 seconds:

    Source        Response Dest    Packet Statistics For      Only For Traffic
  192.168.3.2     192.168.5.2     All Multicast Traffic      From 192.168.3.2
      |          __/  rtt 7    ms   Lost/Sent = Pct  Rate      To 239.5.5.55
      v         /     hop 7    ms   --------------------       --------------------
  192.168.3.1
  192.168.5.1     ?
      |      ^        ttl   0
      v      |        hop 0    ms   -2/0 = --%       0 pps    0/0 = --%  0 pps
  192.168.5.2     ?
      |      \__      ttl   1
      v        \      hop 0    ms       0            0 pps        0      0 pps
  192.168.5.2     192.168.5.2
    Receiver      Query Source


Router>
```

This command tells the router to actually probe the RPF tree by using a similar technique to that used by the *traceroute* program. It presents the results starting at the
top with the source and tracing down to the receiver, which is the router itself, at the
bottom, and shows all of the intermediate router hops. There is a lot of useful information in this output. It tells you, for example, the minimum source TTL value
required to reach each point in the network. And it also shows the multicast forwarding packet statistics at each hop for both this group and for all multicast traffic.
You can use this to determine if you are losing multicast traffic due to congestion at
some point in your network.

Here is another interesting *mstat* output in which the router discovers a TTL boundary:

```
Router#mstat 192.168.1.201 239.5.5.55
Type escape sequence to abort.
Mtrace from 192.168.1.201 to 192.168.254.5 via group 239.5.5.55
From source (?) to destination (?)
```

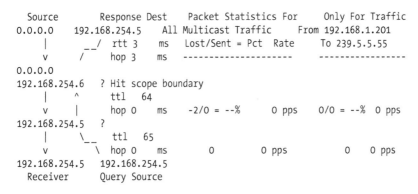

```
Waiting to accumulate statistics......
Results after 10 seconds:

   Source        Response Dest    Packet Statistics For    Only For Traffic
 0.0.0.0       192.168.254.5   All Multicast Traffic    From 192.168.1.201
   |            __/  rtt 3    ms   Lost/Sent = Pct  Rate     To 239.5.5.55
   v          /      hop 3    ms   --------------------     ----------------
 0.0.0.0
 192.168.254.6    ? Hit scope boundary
   |        ^       ttl   64
   v        |       hop 0    ms    -2/0 = --%       0 pps    0/0 = --% 0 pps
 192.168.254.5    ?
   |        \__     ttl   65
   v         \      hop 0    ms        0            0 pps        0     0 pps
 192.168.254.5    192.168.254.5
   Receiver       Query Source

Router#
```

Notice that at the 192.168.254.6 hop, *mstat* discovers that there is a TTL boundary with a threshold value of 64. So you can see that the minimum TTL required to reach the final destination is 65. This is an extremely useful command for isolating multicast routing problems.

23.21 Debugging Multicast Routing

Problem

You want to use debug functions to isolate problem with multicast forwarding.

Solution

Cisco routers have several useful debug features that you can use to isolate multicast problems. The first is a general command that shows how the router maintains its multicast routing tables when it hears from sources and group members:

```
Router#debug ip mrouting
```

You can watch the actual multicast packets for a particular group using the command:

```
Router#debug ip mpacket 239.5.5.55
```

And the other commonly useful multicast debug command looks specifically at IGMP information:

```
Router#debug ip igmp
```

Discussion

As with all debugging commands, you need to be extremely careful because sometimes the sheer volume of the output can overwhelm the router. So it is usually wise to try these commands one at a time, and disable all debugging with the command *undebug all* before trying the next command.

The first debug command, *debug ip mrouting*, shows how the router creates, updates, and deletes multicast routing information:

```
Router#terminal monitor
Router#debug ip mrouting
IP multicast routing debugging is on
Router#
17:20:27: MRT: Create (192.168.5.1/32, 239.5.5.55), RPF Ethernet0/0.0.0.0, PC
0x33A89D8
17:20:43: MRT: Update (*, 224.0.1.40), RPF Null, PC 0x339F96C
17:20:49: MRT: Delete (192.168.3.2/32, 224.0.1.39), PC 0x33AB26A
17:21:43: MRT: Update (*, 224.0.1.40), RPF Null, PC 0x339F96C
17:21:49: MRT: Create (192.168.3.2/32, 224.0.1.39), RPF Ethernet0/192.168.5.1, PC
0x33A89D8
17:22:13: MRT: Delete (*, 224.0.1.1), PC 0x33AB26A
17:22:24: MRT: Create (*, 224.0.1.1), RPF Null, PC 0x33A8890
17:22:46: MRT: Update (*, 224.0.1.40), RPF Null, PC 0x339F96C
17:22:46: MRT: Update (*, 224.0.1.40), RPF Null, PC 0x339F96C
```

In this example, the first line creates a group entry for 239.5.5.55 with the source 192.168.5.1 in response to receiving a multicast packet from this source. You can also see a number of entries here for the Auto-RP groups, 224.0.1.39 and 224.0.1.39. These are the result of routers chatting amongst themselves to ensure that a stable RP exists for the network.

The next command, *debug ip mpacket*, shows individual multicast packets. Looking at packet-level debug traces is always particularly dangerous because of the possibility of overwhelming the router. In this example, we have asked the router to show only the group 239.5.5.55, which we have used as an example throughout this chapter:

```
Router#debug ip mpacket 239.5.5.55
IP multicast packets debugging is on for group 239.5.5.55
May 10 16:18:40.870: IP: s=192.168.5.2 (Ethernet1) d=239.5.5.55 (TokenRing0) len
 114, mforward
May 10 16:18:40.874: IP: s=192.168.5.2 (Ethernet1) d=239.5.5.55 (Ethernet0) len
114, mforward
May 10 16:18:40.878: IP: s=192.168.5.2 (TokenRing0) d=239.5.5.55 len 122, not RP
F interface
May 10 16:18:40.890: IP: s=192.168.254.5 (TokenRing0) d=239.5.5.55 (Ethernet1) l
en 122, mforward
May 10 16:18:40.890: IP: s=192.168.254.5 (TokenRing0) d=239.5.5.55 (Ethernet0) l
en 122, mforward
```

As you can see, a packet was received on interface *Ethernet1* with the source address of 192.168.5.2 for this group. The router immediately turned around and forwarded this packet to interface *TokenRing0* and *Ethernet0*. A short time later, it received another packet for this group with the same source address from *TokenRing0*. However it doesn't forward this packet along because it was not received on the RPF interface. That is, the router looks in its routing table and realizes that this is not the way that it should have received this packet, so it drops it to avoid loops.

The router then receives a multicast packet for this same group on interface *TokenRing0*, but this time with a source address of 192.168.254.5. It forwards this packet over to both *Ethernet1* and *Ethernet0*.

It is important to note that this command tells you nothing about group membership. If devices join or leave this group, you will not see them this way. To do that, you need to look at the output of *debug ip igmp*:

```
Router#debug ip igmp
IGMP debugging is on
17:34:17: IGMP: Send v2 Query on Ethernet0 to 224.0.0.1
17:34:18: IGMP: Send v2 Query on Ethernet1 to 224.0.0.1
17:34:18: IGMP: Set report delay time to 8.6 seconds for 224.0.1.40 on Ethernet1
17:34:18: IGMP: Send v2 Query on TokenRing0 to 224.0.0.1
17:34:19: IGMP: Received v2 Report from 192.168.1.104 (Ethernet0) for 239.5.5.55
17:34:21: IGMP: Received v2 Report from 192.168.5.2 (Ethernet1) or 224.0.1.40
17:34:21: IGMP: Cancel report for 224.0.1.40 on Ethernet1
17:34:23: IGMP: Received v2 Report from 192.168.3.2 (TokenRing0) for 239.5.5.55
17:34:24: IGMP: Received v2 Report from 192.168.3.2 (TokenRing0) for 224.0.1.39
17:34:25: IGMP: Received v2 Report from 192.168.3.2 (TokenRing0) for 224.0.1.1
17:34:26: IGMP: Received v2 Report from 192.168.1.100 (Ethernet0) for 239.255.255.250
17:34:27: IGMP: Received v2 Report from 192.168.1.104 (Ethernet0) for 239.5.5.55
17:34:32: IGMP: Received v2 Report from 192.168.1.104 (Ethernet0) for 239.5.5.55
```

This debug trace shows a couple of interesting events buried in a whole lot of router-to-router multicast chatter, so you have to look carefully at the group addresses to makes sure that you're seeing the interesting data. The group 224.0.0.1 is the All Systems group, which is used for local segment chatter. It is rarely interesting for multicast routing because it is intended to be purely local, and all multicast capable devices are always members. The groups 224.0.1.39 and 224.0.1.40 are used by the Auto-RP protocol to allow routers to share information about the PIM-SM RPs for the network.

So, unless you are trying to debug an Auto-RP problem, the only really interesting information in this trace are the entries for the groups 239.5.5.55 and 239.255.255.250. The device 192.168.1.104 has joined the first group, and sends several IGMP Report packets to make sure that it has successfully joined that group. The device 192.168.1. 100, on the other hand, has been a member of 239.255.255.250 for some time, and it sends only a single packet to ensure that it will continue to receive this group.

A short time later, the device 192.168.1.104 leaves the group 239.5.5.55, as shown in the following trace:

```
17:34:54: IGMP: Received Leave from 192.168.1.104 (Ethernet0) for 239.5.5.55
17:34:54: IGMP: Send v2 Query on Ethernet0 to 239.5.5.55
17:34:55: IGMP: Send v2 Query on Ethernet0 to 239.5.5.55
17:34:57: IGMP: Deleting 239.5.5.55 on Ethernet0
```

Since this was the last known member of this group on this segment, the router responds to the IGMP Leave message with an IGMP Query. It tries twice to see if there are still any other devices interested in continuing to see this group, and then deletes it.

## CHAPTER 24

IP Mobility

24.0 Introduction

The subject of IP Mobility generally comes up first in wireless environments where end users devices could be connected to the network in any number of places. However, the problem is more general that this. A commuter train, for example, might offer its riders Internet access through either wired or wireless connections in the car. The train could then access the network through a series of radio transmitters located along the tracks, defaulting to a satellite connection whenever there is no local radio transmitter. This is an example of a mobile network, as opposed to a single mobile node.

The simplest solution to this problem is to use DHCP and allow the roaming devices to automatically obtain new and locally relevant IP addresses for whatever section of network they are connected to, as we discussed in Chapter 20.

The trouble with the DHCP approach, particularly with mobile nodes, is that it requires all of the applications on the roaming devices to drop all of their network connections, obtain a new address and potentially new server and domain information, and then re-establish communications. This is not always convenient.

A mobile network could, in principle, buffer packets from client devices while obtaining an address for the new network by DHCP. But the time required to get a new DHCP address and resynchronize routing tables is often far too long for seamless operation.

The strongest case for IP Mobility comes from mobile devices such as third-generation cellular telephones. You cannot drop a call when passing from one network region to the next.

There are two solutions to this problem. The first is called IP Mobility and the second, which has more limited applicability, is Local Area Mobility. We will discuss both of these options in this chapter.

IP Mobility, originally defined in RFCs 2002 through 2006, and updated in RFC 3344, allows the roaming device to use its own "home" IP address wherever it goes. The next hop router on the "foreign" network where the device currently finds itself essentially creates a tunnel for the roaming device, sending its traffic back to its designated "home" router.

Terminology

IP Mobility has its own set of unique jargon, so defining some terms will make it easier to discuss how to configure it.

There are three different types of devices in a Mobile IP network configuration:

Mobile Node
> The roaming device, which could be an end node or a router.

Home Agent
> The router on the Mobile Node's home network that is responsible for tunneling its packets while it is away.

Foreign Agent
> The router on the foreign network that the Mobile Node is currently visiting.

The next important concept is the *Care-of Address*. This is an IP address on the Foreign Agent router that the Home Agent can connect to, creating a tunnel for the Mobile Node to use.

The IP Mobility protocol has three main phases:

Agent Discovery
> This protocol has two components. Home and Foreign Agents can advertise themselves over a network link, and Mobile Nodes can send solicitation messages looking for these agent devices. They use the ICMP Router Discovery Protocol (IRDP) for this purpose.

Registration
> The Mobile Node communicates first with the Foreign Agent to obtain a Care-of Address. Then, using the Foreign Agent, it registers this Care-of Address with the Home Agent.

Tunneling
> The Home and Foreign Agents set up a tunnel to carry traffic for the Mobile Node from its home network. This tunnel can be encrypted if desired.

Local Area Mobility

Cisco has developed another limited solution to this problem. Local Area Mobility takes advantage of an Interior Gateway Protocol to transmit a host route for the mobile node throughout the network. In this way, it is not necessary to set up a tunnel between the foreign and home routers.

When hosts on the home network try to communicate with the mobile node, the home router uses Proxy ARP. When the other hosts want to send a packet to the mobile node, they first send an ARP packet to associate a MAC address with its IP address. The home router knows that this device is currently located elsewhere in the network, so it responds to the ARP request on its behalf, and then forwards the packet according to the host route in its routing table.

This method is not practical over an Exterior Gateway Protocol such as BGP because it is common to filter out and remove host routes from BGP routing tables. Further, the Local Area Mobility solution has weaker security, making it inappropriate for untrusted networks.

Cisco developed Local Area Mobility as a temporary alternative to DHCP, useful primarily for situations in which DHCP is not yet fully operational or a significant number of end devices don't support it. And, like DHCP, Local Area Mobility is not particularly useful for fast roaming. Although you can adjust the timers somewhat, by default it takes 15 minutes for the router on the foreign network segment to remove an inactive device from its ARP and IP routing tables.

However, it has one key advantage over DHCP as well as IP Mobility, which is that the roaming device doesn't need to have any specialized software to allow it to roam. This is less of an issue now than it once was, as DHCP support is now built into most commercial operating systems. However, there are still devices on some networks that do not have this capability.

24.1   Local Area Mobility

Problem

You want to set up Local Area Mobility to allow devices to roam throughout your network.

Solution

In this example, the roaming device will have a statically configured address in the 192.168.10.0/24 range. We have to configure the home router to use Proxy ARP for mobile nodes, allowing other locally connected devices in the same range to communicate transparently with the roaming device:

```
RouterHome#configure terminal
Enter configuration commands, one per line.  End with CNTL/Z.
RouterHome(config)#interface FastEthernet0/0
RouterHome(config-if)#ip address 192.168.10.1 255.255.255.0
RouterHome(config-if)#ip proxy-arp
RouterHome(config-if)#ip mobile arp
RouterHome(config-if)#exit
RouterHome(config)#router eigrp 99
RouterHome(config-router)#network 192.168.10.0
RouterHome(config-router)#default-metric 10000 10 255 1 1500
RouterHome(config-router)#redistribute mobile
RouterHome(config-router)#no auto-summary
RouterHome(config-router)#exit
RouterHome(config)#end
RouterHome#
```

Then we have to configure the foreign router, which supports the network segment where our roaming node temporarily finds itself:

```
RouterForeign#configure terminal
Enter configuration commands, one per line.  End with CNTL/Z.
RouterForeign(config)#interface FastEthernet0/0
RouterForeign(config-if)#ip address 192.168.110.1 255.255.255.0
RouterForeign(config-if)#ip proxy-arp
RouterForeign(config-if)#ip mobile arp
RouterForeign(config-if)#exit
RouterForeign(config)#router eigrp 99
RouterForeign(config-router)#network 192.168.100.0
RouterForeign(config-router)#default-metric 10000 10 255 1 1500
RouterForeign(config-router)#redistribute mobile
RouterForeign(config-router)#no auto-summary
RouterForeign(config-router)#exit
RouterForeign(config)#end
RouterForeign#
```

Discussion

As this example shows, there are two steps to configuring Local Area Mobility. The first is to configure the *ip mobile arp* command on all of the interfaces that will support roaming devices either as home or foreign networks:

```
RouterForeign(config)#interface FastEthernet0/0
RouterForeign(config-if)#ip mobile arp
```

This command has two functions. On the home network, it tells the router to use Proxy ARP to support members of the local address range that are represented by a host route in the routing table. On the foreign network, it tells the router to create an ARP table entry and a host route whenever it sees packets from devices that don't belong to this subnet.

We also explicitly enable Proxy ARP on the interface, in case it has been disabled:

```
RouterForeign(config)#interface FastEthernet0/0
RouterForeign(config-if)#ip proxy-arp
```

The second step is to redistribute these mobile host routes into the Interior Gateway Protocol:

```
RouterForeign(config)#router eigrp 99
RouterForeign(config-router)#network 192.168.100.0
RouterForeign(config-router)#default-metric 10000 10 255 1 1500
RouterForeign(config-router)#redistribute mobile
```

In this example, we have used EIGRP as our IGP, but we could have used RIP, IS-IS or OSPF just as easily. We could even have used BGP, although we caution that doing so could be dangerous if you don't control all of the devices that are taking part in BGP. This is because the Local Area Mobility feature will work reliably only if every router can see both the route for the full subnet prefix and the host route for the roaming device. In BGP networks, it is relatively common to try to save network and router resources by filtering out extremely long prefixes like host networks.

For the same reason, we have explicitly disabled EIGRP's auto-summarization feature in this example.

You will notice that we have actually configured both the home and foreign routers essentially identically. In fact we didn't need to use the *redistribute mobile* command on the home router because only the foreign router will actually be supporting roaming end devices. However, in a more general situation it is likely that the home router will also serve as a foreign router some of the time. So, because there is essentially no overhead in configuring this mobile host route redistribution when it's not used, we suggest configuring it on all of the routers that will be supporting Local Area Mobility.

There are a few simple options available with Local Area Mobility. The *ip mobile arp* command accepts arguments to change how long the router keeps unused mobile ARP entries:

```
RouterForeign(config)#interface FastEthernet0/0
RouterForeign(config-if)#ip mobile arp timers 3 9
```

The first numerical argument here is a keepalive timer, which specifies in minutes how often to send ARP packets to see if the mobile device is still there. The second number is a hold time. This is the length of time, in minutes, that the router will maintain the ARP entry for a mobile device without seeing any traffic from this device. Cisco recommends making the hold time at least three times the keepalive time. The default values are 5 minutes and 15 minutes, respectively.

Note that because these timeout periods are relatively long, this solution is not suitable for situations involving active roaming. In fact, it would be faster in such situations to use DHCP. It's useful to remember that Cisco developed the Local Area Mobility feature primarily to be used as a temporary substitute for DHCP. Please refer to Chapter 20 for more information on DHCP.

The *ip mobile arp* command also allows you to specify an ACL to restrict which off-segment source addresses the router is willing to support:

```
RouterForeign(config)#interface FastEthernet0/0
RouterForeign(config-if)#ip mobile arp access-group 15
RouterForeign(config-if)#exit
RouterForeign(config)#access-list 15 permit 192.168.10.0 0.0.0.255
RouterForeign(config)#access-list 15 deny any
```

There are two useful *show* commands with Local Area Mobility. The first is *show ip arp*, which shows the ARP cache, including any addresses learned by means of this feature:

```
RouterForeign#show ip arp FastEthernet0/0
Protocol  Address          Age (min)  Hardware Addr   Type   Interface
Internet  192.168.110.1        -       000e.d7d6.1060  ARPA   FastEthernet0/0
Internet  192.168.10.109       1       00b0.64ab.0580  ARPA   FastEthernet0/0
Internet  192.168.110.9        21      0000.0c75.c684  ARPA   FastEthernet0/0
RouterForeign#
```

It is also useful to look at the routing table for any Mobile or host routes. On the foreign router, they will show up as Mobile routes:

```
RouterForeign#show ip route
Codes: C - connected, S - static, R - RIP, M - mobile, B - BGP
       D - EIGRP, EX - EIGRP external, O - OSPF, IA - OSPF inter area
       N1 - OSPF NSSA external type 1, N2 - OSPF NSSA external type 2
       E1 - OSPF external type 1, E2 - OSPF external type 2
       i - IS-IS, su - IS-IS summary, L1 - IS-IS level-1, L2 - IS-IS level-2
       ia - IS-IS inter area, * - candidate default, U - per-user static route
       o - ODR, P - periodic downloaded static route

Gateway of last resort is not set

C    192.168.110.0/24 is directly connected, FastEthernet0/0
     192.168.10.0/24 is variably subnetted, 2 subnets, 2 masks
M       192.168.10.109/32 [3/1] via 192.168.10.109, 00:17:59, FastEthernet0/0
D       192.168.10.0/24 [90/2172416] via 192.168.55.11, 00:29:43, Serial0/0
C    192.168.55.0/24 is directly connected, Serial0/0
RouterForeign#
```

On any other router, they will appear simply as external redistributed host routes:

```
RouterHome#show ip route
Codes: C - connected, S - static, R - RIP, M - mobile, B - BGP
       D - EIGRP, EX - EIGRP external, O - OSPF, IA - OSPF inter area
       N1 - OSPF NSSA external type 1, N2 - OSPF NSSA external type 2
       E1 - OSPF external type 1, E2 - OSPF external type 2
       i - IS-IS, su - IS-IS summary, L1 - IS-IS level-1, L2 - IS-IS level-2
       ia - IS-IS inter area, * - candidate default, U - per-user static route
       o - ODR, P - periodic downloaded static route

Gateway of last resort is not set

D    192.168.110.0/24 [90/2172416] via 192.168.55.12, 00:31:43, Serial0/0
     192.168.10.0/24 is variably subnetted, 2 subnets, 2 masks
D EX    192.168.10.109/32 [170/2172416] via 192.168.55.12, 00:18:19, Serial0/0
C       192.168.10.0/24 is directly connected, FastEthernet0/0
C    192.168.55.0/24 is directly connected, Serial0/0
RouterHome#
```

Note that if you have a lot of devices roaming using this method, then your routing
tables will have a lot of host routes. Normally, we try to keep routing tables small by
using features such as route summarization to help with routing protocol convergence and to improve route lookup performance. This feature works against such
mechanisms, and consequently doesn't scale well. In general, we prefer DHCP for
this type of semistatic mobility.

See Also

Chapter 20

24.2 Home Agent Configuration

Problem

You want to configure a router to act as a Home Agent for Mobile Nodes.

Solution

The first step in configuring IP Mobility in your network is to set up one or more Home Agent routers, which will act as the virtual home base and support tunnels for your roaming devices:

```
RouterHome#configure terminal
Enter configuration commands, one per line.  End with CNTL/Z.
RouterHome(config)#interface Loopback0
RouterHome(config-if)#ip address 192.168.9.1 255.255.255.255
RouterHome(config-if)#exit
RouterHome(config)#router mobile
RouterHome(config-router)#exit
RouterHome(config)#router eigrp 99
RouterHome(config-router)#redistribute mobile
RouterHome(config-router)#network 192.168.9.0
RouterHome(config-router)#network 192.168.10.0
RouterHome(config-router)#default-metric 10000 10 255 1 1500
RouterHome(config-router)#no auto-summary
RouterHome(config-router)#exit
RouterHome(config)#ip mobile home-agent address 192.168.9.1
RouterHome(config)#ip mobile virtual-network 192.168.10.0 255.255.255.0
RouterHome(config)#ip mobile host 192.168.10.1 192.168.10.254 virtual-network 192.
168.10.0 255.255.255.0
RouterHome(config)#ip mobile secure host 192.168.10.110 spi 100 key ascii cookbook
RouterHome(config)#ip mobile secure host 192.168.10.111 spi 100 key ascii cookbook
RouterHome(config)#ip mobile secure host 192.168.10.112 spi 100 key ascii cookbook
RouterHome(config)#ip mobile secure host 192.168.10.113 spi 100 key ascii cookbook
RouterHome(config)#ip mobile secure host 192.168.10.114 spi 100 key ascii cookbook
RouterHome(config)#ip mobile secure host 192.168.10.115 spi 100 key ascii cookbook
RouterHome(config)#end
RouterHome#
```

 In case you need to adjust access-lists or firewall rules, note that IP Mobility tunnels use IP protocol number 55.

Discussion

A good way to handle IP Mobility in an enterprise network is to configure the roaming pool of addresses and the Home address on Loopback interfaces on the home router. This is how we have handled the configuration in this recipe. This way, if you have a lot of roaming devices, they are easy to identify from their IP addresses. As a side effect of this approach, none of the roaming devices are ever "home" because their home network doesn't really exist on a physical piece of wire anywhere.

The first thing we do in this recipe is to configure a Loopback interface that will be the Home Agent IP address. Because this is where all of the tunnels will terminate, it is sensible to make it a Loopback interface. This way, as long as there is network connectivity between the Home Agent and Foreign Agent routers, the tunnels can continue to operate, allowing you to take advantage of any link redundancy in your network:

```
RouterHome(config)#interface Loopback0
RouterHome(config-if)#ip address 192.168.9.1 255.255.255.255
```

Then we enable IP Mobility functionality on this router. Because IP Mobility introduces routes into the routing table, it is enabled in the same way as any other routing protocol, with a *router* command:

```
RouterHome(config)#router mobile
RouterHome(config-router)#exit
```

There is nothing to configure in the *router* configuration mode. This command just turns on the ability to inject IP Mobile routes into the routing table and allows you to redistribute these routes into other routing protocols, which we do next:

```
RouterHome(config)#router eigrp 99
RouterHome(config-router)#redistribute mobile
RouterHome(config-router)#network 192.168.9.0
RouterHome(config-router)#network 192.168.10.0
RouterHome(config-router)#default-metric 10000 10 255 1 1500
RouterHome(config-router)#no auto-summary
RouterHome(config-router)#exit
```

In this example, we have used EIGRP as our routing protocol, but you could just as easily use any other routing protocol. The Mobile routes are injected into the routing protocol by using the *redistribute mobile* command. Consequently, they will always appear as external routes when viewed elsewhere in the network. Please refer to Chapters 6, 7, 8, and 9 for more information about IP routing and redistribution into different routing protocols.

Next we configure the IP Mobility features that we need on the Home Agent router. First we define the IP address that will serve as the Home Agent address on all of the roaming devices served by this Home Agent:

```
RouterHome(config)#ip mobile home-agent address 192.168.9.1
```

Then we use the *ip mobile virtual-network* and *ip mobile host* commands to define the IP addresses that will be used by the Mobile Nodes:

```
RouterHome(config)#ip mobile virtual-network 192.168.10.0 255.255.255.0
RouterHome(config)#ip mobile host 192.168.10.1 192.168.10.254 virtual-network 192.
168.10.0 255.255.255.0
```

Note that the *virtual-network* command is required here because this 192.168.10.0/24 network does not appear on any physical interface on this router. If we had wanted instead to have a real network segment that supported a mixture of roaming and nonroaming devices, we could have done so by pointing the *ip mobile host* command to the corresponding interface as follows:

```
RouterHome(config)#ip mobile host 192.168.10.10 192.168.10.254 interface
FastEthernet0/1
```

We have made another small change in this command by excluding the devices in the range 192.168.10.1-9. This was done to save space for network devices, which will presumably never roam. Also note that if you are using a physical interface to support the roaming range, then it might make sense to use the router's IP address on this interface as the Home Agent address.

We stress, however, that we prefer to use virtual networks for roaming. The only compelling reason for requiring a mixture of roaming and nonroaming devices in the same address range is to support an ad-hoc mobile infrastructure. We feel that the resource and maintenance requirements for supporting IP Mobility in a network of any size are sufficiently heavy to warrant a more careful network design than this.

Finally, we have configured a list of security keys to be used for authenticating the Mobile Nodes as they connect:

```
RouterHome(config)#ip mobile secure host 192.168.10.110 spi 100 key ascii cookbook
RouterHome(config)#ip mobile secure host 192.168.10.111 spi 100 key ascii cookbook
RouterHome(config)#ip mobile secure host 192.168.10.112 spi 100 key ascii cookbook
RouterHome(config)#ip mobile secure host 192.168.10.113 spi 100 key ascii cookbook
RouterHome(config)#ip mobile secure host 192.168.10.114 spi 100 key ascii cookbook
RouterHome(config)#ip mobile secure host 192.168.10.115 spi 100 key ascii cookbook
```

We have configured a separate line for each Mobile Node, specifying its IP address and an authentication key. You can specify a list of different keys for each host by giving each key a different Security Parameter Index (SPI) value:

```
RouterHome(config)#ip mobile secure host 192.168.10.112 spi 100 key ascii cookbook
RouterHome(config)#ip mobile secure host 192.168.10.112 spi 200 key ascii oreilly
RouterHome(config)#ip mobile secure host 192.168.10.112 spi 300 key ascii 2edition
```

You must then configure the same keys with the same SPI values on the Mobile Node. This allows you to easily update your keys without losing connectivity. When you want to change your key values, you simply add the new keys to your Mobile Nodes and to the Home Agent, and then you go back around and delete the old keys.

In this case, of course, we have set the keys for all of the Mobile Nodes to the same value, cookbook, which we certainly don't recommend doing in a production network.

In larger networks, it can become rather onerous to manually configure all of these keys on the Home Agent routers. So Cisco has made it possible to use AAA to obtain these keys from a central TACACS+ database:

```
RouterHome(config)#aaa new-model
RouterHome(config)#aaa authorization ipmobile default group tacacs+
RouterHome(config)#ip mobile secure mn-aaa spi 200 algorithm md5
```

Please refer to Chapter 4 for more information on TACACS+.

See Also

Chapters 4, 6, 7, 8, and 9

24.3 Foreign Agent Configuration

Problem

You want to configure a Foreign Agent router for IP Mobility to support one or more roaming Mobile Nodes.

Solution

Here is a minimal configuration for a Foreign Agent to support Mobile Nodes:

```
RouterForeign#configure terminal
Enter configuration commands, one per line.  End with CNTL/Z.
RouterForeign(config)#router mobile
RouterForeign(config-router)#exit
RouterForeign(config)#router eigrp 99
RouterForeign(config-router)#network 192.168.110.0
RouterForeign(config-router)#no auto-summary
RouterForeign(config-router)#exit
RouterForeign(config)#interface Ethernet0/0
RouterForeign(config-if)#ip address 192.168.110.1 255.255.255.0
RouterForeign(config-if)#ip irdp
RouterForeign(config-if)#ip mobile foreign-service
RouterForeign(config-if)#exit
RouterForeign(config)#ip mobile foreign-agent care-of Ethernet0/0
RouterForeign(config)#end
RouterForeign#
```

Discussion

Throughout this recipe, when we refer to the Home Agent, we mean the configuration shown in the previous recipe. The Discussion in this recipe follows directly from Recipe 24.2.

The configuration for a Foreign Agent router is considerably simpler than what we saw in Recipe 24.2 for a Home Agent, but there are several points that you have to make sure to cover. The first thing that we have done in the configuration in the Solution section is enable IP Mobility support and configure this router to take part in the same routing protocol as the Home Agent:

```
RouterForeign(config)#router mobile
RouterForeign(config-router)#exit
RouterForeign(config)#router eigrp 99
RouterForeign(config-router)#network 192.168.110.0
RouterForeign(config-router)#no auto-summary
RouterForeign(config-router)#exit
```

Naturally, you could run IP Mobility across a large network, or even across the public Internet, as long as you were able to exchange routing information between the Home and Foreign Agent routers. We show them here as belonging to the same IGP Autonomous System for simplicity.

The one thing that you should note from the EIGRP configuration section is that we have not included a command to redistribute mobile routes into EIGRP. This is because the Home Agent will do all of the redistribution.

Next we configure the interface that will support the Mobile Nodes:

```
RouterForeign(config)#interface Ethernet0/0
RouterForeign(config-if)#ip address 192.168.110.1 255.255.255.0
RouterForeign(config-if)#ip irdp
RouterForeign(config-if)#ip mobile foreign-service
```

The *ip irdp* command enables ICMP Router Discover Protocol, which is defined in RFC 1256. This is a very simple protocol that just sends out ICMP packets onto the network, allowing routers to advertise their services and end nodes to learn about available routers on the network segment. There are two types of IRDP messages. Routers will periodically advertise themselves using Advertisement packets, and other nodes can send IRPD Solicitation packets to try to find an available router. IP Mobility uses IRDP to allow Mobile Nodes to find the address of the Foreign Agent.

Then the *ip mobile foreign-service* command simply allows this interface to act as a Foreign Agent.

Finally, we must configure a *care-of* address for the Foreign Agent. The care-of agent is the address on the Foreign end of the tunnel. The other end of this tunnel will be the Home Agent's advertised address:

```
RouterForeign(config)#ip mobile foreign-agent care-of Ethernet0/0
```

In this case, we use the address of the Ethernet interface that will be supporting the Mobile Nodes. A physical failure of this interface will bring down the tunnel, but it will also make the Foreign Agent router lose contact with the Mobile Node. In this case, losing the tunnel is a good thing.

We note in passing that we didn't configure either a Home Agent address in the Foreign Agent router or a Foreign Agent Care-of address in the Home Agent router. This is because the Foreign Agent is, in principle, capable of accommodating a Mobile Node from any home network. The Mobile Node knows its Home Agent and requests that the Foreign Agent make the connection on its behalf. When it does so, it tells the Home Agent about its own Care-of address. So the Mobile Node must initiate this exchange of information.

Authenticating the Foreign Agent

The configurations shown in this recipe and Recipe 24.2 will in principle allow any Foreign Agent router to connect to any Home Agent router. This is usually acceptable, since the Mobile Node must authenticate anyway. However, you can improve the overall security of the exchange and decrease the likelihood of man-in-the-middle attacks by forcing the Foreign Agent to authenticate with the Home Agent.

To enable this additional level of authentication, you simply configure a security association and a key on the Foreign and Home Agent routers. On the Home Agent router, you do this with the *ip mobile secure foreign-agent* command, and specify the Care-of address on the Foreign Agent router:

```
RouterHome(config)#ip mobile secure foreign-agent 192.168.110.1 spi 100 key ascii
xenophobia
```

On the Foreign Agent router, you configure the same key and SPI, but you use the Home Agent IP address with the *ip mobile secure home-agent* command:

```
RouterForeign(config)#ip mobile secure home-agent 192.168.9.1 spi 100 key ascii
xenophobia
```

See Also

Recipe 24.2; RFC 1256

24.4 Making a Router a Mobile Node

Problem

You want to configure a router to act as a Mobile Node.

Solution

The configuration required to make a router act as a Mobile Node must specify the Home Agent and match its authentication parameters:

```
RouterMobile#configure terminal
Enter configuration commands, one per line.  End with CNTL/Z.
RouterMobile(config)#router mobile
RouterMobile(config-router)#exit
RouterMobile(config)#ip mobile secure home-agent 192.168.9.1 spi 100 key ascii
cookbook
RouterMobile(config)#ip mobile router
RouterMobile(mobile-router)#address 192.168.10.112 255.255.255.0
RouterMobile(mobile-router)#home-agent 192.168.9.1
RouterMobile(mobile-router)#exit
RouterMobile(config)#interface FastEthernet0/0
RouterMobile(config-if)#ip address 192.168.10.112 255.255.255.0
RouterMobile(config-if)#ip irdp
RouterMobile(config-if)#ip mobile router-service roam
RouterMobile(config-if)#ip mobile router-service solicit
RouterMobile(config-if)#exit
RouterMobile(config)#end
RouterMobile#
```

Discussion

Starting in IOS Version 12.2(4)T, Cisco introduced the ability for a router to act as a Mobile Node. This may sound somewhat strange because routers don't generally get up and roam around the network. But, in fact, it makes a great deal of sense to have this capability. For example, in the Introduction to this chapter we mentioned the idea of putting a mobile network on a train. In this example, users on the train can connect to a local network segment and let the router handle the task of roaming from one subnet to the next as it passes a series of access points along the track. This kind of scenario was even noted in the original IP Mobility RFC.

As we previously saw in Recipes 24.2 and 24.3, the first thing you must do is to enable the IP Mobility feature set:

```
RouterMobile(config)#router mobile
RouterMobile(config-router)#exit
```

Next we define the authentication key to allow this Mobile Node to connect to the Home Agent that we defined back in Recipe 24.2:

```
RouterMobile(config)#ip mobile secure home-agent 192.168.9.1 spi 100 key ascii
cookbook
```

Note that the SPI values and keys must match, and the IP address must be the Home Agent address specified in the *ip mobile home-agent address* command on the Home router.

Then we must configure the information that the Mobile Node needs to register with the Foreign and Home Agents:

```
RouterMobile(config)#ip mobile router
RouterMobile(mobile-router)#address 192.168.10.112 255.255.255.0
RouterMobile(mobile-router)#home-agent 192.168.9.1
```

And, finally, we configure the interface that this router will use to connect to the Foreign Agent router:

```
RouterMobile(config)#interface FastEthernet0/0
RouterMobile(config-if)#ip address 192.168.10.112 255.255.255.0
RouterMobile(config-if)#ip irdp
RouterMobile(config-if)#ip mobile router-service roam
RouterMobile(config-if)#ip mobile router-service solicit
```

Note that we have had to configure IRDP here, just as we did in Recipe 24.3. This allows the Mobile Node to solicit the Foreign Agent for its address. We have also configure two *ip mobile router-service* commands to identify that this is the roaming interface and to allow this router to use IRDP to solicit for a Foreign Agent on this interface.

Since this is a router, you could then configure a local interface that will support the users who roam with the router, such as the commuters in the train car mentioned earlier:

```
RouterMobile(config)#interface FastEthernet0/1
RouterMobile(config-if)#ip address 192.168.20.1 255.255.255.0
```

Once the tunnels are established, the router will learn about all foreign networks via the Foreign Agent:

```
RouterMobile#show ip route
Codes: C - connected, S - static, R - RIP, M - mobile, B - BGP
       D - EIGRP, EX - EIGRP external, O - OSPF, IA - OSPF inter area
       N1 - OSPF NSSA external type 1, N2 - OSPF NSSA external type 2
       E1 - OSPF external type 1, E2 - OSPF external type 2
       i - IS-IS, su - IS-IS summary, L1 - IS-IS level-1, L2 - IS-IS level-2
       ia - IS-IS inter area, * - candidate default, U - per-user static route
       o - ODR, P - periodic downloaded static route

Gateway of last resort is 192.168.110.1 to network 0.0.0.0

     192.168.110.0/32 is subnetted, 1 subnets
M       192.168.110.1 [3/1] via 192.168.110.1, 00:24:14, FastEthernet0/0
     192.168.9.0/32 is subnetted, 1 subnets
M       192.168.9.1 [3/1] via 192.168.110.1, 00:24:14, FastEthernet0/0
C    192.168.10.0/24 is directly connected, FastEthernet0/0
C    192.168.20.0/24 is directly connected, Loopback0
M*   0.0.0.0/0 [3/1] via 192.168.110.1, 00:24:14, FastEthernet0/0
RouterMobile#
```

We note in passing that the Home Agent does not, by default, learn about other subnets that the Mobile Router might be supporting. So users on these subnets will have connectivity problems with this minimal configuration. Perhaps the most reliable solution to this problem is to configure iBGP peer relationships between the Mobile Routers and the Home Agent and redistribute this routing information into the IGP. Please refer to Chapter 9 for more information on BGP.

Authenticating with the Foreign Agent

The configurations shown in this recipe and Recipes 24.2 and 24.3 will in principle allow the Mobile Node to use any Foreign Node. However, sometimes this is not desirable. For added security, you can configure the Foreign Node to require an additional layer of authentication between the Mobile Node and itself.

To do this, you would configure the Mobile Node to authenticate with the Foreign Agent as follows:

```
RouterMobile(config)#ip mobile secure foreign-agent 192.168.110.1 spi 200 key ascii
oreilly
```

And you would configure the same SPI and key values on the Foreign Agent router:

```
RouterForeign(config)#ip mobile secure visitor 192.168.10.112 spi 200 key ascii
oreilly
```

Note that if you are going to use this sort of authentication, you must set up authentication on the Mobile node for every possible Foreign Agent that it would connect to, and you must configure the Foreign Agents for every possible Mobile Node that will connect to them. This is unfortunately complicated by the fact that the Mobile

Node can't communicate with an AAA server, so all of these keys must be configured manually on at least the Mobile Node.

See Also

Recipe 24.2; Recipe 24.3; Chapter 9

24.5 Reverse-Tunnel Forwarding

Problem

You want to force all packets to use the tunnel to avoid anti-spoofing ACLs in the network.

Solution

You configure Reverse-Tunnel Forwarding on the Mobile Node so that it requests this feature when it registers with the Foreign Node:

```
RouterMobile#configure terminal
Enter configuration commands, one per line.  End with CNTL/Z.
RouterMobile(config)#ip mobile router
RouterMobile(mobile-router)#reverse-tunnel
RouterMobile(mobile-router)#exit
RouterMobile(config)#end
RouterMobile#
```

Discussion

When a Mobile Node communicates with another device elsewhere on the network (called the Correspondent Node), the inbound traffic follows a path from the Correspondent Node to the Home Agent, through the tunnel to the Foreign Agent, and from there to the Mobile Node. On the way back from the Mobile Node to the Correspondent Node, the packet goes first to the Foreign Agent, which looks at the destination address, and forwards this packet according to its routing table by using the most direct path.

The trouble is that the source IP address in the packet from the Mobile Node to the Correspondent Node doesn't belong to the Foreign Agent router. It is effectively a spoofed source address. Many networks use ACLs to look at the source addresses of packets and make sure that they are received on an interface that leads back to the source network. This is a good security practice because it helps prevent hackers from deliberately spoofing addresses in packets when launching attacks.

If your network includes this sort of security precaution, you must configure what is called Reverse-Tunnel Forwarding. This means simply that packets from the Mobile Node should be sent through the tunnel to the Home Agent, even if it has a better route to the destination device. Then the illegal source address in the packet is hidden from any ACLs until it reaches the Home Agent, which is a legitimate router for this source address.

This feature is negotiated when the Mobile Node connects to the network, which is why it is only necessary to configure it on the Mobile Node:

```
RouterMobile(config)#ip mobile router
RouterMobile(mobile-router)#reverse-tunnel
```

You can then verify that the Foreign Agent is using Reverse-Tunnel Forwarding with the *show ip mobile tunnel* command:

```
outerForeign#show ip mobile tunnel
Mobile Tunnels:

Tunnel0:
    src 192.168.110.1, dest 192.168.9.1
    encap IP/IP, mode reverse-allowed, tunnel-users 1
    IP MTU 1480 bytes
    Path MTU Discovery, mtu: 0, ager: 10 mins, expires: never
    outbound interface Serial0/0
    FA created, fast switching enabled, ICMP unreachable enabled
    105 packets input, 8462 bytes, 0 drops
    0 packets output, 0 bytes
RouterForeign#
```

See Also

Recipe 24.2; Recipe 24.3; Recipe 24.4

24.6 Using HSRP for Home Agent Redundancy

Problem

You want to set up redundant Home Agents to improve network availability for your Mobile Nodes.

Solution

For this recipe, we must configure two nearly identical Home Agent routers. Here is the configuration of the first one:

```
RouterHome1#configure terminal
Enter configuration commands, one per line.  End with CNTL/Z.
RouterHome1(config)#interface FastEthernet0/0
RouterHome1(config-if)#ip address 192.168.9.2 255.255.255.0
RouterHome1(config-if)#standby 1 ip 192.168.9.1
RouterHome1(config-if)#standby 1 name HA-GROUP
RouterHome1(config-if)#exit
RouterHome1(config)#router mobile
RouterHome1(config-router)#exit
RouterHome1(config)#router eigrp 99
RouterHome1(config-router)#redistribute mobile
```

```
RouterHome1(config-router)#network 192.168.9.0
RouterHome1(config-router)#network 192.168.10.0
RouterHome1(config-router)#default-metric 10000 10 255 1 1500
RouterHome1(config-router)#no auto-summary
RouterHome1(config-router)#exit
RouterHome1(config)#ip mobile home-agent address 192.168.9.1
RouterHome1(config)#ip mobile home-agent redundancy HA-GROUP virtual-network
RouterHome1(config)#ip mobile virtual-network 192.168.10.0 255.255.255.0
RouterHome1(config)#ip mobile host 192.168.10.1 192.168.10.254 virtual-network 192.
168.10.0 255.255.255.0
RouterHome1(config)#ip mobile secure home-agent 192.168.9.3 spi 100 key ascii cisco
RouterHome1(config)#ip mobile secure host 192.168.10.110 spi 100 key ascii cookbook
RouterHome1(config)#ip mobile secure host 192.168.10.111 spi 100 key ascii cookbook
RouterHome1(config)#ip mobile secure host 192.168.10.112 spi 100 key ascii cookbook
RouterHome1(config)#ip mobile secure host 192.168.10.113 spi 100 key ascii cookbook
RouterHome1(config)#ip mobile secure host 192.168.10.114 spi 100 key ascii cookbook
RouterHome1(config)#ip mobile secure host 192.168.10.115 spi 100 key ascii cookbook
RouterHome1(config)#end
RouterHome1#
```

And here is the second Home Agent router:

```
RouterHome2#configure terminal
Enter configuration commands, one per line.  End with CNTL/Z.
RouterHome2(config)#interface FastEthernet0/0
RouterHome2(config-if)#ip address 192.168.9.3 255.255.255.0
RouterHome2(config-if)#standby 1 ip 192.168.9.1
RouterHome2(config-if)#standby 1 name HA-GROUP
RouterHome2(config-if)#exit
RouterHome2(config)#router mobile
RouterHome2(config-router)#exit
RouterHome2(config)#router eigrp 99
RouterHome2(config-router)#redistribute mobile
RouterHome2(config-router)#network 192.168.9.0
RouterHome2(config-router)#network 192.168.10.0
RouterHome2(config-router)#default-metric 10000 10 255 1 1500
RouterHome2(config-router)#no auto-summary
RouterHome2(config-router)#exit
RouterHome2(config)#ip mobile home-agent address 192.168.9.1
RouterHome2(config)#ip mobile home-agent redundancy HA-GROUP virtual-network
RouterHome2(config)#ip mobile virtual-network 192.168.10.0 255.255.255.0
RouterHome2(config)#ip mobile host 192.168.10.1 192.168.10.254 virtual-network 192.
168.10.0 255.255.255.0
RouterHome2(config)#ip mobile secure home-agent 192.168.9.2 spi 100 key ascii cisco
RouterHome2(config)#ip mobile secure host 192.168.10.110 spi 100 key ascii cookbook
RouterHome2(config)#ip mobile secure host 192.168.10.111 spi 100 key ascii cookbook
RouterHome2(config)#ip mobile secure host 192.168.10.112 spi 100 key ascii cookbook
RouterHome2(config)#ip mobile secure host 192.168.10.113 spi 100 key ascii cookbook
RouterHome2(config)#ip mobile secure host 192.168.10.114 spi 100 key ascii cookbook
RouterHome2(config)#ip mobile secure host 192.168.10.115 spi 100 key ascii cookbook
RouterHome2(config)#end
RouterHome2#
```

The configurations of the Mobile Router and the Foreign Agent router are identical
to those seen in previous recipes in this chapter.

Discussion

If you plan to configure a large Mobile IP infrastructure, then a natural design would be to have a centralized Home Agent router by using virtual-networks to support a large pool of Mobile Nodes. In this design, it quickly becomes apparent that the Home Agent router itself is a serious single point of failure for the entire Mobile IP network. Fortunately, Cisco provides a way to make the Home Agent redundant.

In this recipe, we modify the Home Agent configuration shown in Recipe 24.2 to allow you to use a pair of dual redundant Home Agent routers. In this example, the two routers are configured in an Active-Standby relationship, so that all traffic uses either one router or the other. Later in this recipe, we will discuss ways to make this an Active-Active relationship instead.

In Recipe 24.2, we configured the Home Agent address on a Loopback interface. The reason for this was simple. Because the tunnels terminate on this address, we wanted to make sure that it was always available. Now, however, we want to be able to flip our tunnels to the backup Home Agent router, which means that we need to put it on a physical interface:

```
RouterHome1(config)#interface FastEthernet0/0
RouterHome1(config-if)#ip address 192.168.9.2 255.255.255.0
RouterHome1(config-if)#standby 1 ip 192.168.9.1
RouterHome1(config-if)#standby 1 name HA-GROUP
```

We have configured HSRP on this interface and assigned the group name HA-GROUP to it. The HSRP virtual IP address for this group is the Home Agent address. On the other router, we have configured a different physical IP address, but the same virtual address and HSRP group:

```
RouterHome2(config)#interface FastEthernet0/0
RouterHome2(config-if)#ip address 192.168.9.3 255.255.255.0
RouterHome2(config-if)#standby 1 ip 192.168.9.1
RouterHome2(config-if)#standby 1 name HA-GROUP
```

This way, the virtual address is available if this Ethernet interface is available on either router. Please refer to Chapter 22 for more information on HSRP.

The rest of the Home Agent configuration is remarkably similar to what we previously saw in Recipe 24.2. So we will just look at the differences, and there are two:

```
RouterHome1(config)#ip mobile home-agent redundancy HA-GROUP virtual-network
RouterHome1(config)#ip mobile secure home-agent 192.168.9.3 spi 100 key ascii cisco
```

These two new commands do two things. The first one associates the HSRP group, HA-GROUP, with the IP Mobility Home Agent and configures it to support a virtual network. The second one configures a security association and authentication key for the relationship between the two redundant Home Agents. This is critical because it is this that allows the two routers to share information about the IP Mobility bindings.

To configure an Active-Active relationship between the two Home Agents, it is necessary to configure two distinct Home Agent addresses. One group of Mobile Nodes will use the first Home Agent address, and another group will use the second address.

First, the interface configuration must be changed to support two HSRP groups with different names and different virtual IP addresses:

```
RouterHome1(config)#interface FastEthernet0/0
RouterHome1(config-if)#ip address 192.168.9.2 255.255.255.0
RouterHome1(config-if)#standby 1 ip 192.168.9.1
RouterHome1(config-if)#standby 1 priority 110
RouterHome1(config-if)#standby 1 preempt
RouterHome1(config-if)#standby 1 name HA-GROUP
RouterHome1(config-if)#standby 2 ip 192.168.9.5
RouterHome1(config-if)#standby 2 priority 90
RouterHome1(config-if)#standby 2 preempt
RouterHome1(config-if)#standby 2 name HA-GROUP2
RouterHome1(config-if)#exit
```

Then the second router is the same, but with a different physical address and different HSRP priority values:

```
RouterHome2(config)#interface FastEthernet0/0
RouterHome2(config-if)#ip address 192.168.9.3 255.255.255.0
RouterHome2(config-if)#standby 1 ip 192.168.9.1
RouterHome2(config-if)#standby 1 priority 90
RouterHome2(config-if)#standby 1 preempt
RouterHome2(config-if)#standby 1 name HA-GROUP
RouterHome2(config-if)#standby 2 ip 192.168.9.5
RouterHome2(config-if)#standby 2 priority 110
RouterHome2(config-if)#standby 2 preempt
RouterHome2(config-if)#standby 2 name HA-GROUP2
RouterHome2(config-if)#exit
```

We have configured HSRP priorities so that during normal operation, the first router will be active for the first virtual IP address and the second router will be active for the second address. We have also configured the *preempt* keyword on both groups so that if one of the routers does fail, they will return to the desired Active-Active relationship after it recovers. Please refer to Chapter 22 for more information on this option.

Then we simply have to configure the routers to advertise the second virtual IP address as a Home Agent address:

```
RouterHome1(config)#ip mobile home-agent redundancy HA-GROUP virtual-network address 192.168.9.1
RouterHome1(config)#ip mobile home-agent redundancy HA-GROUP2 virtual-network address 192.168.9.5
```

And, finally, we must configure some of our Mobile Nodes to point to the first address and some to point to the second address for their respective Home Agents.

See Also

Recipe 24.2; Recipe 24.3; Recipe 24.4; Chapter 22

## CHAPTER 25

IPv6

25.0 Introduction

IPv6 was initially developed to resolve a critical problem with the existing Internet Protocol (commonly called IPv4). An IPv4 address has 4 octets, or 32 bits, to identify every device on the Internet. If each node has a single unique address, then there can be at most 4,294,967,296 (that is, 2^32) devices on the Internet. And that doesn't account for the fact that most routers and many servers have several addresses.

And, in fact, the situation is worse than that because of how IP addresses were originally allocated. With a handful of large organizations using Class A and B addresses, and large blocks of the IPv4 address range set aside for things like multicasting, the Internet Assigned Number Authority (IANA) was quickly running out of addresses. The Internet Engineering Task Force (IETF) went off to create a new version of the IP protocol with larger addresses to fix this problem.

Many options were considered, and in the end they came up with IPv6. Of course, in the meantime, because the available assignable address ranges were rapidly running out, a few simple interim standards such as NAT and CIDR were drafted that effectively saved IPv4 for many years to come.

Today the case for IPv6 is somewhat different. The force driving the new protocol is still based on increasing the number of addresses, but it is now a local rather than a global problem. Several large telephone companies, particularly in Asia, have started to encounter problems in assigning an IP address to every cellular telephone. If they start with a Class A address (such as the ubiquitous 10.0.0.0/8 range from RFC 1918), then they can address at most 16,777,216 devices. So it is easy to see how a national network with many millions of subscribers would quickly exhaust the available addressing. These companies could adopt an elaborate set of overlapping address ranges segregated by NAT, but IPv6 is a much more natural and flexible solution to the problem.

IPv6 Addressing

When the IPv4 address has 32 bits, the IPv6 address is represented by a (hopefully) inexhaustible 128-bit number. The full IPv6 address is written as eight blocks, each containing four hexadecimal numbers. These blocks are separated by colons ":". A hex number represents a 4-bit field, so a group of 4 hex numbers represents 16 bits. So we must have 8 such groups of numbers to make up the full 128 bits of the IPv6 address:

    x:x:x:x:x:x:x:x

As we will discuss in a moment, many types of standard IPv6 address implementations involve a lot of sequential zeroes in the address. When this happens, there are some useful rules that allow us to simplify the address. It's easiest to understand these rules with a concrete example.

Suppose we have this address:

    FEC0:0000:0000:0001:0000:0000:0000:0001/64

We can first delete all of the high order zeroes in each group of four hex numbers.

    FEC0:0:0:1:0:0:0:1/64

Then we can replace the longest set of consecutive zeroes with simply "::":

    FEC0:0:0:1::1/64

This object is now much easier to work with.

Also note that in the example, we have included the prefix size /64, at the end of the address. This convention is identical to the prefix size bit count used in IPv4 addresses. This is not only similar in appearance to the IPv4 CIDR representation of addresses, but it has the same function, allowing routers to establish multiple hierarchical address summarizations in the network.

Addressing Standards

The IANA has allocated several ranges of IPv6 addresses for different purposes. RFC 4294 defines these rules, updating the earlier RFC 3513 document. This document defines three general classes of addresses—Unicast, Multicast and Anycast. In addition, the standard defines several different types of Unicast address. As with IPv4, these different address types are uniquely identified by the first few bits of the address.

A unicast address identifies a single interface on a device. This is essentially the same as in IPv4 addressing, except that sometimes IPv4 addresses can represent two or more interfaces or devices through mechanisms like NAT and HSRP.

A multicast address in IPv6 functions exactly the same as in IPv4. Please refer to Chapter 23 for more information about IPv4 multicast protocols.

Anycast is a relatively new concept with IPv6, although it was proposed as an extension for IPv4 and is actually used in a limited way with the example of an IPv4

Anycast Rendezvous Point for multicast traffic (please refer to Chapter 23 for an example). An anycast address can represent several different interfaces or devices, any one of which may receive the packet. There are IPv4 mechanisms for achieving this effect. The virtual IP address in VRRP and HSRP is effectively an anycast as any of the devices in the group can handle the packet. The VRRP or HSRP protocol simply elects which device is currently handling a particular address on behalf of the group. Similarly, load balancing devices are often used to stand in front of a pool of servers, accepting packets for a single destination address and distributing the connections among the pool.

With IPv6, though, this concept is formalized. Normally people say that the "closest" anycast device will respond, but as the examples in the previous paragraph suggest, there are many other more sophisticated applications for this anycast concept than merely finding the closest of a group of devices.

Perhaps the biggest change is that there is no broadcast in IPv6.

The different types of address are specified by the first several bits, as shown in Table 25-1.

Table 25-1. IPv6 Address types

IPv6 address	Leading bits	IPv4 example	Description
::/128	0000....0000/128 (128 bits of zeroes)		Unspecified address
::1/128	0000...0001/128 (all zeroes except very last bit)	127.0.0.1	Loopback address
FF00::/8	1111 1111000... (8 leading zeroes)	224.0.0.0 through 239.255.255.255	Multicast address
FE80::/10	1111 1110 10...		Link local unicast
FEC0::/10	1111 1110 11...	10.0.0.0/8	Site local unicast (deprecated by IETF)
	Everything else		Global unicast

The Link Local Unicast is an address that is not permitted to "leak" off of the local network segment. The Site Local Unicast is similarly not permitted to leak out of an enterprise network (similar to RFC 1918 addresses). Note, however, that the Site Local Unicast definition is no longer considered part of the IPv6 addressing standard.

In addition, there are standard methods for encapsulating IPv4 addresses inside of IPv6 addresses. The so-called "IPv4-Compatible Address" follows the convention of just putting the IPv4 address into the last 32 bits of the 128-bit IPv6 address and padding all of the higher order bits with zeroes. For example, the address 192.168.11.1 would be written as 0:0:0:0:0:0:C0A8:0B01 or ::C0A8:B01, or following another convenient standard for representing IPv6 address that contain IPv4 address, ::192.168.11.1. Once again, this method is also deprecated because it doesn't match well with newer methods for interoperating IPv4 and IPv6 networks. However, you will sometimes see it in use in older IPv6 implementations.

Another common method for writing IPv4 addresses inside of IPv6 addresses is called "IPv4-Mapped Addressing", and it follows a similar strategy. Once again, the last 32 bits encapsulate the IPv4 address, but in this method, the IPv4 address is padded by 16 binary ones and 80 zeroes. So this time the address 192.168.11.1 becomes 0:0:0:0:0:FFFF:C0A8:0B01, or ::FFFF:C0A8:B01.

Finally, some Cisco documentation talks about so-called Site-Local addressing, which has a binary prefix of 1111 1110 11, or FEC0::/10 in hex. The Site-Local addressing concept has now been deprecated and removed from the IPv6 standard. While individual sites are free to continue using this addressing scheme and manually block these addresses from leaking out of a particular administrative area by means of access-lists, these addresses are now considered to be standard unicast addresses.

IEEE EUI-64 Identifiers

One thing that you will run into quickly in working with IPv6 is the EUI-64 identifier for an interface. The EUI-64 identifier is essentially an extension of the already familiar 48-bit MAC address commonly used on Ethernet interfaces. RFC 4291 defines a way of using this EUI-64 address to build a unique IPv6 address automatically for an interface.

Routing Protocols

Besides the rather large addressing differences already discussed, IPv6 is essentially IP as we already know it. It carries TCP and UDP and other higher layer protocols with no changes to those higher layer protocols. Telnet in IPv6 is Telnet. SMTP is still SMTP, and so forth.

Even the routing protocols that we use to distribute information about where different hosts exist on the network are very familiar from the protocols we have already discussed in this book. There are obviously some differences just due to the differences in addressing. Cisco routers implement several different IPv6 routing protocols, and we will show examples of RIP and OSPF for IPv6 in particular. There is also an IOS implementation of MBGP that allows you to carry IPv6 addressing, which we will discuss briefly in this chapter.

Cisco routers also implement a version of the IS-IS routing protocol for IPv6. However, as we don't cover this protocol for IPv4, we will not cover it for IPv6 either.

EIGRP for IPv6 became available in IOS Version 12.4(6)T, unfortunately putting it out of reach for most currently installed routers.

25.1 Automatically Generating IPv6 Addresses for an Interface

Problem

You want to enable IPv6 and generate addresses automatically.

Solution

There are two methods for generating IPv6 addresses automatically. The first uses the *autoconfig* command:

```
Router1#configure terminal
Enter configuration commands, one per line. End with CNTL/Z.
Router1(config)#ipv6 unicast-routing
Router1(config)#interface FastEthernet0/0
Router1(config-if)#ipv6 address autoconfig
Router1(config-if)#end
Router1#
```

The second method uses the EUI-64 method to automatically generate only the host part of the IPv6 address, combined with a defined network portion:

```
Router1#configure terminal
Enter configuration commands, one per line. End with CNTL/Z.
Router1(config)#ipv6 unicast-routing
Router1(config)#interface FastEthernet0/0
Router1(config-if)#ipv6 address AAAA::/64 eui-64
Router1(config-if)#end
Router1#
```

Discussion

Throughout this chapter you will see the following command frequently:

```
Router1(config)#ipv6 unicast-routing
```

By default, the router will not route IPv6 packets. You can configure interfaces with IPv6 addresses, and you can even use IPv6 applications such as PING and TELNET to communicate to and from these routers. And, somewhat confusingly, you can configure static IPv6 routes to allow the routers to do simple IPv6 networking. But without this command, you cannot enable any IPv6 routing protocols. So, even though we are not using any routing protocols in this recipe, we have enabled the *ipv6 unicast-routing* command because it is a good practice and will help to avoid confusion later on when you do want to run routing protocols.

The first method described in this recipe uses the *autoconfig* command. This does two things. First, it automatically generates a Link-Local address for use on the local network segment. As we discussed in the Introduction to this chapter, Link-Local addresses are valid IPv6 addresses that can be used to communicate with other devices on the segment, but that do not "leak" off of it. So it is not possible to route packets to these addresses.

So why would you want to configure a link-local address on a router? Well, the short answer is that RFC 4291 says that every interface must have one. The rationale is that you don't need a globally scoped address for any situation where the interface in question is neither the source nor the destination for a packet.

For example, suppose you have two routers connected by an Ethernet segment. If the first router recives a packet that it wants via the second router, the next hop address in its routing table doesn't need to be accessible off the segment. And there are many situations like this when the link-local address can be used, either because the packets are exchanged purely between neighbors or because the address doesn't appear in the packet header but is only used for routing decisions:

```
Router1#show ipv6 interface FastEthernet0/0
FastEthernet0/0 is up, line protocol is up
  IPv6 is enabled, link-local address is FE80::20E:D7FF:FED6:4D80
  No global unicast address is configured
  Joined group address(es):
    FF02::1
    FF02::1:FFD6:4D80
  MTU is 1500 bytes
  ICMP error messages limited to one every 100 milliseconds
  ICMP redirects are enabled
  ND DAD is enabled, number of DAD attempts: 1
  ND reachable time is 30000 milliseconds
Router1#
```

The address that the router generates this way uses the standard link-local prefix FE80::/10 and the EUI-64 version of the MAC address for the last 64 bits. We will discuss the EUI-64 encoding in a moment.

The second thing that this command does is check for any available IPv6 DHCP servers. If DHCP is available on the local network segment, then the router will automatically attempt to use this protocol to acquire a more general IPv6 address. If a DHCP server is available, the router will automatically discover and download an appropriate configuration. For more information on DHCP for IPv6, please refer to Recipe 25.3.

The other method shown in the Solution section of this recipe uses the EUI-64 keyword:

```
Router1(config)#interface FastEthernet0/0
Router1(config-if)#ipv6 address AAAA::/64 eui-64
```

In this case, the router will automatically use the MAC address of the interface to generate the host portion of the IPv6 address. In this case, the network portion of the address is AAAA::/64. Then, if we look at the interface with the *show ipv6 interface* command, we can see what the actual address is:

```
Router1#show ipv6 interface FastEthernet0/0
FastEthernet0/0 is up, line protocol is up
```

```
IPv6 is enabled, link-local address is FE80::20E:D7FF:FED6:4D80
Global unicast address(es):
  AAAA::20E:D7FF:FED6:4D80, subnet is AAAA::/64
Joined group address(es):
  FF02::1
  FF02::1:FFD6:4D80
MTU is 1500 bytes
ICMP error messages limited to one every 100 milliseconds
ICMP redirects are enabled
ND DAD is enabled, number of DAD attempts: 1
ND reachable time is 30000 milliseconds
Router1#
```

We can use the *show interface* command to see the 48-bit MAC address for this interface:

```
Router1#show interface FastEthernet0/0
FastEthernet0/0 is up, line protocol is up
  Hardware is AmdFE, address is 000e.d7d6.4d80 (bia 000e.d7d6.4d80)
  Internet address is 192.168.1.3/24
  MTU 1500 bytes, BW 100000 Kbit, DLY 100 usec,
     reliability 255/255, txload 1/255, rxload 1/255
  Encapsulation ARPA, loopback not set
  Keepalive set (10 sec)
  Full-duplex, 100Mb/s, 100BaseTX/FX
  ARP type: ARPA, ARP Timeout 04:00:00
  Last input 00:00:00, output 00:00:00, output hang never
  Last clearing of "show interface" counters never
  Input queue: 0/75/0/0 (size/max/drops/flushes); Total output drops: 0
  Queueing strategy: fifo
  Output queue: 0/40 (size/max)
  5 minute input rate 0 bits/sec, 0 packets/sec
  5 minute output rate 0 bits/sec, 0 packets/sec
     10879 packets input, 839782 bytes
     Received 8284 broadcasts, 0 runts, 0 giants, 0 throttles
     0 input errors, 0 CRC, 0 frame, 0 overrun, 0 ignored
     0 watchdog
     0 input packets with dribble condition detected
     12137 packets output, 908637 bytes, 0 underruns
     0 output errors, 0 collisions, 2 interface resets
     0 babbles, 0 late collision, 0 deferred
     0 lost carrier, 0 no carrier
     0 output buffer failures, 0 output buffers swapped out
Router1#
```

As you can see, the interface is now using the address AAAA:: 20E:D7FF:FED6:4D80. The 48-bit MAC address on this interface is 000e.d7d6.4d80. There is a unique correspondence between the host portion of the IPv6 address and this globally unique Ethernet MAC address. The EUI-64 encoding is defined in RFC 4291. For the full details, we encourage readers to refer to that document, but we will summarize the scheme here.

The IEEE 802 standard 48-bit MAC address used on Ethernet interfaces has a well-defined format. The first 24 bits specify the vendor Organizationally Unique Identifier (OUI), which identifies the manufacturer or the equipment. The remaining 24 bits specify an individual interface. The vendor portion of the MAC address has 2 special bits in locations 7 and 8. Bit 7 is the "scope" indicator. If this bit is equal to zero, then the MAC address has *global scope*, meaning that it can be used anywhere. If it is equal to one, then it has *local scope*, which usually means that it has been redefined for local purposes. Bit 8 is the "individual/group" bit, which specifies whether this MAC address is to be used by a single device or a collection of devices.

The first rule for converting 48-bit MAC addresses to IPv6 EUI-64 format host addresses is to flip the scope bit. If it is zero, make it one, and vice versa. The second rule, which is just required to pad the 48-bit address to 64 bits, is to insert the hex value 0xFFFE in between the vendor and host portions of the MAC address. So, in our case, when the MAC address is 000e.d7d6.4d80, the second octet must change from 0x00 (0000 0000 in binary) to 0x02 (0000 0010 in binary). Then, when we insert the hex value 0xFFFE, we get 020e.d7ff.fed6.4d80. Adding this as the host portion of the address to the prefix that we specified, AAAA::/64, we get AAAA::020E:D7FF:FED6:4D80/64.

The great advantage to this method of addressing is that you can configure exactly the same commands on every device on a segment, and allow each device to ensure that it has a unique IPv6 address. In fact, you can keep your configurations very simple by just having to worry about the prefixes for each network segment.

The disadvantage to this method, however, is that you will not generally know ahead of time what the full IPv6 address for each device is, only that they will be unique. If you use this method, you must do your record keeping after the fact rather than as part of the design process. This implementation method is quite foreign to the usual models of network design for IPv4 networks.

See Also

Recipe 25.3; RFC 4291

25.2 Manually Configuring IPv6 Addresses on an Interface

Problems

You want to manually configure a full IPv6 address on an interface.

Solution

You can configure an IPv6 unicast address on an interface by using a very similar process to how we set up IPv4 addresses in previous chapters of this book:

```
Router1#configure terminal
Enter configuration commands, one per line. End with CNTL/Z.
Router1(config)#ipv6 unicast-routing
Router1(config)#interface FastEthernet0/0
Router1(config-if)#ipv6 address AAAA::1/64
Router1(config-if)#exit
Router1(config)#end
Router1#
```

We can configure an IPv6 Anycast address by using the *anycast* keyword:

```
Router1#configure terminal
Enter configuration commands, one per line. End with CNTL/Z.
Router1(config)#ipv6 unicast-routing
Router1(config)#interface FastEthernet0/0
Router1(config-if)#ipv6 address AAFF::1/64 anycast
Router1(config-if)#exit
Router1(config)#end
Router1#
```

You can specify an IPv6 link-local address by using the *link-local* keyword:

```
Router1#configure terminal
Enter configuration commands, one per line. End with CNTL/Z.
Router1(config)#ipv6 unicast-routing
Router1(config)#interface FastEthernet0/0
Router1(config-if)#ipv6 address FE80::1 link-local
Router1(config-if)#exit
Router1(config)#end
Router1#
```

Discussion

In this recipe, we have manually configured three different types of IPv6 addresses. The first example simply configures a standard globally accessible unicast address. This is similar to the standard IPv4 unicast address:

```
Router1(config)#interface FastEthernet0/0
Router1(config-if)#ipv6 address AAAA::1/64
```

Assigning an address to an address like this also enables IPv6 functionality for the interface:

```
Router1#show ipv6 interface FastEthernet0/0
FastEthernet0/0 is up, line protocol is up
  IPv6 is enabled, link-local address is FE80::20E:84FF:FE24:4E70
  Global unicast address(es):
    AAAA::1, subnet is AAAA::/64
  Joined group address(es):
    FF02::1
    FF02::2
    FF02::1:FF00:1
    FF02::1:FF24:4E70
  MTU is 1500 bytes
  ICMP error messages limited to one every 100 milliseconds
  ICMP redirects are enabled
```

```
ND DAD is enabled, number of DAD attempts: 1
ND reachable time is 30000 milliseconds
ND advertised reachable time is 0 milliseconds
ND advertised retransmit interval is 0 milliseconds
ND router advertisements are sent every 200 seconds
ND router advertisements live for 1800 seconds
Hosts use stateless autoconfig for addresses.
Router1#
```

Even though we have only assigned the single global unicast address, AAAA::1/64, to the interface, it now has a link-local address as well, and it has joined several multicast groups. Because we didn't specify the link-local address, the router has created one for us using the standard FE80::/10 prefix and the EUI-64 host address, which we discussed in Recipe 25.1.

In the second example in the Solution section, we have defined an anycast address on this interface:

```
Router1(config)#interface FastEthernet0/0
Router1(config-if)#ipv6 address AAFF::1/64 anycast
```

This command is currently only available on certain higher end hardware platforms. After applying this command to the same interface that we were discussing a moment ago, we get the following output:

```
Router1#show ipv6 interface FastEthernet0/0
FastEthernet0/0 is up, line protocol is up
  IPv6 is enabled, link-local address is FE80::20E:84FF:FE24:4E70
  Global unicast address(es):
    AAAA::1, subnet is AAAA::/64
    AAFF::1, subnet is AAFF::/64 [ANY]
  Joined group address(es):
    FF02::1
    FF02::2
    FF02::1:FF00:1
    FF02::1:FF24:4E70
  MTU is 1500 bytes
  ICMP error messages limited to one every 100 milliseconds
  ICMP redirects are enabled
  ND DAD is enabled, number of DAD attempts: 1
  ND reachable time is 30000 milliseconds
  ND advertised reachable time is 0 milliseconds
  ND advertised retransmit interval is 0 milliseconds
  ND router advertisements are sent every 200 seconds
  ND router advertisements live for 1800 seconds
  Hosts use stateless autoconfig for addresses.
Router1#
```

The line with this newly configured anycast address is indicated by [ANY].

Anycast addresses can be extremely useful in allowing several different devices to fulfill a single function. A typical expected use for this feature is the ability to give remote users automatic access to your backup site if the primary site fails, without having to rely on DNS to time out. In this case, you would distribute the same anycast address into the global routing tables, but the backup site would have a metric or a BGP AS_PATH that would make it less desirable from anywhere on the network than the primary site. If the primary site becomes unavailable, the backup site would automatically take over as soon as the global routing protocol had flushed the primary site from its tables. This would likely take less time than waiting for DNS to update globally.

Another potential use for Anycast addresses is to offer several equivalent access points into your network. Remote users will simply find the closest access point through the global routing protocol.

Anycast would not function well as a replacement for protocols like HSRP for two reasons. First, when an IPv6 device communicates with its next-hop router, it uses link-local addresses, not a global address. Second, Anycast addresses work best when a routing protocol distributes them. Then the network will automatically determine which single device to send the packets to. If two or more anycast devices were the same distance away, by virtue of being on the same physical segment, and if both devices received the packet, both would assume that they were the only router receiving the packet and would forward it along. This would lead to duplication of every packet, and result in both added network congestion and protocol confusion.

We note in passing that there is some confusion in some of Cisco's documentation regarding legitimate uses for anycast addresses. The 12.4 configuration guide for IPv6 states that anycast address may only be used by routers, not hosts, and that they may not be used as source addresses in any packets. These restrictions were present in RFC 3513, but were removed in RFC 4291, and are no longer part of the IPv6 standard.

The final example in the Solution section shows how to manually configure a link-local address for the segment:

```
Router1(config)#interface FastEthernet0/0
Router1(config-if)#ipv6 address FE80::1 link-local
```

Note that there is no CIDR prefix indicator on link-local addresses. This is because all link-local addresses are assumed to be purely host addresses, and because link-local addresses are not advertised by routing protocols, so the prefix is not relevant.

Now when we look at the *show ipv6* interface command we see an interesting change:

```
Router1#show ipv6 interface FastEthernet0/0
FastEthernet0/0 is up, line protocol is up
  IPv6 is enabled, link-local address is FE80::1
  Global unicast address(es):
    AAAA::1, subnet is AAAA::/64
    AAFF::1, subnet is AAFF::/64 [ANY]
  Joined group address(es):
    FF02::1
    FF02::2
```

```
    FF02::1:FF00:1
  MTU is 1500 bytes
  ICMP error messages limited to one every 100 milliseconds
  ICMP redirects are enabled
  ND DAD is enabled, number of DAD attempts: 1
  ND reachable time is 30000 milliseconds
  ND advertised reachable time is 0 milliseconds
  ND advertised retransmit interval is 0 milliseconds
  ND router advertisements are sent every 200 seconds
  ND router advertisements live for 1800 seconds
  Hosts use stateless autoconfig for addresses.
Router1#
```

Note that the route has replaced the default link-local address with the new one we have defined. These link-local addresses will become more significant in Recipe 25.4 when we start talking about routing protocols.

We should finish this discussion with a brief explanation of the information shown at the end of the *show ipv6 interface* command, the lines that begin "ND". This referes to the IPv6 Neighbor Discovery process.

The IPv6 protocol includes automatic features that allow devices that share a network segment to discover one another. The Neighbor Discovery protocol is extremely simple, and amounts to little more than simply sending ICMP messages. The values shown in the command output indicate how often the router will send these messages. The two most important pieces of information here are the line that says "ND DAD is enabled", and the lines that describe "ND router advertisements".

DAD stands for Duplicate Address Detection, and is exactly that. When this feature is enabled, and it is enabled by default, the router will periodically send out packets testing to see if anybody else on the segment has taken over its address.

ND router advertisements (RA) packets are ICMP packets that the router sends out periodically to advertise itself as a router uses the default parameters, advertising itself as a router every 200 seconds. And, by default, it will retain information about other routers detected this way for 1,800 seconds.

See Also

Recipe 25.1; Recipe 25.4; RFC 3513; RFC 4291

25.3   Configuring DHCP for IPv6

Problem

You want to use the DHCP services built into IOS for distributing IPv6 address information.

Solution

Just as you can configure a router to act as a DHCP server for IPv4 addresses, Cisco's IOS also includes an IPv6 DHCP server function:

```
Router1#configure terminal
Enter configuration commands, one per line. End with CNTL/Z.
Router1(config)#ipv6 dhcp database flash:/DHCPv6-db
Router1(config)#ipv6 local pool VLAN10-pool AAAA:1::/48 64
Router1(config)#ipv6 local pool VLAN11-pool AAAA:11::/48 64
Router1(config)#ipv6 dhcp pool DHCPv6POOL
Router1(config-dhcp)#prefix-delegation AAAA:1::23F6:33BA/64 00030001000E84244E70
Router1(config-dhcp)#prefix-delegation pool VLAN10-pool
Router1(config-dhcp)#dns-server AAAA:1::19
Router1(config-dhcp)#domain-name oreilly.com
Router1(config-dhcp)#exit
Router1(config)#interface FastEthernet0/0
Router1(config-if)#ipv6 address AAAA:1::1/64
Router1(config-if)#ipv6 address FE80::1 link-local
Router1(config-if)#ipv6 nd managed-config-flag
Router1(config-if)#ipv6 nd other-config-flag
Router1(config-if)#ipv6 dhcp server DHCPv6POOL rapid-commit preference 1 allow-hint
Router1(config-if)#exit
Router1(config)#end
Router1#
```

Discussion

DHCP is currently available only on certain higher end routers. The rationale is probably that DHCP for IPv6 will be used primarily for WAN or wireless links in service provider networks, and that customers will continue to use IPv4 internally. However, experience with IPv4 shows that most large networks prefer to deploy DHCP services on dedicated servers because they have more user-friendly management tools and because the memory demands of maintaining dynamic addressing tables for a very large network are rather onerous for a router. Further, dedicated commercial DHCP servers tend to be deployed in clusters to ensure that a failure of any single server will not cause a loss of dynamic address information.

In IPv4 environments, DHCP servers tend to be deployed on routers only for smaller sites where a dedicated server was considered overkill. If a small network wants to deploy IPv6 with DHCP internally, it would be far more convenient to be able to run it on an existing integrated services router. So it is unfortunate that Cisco has opted to only provide DHCP server functionality on higher end routers, where we believe it is less likely to be required.

In our configuration example, the first DHCP command just defines where the router will hold its DHCP database:

```
Router1(config)#ipv6 dhcp database flash:/DHCPv6-db
```

In this case, we have opted to put this database into the named file on the flash partition. However, we could have also opted to store this information on a server as follows:

```
Router1(config)#ipv6 dhcp database tftp://192.168.100.15/DHCPv6-db
```

Next we defined an address pool called VLAN10-pool and assigned it to a DHCP pool:

```
Router1(config)#ipv6 local pool VLAN10-pool AAAA:1::/48 64
Router1(config)#ipv6 dhcp pool DHCPv6POOL
Router1(config-dhcp)#prefix-delegation pool VLAN10-pool
Router1(config-dhcp)#dns-server AAAA:1::19
Router1(config-dhcp)#domain-name oreilly.com
Router1(config-dhcp)#exit
```

You can only assign one address pool to each DHCP pool. So if you intend to support several different networks with your router's DHCP server, you will need to create a distinct DHCP pool for each one.

In this example, all addresses are assigned dynamically from this local pool prefix. However, you can also assign addresses statically by associating the IPv6 address with the DHCP Unique Identifier (DUID), as follows:

```
Router1(config)#ipv6 dhcp pool DHCPv6POOL
Router1(config-dhcp)#prefix-delegation AAAA:1::23F6:33BA/64 00030001000E84244E70
```

The DUID value for a device is a global value for the entire device that is uniquely derived from its first MAC address on the device:

```
Router1#show ipv6 dhcp
This device's DHCPv6 unique identifier(DUID): 00030001000E84244E70
Router1#show interface FastEthernet0/0 | include Hardware
  Hardware is Gt96k FE, address is 000e.8424.4e70 (bia 000e.8424.4e70)
Router1#
```

You can then look at your DHCP pools by using the following command:

```
Router1#show ipv6 dhcp pool DHCPv6POOL
DHCPv6 pool: DHCPv6POOL
  Static bindings:
    Binding for client 00030001000E84244E70
      IA PD: IA ID not specified
        Prefix: AAAA:1::23F6:33BA/64
                preferred lifetime 604800, valid lifetime 2592000
  Prefix pool: VLAN10-pool
                preferred lifetime 604800, valid lifetime 2592000
  DNS server: AAAA:1::19
  Domain name: oreilly.com
  Active clients: 0
Router1#
```

This output shows a single static binding in the pool as well as a dynamic prefix pool. It also shows any additional DHCP options that are being set; in this case, you can see the DNS server address and the domain name.

Finally, the last step in setting up IPv6 DHCP on a router is to associate a DHCP pool with an interface:

```
Router1(config)#interface FastEthernet0/0
Router1(config-if)#ipv6 nd managed-config-flag
Router1(config-if)#ipv6 nd other-config-flag
Router1(config-if)#ipv6 dhcp server DHCPv6POOL rapid-commit preference 1 allow-hint
Router1(config-if)#exit
```

There are three important commands here. First, when you set the *ipv6 nd managed-config-flag* command, the router sends its IPv6 Router Advertisement (RA) packets with a bit that tells any connected devices to use DHCP for dynamic address configuration. Similarly, the *ipv6 nd other-config-flag* command sets another flag in the RA packet that tells devices to get other information besides the address via DHCP. This includes things like DNS server and domain name.

Finally, we associate the DHCP server pool with the interface by using the *ipv6 dhcp server* command.

See Also

Recipe 25.1

25.4   Dynamic Routing with RIP

Problem

You want to use the IPv6 version of RIP to distribute your IPv6 routing information.

Solution

Configuring RIP for IPv6 is somewhat different from how it is configured for IPv4. To enable RIP for IPv6, you must create a routing process. and then assign interfaces to this process:

```
Router1#configure terminal
Enter configuration commands, one per line. End with CNTL/Z.
Router1(config)#ipv6 unicast-routing
Router1(config)#ipv6 router rip RIP_PROC
Router1(config-rtr)#exit
Router1(config)#interface FastEthernet0/0
Router1(config-if)#ipv6 address AAAA:5:1/64
Router1(config-if)#ipv6 rip RIP_PROC enable
Router1(config-if)#exit
Router1(config)#interface Serial0/0
Router1(config-if)#ipv6 address AAAA:1:2/64
Router1(config-if)#ipv6 rip RIP_PROC enable
Router1(config-if)#frame-relay map ipv6 AAAA:1:3 206 broadcast
Router1(config-if)#exit
Router1(config)#end
Router1#
```

Discussion

RIP, whether for IPv4 or IPv6, is not one of our favorite protocols. It's slow to converge, bandwidth intensive, and scales poorly. However, it has a couple of key advantages over other protocols. First, it's easy to understand and easy to configure. Second, because it's easy to understand, it's usually the first protocol to be implemented by programmers. And third, largely because of the second point, it's available on every router you'll ever encounter, making it the lowest common denominator of vendor interoperability.

The IPv6 version of RIP is described in RFC 2080. It has more in common with RIP Version 2 than Version 1, which is necessary because IPv6 is inherently classless and supports multicasts, but not broadcasts. The IPv6 multicast address used by RIP is FF02::9.

The configuration method is somewhat different from the more familiar RIP for IPv4. You first configure a RIP routing process:

```
Router1(config)#ipv6 unicast-routing
Router1(config)#ipv6 router rip RIP_PROC
Router1(config-rtr)#exit
```

This is similar to the IPv4 *router rip* command. It starts the RIP configuration mode, allowing you to make certain customizations. However, in this case we want to use the defaults. The process name, RIP_PROC in this example, is analogous to a routing process ID number used with some routing protocols. It is only significant within the router, and allows you to run more than one RIP process if you want to. Because it is only locally significant, every router can have a different RIP process name without conflict, although we generally don't recommend this, as it can become confusing to manage.

The most obvious difference from configuring RIP for IPv4 is that this version doesn't include the *network* command. Instead, you configure individual interfaces to take part in the routing protocol by using the *ipv6 rip enable* command:

```
Router1(config)#interface FastEthernet0/0
Router1(config-if)#ipv6 address AAAA:5:1/64
Router1(config-if)#ipv6 rip RIP_PROC enable
```

In this network, we have several routers distributing IPv6 routing information using RIP:

```
Router1#show ipv6 route rip
IPv6 Routing Table - 9 entries
Codes: C - Connected, L - Local, S - Static, R - RIP, B - BGP
       U - Per-user Static route
       I1 - ISIS L1, I2 - ISIS L2, IA - ISIS interarea, IS - ISIS summary
       O - OSPF intra, OI - OSPF inter, OE1 - OSPF ext 1, OE2 - OSPF ext 2
       ON1 - OSPF NSSA ext 1, ON2 - OSPF NSSA ext 2
R   AAAA:2::/64 [120/2]
     via FE80::2E0:1EFF:FE7F:9E41, FastEthernet0/0
R   AAAA:95::/64 [120/2]
     via FE80::2E0:1EFF:FE7F:9E41, FastEthernet0/0
R   AAAA:99::/64 [120/2]
     via FE80::20E:D7FF:FED6:1060, FastEthernet0/0
Router1#
```

The information here is similar to IPv4 RIP. Each of the RIP routes specifies a prefix, such as AAAA:2::/64, followed by a pair of numbers enclosed in square brackets, [120/2]. Exactly the same as IPv4 RIP, these two numbers are the administrative distance and the RIP metric, respectively. The administrative distances for IPv6 work exactly the same as for IPv4. The only difference is that there are fewer IPv6 routing protocols. So RIP has a default administrative distance of 120, OSPF uses 110, static routes default to a distance of 1, and connected interfaces are zero.

The next piece of information, though, is unique to IPv6. The next-hop router, indicated by the word via in the output, is the link-local address of the nearest interface on the next-hop router. IPv4 doesn't have a concept of a link-local address. By default, every IPv4 interface has a single globally scoped address. However, it does make a lot of sense to use the link-local address with IPv6 where it is available. This is because in most cases, the end users and their applications don't need to access the intermediate hops along the path to their destination devices. These next-hop addresses are strictly for packet forwarding and are only strictly relevant as a way of specifying a path to that destination. So it is not necessary that they have a global scope.

Note, however, that there are no link-local addresses in the routing table itself. This is because link-local addresses are not meaningful off of the local segment.

You can see what IPv6 routing protocols are running with the *show ipv6 protocols* command:

```
Router1#show ipv6 protocols
IPv6 Routing Protocol is "connected"
IPv6 Routing Protocol is "static"
IPv6 Routing Protocol is "rip RIP_PROC"
  Interfaces:
    Serial0/0
    FastEthernet0/0
  Redistribution:
    None
Router1#
```

As we mentioned earlier, one of the biggest differences from IPv4 is the relative lack of information in the RIP configuration section:

```
Router1(config)#ipv6 router rip RIP_PROC
Router1(config-rtr)#exit
```

This is because Cisco's RIP for IPv6 implementation makes a useful set of default assumptions for things like timers and so forth. Recipe 25.5 shows how to modify these parameters.

One final useful command for IPv6 RIP is *show ipv6 rip next-hops*, which lists all of the neighboring RIP routers:

```
Router1#show ipv6 rip next-hops
RIP process "RIP_PROC", Next Hops
  FE80::2E0:1EFF:FE7F:9E41/FastEthernet0/0 [2 paths]
```

```
FE80::20E:D7FF:FED6:1060/FastEthernet0/0 [7 paths]
FE80::200:CFF:FE75:C684/FastEthernet0/0 [2 paths]
FE80::2E0:1EFF:FE7F:9E41/Serial0/0 [2 paths]
Router1#
```

See Also

RFC 2080; Chapter 6; Recipe 25.5

25.5   Modifying the Default RIP Parameters

Problem

You want to modify the default parameters such as timers and administrative distance for IPv6 RIP.

Solution

There are several customizations that we can make to the default RIP configuration. You can modify the timers by using the *timers* command in the RIP configuration mode:

```
Router1#configure terminal
Enter configuration commands, one per line. End with CNTL/Z.
Router1(config)#ipv6 unicast-routing
Router1(config)#ipv6 router rip RIP_PROC
Router1(config-rtr)#timers 15 60 5 120
Router1(config-rtr)#exit
Router1(config)#end
Router1#
```

You can change the default administrative distance with the *distance* command:

```
Router1#configure terminal
Enter configuration commands, one per line. End with CNTL/Z.
Router1(config)#ipv6 unicast-routing
Router1(config)#ipv6 router rip RIP_PROC
Router1(config-rtr)#distance 100
Router1(config-rtr)#exit
Router1(config)#end
Router1#
```

And, in NBMA networks in particular, it is often necessary to disable the default split-horizon behavior of RIP:

```
Router1#configure terminal
Enter configuration commands, one per line. End with CNTL/Z.
Router1(config)#ipv6 unicast-routing
Router1(config)#ipv6 router rip RIP_PROC
Router1(config-rtr)#no split-horizon
Router1(config-rtr)#exit
Router1(config)#end
Router1#
```

Discussion

You can see the current RIP configuration with the *show ipv6 rip* command. Here is the output of this command before you make any changes to the default configuration:

```
Router1#show ipv6 rip
RIP process "RIP_PROC", port 521, multicast-group FF02::9, pid 125
     Administrative distance is 120. Maximum paths is 16
     Updates every 30 seconds, expire after 180
     Holddown lasts 0 seconds, garbage collect after 120
     Split horizon is on; poison reverse is off
     Default routes are not generated
     Periodic updates 717, trigger updates 3
   Interfaces:
     FastEthernet0/0
     Loopback0
   Redistribution:
     None
Router1#
```

First, we will look at the timers. As you can see, by default RIP sends updates every 30 seconds and routes time out after 180 seconds. The hold-down timer is zero by default, and garbage collection is done every 120 seconds. Now we will look at modifying these timers:

```
Router1(config)#ipv6 router rip RIP_PROC
Router1(config-rtr)#timers 15 60 5 120
```

In this example, we have set the update period to 15 seconds and the timeout interval to 60 seconds. We have also set the holddown timer to 5 seconds, but we will leave the garbage collection period at the default value of 120 seconds:

```
Router1#show ipv6 rip
RIP process "RIP_PROC", port 521, multicast-group FF02::9, pid 125
     Administrative distance is 120. Maximum paths is 16
     Updates every 15 seconds, expire after 60
     Holddown lasts 5 seconds, garbage collect after 120
     Split horizon is on; poison reverse is off
     Default routes are not generated
     Periodic updates 755, trigger updates 3
   Interfaces:
     FastEthernet0/0
     Loopback0
   Redistribution:
     None
Router1#
```

It is important to note that with RIP, these timers are global, applying to updates sent on all RIP interfaces. So, while reducing the timers will improve the convergence time after a topology change, it could also cause serious instability problems if all of the routers in a network do not agree on the timers.

The second example in the Solution section of this recipe changed the administrative distance from the default value of 120 to 100:

```
Router1(config)#ipv6 router rip RIP_PROC
Router1(config-rtr)#distance 100
```

If we look at the routing table now, you can see that the administrative distance is now 100:

```
Router1#show pv6 route rip
IPv6 Routing Table - 14 entries
Codes: C - Connected, L - Local, S - Static, R - RIP, B - BGP
       U - Per-user Static route
       I1 - ISIS L1, I2 - ISIS L2, IA - ISIS interarea, IS - ISIS summary
       O - OSPF intra, OI - OSPF inter, OE1 - OSPF ext 1, OE2 - OSPF ext 2
       ON1 - OSPF NSSA ext 1, ON2 - OSPF NSSA ext 2
R    AAAA:2::/64 [100/2]
     via FE80::2E0:1EFF:FE7F:9E41, Serial0/0
     via FE80::2E0:1EFF:FE7F:9E41, FastEthernet0/0
R    AAAA:99::9:0/112 [100/2]
     via FE80::20E:D7FF:FED6:1060, FastEthernet0/0
<lines deleted for brevity>
Router2#
```

Administrative distance for IPv6 functions exactly the same way as in IPv4. If the router has routing information for the same prefix from two or more sources, it will prefer the one with the lowest administrative distance. In this case, we have set the distance for all RIP routes to 100 so that they will always be used in preference to OSPF routes.

Split horizon means that the router will not send routes back out through the interface through which it learned them. This is normally the right behavior. On an Ethernet segment, for example, with three routers, all of the routers can see one another. So if Router1 advertises a particular prefix, Router2 does not need to re-advertise this same prefix to Router3. In fact, doing so would be potentially dangerous because if Router1 goes down, Router3 will think that Router2 is still a valid next hop for this route.

However, in Nonbroadcast Multiple Access (NBMA) networks, such as Frame Relay and ATM, it is possible to have several downstream routers on an interface, and they can't see one another directly. For example, Router1 may have connectivity to Router2 and Router3, but Router2 cannot directly communicate with Router3. In this case Router1 must readvertise the prefixes that it learns from Router2 through this interface so that Router3 can see them.

In IPv6 RIP, you can only disable split-horizon processing globally:

```
Router1(config)#ipv6 router rip RIP_PROC
Router1(config-rtr)#no split-horizon
```

This is somewhat less than optimal, as this router may have several downstream Frame Relay neighbors and several downstream Ethernet neighbors. Ideally you would want to disable split-horizon only for the Frame Relay interface, as is possible with RIP for IPv4.

In general, IPv4 RIP gives much finer control over parameters such as timers, administrative distance and split-horizon. In IPv4 RIP, you can configure different timers on each interface. You can set different distance values for different prefixes learned from different neighbors, and you can configure split-horizon processes differently on each interface. Unfortunately, Cisco has not yet implemented this level of control for IPv6. Presumably the IPv6 feature set will become richer as the protocol becomes more widely implemented.

See Also

RFC 2080; Chapter 6

25.6 IPv6 Route Filtering and Metric Manipulation in RIP

Problem

You want to manipulate the IPv6 routing table created by RIP.

Solution

There are several types of route filtering available with RIP and IPv6. The first is a simple summary address, which you can configure on the interface that will be sending this summary information:

```
Router1#configure terminal
Enter configuration commands, one per line. End with CNTL/Z.
Router1(config)#interface FastEthernet0/0
Router1(config-if)#ipv6 rip RIP_PROC summary-address AAAA:99::8:0/109
Router1(config-if)#exit
Router1(config)#end
Router1#
```

In addition to summary addresses, RIP can advertise a default route in addition to the routes in its routing table:

```
Router1#configure terminal
Enter configuration commands, one per line. End with CNTL/Z.
Router1(config)#interface FastEthernet0/0
Router1(config-if)#ipv6 rip RIP_PROC default-information originate
Router1(config-if)#exit
Router1(config)#end
Router1#
```

Or, to save network and memory resources, you can configure RIP to advertise only a default route:

```
Router1#configure terminal
Enter configuration commands, one per line. End with CNTL/Z.
Router1(config)#interface FastEthernet0/0
```

```
Router1(config-if)#ipv6 rip RIP_PROC default-information only
Router1(config-if)#exit
Router1(config)#end
Router1#
```

You can filter routes both inbound and outbound with RIP:

```
Router1#configure terminal
Enter configuration commands, one per line. End with CNTL/Z.
Router1(config)#ipv6 prefix-list BLOCK_2E6 seq 5 deny AAAA:2E6::/64 le 128
Router1(config)#ipv6 prefix-list BLOCK_2E6 seq 10 permit ::/0 le 128
Router1(config)#ipv6 prefix-list ALLOW_2222 seq 5 permit AAAA:2222::/64 le 128
Router1(config)#ipv6 prefix-list ALLOW_2222 seq 10 deny ::/0 le 128
Router1(config)#ipv6 router rip RIP_PROC
Router1(config-rtr)#distribute-list prefix-list BLOCK_2E6 in FastEthernet0/0
Router1(config-rtr)#distribute-list prefix-list ALLOW_2222 out FastEthernet0/0
Router1(config-rtr)#exit
Router1(config)#end
Router1#
```

It is also sometimes useful to modify the metrics associated with specific links to help route traffic along the best path, instead of just the path with the fewest hops:

```
Router1#configure terminal
Enter configuration commands, one per line. End with CNTL/Z.
Router1(config)#interface Serial0/0
Router1(config-if)#ipv6 rip RIP_PROC metric-offset 5
Router1(config-if)#exit
Router1(config)#end
Router1#
```

Discussion

The first example in this recipe looks at route summarization on an interface:

```
Router1(config)#interface FastEthernet0/0
Router1(config-if)#ipv6 rip RIP_PROC summary-address AAAA:99::8:0/109
```

To see how this works, we will first create several Loopback interfaces with addresses AAAA:99::9:1/112, AAAA:99::A:1/112, AAAA:99::B:1/112, AAAA:99::C:1/112, AAAA:99::D:1/112, and AAAA:99::E:1/112. We want to replace all of these entries with the single summary route, AAAA:99::8:0/109. Before implementing any summarization, a downstream router has the following routing table:

```
Router9>show ipv6 route rip
IPv6 Routing Table - 14 entries
Codes: C - Connected, L - Local, S - Static, R - RIP, B - BGP
       U - Per-user Static route
       I1 - ISIS L1, I2 - ISIS L2, IA - ISIS interarea, IS - ISIS summary
       O - OSPF intra, OI - OSPF inter, OE1 - OSPF ext 1, OE2 - OSPF ext 2
       ON1 - OSPF NSSA ext 1, ON2 - OSPF NSSA ext 2
R   AAAA:1::/64 [120/11]
     via FE80::2E0:1EFF:FE7F:9E41, Ethernet0
R   AAAA:2::/64 [120/11]
     via FE80::2E0:1EFF:FE7F:9E41, Ethernet0
```

```
R    AAAA:99::9:0/112 [120/11]
       via FE80::20E:D7FF:FED6:1060, Ethernet0
R    AAAA:99::A:0/112 [120/11]
       via FE80::20E:D7FF:FED6:1060, Ethernet0
R    AAAA:99::B:0/112 [120/11]
       via FE80::20E:D7FF:FED6:1060, Ethernet0
R    AAAA:99::C:0/112 [120/11]
       via FE80::20E:D7FF:FED6:1060, Ethernet0
R    AAAA:99::D:0/112 [120/11]
       via FE80::20E:D7FF:FED6:1060, Ethernet0
R    AAAA:99::E:0/112 [120/11]
       via FE80::20E:D7FF:FED6:1060, Ethernet0
Router9>
```

Then, with the summarization configured, the individual routes disappear and are replaced by the single summary route:

```
Router9>show ipv6 route rip
IPv6 Routing Table - 9 entries
Codes: C - Connected, L - Local, S - Static, R - RIP, B - BGP
       U - Per-user Static route
       I1 - ISIS L1, I2 - ISIS L2, IA - ISIS interarea, IS - ISIS summary
       O - OSPF intra, OI - OSPF inter, OE1 - OSPF ext 1, OE2 - OSPF ext 2
       ON1 - OSPF NSSA ext 1, ON2 - OSPF NSSA ext 2
R    AAAA:1::/64 [120/11]
       via FE80::2E0:1EFF:FE7F:9E41, Ethernet0
R    AAAA:2::/64 [120/11]
       via FE80::2E0:1EFF:FE7F:9E41, Ethernet0
R    AAAA:99::8:0/109 [120/11]
       via FE80::20E:D7FF:FED6:1060, Ethernet0
Router9>
```

The ultimate route summarization is a default route. There are two ways to advertise a default route in RIP without needing to introduce any external networks through redistribution. The first method advertises a default route in addition to the existing networks:

```
Router1(config)#interface FastEthernet0/0
Router1(config-if)#ipv6 rip RIP_PROC default-information originate
```

On a downstream router, the routing table now includes an IPv6 default route prefix, ::/0:

```
Router3#show ipv6 route rip
IPv6 Routing Table - 12 entries
Codes: C - Connected, L - Local, S - Static, R - RIP, B - BGP
       U - Per-user Static route
       I1 - ISIS L1, I2 - ISIS L2, IA - ISIS interarea, IS - ISIS summary
       O - OSPF intra, OI - OSPF inter, OE1 - OSPF ext 1, OE2 - OSPF ext 2
       ON1 - OSPF NSSA ext 1, ON2 - OSPF NSSA ext 2
R    ::/0 [120/3]
       via FE80::20E:D7FF:FED6:1060, Serial0/0
       via FE80::20E:D7FF:FED6:4D80, Serial0/0
R    AAAA:2::/64 [120/3]
       via FE80::20E:D7FF:FED6:1060, Serial0/0
```

```
         via FE80::20E:D7FF:FED6:4D80, Serial0/0
R    AAAA:5::/64 [120/2]
         via FE80::20E:D7FF:FED6:4D80, Serial0/0
         via FE80::20E:D7FF:FED6:1060, Serial0/0
R    AAAA:99::8:0/109 [120/2]
         via FE80::20E:D7FF:FED6:1060, Serial0/0
R    AAAA:FE::/64 [120/3]
         via FE80::20E:D7FF:FED6:1060, Serial0/0
         via FE80::20E:D7FF:FED6:4D80, Serial0/0
R    AAAA:2E6::/64 [120/2]
         via FE80::209:7CFF:FEB7:C9E1, Ethernet0/0
Router3#
```

The alternative method is useful for creating *stub* networks, conserving both band-width and memory on downstream routers. This method uses the keyword *only* on the *default-originate* command to indicate that the router should advertise only the default route and no other prefixes:

```
Router1(config)#interface FastEthernet0/0
Router1(config-if)#ipv6 rip RIP_PROC default-information only
```

Now the downstream router no longer shows any of the other prefixes, such as AAAA:FE::/64, and AAAA:2::/64, that originated with the router that introduced the default route. Note, however, that it still sees route prefixes that originated within the same stub network region:

```
Router3#show ipv6 route rip
IPv6 Routing Table - 10 entries
Codes: C - Connected, L - Local, S - Static, R - RIP, B - BGP
       U - Per-user Static route
       I1 - ISIS L1, I2 - ISIS L2, IA - ISIS interarea, IS - ISIS summary
       O - OSPF intra, OI - OSPF inter, OE1 - OSPF ext 1, OE2 - OSPF ext 2
       ON1 - OSPF NSSA ext 1, ON2 - OSPF NSSA ext 2
R    ::/0 [120/3]
         via FE80::20E:D7FF:FED6:1060, Serial0/0
         via FE80::20E:D7FF:FED6:4D80, Serial0/0
R    AAAA:5::/64 [120/2]
         via FE80::20E:D7FF:FED6:4D80, Serial0/0
         via FE80::20E:D7FF:FED6:1060, Serial0/0
R    AAAA:99::8:0/109 [120/2]
         via FE80::20E:D7FF:FED6:1060, Serial0/0
R    AAAA:2E6::/64 [120/2]
         via FE80::209:7CFF:FEB7:C9E1, Ethernet0/0
Router3#
```

A more generic form of route filtering is available by means of *distribute-lists*. This technique is already quite familiar from IPv4. The only real difference here is that the distribute-list command in IPv6 RIP only accepts prefix-lists and not access-lists as arguments. The example in the solutions section actually includes both an inbound and an outbound distribute-list, which we will now look at separately:

```
Router1(config)#ipv6 prefix-list BLOCK_2E6 seq 5 deny AAAA:2E6::/64 le 128
Router1(config)#ipv6 prefix-list BLOCK_2E6 seq 10 permit ::/0 le 128
```

```
Router1(config)#ipv6 router rip RIP_PROC
Router1(config-rtr)#distribute-list prefix-list BLOCK_2E6 in FastEthernet0/0
```

This inbound distribute-list allows whatever IPv6 prefixes are specified by the prefix-list. In this case, we only want to remove a single prefix, and only if it is received on interface *FastEthernet0/0*. If we had left off the interface argument, then the command would apply this prefix-list to filter routes received on all interfaces:

```
Router1(config)#ipv6 router rip RIP_PROC
Router1(config-rtr)#distribute-list prefix-list BLOCK_2E6 in
```

The outbound distribute-list is similar, except that it affects what route prefixes this router will send to downstream neighbors:

```
Router1(config)#ipv6 prefix-list ALLOW_2222 seq 5 permit AAAA:2222::/64 le 128
Router1(config)#ipv6 prefix-list ALLOW_2222 seq 10 deny ::/0 le 128
Router1(config)#ipv6 router rip RIP_PROC
Router1(config-rtr)#distribute-list prefix-list ALLOW_2222 out FastEthernet0/0
```

In this case, we have decided to remove all routes except for AAAA:2222::/64, but only for routing updates sent out through interface *FastEthernet0/0*.

Finally, we can use the *ipv6 rip metric-offset* command to change the way that RIP calculates the distance along a particular path:

```
Router1(config)#interface Serial0/0
Router1(config-if)#ipv6 rip RIP_PROC metric-offset 5
```

This has the effect of increasing the metrics of all routes received on this interface by the specified amount. So a route that previously had a metric value of 2 will now have a metric of 7. This router will also pass along this new metric with all of the associated prefixes to any downstream routers. This feature is most commonly used to force the network to prefer a primary path over a backup path.

See Also

Recipe 25.4

25.7   Using OSPF for IPv6

Problem

You want to distribute your IPv6 routing information using OSPF Version 3.

Solution

Configuring OSPF for IPv6 is similar to the IPv4 configuration:

```
Router1#configure terminal
Enter configuration commands, one per line. End with CNTL/Z.
Router1(config)#ip cef
Router1(config)#ipv6 cef
```

```
Router1(config)#ipv6 unicast-routing
Router1(config)#ipv6 router ospf 1
Router1(config-rtr)#router-id 1.0.0.1
Router1(config-rtr)#area 0 range AAAA:5::/64
Router1(config-rtr)#exit
Router1(config)#interface FastEthernet0/0
Router1(config-if)#ipv6 address AAAA:5::1/64
Router1(config-if)#ipv6 ospf 1 area 0
Router1(config-if)#exit
Router1(config)#end
Router1#
```

Discussion

OSPF Version 3 is a set of relatively straightforward extensions to the existing OSPF Version 2 protocol. These extensions are used purely to allow IPv6 support. The basic operation of OSPF, with its Link State Advertisement (LSA) packets, its strict two-level hierarchy of areas, flooding, Designated Routers, and so forth are exactly the same as what we previously saw for IPv4 in Chapter 8.

OSPFv3 is defined in RFC 2740.

Configuring OSPF for IPv6 has a few more steps than configuring RIP. In particular, CEF must be enabled for both IPv4 and IPv6:

```
Router1(config)#ip cef
Router1(config)#ipv6 cef
```

You then define an OSPF process:

```
Router1(config)#ipv6 router ospf 1
Router1(config-rtr)#router-id 1.0.0.1
Router1(config-rtr)#area 0 range AAAA:5::/64
```

Note that OSPF requires a *router ID* for every router, and that this ID is always a 32-bit IPv4 style address. If your router has IPv4 configured, then it will select a router-id automatically using the same criteria that we discussed in Chapter 8. However, if there are no IPv4 addresses on the router, you must manually configure a router-ID, as OSPF will not work without it.

We have used the *area range* command to define a single area on this router. Once again, OSPF Version 3 area ID numbers are 32-bit values that can be written in IPv4 style dotted decimal notation or as an integer value between 0 and 4,294,967,295, exactly the same as we saw in Chapter 8 when discussing OSPF Version 2 for IPv4.

Finally, we must configure at least one interface to take part in OSPF process number 1:

```
Router1(config)#interface FastEthernet0/0
Router1(config-if)#ipv6 address AAAA:5::1/64
Router1(config-if)#ipv6 ospf 1 area 0
You can view OSPF neighbor relationships using the show ipv6 ospf neighbor command.
Router1#show ipv6 ospf neighbor
```

```
Neighbor ID    Pri  State        Dead Time   Interface ID   Interface
1.0.0.2         1   FULL/DR      00:00:36    3              FastEthernet0/
0
Router1#
```

And you can look at the OSPF routing information with the command *show ipv6 route ospf*:

```
Router1#show ipv6 route ospf
IPv6 Routing Table - 15 entries
Codes: C - Connected, L - Local, S - Static, R - RIP, B - BGP
       U - Per-user Static route
       I1 - ISIS L1, I2 - ISIS L2, IA - ISIS interarea, IS - ISIS summary
       O - OSPF intra, OI - OSPF inter, OE1 - OSPF ext 1, OE2 - OSPF ext 2
       ON1 - OSPF NSSA ext 1, ON2 - OSPF NSSA ext 2
O   AAAA:F::AA:1/128 [110/1]
     via FE80::20E:D7FF:FED6:1060, FastEthernet0/0
OI  AAAA:99::9:0/112 [110/2]
     via FE80::20E:D7FF:FED6:1060, FastEthernet0/0
OI  AAAA:99::A:0/112 [110/151]
     via FE80::20E:D7FF:FED6:1060, FastEthernet0/0
OI  AAAA:99::B:0/112 [110/163]
     via FE80::20E:D7FF:FED6:1060, FastEthernet0/0
OI  AAAA:99::C:0/112 [110/20]
     via FE80::20E:D7FF:FED6:1060, FastEthernet0/0
OI  AAAA:99::D:0/112 [110/893]
     via FE80::20E:D7FF:FED6:1060, FastEthernet0/0
OI  AAAA:99::E:0/112 [110/2]
     via FE80::20E:D7FF:FED6:1060, FastEthernet0/0
Router1#
```

This routing table shows a single intra-area route, designated by the "O" at the start of the line. All of the other routes shown are OSPF interarea routes.

We note in passing that the *area range* command we included in the example is not strictly necessary. The interface *ipv6 ospf area* command instructs the router to include all of the IPv6 prefixes defined on this interface in the specified area anyway. The *area* command is useful, however, when we want to define nondefault characteristics for the area. For example, with this command, we can specify that a particular area is to be a stub or Not So Stubby Area (NSSA) as follows:

```
Router1(config)#ipv6 router ospf 1
Router1(config-rtr)#area 15 stub no-summary
```

All of the same area types that we discussed in Chapter 8 for IPv4 are available for IPv6 as well.

We can also use the *area* command to define virtual links:

```
Router1(config)#ipv6 router ospf 1
Router1(config-rtr)#area 16 virtual-link 1.0.0.5
```

Note that the IPv4 address used in the *area virtual-link* command is the router-id of the destination device.

Several of the familiar OSPF options from OSPFv2 for IPv4 are not currently available for IPv6. For example, the OSPFv3 standard deliberately removes neighbor authentication, relying instead on IPv6's IPSec Authentication Header (AH) and Encapsulating Security Payload (ESP) options.

See Also

RFC 2740; Chapter 8

25.8 IPv6 Route Filtering and Metric Manipulation in OSPF

Problem

You want to manipulate the IPv6 routing tables distributed by OSPF.

Solution

OSPF Version 3 has many of the same features for route filtering and metric manipulation that we previously saw for OSPF Version 2 in Chapter 8. There are two commands for configuring link costs.

The first command changes the costs globally for all links according to their bandwidth values:

```
Router1#configure terminal
Enter configuration commands, one per line. End with CNTL/Z.
Router1(config)#ipv6 router ospf 1
Router1(config-rtr)#auto-cost reference-bandwidth 1000
%OSPFv3: Reference bandwidth is change.
        Please ensure reference bandwidth is consistent across all routers.
Router1(config-rtr)#exit
Router1(config)#end
Router1#
```

The second method changes the costs for individual links:

```
Router1#configure terminal
Enter configuration commands, one per line.  End with CNTL/Z
Router1(config)#interface FastEthernet0/0
Router1(config-if)#ipv6 ospf cost 500
Router1(config)#end
Router1#
```

We can also filter routes in OSPFv3, but only according to the same rules that we previously saw for OSPFv2:

```
Router1#configure terminal
Enter configuration commands, one per line. End with CNTL/Z.
Router1(config)#ipv6 prefix-list BLOCK_99_E seq 5 deny AAAA:99::E:0/112
Router1(config)#ipv6 prefix-list BLOCK_99_E seq 10 permit ::/0 le 128
Router1(config)#ipv6 router ospf 1
```

```
Router1(config-rtr)#distribute-list prefix-list BLOCK_99_E in
Router1(config-rtr)#exit
Router1(config)#end
Router1#
```

Discussion

The first configuration example shown in the Solution section of this recipe sets the global reference bandwidth for OSPF to use in calculating link costs. This command is exactly the same as we previously saw in Chapter 8:

```
Router1(config)#ipv6 router ospf 1
Router1(config-rtr)#auto-cost reference-bandwidth 1000
```

The default reference-bandwidth for OSPFv3 is 100 Mbps. This means that links with a bandwidth of 100 Mbps and higher are assigned an OSPF cost value of 1. Links with lower bandwidths are assigned a cost value equal to this reference bandwidth divided by the interface bandwidth. So, by default a 10 Mbps Ethernet link has a cost of 10, and a 1.554 Mbps T1 link has a cost of 64. Note that the cost value is an integer.

Unfortunately, the default value of 100 Mbps is probably too low for most networks these days, as it fails to distinguish between Fast Ethernet and Gigabit Ethernet, both of which are rather common. So a reasonable starting point for these networks would be to set a reference bandwidth of 10,000, corresponding to a 10 Gigabit backbone link. This has the unfortunate consequence of assigning any link slower than 152 kbps a cost of 65,535, which is the maximum allowed in OSPF.

We discuss this problem in more detail in Chapter 8, since it is generic to OSPF. The way around it is to assign costs to individual links, which you can do using the method shown in the second configuration example:

```
Router1(config)#interface FastEthernet0/0
Router1(config-if)#ipv6 ospf cost 500
```

This example assigns an OSPF link cost of 500 to this interface. Remember that lower-cost paths are preferred when OSPF constructs its shortest-path routing table. So you can also use this command to manually force traffic to use a particular network link preferentially.

As we discussed in Chapter 8, you can block individual prefixes in OSPF, but this doesn't have the same meaning as for RIP:

```
Router1(config)#ipv6 prefix-list BLOCK_99_E seq 5 deny AAAA:99::E:0/112
Router1(config)#ipv6 prefix-list BLOCK_99_E seq 10 permit ::/0 le 128
Router1(config)#ipv6 router ospf 1
Router1(config-rtr)#distribute-list prefix-list BLOCK_99_E in
```

The OSPF algorithm requires that every router in an area must see exactly the same list of link state advertisements. Otherwise there is a serious risk that routing within this area will become unstable and perhaps generate loops. So there is no way to prevent a router from distributing the LSA information that it has received from other routers in the same area.

However, because OSPF keeps the LSA database separate from the routing table, you can use a distribute-list, as we have done in this example, to prevent the router from installing particular routes in its own routing table. In this case, you can see that the route in question, AAAA:99::E:0/112, is in the OSPF database:

```
Router1#show ipv6 ospf database

            OSPFv3 Router with ID (1.0.0.1) (Process ID 1)

            Router Link States (Area 0)

ADV Router      Age       Seq#        Fragment ID  Link count  Bits
1.0.0.1         1687      0x8000000F  0            1           B
1.0.0.2         409       0x80000011  0            1           B

            Net Link States (Area 0)

ADV Router      Age       Seq#        Link ID    Rtr count
1.0.0.2         409       0x8000000D  3          2

            Inter Area Prefix Link States (Area 0)

            Inter Area Prefix Link States (Area 0)

ADV Router      Age       Seq#        Prefix
1.0.0.1         439       0x8000000D  AAAA:1::/64
1.0.0.2         1507      0x8000000D  AAAA:1::/64
1.0.0.2         491       0x8000000D  AAAA:99::E:0/112
1.0.0.2         491       0x8000000D  AAAA:99::D:0/112
<lines deleted for brevity>
But this prefix isn't present in the routing table.
Router1#show ipv6 route AAAA:99::E:0/112
% Route not found
Router1#
```

See Also

Chapter 8; Recipe 25.7

25.9   Route Redistribution

Problem

You want to redistribute IPv6 routes between routing protocols.

Solution

First, we will show an example of redistributing from OSPF into RIPv6:

```
Router1#configure terminal
Enter configuration commands, one per line.  End with CNTL/Z.
Router1(config)#ipv6 router rip RIP_PROC
Router1(config-rtr)#redistribute ospf 1 metric 5
```

```
Router1(config-rtr)#exit
Router1(config)#end
Router1#
```

And here is an example showing redistribution of RIPv6 into OSPF:

```
Router1#configure terminal
Enter configuration commands, one per line.  End with CNTL/Z.
Router1(config)#ipv6 router ospf 1
Router1(config-rtr)#redistribute rip RIP_PROC
Router1(config-rtr)#exit
Router1(config)#end
Router1#
```

You can advertise a default route with OSPF by using the *default-information originate* command:

```
Router1#configure terminal
Enter configuration commands, one per line.  End with CNTL/Z.
Router1(config)#ipv6 router ospf 1
Router1(config-rtr)#default-information originate always
Router1(config-rtr)#exit
Router1(config)#end
Router1#
```

Discussion

Both of these examples show a minimal configuration for redistributing from one routing protocol into another. In a moment we will show some more sophisticated examples, but these examples show the basic requirements. In the first example, we redistribute OSPF routes into RIP:

```
Router1(config)#ipv6 router rip RIP_PROC
Router1(config-rtr)#redistribute ospf 1 metric 5
```

Note that, in this example, we have somewhat arbitrarily set a default metric for RIP to use for all of these redistributed routes. This is because, by default, RIP will attempt to use the existing route metric from OSPF. If we look at the OSPF routing table on this router, you can see that many of the routes that we want to use in the RIP side of the network have metrics that are greater than 15:

```
Router1#show ipv6 route ospf
IPv6 Routing Table - 16 entries
Codes: C - Connected, L - Local, S - Static, R - RIP, B - BGP
       U - Per-user Static route
       I1 - ISIS L1, I2 - ISIS L2, IA - ISIS interarea, IS - ISIS summary
       O - OSPF intra, OI - OSPF inter, OE1 - OSPF ext 1, OE2 - OSPF ext 2
       ON1 - OSPF NSSA ext 1, ON2 - OSPF NSSA ext 2
O   AAAA:F::AA:1/128 [110/1]
     via FE80::20E:D7FF:FED6:1060, FastEthernet0/0
OI  AAAA:99::9:0/112 [110/2]
     via FE80::20E:D7FF:FED6:1060, FastEthernet0/0
OI  AAAA:99::A:0/112 [110/151]
     via FE80::20E:D7FF:FED6:1060, FastEthernet0/0
OI  AAAA:99::B:0/112 [110/163]
     via FE80::20E:D7FF:FED6:1060, FastEthernet0/0
```

```
OI  AAAA:99::C:0/112 [110/20]
      via FE80::20E:D7FF:FED6:1060, FastEthernet0/0
OI  AAAA:99::D:0/112 [110/893]
      via FE80::20E:D7FF:FED6:1060, FastEthernet0/0
OI  AAAA:99::E:0/112 [110/2]
      via FE80::20E:D7FF:FED6:1060, FastEthernet0/0
Router1#
```

If we don't include the *metric* keyword when redistributing, then none of these routes appear on a downstream RIP router because their metrics are all too large:

```
Router9#show ipv6 route rip
IPv6 Routing Table - 10 entries
Codes: C - Connected, L - Local, S - Static, R - RIP, B - BGP
       U - Per-user Static route
       I1 - ISIS L1, I2 - ISIS L2, IA - ISIS interarea, IS - ISIS summary
       O - OSPF intra, OI - OSPF inter, OE1 - OSPF ext 1, OE2 - OSPF ext 2
       ON1 - OSPF NSSA ext 1, ON2 - OSPF NSSA ext 2
R   AAAA:F::AA:1/128 [120/2]
      via FE80::20E:D7FF:FED6:4D80, Ethernet0
R   AAAA:99::9:0/112 [120/3]
      via FE80::20E:D7FF:FED6:4D80, Ethernet0
R   AAAA:99::E:0/112 [120/3]
      via FE80::20E:D7FF:FED6:4D80, Ethernet0
Router9#
```

However, if we just set all of these external routes to have the same default metric of 5, then we see all of the OSPF routes:

```
Router9#show ipv6 route rip
IPv6 Routing Table - 14 entries
Codes: C - Connected, L - Local, S - Static, R - RIP, B - BGP
       U - Per-user Static route
       I1 - ISIS L1, I2 - ISIS L2, IA - ISIS interarea, IS - ISIS summary
       O - OSPF intra, OI - OSPF inter, OE1 - OSPF ext 1, OE2 - OSPF ext 2
       ON1 - OSPF NSSA ext 1, ON2 - OSPF NSSA ext 2
R   AAAA:F::AA:1/128 [120/2]
      via FE80::20E:D7FF:FED6:4D80, Ethernet0
R   AAAA:99::9:0/112 [120/6]
      via FE80::20E:D7FF:FED6:4D80, Ethernet0
R   AAAA:99::A:0/112 [120/6]
      via FE80::20E:D7FF:FED6:4D80, Ethernet0
R   AAAA:99::B:0/112 [120/6]
      via FE80::20E:D7FF:FED6:4D80, Ethernet0
R   AAAA:99::C:0/112 [120/6]
      via FE80::20E:D7FF:FED6:4D80, Ethernet0
R   AAAA:99::D:0/112 [120/6]
      via FE80::20E:D7FF:FED6:4D80, Ethernet0
R   AAAA:99::E:0/112 [120/6]
      via FE80::20E:D7FF:FED6:4D80, Ethernet0
Router9#
```

In the second example, we do a simple redistribution of RIP into OSPF:

```
Router1(config)#ipv6 router ospf 1
Router1(config-rtr)#redistribute rip RIP_PROC
```

Here we can use the default configuration and get useful results. On a downstream OSPF router, you can see that we now have external OSPF routes:

```
Router2#show ipv6 route ospf
IPv6 Routing Table - 22 entries
Codes: C - Connected, L - Local, S - Static, R - RIP, B - BGP
       U - Per-user Static route
       I1 - ISIS L1, I2 - ISIS L2, IA - ISIS interarea, IS - ISIS summary
       O - OSPF intra, OI - OSPF inter, OE1 - OSPF ext 1, OE2 - OSPF ext 2
       ON1 - OSPF NSSA ext 1, ON2 - OSPF NSSA ext 2
OE2  AAAA:FE::/64 [110/20]
     via FE80::20E:D7FF:FED6:4D80, FastEthernet0/0
O    AAAA:2222::2/128 [110/1]
     via FE80::20E:D7FF:FED6:4D80, FastEthernet0/0
Router2#
```

As we previously saw in Chapter 8 when talking about IPv4 OSPF, the default for redistributed routes in OSPF is type 2 external. This type of route is always considered worse than any internal route, and worse than any external route of type 1. The metric for an OSPF type 2 external route is the same everywhere in the network. We could choose to redistribute all RIP routes into OSPF by simply specifying the *metric-type* keyword on the *redistribute* command:

```
Router1(config)#ipv6 router ospf 1
Router1(config-rtr)#redistribute rip RIP_PROC metric-type 1
```

Now the downstream OSPF router shows this route as follows:

```
Router2#show ipv6 route ospf
IPv6 Routing Table - 22 entries
Codes: C - Connected, L - Local, S - Static, R - RIP, B - BGP
       U - Per-user Static route
       I1 - ISIS L1, I2 - ISIS L2, IA - ISIS interarea, IS - ISIS summary
       O - OSPF intra, OI - OSPF inter, OE1 - OSPF ext 1, OE2 - OSPF ext 2
       ON1 - OSPF NSSA ext 1, ON2 - OSPF NSSA ext 2
OE1  AAAA:FE::/64 [110/21]
     via FE80::20E:D7FF:FED6:4D80, FastEthernet0/0
O    AAAA:2222::2/128 [110/1]
     via FE80::20E:D7FF:FED6:4D80, FastEthernet0/0
Router2#
```

When using route redistribution, we generally like to use route tags for the external routes. This is simply an arbitrary number associated with the routing prefix that gets carried with the route throughout the autonomous system. Route tags have several applications, but the most common one is to simply designate the autonomous system boundary router where this external route originated. If you have another router connected to the same external network, then you can use this route tag information to ensure that you don't redistribute the same route back into the original network.

You can specify a tag on the *redistribute* command when redistributing into OSPF:

```
Router1(config)#ipv6 router ospf 1
Router1(config-rtr)#redistribute rip RIP_PROC metric-type 1 tag 123
```

This will affect all routes coming from this RIP process. The tag is visible in the downstream routing table:

```
Router2#show ipv6 route ospf
IPv6 Routing Table - 22 entries
Codes: C - Connected, L - Local, S - Static, R - RIP, B - BGP
       U - Per-user Static route
       I1 - ISIS L1, I2 - ISIS L2, IA - ISIS interarea, IS - ISIS summary
       O - OSPF intra, OI - OSPF inter, OE1 - OSPF ext 1, OE2 - OSPF ext 2
       ON1 - OSPF NSSA ext 1, ON2 - OSPF NSSA ext 2
OE1  AAAA:FE::/64 [110/21], tag 123
       via FE80::20E:D7FF:FED6:4D80, FastEthernet0/0
O    AAAA:2222::2/128 [110/1]
       via FE80::20E:D7FF:FED6:4D80, FastEthernet0/0
Router2#
```

Specifying a route tag in RIPv6 is a little bit more complicated because it requires a *route-map*:

```
Router1(config)#route-map OSPF-2-RIP permit 10
Router1(config-route-map)#set tag 555
Router1(config-route-map)#exit
Router1(config)#ipv6 router rip RIP_PROC
Router1(config-rtr)#redistribute ospf 1 metric 5 route-map OSPF-2-RIP
```

Now the redistributed OSPF routes all appear in the routing table of a downstream RIP device with this tag:

```
Router9#show ipv6 route rip
IPv6 Routing Table - 14 entries
Codes: C - Connected, L - Local, S - Static, R - RIP, B - BGP
       U - Per-user Static route
       I1 - ISIS L1, I2 - ISIS L2, IA - ISIS interarea, IS - ISIS summary
       O - OSPF intra, OI - OSPF inter, OE1 - OSPF ext 1, OE2 - OSPF ext 2
       ON1 - OSPF NSSA ext 1, ON2 - OSPF NSSA ext 2
R    AAAA:F::AA:1/128 [120/6], tag 555
       via FE80::20E:D7FF:FED6:4D80, Ethernet0
R    AAAA:99::9:0/112 [120/6], tag 555
       via FE80::20E:D7FF:FED6:4D80, Ethernet0
R    AAAA:99::A:0/112 [120/6], tag 555
       via FE80::20E:D7FF:FED6:4D80, Ethernet0
R    AAAA:99::B:0/112 [120/6], tag 555
       via FE80::20E:D7FF:FED6:4D80, Ethernet0
R    AAAA:99::C:0/112 [120/6], tag 555
       via FE80::20E:D7FF:FED6:4D80, Ethernet0
R    AAAA:99::D:0/112 [120/6], tag 555
       via FE80::20E:D7FF:FED6:4D80, Ethernet0
R    AAAA:99::E:0/112 [120/6], tag 555
       via FE80::20E:D7FF:FED6:4D80, Ethernet0
Router9#
```

With route-maps you can also construct more complicated examples. Using the *match* command in the route-map, you could, for example, set different tag values for different route prefixes:

```
Router1(config)#ipv6 prefix-list special-prefixes permit AAAA:99::A:0/112
Router1(config)#ipv6 prefix-list special-prefixes permit AAAA:99::B:0/112
Router1(config)#ipv6 prefix-list ANY-IPv6 permit ::/0 le 128
Router1(config)#route-map OSPF-2-RIP permit 5
Router1(config-route-map)#match ipv6 address prefix-list special-prefixes
Router1(config-route-map)#set tag 321
Router1(config-route-map)#exit
Router1(config)#route-map OSPF-2-RIP permit 10
Router1(config-route-map)#match ipv6 address prefix-list ANY-IPv6
Router1(config-route-map)#set tag 555
Router1(config-route-map)#exit
Router1(config)#ipv6 router rip RIP_PROC
Router1(config-rtr)#redistribute ospf 1 metric 5 route-map OSPF-2-RIP
```

Now our downstream RIP router has two different tag values:

```
Router9#show ipv6 route rip
IPv6 Routing Table - 14 entries
Codes: C - Connected, L - Local, S - Static, R - RIP, B - BGP
       U - Per-user Static route
       I1 - ISIS L1, I2 - ISIS L2, IA - ISIS interarea, IS - ISIS summary
       O - OSPF intra, OI - OSPF inter, OE1 - OSPF ext 1, OE2 - OSPF ext 2
       ON1 - OSPF NSSA ext 1, ON2 - OSPF NSSA ext 2
R   AAAA:F::AA:1/128 [120/6], tag 555
     via FE80::20E:D7FF:FED6:4D80, Ethernet0
R   AAAA:99::9:0/112 [120/6], tag 555
     via FE80::20E:D7FF:FED6:4D80, Ethernet0
R   AAAA:99::A:0/112 [120/6], tag 321
     via FE80::20E:D7FF:FED6:4D80, Ethernet0
R   AAAA:99::B:0/112 [120/6], tag 321
     via FE80::20E:D7FF:FED6:4D80, Ethernet0
R   AAAA:99::C:0/112 [120/6], tag 555
     via FE80::20E:D7FF:FED6:4D80, Ethernet0
R   AAAA:99::D:0/112 [120/6], tag 555
     via FE80::20E:D7FF:FED6:4D80, Ethernet0
R   AAAA:99::E:0/112 [120/6], tag 555
     via FE80::20E:D7FF:FED6:4D80, Ethernet0
Router9#
```

The final example in the Solution section of this recipe shows how to advertise a default route with OSPF. Recall that in IPv4, a default route is written as 0.0.0.0/0—that is, an address of all zeroes with a prefix-length of zero. In IPv6 the default route follows the same formula, it is an address of all zeroes and a prefix-length of zero. Since the IPv6 addressing rules allow us to replace the longest string of zeroes with two colons, "::", it follows that an IPv6 address consisting of only zeroes can be written as ::/0.

We can inject a default route into OSPF by using the default-originate command, just as we previously saw in OSPFv2 for IPv4:

```
Router1(config)#ipv6 router ospf 1
Router1(config-rtr)#default-information originate always
```

Then, on a downstream router, we see that this default route is, by default, an external route of type 2:

```
Router2#show ipv6 route ospf
IPv6 Routing Table - 15 entries
Codes: C - Connected, L - Local, S - Static, R - RIP, B - BGP
       U - Per-user Static route
       I1 - ISIS L1, I2 - ISIS L2, IA - ISIS interarea, IS - ISIS summary
       O - OSPF intra, OI - OSPF inter, OE1 - OSPF ext 1, OE2 - OSPF ext 2
       ON1 - OSPF NSSA ext 1, ON2 - OSPF NSSA ext 2
OE2  ::/0 [110/1], tag 1
     via FE80::20E:D7FF:FED6:1060, Serial0/0
OI   AAAA:99::9:0/112 [110/65]
     via FE80::20E:D7FF:FED6:1060, Serial0/0
<routes delete for brevity>
R2011#
```

There are several useful options on the *default-information originate* command. If you want to advertise this route with some other metric, or as a type 1 external route, you simply add the *metric* and *metric-type* keywords to the command as follows:

```
Router1(config)#ipv6 router ospf 1
Router1(config-rtr)#default-information originate always metric 15 metric-type 1
```

And, by associating the default route with a route-map, you can force this router to only advertise itself as a valid default if it sees certain other routes in its routing table:

```
Router1(config)#ipv6 prefix-list OUTSIDE-WORLD seq 5 permit AAAA:99::0/112
Router1(config)#route-map DEFAULT-VALID permit 10
Router1(config-route-map)#match ipv6 address prefix-list OUTSIDE-WORLD
Router1(config-route-map)#exit
Router1(config)#ipv6 router ospf 1
Router1(config-rtr)#default-information originate route-map DEFAULT-VALID
Router1(config-rtr)#exit
```

Here we have defined a route-map that uses a prefix-list to match on a particular external network prefix. If this prefix is present in the routing table, then we know that this router's gateway to the outside world is working, and it is safe to advertise a default route.

See Also

Chapter 6; Chapter 8

25.10 Dynamic Routing with MBGP

Problem

You want to use MBGP to carry IPv6 routing information between autonomous systems.

Solution

MBGP readily carries IPv6 unicast routing information between IPv6 BGP peers:

```
Router1#configure terminal
Enter configuration commands, one per line.  End with CNTL/Z.
Router1(config)#router bgp 65520
Router1(config-router)#no bgp default ipv4-unicast
Router1(config-router)#neighbor AAAA:5::2 remote-as 65522
Router1(config-router)#neighbor AAAA:5::AA9 remote-as 65521
Router1(config-router)#address-family ipv6
Router1(config-router-af)#neighbor AAAA:5::2 activate
Router1(config-router-af)#neighbor AAAA:5::AA9 activate
Router1(config-router-af)#network AAAA:2222::2/64
Router1(config-router-af)#no synchronization
Router1(config-router-af)#exit-address-family
Router1(config-router)#exit
Router1(config)#end
Router1#
```

And you can even run a combination of IPv4 and IPv6 BGP on the same router:

```
Router9#configure terminal
Enter configuration commands, one per line.  End with CNTL/Z.
Router9(config)#router bgp 65521
Router9(config-router)#no bgp default ipv4-unicast
Router9(config-router)#neighbor AAAA:5::1 remote-as 65520
Router9(config-router)#neighbor 192.168.1.103 remote-as 65525
Router9(config-router)#address-family ipv4
Router9(config-router-af)#redistribute connected
Router9(config-router-af)#neighbor 192.168.1.103 activate
Router9(config-router-af)#no auto-summary
Router9(config-router-af)#no synchronization
Router9(config-router-af)#exit-address-family
Router9(config-router)#address-family ipv6
Router9(config-router-af)#neighbor AAAA:5::1 activate
Router9(config-router-af)#network AAAA:FE::1/64
Router9(config-router-af)#network AAAA:BBBB::1/64
Router9(config-router-af)#no synchronization
Router9(config-router-af)#exit-address-family
Router9(config-router)#exit
Router9(config)#end
Router9#
```

Discussion

The first example shows how to configure a router to run BGP between IPv6 peers:

```
Router1(config)#router bgp 65520
Router1(config-router)#no bgp default ipv4-unicast
Router1(config-router)#neighbor AAAA:5::2 remote-as 65522
```

The critical command here is the *no bgp default ipv4-unicast* line. By default, BGP will only distribute IPv4 prefixes to its neighbors. However, when you disable the *default ipv4-unicast* command, you can start to distribute IPv6 routing information as well.

We note in passing that you can configure IPv4 neighbors to pass IPv6 routing information, but this quickly becomes very complicated because the next-hop information is in the wrong protocol. For this reason, we strongly recommend using IPv6 neighbor addresses when passing IPv6 routing prefixes with MBGP.

The next step is to configure one or more *neighbor* statements and to activate them in the *address-family ipv6* configuration block. This way the router knows what sorts of Network Layer Reachability Information (NLRI) to pass to this neighbor. You also configure any network commands in the address-family configuration area:

```
Router1(config)#router bgp 65520
Router1(config-router)#neighbor AAAA:5::2 remote-as 65522
Router1(config-router)#address-family ipv6
Router1(config-router-af)#neighbor AAAA:5::2 activate
Router1(config-router-af)#network AAAA:2222::2/64
Router1(config-router-af)#no synchronization
```

Note that we have included the *no synchronization* command here for the same reasons that we included it in many of the BGP examples in Chapter 9. By default, BGP wants to ensure that all routing is consistent within the Autonomous System. So it wants to see that any prefixes that it distributes using iBGP are also present in the IGP for the AS. In this example, however, we are not redistributing routing information between BGP and the IGP. In fact, we're not even running an IGP. Please refer to Chapter 9 for a more detailed discussion of this command.

In the second example in the Solution section of this recipe, we have configured both IPv4 and IPv6 BGP neighbors:

```
Router9#configure terminal
Enter configuration commands, one per line.  End with CNTL/Z.
Router9(config)#router bgp 65521
Router9(config-router)#no bgp default ipv4-unicast
Router9(config-router)#neighbor AAAA:5::1 remote-as 65520
Router9(config-router)#neighbor 192.168.1.103 remote-as 65525
```

Then we have included *address-family* configuration both IPv4 and IPv6 unicast route prefixes:

```
Router9(config-router)#address-family ipv4
Router9(config-router-af)#redistribute connected
Router9(config-router-af)#neighbor 192.168.1.103 activate
Router9(config-router-af)#no auto-summary
Router9(config-router-af)#no synchronization
Router9(config-router-af)#exit-address-family
Router9(config-router)#address-family ipv6
Router9(config-router-af)#neighbor AAAA:5::1 activate
Router9(config-router-af)#network AAAA:FE::1/64
Router9(config-router-af)#network AAAA:BBBB::1/64
Router9(config-router-af)#no synchronization
Router9(config-router-af)#exit-address-family
```

This means that this router is running BGP for both IPv4 and IPv6 simultaneously. Note that when you do this, the ASN for both protocols is the same.

The commands to look at IPv6 BGP information are slightly different that we previously saw for IPv4 BGP. You can see the status of the neighbor routers with the *show bgp summary* command:

```
Router9#show bgp summary
BGP router identifier 172.16.1.1, local AS number 65521
BGP table version is 19, main routing table version 19
6 network entries using 798 bytes of memory
6 path entries using 432 bytes of memory
4 BGP path attribute entries using 240 bytes of memory
2 BGP AS-PATH entries using 48 bytes of memory
0 BGP route-map cache entries using 0 bytes of memory
0 BGP filter-list cache entries using 0 bytes of memory
BGP using 1518 total bytes of memory
BGP activity 58/50 prefixes, 112/104 paths, scan interval 60 secs

Neighbor        V    AS MsgRcvd MsgSent   TblVer  InQ OutQ Up/Down  State/PfxRcd

AAAA:5::1       4 65520    168     147       19    0    0 01:44:39        4
Router9#
```

You still use the *show ip bgp summary* command to see the pure IPv4 BGP peers:

```
Router9#show ip bgp summary
BGP router identifier 172.16.1.1, local AS number 65521
BGP table version is 12, main routing table version 12
5 network entries using 505 bytes of memory
6 path entries using 288 bytes of memory
5 BGP path attribute entries using 300 bytes of memory
3 BGP AS-PATH entries using 72 bytes of memory
0 BGP route-map cache entries using 0 bytes of memory
0 BGP filter-list cache entries using 0 bytes of memory
BGP using 1165 total bytes of memory
BGP activity 61/50 prefixes, 116/104 paths, scan interval 60 secs

Neighbor        V    AS MsgRcvd MsgSent   TblVer  InQ OutQ Up/Down  State/PfxRcd

192.168.1.103   4 65525     83      83       12    0    0 00:01:43        4
Router9#
```

To look at the BGP table, which contains all BGP routing prefixes, you use the *show bgp* command:

```
Router9#show bgp
BGP table version is 19, local router ID is 172.16.1.1
Status codes: s suppressed, d damped, h history, * valid, > best, i - internal,
              r RIB-failure, S Stale
Origin codes: i - IGP, e - EGP, ? - incomplete

   Network          Next Hop            Metric LocPrf Weight Path
*> AAAA:99::A:0/112 AAAA:5::2                            0 65520 65522 65523 i
```

```
 *> AAAA:99::B:0/112 AAAA:5::2                        0 65520 65522 65523 i

 *> AAAA:99::C:0/112 AAAA:5::2                        0 65520 65522 65523 i

 *> AAAA:FE::1/64    ::              0      32768 i
 *> AAAA:2222::/64   AAAA:5::1       0          0 65520 i
 *> AAAA:BBBB::/64   ::              0      32768 i
 Router9#
```

And you can verify that these IPv6 prefixes have been imported into the routing table
with the command *show ipv6 route bgp*:

```
Router9#show ipv6 route bgp
IPv6 Routing Table - 20 entries
Codes: C - Connected, L - Local, S - Static, R - RIP, B - BGP
       U - Per-user Static route
       I1 - ISIS L1, I2 - ISIS L2, IA - ISIS interarea, IS - ISIS summary
       O - OSPF intra, OI - OSPF inter, OE1 - OSPF ext 1, OE2 - OSPF ext 2
       ON1 - OSPF NSSA ext 1, ON2 - OSPF NSSA ext 2
B   AAAA:99::A:0/112 [20/0]
     via AAAA:5::2
B   AAAA:99::B:0/112 [20/0]
     via AAAA:5::2
B   AAAA:99::C:0/112 [20/0]
     via AAAA:5::2
B   AAAA:2222::/64 [20/0]
     via FE80::20E:D7FF:FED6:4D80, Ethernet0
Router9#
```

See Also

Chapter 9

25.11 Tunneling IPv6 Through an Existing IPv4 Network

Problem

You want to connect two IPv6 networks through an existing IPv4 network that
doesn't natively support IPv6.

Solution

The easiest way to pass IPv6 traffic through a section of IPv4 network that doesn't
offer native IPv6 support is to create a simple GRE tunnel:

```
Router1#configure terminal
Enter configuration commands, one per line.  End with CNTL/Z.
Router1(config)#interface Loopback1
Router1(config-if)#ip address 10.15.1.11 255.255.255.255
```

```
Router1(config-if)#exit
Router1(config)#interface Tunnel1
Router1(config-if)#ipv6 address BBBB:1::1/126
Router1(config-if)#ipv6 rip RIP_PROC enable
Router1(config-if)#tunnel source 10.15.1.11
Router1(config-if)#tunnel destination 172.16.11.9
Router1(config-if)#exit
Router1(config)#end
Router1#
```

And then you configure the device on the other end similarly:

```
Router9#configure terminal
Enter configuration commands, one per line.  End with CNTL/Z.
Router9(config)#interface Loopback1
Router9(config-if)#ip address 172.16.11.9 255.255.255.255
Router9(config-if)#exit
Router9(config)#interface Tunnel1
Router9(config-if)#ipv6 address BBBB:1::2/126
Router9(config-if)#ipv6 rip RIP_PROC enable
Router9(config-if)#tunnel source 172.16.11.9
Router9(config-if)#tunnel destination 10.15.1.11
Router9(config-if)#exit
Router9(config)#end
Router9#
```

Discussion

This example is actually simpler than a lot of GRE tunnel configuration examples because the protocol used to support the tunnel end points is different from the protocol that will be passing through the tunnel. As a result, we can freely use whatever routing protocol we like to distribute the routing information about the tunnel source and destination addresses without worrying about recursive routing problems. For more information on recursive routing, please refer to Chapter 12.

Also, as we mention in Chapter 12, we have deliberately created loopback interfaces to support these tunnel source and destination addresses. This is because we want to make sure that these interfaces never become unavailable due to a link failure. If there is any network path to the tunnel destination, we want to keep the tunnel up.

In the example, we have configured the tunnel interfaces to pass IPv6 routing information using RIP. However, this was just for demonstration purposes. You could use whatever protocol is most convenient for this purpose.

Note that starting in IOS Version 12.3(7)T, Cisco modified the *tunnel destination* command to allow it to accept an IPv6 address. This makes it possible to construct GRE tunnels to carry IPv4 traffic through an existing IPv6 network in exactly the same way that we have tunneled IPv6 traffic through an existing IPv4 network in this recipe.

See Also

Chapter 12

25.12 Translating Between IPv6 and IPv4

Problem

You want to configure a router to act as a gateway between IPv4 and IPv6 networks.

Solution

Cisco includes a protocol translation feature that allows you to interconnect IPv6 and IPv4 networks:

```
Router1#configure terminal
Enter configuration commands, one per line.  End with CNTL/Z.
Router1(config)#ipv6 access-list ALLOWED-NAT-DEVS
Router1(config-ipv6-acl)# permit ipv6 any any
Router1(config-ipv6-acl)#exit
Router1(config)#ipv6 nat prefix ::FFFF:0.0.0.0/96 v4-mapped ALLOWED-NAT-DEVS
Router1(config)#ipv6 nat v6v4 source AAAA:5::AA9 192.168.56.100
Router1(config)#interface FastEthernet0/0
Router1(config-if)#no ip address
Router1(config-if)#ipv6 address AAAA:5::2012/64
Router1(config-if)#ipv6 nat
Router1(config-if)#exit
Router1(config)#interface Serial0/0
Router1(config-if)#ip address 192.168.55.12 255.255.255.0
Router1(config-if)#ipv6 nat
Router1(config-if)#exit
Router1(config)#end
Router1#
```

Discussion

Starting in IOS Version 12.2(13)T, Cisco introduced the ability to use a router as a protocol gateway, translating between IPv6 and IPv4 worlds by means of Network Address Translation with Protocol Translation (NAT-PT). For more information on NAT in general, please refer to Chapter 21.

RFCs 4038 and 4291 include discussions of how to address IPv4 packets that originate in an IPv6 network. The current standard method is called the "IPv4-Mapped IPv6 Address," which works very simply. If an IPv6 device wants to send a packet to an IPv4 device whose address is A.B.C.D, then it uses the IPv6 destination address, ::FFFF:A.B.C.D. We have used this standard in this recipe:

```
Router1(config)#ipv6 access-list ALLOWED-NAT-DEVS
Router1(config-ipv6-acl)#permit ipv6 any any
Router1(config-ipv6-acl)#exit
Router1(config)#ipv6 nat prefix ::FFFF:0.0.0.0/96 v4-mapped ALLOWED-NAT-DEVS
```

The *ipv6 nat prefix* command here defines the IPv6 prefix that will be used when translating IPv4 addresses. By including the keyword *v4-mapped*, we tell the router to simply copy the 4 octets of the IPv4 address into the last 32 bits of the translated

IPv6 address. The *v4-mapped* keyword was introduced in IOS Version 12.3(14)T to ease compliance with RFC 4038.

We have also specified an IPv6 access-list with this command that specifies that all IPv6 devices are allowed to use this rule. If you would prefer to use a more restrictive ACL here, you can easily do so. For example, we might have wanted to specify a single host:

```
Router1(config)#ipv6 access-list ALLOWED-NAT-DEVS
Router1(config-ipv6-acl)#permit ipv6 host AAAA:5::AA9 any
```

Or we might have wanted to specify a range of allowed devices:

```
Router1(config)#ipv6 access-list ALLOWED-NAT-DEVS
Router1(config-ipv6-acl)#permit ipv6 AAAA:5::/64 any
```

For more information on IPv6 access-lists and access-lists in general, please refer to Chapter 19.

The next NAT-PT command configures a static translation between an IPv6 device and the IPv4 address that refers to this device in the IPv4 network. Unfortunately, there is no way to uniquely encode a 128-bit IPv6 address in a 32-bit IPv4 address, so if we want full two-way connectivity between these networks, we must use a static rule. This is defined using the *ipv6 nat v6v4 source* command:

```
Router1(config)#ipv6 nat v6v4 source AAAA:5::AA9 192.168.56.100
```

In this case, we have decided to associate the IPv6 global unicast address, AAAA:5::AA9, with the IPv4 address, 192.168.56.100. Now all incoming IPv4 packets addressed to 192.168.56.100 will be translated into IPv6 packets and forwarded to AAAA:5::AA9. Similarly, all outgoing IPv6 packets with this IPv6 source address will be translated into IPv4 packets with the specified IPv4 source address.

The final step is to associate this NAT-PT rule with router interfaces:

```
Router1(config)#interface FastEthernet0/0
Router1(config-if)#no ip address
Router1(config-if)#ipv6 address AAAA:5::2012/64
Router1(config-if)#ipv6 nat
Router1(config-if)#exit
Router1(config)#interface Serial0/0
Router1(config-if)#ip address 192.168.55.12 255.255.255.0
Router1(config-if)#ipv6 nat
Router1(config-if)#exit
```

In this example, FastEthernet0/0 connects to the IPv6 network, while Serial0/0 connects to the IPv4 network. Both of these interfaces are associated with the NAT-PT rule using the *ipv6 nat* command. Note that there is no "inside" or "outside" NAT interface here as we saw when we looked at NAT for IPv4 in Chapter 21.

You can then look at the NAT-PT translation table with the command *show ipv6 nat translations*:

```
Router1#show ipv6 nat translations
Prot  IPv4 source           IPv6 source
```

```
          IPv4 destination        IPv6 destination
     ---  ---                     ---
          192.168.55.3            ::FFFF:192.168.55.3

     tcp  192.168.56.100,80       AAAA:5::AA9,80
          192.168.55.3,15609      ::FFFF:192.168.55.3,15609

     tcp  192.168.56.100,60215    AAAA:5::AA9,60215
          192.168.55.3,23         ::FFFF:192.168.55.3,23

     ---  192.168.56.100          AAAA:5::AA9
          192.168.55.3            ::FFFF:192.168.55.3

     ---  192.168.56.100          AAAA:5::AA9
          ---                     ---

     Router1#
```

This output shows several mappings between the same addresses. Focusing on the two TCP connections, we see that the external device, 192.168.55.3, made a connection to TCP port 80 (HTTP) on destination device 192.168.56.100, and with an TCP arbitrary source port of 15609. This was translated to an IPv6 destination address of AAAA:5::AA9 on TCP port 80, and a source address of ::FFFF:192.168.55.3, with a TCP source port of 15609 once again.

The second TCP connection started on the IPv6 side. The IPv6 device AAAA:5::AA9 made a TCP connection on port 23 (Telnet) to the IPv6 destination address, ::FFFF:192.168.55.3, using the arbitrary TCP source port of 60215. NAT-PT rewrote this IPv6 packet as an IPv4 packet with a source address of 192.168.56.100 and source port of 60215 with a destination address of 192.168.55.3 on port 23.

In this example, we wanted full two-way connectivity, so we were forced to use a static mapping for the IPv6 side of the network. However, if we know that all connections will originate from the IPv6 network, then we can use Port Address Translation (PAT), and map all internal IPv6 addresses to a single external IPv4 address, such as the IP address on the IPv4 side of the router:

```
Router1(config)#ipv6 nat v6v4 source list ALLOWED-NAT-DEVS interface Serial0/0
overload
```

The *overload* keyword in this command works exactly the same way as in NAT for IPv4, assigning multiple internal addresses to a single external address.

See Also

Chapter 19; Chapter 21; RFC 4038; RFC 4291

## CHAPTER 26

MPLS

26.0 Introduction

Multiprotocol Label Switching (MPLS) is an advanced topic. Before tackling this technology, you should have a good understanding of IP routing, with particular attention to BGP (Chapters 5 and 9, respectively). However, with that caution, MPLS is not as complicated as many of the books on the subject make it appear. There are several basic concepts and protocols that work together to create an MPLS network, and these correspond to the various essential steps required to set up such a network.

And before going into the concepts and protocols of MPLS, it is worth noting that most users of MPLS networks don't ever need to actually configure MPLS. The usual model is that MPLS exists within the core of a network provider's network. The provider delivers some sort of network connection, such as a switched Ethernet port to the customer's premise, and the customer just routes IP traffic into this port. The customer doesn't actually need to know anything about MPLS.

If you are the customer of an MPLS network, there are still some issues worth noting, particularly regarding how to exchange routing protocol information with the MPLS network (Recipes 26.3, 26.5, 26.6, 26.7, and 26.8), and you may be interested in how to use QoS (Recipe 26.9) or how multicast works with MPLS (Recipe 26.11). But in most of these cases, you will need to work with your MPLS network provider to implement the features you want, as everything depends on how they have built their network.

However, there is one important recipe in this chapter that's just for the MPLS customer. Recipe 26.12 talks about how to connect to an MPLS network that doesn't deliver all of the protocols or services you need.

The first basic concept is label switching (sometimes called tag switching) itself. This is essentially just a way of improving routing efficiency through a routed network. In normal IP routing, as a packet bounces along the path from the source to the destination, it passes through a series of routers. Each router receives the packet, opens up the IP header, looks up the destination information in its routing table, and then sends the packet along to the next hop on its path. We have already discussed some of the tricks that routers use to improve the efficiency of this process. For example, the router might generate a fast switching cache so that once it has looked up a destination address in its routing table for one packet, it doesn't need to repeat this process for the next packet in the same data stream.

Label switching takes this concept one step further by marking the packet header with a special number that tells each router how to route the packet. With this information, the router doesn't need to look at the IP packet header at all. It just checks the label and forwards the packet. This may not sound like a significant improvement—after all, how hard is it really to look up an IP address in a routing table? Well, it turns out that in modern high-speed networks where you need to forward billions of packets per second, MPLS offers a significant performance improvement, which is one of the reasons why it has become so popular with network service providers.

MPLS requires the Cisco Express Forwarding (CEF) feature. The routers use CEF to build the MPLS label tables.

The second basic concept of MPLS is the VPN or Virtual Routing and Forwarding (VRF) table. This is particularly important in carrier environments. A network service provider or WAN carrier needs to deliver packets for different customers reliably and flexibly. In the old days, WAN carriers would build large multiplexed networks to provide dedicated leased line bandwidth between customer sites. If they could instead build a simple cost-effective IP network backbone and send all of their customer traffic through this single network, this would clearly save a lot of money and it would be easier to manage.

But there are serious complications to simply attaching all of your customers to the same routed IP network. Suppose two of your customers use the same unregistered IP address ranges? Suppose a customer uses the same IP address range as the network core? You could get around these problems by using NAT at the edges of the network, but then you must rewrite the source and destination addresses of every packet for every customer twice: once when it enters your network and again when it leaves. And that also introduces the management nightmare of maintaining a huge and globally unique address translation table that encompasses the requirements of all of your clients.

MPLS solves this problem in a different way by creating VPNs by means of VRF tables. The VRF is the special routing table that maps a set of MPLS path labels to IP addresses, and associates a set of MPLS edge devices together into VPNs. These MPLS VPNs are similar to the VPNs that we discussed in Chapter 12, in that they allow you to segregate and protect traffic as it passes through a network. But most of the VPNs that we discussed in Chapter 12 were point-to-point. The MPLS VRF concept is more of a community of several end points belonging to the same customer network. It provides fully meshed connectivity between all of these end points.

We can share a routing table among these end points and still have complete separation of the customer networks. Customer A can't access Customer B's network, and can't even see his routing table. And, best of all, this all happens transparently without the need to manually configure everything in the carrier network.

This brings us to the third essential concept, which is Multiprotocol over Border Gateway Protocol (MBGP, sometimes also called MP-BGP). This is a set of extensions to BGP described in RFC 2283. This allows us to define a set of "address families," which correspond to the various customer routing tables included in the VRF tables. Then BGP simply carries the customer routing information between the various customer sites where it can be redistributed into the customer's routing protocol.

In Chapters 6, 7, 8, and 9, we saw that redistributing from one routing protocol to another generally means that the redistributed routes are considered "external." This is a problem, as internal routes are preferred to external routes. So if a customer network intended to use a fast MPLS link as its primary path and some slower leased line or dial backup technology as a backup path, a great deal of unpleasant manual manipulation of the routing protocols and administrative distances would be required. So, in Cisco's implementation, when you redistribute routes from MBGP into an IGP, the IGP considers the routes to be "internal." This sometimes confuses people at first, but it is definitely preferable to the alternative.

Some Terminology

Perhaps the most confusing thing facing experienced IP network engineers who look at MPLS for the first time is the new jargon. In this chapter, we will try to go a little bit easy on the jargon and acronyms, using functional descriptions such as "MPLS router" instead of LSR (for Label Switch Router), valuing greater clarity over compactness. Nonetheless, it is important to review some of the most common terms because many readers will want to refer to other references for information that is beyond the scope of this short chapter:

Label Switch Router (LSR)
    This is any router or switch that supports MPLS on one or more of its interfaces.

Label Switch Path (LSP)
    This is a path that data might take through the MPLS cloud as it passes from one LSR to another. There might be several LSPs between two LSRs, so it is often important to identify the ingress LSR as the starting point of the LSP and the egress LSR as its end point.

Label Distribution Protocol and Tag Distribution Protocol (LDP and TDP)
    These are two functionally similar but incompatible protocols. LDP is an open standard for MPLS, while TDP is a Cisco proprietary standard for Tag Switching. Most Cisco devices are able to automatically sense which protocol the neighboring LSR is using and adapt appropriately.

    Both of these protocols perform the critical function of distributing MPLS label or tag information between adjacent LSRs.

Each of the preceding terms apply to MPLS networking in general—that is, before any VPNs have been overlaid on the network. In a typical MPLS network, however, customer networks are attached at the edges of the network and interconnected by meshes of Virtual Route Forwarding (VRF) VPNs. In such a network the routers break down into four essential functional types. These are shown in Figure 26-1.

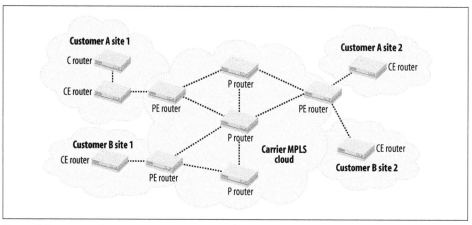

Figure 26-1. Types of routers in an MPLS network

C Router

A C, or Customer Internal Router, is a router that is purely internal to a customer's network. The C router connects to other C routers and to the CE router. It does not connect directly to any P or PE routers. This router does not run MPLS.

CE Router

A CE, or Customer Edge Router, is the connection point between the customer's network and the MPLS network. The CE router talks to PE routers and C routers, but not to the P routers. This router also does not run MPLS.

PE Router

The PE, or Provider Edge Router, is where much of actual work takes place. These routers run MPLS and are part of the carrier's MPLS network, but they also communicate with the customer's CE router and may take part in the customer's routing protocol. PE routers are the end points of the VPNs.

P Router

P, or Provider Internal Routers, are purely internal to the carrier's MPLS network. This router runs MPLS to communicate with the rest of the carrier's network and transport customer packets through VPNs. However, the P router does not see the customer routing tables or VRF information. These are the backbone of the MPLS network, and they talk to PE routers and other P routers.

Benefits of MPLS

We have already mentioned one of the key benefits of MPLS, its speed and efficiency in high-speed networks. Because an MPLS network is built on an IP network, it also has the excellent scaling and stability features of IP networks (assuming, of course, a well-designed underlying IP network).

MPLS relies heavily on IP. The MPLS packet header is essentially an IP packet header, but with an additional "tag" or "label" inserted. This tag information defines a path. The association between these MPLS tags and IP routes are predefined and dynamically updated by the network. The net result is that, when a router receives an MPLS packet, it just needs to look at this tag information to know everything it needs to know about how to forward the packet. This greatly improves network efficiency.

The tag information in the MPLS header also includes three bits called the Experimental Field, or EXP. It is customary to use these bits to carry Quality of Service (QoS) information. So, if the EXP field on each packet is set at the ingress point, the MPLS network can use this information to segregate streams of different priority packets without sacrificing any of the speed advantages that we have already discussed.

Another key benefit of MPLS is Traffic Engineering (TE). Traffic Engineering is a general networking term that simply means that the redundant paths through the network will be used in some more complex way than simply always using the shortest path to the destination.

For example, suppose you have a network that includes two paths between points A and B. By default, if the routing protocol determines that one of these paths has a lower aggregate metric, the network will forward all of the traffic for this destination along this path. Now suppose that this first path is being over-used and packets are being dropped due to congestion. The network engineer may decide to redirect some of this traffic along the second path, reasoning that a slightly greater latency is better than a dropped packet. Whatever the engineer does to achieve this result is generically called Traffic Engineering.

MPLS has a number of built-in features to dynamically facilitate traffic engineering. A detailed discussion of Traffic Engineering would fill several books, so in this chapter we will just show a simple example of a useful Cisco feature called Autoroute, which uses either OSPF or IS-IS to dynamically distribute resource information for Traffic Engineering.

While all of the examples in this chapter use Layer 3 VPNs, MPLS is also capable of running Layer 2 VPNs, which are effectively bridged connections between sites. And MPLS can also do useful things like circuit emulation, in which a legacy medium such as a T1 leased line can be carried through an MPLS network. Cisco implements a feature set called Anything over MPLS (AToM), which allows you to even deliver ATM and Frame Relay circuits to a customer site and transport the traffic through the same MPLS network core.

All of these benefits mean that MPLS is rapidly becoming the underlying architecture of choice for deploying carrier networks for voice and data traffic. In fact, because you can effectively run MPLS over an existing IP network, it is relatively straightforward to convert an existing IP WAN to an MPLS carrier network. It may take a little iterative re-engineering to get the full benefits of MPLS traffic engineering and QoS features in this case, but it inherently provides a mechanism for WAN service providers to phase out old multiplexed carrier networks in favor of more modern and flexible infrastructure.

IOS Versions and Feature Sets

MPLS is not included in all IOS images. The Version 12.4 feature set images are rather complicated, as the names and content depend on the hardware platform. The general rule of thumb is that you need one of the "Advanced," "Service Provider," or "Enterprise" feature sets if you want to use MPLS. For example, for the 2800 series routers, you can run MPLS if you have the "Advanced IP Services" version, any of the "SP Services" versions, or any of the "Enterprise Services" versions (including "Enterprise Services," "Advanced Enterprise Services," "Advanced Enterprise Services with SNA," or "Enterprise Services with Crypto" releases).

If you are unsure, please consult Cisco's Feature Navigator *http://tools.cisco.com/ITDIT/CFN/jsp/index.jsp*.

Structure of This Chapter

This chapter will work a little bit differently than other chapters in this book. Rather than having, for example, a first recipe that sets up all of the features of a basic MPLS network, we will spend the first several recipes showing how to configure each of the essential types of routers in the same simple network. Then we will examine some interesting and useful variations.

We need to do it this way for two reasons. First, there are so many routers involved in even a simple MPLS network that it's more logical to take them individually and explain the configurations one at a time. Second, some of the individual router configurations, particularly for the PE routers, are rather long, and need to be discussed in some depth.

Consequently, we will use the same basic network, shown in Figure 26-2, for all of the recipes in this chapter. The router names and connections used throughout this chapter will be consistent with this picture, although we won't necessarily talk about every router in every recipe, and we will only show those portions of each router configuration that are relevant to the concept being discussed.

In this figure, the C and CE routers can be any type of router running essentially any version of IOS, except when we will note that we are using some special feature. None of the C or CE routers run MPLS. The P and PE routers all run MPLS. The only special device in this picture is the P router called Switch-P2, which is actually

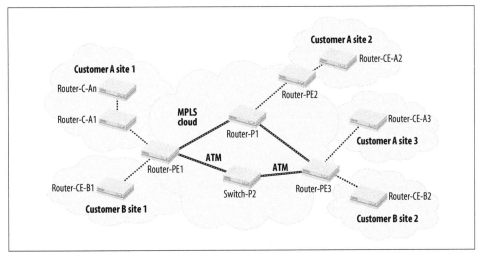

Figure 26-2. Example MPLS network

an ATM switch. In our example, this will be a Cisco Lightstream 1010 that uses OC3 interfaces to connect to Router-PE1 and Router-PE2. The configuration of this device will be discussed in Recipe 26.4. Although we use a Lightstream 1010 for this purpose, any Cisco ATM switch could be readily substituted. We also have the P router called Router-P1, which is a conventional IP router. You don't need ATM for MPLS, although the two protocols do work very well together.

The point of our example is to discuss the issues and features involved in running MPLS over ATM links, which is a relatively common implementation. Because there are so many different varieties of ATM switches, all of which are configured differently, we will not cover configuration of the ATM switch in any detail, and offer the Lightstream 1010 configuration only as a general guide.

26.1   Configuring a Basic MPLS P Router

Problem

You want to set up the core of an MPLS network.

Solution

For the P routers in the core of the MPLS network, the primary requirement is to enable CEF and turn on MPLS on each of the interfaces that will be forwarding MPLS tagged packets. In this example, we have also enabled OSPF as a dynamic routing protocol within the MPLS core:

```
Router-P1#configure terminal
Enter configuration commands, one per line.  End with CNTL/Z.
Router-P1(config)#ip cef
```

```
Router-P1(config)#mpls ip
Router-P1(config)#interface FastEthernet0/0
Router-P1(config-if)#description connection to Router-PE2
Router-P1(config-if)#ip address 10.1.2.11 255.255.255.0
Router-P1(config-if)#mpls ip
Router-P1(config-if)#exit
Router-P1(config)#interface Serial0/0
Router-P1(config-if)#description connection to Router-PE1
Router-P1(config-if)#ip address 10.1.1.14 255.255.255.252
Router-P1(config-if)#mpls ip
Router-P1(config-if)#exit
Router-P1(config)#interface Serial0/1
Router-P1(config-if)#description connection to Router-PE3
Router-P1(config-if)#ip address 10.1.1.10 255.255.255.252
Router-P1(config-if)#mpls ip
Router-P1(config-if)#exit
Router-P1(config)#interface Loopback0
Router-P1(config-if)#ip address 10.0.0.11 255.255.255.255
Router-P1(config-if)#exit
Router-P1(config)#router ospf 99
Router-P1(config-router)#router-id 10.0.0.11
Router-P1(config-router)#network 10.0.0.0 0.255.255.255 area 0
Router-P1(config-router)#exit
Router-P1(config)#end
Router-P1#
```

Discussion

There are several things to note in this example. Firstly, enabling MPLS is simply a matter of enabling CEF globally on the router with the *ip cef* command, and then enabling MPLS on each interface with the *mpls ip* command:

```
Router-P1(config)#ip cef
Router-P1(config)#mpls ip
Router-P1(config)#interface FastEthernet0/0
Router-P1(config-if)#mpls ip
```

In some older references, the interface command for enabling MPLS on an interface is tag-switching ip instead of mpls ip. Both commands are accepted on most 12.x IOS levels. All IOS levels up to and including Version 12.3 automatically rewrite the new command into the old form. More confusingly, some IOS devices, such as the Lightstream 1010, interpret the mpls ip command as the global command and tag-switching ip as the interface command. So, on these devices, you may think that you have enabled MPLS on the interface when you have in fact just re-enabled it globally. So you should recheck your configuration after you have typed it to ensure that it is still what you intended.

We also note in passing that the global command, mpls ip, is often not required, as the router will forward MPLS packets by default when the interface level command is enabled. However, we have included this command here just in case the global forwarding behavior has been disabled. You can disable MPLS packet forwarding for the entire router by simply entering the "no" form of the global command:

```
Router-P1(config)#no mpls ip
```

The next thing to notice is that we have enabled MPLS on a FastEthernet interface and two Serial interfaces. You can run MPLS on a very wide variety of interface types. Later in this chapter, to save on physical connections, we will configure MPLS on Ethernet subinterfaces to allow us to use VLANs. MPLS also works well over ATM, as we will discuss in a subsequent recipe.

When you enable MPLS on an interface, the router automatically starts looking for LDP or TDP packets. Most Cisco devices support both and will auto-sense which one their neighbor is using, and most will run the Cisco proprietary TDP by default, but switch to the open standard LDP if they detect LDP packets coming from the neighbor. So you generally don't need to worry about which one you want to run, the router will automatically select the appropriate protocol.

In the example, we are using OSPF as an Interior Gateway Protocol (IGP) within the MPLS core. Remember that this MPLS core is itself just an IP network, so we need to distribute routing information. You could in principle use any routing protocol you choose for this purpose. However, some ATM switches, notably the Lightstream 1010, only support OSPF for use with MPLS, making it the most natural choice for the MPLS core IGP. For more information on OSPF, please refer to Chapter 8:

```
Router-P1(config)#interface Loopback0
Router-P1(config-if)#ip address 10.0.0.11 255.255.255.255
Router-P1(config-if)#exit
Router-P1(config)#router ospf 99
Router-P1(config-router)#router-id 10.0.0.11
Router-P1(config-router)#network 10.0.0.0 0.255.255.255 area 0
Router-P1(config-router)#exit
```

It is a good general practice to use a real IP address on the device for the OSPF router ID. This is because the OSPF Router-ID appears in the neighbor display, and it is often much easier to troubleshoot problems with your IGP if you can do simple PING and Telnet tests to this address:

```
Router-P1#show ip ospf neighbor
```

```
Neighbor ID    Pri   State      Dead Time   Address      Interface
10.0.0.3         0   FULL/  -    00:00:32    10.1.1.9     Serial0/1
10.0.0.2         0   FULL/  -    00:00:31    10.1.1.13    Serial0/0
10.0.0.4         1   FULL/DR     00:00:36    10.1.2.4     FastEthernet0/0
Router-P1#
```

There are three useful commands for verifying basic functionality of your MPLS P routers. The first simply shows you the status of all of your MPLS interfaces:

```
Router-P1#show mpls interfaces
Interface            IP           Tunnel   Operational
FastEthernet0/0      Yes (tdp)    No       Yes
```

```
Serial0/0              Yes (tdp)    No      Yes
Serial0/1              Yes (tdp)    No      Yes
Router-P1#
```

In this example, you can see that the three interfaces that we configured for MPLS are all listed and flagged as "Operational."

The next command allows you to see information about the LDP or TDP neighbor relationships with each of these neighbors:

```
Router-P1#show mpls ldp neighbor
    Peer TDP Ident: 10.0.0.2:0; Local TDP Ident 10.0.0.11:0
        TCP connection: 10.0.0.2.711 - 10.0.0.11.28185
        State: Oper; PIEs sent/rcvd: 0/82; Downstream
        Up time: 01:04:45
        TDP discovery sources:
          Serial0/0, Src IP addr: 10.1.1.13
        Addresses bound to peer TDP Ident:
          10.0.0.2        10.1.1.2        10.1.1.13
    Peer TDP Ident: 10.0.0.3:0; Local TDP Ident 10.0.0.11:0
        TCP connection: 10.0.0.3.711 - 10.0.0.11.57014
        State: Oper; PIEs sent/rcvd: 0/79; Downstream
        Up time: 01:04:33
        TDP discovery sources:
          Serial0/1, Src IP addr: 10.1.1.9
        Addresses bound to peer TDP Ident:
          10.0.0.3        10.1.1.9        10.1.1.6
    Peer TDP Ident: 10.0.0.4:0; Local TDP Ident 10.0.0.11:0
        TCP connection: 10.0.0.4.711 - 10.0.0.11.21206
        State: Oper; PIEs sent/rcvd: 0/77; Downstream
        Up time: 01:04:50
        TDP discovery sources:
          FastEthernet0/0, Src IP addr: 10.1.2.4
        Addresses bound to peer TDP Ident:
          10.0.0.4        10.1.2.4
Router-P1#
```

This command is particularly useful if the output of the show mpls interfaces command indicated that one or more interfaces were not operational. You can see in this output both the IP address of the neighboring device and a Peer TDP ID. This peer ID value comes from a Loopback interface, if one has been configured, and identifies the entire device. This is particularly useful in situations when you have multiple links between neighboring devices. You will also notice that this display includes the IP address of the nearest interface on the neighboring device, as well as a list of all other addresses used by this device.

This display can also be useful for what it doesn't include. If you are having trouble getting an MPLS interface to become operational, you should check the TDP neighbor command to see if the router has discovered any neighbors at all on this interface. If not, then you might have a connection problem, or perhaps the neighbor is not properly configured for MPLS.

The third extremely useful command on MPLS P routers looks at the MPLS forwarding table:

```
Router-P1#show mpls forwarding-table
Local  Outgoing    Prefix         Bytes tag  Outgoing   Next Hop
tag    tag or VC   or Tunnel Id   switched   interface
16     Pop tag     10.0.0.2/32    7697       Se0/0      point2point
17     Pop tag     10.1.1.0/30    0          Se0/0      point2point
18     Pop tag     10.0.0.3/32    6685       Se0/1      point2point
19     Pop tag     10.1.1.4/30    0          Se0/1      point2point
20     21          10.0.0.1/32    0          Se0/0      point2point
       21          10.0.0.1/32    0          Se0/1      point2point
21     Pop tag     10.0.0.4/32    19700      Fa0/0      10.1.2.4
Router-P1#
```

This output shows you all of the MPLS tags that are currently in use and which interfaces they point to. It is often useful to look at the "Outgoing interface" and "Next Hop" columns to ensure that a given route prefix is taking the path that you expect.

See Also

Chapter 8

26.2 Configuring a Basic MPLS PE Router

Problem

You want to configure a Provider Edge (PE) router to connect your MPLS core to a customer network.

Solution

To configure a PE router, you must set up connections to the MPLS core as well as to one or more customer networks. Further, to distribute customer VRF routing information to other PE routers, you must configure MP-BGP:

```
Router-PE1#configure terminal
Enter configuration commands, one per line.  End with CNTL/Z.
Router-PE1(config)#ip cef
Router-PE1(config)#mpls ip
Router-PE1(config)#interface Serial0/0
Router-PE1(config-if)#description Connection to Router-P1
Router-PE1(config-if)#ip address 10.1.1.13 255.255.255.252
Router-PE1(config-if)#mpls ip
Router-PE1(config-if)#exit
Router-PE1(config)#interface Loopback0
Router-PE1(config-if)#ip address 10.0.0.2 255.255.255.255
Router-PE1(config-if)#exit
Router-PE1(config)#router ospf 99
Router-PE1(config-router)#router-id 10.0.0.2
Router-PE1(config-router)#network 10.0.0.0 0.255.255.255 area 0
```

```
Router-PE1(config-router)#exit
Router-PE1(config)#ip vrf NetworkA
Router-PE1(config-vrf)#rd 100:1
Router-PE1(config-vrf)#route-target export 100:1
Router-PE1(config-vrf)#route-target import 100:1
Router-PE1(config-vrf)#exit
Router-PE1(config)#ip vrf NetworkB
Router-PE1(config-vrf)#rd 100:2
Router-PE1(config-vrf)#route-target export 100:2
Router-PE1(config-vrf)#route-target import 100:2
Router-PE1(config-vrf)#exit
Router-PE1(config)#interface Ethernet0/0
Router-PE1(config-if)#description connection to customer A, site 1
Router-PE1(config-if)#ip vrf forwarding NetworkA
Router-PE1(config-if)#ip address 192.168.1.1 255.255.255.0
Router-PE1(config-if)#exit
Router-PE1(config)#interface Ethernet0/1
Router-PE1(config-if)#description connection to customer B, site 1
Router-PE1(config-if)#ip vrf forwarding NetworkB
Router-PE1(config-if)#ip address 192.168.11.1 255.255.255.0
Router-PE1(config-if)#exit
Router-PE1(config)#router bgp 100
Router-PE1(config-router)#bgp log-neighbor-changes
Router-PE1(config-router)#neighbor 10.0.0.3 remote-as 100
Router-PE1(config-router)#neighbor 10.0.0.3 update-source Loopback0
Router-PE1(config-router)#neighbor 10.0.0.4 remote-as 100
Router-PE1(config-router)#neighbor 10.0.0.4 update-source Loopback0
Router-PE1(config-router)#address-family ipv4 vrf NetworkA
Router-PE1(config-router-af)#no auto-summary
Router-PE1(config-router-af)#no synchronization
Router-PE1(config-router-af)#redistribute connected
Router-PE1(config-router-af)#exit-address-family
Router-PE1(config-router)#adress-family ipv4 vrf NetworkB
Router-PE1(config-router-af)#no auto-summary
Router-PE1(config-router-af)#no synchronization
Router-PE1(config-router-af)#redistribute connected
Router-PE1(config-router-af)#exit-address-family
Router-PE1(config-router)#address-family vpnv4
Router-PE1(config-router-af)#neighbor 10.0.0.3 activate
Router-PE1(config-router-af)#neighbor 10.0.0.3 send-community extended
Router-PE1(config-router-af)#neighbor 10.0.0.4 activate
Router-PE1(config-router-af)#neighbor 10.0.0.4 send-community extended
Router-PE1(config-router-af)#exit-address-family
Router-PE1(config-router)#exit
Router-PE1(config)#end
Router-PE1#
```

We will also show the configuration for the other two PE routers for reference:

```
Router-PE2#configure terminal
Enter configuration commands, one per line.  End with CNTL/Z.
Router-PE2(config)#ip cef
Router-PE2(config)#mpls ip
```

```
Router-PE2(config)#interface FastEthernet0/0
Router-PE2(config-if)#no ip address
Router-PE2(config-if)#exit
Router-PE2(config)#interface FastEthernet0/0.1
Router-PE2(config-if)#description Connection to Router-P1
Router-PE2(config-if)#encapsulation dot1Q 10
Router-PE2(config-if)#ip address 10.1.2.4 255.255.255.0
Router-PE2(config-if)#mpls ip
Router-PE2(config-if)#exit
Router-PE2(config)#interface Loopback0
Router-PE2(config-if)#ip address 10.0.0.3 255.255.255.255
Router-PE2(config-if)#exit
Router-PE2(config)#router ospf 99
Router-PE2(config-router)#router-id 10.0.0.3
Router-PE2(config-router)#network 10.0.0.0 0.255.255.255 area 0
Router-PE2(config-router)#exit
Router-PE2(config)#ip vrf NetworkA
Router-PE2(config-vrf)#rd 100:1
Router-PE2(config-vrf)#route-target export 100:1
Router-PE2(config-vrf)#route-target import 100:1
Router-PE2(config-vrf)#exit
Router-PE2(config)#ip vrf NetworkB
Router-PE2(config-vrf)#rd 100:2
Router-PE2(config-vrf)#route-target export 100:2
Router-PE2(config-vrf)#route-target import 100:2
Router-PE2(config-vrf)#exit
Router-PE2(config)#interface FastEthernet0/0.2
Router-PE2(config-if)#description Connection to customer A, site 2
Router-PE2(config-if)#encapsulation dot1Q 102
Router-PE2(config-if)#ip address 192.168.3.1 255.255.255.0
Router-PE2(config-if)#mpls ip
Router-PE2(config-if)#exit
Router-PE2(config)#router bgp 100
Router-PE2(config-router)#bgp log-neighbor-changes
Router-PE2(config-router)#neighbor 10.0.0.2 remote-as 100
Router-PE2(config-router)#neighbor 10.0.0.2 update-source Loopback0
Router-PE2(config-router)#neighbor 10.0.0.3 remote-as 100
Router-PE2(config-router)#neighbor 10.0.0.3 update-source Loopback0
Router-PE2(config-router)#address-family ipv4 vrf NetworkA
Router-PE2(config-router-af)#no auto-summary
Router-PE2(config-router-af)#no synchronization
Router-PE2(config-router-af)#redistribute connected
Router-PE2(config-router-af)#exit-address-family
Router-PE2(config-router)#address-family vpnv4
Router-PE2(config-router-af)#neighbor 10.0.0.2 activate
Router-PE2(config-router-af)#neighbor 10.0.0.2 send-community extended
Router-PE2(config-router-af)#neighbor 10.0.0.4 activate
Router-PE2(config-router-af)#neighbor 10.0.0.4 send-community extended
Router-PE2(config-router-af)#exit-address-family
Router-PE2(config-router)#exit
Router-PE2(config)#end
Router-PE2#
```

The third PE router looks like this:

```
Router-PE3#configure terminal
Enter configuration commands, one per line.  End with CNTL/Z.
Router-PE3(config)#ip cef
Router-PE3(config)#mpls ip
Router-PE3(config)#interface Serial0/0
Router-PE3(config-if)#description Connection to Router-P1
Router-PE3(config-if)#ip address 10.1.1.9 255.255.255.252
Router-PE3(config-if)#mpls ip
Router-PE3(config-if)#exit
Router-PE3(config)#interface Loopback0
Router-PE3(config-if)#ip address 10.0.0.3 255.255.255.255
Router-PE3(config-if)#exit
Router-PE3(config)#router ospf 99
Router-PE3(config-router)#router-id 10.0.0.3
Router-PE3(config-router)#network 10.0.0.0 0.255.255.255 area 0
Router-PE3(config-router)#exit
Router-PE3(config)#ip vrf NetworkA
Router-PE3(config-vrf)#rd 100:1
Router-PE3(config-vrf)#route-target export 100:1
Router-PE3(config-vrf)#route-target import 100:1
Router-PE3(config-vrf)#exit
Router-PE3(config)#ip vrf NetworkB
Router-PE3(config-vrf)#rd 100:2
Router-PE3(config-vrf)#route-target export 100:2
Router-PE3(config-vrf)#route-target import 100:2
Router-PE3(config-vrf)#exit
Router-PE3(config)#interface Ethernet0/0
Router-PE3(config-if)#description connection to customer A, site 3
Router-PE3(config-if)#ip vrf forwarding NetworkA
Router-PE3(config-if)#ip address 192.168.2.1 255.255.255.0
Router-PE3(config-if)#exit
Router-PE3(config)#interface Ethernet0/1
Router-PE3(config-if)#description connection to customer B, site 2
Router-PE3(config-if)#ip vrf forwarding NetworkB
Router-PE3(config-if)#ip address 192.168.10.1 255.255.255.0
Router-PE3(config-if)#exit
Router-PE3(config)#router bgp 100
Router-PE3(config-router)#bgp log-neighbor-changes
Router-PE3(config-router)#neighbor 10.0.0.2 remote-as 100
Router-PE3(config-router)#neighbor 10.0.0.2 update-source Loopback0
Router-PE3(config-router)#neighbor 10.0.0.4 remote-as 100
Router-PE3(config-router)#neighbor 10.0.0.4 update-source Loopback0
Router-PE3(config-router)#address-family ipv4 vrf NetworkA
Router-PE3(config-router-af)#no auto-summary
Router-PE3(config-router-af)#no synchronization
Router-PE3(config-router-af)#redistribute connected
Router-PE3(config-router-af)#exit-address-family
Router-PE3(config-router)#adress-family ipv4 vrf NetworkB
Router-PE3(config-router-af)#no auto-summary
Router-PE3(config-router-af)#no synchronization
Router-PE3(config-router-af)#redistribute connected
Router-PE3(config-router-af)#exit-address-family
```

```
Router-PE3(config-router)#address-family vpnv4
Router-PE3(config-router-af)#neighbor 10.0.0.2 activate
Router-PE3(config-router-af)#neighbor 10.0.0.2 send-community extended
Router-PE3(config-router-af)#neighbor 10.0.0.4 activate
Router-PE3(config-router-af)#neighbor 10.0.0.4 send-community extended
Router-PE3(config-router-af)#exit-address-family
Router-PE3(config-router)#exit
Router-PE3(config)#end
Router-PE3#
```

Discussion

This is a rather long configuration, but it divides up rather naturally into a few basic components.

First, we have configured the basic MPLS functionality:

```
Router-PE1(config)#ip cef
Router-PE1(config)#mpls ip
Router-PE1(config)#interface Serial0/0
Router-PE1(config-if)#description Connection to Router-P1
Router-PE1(config-if)#ip address 10.1.1.13 255.255.255.252
Router-PE1(config-if)#mpls ip
Router-PE1(config-if)#exit
Router-PE1(config)#interface Loopback0
Router-PE1(config-if)#ip address 10.0.0.2 255.255.255.255
Router-PE1(config-if)#exit
Router-PE1(config)#router ospf 99
Router-PE1(config-router)#router-id 10.0.0.2
Router-PE1(config-router)#network 10.0.0.0 0.255.255.255 area 0
Router-PE1(config-router)#exit
```

Notice that this section of configuration is extremely similar to how we configured the P router in Recipe 26.1.

The next chunk of the router's configuration defines the VPNs. We have created two customer networks called NetworkA and NetworkB. Let's look at the first of these in more detail:

```
Router-PE1(config)#ip vrf NetworkA
Router-PE1(config-vrf)#rd 100:1
Router-PE1(config-vrf)#route-target export 100:1
Router-PE1(config-vrf)#route-target import 100:1
Router-PE1(config-vrf)#exit
```

The first line defines the name of the VRF, in this case NetworkA. Then the rd command defines a "route descriptor" for this VRF. This is really just a numerical tag that MP-BGP will use when propagating the routes associated with this VPN.

The route-target commands then tell MP-BGP which route descriptors to share its routes with. There can only be one route descriptor in a VRF definition, but you can freely share routes among several different route targets. In most cases, however, you will actually want to keep the routes confined to a particular VRF, as we have done in the example.

The route descriptor value is a 48-bit number that is conventionally written in two different ways. We have written the value as 100:1, which is a 16-bit BGP Autonomous System Number (ASN), followed by an arbitrary 32-bit number identifying the client network. The other way to write this value is as a 32-bit dotted decimal value (like an IP address) followed by an arbitrary 16 bit value—for example, 192.168.1.1:100.

MP-BGP then uses these values as a tag that it adds to the client routing prefixes. It's important to note that although it is a good idea to make these RD values meaningful, to MP-BGP they are just a sequence of bits. As long as they are consistent throughout your network, you can use whatever values are meaningful to you. It is not necessary, for example, to make the ASN identical with the BGP ASN, as we have done in this recipe. However, this is often a good practice, particularly if your MPLS network includes multiple ASNs that must be kept straight.

We note also that you can deliberately "leak" routes between VRFs as follows:

```
Router-PE1(config)#ip vrf NetworkA
Router-PE1(config-vrf)#rd 100:1
Router-PE1(config-vrf)#route-target export 100:1
Router-PE1(config-vrf)#route-target import 100:1
Router-PE1(config-vrf)#route-target export 100:2
Router-PE1(config-vrf)#route-target import 100:2
Router-PE1(config-vrf)#exit
```

This is sometimes used by service providers to ensure that their network management VLAN can access customer networks. However, most of the time you want to keep the VRFs separated.

Next we associate the VRF instances with physical interfaces:

```
Router-PE1(config)#interface Ethernet0/0
Router-PE1(config-if)#description connection to customer A, site 1
Router-PE1(config-if)#ip vrf forwarding NetworkA
Router-PE1(config-if)#ip address 192.168.1.1 255.255.255.0
Router-PE1(config-if)#exit
```

You should always input the IP address after the *ip vrf forwarding* command because the router will automatically delete any existing IP addresses when you assign the VRF to an interface.

The IP address in this case is part of the VRF for this customer network. Consequently, devices inside the customer network will be able to PING and route to this address. If this were a real customer and service provider, it would be critical to secure this interface to prevent users from using TELNET or other protocols to gain access to the provider network.

Note also that because two customers could well be using the same IP addresses, the *ip vrf forwarding* command allows you to configure overlapping or even duplicate IP addresses on the PE router, provided the interfaces with conflicting addresses belong to different VRFs.

Notice that we have created the same VRFs on all three PE routers, even though NetworkB only appears on two of them. This VRF is not assigned to any physical interface. You can see which interfaces are associated with each VRF:

```
Router-PE1#show ip vrf
  Name                      Default RD          Interfaces
  NetworkA                  100:1               Ethernet0/0
  NetworkB                  100:2               Ethernet0/1
Router-PE1#
```

If a particular VRF is not assigned to any interface, this command will list it in the output but leave the interface column blank:

```
Router-PE2#show ip vrf
  Name                      Default RD          Interfaces
  NetworkA                  100:1               FastEthernet0/0.2
  NetworkB                  100:2
Router-PE2#
```

The next section of the PE configuration shows the MP-BGP configuration:

```
Router-PE1(config)#router bgp 100
Router-PE1(config-router)#bgp log-neighbor-changes
Router-PE1(config-router)#neighbor 10.0.0.3 remote-as 100
Router-PE1(config-router)#neighbor 10.0.0.3 update-source Loopback0
Router-PE1(config-router)#neighbor 10.0.0.4 remote-as 100
Router-PE1(config-router)#neighbor 10.0.0.4 update-source Loopback0
Router-PE1(config-router)#address-family ipv4 vrf NetworkA
Router-PE1(config-router-af)#no auto-summary
Router-PE1(config-router-af)#no synchronization
Router-PE1(config-router-af)#redistribute connected
Router-PE1(config-router-af)#exit-address-family
Router-PE1(config-router)#adress-family ipv4 vrf NetworkB
Router-PE1(config-router-af)#no auto-summary
Router-PE1(config-router-af)#no synchronization
Router-PE1(config-router-af)#redistribute connected
Router-PE1(config-router-af)#exit-address-family
Router-PE1(config-router)#address-family vpnv4
Router-PE1(config-router-af)#neighbor 10.0.0.3 activate
Router-PE1(config-router-af)#neighbor 10.0.0.3 send-community extended
Router-PE1(config-router-af)#neighbor 10.0.0.4 activate
Router-PE1(config-router-af)#neighbor 10.0.0.4 send-community extended
Router-PE1(config-router-af)#exit-address-family
Router-PE1(config-router)#exit
```

First we define all of the BGP peer relationships in the usual way:

```
Router-PE1(config)#router bgp 100
Router-PE1(config-router)#neighbor 10.0.0.3 remote-as 100
Router-PE1(config-router)#neighbor 10.0.0.3 update-source Loopback0
```

The peer devices indicated are the other PE routers in this network. Since the Remote-AS indicated for each of the peers is the same as this router's BGP AS, they are all internal or iBGP peer relationships. IBGP peer relationships are required because MP-BGP distributes VRF information using extended BGP communities. If you need to break up your BGP network into more than one AS, you can do so, but you must take care to redistribute the VRF tables between the ASBR devices.

The other common way of handling the inherent scaling problems of large numbers of BGP peers in MPLS networks is to use Route Reflectors. We discuss Route Reflectors in Chapter 9.

For improved network stability, we prefer to identify all of our peer IP address with Loopback interfaces rather than physical interfaces. This way, if your PE router has multiple connection points into your MPLS core, a physical failure on one interface won't bring down the network.

Next we must tell MP-BGP about the VRF information that we want it to carry between the PE routers:

```
Router-PE1(config-router)#address-family ipv4 vrf NetworkA
Router-PE1(config-router-af)#no auto-summary
Router-PE1(config-router-af)#no synchronization
Router-PE1(config-router-af)#redistribute connected
Router-PE1(config-router-af)#exit-address-family
```

In this case, the only interface on this router is a member of the VRF that we have called NetworkA is Ethernet0/0, which has an IP address of 192.168.1.1/24. We chose to include this interface using the *redistribute connected* command. Usually in BGP networks we prefer to use a *network* command rather than redistributing connected routes because it will result in a better Origin code. However, MP-BGP doesn't treat redistributed routes in the same way, as we will see later in this chapter. Consequently, the *redistribute connected* command is actually the most convenient way of making sure that every interface associated with this VRF is automatically included in the routing table.

We note in passing that you exit from the *address-family* configuration block using the command *exit-address-family* rather than the simple *exit* command that Cisco usually uses for this purpose. The short form works, but the router will replace it with the long form in the configuration file. We don't know why this is.

Finally, the last section of the configuration example is necessary to allow MP-BGP to carry the VRF routing prefixes:

```
Router-PE1(config-router)#address-family vpnv4
Router-PE1(config-router-af)#neighbor 10.0.0.3 activate
Router-PE1(config-router-af)#neighbor 10.0.0.3 send-community extended
Router-PE1(config-router-af)#neighbor 10.0.0.4 activate
Router-PE1(config-router-af)#neighbor 10.0.0.4 send-community extended
Router-PE1(config-router-af)#exit-address-family
```

The critical command here is send-community extended, which tells MP-BGP to use extended communities.

You can verify basic MPLS connectivity for the connection between the PE and P routers by using the show mpls interfaces command, as we did in Recipe 26.1:

```
Router-PE1#show mpls interfaces
Interface          IP    Tunnel  Operational
Serial0/0          Yes   No      Yes
Router-PE1#
```

And you can see the contents of your VRF tables as follows:

```
Router-PE1#show ip route vrf NetworkA
Codes: C - connected, S - static, I - IGRP, R - RIP, M - mobile, B - BGP
       D - EIGRP, EX - EIGRP external, O - OSPF, IA - OSPF inter area
       N1 - OSPF NSSA external type 1, N2 - OSPF NSSA external type 2
       E1 - OSPF external type 1, E2 - OSPF external type 2, E - EGP
       i - IS-IS, su - IS-IS summary, L1 - IS-IS level-1, L2 - IS-IS level-2
       ia - IS-IS inter area, * - candidate default, U - per-user static route
       o - ODR, P - periodic downloaded static route

Gateway of last resort is not set

     10.0.0.0/32 is subnetted, 1 subnets
B       10.8.8.8 [200/4] via 10.0.0.4, 02:15:54
C    192.168.1.0/24 is directly connected, Ethernet0/0
B    192.168.2.0/24 [200/0] via 10.0.0.3, 02:16:08
B    192.168.3.0/24 [200/0] via 10.0.0.4, 02:15:54
Router-PE1#
```

It is sometimes useful to be able to do PING tests through a customer VLAN. You can do this from your PE routers, although you must take care to specify a source address that is also part of this VRF:

```
Router-PE1#ping vrf NetworkA 192.168.2.9 source 192.168.1.1

Type escape sequence to abort.
Sending 5, 100-byte ICMP Echos to 192.168.2.9, timeout is 2 seconds:
Packet sent with a source address of 192.168.1.1
!!!!!
Success rate is 100 percent (5/5), round-trip min/avg/max = 4/6/8 ms
Router-PE1#
```

In this case, the destination address is a CE router at a different site.

See Also

Recipe 26.1; Chapter 8; Chapter 9

26.3 Configuring Basic MPLS CE Routers

Problem

You want to configure the "customer" CE routers for MPLS.

Solution

CE routers do not require any special software or configuration to work with an MPLS carrier. You just need to ensure that there are appropriate routing table entries to allow sites to communicate across the MPLS network. We will do this with static routes for now:

```
Router-CE-A1#configure terminal
Enter configuration commands, one per line.  End with CNTL/Z.
Router-CE-A1(config)#interface FastEthernet0/0.1
Router-CE-A1(config-if)#encapsulation dot1Q 101
Router-CE-A1(config-if)#ip address 192.168.1.5 255.255.255.0
Router-CE-A1(config-if)#exit
Router-CE-A1(config)#ip route 0.0.0.0 0.0.0.0 192.168.1.1
Router-CE-A1(config)# exit
Router-CE-A1#
```

Discussion

In this example, we used static routes to communicate across the MPLS core. You could also use various routing protocols such as RIP, OSPF, EIGRP, or BGP to communicate between the CE and PE routers. We will discuss these options in more depth in Recipes 26.5, 26.6, 26.7, and 26.8. Another simple solution is to use GRE tunnels between your CE routers. You can then continue to use static routes to carry traffic between the CE and PE routers, but still have the all of the advantages of a routing protocol.

It is important to remember that the customer data passes through the MPLS network in a VLAN tunnel. If you look at any common IP information, such as the Time To Live (TTL) value, in the IP header or the output of a traceroute command, the entire MPLS cloud looks like a single hop:

```
Router-CE-A1#traceroute ip 192.168.2.9

Type escape sequence to abort.
Tracing the route to 192.168.2.9

  1 192.168.1.1 0 msec 4 msec 4 msec
  2 192.168.2.1 4 msec 4 msec 4 msec
  3 192.168.2.9 4 msec *  4 msec
Router-CE-A1#
```

In this case, 192.168.1.1 is the address of the PE router at this site, 192.168.2.1 is the PE router at the other site, and 192.168.2.9 is the address of the CE router at the other site.

We also note that we have used an Ethernet subinterface in this example to associate the PE-CE link with a VLAN. We did this for two reasons. First, the practical reason was that this router was limited in its physical Ethernet interfaces, so if we wanted to connect to other downstream C routers via Ethernet, we could still do so by putting them on a different VLAN. The second reason was to stress that the connection between PE and CE happens at Layer 3, so we can use any Layer 2 technology that is the most convenient. This is, in fact, one of the most attractive features of MPLS. The provider can deliver the service over any available medium. Ethernet is a popular delivery method because it allows the CE router to be essentially any inexpensive access router.

See Also

Recipe 26.5; Recipe 26.6; Recipe 26.7

26.4   Configuring MPLS over ATM

Problem

You want to run MPLS over an ATM network.

Solution

There are really two solutions to this problem, depending on the capabilities of your ATM switches. The first and conceptually simpler solution is to configure your ATM switch to just pass ATM cells, but not to interact with MPLS at the IP layer.

First we will configure the two PE routers to run MPLS over ATM. Note that for these configurations we show only the additional configuration required for the MPLS over ATM functionality. Please refer to Recipe 26.2 for the remainder of the configuration for MPLS PE functionality:

```
Router-PE1#configure terminal
Enter configuration commands, one per line.  End with CNTL/Z.
Router-PE1(config)#ip cef
Router-PE1(config)#mpls ip
Router-PE1(config)#interface ATM1/0
Router-PE1(config-if)#no ip address
Router-PE1(config-if)#exit
Router-PE1(config)#interface ATM1/0.1 mpls
Router-PE1(config-if)#ip address 10.1.1.2 255.255.255.252
Router-PE1(config-if)#mpls ip
Router-PE1(config-if)#exit
Router-PE1(config)#end
Router-PE1#
```

The other PE router's configuration is identical, except for the IP address:

```
Router-PE3#configure terminal
Enter configuration commands, one per line.  End with CNTL/Z.
Router-PE3(config)#ip cef
Router-PE3(config)#mpls ip
Router-PE3(config)#interface ATM1/0
Router-PE3(config-if)#no ip address
Router-PE3(config-if)#exit
Router-PE3(config)#interface ATM1/0.1 mpls
Router-PE3(config-if)#ip address 10.1.1.1 255.255.255.252
Router-PE3(config-if)#mpls ip
Router-PE3(config-if)#exit
Router-PE3(config)#end
Router-PE3#
```

And the ATM switch configuration simply requires connecting two PVCs: one for the MPLS Control-VC and the other for data. We use the defaults of 0/32 for the Control-VC and 1/33 for data for simplicity:

```
Switch-P2#configure terminal
Enter configuration commands, one per line.  End with CNTL/Z.
Switch-P2(config)#interface ATM0/1/2
Switch-P2(config-if)#no ip address
Switch-P2(config-if)#exit
Switch-P2(config)#interface ATM0/1/3
Switch-P2(config-if)#no ip address
Switch-P2(config-if)#atm pvc 0 32 interface ATM0/1/2 0 32
Switch-P2(config-if)#atm pvc 1 33 interface ATM0/1/2 1 33
Switch-P2(config-if)#exit
Switch-P2(config)#end
Switch-P2#
```

The second solution, which is possible on most newer Cisco ATM switches, is to configure the switch to take part in the IP and MPLS packet forwarding as a P router:

```
Router-PE1#configure terminal
Enter configuration commands, one per line.  End with CNTL/Z.
Router-PE1(config)#ip cef
Router-PE1(config)#mpls ip
Router-PE1(config)#interface ATM1/0
Router-PE1(config-if)#no ip address
Router-PE1(config-if)#exit
Router-PE1(config)#interface ATM1/0.1 mpls
Router-PE1(config-if)#ip address 10.1.1.2 255.255.255.252
Router-PE1(config-if)#mpls ip
Router-PE1(config-if)#exit
Router-PE1(config)#end
Router-PE1#
```

Once again, the other PE router's configuration is identical, except for the IP address. However, note that we have changed the IP address this time, as the two routers are no longer on the same subnet:

```
Router-PE3#configure terminal
Enter configuration commands, one per line.  End with CNTL/Z.
```

```
Router-PE3(config)#ip cef
Router-PE3(config)#mpls ip
Router-PE3(config)#interface ATM1/0
Router-PE3(config-if)#no ip address
Router-PE3(config-if)#exit
Router-PE3(config)#interface ATM1/0.1 mpls
Router-PE3(config-if)#ip address 10.1.1.6 255.255.255.252
Router-PE3(config-if)#mpls ip
Router-PE3(config-if)#exit
Router-PE3(config)#end
Router-PE3#
```

The switch configuration then includes the MPLS configuration on the interfaces,
and it also must take part in OSPF:

```
Switch-P2#configure terminal
Enter configuration commands, one per line.  End with CNTL/Z.
Switch-P2(config)#ip cef
Switch-P2(config)#mpls ip
Switch-P2(config)#interface ATM0/1/2
Switch-P2(config-if)#ip address 10.1.1.5 255.255.255.252
Switch-P2(config-if)#mpls ip
Switch-P2(config-if)#exit
Switch-P2(config)#interface ATM0/1/3
Switch-P2(config-if)#ip address 10.1.1.1 255.255.255.252
Switch-P2(config-if)#mpls ip
Switch-P2(config-if)#exit
Switch-P2(config)#interface Loopback0
Switch-P2(config-if)#ip address 10.0.0.1 255.255.255.255
Switch-P2(config-if)#exit
Switch-P2(config)#router ospf 99
Switch-P2(config-router)#router-id 10.0.0.1
Switch-P2(config-router)#network 10.0.0.0 0.255.255.255 area 0
Switch-P2(config-router)#exit
Switch-P2(config)#end
Switch-P2#
```

Discussion

In both of these examples, our ATM switch is a Cisco Lightstream LS1010. This
makes for a convenient example device because these switches are inexpensive and
they run IOS. However, Cisco has terminated support for these switches and recommends that users upgrade to MGX 8800, Catalyst 4500, or Catalyst 6500 series
devices. The configuration for all of these devices is similar in concept, although
some feature different syntaxes for connecting physical interfaces to the Layer 3
switching layer.

MPLS behaves particularly nicely over ATM because there is a standard protocol for
inserting the MPLS tags into the ATM cell header. The result is that the ATM
switches in the middle of the network can handle the MPLS tag switching without
ever having to reassemble the cell payloads into IP packets. Consequently, organizations with existing ATM infrastructure can easily convert to MPLS.

We show two essential methods for running an MPLS network over an ATM switched infrastructure. The first method is to essentially just create end-to-end PVCs between PE routers at the edges of the MPLS cloud. This has two advantages: it's simple to deploy and the ATM switches don't need to support MPLS tagging of ATM cells. However, it has the disadvantage that you must manually create all of your ATM PVCs. Alternatively, you could use ILMI and QSAAL to create these VCs automatically, but you would still need to do a lot of manual configuration to make this work. Neither of these methods scales well to larger networks.

The second method is much more flexible. The switches take part in the IGP, and exchange tag information using either TDP or LDP. Then every new PE router you add to your network will automatically join the MPLS infrastructure, even if it isn't directly connected to an ATM switch.

You can see the TDP neighbor information on the ATM switch with the *show tag-switching tdp neighbor* command:

```
Switch-P2#show tag-switching tdp neighbor
Peer TDP Ident: 10.0.0.2:1; Local TDP Ident 10.0.0.1:2
        TCP connection: 10.1.1.2.11001 - 10.1.1.1.711
        State: Oper; PIEs sent/rcvd: 160/160; Downstream on demand
        Up time: 02:14:39
        TDP discovery sources:
          ATM0/1/3, Src IP addr: 10.1.1.2
Peer TDP Ident: 10.0.0.3:1; Local TDP Ident 10.0.0.1:1
        TCP connection: 10.1.1.6.11001 - 10.1.1.5.711
        State: Oper; PIEs sent/rcvd: 158/158; Downstream on demand
        Up time: 02:14:39
        TDP discovery sources:
          ATM0/1/2, Src IP addr: 10.1.1.6
Switch-P2#
```

Now that we have added a second path to the MPLS network, the routing tables become more interesting. First we'll look at the routing within the MPLS cloud. Note that this output does not show any of the tunneled customer routing tables:

```
Router-PE3#show ip route
Codes: C - connected, S - static, I - IGRP, R - RIP, M - mobile, B - BGP
       D - EIGRP, EX - EIGRP external, O - OSPF, IA - OSPF inter area
       N1 - OSPF NSSA external type 1, N2 - OSPF NSSA external type 2
       E1 - OSPF external type 1, E2 - OSPF external type 2, E - EGP
       i - IS-IS, su - IS-IS summary, L1 - IS-IS level-1, L2 - IS-IS level-2
       ia - IS-IS inter area, * - candidate default, U - per-user static route
       o - ODR, P - periodic downloaded static route

Gateway of last resort is not set

     10.0.0.0/8 is variably subnetted, 10 subnets, 3 masks
O       10.0.0.11/32 [110/65] via 10.1.1.10, 00:39:11, Serial0/0
C       10.1.1.8/30 is directly connected, Serial0/0
O       10.1.1.12/30 [110/66] via 10.1.1.5, 00:39:11, ATM1/0.1
```

```
O       10.0.0.2/32 [110/3] via 10.1.1.5, 00:39:11, ATM1/0.1
O       10.1.2.0/24 [110/11] via 10.1.1.5, 00:39:11, ATM1/0.1
C       10.0.0.3/32 is directly connected, Loopback0
O       10.1.1.0/30 [110/2] via 10.1.1.5, 00:39:11, ATM1/0.1
O       10.0.0.1/32 [110/2] via 10.1.1.5, 00:39:12, ATM1/0.1
O       10.0.0.4/32 [110/66] via 10.1.1.10, 00:39:12, Serial0/0
C       10.1.1.4/30 is directly connected, ATM1/0.1
Router-PE3#
```

If we want to see the client routing tables, we need to include the *vrf* keyword:

```
Router-PE3#show ip route vrf NetworkA
Codes: C - connected, S - static, I - IGRP, R - RIP, M - mobile, B - BGP
       D - EIGRP, EX - EIGRP external, O - OSPF, IA - OSPF inter area
       N1 - OSPF NSSA external type 1, N2 - OSPF NSSA external type 2
       E1 - OSPF external type 1, E2 - OSPF external type 2, E - EGP
       i - IS-IS, su - IS-IS summary, L1 - IS-IS level-1, L2 - IS-IS level-2
       ia - IS-IS inter area, * - candidate default, U - per-user static route
       o - ODR, P - periodic downloaded static route

Gateway of last resort is not set

       10.0.0.0/32 is subnetted, 1 subnets
B         10.8.8.8 [200/4] via 10.0.0.4, 00:41:00
B      192.168.1.0/24 [200/0] via 10.0.0.2, 00:41:15
C      192.168.2.0/24 is directly connected, Ethernet0/0
B      192.168.3.0/24 [200/0] via 10.0.0.4, 00:41:00
Router-PE3#
```

In this case, we see an interesting mixture of customer route prefixes that point to MPLS core IP address destinations. The destinations listed are the iBGP peer addresses of the PE routers. So, for example, the highlighted line shows that the customer route prefix 192.168.1.0/24 in the NetworkA customer network is reachable through the PE router, 10.0.0.2.

The *show mpls forwarding-table* command gives useful information on the MPLS tag information:

```
Router-PE3#show mpls forwarding-table
Local  Outgoing    Prefix           Bytes tag  Outgoing   Next Hop
tag    tag or VC   or Tunnel Id     switched   interface
16     1/36        10.0.0.2/32      0          AT1/0.1    point2point
17     Pop tag     10.0.0.11/32     0          Se0/0      point2point
18     1/34        10.1.1.0/30      0          AT1/0.1    point2point
19     1/37        10.1.1.12/30     0          AT1/0.1    point2point
20     1/35        10.1.2.0/24      0          AT1/0.1    point2point
21     1/33        10.0.0.1/32      0          AT1/0.1    point2point
22     Aggregate   192.168.2.0/24[V] 1976
23     Aggregate   192.168.10.0/24[V]  \
                                    936
24     21          10.0.0.4/32      0          Se0/0      point2point
Router-PE3#
```

This output shows that the tag values 22 and 23 are aggregates. In our network, both of these addresses are customer VRF prefixes that we reach through the same PE router, so they can easily be aggregated through the same path.

Tag value 16 is used for internal MPLS routing to the destination prefix 10.0.0.2/32, which is the loopback address of one of our PE routers. Everything tagged with this value is sent out the ATM interface using a VPI/VCI value of 1/36. Similarly, tag value 24 is used for the destination prefix 10.0.0.4/32, another of our PE routers. In this case the *outgoing tag* value is not an ATM VPI/VCI pair because the outgoing interface is a serial link, which in our network connects to Router-P1. The same command on that router allows us to trace the tag values through the MPLS core:

```
Router-P1#show mpls forwarding-table
Local  Outgoing    Prefix         Bytes tag  Outgoing   Next Hop
tag    tag or VC   or Tunnel Id   switched   interface
16     Pop tag     10.0.0.2/32    7404       Se0/0      point2point
17     Pop tag     10.1.1.0/30    0          Se0/0      point2point
18     Pop tag     10.0.0.3/32    5940       Se0/1      point2point
19     Pop tag     10.1.1.4/30    0          Se0/1      point2point
20     21          10.0.0.1/32    0          Se0/0      point2point
       21          10.0.0.1/32    0          Se0/1      point2point
21     Pop tag     10.0.0.4/32    14342      Fa0/0      10.1.2.4
Router-P1#
```

Here you can see that tag value 21 is indeed used for prefix 10.0.0.4/32, as you would expect. Also, in this output you can see that the next hop device is given as an IP address. All of the other tags that we have looked at so far have been connected via point-to-point media, such as ATM VCs or serial connections. In this case, however, the next hop device is connected through an Ethernet, so the command output lists the next hop device's IP address.

The outgoing tag value is listed as *Pop tag* for this entry. This router is doing something called *Penultimate Hop Popping* (PHP), which means that the second from the last router in the path through the MPLS cloud is removing the MPLS label so that the PE router can process the packet slightly faster. The PE router in this case doesn't need to remove the MPLS information before routing the packet based on the IP header; the previous router has already done the first step for it.

26.5 PE-CE Communication via RIP

Problem

You want to use RIP to exchange routing information between the CE and PE routers.

Solution

You can use RIP to exchange customer routing information between the CE and PE routers at each site. The advantage to doing this is that any customer routes at one site can be automatically propagated to other customer sites. This requires a normal RIP configuration on the CE router:

```
Router-CE-A2#configure terminal
Enter configuration commands, one per line.  End with CNTL/Z.
Router-CE-A2(config)#router rip
Router-CE-A2(config-router)#version 2
Router-CE-A2(config-router)#network 10.0.0.0
Router-CE-A2(config-router)#network 192.168.3.0
Router-CE-A2(config-router)#end
Router-CE-A2#
```

And there must be a matching RIP configuration for this VRF on the PE router:

```
Router-PE2#configure terminal
Enter configuration commands, one per line.  End with CNTL/Z.
Router-PE2(config)#router rip
Router-PE2(config-router)#version 2
Router-PE2(config-router)#address-family ipv4 vrf NetworkA
Router-PE2(config-router-af)#version 2
Router-PE2(config-router-af)#redistribute bgp 100 metric 4
Router-PE2(config-router-af)#network 192.168.3.0
Router-PE2(config-router-af)#exit-address-family
Router-PE2(config-router)#exit
Router-PE2(config)#router bgp 100
Router-PE2(config-router)#address-family ipv4 vrf NetworkA
Router-PE2(config-router-af)#redistribute rip metric 4
Router-PE2(config-router-af)#end
Router-PE2#
```

Discussion

There are a few key points to note in this configuration. First, this just configures RIP between the CE and PE routers at this site. It doesn't configure RIP end-to-end across the MPLS cloud. The customer VRF routing prefixes are carried through the MPLS cloud by BGP. In this case, the customer network is called NetworkA, and the BGP ASN is 100, both of which we previously configured in Recipes 26.1, 26.2, and 26.3. This is important because it means that we could potentially use different routing protocols for the communication between the PE and CE routers at each customer site.

The second important point, which follows from the first one, is that we must only make sure the routing protocol parameters match between the PE and CE routers at this site. In our example, we demonstrate this by setting both routers to RIP Version 2. You could just as easily use RIP Version 1, which we would configure as follows:

```
Router-CE-A2(config)#router rip
Router-CE-A2(config-router)#version 1
```

In this case, we would have to make the corresponding change to the PE router:

```
Router-PE2(config)#router rip
Router-PE2(config-router)#version 1
Router-PE2(config-router)#address-family ipv4 vrf NetworkA
Router-PE2(config-router-af)#version 1
```

The third important point is that on the PE router, you must be careful to configure the PE-to-CE routing protocol for the required VRF only, and *not globally*. This is accomplished using the *address-family ipv4 vrf* command on the PE router:

```
Router-PE2(config-router)#address-family ipv4 vrf NetworkA
```

Note, however, that the CE router doesn't know anything about MPLS or VRF tables, so this router uses the same RIP configuration that we saw in Chapter 6.

The next key issue that we need to point out is that we are using redistribution between BGP and RIP on the PE router. This means that we must redistribute from RIP into BGP, as well as from BGP into RIP, as shown in this excerpt:

```
Router-PE2(config)#router rip
Router-PE2(config-router)#address-family ipv4 vrf NetworkA
Router-PE2(config-router-af)#redistribute bgp 100 metric 4
Router-PE2(config-router-af)#exit-address-family
Router-PE2(config-router)#exit
Router-PE2(config)#router bgp 100
Router-PE2(config-router)#address-family ipv4 vrf NetworkA
Router-PE2(config-router-af)#redistribute rip metric 4
```

In this example, we have set a redistribution metric of 4 in both directions. This is not necessary. By default you can use a RIP metric of 1, but it can be useful to give a higher metric to these redistributed routes, particularly when there are other paths to the remote network.

If we now look at the routing table for this VRF on the PE, we see a mixture of RIP and BGP routes:

```
Router-PE2#show ip route vrf NetworkA
Codes: C - connected, S - static, I - IGRP, R - RIP, M - mobile, B - BGP
       D - EIGRP, EX - EIGRP external, O - OSPF, IA - OSPF inter area
       N1 - OSPF NSSA external type 1, N2 - OSPF NSSA external type 2
       E1 - OSPF external type 1, E2 - OSPF external type 2, E - EGP
       i - IS-IS, su - IS-IS summary, L1 - IS-IS level-1, L2 - IS-IS level-2
       ia - IS-IS inter area, * - candidate default, U - per-user static route
       o - ODR, P - periodic downloaded static route

Gateway of last resort is not set

B     192.168.57.0/24 [200/4] via 10.0.0.2, 00:01:14
B     192.168.5.0/24 [200/4] via 10.0.0.2, 00:02:14
      10.0.0.0/32 is subnetted, 1 subnets
R        10.8.8.8 [120/1] via 192.168.3.8, 00:00:21, FastEthernet0/0.2
B     192.168.1.0/24 [200/0] via 10.0.0.2, 03:53:27
B     192.168.2.0/24 [200/0] via 10.0.0.3, 03:53:27
C     192.168.3.0/24 is directly connected, FastEthernet0/0.2
Router-PE2#
```

And the standard *show ip route* command on the CE router gives us:

```
Router-CE-A2#show ip route
Codes: C - connected, S - static, I - IGRP, R - RIP, M - mobile, B - BGP
```

```
     D - EIGRP, EX - EIGRP external, O - OSPF, IA - OSPF inter area
     N1 - OSPF NSSA external type 1, N2 - OSPF NSSA external type 2
     E1 - OSPF external type 1, E2 - OSPF external type 2, E - EGP
     i - IS-IS, L1 - IS-IS level-1, L2 - IS-IS level-2, ia - IS-IS inter area
     * - candidate default, U - per-user static route, o - ODR
     P - periodic downloaded static route

Gateway of last resort is not set

R    192.168.57.0/24 [120/4] via 192.168.3.1, 00:00:17, Ethernet0
R    192.168.5.0/24 [120/4] via 192.168.3.1, 00:00:17, Ethernet0
     10.0.0.0/32 is subnetted, 1 subnets
C       10.8.8.8 is directly connected, Loopback0
R    192.168.1.0/24 [120/4] via 192.168.3.1, 00:00:17, Ethernet0
R    192.168.2.0/24 [120/4] via 192.168.3.1, 00:00:17, Ethernet0
C    192.168.3.0/24 is directly connected, Ethernet0
Router-CE-A2#
```

In this example, we are also using RIP to communicate between the CE and PE at Site 1 for Customer A. This is where we are getting the prefixes 192.168.1.0/24 and 192.168.57.0/24. However, it is worth noting that 192.168.57.0/24 is actually on an internal C router that is one hop behind the CE router. But looking at the routing table, you can see that all of the RIP routes have exactly the same metric of 4, which was our redistribution metric. So, because of the redistribution, we have actually lost all metric information from the other sites. In a simple network, like the one in our example, this isn't important, but if there were other links between these sites, it might cause routing problems.

If you need to see real metrics between the sites, then the simplest solution using RIP is to use a static route between the CE and PE routers at each site and create a GRE tunnel between your CE routers. On the first CE router you would create a Tunnel interface, add a static route to the CE router at the other site, and then configure RIP to send updates over the Tunnel interface. Note, however, that this doesn't scale very well if you have a large number of CE sites. Because MPLS implicitly meshes the customer sites that are members of the same VRF, the number of tunnels required for N sites is N(N-1)/2. So this is not always a practical solution:

```
Router-CE-A1#configure terminal
Enter configuration commands, one per line.  End with CNTL/Z.
Router-CE-A1(config)#interface Tunnel1
Router-CE-A1(config-if)#ip address 192.168.152.1 255.255.255.252
Router-CE-A1(config-if)#tunnel source 192.168.1.5
Router-CE-A1(config-if)#tunnel destination 192.168.3.8
Router-CE-A1(config-if)#exit
Router-CE-A1(config)#ip route 192.168.3.0 255.255.255.0 192.168.1.0
Router-CE-A1(config)#router rip
Router-CE-A1(config-router)#version 2
Router-CE-A1(config-router)#network 192.168.5.0
Router-CE-A1(config-router)#network 192.168.152.0
Router-CE-A1(config-router)#exit
```

```
Router-CE-A1(config)#end
Router-CE-A1#
```

And on the other CE router, you would configure the other end of the tunnel and a static route to go back to the first site:

```
Router-CE-A2#configure terminal
Enter configuration commands, one per line.  End with CNTL/Z.
Router-CE-A2(config)#interface Tunnel1
Router-CE-A2(config-if)#ip address 192.168.152.2 255.255.255.252
Router-CE-A2(config-if)#tunnel source 192.168.3.8
Router-CE-A2(config-if)#tunnel destination 192.168.1.5
Router-CE-A2(config-if)#exit
Router-CE-A2(config)#ip route 192.168.1.0 255.255.255.0 192.168.3.1
Router-CE-A2(config)#router rip
Router-CE-A2(config-router)#version 2
Router-CE-A2(config-router)#network 10.0.0.0
Router-CE-A2(config-router)#network 192.168.152.0
Router-CE-A2(config-router)#end
Router-CE-A2#
```

Now when we look at the routing table we see more realistic metrics:

```
Router-CE-A2#show ip route
Codes: C - connected, S - static, I - IGRP, R - RIP, M - mobile, B - BGP
       D - EIGRP, EX - EIGRP external, O - OSPF, IA - OSPF inter area
       N1 - OSPF NSSA external type 1, N2 - OSPF NSSA external type 2
       E1 - OSPF external type 1, E2 - OSPF external type 2, E - EGP
       i - IS-IS, L1 - IS-IS level-1, L2 - IS-IS level-2, ia - IS-IS inter area
       * - candidate default, U - per-user static route, o - ODR
       P - periodic downloaded static route

Gateway of last resort is not set

R    192.168.57.0/24 [120/2] via 192.168.152.1, 00:00:23, Tunnel1
R    192.168.5.0/24 [120/1] via 192.168.152.1, 00:00:23, Tunnel1
     10.0.0.0/32 is subnetted, 1 subnets
C       10.8.8.8 is directly connected, Loopback0
     192.168.152.0/30 is subnetted, 1 subnets
C       192.168.152.0 is directly connected, Tunnel1
S    192.168.1.0/24 [1/0] via 192.168.3.1
C    192.168.3.0/24 is directly connected, Ethernet0
Router-CE-A2#
```

For more information on tunnels, please refer to Chapter 12, and for a more detailed example of tunneling between CE routers, please refer to Recipe 26.12.

Finally, it is one of the more interesting quirks of MPLS that this route redistribution between MP-BGP and an IGP on the PE router doesn't behave the way that redistribution normally does. In particular, none of the routes that we redistribute into the IGP appear as external. This will become critically important in situations where you have backup links between your sites because all IGPs prefer internal to external routes by default. If MP-BGP redistributed routes as external, it would be extremely difficult to make a robust IGP design without resorting to tunnels.

See Also

Chapter 6; Chapter 12; Recipe 26.1; Recipe 26.2; Recipe 26.3; Recipe 26.12

26.6   PE-CE Communication via OSPF

Problem

You want to use OSPF to exchange routing information between the CE and PE routers.

Solution

You can use OSPF to exchange customer routing information between the CE and PE routers at each site. For this example, we will configure OSPF for the CE to PE IGP at Customer A's Sites 1 and 2, but not 3, so that we can show some of the idiosyncrasies of MP-BGP route redistribution.

First we will configure the CE routers. We will use two OSPF *network* statements on the router at Site 1. The first, 192.168.1.0/24, allows this router to communicate with the PE router, while the second, 192.168.5.0/24, includes downstream devices in the OSPF network:

```
Router-CE-A1#configure terminal
Enter configuration commands, one per line.  End with CNTL/Z.
Router-CE-A1(config)#router ospf 55
Router-CE-A1(config-router)#network 192.168.1.0 0.0.0.255 area 0
Router-CE-A1(config-router)#network 192.168.5.0 0.0.0.255 area 0
Router-CE-A1(config-router)#end
Router-CE-A1#
```

And the CE router at the second site will use only one *network* statement:

```
Router-CE-A2#configure terminal
Enter configuration commands, one per line.  End with CNTL/Z.
Router-CE-A2(config)#router ospf 55
Router-CE-A2(config-router)#network 192.168.3.0 0.0.0.255 area 0
Router-CE-A2(config-router)#end
Router-CE-A2#
```

For the corresponding configuration on the PE routers, we need to create a new OSPF process that is associated with this VRF, and we need to configure the appropriate redistribution:

```
Router-PE1#configure terminal
Enter configuration commands, one per line.  End with CNTL/Z.
Router-PE1(config)#router ospf 155 vrf NetworkA
Router-PE1(config-router)#redistribute bgp 100 subnets
Router-PE1(config-router)#network 192.168.1.0 0.0.0.255 area 0
Router-PE1(config-router)#exit
Router-PE1(config)#router bgp 100
```

```
Router-PE1(config-router)#address-family ipv4 vrf NetworkA
Router-PE1(config-router-af)#redistribute ospf 155
Router-PE1(config-router-af)#exit-address-family
Router-PE1(config-router)#end
Router-PE1#
```

The configuration on the other PE router is similar:

```
Router-PE2#configure terminal
Enter configuration commands, one per line.  End with CNTL/Z.
Router-PE2(config)#router ospf 155 vrf NetworkA
Router-PE2(config-router)#redistribute bgp 100 subnets
Router-PE2(config-router)#network 192.168.3.0 0.0.0.255 area 0
Router-PE2(config-router)#exit
Router-PE2(config)#router bgp 100
Router-PE2(config-router)#address-family ipv4 vrf NetworkA
Router-PE2(config-router-af)#redistribute ospf 155
Router-PE2(config-router-af)#exit-address-family
Router-PE2(config-router)#end
Router-PE2#
```

Discussion

Before going into this example, we need to remind the reader that these configuration excerpts are not complete. They assume that the routers have already been configured for their CE and PE roles and that MPLS is functioning end-to-end, as shown in Recipes 26.1, 26.2, and 26.3.

Unlike the RIP example shown in Recipe 26.5, this OSPF example does extend the customer OSPF network across the MPLS cloud. However, it does so in a slightly odd way, which you can see from looking at the output of a *show ip route* command on one of the CE routers:

```
Router-CE-A1#show ip route
Codes: C - connected, S - static, I - IGRP, R - RIP, M - mobile, B - BGP
       D - EIGRP, EX - EIGRP external, O - OSPF, IA - OSPF inter area
       N1 - OSPF NSSA external type 1, N2 - OSPF NSSA external type 2
       E1 - OSPF external type 1, E2 - OSPF external type 2, E - EGP
       i - IS-IS, su - IS-IS summary, L1 - IS-IS level-1, L2 - IS-IS level-2
       ia - IS-IS inter area, * - candidate default, U - per-user static route
       o - ODR, P - periodic downloaded static route

Gateway of last resort is not set

     192.168.57.0/32 is subnetted, 1 subnets
O       192.168.57.12 [110/2] via 192.168.5.12, 00:37:06, FastEthernet0/0.2
C    192.168.5.0/24 is directly connected, FastEthernet0/0.2
C    192.168.1.0/24 is directly connected, FastEthernet0/0.1
O E2 192.168.2.0/24 [110/1] via 192.168.1.1, 00:37:06, FastEthernet0/0.1
O IA 192.168.3.0/24 [110/2] via 192.168.1.1, 00:35:00, FastEthernet0/0.1
Router-CE-A1#
```

Looking back at our OSPF configurations, you can see that everything is configured to be a part of Area 0. However, we can actually see three different varieties of OSPF

---

route in this output. The prefix 192.168.57.12/32 is an intraarea route originating from a C router at the same site as this CE router. Of the other two OSPF prefixes, 192.168.2.0/24 is external and 192.168.3.0/24 is considered an interarea route.

The external status for 192.168.2.0/24 is easy to understand, as this route originates from a third site that is also part of this VRF, but not configured for OSPF. In fact, this site is configured using static routes, as shown in Recipe 26.3. So this route really is external to OSPF.

The interarea status for 192.168.3.0/24, however, is a little more confusing because this prefix is injected from OSPF and is part of Area 0. As you can see from the OSPF database, this has happened because the PE router uses a Type 3 LSA (Summary-LSA) when advertising all internal prefixes learned from MP-BGP:

```
Router-CE-A1#show ip ospf database

        OSPF Router with ID (192.168.5.1) (Process ID 55)

            Router Link States (Area 0)

Link ID          ADV Router       Age        Seq#       Checksum Link count
192.168.1.1      192.168.1.1      1161       0x80000004 0x00C2AF 1
192.168.5.1      192.168.5.1      1218       0x80000006 0x0097DE 2
192.168.57.12    192.168.57.12    1470       0x80000004 0x00AE6F 2

            Net Link States (Area 0)

Link ID          ADV Router       Age        Seq#       Checksum
192.168.1.5      192.168.5.1      1218       0x80000002 0x0086F8
192.168.5.12     192.168.57.12    1470       0x80000003 0x00DA16

            Summary Net Link States (Area 0)

Link ID          ADV Router       Age        Seq#       Checksum
192.168.3.0      192.168.1.1      1180       0x80000002 0x001EC4

            Type-5 AS External Link States

Link ID          ADV Router       Age        Seq#       Checksum Tag
192.168.2.0      192.168.1.1      1180       0x80000002 0x009115 3489661028
Router-CE-A1#
```

In a conventional OSPF situation, this prefix would be advertised throughout the area using Type 1 (Router-LSA) or Type 2 (Network-LSA) LSAs. Consequently, even though this prefix is part of the same area, it appears to come from another area.

This is often not a problem, but it can easily become a problem if you have other links between these sites. In this case, OSPF will always favor an intra-area route over an inter-area route, even if the MPLS network is the better path. You could get around this problem using a tunnel, as we did in Recipe 26.5, but OSPF has a more elegant solution using *sham-links*, which became available in IOS Version 12.2(8)T.

In this case, we want to configure an OSPF *sham-link* between the two OSPF PE routers inside the MPLS cloud. The sham link is essentially a tunnel, similar to an OSPF virtual link, except that it has this special function of maintaining LSA types across the cloud. We always recommend using loopback interfaces for the end points of any tunnel because they never go down. Consequently, if there is any path available through the MPLS cloud, the sham link will remain available.

To facilitate this, we will first create new loopback interfaces that are also members of the NetworkA VRF on both PE routers. Because we used the *redistribute connected* command in our MP-BGP configuration for this VRF, we don't need to explicitly add the IP addresses for these interfaces. They will be distributed automatically, saving us a step. Then we will configure the sham link in our OSPF routing instance for this VRF:

```
Router-PE1#configure terminal
Enter configuration commands, one per line.  End with CNTL/Z.
Router-PE1(config)#interface Loopback155
Router-PE1(config-if)#ip vrf forwarding NetworkA
Router-PE1(config-if)#ip address 192.168.155.1 255.255.255.255
Router-PE1(config-if)#exit
Router-PE1(config)#router ospf 155 vrf NetworkA
Router-PE1(config-router)#area 0 sham-link 192.168.155.1 192.168.155.2 cost 10
Router-PE1(config-router)#redistribute bgp 100 subnets
Router-PE1(config-router)#network 192.168.1.0 0.0.0.255 area 0
Router-PE1(config-router)#end
Router-PE1#
```

We must apply the same nearly identical steps on the other PE router:

```
Router-PE2#configure terminal
Enter configuration commands, one per line.  End with CNTL/Z.
Router-PE2(config)#interface Loopback155
Router-PE2(config-if)#ip vrf forwarding NetworkA
Router-PE2(config-if)#ip address 192.168.155.2 255.255.255.255
Router-PE2(config-if)#exit
Router-PE2(config)#router ospf 155 vrf NetworkA
Router-PE2(config-router)#area 0 sham-link 192.168.155.2 192.168.155.1 cost 10
Router-PE2(config-router)#redistribute bgp 100 subnets
Router-PE2(config-router)#network 192.168.3.0 0.0.0.255 area 0
Router-PE2(config-router)#end
Router-PE2#
```

Now when we look at the routing tables on the CE routers, all of the intra-area routes look like intra-area routes:

```
Router-CE-A1#show ip route
Codes: C - connected, S - static, I - IGRP, R - RIP, M - mobile, B - BGP
       D - EIGRP, EX - EIGRP external, O - OSPF, IA - OSPF inter area
       N1 - OSPF NSSA external type 1, N2 - OSPF NSSA external type 2
       E1 - OSPF external type 1, E2 - OSPF external type 2, E - EGP
       i - IS-IS, su - IS-IS summary, L1 - IS-IS level-1, L2 - IS-IS level-2
       ia - IS-IS inter area, * - candidate default, U - per-user static route
       o - ODR, P - periodic downloaded static route

Gateway of last resort is not set
```

```
      192.168.57.0/32 is subnetted, 1 subnets
O        192.168.57.12 [110/2] via 192.168.5.12, 01:25:24, FastEthernet0/0.2
C     192.168.5.0/24 is directly connected, FastEthernet0/0.2
C     192.168.1.0/24 is directly connected, FastEthernet0/0.1
      192.168.155.0/32 is subnetted, 1 subnets
O E2    192.168.155.1 [110/1] via 192.168.1.1, 01:25:24, FastEthernet0/0.1
O E2  192.168.2.0/24 [110/1] via 192.168.1.1, 01:25:24, FastEthernet0/0.1
O     192.168.3.0/24 [110/12] via 192.168.1.1, 01:25:26, FastEthernet0/0.1
Router-CE-A1#
```

We note in passing that this has added one prefix to the routing table, which is the loopback interface we added to the nearest PE router. Some engineers may be tempted to filter this out, as it is a prefix that has been added to the customer's routing table by the MPLS cloud. We discuss methods for filtering OSPF routes in Chapter 8, if the reader is interested in doing this. However, we would also caution against this idea, as it would be very easy for somebody within the customer's network to assign these addresses if they didn't appear in the routing table. This would immediately break the sham link and could cause very strange routing problems that would be difficult to troubleshoot.

See Also

Chapter 8; Recipe 26.1; Recipe 26.2; Recipe 26.3; Recipe 26.5

26.7   PE-CE Communication via EIGRP

Problem

You want to use EIGRP to exchange routing information between your CE and PE routers.

Solution

The solution to this problem is similar to the RIP solution in Recipe 26.5 and the OSPF solution in Recipe 26.6. First we have to enable the routing protocol on the CE routers, which we do in the usual way:

```
Router-CE-A1#configure terminal
Enter configuration commands, one per line.  End with CNTL/Z.
Router-CE-A1(config)#router eigrp 156
Router-CE-A1(config-router)#network 192.168.1.0
Router-CE-A1(config-router)#network 192.168.5.0
Router-CE-A1(config-router)#no auto-summary
Router-CE-A1(config-router)#end
Router-CE-A1#
```

We have disabled EIGRP autosummarization because, for the clarity of the example, we want to see all of the subnets. The other CE router's configuration is similar:

```
Router-CE-A2#configure terminal
Enter configuration commands, one per line.  End with CNTL/Z.
```

```
Router-CE-A2(config)#router eigrp 156
Router-CE-A2(config-router)#network 10.0.0.0
Router-CE-A2(config-router)#network 192.168.3.0
Router-CE-A2(config-router)#no auto-summary
Router-CE-A2(config-router)#end
Router-CE-A2#
```

And then we must configure the PE routers to take part in EIGRP for this VRF:

```
Router-PE1#configure terminal
Enter configuration commands, one per line.  End with CNTL/Z.
Router-PE1(config)#router eigrp 1001
Router-PE1(config-router)#no auto-summary
Router-PE1(config-router)#address-family ipv4 vrf NetworkA
Router-PE1(config-router-af)#redistribute bgp 100 metric 10000 10 255 1 1500
Router-PE1(config-router-af)#network 192.168.1.0
Router-PE1(config-router-af)#no auto-summary
Router-PE1(config-router-af)#autonomous-system 156
Router-PE1(config-router-af)#exit-address-family
Router-PE1(config-router)#exit
Router-PE1(config)#router bgp 100
Router-PE1(config-router)#address-family ipv4 vrf NetworkA
Router-PE1(config-router-af)#redistribute eigrp 156
Router-PE1(config-router-af)#exit-address-family
Router-PE1(config-router)#exit
Router-PE1(config)#end
Router-PE1#
```

The other PE router's configuration is similar:

```
Router-PE2#configure terminal
Enter configuration commands, one per line.  End with CNTL/Z.
Router-PE2(config)#router eigrp 1001
Router-PE2(config-router)#auto-summary
Router-PE2(config-router)#address-family ipv4 vrf NetworkA
Router-PE2(config-router-af)#redistribute bgp 100 metric 10000 10 255 1 1500
Router-PE2(config-router-af)#network 192.168.3.0
Router-PE2(config-router-af)#no auto-summary
Router-PE2(config-router-af)#autonomous-system 156
Router-PE2(config-router-af)#exit-address-family
Router-PE2(config-router)#end
Router-PE2#
```

Discussion

As you should start to expect with MPLS, the CE router configurations don't contain any special commands, and look exactly the same as the nonMPLS configurations that we have discussed elsewhere in this book. The PE configurations are where all of the differences are. The syntax for EIGRP looks very similar to what we saw when using RIP for PE-to-CE routing in Recipe 26.5. First, we configure a global routing process, and then we use the *address-family* command to define how the protocol should behave for each VRF:

```
Router-PE1(config)#router eigrp 1001
Router-PE1(config-router)#no auto-summary
```

```
Router-PE1(config-router)#address-family ipv4 vrf NetworkA
Router-PE1(config-router-af)#redistribute bgp 100 metric 10000 10 255 1 1500
Router-PE1(config-router-af)#network 192.168.1.0
Router-PE1(config-router-af)#no auto-summary
Router-PE1(config-router-af)#autonomous-system 156
Router-PE1(config-router-af)#exit-address-family
```

There are several key things to notice in this configuration. First, we use the *network* command to define which networks will take part in EIGRP. Recall from Chapter 7 that this command defines which interfaces will take part in the protocol, as well as which routing prefixes the EIGRP will distribute.

Second, the *redistribute* command behaves a little bit differently under EIGRP than under other routing protocols. Specifically, there are no default metric values, so you must explicitly define them either in this command, as we have done here or on a separate line using the *metric* command. This is generally true with redistribution in EIGRP, so we ask the reader to refer to Chapter 7 for more details.

The third key point is the *autonomous-system* command:

```
Router-PE1(config-router-af)#autonomous-system 156
```

In the OSPF configuration in Recipe 26.6, we created a separate OSPF routing instance for each VRF. That works for OSPF because the protocol doesn't care about the AS number. However, EIGRP routers will not form adjacencies if they don't have the same AS number. Since different customers using different VRFs could easily have the same AS number, we have to define the AS number that EIGRP will use within each address-family configuration block.

Then, once EIGRP is configured and redistributing routes from BGP, we have to make sure that BGP redistributes the routes from EIGRP so that they are available at the other sites that share this VRF:

```
Router-PE1(config)#router bgp 100
Router-PE1(config-router)#address-family ipv4 vrf NetworkA
Router-PE1(config-router-af)#redistribute eigrp 156
```

Notice that we have redistributed EIGRP by using the customer's AS number, 156, and not the global EIGRP process number, which is 1001 in this example.

We can then look at the customer routing tables from the PE router using the VRF name:

```
Router-PE1#show ip route vrf NetworkA

Routing Table: NetworkA
Codes: C - connected, S - static, R - RIP, M - mobile, B - BGP
       D - EIGRP, EX - EIGRP external, O - OSPF, IA - OSPF inter area
       N1 - OSPF NSSA external type 1, N2 - OSPF NSSA external type 2
       E1 - OSPF external type 1, E2 - OSPF external type 2
       i - IS-IS, su - IS-IS summary, L1 - IS-IS level-1, L2 - IS-IS level-2
       ia - IS-IS inter area, * - candidate default, U - per-user static route
       o - ODR, P - periodic downloaded static route
```

Gateway of last resort is not set

```
D    192.168.57.0/24 [90/158720] via 192.168.1.5, 01:14:20, FastEthernet0/0
D    192.168.5.0/24 [90/30720] via 192.168.1.5, 01:14:20, FastEthernet0/0
     10.0.0.0/32 is subnetted, 1 subnets
B       10.8.8.8 [200/156160] via 10.0.0.4, 00:33:06
C    192.168.1.0/24 is directly connected, FastEthernet0/0
B    192.168.2.0/24 [200/0] via 10.0.0.3, 02:01:42
B    192.168.3.0/24 [200/0] via 10.0.0.4, 00:33:52
Router-PE1#
```

Or we can look at the same information from the CE router using the standard command:

```
Router-CE-A1#show ip route
Codes: C - connected, S - static, I - IGRP, R - RIP, M - mobile, B - BGP
       D - EIGRP, EX - EIGRP external, O - OSPF, IA - OSPF inter area
       N1 - OSPF NSSA external type 1, N2 - OSPF NSSA external type 2
       E1 - OSPF external type 1, E2 - OSPF external type 2, E - EGP
       i - IS-IS, su - IS-IS summary, L1 - IS-IS level-1, L2 - IS-IS level-2
       ia - IS-IS inter area, * - candidate default, U - per-user static route
       o - ODR, P - periodic downloaded static route

Gateway of last resort is not set

D    192.168.57.0/24 [90/156160] via 192.168.5.12, 01:56:04, FastEthernet0/0.2
C    192.168.5.0/24 is directly connected, FastEthernet0/0.2
     10.0.0.0/32 is subnetted, 1 subnets
D       10.8.8.8 [90/158720] via 192.168.1.1, 00:31:26, FastEthernet0/0.1
C    192.168.1.0/24 is directly connected, FastEthernet0/0.1
D EX 192.168.2.0/24 [170/261120] via 192.168.1.1, 01:14:30, FastEthernet0/0.1
D    192.168.3.0/24 [90/30720] via 192.168.1.1, 00:31:47, FastEthernet0/0.1
Router-CE-A1#
```

Notice that the prefixes located at the same site, such as 192.168.57.0/24, look like internal EIGRP routes. Similarly, the entries for prefixes, such as 10.8.8.8/32 and 192.168.3.0/24, which are located at the other EIGRP site, also appear as internal EIGRP routes. But other networks like 192.168.2.0/24 appear as external routes, exactly as we saw in the OSPF example in Recipe 26.6.

Because EIGRP doesn't use the concept of an area as OSPF does, there is no need for the equivalent of a sham link.

See Also

Chapter 7; Recipe 26.5; Recipe 26.6

26.8 PE-CE Communication via BGP

Problem

You want to use BGP to exchange routing information between CE and PE routers.

Solution

Once again, this problem is similar to the RIP, OSPF, and EIGRP examples in Recipes 26.5, 26.6, and 26.7. First we have to enable the routing protocol on the CE routers, which we do by configuring a new AS number on the CE routers. These devices are part of a different AS than the MPLS cloud, so they must have different AS numbers:

```
Router-CE-A1#configure terminal
Enter configuration commands, one per line.  End with CNTL/Z.
Router-CE-A1(config)#router bgp 65535
Router-CE-A1(config-router)#neighbor 192.168.1.1 remote-as 100
Router-CE-A1(config-router)#redistribute ospf 155
Router-CE-A1(config-router)#no synchronization
Router-CE-A1(config-router)#no auto-summary
Router-CE-A1(config-router)#exit
Router-CE-A1(config)#router ospf 155
Router-CE-A1(config-router)#redistribute bgp 65535 subnets
Router-CE-A1(config-router)#network 192.168.5.0 0.0.0.255 area 0
Router-CE-A1(config-router)#end
Router-CE-A1#
```

At this site, we are using the same OSPF configuration as in Recipe 26.6 to facilitate routing within the site, so we must redistribute the OSPF routes into BGP, and vice versa.

We configure the other CE router similarly, but with a different AS number:

```
Router-CE-A2#configure terminal
Enter configuration commands, one per line.  End with CNTL/Z.
Router-CE-A2(config)#router bgp 65534
Router-CE-A2(config-router)#neighbor 192.168.3.1 remote-as 100
Router-CE-A2(config-router)#network 10.8.8.0 mask 255.255.255.0
Router-CE-A2(config-router)#network 192.168.3.0
Router-CE-A2(config-router)#no synchronization
Router-CE-A2(config-router)#no auto-summary
Router-CE-A2(config-router)#end
Router-CE-A2#
```

Then the PE configurations are simply a matter of adding the appropriate *neighbor* commands to the BGP configuration:

```
Router-PE1#configure terminal
Enter configuration commands, one per line.  End with CNTL/Z.
Router-PE1(config)#router bgp 100
Router-PE1(config-router)#address-family ipv4 vrf NetworkA
Router-PE1(config-router-af)#neighbor 192.168.1.5 remote-as 65535
Router-PE1(config-router-af)#neighbor 192.168.1.5 activate
Router-PE1(config-router-af)#end
Router-PE1#
```

The other PE router configuration is similar:

```
Router-PE2#configure terminal
Enter configuration commands, one per line.  End with CNTL/Z.
Router-PE2(config)#router bgp 100
```

```
Router-PE2(config-router)#address-family ipv4 vrf NetworkA
Router-PE2(config-router-af)#neighbor 192.168.3.8 remote-as 65534
Router-PE2(config-router-af)#neighbor 192.168.3.8 activate
Router-PE2(config-router-af)#end
Router-PE2#
```

Discussion

We need to stress that the BGP configurations of the PE routers given here are just the additional commands required to add this CE to PE functionality. The full BGP configuration required to share the VRF information throughout the MPLS cloud is considerably more complicated, and is given in Recipe 26.2. The same is true of the OSPF configuration on the CE router at Site 1. The full OSPF configuration is discussed in Recipe 26.6.

The important new commands here are the ones required for eBGP between the CE and PE routers. On the CE router, we just define a BGP process and include a *neighbor* command pointing to the PE router for this site:

```
Router-CE-A1(config)#router bgp 65535
Router-CE-A1(config-router)#neighbor 192.168.1.1 remote-as 100
Router-CE-A1(config-router)#redistribute ospf 155
```

On the PE router the BGP process is already defined, so we just need to add a *neighbor* command to the *address-family* configuration for this customer's VRF:

```
Router-PE1(config)#router bgp 100
Router-PE1(config-router)#address-family ipv4 vrf NetworkA
Router-PE1(config-router-af)#neighbor 192.168.1.5 remote-as 65535
Router-PE1(config-router-af)#neighbor 192.168.1.5 activate
```

The *neighbor activate* command actually appears automatically by default. You can remove this command to temporarily deactivate this neighbor.

You use the usual *show ip bgp summary* command to view the BGP neighbors on the CE routers:

```
Router-CE-A1#show ip bgp summary
BGP router identifier 192.168.5.1, local AS number 65535
BGP table version is 14, main routing table version 14
5 network entries using 485 bytes of memory
5 path entries using 180 bytes of memory
4 BGP path attribute entries using 240 bytes of memory
1 BGP AS-PATH entries using 24 bytes of memory
0 BGP route-map cache entries using 0 bytes of memory
0 BGP filter-list cache entries using 0 bytes of memory
BGP using 929 total bytes of memory
BGP activity 9/4 prefixes, 9/4 paths, scan interval 60 secs

Neighbor        V    AS MsgRcvd MsgSent   TblVer  InQ OutQ Up/Down  State/PfxRcd
192.168.1.1     4   100      76      73       14    0    0 01:05:51           3
Router-CE-A1#
```

The corresponding command on the PE router must specify the VRF name associated with this customer network:

```
Router-PE1#show ip bgp vpnv4 vrf NetworkA summary
BGP router identifier 10.0.0.2, local AS number 100
BGP table version is 32, main routing table version 32
5 network entries and 5 paths using 925 bytes of memory
8 BGP path attribute entries using 480 bytes of memory
1 BGP AS-PATH entries using 24 bytes of memory
2 BGP extended community entries using 48 bytes of memory
0 BGP route-map cache entries using 0 bytes of memory
0 BGP filter-list cache entries using 0 bytes of memory
BGP activity 12/21 prefixes, 12/5 paths, scan interval 15 secs

Neighbor        V    AS MsgRcvd MsgSent   TblVer  InQ OutQ Up/Down  State/PfxRcd

192.168.1.5     4 65535      73      76       32    0    0 01:05:02           2
Router-PE1#
```

The principle advantage to using BGP like this is that unlike the previous IGP examples, it provides some end-to-end information:

```
Router-CE-A1#show ip bgp
BGP table version is 15, local router ID is 192.168.5.1
Status codes: s suppressed, d damped, h history, * valid, > best, i - internal
Origin codes: i - IGP, e - EGP, ? - incomplete

   Network          Next Hop         Metric LocPrf Weight Path
*> 10.8.8.8/32      192.168.1.1                        0 100 65534 i
*> 192.168.1.0      192.168.1.1           0            0 100 ?
*> 192.168.2.0      192.168.1.1                        0 100 ?
*> 192.168.3.0      192.168.1.1                        0 100 ?
*> 192.168.5.0      0.0.0.0               0        32768 ?
*> 192.168.57.12/32 192.168.5.12          2        32768 ?
Router-CE-A1#
```

In this case, you can see that the prefix 10.8.8.8/32 originates at the site with AS number 65534 before passing through the MPLS cloud, which has AS number 100. This prefix originates internally to BGP because it happens to be a loopback interface on the other CE router. The view from the other CE router is also instructive:

```
Router-CE-A2#show ip bgp
BGP table version is 19, local router ID is 10.8.8.8
Status codes: s suppressed, d damped, h history, * valid, > best, i - internal
Origin codes: i - IGP, e - EGP, ? - incomplete

   Network          Next Hop         Metric LocPrf Weight Path
*> 10.8.8.8/32      0.0.0.0               0        32768 i
*> 192.168.1.0      192.168.3.1                        0 100 ?
*> 192.168.2.0      192.168.3.1                        0 100 ?
*  192.168.3.0      192.168.3.1           0            0 100 ?
*>                   0.0.0.0              0        32768 i
*> 192.168.5.0      192.168.3.1                        0 100 65535 ?
*> 192.168.57.12/32 192.168.3.1                        0 100 65535 ?
Router-CE-A2#
```

Here you can see that the prefix 192.168.57.12/32 originates from the site with AS number 65535 and is received via the MPLS cloud's AS number 100. However, this prefix has an origin code of *incomplete* because it was redistributed into BGP from OSPF at the other site.

This level of information can be useful in some networks. However, because most organizations don't run BGP for their internal routing protocol, you always need to do some route redistribution with this method. Consequently, the MPLS routers will always be Autonomous System Boundary Routers (ASBR), and you will always have to contend with awkward routing over your backup links between sites. For this reason, we generally favor using an IGP such as RIP, OSPF, or EIGRP, as discussed in Recipes 26.5, 26.6, and 26.7. Of these IGPs, OSPF tends to be the most useful because the combination of EIGRP and MPLS is only available in more recent IOS versions, and not on all hardware platforms.

However, some providers only offer a limited range of options for PE-CE routing protocols. And, because the provider has to run BGP inside the MPLS core anyway, it is not uncommon for them to offer BGP as the only PE-CE routing option. If this is the case, and if it presents problems for your IGP design, the only real option is to configure GRE tunnels between your CE routers, as shown in Recipe 26.12. As we note in that recipe, this solution doesn't scale well, but at least it allows you to keep your IGP intact.

See Also

Chapter 9; Recipe 26.2; Recipe 26.5; Recipe 26.6; Recipe 26.7

26.9   QoS over MPLS

Problem

You want to use the Quality of Service (QoS) features of MPLS.

Solution

For this example, we will take a relatively simple view that the PE router will trust the CE router's DSCP/IP Precedence settings and map them to the MPLS EXP traffic priority field in a simple way. So we will focus on the configuration required on the PE and P routers to make use of this information.

First, the PE routers have the dual function of converting DSCP or IP Precedence values to MPLS EXP values and then using this information appropriately when forwarding the packets into the MPLS cloud. In this example, we will do both of these functions in a single policy map.

This MPLS network supports four categories of user traffic: low, medium, and high priority plus a real-time queue, which is indicated with the Expedited Forwarding (EF) DSCP value:

```
Router-PE1#configure terminal
Router-PE1(config)#class-map match-any med-priority
Router-PE1(config-cmap)#match precedence 1
Router-PE1(config-cmap)#match precedence 2
Router-PE1(config-cmap)#exit
Router-PE1(config)#class-map match-any high-priority
Router-PE1(config-cmap)#match precedence 3
Router-PE1(config-cmap)#match precedence 4
Router-PE1(config-cmap)#match precedence 5
Router-PE1(config-cmap)#exit
Router-PE1(config)#class-map match-any realtime-priority
Router-PE1(config-cmap)#match precedence 6
Router-PE1(config-cmap)#match dscp ef
Router-PE1(config-cmap)#exit
Router-PE1(config)#policy-map MPLS-priority
Router-PE1(config-pmap)#class realtime-priority
Router-PE1(config-pmap-c)#priority percent 10
Router-PE1(config-pmap-c)#set mpls experimental topmost 3
Router-PE1(config-pmap-c)#exit
Router-PE1(config-pmap)#class high-priority
Router-PE1(config-pmap-c)#bandwidth percent 10
Router-PE1(config-pmap-c)#queue-limit 20
Router-PE1(config-pmap-c)#set mpls experimental topmost 2
Router-PE1(config-pmap-c)#exit
Router-PE1(config-pmap)#class med-priority
Router-PE1(config-pmap-c)#bandwidth percent 15
Router-PE1(config-pmap-c)#queue-limit 50
Router-PE1(config-pmap-c)#set mpls experimental topmost 1
Router-PE1(config-pmap-c)#exit
Router-PE1(config-pmap)#class class-default
Router-PE1(config-pmap-c)#bandwidth percent 40
Router-PE1(config-pmap-c)#random-detect
Router-PE1(config-pmap-c)#set mpls experimental topmost 0
Router-PE1(config-pmap-c)#exit
Router-PE1(config-pmap)#exit
Router-PE1(config)#interface Serial0/0
Router-PE1(config-if)#service-policy output MPLS-priority
Router-PE1(config-if)#exit
Router-PE1(config)#end
Router-PE1#
```

Then the P routers must carry out the appropriate forwarding policy based on the values found in the MPLS EXP field:

```
Router-P1#configure terminal
Enter configuration commands, one per line.  End with CNTL/Z.
Router-P1(config)#class-map match-any med-priority
Router-P1(config-cmap)#match mpls experimental topmost 1
Router-P1(config-cmap)#exit
Router-P1(config)#class-map match-any high-priority
```

```
Router-P1(config-cmap)#match mpls experimental topmost 2
Router-P1(config-cmap)#exit
Router-P1(config)#class-map match-any realtime-priority
Router-P1(config-cmap)#match mpls experimental topmost 3
Router-P1(config-cmap)#exit
Router-P1(config)#policy-map MPLS-priority
Router-P1(config-pmap)#class realtime-priority
Router-P1(config-pmap-c)#priority percent 10
Router-P1(config-pmap-c)#exit
Router-P1(config-pmap)#class high-priority
Router-P1(config-pmap-c)#bandwidth percent 10
Router-P1(config-pmap-c)#queue-limit 20
Router-P1(config-pmap-c)#exit
Router-P1(config-pmap)#class med-priority
Router-P1(config-pmap-c)#bandwidth percent 15
Router-P1(config-pmap-c)#queue-limit 50
Router-P1(config-pmap-c)#exit
Router-P1(config-pmap)#class class-default
Router-P1(config-pmap-c)#bandwidth percent 40
Router-P1(config-pmap-c)#random-detect
Router-P1(config-pmap-c)#exit
Router-P1(config-pmap)#exit
Router-P1(config)#interface FastEthernet0/0
Router-P1(config-if)#service-policy output MPLS-priority
Router-P1(config-if)#exit
Router-P1(config)#end
Router-P1#
```

Note that in both of these configurations we have applied the *service-policy* command to a single interface. We have done this simply to demonstrate the principles. In a real network, you would want to apply a similar policy to every MPLS-enabled interface.

Discussion

As we discuss in Chapter 11, there are two steps to any QoS deployment, whether over MPLS or traditional networks. The first step is to mark the packets with some sort of priority designation. This is best done at the edges of the network, the PE routers in an MPLS network. This is because the core of the network typically aggregates a large number of access points, so it has higher traffic loads to deal with than the edges.

The second step is then to use this priority marking on each packet to decide how to forward the packet during periods of congestion. If the network is congested, packets will be buffered, with higher priority packets having precedence in the queues. If the congestion is serious enough, some packets will need to be dropped. The priority designations on the packets can be used to help decide which packets to drop first.

Chapter 11 and Appendix B describe the standard IP priority designation using the Differentiated Services Code Point (DSCP) field in the IP packet header. This is a 6-bit field that requests a particular Per-Hop Behavior (PHB) that the network should use when forwarding the packet. The actual PHB is implemented by the network engineer who may decide on a relatively free interpretation.

MPLS has its own QoS marking field contained in the 3-bit Experimental (EXP) field of the MPLS tag. In this recipe we have opted to let the customer decide how they want their network to be prioritized. They are given Table 26.1, showing the correspondence between DSCP/IP Precedence values and the four queues implemented in the MPLS cloud. The MPLS network provider can then set up IP accounting on these four queues and bill a higher per-packet amount for the higher priority queues.

Table 26-1. Example DSCP/IP precedence and MPLS queues

Queue name	DSCP/IP Precedence values	MPLS EXP value	Queueing parameters
Default	All other values	0	55% of bandwidth with WRED
Medium	Precedence: 1, 2	1	15% of bandwidth
High	Precedence: 3, 4, 5	2	10% of bandwidth
Real-time	Precedence: 6 DSCP: AF	3	10% of bandwidth, priority queue

For more complex QoS marking schemes, please refer to Chapter 11. You could, for example, mark packets based on the receiving interface, source, or destination IP addresses, protocol or port numbers, or even using some higher layer application information, if necessary. However, the simple method chosen for this recipe is more in keeping with how MPLS QoS is commonly implemented in practice.

The most convenient way to look at the results of your QoS configuration is with the *show policy interface* command:

```
Router-P1#show policy interface FastEthernet0/0
FastEthernet0/0

  Service-policy output: MPLS-priority

    Class-map: realtime-priority (match-any)
      0 packets, 0 bytes
      5 minute offered rate 0 bps, drop rate 0 bps
      Match: mpls experimental topmost 3
        0 packets, 0 bytes
        5 minute rate 0 bps
      Queueing
        Strict Priority
        Output Queue: Conversation 264
        Bandwidth 10 (%)
        Bandwidth 10000 (kbps) Burst 250000 (Bytes)
        (pkts matched/bytes matched) 0/0
        (total drops/bytes drops) 0/0

    Class-map: high-priority (match-any)
      70 packets, 4277 bytes
      5 minute offered rate 0 bps, drop rate 0 bps
```

```
Match: mpls experimental topmost 2
  70 packets, 4277 bytes
  5 minute rate 0 bps
Queueing
  Output Queue: Conversation 265
  Bandwidth 10 (%)
  Bandwidth 10000 (kbps) Max Threshold 20 (packets)
  (pkts matched/bytes matched) 0/0
  (depth/total drops/no-buffer drops) 0/0/0

Class-map: med-priority (match-any)
  0 packets, 0 bytes
  5 minute offered rate 0 bps, drop rate 0 bps
  Match: mpls experimental topmost 1
    0 packets, 0 bytes
    5 minute rate 0 bps
  Queueing
    Output Queue: Conversation 266
    Bandwidth 15 (%)
    Bandwidth 15000 (kbps) Max Threshold 50 (packets)
    (pkts matched/bytes matched) 0/0
    (depth/total drops/no-buffer drops) 0/0/0

Class-map: class-default (match-any)
  2134 packets, 166141 bytes
  5 minute offered rate 0 bps, drop rate 0 bps
  Match: any
  Queueing
    Output Queue: Conversation 267
    Bandwidth 40 (%)
    Bandwidth 40000 (kbps)
    (pkts matched/bytes matched) 159/11082
    (depth/total drops/no-buffer drops) 0/0/0
     exponential weight: 9
     mean queue depth: 0
```

class	Transmitted pkts/bytes	Random drop pkts/bytes	Tail drop pkts/bytes	Minimum thresh	Maximum thresh	Mark prob
0	460/48177	0/0	0/0	20	40	1/10
1	0/0	0/0	0/0	22	40	1/10
2	0/0	0/0	0/0	24	40	1/10
3	0/0	0/0	0/0	26	40	1/10
4	0/0	0/0	0/0	28	40	1/10
5	0/0	0/0	0/0	30	40	1/10
6	1676/118118	0/0	0/0	32	40	1/10
7	0/0	0/0	0/0	34	40	1/10
rsvp	0/0	0/0	0/0	36	40	1/10

```
Router-P1#
```

In this output, you can see that we have run some test traffic through these queues. Each of the 70 packets seen in the high priority queue was seen with an MPLS Experimental value of 3.

You should also notice that the default queue's WRED output shows that, in addition to the 460 packets with an IP Precedence value of 0, there were 1676 packets with IP Precedence values of 6. How is this possible, if all of the incoming traffic from the PE router with this IP Precedence value is marked for the real-time queue? These are actually OSPF packets generated internally within the MPLS part of the network. Since they haven't been marked with an MPLS experimental value, they are forwarded in the default queue.

See Also

Chapter 11; Appendix B

26.10 MPLS Traffic Engineering with Autoroute

Problem

You want to use the Autoroute feature to automatically maintain traffic-engineered paths through your MPLS network.

Solution

This recipe uses Cisco's *Autoroute* feature for managing Traffic Engineering (TE) with OSPF in an MPLS network. For this method, we must explicitly define all of the traffic paths and associate them with Tunnels on the PE routers:

```
Router-PE1#configure terminal
Enter configuration commands, one per line.  End with CNTL/Z.
Router-PE1(config)#mpls traffic-eng tunnels
Router-PE1(config)#interface Loopback0
Router-PE1(config-if)#ip address 10.0.0.2 255.255.255.255
Router-PE1(config-if)#exit
Router-PE1(config)#interface Tunnel11
Router-PE1(config-if)#ip unnumbered Loopback0
Router-PE1(config-if)#tunnel destination 10.0.0.3
Router-PE1(config-if)#tunnel mode mpls traffic-eng
Router-PE1(config-if)#tunnel mpls traffic-eng autoroute announce
Router-PE1(config-if)#tunnel mpls traffic-eng priority 7 7
Router-PE1(config-if)#tunnel mpls traffic-eng bandwidth 256
Router-PE1(config-if)#tunnel mpls traffic-eng path-option 1 explicit name def-PE3
Router-PE1(config-if)#exit
Router-PE1(config)#interface Tunnel12
Router-PE1(config-if)#ip unnumbered Loopback0
Router-PE1(config-if)#tunnel destination 10.0.0.3
Router-PE1(config-if)#tunnel mode mpls traffic-eng
Router-PE1(config-if)#tunnel mpls traffic-eng autoroute announce
Router-PE1(config-if)#tunnel mpls traffic-eng priority 7 7
Router-PE1(config-if)#tunnel mpls traffic-eng bandwidth 256
Router-PE1(config-if)#tunnel mpls traffic-eng path-option 1 explicit name hi-PE3
Router-PE1(config-if)#exit
```

```
Router-PE1(config)#interface Serial0/0
Router-PE1(config-if)#ip address 10.1.1.13 255.255.255.252
Router-PE1(config-if)#mpls traffic-eng tunnels
Router-PE1(config-if)#tag-switching ip
Router-PE1(config-if)#ip rsvp bandwidth 512
Router-PE1(config-if)#exit
Router-PE1(config)#interface ATM1/0.1 tag-switching
Router-PE1(config-subif)#ip address 10.1.1.2 255.255.255.252
Router-PE1(config-subif)#mpls traffic-eng tunnels
Router-PE1(config-subif)#tag-switching ip
Router-PE1(config-subif)#ip rsvp bandwidth 4000
Router-PE1(config-subif)#exit
Router-PE1(config)#router ospf 99
Router-PE1(config-router)#router-id 10.0.0.2
Router-PE1(config-router)#log-adjacency-changes
Router-PE1(config-router)#network 10.0.0.0 0.255.255.255 area 0
Router-PE1(config-router)#mpls traffic-eng router-id Loopback0
Router-PE1(config-router)#mpls traffic-eng area 0
Router-PE1(config-router)#exit
Router-PE1(config)#ip explicit-path name def-PE3 enable
Router-PE1(cfg-ip-expl-path)#next-address 10.1.1.14
Explicit Path name def-PE3:
    1: next-address 10.1.1.14
Router-PE1(cfg-ip-expl-path)#next-address 10.1.1.9
Explicit Path name def-PE3:
    1: next-address 10.1.1.14
    2: next-address 10.1.1.9
Router-PE1(cfg-ip-expl-path)#exit
Router-PE1(config)#ip explicit-path name hi-PE3 enable
Router-PE1(cfg-ip-expl-path)#next-address 10.1.1.1
Explicit Path name hi-PE3:
    1: next-address 10.1.1.1
Router-PE1(cfg-ip-expl-path)#next-address 10.1.1.6
Explicit Path name hi-PE3:
    1: next-address 10.1.1.1
    2: next-address 10.1.1.6
Router-PE1(cfg-ip-expl-path)#exit
Router-PE1(config)#end
Router-PE1#
```

The other PE router has a similar configuration:

```
Router-PE3#configure terminal
Enter configuration commands, one per line.  End with CNTL/Z.
Router-PE3(config)#mpls traffic-eng tunnels
Router-PE3(config)#interface Loopback0
Router-PE3(config-if)#ip address 10.0.0.3 255.255.255.255
Router-PE3(config-if)#exit
Router-PE3(config)#interface Tunnel11
Router-PE3(config-if)#ip unnumbered Loopback0
Router-PE3(config-if)#tunnel destination 10.0.0.2
Router-PE3(config-if)#tunnel mode mpls traffic-eng
Router-PE3(config-if)#tunnel mpls traffic-eng autoroute announce
```

```
Router-PE3(config-if)#tunnel mpls traffic-eng priority 7 7
Router-PE3(config-if)#tunnel mpls traffic-eng bandwidth 256
Router-PE3(config-if)#tunnel mpls traffic-eng path-option 1 explicit name def-PE1
Router-PE3(config-if)#exit
Router-PE3(config)#interface Tunnel12
Router-PE3(config-if)#ip unnumbered Loopback0
Router-PE3(config-if)#tunnel destination 10.0.0.2
Router-PE3(config-if)#tunnel mode mpls traffic-eng
Router-PE3(config-if)#tunnel mpls traffic-eng autoroute announce
Router-PE3(config-if)#tunnel mpls traffic-eng priority 7 7
Router-PE3(config-if)#tunnel mpls traffic-eng bandwidth 256
Router-PE3(config-if)#tunnel mpls traffic-eng path-option 1 explicit name hi-PE1
Router-PE3(config-if)#exit
Router-PE3(config)#interface Serial0/0
Router-PE3(config-if)#ip address 10.1.1.9 255.255.255.252
Router-PE3(config-if)#mpls traffic-eng tunnels
Router-PE3(config-if)#tag-switching ip
Router-PE3(config-if)#ip rsvp bandwidth 512
Router-PE3(config-if)#exit
Router-PE3(config)#interface ATM1/0.1 tag-switching
Router-PE3(config-subif)#ip address 10.1.1.6 255.255.255.252
Router-PE3(config-subif)#mpls traffic-eng tunnels
Router-PE3(config-subif)#tag-switching ip
Router-PE3(config-subif)#ip rsvp bandwidth 4000
Router-PE3(config-subif)#exit
Router-PE3(config)#router ospf 99
Router-PE3(config-router)#router-id 10.0.0.3
Router-PE3(config-router)#log-adjacency-changes
Router-PE3(config-router)#network 10.0.0.0 0.255.255.255 area 0
Router-PE3(config-router)#mpls traffic-eng router-id Loopback0
Router-PE3(config-router)#mpls traffic-eng area 0
Router-PE3(config-router)#exit
Router-PE3(config)#ip explicit-path name def-PE1 enable
Router-PE3(cfg-ip-expl-path)#next-address 10.1.1.10
Explicit Path name def-PE1:
    1: next-address 10.1.1.10
Router-PE3(cfg-ip-expl-path)#next-address 10.1.1.13
Explicit Path name def-PE1:
    1: next-address 10.1.1.10
    2: next-address 10.1.1.13
Router-PE3(cfg-ip-expl-path)#exit
Router-PE3(config)#ip explicit-path name hi-PE1 enable
Router-PE3(cfg-ip-expl-path)#next-address 10.1.1.5
Explicit Path name hi-PE1:
    1: next-address 10.1.1.5
Router-PE3(cfg-ip-expl-path)#next-address 10.1.1.2
Explicit Path name hi-PE1:
    1: next-address 10.1.1.5
    2: next-address 10.1.1.2
Router-PE3(cfg-ip-expl-path)#exit
Router-PE3(config)#end
Router-PE3#
```

Then we have to configure the P routers, which are somewhat simpler because they don't require tunnels or explicit path definitions. We will show only one P router because they are all essentially the same:

```
Router-P1#configure terminal
Enter configuration commands, one per line.  End with CNTL/Z.
Router-P1(config)#mpls traffic-eng tunnels
Router-P1(config)#interface Loopback0
Router-P1(config-if)#ip address 10.0.0.11 255.255.255.255
Router-P1(config-if)#exit
Router-P1(config)#interface Serial0/0
Router-P1(config-if)#ip address 10.1.1.14 255.255.255.252
Router-P1(config-if)#tag-switching ip
Router-P1(config-if)#mpls traffic-eng tunnels
Router-P1(config-if)#ip rsvp bandwidth 512
Router-P1(config-if)#exit
Router-P1(config)#interface Serial0/1
Router-P1(config-if)#ip address 10.1.1.10 255.255.255.252
Router-P1(config-if)#tag-switching ip
Router-P1(config-if)#mpls traffic-eng tunnels
Router-P1(config-if)#ip rsvp bandwidth 512
Router-P1(config-if)#exit
Router-P1(config)#router ospf 99
Router-P1(config-router)#router-id 10.0.0.11
Router-P1(config-router)#log-adjacency-changes
Router-P1(config-router)#network 10.0.0.0 0.255.255.255 area 0
Router-P1(config-router)#mpls traffic-eng router-id Loopback0
Router-P1(config-router)#mpls traffic-eng area 0
Router-P1(config-router)#exit
Router-P1(config)#end
Router-P1#
```

Discussion

Traffic Engineering (TE) is a large and complicated topic in itself, and a detailed discussion is out of the scope of this book. For more information, we encourage the reader to refer to one of the many books dedicated to MPLS networking.

In this example, we take advantage of OSPF to distribute information about resource utilization within the MPLS cloud. OSPF uses LSP number 10, the so-called Opaque LSP, to flood this information throughout the area. We enable this feature by using the *mpls traffic-eng* OSPF configuration commands:

```
Router-PE3(config)#router ospf 99
Router-PE3(config-router)#router-id 10.0.0.3
Router-PE3(config-router)#log-adjacency-changes
Router-PE3(config-router)#network 10.0.0.0 0.255.255.255 area 0
Router-PE3(config-router)#mpls traffic-eng router-id Loopback0
Router-PE3(config-router)#mpls traffic-eng area 0
```

Since these TE LSPs are only flooded within the area, we have to specify the area to be used. In this case, everything is in Area 0. We have also specified a stable Loopback interface as the source for all TE LSPs to ensure that the information contained in these updates is consistent. Note that although the TE router-id is the same as the main OSPF router ID in this case, this is not always true. Recall from Chapter 8 that the main OSPF router ID is an arbitrary 32-bit value that does not need to be associated with any interfaces on the router.

The bandwidth resource information that the routers send using this method comes from RSVP, which we discuss in greater detail in Chapter 11. We enable RSVP on each MPLS interface and associate with it a maximum reservable bandwidth—512 Kbps, in this case:

```
Router-PE1(config)#interface Serial0/0
Router-PE1(config-if)#ip address 10.1.1.13 255.255.255.252
Router-PE1(config-if)#mpls traffic-eng tunnels
Router-PE1(config-if)#tag-switching ip
Router-PE1(config-if)#ip rsvp bandwidth 512
```

This underscores one of the important features of TE tunnels. You can think of them as bandwidth reserved point-to-point virtual circuits between PE routers, across the MPLS cloud. RSVP handles the bandwidth reservation.

But the big trick to this particular type of MPLS TE is the use of special tunnels between the PE routers:

```
Router-PE1(config)#interface Tunnel11
Router-PE1(config-if)#ip unnumbered Loopback0
Router-PE1(config-if)#tunnel destination 10.0.0.3
Router-PE1(config-if)#tunnel mode mpls traffic-eng
Router-PE1(config-if)#tunnel mpls traffic-eng autoroute announce
Router-PE1(config-if)#tunnel mpls traffic-eng priority 7 7
Router-PE1(config-if)#tunnel mpls traffic-eng bandwidth 256
Router-PE1(config-if)#tunnel mpls traffic-eng path-option 1 explicit name def-PE3
```

In this case, we have defined a tunnel from Router-PE1 to Router-PE3. The *tunnel mode* command specifies that this is to be an MPLS TE tunnel. Recall that in Chapter 12 we looked at other tunnel types such as GRE. This is similar to those tunnels in that it can carry a wide variety of protocols. However it is dynamically generated by the MPLS TE process whenever it is required. The *priority* and *bandwidth* options define parameters that the TE process can use to determine which tunnels and which pathways may be used.

The most interesting command in this tunnel configuration is the last one, which associates this tunnel with an explicit path through the MPLS cloud. In this case, the path is named def-PE3, and it is defined using the *ip explicit-path* command:

```
Router-PE1(config)#ip explicit-path name def-PE3 enable
Router-PE1(cfg-ip-expl-path)#next-address 10.1.1.14
Router-PE1(cfg-ip-expl-path)#next-address 10.1.1.9
```

Usually in IP networking we don't want to explicitly define paths through the network for two main reasons. First, it doesn't scale well, and second, we usually want the routing protocol to select the best path for us. With TE, however, we do want to exercise control over which of many possible paths a particular conversation might take.

In this example, we have defined two flows, one through each of the two available paths, and have named them "def" and "hi" for default and high priority, respectively. You could use this in conjunction with the MPLS QoS functionality discussed in Recipe 26.9 to make sure that high priority traffic is sent through a different physical path through the network than low priority traffic.

The big advantage to using an IGP like OSPF to control these TE tunnels is that we can still have all of the fault tolerance afforded by multiple paths through the network. And, at the same time, we can ensure that all of the available paths are used appropriately to maximize throughput or to balance the internal loading of the network.

You can see which tunnels are in use with the *show mpls traffic-eng tunnels* command:

```
Router-PE1#show mpls traffic-eng tunnels

Name: Router-PE1_t11                        (Tunnel11) Destination: 10.0.0.3
  Status:
    Admin: up          Oper: up     Path: valid       Signalling: connected

    path option 1, type explicit def-PE3 (Basis for Setup, path weight 128)

  Config Parameters:
    Bandwidth: 256       kbps (Global)  Priority: 7  7   Affinity: 0x0/0xFFFF
    Metric Type: TE (default)
    AutoRoute:  enabled   LockDown: disabled  Loadshare: 256      bw-based
    auto-bw: disabled

  InLabel  :  -
  OutLabel : Serial0/0, 18
  RSVP Signalling Info:
      Src 10.0.0.2, Dst 10.0.0.3, Tun_Id 11, Tun_Instance 16
    RSVP Path Info:
      My Address: 10.0.0.2
      Explicit Route: 10.1.1.14 10.1.1.9 10.0.0.3
      Record Route:  NONE
      Tspec: ave rate=256 kbits, burst=1000 bytes, peak rate=256 kbits
    RSVP Resv Info:
      Record Route:  NONE
      Fspec: ave rate=256 kbits, burst=1000 bytes, peak rate=256 kbits
  History:
    Tunnel:
      Time since created: 2 hours, 14 minutes
      Time since path change: 2 hours, 12 minutes
    Current LSP:
      Uptime: 2 hours, 12 minutes

 Name: Router-PE1_t12                        (Tunnel12) Destination: 10.0.0.3
   Status:
     Admin: up          Oper: down    Path: not valid   Signalling: Down
     path option 1, type explicit hi-PE3

   Config Parameters:
     Bandwidth: 256       kbps (Global)  Priority: 7  7   Affinity: 0x0/0xFFFF
```

```
    Metric Type: TE (default)
    AutoRoute: enabled   LockDown: disabled  Loadshare: 256      bw-based
    auto-bw: disabled

  History:
    Tunnel:
      Time since created: 2 hours, 14 minutes
    Path Option 1:
      Last Error: PCALC:: Explicit path has unknown address, 10.1.1.1

LSP Tunnel Router-PE3_t11 is signalled, connection is up
  InLabel  : Serial0/0, implicit-null
  OutLabel :  -
  RSVP Signalling Info:
      Src 10.0.0.3, Dst 10.0.0.2, Tun_Id 11, Tun_Instance 30
    RSVP Path Info:
      My Address: 10.0.0.2
      Explicit Route:  NONE
      Record Route:  NONE
      Tspec: ave rate=256 kbits, burst=1000 bytes, peak rate=256 kbits
    RSVP Resv Info:
      Record Route:  NONE
      Fspec: ave rate=256 kbits, burst=1000 bytes, peak rate=256 kbits
Router-PE1#
```

See Also

Chapters 8, 11, and 12; Recipe 26.9

26.11 Multicast Over MPLS

Problem

You want to pass customer multicast traffic through an MPLS network.

Solution

For this recipe, we must configure Multicast capabilities on all of the different types of routers: C, CE, P, and PE. First, the C and CE routers, which we configure for multicast using exactly the same techniques that we used in Chapter 23:

```
Router-C-An#configure terminal
Enter configuration commands, one per line.  End with CNTL/Z.
Router-C-An(config)#ip multicast-routing
Router-C-An(config)#interface FastEthernet0/0
Router-C-An(config-if)#ip address 192.168.5.12 255.255.255.0
Router-C-An(config-if)#ip pim sparse-dense-mode
Router-C-An(config-if)#exit
Router-C-An(config)#end
Router-C-An#
```

For the CE routers, we need to configure the interfaces that point to both the C and PE routers:

```
Router-CE-A1#configure terminal
Enter configuration commands, one per line.  End with CNTL/Z.
Router-CE-A1(config)#ip multicast-routing
Router-CE-A1(config)#interface FastEthernet0/0.1
Router-CE-A1(config-subif)#encapsulation dot1Q 101
Router-CE-A1(config-subif)#ip address 192.168.1.5 255.255.255.0
Router-CE-A1(config-subif)#ip pim sparse-dense-mode
Router-CE-A1(config-subif)#exit
Router-CE-A1(config)#interface FastEthernet0/0.2
Router-CE-A1(config-subif)#encapsulation dot1Q 111
Router-CE-A1(config-subif)#ip address 192.168.5.1 255.255.255.0
Router-CE-A1(config-subif)#ip pim sparse-dense-mode
Router-CE-A1(config-subif)#exit
Router-CE-A1(config)#end
Router-CE-A1#
```

We will configure a static *IGMP join-group* statement on the *Loopback* interface of the other CE router to allow us to do a simple multicast connectivity demonstration later:

```
Router-CE-A2#configure terminal
Enter configuration commands, one per line.  End with CNTL/Z.
Router-CE-A2(config)#ip multicast-routing
Router-CE-A2(config)#interface Loopback0
Router-CE-A2(config-if)#ip address 10.8.8.8 255.255.255.255
Router-CE-A2(config-if)#ip pim sparse-dense-mode
Router-CE-A2(config-if)#ip igmp join-group 239.1.1.1
Router-CE-A2(config-if)#exit
Router-CE-A2(config)#interface Ethernet0
Router-CE-A2(config-if)#ip address 192.168.3.8 255.255.255.0
Router-CE-A2(config-if)#ip pim sparse-dense-mode
Router-CE-A2(config-if)#exit
Router-CE-A2(config)#end
Router-CE-A2#
```

On the PE routers, we have to configure multicast routing globally for the internal MPLS cloud as well as on each VRF that must support multicasting on the client side. We also need to configure all of the interfaces, including the Loopback interfaces that support MP-BGP, and those that exist within the VRF. Also, we are configuring this particular PE router to be the RP for this VRF. You could just as easily use any of the customer routers for this function, but we do it here to demonstrate the different syntax required:

```
Router-PE1#configure terminal
Enter configuration commands, one per line.  End with CNTL/Z.
Router-PE1(config)#ip multicast-routing
Router-PE1(config)#interface Loopback0
Router-PE1(config-if)#ip address 10.0.0.2 255.255.255.255
Router-PE1(config-if)#ip pim sparse-dense-mode
Router-PE1(config-if)#exit
Router-PE1(config)#interface Serial0/0
```

```
Router-PE1(config-if)#ip address 10.1.1.13 255.255.255.252
Router-PE1(config-if)#ip pim sparse-dense-mode
Router-PE1(config-if)#tag-switching ip
Router-PE1(config-if)#exit
Router-PE1(config)#ip multicast-routing vrf NetworkA
Router-PE1(config)#ip vrf NetworkA
Router-PE1(config-vrf)#rd 100:1
Router-PE1(config-vrf)#route-target export 100:1
Router-PE1(config-vrf)#route-target import 100:1
Router-PE1(config-vrf)#mdt default 239.100.100.1
Router-PE1(config-vrf)#exit
Router-PE1(config)#interface Loopback155
Router-PE1(config-if)#ip vrf forwarding NetworkA
Router-PE1(config-if)#ip address 192.168.155.1 255.255.255.255
Router-PE1(config-if)#ip pim sparse-dense-mode
Router-PE1(config-if)#exit
Router-PE1(config)#interface Ethernet0/0
Router-PE1(config-if)#description connection to customer A, site 1
Router-PE1(config-if)#ip vrf forwarding NetworkA
Router-PE1(config-if)#ip address 192.168.1.1 255.255.255.0
Router-PE1(config-if)#ip pim sparse-dense-mode
Router-PE1(config-if)#exit
Router-PE1(config)#ip pim vrf NetworkA send-rp-announce Loopback155 scope 15
Router-PE1(config)#ip pim vrf NetworkA send-rp-discovery Loopback155 scope 15
Router-PE1(config)#end
Router-PE1#
```

The other PE router is similar to the first one, except that we will omit the RP configuration here. This PE configuration is more typical of situations where some other
router, particularly one of the C routers, takes on the RP role. In general, that is the
preferred arrangement, as it allows the customers greater control over their internal
multicast configurations:

```
Router-PE2#configure terminal
Enter configuration commands, one per line.  End with CNTL/Z.
Router-PE2(config)#ip multicast-routing
Router-PE2(config)#interface Loopback0
Router-PE2(config-if)#ip address 10.0.0.4 255.255.255.255
Router-PE2(config-if)#ip pim sparse-dense-mode
Router-PE2(config-if)#exit
Router-PE2(config)#interface FastEthernet0/0.1
Router-PE2(config-subif)#encapsulation dot1Q 10
Router-PE2(config-subif)#ip address 10.1.2.4 255.255.255.0
Router-PE2(config-subif)#ip pim sparse-dense-mode
Router-PE2(config-subif)#tag-switching ip
Router-PE2(config-subif)#exit
Router-PE2(config)#ip multicast-routing vrf NetworkA
Router-PE2(config)#ip vrf NetworkA
Router-PE2(config-vrf)#rd 100:1
Router-PE2(config-vrf)#route-target export 100:1
Router-PE2(config-vrf)#route-target import 100:1
Router-PE2(config-vrf)#mdt default 239.100.100.1
Router-PE2(config-vrf)#exit
```

```
Router-PE2(config)#interface Loopback155
Router-PE2(config-if)#ip vrf forwarding NetworkA
Router-PE2(config-if)#ip address 192.168.155.2 255.255.255.255
Router-PE2(config-if)#ip pim sparse-dense-mode
Router-PE2(config-if)#exit
Router-PE2(config)#interface FastEthernet0/0.2
Router-PE2(config-subif)#encapsulation dot1Q 102
Router-PE2(config-subif)#ip vrf forwarding NetworkA
Router-PE2(config-subif)#ip address 192.168.3.1 255.255.255.0
Router-PE2(config-subif)#ip pim sparse-dense-mode
Router-PE2(config-subif)#exit
Router-PE2(config)#end
Router-PE2#
```

The P router's configuration is somewhat simpler because it doesn't need to know about what goes on inside the VRFs:

```
Router-P1#configure terminal
Enter configuration commands, one per line.  End with CNTL/Z.
Router-P1(config)#ip multicast-routing
Router-P1(config)#interface FastEthernet0/0
Router-P1(config-if)#ip address 10.1.2.11 255.255.255.0
Router-P1(config-if)#ip pim sparse-dense-mode
Router-P1(config-if)#tag-switching ip
Router-P1(config-if)#exit
Router-P1(config)#interface Serial0/0
Router-P1(config-if)#ip address 10.1.1.14 255.255.255.252
Router-P1(config-if)#ip pim sparse-dense-mode
Router-P1(config-if)#tag-switching ip
Router-P1(config-if)#exit
Router-P1(config)#interface Serial0/1
Router-P1(config-if)#ip address 10.1.1.10 255.255.255.252
Router-P1(config-if)#ip pim sparse-dense-mode
Router-P1(config-if)#tag-switching ip
Router-P1(config-if)#exit
Router-P1(config)#end
Router-P1#
```

Discussion

For this example, we have configured all of the routers for sparse-dense mode PIM because it is the easiest to configure. We could also have used sparse-mode or bidirectional PIM. Please refer to Chapter 23 for more information on multicast configurations.

In the example, we configured Router-CE-A2 to be a member of the multicast group 239.1.1.1. Chapter 23 shows several more sophisticated methods for monitoring multicast networks, but for our purposes here a simple *ping* is sufficient to demonstrate basic multicast functionality:

```
Router-C-An#ping 239.1.1.1

Type escape sequence to abort.
Sending 1, 100-byte ICMP Echos to 239.1.1.1, timeout is 2 seconds:
```

```
Reply to request 0 from 192.168.3.8, 8 ms
Router-C-An#
```

It is worthwhile examining one of the PE router configurations in more detail, as there are several distinct components.

First, we have to enable basic multicast functionality within the MPLS cloud. This means that we must globally enable multicast routing with the *ip multicast-routing* command, and then enable PIM on each of the tag-switching interfaces. We have also enabled PIM on the Loopback interface that supports our MP-BGP peer for this router. This is necessary because MP-BGP is used as a transport mechanism for the Multicast Distribution Tree (MDT) protocol:

```
Router-PE1(config)#ip multicast-routing
Router-PE1(config)#interface Loopback0
Router-PE1(config-if)#ip address 10.0.0.2 255.255.255.255
Router-PE1(config-if)#ip pim sparse-dense-mode
Router-PE1(config-if)#exit
Router-PE1(config)#interface Serial0/0
Router-PE1(config-if)#ip address 10.1.1.13 255.255.255.252
Router-PE1(config-if)#ip pim sparse-dense-mode
Router-PE1(config-if)#tag-switching ip
Router-PE1(config-if)#exit
```

In this case, we have used sparse-dense mode PIM. We could have used sparse mode or bidirectional mode PIM as well, however pure dense mode PIM is not supported within the MPLS cloud. We note in passing, though, that you can use dense-mode PIM on the client side of the network as long as you gateway to one of the supported modes on the CE router.

The next part of the PE configuration enables multicast capabilities for the VRF. Note that we have only enabled multicast routing for NetworkA. The other VRF in this network, NetworkB, is still a pure unicast network:

```
Router-PE1(config)#ip multicast-routing vrf NetworkA
Router-PE1(config)#interface Loopback155
Router-PE1(config-if)#ip vrf forwarding NetworkA
Router-PE1(config-if)#ip address 192.168.155.1 255.255.255.255
Router-PE1(config-if)#ip pim sparse-dense-mode
Router-PE1(config-if)#exit
Router-PE1(config)#interface Ethernet0/0
Router-PE1(config-if)#description connection to customer A, site 1
Router-PE1(config-if)#ip vrf forwarding NetworkA
Router-PE1(config-if)#ip address 192.168.1.1 255.255.255.0
Router-PE1(config-if)#ip pim sparse-dense-mode
Router-PE1(config-if)#exit
```

Here we have enabled PIM on every interface that takes part in this VRF, and we have also globally enabled multicast routing for this VRF by using the *ip multicast-routing vrf* command. Then we have to configure MDT for this VRF:

```
Router-PE1(config)#ip vrf NetworkA
Router-PE1(config-vrf)#rd 100:1
```

```
Router-PE1(config-vrf)#route-target export 100:1
Router-PE1(config-vrf)#route-target import 100:1
Router-PE1(config-vrf)#mdt default 239.100.100.1
```

This configures MDT to use the multicast group 239.100.100.1 to carry multicast traffic through the MPLS cloud for this particular VRF. This default MDT multicast group is also the group that will be used to carry MDT signaling information for this VRF. All PE routers supporting this VRF are members of this group. And, as we have left the MDT configuration at a single default group like this, all user data will be transmitted through the same group. If there are a lot of different multicast groups in the customer network, and not all PE routers are interested in all groups, you can improve the efficiency by defining a list of Data Multicast Distribution Trees, as follows:

```
Router-PE1(config)#ip vrf NetworkA
Router-PE1(config-vrf)#rd 100:1
Router-PE1(config-vrf)#route-target export 100:1
Router-PE1(config-vrf)#route-target import 100:1
Router-PE1(config-vrf)#mdt default 239.100.100.1
Router-PE1(config-vrf)#mdt data 239.200.1.0 0.0.0.255 threshold 28
```

This tells the routers to dynamically spawn new multicast groups from the specified range whenever the amount of multicast traffic on any existing MDT group exceeds the specified threshold. In this example, we have specified the range from 239.200.1.0 through 239.200.1.255, and the threshold for creating new groups is 28 kbps.

Finally, we need an RP somewhere in this VRF. We would usually prefer to configure this functionality on a C router somewhere because it would provide the client with greater control over internal multicast traffic. However, in this example we have configured one of the PE routers as the RP, mostly to show how it can be done:

```
Router-PE1(config)#ip pim vrf NetworkA send-rp-announce Loopback155 scope 15
Router-PE1(config)#ip pim vrf NetworkA send-rp-discovery Loopback155 scope 15
```

We show several RP configuration examples in Chapter 23.

See Also

Chapter 23

26.12 Your Service Provider Doesn't Do What You Want

Problem

As an MPLS customer, you want to implement a feature like multicast or a particular PE-CE routing protocol that your service provider doesn't support.

Solution

Some service providers support only a limited range of MPLS features. The most common missing features are specific routing protocols for PE-CE routing and multicast support. This example will assume that you want to pass OSPF and multicast through an MPLS network that supports only BGP:

```
Router-CE-A1#configure terminal
Enter configuration commands, one per line.  End with CNTL/Z.
Router-CE-A1(config)#ip multicast-routing
Router-CE-A1(config)#interface FastEthernet0/0.1
Router-CE-A1(config-if)#encapsulation dot1Q 101
Router-CE-A1(config-if)#ip address 192.168.1.5 255.255.255.0
Router-CE-A1(config-if)#exit
Router-CE-A1(config)#interface Loopback1
Router-CE-A1(config-if)#ip address 192.168.101.1 255.255.255.255
Router-CE-A1(config-if)#exit
Router-CE-A1(config)#interface Tunnel1
Router-CE-A1(config-if)#ip address 192.168.152.1 255.255.255.252
Router-CE-A1(config-if)#tunnel source 192.168.101.1
Router-CE-A1(config-if)#tunnel destination 192.168.101.2
Router-CE-A1(config-if)#ip pim sparse-dense-mode
Router-CE-A1(config-if)#exit
Router-CE-A1(config)#router bgp 65535
Router-CE-A1(config-router)#neighbor 192.168.1.1 remote-as 100
Router-CE-A1(config-router)#network 192.168.1.0
Router-CE-A1(config-router)#network 192.168.101.1 mask 255.255.255.255
Router-CE-A1(config-router)#no synchronization
Router-CE-A1(config-router)#no auto-summary
Router-CE-A1(config-router)#exit
Router-CE-A1(config)#router ospf 155
Router-CE-A1(config-router)#network 192.168.5.0 0.0.0.255 area 0
Router-CE-A1(config-router)#network 192.168.152.0 0.0.0.255 area 0
Router-CE-A1(config-router)#exit
Router-CE-A1(config)#end
Router-CE-A1#
```

At this site, we are using the same OSPF configuration as in Recipe 26.6 to facilitate routing within the site, but we want to separate the BGP and OSPF parts of the network. BGP will allow us to route between the CE routers and keep the tunnels working, while OSPF will run through the tunnels. So we don't redistribute between BGP and OSPF this time.

We configure the other CE router similarly:

```
Router-CE-A2#configure terminal
Enter configuration commands, one per line.  End with CNTL/Z.
Router-CE-A2(config)#ip multicast-routing
Router-CE-A2(config)#interface Ethernet0
Router-CE-A2(config-if)#ip address 192.168.3.8 255.255.255.0
Router-CE-A2(config-if)#exit
Router-CE-A2(config)#interface Loopback1
Router-CE-A2(config-if)#ip address 192.168.101.2 255.255.255.255
Router-CE-A2(config-if)#exit
Router-CE-A2(config)#interface Tunnel1
Router-CE-A2(config-if)#ip address 192.168.152.2 255.255.255.252
Router-CE-A2(config-if)#tunnel source 192.168.101.2
Router-CE-A2(config-if)#tunnel destination 192.168.101.1
```

```
Router-CE-A2(config-if)#ip pim sparse-dense-mode
Router-CE-A2(config-if)#exit
Router-CE-A2(config)#router bgp 65534
Router-CE-A2(config-router)#neighbor 192.168.3.1 remote-as 100
Router-CE-A2(config-router)#network 192.168.3.0
Router-CE-A2(config-router)#network 192.168.101.2 mask 255.255.255.0
Router-CE-A2(config-router)#no synchronization
Router-CE-A2(config-router)#no auto-summary
Router-CE-A2(config-router)#exit
Router-CE-A2(config)#router ospf 155
Router-CE-A2(config-router)#network 10.8.8.0 0.0.0.255 area 0
Router-CE-A2(config-router)#network 192.168.152.0 0.0.0.255 area 0
Router-CE-A2(config-router)#exit
Router-CE-A2(config)#end
Router-CE-A2#
```

Then the PE configurations are identical to those shown in Recipe 26.8.

Discussion

In the discussion section to Recipe 26.5, we showed a simplified version of this recipe. In that case, we used GRE tunnels to carry RIP between CE routers. Here we use GRE tunnels to carry OSPF and multicast traffic. Also, in Recipe 26.5 we used static routes to define the routing for the loopback interfaces that hold the tunnel source and destination addresses. Here we assume that the MPLS carrier allows BGP and only BGP as a PE-CE routing protocol. So we take advantage of this BGP capability to bring up the tunnels, but we have been careful to keep all other internal customer routing out of the BGP routing tables.

This careful separation of internal and external routing tables serves two purposes. First, it ensures that there are no problems with *recursive routing*. This is a common problem when using tunnels with dynamic routing protocols. It happens when the routing protocol that goes through the tunnel is also carrying the information about the tunnel source and destination addresses. Here, the source and destination addresses are carried by BGP and the internal customer routing tables that traverse the tunnel are carried by OSPF. As long as we avoid redistribution between the two protocols, there are no issues.

The second advantage to doing it this way is that your tunnels will go down in the event of a problem in the MPLS cloud. If there is a failure in the cloud that isolates a site, the tunnel destination address for this site will drop out of the routing tables for all of your other CE routers. The tunnels will then drop, and you'll lose your OSPF neighbor relationships. This is a good thing because it means that you will be able to use standard rerouting mechanisms such as dial backup to recover your network connection.

However, if you allowed the tunnel destination addresses to lead into your OSPF routing tables, you could wind up with a situation in which the network is actually using a secondary path between sites and carrying the tunnel traffic down this alternate path. This is not only disoptimal in terms of routing, but also inherently unstable because OSPF doesn't have a way to discover the failure or subsequent recovery of the primary path.

So why use BGP at all in this case? Why not just use static routes to carry the information about the tunnel end points? The biggest reason is flexibility. If your MPLS service provider is willing to use BGP for carrying your tunnel source and destination addresses for you, then you are free to define as many tunnels as you like, and change them if necessary without notifying the carrier. If you were to use, for example, static routes, then the carrier would have to manually inject these addresses into their MP-BGP routing tables for your VRF. So using a routing protocol here is in everybody's best interests.

With the tunnels up, OSPF establishes neighbor relationships directly between the CE routers:

```
Router-CE-A1#show ip ospf neighbor

Neighbor ID     Pri  State      Dead Time  Address         Interface
192.168.101.2    1   FULL/  -   00:00:36   192.168.152.2   Tunnel1
192.168.57.12    1   FULL/BDR   00:00:39   192.168.5.12    FastEthernet0/0.2
Router-CE-A1#
```

And multicast routing works normally through the tunnel, as if the two CE routers were directly connected to one another. To demonstrate this, we will put a static IGMP Join on the loopback interface of one of the routers:

```
Router-CE-A2#configure terminal
Enter configuration commands, one per line.  End with CNTL/Z.
Router-CE-A2(config)#interface Loopback0
Router-CE-A2(config-if)#ip address 10.8.8.8 255.255.255.255
Router-CE-A2(config-if)#ip pim sparse-dense-mode
Router-CE-A2(config-if)#ip igmp join-group 239.1.2.3
Router-CE-A2(config-if)#end
Router-CE-A2#
```

We can then ping this multicast group to see that multicast routing works as expected through the tunnel:

```
Router-CE-A1#show ip pim neighbor
PIM Neighbor Table
Neighbor        Interface            Uptime/Expires     Ver  DR
Address                                                      Prio/Mode
192.168.152.2   Tunnel1              00:24:49/00:01:26  v2   1 / S
Router-CE-A1#ping 239.1.2.3

Type escape sequence to abort.
Sending 1, 100-byte ICMP Echos to 239.1.2.3, timeout is 2 seconds:

Reply to request 0 from 192.168.152.2, 12 ms
Router-CE-A1#
```

For more information on multicast routing, as well as other multicast configuration options, please refer to Chapter 23.

So this solution does work. Protocols such as OSPF and multicast travel transparently through the MPLS cloud between the CE routers, and the customer's network behaves very much like a conventional WAN. But there are two potential issues with this solution that you should at least be aware of.

The first is that there is overhead to carrying traffic through a tunnel. If the maximum transmission unit (MTU) on the network is 1,500 bytes, you lose 24 bytes to the GRE tunnel packet header. So, between your CE routers, your effective MTU becomes 1,476 bytes. This could result in packet fragmentation and a small performance degradation.

The second potential problem is that this solution doesn't scale well to large numbers of CE routers, as we noted in Recipe 26.5. Since the MPLS network forms a mesh of all of the CE routers that belong to the same VRF, the number of tunnels required to duplicate this mesh for N CE routers is $N(N-1)/2$. For large networks, this quickly becomes unmanageable.

There is a standard solution to this link mesh scaling problem, though, which is simply to avoid a fully meshed network topology. In traditional WAN technologies such as X.25, ATM, and Frame Relay, it is common to deploy the network using a *hub and spoke* topology. This means that the routers at different sites don't all talk directly to one another. Instead, a small number (usually one or two) of routers become the central *hub* routers. The other *spoke* routers talk only to the hub routers. If two spoke routers need to communicate, their packets are relayed through one of the hub routers.

So, for the purposes of this recipe, we would define one or two of our CE routers as hub routers, and the other CE routers as spoke routers. This way, the spoke routers would have only as many tunnel interfaces as there are hub routers. The hub routers, on the other hand, would have tunnel connections to all of the other CE routers. Instead of scaling as $N(N-1)/2$, this now scales like N, which is much more manageable.

See Also

Chapter 12; Chapter 23; Recipe 26.5; Recipe 26.8

Chapter 27, Appendix A, and Appendix B are available for FREE online at *oreilly.com*. Download them here: *http://oreilly.com/go/ ciscoIOS2e*

Index

We'd like to hear your suggestions for improving our indexes. Send email to *index@oreilly.com*.

T

About the Authors

Kevin Dooley is Director of Enterprise Networking at CNG Solutions. He has been designing and implementing networks for longer than he'd like to admit. In that time, he has built large-scale local and wide area networks for several of Canada's largest companies. He holds a Ph.D. in physics from the University of Toronto, numerous Cisco certifications, and is the author of *Designing Large-Scale LANs* (O'Reilly).

Ian J. Brown, CCIE #3372, is a managing consultant at Bell Nexxia in Toronto with more than 12 years of experience in the networking induststry. His areas of expertise include TCP/IP and IP routing, as well as management, security, design, and trouble-shooting for large-scale networks. He has had the privilege of working on some of Canada's largest and most complex networks. In his spare time, Ian enjoys scuba diving, working out, and traveling.

Colophon

The animal on the cover of *Cisco IOS Cookbook*, Second Edition is a black jaguar (*Panthera onca*), sometimes called a black panther. While the color of black (melanastic) jaguars differs from that of the more common golden-yellow variety, they are of the same species. Jaguars of all types are native to the tropics, swamps, and grasslands of Central and South America (and rumored to still exist in parts of the Southwestern U.S.), but the black jaguar is usually found only in dense forests. They are between 4 and 6 feet long and have a long tail that is usually about 30 inches long. Males can weigh up to 250 pounds, while females are considerably smaller and rarely grow to more than 150 pounds. Although black jaguars often appear to be solid black in artistic renditions and photography, their coats still have the dark rings containing even darker spots that are a distinguishing feature of all jaguars. Also notable are their eyes, which are a shiny, reflective yellow.

Jaguars will eat almost any animal, including sloths, pigs, deer, monkeys, and cattle. Their hooked claws allow them to catch fish, frogs, turtles, and even small alligators. Although jaguars sit at the top of the rain forest food chain, humans are a large threat—it's estimated that only 15,000 jaguars are left in the wild, and the species is listed as near threatened. They are hunted for their coats (the black coat is greatly prized), and deforestation threatens their survival.

The black jaguar plays a large role in many South American religions and is often considered a wise and divine animal that is associated with the worlds of magic and spirit. The Aztecs believed that the jaguar was the earthbound representative of their deity, and both the Mayans and Toltecs believed that their sun god became a black jaguar at night in order to pass unseen through the underworld.

The cover image is a 19th-century engraving from the Dover Pictorial Archive. The cover font is Adobe ITC Garamond. The text font is Linotype Birka; the heading font is Adobe Myriad Condensed; and the code font is LucasFont's TheSans Mono Condensed.

Get even more for your money.

Join the O'Reilly Community, and register the O'Reilly books you own. It's free, and you'll get:

- $4.99 ebook upgrade offer
- 40% upgrade offer on O'Reilly print books
- Membership discounts on books and events
- Free lifetime updates to ebooks and videos
- Multiple ebook formats, DRM FREE
- Participation in the O'Reilly community
- Newsletters
- Account management
- 100% Satisfaction Guarantee

Signing up is easy:

1. Go to: oreilly.com/go/register
2. Create an O'Reilly login.
3. Provide your address.
4. Register your books.

Note: English-language books only

To order books online:
oreilly.com/store

For questions about products or an order:
orders@oreilly.com

To sign up to get topic-specific email announcements and/or news about upcoming books, conferences, special offers, and new technologies:
elists@oreilly.com

For technical questions about book content:
booktech@oreilly.com

To submit new book proposals to our editors:
proposals@oreilly.com

O'Reilly books are available in multiple DRM-free ebook formats. For more information:
oreilly.com/ebooks

O'REILLY®

Spreading the knowledge of innovators   oreilly.com

Have it your way.

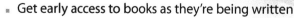